NINTH EDITION

Business

Its Legal, Ethical, and Global Environment

Marianne Moody Jennings

Arizona State University

SOUTH-WESTERN
CENGAGE Learning™

Australia • Brazil • Japan • Korea • Mexico • Singapore • Spain • United Kingdom • United States

SOUTH-WESTERN
CENGAGE Learning™

Business: Its Legal, Ethical, and Global Environment, Ninth Edition
Marianne M. Jennings

Vice President of Editorial, Business:
Jack W. Calhoun

Editor-in-Chief: Rob Dewey

Sr. Acquisitions Editor: Vicky True-Baker

Sr. Developmental Editor:
Laura Bofinger Ansara

Editorial Assistant: Patrick Ian Clark

Marketing Manager: Laura-Aurora Stopa

Sr. Content Project Manager:
Tamborah Moore

Sr. Media Editor: Kristen Meere

Sr. Frontlist Buyer: Kevin Kluck

Marketing Coordinator: Nicole Parsons

Sr. Marketing Communications Manager:
Sarah Greber

Production Service: Edward Dionne/
MPS Limited, a Macmillan Company

Sr. Art Director: Michelle Kunkler

Cover and Internal Designer:
Red Hangar Design, LLC

Cover Image: © George Steinmetz/Corbis

Rights Acquisitions Specialist: John Hill

Photo Researcher: Scott Rosen/
Bill Smith Group

Text Permissions Researcher: Karyn Morrison

For product information and technology assistance, contact us at
Cengage Learning Customer & Sales Support, 1-800-354-9706

For permission to use material from this text or product,
submit all requests online at **www.cengage.com/permissions**
Further permissions questions can be emailed to
permissionrequest@cengage.com

Library of Congress Control Number: 2010938758

ISBN-13: 978-0-538-47054-4

ISBN-10: 0-538-47054-2

South-Western Cengage Learning
5191 Natorp Boulevard
Mason, OH 45040
USA

Cengage Learning products are represented in Canada by
Nelson Education, Ltd.

For your course and learning solutions, visit **www.cengage.com**

Purchase any of our products at your local college store or at our preferred online store **www.cengagebrain.com**

Printed in Canada
1 2 3 4 5 6 7 14 13 12 11 10

To my roots, my mother and father, and to my branches, sprouts, gardeners, and inspiration, my husband and children, Terry, Sarah, Sam, John, and our beloved Claire

Brief Contents

Contents

CHAPTER 3
The Judicial System 76

CHAPTER 4
Managing Disputes: *Alternative Dispute Resolution and Litigation Strategies* 106

Part 2

Business: Its Regulatory Environment   141

CHAPTER 5

Business and the Constitution 142

CHAPTER 6

Administrative Law 180

Part 3

Business Competition and Sales   389

Part 4
Business and Its Employees   563

Part 5

Business Forms and Capitalization

683

Appendices

Preface

A Different World, but the Same Issues

Two editions ago, the seventh edition was published amidst the fallout from the legal, ethical, and, too often, financial collapses of Enron, WorldCom, Adelphia, HealthSouth, Parmalat, Arthur Andersen, Kmart, and others. With Sarbanes–Oxley on the books and new regulatory demands on corporations, we thought perhaps we had turned the corner. But the eighth edition was published as Wall Street and the economy were reeling from the fallout of a subprime mortgage market operating under regulatory radar without a great deal of disclosure on portfolio risk. As the ninth edition goes to press, the SEC has settled a civil suit it brought against Goldman Sachs for allegedly selling securities to clients it was betting against as a short-seller in a scheme that saw its profits reach double-digit billions. Goldman paid a fine of $550 million. In late 2009, Goldman's CEO, Lloyd Blankfein, uttered the same words that Jeffrey Skilling did in 2000: "We are doing God's work." The patterns of business behavior that push the envelope of law and ethics continue. A good portion of New Jersey was indicted on corruption charges, Siemens paid the largest fine in the history of the Foreign Corrupt Practices Act, and BP, in addition to facing its liability from the explosion and leak at the Deepwater Horizon oil rig in the Gulf, anted up the largest fine in OSHA's history for an explosion at its Texas City refinery, where the agency found over 400 violations. The NFL is busy handing out suspensions to quarterbacks who escape criminal prosecution and trying to determine what to do with players who want to return to the game following time in prison. The issues of law and ethics are still at the forefront of business, sports, and government. It has become a tall order just to keep up with all the events!

These companies and organizations and their employees and executives certainly could have benefited from understanding and keeping at the forefront of their decision processes the basics of law and ethics! The legal and ethical environments of business are center stage. Several editions ago, Congress made massive regulatory reform a reality with the passage of the Sarbanes–Oxley legislation on corporate governance, accounting regulation, and criminal penalties. But the SEC missed Bernie Madoff's $50 billion Ponzi scheme for 18 years and Congress passed additional reforms for financial market regulation in 2010. Credit card bills and fees were changed dramatically in 2009 with the passage of major reforms on how much companies can charge in late fees, how much time you have to pay your bills, and how much it will cost you to pay off those charges.

Business is even more international, and we are witnessing the need for thoughtful legal and ethical analysis as companies enter new markets. Google finds itself in a face-off with China over censorship on its search engine. And there are pirates seizing U.S. ships and citizens off the coast of Africa. The world and business continue to change and grow, but law and ethics have retained their role and importance. In fact, now more than ever, we need to understand the legal and ethical issues that affect our businesses and our lives. The knowledge base and even the questions in law and ethics remain the same, but the underlying facts have changed. For example, we still debate the social responsibility role of business. Now we raise that issue in the context of whether Google should do business in China when the Chinese government demands information on users and controls information that is available. We continue to delve into the pros and cons of sending production to other countries. We still have the question of when a contract is formed, but now we face that question with "point and click" technology rather than faxes and letters. We continue to be concerned about our privacy as consumers, but now we wonder who really has access to our Facebook page. We still wonder about the extent of copyright law. Today the movie industry is filing infringement suits against those who use the Internet to download films, free of charge. Their experience repeats that of the music industry 10 years ago.

The world is different, but law and ethics form the constant framework into which we fit the issues of the day. In the materials that follow, you have the chance to understand the marvelous stability of this framework and the ease with which you can apply it to this very different world. Be sure to look for descriptions of the new structure as well as the continuing features in the book such as the "Consider" tutorials, the ethics issues, and the Business Strategy application exercises.

Building the Bridge: Applying Legal and Ethical Reasoning to Business Analysis

I gave my students a midterm exam—a review of what happened with Mattel and its recalled toys that were produced in China with a healthy—well, large, but unhealthy—dose of lead paint used in the production. These students are in the second year of their master's degree studies. They have been trained in economics, marketing, management, and finance. But as they completed their analysis of what went wrong and why with the world's largest toy manufacturer, they had an epiphany. A company can get the finance issues right (Mattel saved 30 percent in production costs by outsourcing to China), have the right brand appeal and great products, and even yield terrific sales figures. However, it can all fall apart over the legal issues. China's standards for paint are different from those of the United States—lead paint is not prohibited there. And the contracts allowed the factories there to use the paint unless the buyer specified otherwise. The law of contracts and the differing legal standards in international business were at the heart of this major setback for a company, one that would cause a 25 percent drop in its stock. And when it comes to problems with safety and toys, the students soon realized that where there is strict liability for products there will also be significant additional financial implications. The students were well trained in economic theory, supply chain management, cash flow issues, and market capitalization. They are very capable *business* students. However, they did not realize until this midterm exam how much of business turns on anticipating the legal issues and getting them resolved correctly. And they also realized that all of our discussions of ethics and social responsibility had a role in doing business. TANSTAAFL—there ain't no such thing as a free lunch when it comes to international outsourcing. There are costs associated with using the much cheaper labor and factories in other countries. And those costs come from legal issues, which, if handled poorly, can affect a company's value and tarnish its brand name.

Why couldn't these students see the interconnection and critical roles of law and ethics in business until this case for their midterm? It was not for lack of exposure to the law. I taught my course "by the book," so to speak. Students could recite the components of a valid contract, rattle off the requirements for bankruptcy, recall from memory the antitrust statutes. Yet, I was coming to realize, this rote knowledge was not enough. One of my best former students, who had gone on to medical school, came to me perplexed about her office lease. She said that the complex in which she wanted to open her practice had a "no advertising" policy. In fact, she said that when she toured the premises with a leasing agent, the leasing agent turned to her and said, "You're not one of those doctors who advertises, are you? Because if you are, we can't lease to you. We have a policy against it." One of my best students, who knew the antitrust statutes well, could not apply them to her everyday business. Worse, perhaps, she could not *recognize* when to apply these statutes: She did not see the antitrust implications of the agent's statements nor the problems with the physicians in the complex taking such an approach to screening tenants.

I reached the conclusion that there were shortcomings in the standard approach to teaching business students law and ethics. Students were not ignorant of the law; rather, they simply lacked the necessary skills to recognize legal and ethical issues and to apply their knowledge of law and ethics to business decision making. As instructors, we were not integrating legal and ethical reasoning with business analysis. My conclusion led me to develop my own materials for classroom use and eventually led to the publication of the first edition of this book. Now in its ninth edition, *Business: Its Legal, Ethical, and Global Environment* brings to the classroom the most integrated approach to learning law and ethics available in the market today. Throughout every chapter and in every feature, students and instructors are continually reminded of how various legal and ethical principles apply in business contexts. For all areas of law and ethics, this book answers the question: How does this concept affect a business? This book builds a bridge for the student between knowledge of law and ethics and application of both in business. My 34 years of teaching law and ethics finally brought this realization: business ethics is not easily grasped nor practiced in business because we depersonalize ethical issues. If we just allow the company or organization to make the decision, our ethics are not in question; the company's are. The ethical issues in the book require students to bring ethical issues into their lives, their circumstances, their world. This feature also forces them to answer this question in a wide variety of contexts: "If it were you, and you were faced with the dilemma and required to make a decision, what would you do?"

Strengthening the Bridge: New Content, Business Applications, and Learning Aids

For the ninth edition, *Business: Its Legal, Ethical, and Global Environment* has undergone further refinement. New content has been added, new business applications have been integrated into every chapter, and the learning aids have been modified and refocused to help students understand and apply legal and ethical concepts.

New Content

The ninth edition of *Business: Its Legal, Ethical, and Global Environment* continues to meet its goal of helping students with their understanding of how law and ethics apply to the business world. The organizational structure continues from the eighth edition because the changes made then were well received. In general, each part begins with an overview that helps students see the importance of the various aspects of law in business management and operations. Part I offers the student an overview of the legal, ethical, and judicial environments of business. Part II covers the regulatory environments of business. Part III, which covers the law and ethics of competition and sales, has been reorganized to provide a more logical flow of material. Part IV covers the legal and ethical issues of business and employees. Part V covers the law and ethical dilemmas of business organization and capitalization, including coverage of financial market reforms following 2008's collapses. Sarbanes–Oxley and Dodd–Frank cross over all parts of the book because of their expansive reach into business credit and governance. All aspects of these massive federal regulatory reforms are covered in the book.

Ethics

Business Ethics and Social Responsibility (Chapter 2) offers new examples and insights on the application of ethics to business decision making. Chapter 2 is chock full of the examples the last two years have netted—from the 41 New York City Marathon runners who took the subway during the race in order to gain a better time to an entertaining and informative "Guess Who?" quiz on the companies that collapsed and the irony of their conduct and statements. Ethics coverage is also integrated throughout all chapters.

Business Applications

Biography

Each chapter contains a biography. Biographies provide students with business history through the study of individuals and companies involved with the area of law and ethics covered in the chapter. For example, Chapter 3 has a biography on the first Hispanic Supreme Court justice, Sonia Sotomayor. Chapter 21 provides the story of Bernie Madoff and the18-year $50-billion Ponzi scheme that took Kevin Bacon and Kyra Sedgwick for all they were worth. Mr. Madoff even managed to snooker Steven Spielberg out of a chunk of change.

For the Manager's Desk

Each chapter also contains at least one For the Manager's Desk. These readings provide students with excerpts from various business publications, including *Forbes*, the *Wall Street Journal*, *Fortune*, and *Corporate Finance Review*, as well as other publications, such as *National Law Journal*, *American Business Law Journal*, and the *Real Estate Law Journal*. These readings, some short and others in-depth, offer students the opportunity to see how business interrelates with ethics and law.

Learning Aids

. . . . and the Law

Each chapter also contains a new feature to further integrate law and ethics with the other "silos" of business. The " . . . and the Law" feature puts law and ethics in the context of economics, human resources, public policy, strategy, finance, and other areas to illustrate the ways knowledge of the where and how for the fit of law and ethics can help make better managers and better decisions. For example, Chapter 8 (Criminal Law) presents the issue of what companies can and should do when executives are charged with crimes. What is the company's responsibility for their legal representation? If the company provides lawyers for its executives, does the government see that as a failure to cooperate with an investigation? And what about the attorney-client privilege? Chapter 11 (Environmental Regulation and Sustainability) presents questions about the activities and role of PETA and environmental activism. Chapter 21 (Securities Law) deals with Goldman, its approach to management and incentives, and whether its driven staff crossed some legal and ethical lines in their zeal to be "filthy rich by 40." These " . . . and the Law" features consist of the situations and events that really force us to think through issues applying all the principles from business disciplines to understand more fully the depth and breadth of management issues.

Case Headlines

Every court case has a case headline that summarizes what issues are involved in the case. In Managing Disputes: Alternative Dispute Resolution and Litigation Strategies (Chapter 4), students read *Wal-Mart Stores, Inc. v Johnson*, a case that addresses the issue of our obligations regarding evidence for a potential civil suit. In the case, a customer is injured when a papier-mâché reindeer falls from an upper shelf and lands on his head and shoulders. The case title is memorable: "'Reining' Deer at the Local Walmart." And who could resist the *Quon v Arch Wireless* case opener of "Text Me, If You Dare," as a way of introducing a vivid precedent on an employer's right to view employees' text messages. The vivid one-line description and colorful facts of the case, a common thread throughout the case choices in the text, help students internalize the rules and lessons about not destroying evidence for a potential lawsuit.

Chapter Openers

Chapters begin with an opening problem, titled "Consider". . ., which presents a legal dilemma relevant to the chapter's discussion and similar to those business managers need to handle. These are revisited and answered in the body of the chapter. For example, Chapter 15's opening "Consider" presents the case of an adult bookstore with the name "Victor's Little Secret," and the resulting litigation when Victoria's Secret cried "Foul!" over the use of its good name. Chapter 10 has a new opening: a product liability case on a towline used to haul someone in an inner tube behind a boat. That short intro serves as a way to get students into the materials; they want to know the answer because a good many of them have used such a towline or, perhaps, been in the inner tube. Moreover, answers to these opening "Considers" are referenced in the text and clearly marked. Next, opening statements discuss the major topics of the chapter and present the general goals for the chapter in the form of questions to be answered. Finally, quotations, often humorous, pique students' interest and focus the chapter on the major issues.

Chapter Summary

Each chapter concludes with a summary that reinforces the major concepts of the chapter. Each summary is constructed around the key questions introduced at the start of the chapter and key terms presented throughout the chapter.

Business Strategy Applications

Each chapter has a business strategy connection designed to help students understand where law and ethics fit in developing effective business strategies. For example, one Chapter 13 strategy piece deals with contract rights and high-powered talent. This feature shows how important good contract negotiations and solid terms are to reining in high-powered talent that may be affecting the company's brand image. The Chapter 17 strategy feature focuses on the content and role of an employee handbook.

Organization and Features: A Structure to Guide Students to Reasoning and Analysis

The classic features have been updated and strengthened. The organization has been retained to continue to meet student needs in the classroom.

Organization

As noted, there are five parts in the book, which serve to organize the materials around business operations. Every chapter integrates international and ethical topics.

Part I

In four chapters, Part I offers an introduction to law, an introduction to business ethics and the judicial system, and a discussion of litigation and alternative dispute resolution. Part I provides students with a foundation in law and ethics, as well as legal and ethical reasoning, necessary for the areas of law in the chapters that follow. By being brief (four chapters), Part I offers instructors an early and logical break for exams.

Part II

In seven chapters, Part II covers the regulatory environment of business, including the following topics: constitutional law, administrative and international law, business crimes and business torts, product advertising and liability, and environmental regulation. At the completion of Parts I and II, students have a grasp of the legal system, ethical boundaries, and the laws that affect business operational decisions, even those in cyberspace.

Part III

The five chapters in Part III present students with the legal and ethical issues surrounding competition and sales. Part III includes the following topics: intellectual property; trade restraints and antitrust laws; contract and sales law; and financing of sales and leases, including credit disclosure requirements. From the negotiation of price to the collection of accounts, this segment of the book covers all aspects of selling business products and services. This section is structured so that the contracts discussion precedes the complexities of property and competition.

Part IV

The three chapters in Part IV discuss the contractual and regulatory aspects of employer and employee relationships. Topics include agency law and employee conduct, management of employee welfare, and employment discrimination.

Part V

In Part V, students study the advantages and disadvantages of various business organizations and the regulation of the capital markets. The two chapters in Part V include the following topics: business organization, securities laws, and business combinations.

Features

Court Cases

Edited court language cases provide in-depth points of law, and many cases include dissenting and concurring opinions. Case questions follow to help students understand the points of law in the case and think critically about the decision. The courts have been active since the last edition, and there are many 2008–2010 case decisions throughout the book. Students will be able to study the Fourth Amendment in the context of whether a police officer can search your car on a traffic stop. And what happens when employees work so many shifts, and are so tired, that they have accidents as they return home from work? Are their employers liable? What happens when a young man saves his Pepsi points to claim a Harrier Jet that he sees in a Pepsi spoof ad for "Pepsi stuff"? Does he get his jet?

Consider...

"Consider" problems, along with "Ethical Issues" and "Business Planning Tips," have been a part of every chapter since the first edition. "Considers," often based on real court cases, ask students to evaluate and analyze the legal and ethical issues discussed in the preceding text. Because these issues are integrated into the text, students must address and think critically about these issues as they encounter them. Through interactive problems, students learn to judge case facts and determine the consequences. The "Considers" bring the most current topics into the book and the classroom. Students will be able to determine whether *Weekly Standard* editor Fred Barnes was defamed by Michael Moore. They can determine the relationship between the First Amendment and the Section 527 political organizations and their relationships to corporations.

Thinking, Applying, and Answering: "Consider" Tutorials—A Guide for Reasoning

One "Consider" per chapter is solved for the students in a methodical walk-through that helps them understand how to apply the legal principles or case precedent that they have just studied. The facts of the case or hypothetical are presented and the students are asked to recall what they have just learned. Next, students are walked through applying those principles to the current facts. Finally, they are given the answer and the reason that answer is consistent with their thinking and applying.

Ethical Issues

The "Ethical Issues" feature appears in every chapter and presents students with real-world ethical problems to grapple with. "Ethical Issues" help integrate coverage of ethics into every chapter. The ethical issues also include personal and real-life examples that help students relate to the pervasive nature of ethical dilemmas that they do and will continue to face.

Business Planning Tips

Students are given sound business and legal advice through "Business Planning Tips." With these tips, students not only know the law, but also know how to anticipate issues and ensure compliance.

Cyberlaw

Many chapters also include a segment on cyberlaw. These chapter-by-chapter materials, marked by an icon, give students the chance to see how new technology fits into the existing legal framework.

Exhibits

Exhibits include charts, figures, and business and legal documents that help highlight or summarize legal and ethical issues from the chapter. With the credit and financial market reforms and the changes in criminal penalties under Sarbanes–Oxley, many of the charts are either new or updated.

End-of-Chapter Problems

Many end-of-chapter problems have been updated and now focus more on actual cases. There are new chapter problems throughout the book of varied lengths for different instructor needs.

The Informed Manager: Who Should Use This Book?

With its comprehensive treatment of the law, integrated business applications, and full-color design, *Business: Its Legal, Ethical, and Global Environment* is well suited for both undergraduate and MBA students. The book is used extensively in undergraduate education programs around the country. In addition, this edition has been class-tested with MBA students, and it is appropriate for MBA and executive education programs.

A Note on AACSB Standards

The strong presence of ethics, social responsibility, international law and issues, and the integration of other business disciplines make the book an ideal fit for meeting AACSB standards and curriculum requirements. The AACSB standards emphasize the need for students to have an understanding of ethical and global issues. The ninth edition continues with its separate chapter on ethics as well as ethical issues and dilemmas for student discussion and resolution in every chapter. The separate chapter on international law continues its expanded coverage from the last edition, and each chapter has a segment devoted to international law issues. The ninth edition includes readings on language issues in contracts, women as executives in other cultures, the role of lawyers in other countries, and attitudes outside the United States on insider trading and antitrust laws.

This edition presents students with the legal foundation necessary for business operations and sales but also affords the students the opportunities to analyze critically the social and political environments in which the laws are made and in which businesses must operate. An examination of the lists of companies and individuals covered in the biographies, and of the publications from which the

For the Manager's Desk readings are taken, demonstrates the depth of background the ninth edition offers in those areas noted as critical by the AACSB. The materials provide a balanced look at regulation, free enterprise, and the new global economy.

Supplements

Business: Its Legal, Ethical, and Global Environment offers a comprehensive and well-crafted supplements package for both students and instructors. Contact your Cengage Learning/South-Western Legal Studies in Business sales representative for more details, or visit www.cengagebrain.com.

Access to Companion Site Resources.   To access additional course materials and companion resources, please visit **www.cengagebrain.com.** At the CengageBrain .com home page, search for the book's ISBN (found on the back cover of your book) using the search box at the top of the page. This will take you to this book's product page, where free companion resources can be found. Instructors should go to login .cengage.com and log in to access instructor-specific resources.

Weekly Ethics and Law Updates.   Available at **mariannejennings.com,** the weekly update contributed by the author offers at least 12 current events per month for discussion and analysis. The update features new decisions, new statutes, new regulations, new ethical dilemmas, and a host of examples and cites to current periodicals. The ninth edition includes references to these updates in the text.

Student Study Guide.   (ISBN: 0-538-47219-7) Written under the guidance of the author, the Study Guide provides the following for each chapter: an outline; chapter outlines, key terms; and matching, multiple choice, fill-in-the-blank, and short answer questions.

Instructor's Manual.   (ISBN: 0-538-47220-0) The Instructor's Manual, written by the author, provides the following for each chapter: a detailed outline; answers to "Considers", Ethical Issues, and case problems; briefs of all cases; supplemental readings; and interactive/cooperative learning exercises.

Test Bank.   (ISBN: 0-538-47221-9) The printed Test Bank for instructors includes more than 1,500 questions in true/false, multiple-choice, and essay format. Answers to questions provide a subject word for easy identification and a classification indicating if they are intended for review of concepts or for analysis and application of concepts. Instructors may access Test Bank files in Microsoft Word after logging on to login.cengage.com, or access them on the Instructor's Resource CD.

ExamView Testing Software—Computerized Testing Software.   This testing software contains all of the questions in the printed test bank. This program is an easy-to-use test creation software compatible with Microsoft Windows. Instructors can add or edit questions, instructions, and answers; and select questions by previewing them on the screen, selecting them randomly, or selecting them by number. Instructors can also create and administer quizzes online, whether over the Internet, a local area network (LAN), or a wide area network (WAN). ExamView is available on the Instructor's Resource CD.

Microsoft PowerPoint Lecture Review Slides. Developed by the author, these PowerPoint slides are available for use by students as an aid to note taking, and by instructors for enhancing their lectures. Instructors may access these PowerPoint files after logging on to login.cengage.com, or access them on the Instructor's Resource CD.

Business Law CourseMate. Cengage Learning's Business Law CourseMate brings course concepts to life with interactive learning, study, and exam preparation tools that support the printed textbook. CourseMate includes an interactive e-book and interactive teaching and learning tools—quizzes, flashcards, videos, Engagement Tracker, and more. Engagement Tracker is a first-of-its-kind tool that monitors student engagement in the course. This intuitive online reporting tool makes it easy for you to evaluate use of study resources, monitor time-on-task, and track progress for the entire class or for individual students. Instantly see what concepts are the most difficult for your class and identify which students are at risk throughout the semester. A student access code is provided when Business Law CourseMate is bundled with a new textbook, or can be purchased at www.cengagebrain.com

Business Law Digital Video Library. This dynamic video library features more that 60 video clips that spark class discussion and clarify core legal principles. The library is organized into five series: Legal Conflicts in Business (includes specific modern business and e-commerce scenarios); Ask the Instructor (presents straightforward explanations of concepts for student review); Drama of the Law (features classic business scenarios that spark classroom participation); Real World Legal (explores conflicts that arise in a variety of business environments), and LawFlix (contains clips from many popular films). Access for students is free when bundled with a new textbook, or can be purchased at www.cengagebrain.com.

Student Guide to the Sarbanes–Oxley Act. This brief overview for business students explains the Sarbanes–Oxley Act, what is required of whom, and how it might affect students in their business life. This guide is available as an optional package with the text.

Cengage Learning's Global Economic Watch: The Impact on Business Law. Cengage Learning's Global Economic Watch adds current events into your studies through a powerful, continuously updated online suite of content, discussion forums, and more. Included in the Business portal of the Watch is a Business Law module that serves as a primer on the subprime mortgage crisis, written by Marianne M. Jennings. This easy-to-read overview covers everything from commercial paper and negotiability to underwater mortgages to the CDO instruments on Wall Street—in a way that allows students to understand what went wrong and why. Instructor resources include PowerPoints that help students understand how individual ethical choices and compliance with the law have an impact on economic systems.

Customize your text with the online Business Law module of the Global Economic Watch. Ask your Cengage/South-Western Legal Studies in Business sales representative for details, or learn more at **www.cengage.com/thewatch.**

About the Author

Professor Marianne Jennings is a member of the Department of Management in the W. P. Carey School of Business at Arizona State University and is a professor of legal and ethical studies in business. At ASU, she teaches graduate courses in the MBA program in business ethics and the legal environment of business. She served as director of the Joan and David Lincoln Center for Applied Ethics from 1995 to 1999. From 2006 to 2007, she served as the faculty director for the MBA Executive Program. Professor Jennings earned her undergraduate degree in finance and her JD from Brigham Young University. Her internships were with the Federal Public Defender and the U.S. Attorney in Nevada, and she has done consulting work for law firms, businesses, and professional groups including AES, Boeing, Dial Corporation, Mattel, Motorola, CFA Institute, Southern California Edison, the Arizona Auditor General, the cities of Phoenix, Mesa, and Tucson, the Institute of Internal Auditors, Coca-Cola, DuPont, Blue Cross Blue Shield, Motorola, Mattel, Pepsi, Hy-Vee Foods, IBM, Bell Helicopter, Amgen, Raytheon, and VIAD.

Professor Jennings has authored hundreds of articles in academic, professional, and trade journals. Currently she has six textbooks and monographs in circulation. In addition to this, the ninth edition of her textbook *Business: Its Legal, Ethical and Global Environment,* the seventh edition of her textbook *Case Studies in Business Ethics* will be published in January 2011. Her first textbook, *Real Estate Law,* had its ninth edition published in January 2010. In 1997 she was added as a co-author to *Anderson's Business and the Legal Environment,* a text whose 21st edition was published in January 2010. Her book *Business Strategy for the Political Arena* was selected in 1985 by *Library Journal* as one of its recommended books on business–government relations. *A Business Tale: A Story of Ethics, Choices, Success, and a Very Large Rabbit,* a fable about business ethics, was chosen by *Library Journal* in 2004 as its business book of the year. *A Business Tale* was also a finalist for two other literary awards for 2004. In 2000 her book on corporate governance was published by the *New York Times* MBA Pocket Series. Professor Jennings's book on long-term success, *Building a Business Through Good Times and Bad: Lessons from Fifteen Companies, Each with a Century of Dividends,* was published in October 2002 and has been used by Booz Allen Hamilton for its work on business longevity. Her latest book, *The Seven Signs of Ethical Collapse,* was published by St. Martin's Press in July 2006. Her books have been translated into five languages.

Her columns have been syndicated around the country, and her work has appeared in the *Wall Street Journal,* the *Chicago Tribune,* the *New York Times,* the *Washington Post,* and *Reader's Digest.* A collection of her essays, *Nobody Fixes Real Carrot Sticks Anymore,* first published in 1994, is still in print. She was given an Arizona Press Club award in 1994 for her work as a feature columnist. She has been a commentator on business issues on *All Things Considered* for National Public Radio.

She has conducted more than 300 workshops and seminars in the areas of business, personal, government, legal, academic, and professional ethics. She was named professor of the year in the College of Business in 1981, 1987, 2000, and 2010 and was the recipient of a Burlington Northern teaching excellence award in 1985. In 1999, she was given best article awards by the Academy of Legal Studies in Business and the Association for Government Accountants. She was given best article awards by the Institute of Internal Auditors and the Association of Government Accountants in 2001 and 2004. She has been a Dean's Council of 100 Distinguished Scholar since 1995. In 2000, the Association of Government Accountants inducted her into its Speakers' Hall of Fame. In 2005, she was named an All-Star Speaker by the Institute of Internal Auditors. In 2006 her article, "Ethics and Investment Management: True Reform," was selected by the United Kingdom's *Emerald Management Review* from 15,000 articles in 400 journals as one of the top 50 articles of 2005.

She is a contributing editor for the *Real Estate Law Journal, New Perspectives, The Smart Manager,* and the *Corporate Finance Review.* She was appointed to the Board of Editors for the *Financial Analysts Journal* in 2007. She served as editor-in-chief of the *Journal of Legal Studies Education* during 2003–2004. During 1984–1985, she served as then–Governor Bruce Babbitt's appointee to the Arizona Corporation Commission. In 1999 she was appointed by Governor Jane Dee Hull to the Arizona Commission on Character. During 1986–1988, she served as Associate Dean in the College of Business. From 1986 to 1987, she served as ASU's faculty athletic representative to the NCAA and PAC-10. From 1999 to 2009, she served as president of the Arizona Association of Scholars.

She is a member of 12 professional organizations, including the State Bar of Arizona, and has served on four boards of directors, including Arizona Public Service (now Pinnacle West Capital) (1987–2000), Zealous Capital Corporation, and the Center for Children with Chronic Illness and Disability at the University of Minnesota. She served as chair of the Bonneville International Advisory Board for KHTC/KIDR from 1994 to 1997 and was a weekly commentator on KGLE during 1998. She was appointed to the board of advisors for the Institute of Nuclear Power Operators in 2004. She has appeared on CNBC, *CBS This Morning*, the *Today Show*, and *CBS Evening New*s.

Since 1976, she has been married to Terry H. Jennings, Maricopa County Attorney's Office Deputy County Attorney, with whom she has had five children Sarah, Sam, and John, and the late Claire and Hannah Jennings.

Acknowledgments

By its ninth edition, a book has evolved to a point of trademark characteristics. This book is known for its hands-on examples and readings for business managers. That trademark evolves because of the efforts of many. There are the reviewers and adopters of the text who provide ideas, cases, and suggestions for improvement and inclusion. For this edition, the following colleagues offered their seasoned advice:

Mark S. Blodgett, *Suffolk University*
Robert H. Breakfield, *Winthrop University*
Kathryn Coulter, *Mount Mercy University*
Jonathan J. Darrow, *Plymouth State University*
Christopher Esgar, *Penn State University*
Elizabeth Gringerich, *Valparaiso University*
Robert Kenny, *Rider University*
Paul M. Klein, *Duquesne University*
Nancy Lasher, *College of New Jersey*
Sue Mota, *Bowling Green State University*
Gail P. Petravick, *Bradley University*
Steven Lance Popejoy, *University of Central Missouri*
Russell L. Welch, *University of North Texas*
Amy Oakes Wren, *Louisiana State University, Shreveport*

Any edition of a book bears the mark of the editors who work to design, refine, market, and produce it. Six editions ago, Rob Dewey saw potential for the book and applied his enthusiasm and market insights to mold a somewhat ugly duckling into a four-color swan. The book also carries the imprimatur of Steve Silverstein, who confronted me with a profound question, "Why can't those in business see these ethical dilemmas when they are in the midst of them?" His question forced me back to the drawing board and resulted in the more personal ethical dilemmas. Laura Bofinger, new to the eighth edition and continuing on to the ninth edition as Laura Ansara, remains the voice of clarity as she hones the features and brings consistency. Laura doesn't just edit; she learns and discusses the material. She has brought a steady hand of schedule to this whole process. She reasons with the often-overpowering left side of my brain. Tamborah Moore, the production editor, once again brought her eye for detail, her experience, and her insightful questions to the long haul of copyedit and page proofs. Kris Tabor has been with me since the first edition, helping with word processing, IMs, study guides, test banks, and venting. We mark 24 years of a terrific partnership with this edition.

This book also carries the unmistakable liveliness of an author who shares her life with helpful and delightful children and one tolerant husband. Since the first edition of this book, I have added four children to our first, witnessed one graduate from college, grieved over the loss of two, and seen the others grow up all too quickly in a household in which "Mom, the UPS guy is here with page proofs" was their first spoken sentence. My family consists of the most charming people I know. They have brought me stories, pop culture, and good sense with their, "Get real, Mom!" Even from their now–globally dispersed positions they call and ask, "How's the writing going?" Their vibrancy is found in the color and charm of these pages. I am grateful for their unanimous and unwavering support for my work. Finally, I am grateful to my parents who taught me through their words and examples of the importance and rewards of ethics and hard work.

Marianne Moody Jennings

Part 1

Business: Its Legal, Ethical, and Judicial Environment

Simply stated, you cannot run a successful business without knowing the law. What is legal? Where can I find the laws I need to know? How do I make decisions about legal conduct that is morally or ethically troublesome to me? What if I have a disagreement with a customer, employee, or shareholder? How and where can I resolve our differences?

This portion of the book explains what law is, where it can be found, how it is applied, and how legal disputes are resolved. But beyond the legal environment of a business, there are the ethical issues. Just because what you are doing is legal does not mean it is ethical. And why should a manager make ethical choices and behave honorably in business? Law and ethics are inextricably intertwined. A commitment to both is part of a sustainable business model.

Introduction to Law

Most people understand the law through personal experiences. Some are exposed to law through traffic tickets. Others encounter the law when a problem arises with a landlord or lease. Many wonder about their rights when their e-mail is flooded with advertisements. In recent years, many came to understand the law as they faced foreclosures on their homes and needed to know their rights. Their understanding of the law may be limited by the anger they feel about the spam or the traffic ticket. However, without traffic laws, the roads would be a study in survival of the fittest. The law is your source of assurance that if you face a foreclosure, you will have not only rights but also time to respond to your lender's actions. Each day businesses find and face legal and ethical issues in everything from privacy rights on Facebook to proper documentation of employees' citizenship.

The types of laws and the penalties for violating them vary from state to state and from city to city; but, however much they vary, laws are everywhere and at every level of government. Indeed, law is a universal, necessary foundation of an orderly society. Law helps maintain order, imposing on us certain minimum standards of conduct. When we fall short of those standards, we risk penalties. Law is made up of rules that control people's conduct and their interrelationships. Traffic laws control not only our conduct when we are driving but also our relationships with other drivers using the roads. In some instances, traffic laws give other drivers a right-of-way and we are liable to them for any injuries we cause by not following those laws.

This chapter offers an introduction to law. How is law defined? What types of laws are there? What are the purposes and characteristics of law? Where are laws found, and who enacts them? ▮

UPDATE ⬉
For up-to-date legal news, go to
mariannejennings.com

This country's planted thick with laws from coast to coast . . . and if you cut them down . . . d'you really think you could stand upright in the winds that would blow then?

A Man for All Seasons, Act I

CONSIDER...

Gottfrid Svartholm Warg, Peter Sunde, Fredrik Neij, and Carl Lundstrom are four Swedish lads who operated the Pirate Bay website. Pirate Bay allowed its users to have free access to copyrighted movies, music, and more. The site had 22 million users and was based in Sweden, a signatory country to the mutual agreement among countries for enforcement of each other's copyright laws. U.S. music companies and filmmakers asked the Swedish government to take action against Pirate Bay for its role in facilitating copyright infringement. When the Swedish government brought criminal copyright charges against Pirate Bay, the four lads said that they were just promoting free information, that they did not actually "host" any of the copyrighted materials, and that they did not profit from the exchange of music and films. "We earn $1,000,000 per year from advertising placed on the site, not from users." Is there copyright infringement? What laws apply?

Definition of Law

Philosophers and scholars throughout history have offered definitions of law. Aristotle, the early Greek philosopher, wrote that "the law is reason unaffected by desire" and "law is a form of order, and good law must necessarily mean good order." Oliver Wendell Holmes Jr., a U.S. Supreme Court justice of the early twentieth century, said, "[L]aw embodies the story of a nation's development through many centuries." Sir William Blackstone, the English philosopher and legal scholar, observed that law was "that rule of action which is prescribed by some superior and which the inferior is bound to obey." *Black's Law Dictionary* defines law as "a body of rules of action or conduct prescribed by the controlling authority, and having legal binding force." Law has been defined at least once by every philosopher, statesman, and police officer.

Law is simply the body of rules governing individuals and their relationships. Most of these rules become law through a recognized governmental authority. Laws give us basic freedoms, rights, and protections. Law also offers a model of conduct for members of society in their business and personal lives and gives them certainty of expectation. Plans, businesses, contracts, and property ownership are based on the expectation that the law will provide consistent protection of rights. Without such constancy in legal boundaries, society would be a mass of chaos and confusion.

Classifications of Law

Public versus Private Law

Public law includes those laws enacted by some authorized governmental body. State and federal constitutions and statutes are all examples of public laws, as are the state incorporation and partnership procedures, county taxation statutes, and local zoning laws.

Private law, on the other hand, is developed between two individuals. For example, landlords usually have regulations for their tenants, and these regulations are private laws. Homeowners' associations have developed an important body of private law that regulates everything from the type of landscaping for homes in a subdivision to whether homeowners can erect basketball hoops in their driveways. The terms of a contract are a form of private law for the contracting parties. Although the requirements for forming and the means for enforcing that contract may be a matter of public law, the terms for performance are the private law the parties agree to as the rules for governing their relationships. Employer rules in a corporation are also examples of private law; as long as those rules do not infringe any public rights or violate any statutory or constitutional protections, those rules define a private law relationship between employer and employee. For example, an employer rule that managers cannot have affairs with their direct reports is a private law rule and a common one in corporations.

Criminal versus Civil Law

A violation of a **criminal law** is a wrong against society. A violation of a **civil law** is a wrong against another person or persons. Criminal violations have penalties such as fines and imprisonment. When you run a red light, you have committed a criminal violation and owe society a penalty, such as a fine or imprisonment. Violations of civil laws, on the other hand, require restitution: Someone who violates a civil law must compensate the harmed party. If you do run a red light and strike and injure a pedestrian, your criminal case is society's remedy. The civil wrong in the same action requires you to pay damages to that pedestrian.

If you drive while intoxicated, you are breaking a criminal law and are subject to a fine, jail term, or license suspension. If you have an accident while driving intoxicated, you commit a civil wrong against anyone you injure. People who are injured as a result of your driving while intoxicated can file a civil suit against you to recover for injuries to their persons and property (cars).

Other differences also distinguish civil laws from criminal laws and their enforcement. For example, different rights and procedures are used in the trials of criminal cases (see Chapter 8 for more details).

Substantive versus Procedural Law

Substantive laws are those that give rights and responsibilities. **Procedural laws** provide the means for enforcing substantive rights. For example, if Zeta Corporation has breached its contract to buy 3,000 microchips from Yerba Corporation, Yerba has the substantive right to expect performance and may be able to collect damages for breach of contract by bringing suit. The laws governing how Yerba's suit is brought and the trial process are procedural laws. Procedural laws are also used in criminal cases, such as grand jury proceedings or arraignments and pleas (see Chapter 8 for more information).

Common versus Statutory Law

The term **common law** has been in existence since 1066, when the Normans conquered England and William the Conqueror sought one common set of laws for governing a then-divided England. The various customs of each locality were conglomerated so that all fiefdoms could operate under a "common" system of law. The common law came about as judges in different areas settled disputes in similar ways by consulting their fellow judges on their previous decisions before making decisions. This principle of following other decisions is referred to as *stare decisis,* meaning "let the decision stand." This process of legal reasoning is still followed today. The courts use the judicial decisions of the past in making their judgments in order to provide the consistency and constancy of the law.

As much of an improvement as it was, the common law was still just uncodified law. Because of increased trade, population, and complexities, the common law needed to be supplemented. As a result, **statutory law,** which is passed by some governmental body and written in some form, was created.

Today, in the United States, we have common law and statutory law. Some of our common law still consists of principles from the original English common law. For example, how we own and pass title to real property are areas largely developed from English common law. The body of common law continues to grow, however: the judicial system's decisions constitute a form of common law that is used in the process of *stare decisis.* Courts throughout the country look to other courts' decisions when confronted with similar cases.

Statutory law exists at all levels of government—federal, state, county, city, borough, and town. Our statutory law varies throughout our nation because of the cultural heritages of various regions. For example, the southwestern states have marital property rights statutes—often referred to as community property laws—that were influenced by the Spanish legal system implemented in Mexico. The northeastern states have different marital property laws that were influenced by English laws on property ownership. Louisiana's contract laws are based on French principles because of the early French settlements there.

Law versus Equity

Equity is a body of law that attempts to do justice when the law does not provide a remedy, when the remedy is inadequate, or when the application of the law is terribly unfair. Equity, which originated in England, came into being because the technicalities of the common law often resulted in unresolved disputes or unfair resolutions. The monarchy allowed its chancellor to hear those cases that could not be resolved in the common law courts; eventually, a separate set of equity courts developed that were not bound by rigid common law rules. These courts could get more easily to the heart of a dispute. Over time, they developed remedies not available under common law. Common law, for example, usually permitted only the recovery of monetary damages. Courts of equity, on the other hand, could issue orders, known as **injunctions,** prohibiting certain conduct or ordering certain acts.

The equitable remedies available in the **courts of chancery** were gradually combined with the legal remedies of the common law courts so that now parties can have their legal and equitable remedies determined by the same court.

Today's courts award equitable remedies when the legal remedy of money damages would be inadequate. For example, in the copyright infringement cases that appear later in this chapter, the recording and motion picture industries brought suit seeking an injunction against the individuals and companies that provided the technological means for making individual copies of movies and songs. The record companies, the movie producers, and the artists could never be adequately compensated with money for these forms of infringement because the continued activity causes the loss of their exclusive copyrights. The remedy that they sought and were given was an injunction that, within certain parameters, ordered a halt to the sites and programs that facilitated the unauthorized downloading of copyrighted materials.

Purposes of Law

Keeping Order

Laws carry some form of penalty for their violation. Antitrust violations carry a fine or imprisonment or both. Violations of civil laws also carry sanctions. If an employer discriminates against you by refusing to give you a raise or promotion because of your age, gender, or race, you can seek money damages. A driver who injures another while driving intoxicated can be prosecuted but must also pay for the damages and the costs of the injuries the other person experiences. These civil and criminal penalties for violations of laws prevent feuds and the use of primitive methods for settling disputes, such as force.

In the past five years, Congress has been particularly active in passing legislation that targets terrorist activities as a means of keeping order and safety in the United States. The USA Patriot Act addresses a variety of legal issues from search warrants to reporting requirements for banks and others engaged in high-dollar transactions (see Chapters 8, 15, and 21). The purpose of these changes under the act was to provide the means to curb terrorist activities through early detection of plots and the control of funds used for financing terrorist activities.

Influencing Conduct

Laws also influence conduct in a society. For example, securities laws require companies to make certain disclosures about those securities before they can be sold to the public. The antitrust laws passed in the early twentieth century prohibited some methods of competition, such as price fixing, and limited others, such as mergers (see Chapter 16). These types of laws changed the way businesses operate.

Honoring Expectations

Businesses commit resources, people, and time to ventures, expansion, and product development with the expectation that the contracts for those commitments will be honored and enforced according to existing law. Investors buy stock with the knowledge that they will enjoy some protection of that investment through the laws that regulate both the securities themselves and the companies in which they have invested. Laws allow prior planning based on the protections inherent in the law.

Promoting Equality

Laws have been used to achieve equality in those aspects of life in which equality is not a reality. For example, the equal-right-to-employment acts (see Chapter 19) were passed to bring greater equality to the job market. The social welfare programs of state and federal governments were created to further the cause of economic justice. The antitrust laws attempt to provide equal access to the free enterprise system.

Law as the Great Compromiser

A final and important purpose of law is to act as the great compromiser. Few people, groups, or businesses agree philosophically on how society, business, or government should be run. Law serves to mesh different views into one united view so that all parties are at least partially satisfied. When disputes occur, the courts impose the law upon the parties in an attempt to strike a compromise between two opposing views. The U.S. Supreme Court has provided compromises for the rights of businesses to be involved in the political process and make donations to candidates (see Chapter 5). In the relationship between freedom of speech and advertising regulation, the law serves as the mediator.

Characteristics of Law

Flexibility

As society changes, the law must change with it. When the United States was an agricultural nation, the issues of antitrust, employment discrimination, and securities fraud rarely arose. However, as the United States became an industrialized nation, those areas of law expanded, and they continue to expand today. As the United States further evolves into a technological and information-based society, still more areas of law will be created and developed. The area of computer fraud, for example, was unknown 30 years ago; today, most states have criminal statutes to cover such theft (see Chapter 8). The introduction of the fax machine required courts to reexamine how offers and acceptances of contracts are made, and the Internet has resulted in legislation allowing electronic signatures to have the same force and effect as signatures on paper (see Chapter 12).

CYBERLAW

Circumstances change through technology, sociology, and even biology. The law must address those changes. In the chapter's opening "Consider," those who benefited and those who were affected struggled with the newfound technology of peer-to-peer file sharing. Downloading quality music via the Internet was now possible, and the issues of copyright protection and infringement became confusing because songs could be copied in a new way. Changing circumstances resulted in judicial review of a previously unaddressed issue.

Consistency

Although the law must be flexible, it still must be predictable. Law cannot change so suddenly that parties cannot rely on its existence or protection. Being able to predict the outcome of a course of conduct allows a party to rely on a contract or dissuades a party from the commission of a crime. For a contract, a judicial remedy can be ordered for breach or nonperformance; for a crime, a prescribed punishment is the result.

Pervasiveness

The law must be pervasive and cover all necessary areas, but at the same time, it cannot infringe individual freedoms or become so complex that it is difficult to enforce. For example, laws cover the formation, operation, and dissolution of corporations. Laws govern corporate management decisions on expanding, developing, and changing the nature of the corporation. Laws also ensure that shareholders' rights are protected. The corporation has great flexibility in management, as long as it stays within these legal boundaries.

CYBERLAW

In the two following cases, the courts struggle as they try to honor the law's purposes of keeping order and honoring expectations while also grappling with the unique issues raised by modern technology and its applications and use in the context of balancing those purposes. The principle of *stare decisis* is at work in these two cases (see Chapter 3). Case 1.1, the *Sony* case, is briefed in Exhibit 1.1. A **brief** is a tool used by lawyers, law students, and judges to help them summarize a case and focus on its facts and the key points of the decision by the court. Case 1.2, the *Grokster* case, provides a fact pattern similar to that of the "Consider" problem posed at the beginning of the chapter.

| CASE 1.1 | *Sony Corporation of America v Universal City Studios, Inc.*
464 U.S. 417 (1984) |

Tape Delay: Contributory Infringement or Fair Use?

FACTS

Sony Corporation (petitioner) manufactures millions of Betamax video tape recorders (VTRs) and sells them through retail establishments (also included as petitioners in the case). The Betamax can record a broadcast off one station while the TV set is tuned to another channel. Tapes can be erased and reused. A timer in the Betamax can be used to activate and deactivate the equipment at predetermined times so the viewer/owner can record programs while not at home.

Universal City Studios, Inc. and Walt Disney Productions (respondents) produce and hold the copyrights on a substantial number of motion pictures and other audiovisual works. They can earn additional returns on these works by licensing limited showings on cable and network television, by selling syndicated rights for repeated airings on local TV, and by marketing programs on prerecorded videotapes or video discs.

Universal and Walt Disney brought a copyright infringement action against Sony and its retailers in federal district court. Universal and Walt Disney claimed that Betamax consumers were using their machines to record copyrighted works from commercially sponsored television. Evidence submitted by both parties indicated that most Betamax owners used their machines for "time-shifting," which is the practice of recording a program to view it at a later time and then erase it. Consumers used time-shifting to see programs they would otherwise miss because they were not at home, were otherwise occupied, or were viewing another station.

Universal and Walt Disney requested money damages, an accounting for profits, and an injunction against the manufacture and marketing of Betamax.

The district court found there was no infringement and denied relief. The court of appeals held that Universal and Walt Disney were entitled to enjoin the sales of Betamax VTRs or to collect a royalty on each sale. Sony appealed.

JUDICIAL OPINION

STEVENS, Justice

From its beginning, the law of copyright has developed in response to significant changes in technology. Indeed, it was the invention of a new form of copying equipment—the printing press—that gave rise to the original need for copyright protection.

We are guided by Justice Stewart's exposition of the correct approach to ambiguities in the law of copyright: "The limited scope of the copyright holder's statutory monopoly, like the limited copyright duration required by the Constitution, reflects a balance of competing claims upon the public interest: Creative work is to be encouraged and rewarded, but private motivation must ultimately serve the cause of promoting broad public availability of literature, music, and the other arts. . . ."

The Copyright Act does not expressly render anyone liable for infringement committed by another. In contrast, the Patent Act expressly brands anyone who "actively induces infringement of a patent" as an infringer, 35 U.S.C. § 271(b), and further imposes liability on certain individuals labeled "contributory" infringers. . . . The absence of such express language in the copyright statute does not preclude the imposition of liability for copyright infringements on certain parties who have not themselves engaged in the infringing activity. For vicarious liability is imposed in virtually all areas of the law, and the concept of contributory infringement is merely a species of the broader problem of identifying the circumstances in which it is just to hold one individual accountable for the actions of another.

As the District Court correctly observed, however, "the lines between direct infringement, contributory infringement, and vicarious liability are not clearly drawn. . . ." The lack of clarity in this area may, in part, be attributable to the fact that an infringer is not merely one who uses a work without authorization by the copyright owner, but also one who authorizes the use of a copyrighted work without actual authority from the copyright owner.

Petitioners in the instant case do not supply Betamax consumers with respondents' works; respondents do. Petitioners supply a piece of equipment that is generally capable of copying the entire range of programs that may be televised: those that are uncopyrighted, those that are copyrighted but may be copied without objection from the copyright holder, and those that the copyright holder would prefer not to have copied. The Betamax can be used to make authorized or unauthorized uses of copyrighted works, but the range of its potential use is much broader.

The only contact between Sony and the users of the Betamax that is disclosed by this record occurred at the moment of sale. The District Court expressly found that "no employee of Sony had either direct involvement with the allegedly infringing activity or direct contact with purchasers of Betamax who recorded copyrighted works off-the-air."

If vicarious liability is to be imposed on petitioners in this case, it must rest on the fact that they have sold equipment with constructive knowledge of the fact that their customers may use that equipment to make unauthorized copies of copyrighted material. There is no precedent in the law of copyright for the imposition of vicarious liability on such a theory.

When a charge of contributory infringement is predicated entirely on the sale of an article of commerce that is used by the purchaser to infringe a patent, the public interest in access to that article of commerce is necessarily implicated. A finding of contributory infringement does not, of course, remove the article from the market altogether; it does, however, give the patentee effective control over the sale of that item. Indeed, a finding of contributory infringement is normally the functional equivalent of holding that the disputed article is within the monopoly granted to the patentee. For that reason, in contributory infringement cases arising under the patent laws the Court has always recognized the critical importance of not allowing the patentee to extend his monopoly beyond the limits of his specific grant.

The staple article of commerce doctrine must strike a balance between a copyright holder's legitimate demand for effective—not merely symbolic—protection of the statutory monopoly, and the rights of others freely to engage in substantially unrelated areas of commerce. Accordingly, the sale of copying equipment, like the sale of other articles of commerce, does not constitute contributory infringement if the product is widely used for legitimate, unobjectionable purposes. Indeed, it need merely be capable of substantial noninfringing uses.

The question is thus whether the Betamax is capable of commercially significant noninfringing uses. In order to resolve that question, we need not explore all the different potential uses of the machine. . . .

Of course, the fact that other copyright holders may welcome the practice of time-shifting does not mean that respondents should be deemed to have granted a license to copy their programs. In this case, the record makes it perfectly clear that there are many important producers of national and local television programs who find nothing objectionable about the enlargement in the size of the television audience that results from the practice of time-shifting for private home use. The

CONTINUED

seller of the equipment that expands those producers' audiences cannot be a contributory infringer if, as is true in this case, it has had no direct involvement with any infringing activity.

If the Betamax were used to make copies for a commercial or profit-making purpose, such use would presumptively be unfair. The contrary presumption is appropriate here, however, because the District Court's findings plainly establish that time-shifting for private home use must be characterized as a noncommercial, nonprofit activity. Moreover, when one considers the nature of a televised copyrighted audiovisual work, and that time-shifting merely enables a viewer to see such a work which he had been invited to witness in its entirety free of charge, the fact that the entire work is reproduced does not have its ordinary effect of militating against a finding of fair use.

The timeshifter no more steals the program by watching it once than does the live viewer, and the live viewer is no more likely to buy pre-recorded videotapes than is the timeshifter. Indeed, no live viewer would buy a pre-recorded videotape if he did not have access to a VTR.

Today, the larger the audience for the original telecast, the higher the price plaintiffs can demand from broadcasters from rerun rights. There is no survey within the knowledge of this court to show that the rerun audience is comprised of persons who have not seen the program. In any event, if ratings can reflect Betamax recording, original audiences may increase and, given market practices, this should aid plaintiffs rather than harm them.

Of course, plaintiffs may fear that the Betamax will keep the tapes long enough to satisfy all their interest in the program and will, therefore, not patronize later theater exhibitions. It should also be noted that there is no evidence to suggest that the public interest in later theatrical exhibitions of motion pictures will be reduced any more by Betamax recording than it already is by the television broadcast of the film.

. . . [We] must conclude that this record amply supports the District Court's conclusion that home time-shifting is fair use. . . . [T]he Court of Appeals erred in holding that the statute as presently written bars such conduct.

Reversed.

CASE QUESTIONS

1. What is "time-shifting"?

2. What is the significance of the fair use doctrine in the court's decision?

3. What is the standard for imposing "vicarious liability for infringement"? What does the court examine in determining copyright vicarious infringement liability?

4. Has Sony infringed the rights of Universal and Walt Disney? Explain your answer.

EXHIBIT 1.1   Sample Case Brief

Name of case:	*Sony Corporation of America v Universal City Studios, Inc.*
Court:	U.S. Supreme Court
Citation:	464 U.S. 417 (1984)
Parties and their roles:	Sony Corporation (petitioner and defendant); Universal Studios, Inc. and Walt Disney Productions (plaintiffs and respondents)
Facts:	*Sony* manufactures video tape recorders (VTRs) that can record programs in homes. Universal and Walt Disney produce movies. They claimed that Sony's VTRs were being used to copy their protected and copyrighted films and that they were therefore entitled to some payment for this type of machine use.
Issues:	Do Sony's VTR and its use by its customers infringe on the filmmakers' copyright?
Lower court decision:	The district court found no infringement. The court of appeals found for Universal and Walt Disney and held that they were entitled to either halt the sales of the VTRs or collect a royalty on each.
Decision:	No infringement by Sony.

Reasoning:	Congress did not give absolute control over all uses of copyright materials. Some uses (fair uses) are permitted. Consumer uses of the machines for time-shifting to watch shows at another time were not only noncommercial, but they were beneficial to those who produced and advertised on the shows because they permitted greater audience exposure. Further, Sony could not be held vicariously liable for infringement using its equipment when it was not a party to such activity and the equipment had valuable uses apart from infringement.

CASE 1.2

Metro-Goldwyn-Mayer Studios Inc. v Grokster, Ltd.
545 U.S. 913 (2005)[1]

Copyright Infringement? Really, It's Just a Little Peer-to-Peer File Sharing

FACTS

Grokster, Ltd., and StreamCast Networks, Inc. (Respondents/defendants) distribute free software products that allow computer users to share electronic files through peer-to-peer networks. With no central computer server required in these networks, the high-bandwidth capacity server storage space issues disappear. Since copies of a file (particularly a popular one) are available on many users' computers, file requests and retrievals move faster than on other types of networks, and can take place between any computers that remain connected to the network without risk of a server glitch. Peer-to-peer networks are used by universities, government agencies, corporations, and libraries to store and distribute electronic files.

Grokster and StreamCast software users have generally used the software networks for sharing copyrighted music and video files without authorization. A group of copyright holders (MGM for short, but including motion picture studios, recording companies, songwriters, and music publishers) (Petitioners) sued Grokster and StreamCast for their users' copyright infringements through the distribution of their software that allows users to reproduce and distribute copyrighted works in violation of the Copyright Act.

Grokster and StreamCast do not know when files are copied, but MGM commissioned a statistician to conduct a systematic search, and his study showed that nearly 90 percent of the files available for download were copyrighted works. . . . [t]he probable scope of copyright infringement is staggering. Grokster and StreamCast dispute this figure and argue that free copying even of copyrighted works may be authorized by the rightholders. They also argue that potential noninfringing uses of their software are significant, although infrequent in use. Some musical performers have gained new audiences by distributing their copyrighted works for free across peer-to-peer networks, and some distributors of unprotected content have used peer-to-peer networks to disseminate files, Shakespeare being an example. StreamCast has given Morpheus users the opportunity to download the briefs in this very case, though their popularity has not been quantified.

StreamCast gave away a software program of a kind known as OpenNap, designed as compatible with the Napster program. The OpenNap program was engineered "to leverage Napster's 50 million user base."

One StreamCast proposed ad read: "Napster Inc. has announced that it will soon begin charging you a fee. That's if the courts don't order it shut down first. What will you do to get around it?" Another proposed ad touted StreamCast's software as the "#1 alternative to Napster" and asked "[w]hen the lights went off at Napster . . . where did the users go?" StreamCast even planned to flaunt the illegal uses of its software; when it launched the OpenNap network, the chief technology officer of the company averred that "[t]he goal is to get in trouble with the law and get sued. It's the best way to get in the new[s]." Grokster launched its own OpenNap system called Swaptor and inserted digital codes into its website so that computer users using Web search engines to look for "Napster" or "[f]ree filesharing" would be directed to the Grokster website, where they could download the Grokster software.

Grokster and StreamCast receive no revenue from users, who obtain the software itself for nothing.

CONTINUED

Instead, both companies generate income by selling advertising space, and they stream the advertising to Grokster and Morpheus users while they are employing the programs. As the number of users of each program increases, advertising opportunities become worth more. While there is doubtless some demand for free Shakespeare, the evidence shows that free access to copyrighted work is most important to users.

The District Court held that those who used the Grokster and Morpheus software to download copyrighted media files directly infringed MGM's copyrights, but granted summary judgment in favor of Grokster and StreamCast as to any liability arising from distribution of the then current versions of their software. The Court of Appeals affirmed. MGM appealed.

JUDICIAL OPINION

SOUTER, Justice

The question is under what circumstances the distributor of a product capable of both lawful and unlawful use is liable for acts of copyright infringement by third parties using the product. . . .

Digital distribution of copyrighted material threatens copyright holders as never before, because every copy is identical to the original, copying is easy, and many people (especially the young) use file-sharing software to download copyrighted works. As the case has been presented to us, these fears are said to be offset by the different concern that imposing liability, not only on infringers but on distributors of software based on its potential for unlawful use, could limit further development of beneficial technologies.

The argument for imposing indirect liability in this case is, however, a powerful one, given the number of infringing downloads that occur every day using StreamCast's and Grokster's software. When a widely shared service or product is used to commit infringement, it may be impossible to enforce rights in the protected work effectively against all direct infringers, the only practical alternative being to go against the distributor of the copying device for secondary liability on a theory of contributory or vicarious infringement.

In *Sony Corp. v Universal City Studios*, 464 U.S. at 434, this Court addressed a claim that secondary liability for infringement can arise from the very distribution of a commercial product. . . . Because the VCR was "capable of commercially significant noninfringing uses," we held the manufacturer could not be faulted solely on the basis of its distribution.

In sum, where an article is "good for nothing else" but infringement, there is no legitimate public interest in its unlicensed availability, and there is no injustice in presuming or imputing an intent to infringe. . . . Conversely, the doctrine absolves the equivocal conduct of selling an item with substantial lawful as well as unlawful uses, and limits liability to instances of more acute fault than the mere understanding that some of one's products will be misused. It leaves breathing room for innovation and a vigorous commerce.

Grokster and StreamCast reply by citing evidence that their software can be used to reproduce public domain works, and they point to copyright holders who actually encourage copying. Even if infringement is the principal practice with their software today, they argue, the noninfringing uses are significant and will grow.

Because the Circuit found the StreamCast and Grokster software capable of substantial lawful use, it concluded on the basis of its reading of *Sony* that neither company could be held liable, since there was no showing that their software, being without any central server, afforded them knowledge of specific unlawful uses.

This view of *Sony*, however, was in error, converting the case from one about liability resting on imputed intent to one about liability on any theory.

. . . Nothing in *Sony* requires courts to ignore evidence of intent if there is such evidence, and the case was never meant to foreclose rules of fault-based liability derived from the common law.

The classic case of direct evidence of unlawful purpose occurs when one induces commission of infringement by another, or "entic[es] or persuad[es] another" to infringe, Black's Law Dictionary 790 (8th ed. 2004), as by advertising. Thus at common law a copyright or patent defendant who "not only expected but invoked [infringing use] by advertisement" was liable for infringement "on principles recognized in every part of the law."

For the same reasons that *Sony* took the staple-article doctrine of patent law as a model for its copyright safe-harbor rule, the inducement rule, too, is a sensible one for copyright. We adopt it here, holding that one who distributes a device with the object of promoting its use to infringe copyright, as shown by clear expression or other affirmative steps taken to foster infringement, is liable for the resulting acts of infringement by third parties. We are, of course, mindful of the need to keep from trenching on regular commerce or discouraging the development of technologies with lawful and unlawful potential. The inducement rule, instead, premises liability on purposeful, culpable expression and conduct, and thus does nothing to compromise legitimate commerce or discourage innovation having a lawful promise.

Here, the summary judgment record is replete with other evidence that Grokster and StreamCast, unlike the manufacturer and distributor in *Sony*, acted with a purpose to cause copyright violations by use of software suitable for illegal use.

. . . [e]ach company showed itself to be aiming to satisfy a known source of demand for copyright infringement, the market comprising former Napster users. StreamCast's internal documents made constant reference to Napster, it initially distributed its Morpheus software through an OpenNap program compatible with Napster, it advertised its OpenNap program to Napster users, and its Morpheus software functions as Napster did except that it could be used to distribute more kinds of files, including copyrighted movies and software programs. Grokster's name is apparently derived from Napster, it too initially offered an OpenNap program, its software's function is likewise comparable to Napster's, and it attempted to divert queries for Napster onto its own Web site. Grokster and StreamCast's efforts to supply services to former Napster users, deprived of a mechanism to copy and distribute what were overwhelmingly infringing files, indicate a principal, if not exclusive, intent on the part of each to bring about infringement.

[Neither company] attempted to develop filtering tools or other mechanisms to diminish the infringing activity using their software. As the record shows, the more the software is used, the more ads are sent out and the greater the advertising revenue becomes. Since the extent of the software's use determines the gain to the distributors, the commercial sense of their enterprise turns on high-volume use, which the record shows is infringing. This evidence alone would not justify an inference of unlawful intent, but viewed in the context of the entire record its import is clear. . . . The unlawful objective is unmistakable.

We hold that one who distributes a device with the object of promoting its use to infringe copyright, as shown by clear expression or other affirmative steps taken to foster infringement, is liable for the resulting acts of infringement by third parties. The judgment of the Court of Appeals is vacated, and the case is remanded for further proceedings consistent with this opinion.

CASE Q UESTIONS

1. What is the difference between Sony's Betamax and Grokster's software program?

2. What did Grokster argue as a means for avoiding vicarious liability for copyright infringement? What is the significance of "other lawful means of use"?

3. List the critical facts that tipped the Court's decision against Grokster.

CONSIDER...   1.1

The USENET network, created over 20 years ago by USENET.com, Inc., is a global system of online bulletin boards on which users, also called subscribers (who pay between $4.95 and $18.95 per month), may post their own messages or read messages posted by others. Articles are also posted to the bulletin boards and are called "newsgroups." Users can make search requests for articles. Once an article is retrieved, software converts the text file into binary content, a process that is automated and virtually invisible to the user. Music files can be transmitted via this process as well. Unlike other forms of file-sharing networks, articles on the USENET are saved to news servers instead of another end user's personal computer; a user accesses these articles and content files by connecting to these central servers. Based on a statistical analysis, over 94 percent of all content files offered in these binary newsgroups were found to be infringing on copyrighted music or articles. USENET marketed its service as "a safe alternative to peer-to-peer file sharing services that are being shut down." Internal communications at the company showed that owners reflected when Napster and Kazaa began to have problems from copyright owners' enforcement of their rights that "[t]his made the way for Usenet to get back in the game." USENET's marketing specialist described the company service as being targeted to "people who want to get free music, ilegal [sic] or not." Several publishers, music companies, and film producers have filed a vicarious copyright infringement suit against USENET. USENET maintains that it did not participate in infringement activities, it did not know about infringing activities, and that its service had uses other than the downloading of copyrighted materials, i.e., it was a means for exchanging ideas, posting comments, and referring others to sites for reading articles. Who is correct? Is USENET involved in infringement?

CONTINUED

THINK: Before answering this problem, review the decisions in the *Sony* and *Grokster* cases. Recall the following.

1. We can record movies and songs for private, noncommercial use or fair use.

2. Technology that permits copying of copyrighted materials is not an automatic violation of copyright law if

    a. The technology has other uses.

    b. The developer would have no way to know who was using its product for infringement.

3. It is possible for a company and officers who develop technology that permits recording of copyrighted materials to be "vicariously liable" for infringement if they are aware that their technology or product is used for infringement, they benefit from the infringement uses, and they take no steps to halt the infringement despite the capability to do so.

APPLY: The use of the Sony Betamax for recording TV programs for individual use was fair use under the copyright laws. The mass sharing of copyrighted music via the Grokster and StreamCast programs was found to be more than fair use. Further, the court determined that the Grokster folks were promoting their programs as a substitute for the original Napster technology that had been outlawed for copyright infringement.

ANSWER: You can answer this "Consider" by reviewing the issues these facts have in common with the facts from the *Sony* and *Grokster* cases. Think through the following questions: Does the company still make the copying possible? Will the copying be done for more than personal use? Would consumers not buy copyrighted materials as a result? How does USENET view its service? What difference do USENET's subscriber fees make? Are there other uses for the technology the company provides? Once you have answered these questions, you have your answer. Lack of knowledge about what users are doing may not be enough to provide copyright infringement liability immunity for USENET. As you think about the answer to this "Consider," refer back to the chapter opening "Consider" and develop your conclusions on whether the "pirates" were involved in vicarious copyright infringement. [*Arista Records LLC v Usenet.com, Inc.*, 633 F.Supp.2d 124 (S.D.N.Y. 2009) and *Arista Records, LLC v Lime Group LLC*, 2010 WL 2291485 (S.D.N.Y.)]

For the Manager's Desk

Re: Grokster Friends and Foes

One of the interesting pieces of background information on the *Grokster* case is the parties, in addition to MGM and Grokster, who filed *amicus curiae* (friend of the court) briefs in the case.

Managers in many companies and industries realized their strategic interests in the outcome of this case. Looking at the following list, discuss whose position you believe these parties took when they wrote their briefs in support.

a. Intellectual Property and Technology Law Professors for the U.S. Public Policy Committee of the Association for Computing Machinery

b. The American Library Association

c. The Consumer Electronics Association

d. Intel Corporation

e. Cellular Telecommunications & Internet Association

f. The American Civil Liberties Union

g. Office of the Commissioner of Baseball; the National Basketball Association; the National Football League

h. Don Henley, Glenn Frey, Joe Walsh, and Timothy B. Schmit (the Eagles); Jimmy Buffett; Kenny "Babyface" Edmonds; Mickey Hart and Bill Kreutzmann (of the Grateful Dead); Sheryl Crow; and Kix Brooks

i. Napster, LLC; Tennessee Pacific Group, LLC, d/b/a Pass Along Networks; Wurld Media, Inc.; and Virtual Music Stores Ltd.

BUSINESS STRATEGY

The Dangers of Lawsuits as a Strategy

Another important lesson of both the *Sony* and *Grokster* cases is the importance of business strategy. The VTR was the beginning of Blockbuster, video rentals, and a new revenue stream for Universal, Disney, and all other filmmakers. The possibilities still seem endless as the technology has evolved into DVD and online purchases. DVD films include commentary from directors and additional scenes cut from the original film.

The free downloading of songs was curbed by copyright laws, and the law is one business tool that can be used to enforce rights and protect stability. However, sometimes the law is a stopgap measure or even something that interferes with the strategic planning for technological changes. Litigation is often not the best resolution for a problem. Here, both industries needed to look at the technology's possibilities and use it, not try to stop it. By 2006, online song purchases were the most popular method for purchasing music. Fueled by Apple and its iTunes site, the focus of the music industry has shifted completely. The litigation and infringement were symptoms of a lack of vision and strategy within the industry for technology's new ways for buying music.

Ethical Issues

What do you think of the ethics of peer-to-peer file sharing? Is peer-to-peer file sharing the same as copyright infringement? Who is harmed by the activity? Who is helped? What would happen if there were no compensation for music composers and lyricists?

The Theory of Law: Jurisprudence

Law is the compromise of conflicting ideas. Not only do people differ in their thinking on the types of specific laws, they also differ on the theory behind the law or the values a legal system should try to advance or encourage. Many can agree on the definition of law and its purposes but still differ on how those purposes are best accomplished. The incorporation of theories or values into the legal process is, perhaps, what makes each society's laws different and causes law to change as society changes its values. These different theories or value bases for law are found in an area of legal study called **jurisprudence,** a Latin term meaning "wisdom of the law." In many cases, how the law should work is unclear. Conflicting philosophical views often come together in litigation. Judges and lawmakers must struggle to do the best good for the most members of society. The Manager's Desk called "A Primer on Jurisprudence" provides a brief overview on the philosophy of law from some scholars of jurisprudence. As you read through the various philosophical views, you will be able to see that issues arise with the uniform application of laws to all situations. The moral view of law shapes our responses to and actions in those situations.

BUSINESS PLANNING TIP

Failure to anticipate technological changes results in significant revenue losses under contracts for copyrighted works or patented products. For example, many actors, writers, and others involved with television shows of the 1950s and 1960s do not enjoy the royalties from their shows,
which run in what seems to be perpetual syndication on networks such as TV Land and Nick at Nite that feature only television shows of other generations. Those involved in the production of these shows did not foresee what technology would permit. Walt Disney and Universal did not anticipate the VTR and its capability.

Technology clauses in royalty agreements for patents and copyrights that cover any future means of distribution, whether by wire, sound, or satellite, provide an open-ended agreement for royalty coverage from evolving technology distributions and uses.

For the Manager's Desk

Re: A Primer on Jurisprudence (Legal Philosophy in a Nutshell; Five Minutes of Legal Philosophy)

First Minute: Positive Law

"An order is an order," the soldier is told. "A law is a law," says the jurist. The soldier, however, is required neither by duty nor by law to obey an order that he knows to have been issued with a felony or misdemeanor in mind, while the jurists, since the last of the natural law theorists among them disappeared a hundred years ago, have recognized no such exceptions to the validity of a law or to the requirement of obedience by those subject to it. A law is valid because it is a law, and it is a law if in the general run of cases it has the power to prevail.

In the end the positivistic theory equates the law with power; there is law only where there is power.

Second Minute: Benefiting People

There have been attempts to supplement or replace this tenet with another: Law is what benefits the people. That is, arbitrariness, breach of contract, and illegality, provided only that they benefit the people, are law. Practically speaking, that means that every whim and caprice of the despot, punishment without laws or judgment, lawless killing of the sick—whatever the state authorities deem to benefit the people—is law. That *can* mean that the private benefit of those in power is regarded as a public benefit.

No, this tenet should not be read as, Whatever benefits the people is law. Rather, it is the other way around: Only what is law benefits the people.

Third Minute: Justice

Law is the will to justice, and justice means: To judge without regard to person, to treat everyone according to the same standard.

If one applauds the assassination of political opponents and orders the murder of those of another race while meting out the most cruel, degrading punishments for the same acts committed against those of one's own persuasion, that is neither justice nor law.

If laws consciously deny the will to justice, if, for example, they grant and deny human rights arbitrarily, then these laws lack validity, the people owe to them no obedience, and even the jurists must find the courage to deny their legal character.

Fourth Minute: Safety and Certainty

Surely laws as such, even bad laws, have value nonetheless—the value of safety regarding the law against doubt. And surely, owing to human imperfection, the three values of law—public benefit, legal certainty, and justice—cannot always be united harmoniously in laws. It remains, then, only to consider whether validity is to be granted to bad, detrimental, or unjust laws for the sale of legal certainty or whether it is to be denied them because they are unjust or socially detrimental.

One thing, however, must be indelibly impressed on the consciousness of the people and the jurists: There can be laws that are so unjust, so socially detrimental, that their validity, indeed their very character as laws, must be denied.

Fifth Minute: Natural Law

There are, therefore, principles of law that are stronger than any statute, so that a law conflicting with these principles is devoid of validity. One calls these principles the *natural law* or the *law of reason*. To be sure, their details remain somewhat doubtful, but the work of the centuries has established a solid core of them and they have come to enjoy such a far-reaching consensus in the declaration of human and civil rights that only the deliberate skeptic can still entertain doubts about some of them.

In religious language, the same thoughts have been recorded in Biblical passages. On the one hand, it is written that you are to obey the authorities who have power over you. But then on the other, it is also written that you are to obey God before man—and this is not simply a pious wish, but a valid proposition of law. The tension between these two directives cannot, however, be relieved by appealing to a third—say, to the maxim Render unto Caesar the things that are Caesar's and unto God the things that are God's. For this directive, too, leaves the boundary in doubt. Rather, it leaves the solution to the voice of God, which speaks to the conscience of the individual only in the exceptional case.

Discussion Questions

1. What is the positivist's view of law? Does it matter to a positivist whether a law is just?

2. What type of law is stronger than any statute? What are its origins? Do you have an example of a principle today that would fit into this type of law?

3. If a law is unjust, is obedience to that law necessary? How should people respond or react to unjust laws? Is civil disobedience justified?

4. What does the author conclude about the boundaries of law and these philosophical issues?

Source: "Funf Minuten Rechtsphilosophie," by Gustave Radbruch, translated by Stanley L. Paulson, in *Rechtsphilosophie,* and edited by Erik Wolf and Hans-Peter Schneider (Stuttgart: K. F. Koehler Verlag, 1973), pp. 327–329. Reprinted with permission of K. F. Koehler Verlag.

Justice Oliver Wendell Holmes, in "The Common Law," had a different view of the theory of law than that expressed in "A Primer on Jurisprudence." In his famous essay written in 1918, at the height of World War I, Holmes rejected the notion of natural law. His essay began with the famous phrase, "The life of the law has not been logic; it has been experience." Holmes's opinion is that our interactions with each other constitute the foundation of law.

> *The jurists who believe in natural law seem to be in that naive state of mind that accepts what has been familiar and accepted by them and their neighbors as something that must be accepted by all men everywhere. No doubt it is true that, so far as we can see ahead, some arrangements and the rudiments of familiar institutions seem to be necessary elements in any society that may spring from our own and that would seem to us to be civilized—some form of permanent association between the sexes—some residue of property individually owned—some mode of binding oneself to a specified future conduct—at the bottom of it all, some protection for the person.*
>
> *It is true that beliefs and wishes have a transcendental basis in the sense that their foundation is arbitrary. You cannot help entertaining and feeling them, and there is an end of it.*
>
> *If they live in society, so far as we can see, there are further conditions. If I do live with others they tell me what I must do if I wish to remain alive. If I do live with others they tell me what I must do and abstain from doing various things or they will put the screws to me.[2]*

Roscoe Pound, another legal philosopher and dean of Harvard Law School for 20 years, had a different view of jurisprudence from Justice Holmes. His view was that law exists as the result of those who happen to be in power. In 1941, Pound wrote his famous credo, called "My Philosophy of Law."

> *I think of law as in one sense a highly specialized form of social control in a developed politically organized society—a social control through the systematic and orderly application of the force of such a society. Moreover, it operates through a judicial process and an administrative process, which also go by the name of law. . . .[3]*

CONSIDER...   1.2

Apply the theories of jurisprudence to the following situations.

1. Maj. Gen. Antonio M. Taguba led an investigation of the conduct of U.S. soldiers in the Abu Ghraib prison in Iraq. The 54-page report documented brutal treatment of Iraqi prisoners, torture, and humiliation, all in violation of either the Geneva Convention for the treatment of prisoners of war or the standards of the Red Cross. Gen. Taguba referred to the treatment of the prisoners as consisting of "egregious acts and grave violations of international law."[4] One of the findings of the report is that the soldiers serving as prison guards had little training. General Taguba recommended training for soldiers in when to disobey orders. A fellow officer said of General Taguba, "If you want the truth; he's going to tell you the truth. He's a stand-up guy."[5]

    General Taguba's father was Staff Sgt. Tomas Taguba, a man who fought in the Battle of Bataan and was taken prisoner by the Japanese. He escaped from prison there and joined the fighters in Japan who opposed the government.

    Based on these brief descriptions of these two men, what philosophy of law do you think they would follow?

2. A supervisor has ordered an employee to inflate the company's earnings for the quarter so that their unit can meet their goals and attain their bonuses. Must the employee obey?

3. Is a businessperson who believes the tax system to be unconstitutional justified in refusing to pay taxes? How will society react to such a position?

4. Is there any example of a law that is accepted by everyone in society? What about the laws against speeding? What about the laws that restrict who can marry? What happens, according to the philosophers, when there is no common agreement on what the law should be?

Sources of Law

Laws exist in different forms at every level of government. As discussed earlier, law exists not only in statutory form but also in its common law form through judicial decisions. Statutory law exists at all levels of government. Statutes are written laws enacted by some governmental body with the proper authority—legislatures, city governments, and counties—and published and made available for public use and knowledge. These written statutes are sometimes referred to as codified law, and their sources, as well as constitutions, are covered in the following sections.

Constitutional Law

The U.S. Constitution and the constitutions of the various states are unique forms of law. **Constitutions** are not statutes because they cannot be added to, amended, or repealed with the same ease as can statutes. Constitutions are the law of the people, and are changed only by lengthier and more demanding procedures than those used to repeal statutes.

Constitutions tend to protect general rights, such as speech, religion, and property (see Chapter 5 for a more complete discussion). They also provide a framework for all other forms of laws. The basic rights and protections afforded in them cannot be abridged or denied by the other sources of law. In other words, a statute's boundaries are formed by constitutionally protected rights. Exhibit 1.2 is an illustration of the sources of law; constitutional law is at the base of the pyramid diagram because of its inviolate status.

Statutory Law at the Federal Level

Congressional Law

Congress is responsible for statutory law at the federal level. The laws passed by Congress become part of the **United States Code (U.S.C.).** Examples of such laws are the 1933 and 1934 Securities Acts (see Chapter 21), the Sherman Act and other antitrust laws (see Chapter 16), the Equal Employment Opportunity Act (see Chapter 19), the National Labor Relations Act (see Chapter 18), the Truth-in-Lending Act (see Chapter 14), the USA Patriot Act (see Chapters 8 and 21), and the Internal Revenue Code (see Chapter 20).

Statutes from the U.S.C. are referenced or *cited* by a standard form of legal shorthand, often referred to as a **cite** or **citation.** The number of the title is put in front of "U.S.C." to tell which volume of the Code to go to. For example, "15 U.S.C." refers to Title 15 of the U.S. Code (Title 15 happens to cover securities). There may be more than one volume that is numbered "15," however. To enable you to find the volume you need, the reference or cite has a section (§) number

EXHIBIT 1.2   Sources of Law

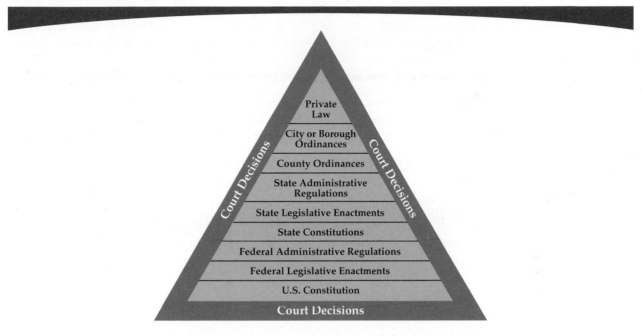

following it. This section number is the particular statute referenced, and you must look for the volume of Title 15 that contains that section. For example, the first volume of Title 15 contains §§ 1–11. A full reference or cite to a United States Code statute looks like this: 15 U.S.C. § 77. When a U.S.C. cite is given, the law cited will be a federal law passed by Congress.

Executive Orders

Executive orders are laws of the executive branch of the federal government and deal with those matters under the direct control of that branch. For example, on his second day as president, Bill Clinton issued an executive order reversing George H. W. Bush's (41) "gag rule" on abortion counseling. The same order also reversed a previous executive order banning the use of federal funds for research involving fetal tissue obtained from abortions. During his first 100 days in office, George W. Bush (43) issued an executive order banning the use of federal funds for abortion in other countries receiving U.S. financial assistance. On his second day in office, Barack Obama issued an executive order prohibiting the use of waterboarding in questioning military combatants who are in U.S. custody.

Federal Administrative Regulations

The federal government has administrative agencies that serve the functions of promulgation of rules for developing specifics such as forms and time requirements for carrying out the legislative enactments of Congress in addition to enforcing both the laws and regulations (see Chapter 6 for more details). Examples of federal agencies include the Environmental Protection Agency (EPA), the Equal Employment Opportunity Commission (EEOC), and the Securities and Exchange Commission (SEC).

Federal regulations are found in the Code of Federal Regulations (CFR), a set of paperback volumes that is published once each year. A citation from the CFR has a structure similar to that of a U.S.C. cite. For example, 12 C.F.R. §226 is volume 12 of the CFR and section 226 is a section that deals with credit disclosure rights.

Statutory Law at the State Level

As noted on p. 18, each state has its own constitution. State constitutions cannot circumvent or cancel any of the rights afforded under the U.S. Constitution. These state constitutions provide the authority for the state statutory law structure.

Legislative Law and State Codes

Each state has its own code containing the laws passed by its legislature. **State codes** contain the states' criminal laws, laws for incorporation, laws governing partnerships, and contract laws. Much of the law that affects business is found in these state codes. Some of the laws passed by the states are **uniform laws,** which are drafted by groups of businesspeople, scholars, and lawyers in an effort to make interstate business less complicated. For example, the **Uniform Commercial Code (UCC),** which has been adopted in 49 states, governs contracts for the sale of goods, commercial paper, security interests, and other types of commercial transactions. Having this uniform law in the various states gives businesses the opportunity to deal across state lines with some certainty. Other uniform acts passed by many state legislatures include the Uniform Partnership Act (Revised), the Uniform Residential Landlord and Tenant Act, the Model Business Corporation Act, and the Uniform Probate Code.

State Administrative Law

Just as at the federal level, state governments have administrative agencies with the power to pass regulations dealing with the statutes and powers given by the state legislatures. For example, most states have an agency to handle incorporations and the status of corporations in the state. Most states also have a tax agency to handle income or sales taxes in the state.

Local Laws of Cities, Counties, and Townships

In addition to federal and state statutes, local governments can pass **ordinances** or statutes within their areas of power or control. For example, cities and counties have the authority to handle zoning issues, and the municipal code outlines the zoning system and whatever means of enforcement and specified penalties apply. These local laws govern lesser issues, such as dog licensing, curfews, and loitering.

Private Laws

Private laws are a final source of written law and are found, for example, in contracts and landlord regulations. These private laws are enforceable provided they are not inconsistent with rights and protections afforded under the other sources of law (see Chapters 3 and 4).

Court Decisions

Looking at Exhibit 1.2, you can see that all of the sources of law just covered are surrounded in the pyramid by the term *Court Decisions.* Often the language in a statute is unclear, or perhaps whether the statute or ordinance applies in a particular situation is unclear. When these ambiguities or omissions occur in the statutory language, courts provide interpretation or clarification of the law when disputing parties bring suit. These court decisions are then read along with the statutory language in order to give a complete analysis of the scope and intent of the statute. The *Sony* and *Grokster* cases illustrate the interpretation of copyright laws in cases involving infringement with new technologies.

Introduction to International Law

Businesses now operate in a global market. Companies headquartered in Japan have factories in the United States, and U.S. firms have manufacturing plants in South America. Trade and political barriers to economic development no longer exist. An international market requires businesses to understand laws beyond those of the United States.

International law is not a neat body of law like contract law or the UCC. Rather, it is a combination of the laws of various countries, international trade customs, and international agreements. Article 38(1) of the Statute of the International Court of Justice (a court of the United Nations that countries consent to have resolve disputes) is a widely recognized statement of the sources of international law:

(a) *international conventions, whether general or particular, establishing rules expressly recognized by the contesting states;*

(b) *international custom as evidence of a general practice accepted as law;*

(c) *the general principles of law recognized by civilized nations;*

(d) *judicial decisions and the teachings of the most highly qualified publicists of the various nations, as subsidiary means for the determination of rules of law.*

Custom

Every country has its boundaries for allowable behavior, and these boundaries are unwritten but recognized laws. The standards of behavior are reflected in statements made by government officials. Among countries that have the same standards of acceptable behavior, there exists an international code of custom. Custom develops over time and through repeated conduct. For example, the continental shelf sea territorial standard came into existence in 1945 when President Harry S. Truman, in the Truman Declaration, established mileage boundary lines. Most countries accepted the declaration because it reflected their customary operations. By 1958, the standard had become a part of the Geneva Convention.

Each individual country has its own customs peculiar to business trade. Businesses operating in various countries must understand those customs in negotiating contracts and conducting operations within those countries. For example, unlike the United States, most countries do not offer a warranty protection on goods and instead follow a philosophy of *caveat emptor*, "Let the buyer beware." Other countries also do not recognize the extensive rules of insurance and risk followed here with respect to the shipment of goods. Multinational firms must make provisions for protection of shipments in those countries with different standards.

At one time, the customs of China with respect to intellectual property, most particularly computer software, lagged behind those of Europe and the United

States. Chinese custom was to separate infringement into two categories: ordinary acts and serious acts. Ordinary infringement is not regarded as a legal issue and requires only that the party apologize, destroy the software, and not engage in infringement again. Courts were rarely involved in ordinary infringement cases. However, the U.S. government demanded more protection for its copyright holders by imposing trade sanctions, and China eventually agreed to revise its customs and laws to afford protection. In this case, China's customs had to be changed to provide protection similar to that afforded in other countries.

Treaties

A **treaty** is an agreement between or among nations on a subject of international law signed by the leaders of the nations and ratified by the nations' governing bodies. In the United States, treaties are ratified by the Senate and are included in the pyramid (Exhibit 1.2) as federal legislative enactments.

Treaties can be between two nations—**bilateral treaties**—or **multilateral treaties,** those that are made among several nations. Other treaties, recognized by almost all nations, are called general or **universal treaties.** Universal treaties are a reflection of widely followed standards of behavior. For example, the Geneva Convention is a universal treaty covering the treatment of prisoners of war. The Vienna Convention is a universal treaty covering diplomatic relations. The Warsaw Convention is a treaty that addresses issues of liability for injuries to passengers and property during international air travel.

Private Law in International Transactions

Those businesses involved in multinational trade and production rely heavily on private law to assure performance of contractual obligations. Even though each country has a different set of laws, all of them recognize the autonomy of parties in an international trade transaction and allow the parties to negotiate contract terms that suit their needs, as long as none of the terms is illegal. **Party autonomy** allows firms to operate uniformly throughout the world if their contracts are recognized as valid in most countries. For example, most international trade contracts have a choice-of-law clause whereby the parties decide which country's law will apply to their disputes under the contract.

International Organizations

Some international organizations provide the means for facilitating multinational commercial transactions. For example, the World Trade Organization (WTO) (see Chapter 7 for more details) provides a Dispute Settlement Body (DSB), a forum for resolving trade disputes related to multilateral treaties.

The Doctrines of International Law

There are a number of principles of international law that are widely accepted and honored by most countries. These include the **act of state doctrine,** a theory that protects governments from reviews of their actions by courts in other countries. In any action in which the government of a country has taken steps to condemn or confiscate property, the courts of other countries will not interfere (see Chapter 7 for a full discussion of this and other doctrines of international law).

For the Manager's Desk

Re: How International Ice Skating Scandals Are Resolved

In an example of private law at work, the International Olympic Committee (IOC) dealt with issues of vote exchanges among judges for the pairs figure skating competition. Canadian skaters David Pelletier and Jamie Sale were awarded a silver medal after what was called "the performance of a lifetime" in the competition. Their performance was flawless, although not as difficult as that of Elena Berezhnaya and Anton Sikharulidze, who were awarded the gold medal despite several errors in their performance.

The French judge on the panel, Marie Reine Le Gougne, said she was pressured by the Russians to rank the Russian team first. There may have been a quid pro quo arrangement with the French to assure the Russian vote for the French

competitors in ice dancing if the Russians could have the French vote in pairs.

Following public outcry and an investigation, the IOC awarded a second gold medal to the Canadian skaters. The decision was based on IOC rules, internal policies, and an internal fact-finding group. No criminal laws were broken, and it was up to the private body to take appropriate action for rules violations.

What ethical issues do you see in these events? Was the remedy appropriate? Would you have accepted the gold medal if you were the Canadian team?

Source: Selena Roberts, "Canadian Skaters Awarded Share of Olympic Gold; French Judge Suspended, Her Scoring Thrown Out," *New York Times,* February 16, 2002, A1, B21.

Trade Law and Policies

The importance of trade laws, tariffs, and policies has increased directly with the rising numbers of international business transactions. For example, the U.S. trade representative, once a dignitary position, has been upgraded to a cabinet-level position. Although Congress is responsible for enacting trade laws, and various federal agencies are responsible for their administration, the U.S. trade representative assumes responsibility for negotiating trade agreements with foreign countries. The laws passed by Congress include import restrictions, tariffs, and enactments such as the Buy American Act (41 U.S.C. §§ 10a–10d [1987]), which requires federal agencies to give preference to U.S. suppliers in their procurement of goods and services. Chapter 7 provides additional details on trade laws, tariffs, restrictions, and trade agreements.

Uniform International Laws

Because trade barriers have been largely eliminated, contracts have been and are being formed between and among businesses from virtually all nations. However, not all nations have the same approach to contracts. Indeed, some nations have no contract laws or commercial codes. In an attempt to introduce uniformity in international contract law, the UN developed its Contracts for the International Sale of Goods (CISG), which has been adopted widely and allows businesses to opt in or out of its application in adopting countries. Similar to the UCC (see Chapter 12), the CISG has provisions on formation, performance, and damages. More information on the CISG can be found in Chapters 7, 12, and 13.

The European Union

Once referred to as the Common Market, and later known as the European Community (EC), the European Union (EU) is a tariff-free group of European countries that have joined together to enjoy the benefits of barrier-free trade.

Formed in 1992, the single economic community requires member nations to subscribe to the same monetary standard, the elimination of immigration and customs controls, universal product and job safety standards, uniform licensing of professionals, and unified taxation schedules. The EU continues to evolve to trade as one country with the introduction of the euro, its single currency. More details on the governance of the EU and its laws can be found in Chapter 7.

B I O G R A P H Y

The Firestorm of Controversy Over a State Legislative Enactment: Arizona Senate Bill 1070

On April 21, 2010, Arizona Governor Jan Brewer signed Arizona Senate Bill 1070, a state legislative enactment that has been described as the "broadest and strictest immigration measure in generations."[a] From the moment of its passage, the law created a firestorm of controversy, including boycotts passed by the cities of Los Angeles, California; Seattle, Washington; and Columbus, Ohio, which prohibited city agencies and divisions from doing business with Arizona. Arizona fired back with a letter from its public utility commission reminding the mayor of Los Angeles that Arizona power plants generated 25 percent of the electricity for his city and asking him to include the power contracts as part of his boycott, a move that would result in brownouts in Los Angeles. The Phoenix Suns players wore jerseys for one of their May playoff games that read, "Los Suns." Los Angeles Lakers coach Phil Jackson, coach of the Suns' opposition team, spoke out and reflected that sports franchises should stay away from political issues and let fans enjoy the sport. The Lakers had protesters outside their arena the following night who demanded a retraction from Mr. Jackson.

The emotionally charged discussion of the bill overlooked both its actual language and the constitutional issues. Little Arizona Senate Bill 1070 is a biography of the sources of law and interaction among the layers of the pyramid in Exhibit 1.2. Below are some of the law's provisions and the legal questions that have resulted.

1. Provision of the law:

    Cooperation and assistance in enforcement of immigration laws; indemnification[b]

    A. No official or agency of this state or a county, city, town or other political subdivision of this state may adopt a policy that limits or restricts the enforcement of federal immigration laws to less than the full extent permitted by federal law.

    Issue: Can the state control the laws of counties, cities, and towns?

    Issue: What authority do counties, cities, and towns have to pass laws that are different from state laws? From federal laws?

2. Provision of the law:

    Trespassing by illegal aliens; assessment; exception; classification[c]

    A. In addition to any violation of federal law, a person is guilty of trespassing if the person is both: present on any public or private land in this state in violation of 8 United States Code Section 1304(e) or 1306(a).

    Issue: Can the state make the violation of a federal law a crime in the state as well?

    Issue: Is the enforcement of immigration laws exclusively a federal responsibility or do the states have authority?

    Issue: When can a state also regulate areas that are already regulated by federal law?

3. Provision of the law:

    Smuggling; classification; definitions[d]

    A. It is unlawful for a person to intentionally engage in the smuggling of human beings for profit or commercial purpose.

    B. A violation of this section is a class 4 felony.

    Issue: Can a state pass laws that would affect an area already regulated by the federal government but which address an issue not covered under federal law?

    Issue: Are crimes and criminal statutes within the jurisdiction of state legislatures?

4. Provision of the law:

    Unlawful stopping to hire and pick up passengers for work; unlawful application, solicitation or employment; classification; definitions[e]

    A. It is unlawful for an occupant of a motor vehicle that is stopped on a street, roadway or highway to attempt to hire or hire and pick up passengers for work at a different location if the motor vehicle blocks or impedes the normal movement of traffic.

    B. It is unlawful for a person to enter a motor vehicle that is stopped on a street, roadway or highway in order to be hired by an occupant of the motor vehicle and to be transported to work at a different location if the motor vehicle blocks or impedes the normal movement of traffic.

    Issue: Which level of government has the authority to regulate traffic and vehicles?

    Issue: Is the purpose of this new law health and public welfare?

    Issue: Does this section conflict with federal law?

5. Provision of the law:

    A. For any lawful contract made by a law enforcement official or agency of this state or a county, city, town, or other political subdivision of this state where reasonable suspicion exists that the person is an alien who is unlawfully present in the United States, a reasonable attempt shall be made, when practicable, to determine the immigration status of the person. The person's immigration status shall be verified with the federal government pursuant to 8 United States Code Section 1373(c).[f]

    Issue: Can a state require local law enforcement officials to follow state law?

    Issue: Can state law enforcement officials refer individuals to the federal government for enforcement?

    Issue: Can states enforce federal laws?

[a]Randal C. Archibald, "Arizona Enacts Stringent Law on Immigration," *New York Times,* April 23, 2010, p. A1.
[b]A.R.S. §11-1051 (2010).
[c]A.R.S. §13-1509 (2010).
[d]A.R.S. §13-2319(2010).
[e]A.R.S. §13-2928(2010).
[f]A.R.S. §11-1051(2010).

Summary

How is law defined?

- Law is a form of order. Law is the body of rules of society governing individuals and their relationships.

What types of laws are there?

- Public law—codified law; statutes; law by government body

- Private law—rules created by individuals for their contracts, tenancy, and employment

- Civil law—laws regulating harms and carrying damage remedies

- Criminal law—laws regulating wrongful conduct and carrying sentences and fines

- Statutory law—codified law

- Common law—law developed historically and by judicial precedent

- Substantive laws—laws giving rights and responsibilities

- Procedural laws—laws that provide enforcement rights

What are the purposes of law?

- Keep order; influence conduct; honor expectations; promote equality; offer compromises

What are the characteristics of law?

- Flexibility; consistency; pervasiveness

- Jurisprudence—theory of law

Where are laws found and who enacts them?

- Constitution—document that establishes structure and authority of a government

- Federal statutes—laws passed by Congress: the U.S. Code

- State statutes—laws passed by state legislatures, including uniform laws on contracts and business organizations

- Ordinances—local laws passed by cities, counties, and townships

What are the sources of international law?

- Customs—the standards of conduct and norms in a country

- Treaties—agreements between and among nations regarding their political and commercial relationships
- Private law—party autonomy recognized in all nations
- International doctrines—widely accepted principles of law followed in most countries
- European Union—group of nations working collectively for uniform laws and barrier-free trade
- Uniform laws—Contracts for the International Sale of Goods (CISG)

Questions and Problems

1. Bryant Gunderson is a sole proprietor with a successful bungee-jumping business. He is considering incorporating his business. What levels and sources of law would affect and govern the process of incorporation?

2. Jeffrey Stalwart has just been arrested for ticket scalping outside the Great Western Forum in Los Angeles. Jeffrey sold a ticket to an Alanis Morrissette concert to an intense fan for $1,200; the face value of the ticket was $48. Ticket scalping in Los Angeles is a misdemeanor. Will Jeffrey's court proceedings be civil or criminal?

3. In 1933, Walt Disney Company entered into a contract with Irving Berlin, Inc., assigning musical copyrights in exchange for a share of Berlin revenues. The agreement exempted from copyright protection Disney's use of the assigned music in motion pictures. The music was used in several Disney feature-length cartoons (*Snow White* and *Pinocchio*) that were later made available for sale on videocassette. Mr. Berlin's heirs brought suit, alleging infringement. Was this new technology an infringement? Could videocassettes have been anticipated? (*Bourne* v *Walt Disney Co.*, 68 F.3d 621 [2d Cir. 1995].)

4. Define and contrast the following:
  a. Civil law and criminal law
  b. Substantive law and procedural law
  c. Common law and statutory law
  d. Private law and public law

5. During the 2001 baseball season, Barry Bonds, a player with the San Francisco Giants, hit 73 home runs in one season, a new record that went beyond the 72 set by Mark McGwire in 2000. Mr. Bonds made his record-breaking home run in San Francisco. When he hit the home run, the ball went into the cheap seats. All agree that Alex Popov had his glove on the home-run ball. However, Patrick Hayashi ended up with the ball.

Mr. Popov filed suit alleging that Mr. Hayashi assaulted Mr. Popov in order to get the ball. A substantial amount of videotape shows Mr. Popov's "gloving" of the ball. Mr. Popov says the ball belongs to him because he held that ball in a "Sno-cone position" and others wrested it from his control.

Mark McGwire's ball from his record-breaking home run sold for $3 million. The battle for the Bonds home-run ball carries high financial stakes. What areas of law will be involved in the judge's determination of who gets the baseball? (Peter Page, "Ownership of historic baseball is in extra innings," National Law Journal, November 12, 2001.)

6. Perfect 10 is the publisher of the eponymous adult entertainment magazine and the owner of the website perfect10.com. Perfect10.com is a subscription site where consumers pay a membership fee in order to gain access to content on the website. Perfect 10 has created approximately 5,000 images of models for display in its website and magazine. Many of the models in these images have signed releases assigning their rights of publicity to Perfect 10. Perfect 10 also holds registered U.S. copyrights for these images and owns several related, registered trademark and service marks.

CWIE provides web hosting and related Internet connectivity services to the owners of various websites. For a fee, CWIE provides "ping, power, and pipe" services to their clients by ensuring the "box" or server is on, ensuring power is provided to the server, and connecting the client's service or website to the Internet via a data center connection. CCBill allows consumers to use credit cards or checks to pay for subscriptions or memberships to e-commerce venues.

Perfect 10 sent letters and e-mails to CCBill and CWIE stating that CCBill and CWIE clients were infringing Perfect 10 copyrights. CCBill and CWIE took no action against their customers following the complaint. Perfect 10 filed suit against CCBill and CWIE for vicarious copyright infringement. Could CCBill and CWIE be liable for infringement? Apply what you have learned of the principles of law in this area from the *Grokster* and *Sony* cases. (*Perfect 10, Inc. v CCBill LLC*, 481 F.3d 751 [9th Cir. 2007])

7. Around 5:00 a.m. on January 1, 2004, Matthew Schmucker, who was eighteen at the time, was traveling alone in a horse and buggy near the intersection of Indiana State Road 37 and Notestine Road in Harlan, Indiana. He was intoxicated at the time and failed to stop at an intersection, thereby colliding with the side of a 2003 Dodge Stratus carrying David Candon and Monica Young, who is now paralyzed from the neck down as a result of the accident. Schmucker was charged with being a minor in possession of alcohol and failing to stop at a throughway. Candon, Young, and their children, who were in the car at the time of the auto/buggy collision, brought suit against Schmucker. Schmucker declared bankruptcy and asked to be discharged from his obligations to Candon and Young. Candon and Young argued that the injury was a "willful and malicious injury by a vessel" under the bankruptcy code and was thus a nondischargeable debt. Schmucker said a horse and buggy is not a vessel. Discuss the role of the court in this case. What would the court look to in making its decision? What is the impact of the court's decision on the ability of the family to recover for injuries? *Young v Schmucker*, 409 B.R. 477 (N.D. Ind. 2008)

8. Ms. Paris Hilton, a well-known celebrity with a ubiquitous presence on television and in *People* magazine, had her driver's license suspended by the state of California because of driving under the influence (DUI) or while intoxicated (DWI). She was then pulled over by officers for DUI while driving with a suspended license.

Following a hearing on the second traffic stop, a judge sentenced Ms. Hilton to 45 days in jail for failure to honor the terms of her DUI probation, including driving while intoxicated. List all the types of laws that apply to Ms. Hilton in her situation and also where the specific California laws would appear on the pyramid of the sources of law. If Ms. Hilton asked for a pardon or commutation of her sentence by the governor of California, would the law allow it?

9. Classify the following subject matters as substantive or procedural laws:
   a. Traffic law on speeding
   b. Small claims court rules
   c. Evidence
   d. Labor law
   e. Securities

10. Mercury Corporation manufactures solar panels for residential use. Mercury is experiencing some sales resistance because homeowners fear that trees and buildings will block the sunlight from their solar panels. At this time, no law in Mercury's state protects light for solar panels. What governmental bodies could pass protective legislation?

Economics, Ethics, and the Law

The Cost of Corporate Wrongdoing

Read and analyze "Paying the Piper: An Empirical Examination of Longer-Term Financial Consequences of Illegal Corporate Behavior," 40 *Academy of Management Journal* 129 (1997), by Melissa S. Baucus and David A. Baucus. Then answer the following questions.

a. What financial impact does illegal corporate behavior have on a company?

b. How long does a company feel the impact of illegal behavior?

c. How does the market react to illegal corporate behavior?

d. What are the financial costs of violating the law?

Notes

1. On remand, the federal district court granted summary judgment to the plaintiffs. *Metro-Goldwyn-Mayer Studios Inc. v Grokster, Ltd.*, 454 F.Supp.2d 966 (C.D. Cal. 2006). The court later granted a permanent injunction against Grokster. 518 F.Supp.2d 1197 (C.D. Cal. 2007).

2. Essay by Oliver Wendell Holmes; reprinted with permission from 32 *Harvard Law Review* 40 (1918). Copyright © 1918 by The Harvard Law Review Association.

3. From *My Philosophy of Law* by Roscoe Pound. © 1941 West Publishing Corporation. Reprinted with permission of West Group.

4. Douglas Jehl, "Head of Inquiry on Iraq Abuses Now in Spotlight," *New York Times*, May 11, 2004, A1, A12.

5. *Id.*

Business Ethics and Social Responsibility

The dawn of the new century brought us the scandals of Enron, WorldCom, Adelphia, Tyco, HealthSouth, and others, and the resulting Sarbanes-Oxley reforms (see Chapters 8, 20, and 21), But the new regulations and stiffer criminal penalties for white-collar crime did not stop over 250 companies from backdating stock options for their executives, a practice that required restatements of income and resulted in shareholder losses in their finances and trust. In the government sector, we lost governors, senators, mayors, and presidential candidates to various kickback and personal scandals. In 2008, two 150-year-old Wall Street firms collapsed and, as a result, the banking and insurance industries teetered and the economy faltered. We learned that the portfolios of the collapsed firms were chock full of high-risk mortgage securities that had been represented as AAA quality. While we were reeling, Bernie Madoff delivered the news of his 18-year $50 billion Ponzi scheme, the largest in U.S. history. College and university financial aid officers were the center of a nationwide investigation into their acceptance of consulting fees, stock options, and substantial gifts from student loan companies that then gained preferred status on those campuses. A 2008 Josephson Institute study found that 82 percent of high-school students copied others' homework and 64 percent of them cheated on tests.[1]

What happened to ethics? Is doing business just a matter of lying and getting away with it? Does anybody really care about ethics in business now? Has society drifted, and is business conduct just a reflection of changing ethical norms? And what does it mean to be ethical in our lives and in business? This chapter discusses these questions and answers several others: What is ethics? How does ethics affect me? What is business ethics? Why is business ethics important? What ethical standards should a business adopt? How do employees recognize ethical dilemmas? How are ethical dilemmas resolved? How does a business create an ethical atmosphere? ■

UPDATE ⬉
For up-to-date news on ethical issues, go to
mariannejennings.com

Goodness is the only investment that never fails.

Henry D. Thoreau
Walden, "Higher Laws"

A bad reputation is like a hangover. It takes a while to get rid of, and it makes everything else hurt.

James Preston
Former CEO, Avon

There is a big difference between what we have the right to do and what is right.

Hon. Justice Potter Stewart
Associate Justice, U.S. Supreme Court, 1958–1981

$$P = f(x)$$

The probability of an ethical outcome is a direct function of the amount of money involved; the more money, the less likely the ethical outcome.

CFA Institute

CONSIDER...

1. Who said, "I have done absolutely nothing wrong"?

2. What CEO said, "In today's regulatory environment, it's virtually impossible to violate the rules. It's impossible for a violation to go undetected, certainly not for a considerable period of time"?

3. What CEO said, "We are the good guys. We are on the side of angels"?

4. Who said, "Go after the men who seek out prostitutes"?

5. What company had a 64-page, award-winning code of ethics?*

ISTOCKPHOTO.COM/MAREK ULIASZ

*ANSWERS: 1. Former Illinois governor Rod Blagojevich, charged with attempting to fill President Obama's Senate seat in exchange for favors and perks and convicted of lying to the FBI. 2. Bernie Madoff, former CEO of Bernard L. Madoff Investment Securities LLC, a firm that perpetrated a $50-billion Ponzi scheme. 3. Jeffrey Skilling, former CEO of Enron, and Lloyd Blankfein, CEO of Goldman Sachs. 4. Former New York governor Eliot Spitzer, in 2004, when he was establishing a task force as New York attorney general to halt prostitution in New York. Mr. Spitzer resigned when his longstanding relationship with a call girl was uncovered in a sting operation. 5. Enron.

The chapter's opening Consider teaches us that often we look at what companies and business executives say and do and the fact that the companies are doing well, and assume that they must all have high ethical standards. The quotes are ironic because these individuals and/or their companies then crossed the ethical lines they touted as standards.

We look at these individuals' behaviors and wonder why they thought they could get away with their poor ethical choices, or why they believed they were immune from the laws and our ethical standards. We like to think of ourselves as so different from those who cross ethical and/or legal lines. But all of them were college graduates, nearly all with business degrees. All of them were respected by their friends and were active in community projects and institutions. These individuals were "good" people, but they lost sight of personal ethics, business ethics, and the importance of ethics in success. Before they committed their business crimes, the worst that could have been said about many white-collar criminals who are serving 6-month to 25-year prison sentences is that they had parking and speeding tickets. Keeping ethics with us, in life and in business, can help us avoid the kinds of mistakes that so many bright and capable business-people have made. But, we wonder, what are ethics? How do we know when we have them? How do we keep them when we face pressures, whether on an important exam or in meeting the quarterly numbers or our sales quota at work? This chapter answers these questions.

What Is Ethics?

When we read that House Ways & Means Committee Chair and Congressman Charlie Rangel accepted a trip from companies seeking legislative favors, we label Mr. Rangel's conduct "unethical," as did the House Ethics Committee. When we read that Zachery Kouwe, a former reporter with the *New York Times,* lifted large segments of his articles from other reporters' work at the *Wall Street Journal* and Reuters, the articles describing his resignation use the term *unethical*. When we read that a Standard & Poor's analyst wrote in an e-mail to colleagues, "Let's hope we are all wealthy and retired by the time this house of cards falters," we feel that we have been duped.[2]

"It's Just Not Right!"

We read about these types of situations in the newspaper each day. From politics to journalism to business, references to ethics run through the stories. But we also face ethical dilemmas ourselves. Two students purchase tickets at a theater to see *Avatar,* and when they emerge from the theater they realize they are in an open area with access to other theaters. If they wanted to, they could slip into *The Blind Side* or *Up in the Air* and see another movie without paying for another ticket. "Who's to know?" they might think. "Hollywood makes too much money anyway." "It doesn't really hurt anyone." These thoughts are similar to those that may have run through the minds of the congressman, the reporter, and the analyst who did not reveal the real risk factors. Although we may believe we are different from busi-ness executives and others involved in scandals, we all face ethical dilemmas each day. Do I tell the clerk that he gave me too much change? Do I tell the lender on my loan application that my salary was just cut 25 percent? Do I go back to pay for the laundry detergent that slipped through on the bottom of my cart? Do I do what my boss says when he tells me to increase the number of people who attended an event that we catered so that we make more money? Do I tell a potential buyer of my car about the hairline crack in the engine block? Do I tell my clients that I am selling off the investments I am trying to get them to buy?

The fact pattern changes slightly. The parties' names and the subject matter vary, but the ethical issues are the same. Some conduct is more harmful, such as those situations in which a criminal statute is violated. Still, regardless of the law, we look at the conduct of Mr. Rangel, Mr. Kouwe, the analysts and their ratings, the students in the theater, the catering company employee, and the seller of the car, and we conclude, "It's just not right!" We probably agree that they all behaved unethically. We may not be able to zero in on what bothers us about their conduct, but we know an ethics violation, or an ethical breach, when we see one.

Normative Standards: How We Behave to Keep Order

But what do we mean when we say that someone has acted unethically? Ethical standards are not the standards of the law. In fact, they are a higher standard. Sometimes referred to as *normative standards* in philosophy, ethical standards are the generally accepted rules of conduct that govern society. Ethical rules are both standards and expectations for behavior, and we have developed them for nearly all aspects of life. For example, no statute in any state makes it a crime for someone to cut in line in order to save the waiting time involved by going to the end of the line. But we all view those who "take cuts in line" with disdain. We sneer at those cars that sneak along the side of the road to get around a line of traffic as we sit and wait our turn. We resent those who tromp up to the cash register in front of us, ignoring the fact that we were there first and that our time is valuable too.

On Line-Cutting and Ethics

If you have ever resented a line-cutter, you understand ethics and have applied ethical standards in life. Waiting your turn in line is a societal expectation. "Waiting your turn" is not an ordinance, a statute, or even a federal regulation. "Waiting your turn" is an age-old principle developed because it was fair to proceed with first in time, first to be served. "Waiting your turn" exists because large groups wait for the same road, theater tickets, or fast food at noon in a busy downtown area. We recognize that lines ensure order and that waiting your turn is the just way to allocate the limited space and time allotted for the traffic, the tickets, or the food. "Waiting your turn" is an expected but unwritten behavior that plays a critical role in an orderly society.

So it is with ethics. Ethics consists of those unwritten rules we have developed for our interactions with each other. These unwritten rules govern us when we share resources or honor contracts. "Waiting your turn" is a higher standard than the laws passed to maintain order. Those laws apply when individuals use physical force or threats to push to the front of the line. Assault, battery, and threats are forms of criminal conduct for which the offenders can be prosecuted. But the law does not apply to the stealthy line-cutter who simply sneaks to the front, perhaps using a friend and a conversation as a decoy. No laws are broken, but the notions of fairness and justice are offended by one individual putting him- or herself above others and taking advantage of others' time and position.

Because line-cutters violate the basic procedures and unwritten rules for line formation and order, they commit an ethical breach. We don't put line-cutters in jail, but we do refer to them as unethical. Other examples of unethical behavior also carry no legal penalty. A married person who commits adultery does not commit a crime but does create a breach of trust with his or her spouse. We do not put adulterers in jail, but we do label their conduct with adjectives such as *unfaithful*, and even use a lay term to describe adultery: *cheating*.

Speaking of cheating, looking at someone else's paper during an exam is not a criminal violation. If you cheat on a test, your professor may sanction you and your college may impose penalties, but the county attorney will not prosecute you for cheating. Your conduct is unethical because you did not earn your standing and grade under the same set of rules applied to the other students. Just like the line-cutter, your conduct is not fair to those who spent their time studying. Your cheating is unjust because you are getting ahead using someone else's work.

For the Manager's Desk

Re: A State of the Union on Academic Ethics

Ethics is not so difficult to understand, but it is difficult to practice. Data are available on the ethics of everyone from school-age children to graduate school students. In 1992, the Josephson Institute found that 61 percent of high school students reported that they had cheated at least once during a school year. By 2008, that number had risen slightly to 64 percent.[†] According to Duke University's Center for Academic Integrity (now relocated to Clemson University), about 75 percent of college students confess that they have cheated in some way in college.[††] The rate for graduate students is 50 percent. They describe taking notes and answers into exams, copying others' work, downloading and buying term papers from the Internet, and not contributing to team projects but still receiving credit for them. Graduate students at Columbia University extended the time clock for an online exam. Harvard Business School candidates tapped into the school's admission database. Thirty-four students at Duke's Fuqua Business School faced discipline for collaborating on a take-home exam.

[†]See http://www.josephsoninstitute.org.
[††]Professor Donald McCabe of Rutgers University has conducted surveys on academic integrity for many years. His latest survey involved 4,500 student respondents nationwide. See http://www.academicintegrity.org, the website for the Center for Academic Integrity at Clemson University, for more information.

These examples of cutting in line, committing adultery, and cheating on exams bring certain common adjectives to our minds: "That's not *fair!*" "That was *dishonest!*" "That was *unjust!*" You have just defined ethics for yourself. Ethics is more than common, or normative, standards of behavior. Ethics is honesty, fairness, and justice. The principles of ethics, when honored, ensure that the playing field is level, and that when we win we do so by using our own work and ideas. Being ethical means being honest and fair in our interactions with each other, whether personally or in business.

CONSIDER...   2.1

Why do we worry about ethics in school? What is the point of teaching young people to be honest? Why do we impose penalties for cheating? How does cheating affect those who do not cheat? What are some of the long-term consequences if those who cheat are permitted to pass courses, graduate with honors, and pursue careers in their fields? What happens when the 75 percent figure reaches 100 percent?

Ethical Issues

Gerry Roscoe was the "Outstanding Graduating Senior" for the class of 2010 at State University. By tradition, the graduate chosen for this honor speaks at the commencement ceremonies for the university. Gerry was scheduled to give the student commencement address and had a job awaiting him on Wall Street at one of the nation's largest investment banking firms.

Jill Swain and Eric Bourdeaux were also graduating seniors who knew Gerry. Jill and Eric knew that at least twice, Gerry had taken exams for others. One was a final exam during their sophomore year. The class was an economics course with 500 students. The exam was held in a large lecture hall and proctored by graduate students. ID was not required, and Gerry took the exam twice, once for his section and at another time for a friend who was having trouble with the course. Without a B on the midterm, Gerry's friend would have failed the course and lost his scholarship. The second instance involved a final exam in finance. Finance 300 had been taught in sections of 50 students, but a common final was given with, again, 500 students in the room. The exam was proctored by one finance professor and graduate students. Gerry had taken Finance 300 one year before his girlfriend, Anissa Foulger, had, and she struggled through the course. She needed a B on the final exam in order to pass the course. If she did not pass, she jeopardized her transfer to a college in New York upon Gerry's graduation and employment there. Jill and Eric saw Gerry enter the common final for Finance 300, and he explained that he was taking the final for Anissa: "You understand. Everything is off if she doesn't make it through. She doesn't need this stuff. She is going into advertising. I can take it for her and she'll get her B."

If you were Jill or Eric, what would you have done at the time of the exams? What would you do now that Gerry has been given this "Outstanding Graduating Senior" honor? Does his dishonesty really hurt anyone? Wasn't Gerry just being noble by taking the exam for his friend? For his girlfriend? Is it any of your business? How is anyone harmed by what Gerry did?

What Is Business Ethics?

Many have referred to "business ethics" as an oxymoron. The little jibe suggests that it is impossible to be in business and be ethical. Some see the pursuit of profit as being at odds with ethics. However, the term *business ethics* is actually a complex one with many layers of meaning. The first layer consists of basic values (covered in the following section) such as being honest, keeping promises, and not taking things that do not belong to you. Another layer consists of notions of fairness (also covered in the next section) such as how we treat others, including customers and employees who report to us. Still a third layer consists of issues related to how a business interacts with the community, the environment, and its neighbors.

The three layers of business ethics bring back into the purely quantitative models of business the elements of a fair playing field. Business ethics involve the study of fairness and moral standards amidst the pressure of earning a profit and providing returns to shareholders and others who have invested in the business.

A business faces the special problem of having to develop ethical standards for a group of people who work together toward the common goal of profit for the firm. Individuals in the group have personal ethical standards, but too often employees find that the ethical standards imposed by managers at the top of a company result in possible harm to those at the bottom or to others outside the firm. An employee may feel compelled to resolve the conflict between loyalty to an employer and the performance of an illegal or unethical act ordered by that employer by simply following the employer's direction. In other words, in developing standards of business ethics, an employee has personal economic interests in continuing employment that may compromise personal ethical standards. Businesses face the additional challenges of developing business standards that are consistent with individual standards and helping employees understand that their personal standards of honesty and fairness need not be different at work. To accomplish this meshing, business managers should understand the various sources of ethical standards.

Ethical Standards: Positive Law and Ethics

Ethical standards can be derived from different sources, and ethicists often debate the origins of these standards. One theory is that our ethical standards are the same as actual or positive law, and that our ethical decisions are made simply upon the basis of whether an activity is legal. **Positive law,** or codified law, establishes the standard for ethical behavior. But compliance with positive law is not always ethical. For example, Enron created more than 3,000 off-the-book entities in order to transfer its debt to them. If Enron owned less than 50 percent of these entities, it did not have to disclose that debt or its transfer on its financial statements. The result was that Enron's financial statements made the company look healthy even while it was self-destructing. Most of the executives felt they were complying with not just the law but also the accounting standard that applied, a rule known as FASB (Financial Accounting Standards Board) 125. But when all of the off-the-book companies were found, and some 800 of them were located in the Cayman Islands, everyone referred to the conduct as "unethical." Professor Richard Leftwich summed it all up: "It takes FASB two years to issue a ruling and the investment bankers two weeks to figure out a way around it." Even without a violation of the letter of the law, a violation of the spirit of the law presents an ethical dilemma.

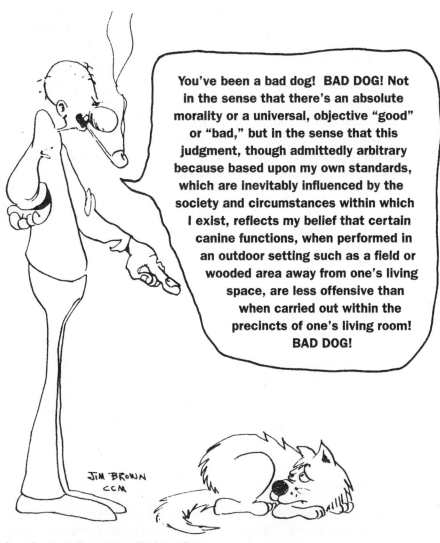

Source: Reprinted with permission of Jim Brown © 1991.

Ethical Standards: Natural Law and Ethics

Others believe that our ethical standards are derived from a higher source and that they are universal. Often labeled **natural law,** this school of ethical thought supports the notion that some standards do not exist because of law (and, indeed, may exist despite laws). For example, at one time the United States permitted slavery. Even though the positive law allowed the activity and the standard of positive law considered slave ownership ethical, natural law dictated that the deprivation of others' rights was unethical.

Ethical Standards: Moral Relativism and Ethics

Moral relativism (also called *situational ethics*) establishes moral standards according to the situation in which the dilemma is faced. Violation of the law, for example, is permitted if you are stealing to provide food for your starving family. Under moral relativism, adultery is justified when you are caught in an unhappy marriage, as is the business situation in which you engage in lying to avoid offending a coworker or a customer. Bribery is illegal in the United States, and most companies even have firm policies against accepting gifts, because doing so may create conflicts of interest; but some companies still use a relativist approach and argue that being competitive in international markets is different. They adhere to a philosophy of "When in Rome, do as the Romans do," following the standards and customs in a given country even though those same behaviors in the United States would be unacceptable and even illegal.

Ethical Standards: Religion and Ethics

A final source of moral standards is religious beliefs or divine revelation. The source of standards can be the Bible, the Koran, or any inspired book or writing that is the cornerstone of a religion or faith and believed to have resulted from divine revelation.

What Are the Categories of Ethical Dilemmas?

Regardless of the root or source of a company or individual's ethical standards, certain categories of conduct involve ethical issues. The following 12 categories were developed and listed in *Exchange*, the magazine of the Brigham Young University School of Business.

Taking Things That Don't Belong to You

Everything from the unauthorized use of the Pitney-Bowes postage meter at your office for mailing personal letters to exaggerations on travel expenses to the downloading of music from the Internet without authorization belongs in this category of ethical violations. Using someone else's property without permission or taking property under false pretenses still means taking something that does not belong to you. A CFO (chief financial officer) of a large electric utility reported that, after taking a cab from LaGuardia International Airport to his midtown Manhattan hotel, he asked for a receipt. The cab driver handed him a full book of blank receipts and drove away. Apparently, the problem of accurately reporting travel expenses involves more than just employees.

Saying Things You Know Are Not True

A salesperson who tells a potential customer that a product carries a "money-back guarantee" when the salesperson knows that only an exchange is possible has said something that is not true, committed an ethical breach and possibly a violation of the law, and misled the customer. If a car dealer assures a customer that a car has not been in an accident and it has, an ethical breach has occurred. If a homeowner tells a buyer that a home has all-copper plumbing in order to ensure a sale, and the home has plastic plumbing in some parts, that false statement is an ethical breach too.

Giving or Allowing False Impressions

An urban legend that has circulated among marketing departments around the country is the story of an infomercial that offered two CDs with the hits of the 1980s on them. The infomercial emphasized over and over again, "All songs by original artists." Even the CDs carried the line, "All songs by original artists." When purchasers read the label with a closer eye and listened to the CDs, they discovered that all the songs were performed by one group, a group called "The Original Artists." While technically true, the advertising left a false impression with customers who assumed they would be buying songs as performed by the recording artists who made the songs popular.

 Ethical Issues

The temptation is remarkable. The run is long. The body screams, "No more!" So, it happened again in the New York City Marathon for 2008. Cheating on this form of a physical final examination became international news when, in 1979, Boston Marathon runner and winner Rosie Ruiz combined her running with a hitch on the train to earn first place. She repeated the ploy in the 1980 Boston Marathon, when her creative approach was discovered.

The New York Road Runners Club, the sponsors and managers of the New York City Marathon, disclosed multiple subway riders in their 2008 race on the eve of the 2009 Marathon with the hope of discouraging the 42,000 runners to go the distance, the real distance. For 2008, there were 71 runners disqualified from the race, 46 of them for taking the subway in order to go the distance. The club discovers these free-riders when it investigates what it believes to be odd times for runners who have not been able or should not be able to achieve their recorded times. In at least two situations, the runners who took the subway also took first place in their age categories and deprived the real winners of their Tiffany trophies as well as the thrill of quaffing the elixir of victory on the day of the marathon. The real winners in these age categories from 2008 were not notified of their victories until July 2009 because of the time the investigations take.

A spokesperson from the Road Runners Club said that the greatest temptation in the race comes when the runners enter Manhattan via the Queensboro Bridge. That entry to the city is close to Central Park and the finish line, but the race first takes a turn there for another 10 miles into Harlem and the Bronx. Most cheaters simply skip those boroughs and head right into Central Park and the finish line.

Are there any laws that govern this situation with the runners? Discuss the ethical issues of the runners. Is anyone really hurt if runners cheat?

Buying Influence or Engaging in Conflict of Interest

A company awards a construction contract to a firm owned by the father of the state attorney general while the state attorney general's office is investigating that company. A county official who has the responsibility for selecting the contractor who will build the county's new baseball stadium travels around the country at the contractor's expense to view existing stadium sites. The county official should see as many sites and samples of work as there are bidders on the new stadium, but when the contractors pay, there is an ethical issue. A physician researcher whose work concludes that a company's product is meritorious needs to disclose the consulting fees he receives from that company.

All of these examples illustrate conflicts of interest. Those involved in situations such as these often protest, "But I would never allow that to influence me." That they have to insist they are not or would not be influenced is evidence of the conflict. Whether the conflict can or will influence those it touches is not the issue, for neither party can prove conclusively that a *quid pro quo* was not intended. The possibility exists, and it creates suspicion.

CONSIDER...   2.2

New York attorney general Andrew Cuomo uncovered some interesting practices in the field of student lenders and college loan officers. Several universities—University of Texas (UT), University of Southern California (USC), Columbia University, and Johns Hopkins—suspended their top financial aid administrators after they discovered that the administrators had conflicts of interest related to the lending companies they had listed as "preferred lenders" for the students attending their institutions. The University of Pennsylvania, New York University, and Syracuse University all reached settlements with law enforcement officials on loan kickback arrangements.

Part of the agreements, in which the universities admitted no wrongdoing, required the schools to refund $3.27 million to students because of revenue-sharing agreements with the lenders. Citibank, also a student lender, agreed to pay $2 million into the same fund. In addition to refunds, the money will be used to provide training for students on the student loan industry and their options.

The investigation, triggered by a whistle-blower's report to Mr. Cuomo and involving 100 colleges and universities and six student lenders, discovered the following types of activities by the campus financial aid officers:

- David Charlow, dean of student affairs at Columbia, owned 7,500 shares and 2,500 warrants in Educational Lending Group, Inc., the parent company of Student Loan Xpress. The company did disclose the ownership interest in its SEC filings. Mr. Charlow was quoted on the Student Loan Xpress website as saying, "We have worked with the Student Loan Xpress team for many years because they consistently meet the very high standards for service that our students and parents expect not only from our university, but also from our partners."*

- Lawrence Burt, vice president of student affairs and director of the office of student financial services at UT–Austin, owns 1,500 shares and 500 warrants in Educational Lending Group. Mr. Burt said that "his ownership of stock in the company did not influence his decision about whether to place it on the list." Mr. Burt said he bought

CONTINUED

the shares at a time when the company did not make direct loans to students but only consolidated existing loans. He said that he purchased the shares on the recommendation of a friend as a high-risk investment with potential. "I did not do anything wrong," was Mr. Burt's only comment.**

- Catherine Thomas, associate dean and director of financial aid at USC, is also listed as a stock and warrant owner in a preferred student lender.

- Ellen Frishberg, financial aid director at Johns Hopkins, took a total of $130,000 in consulting fees from a preferred lender, only half of which was disclosed to the university.

- In addition to the revenue-sharing agreements, the investigations have also revealed other activities on the parts of the student lenders such as their sponsorships of the meetings of the National Association of Student Financial Aid Administrators (NASFAA) with exhibitor fees totaling $650,000.

The NASFAA has long been debating the issue of the ties between its members and the student lenders. In response to the investigation and the stock ownership issues, the NASFAA issued the following statement:

It would be inappropriate for a school to place a lender on a preferred lender list in exchange for shares of stock. We would also note that if the financial aid administrator purchased the stock with their own funds, their ownership of the shares may not be evidence of improper conduct, but would certainly present the appearance of a conflict of interest.†

In 2003, a task force created by NASFAA proposed that NASFAA submit a law to Congress that would limit gifts and other perks from lenders to loan administrators to $50. A member of the task force said, "We were inclined to believe that a little bit of sunshine probably modifies behavior."†† But, by a 13–12 vote, the NASFAA board rejected the task force's proposal.

As the Cuomo investigation progressed, the various state officials also discovered interconnections with the U.S. Department of Education (DOE), the agency that must approve a student loan company's status for a presence on campus. For example, the general counsel for the College Loan Corporation was formerly the general counsel for the DOE. The current executive vice president of U.S. Education Finance Group was formerly a deputy assistant secretary in the Office of Postsecondary Education in the DOE. The doors are open both ways, with executives flowing back and forth between the department and the student loan companies.‡

Steps for Analyzing Ethical Dilemmas and Case Studies in Business

1. Make sure you have a grasp of all the available facts.

2. List any information you would like to have but don't and what assumptions you would have to make, if any, in resolving the dilemma.

3. Take each person involved in the dilemma and list the concerns they face or might have. Be sure to consider the impact on those not specifically mentioned in the case. For example, product safety issues don't involve just engineers' careers and company profits; shareholders, customers, customers' families, and even communities supported by the business are affected by a business decision on what to do about a product and its safety issue.

4. Develop a list of resolutions for the problem. Apply the various models for reaching this resolution. As you apply the various models to the dilemma, you may find additional insights for questions 1, 2, and 3. If the breach has already occurred, consider the possible remedies and develop systemic changes so that such breaches do not occur in the future.

5. Evaluate the resolutions for costs, legalities, and impact. Try to determine how each of the parties will react to and be affected by each of the resolutions you have proposed.

6. Make a recommendation for the actions that should be taken.

Some Help for You on the Student Loan Case

THINK: To help in your analysis, consider the following list of the parties affected by this dilemma.

*   The financial aid officials: Their independence and the credibility of their recommendations for lenders for students are affected if the officials are faced with an actual conflict or the appearance of a conflict.

*   Although the colleges and universities may not have known of their employees' conduct, they are affected by the disclosures and they are experiencing a financial impact.

*   Students and their families: They lose trust.

*   Lenders' credibility is affected by the undisclosed conflict and controversy.

*   Lenders who did not participate in the gifts and programs were disadvantaged.

*   The federal government may experience losses because it underwrites the student loans.

*   Taxpayers must then subsidize the federal student loan programs' losses.

APPLY: To further assist you in your analysis, consider the following categories:

*   Conflict of interest: Financial aid officers had an economic interest in the lenders doing well and that interest was at odds with their roles as objective evaluators of lenders for their institutions.

*   Giving or allowing false impressions: The financial aid officers played the role of objective observers when they were really investors or had a financial interest in the lenders.

ANSWER: Because the conduct has already occurred, your role becomes one of recommendation. You need to provide a recommendation that affords protection to all the parties listed as affected by the conduct. For example, to protect the credibility of the colleges and universities, a policy on accepting gifts will need to be developed, as well as one for disclosures of conflicts of interest, including any investments university financial aid officials hold with the lenders. That policy may require not only disclosure but also prohibitions on certain types of conduct (such as stock ownership) if the conflict seems too difficult to overcome. Two approaches can be taken in regard to a conflict of interest: (1) don't do it, or (2) disclose the conflict to those affected. Sometimes disclosure is insufficient and one party must not engage in the conduct. Regulators may force these new standards on colleges and universities.

* John Hechinger, "Probe Into College-Lender Ties Widens," *Wall Street Journal*, April 5, 2007, pp. D1, D2.
** Jonathan D. Glater, "Student Loans Led to Benefits by College Aides," *New York Times*, April 5, 2007, pp. A1, A13.
† *Id.*
†† David Armstrong and Daniel Golden, "Trade Group Saw Possible Conflicts in Student Loans," *Wall Street Journal*, April 11, 2007, pp. A1, A11.
‡ Jonathan D. Glater and Karen W. Arenson, "Federal Official in Student Loans Held Loan Stock," *New York Times*, April 6, 2007, pp. A1, A14; Kathy Chu, "3 top financial aid chiefs suspended," *USA Today*, April 6, 2007, p. 1B.

Hiding or Divulging Information

Taking your firm's product development or trade secrets to a new place of employment constitutes an ethical violation: divulging proprietary information. Failing to disclose the results of medical studies that indicate that your firm's new drug has significant side effects is an ethical violation: hiding information that the product could be harmful to purchasers.

Taking Unfair Advantage

New credit card regulations went into effect in 2010 because so many businesses took unfair advantage of customers on payment due dates, late fees, and increases in interest rates. Not all of the charges were spelled out clearly in the credit card terms prior to the regulatory changes. These new credit disclosure requirements and other truth-in-lending provisions all resulted because businesses misled consumers who could not easily follow the jargon of long and complex agreements.

CONSIDER... 2.3

Ross Klein and Amar Lalvani, two former employees of Starwood Hotels & Resorts Worldwide, were hired by Hilton Hotels Corporation in the summer of 2008. Starwood filed a suit that alleges that its two former employees took with them more than 100,000 electronic documents that contained proprietary information that Hilton then used.

Starwood's suit also alleges that its preliminary work on its planned new chain was taken by the former employees to Hilton and that its concepts made their way into Hilton's new Denizen brand. The suit maintains that the two employees sent the documents to Hilton via e-mail and through document shipments.

Starwood uncovered the alleged theft through serendipity. Starwood had begun an arbitration proceeding against Hilton for its recruitment of eight Starwood employees. While Hilton's in-house legal counsel was preparing for that arbitration, he discovered bundles of Starwood documents in the files of Mr. Klein and other Hilton employees. Hilton then sent the electronic files and documents, eight boxes of materials in total, back to Starwood. Hilton's general counsel said in a cover letter that he did not think the information was proprietary or confidential but that he was sending the materials back as a precaution.

Evaluate the ethics of Hilton in hiring the two men from Starwood.

Committing Acts of Personal Decadence

While many argue about the ethical notion of an employee's right to privacy, it has become increasingly clear that personal conduct outside the job can influence performance and company reputation. A company driver must abstain from substance abuse because of safety issues. Even the traditional company summer picnic has come under scrutiny as the behavior of employees at and following these events has brought harm to others in the form of alcohol-related accidents.

Perpetrating Interpersonal Abuse

A manager sexually harasses an employee. Another manager is verbally abusive to an employee. Still another manager subjects employees to humiliating correction in the presence of customers. In some cases, laws protect employees. But at the heart of this category is unfair treatment.

Permitting Organizational Abuse

Many U.S. firms with operations overseas, such as Walmart, Levi Strauss, Apple, and Nike, have faced issues of organizational abuse. The unfair treatment of workers in international operations appears in the form of child labor, demeaning wages, and excessive working hours. Even though a business cannot change the culture of another country, it can perpetuate—or alleviate—abuse through its operations there.

Violating Rules

Many rules, particularly those in large organizations that tend toward bureaucracy from a need to maintain internal controls or follow lines of authority, seem burdensome to employees trying to serve customers and other employees. Stanford University experienced difficulties in this area of ethics when it allocated as overhead for federal grants miscellaneous university expenses. Questions arose about the propriety of the allocations of costs to the federal government for non-research activities. The rules for the administration of federal grant monies used for overhead were not followed. The results not only constituted an ethical violation but also caused damage to Stanford's reputation and necessitated the hiring of a new president for the university because of the loss of trust among government regulators as well as donors and alumni.

Condoning Unethical Actions

In this breach of ethics, the wrong results from the failure to report the wrong. What if you witnessed a fellow employee embezzling company funds by forging his signature on a check that was supposed to be voided? Would you report that violation? A winking tolerance of others' unethical behavior is in itself unethical. Suppose that as a product designer, you were aware of a fundamental flaw in your company's new product—a product predicted to catapult your firm to record earnings. Would you pursue the problem to the point of halting the distribution of the product? Would you disclose what you know to the public if you could not get your company to act? Toyota experienced the cost of employees not passing along information about customer accidents and complaints when it recalled 8.5 million vehicles, answered class-action suits, and repaired relationships with government regulators over its alleged failure to disclose important data and issues about its cars' safety. One former employee of Lehman Brothers, whose sales efforts and structuring of securities investments "helped lead to the demise of the bank he loved and to an economic unraveling worldwide confessed, 'I have blood on my hands.'"[3] His remorse comes from his failure to speak up and raise his concerns about the ethical issues he saw even as he was rewarded for his work.

Balancing Ethical Dilemmas

In some situations, the answers are neither right nor wrong; rather, the situations present dilemmas to be resolved. For example, Google has struggled for two years with its decision to do business in the People's Republic of China because of known human rights violations and censorship by the government there. Its eventual decision was to remain in China despite the government's censorship of its search engine there. Other companies debated whether to do business in South

Africa when that country's government followed a policy of apartheid. In some respects, the presence of these companies would help by advancing human rights and, certainly, by improving the standard of living or communications for at least some international operations workers. On the other hand, their presence could help such governments sustain themselves by enabling them to point to economic successes despite human rights violations.

Resolution of Business Ethical Dilemmas

So far, you know what business ethics is and you have a list of the areas that cover most ethical dilemmas. But if you were faced with an ethical dilemma, how would you resolve it? The resolution of ethical dilemmas in business is often difficult, even in firms with codes of ethics and cultures committed to compliance with ethical models for decision making. Managers need guidelines for making ethical choices. Several prominent scholars in the field of business ethics have developed models for use as guides in difficult situations. This section covers those models.

Blanchard and Peale

The late Dr. Norman Vincent Peale and management expert Kenneth Blanchard offer three questions that managers should ponder in resolving ethical dilemmas: "Is it legal?" "Is it balanced?" "How does it make me feel?" If the answer to the first question, "Is it legal?" is no, for business ethics purposes, your ethical analysis is done. While there is room for conscientious objection to many laws on a moral basis, a manager is not given the authority to break the law, and agencies such as the IRS and SEC are not known for helping companies ease their consciences through refusals to pay taxes or file required securities disclosures and reports. The Hewlett-Packard board hired private investigators to determine the source of leaks about its board meetings, activities, and decisions. The investigators hired (actually a subcontractor of a contractor) used a technique known as "pretexting" in the trade. They posed as others in order to obtain access to phone records of directors and reporters to determine who was calling whom, an activity prohibited by a California statute.[4] Eventually, the investigators as well as some within the company, including HP's ethics officer, were charged with violations. These managers failed to stop when the answer to the question of legality was "no."

Answering the second question, "Is it balanced?" requires a manager to step back and view a problem from other perspectives—those of other parties, owners, shareholders, or the community. For example, an M&M/Mars cacao buyer was able to secure a low price on cacao for his company because of pending government takeovers and political disruption. M&M/Mars officers decided to pay more for the cacao than the negotiated figure. Their reason was that someday their company would not have the upper hand, and then they would want to be treated fairly when the price became the seller's choice.

Answering "How does it make me feel?" requires a manager to do a self-examination of the comfort level of a decision. Some decisions, though they may be legal and may appear balanced, can still make a manager uncomfortable. For example, many managers feel uncomfortable about the "management" of earnings when inventory and shipments are controlled to maximize bonuses or to produce a particularly good result for a quarter. Although they have done nothing illegal, managers who engage in such practices often suffer such physical effects as insomnia and appetite problems. Known as the element of conscience, this test for ethics requires businesspeople to find the source of their discomfort in a particular dilemma or proposed decision.

The Front-Page-of-the-Newspaper Test

One simple ethical model requires only that a decision maker envision how a reporter would describe a decision on the front page of a local or national newspaper. When Salomon Brothers illegally cornered the U.S. government's bond market, the *BusinessWeek* headline read, "How Bad Will It Get?" Nearly two years later, a follow-up story on Salomon's crisis strategy was headlined "The Bomb Shelter That Salomon Built." During the aftermath of the bond market scandal, the interim chairman of Salomon, Warren Buffett, told employees, "Contemplating any business act, an employee should ask himself whether he would be willing to see it immediately described by an informed and critical reporter on the front page of his local paper, there to be read by his spouse, children, and friends. At Salomon we simply want no part of any activities that pass legal tests but that we, as citizens, would find offensive."[5]

There are other examples such as that involving the airline Gulfstream Air, which had provided the training for the pilots who were then involved in two fatal commercial crashes. The FAA discovered that Gulfstream had falsified the records for the hours the pilots had trained and flown. The headline read, "Airline Is Fined $1.3M for Fake Data."[6] The harsh headline brings a different perspective to the conduct. When Wall Street firms were reporting multibillion-dollar losses due to their highly leveraged portfolios of risky instruments, the headline on the cover of *Fortune* magazine read, "What Were They Smoking?" (November 26, 2007).

Laura Nash and Perspective

Business ethicist Laura Nash has developed a series of questions that business managers should ask themselves as they evaluate their ethical dilemmas. One of the questions is, "How would I view the issue if I stood on the other side of the fence?" For example, in 1993, federal guidelines required meat to be cooked to 140 degrees Fahrenheit. At that time, however, the state of Washington proposed imposing a higher temperature requirement of 155 degrees. Burger King cooked its hamburgers to 160 degrees and Wendy's, Hardee's, and Taco Bell cooked their meat to 165 degrees.

Health and food industry experts supported a minimum cooking temperature of 155 degrees to be certain *E. coli* bacteria are eliminated. Jack-in-the-Box followed the legal minimum of 140 degrees. Would you want that information as a consumer? Given the trend toward higher temperatures and the pending regulation, would you want your meat cooked to a higher temperature? Although the cooking temperature was legal, an ethical issue arises in continuing to follow only the law when health experts are concerned about the adequacy of the law. Jack-in-the-Box did, in fact, experience an *E. coli* outbreak: one child died and 300 other customers became ill.[7]

Other questions in the Nash model include, "Am I able to discuss my decision with my family, friends, and those closest to me?" "What am I trying to accomplish with my decision?" "Will I feel as comfortable about my decision over time as I do today?" The Nash model forces managers to seek additional perspectives as decisions are evaluated and implemented. For example, when William Aramony served as the CEO of United Way, he enjoyed such perks as an annual salary of close to $400,000, flights on the Concorde, and limousine service. Even though these benefits were about the same as those of other CEOs managing comparable assets, it would still be difficult to justify such benefits to a donor who earns $22,000 a year and has pledged 5 percent of it to United Way.

The *Wall Street Journal* Model

The *Wall Street Journal* model for resolution of ethical dilemmas consists of compliance, contribution, and consequences. Like the Blanchard–Peale model, any proposed conduct must first be in compliance with the law. The next step requires an evaluation of a decision's contributions to the shareholders, the employees, the community, and the customers. For example, furniture manufacturer Herman Miller, in a decision that was prescient in relation to the sustainability initiatives of 2010, decided both to invest in equipment that would exceed the requirements for compliance with the 1990 Clean Air Act and to refrain from using rain forest woods in producing its signature Eames chair. The decision was costly to the shareholders at first, but ultimately they, the community, and customers enjoyed the benefits.

Finally, managers are asked to envision the consequences of a decision, such as whether headlines that are unfavorable to the firm may result. The initial consequence of Miller's decisions was a reduction in profits because of the costs of the changes. However, the long-term consequences were the respect of environmental regulators, a responsive public committed to rain forest preservation, and Miller's longstanding recognition as one of America's top 20 corporate citizens.

Other Models

Of course, much simpler models for making ethical business decisions are available. One stems from Immanuel Kant's categorical imperative, loosely similar to the Golden Rule: "Do unto others as you would have them do unto you." Treating others or others' money as we would want to be treated is a powerful evaluation technique in ethical dilemmas. See Exhibit 2.5 and p. 66 for more discussion.

Why We Fail to Reach Good Decisions in Ethical Dilemmas

Very often, we look at the harmful and wrong conduct of corporate executives and wonder, "Where were their minds, and what were they thinking when they decided to engage in such bad behavior?" Often those involved did not walk through the steps in resolving ethical dilemmas discussed earlier. But they probably also slipped into rationalizations rather than analysis. The following sections provide a list and summary of each of the frequent statements of rationalization that we use to avoid facing ethical dilemmas (see Exhibit 2.1).

EXHIBIT 2.1   The Language of Rationalization

"Everybody else does it."

"If we don't do it, someone else will."

"That's the way it has always been done."

"We'll wait until the lawyers tell us it's wrong."

"It doesn't really hurt anyone."

"The system is unfair."

"If you think this is bad—you should have seen . . . "

"I was just following orders."

"It's a gray area."

"Everybody Else Does It"

When 15-year-old Jonathan Lebed was caught using many different screen names to post notices about the value of stocks he had purchased so that he could pump up their value and then sell them, he had made more than $800,000 by taking advantage of others who believed the false notices posted. His father said that he was proud of his son because his son was doing what all the other analysts and investment firms on Wall Street were doing. "Everybody else does it" is a rationalization, but it is not an analysis of the ethical issues involved in conduct.

"If We Don't Do It, Someone Else Will"

The rationalization of competition is one that finds us reasoning that if someone is going to do it and make money, it might as well be us. For Halloween 1994, O. J. Simpson masks and plastic knives and Nicole Brown Simpson masks and costumes complete with slashes and bloodstains were offered for sale. When Nicole Simpson's family objected to this violation of the basic standard of decency, a costume-shop owner commented that if he didn't sell the items, someone down the street would. Although nothing about the marketing of the costumes was illegal, ethical issues abound surrounding earning a profit from an event as heinous as the brutal murder of a young mother.

"That's the Way It Has Always Been Done"

Corporate or business history and business practices are not always sound. The fact that for years nothing has changed in a firm may indicate the need for change and an atmosphere that invites possible ethical violations. For example, until the changes in the law with the passage of Sarbanes-Oxley (SOX), firms that audited companies also provided consulting services for those companies. The consulting services were often worth as much or more to the audit firms than the audit work. To keep the consulting contracts, the audit firms often "went along" with management decisions on financial statement disclosures. SOX changed the way things had always been done, and now audit firms cannot also provide consulting services for their audit clients. A conflict of interest existed, but everybody was doing it, and corporations and audit firms had always had multiple service relationships. Again, unquestioning adherence to a pattern of practice or behavior often indicates an underlying ethical dilemma. For more discussion of auditor independence and SOX, see Chapters 20 and 21.

"We'll Wait until the Lawyers Tell Us It's Wrong"

Lawyers are trained to provide only the parameters of the law. In many situations, they offer an opinion that is correct in that it does not violate the law. Whether the conduct they have judged as legal is also ethical is a different question. Allowing law and lawyers to control a firm's destiny ignores the opportunity to make wise and ethical choices. For example, lawyers disagreed over whether the downloading of music over the Internet was a violation of copyright law. However, whether the downloading was legal does not answer the question of whether gaining access to and using someone else's intellectual property without permission or compensation was ethical.

"It Doesn't Really Hurt Anyone"

When we are the sole rubbernecker on the freeway, traffic remains unaffected. But if everyone rubbernecks, we have a traffic jam. If all of us made poor ethical choices, we would cause significant harm. A man interviewed after he was arrested for defrauding insurance companies through staged auto accidents remarked, "It didn't really hurt anyone. Insurance companies can afford it." The second part of his statement is accurate. The insurance companies can afford it—but not without cost to someone else. Such fraud harms all of us because we must pay higher premiums to allow insurers to absorb the costs of investigating and paying for fraudulent claims.

"The System Is Unfair"

Often touted by students as a justification for cheating on exams, this rationalization eases our consciences by telling us we are cheating only to make up for deficiencies in the system; yet just one person cheating can send ripples through an entire system. The credibility of grades and the institution come into question as students obtain grades through means beyond the system's standards. In countries in which corruption is a way of life and government employees award contracts and rights to do business on the basis of payments rather than on the merits of a given company or its proposal, the bribery only results in greater unfairness within and greater costs to those countries. Many economists have noted that a country's businesses and economy will not progress without some fundamental assurance of trust that comes through a belief that there is a level playing field where the quality of products and services matter.

"I Was Just Following Orders"

In many criminal trials and disputes over responsibility and liability, managers disclaim their responsibility by stating, "I was just following orders." Sometimes, individuals cannot follow the directions of supervisors because they have been asked to do something illegal or immoral. Judges who preside over the criminal trials of war criminals often remind defendants that an order is not necessarily legal or moral. Values require us to question or depart from orders when others will be harmed or wronged. When the allegations of prisoner abuse in Iraq emerged, along with photos, one of the first defenses raised by lawyers for the soldiers being court-martialed for their role in the abuses was, "I was just following orders." Sometimes following orders is not the ethical thing to do.

"You Think This Is Bad, You Should Have Seen . . . "

This rationalization finds employees looking back at earlier times and reminding others that the company's safety policies or accounting practices used to be much worse. At one company, when some employees objected to backdating contracts to slip the earnings into the quarter, some employees reassured them by saying, "At least we're not using the 35-day month we used to use to meet targets."

"It's a Gray Area"

The gray area is a comfort level for us when we are in the midst of an ethical dilemma. Once we enter the gray area, we have a fine line that crosses into illegality and also an opportunity to explore an issue beyond bare legal requirements. An attorney for former HP general counsel Ann Baskins says that Ms. Baskins now realizes that she should have focused on questioning whether the pretexting was ethical, not just on whether it was legal. "She regrets that she did not do so."[8] Kevin Hunsaker, a deputy general counsel and chief ethics officer, asked internal HP security employees about the legality of the pretexting operations, and one responded, "I think it's on the edge, but above board." Hunsaker responded with what have become the infamous words in the investigation, "I shouldn't have asked." On the edge and in a gray area often lands us in legal difficulty and controversy. Even though many of the charges were dismissed or reduced, five individuals, including Mr. Hunsaker, were charged with criminal misconduct in the HP pretexting case and the company paid a $14 million fine to settle the charges.

Ethical Issues

Indy driver Danica Patrick gave an interview to *Sports Illustrated* writer and radio host Dan Patrick, a transcript of which follows.

> *Dan: If you could take a performance-enhancing drug and not get caught, would you do it if it allowed you to win Indy?*
>
> *Danica: Well then it's not cheating, is it? If nobody finds out?*
>
> *Dan: So you would do it?*
>
> *Danica: Yeah, it would be like finding a grey area. In motorsports we work in the grey areas a lot. You're trying to find where the holes are in the rule book.*[9]

After the interview, in an interview with *USA Today*, Ms. Patrick indicated that she was just joking. The head of the USADA (U.S. Anti-Doping Agency) called the interview "totally irresponsible," and added, "Although joking about the use of dangerous and unhealthy drugs that cheaters use to rob clean athletes of their dreams is no laughing matter."[10]

Identify the rationalizations in Ms. Patrick's statements. Why do you think she answered the questions as she did? Was the joke still an ethical issue?

Social Responsibility:
Another Layer of Business Ethics

So far in this chapter we have covered two layers of business ethics: the basic categories, and notions of fairness. A third layer of ethics focuses on relationships and conflicts among relationships.

In some ethical dilemmas in business, the interests of the shareholders might be different from the interests of the employees. Lower wages bring higher profits and returns, at least temporarily, to shareholders, but is shipping work overseas to countries where the wages are low taking unfair advantage? In this third layer of business ethics, we look at the interests of those who are affected by business decisions, often called the stakeholders of the business. For example, suppose the business discovers that its air pollution control equipment is not state-of-the-art technology and that, although no laws are being violated, more pollution is being released than is necessary. To correct the problem, its factory must be shut down for a minimum of three months. The pollution will harm the air and the community, but the shutdown will harm the workers and the shareholders. The business must consider the needs and interests of all its stakeholders in resolving the ethical dilemma it faces. Much discussion and disagreement continue to surround this particular issue. In the following interview excerpt, economist Milton Friedman offers a different perspective on this ethical dilemma.

> Q: Quite apart from emission standards and effluent taxes, shouldn't corporate officials take action to stop pollution out of a sense of social responsibility?
>
> Milton Friedman: *I wouldn't buy stock in a company that hired that kind of leadership. A corporate executive's responsibility is to make as much money for the shareholders as possible, as long as he operates within the rules of the game. When an executive decides to take action for reasons of social responsibility, he is taking money from someone else—from the stockholders, in the form of lower dividends; from the employees, in the form of lower wages; or from the consumer, in the form of higher prices. The responsibility of a corporate executive is to fulfill the terms of his contract. If he can't do that in good conscience, then he should quit his job and find another way to do good. He has the right to promote what he regards as desirable moral objectives only with his own money. If, on the other hand, the executives of U.S. Steel undertake to reduce pollution in Gary for the purpose of making the town attractive to employees and thus lowering labor costs, then they are doing the stockholders' bidding. And everyone benefits: The stockholders get higher dividends; the customer gets cheaper steel; the workers get more in return for their labor. That's the beauty of free enterprise. . . . To the extent that pollution caused by the U.S. Steel plant there is confined to that city and the people there are truly concerned about the problem, it's to the company's advantage to do something about it. Why? Because if it doesn't, workers will prefer to live where there is less pollution, and U.S. Steel will have to pay them more to live in Gary, Indiana.*[11]

Ethical Postures for Social Responsibility

Often, decisions in dilemmas that involve stakeholders depend on the overall attitude of a company and its perspective on the role of business in society. The ethical perspective of a business often sets the tone for its operations and employees' choices. Historically, the philosophical debate over the role of business in society has evolved into four schools of thought on ethical behavior based on the responses

EXHIBIT 2.2 Social Responsibility of Corporations

	MORAL QUESTION: WHOSE INTEREST SHOULD THE CORPORATION SERVE?	POLICY QUESTION: BEST WAY TO SERVE INTEREST IF THE CORPORATION IS RESPONSIVE TO:
Inherence	Shareholders only	Shareholders only
Enlightened self-interest	Shareholders only	Larger society
Invisible hand	Larger society	Shareholders only
Social responsibility	Larger society	Larger society

Source: Adapted with permission of *American Business Law Journal*, from Daryl Hatano, "Should Corporations Exercise Their Freedom of Speech Rights?" 22 *American Bus. L.J.* 165 (1984).

to two questions: (1) Whose interest should a corporation serve? (2) To whom should a corporation be responsive in order to best serve that interest? These questions have only two answers—"shareholders only" and "the larger society"—and the combination of those answers defines the school of thought. The following discussion is summarized in Exhibit 2.2.

Inherence

According to the inherence school of thought, managers answer only to shareholders and act only with shareholders' interests in mind. This type of manager would not become involved in any political or social issues unless it was in the shareholders' best interests to do so, provided the involvement did not backfire and cost the firm sales. Milton Friedman's philosophy, as previously expressed, is an example of inherence. To understand how a business following the inherence school of thought would behave, consider the issue of a proposed increase in residential property taxes for school funding. A business that subscribes to the inherence school would support a school tax increase only if the educational issue affected the company's performance and only if such a position did not offend those who opposed the tax increase.

Enlightened Self-Interest

According to this school of thought, the manager is responsible to the shareholders but serves them best by being responsive to the larger society. Enlightened self-interest is based on the view that, in the long run, business value is enhanced if business is responsive to the needs of society. In this school, managers are free to speak out on societal issues without the constraint of offending someone, as in inherence. Businesses would anticipate social changes and needs and be early advocates for change. For example, many corporations today have instituted job sharing, child-care facilities, and sick-child care in response to the changing structure of the American family and workforce. This responsiveness to the needs of the larger society should also be beneficial to shareholders because it enables the business to retain a quality workforce.

The Invisible Hand

The invisible hand school of thought is the opposite of enlightened self-interest. According to this philosophy, business ought to serve the larger society and it does this best when it serves the shareholders only. Such businesses allow government to set the standards and boundaries for appropriate behavior and simply adhere to these governmental constraints as a way of maximizing benefits to their shareholders. They become involved in issues of social responsibility or in political issues only when society lacks sufficient information on an issue to make a decision. Even then, their involvement is limited to presenting data and does not extend to advocating a particular viewpoint or position. This school of thought holds that it is best for society to guide itself and that businesses work best when they serve shareholders within those constraints.

Social Responsibility

In the social responsibility school of thought, the role of business is to serve the larger society by responding to society's needs as a first priority. A business following this school of thought would advocate full disclosure of product information to consumers in its advertising and would encourage political activism on the part of its managers and employees on all issues, not just those that affect the corporation. These businesses adhere to the belief that their sense of social responsibility contributes to their long-term success.

Why Business Ethics?

Now that you have background on the types of ethical issues businesses face, background on social responsibility, and a framework for analysis of ethical issues, you may still be skeptical: "But why should a business worry about these things beyond just complying with the law? Why not just maximize under the system?" Some compelling reasons promote choosing ethical behavior, as discussed in the following sections.

Personal Accountability and Comfort: Business Ethics for Personal Reasons

Before looking at business data on the value of ethics, it is important to realize that the choices we make in our business lives must still feel personally comfortable. And it would be misleading to say that every ethical business is a profitable business. First, not all ethical people are good managers or possess the necessary skills for making a business a success; but many competent businesspeople have suffered for being ethical, and many others seem to survive despite their lack of ethics. Columnist Dave Barry noted that every time an oil spill occurs, the oil companies ready themselves for the higher prices and profits that come because all that oil is lost at sea. Despite his conviction and jail term related to junk bond sales in the 1980s, Michael Milken earned a $50 million fee for helping Ted Turner negotiate a merger with Time Warner.[12] Many whistle-blowers, although highly respected, have been unable to find employment in their industries. If ethical behavior does not guarantee success, then why have ethics? The answer has to do with personal ethics applied in a business context. One investment banker who worked on Drexel Burnham's trading desk during the Michael Milken days of that firm and who is now chairman of GoldTree Asset Management said, "Just to be able to sit on the desk and see the calls start at 4:15 in the morning, Boesky and Perelman and Diller and Murdoch . . . "[13] But Mr. Wagner said that he took not just the memories of the power of Drexel with him but a powerful lesson as well:

"There's a difference between being very competitive and can-do, and winning at all costs. All costs is costly."

Business ethics is really nothing more than a standard of personal behavior applied to a group of people working together to make a profit. Some people are ethical because it enables them to sleep better at night. Some people are ethical because of the fear of getting caught. But being personally ethical is a justification for business ethics—it is simply the correct thing to do. Bowen McCoy's "The Parable of the Sadhu" focuses on business ethics for personal reasons.

For the Manager's Desk

Re: The Parable of the Sadhu

[In 1982], as the first participant in the new six-month sabbatical program that Morgan Stanley has adopted, I enjoyed a rare opportunity to collect my thoughts as well as do some traveling. I spent the first three months in Nepal, walking 600 miles through 200 villages in the Himalayas and climbing some 120,000 vertical feet. On the trip my sole Western companion was an anthropologist who shed light on the cultural patterns of the villages we passed through.

During the Nepal hike, something occurred that has had a powerful impact on my thinking about corporate ethics. Although some might argue that the experience has no relevance to business, it was a situation in which a basic ethical dilemma suddenly intruded into the lives of a group of individuals. How the group responded I think holds a lesson for all organizations no matter how defined.

The Sadhu

The Nepal experience was more rugged and adventuresome than I had anticipated. Most commercial treks last two or three weeks and cover a quarter of the distance we traveled.

My friend Stephen, the anthropologist, and I were halfway through the 60-day Himalayan part of the trip when we reached the high point, an 18,000-foot pass over a crest that we'd have to traverse to reach the village of Mukinath [sic], an ancient holy place for pilgrims.

Six years earlier I had suffered pulmonary edema, an acute form of altitude sickness, at 16,500 feet in the vicinity of Everest base camp, so we were understandably concerned about what would happen at 18,000 feet. Moreover, the Himalayas were having their wettest spring in 20 years; hip-deep powder and ice had already driven us off one ridge. If we failed to cross the pass, I feared that the last half of our "once in a lifetime" trip would be ruined.

The night before we would try the pass, we camped at a hut at 14,500 feet. In the photos taken at the camp, my face appears wan. The last village we'd passed through was a sturdy two-day walk below us, and I was tired.

During the late afternoon, four backpackers from New Zealand joined us, and we spent most of the night awake, anticipating the climb. Below we could see the fires of two other parties, which turned out to be two Swiss couples and a Japanese hiking club.

To get over the steep part of the climb before the sun melted the steps cut in the ice, we departed at 3:30 A.M. The New Zealanders left first, followed by Stephen and myself, our porters and Sherpas, and then the Swiss. The Japanese lingered in their camp. The sky was clear, and we were confident that no spring storm would erupt that day to close the pass.

At 15,500 feet, it looked to me as if Stephen were shuffling and staggering a bit, which are symptoms of altitude sickness. (The initial stage of altitude sickness brings a headache and nausea. As the condition worsens, a climber may encounter difficult breathing, disorientation, aphasia, and paralysis.) I felt strong, my adrenaline was flowing, but I was very concerned about my ultimate ability to get across. A couple of our porters were also suffering from the height, and Pasang, our Sherpa sirdar (leader), was worried.

Just after daybreak, while we rested at 15,500 feet, one of the New Zealanders, who had gone ahead, came staggering down toward us with a body slung across his shoulders. He dumped the almost naked, barefoot body of an Indian holy man—a sadhu—at my feet. He had found the pilgrim lying on the ice, shivering and suffering from hypothermia. I cradled the sadhu's head and laid him out on the rocks. The New Zealander was angry. He wanted to get across the pass before the bright sun melted the snow. He said, "Look, I've done what I can. You have porters and Sherpa guides. You care for him. We're going on!" He turned and went back up the mountain to join his friends.

I took a carotid pulse and found that the sadhu was still alive. We figured he had probably visited the holy shrines at Mukinath [sic] and was on his way home. It was fruitless to question why he had chosen this desperately high route instead of the safe, heavily traveled caravan route through the

CONTINUED

Kali Gandaki gorge. Or why he was almost naked and with no shoes, or how long he had been lying in the pass. The answers were not going to solve our problem.

Stephen and the four Swiss began stripping off outer clothing and opening their packs. The sadhu was soon clothed from head to foot. He was not able to walk, but he was very much alive. I looked down the mountain and spotted below the Japanese climbers marching up with a horse.

Without a great deal of thought, I told Stephen and Pasang that I was concerned about withstanding the heights to come and wanted to get over the pass. I took off after several of our porters who had gone ahead.

On the steep part of the ascent where, if the ice steps had given way, I would have slid down about 3,000 feet, I felt vertigo. I stopped for a breather, allowing the Swiss to catch up with me. I inquired about the sadhu and Stephen. They said that the sadhu was fine and that Stephen was just behind. I set off again for the summit.

Stephen arrived at the summit an hour after I did. Still exhilarated by victory, I ran down the snow slope to congratulate him. He was suffering from altitude sickness, walking fifteen steps, then stopping, walking fifteen steps, then stopping. When I reached them, Stephen glared at me and said: "How do you feel about contributing to the death of a fellow man?"

I did not fully comprehend what he meant.

"Is the sadhu dead?" I inquired.

"No," replied Stephen, "but he surely will be!"

After I had gone, and the Swiss had departed not long after, Stephen had remained with the sadhu. When the Japanese had arrived, Stephen had asked to use their horse to transport the sadhu down to the hut. They had refused. He had then asked Pasang to have a group of our porters carry the sadhu. Pasang had resisted the idea, saying that the porters would have to exert all their energy to get themselves over the pass. He had thought they could not carry a man down 1,000 feet to the hut, reclimb the slope, and get across safely before the snow melted. Pasang had pressed Stephen not to delay any longer.

The Sherpas had carried the sadhu down to a rock in the sun at about 15,000 feet and had pointed out the hut another 500 feet below. The Japanese had given him food and drink. When they had last seen him he was listlessly throwing rocks at the Japanese party's dog, which had frightened him.

We do not know if the sadhu lived or died.

For many of the following days and evenings Stephen and I discussed and debated our behavior toward the sadhu. Stephen is a committed Quaker with deep moral vision. He said, "I feel that what happened with the sadhu is a good example of the breakdown between the individual ethic and the corporate ethic. No one person was willing to assume ultimate responsibility for the sadhu. Each was willing to do his bit just so long as it was not too inconvenient. When it got to be a bother, everyone just passed the buck to someone else and took off. Jesus was relevant to a more individualist stage of society, and how do we interpret his teaching today in a world filled with large, impersonal organizations and groups?"

I defended the larger group, saying, "Look, we all cared. We all stopped and gave aid and comfort. Everyone did his bit. The New Zealander carried him down below the snow line. I took his pulse and suggested we treat him for hypothermia. You and the Swiss gave him clothing and got him warmed up. The Japanese gave him food and water. The Sherpas carried him down to the sun and pointed out the easy trail toward the hut. He was well enough to throw rocks at a dog. What more could we do?"

"You have just described the typical affluent Westerner's response to a problem. Throwing money—in this case food and sweaters—at it, but not solving the fundamentals!" Stephen retorted.

"What would satisfy you?" I said. "Here we are, a group of New Zealanders, Swiss, Americans, and Japanese who have never met before and who are at the apex of one of the most powerful experiences of our lives. Some years the pass is so bad no one gets over it. What right does an almost naked pilgrim who chooses the wrong trail have to disrupt our lives? Even the Sherpas had no interest in risking the trip to help him beyond a certain point."

Stephen calmly rebutted, "I wonder what the Sherpas would have done if the sadhu had been a well-dressed Nepali, or what the Japanese would have done if the sadhu had been a well-dressed Asian, or what you would of done, Buzz, if the sadhu had been a well-dressed Western woman?"

"Where, in your opinion," I asked instead, "is the limit of our responsibility in a situation like this? We had our own well-being to worry about. Our Sherpa guides were unwilling to jeopardize us or the porters for the sadhu. No one else on the mountain was willing to commit himself beyond certain self-imposed limits."

Stephen said, "As individual Christians or people with a Western ethical tradition, we can fulfill our obligations in such a situation only if (1) the sadhu dies in our care, (2) the sadhu demonstrates to us that he could undertake the two-day walk down to the village, or (3) we carry the sadhu for two days down to the village and convince someone there to care for him."

"Leaving the sadhu in the sun with food and clothing, while he demonstrated hand-eye coordination by throwing a rock at a dog, comes close to fulfilling items one and two," I answered. "And it wouldn't have made sense to take him to the village, where the people appeared to be far less caring than the Sherpas, so the third condition is impractical. Are you really saying that, no matter what the implications, we should, at the drop of a hat, have changed our entire plan?"

The Individual versus the Group Ethic

Despite my arguments, I felt and continue to feel guilt about the sadhu. I had literally walked through a classic moral dilemma without fully thinking through the consequences. My excuses for my actions include a high adrenaline flow, a superordinate goal, and a once-in-a-lifetime opportunity—factors in the usual corporate situation, especially when one is under stress.

Real moral dilemmas are ambiguous, and many of us hike right through them, unaware that they exist. When, usually after the fact, someone makes an issue of them, we tend to resent his or her bringing it up. Often, when the full import of what we have done (or not done) falls on us, we dig into a defensive position from which it is very difficult to emerge. In rare circumstances we may contemplate what we have done from inside a prison.

Had we mountaineers been free of physical and mental stress caused by the effort and the high altitude, we might have treated the sadhu differently. Yet isn't stress the true test of personal and corporate values? The instant decisions executives make under pressure reveal the most about personal and corporate character. Among the many questions that occur to me when pondering my experience are: What are the practical limits of moral imagination and vision? Is there a collective or institutional ethic beyond the ethics of the individual? At what level of effort or commitment can one discharge one's ethical responsibilities?

Not every ethical dilemma has a right solution. Reasonable people often disagree; otherwise there would be no dilemma. In a business context, however, it is essential that managers agree on a process for dealing with dilemmas.

The sadhu experience offers an interesting parallel to business situations. An immediate response was mandatory. Failure to act was a decision in itself. Up on the mountain we could not resign and submit our résumé to a headhunter. In contrast to philosophy, business involves action and implementation—getting things done. Managers must come up with answers to problems based on what they see and what they allow to influence their decision-making processes. On the mountain, none of us but Stephen realized the true dimensions of the situation we were facing.

One of our problems was that as a group we had no process for developing a consensus. We had no sense of purpose or plan. The difficulties of dealing with the sadhu were so complex that no one person could handle it. Because it did not have a set of preconditions that could guide its action to an acceptable resolution, the group reacted instinctively as individuals. The cross-cultural nature of the group added a further layer of complexity. We had no leader with whom we could identify and in whose purpose we believed. Only Stephen was willing to take charge, but he could not gain adequate support to care for the sadhu.

Some organizations do have a value system that transcends the personal values of the managers. Such values, which go beyond profitability, are usually revealed when the organization is under stress. People throughout the organization generally accept its values, which, because they are not presented as a rigid list of commandments, may be somewhat ambiguous. The stories people tell, rather than printed materials, transmit these conceptions of what is proper behavior.

For twenty years I have been exposed at senior levels to a variety of corporations and organizations. It is amazing how quickly an outsider can sense the tone and style of an organization and the degree of tolerated openness and freedom to challenge management.

Organizations that do not have a heritage of mutually accepted, shared values tend to become unhinged during stress, with each individual bailing out for himself. In the great takeover battles we have witnessed during past years, companies that had strong cultures drew the wagons around them and fought it out, while other companies saw executives, supported by their golden parachutes, bail out of the struggles.

Because corporations and their members are interdependent, for the corporation to be strong the members need to share a preconceived notion of what is correct behavior, a "business ethic," and think of it as a positive force, not a constraint.

As an investment banker I am continually warned by well-meaning lawyers, clients, and associates to be wary of conflicts of interest. Yet if I were to run away from every difficult situation, I wouldn't be an effective investment banker. I have to feel my way through conflicts. An effective manager can't run from risk either; he or she has to confront and deal with risk. To feel "safe" in doing this, managers need the guidelines of an agreed-on process and set of values within the organization.

After my three months in Nepal, I spent three months as an executive-in-residence at both Stanford Business School and the Center for Ethics and Social Policy at the Graduate Theological Union at Berkeley. These six months away from my job gave me time to assimilate twenty years of business experience. My thoughts turned often to the meaning of the leadership role in any large organization. Students at the seminary thought of themselves as antibusiness. But when I questioned them they agreed they distrusted all large organizations, including the church. They perceived all large organizations as impersonal and opposed to individual values and needs. Yet we all know of organizations where people's values and beliefs are respected and their expressions encouraged. What makes the difference? Can we identify the difference and, as a result, manage more effectively?

The word "ethics" turns off many and confuses more. Yet the notions of shared values and an agreed-on process for dealing with adversity and change—what many people mean when they talk about corporate culture—seem to be at the heart of the ethical issue. People who are in touch with their own core beliefs and the beliefs of others and are sustained by them can be more comfortable living on the cutting edge.

At times, taking a tough line or a decisive stand in a muddle of ambiguity is the only ethical thing to do. If a manager is indecisive and spends time trying to figure out the "good" thing to do, the enterprise may be lost.

Business ethics, then, has to do with authenticity and integrity of the enterprise. To be ethical is to follow the business as well as the cultural goals of the corporation, its owners, its employees, and its customers. Those who cannot serve the corporate vision are not authentic business people and, therefore, are not ethical in the business sense.

At this stage of my own business experience I have a strong interest in organizational behavior. Sociologists are keenly studying what they call corporate stories, legends, and heroes as a way organizations have of transmitting the value

CONTINUED

system. Corporations such as Arco have even hired consultants to perform an audit of their corporate culture. In a company, the leader is the person who understands, interprets, and manages the corporate value system. Effective managers are then action-oriented people who resolve conflict, are tolerant of ambiguity, stress, and change, and have a strong sense of purpose for themselves and their organizations.

If all this is true, I wonder about the role of the professional manager who moves from company to company. How can he or she quickly absorb the values and culture of different organizations? Or is there, indeed, an art of management that is totally transportable? Assuming such fungible managers do exist, is it proper for them to manipulate the values of others?

What would have happened had Stephen and I carried the sadhu for two days back to the village and become involved with the villagers in his care? In four trips to Nepal my most interesting experiences occurred in 1975 when I lived in a Sherpa home in the Khumbu for five days recovering from altitude sickness. The high point of Stephen's trip was an invitation to participate in a family funeral ceremony in Manang. Neither experience had to do with climbing the high passes of the Himalayas. Why were we so reluctant to try the lower path, the ambiguous trail? Perhaps because we did not have a leader who could reveal the greater purpose of the trip to us.

Why didn't Stephen with his moral vision opt to take the sadhu under his personal care? The answer is because, in part, Stephen was hard-stressed physically himself, and because, in part, without some support system that involved our involuntary and episodic community on the mountain, it was beyond his individual capacity to do so.

I see the current interest in corporate culture and corporate value systems as a positive response to Stephen's

pessimism about the decline of the role of the individual in large organizations. Individuals who operate from a thoughtful set of personal values provide the foundation of a corporate culture. A corporate tradition that encourages freedom of inquiry, supports personal values, and reinforces a focused sense of direction can fulfill the need for individuality along with the prosperity and success of the group. Without such corporate support, the individual is lost.

That is the lesson of the sadhu. In a complex corporate situation, the individual requires and deserves the support of the group. If people cannot find such support from their organization, they don't know how to act. If such support is forthcoming, a person has a stake in the success of the group, and can add much to the process of establishing and maintaining a corporate culture. It is the management's challenge to be sensitive to individual needs, to shape them, and to direct and focus them for the benefit of the group as a whole.

For each of us the sadhu lives. Should we stop what we are doing and comfort him; or should we keep trudging up toward the high pass? Should I pause to help the derelict I pass on the street each night as I walk by the Yale Club en route to Grand Central Station? Am I his brother? What is the nature of our responsibility if we consider ourselves to be ethical persons? Perhaps it is to change the values of the group so that it can, with all its resources, take the other road.

Discussion Question

Consider the closing questions Mr. McCoy poses. How do they apply to you personally and to businesses?

Ethical Issues

In 2006, David Sharp, 34, from Britain, was not handling a climb to Mt. Everest well. He was a victim of oxygen deprivation and eventually collapsed on the ground. Forty other climbers passed him by and, unable to move, Mr. Sharp froze to death. Those who passed him by indicated that the conditions are rugged and that climbers know going in that they may have to pay the ultimate price.

Lincoln Hall, 50, from Australia, was discovered by an American guide after he had spent a night on the freezing mountainside. The MyHeroProject describes Mr. Hall's condition as follows, "He was sitting on the trail with his jacket around his waist, wearing no hat or gloves. The group stopped to investigate and found he was suffering from symptoms of edema, frostbite and dehydration. He was alone and hallucinating; and generally incoherent in

his responses to their offers of help. He was without any of the proper equipment for survival in such conditions. Apparently, Mr. Hall had collapsed the previous day on his way down from the summit."

Mr. Dan Mazur and his team abandoned their climb and stayed with Mr. Hall until rescuer sherpas could come to help. Mr. Hall's team assumed that he was dead and had called his wife the evening before to tell her.

In the years since 1953, 3,000 climbers have made it to the Everest summit, but 200 climbers have died. A climb with a guide costs about $60,000. What do you think makes the difference in the decision process between those who stop to help and those who continue their climbs?

Importance of Values
in Business Success

As you learn in other disciplines, from economics to management, business is driven by the bottom line. Profits control whether the firm can obtain loans or gain investors and serve as the sole indicator of the firm's success—and, in most cases, its employees' success, as well. Indeed, business firms can be defined as groups of people working together to obtain maximum profits. The pursuit of the bottom line, however, can occasionally distort the perspective of even the most conscientious among us. The fear of losing business and, consequently, losing profits and capital support can persuade people to engage in conduct that, although not illegal, is unethical. But those who pursue only the bottom line fail to recognize that a successful business is more like a marathon than a sprint, requiring that ethical dilemmas be resolved with a long-term perspective in mind. Indeed, those firms that adhere to ethical standards perform better financially over the long run.

A 1997 study on the relationship between corporate behavior and financial performance concluded that firms involved in regulatory or criminal violations or product liability litigation because of an unsafe product experience lower returns and slower sales growth even five years after their problems in these areas occur.[14]

The Tylenol tampering incident of 1982 offers one of the most telling examples of the rewards of being ethical. When Tylenol capsules were discovered to have been tainted with deadly poison, Tylenol's manufacturer, McNeil Consumer Products Company, a subsidiary of Johnson & Johnson, followed its code of ethics, which required it to put the interests of the consumer first. In what many financial analysts and economists considered to be a disastrous decision and a dreadful mistake, McNeil recalled all Tylenol capsules from the market—31 million bottles with a retail value of about $100 million. A new and safer form of a noncapsule Tylenol caplet was developed, and within a few months Tylenol regained its majority share of the market. The recall had turned out to be neither a poor decision nor a financial disaster. Rather, the company's actions enhanced its reputation and served to create a bond between Tylenol and its customers that was based largely on trust and respect for the integrity of the company and the product.[15] (See "Leadership's Role in Ethical Choices" for further discussion of this issue.)

In contrast to the positive nature of ethical behavior is unethical behavior. For example, companies in investment banking and mortgage industries collapses have been reeling from the revelations about their lack of candor in selling and buying mortgages and mortgage instruments and now struggle to regain credibility. Beech-Nut suffered tremendous earnings losses as a result of the discovery that its baby food "apple juice" did not in fact contain any real apple juice. Nestlé endured many consumer boycotts since the early 1970s as a result of its intense—and what came to be perceived by the public as exploitative and unethical—marketing of infant formula in then–Third World nations, where the lack of sanitation, refrigeration, and education led to serious health problems in infants given the formula. In 1989, nearly 20 years after the infant formula crisis, Nestlé's new "Good Start" formula was slow in market infiltration and, because of continuing consumer resistance, did not perform as well as its quality and innovativeness would have predicted. Nestlé has never gained the market share or reputation its quality product deserves. As the Nestlé experience illustrates, a firm's reputation for ethical behavior is the same as an individual's reputation: It takes a long time to gain, but it can be lost instantly as the result of one bad choice.

BP, the oil and natural gas company, was performing well with operations in 100 countries, 96,000 employees, and nearly 24,000 retail service stations around the world. As the second-largest oil company in the world and one of the world's 10 largest corporations, BP had also been a perennial favorite of NGOs and environmental groups. For example, *Business Ethics* named BP the world's most admired company and one of its top corporate citizens. Green Investors named BP its top company because of BP's continuing commitment to investment in alternative energy sources. But BP had issues percolating as it gained these recognitions. In 2005, an explosion at one of BP's refineries, located in Texas City, Texas, resulted in the death of 15 employees and injuries to 170 others. Both an internal investigation and a government report indicated that the accident would have been avoidable if the company had not cut maintenance costs at the expense of safety. The accident followed on the heels of charges that the company's traders were manipulating the price of propane in the markets by holding back on supplies.

Also, the company's oil fields at Prudhoe Bay, Alaska, burst in 2006, resulting in a 267,000-gallon oil spill on pristine Alaskan tundra.[16] Industry standards require "smart-pigging" (ultrasonic checking) of pipelines every five years to detect weaknesses or corrosion. At the time of the March 2006 spill, BP disclosed that it had not done smart-pigging on the Prudhoe Bay line since 1998 and that the pipes had not been cleaned since 1992. The BP field manager at Prudhoe Bay said, following the spill, "If we had it to do over again, we would have been pigging those lines."[17] The line had to be closed down and, again, an internal report revealed that the cost-cutting drive at BP affected the decisions in the oil fields. Following the oil spill, BP's stock price fell more than 15 percent in three months.

Oil production dropped 75 percent and BP spent $1 billion to fix the Texas refinery. One expert noted at that time that it would take years for BP to recover financially and even longer to restore its credibility with the market and regulators. That prescient remark has proved to be even more true after BP's Deepwater Horizon in the Gulf of Mexico well sprung a "leak" and began gushing oil in April 2010. Evidence has emerged that BP used shortcuts in the critical path for digging the offshore well. There is also evidence that the decisions BP made were not industry practice for the nature and depth of this well. BP's stock price fell over 50 percent in the month following the Deepwater Horizon accident. A federal ban on offshore oil was enjoined by a court but another was attempted and the entire oil industry was feeling the impact of BP's actions and choices.

As General Motors prepared to release its Chevrolet Malibu for production in 1976, an engineer drafted a memo about some issues with the placement of the car's gas tank and the likelihood of its explosion in the event of a rear-end collision. The memo discussed both the potential liability for such accidents and the costs of modifying the design. The Malibu went forward without production and design changes. By 1981, the company faced some litigation related to rear-end collisions involving the Malibu and gas tank explosions. A lawyer working on the cases found the 1976 memo and explained the need to keep the engineer's thoughts and analysis from being disclosed. In December 1999, a jury awarded the victims of a Malibu rear-end collision and explosion more than $107 million compensatory damages and $4.8 billion punitive damages (later reduced to $1.2 billion on appeal) and explained that its high damage verdict was directly attributable to the memo, the knowledge, and the failure to disclose that information or take corrective action.

The poor value choices of the aforementioned firms resulted in tremendous financial setbacks and, in some cases, destruction. The core values of a firm give it long-standing profitability. "The Tony Bennett Factor" (p. 57) offers some insight into longevity, profitability, and values.

For the Manager's Desk

Re: The Tony Bennett Factor

I had blocked out the background noise offered courtesy of MTV and my teenager, but I glanced up and saw Tony Bennett. My parents raised me on Tony Bennett LPs back in the '50s. "I Left My Heart in San Francisco" enjoyed hours of play in Tyrone, Pa. And here he was back, "Tony Bennett Unplugged." Mr. Bennett has not changed. Yet his success has spanned generations. Suddenly my work with a colleague, Prof. Louis Grossman, had new meaning. We had been studying business longevity, trying to determine what makes some businesses survive so successfully for so long.

Prof. Grossman and I began our study when we spotted a 1982 full-page ad in this newspaper placed by Diamond Match Co. The ad touted the company's 100 years of consistent dividend payments. Today's standards tell us that 100 quarters of dividend payments would be stellar. What kind of company was this? Were there others?

We discovered seven other industrial firms that could boast of making at least an annual dividend payment for a string of 100 years or more: Scovill, Inc.; Ludlow Corp.; Stanley Works; Singer Co.; Pennwalt, Inc.; Pullman, Inc.; and Corning Glass Works. Pullman, Ludlow and Stanley had unbroken chains of a century of quarterly dividend payments as well.

Mr. Bennett and our eight companies have survival in common. These survivors' tools make management theories of today seem trite. They had no shifting paradigms. No buzzwords.

Mr. Bennett recognized his strength as a balladeer and stuck with it, through everything from the Beatles to Hootie and the Blowfish. Although each of our companies recognized the importance of diversification, they all held fast to a WBAWI—or "what business are we in?"—philosophy. They knew their strengths, developed strong market presences based on those strengths, and never forgot their roots. Mr. Bennett never performed without singing "I Wanna Be Around." Singer never left its sewing machines. Pullman never deserted its train cars. Diamond held on to its matches.

The firms diversified only when their strengths allowed. Scovill began as a brass button manufacturer and backed into brass manufacturing because it knew brass. Scovill bought Hamilton Beach because Hamilton Beach was a major brass purchaser. Scovill understood this customer's business.

Other companies have forgotten the WBAWI lesson and paid the price. Sears abandoned its catalog, insurance and real estate businesses and now struggles to find a retail presence. IBM has suffered for not understanding its business was the workplace, not mainframe computers. Its Lotus takeover shows it may recognize the PC as the workplace.

All Mr. Bennett needs are a microphone and a pianist to make music. All eight of our companies were low-cost producers. All eight were cost conscious. Scovill executive vice presidents with worldwide responsibilities shared a secretary. Spartan company headquarters were the rule for these firms. There were barely six-figure salaries for executives. By contrast, IBM's Louis Gerstner hired an executive chef at $120,000 just last month.

Mr. Bennett has used the same musical arranger for nearly 30 years. Our eight companies' management team histories are in direct contrast to the executive recruiting practices in vogue today. Scovill, founded during the Jefferson administration in 1803, had only 12 CEOs during its 100-year dividend run. Three of the companies (Singer, Stanley and Diamond) had CEOs who served for more than 40 years. Seven of the companies never had a CEO serve for fewer than 10 years. They were not afraid of home-grown management. Their officers and CEOs came up through the ranks. Management succession is found in all eight companies.

Perhaps this information demonstrates the importance of continuity and stability. The executives appreciated the tension between short-term results and long-term performance, but the short term did not control decision making. Donald Davis, chairman and CEO of Stanley Works, put it this way: "The tension is always there. One of the top management's toughest jobs really is to mediate between the two viewpoints—short-term profit results now versus investment for future development."

Mr. Bennett did and does spend time on the road in concert, in direct contact with audiences—no mega-tours, just constant gigs. And a full century before we heard of customer service, these firms sent their sales forces and vice presidents alike out on the road to talk directly with customers. They had interesting marketing studies: one-on-one feedback. Sales calls, follow-ups, replacements, and refunds allowed them to remain in the customers' minds and good graces.

One officer said it best: "Anyone can read the monthly financial reports: What we need to do is to interpret them so we can spot trends. We call on customers, on suppliers, we look at the bottom line of course, but we know how that line reached the bottom."

Mr. Bennett has never made a bad recording or disappointed during a live performance. Our eight firms had strong commitments to integrity. Their mantra was: "If there's integrity, there will be quality and profits." Their integrity manifested itself in more than just quality. Frederick T. Stanley, founder of Stanley Works, spoke of the intricate balance between automation and employees: "Machines are no better than the skill,

CONTINUED

care, ingenuity and spirit of the men who operate them. We can achieve perfect harmony when shortening of an operation provides mutual advantages to the workman and the producers." Ethics before its time. Re-engineering done correctly in the 1800s. Nothing at the expense of the customer or the employee.

Our firms were no less remarkable than Mr. Bennett and his success with Generation X—his third generational conquest. The sad part of their stories is what happened following the takeover battles of the '80s. But that is a story for another time. For now, it is reassuring to realize that cost-consciousness, focus, customer service, home-grown management and integrity are keys to longevity. Today's management fads seem as shallow as Ice T (aka Ice-T) and Madonna. There is a simple Tony Bennett factor in success that makes today's fads much easier to debunk and infinitely easier to question.

Source: "The Tony Bennett Factor" reprinted with permission of *The Wall Street Journal*, Louis Grossman, and Marianne M. Jennings, from *The Wall Street Journal*, June 26, 1995, p. A12. Copyright © 1995 Dow Jones & Company, Inc. All rights reserved.

Ethics as a Strategy

Ethical behavior not only increases long-term earnings; it also enables businesses to anticipate and plan for social needs and cultural changes that require the firm or its product to evolve. One of the benefits of a firm's ethical behavior and participation in community concerns is the goodwill that such involvement fosters. Conversely, the absence of that goodwill and consequent loss of trust can mean the destruction of the firm.

When methyl isocyanate gas leaked from the Union Carbide plant in Bhopal, India, in 1984, the deadly gas left more than 2,500 dead and 200,000 injured. Investigations revealed that the plant had experienced problems with some of the equipment designed to prevent such leaks. Although actual liability issues were hotly debated in court, many ethical questions were raised regarding the plant and Union Carbide. Was it a wise decision to build the plant in a country with little expertise in the relevant technology? Did the people in the town know of the potential dangers of the plant? Why was a city of shacks allowed to be erected so close to the plant?

According to the Indian government, the plant had been operated well within legal and regulatory requirements, and Union Carbide's management had been cooperative in installing any additional equipment needed. Should Union Carbide have done more than was legally required? Did the plant operators need more training for such emergencies? Finally, the Bhopal incident raises many questions about the relationship between U.S. businesses and their operations in developing countries that may not be prepared to deal with the latest technologies and may not be fully informed about the associated risks. And the effect on Union Carbide's market capitalization continued for years following the accident. Union Carbide really never recovered from the damage to its reputation despite the fact that several reports conclude the accident was the result of a deliberate act of sabotage. Eventually Dow acquired Union Carbide and the curse of the Union Carbide accident ended as the company was absorbed. Reputations and conduct move markets.

The Value of a Good Reputation

A reputation, good or bad, stays with a business or an individual for a long time. Richard Teerlink, the former CEO of Harley-Davidson, has said, "A reputation, good or bad, is tough to shake." Once a company makes poor ethical choices, it carries the baggage of those choices despite successful and sincere efforts to reform. Salt Lake City struggled to regain its credibility as the trials from the bribery allegations surrounding its winning the bid for the 2002 Winter Olympics progressed and companies withdrew sponsorships. Businesses were, at that time, unsure about the reputations and trustworthiness of those running the Salt Lake City Olympic operations. It took new leadership and a commitment to high ethical standards from Mitt Romney, who went on to become a two-term governor of Massachusetts and presidential candidate in 2008, to restore confidence in the Salt Lake City 2002 Winter Olympics.

Leadership's Role in Ethical Choices

George Fisher, the former CEO of Motorola and Kodak, has defined leadership as the ability to see around corners. In other words, a leader sees a problem before it becomes a legal issue or liability and fixes it, thus saving company time and money. All social, regulatory, and litigation issues progress along a timeline. As the issue is brought to the public's attention, either by stories or by the sheer magnitude of the problem, the momentum for remedies and reforms continues until behavior is changed and regulated. Ethical choices afford firms opportunities to take positions ahead of the curve. Firms can choose to go beyond the law and perhaps avoid regulation that might be costly or litigation that can be devastating. For example, the issues relating to the problems with asbestos dust in the lungs of asbestos workers and installers were clear in the 1930s. More studies needed to be done, but there was sufficient evidence to justify lung protection for workers and the development of alternative forms of insulation. However, the first litigation relating to asbestos and asbestos workers did not arise until 1968. For that 30-year period, those in the business of producing and selling asbestos insulation products had the opportunity to take preventive actions. They chose to wait out the cycle. The results were a ban on asbestos and litigation at levels that forced the largest producer, Johns-Manville (now Manville), into bankruptcy. Leadership choices were available in the 1930s for offering warnings, providing masks, and developing alternative insulators. Johns-Manville chose to continue its posture of controlling information releases and studies. The liability issue progressed to a point of no choice other than bankruptcy and reorganization.

Every business regulation that exists today controls business conduct in an area that was once not subject to control but, rather, provided an opportunity for businesses to self-regulate by making good value choices. Problems resulting from a lack of candor in payday loans and in the so-called subprime loan market have surfaced at all levels of our economy. "We made so much money, you couldn't believe it. And you didn't have to do anything. You just had to show up,"[18] was the comment of Kal Elsayed, a former executive at New Century Financial, a mortgage brokerage firm based in Irvine, California. With his red Ferrari, Mr. Elsayed enjoyed the benefits of the growth in the subprime mortgage market. However, those risky debtors, whose credit histories spelled trouble, defaulted on their loans. New Century Financial declared bankruptcy under the weight of its portfolio of $39.4 billion in subprime loans. "Subprime mortgage lending was easy until the market changed" is the hindsight comment of mortgage brokers and analysts. And the Wall Street instruments tied to those mortgages carried the defaults throughout the economy. The mortgage lending market is now greatly controlled and limited by state and federal regulations. Wall Street firms not under federal controls are nevertheless subject to increased regulation.[19] Ethical choices give businesses the freedom to make choices before regulators mandate them. Breaches of ethics bring about regulation and liability with few

EXHIBIT 2.3   Leadership and Ethics: Making Choices before Liability and Regulation

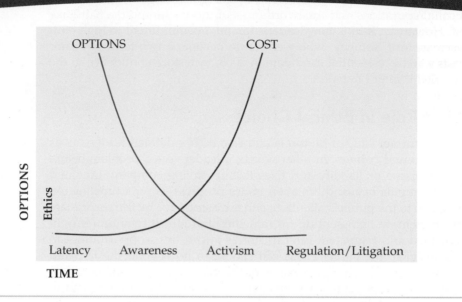

Source: Adapted from James Frierson, "Public Policy Forecasting: A New Approach," *SAM Advanced Management Journal*, Spring 1985, pp. 18–23.

opportunities to choose and less flexibility. The notions of choices and leadership are diagrammed in Exhibit 2.3, which is explained in the following discussion.

Every issue progresses along a cycle that begins with a *latency* phase, in which the industry is aware of a problem. The use of private information about consumers' buying patterns was well known in the marketing industry, but few consumers were aware of that use. The *awareness* stage begins when the popular press reports on an issue and raises questions. Once the public has knowledge of a problem, it responds by demanding assurance that the problem either is resolved or is not really an issue—or by calling for reform. The *activism* stage is one in which members of the public ask for either voluntary or regulatory reform. If voluntary reform is not forthcoming, those affected may sue or lobby for reform, or both. For example, a group of parents, police officers, and shareholders protested Time Warner's production of "Cop Killer," a song by the rap music artist Ice T (a.k.a. Ice-T.) The public outcry was strong both in the press and at Time Warner's shareholder meeting. Congress was considering holding hearings on record labels and record content. Time Warner eventually made a choice to voluntarily withdraw the song, later in the regulatory cycle when public outcry was strong but still in time to avert regulation.

During 2004, the public again became active in demanding changes in the content of entertainment when Janet Jackson and Justin Timberlake's performance at the halftime show at the Super Bowl resulted in partial nudity on prime-time television. In 2007, CBS Radio and MSNBC pulled the Don Imus show because of questionable comments he made. Entertainment and television executives undertook voluntary controls to prevent government controls. The televised Academy Awards are on a five-second delay so that any mishaps can be edited out before broadcast. Some artists are not permitted to appear on awards shows because of their past behaviors on similar shows. Voluntary self-control averts government regulation.

Few people realize one aspect of the Tylenol poisonings case (noted earlier in the chapter), which is that the issue of tamper-proof packaging had been a concern in the industry long before the poisonings involving Tylenol occurred. Those in the industry were concerned that packaging that did not signal unauthorized entry so that a buyer could spot tampering could open the door to the tragedy that eventually occurred. However, no one in the industry, despite knowledge of this issue, took steps to create tamper-proof packaging. The law did not require such a step; additional costs were associated with the packaging and retooling production; and some were worried that they would be at a competitive disadvantage if their products were harder to use than those that did not have the tamper-proof packages. By not solving the problem voluntarily, companies faced unpleasant results: first, the tragedy of the deaths, and second, additional regulations and costs imposed as the government required tamper-proof packaging.

Nonetheless, Johnson & Johnson and McNeil enjoyed decades of goodwill and deferential treatment arising from their recall. The companies had a near immunity from questions about their products and practices until 2010, when the companies' conduct differed substantially from the 1982 recall. In 2010, the FDA found metal particles in the company's liquid Infant's Tylenol. That can happen in production, but they key is to stop production, issue a recall, and 'fess up. Instead, however, one officer has resigned and the FDA is poised to levy criminal penalties against McNeil over the company's lack of cooperation, mishandling of materials, lax documentation, and failure to follow up on customer complaints.[20] An April 2010 FDA site visit to one plant found 20 violations of the agency's good manufacturing processes. One violation was releasing seven batches of cherry-flavored Infants' Tylenol after employees had found metal from processing pistons in the product.

Perhaps the most troubling McNeil conduct came to light in a congressional hearing. Documents seem to indicate that the company hired contractors to go out and purchase all the Tylenol products affected by production problems so that a recall did not have to be issued.[21] The company seems to have drifted from its 1980s standard, which resulted in it being held in such high esteem by regulators and consumers, and the result will be significant penalties as well as litigation by the parents of the children who became ill from the metal-laced Tylenol.

Creation of an Ethical Culture in Business

The Tone at the Top and an Ethical Culture

Employees work under the pressures of meeting quarterly and annual goals and can make poor choices if the company's priority with respect to values and ethics is not made clear. Employees must see that those who evaluate and pay them really do care about ethics. Employees are convinced that ethics is important when they see officers comply with all of the provisions in the company code of ethics. They see the right tone at the top when ethical employees are rewarded and unethical conduct is punished. The tone at the top comes from actions by officers and executives that show they "walk the talk" about ethics.

Sarbanes-Oxley, Sentencing, and an Ethical Culture

Following the collapses of Enron, WorldCom, and other companies noted in the chapter's opening Consider, Congress passed the most extensive reforms of corporate governance and financial reporting since the enactment of the 1933 and 1934 securities laws following the 1929 stock market crash. Although SOX imposes many requirements on accountants, lawyers, directors, and officers (covered in Chapters 8, 20, and 21), it also mandates the Federal Sentencing Commission to examine the types of things companies could do that would improve the ethical culture, thereby reducing the risk of misconduct and earning sentence reductions for companies that attempt to create an ethical culture but still have an ethical or legal lapse.

The Sentencing Commission determined that factors such as the following would be helpful in setting the tone of the company:

- A code of ethics
- Training for employees in the code and in ethics
- A means for employees to report misconduct anonymously
- Follow-up on reports employees make on misconduct
- Action by the board, including follow-up and monitoring, on complaints and reports made by employees
- Self-reporting and investigation of legal and ethical issues
- Sanctions and terminations for those within the company who violate the law and company rules, including officers
- A high-ranking officer, with the ability to communicate with the CEO and board, who is responsible for the code of ethics and ethics training in the company

The guidelines for company practices incorporate the factors most experts agree are critical to setting an ethical culture in a company.

Reporting Lines: An Anonymous Ethics Line for an Ethical Culture

Most companies have either an ombudsperson or a hotline, or both, to which employees can anonymously report ethical violations. The anonymous reporting line is a minimum requirement for companies in this post–SOX era. In addition to encouraging employees to discuss issues with their supervisors, most companies now have some means by which employees can raise issues anonymously because of fear and concern that their jobs are at stake. Under the sentencing guidelines, companies that can show they fostered an atmosphere of education and discussion in which employees were encouraged to come forward will fare much better in terms of fines and other punishments if any missteps occur. Many companies have developed ethical news bulletins to offer employees examples of and guidelines on ethical dilemmas. DuPont delivers an ethics bulletin to employees through its e-mail system. Blue Cross Blue Shield has given employees Slinky toys for their desks with the hotline reporting number on them so that as employees think and perhaps use the Slinky to relieve pressure and stress, they will be reminded to report any problems. The federal government has an ethics encyclopedia online for its employees to use.

BUSINESS PLANNING TIP

In the past, company ethics officers tended to come from HR and PR. Now, ethics officers at companies have unprecedented power. They are given full access to speak to all employees, have direct lines to boards and CEOs, and appear to have an edge in knowing how to question employees in terms of halting activities. A number of former prosecutors have become ethics officers at companies that have experienced legal or ethical difficulties:

- Richard C. Breeden, former SEC chairman, was an outside monitor at KPMG and is now the CEO of Breeden Capital Management LLC.

- Eric R. Dinallo, formerly with Eliot Spitzer at the New York attorney general's office, was chief compliance officer at Morgan Stanley from 2003 to 2006. Since 2006 he has been general counsel for Willis Group Holdings, an insurance broker.

- Beth L. Golden, also formerly with Spitzer's office, was chief compliance officer at Bear Stearns until its collapse in 2008 and subsequent acquisition by JP Morgan.

- Mari B. Maloney, formerly with the National Association of Securities Dealers (NASD) (now Financial Industry Regulatory Authority, FINRA) and the Manhattan DA's office, was chief compliance officer at AIG and is now the chief compliance officer at Standard & Poor's.

BUSINESS STRATEGY

The Ethical Culture

```
                    Leadership
                    by Example
     _____

              Company Policies and
             Compensation Systems
               Reward Ethical and
                 Moral Behavior
     _____

                  Ethics Codes
       Ethics Training: Annual/Scenarios
       Investigations/Enforcement/Feedback
```

A strategic pyramid can help in understanding how to implement an ethical culture. At the base of the pyramid are the facial trappings of ethics: codes. Even Enron had a 64-page, award-winning code of ethics. Some companies have progressed beyond annual training seminars to regular ethics scenarios circulated throughout the company for employees to consider and discuss before the ethics office offers its insights and guidance on the hypothetical or reality-based scenario that has been presented. In the investigations portion, some companies provide employees with data on number of questions/reports made, the investigations, and the outcomes (within the bounds of privacy constraints). An example: "The ethics office investigated 323 matters and employee disciplinary action was taken in 175 of those matters. The form of discipline included terminations, warnings, loss of bonus [and whatever other sanctions were imposed]." The purpose of this data-based feedback is to let employees know, particularly those who reported anonymously and wish to remain anonymous, of the ethics office activity, the results of investigations, and, perhaps most importantly, the enforcement.

The next layer involves compensation for and recognition of the role of individuals' moral development and the differing roles employees play in terms of organizational behavior parameters in moving the company toward ethical behavior and an ethical culture.

The final or top layer, and the area conquered by so few companies, requires leadership at the executive level and dramatic shifts in both internal and external policies and behaviors of the company. Exploring these top two layers can provide ethics officers and ethics programs within companies with the next step in the evolution of not just "best practices in ethics programs," but in the creation of an ethical culture.

Source: Adapted from Marianne M. Jennings, "Taking Ethics Programs to the Next Level: Why CFOs Are Critical," *Corporate Finance Review* 10, no. 3 (2005), pp. 38–42.

The encyclopedia is filled with examples of government employees' misconduct and the sanctions they received.

Developing an Ethics Stance

Both individuals and firms should decide up front what types of conduct they would never engage in and be certain that the rules are in writing, that everyone understands the rules, and that the rules will be enforced uniformly. Individuals can vary in their responses to various ethical dilemmas. For example, a woman who had taken $12,000 from her employer was terminated immediately upon the company's discovery of the embezzlement. At the company's next board meeting, the board members discussed the issue and had varying views. One director felt that taking something that does not belong to you is wrong and that termination was the appropriate action. Another director said that his remedy would be determined by whether the money was taken all at once or over a period of time. Another director said that his remedy would be determined according to why the employee took the money. Still another director noted that perhaps the employee did not understand that this type of action is wrong. The directors varied in their views on ethics. One is pragmatic—it is simply wrong. Another applies a relative approach—why did she take the money? Exhibit 2.4 diagrams the ethical stances of the directors.

Knowing where you stand as a company sends clear signals to employees. Knowing where you stand as an individual sends clear signals for the behavior of those around you. Taking a position on a set of values helps a company avoid the either/or conundrum in which tough situations are boiled down to something

EXHIBIT 2.4 Your Ethics Stance: The Embezzling Employee

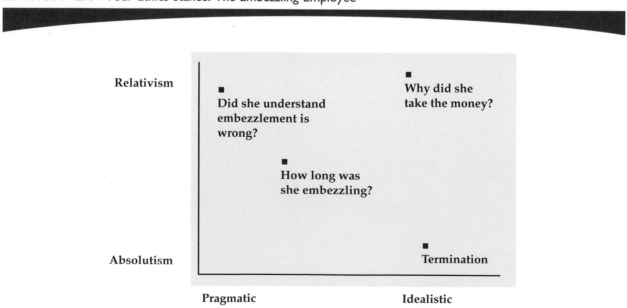

Source: Developed from Professor Patricia Pattison's presentation, "Teaching Ethics," Academy of Legal Studies in Business Annual Meeting, August 11–15, 1994, Dallas, Texas; and adapted from "Teaching Ethics" by D. R. Forsych, *Journal of Personality and Social Psychology*.

such as, "Either we release this product now with its flaws and meet the deadline and start getting earnings, or we don't and the company collapses." A value-based decision is one that says, "We as a company do not cheat our customers with poorly designed or manufactured products, and we don't hurt them with defective ones. Because of that value, we retool quickly to correct the problem and get the product out there as soon as possible." With this value-based decision, the company also makes a good business decision, for it has chosen to avoid the often-destructive costs of releasing a defective product despite knowledge of that defect. The GM Malibu case discussed earlier represents the destructive costs of deciding not to take action based on values but, rather, taking action based only on immediate returns.

Being Careful About Pressure and Signals

Doing the right and ethical thing often gets lost in the pressures employees felt with respect to goals and number quotas. These types of signals create a pressured environment in which employees fall into ethical lapses that often lead to illegal behavior. Just the disparity between the amount of time devoted to discussion of results versus ethics is a signal. For example, most employees will say that they discuss performance goals every day and then add, "Without fail, we sign off on the ethics policy once each year!" The signal, however unwitting, is that performance matters most.

In the subprime mortgage meltdown that affected so many Wall Street investment houses, there were clear differences between the firms that collapsed and those that survived. Stan O'Neal at Merrill Lynch, a company that led the pack with over $25 billion in losses and an eventual takeover, was an indefatigable "numbers guy" who took Merrill from its position of being a safe, trading house to a leveraged player, and O'Neal expected employees to produce results. One Merrill executive noted the pressure, "It got to the point where you didn't want to be in the office on Goldman earnings days." The pressure for goals was so intense that no one really questioned the numbers and how they were getting the results. Merrill employees called operations meetings "staged." The result was Merrill's demise, even as employees became concerned but were pressured to just keep going despite the clear consequences.

Ethical Issues in International Business

The global market presents firms with more complex ethical issues than they would experience if operations were limited to one country and one culture. Moral standards vary across cultures. In some cases, cultures change and evolve to allow conduct that was not previously acceptable. For example, tipping hospital employees is common practice in some countries. In the United States, such behavior could be illegal in the case of government-run hospitals.

In many executive training seminars for international business, executives are taught to honor customs in other countries and to "Do as the Romans do." Employees are often confused by this direction.

A manager for a U.S. title insurer provides a common example. He complained that if he tipped employees in the United States, such as employees at public recording agencies, for their expediting property filings, the manager would not only be violating the company's code of ethics but could be charged with violations of the Real Estate Settlement Procedures Act and state and federal antibribery provisions. Yet that same type of practice is permitted, recognized, and encouraged in other countries as a cost of doing business. Paying a regulatory agency in the United States to expedite a licensing process would be bribery of a public official. Yet many businesses maintain that they cannot obtain such authorizations to do business in other countries unless such payments are made. So-called grease or facilitation payments are permitted under the Foreign Corrupt Practices Act (see Chapter 7), but legality does not necessarily make such payments ethical.

An inevitable question arises when custom and culture clash with ethical standards and moral values adopted by a firm. Should the national culture or the company code of ethics control? Typical business responses to the question of whether cultural norms or company codes of ethics should control in international business operations are: Who am I to question the culture of another country? Who am I to impose U.S. standards on all the other nations of the world? Isn't legality the equivalent of ethical behavior? The attitude of businesses is one that permits ethical deviations in the name of cultural sensitivity. Many businesses fear that the risk of offending those in other countries is far too high to impose U.S. ethical standards on the conduct of business in other countries.

Part of the misunderstanding about ethics in international business on the part of U.S.-based businesses is that ethical standards in the United States vary significantly from the ethical standards in other countries. Operating under this misconception can create a great deal of ethical confusion among employees. Strategically, businesses and their employees are more comfortable when they operate under uniform standards. What is known as the "Golden Rule" in the United States actually has existed for some time in other religions and cultures and among philosophers. Exhibit 2.5 offers a list of how this simple rule is phrased in different writings. The principle is the same even if the words vary slightly.

EXHIBIT 2.5 A Possible Uniform Standard for Ethical Choices

Categorical imperative: How would you want to be treated?

   Would you be comfortable with a world with your standards?

Christian principle: The Golden Rule

   And as ye would that men should do to you, do ye also to them likewise. (Luke 6:31)

   Thou shalt love . . . thy neighbor as thyself. (Luke 10:27)

Confucius: What you do not want done to yourself, do not do to others.

Aristotle: We should behave to our friends as we wish our friends to behave to us.

Judaism: What you hate, do not do to anyone.

Buddhism: Hurt not others with that which pains thyself.

Islam: No one of you is a believer until he loves for his brother what he loves for himself.

Hinduism: Do nothing to thy neighbor which thou wouldst not have him do to thee.

Sikhism: Treat others as you would be treated yourself.

Plato: May I do to others as I would that they should do unto me.

The successful operation of commerce depends on the ethical roots of business. A look at the three major parties in business explains this point. These parties are the risk-takers, the employees, and the customers. Risk-takers—those furnishing the capital necessary for production—are willing to take risks on the assumption that customers will judge their products as valuable. Employees are willing to offer production input, skills, and ideas in exchange for wages, rewards, and other incentives. Consumers and customers are willing to purchase products and services as long as they receive value in exchange for their furnishing, through payment, costs, and profits to the risk-takers and employees. To the extent that the interdependency of the parties in the system is affected by factors outside of their perceived roles and control, the intended business system does not function on its underlying assumptions.

CONSIDER... 2.4

Transparency International publishes an annual index of perceptions of corruption. Business executives are asked to rank countries on a scale from 1 to 10, with 10 being the least corrupt. The results for 2009 are as follows.

Corruption Perceptions Index (Transparency International, 2009)

LEAST Corrupt		MOST Corrupt	
• New Zealand	9.4	• Somalia	1.1
• Denmark	9.3	• Afghanistan	1.3
• Singapore	9.2	• Myanmar	1.4
• Sweden	9.2	• Sudan	1.5
• Switzerland	9.0	• Iraq	1.5
• Finland	8.9	• Chad	1.6
• Netherlands	8.9	• Uzbekistan	1.7
• Australia	8.7	• Turkmenistan	1.8
• Canada	8.7	• Iran	1.8
• Iceland	8.7	• Haiti	1.8
• Norway	8.6	• Guinea	1.8
• Hong Kong	8.2	• Equatorial Guinea	1.8
• Luxembourg	8.2	• Burundi	1.8
• Germany	8.0	• Venezuela	1.9
• Ireland	8.0	• Kyrgyzstan	1.9
• Austria	7.9	• Guinea-Bissau	1.9
• Japan	7.7	• Democratic Rep of Congo	1.9
• United Kingdom	7.7	• Congo Brazzaville	1.9
• USA	7.5	• Angola	1.9
• Barbados	7.4	• Tajikistan	2.0
• Belgium	7.1		

Why do you think the index appears as it does? Do you see a correlation between economic development or its absence and corruption?

Source: Reprinted from CORRUPTION PERCEPTION INDEX LIST. Copyright 2009 Transparency International: the global coalition against corruption. Used with permission. For more information, visit http://www.transparency.org.

EXHIBIT 2.6 The Interdependence of Trust, Business, and Government

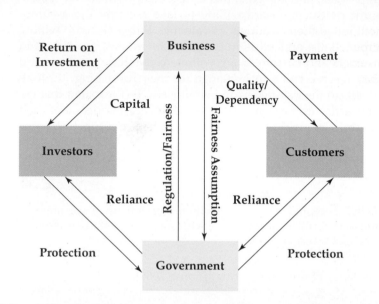

Although the roots of business have been described as primarily economic, this economic system cannot survive without recognition of some fundamental values. Some of the inherent—indeed, universal—values built into our capitalistic economic system, as described here, are as follows: (1) the consumer is given value in exchange for the funds expended; (2) employees are rewarded according to their contribution to production; and (3) the risk-takers are rewarded for their investment in the form of a return on that investment. Exhibit 2.6 depicts this relationship. Everyone in the system must be ethical. An economic system is like a four-legged stool. If corruption seeps into one leg, the economic system is off balance. In international business, often the government slips into corruption, with bribes controlling which businesses are permitted to enter the country and who is awarded contracts in that country. In the United States, the SOX wave of reforms at the federal level was the result of perceived corruption by businesses in their economic operations. The 2007 Congressional ethics reforms focused on government corruption.

To a large extent, all business is based on trust. The tenets for doing business are dissolved as an economy moves toward a system in which one individual can control the market in order to maximize personal income.

Suppose, for example, that the sale of a firm's product is determined not by perceived consumer value but, rather, by access to consumers, which is controlled by government officials. That is, your company's product cannot be sold to consumers in a particular country unless and until you are licensed within that country. Suppose further that the licensing procedures are controlled by government officials and that those officials demand personal payment in exchange for your company's right to even apply for a business license. Payment size may be arbitrarily determined by officials who withhold portions for themselves. The basic values of the system have been changed. Consumers no longer directly determine the demand.

Beyond just the impact on the basic economic system, ethical breaches involving grease payments introduce an element beyond a now-recognized component in economic performance: consumer confidence in long-term economic performance. Economist Douglas Brown has described the differences between the United States and other countries in explaining why capitalism works here and not in all nations. His theory is that capitalism depends on an interdependent system of production. For economic growth to proceed, consumers, risk-takers, and employees must all feel confident about the future, about the concept of a level playing field, and about the absence of corruption. To the extent that consumers, risk-takers, and employees feel comfortable about a market driven by these basic assumptions, the investment and commitments necessary for economic growth via capitalism will be made. Significant monetary costs are incurred by business systems based on factors other than customer value, as discussed earlier. In developing countries where "speed" or grease payments are required and corrupt government officials are in control, the actual money involved may not be significant in terms of the nation's culture. Such activities and payments introduce an element of demoralization and cynicism that thwarts entrepreneurial activity when these nations most need risk-takers to step forward.

Bribes and *guanxi* (gifts) in China given to establish connections with the Chinese government are estimated at 3 to 5 percent of operating costs for companies, totaling $3 billion to $5 billion of 1993's foreign investment. But China incurs costs from the choices government officials make in return for payments. For example, *guanxi* are often used to persuade government officials to transfer government assets to foreign investors for substantially less than their value. Chinese government assets have fallen more than $50 billion in value during the same period of economic growth, primarily because of the large undervaluation by government officials in these transactions with foreign companies. China's economy was adrift because of this underlying corruption. Economic progress began with graft's elimination.

Perhaps Italy and Brazil provide the best examples of the long-term impact of foreign business corruption. Although the United States, Japan, and Great Britain have scandals such as the savings and loan failures, political corruption, and insurance regulation, these forms of misconduct do not indicate corruption that pervades entire economic systems. The same cannot be said about Italy. Elaborate connections between government officials, the Mafia, and business executives were unearthed in the 1990s. As a result, half of Italy's cabinet resigned at one time, and hundreds of business executives were indicted. It has been estimated that the interconnections of these three groups cost the Italian government $200 billion, as well as compromising the completion of government projects.

In Brazil, the level of corruption has led to a climate of murder and espionage. Many foreign firms have elected not to do business in Brazil because of so much uncertainty and risk—beyond the normal financial risks of international investment. Why send an executive to a country where officials may use force when soliciting huge bribes?

The *Wall Street Journal* offered an example of how Brazil's corruption has damaged the country's economy despite growth and opportunity in surrounding nations. The governor of the northeastern state of Paraiba in Brazil, Ronaldo Cunha Lima, was angry because his predecessor, Tarcisio Burity, had accused

Mr. Lima's son of corruption. Mr. Lima shot Mr. Burity twice in the chest while Mr. Burity was having lunch at a restaurant. The speaker of Brazil's Senate praised Mr. Lima for his courage in doing the shooting himself as opposed to sending someone else. Mr. Lima was given a medal by the local city council and granted immunity from prosecution by Paraiba's state legislature. No one spoke for the victim, and the lack of support reflected a culture controlled by self-interest that benefits those in control. Unfortunately, these self-interests preclude economic development.

Economists in Brazil document hyperinflation and systemic corruption. A Sao Paulo businessman observed, "The fundamental reason we can't get our act together is we're an amoral society." This businessperson probably understands capitalism. Privatization that has helped the economies of Chile, Argentina, and Mexico cannot take hold in Brazil because government officials enjoy the benefits of generous wages and returns from the businesses they control. The result is that workers are unable to earn enough even to clothe their families, 20 percent of the Brazilian population lives below the poverty line, and crime has reached levels of nightly firefights. Brazil's predicament occurred over time, as graft, collusion, and fraud became entrenched in the government-controlled economy.[22]

BIOGRAPHY

The Enron Tragedy for the Officer Who Got Out on Time: Cliff Baxter

Clifford Baxter, the son of a police officer, held his undergraduate degree from NYU and his MBA from Columbia. Mr. Baxter rose through the ranks of Enron to become its vice chairman. He was a model Houston citizen with a wife and two children and was heavily involved in community service. Ironically, his passion was Junior Achievement, a friend said, through which he hoped to help make sure that young people "understood the values of the free enterprise system."* Mr. Baxter left Enron in August 2001, shortly after Sherron Watkins, the famous whistle-blower, sent her memo on concerns about Enron's financial position to Chairman Ken Lay. She had indicated in that memo that Mr. Lay should talk to Mr. Baxter if he wanted verification of the teetering financial condition of the company. Mr. Baxter sold most of his Enron stock at that time; thus, he avoided losing everything (as most Enron employees did) when the stock price dropped from $83 per share to just pennies per share. Mr. Baxter sold 577,000 shares of Enron stock between October 1998 and early 2001, for a total of $35.2 million. Enron released a statement upon Mr. Baxter's departure that he had taken early retirement to spend more time with his family. Enron began its long collapse in the fall of 2001 and by the end of the year, the company was in bankruptcy. Most of the senior officers in the company were indicted. However, Mr. Baxter was found dead in his 2001 Mercedes of a self-inflicted gunshot wound just a few miles from his suburban Houston home.[†]

What do you learn from this tragic story? What do you think caused Mr. Baxter to commit suicide? Wasn't it enough that he quit his job? Do you think the millions that he made by selling his stock affected him?

Source: Adapted from Jim Yardley and Sheila K. Dewan, "Despite His Qualms, Scandal Engulfed Executive," *New York Times,* January 27, 2002, p. 27; Jim Yardley, "Critic Who Quit Top Enron Post Is Found Dead," *New York Times,* January 26, 2002, p. A1; and Mary Babineck, "Deceased Enron Executive Earned Respect in the Ranks," *Houston Chronicle,* January 26, 2002. Accessed online March 5, 2010, at http://www.chron.com.

*Jim Yardley and Sheila K. Dewan, "Despite His Qualms, Scandal Engulfed Executive," *New York Times,* January 27, 2002, p. 27.
†Elissa Gootman, "Hometown Remembers Man Who Wore His Success Quietly," *New York Times,* January 30, 2002, p. A1.

Summary

What is ethics?

- Behavior beyond the law
- Day-to-day nature of ethics

What is business ethics?

- Ethical standards—normative standards of behavior set by culture
- Ethical standards—standards of behavior set by natural law
- Ethical standards—moral relativism; moral standards by situation
- Ethical standards—religion and ethics

What are the categories of ethical dilemmas in business?

- Taking things that don't belong to you
- Saying things you know are not true
- Giving or allowing false impressions
- Buying influence or engaging in conflict of interest
- Hiding or divulging information
- Taking unfair advantage
- Committing acts of personal decadence
- Perpetrating interpersonal abuse
- Permitting organizational abuse
- Violating rules
- Condoning unethical actions
- Balancing ethical dilemmas

How do employees resolve ethical dilemmas?

- Blanchard and Peale
- Front-page-of-the-newspaper test
- *Wall Street Journal* and stakeholders
- Laura Nash and perspective
- Categorical imperative

Why do we fail to reach good ethical decisions?

- "Everybody else does it."
- "If we don't do it, someone else will."

- "That's the way it has always been done."
- "We'll wait until the lawyers tell us it's wrong."
- "It doesn't really hurt anyone."
- "The system is unfair."
- "I was just following orders."
- "You think that's bad, you should've seen . . . "
- "It's a gray area."

What is social responsibility and how does a business exercise it?

- Positive law—codified law
- Inherence—serves shareholders' interests
- Enlightened self-interest—serves shareholders' interests by serving larger society
- Invisible hand—serves larger society by serving shareholders' interests
- Social responsibility—serves largest society best by serving larger society

Why is business ethics important?

- Profit
- Leadership
- Reputation
- Strategy

How does a business create an ethical atmosphere?

- Tone at the top
- SOX and corporate sentencing guidelines
- Code of ethics
- Reporting hotlines
- Ethical posture and developing an ethical stance

What are the ethical issues in international business?

- Corruption issues
- Economic systems and ethics

Questions and Problems

1. E. & J. Gallo, the world's largest winery, announced that it would stop selling its Thunderbird and Night Train Express wines in the Tenderloin, the skid row of San Francisco, for six months. Gallo took the action after meeting with an activist group called Safe and Sober Streets, which has asked grocers to remove the high-alcohol wine from the district, where citizens say drunks create a menace. One retailer in the district said, "If I don't sell this, I will have to close my doors and go home."

Discuss the actions of E. & J. Gallo and the dilemma of the retailers in the district. Be sure to discuss the type of philosophy each of them holds with respect to social responsibility and ethical dilemmas.

2.   Paul Backman is the head of the purchasing department for L. A. East, one of the "Baby Bells" that came into existence after the divestiture of AT&T. Mr. Backman and his department purchase everything for the company, from napkins to wires for equipment lines.

S. C. Rydman is an electronics firm and has been a major supplier for L. A. East since 1984. Rydman is also the cosponsor of an exhibit at Wonder World, a theme park in Florida.

Rydman's vice president and CFO, Gunther Fromme, visited Mr. Backman in his office on April 3, 2004. Rydman had no bids pending at that time, and Mr. Fromme told Mr. Backman that he was there "for goodwill." Mr. Fromme explained that Rydman had a block of rooms at Wonder World because of its exhibit there and that Mr. Backman and his group could use the rooms at any time, free of charge.

Should Mr. Backman and his employees use the block of rooms? Why or why not?

3.   The Association for Competitive Technology (ACT) is a trade group funded largely by Microsoft Corporation. During Microsoft's antitrust trial, ACT was active in public relations.

Lawrence J. Ellison, chairman of Oracle Corporation, a software manufacturer and Microsoft competitor, was concerned that the public might not understand that ACT was funded by Microsoft and was not truly an independent group. Mr. Ellison and Bill Gates, the chairman of Microsoft, were known as fierce competitors and often referred to as each other's nemesis. Through Oracle, Mr. Ellison hired Group International, a private investigation firm headed by Terry Lenzner (who became famous for his work on the Watergate investigation during the Nixon administration and also for his work with President Clinton's lawyers during the Paula Jones civil suit for sexual harassment). Group International was to find information tying Microsoft to ACT. Mr. Ellison described his hiring of Group International as his "civic duty."

Shortly after Group International was hired by Oracle, janitors working the night shift at the offices of ACT were offered $50–$60 each by Blanca Lopez, a woman who worked for Lenzner, if they would turn over ACT's trash to her rather than dumping it. The janitors refused, and Ms. Lopez returned the next evening and offered them $500 each for the trash plus $200 extra to the supervisor if he could convince the janitors to cooperate. All of the staff declined. Ms. Lopez left them her card, explained that she was working on a

criminal case, and asked them to call if they changed their minds.

When the janitors disclosed what had happened and the investigator was traced back to Mr. Ellison, he said, "All we did was to try to take information that was hidden and bring it into the light. I don't think that's arrogance. That's a public service."

Mr. Ellison also offered to box up all of Oracle's trash and send it to Mr. Gates in Redmond, Washington, noting, "We believe in full disclosure."

Do you think what Oracle did was legal? Do you think it was ethical? How do you evaluate Mr. Ellison's claim that he was performing a civic responsibility? In 2010, Mr. Ellison came out publicly to support former HP CEO, Mark Hurd, who was asked by the HP board to resign because of questions about his personal relationship with a company contractor and issues in his expense claims. Mr. Ellison said Mr. Hurd's personal life was not an issue in managing HP. Does his position follow his statements about transparency?

4.   Kenneth Branch was an employee with Lockheed Martin in 1996. At that time Lockheed Martin was competing head-to-head with the Boeing Company for a government contract worth $5 billion. Mr. Branch interviewed for a job in Boeing's rocket division in 1996 and began employment at Boeing in January 1997.*

The government awarded the contract to Boeing. An internal investigation by Boeing revealed that Mr. Branch and his supervisor, William Erskine, had thousands of pages of proprietary documents from Lockheed Martin, including detailed information about Lockheed Martin's costs and specifications for the rocket contract. Boeing turned over 11 boxes of documents to Lockheed in 2003, some of which were marked "Proprietary."

Applying the model you learned in Consider 2.2, determine whether there were any ethical breaches in Boeing's conduct.

The author has performed consulting work for Boeing on changing its ethical culture. Why is this disclosure important in this text? Why is this disclosure important to you?

5.   Paul Wolfowitz was the head of the World Bank from June 1, 2005 through mid-2007. At the time he became president of the bank, Mr. Wolfowitz was romantically involved with an executive at the bank, Shaza Riza. Mr. Wolfowitz went to the board with an ethics question about their relationship and her employment, and the bank board advised that Ms. Riza be relocated to a position beyond Mr. Wolfowitz's influence because of their relationship and also because she could

*Anne Marie Squeo and Andy Pasztor, "U.S. Probes Whether Boeing Misused a Rival's Documents," *Wall Street Journal*, May 5, 2003, pp. A1, A7

no longer be promoted at the bank. On August 11, 2005, Mr. Wolfowitz wrote a memo to Xavier Coll, the bank's vice president of human resources, and suggested the following: *"I now direct you to agree to a proposal which includes the following terms and conditions:"* The terms and conditions included Ms. Riza's future at the bank when Mr. Wolfowitz was no longer heading it as well as an obligation to find her other employment. Ms. Riza now earns $193,590 per year at a nonprofit organization, following a stint at the State Department at World Bank expense. She earned $132,000 at the World Bank (a salary that was tax-free because of diplomatic status). Using the categories of ethical dilemmas that you studied, evaluate Mr. Wolfowitz's conduct. What ethical issues do you see? Did Mr. Wolfowitz act properly? What should the board have done? The overarching goal of Mr. Wolfowitz's tenure as head of the World Bank was eliminating corruption in all countries that deal with the bank. What effect did his personal conduct have on that goal?

6. Richard M. Scrushy, the former CEO of HealthSouth and now a convicted felon (bribery), was the subject of a probation hearing. Prosecutors said that Mr. Scrushy was trying to leave the country in February 2007 via his 92-foot yacht, the *Chez Soiree*. The yacht journey was nixed when bad weather hit the Alabama coast. Mr. Scrushy protested the allegations, testifying that he had permission to travel to South Florida as part of a vacation that had been approved for him and his family (including going to Disney World). He said he did not tell the probation officer about the trip to Miami because her questions were not specific enough, "I can't answer the question unless she asks me."[23] The federal magistrate said that Mr. Scrushy was being "coy" with his probation officers. Discuss whether Mr. Scrushy breached any ethical standards with his conduct and interpretation of the terms of his probation.

7. Marilee Jones, the dean of admissions of MIT, resigned in 2007 after 28 years as an administrator in the admissions office. The dean for undergraduate education received information questioning Ms. Jones's academic credentials. Her résumé, used when she was hired by MIT, indicated that she had degrees from Albany Medical College, Union College, and Rensselaer Polytechnic Institute. In fact, she had no degrees from any of these schools or from anywhere else. She had attended Rensselaer Polytechnic as a part-time nonmatriculated student during the 1974–75 school year but the other institutions had no record of any attendance at their schools. When Ms. Jones arrived at MIT for her entry-level position in 1979, a degree was probably not required. She then progressed through the ranks of the admissions office and, in 1997, she was appointed dean of admissions. She explained that she wanted to disclose her lack of degrees at that point but that she had gone on for so long that she did not know how to come clean with the truth.

Ms. Jones had been on a national book tour from 2006–2007 promoting her book, *Less Stress, More Success: A New Approach to Guiding Your Teen Through College Admissions and Beyond*. The book advises, "Holding integrity is sometimes very hard to do because temptation may be to cheat or cut corners. But just remember that 'what goes around comes around,' meaning that life has a funny way of giving back what you put out."

Ms. Jones was known around the campus for her sense of humor as well as her common sense and outspokenness. She resigned because the chancellor, Philip M. Clay, said, "There are some mistakes people can make for which 'I'm sorry' can be accepted, but this is one of those matters where the lack of integrity is sufficient all by itself."

In her letter of resignation, Ms. Jones said she "did not have the courage to correct my resume." Apply what you have learned in this chapter to help analyze what went wrong with Ms. Jones's decision process. What mistakes did she make through the whole process in her actions and responses?

8. James J. Cramer is the host of CNBC's *Mad Money*. He was interviewed for TheStreet.com, and the video showed up on YouTube. On the video Mr. Cramer explained how he was able to make real money by manipulating markets. He said that if he wanted to make a stock look bad, he would spread negative information to a "bozo reporter" at the *Wall Street Journal*. He also noted that Bob Pisani of CNBC is another "useful conduit" for negative information. "No one else in the world would ever admit it, but I don't care."[24] After CNBC pulled the YouTube video, Mr. Cramer appeared on the Don Imus radio program and said that he did not do any of those things. He also said that Mr. Pisani is one of the best, but he failed to answer the question Mr. Imus asked, "Who's the bozo at the *Wall Street Journal*?"

If what Mr. Cramer said was true, evaluate his ethics. If what he said was false, evaluate his ethics.

9. Heinz Ketchup holds 54 percent of the U.S. ketchup market, and 9 of every 10 restaurants feature Heinz ketchup. However, Heinz has learned that many restaurant owners simply refill Heinz bottles with cheaper ketchup, thereby capitalizing on the Heinz name without the cost. One restaurant owner explains, "It's just ketchup. The customers don't notice." There are no specific health regulations that apply, and owners are not breaking the law by refilling the bottles. Do you think this practice is ethical?

10. Gerald Grinstein, the former CEO of Delta Air Lines, refused to take any bonuses, stock options, or extra compensation for 2006 and instead would only take his base salary of $338,000. Grinstein arranged to have $1 billion distributed to about 39,000 non-unionized employees and 1,000 managers within 12 to 15 months after the airline emerged from bankruptcy. "I'm the dawning of the old age," was the comment the 74-year-old CEO made when asked why he was taking such an unprecedented step.[25] Grinstein is giving up an estimated $10 million. He also added, "Corporate pay packages have gotten out of control.

It has become a salary derby out there." Grinstein still arranged to have bonuses for top executives if they hit certain profit targets and explained, "You have got to have a program that attracts executives but at the same time you've got to take care of the relationships with frontline employees."[26] Apply the various schools of social responsibility to Mr. Grinstein and decide which he followed. Think about the regulatory cycle's application to the issue of CEO pay. What do you think regulators will do?

Economics, Ethics, and the Law

Adam Smith, in what has been called the seminal work in free-market economics, wrote, "It is not from the benevolence of the butcher, the brewer, or the baker, that we can expect our dinner, but from their regard to their own interest."[27] Self-interest, then, is what Smith believed to be the motivator for economic engagement and growth. Is there a difference between self-interest and selfishness? Where would social responsibility fit in the Smith view of the relationship between ethics and economics? However,

17 years before writing *Wealth of Nations*, Smith wrote *The Theory of Moral Sentiments*, and included the following observation about ethics and business: "How selfish soever man may be supposed, there are evidently some principles in his nature which interest him in the fortune of others and render their happiness necessary to him though he derives nothing from it except the pleasure of seeing it."[28] What does this quote reveal about Smith's attitudes toward social responsibility?

Notes

1. www.josephsoninstitute.org, accessed March 5, 2010. For information on cheating in college, see Donald L. McCabe, Kenneth D. Butterfield, and Linda Klebe Treviño, "Academic Dishonesty in Graduate Business Programs: Prevalence, Causes, and Proposed Action," 5 *Academy of Management Learning and Education* 294 (2006).

2. Email No. 2: Analytical Manager to Senior Analytical Manager (Dec. 15, 2006, 8:31 PM). Report of Issues Identified in the Commission Staff's Examinations of Select Credit Rating Agencies By the Staff of the Securities and Exchange Commission July 8, 2008, FN 8, at p. 12.

3. Louise Story and Landon Thomas, Jr., "Tales From Lehman's Crypt," *New York Times*, Sept. 12, 2009, p. SB1.

4. Steve Stecklow et al., "Sonsini Defended HP's Methods in Leak Inquiry," *Wall Street Journal*, September 8, 2006, p. A1.

5. Leah Nathan Spiro, "The Bomb Shelter Salomon Built," *BusinessWeek*, September 9, 1991, pp. 78–80.

6. Alan Levin, "Airline Is Fined $1.3M for Fake Data," *USA Today*, May 22, 2009, p. 3A.

7. Catherine Yang and Amy Barrett, "In a Stew Over Tainted Meat," *BusinessWeek*, April 12, 1993, p. 36.

8. Sue Reisinger, "Runaway Train Hits H-P's GC," *National Law Journal*, December 18–25, 2006, pp. 8–9.

9. Danpatrick.com. www.sportsillustrated.cnn.com, accessed June 2, 2009.

10. Eddie Pells, AP wire story, June 2, 2009.

11. From "Interview: Milton Friedman," *Playboy*, February 1973. © 1973 *Playboy*.

12. Mr. Milken was required by the Securities and Exchange Commission to pay a fine for his involvement in the negotiations (see Chapter 21).

13. Mr. Wagner is referring to Ivan Boesky, another financier who served a prison sentence; Ron Perelman, the chairman of Revlon, Inc.; Barry Diller, former chairman of Paramount and Fox and owner of the Home Shopping Network; and Rupert Murdoch, the media mogul who now owns Fox. Jenny Anderson, "The Drexel Diaspora," *New York Times*, Feb. 6, 2005, 3-1, Money & Business.

14. Melissa S. Baucus and David A. Baucus, "Paying the Piper: An Empirical Examination of Longer-Term Financial Consequences of Illegal Corporate Behavior," 40 *Academy of Management Journal* 129 (1997).

15. Sadly, in 2010, the FDA was considering charges against McNeil for its failure to recall a line of Tylenol Infant Drops when the company discovered metal pieces in the product. The charges would be based on the company's attempted surreptitious buy-out of the product by contractors in lieu of a public recall.

16. For complete information about BP's presence in Alaska and its contribution to the economic base there, go to http://alaska.bp.com.

17. Chris Woodward, Paul Davidson, and Brad Heath, "BP Spill Highlights Aging Oil Field's Increasing Problems," *USA Today*, August 14, 2006, pp. 1B, 2B.

18. Julie Creswell and Vikas Bajas, "A Mortgage Crisis Begins to Spiral, and the Casualties Mount," *New York Times*, March 5, 2007, pp. C1, C4.

19. For a summary of the state legislation on predatory lending practices, see Therese G. Franzén and Leslie M. Howell, "Predatory Lending Legislation in 2004," 60 *Business Lawyer* 677 (2005).

20. Jonathan D. Rockoff, "J&J Lapses Are Cited In Drugs for Kids," *Wall Street Journal*, May 27, 2010, p. B1.

21. Natasha Singer, "Johnson & Johnson Seen as Uncooperative on Recall Inquiry," *New York Times*, June 11, 2010, p. B1.

22. Barnaby J. Feder, "An Abrupt Departure Is Seen as a Harbinger," *New York Times*, May 1, 2002, pp. C1, C2.

23. Andrew Backover, "Report Slams Culture at WorldCom," *USA Today*, November 5, 2002, p. 1B.

24. *Id.*

25. Annual report for 1998, posted at http://www.worldcom.com. (*Note:* Because WorldCom no longer exists, company information can be found only in the Edgar database at http://www.sec.gov.)

26. Bernard Ebbers's letter to shareholders in the annual report for 1999, posted at http://www.worldcom.com. (*Note:* Because WorldCom no longer exists, information about the company can be found only in the Edgar database at http://www.sec.gov.)

27. Adam Smith, *An Inquiry into the Nature and Causes of the Wealth of Nations.* (1776). Book 1, Chapter 2, Paragraph 2, Edited by Edwin Cannan. Chicago: University of Chicago Press, 1976. Accessed online March 5, 2010 at http://www.econlib.org/library/Smith/smWN.html.

28. *The Theory of Moral Sentiments* (1759). Part 1, Section 1, Chapter 1, Paragraph 1, Edited by D. D. Raphael and A. L. Macfie. Oxford: Clarendon Press; New York: Oxford University Press, 1976. Accessed online March 5, 2010 at http://www.econlib.org/library/Smith/smMS.html.

The Judicial System

O ur introduction to law included discussions of statutory law and common law. With so many statutes at so many levels, you perhaps might think that statutory law is a complete source of law. However, sometimes statutes need interpretation. Someone must determine when, how, and to whom statutes apply. Statutory law is not even half of all the law. The bulk of the law is found in judicial decisions. These decisions contain statutory interpretations and common law. This chapter covers the parties involved in these decisions as well as the courts that make them— what they decide, when they can decide, and how those decisions are made. ■

**For as thou urgest justice, be assured thou shalt
have justice, more than thou desirest.**

Portia
The Merchant of Venice, Act IV, Scene I

UPDATE ➤
For up-to-date legal news, go to
mariannejennings.com

CONSIDER...

Gail Lindgren is an entrepreneur who runs a small business called Moonbeams, based in West Des Moines, Iowa. Ms. Lindgren designed and began selling JEANJANGLES, jewelry that hangs from the belt loops on jeans. Ms. Lindgren obtained a patent for the trinkets and, in addition to storming the Iowa jeans-wearing market, sold the JEANJANGLES on her website, http://www.jeanjangles.com (the company's original website). A California company, GDT, began selling "Jeans for the Hip," called JEAN JEWEL. Ms. Lindgren became aware of GDT, its website, and its product when *People* magazine did a feature

story on the jean trinkets and friends called to congratulate her on her national success. Ms. Lindgren filed suit in federal district court in Iowa against GDT for infringement. GDT maintains that it has never been to Iowa, has no stores in Iowa, has no salespeople or other employees in Iowa, and cannot be required to come to Iowa to defend a lawsuit. Ms. Lindgren says that GDT has a website and is selling its jewels to residents in Iowa and must come to Iowa to defend a suit there because it is doing business there. Who is correct?

Types of Courts

All U.S. court systems include two different types or levels of courts: trial courts and appellate courts.

Trial Courts

A **trial court** is the place in the judicial system where the facts of a case are presented. This court is where the jury sits if the case is a jury trial. Here the evidence and witnesses are presented and the first decision in the case is made, by either judge or jury. The procedures for trials and trial courts are covered in Chapter 4.

Appellate Courts

At least one other court, an **appellate court,** reviews the conduct during the trial of the judge, the lawyers, the witnesses, and the jury. This process of review helps assure that the lower court applied the law correctly and followed the rules of procedure. Further, this review system provides uniformity. In some appeals, the appellate court issues published opinions, which can then be referred to and used as resources in deciding future cases. However, in many cases the appellate court issues unpublished opinions. Unpublished opinions have become a controversial issue; and although no law prohibits citing such opinions, a cite should always make clear that the opinion is an unpublished one.

How Courts Make Decisions

The Process of Judicial Review

Appellate courts do not hold trials. Rather, they review what has been done by trial courts to determine whether the trial court, also referred to as the lower court, made an error in applying the substantive or procedural law in the case through the process of **judicial review.**

The appellate court atmosphere is different from that of the trial court. No witnesses, no jury, and no testimony play a role. No new evidence is considered; only the evidence presented at trial is reviewed. The court reviews a transcript of the trial along with all the evidence presented at trial to determine whether an error was made.

In addition to the transcript and evidence, each of the parties to a case can present the appellate court with a **brief,** which is a summary of the case and the legal issues being challenged on appeal. The appellate brief is each side's summary of why the trial court decision or procedures were correct or incorrect. The parties make their arguments for their positions in the brief and support them with statutes and decisions from other cases. The brief serves as a summary of the major points of error the parties allege occurred during the trial. This type of brief, called an **appellate brief,** is very detailed. In fact, many refer to "briefs" as a misnomer because they are generally quite lengthy. Note that these briefs differ from the case brief presented in Exhibit 1.1.

Many appellate courts permit the attorneys for the opposing parties to make timed oral arguments in their cases. An **oral argument** is a summary of the points that have been made in each party's brief. The judge can also ask questions of the attorneys at that time. At the trial level, one judge makes all decisions. At the appellate level, more than one judge reviews the actions of the lower court in a case. The typical number is three, but, in the case of state supreme courts and the U.S. Supreme Court, the full bench of judges on the court hears each case. For example, in U.S. Supreme Court decisions, all nine justices review the cases before the Court unless they have recused (disqualified) themselves because of some conflict.

The panel of appellate judges reviews the case and the briefs, hears the oral argument, and then renders a decision. The decision in the case could be unanimous or could be a split vote, such as 2 to 1. In the case of a split vote, a justice who is not in the majority will frequently draft a **dissenting opinion,** which is the judge's explanation for a vote different from that of the majority.

Checking for Error

A **reversible error** is one that might have affected the outcome of the case or influenced the decision made. Examples of reversible errors include the refusal to allow some evidence to be admitted that should have been admitted, the refusal to allow a particular witness to testify, and misapplication of the law.

When a reversible error has been made, the appellate court **reverses** the lower court's decision. However, in some cases, the appellate court will also **remand** the case, which means the court sends the case back to the trial court for further proceedings. For example, when the court orders a reversal because some evidence should have been admitted that was not, the case is remanded for a new trial with that evidence admitted (i.e., allowed).

If the appellate court does not find a reversible error, it simply **affirms** the decision of the lower court. The fact that a decision has been affirmed does not mean no mistakes were made at the trial; rather, it means that none of the mistakes was a reversible error. The appellate decision is written by a member of the court who has voted with the majority. The decision explains the facts and the reasons for the court's reversal, remand, or affirmation.

In some appellate cases, the court will **modify** the decision of a lower court. The full case is neither reversed nor affirmed; instead, a portion or portions of the case are reversed or modified. For example, a trial court verdict that found a defendant negligent might be affirmed, but the appellate court could also hold that the damages awarded were excessive. In this type of decision, the case is remanded for a redetermination of damages at the trial court level.

Statutory Interpretation

In addition to checking for error, appellate courts render interpretations of statutes. Often, statutes seem perfectly clear until a new factual situation not covered by the statute arises.

The Doctrine of *Stare Decisis*

Judicial review by appellate courts of lower court decisions by appellate courts provides the database for the doctrine of *stare decisis*, a Latin term meaning "let the decision stand." The decisions of the appellate courts are written and often published so that they may be analyzed, reviewed, and perhaps applied in the future.

Setting Precedent

When reviewing the decisions of lower courts, courts examine their own previous decisions, along with decisions of other courts on the same topic. This process of examining other decisions for help in a new case uses case **precedent,** which is the doctrine of *stare decisis*. Judges examine all prior cases in the same area of law or related to a statute to determine whether the issue has already been decided and, if so, whether the current case should be decided in the same way. Following case precedent does not mean similar cases will be decided identically; several factors influence the weight given to precedent.

The Quality of Precedent

Where the case originated is one of the factors that influence the use of precedent in a case. In federal courts, precedent from other federal courts is strongest when the case involves federal issues.

In state courts, prior decisions within a particular state's own court system are given greater weight than decisions from other states' courts. One state's courts are not obliged to follow the precedent of another state's courts; they are free to examine it and use it, but, as with all precedent, it is not a mandatory requirement to follow another state's decisions.

The Purposes of Precedent

The purposes of precedent are the same as the purposes of law. Law offers some assurance of consistency and reliability. The judiciary recognizes these obligations in applying precedent. Stability and predictability are necessary in the way law functions. No exact formula applies when deciding a case, but consistency is a key element in the use of precedent.

In addition to consistency, however, judges must remember the law's need for flexibility. As new twists in facts arise and technology develops, the judiciary must adapt the law to those changes. For example, in Chapter 1, the *Sony* and *Grokster* cases illustrated the need for a reexamination of the scope of a law because of evolved technology and its role in copyright law and protections.

The Interpretation of Precedent

Using precedent involves more than just finding similar cases. Every case decision has two parts. One is the actual rule of law, which technically is the precedential part. However, judges never offer just a rule of law in a case. The rule of law is given at the end of the case decision after a full discussion of reasoning and precedent. This discussion is called the *dicta* of the case, which includes case precedent of benefit to each party. In some instances, the rule of law may benefit one party while the *dicta* benefit the other party.

A dissenting opinion is *dicta* and is often quoted in subsequent cases to urge a court to change existing precedent. Application of precedent is not a scientific process, and it often leaves much room for interpretation and variation.

CONSIDER...   3.1

The following rule appears in State University's current catalog:

> *A course in which a grade of C or better has been earned may not be repeated. The second entry will not be counted in earned hours or grade point index for graduation.*

Rod took his business math course and earned a C. Not satisfied with his grade but unaware of the catalog regulation, Rod took the math course again and this time earned a D. The registrar has entered the D grade in Rod's cumulative average. Rod objects based on the catalog rule, but the registrar says the rule applies only if a higher grade is earned. What should Rod do? Should the grade count?

Discussion

The purpose of the university regulation was to prevent students from retaking courses to earn a higher grade point average (GPA). In the factual situation, the student earned a lower grade. The registrar entered the lower grade hoping to create a deterrent for students retaking courses when they had a C or better. However, it is clear that a second grade, whether higher or lower, should not be entered.

Here's another follow-up question for you to solve on your own. Suppose that the registrar has always counted the lower grades in the cumulative GPA. Does Rod still have an effective argument? Is the registrar using a strained interpretation of the regulation?

When Precedent Is Not Followed

Precedent may not be followed for several reasons. Some of those reasons have already been given: the precedent is from another state, or the precedent is interpreted differently because of the *dicta* in that precedent. Precedent is also not followed when the facts of cases can be "distinguished," which means that the context of the facts in one case is different enough from those in other cases that the precedent cannot be applied. For example, suppose that a court decided that using roadblocks to stop motorists to check for drunk drivers is constitutional. Another court then decides that using roadblocks just to check for drivers' licenses is not constitutional. The first case can be distinguished because of the purpose of the roadblocks: to prevent a hazardous highway condition. The court may not see the same urgency or safety issue in roadblocks used for checking for drivers' licenses. The precedent can be distinguished.

The theories of law discussed in Chapter 1 may also control whether precedent is applied. For example, a court may not follow a precedent because of a moral reason or because of the need to change the law on the basis of what is moral or what is right. A precedent may also be abandoned on an economic theory; in this case, the court changes the law to do the most good for the most people. For example, a factory may be a nuisance because of the noise and pollution it creates, and ample case law probably supports shutting down the factory as a nuisance. However, the factory may also be the town's only economic support, and its shutdown will mean unemployment for virtually the whole town. In balancing the economic factors, the nuisance precedent may not be followed or it may be followed in only a modified way.

Courts struggle with issues of fact and law and with changes in society as they apply precedent and consider modifications.

Parties in the Judicial System (Civil Cases)

Plaintiffs

Plaintiffs are the parties who initiate a lawsuit and are seeking some type of recovery. In some types of cases those who initiate the court action are called petitioners (such as in an action for divorce). Plaintiffs file their suits in the appropriate court, and this filing step begins the litigation process.

Defendants

Plaintiffs seek recovery from **defendants,** who are named in the suit as having committed some violation of the law or the rights of the plaintiff. Another name for a defendant is **respondent.**

Lawyers

In most cases, each of the parties is represented by a **lawyer.** Lawyers have other functions besides representing clients in a lawsuit. Many lawyers offer "preventive" services. Lawyers draft contracts, wills, and other documents to prevent legal problems from arising. One role that lawyers play is advising clients in advance in order to minimize clients' legal problems and costs.

The attorney–client relationship is a fiduciary one that carries a protected privilege. The attorney is expected to act in the best interests of the client and can do so without the fear of having to disclose the client's thoughts and decisions. The **attorney–client privilege** keeps the relationship confidential and assures that others (even an adversary in a lawsuit) have limited access to lawyer–client conversations. One of the key areas of discussion, debate, and reform under Sarbanes-Oxley (SOX) related to imposing upon corporate lawyers the duty to report fraud and other financial misdeeds of their client companies. Lawyers were concerned about the need for client confidentiality, and regulators and investors were concerned that lawyers have remained silent as financial frauds have been ongoing in companies. Although the final SOX rules do not require lawyers to blow the whistle on their clients, they are required to take steps to notify the audit committee and board about misconduct, and ultimately resign if the conduct is not changed and rectified. (For more details of the role of general counsel, the privilege, and corporations under SOX provisions, refer to Chapters 8, 20, and 21.)

Under the American Bar Association's Model Rules for Professional Responsibility, attorneys are obligated to represent clients with persuasive force.

An attorney who agrees to represent a client must represent that client to the best of the lawyer's ability. Because of the privilege, many lawyers know that their clients actually did commit a crime or breach a contract. However, the client's confession to an attorney is confidential. Even with knowledge of a client's guilt, an attorney must represent the client in a manner that gives the client all rights and protections under the law. There is a difference between a client's confession to a crime and the proof required for conviction of that crime. A lawyer's obligation is to see that the other side meets its burdens and responsibilities in proving a case against the client. Lawyers *do* represent guilty people. Their role is to, as many lawyers phrase it, "keep the system clean." Protecting the rights of the guilty is required in order to ensure that the rights of the innocent are also preserved. However, lawyers are not required to remain silent under the privilege if a client is about to commit a crime. A lawyer representing a client accused of murder cannot disclose that the client confessed. However, a lawyer whose client vows to kill someone must make a disclosure in order to prevent a crime.

Lawyers and their titles and roles vary from country to country. Great Britain and most of Canada have *solicitors* and *barristers*. Solicitors prepare legal documents, give legal advice, and represent clients in some of the lesser courts. Barristers are the only "lawyers" who can practice before higher courts and administrative agencies. Quebec and France have three types of lawyers: the *avocat*, who can practice before the higher courts and give legal advice; the *notaire*, who can handle real property transactions and estates and

BUSINESS PLANNING TIP

Be careful and protect your lawyer–client privilege. Business letters and memos to lawyers should be marked as privileged and include limitations on access to those letters and memos. If you reveal information to someone other than your lawyer, you may lose your privilege on that information. Holding a conversation or meeting with your lawyer with others present may cost you your privilege, too. Privileged communications should be with your lawyer(s) only.

For the Manager's Desk

Re: The Privilege of Lawyers

To whom does the attorney–client privilege belong? An attorney who is employed as general counsel for a corporation, or a lawyer representing that corporation in a particular matter, owes a duty to the corporation. The corporation, in those circumstances, is the client. Employees are not. The privilege, therefore, applies to corporate client communications. Even though officers and employees provide the attorney with the information about what the corporation did, the lawyer does not represent those officers and employees. In most situations, the interests of the officers and employees are the same as those of the corporation, and a lawyer can work closely with the officers and employees to represent the corporation. However, in some circumstances the corporation's interests are different from those of the employees. For example, suppose that a general counsel for a corporation learned that its officers had engaged in price-fixing. (See Chapter 8 for more discussion of criminal prosecutions of officers of a corporation and Chapter 16 for discussion of price-fixing and antitrust violations.) The general counsel would discuss the issue with the board (see Chapter 20) and perhaps conclude that it is best to disclose what has happened to the Justice Department. The officers involved might object, but they are not protected by any privilege with the corporation's attorney. The attorney is protecting a client, the company, by disclosing the misconduct and perhaps providing assurance that the board was unaware of the price-fixing, which would then reduce any penalties the company might be required to pay. The issue of client confidentiality for corporate officers' discussions with corporate counsel continues to be a contentious issue that is on a path to the U.S. Supreme Court. In *U.S. v Nicholas*, 606 F. Supp.2d 1109 (C.D. Cal. 2009), a federal judge ruled that the privilege would apply to those officers unless the lawyer made it clear that he or she was representing only the corporation. However, in *U.S. v Ruehle*, 583 F.3d 600 (9th Cir. 2009), a case that involved officer discussions with counsel about backdating stock options, the court held that there was no confidentiality privilege for those discussions.

can prepare some legal documents; and the *juriste* (legal counselor), who can give advice and prepare legal documents. In Germany, a lawyer who litigates is called *Rechtsanwalt* and a lawyer who advises clients but does not appear in court is called *Rechtsbeistand.* Japan has only one class of lawyers, called *Bengosh,* but does have the *Shiho-Soshi,* a type of advanced notary with the authority to incorporate companies, prepare documents, and create wills. In Italy, the two types of lawyers—whose roles are similar to those in the dual British system—are *avocati* and *procuratori.*

Judges

Judges control the proceedings in a case and, in some instances, the outcome. Trial judges control the trial of a case, from presiding over the selection of a jury to ruling on evidence questions. (See Chapter 4 for more details on trial procedures.) Appellate judges review the work of trial court judges. They do not actually hear evidence. Rather, they review the record of the case to determine whether there has been reversible error.

Judges are selected in various ways throughout the country. Some judges are elected to their offices. Some states have merit appointment systems wherein judges are appointed on the basis of their qualifications. In some states, judges are appointed by elected officials subject to the approval of the legislature. In some states with appointed judges, the judges are put on the ballot every other year (or at some other interval) for retention; voters in these states do not decide whom they want as judges but do decide whether they want to keep them once they are in office. Federal judges are appointed by the president with Senate approval.

Name Changes on Appeal

The lawyers and the parties stay in the "game" even after a case is appealed. However, the names of the parties do change on appeal. The party appealing the case is called the **appellant.** Some courts also call the party appealing a case the **petitioner.** The other party (the one not appealing) is called the **appellee** or **respondent.**

Some states change the name of the case if the party appealing the case is the defendant. For example, suppose that Smith sues Jones for damages in a car accident. The name of the case at trial is *Smith v Jones.* Smith is the plaintiff, and Jones is the defendant. If Smith wins the case at trial and Jones decides to appeal, Jones is the appellant and Smith is the appellee. In some courts, the name of the case on appeal becomes *Jones v Smith.* Other courts leave the case name the same but still label Jones the appellant and Smith the appellee.

The Concept of Jurisdiction

Courts are found at every level of government, and every court handles a different type of case. In order for a court to decide or try a particular case, both parties to the case and the subject matter of the case must be within the established powers of the court. The established powers of a court make up the court's **jurisdiction.** *Juris* means law, and *diction* means to speak.

Jurisdiction is the authority or power of a court to speak the law. Some courts can handle bankruptcies, whereas others may be limited to traffic violations. Some courts handle violations of criminal laws, whereas others deal only with civil matters. The subject matter of a case controls which court has jurisdiction. For example, a case involving a federal statute belongs in a federal district court by its subject matter; however, federal district courts are found in every state. **In personam jurisdiction,** or jurisdiction over the person, controls which of the federal district courts will decide the case. Determining which court can be used is a two-step process; subject matter and *in personam* jurisdiction must fit in the same court.

Subject Matter Jurisdiction of Courts: The Authority Over Content

The two general court systems in the United States are the federal court system (see Exhibit 3.1) and the state court system.

The Federal Court System

The Trial Court of the Federal System

The **federal district court** is the general trial court of the federal system. However, federal district courts are limited in the types of cases they can hear; that is, their subject matter jurisdiction is limited. Federal district courts can hear three types of cases: those in which the United States is a party, those that involve a federal question, and those that involve diversity of citizenship.

Jurisdiction When the United States Is a Party

Any time the U.S. government is a party in a lawsuit, it will want to be tried in its own court system—the federal system. The United States is a party when it brings

EXHIBIT 3.1   The Federal Court System

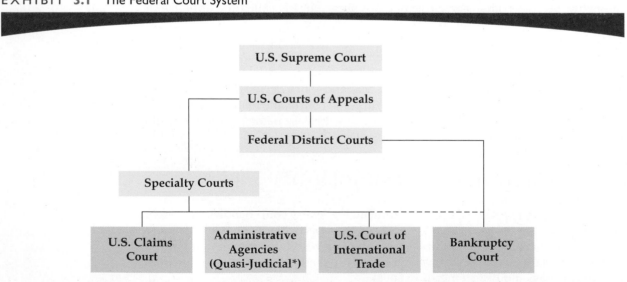

*For example, the Federal Trade Commission (FTC) or the National Labor Relations Bureau (NLRB).

suit or when it is the defendant named in a suit. For example, if a victim of a plane crash names the Federal Aviation Administration (FAA) in a suit, the United States is a defendant and the federal system again has jurisdiction. When the United States is a party in a case, the federal district court has exclusive jurisdiction.

Federal Jurisdiction for a Federal Question

The federal district court has jurisdiction over cases involving federal questions. For example, if a business is suing for treble damages (a remedy of three times the amount of damages experienced) under the federal antitrust laws (see Chapter 16), the case involves a federal question and may be brought in federal district court. A suit charging a violation of the Equal Protection Clause of the U.S. Constitution (see Chapter 5 for more details) also involves a federal question and can be brought in federal district court. Prosecutions for federal crimes also involve federal questions, and the United States will be a party as the prosecutor; these criminal cases are tried in federal district court.

Many federal questions can also be heard by a state court. For example, most state constitutions include the same Fifth Amendment protections included in the U.S. Constitution. A plaintiff often has a choice between federal and state court, and the decision to proceed in one forum as opposed to the other may be a strategic one based on the nature of the case, rules of procedure, and other factors related to differences between the two court systems.

Jurisdiction by Diversity

Most of the civil cases in federal district court are not there because they are federal questions or because the United States is a party. Most civil cases are in federal district court because the plaintiff and defendant are from different states and their case involves damage claims in excess of $75,000. Cases in which the parties are from different states qualify for **diversity of citizenship** status, and federal district courts have the authority to hear these diversity cases. That authority is not exclusive; a state court can also hear diversity cases as long as neither party chooses to exercise the right to a federal district court trial. In diversity cases, state and federal courts have **concurrent jurisdiction.** Concurrent jurisdiction means that two courts have the authority to hear a case. By contrast, **exclusive jurisdiction** means that only one court has the authority to hear the case. For example, federal district courts have exclusive jurisdiction over cases in which the United States has charged an individual or corporation with a federal crime.

Federal courts decide controversies among citizens of different states for reasons that go back to fears about state court judges giving preferential or favorable treatment to citizens of their state, as opposed to nonresident parties. If the case is held in one side's state court, that side might have an unfair advantage or built-in prejudice because of the location of the court.

When corporations are parties to suits, the diversity issue is more complex. The citizenship of a corporation can be its state of incorporation or the state in which its principal office is located. This citizenship test is used for subject matter jurisdiction. The citizenship test for *in personam* jurisdiction has been greatly expanded.

It is important to understand that when a federal court tries a case on the basis of diversity, it is simply trying the case under the same state laws but without the local prejudice that might exist in a state court. In other words, federal courts do not rule under a different set of laws; they simply apply the state law in a different setting.

Limited Jurisdiction: The Special Trial Courts of the Federal System

Not all cases in which the United States is a party or in which a federal question is involved are decided in federal district courts. The federal system also has specialized trial courts to handle limited matters. For example, the jurisdiction of the Tax Court in the federal system is limited to tax issues. If you challenge the Internal Revenue Service because it would not allow one of your deductions, your case would be heard in Tax Court. The bankruptcy courts make up a well-used limited court system within the federal system and have exclusive jurisdiction over all bankruptcies. No other court can handle a bankruptcy or bankruptcy issues, and bankruptcy courts do not handle any other type of trial or suit.

The U.S. Claims Court is another specialized federal court: It handles disputes that involve government contracts and other claims against the federal government, such as eminent domain issues. (See Chapter 5 for more discussion of eminent domain and "takings.")

The U.S. Court of International Trade is a specialized court that focuses on international trade transactions regulated by federal agencies in various ways and also on customs issues.

Another court that is often discussed along with the federal system is the Indian Tribal Court. This court, the court of the Native American nations, has exclusive jurisdiction over criminal and civil matters on the reservations. Indian tribal courts are unique because of their limited jurisdiction and their exclusivity, which arises from their sovereign nature.

The Structure of the Federal District Court System

Each state has at least one federal judicial district. The number of federal districts in each state is determined by the state's population and caseload. States such as Wyoming and Nevada have only one federal district each, whereas states such as Illinois and New York have many. The number of courts and judges in each federal district is also determined by the district's population and caseload. Even in those states with just one district, the district has several judges and multiple courtrooms for federal trials. Ninety-four federal districts serve the 50 states, the District of Columbia, and Puerto Rico. Three territories of the United States (Guam, the Virgin Islands, and the Northern Mariana Islands) also have district courts, including a bankruptcy court.

The Importance of Federal District Court Decisions

The subject matter of cases that qualify for federal district court jurisdiction is important. These cases involve the interpretation of federal statutes, and often the resolution of constitutional issues. Because of the importance of these decisions, the opinions of federal district judges are published in a reporter series called the *Federal Supplement,* which reprints most opinions issued by federal district judges in every federal district. (Decisions of the Court of International Trade are also found in the *Federal Supplement.*) Cases in the *Federal Supplement* provide excellent precedent for interpretation and application of federal statutes. In addition to the system for citing statutes (see Chapter 1), a specific system is used for citing case opinions. Such a system is necessary so that precedent can be found easily for use in future cases.

All case cites consist of three elements: an abbreviation for the reporter, the volume number, and the page number. The abbreviation for the *Federal Supplement* is "F.Supp." or, for the second series, after volume 999, "F.Supp.2d." The volume number always appears in front of the abbreviation, and the page number appears after it. A formal cite includes in parentheses the federal district in which the case was decided and the year the case was decided. A sample federal district court cite of a case decided in the D.C. district that dealt with the First Amendment issues in corporate political involvement looks like this:

Citizens United v Federal Election Com'n, 530 F.Supp.2d 274 (D.D.C. 2008)

This method of uniform citation not only helps ease the burden of research but also provides an automatic way to know where a case came from and how it can be used.

The Appellate Level in the Federal System

Cases decided in federal district court and the specialized trial courts of the federal system can be appealed. These cases are appealed to the U.S. courts of appeals (formerly called the U.S. circuit courts of appeals).

Structure. All of the federal district courts are grouped into **federal circuits** according to their geographic location. Exhibit 3.2 is a map that shows the 13 federal circuits. Note that eleven of the circuits are geographic groupings of states; the

EXHIBIT **3.2** The 13 Federal Judicial Circuits

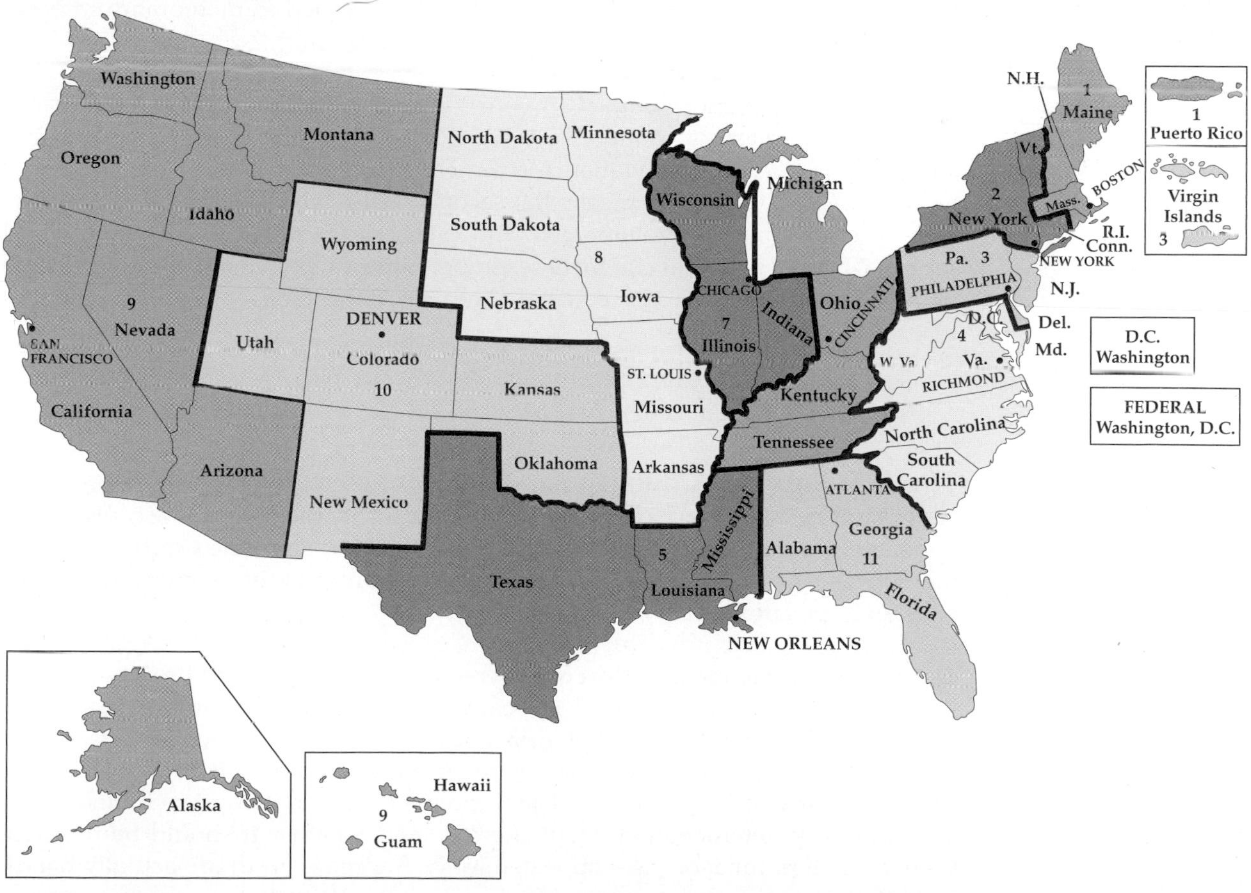

Source: Reprinted with permission and courtesy of West Publishing Company.

twelfth circuit is the District of Columbia, and the thirteenth is a nongeographic circuit created to handle special cases such as those involving patent disputes and issues, and appeals from the Court of Claims and Court of International Trade. Some scholars and members of Congress have proposed creating a fourteenth circuit by dividing the very large Ninth Circuit.

Each circuit has its own court of appeals. The office of the court's clerk is located in the city named in each of the federal circuits in Exhibit 3.2. The number of judges for each of the federal circuits varies according to caseload. However, most cases are heard by a panel of three of the circuit judges. It is rare for a case to be heard *en banc* (by the "whole bench," meaning all the judges in that circuit). One of the more famous cases to be heard *en banc* following a three-judge panel decision involved a father's challenge to his child being required to recite the Pledge of Allegiance because the phrase "under God" was in the pledge: *Elk Grove Unified School Dist. v Newdow*, 292 F.3d 597 (9th Cir. 2002) and 313 F.3d 500 (9th Cir. 2002) with *en banc* rehearing denied, 328 F.3d 466 (9th Cir. 2003).[1]

Procedures.   The U.S. courts of appeals are appellate courts and operate by the same general procedures discussed earlier in the chapter. An appeal consists of a record of the trial in the court below (here, the federal district court), briefs, and possible oral argument. The standard for reversal is reversible error. Because the right of appeal is automatic, the appellate courts have tremendous caseloads. A full opinion is not given in every case. In the cases that are affirmed, the opinion may consist of that one word. Other decisions are issued as memorandum opinions for the benefit of the parties but not for publication.

Opinions.   The opinions of the U.S. courts of appeals are published in the *Federal Reporter*. The system of citation for these cases is the same as for federal district court opinions. The abbreviation for the *Federal Reporter* is "F." (or sometimes "F.2d" or "F.3d"; the "2d" means the second series, which was started after the first "F" series reached volume 300. and this series is now followed by a third series—"F.3d"). A formal cite includes in parentheses the federal circuit and date of the decision. A sample U.S. court of appeals cite, the appeal of a tobacco liability case, would look like this:

Good v Altria Group, Inc.
501 F.3d 29 (1st Cir. 2007)

The U.S. Supreme Court

A decision by a U.S. court of appeals is not necessarily the end of a case. One more appellate court is part of the federal system—the **U.S. Supreme Court.** However, the Supreme Court's procedures and jurisdiction are slightly different from those of other appellate courts.

Appellate Jurisdiction and Process.   The Supreme Court handles appeals from the U.S. courts of appeals. This appeal process, however, is not an automatic right. The Supreme Court must first decide whether a particular case merits review. That decision is announced when the Court issues a *writ of certiorari* for those cases it will review in full. The Supreme Court, in its writ, actually makes a preliminary determination about the case and whether it should be decided. Only a small number of cases appealed to the Supreme Court are actually heard. In 1945, 1,460 cases were appealed to the Court. By 1960, that number had grown

For the Manager's Desk

Re: A Look at What Appellate Courts Do

The following chart, organized by federal circuits, shows the percentage of lower court decisions the U.S. Supreme Court reversed in 2009.

CIRCUIT	CASES TAKEN	CASES REVERSED	REVERSAL RATE
1st	4	2	50%
2nd	9	7	77.8%
3rd	2	1	50%
4th	5	5	100%
5th	5	3	60%
6th	5	5	100%
7th	1	1	100%
8th	4	4	100%
9th	16	13	81.3%
10th	2	2	100%
11th	3	0	0%

to 2,313. Now the number averages about 7,000 each year, with 2008 (the latest year available from the Court) having 7,738 cases. The court grants *certiorari* in about 100 cases and hears oral arguments and issues written opinions in about 70 to 80 cases. For example, in the 2008 term, the Supreme Court heard oral arguments in 87 cases and issued 70 written opinions. All of the Supreme Court opinions issued in one year total about 5,000 pages, including the majority, concurring, and dissenting opinions.

The court grants *writs of certiorari* in cases as a matter of discretion. *Certiorari* may be granted because of a conflict among the circuits about the law, such as the differing decisions among the circuits on the Second Amendment, or because the case presents a major constitutional issue, such as with corporate political donations. This *writ of certiorari* procedure also applies to other sources of appellate cases, such as those coming up through state supreme courts, which can be appealed to the U.S. Supreme Court. For example, in 2000, the U.S. Supreme Court granted *certiorari* on George W. Bush's appeal of a Florida Supreme Court decision on recounting the Florida ballots in the November 2000 presidential election. That case, because of its significance and its interpretation of statutory law and the role of judicial review, was granted *certiorari* and was then heard and decided by the court with an issued opinion.

The U.S. Supreme Court also acts as a trial court (called a court of **original jurisdiction**) in certain cases. When one state is suing another state, the U.S. Supreme Court becomes the states' trial court. For example, the water dispute among California, Arizona, Colorado, and Nevada has been tried over a period of years by the U.S. Supreme Court. The Court also handles the trials (on espionage charges, for example) of ambassadors and foreign consuls.

Structure.   The U.S. Supreme Court consists of nine judges, who are nominated as justices to the Court by the president and confirmed by the Senate. The appointment runs for a lifetime. A president who has the opportunity to appoint a Supreme Court justice is shaping the structure of the Court and the resulting decisions. For this reason, the U.S. Supreme Court is often labeled "conservative" or "liberal." The makeup of the bench controls the philosophy and decisions of the Court.

Opinions.   Because the Court is the highest in the land, its opinions are precedent for every other court in the country. The importance of these opinions has resulted in three different volumes of reporters for U.S. Supreme Court opinions. The first is the *United States Reports* (abbreviated "U.S."). These reports are put out by the U.S. Government Printing Office and are the official reports of the Court. Because these reports are often slow to be published, two private companies also publish opinions in the *Supreme Court Reporter* (abbreviated "S. Ct.") and the *Lawyer's Edition* (abbreviated "L. Ed." or "L. Ed. 2d"). The three-part cite for *Arthur Andersen, LLP v U.S.* (the Court's decision on document destruction at the defunct accounting firm) follows:

544 U.S. 695 (2005)
125 S.Ct. 2129 (2005)
161 L.Ed.2d 1008 (2005)

The State Court Systems

Although each state court has a different structure for its court system and the courts may have different names, the basic structure in each state is similar to the federal system. Exhibit 3.3 provides a diagram of a sample state court system.

State Trial Courts

Each state has its own general trial court. This court is usually called a circuit, district, county, or superior court. It is the court in which nondiversity civil cases are heard and state criminal cases are tried.

EXHIBIT 3.3   Typical State Court System

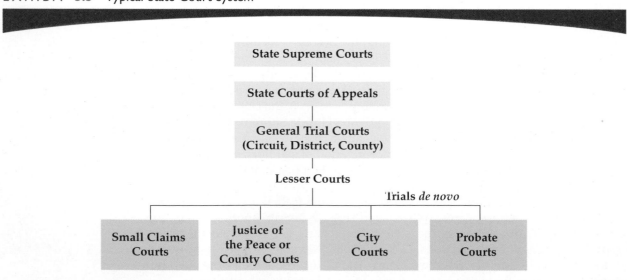

In addition to its general trial court, each state also has its own group of "lesser courts." They are courts with **limited jurisdiction** and are comparable to the specialty courts of the federal system. For example, most states have a **small claims court** in which civil cases with minimal damage claims are tried. In a true small claims court attorneys are not used. Parties represent themselves before a judge. Such a setting offers parties the chance to have a judge arrive at a solution without the expense of attorneys. The amount recoverable in small claims court is indeed small: $200–$5,000 is the typical range.

Most states also have a lesser court that allows the participation of lawyers but limits the amount that can be recovered. The idea is to take the burden of lesser cases away from the usually overburdened general trial courts. These courts are called **justice of the peace courts** or **county courts.**

Most cities also have their own trial courts, which are limited in their jurisdiction to the trial of lesser crimes, such as violations of city ordinances. Many states call these courts **traffic courts** because city ordinances involve so many traffic regulations.

In addition to these courts, some states have specialized courts to handle matters that are narrow in their application of law but frequent in occurrence. For example, although probating (processing) a will and an estate involves narrow issues of law, the supply of this type of case is constant. Many states have special courts to handle this and related matters, such as guardianships for incompetent persons.

Many of the lesser courts allow appeals to a general state trial court for a new trial (**trial de novo**) because not all judges in these lesser courts are lawyers, and constitutional protections require a right of *de novo* appeal in those situations.

State Appellate Courts

State appellate courts serve the same function as the U.S. courts of appeals. The court system provides an automatic right of review in these courts. Some states have two appellate-level courts to handle the number of cases being appealed. The opinions of these courts are reported in the state's individual reporter, which contains the state's name and some indication that an appellate court decided the case. For example, state appellate decisions in Colorado are reported in *Colorado Appeals Reports* (abbreviated "Colo. App."). These opinions are also reported in a **regional reporter.** All states are grouped into regions, and opinions of state appellate courts are grouped into the reporter for that region. Exhibit 3.4 presents the various regions and state groupings. For example, Nevada is part of the Pacific region, and its appellate reports are found in the *Pacific Reporter* (abbreviated "P.," "P.2d," or "P.3d"). The following is a cite from a Georgia state appellate court decision—a case dealing with an estranged spouse's consent for a home search that was later appealed to the U.S. Supreme Court:

   Randolph v State, 590 S.E.2d 834 (Ga. Ct. App. 2003)

State Supreme Courts

State supreme courts are similar in their function and design to the U.S. Supreme Court. These courts do not hear every case because the right of appeal is not automatic. These supreme courts have some discretion in deciding which cases they will hear. State supreme courts also act as trial courts in certain types of cases and so are also courts of original as well as appellate jurisdiction. For example, if two counties within a state have a dispute, the state supreme court would take the trial to ensure fairness. A state supreme court's decision is not necessarily the end

EXHIBIT 3.4 National Reporter System Regions

Pacific (P. or P.2d)	Northwestern (N.W. or N.W.2d)	Northeastern (N.E. or N.E.2d)	Southeastern (S.E. or S.E.2d)
Alaska	Iowa	Illinois	Georgia
Arizona	Michigan	Indiana	North Carolina
(California)	Minnesota	Massachusetts	South Carolina
Colorado	Nebraska	(New York)	Virginia
Hawaii	North Dakota	Ohio	West Virginia
Idaho	South Dakota	**Atlantic (A. or A.2d)**	**Southern (So. or So.2d)**
Kansas	Wisconsin	Connecticut	Alabama
Montana	**Southwestern (S.W. or S.W.2d)**	Delaware	Florida
Nevada	Arkansas	District of Columbia	Louisiana
New Mexico	Kentucky	Maine	Mississippi
Oklahoma	Missouri	Maryland	
Oregon	Tennessee	New Hampshire	
Utah	Texas	New Jersey	
Washington		Pennsylvania	
Wyoming		Rhode Island	
		Vermont	

Note: California and New York each have their own reporter system.
Source: The national reporter system was developed by West Publishing Company. Reprinted with permission of West Publishing Company.

because there is the possibility of an appeal to the U.S. Supreme Court if the case also involves a federal question or an issue of constitutional rights.

The opinions of state supreme courts are significant and are reported in the regional reporters discussed earlier. Many states also have their own reporters for state supreme court opinions. For example, California has the *California Reporter*. The state supreme court reporters are easily recognized because their abbreviations are the abbreviation of each state's name. The following cite is for the state supreme court decision in the *Randolph* case:

> *State v Randolph*, 604 S.E.2d 835 (Ga. 2004)

Judicial Opinions

Although the published opinions of the courts just discussed vary in their places of publication, the format is the same. Exhibit 3.5 shows a sample page from a reporter, with each part of the excerpt identified. Opinions are reported consistently in this manner so that precedent can be found and used easily through the research keys highlighted at the beginning.

Venue

The concept of jurisdiction addresses the issue of which court system has the authority to try a case. The concept of **venue** addresses the issue of the location

EXHIBIT 3.5   Sample Page of a Case in a National Reporter

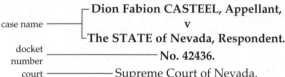

CASTEEL v STATE ——————————————— case name
Cite as 131 P.3d 1 (Nev. 2006) ——————————— case cite

case name ——— ┌─ **Dion Fabion CASTEEL, Appellant,**
                v
               └─ **The STATE of Nevada, Respondent.**

docket —————————————— **No. 42436.**
number

court ——————— Supreme Court of Nevada.

March 30, 2006.

Rehearing Denied May 17, 2006.

Reconsideration en banc Denied
June 12, 2006.

Background: Defendant was convicted in the Eighth Judicial District Court, Clark County, Joseph T. Bonaventure, J., of 10 counts of sexual assault of a minor and 12 counts of use of a minor under age of 14 in production of pornography. He appealed.

Holdings: The Supreme Court, Maupin, J., held that:

1. consent to search of apartment given by defendant's live-in girlfriend authorized police officers to search apartment;

2. girlfriend had authority to consent to officers' search of defendant's gym bag;

3. trial court's findings supported its conclusion that defendant was not in custody for *Miranda* purposes when he was interrogated by officer; but

4. defendant could be convicted only of four counts of use of a minor under age of 14 in production of -pornography.

decision
of the —— Affirmed in part, reversed in part, and
court   remanded.

decision   ┌─ **1. Searches and Seizures 177**
issue   Consent to search of apartment given
research   by defendant's live-in girlfriend autho-
tool   rized police officers to search apartment;
           girlfriend had equal control over apart-
           ment, which she shared with defendant.
           └─ U.S.C.A. Const.Amend. 4.

2. Criminal Law 1139

Appellate court reviews the lawfulness of a search de novo because such a review requires consideration of both factual circumstances and legal issues. U.S.C.A. Const.Amend. 4.

3. Searches and Seizures 177

A warrantless search is valid if police officers acquire consent from a cohabitant who possesses common authority over the property to be searched. U.S.C.A. Const.Amend. 4.

4. Searches and Seizures 186

Defendant's live-in girlfriend had authority to consent to police officers' search of his gym bag, which was located in closet inside apartment that he shared with girl-friend; girlfriend gave officers valid consent to search apartment, and defendant apparently took no special steps to secure privacy interest in gym bag and did not deny girl-friend all access to apartment, given that both girlfriend and minor victim knew contents of gym bag and knew that it could be found in closet. U.S.C.A. Const.Amend. 4.

5. Searches and Seizures 177

A warrantless search is valid based on the consent of one occupant, despite the physical presence of the nonconsenting occupant. U.S.C.A. Const.Amend. 4.

Philip J. Kohn, Public Defender, and   ┐
Sharon G. Dickinson and Jordan S. Savage,
Deputy Public Defenders, Clark County,
for Appellant.   │
George Chanos, Attorney General,   │
Carson City; David J. Roger, District   ├── attorneys for
Attorney, James Tufteland, Chief Deputy   parties
District Attorney, and Ross J. Miller,   │
Deputy District Attorney, Clark County, for
Respondent.   ┘

Before MAUPIN, GIBBONS and
HARDESTY, JJ.

judge
MAUPIN, J. ——————————————— deciding
                                case

In this appeal, we hold that a warrant-┐
less search of a residence is valid based
on the consent of one occupant where
the other occupant fails to object. We also
resolve questions concerning custody for   ├── opinion
purposes of *Miranda v Arizona*.[1] Finally, we
conclude that only 4 counts of production
of child pornography may stand because
the State failed to prove production depict-
ing separate sexual performances.   ┘

BUSINESS STRATEGY

Strategic Punitive Damages

In May 2001, Boeing Company announced that it was moving its corporate headquarters from Seattle, Washington, to Chicago, Illinois. When the announcement was made, many plaintiffs' lawyers for airline crash victims cheered. Cook County courts traditionally have juries drawn from blue-collar workers who tend to be tough on business. One lawyer said, "Any case in Cook County is worth more than it would be in most places on earth." Cook County is home to a 1994 settlement of $252 million awarded to one family as a result of its losses from a US Airways plane crash. The settlement remains the largest in aviation history.

Most airline crash suits are brought in federal district court because of the diversity of citizenship of the parties, the passengers, and the airlines. Which federal court remains a venue issue, and most courts will allow cases to be filed where the defendant is located; in the case of an airline, that venue is where it is headquartered. So, plaintiffs in airline crashes can now file in Cook County, Boeing's new residency for purposes of federal district court diversity.

In choosing a business location, the common strategic factors are often taxes, workforce, education resources, transportation, and climate. Businesses should add one more strategic factor: litigation climate.

Source: Blake Morrison, "Crash Lawyers Like Boeing Move," *USA Today*, May 16, 2001, p. 1A.

of the court in the system. For example, a criminal case in which a defendant is charged with a felony can be tried in any of a state's general trial courts. Heavy media coverage, however, may result in a judge's changing the venue of a case from the place where the crime was committed to another trial court in an area where there is less publicity about the case and it is easier to obtain an impartial jury. However, the bar is a tall one for establishing the need for a change of venue. In *Skilling v U.S.*, 130 S.Ct. 2896 (2010), the U.S. Supreme Court held that the daily and ongoing coverage of Enron's collapse and the role of former CEO Jeffrey Skilling in that collapse were not enough to require that Mr. Skilling's trial for criminal fraud be moved from Houston, where the company was headquartered, to another federal court in Texas or outside the state.

In Personam Jurisdiction of Courts: The Authority Over Persons

Once the proper court for the subject matter in a case is determined, only half the job is done. For example, a case may involve a million-dollar claim between citizens of different states, in which case a federal district court has subject matter jurisdiction over the parties. So which of the 94 federal district courts will hear the case? The case will be heard by the federal district court with *in personam* jurisdiction over the parties. Subject matter jurisdiction is one issue; the other jurisdictional issue is power over the parties involved in the case.

The various criteria for determining *in personam* jurisdiction are examined here and are outlined in Exhibit 3.6.

EXHIBIT 3.6 Personal Jurisdiction

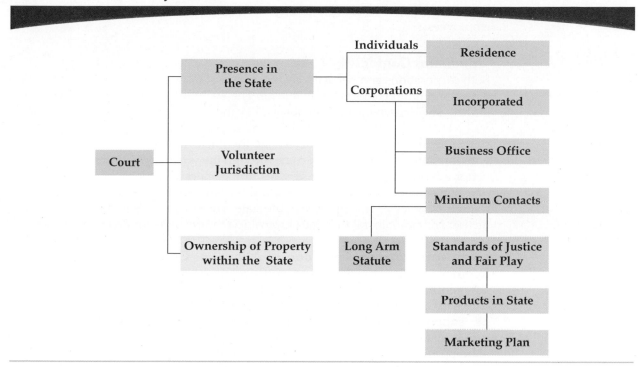

Ownership of Property within the State

A party who owns real property in a state is subject to the jurisdiction of that state's courts for litigation related to that property. Actually, this type of jurisdiction gives the court authority over the person because the person owns a thing in the state. Technically, this type of jurisdiction through property ownership is called **in rem jurisdiction.**

Volunteer Jurisdiction

A court has jurisdiction over a person who agrees to be subject to that court. In some contracts, for example, the parties agree that any lawsuits will be brought in the seller's state. The seller's state courts then have jurisdiction over that volunteer buyer. Most Internet contracts have a venue clause.

Presence in the State

The third and final way a state court can take jurisdiction is by the "presence" of a party in the state, which is determined by different factors.

Residence

Individuals are present in a state if they have a residence in that state. Different definitions of residency are used for tax and election laws, but the requirement here is simply that the person live in the state some time during any given year.

Corporations are residents of the states in which they are incorporated. A corporation is also a resident of any state in which it has a business office with employees.

"Minimum Contacts"

Both corporations and residents can be subject to a state court's jurisdiction if they have "minimum contacts" in that state. The standard for **minimum contacts** is a fairness standard, which was established by the U.S. Supreme Court in *International Shoe v Washington*, 326 U.S. 310 (1945). This decision requires states to notify out-of-state defendants of a suit and determine that those defendants have some contact with the state. Such contact can come through the voluntary acts of shipping product or advertising products or services in the state. The courts look at the extent of involvement in the state as a standard for fairness. However, fairness does not require an office or an employee in the state. These standards for *in personam* jurisdiction are more liberal than the citizenship requirements for diversity actions.

Long-Arm Statutes: The Tools of Minimum Contacts

In order to follow the Supreme Court's ruling on fairness, all of the states have adopted **long-arm statutes.** These statutes are appropriately named: They give courts the power to extend their "arms of jurisdiction" into other states. For example, suppose that Zeta Corporation is incorporated in Ohio and has its manufacturing plant there. Zeta ships its glass baking dishes to every state in the country, although it has no offices anywhere except in Ohio. Joan Berferd, who lives in Alabama, is injured when one of Zeta's baking dishes explodes. Can the Alabama courts allow Berferd to file suit there and require Zeta to come to Alabama to defend the suit? Yes, because a long-arm statute is fair if it covers businesses shipping products to the state. Zeta entered the Alabama market voluntarily and must be subject to the Alabama courts. Long-arm statutes generally cover businesses with offices in the state, businesses shipping products into the state, and businesses that cause a **tort** to be committed in that state.

Lindgren v GDT, LLC (Case 3.1) deals with a long-arm issue and provides an answer for the chapter's opening "Consider."

CASE 3.1

Lindgren v GDT, LLC
312 F.Supp.2d 1125 (S.D. Iowa 2004)

Jangling Jewels on the Internet: Can the Court Loop Them In?

FACTS

Gail Lindgren is an entrepreneur who runs a small business called Moonbeams based in West Des Moines, Iowa. In 1997, Ms. Lindgren designed and began selling JEANJANGLES, for which she obtained a patent in 2000. JEANJANGLES are designed to hang from the belt loop and are made from sterling silver or gold-filled wire, with pieces incorporating such items as gold nuggets, glass, or abalone. Prices range from $18 to $58. JEANJANGLES may be purchased from

Ms. Lindgren's website, http://www.jeanjangle.com, or from Teacups and Tiaras in West Des Moines, Iowa and its online store.

A California company, GDT, began selling "Jeans for the Hip," also called JEAN JEWEL. GDT filed a trademark application for JEAN JEWEL on May 21, 2002. GDT's jewelry is made from sterling silver or gold and may contain semi-precious stones or glass. Prices range from $55 to $835. GDT maintains a Web site, http://www.jeanjewel.com, which began selling JEAN JEWEL merchandise in June 2003. From GDT's website, consumers can create a personal JEAN JEWEL account, browse product offerings, place orders, and have the product shipped to them anywhere in the world, including Iowa. An online order will be delivered by FedEx and "will arrive within 1–3 days after it is shipped anywhere in the continental U.S." JEAN JEWEL merchandise is also available at foreign and domestic retail outlets, although not in Iowa. GDT's principal place of business is Pacific Palisades, California.

Ms. Lindgren became aware of GDT, its website, and its product when *People* magazine did a feature story on the jean trinkets and friends called to congratulate her on her national success. There was further product confusion when singer Lance Bass of N'Sync referred to the California products during a national radio interview that had listeners thinking again that Ms. Lindgren's product was enjoying newfound notoriety. Ms. Lindgren filed suit in federal district court in Iowa against GDT for infringement. GDT maintains that it has never been to Iowa, has no stores in Iowa, has no salespeople or other employees in Iowa, no production facilities there, owns no real property there, and, therefore, cannot be required to come to Iowa to defend a lawsuit. Ms. Lindgren says that GDT has a website and is selling its jewels to residents in Iowa and must come to Iowa to defend a suit because it is doing business there. GDT filed a motion to dismiss the case for lack of *in personam* jurisdiction.

JUDICIAL OPINION

LONGSTAFF, Chief Judge

Due process requires that, in order to subject a non-resident to the jurisdiction of a state's courts, the non-resident must have "certain minimum contacts with it such that the maintenance of the suit does not offend 'traditional notions of fair play and substantial justice.'" *Int'l Shoe Co. v Washington*, 326 U.S. 310, 316, 66 S.Ct. 154, 90 L.Ed. 95 (1945).

The application of [the minimum contacts] rule will vary with the quality and nature of the defendant's activity, but it is essential in each case that there be some act by which the defendant purposefully avails itself of the privilege of conducting activities within the forum State, thus invoking the benefits and protections of its laws. *Hanson v Denckla*, 357 U.S. 235, 253, 78 S.Ct. 1228, 2 L.Ed.2d 1283 (1958). The Supreme Court repeatedly has applied the "purposefully avails" requirement of *Hanson*. The contacts with the forum state must be more than "'random,' 'fortuitous,' or 'attenuated.'"

The personal jurisdiction issue in this case is a close question. As the Supreme Court has noted, the determination of whether minimum contacts exist "is one in which few answers will be written 'in black or white. The greys are dominant and even among them the shades are innumerable.'"

The Eighth Circuit recently has indicated that when specific jurisdiction is premised on defendant's Web site contacts with the forum, the appropriate analytical framework is that of *Zippo Manufacturing Co. v Zippo Dot Com. Inc.*, 952 F.Supp. 1119, 1124 (W.D. Pa. 1997). The *Zippo* court observed that "the likelihood that personal jurisdiction can be constitutionally exercised is directly proportionate to the nature and quality of the commercial activity that an entity conducts over the Internet." The court employed a "sliding scale" to measure the nature and quality of the commercial activity central to its personal jurisdiction analysis. It noted:

> At one end of the spectrum are situations where a defendant clearly does business over the Internet. If the defendant enters into contracts with residents of a foreign jurisdiction that involve the knowing and repeated transmission of computer files over the Internet, personal jurisdiction is proper. At the opposite end are situations where a defendant has simply posted information on an Internet Web site which is accessible to users in foreign jurisdictions. A passive Web site that does little more than make information available to those who are interested in it is not grounds for the exercise [of] personal jurisdiction. The middle ground is occupied by interactive Web sites where a user can exchange information with the host computer. In these cases, the exercise of jurisdiction is determined by examining the level of interactivity and commercial nature of the exchange of information that occurs on the Web site

In the present case, GDT's site consists primarily of single point-of-sale transactions rather than . . . continuous, long-term contracts. While GDT's site allows visitors to establish an online account, the account is for convenience purposes only and entails no continuing obligations.

Prior to the filing of this action, GDT's only conduct directed at Iowa was the state's inclusion on a drop-down menu on the shipping page of GDT's Web site. The shipping page enabled shipment around the world—to Uzbekistan or Palau, if the customer so indicated. Shipments were contracted to FedEx as the third-party carrier, with the costs to be paid by the consumer. While GDT's Web site is both commercial and highly interactive, the site is arguably no more directed at Iowa than at Uzbekistan. "The fact

CONTINUED

that someone who accesses defendants' Web site can purchase a [JEAN JEWEL] does not render defendants' actions 'purposely directed' at this forum." As GDT's Web site could be accessed anywhere, including Iowa, its existence does not demonstrate an intent to purposefully target Iowa.

There is no evidence that GDT took any purposeful action towards Iowa—it did not direct any paid advertising to Iowa or solicit Iowa residents to visit its Web site. It merely processed the orders from Iowa customers who visited its site. Furthermore, under both the California and Iowa versions of the U.C.C., the sales were made F.O.B. seller with the carrier acting as the buyer's agent. Title thus passed to the buyer in California when GDT delivered the items to FedEx for shipment. Consequently, the Internet sales were clearly made in California, and are an insufficient basis for personal jurisdiction over GDT in Iowa.

Here, Lindgren asserts that because the alleged confusion occurred in Iowa, and her principal place of business is in Iowa, the "brunt" of the injury is felt here. Additionally, she argues that her registration of the JEANJANGLES name put GDT on constructive notice that infringement of that name would harm her in Iowa.

GDT did not intentionally direct its activities at Iowa knowing that Lindgren could be harmed through its Web site. Lindgren contends that GDT had constructive notice, based on the presence of JEANJANGLES in the federal trademark database, that its JEAN JEWEL mark could infringe her trademark rights in Iowa. This contention, however, is undermined by the fact that the U.S. Patent and Trademark Office (USPTO) issued a Notice of Allowance for GDT's mark on September 16, 2003, signifying that the mark survived the trademark opposition period and has consequently been allowed for registration. Absent additional minimum contacts and evidence

that defendant expressly aimed their conduct at Iowa, the "effects test" does not support personal jurisdiction over GDT in Iowa.

Lindgren submits that GDT's use of the JEAN JEWEL mark to identify their Web site and products has caused actual confusion in the marketplace. Yet the only evidence of harm to Lindgren are the post-filing Internet sales. Even if the Court were to consider the post-filing sales to Iowa residents, those California purchases are not sufficient to subject GDT to personal jurisdiction in Iowa. They are, however, sufficient to confer personal jurisdiction over GDT in California. This Court recognizes that Iowa has a strong interest in providing a forum to protect its citizens from trademark infringement and unfair competition, and that Lindgren would no doubt be inconvenienced if forced to litigate her claim in California. These considerations do not, however, obviate the requirements of due process.

Viewing the circumstances of this case as a whole, Lindgren has failed to make a *prima facie* case of personal jurisdiction over GDT. GDT lacks minimum contacts with Iowa and considerations of fairness and justice do not warrant an exercise of personal jurisdiction by this Court. Although this Court lacks jurisdiction, it finds that Lindgren's claims may continue in the Central District of California, Western Division. Therefore, GDT's Motion to Dismiss is DENIED.

CASE QUESTIONS

1. Who developed the jeans jewelry first? Did either company cross the other in the federal records for patents and trademark registration?

2. What is the scope of Iowa's long-arm statute?

3. Can GDT be required to come to Iowa and defend the suit?

Ethical Issues

Evaluate the ethics of GDT in capitalizing on Lindgren's idea and market.

Would you purchase GDT's product? Why or why not? Suppose you were offered a counterfeit Burberry purse for $25. The purse looks just like the store originals that cost $480. You could give it as a gift or resell it for as much as $75. Would you buy the purse? Why or why not? What difference does it make whether the purse is real or counterfeit? Is it your role to police trademark counterfeiters?

CONSIDER...   3.2

Gerald Pecoraro was 14 years old and a resident of Nebraska when, in 1965, his parents sent him to Sky Ranch for Boys, Inc. in South Dakota. Father Donald Murray, now deceased, was the director of Sky Ranch at that time. Mr. Pecoraro alleged that Father Murray sexually assaulted him on three occasions in 1965 and 1966: twice at Sky Ranch in South Dakota and once in a hotel room in Chicago, Illinois. After the third assault, Mr. Pecoraro and another boy approached one of their counselors at Sky Ranch and told the counselor that Father Murray had sexually assaulted them.

Several months later Omaha police arrested Mr. Pecoraro while he was a passenger in a stolen vehicle. He was sent to the Nebraska State Training School (NSTS) in Kearney, Nebraska. Father Murray then contacted NSTS, informed officials there that Sky Ranch had re-opened, and requested custody of Mr. Pecoraro. NSTS agreed. Father Murray flew the Sky Ranch airplane to Kearney, picked up Mr. Pecoraro, stopped in Omaha for another fund-raising dinner, then took Mr. Pecoraro to a different ranch in Aladdin, Wyoming, for the summer. He later moved Mr. Pecoraro to a private residence in Belle Fourche, South Dakota, for about one year. Mr. Pecoraro eventually fled South Dakota and filed suit in the Federal District of Nebraska, naming Sky Ranch, the Sky Ranch Foundation, Inc., and the Diocese as defendants, alleging that all three were vicariously liable for Father Murray's conduct. The defendants in the suit moved to dismiss for lack of *in personam* jurisdiction. What should the court do?

Steps for Analyzing This Case Study

THINK:

1. Determine how much of a presence Sky Ranch, the foundation, and the diocese had in Nebraska.

2. List the contacts each had with folks in Nebraska.

3. Determine whether the diocese, foundation, or ranch had tried to enter Nebraska.

4. Determine whether there will be any suit or remedy if the case must be moved to South Dakota.

APPLY: The ranch had contact because the priest flew the ranch's plane into Nebraska. The foundation had contacts because it held fundraisers there. However, the diocese did not enter Nebraska. The diocese was responsible for the priest, but it did not voluntarily enter Nebraska. If the case is not heard in Nebraska, the young man may not have the means to pursue the case in South Dakota. On the other hand, all of the events occurred outside of Nebraska, mostly in South Dakota.

ANSWER: The facts of this case provide a sufficient basis for granting jurisdiction over the ranch and the foundation but not over the diocese. The ranch and foundation can be required to come to Nebraska to defend the suit. Litigation against the diocese must be in South Dakota. [*Pecoraro v Sky Ranch for Boys, Inc.*, 340 F.3d 558 (8th Cir. 2003)]

The International Courts

The decisions of international courts provide precedent for parties involved in international trade. However, one of the restrictions on international court decisions is that the decision binds only the immediate parties to the suit on the basis of their factual situation. International courts do not carry the enforcement power or authority of courts in the U.S. federal and state systems. They are consensual courts and are used only when the parties agree to use them.

The **International Court of Justice** (ICJ) is the most widely known international court. It was first established as the Permanent Court of International Justice (PCIJ) in 1920 by the League of Nations. In 1945, the United Nations (UN) changed the name and structure of the court. The ICJ is made up of 15 judges, no more than 2 of whom can be from the same nation, who are elected by the General Assembly of the UN. The court has been described as having **contentious jurisdiction,** which is to say that the court's jurisdiction is consensual: When a dispute occurs, the parties can agree to submit the dispute to the ICJ.

In addition to the ICJ, other international courts include the European Union's **Court of Justice of European Communities** and the **European Court of Human Rights,** as well as the **Inter-American Court of Human Rights.** Jurisdiction in these courts is also consensual.

The decisions of these courts and decisions from individual countries' courts dealing with international law issues can be found in *International Law Reports.*

In recent years, London's Commercial Court, established more than 100 years ago, has become a popular forum for the resolution of international commercial disputes. Over half the cases in this court involve foreign enterprises. Some companies choose London's Commercial Court as the forum for their disputes for several reasons, even though neither they nor their transactions have any connection with England. First, the court has the advantage of being a neutral forum. Second, for U.S. firms, the use of the English language in the court is important. Third, the court has a wide range of experience in international disputes, from shipping contracts to joint trading ventures. Fourth, the judges on the court were all once commercial litigators themselves and bring their depth of experience to the cases. Fifth, the court is known for its rapid calendar, moving cases along quickly. Major cases are heard within one year from the service of summons. Finally, the court has used a variety of creative remedies. The Commercial Court has issued pretrial injunctions to freeze assets, and its ties to the English government afford the injunctions international recognition. Perhaps the most famous of the Commercial Court's cases is its handling of the 20 class actions against Lloyd's of London.

> ## BUSINESS PLANNING TIP
>
> With national and international business transactions becoming so frequent, many contracts now include "forum selection" clauses. These portions of a contract stipulate that if litigation is required, a particular court in a particular state or country will have jurisdiction over both parties. For example, a franchisor might have the forum selection clause provide that all litigation by franchisees would be in the state and city where the franchisor's principal office is located. Checking a contract carefully for these clauses will enable you to decide, before signing, whether you want to agree to travel to another state or country if litigation becomes necessary.

Jurisdictional Issues in International Law

The jurisdiction of courts within a particular country over businesses from other countries is a critical issue in international law. A common subject in international disputes is whether courts in the United States, for example, can require foreign companies to defend lawsuits within the United States.

Conflicts of Law in International Disputes

The courts and judicial systems of countries around the globe vary, as do the procedural aspects of litigation. For example, Japan has no discovery process that permits the parties to examine each other's documents and witnesses prior to trial (see Chapter 4 for more details on discovery and the Japanese court system), and the United States permits lawyers to collect contingency fees and also permits broader tort recovery than would be available in most other countries.

Because of liberal discovery and recovery rules in the United States, many plaintiffs injured in other countries by products manufactured by U.S.-based firms want to bring suit in the United States to take advantage of our judicial system's processes and rules. However, the California Supreme Court has ruled in *Stangvik v Shiley, Inc.*, 819 P.2d 14 (Cal. 1991) that if a plaintiff's home country provides an adequate forum for a dispute, the case cannot be brought in the United States. The suit involved family members of various patients who had died when their heart valves, manufactured by Shiley of Irvine, California, failed. The decision of the California Supreme Court required the plaintiffs to return to their home countries, where the recovery would be substantially less. However, states do differ on their conclusions about *forum non conveniens*; see *Ison v E.I. DuPont de Nemours and Co., Inc.*, 729 A.2d 832 (Del. 1999).

B I O G R A P H Y

Third Woman and First Hispanic on the High Court

Justice Sonia Sotomayor is the first Hispanic justice on the court and her story is one of remarkable achievement. Born in the Bronx, New York, on June 25, 1954, to immigrant parents from Puerto Rico, she grew up in public housing. She earned a BA in 1976 from Princeton University, graduating *summa cum laude*. In 1979, she earned a JD from Yale Law School where she served as an editor of the *Yale Law Journal*. She was an Assistant District Attorney in the New York County District Attorney's Office from 1979–1984 and an associate and then partner at Pavia & Harcourt in New York City. In 1991, President George H.W. Bush nominated her to the U.S. District Court, Southern District of New York, and she served

in that role until 1998, when President Clinton nominated her as a judge on the United States Court of Appeals for the Second Circuit. She served there until President Barack Obama nominated her as an Associate Justice of the Supreme Court, a role she assumed on August 8, 2009. One of her former law clerks said of Justice Sotomayor, "She grew up in a situation of disadvantage, and was able, by virtue of the system operating in such a fair way, to accomplish what she did. I think she sees the law as an instrument that can accomplish the same thing for other people, a system that, if administered fairly, can give everyone the fair break they deserve, regardless of who they are."[2]

Summary

What is the judicial process?

- Judicial review—review of a trial court's decisions and verdict to determine whether any reversible error was made

- Appellate court—court responsible for review of trial court's decisions and verdict

- Brief—written summary of basis for appeal of trial court's decisions and verdict

- Reversible error—mistake by trial court that requires a retrial or modification of a trial court's decision

- Options for appellate court:
  - Reverse—change trial court's decision

- Remand—return case to trial court for retrial or reexamination of issues

- Affirm—uphold trial court's decisions and verdict

- Modify—overturn a portion of the trial court's verdict

- *Stare decisis*—Latin for "let the decision stand"; doctrine of reviewing, applying, and/or distinguishing prior case decisions

- Case opinion—written court decision used as precedent; contains *dicta* or explanation of reasoning and, often, a minority view or dissenting opinion

Who are the parties in the judicial system?

- Plaintiffs/petitioners—initiators of litigation
- Defendants/respondents—parties named as those from whom plaintiff seeks relief
- Lawyers—officers of the court who speak for plaintiffs and defendants
- Attorney–client privilege—confidential protections for client conversations
- Appellant—party who appeals lower court's decision
- Appellee—party responding in an appeal

What factors decide jurisdiction?

- **The power of the court to hear cases**
  - Subject matter jurisdiction—authority of court over subject matter
  - Jurisdiction over the parties: *in personam* jurisdiction
  - Voluntary
  - Through property
  - Presence in the state: minimum contacts
  - Residence
  - Business office

What are the courts and court systems?

- **Federal court system**
  - Federal district court—trial court in federal system; hears cases that involve a federal question, the United States as a party, or a plaintiff and defendant from different states (diversity of citizenship) and $75,000 or more at issue; opinions reported in *Federal Supplement*
  - Limited jurisdiction courts—bankruptcy courts, court of claims
  - U.S. Courts of Appeals—federal appellate courts in each of the circuits; opinions reported in *Federal Reporter*
  - U.S. Supreme Court—highest court in United States; requires writ of *certiorari* for review; acts as trial court (original jurisdiction) for suits involving states and diplomats
- **State court system**
  - Lesser courts—small claims, traffic courts, justice of the peace courts
  - State trial courts—general jurisdiction courts in each state
  - State appellate courts—courts that review trial court decisions
  - State supreme courts—courts that review appellate court decisions
- **International courts**
  - Voluntary jurisdiction
  - International Court of Justice—UN court; contentious (consensual) jurisdiction; reported in *International Law Reports*
  - London Commercial Court—voluntary court of arbitration

Questions and Problems

1. The brokerage firm of E. F. Hutton was charged with federal criminal violations of interstate funds transfers. In reviewing the case, the lawyers for the government discovered internal memoranda from and between branch managers in several states that outline a process for check kiting (a literal stringing together of checks and deposits) that enabled E. F. Hutton to earn interest on phantom deposits. Where will the case be tried? Which court system? Which court? Why?

What are the lawyers' obligations with respect to the documents? What is the company's obligation? If you were a manager at E. F. Hutton, would you voluntarily disclose the documents to the government?

2. Pharmaceutical manufacturer Merck is experiencing ongoing litigation over its drug Vioxx because of customers who say they had cardiovascular side effects from taking the anti–arthritis pain drug. As of mid-2007, Merck was facing 9,500 lawsuits that a federal judge ruled could not be tried as class actions because of the different health issues among the plaintiffs who were bringing the suits against Merck. A jury in a federal court in New Orleans cleared Merck of any responsibility for the death of Richard Irvin, a Florida resident who had a fatal heart attack one month after he began to take Vioxx. In 2005, Merck won one state court verdict in New Jersey and lost another state court trial in Texas. Why would some of the cases be tried in state court and some be tried in federal court? Explain the differing decisions.

3. N-the-Water Publishing, Inc. dba Still N the Water Publishing produces hip-hop and rap music through sampling, the process of copying portions of prior master sound recordings directly onto new sound recordings and then rapping on top of the new sound recording. Bridgeport Music is the owner of the copyright for the music that Still N the Water has used for its rap and hip-hop song productions. Bridgeport is headquartered in Nashville, Tennessee, and Still N the Water is part of a series of record companies based in Florida and Texas. Bridgeport brought suit against Still N the Water in federal district court in Tennessee. Under Tennessee's long-arm statute, jurisdiction may be asserted on "any basis not inconsistent with the constitution of this state or of the United States" [Tenn. Code Ann. § 20–2–214(a)(6)]. Still N the Water sells CDs in all 50 states, with sales spread equally among the states and marketing plans for each of the states.

Can Still N the Water be required to come to Tennessee to defend the lawsuit? [*Bridgeport Music, Inc. v Still N The Water Pub.* 327 F.3d 472 (6th Cir. 2003); *cert. denied* 540 U.S. 948 (2003).]

4. The domain name aol.org was registered by Korea DNS, a South Korean entity, on September 3, 2001, and subsequently transferred first to an individual, Sujin Jeon, and thereafter to an individual listed simply as "Will E." Here in the United States, the domain name AOL.COM is registered to its parent company and owner, Time Warner/AOL. That name has been held since 1996. On July 30, 2002, America Online, the original holder of registered United States trademarks for AOL and AOL.COM, filed suit against the Korean company and individuals for infringement and violation of the Anticybersquatting Act. The Korean defendants filed a motion to dismiss on the grounds that the federal district court in Virginia, where AOL had filed suit and where its company headquarters are situated, did not have *in personam* jurisdiction over aol. org because it had no presence in the United States. Should the motion to dismiss be granted? [*America Online, Inc. v Aol.Org,* 259 F.Supp.2d 449 (E.D. Va. 2003)]

5. Determine which court(s) would have jurisdiction over the following matters:

   a. The sale of securities without first registering them with the Securities and Exchange Commission, as required under 15 U.S.C. § 77 *et seq.*

   b. A suit between a Hawaiian purchaser of sunscreen lotion and its California manufacturer for severe sunburn that resulted in $65,000 in medical bills

6. Where will the following cases be tried?

   a. A will contest that challenges the validity of a will

   b. A suit by a homeowner against his building contractor for $1.5 million for the failure to provide termite protection on the home the contractor built

   c. A suit by a defense contractor against the U.S. Army for nonpayment on drones delivered to Iraq

7. A Delaware banking corporation was named as trustee for the large estate of a wealthy individual in that individual's will. The beneficiaries of the trust are the deceased's two children, one of whom lives in Pennsylvania and the other in Florida. The bank does business in Delaware only. Can the beneficiary in Florida successfully require the bank to submit to the jurisdiction of Florida courts? [*Hanson v Denckla,* 357 U.S. 235 (1958)]

8. Eulala Shute lived in Arlington, Washington, and through a local travel agent purchased a seven-day Carnival cruise. The cruise began in Los Angeles, went to Puerto Vallarta, Mexico, and then returned to Los Angeles. Carnival Cruise Lines, Inc., the owner of the ship and the firm responsible for the cruise, is a corporation based in Miami, Florida. While the cruise ship was in international waters off of Mexico, Shute tripped and fell on a deck mat during a guided tour of the ship's galley.

Shute filed suit in federal district court in the state of Washington against Carnival to recover for her injuries. Could the Washington court take *in personam* jurisdiction over Carnival? [*Carnival Cruise Lines, Inc. v Shute,* 499 U.S. 585 (1991)]

9. Centurion Wireless, Inc., is a Nebraska corporation that designs and engineers antennas and power products for telecommunications and information technology purposes. Hop-On is a Nevada corporation selling, among other products, disposable cellular phones. Hop-On's employee Melyssa Banda contacted Centurion by phone or e-mail in relation to designing an antenna for a cellular phone. The parties then entered into a contract entitled "Statement of Work," signed by in Lincoln, Nebraska, by Steve Bowles, Centurion's vice president of sales, in which Centurion agreed to design, develop, and integrate an antenna design for Hop-On and provide up to 100 prototype antennae. In addition, the contract provided that more prototype antennae could be sold at a per-unit price. Centurion was to be paid $10,000 by February 15, 2002. Centurion also agreed not to sell the antenna design to any other cellular phone manufacturer.

Centurion completed its work and made offers to manufacture up to 3 million antennas, but Hop-On declined. Centurion alleges that Hop-On then offered to buy the design, but the parties could not agree on a price. Centurion's final offer was to sell the antenna design for $45,000.

On April 7, 2003, Centurion was contacted by Banda, the former vice-president of Hop-On, and informed that even though Hop-On had not purchased the antenna design, it had copied and used it in their phones. Hop-On's phones, which used the Centurion antenna design, were sold at Walgreens stores in California. Hop-On operates a website at Hop-On.com, which provides some information about phones and contact information. Centurion filed suit against Hop-On in Nebraska for copyright infringement, conversion, and unjust enrichment. Hop-On filed a motion to dismiss because of Nebraska's lack of jurisdiction over it. Does the Nebraska court have jurisdiction? Why or why not? [*Centurion Wireless Technologies, Inc. v Hop-On Communications, Inc.*, 342 F.Supp.2d 832 (D. Neb. 2004)]

10.   The words "I've fallen and I can't get up!" were part of a TV commercial for a device whose marketing was directed at the elderly and whose appeal was that the device was hooked to communication links with emergency care providers. In fact, the device provided a link, but not a direct link, to a 911 number; some interlink delay would occur in notifying emergency personnel. The devices, worn around the neck, were in fact a means of affecting communication when the wearer could not get to a phone. However, the device was not directly linked to a 911 number.

Officials in Arizona brought charges against the company for deceptive advertising. Standards in Arizona require proof only that someone could be misled by the commercials; actions against advertisers do not require proof that someone was actually misled. The devices have been a help to many people, bringing assistance to those who would otherwise, because of temporary or permanent mobility impairment, be unable to call for help. Officials in other states did not find the ads misleading. Does Arizona have jurisdiction?

If you were an official for the company, would you change all of your ads or modify only those in Arizona? Were the ads unethical?

Ethics and the Law

Timothy J. Mayopoulos was the general counsel for Bank of America (B of A) until shortly before its merger/acquisition of Merrill Lynch was approved by B of A shareholders. Mr. Mayopoulos was fired from his position on the day he met with the board and the board was told that Merrill had heretofore undisclosed losses that had not been disclosed to B of A shareholders. He was escorted out of the Charlotte, North Carolina, B of A headquarters by security personnel and was not permitted to return to his office and collect his belongings. The merger was approved and the shareholders brought suit for the bank's failure to disclose the full scope of the Merrill losses.

Mr. Mayopoulos gave testimony to New York Attorney General Andrew Cuomo, the official who has been investigating whether information about the scope of the losses was withheld prior to the shareholder vote on the Merrill merger/acquisition. Mr. Mayopoulos, however, declined to disclose to Mr. Cuomo's office the content of the advice he gave to the bank, citing legal ethics rules.

Mr. Cuomo asked B of A to waive "the privilege" because its refusal was hindering his office's ability to investigate what happened in the days leading up to the merger/acquisition. B of A initially refused to waive its attorney–client privilege. However, when an SEC investigation began, the bank waived the privilege and then settled the SEC case for a $150 million fine. The shareholder litigation is ongoing

B of A's then–CEO, Kenneth D. Lewis, testified that Mr. Mayopoulos was fired because B of A had more executives than it needed following the merger.

Mr. Mayopoulos is now general counsel for Fannie Mae, but, in an ironic note, Mr. Mayopoulos still resides in Charlotte, North Carolina on the same street as Mr. Lewis. The neighborhood block parties during the summer of 2009 must have been tense.

What is the lawyer–client privilege and when does it apply? Does it apply to general counsel as well as to outside counsel? When is the privilege waived? Why do you think Mr. Mayopoulos stood so firm on his refusal to answer questions about what happened in the days leading up to the merger and his termination? What do you think really happened in the lead-up to the merger?

FOR MORE INFORMATION

Louise Story, "Bank Firing of Counsel Is Examined," *New York Times*, September 9, 2009, p. C1.

Dan Fitzpatrick, "New York Nears Charges on Merrill Deal," *Wall Street Journal*, September 9, 2009, p. C1.

Notes

1. The U.S. Supreme Court ruled that Mr. Newdow lacked standing to challenge the "under God" clause in the pledge of allegiance because he was not the custodial parent of his daughter. 542 U.S. 1 (2004). The other cites for this case are 124 S.Ct. 2301(2004) and 159 L.Ed.2d 98(2004).

2. Jeffrey Rosen, "The Case Against Sotomayor," *The New Republic*, May 4, 2009.

Managing Disputes:
Alternative Dispute Resolution and Litigation Strategies

A federal judge, faced with two hostile lawyers in a case, found that he was refereeing a dispute between the two over where to hold the deposition of a witness.[1] Both wanted neutral territory. The judge proposed the steps of the federal courthouse. One lawyer proposed a conference room in the office building where they both work (four floors apart), while the other proposed going down the street from their offices to the court reporter's office to hold the deposition there. Judge Gregory A. Presnell of the district of Orlando ordered the parties to use "rock, paper, and scissors" to determine the site, noting that his innovation was "a new form of alternative dispute resolution."

Daniel Pettinato, the lawyer for the plaintiff in the case, said that he had been training with his five- and nine-year-old daughters for the event. They were encouraging him to open with "rock" because, as they said, "everyone opens with rock," and Mr. Pettinato said his case was "as solid as a rock." The director of the USA Rock Paper Scissors League, the LA-based governing body for the childhood sport, said that opening with paper was better. The lawyer for the defendant, D. Lee Craig, had no comment.

The study of business regulation to this point has involved an overview of ethics, law, and the courts responsible for enforcing, interpreting, and applying the law. This chapter focuses on disputes and answers the following questions: How can businesses best resolve disputes? What strategies should a business follow if litigation is inevitable? How do courts proceed with litigation?

The parties needed a better way to resolve their differences. This chapter offers some insights. ■

UPDATE
For up-to-date news on law, ethics, and economics, go to
mariannejennings.com

> **If I were asked where I place the American aristocracy, I should reply without hesitation that it occupies the judicial bench and bar.**
>
> Alexis de Tocqueville
> *(1805–1859)*

CONSIDER...

Ophthalmologists Lewis Frazee and Robert Selkin formed American Laser Vision (ALV), which opened laser vision correction centers in Texas and Oklahoma. ALV signed contracts with The Laser Vision Institute (LVI) to have LVI operate the eye centers by providing management, nonmedical staff, and equipment. ALV would provide the surgeons: Drs. Frazee and Selkin. LVI was to pay ALV a fee for each surgery performed. Their agreement provided that any disputes would be submitted to arbitration. After a few months, Dr. Selkin complained about the LVI staff, so

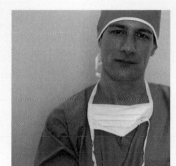

he quit performing surgeries at LVI and began doing surgeries at other clinics in other states. Dr. Selkin bought out Frazee's interest in ALV and then filed an arbitration claim against LVI for $4 million in lost surgery fees and other damages. After a three-day hearing, the arbitrator awarded Dr. Selkin $1.8 million. LVI filed suit to have the award set aside because the arbitrator failed to recognize that Dr. Selkin was in breach, was making money elsewhere, and never gave LVI a chance to deal with staff issues. What can and should the court do with the arbitration award?

What Is Alternative Dispute Resolution?

Alternative dispute resolution (ADR) offers parties alternative means of resolving their differences outside actual courtroom litigation and the costly preparation for it. ADR ranges from informal options, such as a negotiated settlement between the CEOs of companies, to the formal, written processes of the American Arbitration Association. These processes may be used along with litigation or in lieu of litigation.

Types of Alternative Dispute Resolution

Arbitration

Nature of Arbitration

Arbitration is the oldest form of ADR and was once the most popular form of alternative dispute resolution, but its increasing costs and time commitment have found businesses and lawyers labeling it "no different from litigation." Mandatory arbitration clauses have even been abandoned by the American Institute of Architects, a pioneer in ADR that had the mandatory clauses in its model contract from 1888 through 2010. The AIA has moved to mandatory mediation. Bank of America has eliminated mandatory arbitration from its credit card, bank account, and auto loan contracts. Because of this shift in ADR, arbitration is no longer the preferred method for business dispute resolution.

The one remaining area of growth in arbitration is through state courts, which, in order to encourage ADR, now impose mandatory arbitration in all cases involving amounts below a certain dollar limit, generally $25,000 or $50,000. In Arizona, these mandatory arbitration proceedings are arbitrated by lawyers in the state, who are required to accept such assignments on a rotating basis either for a fee or as part of their *pro bono* activities. Such mandatory arbitration requirements have reduced the civil caseloads in many states by as much as 50 percent.

Binding vs. Nonbinding vs. Mandatory Arbitration

An agreement to submit to arbitration is an enforceable clause in consumer and commercial contracts. The parties may also agree to submit to arbitration after their dispute arises even though they do not have such a clause in their contract. Arbitration can be binding or nonbinding. **Binding arbitration** means that the decision of the arbitrators is final. Appeals of the decision are limited (see discussion that follows). **Nonbinding arbitration** is a preliminary step to litigation. If one of the parties is not satisfied with the result in the arbitration, the case may still be litigated.

A contract can also require arbitration, something known as mandatory arbitration. Under mandatory arbitration, the parties cannot choose court action first. Mandatory arbitration clauses have been a focus of court challenges, but the courts have been firm in their support of the clauses. In addition, the Federal Arbitration Act (FAA) permits mandatory arbitration in consumer contracts and has been upheld by the U.S. Supreme Court [*Green Tree Financial Corp. v Randolph*, 531 U.S. 79 (2000)].

Arbitration Procedures

Once the parties agree to arbitrate, they usually notify the American Arbitration Association (AAA) (http://www.adr.org), which for a fee will handle all the steps in the arbitration. The AAA is the largest ADR provider in the country for commercial disputes and the National Arbitration Forum is the largest for consumer contracts.

The parties submit names for arbitration and a mutually agreeable arbitrator or panel is appointed. A hearing date is set at a mutually agreeable time. Between the time the date is set and the actual hearing, the parties have the responsibility of gathering their evidence and necessary witnesses. The parties are, in effect, doing their preparation or discovery (see pages 126–130). The parties can also request that the other party bring certain documents to the hearing. Some arbitrators are given subpoena power in certain states; that is, they have the power to require the production of documents or to have a witness testify.

The parties need not have lawyers but have the right to use one under AAA rules. AAA rules require notification to the other parties about the use and identity of counsel. Although the atmosphere is more relaxed, an arbitration hearing parallels a trial. Each of the parties has the opportunity to present evidence and witnesses. Each has the right to cross-examination and a closing statement. Some of the emotion of a trial is missing because, although emotional appeal influences juries, an expert arbitrator is not likely to be swayed by it. After the close of the hearing, the arbitrator has 30 days to make a decision.

In binding arbitration, the arbitrator's award is final. The award and decision cannot be changed, modified, or reversed. Only the parties can agree to have the case reopened; the arbitrator cannot do so. The courts are strict in their hands-off policy on private arbitration decisions that result from the parties' contractual agreement to submit to arbitration. The grounds for setting aside an arbitration finding under federal law are (1) the award resulted from corruption, fraud, or undue influence; (2) partiality or corruption occurred among the arbitrators; (3) the arbitrators were guilty of misconduct, which prejudiced the rights of one of the parties; or (4) the arbitrators exceeded their powers. Case 4.1 involves a decision that reflects judicial restraint on arbitration decisions and also provides an answer to the opening "Consider."

CASE 4.1

American Laser Vision, P.A. v Laser Vision Institute, L.L.C.
487 F.3d 255 (5th Cir. 2007)

Arbitrators Don't Need Laser Precision to Be Right

FACTS

In 2000, ophthalmologists Lewis Frazee and Robert Selkin formed American Laser Vision (ALV), which opened laser vision correction centers in Texas and Oklahoma. Drs. Frazee and Selkin were each 50-percent shareholders of ALV. In early 2002, ALV signed a series of contracts with The Laser Vision Institute (LVI). Under those contracts, LVI would operate the eye centers by providing management, nonmedical staff, and equipment, and ALV would provide the surgeons: Drs. Frazee and Selkin. According to the agreements, LVI was to pay ALV a fee for each surgery performed. In practice, however, LVI paid Drs. Frazee and Selkin individually for the surgeries each doctor performed. The contracts specifically prohibited LVI from interfering with the surgeons' professional judgment and care of patients. ALV and LVI also entered into subleases whereby LVI would pay rent to ALV for the offices, make equipment payments to vendors, and fulfill other obligations relating to the subleased office space. Finally, the agreements provided that any disputes would be settled by arbitration.

Drs. Frazee and Selkin performed surgeries from February through May. In June, Dr. Selkin stopped performing surgeries at the LVI facility because, as he wrote to LVI in a series of letters, LVI staff were interfering with the treatment of patients and his professional judgment by: giving patients instructions that conflicted with his orders; using an improper solution to clean surgical supplies; changing post-operative

prescriptions without his knowledge; instructing employees not to perform maintenance duties that Dr. Selkin requested; switching patients to Dr. Frazee if Dr. Selkin felt they were bad candidates for surgery; and misrepresenting to patients the risks and benefits of surgery. Dr. Selkin never met with LVI about his concerns, but he did work during this time at similar centers in North Carolina and Tennessee earning substantial fees.

Dr. Selkin then bought out Dr. Frazee's interest in ALV and pursued a breach of contract claim by ALV against LVI, seeking an arbitral award of $4,031,241.55 for damages from 2002–2005. ALV sought $3,524,966.67 for lost surgery revenue due to Selkin's departure, $34,226.84 for surgeries allegedly performed but not yet paid, and about $500,000 for the sublease and equipment claims.

The arbitrator recognized that the contract was between LVI and ALV, but treated the contract as if it were between LVI and Dr. Selkin because LVI paid Drs. Selkin and Frazee directly. The arbitrator also "sustained" LVI's objection to Dr. Selkin's figures for fees for 2004–2005, agreeing that they were unduly speculative. After a three-day hearing, the arbitrator concluded that LVI breached the professional service and sublease agreements and awarded ALV $1,842,220.39 in damages, plus interest, attorneys' fees, and costs. Although the parties had agreed that the arbitrator need not file findings or otherwise explain his decision, LVI asked the arbitrator to explain the award. The arbitrator declined. LVI filed suit in federal district court, and the court granted ALV's motion for

CONTINUED

summary judgment and denied LVI's request to vacate the arbitration award. LVI appealed.

PER CURIAM

Judicial review of an arbitration award is "exceedingly deferential." Vacatur is available "only on very narrow grounds," and federal courts must "defer to the arbitrator's decision when possible." An award must be upheld as long as it "is rationally inferable from the letter or purpose of the underlying agreement." Even "the failure of an arbitrator to correctly apply the law is not a basis for setting aside an arbitrator's award." "It is only when the arbitrator strays from interpretation and application of the agreement and effectively 'dispense[s] his own brand of industrial justice' that his decision may be unenforceable." Moreover, "the arbitrator's selection of a particular remedy is given even more deference than his reading of the underlying contract," and "the remedy lies beyond the arbitrator's jurisdiction only if there is no rational way to explain the remedy . . . as a logical means of furthering the aims of the contract."

LVI argues first that the arbitrator disregarded the plain meaning of the contracts by construing them as between Selkin and LVI, not ALV and LVI, and considering the losses of Selkin personally, not those of ALV. We are not persuaded. The record shows that the arbitrator was quite aware of the factual nuances of the case, the identities of the parties, and the flow of money.

LVI next argues that, if the arbitrator correctly analyzed only the losses accruing to ALV, then he completely ignored the notice and cure provisions because Selkin never attempted to provide notice and accept cure and, more importantly, ALV through Frazee provided notice and accepted cure of whatever problems may have existed. As the district court recognized, however, Frazee alone could not bind ALV when Selkin was still the President and co-owner. And the arbitrator heard evidence about Selkin's attempts to provide notice and accept cure—which, if one considers Frazee to have implicitly consented to such acts because he was aware of them, means ALV was attempting to provide notice and accept cure—and there is evidence that those attempts were rebuffed, or at a minimum not satisfied by LVI. In any event, the arbitrator could have found that LVI had notice of the problems forming the basis of this entire dispute.

Third, LVI challenges the actual amount of the award. It argues that even if ALV might legitimately recover damages for the sublease breaches, and even if ALV recovered all such damages that it requested, the arbitrator also must have awarded about $1.3 million in lost income damages for 2002–2003. First, LVI contends, this represents damages to Selkin, not ALV. As we have noted, however, the arbitrator understood the distinction. Second, it contends, either ALV failed to mitigate its damages by not hiring another doctor or Selkin fully mitigated all damages flowing to ALV with his high earnings in North Carolina and Tennessee. The first argument ignores the nature of LVI's breach—Selkin refused to continue working because LVI was allegedly interfering in his practice, and it wasn't unreasonable for the arbitrator to conclude that, under those facts, ALV was not obligated to hire another surgeon until LVI addressed its allegedly substandard performance. The second argument fails because the arbitrator did not award ALV the full amount of lost income damages it sought. Moreover, he heard testimony regarding the possibility that Selkin could have performed surgeries in North Carolina and Tennessee while also performing them for ALV in Texas. Indeed, the record reveals that the arbitrator dealt extensively with this possibility and recognized its difficulties.

LVI also urges that, at a minimum, we should remand for the arbitrator to clarify the nature of his award. Remand is rare, appropriate only "when an award is patently ambiguous, when the issues submitted were not fully resolved, or when the language of the award has generated a collateral dispute." None of those situations is present here. Although, as explained above, the exact basis for the award is unclear, the parties agreed that the arbitrator need not state his reasons.

We will not second-guess multiple, implicit findings and conclusions underpinning the award. We do not decide if the award was free from error. We decide only that it is not the kind of extraordinary award that ineluctably leads to the conclusion that the arbitrator was "dispensing his own brand of industrial justice." There are advantages and disadvantages in contracting for private resolution of a dispute announced without explanation of reason. When a party does so and loses, federal courts cannot rewrite the contract and offer review the party contracted away.

AFFIRMED.

CASE QUESTIONS

1. List the areas of arbitrariness LVI raised regarding the arbitrator's decision.

2. How does the court respond to the concerns raised about the arbitrator's decision?

3. What is the standard for setting aside an arbitration decision?

For the Manager's Desk

Re: Understanding the Disillusionment with ADR

The issues lawyers raise about arbitration include the following:

- Increasingly, arbitrations are as time-consuming and costly as trials.

- Too many arbitrators are allowing extensive discovery.

- Some arbitrators are requiring $40,000 retainers just for agreeing to begin hearing a case.

- The panel of arbitrators may consist of people who, while knowledgeable in their fields, are beholden to the industry, such as an engineer siding with an engineer defendant.

Some businesses are revisiting their mandatory arbitration clauses because they are looking at some of the arbitration decisions and saying, "Maybe the court system isn't so bad—at least you get due process at some point."

The concern of many lawyers and court administrators is the loss of common law and statutory interpretation when too many cases opt for the ADR route, which does not include published decisions or rationale.

What are the theoretical benefits of arbitration? What are its drawbacks?

Source: Michael Orey, "The Vanishing Trial," *BusinessWeek*, April 30, 2007, pp. 38–39.

CONSIDER...   4.1

Prestige Ford is an automobile dealership located in Garland, Texas. Ford Dealer Computer Services (DCS), located in Houston, Texas, sells computer systems that are designed to assist Ford dealers in managing their operations. On January 28, 1993, Prestige Ford entered into a written contract with DCS under which DCS agreed to provide Prestige with hardware, software, and maintenance related to one of its computer systems. The contract's initial five-year term was extended for an additional five years, amounting to a total contract period of ten years, commencing at the installation date. There was an arbitration clause in the contract that required the parties to follow AAA rules and processes.

In September 1997, Prestige Ford terminated the agreement with DCS because it said the computer system DCS had provided did not operate correctly and because DCS was unable to perform maintenance for the system in a timely fashion. In July of 1998, DCS filed a claim in arbitration against Prestige Ford. Prior to the arbitration hearing, Prestige Ford filed five separate motions to obtain DCS documents. The arbitration panel heard oral argument on the motions and denied them.

The arbitration hearing was held in Austin, Texas, from August 6, 2001 through August 14, 2001. The arbitration panel found that Prestige breached its contract, and awarded DCS $101,752.32 in damages. The panel also found that Prestige Ford had not established any breach of contract or lack of adequate performance by DCS. The panel also awarded DCS $337,459.76 in costs and attorney fees.

Following the panel's decision, Prestige Ford filed suit to vacate the award because it had not been given a chance to see the evidence it needed from DCS and that the damages were excessive. The district court refused to set aside the decision. Was the court correct? Should the arbitration decision stand? Isn't discovery of evidence a necessary part of any case? [*Prestige Ford v Ford Dealer Computer Services, Inc.*, 324 F.3d 391 (5th Cir. 2003)]

Mediation

Other forms of ADR are readily available and relatively inexpensive, especially when compared to arbitration. **Mediation** is one such alternative. Mediation is a process in which both parties meet with a neutral mediator who listens to

BUSINESS PLANNING TIP

Mediation has been a popular form of dispute resolution among business-to-business (B2B) e-commerce companies. Amazon.com and eBay have used mediation regularly in the resolution of disputes.

each side explain its position. The mediator is trained to get the parties to respond to each other and their concerns. The mediator helps break down impasses and works to have the parties arrive at a mutually agreeable solution. Unlike an arbitrator, the mediator does not issue a decision; the role of the mediator is to try to get the parties to agree on a solution. Mediation is completely confidential. What is said to the mediator cannot be used later by the parties or their lawyers if litigation becomes necessary. Mediation does not require that the parties be represented by lawyers. Mediation is not binding unless the parties have agreed to be bound by the decision.

Medarb

Mediation arbitration (medarb) is a recent creation in which the arbitrator begins by attempting to negotiate between the two parties. If the arbitrator is unable to reach a settlement, the case proceeds to arbitration with the same party serving as arbitrator. One percent of the AAA's cases each year are decided by a medarb process.

The Minitrial

In a **minitrial,** the parties have their lawyers present the strongest aspects of their cases to senior officials from both companies in the presence of a neutral advisor or a judge with experience in the field. At the end of the presentations by both parties, the neutral advisor can provide several forms of input, which are controlled by the parties. The advisor may be asked to provide what his or her judgment would be in the case, or the advisor may be asked to prepare a settlement proposal based on the concerns and issues presented by the parties. Minitrials are more adversarial than mediation, but they are confidential; and the input from a neutral but respected advisor may help bring the parties together. A minitrial is not binding.

Rent-a-Judge

Many companies and individuals are discovering that the time that elapses between the filing of a lawsuit and its resolution is too great to afford much relief. As a result, a kind of private court system, known as **rent-a-judge,** is developing in which parties may have their case heard before someone with judicial experience without waiting for the slower process of public justice. These private courts are like "Judge Judy" without the television cameras. The parties pay filing fees and pay for the judges and courtrooms. These private courts also offer less expensive settlement conferences to afford the parties a chance at mediation prior to their private hearing. This and the other methods of ADR previously discussed offer the opportunity to obtain final dispositions of cases more quickly and at less cost.

Summary Jury Trials

Under this relatively new method of ADR, the parties are given the opportunity to present summaries of their evidence to a judge and jurors. The jurors then give an advisory verdict to start the settlement process. If the parties are unable to agree on a settlement, a formal trial proceeds. This means of resolution gives the parties an idea of a jury's perception and assists in setting guidelines for settlement. A **summary jury trial** occurs late in the litigation process, after the costs of **discovery** have been incurred. It can, however, save the expense of a trial.

Early Neutral Evaluation

Early neutral evaluation requires another attorney to meet with the parties, receive an assessment of the case by both sides, and then provide an evaluation of the merits of the case. The attorney, who is either a paid consultant or a volunteer through the state bar association, renders an opinion on the resolution of the case. The idea in this method of resolution is to encourage settlement. Because early neutral evaluation occurs before the discovery phase of the case, it can save time and money if the parties are able to settle.

Peer Review

Peer review has become popular particularly for disputes between employers and employees and is used by Darden Industries (Red Lobster, Olive Garden), TRW Inc., Rockwell International Corp., and Marriott International, Inc. Peer review, which is generally conducted within three weeks of demand, is a review by coworkers of the action taken against an employee (demotion, termination, discipline). These panels of fellow employees (one chosen by management, one chosen by the employee, and one chosen randomly) can take testimony, review documents, and make decisions that can include an award of damages.

Employers say that sometimes their decisions are reversed in peer review, but Darden Industries indicates that peer review has reduced employee litigation and legal fees. Of the 100 disputes handled each year in peer review, only 10 proceed to litigation.

Experiments in the use of peer review for customers, contractors, and physicians are ongoing around the country. Many see the perception of fairness as an important quality that has resulted in the growth of the use of peer review.

For the Manager's Desk

Re: Southwest Airlines and Creative Dispute Resolution

In 1991, Dallas-based Southwest Airlines began a marketing campaign using the slogan "Just Plane Smart." Greenville-based Stevens Aviation had been using the slogan "Plane Smart" to market its airline service business. Following posturing by lawyers, Kurt Herwald, the chairman of Stevens Aviation, called Herb Kelleher, then chairman of Southwest Airlines, and offered to arm wrestle for the rights to the slogan. Mr. Kelleher rented a wrestling auditorium, sold tickets to the event, and offered the proceeds to charity.

Mr. Kelleher, then 61, lost to Mr. Herwald, then 38, who is also a weightlifter. Mr. Herwald said, "Just to show sympathy for the elderly and that there's no hard feelings, we've decided to allow Southwest Airlines to continue using our slogan." After the event, a commentator noted, "Not only did the companies save a court battle that would have taken years and cost several hundred thousand dollars, they gained loads of free publicity. They also made donations to charities."

Resolution of International Disputes

Arbitration has been used in the international business arena since 1922. The **International Chamber of Commerce** (ICC) is a private organization that handles arbitration cases from parties in 123 countries. In 2009, the Arbitration Court of the ICC handled 817 requests for arbitration and issued 415 arbitration awards. Most requests for ICC arbitration come from 128 countries, and the typical subject matters are trade transactions, contracts, intellectual property, agency, and corporate law. The following statistics were taken from the ICC's annual report for 2006.

- Arbitrators of 73 different nationalities were appointed or confirmed under the ICC Rules.
- Hearings were held in 53 different countries.
- The amount in dispute exceeded $1 million (U.S.) in 77.1 percent of new cases.

The ICC process is similar to that discussed earlier for the American Arbitration Association. The award of the ICC is final, and payment must be made at the location of the hearing.

The ICC also provides mediation, referred to as conciliation, services. In conciliation, the court assigns an expert to work with the parties to try to achieve a settlement of the case.

In addition to the ICC, the World Bank has established the International Center for Settlement of Investment Disputes (ICSID). The ICSID is an arbitral organization created specifically to hear disputes between investors and the nations in which they have made investments. This arbitration forum was created because of investors' fears that the courts of the nation in which they have invested may favor the government of that nation.

The American Arbitration Association created the International Centre for Dispute Resolution (ICDR), with offices in New York City, Dublin, and Mexico City to provide an international AAA service for global U.S.-based companies that face contract and other types of disputes in their international operations. The ICDR has partnering agreements with 62 ADR organizations in 43 countries and uses those partnerships to manage disputes that occur primarily in other countries. The United Nations Commission on International Trade Law (UNCITRAL) adopted a Model Law for Arbitration that deals with where arbitration should be held (the parties can decide) and which country's laws should apply.

Litigation Versus ADR: The Issues and Costs

Speed and Cost

Speed and cost are two compelling reasons businesses turn to ADR to resolve disputes. Costs of ADR have increased substantially over the past five years, but the speed still remains an important issue for many businesses.

Protection of Privacy

Whatever matter is in dispute can be kept private if referred directly to ADR, which means that no public court documents are available for examination. Even when a suit is filed, the negotiated settlement achieved through alternative means can be kept private to protect the interests of the parties. When Dillard's, a national department store chain, and Joseph Home Company, a department store based in Pittsburgh, were litigating over Dillard's conduct in a Home's takeover, the parties' dispute centered on whether Dillard's was conducting due diligence in obtaining access to Home's facilities and records, or whether Dillard's was actually running the stores in an attempt to drive down the acquisition price. The business press reported on the litigation and the underlying dispute. The information was not flattering to either party. Dillard's was portrayed as a large firm taking advantage of a small chain and engaging in unethical conduct when it was supposed to be obtaining just financial information prior to finalizing the acquisition (a process called due diligence). Home's was portrayed as naive and inept. Dillard's and Home's settled the dispute, and both agreed to keep the terms of the settlement confidential. As a result, the public litigation ended, and the focus on alleged misconduct changed because of the settlement and its private nature.

Creative Remedies

Often, without the constraints of court jurisdiction and the restraints of legal boundaries, a creative remedy can be crafted that helps both sides. For example, Intel, a computer chip manufacturer, experienced ongoing disputes with employees who left the company to begin their own businesses with products and in areas that would compete with Intel. Intel's concern was whether the departing employees were taking with them technology that had been developed at and belonged to Intel. Using only the courts, Intel would have found itself in lengthy, expensive, and complex litigation over engineering and developmental issues. Such litigation is costly not only in a monetary sense but also to the morale of employees charged with product development. Constant legal battles with former employees are not healthy for a corporate image within a company or from the outside.

After filing suit against one group of employees, Intel agreed, along with the former employees, to have an expert oversee the former employees' work in their business. The expert would have knowledge of Intel's product development efforts that the employees had been involved with and would agree to notify all sides if the new company was infringing on any of Intel's patents. The expert agreed to oversee the new company's work for one year, at which point technology would make obsolete anything developed by the former employees while they were still at Intel. This creative solution permitted the former employees to operate their business, but it also provided Intel officials with the reassurance that their intellectual property was not being taken.

Judge and Jury Unknowns

Even though a good case and preparation are often offered as explanations for victory in a lawsuit, many good cases are lost

BUSINESS PLANNING TIP

Businesses such as Intel have now taken litigation strategy to a prevention stage. Intel and other firms, particularly those in high-tech and product development fields, now offer departing employees a partnership if they are leaving to start their own firms. The company provides a sort of incubator for the departing employee to get started in business. The company is an investor and will share in the returns the new product brings. The strategy here: Why try to beat them in litigation when you can join them with an investment?

despite excellent preparation. Various unknowns characterize all forms of litigation and ADR. The unknowns are judges, juries, and arbitrators and their perceptions and abilities. Research shows that 80 percent of all jurors make up their minds about a case after only the opening statements in a trial have been made. Further research has shown that juries use their predetermined ideas in reaching a verdict. Finally, research shows that juries employ hindsight bias in their deliberation processes; that is, juries view the outcome of a set of facts and conclude that one party should have done more. Knowing that someone was injured often clouds our ability to determine whether that person should have been able to prevent the injury.

Based on information about juries, many businesses opt for a trial in which a judge, not a jury, renders a decision. However, research with judges has demonstrated that even their case judgments are affected by predetermined ideas and hindsight bias, although to a lesser extent than those of jurors. "The Wild Card in Complex Business Litigation: The Jury" provides background information on the risks that juries pose for businesses in litigation.

For the Manager's Desk

Re: The Wild Card in Complex Business Litigation: The Jury

Former Chief Justice Warren Burger was one of the most vocal critics on the issue of mandatory jury trials in complex civil cases, with his feelings that juries waste time and are often incapable of understanding the issues presented to them and the application of the law to the case. Most criticisms regarding the use of juries in complex suits are focused on civil cases and not on criminal prosecutions.

In the 1978 IBM antitrust case, a jury heard five months of testimony on IBM's alleged monopolization of various market segments in the computer industry. The jury was deadlocked, and an interview with one of the jurors afterward gave some indication of the level of comprehension that resulted from the trial. The concept of "interface" was critical in the trial since the ability to interface would largely control whether there was ease of market entry and product compatibility.

Stephen J. Adler documents the following exchange in the case in *The Jury*:

Judge: "What is software?"

Juror: "That's the paper software."

Asked to define "interface," the juror said: "Well, if you take a blivet, turn it off one thing and drop it down, it's an interface change, right?"

The judge asked a second juror, "What about barriers to entry?"—to which she answered, "I would have to read about it."

A mistrial was declared.

Additional difficulties arise with finding available jurors. Complex civil suits are quite lengthy, a problem that continues to grow. Trials are simply getting longer, as evidenced by the following statistics: in 1968, 26 percent of the civil trials in federal district courts took one day; today that statistic is down to 14 percent; and in 1968, 75 cases lasted 10 days or more, and today that number is 359 cases. The question that arises about the jurors is, in cases like the five-month IBM trial, who were these people who were able to spend every day for five months sitting on a jury? Many critics noted that the result is an overabundance of retired individuals, housewives, and the unemployed, and an absence of professionals and businesspeople who might have some experience with the issues. A cultural and financial gap is created when a jury has limited cross-sectional representation. The perceptions of individuals differ according to their circumstances. For example, the American Bar Association's study of juror deliberations indicated the verdict figures in a trade secret case ranged from $1 to $1.5 million, and one juror commented as follows:

"When you start talking millions, I can't relate to that. It doesn't mean anything to me. I have trouble paying $8 for parking every day."

Source: Adapted from Marianne Jennings and Chris P. Neck, "The Wild Card in Complex Business Litigation: The Jury." Reprinted with permission from *Commercial Law Journal* 96, No. 1, p. 45. Copyright © 1991 by the Commercial Law League of America. All rights reserved.

EXHIBIT 4.1 Benefits of ADR versus Litigation

LITIGATION	ALTERNATIVE DISPUTE RESOLUTION
Technical discovery rules	Open lines of communication
Judicial constraints of precedent	Parties can agree to anything
Remedies limited (by law and precedent)	Creative remedies permitted
Backlog	Parties set timetable
Public proceeding	Privacy
Control by lawyers	Control by parties (or mediator/arbitrator)
Expensive	Cheaper
Strict procedures/timing	More flexibility
Judge/jury unknowns	Parties select mediator/arbitrator
Those who can afford to stay in win	Positions examined for validity
Judicial enforcement tools	Enforcement by good faith

Absence of Technicalities

Under ADR, the parties have the opportunity to tell their stories. The strict procedural rules and evidentiary exclusions do not apply in these forums, and many companies feel more comfortable because ADR seems to be more of a search for the truth than a battle of processes. A mediator can serve as a communication link between the parties and help them focus on issues and concerns. As one mediator described ADR, "If you've done your job . . . everyone goes home with big smiles."

Exhibit 4.1 provides a list of the benefits of ADR versus litigation.

For the Manager's Desk

Re: A Checklist for When to Litigate

Costs

Every lawsuit costs time and money. Costs of litigation include but by no means end with attorneys' fees, and other significant costs are often not considered before a business decides to become embroiled in a legal battle.

Legal Costs

The total legal fee must be considered in every case of possible litigation. A lawyer should be required to give an estimate of fees for any suit before the suit begins. The estimate should always include discovery costs. . . .

Time Costs (Hidden Downtime)

Litigation costs time as well as money. Indeed, in many cases, the loss of time can be more devastating to a firm than the

financial loss. If a firm takes part in major litigation, chances are that its officers and possibly its directors will be involved in depositions, other forms of pretrial discovery and paperwork, and eventually in the trial itself. This involvement inevitably diverts the attention of the officers from their normal duties. . . .

Image Costs

If a lawsuit attracts the attention of the media, a firm may incur money and time costs stemming from public relations. Someone must be available to explain the firm's position to reporters and perhaps initiate an affirmative campaign to minimize negative publicity about the suit.

Capital Costs

Auditors require that pending litigation be listed in the financial reports of the company. Ongoing litigation that carries the

CONTINUED

potential for great financial loss to a business can have a negative effect on the firm's financial rating and the ability to raise capital.

Costs of Alternatives to Litigation

The costs of litigation should be compared with the costs of alternatives to litigation. For example, it may not add much to potential litigation costs to submit a case to arbitration before pursuing full litigation. Such arbitration may produce a settlement that makes the trip to court unnecessary.

Costs of Not Litigating

There are costs for litigating, but there are also costs for not litigating. If the stakes are high enough, litigation may be worth pursuing regardless of the expense. For example, if a suit challenges the land records and thus the title to the land on which the business is located, the cost of not responding to the suit may be the loss of the property and the expense of reestablishing the business at another site. In a trademark or trade name suit, the cost may be a product or company name or label. In a patent infringement case, the failure to sue an infringer may undermine a company's sales and its exclusivity in the marketplace.

Sometimes the price of not litigating or of not responding vigorously to litigation can be a firm's very existence. For example, the product liability suits involving Johns-Manville and the other makers of asbestos threatened the lives of those firms because they involved the only product the firms made.

Public Relations Issues

Litigation is not a private matter. In every city, at least one reporter is assigned to the clerk's office in the state and federal courts for the purpose of checking on suits filed.

Many an electric bill goes unpaid simply because it is not good public relations for a utility company to appear in the newspapers and on television as the "bad guy" when a retired widow explains that the big power company has just filed suit because she has no money to pay her bill. . . .

Jury Appeal

When considering the effects of publicity on a case, a company should also consider the closely related matter of jury appeal. In some cases it will not matter how correct a business may be, how much of a remedy the law provides, or how wrong the other side is; the jury will simply side with the "little guy," and the business will have no chance of succeeding in the courtroom. For example, the Arthur Murray Dance Studios once fully litigated a case in which a man who had been severely injured in a car accident and was unable to complete the lessons in his contract with Arthur Murray (some 2,734 lessons, for which he had paid $24,812.40) sought to recover his payments on the grounds that performance had become impossible. It is difficult to build jury appeal into such a case.

Discussion Questions

1. List the factors you should consider as you make a decision to litigate.

2. At the awards show for the Academy of Motion Picture Arts and Sciences (Academy), a character dressed as Snow White appeared in the opening musical number and sang with actor Rob Lowe. Walt Disney, Inc., had not given the Academy permission to use the Snow White likeness, a trademarked Disney character. If you were the Walt Disney Corporation, would you sue the Academy?

3. List concerns you would have as an employer litigating a sexual harassment case.

Source: Frank Shipper and Marianne Jennings. *Avoiding and Surviving Lawsuits: The Executive Guide to Strategic Legal Planning for Business,* Jossey-Bass Publishing, Inc., pp. 59–73. Copyright © 1989. Excerpted and reprinted with permission of the authors.

When You Are in Litigation

At times, a business must face litigation and ADR is not possible. This portion of the chapter explains the language, process, and strategies of civil litigation.

How Does a Lawsuit Start?

Lawsuits are based on feelings. Whether rights have actually been violated and what damages were caused as a result are the questions addressed through the trial process. The only restriction on the filing of a suit is that the plaintiff's claim of right must be based on some statutory law or common law.

People begin lawsuits. The judicial system does not unilaterally undertake the enforcement of civil rights. Individuals must assume responsibility for protecting their rights. The judicial system determines what and whose rights have been violated.

EXHIBIT 4.2   The Trial Process

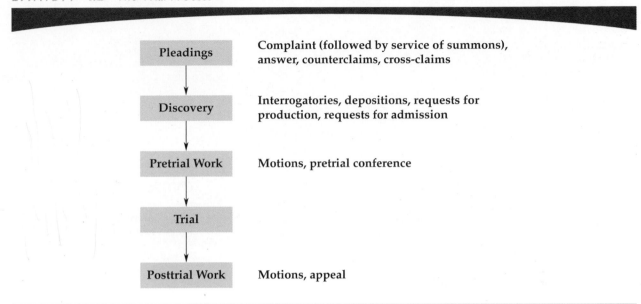

Pleadings	**Complaint (followed by service of summons), answer, counterclaims, cross-claims**
Discovery	**Interrogatories, depositions, requests for production, requests for admission**
Pretrial Work	**Motions, pretrial conference**
Trial	
Posttrial Work	**Motions, appeal**

Although procedures vary from state to state, the following sections offer a general discussion of the procedures involved in a civil lawsuit. Exhibit 4.2 summarizes the trial process.

The Complaint (Petition)

The first step in a lawsuit is the filing of a document called a **complaint** or **petition.** The plaintiff must file the petition or complaint within certain time limits each state has for filing suit. These time limits are called **statutes of limitations.** They vary depending on the type of rights involved in a suit. The typical statute of limitations for personal injuries is two years; the typical limitation for contracts is four years.

A complaint is a general statement of the plaintiff's claim of rights. For example, if a plaintiff is suing for a breach of contract, the complaint must describe the contract, when it began, and what the defendant did that the plaintiff says is a breach. Exhibit 4.3 shows a sample complaint in a suit over a car accident.

The complaint need not have every detail described in it. The standard for a valid complaint is that it must be definite enough in its description of what happened for the defendant to understand why the suit has been brought.

All complaints must establish the subject matter jurisdiction of the court (see Chapter 3 for a discussion of this concept). For example, for a federal district court action, the complaint would have to allege either diversity of citizenship between the parties and a damage claim of more than $75,000, or that a federal question is involved.

In some cases, the complaint is filed by a group of plaintiffs who have the same cause of action against one defendant. These types of suits, called **class action suits,** are typically filed in antitrust cases, shareholder actions against corporations, and employment discrimination cases. The class action suit enables a group of plaintiffs to share one lawyer and minimize litigation expenses while at the same time preserving their individual rights. Perhaps the most widely publicized type of class

EXHIBIT 4.3 Sample Complaint

Reed C. Tolman, Esq. (006502)
TOLMAN & OSBORNE, PC.
1400 E. Southern, Suite 625
Tempe, Arizona 85282
Attorneys for Plaintiffs

SUPERIOR COURT OF ARIZONA

MARICOPA COUNTY

CRAIG CONNER and KATHY CONNER,)
husband and wife, individually)
and on behalf of their minor)
son, CASEY CONNER,)
)
Plaintiffs,)
)
v.)
)
CARMEN A. CHENAL and THOMAS K.)
CHENAL, wife and husband,)
)
Defendants.)
_____)

CV92–91319

COMPLAINT
(Tort—Motor Vehicle)

For their complaint, plaintiffs allege:

1. Plaintiffs and defendants are residents of Maricopa County, Arizona.

2. This Court has jurisdiction over the subject matter under the Arizona Constitution, Art. 6, § 14.

3. Casey Conner is the minor son of Craig and Kathy Conner.

4. Carmen A. Chenal and Thomas K. Chenal are wife and husband. At all times relevant hereto, Carmen A. Chenal was acting for and on behalf of the marital community of which she is a member.

5. On or about July 20, 1990, defendant Carmen A. Chenal was driving her motor vehicle in the vicinity of Primrose Path and Cave Creek Road in Carefree, Arizona. At the time, Casey Conner was a passenger in the back seat of defendants' vehicle, a 1976 Mercedes, ID No.11603312051326.

6. At all times relevant hereto, defendant Carmen A. Chenal had a duty to care properly for the safety of Casey Conner. That duty included the responsibility to place Casey in an appropriate and functioning seat belt.

7. Prior to the accident that resulted in injuries to Casey Conner, Carmen A. Chenal knew that the right rear door of her vehicle was damaged and not functioning properly.

8. Despite the duty Carmen A. Chenal had to care properly for the safety of Casey Conner, and despite her knowledge of a malfunctioning right rear door, Carmen A. Chenal negligently failed to place Casey in an appropriate and functioning seatbelt and negligently and carelessly operated her vehicle in such a way that the right rear door opened and allowed Casey to be ejected from the vehicle while the vehicle was in operation.

9. Carmen A. Chenal's failure to exercise reasonable care for the safety of Casey and the failure to operate her vehicle in a careful and safe manner proximately caused Casey to suffer personal injuries.

10. As a result of Casey Conner's injuries, he has experienced physical and psychological suffering, and his parents have incurred medical and other expenses, as well as lost earnings.

WHEREFORE, plaintiffs request judgment against defendants for compensatory damages in an amount to be determined at trial.

DATED: this _____ day of July, 1992.
TOLMAN & OSBORNE

By: _____
Reed C. Tolman
1400 E. Southern
Suite 625
Tempe, Arizona 85282

Source: Complaint appears courtesy of Tolman & Osborne, P.C., Tempe, AZ 85282.

action lawsuit is the suit that results when a large jet airliner crashes and causes multiple deaths and injuries. All the plaintiffs were injured in the same event, and the defendant then litigates once with a group of plaintiffs. (See Chapter 10 for more information on product liability class action litigation.)

Another form of class action suit is the **derivative suit,** in which shareholders sue a corporation to recover damages for actions taken by the corporation. (See Chapter 20 for more information.)

The final paragraphs of a complaint list the damages or remedies the plaintiff wants. The damages may be a **legal remedy** such as money, in which case a dollar amount is specified. The plaintiff may seek an **equitable remedy,** such as specific performance in the case of an action for breach of contract. **Specific performance** is an order of the court requiring a defendant to perform on a contract. In some cases, the plaintiffs just want the defendants to stop violating their rights. In those complaints, plaintiffs ask for **injunctions,** which are court orders requiring the defendant to stop doing the act complained of. In an action for nuisance, for example, an injunction orders the defendant to stop engaging in the conduct that causes the nuisance or orders the defendant to comply with a law or a previous decision. As another example, an injunction could order a website to stop infringement of copyright music or material.

The Summons

The complaint or petition of the plaintiffs is filed with the clerk of the appropriate court—that is, the court with subject matter jurisdiction, *in personam* jurisdiction, and venue. The defendant, however, will not know of the suit just because it is filed. The second step in a lawsuit is serving the defendant with a copy of the complaint and a **summons,** which is a legal document that tells the defendant of the suit and explains the defendant's rights under the law. Those rights include the opportunity to respond and the grant of a limited amount of time for responding. Exhibit 4.4 shows a sample summons.

A summons must be delivered to the defendant. Some states require that the defendant be given the papers personally. Other states allow the papers to be given to some member of the defendant's household or, in the case of a business, to an agent of that business. (See Chapter 17 for a discussion of an agent's authority to receive the papers notifying the business of a lawsuit.)

The summons is delivered by an officer of the court (such as a sheriff or magistrate) or by private firms licensed as **process servers.** Once the defendant is served, the server must file an affidavit with the court to indicate when and where the service was made. In rare circumstances, courts allow service of process by mail or by publishing the summons and complaint. These circumstances, however, are limited and are carefully supervised by the courts.

The Answer

The parties' positions in a case are found in the **pleadings.** The complaint or petition is a pleading. The defendant's position is found in the **answer,** another pleading in a case. The defendant must file an answer within the time limits allowed by the court or risk default. The time limits are typically 20 days for in-state defendants and 30 days for out-of-state defendants. A failure to answer, or a **default,** is like a forfeit in sports: The plaintiff wins because the defendant failed to show up. The plaintiff can then proceed to a judgment to collect damages.

EXHIBIT 4.4 Sample Summons

Name:
Address:
City, State, Zip:
Telephone:
State Bar Code:
Client:

ARIZONA SUPERIOR COURT, County of

ACTION NO:

SUMMONS

THE STATE OF ARIZONA TO THE DEFENDANTS:

YOU ARE HEREBY SUMMONED and required to appear and defend, within the time applicable, in this action in this court. If served within Arizona, you appear and defend within 20 days after the service of the Summons and Complaint upon you, exclusive of the day of service. If served out of the State of Arizona—whether by direct service, by registered or certified mail, or by publication you shall appear and defend within 30 days after the service of the Summons and Complaint upon you is complete, exclusive of the day of service. Where process is served upon the Arizona Director of Insurance as an insurer's attorney to receive service of legal process against it in this state, the insurer shall not be required to appear, answer or plead until expiration of 40 days after date of such service upon the Director. Service by registered or certified mail without the State of Arizona is complete 30 days after the date of receipt by the party being served. Service by publication is complete 30 days after the date of first publication. Direct service is complete when made. Service upon the Arizona Motor Vehicle Superintendent is complete 30 days after filing the Affidavit of Compliance and return receipt or Officer's Return. RCP 4; ARS §§ 20-222, 28-502, 28-503.

Copies of the pleadings filed herein may be obtained by contacting the Clerk of Superior Court,
——————————— County, located at ——————————————————————————————— ,
Arizona. RCF 4.1 (e).

SUMMONS
(Continued on Reverse Side)   1-1 ©LawForms 10-92 1-93

YOU ARE HEREBY NOTIFIED that in case of your failure to appear and defend within the time applicable, judgment by default may be rendered against you for the relief demanded in the Complaint.

YOU ARE CAUTIONED that in order to appear and defend, you must file an Answer or proper response in writing with the Clerk of this Court, accompanied by the necessary filing fee, within the time required, and you are required to serve a copy of any Answer or response upon the Plaintiffs' attorney. RCP 10(D); ARS 12-311; RCP5.

The name and address of plaintiffs' attorney is:

SIGNED AND SEALED this date :_____

. . . .
Clerk

Method of Service: By . . . .
☐ Private Process Service   Deputy Clerk
☐ Sheriff or Marshall
☐ Personal Service
☐ Registered/Certified Mail (out of State)

SUMMONS   1-1 ©LawForms 11-67, 3-84, 1-93

Source: Form appears courtesy of National LawForms, Inc., Phoenix, AZ.

The defendant's answer can do any or all of several different things. The defendant may admit certain facts in the answer. Although it is rare for a defendant to admit the wrong alleged by the plaintiff, the defendant might admit parts of the plaintiff's complaint, such as those that establish jurisdiction and venue. If the plaintiff already has correct venue, fighting that issue is costly, and admitting jurisdiction is a way to move on with the case. If, however, the court lacked *in personam* jurisdiction over the defendant, the defendant could deny the jurisdiction. (See Chapter 3 for more discussion of *in personam* jurisdiction.)

A denial is a simple statement in the answer whereby the defendant indicates that the allegation is denied. An answer might also include a statement that the defendant does not know enough to admit or deny the allegations in the complaint and might include a demand for proof of those allegations.

An answer might also include a **counterclaim,** with which the defendant, in effect, countersues the plaintiff, alleging a violation of rights and damages against the plaintiff. The plaintiff must respond to the counterclaim using the same answer process of admitting or denying the alleged wrong. Exhibit 4.5 shows a sample answer.

The answer must be filed with the clerk of the court and a copy sent to the plaintiff. With the exception of amendments to these documents, the pleadings are now complete.

Seeking Timely Resolution of the Case

The fact that a suit has been filed does not mean that the case will go to trial. A great majority of suits are disposed of before trial because of successful motions to end them. **Motions** are requests to the court that it take certain action. Motions usually involve filed documents and include citations to precedent that support granting the motion. Often the judge will have the attorneys present oral arguments for and against the motion, after which the court then issues a ruling on the motion.

Motion for Judgment on the Pleadings

Either in the answer or by separate motion, a defendant can move for judgment based just on the content of the pleadings. The theory behind a **motion for judgment on the pleadings** is that the plaintiff has no cause of action even if everything the plaintiff alleges is true. For example, a plaintiff could file suit claiming the defendant is an annoying person; but unless the defendant is annoying to the extent of invading privacy or not honoring contracts, the plaintiff has no right of recovery. The defendant in this case could win a motion for judgment on the pleadings because the law (perhaps unfortunately) does not provide a remedy for annoying people. A denial of a motion for judgment on the pleadings does not imply victory for the plaintiff. It simply means that the case will proceed with the next steps.

Motion to Dismiss

A **motion to dismiss** can be filed any time during the proceedings but usually is part of the defendant's answer. Such a motion can be based on the court's lack of subject matter or *in personam* jurisdiction. Again, if the case is not dismissed, it does not mean that the plaintiff wins; it just means that the case will proceed to the next steps and possibly trial.

Motion for Summary Judgment

A **motion for summary judgment** has two requirements. Summary judgment is appropriate only when (1) the moving party is entitled to a judgment under

EXHIBIT 4.5   Sample Answer

Grand, Canyon & Rafts
12222 W. Camelback
Phoenix, Arizona
555-5555
Attorneys for Defendant

SUPERIOR COURT OF ARIZONA

MARICOPA COUNTY

CRAIG CONNER and KATHY CONNER,)
husband and wife, individually   )
and on behalf of their minor   )
son, CASEY CONNER,   )
)
                    Plaintiffs,   )
)
              v.   )
)
CARMEN A. CHENAL and THOMAS K.)
CHENAL, wife and husband,   )
)
                    Defendants.   )
_____)

CV92-91319

ANSWER

For their answer, defendants respond to plaintiffs'
complaint as follows:

1. Admit paragraph one.
2. Admit paragraph two.
3. Have no knowledge to admit or deny paragraph three.
4. Have no knowledge to admit or deny paragraph four.
5. Admit paragraph five.
6. As for paragraphs 6 through 10, inclusive of plaintiffs'
complaint, defendants have no knowledge of the statements alleged and
deny all statements made therein.

Defendents deny any and all parts of plaintiffs' complaints
not specifically mentioned herein.

DATED this _____ day of August, 1992.
            Grand, Canyon & Raft

By: _____
            Robert C. Canyon
            12222 W. Camelback
            Phoenix, Arizona

BUSINESS STRATEGY

Walmart: The Most-Sued Company in America

WalMart manages approximately 10,000 open lawsuits each year. The retail giant has been sued, on average over the years, about 13 times per day every day of the year. Most experts have concluded that Walmart is sued more than any other entity except the U.S. government. There is even a Walmart Litigation Project lawsuit that provides sample complaints for lawyers who are filing suit against Walmart.

Walmart is unique in that it has taken the position of fighting the suits brought against it. Most corporations take a cost-benefit analysis approach and settle most lawsuits because it is cheaper for them to do so. Walmart, however, is working to change the nature of litigation against corporations and fights most suits aggressively. The result of its stance is that the number of suits has leveled off despite Walmart's increasing size and number of stores.

The types of lawsuits Walmart has pending or has experienced include the following:

- Slip-and-fall cases where customers have been injured in a Walmart store
- One case brought by the family of a woman shot by her husband, who had purchased the rifle at Walmart
- Class action employment suits alleging discrimination
- Failure to report safety violations
- Wrongful-termination-of-employment cases
- Unpaid overtime litigation brought by employees
- Shoppers injured in a "Furby" stampede when the toy was in demand at Christmas time

Walmart also employs several different litigation strategies.

- It hires outside lawyers and pays them a flat fee.

- It has cases moved to federal district court, where judges are not elected.
- It settles those cases where the company or employees have done something wrong, but it fights ferociously in cases of no fault.

However, Walmart has also experienced some litigation difficulties over the disclosure of evidence in the discovery process. (See Case 4.2, *Wal-Mart Stores, Inc. v Johnson*, later in this chapter.) Once a company has evidence regarding a product, a contract, or conduct of employees, it is costly and illegal to try to hide that information before or during litigation.

Walmart has experienced sanctions and bad publicity from a number of lawsuits in which it is a defendant for its alleged failure to be forthcoming with discovery requests and documents.

McClung v Delta Square Limited Partnership, 937 S.W.2d 891 (Tenn. 1996), illustrates Walmart's discovery issues. After the case was tried, the husband of a woman who was killed after being abducted from the parking lot at a Walmart store learned that Walmart had conducted a study and pilot program showing that store parking lots could be made safer with relatively little cost just by adding safety patrols. The study was not released to the husband during the litigation. When the report surfaced in other cases, plaintiffs' lawyers had the report in hand even as Walmart denied in discovery requests that the report existed. Walmart was sanctioned $18 million in one case for its failure to reveal the report.

Sources: Adapted from Richard Willing, "Lawsuits Follow Growth Curve of Wal-Mart," *USA Today*, August 14, 2001, pp. A1, A2, and Bob Van Voris, "Wal-Mart Mending Its Ways?" *National Law Journal*, January 22, 2001, pp. A1, A8.

the law and (2) no issues of fact remain disputed. Actions brought on the basis of motor vehicle accidents, for example, always involve different witnesses' testimonies and variations in facts. These types of cases cannot be decided by summary judgment. In other cases, however, the parties do not dispute the facts but differ on the applications of law. Consider, for example, a dispute involving a contract for the repair of a computer, including service and parts. Different laws govern contractual provisions for services and provisions for goods. The parties do not dispute the facts: They agree goods and services are covered in the contract. At issue is the question about which law applies, and a summary judgment appropriately will resolve it. A suit may involve other factual disputes about contract performance, but the partial summary judgment will determine which contract law will apply.

How a Lawsuit Progresses: Discovery

Trials in the United States are not conducted by ambush. Before the trial, the parties engage in a mandatory process of mutual disclosure of all relevant documents and other evidence. This court-supervised process of gathering evidence is called **discovery.** Under procedural rules that govern discovery, the parties must provide to each other lists of witnesses, all relevant documents, tangible evidence, and statements related to the case. Under the old discovery rules, the expense and difficulty of discovery techniques often meant the search for the truth was a cat-and-mouse game won by those with the most funds. Armed with the evidence from a full-disclosure approach, the parties to a case are more prepared, and perhaps more inclined, to negotiate a settlement. Discovery rules provide for sanctions (penalties) for not turning over relevant documents at the start of a case. Sanctions can include fines against the party who withheld the evidence, findings of contempt against the lawyers, including fines, and the exclusion of responses to the withheld evidence. The following sections cover the traditional tools of discovery.

Requests for Admissions and Interrogatories

A **request for admissions** asks the other side to admit a certain fact. **Interrogatories** ask questions about facts. The parties have some incentive to admit the facts requested if they are true because if these facts are denied and then proved at trial, the party who had to prove those true facts can recover the costs of proof. Requests for admissions request the other party to admit that a document is authentic. For example, the parties might have a dispute about the amount due under a contract but should be willing to admit that they signed the contract and that it is authentic. These requests for admission reduce the length of trials.

Depositions

Depositions are the oral testimony of parties or witnesses that are taken under oath but outside the courtroom and before the trial. They can be taken long before a trial and help preserve a witness's or party's recollection. Depositions are also helpful in determining just how strong a case is. It is far better to discover damaging information in a deposition than to have surprises at trial.

Requests for Production

A **request for production** requires the other side to produce requested documents. For example, if a business is suing to recover lost profits, the defendant will probably want to request the income statements and perhaps the income tax returns of that business in order to prepare for the presentation of damages issues at trial. A request for production can include medical records as well as tangible evidence. In *Wal-Mart Stores, Inc. v Johnson* (Case 4.2), the failure to produce physical evidence that was part of an accident resulted in sanctions for a store.

CASE 4.2	*Wal-Mart Stores, Inc. v Johnson* 106 S.W.3d 718 (Tx. 2003)

"Reining" Deer at the Local Wal-Mart

FACTS

While stocking merchandise, a Wal-Mart employee accidentally knocked at least one and possibly more decorative reindeer from a high shelf onto Monroe Johnson's head and arm. Mr. Johnson's fiancée, now his wife, was with him and heard but did not see the accident. When she went to investigate, she found her fiancé dazed but still standing, with a cut on one arm and several reindeer lying at his feet. At the scene, Mr. Johnson told Phyllis McClane, a Wal-Mart supervisor who had come to investigate, that he was not hurt. After a Wal-Mart employee cleaned and bandaged his cut, Mr. Johnson and his fiancée left the store.

During her investigation, Ms. McClane took notes, photographed the reindeer, and obtained a written statement from the employee who caused the accident. She recorded the results of her investigation on a Wal-Mart form entitled "Report of Customer Incident." She attached the photo and the employee's statement, sending copies to the District Manager and claim management personnel. According to the incident report, Mr. Johnson neither threatened to sue nor indicated that Wal-Mart should pay any medical costs or other damages. After completing the report, Ms. McClane discarded her notes.

That evening, Mr. Johnson's neck and arm began to hurt, and he could not sleep. The next day, his doctor prescribed muscle relaxers, pain killers, and physical therapy. Still in pain six months later, Mr. Johnson and his wife sued Wal-Mart. While suit was pending, Mr. Johnson consulted three more physicians and tried additional treatments without success. About seventeen months after the accident, a surgeon performed an anterior cervical discectomy and fusion on Mr. Johnson's neck.

During discovery, the Johnsons asked whether Wal-Mart still possessed the reindeer that fell on him. Wal-Mart did not, but the company offered to provide a "reasonable facsimile." The Johnsons did not want the facsimile, and the trial court prohibited Wal-Mart "from introducing into evidence a reasonable facsimile of the reindeer made the basis of this lawsuit."

At trial, the parties offered sharply divergent evidence about the composition and weight of the reindeer in question. Mr. Johnson testified that they were made of wood, each weighing as much as ten pounds. Ron Wheeler, the store manager, countered that the reindeer were made of papier-mâché and weighed only five to eight ounces each. Wal-Mart argued that such flimsy reindeer could not have proximately caused Mr. Johnson's neck problems, which it claimed resulted from an automobile accident years earlier. Mr. Wheeler also testified that Wal-Mart could not produce any of the reindeer because they had all been sold or, if broken, thrown away. Only the photograph of the reindeer was introduced in evidence, but its quality was too poor to substantiate or rebut either party's description.

Based on Wal-Mart's failure to keep the reindeer, the judge gave the following jury instruction (see p. 134 for more information on jury instructions).

You are instructed that, when a party has possession of a piece of evidence at a time he knows or should have known it will be evidence in a controversy, and thereafter he disposes of it, makes it unavailable, or fails to produce it, there is a presumption in law that the piece of evidence, had it been produced, would have been unfavorable to the party who did not produce it. If you find by a preponderance of the evidence that Wal-Mart had possession of the reindeer at a time it knew or should have known they would be evidence in this controversy, then there is a presumption that the reindeer, if produced, would be unfavorable to Wal-Mart.

The jury found for Mr. and Mrs. Johnson and awarded damages. Wal-Mart did not appeal the award or the damages. Rather, Wal-Mart appealed the jury instruction. The court of appeals affirmed, and Wal-Mart appealed again.

JUDICIAL OPINION

PHILLIPS, Chief Justice

Evidence may be unavailable for discovery and trial for a variety of reasons. Evidence may be lost, altered or destroyed wilfully [*sic*] and in bad faith or it may be lost for reasons completely innocent. Sometimes, lost evidence may be easily replicated, or it may be so marginal that it has little or no effect on the outcome of the case. On other occasions, the loss or destruction of evidence may seriously impair a party's ability to present its case. A trial judge should have discretion to fashion an appropriate remedy to restore the parties

CONTINUED

to a rough approximation of their positions if all evidence were available.

In this case, the trial court decided to remedy what it perceived to be Wal-Mart's misconduct by giving a spoliation instruction. The instruction informed the jury that it must presume that the missing reindeer would have harmed Wal-Mart's case if the jury concluded that Wal-Mart disposed of the reindeer after it knew or should have known that they would be evidence in the case. Such an instruction is a common remedy for spoliation, with roots going back to the English common law.

Our courts of appeals have generally limited the use of the spoliation instruction to two circumstances: [1] the deliberate destruction of relevant evidence and [2] the failure of a party to produce relevant evidence or to explain its non-production.

Although the parties argue their respective positions under this second circumstance at length, we need not decide whether a spoliation instruction is justified when evidence is unintentionally lost or destroyed, or if it is, what standard is proper. Rather we begin and end our analysis here with the issue of duty, the initial inquiry for any complaint of discovery abuse. Before any failure to produce material evidence may be viewed as discovery abuse, the opposing party must establish that the non-producing party had a duty to preserve the evidence in question.

Wal-Mart argues that it had no duty to preserve the reindeer as evidence because it had no notice that they would be relevant to a future claim. Specifically, Wal-Mart contends that it did not learn of the Johnsons' claim until all of the reindeer had been disposed of in the normal course of business. The Johnsons point out that Wal-Mart's extensive investigation on the day of the accident indicates its awareness of both the potential claim and the reindeer's importance to it. Wal-Mart responds that it routinely investigates all accidents on its premises, and this particular investigation revealed that Johnson had not been seriously injured and never

indicated that he might seek legal relief. We agree that nothing about the investigation or the circumstances surrounding the accident would have put Wal-Mart on notice that there was a substantial chance that the Johnsons would pursue a claim.

Thus, as a foundation for the submission of the spoliation instruction in this case, the Johnsons had to show that Wal-Mart disposed of the reindeer after it knew, or should have known, that there was a substantial chance there would be litigation and that the reindeer would be material to it. We therefore agree with Wal-Mart that the trial court abused its discretion when it submitted the spoliation instruction to the jury because the Johnsons failed to establish that Wal-Mart had a duty to preserve the reindeer.

While we do not lightly reverse a judgment because of an erroneous instruction, we believe an unnecessary spoliation instruction is particularly likely to cause harm. Because the instruction itself is given to compensate for the absence of evidence that a party had a duty to preserve, its very purpose is to "nudge" or "tilt" the jury. Thus, if a spoliation instruction should not have been given, the likelihood of harm from the erroneous instruction is substantial, particularly when the case is closely contested.

We hold that the trial court erred in submitting the spoliation instruction in this case and that the spoliation instruction was harmful and probably caused the rendition of an improper judgment. Accordingly, we reverse the court of appeals' judgment and remand this case to the trial court for further proceedings.

CASE QUESTIONS

1. Describe the accident that led to the litigation.
2. What happened to the notes on the accident? The reindeer?
3. When does the duty to preserve evidence arise?
4. Why does the court worry about "tilting" or "nudging" the jury in the case?

CONSIDER...   4.2

The obstruction of justice trial against the accounting firm of Arthur Andersen found the prosecution using the following types of evidence:

- Testimony from partners, employees, and consultants with Andersen
- E-mails between and among Andersen partners, employees, and consultants, both saved and deleted e-mails were introduced into evidence
- A videotape of a partner making a presentation to employees on the pending SEC investigation in which he urged employees to get rid of excess files so that "nosy plaintiffs' lawyers" wouldn't be able to find damaging evidence

- The statistics on the e-mail deletions by Andersen employees, including the peak in e-mail deletions following the presentation that was shown on video and the instruction to get rid of unnecessary files
- The articles clipped and saved by Andersen employees relating to Enron and SEC investigations

What would the government need to show to establish that Andersen had engaged in spoliation through their e-mail deletions?

THINK: In the *Wal-Mart* case, the court held that the reindeer would have needed to be destroyed by employees knowing that a suit was pending.

APPLY: What is different in this Andersen situation? What is the same?

ANSWER: The evidence shows that the Andersen employees had been briefed on at least the investigations, a likely source of litigation. With the investigations pending, the destruction of e-mails and other documents at that time meets the test for spoliation.

 # Ethical Issues

Evaluate the ethics of the Andersen employees. Why do you think they followed orders to destroy the e-mails and other documents so willingly? Is "I was just following orders" a defense in criminal and civil cases? Is it a justification for conduct?

Limitations on Discovery

Discovery has the general limitation of relevance. Only things that are evidence or could lead to the discovery of evidence are discoverable. However, discovery also has a specific limitation. Discovery cannot require the production of **work product,** which consists of the attorney's legal research, comments or reactions to a witness, thoughts, analysis, and case or trial strategy. Discovery affords the parties the right to know all the evidence (if it asks for it), but it does not give them the right to know how that evidence will be used or what legal precedent supports a party's position.

Certain evidence in cases is not discoverable. Communications between lawyers and their clients is protected by a privilege and, except in certain limited circumstances, cannot be discovered or used by the opposition. (See Chapter 3 for a complete discussion of privilege.)

Cyber Law and Discovery

Businesses are required to preserve their business records. The so-called smartphones, such as the BlackBerry and iPhone, create problems because smartphones can be configured in different ways, sometimes with very limited archiving capability. In certain configurations, a message deleted from a BlackBerry is lost forever. There are programs that permit hackers to download everything from a smartphone in about 30 seconds. There is a risk of everything from corporate espionage to the loss of privilege on documents that become public via hackers or theft.

The *National Law Journal* advises that companies should develop policies on the use of smartphones by executives, policies that cover the following:

CYBERLAW

- Configuration of smartphones, access, and archiving. For example, the executive branch of the federal government has configured the smartphones of government officials so that the messages are archived (as required by law for government business) and then stored by a contractor who then manages and indexes the messages so that they are not lost.

CONTINUED

- The requirement of a password for access to the phone
- Policies on what may or may not be discussed using the smartphone technology
- Disclosure of risks of communication via smartphone to clients and customers
- Policies on deletion of messages on smartphones

List the discovery and record-keeping issues you see with smartphones.

Source: William A. McComas, "Risky for All Executives," *National Law Journal,* January 5, 2009, p. 26.

Resolution of a Lawsuit: The Trial

If a case is not settled (and many are settled literally on the courthouse steps), the trial begins.

The Type of Trial—Jury or Nonjury

Occasionally, the parties agree not to have a jury trial and instead have a trial to the court. In these cases, the judge acts as both judge and jury—both running the trial and determining its outcome. In highly technical cases it is sometimes better for both sides to have a knowledgeable judge involved than to try to explain the complexities of the case to a jury of laypersons.

If the parties do not agree on a nonjury trial, then certain types of cases carry a constitutional right to a trial by jury. The Seventh Amendment of the U.S. Constitution covers the jury requirement in civil trials:

> In suits at common law, where the value in controversy shall exceed twenty dollars, the right of trial by jury shall be preserved, and no fact tried by a jury shall be otherwise re-examined in any court of the United States other than according to the rules of common law.

Although this right is limited to what existed at common law at the time the U.S. Constitution was adopted, many states have expanded the right under their state constitutions. The absolute right to a jury exists in criminal cases as covered in Article III and the Fifth and Sixth Amendments of the U.S. Constitution.

The size of a jury varies; some states require only six jurors. A jury may have 12 to 18 members, which include alternates, particularly in long trials, to ensure that a panel of 12 participates fully in the trial.

The pool of potential jurors and the selection of those jurors are resolved before trial. Usually, voting lists, alone or combined with other lists (e.g., rosters of licensed drivers), are used as pools for potential jurors. People on these lists are randomly notified of a period of time during which they should report for jury duty. Many states excuse from jury duty certain individuals, such as doctors and emergency workers, because of the needs they serve in society. Students are often excused if they are summoned for duty during the semester because of their peculiar obligations and time limitations on completing classes. Judges also usually have the power to excuse certain individuals who would experience hardship if they were required to serve. For example, a sole proprietor of a service business would have no income during the time of jury service and would probably be excused on a hardship basis.

Many more jurors than are actually needed are summoned to serve. These extra numbers are required because all the parties to a dispute participate in the selection of a jury. Once a pool is available, the court begins the process of *voir dire,* which determines whether a potential juror is qualified to serve. Most states have

BUSINESS PLANNING TIP

When in doubt, don't. That is, if you have any question about litigation or an investigation, do not destroy e-mails, documents, or tangible evidence.

Every company should have a document retention and file purging policy. Employees should follow the timelines on retention and destruction. Even when the designated time for destruction has arrived, any doubt about pending litigation, investigations, or regulatory issues means the documents should be retained.

jurors complete a questionnaire on general topics so that the selection process can move quickly. The questionnaire covers personal information—age, occupation, and so on. The questionnaire might also ask whether the person has ever been a juror, a party to a lawsuit, or a witness.

A juror can be removed from a jury panel for two reasons. First, a juror can be removed for cause, which means the juror is incapable of making an impartial decision in the case. If a juror is related to one of the attorneys in the case, for example, the juror would be excused for cause. Some jurors reveal their biases or prejudices, such as racial prejudice, in the questionnaire they are required to complete. Others may express strong feelings of animosity toward the medical profession. Clearly, the removal of such jurors for cause in cases involving civil rights and malpractice suits, respectively, is an important part of trial strategy.

CONSIDER... 4.3

Winona Ryder was arrested for shoplifting from Saks Fifth Avenue. The charges against her included theft and burglary for taking $5,600 in merchandise from Saks's Beverly Hills store.

The jury selection process in the trial uncovered the fact that Peter Guber, a Hollywood executive who was in charge of three films that starred Ms. Ryder (*Bram Stoker's Dracula, The Age of Innocence, Little Women*), was among the pool of jurors. When questioned by the judge, Mr. Guber assured him that he could be impartial in judging the evidence. Mr. Guber was allowed to remain on the jury.

What argument could the prosecution have made against keeping Mr. Guber? What argument could the defense have made against Mr. Guber? What process could each side have used to have him removed from the jury?

Source: Rick Lyman, "For the Ryder Trial, a Hollywood Script," *New York Times*, November 3, 2002, p. SL-1.

Sometimes a juror cannot be excused for cause but an attorney feels uncomfortable about the juror or the juror's attitudes. In these circumstances, the lawyer issues a **peremptory challenge,** which excuses the juror. The peremptory challenge is the attorney's private tool. However, the use of peremptory challenges is limited. All states have a statute or court rule limiting the number of peremptory challenges an attorney may use in a trial. The U.S. Supreme Court ruled that the use of peremptory challenges is subject to some limitations. The Court indicated that such a challenge cannot be based on either race or gender. If the trial judge suspects that either of these factors may have induced one of the lawyers to seek a peremptory challenge, the lawyer will be required to produce a plausible explanation for the use of the peremptory challenge that is unrelated to race or gender.

Jury selection is an art and a science. Jury consulting firms specialize in providing data to attorneys for jury selection. These firms do thorough checks of the potential jurors' backgrounds and offer statistics on the reactions of certain economic and social groups to trials and trial issues. Much about a case at trial is uncontrollable, but jury selection is a part of the process that, with thorough preparation, can increase the likelihood of desired results by ensuring an optimally favorable jury panel.

Jury or trial consultants perform jury profiles, find surrogate juries, and often conduct mock trials. The use of trial consultants has increased dramatically since the 1970s, and membership in the American Society of Trial Consultants has grown from 19 members in 1983 to 250 members today. Jury consultants were

For the Manager's Desk

Re: Jury Selection in High-Profile Cases

Even though the criminal rape charges against him were eventually dismissed, NBA basketball star Kobe Bryant's trial still had progressed to the point of jury selection. As part of the *voir dire* questions for the potential Bryant jurors, the 276 jury panelists were asked the following as part of their 82-question background sheet:

- Have you received any training in law, law enforcement, or criminology?
- What are your feelings about the sexual assault laws in Colorado?
- Do you think that people who make a lot of money are treated better by our court system than other people?
- Have you or anyone close to you ever felt in danger of being sexually assaulted by another person, including a stranger, acquaintance, or family member?

- Have you ever been afraid of or had any negative experience with an African American individual?
- In your opinion, in general do African Americans in our society experience (check one): a great deal of racial discrimination; some amount of racial discrimination; or no racial discrimination?
- How do you feel about interracial relationships?
- Do you have particularly strong feelings about, or have you or anyone close to you ever been affected by or involved in, a situation of marital infidelity? [At the time of the alleged rape, Mr. Bryant was married and had one child.]
- Which of the following best describes your opinion of professional basketball players: very positive; positive; negative; very negative?

---

used to assist in defense victories in the Sean "Puffy" Combs shooting trial and the O. J. Simpson double homicide trial.[2]

Trial Language

It is often difficult to piece together all the witnesses and evidence in a trial. A lengthy trial may leave the jurors confused. The attorney for each party, therefore, is permitted to make an **opening statement** that summarizes what that party hopes to prove and how it will be proved. Most attorneys also mention the issue of **burden of proof,** which controls who has the responsibility for proving what facts. Although the plaintiff has the burden of proving a case, the defendant has the burden of proving the existence of any valid defenses. Various standards are used for meeting the burden of proof. In criminal cases, the standard is proof beyond a reasonable doubt. In civil cases, the standard is proof by a preponderance of the evidence, or more likely than not.

Because the plaintiff has the burden of proof, the plaintiff presents his or her case and evidence first. The attorney for the plaintiff decides the order of the witnesses; questioning of these witnesses under oath is called **direct examination.** Although the defense cannot present witnesses during this part of the trial, it can question the plaintiff's witnesses after their direct examination is completed. The defense questioning of plaintiff witnesses is called **cross-examination,** after which, the plaintiff may again pose questions to clarify under **redirect examination.**

By the end of the case, the plaintiff must show enough evidence to establish a **prima facie case,** one in which the plaintiff has offered some evidence on all the elements required to be established for recovery. Although the evidence may be subjected to credibility questions and challenged by defense evidence, some proof is required for each part of the claim. If the plaintiff does not meet this standard, the defendant can and may make a motion for a **directed verdict.** This motion for a directed verdict is made outside the jury's hearing and argued to the judge. If it is not granted, the trial proceeds with the defendant's case.

The defendant then has the same opportunity to present witnesses and evidence. Throughout the trial, the judge will apply the rules of evidence to determine what can and cannot be used as evidence. All trials have some form of witness testimony. However, tangible evidence is also often presented. In a contracts case, for example, a great deal of paper evidence—letters, memos, and cost figures—is likely.

One of the evidentiary issues that has been debated and litigated over the past few years is the use of expert testimony in cases. The issue the courts face is determining whether the expert's testimony reflects scientific knowledge or whether the testimony is contrived for the trial (often called "junk science"). In *Daubert v Merrell Dow Pharmaceuticals, Inc.*, 509 U.S. 579 (1993), the U.S. Supreme Court provided guidance for the standards judges should use in determining whether the studies and testimony of experts and their experiments and analysis should be allowed as evidence in a case. One expert, who was testifying in a suit against Merrell Dow (defendant) about birth defects allegedly caused by pregnant women's use of the anti-nausea drug Bendectin, filed an affidavit in the case stating that the use of Bendectin during the first trimester had not been shown to be a risk factor for birth defects. On the other hand, eight experts for the plaintiff parents in the case concluded, based on animal and epidemiological studies, that Bendectin can cause birth defects. The court ruled that the decision to admit the expert's evidence must be based on an examination of the study methodology as well as whether the expert's work had been subjected to peer review, the means that academics use for testing the validity of new studies and theories. The court noted that studies developed for purposes of the litigation require higher levels of scrutiny than studies that existed under the expert's work prior to the litigation. However, the expert's work does not require general acceptance and still will be subject to the scrutiny of the opposing parties' experts as well as the rigor of cross-examination.

CONSIDER...   4.4

Karsten Manufacturing Corporation filed suit against the Professional Golf Association (PGA) because the PGA had proposed a ban of Karsten's U-groove Ping brand clubs from professional play. Karsten hired Richard Smith, then an Arizona State University finance professor, to develop an economic model to correlate professional and consumer usage. Professor Smith's model showed that if pros play with Ping clubs, a proportionate number of duffers will play with them. If the pros cannot use Ping clubs, Karsten is out of business because amateur golfers will not purchase Karsten products. Professor Smith said he conducted valid regression analysis. The attorney for the PGA, Larry Hammond, called it "junk science" that interferes with the real issues in the case. Should the Smith model be admitted? Does it make a difference that the model was developed only for the case? Does it make a difference that Professor Smith's consulting firm was paid more than $1 million for the model?

The forms and types of evidence that can be used at trial are subject to some restrictions. Most people are familiar with the hearsay rule of evidence. Hearsay is evidence offered by a witness who does not have personal knowledge of the information being given but just heard it from someone else. For example, suppose that Arkansas Sewing and Fit Fabric are involved in contract litigation. Fit Fabric says there was no contract. Arkansas Sewing has a witness who overheard the president of Fit Fabric talking to someone on a plane saying he had a contract with Arkansas Sewing but had no intention of performing on it. The witness's testimony of the airplane conversation is hearsay and cannot be used to prove the contract existed. The reason for the hearsay rule is to keep evidence as reliable as possible. The person testifying about the hearsay may not know of the circumstances or background of the conversation and is testifying only to what someone else said.

Once the evidence is presented and the parties are finished with their cases, the parties have one final "go" at the jury. The parties are permitted to make **closing arguments,** which review the presented evidence, highlight the important points for the jurors, and point out the defects in the other side's case. After the cases and closing arguments are presented, the jurors are given their **instructions.** These instructions tell the jurors what the law is and how to apply the law to the facts presented. The instructions are developed by the judge and all the attorneys in the case.

Jury deliberations are done privately; they cannot be recorded, and no one can attend the deliberations except the jurors. Jurors can, but are not required to, discuss what happened during the deliberations after they are ended and a decision is returned to the court.

The U.S. Supreme Court has ruled that jury verdicts need not be unanimous. A state can adopt a rule that requires only a simple majority or three-fourths of the jury to agree on a verdict. In those states requiring unanimous verdicts, it is not unusual for juries to be unable to agree on a verdict. The jurors have then reached

For the Manager's Desk

Re: The "Googling" Jurors

Defense lawyers are calling it the first "Google Mistrial." A federal judge in Florida had to declare a mistrial after a juror told that judge that he had been doing research on the Internet about the drug trial in which he was serving as a juror. The Internet surfing was a direct violation of the judge's instructions to the jurors to not read information about the case or discuss it with others. When the judge declared the mistrial, eight other jurors confessed that they had been doing the same thing. After the mistrial was declared, the jurors shared with the defense attorney in the case that he was on the verge of winning the case.

Google may be the least of the problems judges and lawyers are grappling with. A judge in Arkansas is reviewing a request for a $12.6 million jury verdict against a company from one of the company's lawyers based on the discovery that one of the jurors was using Twitter to send out postings on how the trial was proceeding. An excerpt from the posting appears below:

"oh, and nobody buy Stoam. Its bad mojo and they'll probably cease to Exist now that their wallet is $12m lighter. . . . So,

Jonathan, what did you do today? Oh nothing really, I just gave away TWELVE MILLION DOLLARS of somebody else's money." *

Jurors are using BlackBerries and iPhones to gather and send out information as they are serving on juries. Some jurors are using Facebook to announce when verdicts are coming.

Judges have been warning jurors for some time about not using the Internet to find additional information about a case. However, their universal access to the Internet through their phones has proved to be tempting. One juror even looked up evidence that had been excluded by the judge in the case. When asked why he violated the judge's order, the juror said simply, 'Well, I was curious."

What is the problem with jurors using Google to investigate their cases?

*John Schwartz, "As Jurors Turn to Google and Twitter, Mistrials Are Popping Up," *New York Times,* March 18, 2009, p. A1.

a deadlock, which is called a **hung jury.** If a trial results in a hung jury, the case can be retried.

The result of jury deliberations is the **verdict.** The verdict is given to the judge and is usually read by the judge's clerk.

Even after the verdict, the case is not over. The losing party can make several motions to get around the verdict. One such motion is for a new trial, wherein the attorney argues the need and reason for a new trial to the judge.

Another motion after the verdict, one that a judge is less likely to grant, is a motion for a **judgment NOV.** *NOV* stands for *non obstante veredicto,* which means "notwithstanding the verdict." In other words, the moving attorney is asking the trial judge to reverse the decision of the jury. The basis for granting a judgment NOV is that the jury's verdict is clearly against the weight of the evidence. Occasionally, juries are swayed by the emotion of a case and do not apply the law properly. It is, however, a strong show of judicial authority for a judge to issue a judgment NOV, and they are rare.

Even if no motions are granted, the case still may not be over; it can go to an appellate court for review. Such an appeal must be done within a specified time limit in each state. Here the trial has come full circle to the principle of judicial review and *stare decisis.* Exhibit 4.6 summarizes the steps in civil litigation.

Issues in International Litigation

As noted earlier, international courts have no enforcement powers. They serve as avenues for voluntary mediation. However, courts in each nation in which a firm is doing business would have jurisdiction over that firm in the nation's court system. In a recent infringement dispute over Mattel's "Barbie" and the French doll "Sindy," the parties litigated in London, where both firms were doing business and the dolls were selling well.

Among the critical questions that arise in international litigation are the following: Which set of laws applies? What court is the appropriate forum for a lawsuit that involves citizens of different countries? For example, many non–U.S. citizens who are injured in their own countries by products made by U.S. firms will generally be able to recover more under the product liability and tort laws of the United States. In *Piper Aircraft Co. v Reyno,* 454 U.S. 235 (1981), the pilot and five passengers were killed when a charter flight from Blackpool to Perth, Scotland, crashed in the Scottish highlands. The pilot and passengers were traveling in a twin-engine Piper Aztec, an aircraft manufactured in Pennsylvania by Piper Aircraft Co. The British Department of Trade conducted an investigation of the crash and determined that its cause was mechanical failure. The relatives and estates of the passengers brought suit in the United States against Piper Aircraft. Scottish law does not recognize strict tort liability (see Chapter 10), and U.S. laws on liability and damages are far more favorable than those of Scotland. The U.S. Supreme Court held that the case was properly heard in Scotland because the accident was in Scotland and all the parties in the case were either English or Scottish.

A similar ruling was made with respect to the 2,500 victims of the Union Carbide gas leak in Bhopal, India. Some of the victims filed suit in the United States because the law and damages provisions here afforded them much greater relief. Their suit was dismissed to India, and the court added that Union Carbide would be required to submit to the jurisdiction of Indian courts and to follow discovery rules of the United States.

EXHIBIT 4.6 Steps in Civil Litigation

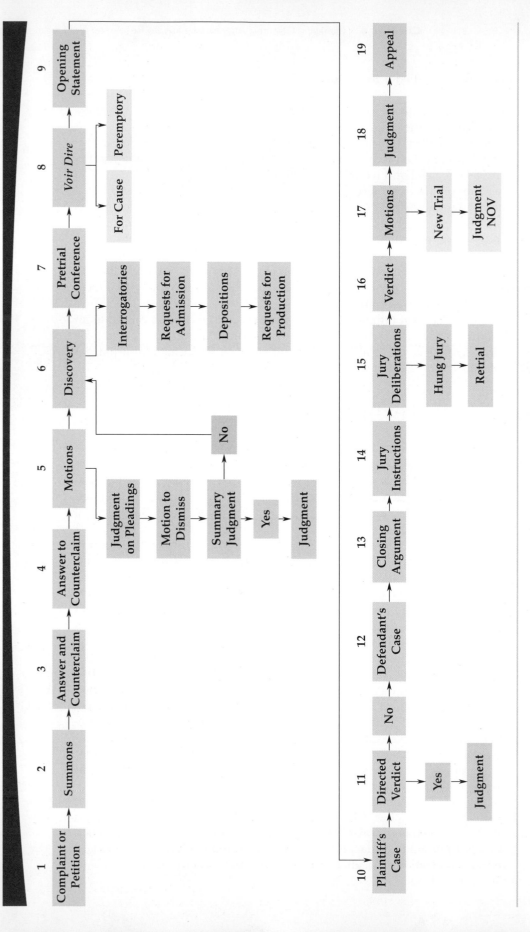

B I O G R A P H Y

The Lawyer's Lawyer Who Bribed a Judge

Class-action lawyer Dickie Scruggs played himself in the 1999 movie "The Insider," which starred Russell Crowe as Jeffrey Wigand, the tobacco industry whistle-blower who obtained a $206 billion settlement from the tobacco companies. Mr. Scruggs used Mr. Wigand as a key witness in his multistate litigation against the tobacco companies. His suits changed forever the way the tobacco companies did business and his fee for the case was $1 billion. Mr. Scruggs was the lawyer every lawyer wanted to be—one of his large verdicts served to help millions and changed the fabric of society. However, almost a decade after "The Insider" premiered, Scruggs would be the lawyer in every lawyer's nightmare. Mr. Scruggs entered a guilty plea to bribery and was sentenced to five years in prison for his role in an attempt to bribe a federal judge.

Mr. Scruggs had been representing insurance claimants against insurers for their damages from Hurricane Katrina. The judge presiding over the case contacted the FBI about a bribery attempt. One of the four lawyers working with Scruggs was approached by the FBI and agreed to wear a wire to catch Scruggs. The content of the tapes revealed the lawyers' clumsy attempts to buy a federal judge. Zachary Scruggs, Dickie's son, also entered a guilty plea. All of the remaining lawyers involved in the bribery scheme entered guilty pleas as well.

Those in the legal profession were baffled because Scruggs's extraordinary talent gave him what he needed to win any case. "He didn't need to cheat," was the comment of a representative from the American Trial Lawyers Association. Scruggs's words at his sentencing were poignant: "I could not be more ashamed to be where I am today, mixed up in a judicial bribery scheme. . . . I realized I was getting mixed up in it. And I will go to my grave wondering why. I have disappointed everyone in my life—my wife, my family, my son, particularly. . . . I deeply regret my conduct. It is a scar and a stain on my soul that will be there forever."

Source: Abha Bhattarai, "Class-Action Lawyer Given 5 Years in a Bribery Case," *New York Times,* June 28, 2008, B3.

© YURY KUZMIN/ISTOCKPHOTO.COM

Summary

How can businesses resolve disputes?

- Alternative dispute resolution (ADR)—means of resolving disputes apart from court litigation

Types of ADR:

- Arbitration—hearing with relaxed rules of evidence
- Mediation—third party acts as go-between
- Conciliation—international term for mediation
- Medarb—combination of mediation and arbitration
- Minitrial—private judge and courtroom; shortened trial
- Rent-a-judge—disputes resolved by hired judge
- Summary jury trial—advisory verdict by jurors in a mock trial
- Early neutral evaluation—third-party evaluation before litigation proceeds
- International Chamber of Commerce (ICC)—voluntary international court that offers arbitration in international disputes

What strategies should businesses follow if litigation is inevitable?

- Evaluate cost, including the unknowns such as jury reaction

- Consider privacy and creative remedies

How do courts proceed with litigation?

- Complaint—plaintiff's statement of a case
- Summons—document to serve defendant with lawsuit
- Answers—defendant's response to complaint
- Statute of limitations—time limit for filing suit
- Discovery—advance disclosure of evidence in case
- Production—obtain and produce document
- Deposition—questioning of witnesses under oath
- Interrogatories—information questions to other party
- Admissions—acknowledgment of facts in a case
- Trial—court proceeding for hearing evidence
- *Voir dire*—jury selection method to screen for bias
- Opening statements—frame by parties' lawyers of the case
- Plaintiff's case—facts for proving complaint presented
- Defendant's case—defenses to allegations presented
- Evidence—testimony and documents presented in the case; no hearsay

Questions and Problems

1. Anna's Dresses, Inc., was delinquent in its payment to one of its suppliers. Anna's intended to pay them, but it had a cash-flow problem and chose to pay rent to its landlord so as not to be evicted from its store rather than make a payment to the supplier. Anna's president is served with a complaint for breach of contract and a summons. The complaint lists the supplier as the plaintiff. What has happened? What must Anna's do now?

2. In the Johns-Manville asbestos litigation, Samuel Greenstone, an attorney for 11 asbestos workers, settled their claims for $30,000 and a promise that he would not "directly or indirectly participate in the bringing of new actions against the Corporation." The 1933 case settlement was documented in the minutes of Johns-Manville's board meeting. Could the information in the minutes be used in later litigation against Johns-Manville? How could a plaintiff's attorney obtain the information? Do you feel Mr. Greenstone made an ethical decision in his agreement? Wasn't his loyalty to his 11 clients and his obligation to obtain compensation for them? Would you have agreed to the no-further-participation-in-a-lawsuit clause? Would you, if you had been an executive at Johns-Manville, have supported the clause?

3. Suppose that your company had received a letter complaint about one of the prescription drugs that it sells. The customer and his physician have complained that there were cardiovascular effects from use of the drug over the past 12 months. You know about the complaint and you also have e-mails from one of your friends in the company, a research scientist who was in your fraternity in college, that indicate he sees some cardiovascular side effects from the same drug. If you deleted the e-mail, would it be spoliation?

What would be required to prove spoliation in this case?

4. After she was found guilty of obstruction of justice and conspiracy (see Chapter 8) lawyers for Martha Stewart filed a motion for a new trial on the grounds that a juror on the case had possible undisclosed bias. The defense lawyers pointed out that juror Chappel Hartridge had checked "No" on the juror questionnaire when asked whether he had been accused of, charged with, or convicted of a crime. The lawyers for Ms. Stewart filed an affidavit from a former girlfriend of Mr. Hartridge's who indicated that he had been arrested and arraigned on charges of assaulting her. Mr. Hartridge's former girlfriend ultimately dropped the charges against him. What bias do you think Ms. Stewart's lawyers alleged? Are they right? Should the juror have been eliminated for cause? [*U.S. v Stewart*, 317 F.Supp.2d 432 (S.D.N.Y.2004)]

5. A discrimination suit by a former flight attendant against Atlantic East Airlines is going to trial. Jury selection has begun. An executive from Atlantic East

notices that a member of the potential juror panel was a flight attendant responsible for pregnancy leave reforms among airline flight attendants during the early 1980s. This potential juror is no longer a flight attendant and is raising two small children at home. The executive informs Atlantic East's lawyer. Can the lawyer do anything to prevent the woman from sitting on the jury?

6. Applegate is in litigation with Magnifium over a contract breach. Applegate has been approached by a former janitor for Magnifium who can testify regarding conversations about the contract between Magnifium executives. The janitor heard them when the executives had stayed late at work and he was cleaning. Can Applegate use the statements at trial?

7. Robert Joiner began work as an electrician in the Water & Light Department of Thomasville, Georgia, in 1973. Mr. Joiner worked with and around electrical transformers that contained a fluid. In 1983, the city of Thomasville discovered that this fluid contained polychlorinated biphenyls (PCBs), a substance considered hazardous.

Mr. Joiner was diagnosed with lung cancer in 1991 and filed suit against General Electric, the manufacturer of the transformers, for negligence and product liability. Mr. Joiner had been a smoker, his parents were smokers, and his family had a history of lung cancer.

Mr. Joiner offered expert testimony on studies involving the injection of PCB into the stomachs of infant mice and resulting cancer. The experts had no epidemiological studies on PCB exposure. Should the expert testimony be admitted? [*General Electric Co. v Joiner*, 522 U.S. 136 (1997)]

8. The ABC News program *Day One* ran two reports, on February 28 and March 7, 1995, which left viewers with the impression that Philip Morris Company was spiking its cigarettes with nicotine to make them more addictive. Philip Morris filed a $10 billion defamation suit against Capital Cities/ABC, Inc. for defamation on March 24, 1995. The suit alleged that the "spiking" report was untrue. An ABC News spokesperson said in response to the suit, "ABC News stands by its reporting on this issue."

Philip Morris is based in New York; the suit was filed in Richmond, Virginia; and a news conference to announce the suit was held in Washington, D.C., on the day hearings were to begin to determine whether the FDA should regulate nicotine as a drug. Philip Morris was not the primary target of the *Day One* report, but it was mentioned by name in the broadcasts. Philip Morris did not ask ABC for a retraction prior to filing suit.

J. D. Lee, a Knoxville, Tennessee, plaintiff's attorney who has had experience litigating against tobacco companies, noted that the prospect of getting his hands on Philip Morris's internal documents in such a suit made him gleeful: "I would have a field day with Philip Morris."

By September 1995, ABC and Philip Morris had settled the suit. ABC issued the following public apology and agreed to pay attorneys' fees for Philip Morris.

It is the policy of ABC News to make corrections where they are warranted. On February 28 and March 7, 1995, the ABC program, Day One, aired segments dealing with the tobacco industry. Philip Morris filed a defamation lawsuit alleging that the segments wrongly reported that, through the introduction of significant amounts of nicotine from outside sources, Philip Morris "artificially spikes" and "fortifies" its cigarettes with nicotine, and "carefully controls" and "manipulates" nicotine for the purpose of "addicting" smokers. Philip Morris states that it does not add nicotine in any measurable amount from any outside source for any purpose in the course of its manufacturing process, and that its finished cigarettes contain less nicotine than is found in the natural tobacco from which they are made.

ABC does not take issue with those two statements. We now agree that we should not have reported that Philip Morris adds significant amounts of nicotine from outside sources. That was a mistake that was not deliberate on the part of ABC, but for which we accept responsibility and which requires correction. We apologize to our audience and Philip Morris.

ABC and Philip Morris continue to disagree about whether the principal focus of the reports was on the use of nicotine from outside sources. Philip Morris believes that this was the main thrust of the programs. ABC believes that the principal focus of the reports was whether cigarette companies use the reconstituted tobacco process to control the levels of nicotine in cigarettes in order to keep people smoking. Philip Morris categorically denies that it does so. ABC thinks the reports speak for themselves on this issue and is prepared to have the issue resolved elsewhere.

ABC and Philip Morris have agreed to discontinue the defamation action.

What do you think of Philip Morris's decision to litigate? Would you have made the same decision? Was it a public relations tactic as well as an enforcement of rights? What motivation did both sides have for settling the case? Evaluate the ethics of ABC News in running the story. Evaluate the ethics of Philip Morris in filing suit without first approaching ABC for a retraction.

9. The SEC investigation of Tyco International for possible securities law violations produced several e-mails. The e-mails focused on two concerns about the company: accounting improprieties and the use of company funds by then-CEO Dennis Kozlowski. The e-mails were written by outside lawyers from the firm of Wilmer Cutler to former Tyco General Counsel Mark Belnick. The e-mails are as follows.

March 23, 2000: E-mail from a Wilmer Cutler Partner, Lewis Liman, to Mark Belnick

There are payments to a woman whom the folks in finance describe to be Dennis's girlfriend. I do not know Dennis's situation, but this is an embarrassing fact.

(Note: The payments were later verified as being made from the Key Employee Loan Account to Karen Mayo, who subsequently became Karen Kozlowski, who has now divorced the imprisoned Mr. Kozlowski.)

May 25, 2000: E-mail from a Wilmer Cutler Partner, William McLucas, to Mark Belnick

We have found issues that will likely interest the SEC; creativeness is employed in hitting the forecasts.

There is also a bad letter from the Sigma people just before the acquisition confirming that they were asked to hold product shipment just before closing. . . .

(This e-mail also went on to suggest that there was, in regard to Tyco's financial reports, "something funny which is likely apparent if any decent accountant looks at this.")

Although Mr. McLucas and Mr. Liman could not comment because of attorney–client privilege, others indicate that they followed up on the e-mails and asked officials at Tyco to correct the concerns and problems raised in the e-mails.

Are the e-mails privileged? How did the SEC gain access to them? Can they be used as evidence? Are they discoverable? (Laurie P. Coehn and Mark Maremont, "E-Mails Show Tyco's Lawyers Had Concerns," (*Wall Street Journal,* December 27, 2002, pp. C1, C5)

10. In October 1995, Saint Clair Adams applied for a job at Circuit City Stores, Inc., a now-defunct national retailer of consumer electronics. Mr. Adams signed an employment application that included the following provision.

I agree that I will settle any and all previously unasserted claims, disputes or controversies arising out of or relating to my application or candidacy for employment, employment and/or cessation of employment with Circuit City, exclusively by final and binding arbitration before a neutral Arbitrator. By way of example only, such claims include claims under federal, state, and local statutory or common law, such as the Age Discrimination in Employment Act, Title VII of the Civil Rights Act of 1964, as amended, including the amendments of the Civil Rights Act of 1991, the Americans with Disabilities Act, the law of contract and the law of tort.

Mr. Adams was hired as a sales counselor in Circuit City's store in Santa Rosa, California.

Two years later, Mr. Adams filed an employment discrimination lawsuit against Circuit City in state court, asserting claims under California's Fair Employment Act. Circuit City filed suit in the U.S. District Court seeking to stop the state court action and to compel arbitration under the FAA. Mr. Adams says the arbitration clause violates his statutory rights for protection against employment discrimination and that he has the right to go to court, not arbitration. Who is correct? Can Mr. Adams be required to submit to arbitration? [*Circuit City Stores, Inc. v Adams*, 532 U.S. 105 (2001)]

Economics, Public Policy, and the Law

Japan's Changing Legal System

Many businesspeople have argued that too many lawyers and lawsuits hurt the United States in the competitive international market. However, Japan is a country that has been moving toward the U.S. model for the role of lawyers in the judicial system even as it preserves some limitations on the standards for civil recovery and the types of recoveries available in those cases.

Lifting Limits on the Number of Lawyers

Prior to 2000, in order to become a *bengoshi* (lawyer) in Japan, an individual had to win a slot at the Legal Training and Research Institute. This government-run school accepted only 2 percent of the 35,000 annual applicants. As a result, only 400 new *bengoshi* were added each year to Japan's bar. However, in 2000, the government allowed the opening of private law schools that are operated in a manner similar to those in the United States. With more slots available for education, there are now 29,000 lawyers in Japan, a more-than-double increase from the 14,336 lawyers there in 1992. There is also increased competition among lawyers. Japan now permits lawyer advertising. Japanese law firms are also now permitted to merge with other firms to increase the services offered and compete effectively.

Limits on Recovery

Japanese courts allow recovery only for actual losses. There is no recovery for mental anguish. Class actions are rare in Japan and it is very difficult to get a court's approval to go forward with such a suit. The Toyota recall of so many cars in the sudden acceleration issues of 2010 resulted in great activity in Japanese courts for class actions and recovery.

Costs to Plaintiffs

Plaintiffs are required to pay money to their lawyers up front. The amount required is 8 percent of the recovery sought plus the nonrefundable filing fee.

Limits on Damage Awards

Judges, not juries, determine damages, and even in wrongful death cases the damages may not include punitive damages.

Encouragement of Settlement and Cultural Disdain for Confrontation

In Japan, a cultural pride exists in being able to resolve disputes outside the courtroom; those who must litigate are looked down upon. However, the Japanese culture and judicial system are moving toward the use of litigation as a means of correcting company behaviors. One financial analyst concluded that litigation is good as he discussed the Toyota issues: "Toyota has been arrogant. It's good that lawsuits are taking place now so Toyota will go through soul-searching."[3]

Discussion Questions

1. Should the United States move more toward some of the rules of the Japanese litigation system as Japan moves toward ours? Why or why not? Are there benefits to the openness of one and the limitedness of the other? What are they?

2. In the English court system, the loser pays court costs and the costs of the other party involved in the litigation. Should such a rule be adopted in the United States? For all cases? Would you be less willing to pursue a case for yourself or your company if you knew that you would be required to pay if you lost the case?

Sources: Michele Galen et al., "Guilty," *BusinessWeek*, April 13, 1992, pp. 60–66; *ABA Report on International Lawyers* (1990); Yuka Hayashi, "Japanese Culture Shifting on Suits," *Wall Street Journal*, February 23, 2010, p. A4.

Notes

1. Adam Liptak, "Lawyers Won't End Squabble, So Judge Turns to Child's Play," *New York Times*, June 9, 2006, p. A20.

2. Bob Van Voris, "Voir Dire Tip: Pick Former Juror," *National Law Journal*, November 1, 1999, pp. A1, A6.

3. Yuka Hayashi, "Japanese Culture Shifting on Suits," *Wall Street Journal*, February 23, 2010, p. A4.

Part 2

Business: Its Regulatory Environment

A business is regulated by everything from the U.S. Constitution to the rules of the Consumer Product Safety Commission. Managers must know codified law as well as the law that develops as cases are litigated and new issues of liability arise. The regulatory environment of business includes penalties for criminal conduct and punitive damages for knowing injuries to customers. Part 2 describes the laws that regulate businesses and business operations, the sanctions that are imposed for violation of these laws, and the manner in which businesses can make compliance with the law a key part of their values.

Business and the Constitution

T he U.S. Constitution is a remarkable document. It was drafted by a group of independent states more than 200 years ago in an attempt to unify the states into one national government that could function smoothly and efficiently without depriving those independent states of their rights. The fact that it has survived so many years with so few changes indicates the flexibility and foresight built into the document.

This chapter covers the application of the U.S. Constitution to business. Several questions are answered: What are the constitutional limitations on business regulation? Who has more power to regulate business—the states or the federal government? What individual freedoms granted under the Constitution apply to businesses? ■

Some men look at constitutions with sanctimonious reverence, and deem them like the ark of the covenant, too sacred to be touched. . . . I am certainly not an advocate for frequent and untried changes in laws and constitutions. . . . But . . . laws and institutions must go hand in hand with the progress of the human mind.

Thomas Jefferson

The history of the United States has been written not merely in the halls of Congress, in the Executive offices and on the battlefields, but to a great extent in the chambers of the Supreme Court of the United States.

Charles Warren

UPDATE ⬉
For up-to-date legal and ethics news, go to
mariannejennings.com

CONSIDER...

In 1996, Nike was inundated with allegations about its labor practices in shoe factories around the world. Nike responded to the negative reports and allegations with a series of press releases, ads, and op-ed pieces in newspapers around the country. In addition, Nike commissioned a report from former Atlanta mayor and U.S. ambassador Andrew Young on the condition of its factories around the world. Mr. Young issued a report in 1997 that reflected favorably on Nike and its labor practices. Nike cited the report in op-ed pieces, most particularly in a letter to the editor of the *New York Times* in response to a negative op-ed piece there on Nike's labor practices.

Marc Kasky filed suit against Nike in California alleging that the op-ed pieces, and letters in response to negative op-ed pieces about Nike, violated the False Advertising Law of California. The act permits state agencies to take action to fine corporate violators of the act as well as obtain remedies such as injunctions to halt the ads.

Nike challenged the suit on the grounds that such an interpretation and application of the advertising regulation violated its rights of free speech. The lower court agreed with Mr. Kasky and held that the advertising statute applied to Nike's defense of its labor practices, even on the op-ed pages of newspapers. Nike appealed to the U.S. Supreme Court. How should the court rule? Does the action under California law violate Nike's free speech rights?

The U.S. Constitution

An Overview of the U.S. Constitution

Although virtually all constitutional issues and all court decisions on those issues are complicated and detailed, the **U.S. Constitution** itself is a simple and short document. Contained within it is the entire structure of the federal government, its powers, the powers of the states, and the rights of all citizens. The exact language of the U.S. Constitution is presented in Appendix A.

Articles I, II, and III—The Framework for Separation of Powers

The first three articles of the U.S. Constitution set up the three branches of the federal government. Article I establishes the **legislative branch.** The two houses of Congress—the House of Representatives and the Senate—are created, their method of electing members is specified, and their powers are listed.

Article II creates the **executive branch** of the federal government. The office of president, along with its qualifications, manner of election, term, and powers are specified.

Article III establishes the **judicial branch** of the federal government. This article creates only the U.S. Supreme Court and establishes its jurisdiction. Congress, however, is authorized to establish inferior courts, which it has done in the form of federal district courts, specialized federal courts, and U.S. courts of appeals (see Chapter 3, Exhibit 3.1).

The first three articles establish the nature of the federal government as involving the **separation of powers.** Each of the branches of government is given unique functions that the other branches cannot perform, but each branch also has curbing powers on the other branches through the exercise of its unique powers. For example, the judicial branch cannot pass laws, but it can prevent a law passed by Congress from taking effect by judicially interpreting the law as unconstitutional. The executive branch does not pass legislation but has veto power over legislation passed by Congress. The executive branch has responsibility for foreign relations and treaty negotiation. However, those treaties do not take effect until the Senate ratifies them. This system of different powers that can be used to curb the other branches' exercise of power is called a system of **checks and balances.**

The drafters of the U.S. Constitution designed the federal government this way to avoid the accumulation of too much power in any one branch of government. In *Nixon v Administrator of General Services*, 433 U.S. 425 (1977), the Supreme Court held that former President Nixon was required to turn over to Congress any records and materials of the executive branch that were relevant to the congressional inquiry into the Watergate scandal (a break-in at the Democratic Party's national headquarters that was masterminded by members of the Nixon administration). In *Clinton v Jones*, 520 U.S. 681 (1997), the Supreme Court ruled that even the president is subject to the laws of the land and is accountable for civil wrongs alleged by private citizens. In the case, Paula Corbin Jones alleged that Mr. Clinton had sexually harassed her while he was governor of Arkansas. The Court ruled that the president cannot be above the law or judicial process when he has violated the rights of a citizen in his private conduct and wrote, ". . . even the sovereign is subject to God and the law."

Other Articles

Article IV deals with states' interrelationships. Article V provides the procedures for constitutional amendments. Article VI is the **Supremacy Clause** (discussed later in this chapter), and Article VII simply provides the method for state ratification of the Constitution.

For the Manager's Desk

Re: The President, Justice Alito, Congress, and the Balance of Powers

During President Obama's State of the Union address on January 27, 2009, he made reference to *Citizens United v Federal Election Commission* 130 S.Ct. 876 (2010) (see pp. 166–168). The decision dealt with the constitutionality of portions of the McCain–Feingold campaign and campaign contributions law. The president made the following statements about the decision:

"With all due deference to separation of powers, last week the Supreme Court reversed a century of law that, I believe, will open the floodgates for special interests, including foreign corporations, to spend without limit in our elections. Well I don't think American elections should

be bankrolled by America's most powerful interests, or worse, by foreign entities. They should be decided by the American people, and that's why I'm urging Democrats and Republicans to pass a bill that helps to right this wrong."

Following the statement, U.S. Supreme Court Justice Alito could be seen (as he was picked up by the cameras) shaking his head and mouthing what appears to be "not true" or "definitely not true."

What can be done with regard to the decision? Who was right on what the decision did—Mr. Obama or Justice Alito? (See p. 166.)

The Bill of Rights

In addition to the seven articles, the U.S. Constitution has 27 amendments, the first 10 of which are the **Bill of Rights.** Although these rights originally applied only to federal procedures, the **Fourteenth Amendment** extended them to apply to the states as well. These amendments establish rights from freedom of speech (First Amendment) to the right to a jury trial (Sixth Amendment) to protection of privacy from unlawful searches (Fourth Amendment) to due process before deprivation of property (Fifth Amendment). The amendments as they apply to businesses are covered later in this chapter and in Chapter 8.

The Role of Judicial Review and the Constitution

The Supreme Court and its decisions are often in the news because the cases decided by the Court are generally significant ones that provide interpretations of the U.S. Constitution and also define the extent of the rights we are afforded under it. The role of the U.S. Supreme Court is to decide what rights are provided by the general language of the U.S. Constitution. For example, the Fifth Amendment guarantees that we will not be deprived of our life, liberty, or property without "due process of law." Due process of law, interpreted by the courts many times now, includes such rights as the right to a hearing before a mortgage foreclosure, or at least the right of notice before property is sold after repossession as a result of nonpayment of the underlying debt.

The First Amendment protects the simple right to freedom of speech, but the Supreme Court has been faced with issues such as whether restrictions on membership in student clubs at state universities are an infringement of the First Amendment.[1] The Fourth Amendment, the "privacy amendment," protects us from warrantless searches. This general idea has been analyzed in the context of garbage taken from cans waiting for pickup on the street and unannounced inspections of company workplaces by OSHA regulators (see Chapter 18 for more information on OSHA).

The U.S. Supreme Court has the responsibility of determining the extent and scope of the rights and protections afforded by the U.S. Constitution. In addition, the Supreme Court plays the unique role of reviewing the actions of the other branches of government. The Court is a crucial part of the checks-and-balances system set up in our Constitution. As noted in the Manager's Desk feature on p. 144, the court recently dealt with the issue of the constitutionality of legislation passed by Congress.

Constitutional Limitations of Economic Regulations

The Commerce Clause

The **Commerce Clause** is found in Article I, Section 8, Part 3 of the U.S. Constitution and provides Congress with the power "[t]o regulate Commerce with foreign Nations, and among the several States. . . . " Although the language is short and simple, the phrase "among the several states" has created much controversy. The clause limits Congress to the regulation of interstate commerce. Local commerce and intrastate commerce are left to the states for regulation. Defining interstate commerce has been the task of the courts. The standards are defined from two perspectives: federal regulation of state and local commerce, and state and local regulation of interstate commerce.

Standards for Congressional Regulation of State and Local Business Activity

The issue, as defined by the U.S. Supreme Court, is whether the situation involves sufficient interstate contact or effects for the application of federal standards. The Constitution gives Congress authority to regulate interstate matters and vests all the remaining regulatory authority in the states.

The U.S. Supreme Court has defined the extent of interstate commerce. The Court initially gave a very narrow interpretation to the scope of the Commerce Clause. For activity to be subject to federal regulation there had to be a "direct and immediate effect" on interstate commerce. In 1918, the Court ruled that manufacturing was not "commerce" (because it was solely intrastate) and struck down an act of Congress that attempted to regulate goods manufactured in plants using child labor [*Hammer v Dagenhart*, 247 U.S. 251 (1918)]. During the 1930s, Congress and President Roosevelt bumped heads with the Court many times in their attempts to legislate a recovery from the Depression. The Court consistently refused to validate federal legislation dealing with manufacturing, operations, and labor [*Schechter Poultry v United States*, 295 U.S. 495 (1935); *Carter v Carter Coal*, 298 U.S. 238 (1936)]. Roosevelt refused to accept the roadblock to his legislation and initiated his court-packing plan to increase the number of members of the court with Roosevelt appointees.

The Court responded in *NLRB v Laughlin Steel*, 336 U.S. 460 (1940), by ruling that intrastate activities, even though local in character, may still affect interstate commerce and thus be subject to federal regulation. The "affectation" doctrine thus expanded the authority of the federal government in regulating commerce. In the words of the Court, "If it is interstate commerce that feels the pinch, it does not matter how local the squeeze" (336 U.S. at 464). The Commerce Clause has had a critical role in the elimination of discrimination because the Court's liberal definition of what constitutes interstate commerce has permitted the application of federal civil rights laws to local economic activities. However, some recent refinements limit federal authority. *U.S. v Morrison* (Case 5.1) is a landmark case that limited federal regulation.

CASE 5.1   *U.S. v Morrison*
529 U.S. 598 (2000)

Economic Impact Is Not the Same as Commerce: Violence Is Intrastate Activity

FACTS

Christy Brzonkala (petitioner) enrolled at Virginia Polytechnic Institute (Virginia Tech) in the fall of 1994. In September of that year, Ms. Brzonkala met Antonio Morrison and James Crawford (respondents), who were both students at Virginia Tech and members of its varsity football team. Ms. Brzonkala alleges that, within 30 minutes of meeting Mr. Morrison and Mr. Crawford, they assaulted and repeatedly raped her. After the attack, Mr. Morrison allegedly told Ms. Brzonkala, "You better not have any . . . diseases." The court omitted portions of the quotes from the briefs in issuing its opinion, stating only that they "consist of boasting, debased remarks about what Morrison would do to women, vulgar remarks that cannot fail to shock and offend."

Ms. Brzonkala became severely emotionally disturbed and depressed. Shortly after the rape, Ms. Brzonkala stopped attending classes and withdrew from the university.

In early 1995, Ms. Brzonkala filed a complaint under Virginia Tech's Sexual Assault Policy. During the school-conducted hearing on her complaint, Mr. Morrison admitted having sexual contact with her despite the fact that she had twice told him "no." After the hearing, Virginia Tech's Judicial Committee found insufficient evidence to punish Mr. Crawford, but found Mr. Morrison guilty of sexual assault and sentenced him to immediate suspension for two semesters.

Virginia Tech's dean of students upheld the judicial committee's sentence. However, in July 1995, Virginia Tech informed Ms. Brzonkala that Mr. Morrison intended to initiate a court challenge to his conviction under the Sexual Assault Policy. University officials told her that a second hearing would be necessary to remedy the school's error in prosecuting her complaint under that policy, which had not been widely circulated to students. The university conducted a second hearing and the Judicial Committee again found Mr. Morrison guilty and sentenced him to an identical two-semester suspension. This time, however, the description of Mr. Morrison's offense was changed from "sexual assault" to "using abusive language."

Mr. Morrison appealed his second conviction. Virginia Tech's senior vice president and provost set aside Mr. Morrison's punishment. She concluded that it was "excessive when compared with other cases where there has been a finding of violation of the Abusive Conduct Policy." Virginia Tech did not inform Ms. Brzonkala of this decision. After learning from a newspaper that Mr. Morrison would be returning to Virginia Tech for the fall 1995 semester, she dropped out of the university.

In December 1995, Ms. Brzonkala sued Mr. Morrison, Mr. Crawford, and Virginia Tech in Federal District Court. Her complaint alleged that Mr. Morrison's and Mr. Crawford's attack violated 42 U.S.C. § 13981, the Violence Against Women Act (VAWA). Mr. Morrison and Mr. Crawford moved to dismiss the complaint on the grounds that § 13981's civil remedy is unconstitutional.

The district court held that Congress lacked authority for the enactment of VAWA and dismissed the complaint against Mr. Morrison and Mr. Crawford. The court of appeals affirmed and Ms. Brzonkala appealed.

JUDICIAL OPINION

REHNQUIST, Chief Justice

[We] consider the constitutionality of 42 U.S.C. § 13981, which provides a federal civil remedy for the victims of gender-motivated violence.

Section 13981 was part of the Violence Against Women Act of 1994. It states that "[a]ll persons within the United States shall have the right to be free from crimes of violence motivated by gender" 42 U.S.C. § 13981(b). To enforce that right, subsection (c) [permits recovery of punitive and other damages in federal court].

Since *U.S. v Lopez*, 514 U.S. 564 (1995) most recently canvassed and clarified our case law governing . . . Commerce Clause regulation, it provides the proper framework for conducting the required analysis of § 13981. In *Lopez*, we held that the Gun-Free School Zones Act of 1990, 18 U.S.C. § 922(q)(1)(A), which made it a federal crime to knowingly possess a firearm in a school zone, exceeded Congress' authority under the Commerce Clause.

First, we observed that § 922(q) was "a criminal statute that by its terms has nothing to do with 'commerce' or any sort of economic enterprise, however broadly one might define those terms." Reviewing our case law, we noted that "we have upheld a wide variety of congressional Acts regulating intrastate economic activity where we have concluded that the activity substantially affected interstate commerce." Although we cited only a few examples, including *Wickard v Filburn*, 317 U.S. 111, 63 S.Ct. 82, 87 L.Ed. 122 (1942); *Katzenbach v McClung*, 379 U.S. 294, 85 S.Ct. 377, 13 L.Ed.2d 290 (1964); and *Heart of Atlanta Motel*, we stated that the pattern of analysis is clear. "Where economic activity substantially affects interstate commerce, legislation regulating that activity will be sustained."

Both petitioners and Justice SOUTER's dissent downplay the role that the economic nature of the regulated activity plays in our Commerce Clause analysis. But a fair reading of *Lopez* shows that the noneconomic, criminal nature of the conduct at issue was central to our decision in that case. The possession of a gun in a local school zone is in no sense an economic activity that might, through repetition elsewhere, substantially affect any sort of interstate commerce. *Lopez*'s review of Commerce Clause case law demonstrates that in those cases where we have sustained federal regulation of intrastate activity based upon the activity's substantial effects on interstate commerce, the activity in question has been some sort of economic endeavor.

[O]ur decision in *Lopez* rested in part on the fact that the link between gun possession and a substantial effect on interstate commerce was attenuated. The United States argued that the possession of guns may lead to violent crime, and that violent crime "can be expected to

CONTINUED

affect the functioning of the national economy . . ." The Government also argued that the presence of guns at schools poses a threat to the educational process, which in turn threatens to produce a less efficient and productive workforce, which will negatively affect national productivity and thus interstate commerce.

We rejected these "costs of crime" and "national productivity" arguments because they would permit Congress to "regulate not only all violent crime, but all activities that might lead to violent crime, regardless of how tenuously they relate to interstate commerce."

With these principles underlying our Commerce Clause jurisprudence as reference points, the proper resolution of the present cases is clear. Gender-motivated crimes of violence are not, in any sense of the phrase, economic activity.

In contrast with the lack of congressional findings that we faced in *Lopez*, § 13981 is supported by numerous findings regarding the serious impact that gender-motivated violence has on victims and their families. "'[S]imply because Congress may conclude that a particular activity substantially affects interstate commerce does not necessarily make it so.'" Rather, "'[w]hether particular operations affect interstate commerce sufficiently to come under the constitutional power of Congress to regulate them is ultimately a judicial rather than a legislative question, and can be settled finally only by this Court.'"

Given these findings and petitioners' arguments, the concern that we expressed in *Lopez* that Congress might use the Commerce Clause to completely obliterate the Constitution's distinction between national and local authority seems well founded. The reasoning that petitioners advance seeks to follow the but-for causal chain from the initial occurrence of violent crime (the suppression of which has always been the prime object of the States' police power) to every attenuated effect upon interstate commerce. If accepted, petitioners' reasoning would allow Congress to regulate any crime as long as the nationwide, aggregated impact of that crime has substantial effects on employment, production, transit, or consumption. Indeed, if Congress may regulate gender-motivated violence, it would be able to regulate murder or any other type of violence since gender-motivated violence, as a subset of all violent crime, is certain to have lesser economic impacts than the larger class of which it is a part.

Petitioners' reasoning, moreover, will not limit Congress to regulating violence but may, as we suggested in *Lopez*, be applied equally as well to family law and other areas of traditional state regulation since the aggregate effect of marriage, divorce, and childrearing on the national economy is undoubtedly significant. Congress may have recognized this specter when it expressly precluded § 13981 from being used in the family law context. Under our written Constitution, however, the limitation of congressional authority is not solely a matter of legislative grace.

The Constitution requires a distinction between what is truly national and what is truly local. In recognizing this fact we preserve one of the few principles that has been consistent since the Clause was adopted. The regulation and punishment of intrastate violence that is not directed at the instrumentalities, channels, or goods involved in interstate commerce has always been the province of the States.

Affirmed.

DISSENTING OPINION

Justice SOUTER, with whom Justice STEVENS, Justice GINSBURG, and Justice BREYER join, dissenting

Our cases, which remain at least nominally undisturbed, stand for the following propositions. Congress has the power to legislate with regard to activity that, in the aggregate, has a substantial effect on interstate commerce. The fact of such a substantial effect is not an issue for the courts in the first instance, but for the Congress, whose institutional capacity for gathering evidence and taking testimony far exceeds ours.

One obvious difference from *United States v Lopez*, 514 U.S. 549, 115 S.Ct. 1624, 131 L.Ed.2d 626 (1995), is the mountain of data assembled by Congress, here showing the effects of violence against women on interstate commerce. Passage of the Act in 1994 was preceded by four years of hearing, which included testimony from physicians and law professors; from survivors of rape and domestic violence; and from representatives of state law enforcement and private business. The record includes reports on gender bias from task forces in 21 States, and we have the benefit of specific factual findings in the eight separate Reports issued by Congress and its committees over the long course leading to enactment.

Indeed, the legislative record here is far more voluminous than the record compiled by Congress and found sufficient in two prior cases upholding Title II of the Civil Rights Act of 1964 against Commerce Clause challenges. In *Heart of Atlanta Motel, Inc. v United States*, 379 U.S. 241, 85 S.Ct. 348, 13 L.Ed.2d 258 (1964), and *Katzenbach v McClung*, 379 U.S. 294, 85 S.Ct. 377, 13 L.Ed.2d 290 (1964), the Court referred to evidence showing the consequences of racial discrimination by motels and restaurants on interstate commerce. Congress had relied on compelling anecdotal reports that individual instances of segregation cost thousands to millions of dollars.

All of this convinces me that today's ebb of the commerce power rests on error, and at the same time leads me to doubt that the majority's view will prove to be enduring law.

CASE QUESTIONS

1. What does VAWA do, and how did Congress establish the connection of VAWA to commerce?

2. What does the majority opinion say the test for the constitutionality of federal regulation under the Commerce Clause is?

3. What does the dissenting opinion say the test for the constitutionality of federal regulation under the Commerce Clause should be?

4. Is VAWA constitutional? What rights does Ms. Brzonkala have other than those afforded by VAWA?

CONSIDER... 5.1

Ollie's Barbecue is a family-owned restaurant in Birmingham, Alabama, specializing in barbecued meats and homemade pies, with a seating capacity of 220 customers. It is located on a state highway 11 blocks from an interstate highway and a somewhat greater distance from railroad and bus stations. The restaurant caters to a family and white-collar trade, with a takeout service for "Negroes." (*Note:* The court uses this term in the opinion on the case.)

In the 12 months preceding the passage of the Civil Rights Act, the restaurant purchased locally approximately $150,000 worth of food, $69,683 or 46 percent of which was meat that it bought from a local supplier who had procured it from outside the state.

Ollie's has refused to serve Negroes in its dining accommodations since its original opening in 1927, and since July 2, 1964, it has been operating in violation of the Civil Rights Act. A lower court concluded that if it were required to serve Negroes, it would lose a substantial amount of business.

The lower court found that the Civil Rights Act did not apply because Ollie's was not involved in "interstate commerce." Will the Commerce Clause permit application of the Civil Rights Act to Ollie's?

THINK: What did the *Morrison* case require for the Commerce Clause to allow Congressional action on intrastate activities? If Congress was to have the authority to regulate seemingly intrastate activities, there had to be some underlying economic activity and, whatever that economic activity was, it had to have some relation to or an impact on interstate activity.

APPLY: What is different about Ollie's Barbecue's activities and the activities cited in support of the federal legislation on violence against women?

Ollie's Barbecue is a commercial enterprise involved in producing and selling food. This is economic activity, and *Morrison* found that the underlying activity being regulated must be economic in nature before the findings of interstate economic activity can be made.

Ollie's has an impact on interstate commerce because it orders goods in interstate commerce, and it serves travelers who are moving from state to state. The impact may be smaller than that outlined in Congress for VAWA, but it is all pure economic activity.

ANSWER: Congress had the authority under the Commerce Clause to pass the Civil Rights Act and have it apply to intrastate businesses such as Ollie's Barbecue. [*Katzenbach v McClung,* 379 U.S. 294 (1964).]

Standards for State Regulation of Interstate Commerce

The Commerce Clause also deals with issues beyond those of federal power. The interpretation of the clause involves how much commerce the states can regulate without interfering in the congressional domain of interstate commerce. In answering this question, the courts are concerned with two factors:

Ethical Issues

The days of discrimination are not over yet. Several large restaurant chains have entered into consent decrees and other settlements with federal agencies over charges that, for example, their employees did not wait on members of protected classes who entered their restaurants. The employees and management did not prohibit the potential customers from entering the restaurants, but made them wait so long that they left.

Suppose that you work as a server at a restaurant where the manager has instructed you to wait before serving either Latino or African American customers. His instructions are, "If you wait 20 minutes before going to their tables, I can almost guarantee they will leave. We don't have to do anything in violation of the law. We can just be slow."

Would you follow the manager's instructions? Why or why not? What are the consequences of following his instructions? What are the consequences of not following them? Is anyone really hurt if you refuse to follow his instructions?

---

(1) whether federal regulation supersedes state involvement, and (2) whether the benefits achieved by the regulation outweigh the burden on interstate commerce. These two factors are meant to prevent states from passing laws that would give local industries and businesses an unfair advantage over interstate businesses. In some circumstances, however, the states can regulate interstate commerce. Those circumstances occur when the state is properly exercising its **police power.**

What Is the Police Power?   The police power is the states' power to pass laws that promote the public welfare and protect public health and safety. Regulation of these primary concerns is within each state's domain. It is, however, inevitable that some of the laws dealing with public welfare and health and safety will burden interstate commerce. Many of the statutes that have been challenged constitutionally have regulated highway use. For example, some cases have tested a state's power to regulate the length of trucks on state highways [*Raymond Motor Transportation v Rice*, 434 U.S. 429 (1978)]. In *Bibb v Navajo Freight Lines, Inc.*, 359 U.S. 520 (1959), the Supreme Court analyzed an Illinois statute requiring all trucks using Illinois roads to be equipped with contour mudguards. These mudguards were supposed to reduce the amount of mud splattering the windshields of other drivers and preventing them from seeing. Both cases revolved around the public safety purpose of the statutes.

The Balancing Test.   A statute is not entitled to constitutional protection just because it deals with public health, safety, or welfare. Although the courts try to protect the police power, that protection is not automatic. The police power is upheld only so long as the benefit achieved by the statute does not outweigh the burden imposed on interstate commerce. Each case is decided on its own facts. States present evidence of the safety benefits involved, and the interstate commerce interests present evidence of the costs to and effects on interstate commerce. The question courts must answer in these constitutional cases is whether the state interest in public health, welfare, or safety outweighs the federal interest in preventing interstate commerce from being unduly burdened. In performing this balancing test, the courts of course examine the safety, welfare, and health issues. However, the courts also examine other factors, such as whether the regulation or law provides an unfair advantage to intrastate or local businesses. For example, a prohibition on importing citrus fruits into Florida would give in-state growers an undue advantage.

Courts also examine the degree of the effect on interstate commerce. State statutes limiting the length of commercial vehicles would require commercial truck lines to buy different trucks for certain routes, or in some cases to stop at a state's border to remove one of the double trailers being pulled. Such stops can have a substantial effect on interstate travel. On the other hand, a state law that requires travelers to stop at the border for a fruit and plant check is not as burdensome: Only a stop is required, and the traveler would not be required to make any further adjustments. Also, the state's health interest is great; most fruit and plant checks are done to keep harmful insects from entering the state and destroying its crops. In the *Bibb* case, the courts found that the evidence of increased safety was not persuasive enough to outweigh the burden on interstate commerce.

Another question courts answer in their analysis is whether the state could accomplish its health, welfare, or safety goal in any other way with less of a burden on interstate commerce. Suppose a state has a health concern about having milk properly processed. One way to cover the concern is to require all milk to be processed in state. Such a regulation clearly favors that state's businesses and imposes a great burden on out-of-state milk producers. The same result, however, could be produced by requiring all milk sellers to be licensed. The licensing procedure would allow the state to check the milk-processing procedures of all firms and accomplish the goal without imposing such a burden on out-of-state firms. In the *Granholm v Heald* case (Case 5.2), the court dealt with states' regulation of imported wines versus its differing regulation of their domestic wine producers.

CASE 5.2

Granholm v Heald
544 U.S. 460 (2005)

Whining About Wine

FACTS

The regulations and statutory frameworks in both New York and Michigan prohibit out-of-state wine producers from selling their wines directly to consumers there. In-state wineries can sell directly to consumers. Out-of-state wine producers are required to pay wholesaler fees and cannot compete with in-state wine producers on direct-to-consumer sales. The direct-to-consumer sales avenue, especially through the Internet, has been a means for small wineries to compete.

Several out-of-state wine producers as well as consumers in both Michigan and New York filed suit in their federal districts challenging these laws that prohibit direct shipment. The Sixth Circuit Court of Appeals held that the out-of-state restrictions violated the Commerce Clause. The state of Michigan appealed. In the New York case, the Second Circuit Court of Appeals upheld the New York statute as constitutional. Michigan and the wine producers from the New York case appealed.

JUDICIAL OPINION

KENNEDY, Justice
Under Michigan law, wine producers, as a general matter, must distribute their wine through wholesalers. There is, however, an exception for Michigan's approximately 40 in-state wineries, which are eligible for "wine maker" licenses that allow direct shipment to in-state consumers.

CONTINUED

New York's licensing scheme is somewhat different. It channels most wine sales through the three-tier system, but it too makes exceptions for in-state wineries. As in Michigan, the result is to allow local wineries to make direct sales to consumers in New York on terms not available to out-of-state wineries. Wineries that produce wine only from New York grapes can apply for a license that allows direct shipment to in-state consumers. These licensees are authorized to deliver the wines of other wineries as well, but only if the wine is made from grapes "at least seventy-five percent the volume of which were grown in New York state." An out-of-state winery may ship directly to New York consumers only if it becomes a licensed New York winery, which requires the establishment of "a branch factory, office or storeroom within the state of New York."

We consolidated these cases and granted certiorari on the following question: "Does a State's regulatory scheme that permits in-state wineries directly to ship alcohol to consumers but restricts the ability of out-of-state wineries to do so violate the . . . Commerce Clause . . . ?"

State laws violate the Commerce Clause if they mandate "differential treatment of in-state and out-of-state economic interests that benefits the former and burdens the latter." This rule is essential to the foundations of the Union. The mere fact of nonresidence should not foreclose a producer in one State from access to markets in other States. States may not enact laws that burden out-of-state producers or shippers simply to give a competitive advantage to in-state businesses. This mandate "reflect[s] a central concern of the Framers that was an immediate reason for calling the Constitutional Convention: the conviction that in order to succeed, the new Union would have to avoid the tendencies toward economic Balkanization that had plagued relations among the Colonies and later among the States under the Articles of Confederation."

Laws of the type at issue in the instant cases contradict these principles. They deprive citizens of their right to have access to the markets of other States on equal terms. The perceived necessity for reciprocal sale privileges risks generating the trade rivalries and animosities, the alliances and exclusivity, that the Constitution and, in particular, the Commerce Clause were designed to avoid. The current patchwork of laws—with some States banning direct shipments altogether, others doing so only for out-of-state wines, and still others requiring reciprocity—is essentially the product of an ongoing, low-level trade war. Allowing States to discriminate against out-of-state wine "invite[s] a multiplication of preferential trade areas destructive of the very purpose of the Commerce Clause."

The discriminatory character of the Michigan system is obvious. Michigan allows in-state wineries to ship directly to consumers, subject only to a licensing requirement. Out-of-state wineries, whether licensed or not, face a complete ban on direct shipment. The differential treatment requires all out-of-state wine, but not all in-state wine, to pass through an in-state wholesaler and retailer before reaching consumers. These two extra layers of overhead increase the cost of out-of-state wines to Michigan consumers. The cost differential, and in some cases the inability to secure a wholesaler for small shipments, can effectively bar small wineries from the Michigan market.

The New York regulatory scheme differs from Michigan's in that it does not ban direct shipments altogether. Out-of-state wineries are instead required to establish a distribution operation in New York in order to gain the privilege of direct shipment. This, though, is just an indirect way of subjecting out-of-state wineries, but not local ones, to the three-tier system.

It comes as no surprise that not a single out-of-state winery has availed itself of New York's direct-shipping privilege. We have no difficulty concluding that New York, like Michigan, discriminates against interstate commerce through its direct-shipping laws.

Affirmed as to judgment of the Sixth Circuit Court of Appeals; reversed and remanded as to judgment of the Second Circuit Court of Appeals.

Note: Strong dissent in the case indicated that because of the Twenty-First Amendment the federal government (and the court) could not be involved in state liquor regulation.

CASE QUESTIONS

1. What do the Michigan and New York statutes require?

2. Why did the U.S. Supreme Court grant *certiorari* in the cases? Why do you think the court heard and decided the two cases together?

3. What is the economic impact of the statutes on wineries, both in- and out-of-state? On wholesalers? On consumers?

Congressional Regulation of Foreign Commerce

The Commerce Clause also grants Congress the power to regulate foreign commerce. The case of *Gibbons v Ogden*, 9 Wheat. 1 (1824), defined foreign commerce as any "commercial intercourse between the United States and foreign nations." This power to regulate applies regardless of where the activity originates and where it ends. For example, many international trade transactions begin and end in the city of New York. Although the paperwork and delivery of the goods may be solely within one state (here within one city), the foreign commerce power is not restricted by intrastate standards. If the transaction involves foreign commerce, congressional regulation can apply regardless of the place of transaction.

Constitutional Standards for Taxation of Business

Article I, Section 8, Paragraph 1 of the Constitution gives Congress its powers of taxation: "The Congress shall have Power To lay and collect Taxes, Duties, Imposts and Excises. . . . " In addition, the Sixteenth Amendment to the Constitution gives this power: "The Congress shall have power to lay and collect taxes on incomes, from whatever source derived, without apportionment among the several States, and without regard to any census or enumeration."

It has been said that taxes are the price we pay for a civilized society. The U.S. Supreme Court has consistently upheld the authority of Congress, and local governments as well, to impose taxes. However, one area in taxation still results in considerable litigation. This area involves state and local taxation of interstate commerce. Interstate businesses are not generally exempt from state and local taxes just because they are interstate businesses. However, the taxes imposed on these businesses must meet certain standards

First, the tax cannot discriminate against interstate commerce. A tax on milk could not be higher for milk that is shipped in from out of state than for milk produced within the state.

Second, the tax cannot unduly burden interstate commerce. For example, a tax on interstate transportation companies that is based on the weight of their trucks as measured upon entering and leaving the states would be a burdensome tax.

Third, some connection—"a sufficient **nexus**"—between the state and the business being taxed must be established. The business must have some activity in the state, such as offices, sales representatives, catalog purchasers, or distribution systems.

Finally, the tax must be apportioned fairly. This standard seeks to avoid having businesses taxed in all 50 states for their property. It also seeks to avoid having businesses pay state income tax on all their income in all 50 states. Their income and property taxes must be apportioned according to the amount of business revenues in each state and the amount of property located in that state. General Motors does not pay an inventory tax to all 50 states on all of its inventory, but it does pay an inventory tax on the inventory it holds in each state. Perhaps the most significant decision on state taxation in recent years is the U.S. Supreme Court case on catalog sales, *Quill Corporation v North Dakota,* summarized in Case 5.3.

BUSINESS PLANNING TIP

Know state taxation laws before you decide where to locate a plant, office, or warehouse. For example, Nevada does not have an inventory tax, so many manufacturers have large warehouse facilities there, including Spiegel and Levi Strauss. Other states have no sales tax but have high property tax rates. Still other states have high sales tax and low income tax rates. Structuring a nationwide business requires an understanding of intrastate as well as interstate taxes.

CASE 5.3

Quill Corporation v North Dakota
504 U.S. 298 (1992)

Is North Dakota a Taxing State?

FACTS

Quill is a Delaware corporation with offices and ware-houses in Illinois, California, and Georgia. None of its employees works or lives in North Dakota, and it owns no property in North Dakota.

Quill sells office equipment and supplies; it solicits business through catalogs and flyers, advertisements in national periodicals, and telephone calls. Its annual national sales exceed $200 million, of which almost $1 million are made to about 3,000 customers in North Dakota. The sixth largest vendor of office supplies in the state, it delivers all of its merchandise to its North Dakota customers by mail or common carriers from out-of-state locations.

As a corollary to its sales tax, North Dakota imposes a use tax upon property purchased for storage, use, or consumption within the state. North Dakota requires every "retailer maintaining a place of business in" the state to collect the tax from the consumer and remit it to the state. In 1987, North Dakota amended its statu-tory definition of the term "retailer" to include "every person who engages in regular or systematic solicitation of a consumer market in th[e] state." State regulations in turn define "regular or systematic solicitation" to mean three or more advertisements within a 12-month period. Thus, since 1987, mail-order companies that engage in such solicitation have been subject to the tax even if they maintain no property or personnel in North Dakota.

Quill has taken the position that North Dakota does not have the power to compel it to collect a use tax from its North Dakota customers. Consequently, the state, through its tax commissioner, filed an action to require Quill to pay taxes (as well as interest and penalties) on all such sales made after July 1, 1987. The trial court ruled in Quill's favor on a motion for summary judg-ment. The North Dakota Supreme Court reversed, and Quill appealed.

JUDICIAL OPINION

STEVENS, Justice

This case, like *National Bellas Hess, Inc. v Department of Revenue of Ill.*, 386 U.S. 753, 87 S.Ct. 1389, 18 L.Ed.2d 505 (1967), involves a State's attempt to require an out-of-state mail-order house that has neither outlets nor sales representatives in the State to collect and pay a use tax on goods purchased for use within the State. In *Bellas Hess* we held that a similar Illinois statute violated the Due Process Clause of the Fourteenth Amendment and created an unconstitutional burden on interstate com-merce. In particular, we ruled that a "seller whose only connection with customers in the State is by common carrier or the United States mail" lacked the requisite minimum contacts with the State.

In this case the Supreme Court of North Dakota declined to follow *Bellas Hess* because "the tremendous social, economic, commercial, and legal innovations" of the past quarter-century have rendered its holding "obsole[te]."

The Due Process Clause "requires some definite link, some minimum connection, between a state and the person, property or transaction it seeks to tax," and that the "income attributed to the State for tax purposes must be rationally related to 'values connected with the taxing State.'" Prior to *Bellas Hess*, we had held that that require-ment was satisfied in a variety of circumstances involv-ing use taxes. For example, the presence of sales person-nel in the State, or the maintenance of local retail stores in the State, justified the exercise of that power because the seller's local activities were "plainly accorded the protection and services of the taxing State." We expressly declined to obliterate the "sharp distinction . . . between mail order sellers with retail outlets, solicitors, or prop-erty within a State, and those who do no more than com-municate with customers in the State by mail or common carrier as a part of a general interstate business."

Our due process jurisprudence has evolved sub-stantially in the 25 years since *Bellas Hess*, particularly in the area of judicial jurisdiction. Building on the seminal case of *International Shoe Co. v Washington*, 326 U.S. 310, 66 S.Ct. 154, 90 L.Ed. 95 (1945), we have framed the relevant inquiry as whether a defendant had minimum contacts with the jurisdiction "such that the mainte-nance of the suit does not offend 'traditional notions of fair play and substantial justice.'"

Applying these principles, we have held that if a foreign corporation purposefully avails itself of the ben-efits of an economic market in the forum State, it may subject itself to the State's *in personam* jurisdiction even if it has no physical presence in the State.

Comparable reasoning justifies the imposition of the collection duty on a mail-order house that is engaged in continuous and widespread solicitation of business within a State. In "modern commercial life" it matters little that such solicitation is accomplished by a deluge of catalogs rather than a phalanx of drummers: the requirements of due process are met irrespective of a corporation's lack of physical presence in the taxing State. Thus, to the extent that our decisions have indicated that the Due Process Clause requires physical presence in a State for the imposition of duty to collect a use tax, we overrule those holdings as superseded by developments in the law of due process.

In this case, there is no question that Quill has purposefully directed its activities at North Dakota residents. We therefore agree with the North Dakota Supreme Court's conclusion that the Due Process Clause does not bar enforcement of that State's use tax against Quill.

Affirmed.

Justice WHITE, concurring in part and dissenting in part.

[o]ur holding in *Bellas Hess* relied on both the Due Process Clause and the Commerce Clause. Although the "two claims are closely related," the Clauses pose distinct limits on the taxing powers of the States. Accordingly, while a State may, consistent with the Due Process Clause, have the authority to tax a particular taxpayer, imposition of the tax may nonetheless violate the Commerce Clause.

. . . [a]lthough in our cases subsequent to *Bellas Hess* and concerning other types of taxes we have not adopted a similar bright-line, physical-presence requirement, our reasoning in those cases does not compel that we now reject the rule that *Bellas Hess* established in the area of sales and use taxes. To the contrary, the continuing value of a bright-line rule in this area and the doctrine and principles of *stare decisis* indicate that the *Bellas Hess* rule remains good law. For these reasons, we disagree with the North Dakota Supreme Court's conclusion that the time has come to renounce the bright-line test of *Bellas Hess*. No matter how we evaluate the burdens that use taxes impose on interstate commerce, Congress remains free to disagree with our conclusions.

Reversed.

CASE QUESTIONS

1. Did Quill Corporation own any property in North Dakota? Were any Quill offices or personnel located in North Dakota?

2. How did Quill come to have customers in North Dakota?

3. Will Quill be subject to North Dakota's use tax? Why or why not? What relationship does the Court see between the Due Process and Commerce Clauses?

CONSIDER... 5.2

JCPenney, a retail merchandiser, has its principal place of business in Plano, Texas. It operates retail stores in all 50 states, including 10 stores in Massachusetts, and a direct-mail catalog business.

Each year Penney issued three major seasonal catalogs, as well as various small sale or specialty catalogs, that described and illustrated merchandise available for purchase by mail order. The planning, artwork, design, and layout for these catalogs were completed and paid for outside of Massachusetts, primarily in Texas, and Penney contracted with independent printing companies located outside Massachusetts to produce the catalogs. The three major catalogs were generally printed in Indiana, while the specialty catalogs were printed in South Carolina and Wisconsin. None of the materials used in printing the catalogs was purchased in Massachusetts.

The catalogs advertised a broader range of merchandise than was available for purchase in Penney's retail stores. Purchases of catalog merchandise were made by telephoning or returning an order form to Penney at a location outside Massachusetts, and the merchandise was shipped to customers from a Connecticut distribution center.

The Massachusetts Department of Revenue audited JCPenney in 1995 and assessed a use tax, penalty, and interest on the catalogs that had been shipped into Massachusetts. The use tax is imposed in those circumstances "in which tangible personal property is sold inside or outside the Commonwealth for storage, use, or other consumption within the Commonwealth." The Department charged JCPenney a tax of $314,674.62 on the catalogs used by Penney's Massachusetts customers. JCPenney said such a tax was unconstitutional in that it had no control or contact with the catalogs in the state. Can the state impose the tax? [*Commissioner of Revenue v J.C. Penney Co., Inc.*, 730 N.E.2d 266 (Mass. 2001)]

State versus Federal Regulation of Business—Constitutional Conflicts: Preemption and the Supremacy Clause

Although the Constitution has sections that deal with the authority of the federal government and some that deal with state and local governments, some crossovers in between state and federal laws still occur. For example, both state and federal governments regulate the sale of securities and both have laws on the sale of real property. Such crossovers create conflicts and a constitutional issue of who has the power to regulate. These conflicts between state and federal laws are governed by Article VI of the Constitution, sometimes called the **Supremacy Clause,** which provides: "This Constitution, and the Laws of the United States which shall be made in Pursuance thereof; and all Treaties made, or which shall be made, under the Authority of the United States, shall be the supreme Law of the Land. . . . "

The Supremacy Clause provides that when state and local laws conflict with federal statutes, regulations, executive orders, or treaties, the federal statute, regulation, executive order, or treaty controls the state or local law. However, in a variety of cases, a state law does not directly conflict with the federal law. Sometimes, the federal government just has extensive regulations in a particular area. In those areas of extensive federal regulation, the issue of which laws control can be resolved in Congress, which specifies its intent in an act. For example, Congress has provided that many federal workplace safety laws can be circumvented by state law as long as the state law provides as much employee protection as the federal laws. In other words, Congress allows the states to regulate the field in some instances and sets the standards for doing so. Most statutes, however, do not

BUSINESS STRATEGY

The Taxing Business of the Internet

The so-called bricks-and-mortar retailers such as Federated Department Stores and Macy's supported state officials' drive to collect taxes on online sales because they already do so on their online sales and would like to level the playing field with their online competitors. Required to collect the taxes because their store facilities are in all states, chains such as JCPenney complain that the processes and formulas for collection are complex and increase their costs of doing business. Retailers such as Target, Wal-Mart, and Circuit City, part of the e-Fairness Coalition, argue that with their thin margins, giving e-retailers a pass on the 6–8 percent sales taxes is the difference between success and demise on the Internet.

The online retailers see such taxes as a cost increase. The states see the lost sales tax revenue. In fact, Wal-Mart and Office Depot settled their Michigan state tax audits by agreeing to pay $2.4 million in sales tax. A study from the University of Tennessee puts the lost sales tax revenue for online sales for all the states at about $18 billion as of 2006. About one-third of the states have adopted a uniform system for taxing online sales as a result of efforts by a group of businesses and state officials working together (Architects of the Streamlined Sales Tax Project). Their group was formed with the recognition that the tax was inevitable and that they were best served by helping to shape its structure, reporting, and enforcement.

Sources: Norm Alster, "So Many Online Sales, So Little in Tax Revenue," *New York Times,* January 26, 2003, p. BU4; and Robert Guy Matthews, "Some States Push to Collect Sales Tax from Internet Stores," *Wall Street Journal,* September 30, 2005, pp. B1, B4.

include the congressional intent on **preemption.** Whether a field has been preempted is a question of fact, of interpretation, and of legislative history. The question of preemption is determined on a case-by-case basis using the following questions:

1. What does the legislative history indicate? Some hearings offer clear statements of the effect and scope of a federal law.

2. How detailed is the federal regulation of the area? The more regulation there is, the more likely a court is to find preemption. Volume itself indicates congressional intent.

3. What benefits exist from having federal regulation of the area? Some matters are more easily regulated by one central government. Airlines fly across state lines, and if each state had different standards there would be no guarantee of uniform standards. The regulation of aircraft and their routes is clearly better handled by the federal government.

4. How much does a state law conflict with federal law? Is there any way that the two laws can coexist?

Altria Group, Inc. v Good, (Case 5.4) deals with a preemption issue.

CASE 5.4

Altria Group, Inc. v Good
129 S.Ct. 538 (2008)

A Smokin' Ad Campaign

FACTS

A group of smokers (Respondents) brought suit against tobacco producer Altria, alleging that they were misled by the Altria and other cigarette producers' (Petitioners) ads and labels on its cigarettes touting "light" and "low-tar." By covering filter ventilation holes with their lips or fingers, taking larger or more frequent puffs, and holding the smoke in their lungs for a longer period of time, smokers of "light" cigarettes unknowingly inhale as much tar and nicotine as do smokers of regular cigarettes. "Light" cigarettes are in fact more harmful because the increased ventilation that results from their unique design features produces smoke that is more mutagenic per milligram of tar than the smoke of regular cigarettes. The smokers argued that the tobacco companies violated the Maine Unfair Trade Practices Act (MUTPA) by fraudulently concealing that information and by affirmatively representing, through the use of "light" and "lowered tar and nicotine" descriptors, that their cigarettes would pose fewer health risks.

The District Court entered summary judgment in favor of the tobacco companies on the ground that the' state-law claim is pre-empted by the Federal Cigarette

Labeling and Advertising Act. The Court of Appeals reversed that judgment, and the U.S. Supreme Court granted certiorari to review its holding that the Labeling Act neither expressly nor impliedly pre-empts state law.

JUDICIAL OPINION

STEVENS, Justice

Congress enacted the Labeling Act in 1965 in response to the Surgeon General's determination that cigarette smoking is harmful to health. The Act required that every package of cigarettes sold in the United States contain a conspicuous warning, and it pre-empted state laws that added to the federally prescribed warning. Congress amended the Labeling Act a few years later by enacting the Public Health Cigarette Smoking Act of 1969. The amendments strengthened the language of the prescribed warning, and prohibited cigarette advertising in "any medium of electronic communication subject to [FCC] jurisdiction." They also broadened the Labeling Act's pre-emption provision. The Labeling Act has since been amended further to require cigarette manufacturers to include four more explicit warnings in their packaging and advertisements on a rotating basis.

CONTINUED

Together, the labeling requirement and preemption provisions express Congress' determination that the prescribed federal warnings are both necessary and sufficient to achieve its purpose of informing the public of the health consequences of smoking. Because Congress has decided that no additional warning statement is needed to attain that goal, States may not impede commerce in cigarettes by enforcing rules that are based on an assumption that the federal warnings are inadequate. Although both of the Act's purposes are furthered by prohibiting States from supplementing the federally prescribed warning, neither would be served by limiting the States' authority to prohibit deceptive statements in cigarette advertising.

In 1966, following the publication of the Surgeon General's report on smoking and health, the FTC issued an industry guidance stating its view that "a factual statement of the tar and nicotine content (expressed in milligrams) of the mainstream smoke from a cigarette," as measured by Cambridge Filter Method testing, would not violate the FTC. The Commission made clear, however, that the guidance applied only to factual assertions of tar and nicotine yields and did not invite "collateral representations . . . made, expressly or by implication, as to reduction or elimination of health hazards." In 1970, the FTC considered providing further guidance, proposing a rule that would have required manufacturers to disclose tar and nicotine yields as measured by Cambridge Filter Method testing. The leading cigarette manufacturers responded by submitting a voluntary agreement under which they would disclose tar and nicotine content in their advertising.

. . . [t]he FTC has in fact never required that cigarette manufacturers disclose tar and nicotine yields, nor has it condoned representations of those yields through the use of "light" or "low tar" descriptors.

This history shows that, contrary to petitioners' suggestion, the FTC has no longstanding policy authorizing collateral representations based on Cambridge Filter Method test results. Rather, the FTC has endeavored to inform consumers of the comparative tar and nicotine content of different cigarette brands and has in some instances prevented misleading representations of Cambridge Filter Method test results. The FTC's failure to require petitioners to correct their allegedly misleading use of "light" descriptors is not evidence to the contrary; agency nonenforcement of a federal statute is not the same as a policy of approval.

We conclude that the Labeling Act does not preempt state-law claims like respondents' that are predicated on the duty not to deceive. We also hold that the FTC's various decisions with respect to statements of tar and nicotine content do not impliedly pre-empt respondents' claim. Respondents still must prove that petitioners' use of "light" and "lowered tar" descriptors in fact violated the state deceptive practices statute, but neither the Labeling Act's pre-emption provision nor the FTC's actions in this field prevent a jury from considering that claim. Accordingly, the judgment of the Court of Appeals is affirmed, and the case is remanded for further proceedings consistent with this opinion.

Justice THOMAS, with whom THE CHIEF JUSTICE, Justice SCALIA, and Justice ALITO join, dissenting.

Respondents' lawsuit under the Maine Unfair Trade Practices Act (MUTPA), is expressly pre-empted under § 5(b) of the Labeling Act. The civil action is premised on the allegation that the cigarette manufacturers misled respondents into believing that smoking light cigarettes would be healthier for them than smoking regular cigarettes. A judgment in respondents' favor will thus result in a "requirement" that petitioners represent the effects of smoking on health in a particular way in their advertising and promotion of light cigarettes. Because liability in this case is thereby premised on the effect of smoking on health, I would hold that respondents' state-law claims are expressly pre-empted by § 5(b) of the Labeling Act. I respectfully dissent.

CASE QUESTIONS

1. What are the differences between the Maine law and the federal law and regulations?

2. What problems do you see for cigarette manufacturers if they are held liable under state labeling law?

3. What are the dissent's concerns about the decision to allow the state suit to go forward?

Ethical Issues

Evaluate the ethics of the low-tar or "light" cigarettes. Why do you think the low-tar or "light" cigarettes were developed? What does the Maine law do to address the ethical issues?

Application of the Bill of Rights to Business

Certain of the amendments to the U.S. Constitution have particular significance for business, especially the First Amendment on freedom of speech and the Fourteenth Amendment for its issues of substantive and procedural due process and equal protection. The Fourth, Fifth, and Sixth Amendments on criminal procedures also have significance for business; those issues are covered in Chapter 8.

Commercial Speech and the First Amendment

The area of First Amendment rights and freedom of speech is complicated and full of significant cases. The discussion here is limited to First Amendment rights as they apply to businesses. The speech of business is referred to as **commercial speech**, which is communication used to further the economic interests of the speaker. Advertising is clearly a form of commercial speech.

First Amendment Protection for Advertising

Until the early 1970s, the U.S. Supreme Court held that commercial speech was different from the traditional speech afforded protection under the First Amendment. The result was that government regulation of commercial speech was virtually unlimited. The Court's position was refined in the 1970s, however, to a view that commercial speech was entitled to First Amendment protection but not on the same level as noncommercial speech. Commercial speech was not an absolute freedom; rather, the benefits of commercial speech were to be weighed against the benefits achieved by government regulation of that speech. Several factors are examined in performing this balancing test.

1. Is a substantial government interest furthered by restricting the commercial speech?

2. Does the restriction directly accomplish the government interest?

3. Is there any other way to accomplish the government interest? Can it be accomplished without regulating commercial speech? Are the restrictions no more extensive than necessary to serve that interest?

These standards clearly provide authority for regulation of fraudulent advertising and advertising that violates the law. For example, if credit terms are advertised, Regulation Z requires full disclosure of all terms (see Chapter 14 for more details). This regulation is acceptable under the standards just listed. Further, restrictions on where and when advertisements are made are permissible. For example, cigarette ads are not permitted on television, and such a restriction is valid.

Exhibit 5.1 illustrates the degrees of protection afforded business speech. The overlapping area represents those cases in which the need to disseminate information conflicts with regulations on ad content or form.

The 1970s brought in the overlapping area of the diagram with cases that reformed the commercial speech doctrine by limiting restrictions on professional advertising. In *Virginia State Board of Pharmacy v Virginia Citizens Consumer Council, Inc.*, 425 U.S. 748 (1976), the Supreme Court dealt with the issue of the validity of a Virginia statute that made it a matter of "unprofessional conduct" for a pharmacist to advertise the price or any discount of prescription drugs. In holding the statute

EXHIBIT 5.1 Commercial Speech: First Amendment Protections and Restrictions

First
Amendment

Full Protection
of Commercial
Speech

Political
Speech by
Business

Speech on
Social Issues
and Business
Operations:
Nike;
Professions

Government
Regulation
of
Commercial
Speech

Business
Advertising

unconstitutional, the Court emphasized the need for the dissemination of information to the public. In a subsequent case, the Court applied the same reasoning to advertising by lawyers [*Bates v State Bar of Arizona*, 433 U.S. 350 (1977)].

An evolving area that is part of the overlapping portion of the two circles is that of corporate speech in defense of corporate decisions and policies—speech by corporations that is neither political speech nor advertising, but rather explains and defends corporate policies such as animal testing, outsourcing production to other countries, and environmental policies. The issues the companies are discussing have social and political implications, but they relate directly to the corporation's business and/or operations. Can the government regulate this form of speech? *Nike, Inc. v Kasky* (Case 5.5) addresses such speech and provides the answers to the chapter's opening "Consider."

CASE 5.5 *Nike, Inc. v Kasky*
539 U.S. 654 (2003)

The Shoe and Mouth *Writ of Certiorari*

FACTS

Beginning in 1996, Nike was besieged with a series of allegations that it was mistreating and underpaying workers at foreign facilities. Nike responded to these charges in numerous ways, such as by sending out press releases, writing letters to the editors of various newspapers around the country, and mailing letters to university presidents and athletic directors. In addition, in 1997, Nike commissioned a report by former Ambassador to the United Nations Andrew Young on the labor conditions at Nike production facilities. After visiting 12 factories, "Young issued a report that commented favorably on working conditions in the factories and found no evidence of widespread abuse or mistreatment of workers."

In April 1998, Marc Kasky (respondent) a California resident, sued Nike for unfair and deceptive practices under California's Unfair Competition Law, Cal. Bus. & Prof. Code Ann. § 17200 et seq. (West 1997), and False Advertising Law, § 17500 *et seq.* Mr. Kasky said Nike's statements in its materials and op-ed contained false information.

Nike contended that Mr. Kasky's suit was absolutely barred by the First Amendment. The trial court dismissed the case. Mr. Kasky appealed, and the California Court of Appeal affirmed, holding that Nike's statements "form[ed] part of a public dialogue on a matter of public concern within the core area of expression protected by the First Amendment."

On appeal, the California Supreme Court reversed and remanded for further proceedings. Nike appealed. The Supreme Court granted *certiorari* but later dismissed the case with a ***per curiam*** opinion (an unsigned opinion that comes from the majority of the court) that indicated only that *certiorari* was granted improvidently.

JUDICIAL OPINION

PER CURIAM

The writ of *certiorari* is dismissed as improvidently granted.

Justice STEVENS, with whom Justice GINSBURG joins, and with whom Justice SOUTER joins

We granted *certiorari* to decide two questions: (1) whether a corporation participating in a public debate may "be subjected to liability for factual inaccuracies on the theory that its statements are 'commercial speech' because they might affect consumers' opinions about the business as a good corporate citizen and thereby affect their purchasing decisions"; and (2) even assuming the California Supreme Court properly characterized such statements as commercial speech, whether the "First Amendment, as applied to the states through the Fourteenth Amendment, permit[s] subjecting speakers to the legal regime approved by that court in the decision below." Today, however, the Court dismisses the writ of *certiorari* as improvidently granted.

In my judgment, the Court's decision to dismiss the writ of *certiorari* is supported by three independently sufficient reasons: (1) the judgment entered by the California Supreme Court was not final within the meaning of 28 U.S.C. § 1257; (2) neither party has standing to invoke the jurisdiction of a federal court; and (3) the reasons for avoiding the premature adjudication of novel constitutional questions apply with special force to this case.

Nike argues that this case fits within the . . . category of such cases . . . in which "the federal issue has been finally decided in the state courts with further proceedings pending in which the party seeking review" might prevail on nonfederal grounds, "reversal of the state court on the federal issue would be preclusive of any further litigation on the relevant cause of action," and "refusal immediately to review the state-court decision might seriously erode federal policy."

In Nike's view, this case fits within the category because if this Court holds that Nike's speech was noncommercial, then "reversal of the state court on the federal issue would be preclusive of any further litigation on the relevant cause of action." Notably, Nike's

argument assumes that all of the speech at issue in this case is either commercial or noncommercial and that the speech therefore can be neatly classified as either absolutely privileged or not.

Theoretically, Nike is correct that we could hold that all of Nike's allegedly false statements are absolutely privileged even if made with the sort of "malice" defined in *New York Times Co. v Sullivan*, 376 U.S. 254, 84 S.Ct. 710, 11 L.Ed.2d 686 (1964), thereby precluding any further proceedings or amendments that might overcome Nike's First Amendment defense. However, the Court could also take a number of other paths that would neither preclude further proceedings in the state courts, nor finally resolve the First Amendment questions in this case. For example, if we were to affirm, Nike would almost certainly continue to maintain that some, if not all, of its challenged statements were protected by the First Amendment and that the First Amendment constrains the remedy that may be imposed. Or, if we were to reverse, we might hold that the speech at issue in this case is subject to suit only if made with actual malice, thereby inviting respondent to amend his complaint to allege such malice. Or we might conclude that some of Nike's speech is commercial and some is noncommercial, thereby requiring further proceedings in the state courts over the legal standards that govern the commercial speech, including whether actual malice must be proved.

In short, because an opinion on the merits in this case could take any one of a number of different paths, it is not clear whether reversal of the California Supreme Court would "be preclusive of any further litigation on the relevant cause of action [in] the state proceedings still to come." Nor is it clear that reaching the merits of Nike's claims now would serve the goal of judicial efficiency. For, even if we were to decide the First Amendment issues presented to us today, more First Amendment issues might well remain in this case, making piecemeal review of the Federal First Amendment issues likely.

[T]he Court will not anticipate a question of constitutional law in advance of the necessity of deciding it. The novelty and importance of the constitutional questions presented in this case provide good reason for adhering to that rule.

This case presents novel First Amendment questions because the speech at issue represents a blending of commercial speech, noncommercial speech and debate on an issue of public importance. On the one hand, if the allegations of the complaint are true, direct communications with customers and potential customers that were intended to generate sales—and possibly to maintain or enhance the market value of Nike's stock—contained significant factual misstatements. The

CONTINUED

regulatory interest in protecting market participants from being misled by such misstatements is of the highest order. That is why we have broadly (perhaps overbroadly) stated that "there is no constitutional value in false statements of fact." On the other hand, the communications were part of an ongoing discussion and debate about important public issues that was concerned not only with Nike's labor practices, but with similar practices used by other multinational corporations. Knowledgeable persons should be free to participate in such debate without fear of unfair reprisal. The interest in protecting such participants from the chilling effect of the prospect of expensive litigation is therefore also a matter of great importance. That is why we have provided such broad protection for misstatements about public figures that are not animated by malice. See *New York Times Co. v Sullivan*, 376 U.S. 254, 84 S.Ct. 710, 11 L.Ed.2d 686 (1964).

Whether similar protection should extend to cover corporate misstatements made about the corporation itself, or whether we should presume that such a corporate speaker knows where the truth lies, are questions that may have to be decided in this litigation. The correct answer to such questions, however, is more likely to result from the study of a full factual record than from a review of mere unproven allegations in a pleading. Indeed, the development of such a record may actually contribute in a positive way to the public debate. In all events, I am firmly convinced that the Court has wisely decided not to address the constitutional questions presented by the *certiorari* petition at this stage of the litigation.

Accordingly, I concur in the decision to dismiss the writ as improvidently granted.

DISSENTING OPINION

Justice BREYER, with whom Justice O'CONNOR joins, dissenting

The communications at issue are not purely commercial in nature. They are better characterized as involving a mixture of commercial and noncommercial (public-issue-oriented) elements. The document least likely to warrant protection—a letter written by Nike to university presidents and athletic directors—has several commercial characteristics. As the California Supreme Court implicitly found, it was written by a "commercial speaker" (Nike), it is addressed to a "commercial audience" (potential institutional buyers or contractees), and it makes "representations of fact about the speaker's own business operations" (labor conditions).

But that letter also has other critically important and, I believe, predominant noncommercial characteristics with which the commercial characteristics are "inextricably intertwined." For one thing, the letter appears outside a traditional advertising format, such as a brief television or newspaper advertisement. It does not propose the presentation or sale of a product or any other commercial transaction. Rather, the letter suggests that its contents might provide "information useful in discussions" with concerned faculty and students.

For another thing, the letter's content makes clear that, in context, it concerns a matter that is of significant public interest and active controversy, and it describes factual matters related to that subject in detail. In particular, the letter describes Nike's labor practices and responds to criticism of those practices, and it does so because those practices themselves play an important role in an existing public debate. This debate was one in which participants advocated, or opposed, public collective action. The First Amendment's protections of speech and press were "fashioned to assure unfettered interchange of ideas for the bringing about of political and social changes." That the letter is factual in content does not argue against First Amendment protection, for facts, sometimes facts alone, will sway our views on issues of public policy.

I do not deny that California's system of false advertising regulation—including its provision for private causes of action—furthers legitimate, traditional, and important public objectives.

If permitted to stand, the state court's decision may well "chill" the exercise of free speech rights. Continuation of this lawsuit itself means increased expense, and, if Nike loses, the results may include monetary liability (for "restitution") and injunctive relief (including possible corrective "counterspeech"). The range of communications subject to such liability is broad; in this case, it includes a letter to the editor of *The New York Times*. The upshot is that commercial speakers doing business in California may hesitate to issue significant communications relevant to public debate because they fear potential lawsuits and legal liability.

This concern is not purely theoretical. Nike says without contradiction that because of this lawsuit it has decided "to restrict severely all of its communications on social issues that could reach California consumers, including speech in national and international media." It adds that it has not released its annual Corporate Responsibility Report, has decided not to pursue a listing in the Dow Jones Sustainability Index, and has refused "dozens of invitations . . . to speak on corporate responsibility issues."

The position of at least one *amicus*—opposed to Nike on the merits of its labor practice claims but supporting Nike on its free speech claim—echoes a famous sentiment reflected in the writings of Voltaire: "I do not agree with what you say, but I will fight to the end so that you may say it."

I respectfully dissent from the Court's contrary determination.

CASE QUESTIONS

1. What speech of Nike's is targeted?
2. Who is objecting to Nike's speech and how is the objection being voiced?
3. Why does the Supreme Court refuse to decide the case after taking *certiorari?*

4. Why does the dissenting justice believe the court should decide the case?

AFTERMATH: Nike settled the case with terms undisclosed by any of the parties. The case cannot now reach the point of justiciability in order for the Supreme Court to hear it and make a determination on this form of corporate speech. Another case will be required.

First Amendment Rights and Profits from Sensationalism

In the past few years, a number of book publishers and movie producers have pursued criminal figures for the rights to tell the stories of their crimes in books, television programs, and movies. Many of the victims of the crimes and their families have opposed such moneymaking ventures as benefits that encourage the commission of crimes. The state of New York, for example, passed a statute requiring that earnings from sales of such stories be used first to compensate victims of the crimes. Statutes such as the one in New York create dilemmas between First Amendment rights and public policy issues concerning criminal activities. In *Simon & Schuster, Inc. v Members of the New York State Crime Victims Board,* 502 U.S. 105 (1991), the U.S. Supreme Court addressed the constitutionality of New York's statute. Simon & Schuster had entered into a contract in 1981 with organized crime figure Henry Hill (who was arrested in 1980) and author Nicholas Pileggi for a book about Mr. Hill's life, *Wiseguy,* a book full of colorful details and the day-to-day workings of organized crime, primarily in Mr. Hill's first-person narrative. Throughout *Wiseguy,* Mr. Hill frankly admits to having participated in an astonishing variety of crimes.

The book was also a commercial success: Within 19 months of its publication, more than 1 million copies were in print. A few years later, the book was converted into a film called *Goodfellas,* which won a host of awards as the best film of 1990.

When the Crime Victims Board requested that Simon & Schuster turn over all monies paid to Mr. Hill and that all future royalties be payable not to Mr. Hill but to the statutorily prescribed escrow account, Simon & Schuster brought suit maintaining that the so-called "Son of Sam law" violated the First Amendment. The U.S. Supreme Court agreed and held that the statute was overly broad, would have a chilling effect on authors and publications, and required a redrafting of the statute to tailor its scope more narrowly so it could still accomplish the public purpose.

First Amendment Rights and Corporate Political Speech

Not all commercial speech is advertising. Some businesses engage in **corporate political speech.** Corporate political speech takes form in three generalized ways:

1. Through financial support such as employee and PAC donations to political candidates
2. Through financial support such as party donations
3. Through direct communications and ads about issues, ballot propositions, and funding proposals (such as bond elections)

Ethical Issues

Orenthal James (O. J.) Simpson was charged with murder in June 1994 in the double homicide of his ex-wife, Nicole Brown Simpson, and her friend Ronald Goldman.

Because Mr. Simpson was charged with a capital crime, he was incarcerated upon being charged. California's version of the Son of Sam law prevents profits from crimes only after there has been a conviction. Mr. Simpson authored a book, *I Want to Tell You*, while he was incarcerated and his nine-month trial progressed. Mr. Simpson also signed autographs and sports memorabilia and sold them from the Los Angeles County jail. Mr. Simpson's cottage industry from jail netted him in excess of $3 million. Could a law that passes constitutional muster be implemented to prevent crime-related profits like those Mr. Simpson was able to obtain?

Mr. Simpson was acquitted of the murders. Following his acquittal, prosecutors in the case, Christopher Darden, Marcia Clark, and Hank Goldberg, signed multimillion-dollar book contracts to write about their experiences during the trial. Alan Dershowitz, the late Johnnie Cochran, and Robert Shapiro, members of the Simpson defense team, signed six-figure contracts to write books about the trial from the defense perspective. Daniel Petrocelli, the lawyer who represented the Goldmans in their civil suit against Mr. Simpson, also wrote a book, *Triumph of Justice: The Final Judgment on the Simpson Saga.*

In 2007, a book by Mr. Simpson, *If I Did It,* was released by the Goldman family. The Goldmans acquired the rights to the Simpson book because of their $33 million judgment against Mr. Simpson following the civil case for wrongful death. They were assigned the rights to the book's royalties as a means of collecting the judgment. Upon its release, the book soared to number 1 on Amazon.com even as Mr. Simpson was arrested in Las Vegas for his alleged role in a robbery of sports paraphernalia.

Is it moral to profit from a crime and a trial? Are these book contracts a form of making money from the deaths of two people? Many publishers refused to publish the *If I Did It* book, and networks refused to air interviews with Mr. Simpson about the book. Would you have declined the book for publication? The interview that would have brought in ad revenues?

For more than a century, both legislators and courts have grappled with the balancing of First Amendment rights and the influence of money in election campaigns. "More than a century ago the 'sober-minded Elihu Root' advocated legislation that would prohibit political contributions by corporations in order to prevent 'the great aggregations of wealth from using their corporate funds, directly or indirectly,' to elect legislators who would 'vote for their protection and the advancement of their interests as against those of the public.'" [*United States v Automobile Workers*, 352 U.S. 567, 571, 77 S.Ct. 529, 1 L.Ed. 2d 563 (1957).]

As a result, Congress, state legislatures, and the U.S. Supreme Court have all addressed corporate speech in all three of these categories. The first legislative prohibition came in 1907 when the Tillman Act completely banned corporate contributions of "money . . . in connection with" any federal election. Since that time corporations have been banned from making direct political donations to political candidates. In 1925 Congress extended the prohibition of contributions "to include 'anything of value,' and made acceptance of a corporate contribution as well as the giving of such a contribution a crime." (Federal Corrupt Practices Act, 1925, §§ 301, 313, 43 Stat. 1070, 1074.) With corporate donations in tow, Congress realized through several election cycles that union contributions were equally as plentiful and powerful as corporate ones. Congress first restricted union contributions in 1940 with the passage of the Hatch Act. Congress later prohibited "union contributions in connection with federal elections . . . altogether." (18 U.S.C. § 610.) During the passage of these limitations, political action committees (PACs) began. PACs are independent of corporations and labor unions, although they may be formed by those affiliated with both. For example, Coors Brewing has its corporate PAC, known as the Six Pac. Employees of companies and members of labor unions make donations to their PACs. Other PACs include trade association PACs (such as the American Medical Association and the American Association of Trial Lawyers), cooperative PACs, and PACs formed along ideological lines, such as the Right-to-Life PAC or Emily's List (Early Money Is Like Yeast, a PAC that supports pro-choice candidates from the early primary stages of an election cycle).

As the Supreme Court has noted in its opinions on the topic of donations, "Money is like water and it always finds an outlet," and the donations and PAC

BUSINESS STRATEGY

Where the Money Flows

A look at the following list of top corporate and trade PACs (hard dollars, not including soft dollars) indicates that those businesses whose markets or prices are controlled by the government are the most active political voices. Why do you think these particular PACs are so active?

Rank/Name (2008 Election)
Top 20 PAC Contributors to Candidates, 2007–2008

PAC NAME	TOTAL AMOUNT	DEM PCT	REPUB PCT
National Assn of Realtors	$4,020,900	58%	42%
Intl Brotherhood of Electrical Workers	$3,344,650	98%	2%
AT&T Inc.	$3,108,200	47%	52%
American Bankers Assn	$2,918,143	43%	57%
National Beer Wholesalers Assn	$2,869,000	53%	47%
National Auto Dealers Assn	$2,860,000	34%	66%
International Assn of Fire Fighters	$2,734,900	77%	22%
Operating Engineers Union	$2,704,067	87%	13%
American Assn for Justice	$2,700,500	95%	4%
Laborers Union	$2,555,350	92%	8%
Honeywell International	$2,515,616	52%	48%
National Assn of Home Builders	$2,480,000	46%	54%
Air Line Pilots Assn	$2,422,000	85%	15%
Credit Union National Assn	$2,362,899	54%	46%
Machinists/Aerospace Workers Union	$2,321,842	97%	3%
Plumbers/Pipefitters Union	$2,316,559	95%	5%
Service Employees International Union	$2,285,850	94%	6%
American Federation of Teachers	$2,283,250	99%	1%
Teamsters Union	$2,248,950	97%	3%
National Air Traffic Controllers Assn	$2,210,475	80%	20%

Sources: www.fec.gov.

activity became a concern. As a result, in 1972 and 1974, Congress passed and amended the Federal Election Campaign Act (FECA), which limited individual donations; required reporting and public disclosure of contributions and expenditures exceeding certain limits; and established the Federal Election Commission (FEC) to administer and enforce the legislation [2 U.S.C. § 431(8)(A)(i)].

The limitations in FECA were challenged and the U.S. Supreme Court ruled on their constitutionality in *Buckley v Valeo,* 424 U.S. 1 (1976). The court struck down the expenditure limitations of the federal law but upheld the $1,000 donation limitation as being sufficiently narrowly tailored to address the corruption concerns without infringing on the speech elements of donation. Individuals remained free to spend as much as they wanted on their own campaigns for federal office. FECA does not apply to state and local elections.

In *First National Bank of Boston v Bellotti,* 435 U.S. 765 (1978), the U.S. Supreme Court developed what has become known as the *Bellotti* doctrine, which gives corporations the same degree of First Amendment protection for their political speech that individuals enjoy in their political speech. Although commercial speech can be regulated, political speech enjoys full First Amendment rights. That is, when a corporation takes a position on a proposed ballot initiative, its right to participate in public discussion of that issue cannot be restricted.

Under FECA, contributions made with funds that are subject to the act's disclosure requirements and source and amount limitations are thus known as "federal dollars" or "hard dollars." Corporations and unions, as well as individuals who had already made the maximum permissible contributions to federal candidates, could still contribute "nonfederal money"—also known as "soft money"—to political parties for activities intended to influence state or local elections. The FEC ruled that political parties could fund mixed-purpose activities—including get-out-the-vote drives and generic party advertising—in part with soft money. In 1995, the FEC concluded that the parties could also use soft money to defray the costs of "legislative advocacy media advertisements," even if the ads mentioned the name of a federal candidate, as long as they did not expressly advocate the candidate's election or defeat.

The so-called soft money donations became extensive. In 2002, the political parties raised almost $300 million—60 percent of their total soft-money fundraising—from just 800 donors, each of which contributed a minimum of $120,000. As a result, Congress passed the Bipartisan Campaign Reform Act of 2002 (BCRA, 2 U.S.C.A. § 431 et seq.). Often referred to as the McCain–Feingold law, Title I of the BCRA regulates the use of soft money by political parties, officeholders, and candidates.

CASE 5.6　　*Citizens United v Federal Election Commission*
130 S.Ct. 876 (2010)

Hillary: It's a Movie! It's A Campaign! It's Free Speech!

FACTS

Citizens United is a nonprofit corporation with an annual budget of about $12 million, most of which comes from donations by individuals.

In January 2008, Citizens United released a film entitled *Hillary: The Movie.* It is a 90-minute documentary about then-Senator Hillary Clinton, who was a candidate in the Democratic Party's 2008 Presidential primary elections. *Hillary* mentions Senator Clinton by name and depicts interviews with political commentators and other persons, most of them quite critical of Senator Clinton. *Hillary* was released in theaters and on DVD, but Citizens United wanted to increase distribution by making it available through video-on-demand.

In December 2007, a cable company offered, for a payment of $1.2 million, to make *Hillary* available on a video-on-demand channel called "Elections '08." Citizens United was prepared to pay for the video-on-demand; and to promote the film, it produced two 10-second ads and one 30-second ad for *Hillary.* Each ad includes a short (and, in our view, pejorative) statement about Senator Clinton, followed by the name of the movie and the movie's Web site address. Citizens United desired to promote the video-on-demand offering by running advertisements on broadcast and cable television.

BCRA § 203(§441) prohibits any "electioneering communication." An electioneering communication is defined as "any broadcast, cable, or satellite communication" that "refers to a clearly identified candidate for Federal office" and is made within 30 days of a primary or 60 days of a general election. The Federal Election Commission's (FEC) regulations further define an electioneering communication as a communication that is "publicly distributed." "In the case of a candidate for nomination for President . . . *publicly distributed* means" that the communication "[c]an be received by 50,000 or more persons in a State where a primary election . . . is being held within 30 days." Corporations and unions are barred from using their general treasury funds for express advocacy or electioneering communications. They may establish, however, a "separate segregated fund" (known as a political action committee, or PAC) for these purposes. The moneys received by the segregated fund are limited to donations from stockholders and employees of the corporation or, in the case of unions, members of the union.

Citizens United wanted to make *Hillary* available through video-on-demand within 30 days of the 2008 primary elections. It feared, however, that both the film and the ads would be covered by § 441b's ban on corporate-funded independent expenditures, thus subjecting the corporation to civil and criminal penalties. In December 2007, Citizens United sought declaratory and injunctive relief against the FEC. It argued that (1) § 441b is unconstitutional as applied to *Hillary;* and (2) BCRA's disclaimer and disclosure requirements are unconstitutional as applied to *Hillary* and to the three ads for the movie.

The District Court denied Citizens United's motion for a preliminary injunction, *(per curiam),* and then granted the FEC's motion for summary judgment. The court held that § 441b was facially constitutional, and that § 441b was constitutional as applied to *Hillary* because it was "susceptible of no other interpretation than to inform the electorate that Senator Clinton is unfit for office, that the United States would be a dangerous place in a President Hillary Clinton world, and that viewers should vote against her." The court also rejected Citizens United's challenge to BCRA's disclaimer and disclosure requirements. It noted that "the Supreme Court has written approvingly of disclosure provisions triggered by political speech even though the speech itself was constitutionally protected under the First Amendment." Citizens United appealed to the U.S. Supreme Court, where the case was argued twice, once following the retirement of Justice David Souter and the addition of Justice Sotomayor.

JUDICIAL OPINION

Kennedy, Justice

The narrative [of *Hillary*] may contain more suggestions and arguments than facts, but there is little doubt that the thesis of the film is that she is unfit for the Presidency.

Citizens United argues that *Hillary* is just "a documentary film that examines certain historical events." We disagree. The movie's consistent emphasis is on the relevance of these events to Senator Clinton's candidacy for President. The narrator begins by asking "could [Senator Clinton] become the first female President in the history of the United States?" And the narrator reiterates the movie's message in his closing line: "Finally, before America decides on our next president, voters should need no reminders of . . . what's at stake—the well-being and prosperity of our nation."

Courts, too, are bound by the First Amendment. We must decline to draw, and then redraw, constitutional lines based on the particular media or technology used to disseminate political speech from a particular speaker.

The law before us is an outright ban, backed by criminal sanctions. Section 441b makes it a felony for all corporations—including nonprofit advocacy corporations—either to expressly advocate the election or defeat of candidates or to broadcast electioneering communications within 30 days of a primary election and 60 days of a general election. Thus, the following acts would all be felonies under § 441b: The Sierra Club runs an ad, within the crucial phase of 60 days before the general election, that exhorts the public to disapprove of a Congressman who favors logging in national forests; the National Rifle Association publishes a book urging the public to vote for the challenger because the incumbent U.S. Senator supports a handgun ban; and

CONTINUED

the American Civil Liberties Union creates a Web site telling the public to vote for a Presidential candidate in light of that candidate's defense of free speech. These prohibitions are classic examples of censorship.

Section 441b's prohibition on corporate independent expenditures is thus a ban on speech. Were the Court to uphold these restrictions, the Government could repress speech by silencing certain voices at any of the various points in the speech process. If § 441b applied to individuals, no one would believe that it is merely a time, place, or manner restriction on speech. Its purpose and effect are to silence entities whose voices the Government deems to be suspect.

Speech is an essential mechanism of democracy, for it is the means to hold officials accountable to the people.

The First Amendment protects speech and speaker, and the ideas that flow from each. The Court has recognized that First Amendment protection extends to corporations. This protection has been extended by explicit holdings to the context of political speech. Under the rationale of these precedents, political speech does not lose First Amendment protection "simply because its source is a corporation. . . ." Government lacks the power to ban corporations from speaking.

It is irrelevant for purposes of the First Amendment that corporate funds may "have little or no correlation to the public's support for the corporation's political ideas." All speakers, including individuals and the media, use money amassed from the economic marketplace to fund their speech. The First Amendment protects the resulting speech, even if it was enabled by economic transactions with persons or entities who disagree with the speaker's ideas.

There is simply no support for the view that the First Amendment, as originally understood, would permit the suppression of political speech by media corporations. The Framers may not have anticipated modern business and media corporations. Yet television networks and major newspapers owned by media corporations have become the most important means of mass communication in modern times. The First Amendment was certainly not understood to condone the suppression of political speech in society's most salient media. It was understood as a response to the repression of speech and the press that had existed in England and the heavy taxes on the press that were imposed in the colonies. The great debates between the Federalists and the Anti-Federalists over our founding document were published and expressed in the most important means of mass communication of that era—newspapers owned by individuals.

When Government seeks to use its full power, including the criminal law, to command where a person may get his or her information or what distrusted source he or she may not hear, it uses censorship to control thought. This is unlawful. The First Amendment confirms the freedom to think for ourselves.

When word concerning the plot of the movie *Mr. Smith Goes to Washington* reached the circles of Government, some officials sought, by persuasion, to discourage its distribution. [I]t, like *Hillary,* was speech funded by a corporation that was critical of Members of Congress. *Mr. Smith Goes to Washington* may be fiction and caricature; but fiction and caricature can be a powerful force.

Modern day movies, television comedies, or skits on Youtube.com might portray public officials or public policies in unflattering ways. Yet if a covered transmission during the blackout period creates the background for candidate endorsement or opposition, a felony occurs solely because a corporation, other than an exempt media corporation, has made the "purchase, payment, distribution, loan, advance, deposit, or gift of money or anything of value" in order to engage in political speech. Speech would be suppressed in the realm where its necessity is most evident: in the public dialogue preceding a real election. Governments are often hostile to speech, but under our law and our tradition it seems stranger than fiction for our Government to make this political speech a crime. Yet this is the statute's purpose and design.

"The First Amendment underwrites the freedom to experiment and to create in the realm of thought and speech. Citizens must be free to use new forms, and new forums, for the expression of ideas. The civic discourse belongs to the people, and the Government may not prescribe the means used to conduct it."

The judgment of the District Court is reversed with respect to the constitutionality of § 441b's restrictions on corporate independent expenditures.

CASE QUESTIONS

1. Why does the Court say it cannot be involved in ongoing monitoring of political ads, documentaries, and other forms of communication?

2. Why are independent expenditures by corporations different from corporate donations and funding of candidates?

3. Are time restrictions and unflattering portraits grounds for regulating political speech? Why or why not?

The BCRA was immediately challenged by 11 different parties in different federal courts, and the cases were consolidated and eventually heard by the U.S. Supreme Court in *McConnell v Federal Election Comm'n,* 540 U.S. 93 (2003). The Supreme Court, in a 500-page opinion (including the dissents), upheld most of the then-new law, but the court was forced to revisit the constitutionality in *Citizens United v FEC,* the decision that the president urged Congress to reverse (see p. 144).

Eminent Domain: The Takings Clause

The right of a governmental body to take title to property for a public use is called **eminent domain.** This right is established in the Fifth Amendment to the Constitution and may also be established in various state constitutions. Private individuals cannot require property owners to sell their property, but governmental entities can require property owners to transfer title for public projects for the public good. The Fifth Amendment provides that "property shall not be taken for a public use without just compensation." For a governmental entity to exercise properly the right of eminent domain, three factors must be present: public purpose, taking (as opposed to regulating), and just compensation.

Public Purpose

To exercise eminent domain, the governmental authority must establish that the taking is necessary for the accomplishment of a government or public purpose. When eminent domain is mentioned, we think of the use of property for highways and schools. However, the right of the government to eminent domain extends much further. For example, the following uses have been held to constitute public purposes: the condemnation of slum housing (for purposes of improving city areas), the limitation of mining and excavation within city limits, the declaration of property as a historic landmark, and the taking of property to provide a firm that is a town's economic base with a large enough tract for expansion. According to the U.S. Supreme Court, the public purpose requirement for eminent domain is to be interpreted broadly, and "the role of the judiciary in determining whether that power is being exercised for a public purpose is an extremely narrow one" [*United States ex rel. TVA v Welch,* 327 U.S. 546 (1946)]. The *Kelo v City of New London* case (Case 5.7) was the U.S. Supreme Court decision that changed the eminent domain landscape, as it were.

CASE 5.7	*Kelo v City of New London* 545 U.S. 469 (2005)

Yes, Actually, They Can Take That Away From You

FACTS

In 1978, the city of New London, Connecticut, undertook a redevelopment plan for purposes of creating a redeveloped area in and around the existing park at Fort Trumbull. The plan sought to develop the related ambience a state park should have, including the absence of pink cottages and other architecturally eclectic homes. Part of the redevelopment plain was the city's deal with Pfizer Corporation for the location of its research facility in the area. The preface to

CONTINUED

the city's development plan included the following statement of goals and purpose:

> To create a development that would complement the facility that Pfizer was planning to build, create jobs, increase tax and other revenues, encourage public access to and use of the city's waterfront, and eventually "build momentum" for the revitalization of the rest of the city, including its downtown area.

The affected property owners, including Susette Kelo, live in homes and cottages (15 total) located in and around other existing structures that will be permitted to stay in the area for the proposed new structures (under the city's economic development plan) that will be placed there primarily by private land developers and corporations. The city was assisted by a private, nonprofit corporation, the New London Development Corporation (NLDC), in the development of the economic plan and the ferrying of it through the various governmental processes, including that of city council approval. The central focus of the plan was getting Pfizer to the Fort Trumbull area (where the homeowners and their properties were located) with the hope of a resulting economic boost such a major corporate employer can bring to an area.

Kelo and the other landowners whose homes would be razed to make room for Pfizer and the accompanying and resulting economic development plan filed suit challenging New London's legal authority to take their homes. The trial court issued an injunction preventing New London from taking certain of the properties but allowing others to be taken. The appellate court found for New London on all the claims, and the landowners (petitioners) appealed.

JUDICIAL OPINION

STEVENS, Justice

Two polar propositions are perfectly clear. On the one hand, it has long been accepted that the sovereign may not take the property of A for the sole purpose of transferring it to another private party B, even though A is paid just compensation. On the other hand, it is equally clear that a State may transfer property from one private party to another if future "use by the public" is the purpose of the taking; the condemnation of land for a railroad with common-carrier duties is a familiar example. Neither of these propositions, however, determines the disposition of this case.

The disposition of this case therefore turns on the question whether the City's development plan serves a "public purpose." Without exception, our cases have defined that concept broadly, reflecting our long-standing policy of deference to legislative judgments in this field.

In *Berman v Parker*, 348 U.S. 26, 75 S.Ct. 98, 99 L.Ed. 27 (1954), this Court upheld a redevelopment plan targeting a blighted area of Washington, D.C., in which most of the housing for the area's 5,000 inhabitants was beyond repair. Under the plan, the area would be condemned and part of it utilized for the construction of streets, schools, and other public facilities. The remainder of the land would be leased or sold to private parties for the purpose of redevelopment, including the construction of low-cost housing.

The owner of a department store located in the area challenged the condemnation, pointing out that his store was not itself blighted and arguing that the creation of a "better balanced, more attractive community" was not a valid public use. Writing for a unanimous Court, Justice Douglas refused to evaluate this claim in isolation, deferring instead to the legislative and agency judgment that the area "must be planned as a whole" for the plan to be successful. The Court explained that "community redevelopment programs need not, by force of the Constitution, be on a piecemeal basis—lot by lot, building by building." "We do not sit to determine whether a particular housing project is or is not desirable. The concept of the public welfare is broad and inclusive. . . . The values it represents are spiritual as well as physical, aesthetic as well as monetary. It is within the power of the legislature to determine that the community should be beautiful as well as healthy, spacious as well as clean, well-balanced as well as carefully patrolled. In the present case, the Congress and its authorized agencies have made determinations that take into account a wide variety of values. It is not for us to reappraise them. If those who govern the District of Columbia decide that the Nation's Capital should be beautiful as well as sanitary, there is nothing in the Fifth Amendment that stands in the way."

In *Hawaii Housing Authority v Midkiff*, 467 U.S. 229, 104 S. Ct. 2321, 81 L.Ed.2d 186 (1984), the Court considered a Hawaii statute whereby fee title was taken from lessors and transferred to lessees (for just compensation) in order to reduce the concentration of land ownership. We unanimously upheld the statute and rejected the Ninth Circuit's view that it was "a naked attempt on the part of the state of Hawaii to take the property of A and transfer it to B solely for B's private use and benefit." Reaffirming *Berman*'s deferential approach to legislative judgments in this field, we concluded that the State's purpose of eliminating the "social and economic evils of a land oligopoly" qualified as a valid public use.

Those who govern the City were not confronted with the need to remove blight in the Fort Trumbull area, but their determination that the area was sufficiently distressed to justify a program of economic rejuvenation is entitled to our deference. The City has carefully formulated an economic development plan that it believes will provide appreciable benefits to the community, including—but by no means limited to—new jobs and increased tax revenue. To effectuate this plan, the City has invoked a state statute that specifically authorizes the use of eminent domain to promote economic development. Given the comprehensive character of the plan, the thorough deliberation that preceded its adoption, and the limited scope of our review, it is appropriate for us, as it was in *Berman*, to resolve the challenges of the individual owners, not on a piecemeal basis, but rather in light of the entire plan. Because that plan unquestionably serves a public purpose, the takings challenged here satisfy the public use requirement of the Fifth Amendment.

Petitioners contend that using eminent domain for economic development impermissibly blurs the boundary between public and private takings. Again, our cases foreclose this objection. We cannot say that public ownership is the sole method of promoting the public purposes of community redevelopment projects. It is further argued that without a bright-line rule nothing would stop a city from transferring citizen A's property to citizen B for the sole reason that citizen B will put the property to a more productive use and thus pay more taxes. Such a one-to-one transfer of property, executed outside the confines of an integrated development plan, is not presented in this case. While such an unusual exercise of government power would certainly raise a suspicion that a private purpose was afoot, the hypothetical cases posited by petitioners can be confronted if and when they arise. They do not warrant the crafting of an artificial restriction on the concept of public use.

Just as we decline to second-guess the City's considered judgments about the efficacy of its development plan, we also decline to second-guess the City's determinations as to what lands it needs to acquire in order to effectuate the project. "It is not for the courts to oversee the choice of the boundary line nor to sit in review on the size of a particular project area. Once the question of the public purpose has been decided, the amount and character of land to be taken for the project and the need for a particular tract to complete the integrated plan rests in the discretion of the legislative branch."

The judgment of the Supreme Court of Connecticut is affirmed.

DISSENTING OPINION

O'CONNOR, Justice, joined by Justices SCALIA, THOMAS and REHNQUIST

Under the banner of economic development, all private property is now vulnerable to being taken and transferred to another private owner, so long as it might be upgraded—i.e., given to an owner who will use it in a way that the legislature deems more beneficial to the public—in the process. To reason, as the Court does, that the incidental public benefits resulting from the subsequent ordinary use of private property render economic development takings "for public use" is to wash out any distinction between private and public use of property—and thereby effectively to delete the words "for public use" from the Takings Clause of the Fifth Amendment. Accordingly I respectfully dissent.

Where is the line between "public" and "private" property use? We give considerable deference to legislatures' determinations about what governmental activities will advantage the public. But were the political branches the sole arbiters of the public-private distinction, the Public Use Clause would amount to little more than hortatory fluff. An external, judicial check on how the public use requirement is interpreted, however limited, is necessary if this constraint on government power is to retain any meaning.

Even if there were a practical way to isolate the motives behind a given taking, the gesture toward a purpose test is theoretically flawed. If it is true that incidental public benefits from new private use are enough to ensure the "public purpose" in a taking, why should it matter, as far as the Fifth Amendment is concerned, what inspired the taking in the first place? And whatever the reason for a given condemnation, the effect is the same from the constitutional perspective—private property is forcibly relinquished to new private ownership.

CASE QUESTIONS

1. What is different from this case and a case in which property is taken for a freeway?

2. What is the concern of the dissent about the decision?

3. Why does the majority state that the courts should be reluctant to get involved in local government eminent domain activities?

The impact of the *Kelo* case has been substantial. The decision unleashed new uncertainty in the minds of landowners and paved the way for legislative reforms that curb eminent domain powers at the state and local levels. Following the November 2006 general elections, nearly one-half of the states had passed ballot propositions limiting the exercise of eminent domain, adopted constitutional amendments restricting economic development eminent domain, or passed legislation with similar limitations.[2]

Taking or Regulating

For a governmental entity to be required to pay a landowner compensation under the doctrine of eminent domain there must be a taking of the property. Mere regulation of the property does not constitute a taking, as determined by *Village of Euclid, Ohio v Ambler Realty Co.,* 272 U.S. 365 (1926). Rather, a taking must go so far as to deprive the landowner of any use of the property. In the landmark case of *Pennsylvania Coal v Mahon,* 260 U.S. 393 (1922), the Supreme Court established standards for determining a taking as opposed to mere regulation. At that time Pennsylvania had a statute that prohibited the mining of coal under any land surface where the result would be the subsidence of any structure used as a human habitation. The owners of the rights to mine subsurface coal brought suit challenging the regulation as a taking, and the Supreme Court ruled in their favor, holding that the statute was more than regulation and, in fact, was an actual taking of the subsurface property rights.

Because of the vast amount of technology that has developed since that case was decided, many new and subtly different issues affect what constitutes a taking. For example, in some areas the regulation of cable television companies is an infringement on air rights. Such specialized areas of real estate rights are particularly difficult to resolve. In *Loretto v Teleprompter Manhattan CATV Corp.,* 458 U.S. 100 (1982), the U.S. Supreme Court held that the small invasion of property by the placement of cable boxes and wires did constitute a taking, albeit very small, and required compensation of the property owners for this small but permanent occupation of their land.

The issue of taking has arisen because of local zoning restrictions on development. These restrictions focus on beaches, wetlands, and other natural habitats. For example, in *Nollan v California Coastal Commission,* 483 U.S. 825 (1987), the Nollans sought permission from the California Coastal Commission to construct a home on their coastal lot where they currently had only a small bungalow. The commission refused to grant permission to the Nollans for construction of their home unless they agreed to give a public easement across their lot for beach access. The Supreme Court held that the demand by the commission for an easement was a taking without compensation and, in effect, prevented the Nollans from using their property until they surrendered their exclusive use.

Yet another issue that arises in taking occurs when regulations take effect after owners have acquired land but before it is developed. In *Lucas v South Carolina Coastal Council,* 505 U.S. 1003 (1992), the U.S. Supreme Court declared that *ex post facto* legislation that prevents development of previously purchased land is a taking. In *Lucas,* David Lucas purchased for $975,000 two residential lots on the Isle of Palms in Charleston County, South Carolina. In 1988, the South Carolina legislature enacted the Beachfront Management Act, which barred any permanent habitable structures on coastal properties. The court held South Carolina was required to compensate Mr. Lucas because his land was rendered useless.

Just Compensation

The final requirement for the proper exercise by a governmental entity of the right of eminent domain is that the party from whom the property is being taken be given **just compensation.** The issue of just compensation is difficult to determine and is always a question of fact. Basic to this determination is that the owner is to be compensated for loss and that the compensation is not measured by the governmental entity's gain. In *United States v Miller*, 317 U.S. 369 (1943), the Supreme Court held that in cases where it can be determined, fair market value is the measure of compensation; and, in *United States ex rel. TVA v Powelson*, 319 U.S. 266 (1943), the Supreme Court defined fair market value to be "what a willing buyer would pay in cash to a willing seller."

Possible problems in applying these relatively simple standards include peculiar value to the owner, consequential damages, and greater value of the land because of the proposed governmental project. Basically, the issue of just compensation becomes an issue of appraisal, which is affected by all the various factors involved. In determining just compensation, the courts must consider such factors as surrounding property values and the owner's proposed use.

Procedural Due Process

Both the Fifth and the Fourteenth Amendments require state and federal governments to provide citizens (businesses included) due process under the law. **Procedural due process** is a right that requires notice and the opportunity to be heard before rights or properties are taken away from an individual or business. Most people are familiar with due process as it exists in the criminal justice system: the right to a lawyer, a trial, and so on (Chapter 8). However, procedural due process is also an important part of civil law. Before an agency—whether state or federal—can take away a business license, suspend a license, or impose a fine for a violation, it must ensure due process.

Businesses encounter the constitutional protections of due process in their relationships with customers. For example, the eviction of a nonpaying tenant cannot be done unilaterally. The tenant has the right to be heard in the setting of a hearing. The landlord must file an action against the tenant, and the tenant will have the opportunity to present defenses for nonpayment of rent. The Due Process Clause of the U.S. Constitution provides protection for individuals before their property is taken. Property includes land (as in the case of eminent domain, discussed previously); rights of possession (tenants and leases); and even intangible property rights. For example, students cannot be expelled from schools, colleges, or universities without the right to be heard. Students must have some hearing before their property rights with respect to education are taken away.

All proceedings designed to satisfy due process requirements must provide notice and the right to be heard and present evidence (see Chapter 6 for more details). If these rights are not afforded, the constitutional right of due process has been denied and the action taken is rescinded until due process requirements are met. Suppose that OSHA charges a company with safety violations in its plants. Before a fine or order can be imposed, procedural due process requires that the company have the right to be heard and to present evidence on the violations. In court cases, a matter reduced to a judgment entitles the victorious side to collect on that judgment. However, under due process, even the proceedings for collection allow the losing party or debtor to be notified of the proceedings and to be heard.

CONSIDER...   5.3

When the Crafts moved into their residence in October 1972, they noticed two separate gas and electric meters and only one water meter serving the premises. The residence had been used previously as a duplex. The Crafts assumed, based on information from the seller, that the second set of meters was inoperative.

In 1973, the Crafts began receiving two bills: their regular bill and another with an account number in the name of Willie C. Craft, as opposed to Willie S. Craft. In October 1973, after learning from a Memphis Light, Gas & Water (MLG&W) meter reader that both sets of meters were running in their home, the Crafts hired a private plumber and electrical contractor to combine the meters into one gas and one electric meter. Because the contractor did not combine the meters properly, they continued to receive two bills until January 1974. During this time, the Crafts' utility service was terminated five times for nonpayment.

Mrs. Craft missed work several times to go to MLG&W offices to resolve the "double billing" problem. She sought explanations on each occasion but was never given an answer.

In February 1974, the Crafts and other MLG&W customers filed suit for violation of the Due Process Clause. The district court dismissed the case. The court of appeals reversed, and MLG&W appealed.

Have the Crafts been given due process? [*Memphis Light, Gas & Water Div. v Craft*, 436 U.S. 1 (1978)]

Substantive Due Process

Procedural rules deal with how things are done. All rules on the adjudication of agency charges are procedural rules. Similarly, all rules for the trial of a civil case, from discovery to jury instructions, are also procedural. These rules exist to make sure the substantive law is upheld. **Substantive law** consists of rights, obligations, and behavior standards. Criminal laws are substantive laws, and criminal procedure rules are procedural laws. **Substantive due process** is the right to have laws that do not deprive businesses or citizens of property or other rights without justification and reason. For example, a law cannot be so vague that you would not understand when you are violating it. The constitutional doctrine of "void for vagueness" and the resulting denial of due process have been reactivated by the courts over the past few years. For example, in *Gonzales v Carhart*, 550 U.S. 124 (2007), the Court dealt with a federal statute that prohibited partial-birth abortions. The issue in that case was whether the terms in the statute on what constitute a partial-birth abortion were so ill defined that enforcement was left entirely to the discretion of officials, which resulted in a lack of due process. In *Fox Television Stations, Inc. v FCC*, 613 F.3d 317 (9th Cir. 2010), the Ninth Circuit dealt with a similar issue that involved the FCC's discretion in determining what were and were not expletives in its decisions to assess fines against broadcasters when, for example, Bono, Paris Hilton, or Cher utter a certain word during live broadcasts (such as music award ceremonies). In these situations, the FCC had assessed fines against several broadcast networks for their failure to censor the artists and stars. The Ninth Circuit held that the FCC could not describe its standards for expletives and indecency with enough specificity to place broadcasters on notice, and that their flexible standards substantively violated the broadcasters' due process under their First Amendment rights.[3]

Equal Protection Rights for Business

The Fourteenth Amendment grants citizens the right to the **equal protection** of the law. Lawmakers, however, are often required to make certain distinctions in legislating and regulating that result in classes of individuals being treated differently.

Such different or **disparate treatment** is justified only if some rational basis for it is determined. In other words, a rational connection is necessary between the classifications and the achievement of some governmental objective. Most classifications survive the rational basis test. An example of a classification that would not survive is one requiring the manufacturers of soft drinks to use only nonbreakable bottles for their product but allowing juice manufacturers to use glass bottles; this classification is irrational. If a public safety concern is raised about glass bottles, it must apply equally to all beverage manufacturers.

The Role of Constitutions in International Law

Although the U.S. Constitution is the basis for all law in the United States, not all countries follow a similar system of governance. The incorporation of other systems (such as a constitution or code) depends on a nation's history, including its colonization by other countries and those countries' forms of law. The United States and England (and countries established through English colonization) tend to follow a pattern of establishing a general set of principles, as set forth in a constitution, and of reliance on custom, tradition, and precedent for the establishment of law in particular legal areas.

In countries such as France, Germany, and Spain (and nations colonized through their influences), a system of law that is dependent on code law exists. These countries have specific codes of law that attempt to be all-inclusive and cover each circumstance that could arise under a particular provision. These nations do not depend on court decisions, and often the application of the law leads to inconsistent results because of the lack of dependence on judicial precedent.

Approximately 27 countries follow Islamic law in some way. When Islamic law is the dominant force in a country, it governs all aspects of personal and business life. The constitutions in these lands are the tenets of the nation's religion.

CONSIDER...   5.4

Following a boom in cruise ship construction, ships are now looking for ports at which they can dock in order to begin voyages, most of which start in the United States. With so many new ships, the companies are trying to establish connections with cities that are not ordinarily considered for cruise ship docks. The companies pursue these alternatives because the traditional docking cities of New York, Seattle, Miami, Los Angeles, and Houston have become crowded with cruise ship traffic. The result has been a burden on the facilities and staff at the ports.

Most cruise ship lines are incorporated outside of the United States, do not pay federal income taxes, and are not subject to state income taxes even though the bulk of their passengers come from the United States. (See "Constitutional Standards for Taxation of Business" earlier in this chapter.)

Can the ships be taxed to cover the harbor expenses? Can they be required by states and cities to pay docking fees, or are they internationally exempt companies?

Source: Nicole Harris, "Big Cruise Ships Cause Traffic Jams in Ports," *Wall Street Journal,* August 20, 2003, pp. B1, B6.

B I O G R A P H Y

John Glover Roberts: Third-Youngest Chief Justice of The U.S. Supreme Court

When he was sworn in on September 29, 2005, as the Chief Justice of the United States Supreme Court, John G. Roberts brought a unique perspective and depth of experience.

Justice Roberts's family moved from Buffalo, New York, where he was born in 1955, to Indiana where he worked summers in the steel mills and graduated with honors from his high school. There, he was also the captain of his high school football team despite being, by his own account, "a slow-footed linebacker." He finished his undergraduate degree in history at Harvard, *summa cum laude*, in just three years, paying his way by working summers in the Indiana steel mills once again. His honors thesis, which was titled "Marxism and Bolshevism: Theory and Practice," won the award for best essay in 1976. He immediately went on to Harvard Law School, where he was managing editor of the *Harvard Law Review* and graduated in 1979 *magna cum laude*. Following his graduation from Harvard Law School, Mr. Roberts served as a law clerk for Judge Henry T. Friendly of the Second Circuit Federal Court of Appeals. From there he spent 1980–1981 as a clerk for U.S. Supreme Court Justice William Rehnquist. Shortly after Mr. Roberts left to go to the Justice Department, Mr. Rehnquist was named Chief Justice.

Following service in the Justice Department from 1981 to 1982, Mr. Roberts became associate general counsel to the White House during the Reagan administration. In 1986, he left the White House and went into private practice. Mr. Roberts argued his first case before the U.S. Supreme Court in 1989. After winning that case on a double-jeopardy issue as a court-appointed lawyer, Mr. Roberts was appointed as Principal Deputy Solicitor General of the United States, a position he would hold until 1992 when he was nominated by President Bush (41) to the Second Circuit Court of Appeals. With the political winds changing at that time, Mr. Roberts's nomination "languished" in the Senate and he returned to private practice. He argued 39 cases before the U.S. Supreme Court, a number that ranks him as one of the country's top five lawyers for appearances at the high court. In 2001, President Bush (43) nominated Mr. Roberts to the D.C. Circuit Court of Appeals, and his nomination was finally approved by the Senate in 2003. After Judge Roberts had served two years there, President Bush nominated him to fill the vacancy created by Sandra Day O'Connor's resignation. However, during Judge Roberts's Supreme Court confirmation process, his former boss and mentor, Chief Justice William Rehnquist, died. President Bush nominated Judge Roberts for Chief Justice rather than Associate Justice, and he was confirmed by the Senate with a 78–22 vote, a departure from previous near-unanimous confirmation of high court nominees.

Known for his clear writing style and warm personality, the Chief Justice shared, during his confirmation hearings, a story on one of his losses at the high court. He lost a case before the court on a 9–0 vote. When a client called to ask how it was possible that they could lose their case by a 9–0 vote, then-Judge Roberts said that he responded, "Because they only have nine justices on the U.S. Supreme Court!"

Summary

What is the Constitution?

- U.S. Constitution—document detailing authority of U.S. government and rights of its citizens

What are the constitutional limitations on business regulations?

- Commerce Clause—portion of the U.S. Constitution that controls federal regulation of business; limits

Congress to regulating interstate and international commerce

- Intrastate commerce—business within state borders

- Interstate commerce—business across state lines

- Foreign commerce—business outside U.S. boundaries

Who has more power to regulate business—the states or the federal government?

- Supremacy Clause—portion of the U.S. Constitution that defines relationship between state and federal laws

- Taxation—authority to tax interstate businesses

What individual freedoms granted under the Constitution apply to businesses?

- Bill of Rights—first 10 amendments to the U.S. Constitution, providing individual freedoms and protection of individual rights

- First Amendment—freedom-of-speech protection in U.S. Constitution

- Commercial speech—ads and other speech by businesses

- Corporate political speech—business ads or positions on candidates or referenda

- Due process—constitutional guarantee against the taking of property or other governmental exercise of authority without an opportunity for a hearing

- Equal protection—constitutional protection for U.S. citizens against disparate treatment

- Substantive due process—constitutional protection against taking of rights or property by statute

Questions and Problems

1. Diana Levine went for her usual treatment for a migraine headache at her local clinic on April 7, 2000. There she received an intramuscular injection of Demerol for her headache and Phenergan for her nausea. Because the combination did not provide relief, she returned later that day and received a second injection of both drugs. This time, the physician assistant administered the drugs by the IV-push method, and the drugs, including Phenergan, entered Levine's artery, either because the needle penetrated an artery directly or because the drug escaped from the vein into surrounding tissue (a phenomenon called "perivascular extravasation"). As a result, Levine developed gangrene, and doctors amputated first her right hand and then her entire forearm. In addition to her pain and suffering, Levine incurred substantial medical expenses and the loss of her livelihood as a professional musician. When Levine filed suit against Wyeth, the drug's manufacturer, a Vermont jury found that Wyeth had failed to provide an adequate warning of that risk and awarded damages to compensate her for the amputation of her arm. The FDA had approved the warnings on Phenergan's label concurrently with its approval of Wyeth's new drug application in 1955 and again when the company applied later for changes in the drug's labeling.

The jury awarded total damages of $7,400,000, which the court reduced to account for Levine's earlier settlement with the health center and clinician. Wyeth appealed on the grounds that the FDA's regulation was extensive and preempted state tort laws. Will the court uphold her state-court damage award? [*Wyeth v Levine*, 129 S.Ct. 1187 (2009)]

2. Mrs. Florence Dolan owned a plumbing and electric supply store on Main Street in Portland, Oregon. Fanno Creek flows through the southeastern corner of Mrs. Dolan's lot, on which her store is located. She applied to the city for a permit to redevelop her lot. Her plans included the addition of a second structure.

The City Planning Commission granted Mrs. Dolan's permit but included the following requirement:

Where landfill and/or development is allowed within and adjacent to the 100-year floodplain, the city shall require the dedication of sufficient open land area for greenway adjoining and within the floodplain. This area shall include portions at a suitable elevation for the construction of a pedestrian/bicycle pathway within the floodplain in accordance with the adopted pedestrian/bicycle plan.

Mrs. Dolan maintained that the requirements were a taking of her property because she would be required to reserve a portion of her property for the pedestrian/bike path, and her plans would have to be redone to accommodate the city's requirements. The city maintains that its requirements are all simply part of a redevelopment plan for the city and a means of working with the floodplain created by Fanno Creek. Mrs. Dolan says the city has imposed additional expense and forced her to dedicate a large portion of her lot to public use. Who is correct? Is Portland taking property from Mrs. Dolan? Is the city required to pay compensation to her? [*Dolan v City of Tigard*, 512 U.S. 374 (1994)]

3. The Heart of Atlanta Motel, which has 216 rooms available to transient guests, is located on Courtland Street, two blocks from downtown Peachtree Street in

Atlanta, Georgia. It is readily accessible to interstate highways 75 and 85 and state highways 23 and 41. The motel does advertise outside Georgia through various national advertising media, including magazines of national circulation; it maintains more than 50 billboards and highway signs within the state, soliciting patronage for the motel; it accepts convention trade from outside Georgia; and approximately 75 percent of its registered guests are from out of state.

Prior to passage of Title II of the Civil Rights Act, the motel had followed a practice of refusing to rent rooms to Negroes, and it alleged that it intended to continue to do so. The motel filed suit, challenging Congress for passing this act in excess of its power to regulate commerce under Article I, Section 8, Part 3 of the Constitution of the United States.

Section 201 of Title II provides: "All persons shall be entitled to the full and equal enjoyment of the goods, services, facilities, privileges, advantages, and accommodations of any place of public accommodation, as defined in this section, without discrimination or segregation on the ground of race, color, religion, or national origin." Section 201(b) covers four classes of business establishments, each of which "serves the public" and "is a place of public accommodation": *any inn, hotel, motel, or other establishment which provides lodging; (2) any restaurant, cafeteria; (3) any motion picture house; and (4) any establishment which is physically located within the premises of any establishment otherwise covered by this subsection.*

Is Title II of the Civil Rights Act constitutional? Is this case different from Ollie's Barbecue? From *Morrison?* [*Heart of Atlanta Motel, Inc. v U.S.*, 379 U.S. 241 (1964)]

4. Bruce Church, Inc. is a company engaged in extensive commercial farming in Arizona and California. A provision of the Arizona Fruit and Vegetable Standardization Act requires that all cantaloupes grown in Arizona "be packed in regular compact arrangement in closed standard containers approved by the supervisor." Arizona, through its agent Pike, issued an order prohibiting Bruce Church from transporting uncrated cantaloupes from its ranch in Parker, Arizona, to nearby Blythe, California, for packing and processing.

It would take many months and $200,000 for Bruce Church to construct a processing plant in Parker. Further, Bruce Church had $700,000 worth of cantaloupes ready for transportation. Bruce Church filed suit in federal district court challenging the constitutionality of the Arizona statutory provision on shipping cantaloupes. The court issued an injunction against the enforcement of the act on the grounds that it was an undue hardship on interstate commerce. Will the regulation withstand Commerce Clause scrutiny? [*Pike v Bruce Church, Inc.*, 397 U.S. 137 (1970)]

5. The International Longshoremen's Association refused to unload cargo shipped from the Soviet Union as a way of protesting the Soviet invasion of Afghanistan. Allied International, an importer of Soviet wood products, could not get its wood unloaded when its ship arrived in Boston. Allied sued on the basis of the National Labor Relations Act, claiming the conduct was an unlawful boycott. The union claims no commerce is involved and that federal law does not apply. Is there commerce? Does the National Labor Relations Act apply? [*International Longshoremen's Association v Allied International, Inc.*, 456 U.S. 212 (1982)]

6. For the past 62 years, Pacific Gas & Electric (PG&E) has distributed a newsletter in its monthly billing envelopes. The newsletter, called *Progress,* reaches more than 3 million customers and contains tips on conservation, utility billing information, public interest information, and political editorials.

A group called TURN (Toward Utility Rate Normalization) asked the Public Utility Commission (PUC) of California to declare that the envelope space belonged to the ratepayers and that TURN was entitled to use the *Progress* space four times each year. The PUC ordered TURN's request, and PG&E appealed the order to the California Supreme Court. When the California Supreme Court denied review, PG&E appealed to the U.S. Supreme Court, alleging a violation of its First Amendment rights. Is PG&E correct? [*Pacific Gas & Electric v Public Utility Commission of California*, 475 U.S. 1 (1986)]

7. The Minnesota legislature enacted a 1977 statute banning the retail sale of milk in plastic nonreturnable, nonrefillable containers but permitting such sale in other nonrefillable containers, such as paperboard milk cartons. Clover Leaf Creamery brought suit challenging the constitutionality of the statute under the Equal Protection Clause, alleging that there was no rational basis for the statute. The Minnesota legislature's purpose in passing the statute was to control solid waste, arguing that plastic containers take up more space in solid waste disposal dumps. The Minnesota Supreme Court found evidence to the contrary: The jugs took up less space and required less energy to produce. On appeal to the U.S. Supreme Court, can the statute survive a constitutional challenge? Is there a "rational basis" for the statute? What effect does the evidence to the contrary have on the statute's constitutionality? [*Minnesota v Clover Leaf Creamery*, 449 U.S. 456 (1981)]

8. Iowa passed a statute restricting the length of vehicles that could use its highways. The length chosen was 55 feet. Semi trailers are generally 55 feet long; double or twin tracks (one cab pulling two trailers) are 65 feet long. Other states in the Midwest have adopted the 65-foot standard. Consolidated Freightways brought suit, challenging the Iowa statute as an unconstitutional burden on interstate commerce. The Iowa statute meant Consolidated could not use its twins in Iowa. The Iowa legislature claims the 65-foot doubles are more dangerous than the 55-foot singles. However, the statute did provide a border exception: Towns and cities along Iowa borders could make an exception to the length requirements to allow trucks to use their city and town roads. Can Iowa's statute survive a constitutional challenge? Is the statute an impermissible burden on interstate commerce? [*Kassel v Consolidated Freightways Corp.*, 450 U.S. 662 (1981)]

9. In 1989, the city of Cincinnati authorized Discovery Network, Inc., to place on public property 62 freestanding news racks for distributing free magazines that consisted primarily of advertising for Discovery Network's service. In 1990, the city became concerned about the safety and attractive appearance of its streets and sidewalks and revoked Discovery Network's permit on the grounds that the magazines were commercial handbills whose distribution was prohibited on public property by a preexisting ordinance. Discovery Network argues that the prohibition is an excessive regulation of its commercial speech and a violation of its rights. The city maintains the elimination of the news racks decreases litter and increases safety. Is the ban on news racks constitutional? [*City of Cincinnati v Discovery Network, Inc.*, 507 U.S. 410 (1993)]

10. In March 2010, the attorneys general of 14 states filed suit against the U.S. Department of Health and Human Services in federal district court to challenge the constitutionality of the Patient Protection and Affordable Care Act, signed into law on March 23, 2010. The suit alleges that the Act exceeds the powers of the United States under Article I of the Constitution and violates the Tenth Amendment to the Constitution.

In addition, the suit alleges that the tax penalty required under the Act constitutes an unlawful capitation or direct tax, in violation of Article I, Sections 2 and 9 of the Constitution of the United States.

The suit also alleges that the Act is an unprecedented encroachment on the sovereignty of the states. Review the provisions of the Constitution cited and the discussion of the powers of the state and federal governments that you studied in this chapter and discuss whether there is a constitutional basis for the suit. Why would businesses be concerned about the new health care law?

Economics and the Law

There is a bittersweet end to the *Kelo* case. The land being taken by New London for private development, including Susette Kelo's little pink house, was taken for purposes of retaining Pfizer's continuing presence in the city as well as expansion of its research park. However, on November 10, 2009, Pfizer announced that it was closing its research and development headquarters in New London.

Ms. Kelo and others lost their homes. New London spent $87 million razing the homes to make way for Pfizer. Now, the area stands vacant, an area that will become a center for criminal activity.

Who are the stakeholders in eminent domain cases? Who is affected by the takings? What lessons do we glean about business and government partnerships?

Notes

1. *Christian Legal Society Chapter of the University of California, Hastings College of the Law v Martinez*, 130 S.Ct. 2971.

2. Florida, Georgia, Louisiana, Michigan, New Hampshire, North Dakota, and South Carolina passed constitutional amendments. Florida, Georgia, Michigan, and New Hampshire, along with Alabama, Alaska, Colorado, Illinois, Kansas, Maine, Minnesota, Missouri, Nevada, Pennsylvania, South Dakota, Utah (had reform prior to Kelo), Vermont, West Virginia, Wisconsin, and Texas, passed legislation limiting eminent domain reforms. The ballot states are Oregon, California, Idaho, Washington, Montana, and Arizona. Oregon has already

codified its ballot proposition. In November 2005, the U.S. House of Representatives passed the Private Property Rights Protection Act of 2005 (also known as House Resolution 4128) by a vote of 376 to 38. The bill died in the Senate.

3. The case has been floating around the federal courts, including the U.S. Supreme Court, since 2002. This Ninth Circuit decision is expected to be appealed to the U.S. Supreme Court. One aspect of the case—on administrative law (the standard of arbitrary and capricious rulemaking)—was decided in 2009. This standard is covered in Chapter 6.

Administrative Law

The regulations of administrative agencies at the federal and state levels affect the day-to-day operations of all businesses. From permits to labor regulations, every business is affected. Agencies are the enforcement arm of governments. Created by one of the branches of government, they affect the way businesses operate. This chapter answers the following questions: What is an administrative agency? What does it do? What laws govern the operation of administrative agencies? How do agencies pass rules? How do agencies enforce the law? ■

Lord's Prayer	**66 words**
Gettysburg Address	**286 words**
Declaration of Independence	**1,322 words**
Federal regulations on the sale of cabbage	**26,911 words**
Internal Revenue Code	**6,200,000 words**

DO NOT REMOVE UNDER PENALTY OF LAW.

Warning printed on tags required on mattresses sold in the United States

THIS TAG NOT TO BE REMOVED EXCEPT BY THE CONSUMER.

Modified warning tag required on mattresses so that agency could reduce the number of calls from citizens about removing their mattress tags

UPDATE ➹
For up-to-date legal and ethical news, go to
mariannejennings.com

CONSIDER...

A. Duda & Sons, Inc. has a plaque posted in the lobby of its company headquarters that reads, "But seek ye first the Kingdom of God, and his righteousness and all these things shall be added unto you." An employee complained to the Equal Employment Opportunity Commission (EEOC) about the plaque, stating that it constituted religious harassment in the workplace.

At the Montgomery County Middle School, the name of its December music event was changed from "Christmas Concert" to "Winter Concert" when a teacher complained that the use of the word "Christmas" constituted religious harassment.

Based on these complaints and others (a total of 538 religious harassment complaints), the EEOC proposed rules on religious harassment that prohibited verbal or physical contact that "denigrates or shows hostility or aversion toward individual because of his/her religion . . . or that of his/her relatives, friends or associates."

An executive in a Florida hospital asked, "These rules could prevent an employee from wearing a necklace with a crucifix to work. Would I have to control Bible reading by my employees when they're having a break? The rules are unmanageable. Where do I turn? How can I raise my concerns about them?"

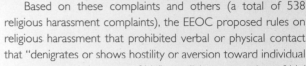

What Are Administrative Agencies?

An **administrative agency** is best defined by what it is not: It is not a legislative or judicial body. An administrative agency is a statutory creation within the executive branch with the power to make, interpret, and enforce laws. Such agencies exist at practically every level of government, and their names vary considerably. Exhibit 6.1 is a list of all the federal administrative agencies.

States also have administrative agencies that are responsible for such things as the licensing of professions and occupations. Architects, contractors, attorneys, accountants, cosmetologists, doctors, dentists, real estate agents, and nurses are all professionals whose occupations are regulated in most states by some administrative agency. Utility and worker compensation regulation are also handled by administrative agencies in each of the states.

All these agencies at every level of government derive their authority from the legislative body responsible for their creation. Congress creates federal agencies; state legislatures create state agencies; and city governments create their cities' administrative agencies.

The structures of agencies may differ significantly, but most will have an organizational chart to show how different departments operate. Exhibit 6.2 is an organizational chart for the Securities and Exchange Commission (SEC). The SEC consists of five commissioners, six divisions, and eleven regional offices.

Legislators begin the creation of an administrative agency with the recognition of a problem and the passage of a law designed to remedy the problem. The enacted law gives the overview—what the legislature wants to accomplish and the penalties for noncompliance with the law. The law may also establish an

EXHIBIT 6.1   Major Federal Administrative Agencies*

EXECUTIVE OFFICE OF THE PRESIDENT

Executive Departments

Department of Agriculture
Department of Commerce
Department of Defense
Office of the Secretary of Defense
Department of the Air Force
Department of the Army
Department of the Navy
Department of Education
Department of Energy
Department of Health and Human Services
Department of Homeland Security
Department of Housing and Urban Development (HUD)
Department of the Interior
Department of Justice

Department of Labor
Department of State
Department of Transportation
Department of the Treasury

Selected Independent Agencies

Civil Aeronautics Board (CAB)
Commodity Futures Trading Commission (CFTC)
Consumer Product Safety Commission (CPSC)
Environmental Protection Agency (EPA)
Equal Employment Opportunity Commission (EEOC)
Federal Aviation Administration (FAA)
Farm Credit Administration (FCA)
Federal Communications Commission (FCC)
Federal Deposit Insurance Corporation (FDIC)
Federal Election Commission (FEC)

Federal Emergency Management Agency (FEMA)
Federal Labor Relations Authority (FLRA)
Federal Maritime Commission (FMC)
Federal Mine Safety and Health Review Commission
Federal Reserve System
Federal Trade Commission (FTC)
General Services Administration (GSA)
Interstate Commerce Commission (ICC)
National Aeronautics and Space Administration (NASA)
National Credit Union Administration (NCUA)
National Highway Traffic Safety Administration (NHTSA)
National Labor Relations Board (NLRB)

National Science Foundation (NSF)
National Transportation Safety Board (NTSB)
Nuclear Regulatory Commission (NRC)
Occupational Safety and Health Administration (OSHA)
Overseas Private Investment Corporation (OPIC)
Patent and Trademark Office
Pension Benefit Guaranty Corporation
Securities and Exchange Commission (SEC)
Selective Service System (SSS)
Small Business Administration (SBA)
Tennessee Valley Authority (TVA)
U.S. Metric Board
U.S. Postal Service (USPS)
Veterans Administration (VA)

* Historical agencies are listed here and in CFR for topical and historical purposes. Current agency structures may include absorption of older agencies.

administrative agency with the power to adopt rules to deal with the problems of enforcement of the statute. The law, referred to as an **enabling act,** gives the agency the power to deal with the issues and problems the act addresses.

Roles of Administrative Agencies

Specialization

Administrative agencies are specialists in their particular areas of law, and this type of specialization is needed because of both the complexities of law and the areas of regulation. For example, securities regulation involves both the complexity of financial reporting as well as the underlying technical accounting rules. The SEC has a special division headed by its chief accountant, and that

EXHIBIT **6.2** SEC Organizational Chart

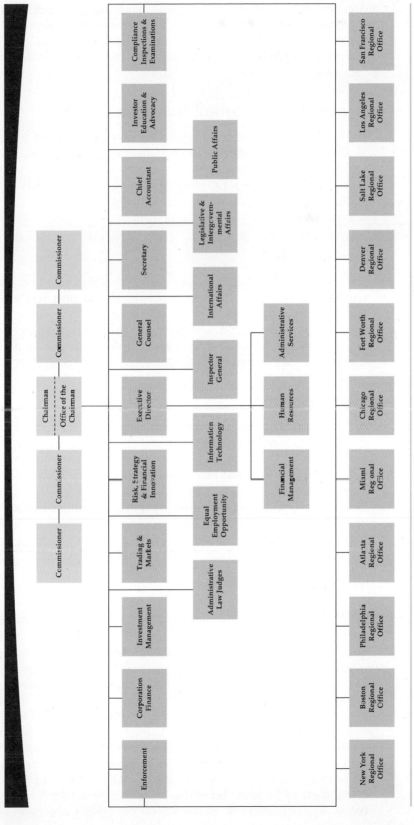

division deals with all current and evolving accounting and financial reporting issues. The people who work as staff members in these agencies are chosen for their knowledge and experience, which helps them provide protection for the public as well as an understanding of the issues members of the regulated industries face.

Protection for Small Business

An individual or competitor who finds a false advertisement in a newspaper would probably not take the time or effort to bring a private suit to collect damages for the false advertisement. But an agency created to oversee truth in advertising would undertake routine enforcement against such advertisements, affording small business competitors and consumers the protection and rights they might not otherwise have.

Faster Relief

If enforcement of all government regulations depended on court hearings, courts would be backlogged and the goals of swift action and enforcement defeated. Administrative agencies help expedite investigations and enforcement and penalties for violations. In addition, administrative agencies serve as review boards for granting licenses. License and permit applications can be done far more quickly than they could be handled legislatively.

Due Process

Administrative agencies provide the opportunity to be heard, a form of due process before property, rights, or income is taken. *Goldberg v Kelly*, 397 U.S. 254 (1970), was the seminal judicial decision responsible for creating administrative agency procedures that provide timely due process. In *Goldberg*, the Supreme Court ruled that before a benefit (such as aid to dependent children) could be taken away, the agency must present its evidence and allow those who have been receiving the aid an opportunity to respond. Administrative hearings provide citizens and businesses with a process for seeing the evidence against them and presenting their side of the story (see Chapter 5 for more insight on due process).

Social Goals

Some experts see administrative agencies as a means for accomplishing social goals that might otherwise be delayed or debated until no resolution could be reached. For example, the Environmental Protection Agency is assigned the goal of creating a cleaner environment. If Congress had to debate every permit for a factory or rule on discharges, the goal might be lost in the political arena. Further, having judicial review and determination of these issues would result in a delay that might make the goal moot. Administrative agencies can function independently of the judicial and legislative branches (however, see the *Massachusetts v EPA* case later in the chapter). Often, these agencies are created in response to a pressing social issue. For example, the Department of Homeland Security was established to combine several agencies to allow more coordinated responses to terrorism, such as the attacks on the World Trade Center and Washington, D.C., in

2001, as well as natural disasters. The goal was a more centralized means of information distribution and relief.

Laws Governing Administrative Agencies

Apart from their enabling acts, administrative agencies are also subject to some general laws on the functioning of agencies. This section covers those laws.

Administrative Procedures Act

This act was the first to deal with administrative agency procedures. It was passed in 1946 after some agencies had been in existence long enough for some standard procedures to be established. The **Administrative Procedures Act (APA)** requires agencies to follow certain uniform procedures in making rules (those procedures are covered later in this chapter). The APA has been amended a number of times by the Freedom of Information Act, the Federal Privacy Act, and the Government in the Sunshine Act, among others.

Freedom of Information Act

The **Freedom of Information Act (FOIA)** allows access to certain information federal agencies possess and requires that the agencies publicly disclose their procedures and decisions. The types of procedures that must be publicly disclosed relate to agencies' structures: where the central and regional offices are located and which office or office division will respond to requests for information. Agencies must also publish their rules, regulations, procedures, policy statements, and reports.

Some agency information, not published but available to the public, can be obtained by an **FOIA request**, which must be written and must describe the documents sought. For example, you could request the results of the Federal Trade Commission's study of coaching programs for college entrance exams. The agency can charge for time and for copying costs in processing the request, although these charges must be published and applied uniformly to all requests. Agencies can waive fees for nonprofit public interest groups.

If an agency wrongfully refuses to supply the information requested, the party requesting it can bring a court action to enforce the request, with all costs paid by the agency.

Some information is exempt from FOIA requests. The nine categories of exemptions would include, for example, requests that would reveal trade secrets or information about government workers' personnel records.

Agencies can also waive exemptions. Some requests have resulted in court cases brought by the parties protected by the exemptions. For example, suppose that one company requests the government bid contract submitted by another company (its competitor for the bid) to the Department of Defense. The bidding company could bring suit to stop the disclosure. Such suits are called "reverse FOIA suits." However, the U.S. Supreme Court held in *Chrysler Corp. v Brown*, 441 U.S. 281 (1979), that the right to stop or grant disclosure rests with the agency and not with the party who supplied the information to the agency.

Ethical Issues

Is the FOIA a means for legal industrial espionage? Could a competitor use an FOIA request as a means of gaining information about another firm that would not otherwise be available? For example, one firm could determine whether another is having product liability safety problems with its product and could alter its product to prevent such problems. Should any further controls be placed on FOIA requests?

Federal Privacy Act

In 1974, Congress passed the **Federal Privacy Act (FPA)** to reduce exchanges of information between agencies about persons (individuals and businesses). The FPA prohibits federal agencies from communicating any records to another agency or person without first obtaining the consent of the person whose record is being communicated. The FPA protects all records about individuals that might be in the possession of the agency, including medical and employment histories.

Because law enforcement agencies would have a difficult time trying to conduct investigations if they had to get permission from the individuals being investigated in order to obtain information, law enforcement agencies are exempt from the FPA. Congress can also obtain information without consent. Routine agency tasks are also exempt from the prior permission requirement. For example, employees of the SEC need constant access to information about stock sales by corporate directors so that the SEC can perform its role of preventing insider trading.

Government in the Sunshine Act

The **Government in the Sunshine Act** is often called an **open meeting law.** Its purpose is to require prior public notice of meetings of those agencies with heads appointed by the president. All the agencies with the word *commission* in their names have agency heads appointed by the president.

This open meeting law applies only to meetings between or among agency heads. For example, when the commissioners of the FTC meet together, that meeting must be public and held only after there has been prior notice. Staff members can hold meetings in private without giving notice. Meetings on law enforcement investigations are also exempt.

Ethical Issues

In 1997, the Internal Revenue Service (IRS) disciplined employees who, out of curiosity, were looking up tax returns of famous people. The employees were not working on the taxpayers' returns; they were not obtaining information for investigations; they were simply checking to see who made how much income. The IRS fired 23 employees, disciplined 349, and provided counseling for 472. During 1996 and 1997, the IRS investigated 1,515 cases of snooping among its 102,000 employees.

Is this practice so bad? What is wrong with just looking at data accessible at work? The IRS employees said they did not disclose the data and therefore didn't violate federal privacy laws. Are ethics and laws the same thing?

For the Manager's Desk

Re: The Size and Scope of Federal Regulation

A study by Professor John W. Dawson and John L. Seater reveals that the CFR has increased in size, from 19,335 pages in 1949 to 134,261 in 2005. The two professors also make the following observations about the CFR during this time period:

> The fastest percentage growth occurred in the early 1950s. High growth also occurred in the 1970s even though there was extensive deregulation in transportation, telecommunications, and energy. Deregulation in that period was more than offset by increased regulation in other areas, notably pertaining to the environment and occupational safety. Total pages decreased in only one year, 1985.[1]

The passage of the Dodd–Frank Wall Street Reform and Consumer Protection Act has resulted in the creation of a new federal agency, the Bureau of Consumer Financial Protection, and will require 234 new federal rulemaking processes at 11 federal agencies including the Federal Reserve, the FTC, the SEC, the Treasury Department, the FDIC, and the Commodities Futures Trading Commission.

For an economic analysis of the impact of regulation, go to http://www.cei.org. For an analysis of the new legislation, go to www.financialservices.house.gov and click on the Dodd-Frank tab.

Federal Register Act

Although the **Federal Register Act (FRA)** is not a part of the APA, its provisions are necessary for all the acts under the APA to work. The FRA created the **Federal Register System,** which oversees publication of federal agency information. This system provides the means for Sunshine Act notices and publication of agency rules and procedures.

Three publications make up the Federal Register System. The first is the *U.S. Government Manual.* This publication is reprinted each year and lists all federal agencies and their regional offices along with addresses. In addition, the *Manual* contains statistics about the agencies and their sizes.

The second publication of the Federal Register Act is the *Code of Federal Regulations.* (The U.S. Code is covered in Chapter 1.) The *Code of Federal Regulations* contains all the regulations of all the federal agencies. The volumes are in paperback, and the entire Code is republished each year because of tremendous changes in the regulations.

The third publication under the Federal Register System provides a daily update on changes in the regulations. This publication, called the *Federal Register,* is published every government working day and contains proposed regulations, notices of meetings (under the Government in the Sunshine Act), notices of hearings on proposed regulations, and the final versions of amended or new regulations. The *Federal Register* totals about 70,000 pages a year, or about 250 pages every working day.

The Functions of Administrative Agencies and Business Interaction

Administrative agencies have three functions: promulgating regulations, enforcing rules, and adjudicating rules. Businesses will find themselves interacting with agencies in all three areas of operation.

Providing Input When Agencies Are Promulgating Regulations

The legislative function of administrative agencies has two forms: **formal rulemaking** and **informal rulemaking.** Some agencies combine them into a type of rulemaking that is a cross between formal and informal—**hybrid rulemaking.** This section focuses on formal rulemaking.

Formal Rulemaking

Exhibit 6.3 diagrams the steps involved in formal rulemaking.

Congressional Enabling Act

Congress is responsible for passing statutes designed to remedy a perceived problem that is within federal jurisdiction. As legislation progresses through Congress, constituents have an opportunity to voice their views and concerns about problem areas.

After the 1929 stock market crash, Congress perceived problems with the way securities were being sold and traded on the national exchanges. To correct some of the problems and abuses in the trading of securities, Congress passed the 1933 and 1934 Securities Acts (see Chapter 21 for more details), the first of which created the SEC as the administrative agency responsible for the enforcement of the two acts. The following is an excerpt from the 1933 Securities Act, the enabling act for the SEC.

> (a) *There is hereby established a Securities and Exchange Commission (hereinafter referred to as the "Commission") to be composed of five commissioners to be appointed by the President by and with the advice and consent of the Senate. Not more than three of such commissioners shall be members of the same political party and in making appointments members of different political parties shall be appointed alternately as nearly as may be practicable. . . .*

EXHIBIT **6.3**   Steps in Formal Rulemaking by Administrative Agencies

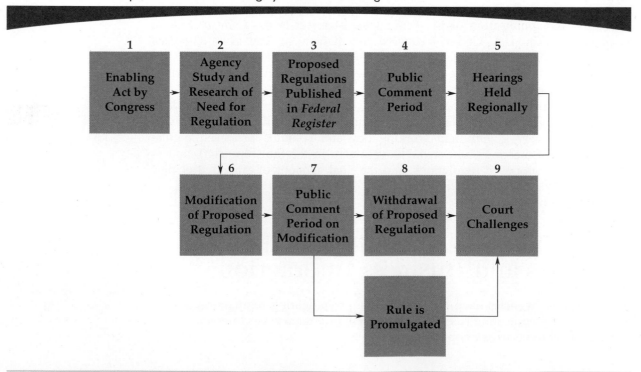

(b) *The Commission is authorized to appoint and fix the compensation of such officers, attorneys, examiners, and other experts as may be necessary for carrying out its functions under this chapter. . . .*

Agency Research of the Problem

Any regulation passed by an administrative agency must have some purpose and evidence to show that the regulation will accomplish the purpose. Rules passed without some study and evidence supporting their need or effectiveness could be challenged as "arbitrary and capricious" (discussed later in this chapter) by the persons or industries affected by the questioned rules.

Agency staff can perform the study, or the agency can hire outside experts to conduct it. The study will examine issues such as whether the regulation will be cost effective. Some regulations may cost billions of dollars for industries to follow. Regulation Z, for example, requires lenders to send out a substantial amount of paperwork; the preparation of the paperwork and the cost of mailing, along with personnel costs for the work involved, are tremendous. However, full knowledge of the cost of consumer debt is an important goal specified by Congress in the Consumer Credit Protection Act. The study focuses not only on monetary costs but also on the problems the regulation is trying to correct and the cost of those problems to the individual and to society.

Proposed Regulations

Based on the needs and costs shown by the completed study, the agency will publish its proposed rules or rule changes in the *Federal Register*. To be valid, the notice in the *Federal Register* must contain certain information. If notice is not given or is given improperly, a court can set aside the action taken by the agency and require the rulemaking process to be repeated with proper notice.

Although not required to do so, some agencies provide background information in the notice so that some history and the function of the rules are given. In addition to publishing the notice of proposed rules in the *Federal Register*, an agency is required under the **Regulatory Flexibility Act** to publish a notice in the publications of those trades and industries that will be affected by the rule. For example, the regulation governing disclosures of sales of used vehicles was published in automobile dealers associations' publications. Exhibit 6.4 is a sample of a proposed rule publication on bunk beds.

EXHIBIT 6.4   Sample Proposed CPSC Rule on Bunk Beds

CONSUMER PRODUCT SAFETY COMMISSION

ACTION: Bunk Beds; Advance Notice of Proposed Rulemaking; Request for Comments and Information

15 CFR CHAPTER II

AGENCY: Consumer Product Safety Commission

SUMMARY: The Commission has reason to believe that unreasonable risks of injury and death may be associated with bunk beds constructed so that children can become entrapped in the beds' structure or become wedged between the bed and a wall.

This advance notice of proposed rulemaking (ANPR) initiates a rulemaking proceeding that could result in a rule mandating bunk bed performance requirements to reduce this hazard. This rule could be issued under either the Federal Hazardous Substances Act (FHSA) or the Consumer Product Safety Act (CPSA).

The Commission solicits written comments from interested persons concerning the risks of injury and death associated with bunk beds, other possible ways to address these risks, and the economic impacts of the various regulatory alternatives. The Commission also invites interested persons to submit an existing standard, or a statement of intent to modify or develop a voluntary standard, to address the risks of injury and death.

The Public Comment Period

One of the purposes for publishing proposed rules is to allow the public an opportunity to review and provide input on the proposed rules. The period during which the agency accepts comments on the rule is called the **public comment period.** Under the APA, the public comment period cannot be fewer than 30 days, but most agencies make the public comment period much longer.

Private citizens, government officials, industry representatives, businesspeople, and corporations can all send in comments. With this opportunity, businesses can provide information and express concerns about proposals. A comment to an agency on a proposed rule need not use a formal format; most just appear in letter form. Anyone who wishes to challenge the validity of a federal regulation after it becomes law must participate in the comment period and voice his or her concerns at that time.

EXHIBIT 6.5 Comments in Favor of the Proposed Rule on Bunk Beds

The CPSC received hundreds of copies of this form letter:

I am writing in regard to the advanced notice of rulemaking pertaining to bunk beds. I truly feel there should be a mandatory standard in the design and construction of bunk beds.

If one child dies due to unsafe bunk bed design and manufacture, this questions whether voluntary standards in the industry are sufficient to protect our children. Due to the fact that there were more than 54 fatalities and over 100,000 injuries from 1990 to 1995, I feel that is overwhelming evidence that mandatory standards **must** be passed to ensure that this tragedy does not strike another American family.

EXHIBIT 6.6 Comments That the Proposed Rules Are Not Enough

From the American Academy of Pediatrics

I am writing to support the creation of a mandatory standard to address children's entrapment in bunk beds.

More than 500,000 bunk beds have been recalled by the U.S. Consumer Product Safety Commission since November 1994, and despite the current voluntary standard, an estimated 50,000 non-conforming bunk beds are sold for residential use in the United States each year. On average, 10 entrapment deaths occur each year, almost all on non-conforming beds.

The Academy supports the requirement for a continuous guardrail along the entire wall side of the bed, and the requirement that all openings of end structures, and not just those within 9 inches of the sleeping surface of the lower mattress, be designed to preclude entrapment.

The Academy also believes that the mandatory standard can be strengthened further. Because bunk beds are often placed in the corner of a room, the end structures of the upper bunk should extend at least 5 inches above the mattress along their entire length to prevent children from slipping between the bed and the wall and becoming entrapped. The proposed rule presumably does not require a 5-inch minimum height along the entire length of the end structures to allow for access to a ladder. This is the same reason the continuous guardrail is not required on the side of the bed. However, closing these gaps may actually decrease the likelihood of falls.

EXHIBIT 6.7 Comments Opposing the Proposed Rule

From the International Mass Retail Association (IRMA)

IRMA urges the CPSC to review alternative measures to reduce bunk bed entrapment hazards, rather than pursuing a mandatory standard that will likely have no significant impact on the high compliance that already exists in the industry with the voluntary bunk bed design.

Product safety is an important concern to the nation's mass retailers, and for that reason, mass retailers actively strive to comply with all industry-recognized product voluntary standards. Potential liability stemming from products that do not meet widely-recognized voluntary standards also serves as an added incentive for retailers to sell compliant products.

Rather than taking the drastic step of implementing a mandatory rule, CPSC would be better advised to seek changes in the standard to address the few entrapment incidents in compliant bunk beds. The agency might also examine conducting a stepped-up education campaign aimed to make consumers, retailers and manufacturers more aware of the voluntary standard.

Some agencies hold public hearings on proposed regulations. The purpose of the hearings is to take input on the proposals and consider additional evidence and factors relevant in promulgating the final version of the rule.

Exhibits 6.5, 6.6, and 6.7 are examples of letters sent to the CPSC offering input on the proposed rule on bunk beds that is found in Exhibit 6.4.

CONSIDER... 6.1

This chapter's opening "Consider" described the EEOC's proposed guidelines on religious harassment in the workplace and the business concerns about those guidelines.

The U.S. Senate passed a resolution 94–0 urging the EEOC to drop the guidelines. The general public became actively involved in the rulemaking. Religious and business groups flooded the EEOC with more than 100,000 letters of protest.

Attorneys who examined the proposed rules issued opinions for their business clients that concluded the only way to avoid religious harassment lawsuits by employees or customers under the proposed rules was to ban all religious expression in the workplace, including the wearing or display of a yarmulke or a cross. The attorneys further concluded that banning such personal expression, a form of speech, would result in a flood of First Amendment suits.

The EEOC withdrew the proposed rules. EEOC spokesman Mike Widomski explained that "the public outcry and the number of comments that were received" triggered the reversal.

Public comments and input have an impact in the regulatory process. Is this process reasonable? How do you feel about this particular rulemaking situation? Do you believe allowing comments is a fair process?

One of the important distinctions between the legislative process and the regulatory rulemaking process is the nature of the role of those involved. Legislators, such as representatives and senators, can accept campaign contributions and meals from lobbyists. However, those who work in administrative agencies fulfill both rulemaking and enforcement roles and cannot accept such gifts. Case 6.1 illustrates what can happen when businesses and regulators cross the fine line on influence. *U.S. v Sun-Diamond Growers of California* (Case 6.1) is a criminal prosecution for alleged bribery of officials in order to persuade them to abandon or change proposed regulations before the agency.

CASE 6.1

U.S. v Sun-Diamond Growers of California
526 U.S. 398 (1999)

Gratitude Can't Be in Cash or Kind or Can It?

FACTS

Sun-Diamond Growers (Respondent) is a trade association that engaged in marketing and lobbying activities on behalf of its member cooperatives, which were owned by approximately 5,000 individual growers of raisins, figs, walnuts, prunes, and hazelnuts. The United States (Petitioner) is represented by Independent Counsel Donald Smaltz, who, as a consequence of his investigation of former Secretary of Agriculture Michael Espy (see p. 208), charged Sun-Diamond with making illegal gifts to Mr. Espy in violation of § 201(c)(1)(A). That statute provides, in relevant part, that anyone who

otherwise than as provided by law for the proper discharge of official duty . . . directly or indirectly gives, offers, or promises anything of value to any public official, former public official, or person selected to be a public official, for or because of any official act performed or to be performed by such public official, former public official, or person selected to be a public official . . . shall be fined under this title or imprisoned for not more than two years, or both.

Count One of the indictment charged Sun-Diamond with giving Mr. Espy approximately $5,900 in illegal gratuities: tickets to the 1993 U.S. Open Tennis Tournament (worth $2,295), luggage ($2,427), meals ($665), and a framed print and crystal bowl ($524). The indictment alluded to two matters in which Sun-Diamond had an interest in favorable treatment from the Secretary at the time it bestowed the gratuities. First, Sun-Diamond's member cooperatives participated in the Market Promotion Plan (MPP), a grant program administered by the Department of Agriculture to promote the sale of U.S. farm commodities in foreign countries.

Second, Sun-Diamond had an interest in the federal government's regulation of methyl bromide, a low-cost pesticide used by many individual growers. In 1992, the Environmental Protection Agency announced plans to promulgate a rule to phase out the use of methyl bromide in the United States. The jury convicted Sun-Diamond, and the District Court sentenced the respondent on this count to pay a fine of $400,000. The Court of Appeals reversed the conviction on Count One and remanded for a new trial, stating

Given that the "for or because of any official act" language in § 201(c)(1)(A) means what it says, the jury instructions invited the jury to convict on materially less evidence than the statute demands—evidence of gifts driven simply by Espy's official position.

The Supreme Court granted *certiorari.*

JUDICIAL OPINION

SCALIA, Justice

Talmudic sages believed that judges who accepted bribes would be punished by eventually losing all knowledge of the divine law. The Federal Government, dealing with many public officials who are not judges, and with at least some judges for whom this sanction holds no terror, has constructed a framework of human laws and regulations defining various sorts of impermissible gifts, and punishing those who give or receive them with administrative sanctions, fines, and incarceration. One element of that framework is 18 U.S.C. § 201(c)(1)(A), the "illegal gratuity statute," which prohibits giving "anything of value" to a present, past, or future public official "for or because of any official act performed or to be performed by such public official." In this case, we consider whether conviction under the illegal gratuity statute requires any showing beyond the fact that a gratuity was given because of the recipient's official position.

Bribery requires intent "to influence" an official act or "to be influenced" in an official act, while illegal gratuity requires only that the gratuity be given or accepted "for or because of" an official act. In other words, for bribery there must be a *quid pro quo*—a specific intent to give or receive something of value in exchange for an official act. An illegal gratuity, on the other hand, may constitute merely a reward for some future act that the public official will take (and may already have determined to take), or for a past act that he has already taken.

The District Court's instructions in this case, in differentiating between a bribe and an illegal gratuity, correctly noted that only a bribe requires proof of a *quid pro quo*. The point in controversy here is that the instructions went on to suggest that § 201(c)(1)(A), unlike the bribery statute, did not require any connection between respondent's intent and a specific official act.

In our view, this interpretation does not fit comfortably with the statutory text, which prohibits only gratuities given or received "for or because of any official act performed or to be performed." It seems to us that this means "for or because of some particular official act of whatever identity"—just as the question

"Do you like any composer?" normally means "Do you like some particular composer?"

Why go through the trouble of requiring that the gift be made "for or because of any official act performed or to be performed by such public official," and then defining "official act" (in § 201(a)(3)) to mean "any decision or action on any question, matter, cause, suit, proceeding or controversy, which may at any time be pending, or which may by law be brought before any public official, in such official's official capacity," when, if the Government's interpretation were correct, it would have sufficed to say "for or because of such official's ability to favor the donor in executing the functions of his office"? The insistence upon an "official act," carefully defined, seems pregnant with the requirement that some particular official act be identified and proved.

Besides thinking that this is the more natural meaning of § 201(c)(1)(A), we are inclined to believe it correct because of the peculiar results that the Government's alternative reading would produce. It would criminalize, for example, token gifts to the President based on his official position and not linked to any identifiable act—such as the replica jerseys given by championship sports teams each year during ceremonial White House visits. Similarly, it would criminalize a high school principal's gift of a school baseball cap to the Secretary of Education, by reason of his office, on the occasion of the latter's visit to the school. That these examples are not fanciful is demonstrated by the fact that counsel for the United States maintained at oral argument that a group of farmers would violate § 201(c)(1)(A) by providing a complimentary lunch for the Secretary of Agriculture in conjunction with his speech to the farmers concerning various matters of USDA policy—so long as the Secretary had before him, or had in prospect, matters affecting the farmers. Of course the Secretary of Agriculture *always* has before him or in prospect matters that affect farmers, just as the President always has before him or in prospect matters that affect college and professional sports, and the Secretary of Education matters that affect high schools.

All of the regulations, and some of the statutes, contain exceptions for various kinds of gratuities given by various donors for various purposes. Many of those exceptions would be snares for the unwary, given that there are no exceptions to the broad prohibition that the Government claims is imposed by § 201(c)(1). More important for present purposes, however, this regulation, and the numerous other regulations and statutes littering this field, demonstrate that this is an area where precisely targeted prohibitions are commonplace, and where more general prohibitions have been qualified by numerous exceptions. Given that reality, a statute in this field that can linguistically be interpreted to be either a meat axe or a scalpel should reasonably be taken to be the latter. Absent a text that clearly requires it, we ought not expand this one piece of the regulatory puzzle so dramatically as to make many other pieces misfits.

We hold that, in order to establish a violation of 18 U.S.C. § 201(c)(1)(A), the Government must prove a link between a thing of value conferred upon a public official and a specific "official act" for or because of which it was given. We affirm the judgment of the Court of Appeals, which remanded the case to the District Court for a new trial on Count One.

Reversed and remanded.

CASE QUESTIONS

1. Are administrative agency employees permitted to accept gifts from those affected by their regulations and policies?

2. What is required for proof of criminal wrongdoing in making a gift?

3. What happens with the conviction, and why?

Deciding What to Do with the Proposed Regulation

After the comment period is over, the agency has three choices about what to do with the proposed rules. The first choice is simply to adopt the rules. The second choice is to modify the proposed rules and go through the process of public comment again. If the modification is minor, however, the APA allows the agency to adopt a modified version of the rule without going through the public comment period again. The final choice of the proposing agency is to withdraw the rule. Some rules have so many comments pointing out their impracticability, inflexibility, or prematurity that they are withdrawn from the promulgation process. For example, the Federal Trade Commission withdrew its proposed rules on regulating advertisements during children's programming hours because of strong industry opposition, the existence of a private industry code already controlling the area, and complicated legal issues involved in the regulation of commercial speech. Subsequently, modified rules were proposed and adopted.

Ethical Issues

Three Chippewa Indian tribes submitted applications to the U.S. Department of the Interior seeking approval to convert a greyhound racing facility in Hudson, Wisconsin, to an off-reservation casino.

On June 8, 1995, the Indian Gaming staff in the department issued a draft report recommending approval of the Chippewa application.

While final decision on the application was pending in the agency, Harold Ickes (then White House Deputy Chief of Staff for Policy and Political Affairs) received a letter from Patrick O'Connor, a lobbyist for tribes that opposed the Chippewa application. The O'Connor letter explained the significance of the Chippewa decision, that the opposition tribes were important contributors to the Democratic Party, and that the Chippewa tribes were Republican supporters. In addition, Donald Fowler, the Democratic National Committee chairman, met with Mr. Ickes and "discussed the basis for the opposition to creating another gaming casino." Further, there were faxes regarding the application between White House staff and Department of the Interior staff.

On June 27, 1995, the Chippewa application was denied. The decision cited "community opposition" but did not incorporate or discuss the lengthy and detailed reports the staff had prepared for its June 8 recommendation of approval.

Interior Secretary Bruce Babbitt told Paul Eckstein, a lawyer for the Chippewa and a lifetime friend of Mr. Babbitt, that Mr. Ickes required him to issue the decision on June 27.

What ethical issues arise when political activities cross into administrative proceedings? How would the Chippewa perceive this series of events?

Court and Legislative Challenges to Proposed Rules

Those parties who made comments on the rules during their proposal stage can challenge the validity of the rules in court. An administrative rule can be challenged on several different grounds.

The Arbitrary and Capricious Standard for Challenging an Agency Action

The first ground on which to challenge an agency rule is that it is arbitrary, capricious, an abuse of discretion, or in violation of some other law. This standard is generally applied to informal rulemaking and simply requires the agency to show evidence to support the proposed rule. Without such evidence, the rule can be held to be **arbitrary and capricious.** *Motor Vehicles Manufacturers Ass'n. v State Farm Mutual Insurance Co.* (Case 6.2) addresses the issue of whether an agency's action is arbitrary and capricious.

CASE 6.2   *Motor Vehicles Manufacturers Ass'n v State Farm Mutual Insurance Co.*
463 U.S. 29 (1983)

Fasten Your Seatbelts: Rulemaking Is a Rough Ride

FACTS

The Department of Transportation (DOT), charged with the enforcement of the National Traffic and Motor Vehicle Safety Act of 1966 and the task of reducing auto accidents, passed Standard 208 in 1967. Standard 208 is the seatbelt requirement for motor vehicles, and its original form simply required that all cars be equipped with seatbelts. It soon became clear to the DOT that people did not use the belts, so the department began a study of passive restraint systems, which do not require any action on the part of the occupant other than operating the vehicle. The two types considered were automatic seatbelts and airbags. Studies showed that these devices could prevent approximately 12,000 deaths a year and over 100,000 serious injuries.

© JODIE COSTON/ISTOCKPHOTO.COM

© MILOUSSK/SHUTTERSTOCK

In 1972, after many hearings and comments, the Department of Transportation passed a regulation requiring some type of passive restraint system on all vehicles manufactured after 1975. The regulation allowed an ignition interlock system, which requires car occupants to have their seatbelts fastened before a car could be started. Congress, however, revoked the requirement of the ignition interlock.

Because of changes in directors of the DOT and the unfavorable economic climate in the auto industry, the requirements for passive restraints were postponed. In 1981, the department proposed a rescission of the passive restraint rule. After receiving written comments and holding public hearings, the agency concluded there was no longer a basis for reliably predicting that passive restraints increased safety levels or decreased accidents. Further, the agency found it would cost $1 billion to implement the rule, and they were unwilling to impose such substantial costs on auto manufacturers.

State Farm filed suit on the rescission of the rule on the basis that it was arbitrary and capricious. The court of appeals held that the rescission was, in fact, arbitrary and capricious. Auto manufacturers appealed.

JUDICIAL OPINION

WHITE, Justice

The ultimate question before us is whether NHTSA's [National Highway Traffic Safety Administration] rescission of the passive restraint requirement of Standard 208 was arbitrary and capricious. We conclude, as did the Court of Appeals, that it was.

The first and most obvious reason for finding the rescission arbitrary and capricious is that NHTSA apparently gave no consideration whatever to modifying the Standard to require that airbag technology be utilized. Standard 208 sought to achieve automatic crash protection by requiring automobile manufacturers to install either of two passive restraint devices: airbags or automatic seatbelts. There was no suggestion in the long rulemaking process that led to Standard 208 that if only one of these options were feasible, no passive restraint standard should be promulgated. Indeed, the agency's original proposed standard contemplated the installation of inflatable restraints in all cars. Automatic belts were added as a means of complying with the standard because they were believed to be as effective as airbags in achieving the goal of occupant crash protection.

The agency has now determined that the detachable automatic belts will not attain anticipated safety benefits because so many individuals will detach the mechanism. Even if this conclusion were acceptable in its entirety, standing alone it would not justify any more than an amendment of Standard 208 to disallow compliance by means of the only technology which will not provide effective passenger protection. It does not cast doubt on the need for a passive restraint standard or upon the efficacy of airbag technology. In its most recent rulemaking, the agency again acknowledged the life-saving potential of the airbag.

Given the effectiveness ascribed to airbag technology by the agency, the mandate of the Safety Act to achieve traffic safety would suggest that the logical response to the faults of detachable seatbelts would be to require the installation of airbags. At the very least this alternative way of achieving objectives of the Act should have been addressed and adequate reasons given for its abandonment. But the agency not only did not require compliance through airbags, it did not even consider the possibility in its 1981 rulemaking. Not one sentence of its rulemaking statement discusses the airbags-only option. We have frequently reiterated that an agency must cogently explain why it had exercised its discretion in a given manner.

For nearly a decade, the automobile industry waged the regulatory equivalent of war against the airbag and lost—the inflatable restraint was proven sufficiently effective. Now the automobile industry has decided to employ a seatbelt system which will not meet the safety objectives of Standard 208. This hardly constitutes cause to revoke the standard itself. Indeed the Motor Vehicle Safety Act was necessary because the industry was not sufficiently responsive to safety concerns. The Act intended that safety standards not depend on current technology and would be "technology-forcing" in the sense of inducing the development of superior safety design.

It is not infrequent that the available data does not settle a regulatory issue and the agency must then exercise its judgment in moving from the facts and probabilities on the record to a policy conclusion. Recognizing that policy making in a complex society must account for uncertainty, however, does not imply that it is sufficient for an agency to merely recite the terms "substantial uncertainty" as a justification for its actions. The agency must explain the evidence which is available, and must offer a "rational connection between the facts found and the choice made."

In this case, the agency's explanation for rescission of the passive restraint requirement is not sufficient to enable us to conclude that the rescission was the product of reasoned decision making. We start with the accepted ground that if used, seatbelts unquestionably would save many thousands of lives and would prevent tens of thousands of crippling injuries. Unlike recent regulations we have reviewed, the safety benefits of wearing seatbelts are not in doubt and it is not challenged that were those benefits to accrue, the monetary costs of implementing the standard would be easily justified.

CONTINUED

Since 20 to 50 percent of motorists currently wear seatbelts on some occasions, there would seem to be grounds to believe that seatbelt use by occasional users will be substantially increased by the detachable passive belts. Whether this is the case is a matter for the agency to decide, but it must bring its expertise to bear on the question.

An agency's view of what is in the public interest may change, either with or without a change in circumstances. But an agency changing its course must supply a reasoned analysis. We do not accept all of the reasoning of the Court of Appeals but we do conclude that the agency has failed to supply the requisite "reasoned analysis" in this case. Accordingly, we remand the matter to the NHTSA for further consideration consistent with this opinion.

CASE QUESTIONS

1. What regulation is at issue in the case?
2. Give the history of the regulation and its modifications over the years.
3. What was done with the regulation to result in this judicial decision?
4. Who challenged the agency's actions, and what were the reasons for this challenge?
5. Is the agency's action valid? Why or why not?

For the Manager's Desk

Re: The Airbag Issue That Does Not Go Away

The issue of passive restraints in vehicles and the Department of Transportation (DOT)'s rejection of them resurfaced in 1996. Following the *State Farm* case, passive restraint systems, including airbags, were mandated in passenger vehicles. However, in 1996, evidence of a problem—noted by General Motors in a 1979 comment to DOT and in DOT studies in 1981—emerged: Children were killed in auto accidents when the airbags in the vehicles in which they were riding deployed.

Engineers discovered that the force of an inflating bag (up to 200 mph) was sufficient to snap a child's neck or deform a child's head. In several of the accidents, children were decapitated by the inflated bags. Children involved in the accidents were properly restrained in their seatbelts or car seats. The cause of the 50 injuries or deaths involving children between 1991 and 1996 was the passenger-side airbag. Over a six-month period, the National Highway Traffic Safety Administration (NHTSA) studied the issue and considered the following options:

1. Elimination of airbags
2. Installation of switches to turn off passenger-side airbags
3. Warnings in vehicles on the dangers of passenger-side airbags
4. Recommendation that all children ride in the back seat of vehicles

Insurers and auto manufacturers opposed elimination of airbags and switches for fear of liability and misuse of switches. Consumers favored switches. NHTSA, following input, required warnings in all vehicles about airbags but did not require switches. The warning labels (three in all new cars) must be posted on the dashboard as well as on each side of the car visor. The dashboard label reads as follows:

> *WARNING*
>
> *Children may be KILLED or INJURED by Passenger Airbag.*
> *The back seat is the safest place for children 12 and under.*
> *Make sure all children use seat belts or child seats.*

Later, NHTSA took feedback on a proposed rule to permit switches, a rule that was promulgated and is now in effect.

However, the airbag continues to be a lightning rod for discussion and controversy. One of the key researchers who testified of the need for airbags over 20 years ago recently testified that he was wrong and that passenger-side airbags don't save enough lives to justify their risk and expense. John Graham, the director of Harvard's Center for Risk Analysis, announced his change of heart at a National Transportation Safety Board hearing.

In 2000, Congress directed the DOT to develop guidelines for airbags that would satisfy the safety requirements but would not result in injury to smaller occupants in cars. The NHTSA published a final rule in December 2001 that required airbags and deployment at 25 mph, but several consumer groups challenged the final rule as creating additional safety problems for vehicle occupants and being promulgated in defiance of existing evidence and studies, making the rules "arbitrary and capricious." The NHTSA continued with the rule, and the consumer groups took the agency to court. In the case [*Public Citizen, Inc. v Mineta*, 374 F.3d 1251 (D.C. Cir. 2004)], the court concluded that experts and consumers can disagree on the agency's rule, but as long as the agency's position is supported by research, evidence, and comments, it is neither arbitrary nor capricious.

BUSINESS STRATEGY

Why Insurers Pursue Federal Safety Regulations

In the *State Farm* case, it is an insurer, not an auto manufacturer, who is challenging the proposed regulation (or lack thereof). Certainly the insurer does not carry the responsibility of implementing the safety designs or perfecting the technology. However, because the implementation of such safety features helps reduce claims for accident injuries and damages, the insurer has a business interest in seeing that the regulations are passed. Businesses, like the insurers here, often must become involved in regulatory proceedings for rules that might not regulate them directly but will benefit or cost them indirectly. In regulatory proceedings, businesses that will experience indirect impact often take a position and use the process to their business benefit.

The Substantial Evidence Standard for Challenging an Agency Action   A second theory for challenging an agency's regulation is that the regulation is unsupported by substantial evidence. This **substantial evidence test** is applied in the review of formal and hybrid rulemaking. Where the arbitrary and capricious standard simply requires some proof or basis for the regulation, substantial evidence requires that more convincing evidence exist in support of the regulation than against it. A third ground on which to challenge an agency's regulation involves the rule that a regulation can be set aside if the agency did not comply with the APA requirements of notice, publication, and public comment or input. The procedures for rulemaking must be followed in order for the regulatory process and resulting rules to be valid. An agency that seeks public comment for the purposes of drafting regulations cannot then turn the proposed regulations into agency rules after the comment period. The promulgated rules must be the result of the proceedings.

CONSIDER...   6.2

Hornbeck Offshore Services, LLC, and other entities that provide a myriad of services to support offshore oil and gas drilling, exploration, and production activities in the Gulf of Mexico's Outer Continental Shelf brought suit against the Department of the Interior (DOI) to challenge the six-month moratorium on offshore drilling operations of new and currently permitted deepwater wells that was imposed on May 28, 2010 by DOI and the Minerals Management Service.

The government moratorium was imposed in reaction to the Deepwater Horizon drilling platform blowout on April 20, 2010, and the resulting devastation. In response to this unprecedented disaster, President Obama formed a bipartisan commission—the National Commission on the BP Deepwater Horizon Oil Spill and Offshore Drilling—to investigate the facts and circumstances that led to the blowout. Mr. Obama also ordered the Secretary of the Interior to conduct a thorough review of the Deepwater Horizon blowout and to report, within 30 days, whether additional protections and precautions were necessary for oil and gas exploration and production operations on the outer continental shelf.

Following consultation with respected experts from state and federal governments, academic institutions, and industry and advocacy organizations, the Secretary issued a report and recommended a six-month moratorium on permits for new wells being drilled

CONTINUED

using floating rigs as well as an immediate halt of drilling operations on the 33 existing wells. The Secretary's Summary stated that "the recommendations contained in this report have been peer-reviewed by seven experts identified by the National Academy of Engineering." The experts objected to the Secretary's characterization, calling it a "misrepresentation" and factually incorrect. Although the experts agreed with the safety recommendations contained in the body of the report, five of the National Academy experts and three of the other experts stated publicly that they "do not agree with the six month blanket moratorium" on drilling and had recommended a more limited kind of moratorium. They also filed affidavits stating that the blanket moratorium was added after their final review and was never agreed to by them. The draft reviewed by the experts, for example, recommended a six-month moratorium on exploratory wells deeper than 1000 feet (not 500 feet) to allow for implementation of suggested safety measures.

What should the judge do with the moratorium imposed by the agency? Should it be upheld?

THINK: The decision in the *State Farm* case, as well as the arbitrary and capricious and substantial evidence doctrines, require that any agency action, whether a promulgation of a rule or its withdrawal, be supported by evidence and APA processes. That process requires some evidence related to the action taken or rule promulgated. There must be a full public airing of the issues.

APPLY: In this case study, the report of the experts has been changed and the experts have filed affidavits indicating that the use of their report with that content is misrepresentation. There are questions about the evidentiary foundation for the agency's decision.

ANSWER: The purpose of the APA requirements is to curb the emotion of the moment and ensure that agencies do not take action without having followed a process for input and before obtaining evidence that the actions take are necessary. The court concluded that the DOI had made no effort to justify the moratorium explicitly and that it had not discussed in its finding any irreparable harm that would warrant a suspension of operations. Some excerpts from the court's opinion follow. Make a list of the kinds of factors the court looks at to determine whether an agency's action is arbitrary and capricious.

"The APA cautions that an agency action may only be set aside if it is 'arbitrary, capricious, an abuse of discretion, or not otherwise not in accordance with law.' . . . After reviewing the Secretary's Report, the Moratorium Memorandum, and the Notice to Lessees, the Court is unable to divine or fathom a relationship between the findings and the immense scope of the moratorium. The Report, invoked by the Secretary, describes the offshore oil industry in the Gulf and offers many compelling recommendations to improve safety. But it offers no time line for implementation, though many of the proposed changes are represented to be implemented immediately. The Report patently lacks any analysis of the asserted fear of threat of irreparable injury or safety hazards posed by the thirty-three permitted rigs also reached by the moratorium. It is incident-specific and driven: Deepwater Horizon and BP only. None others. While the Report notes the increase in deepwater drilling over the past ten years and the increased safety risk associated with deepwater drilling, the parameters of "deepwater" remain confused. And drilling elsewhere simply seems driven by political or social agendas on all sides. The Report seems to define "deepwater" as drilling beyond a depth of 1000 feet by referencing the increased difficulty of drilling beyond this depth; similarly, the shallowest depth referenced in the maps and facts included in the Report is "less than 1000 feet." But while there is no mention of the 500 feet depth anywhere in the Report itself, the Notice to Lessees suddenly defines "deepwater" as more than 500 feet. . . . The Court cannot substitute its judgment for that of the agency, but the agency must "cogently explain why it has exercised its discretion in a given manner. It has not done so." The DOI later withdrew the moratorium. [*Hornbeck Offshore Services, LLC v Salazar,* 696 F.Supp. 2d 627 (E.D. La. 2010); 2010 WL 3825385 (5th Cir. 2010).]

The Constitutional Standard for Challenging an Agency's Action   Another basis for challenging a regulation is that the regulation is unconstitutional. Many challenges based on constitutional grounds deal with regulations that give an agency authority to search records or that impose discriminatory requirements for licensing professionals. For example, a requirement of a minimum residency period before allowing an applicant to become licensed in a particular profession has been challenged successfully. Zoning board regulations that discriminate against certain classes or races as to the use of property have also been successfully challenged as unconstitutional. Further, broadcasters often depend on freedom of speech—the First Amendment—to challenge new Federal Communication Commission (FCC) regulations. *FCC v Fox Television Stations, Inc.*, 129 S.Ct. 1800 (2009).

The *Ultra Vires* Standard for Challenging an Agency's Action   Another theory for challenging a regulation in court is *ultra vires,* a Latin term meaning "beyond its powers." An *ultra vires* regulation is one that goes beyond the authority given to the agency in its enabling act. Although most agencies stay clearly within their authority, if an agency tries to change the substance and purpose of the enabling act through regulation, the regulations would be *ultra vires.* For example, the intent of the 1933 Securities Act was to provide full disclosure to investors about a securities sale. The SEC could not, on the basis of its authority, pass a rule that eliminated securities registration in favor of an unregulated securities market. In *Massachusetts v EPA* (Case 6.3), the court dealt with greenhouse gases as well as their regulation within the context of challenges to the EPA based on *ultra vires,* substantial evidence, and the administrative regulation process. (Uniquely, the agency's defense was that the actions groups were demanding were *ultra vires.*)

CASE 6.3	*Massachusetts v EPA* 549 U.S. 497 (2007)

Who Has Jurisdiction Over Hot Air? Congress? EPA? The Supreme Court?

FACTS

On October 20, 1999, a group of 19 private organizations (petitioners) filed a rulemaking petition asking EPA to regulate "greenhouse gas emissions from new motor vehicles under § 202 of the Clean Air Act." Petitioners maintained that greenhouse gas emissions have significantly accelerated climate change; and that "carbon dioxide remains the most important contributor to [man-made] forcing of climate change."

Fifteen months after the petition was filed, the EPA requested public comment on "all the issues raised in [the] petition," adding a "particular" request for comments on "any scientific, technical, legal, economic or other aspect of these issues that may be relevant to EPA's consideration of this petition," including whether there was global warming due to carbon emissions. The EPA received more than 50,000 comments over the next five months.

On September 8, 2003, EPA entered an order denying the rulemaking petition because (1) the Clean Air Act does not authorize EPA to issue mandatory regulations to address global climate change; and (2) even if the agency had the authority to set greenhouse gas emission standards, it would be unwise to do so at this time. Massachusetts, other states, and private organizations filed suit challenging the EPA denial as arbitrary and capricious, violative of the APA, and *ultra vires* because of statutory mandates for EPA action. The court of appeals dismissed the appeal from the agency denial and the Supreme Court granted *certiorari.*

JUDICIAL OPINION

STEVENS, Justice

In concluding that it lacked statutory authority over greenhouse gases, EPA observed that Congress "was

CONTINUED

well aware of the global climate change issue when it last comprehensively amended the [Clean Air Act] in 1990," yet it declined to adopt a proposed amendment establishing binding emissions limitations. Congress instead chose to authorize further investigation into climate change. In essence, EPA concluded that climate change was so important that unless Congress spoke with exacting specificity, it could not have meant the agency to address it.

According to the climate scientist Michael MacCracken, "qualified scientific experts involved in climate change research" have reached a "strong consensus" that global warming threatens (among other things) a precipitate rise in sea levels by the end of the century.[2]

While it may be true that regulating motor vehicle emissions will not by itself *reverse* global warming, it by no means follows that we lack jurisdiction to decide whether EPA has a duty to take steps to *slow* or *reduce* it. Because of the enormity of the potential consequences associated with man-made climate change, the fact that the effectiveness of a remedy might be delayed during the (relatively short) time it takes for a new motor-vehicle fleet to replace an older one is essentially irrelevant.

We find such action is " . . . arbitrary, capricious, an abuse of discretion, or otherwise not in accordance with law."

. . . The first question is whether § 202(a)(1) of the Clean Air Act authorizes EPA to regulate greenhouse gas emissions from new motor vehicles in the event that it forms a "judgment" that such emissions contribute to climate change.

The Clean Air Act's sweeping definition of "air pollutant" includes "*any* air pollution agent or combination of such agents, including *any* physical, chemical . . . substance or matter which is emitted into or otherwise enters the ambient air . . ." § 7602(g) (emphasis added). On its face, the definition embraces all airborne compounds of whatever stripe, and underscores that intent through the repeated use of the word "any." Carbon dioxide, methane, nitrous oxide, and hydrofluorocarbons are without a doubt "physical [and] chemical . . . substance[s] which [are] emitted into . . . the ambient air." The statute is unambiguous. If EPA makes a finding of endangerment, the Clean Air Act requires the agency to regulate emissions of the deleterious pollutant from new motor vehicles. Under the clear terms of the Clean Air Act, EPA can avoid taking further action only if it determines that greenhouse gases do not contribute to climate change or if it provides some reasonable explanation as to why it cannot or will not exercise its discretion to determine whether they do. To the extent that this constrains agency discretion to pursue other priorities of the Administrator or the President, this is the congressional design.

EPA finally argues that it cannot regulate carbon dioxide emissions from motor vehicles because doing so would require it to tighten mileage standards, a job (according to EPA) that Congress has assigned to DOT. But that DOT sets mileage standards in no way licenses EPA to shirk its environmental responsibilities. EPA has been charged with protecting the public's "health" and "welfare," a statutory obligation wholly independent of DOT's mandate to promote energy efficiency. The two obligations may overlap, but there is no reason to think the two agencies cannot both administer their obligations and yet avoid inconsistency.

Because greenhouse gases fit well within the Clean Air Act's capacious definition of "air pollutant," we hold that EPA has the statutory authority to regulate the emission of such gases from new motor vehicles.

. . . the use of the word "judgment" is not a roving license to ignore the statutory text. It is but a direction to exercise discretion within defined statutory limits.

Nor can EPA avoid its statutory obligation by noting the uncertainty surrounding various features of climate change and concluding that it would therefore be better not to regulate at this time. If the scientific uncertainty is so profound that it precludes EPA from making a reasoned judgment as to whether greenhouse gases contribute to global warming, EPA must say so. That EPA would prefer not to regulate greenhouse gases because of some residual uncertainty-which, contrary to Justice SCALIA's apparent belief, is in fact all that it said, is irrelevant. The statutory question is whether sufficient information exists to make an endangerment finding.

In short, EPA has offered no reasoned explanation for its refusal to decide whether greenhouse gases cause or contribute to climate change. Its action was therefore "arbitrary, capricious . . . , or otherwise not in accordance with law." We need not and do not reach the question whether on remand EPA must make an endangerment finding, or whether policy concerns can inform EPA's actions in the event that it makes such a finding. We hold only that EPA must ground its reasons for action or inaction in the statute.

The judgment of the Court of Appeals is reversed, and the case is remanded.

DISSENTING OPINION

Chief Justice ROBERTS, with whom Justice SCALIA, Justice THOMAS, and Justice ALITO join, dissenting.

Global warming may be a "crisis," even "the most pressing environmental problem of our time." Indeed, it may ultimately affect nearly everyone on the planet in some potentially adverse way, and it may be that governments have done too little to address it. It is not a problem, however, that has escaped the attention of policymakers in the Executive and Legislative Branches of our Government, who continue to consider regulatory, legislative, and treaty-based means of addressing global climate change.

Apparently dissatisfied with the pace of progress on this issue in the elected branches, petitioners have come to the courts claiming broad-ranging injury, and attempting to tie that injury to the Government's alleged failure to comply with a rather narrow statutory provision. I would reject these challenges as nonjusticiable. Such a conclusion involves no judgment on whether global warming exists, what causes it, or the extent of the problem. Nor does it render petitioners without recourse. This Court's standing jurisprudence simply recognizes that redress of grievances of the sort at issue here "is the function of Congress and the Chief Executive," not the federal courts. I would vacate the judgment below and remand for dismissal of the petitions for review.

Justice SCALIA, with whom THE CHIEF JUSTICE, Justice THOMAS, and Justice ALITO join, dissenting.

EPA's interpretation of the discretion conferred by the statutory reference to "its judgment" is not only reasonable, it is the most natural reading of the text. The Court nowhere explains why this interpretation is incorrect. . . . Although there have been substantial advances in climate change science, there continue to be important uncertainties in our understanding of the factors that may affect future climate change and how it should be addressed.

[The] Court invents a multiple-choice question that the EPA Administrator must answer when a petition for rulemaking is filed. The Administrator must exercise his judgment in one of three ways: (a) by concluding that the pollutant *does* cause, or contribute to, air pollution that endangers public welfare (in which case EPA is required to regulate); (b) by concluding that the pollutant *does not* cause, or contribute to, air pollution that endangers public welfare (in which case EPA is *not* required to regulate); or (c) by "provid[ing] some reasonable explanation as to why it cannot or will not exercise its discretion to determine whether"

greenhouse gases endanger public welfare, (in which case EPA is *not* required to regulate).

I am willing to assume, for the sake of argument, that the Administrator's discretion in this regard is not entirely unbounded-that if he has no reasonable basis for deferring judgment he must grasp the nettle at once. The Court, however, with no basis in text or precedent, rejects all of EPA's stated "policy judgments" as not "amount[ing] to a reasoned justification." Judgment can be delayed *only* if the Administrator concludes that "the scientific uncertainty is [too] profound." The Administrator is precluded from concluding *for other reasons* "that it would . . . be better not to regulate at this time." Such other reasons—perfectly valid reasons— were set forth in the agency's statement.

I simply cannot conceive of what else the Court would like EPA to say.

The Court's alarm over global warming may or may not be justified, but it ought not distort the outcome of this litigation. This is a straightforward administrative-law case, in which Congress has passed a malleable statute giving broad discretion, not to us but to an executive agency. No matter how important the underlying policy issues at stake, this Court has no business substituting its own desired outcome for the reasoned judgment of the responsible agency.

CASE QUESTIONS

1. What authority is given to the EPA by statute? Why does the EPA not want to exercise authority over greenhouse gases?

2. Why does the majority conclude that greenhouse gases are included within that authority?

3. List the arguments the dissent makes against requiring the EPA to take action on greenhouse gases. What do you learn about the role of the issue of global warming in the dissent's analysis of the case versus the analysis of the majority?

Proactive Business Strategies in Regulation

Some administrative regulations can be eliminated through the use of legislation. In an enabling act called a **sunset law,** Congress creates an agency for a limited period of time during which the agency must establish its benefits and other justification for its continuation. The enabling act may provide for an audit to determine effectiveness after the agency has been in existence for two years. Without renewal by Congress, the "sun sets" on the agency and it is terminated. Some businesses lobby for the creation of sunset agencies to better control the number of agencies and their effectiveness.

Some agencies' power is controlled through congressional purse strings. With **zero-based budgeting,** the agency does not automatically receive a budget amount but rather starts with a zero budget each year and then is required to justify all its needs for funds. This type of control gives Congress some say each year in how the agency is operating. For example, the budget could be renewed only on the condition that the agency not promulgate certain regulations opposed by Congress.

Another tool for curbing regulation that has been used in recent years has been action by the executive branch. For example, former President George H. W. Bush (41) imposed a 90-day moratorium on all new regulations in 1992. During this period, regulators were not permitted to promulgate new regulations. Additionally, the Negotiated Rulemaking Act of 1990 helps businesses work with regulators and permits agencies to develop new methods for resolving controversies outside of the traditional rulemaking process.

Informal Rulemaking

The process for informal rulemaking is the same as that for formal rulemaking, with the exception that no public hearings are held on the rule. The only input from the public comes in the form of comments, using the same procedures discussed earlier.

Business Rights in Agency Enforcement Action

Administrative agencies not only make the rules; they enforce them. In so doing, the agencies are also responsible for adjudicating disputes over the scope or interpretation of the rules. Exhibit 6.8 is a chart of the steps involved in agency enforcement and adjudication.

EXHIBIT 6.8   Steps for Administrative Agency Enforcement and Adjudication

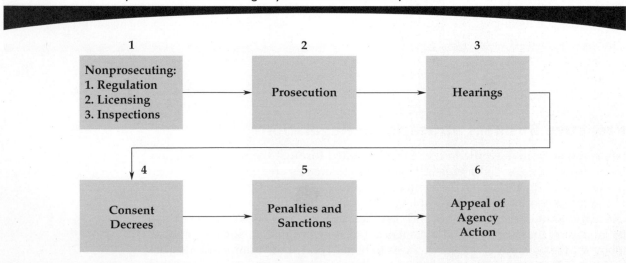

Licensing and Inspections

Much of an administrative agency's role in enforcement is carried out by requiring the submission of certain types of paperwork. Many agencies issue licenses or permits as a way to enforce the law. For example, state administrative agencies may require building contractors to be licensed so that their dues can finance a recovery fund for the victims of bankrupt or negligent contractors. The idea behind the licensing and permit method of enforcement is to curtail illegal activity up front and also to have records in case problems arise.

Agencies also have the authority to conduct inspections, such as when an agency responsible for restaurant licenses inspects restaurant facilities to check for health code violations. The Occupational Safety and Health Administration (OSHA) at the federal level has the authority to inspect plants to check for violations of OSHA standards. This power of inspection at unannounced times is an enforcement tool by itself and provides strong incentive to comply with regulations. A business can refuse an inspection, but an agency can obtain a warrant and return for a mandatory inspection.

Prosecution of Businesses

Administrative agencies are also given the authority to prosecute violators. These agency prosecutions, however, are not traditional criminal prosecutions; the sanctions imposed for agency violations are not jail terms but rather fines, penalties, and injunctions, which are civil penalties, not criminal ones. For example, in the case of false advertising—a violation of Federal Trade Commission (FTC) rules— the agency could impose restitution as a sanction: The violator would have to reimburse all those individuals who bought the product based on false advertising. In some cases, an agency may merely want a violator to stop certain conduct and promise not to engage in that type of conduct again.

Beginning Enforcement Steps

Regardless of the remedy an agency seeks, all action begins when the agency issues a **complaint** against the violating party. The complaint describes when and what the company did and why it is a violation.

Once a complaint is filed, an agency can negotiate with a party for an order or proceed to a hearing to obtain an order from an administrative law judge. The remedies in an order vary according to the type of violation and whether it is ongoing. The FTC could, and typically does, order companies running deceptive ads to stop using the ads and promise not to use them again in the future. These sanctions usually come in the form of an **injunction,** which is a court order that prohibits specifically described conduct. Many statutes are unclear about the extent of authority an agency is given in enforcement proceedings and what types of sanctions an agency can impose for violations. The authority to assess civil penalties, for example, varies from agency to agency.

Consent Decrees

Rather than go through a hearing and the expense of the administrative process, some companies agree to penalties proposed by an agency. They do so in a document called a **consent decree,** which is comparable to a *nolo contendere* plea in the criminal system. The party does not admit or deny a violation but simply

EXHIBIT 6.9   Excerpts from an FTC Consent Decree

In the matter of the National Media Group, Inc. et al. Consent Order, etc., in regard to Alleged Violation of The Federal Trade Commission Act

This consent order, among other things, requires a King of Prussia, Pa. firm and a corporate officer engaged in the advertising and sale of "Acne-Statin," an acne "treatment," to cease disseminating or causing the dissemination of advertisements that represent that Acne-Statin cures acne, eliminates or reduces the bacteria and fatty acids responsible for acne blemishes, and is superior to all other acne preparations and soap for the antibacterial treatment of acne. . . . Additionally, they are required to establish an independent, irrevocable trust account containing sixty thousand dollars ($60,000) to be used to pay half of all requests for restitution by Acne-Statin purchasers; and obligated to conduct and be totally responsible for the administration of the restitution program.

(The original complaint appeared here.)

Order

It is ordered, That respondents, The National Media Group, Inc. a corporation . . . and the corporate respondent's officers, agents, representatives, and employees . . . do forthwith cease and desist from:

A. *Disseminating or causing the dissemination of any advertisement by means of the United States mails or by any means in or affecting commerce . . . which directly or indirectly:*

  1. *Represents that use of Acne-Statin will cure acne or any skin condition associated with acne.*

  2. *Represents that Acne-Statin will eliminate or reduce the bacteria responsible for pimples, blackheads, whiteheads, or other acne blemishes or any skin condition associated with acne.*

  3. *Represents that Acne-Statin will eliminate or reduce the fatty acids responsible for pimples, blackheads, whiteheads, other acne blemishes or any skin condition associated with acne.*

  4. *Represents that Acne-Statin is superior to prescription or over-the-counter antibacterial acne preparations in the treatment of acne.*

  5. *Represents that Acne-Statin is superior to soap in the antibacterial treatment of acne.*

It is further ordered, That:

A. *Within thirty (30) days of final acceptance of this consent order by the Federal Trade Commission (hereinafter the "Commission"), respondent, The National Media Group, Inc., shall establish an interest-bearing trust account containing the sum of sixty thousand dollars ($60,000), for the purpose of paying restitution to Acne-Statin purchasers. . . .*

negotiates a settlement with the administrative agency. The negotiated settlement includes the same types of sanctions the agency would have the power to impose if the case went to a hearing. The agency may be willing to give up a little in exchange for the violator's willingness to settle and save the agency the time and costs of full prosecution. The consent decree is a contract between the charged party and the regulatory agency. Exhibit 6.9 provides an example of an FTC consent decree.

Hearings

If the parties cannot reach an agreement through a consent decree, the question of violations and penalties will go to an administrative hearing, which is quite different from the litigation procedures described in Chapter 4. This type of hearing does not involve a jury. The plaintiff or prosecutor is the administrative agency, represented by one of its staff attorneys. The defendant is the person or company accused of violating an administrative regulation. The judge is called an **administrative law judge (ALJ)** at the federal level, and is called a **hearing examiner** or **hearing officer** in some state-level agencies. The defendant can be represented by an attorney.

An ALJ has all the powers of a judge. He or she conducts the hearing, rules on evidentiary and procedural questions, and administers oaths. The ALJ also has certain unique powers, such as the ability to hold settlement conferences between the parties. The ALJ also has the responsibility of making the decision in the case. That decision is cast in the form of a written opinion that consists of findings of facts, conclusions of law, and an order specifying the remedies and sanctions.

The ALJ also has the ethical responsibilities of a trial judge; that is, the judges are prohibited from having *ex parte* **contacts,** which are contacts with one side or one of the parties in the dispute without the knowledge of the others. Staff members of the agency are prohibited from supplying information to the ALJ except when they are witnesses or attorneys in the hearings.

Administrative hearings can have as participants more than just the agency and the party charged with a violation. Other parties with an interest in the case can intervene. These **intervenors** file motions to intervene and are usually permitted to do so at any time before the start of a hearing. Typical intervenors are industry organizations: Should the FCC hold hearings on charges against a television station on the content of ads on the station, the National Association of Broadcasters would probably want to intervene in the hearing.

The rules of evidence and procedure are somewhat relaxed in administrative hearings. Agencies involved in the hearings can issue subpoenas for documents, but the subpoenas can only be enforced by the courts. All of the investigation and adjudication processes of administrative agencies are subject to the constitutional standards of due process, which include the following rights: right to notification of the charges; right to notification of the hearing day; right to present evidence; right to be represented by an attorney; right to an impartial judge; right to a decision based on the law or regulation; and right to cross-examine the witnesses of the agency or intervenors.

Administrative Law of Appeals

Once the ALJ has issued a decision, the decision can be appealed. However, the appellate process in administrative law is slightly different. The first step in an appeal of an ALJ decision is not to a court but to the agency itself. This step gives the agency a chance to correct a bad decision before the courts become involved.

The appeal is to the next higher level in the agency. For example, in the FTC an appeal of an ALJ's decision goes to the five commissioners of the FTC for reconsideration.

In some agencies, the structure is such that appeals may be made to more than one person in the structure. Those appealing an ALJ decision, however, must go through all the required lines of authority in the agency before they can go to court. This process is known as **exhausting administrative remedies.** An appeal made before administrative remedies are completed will be rejected for the failure to exhaust available administrative processes and remedies.

The exhaustion rule does allow some exceptions. A decision by a zoning board to allow construction of a building project could go directly to court because, if the building is started but the decision to allow construction later overruled, the builder is damaged. Alternatively, if the building is not started, other purchasers of the land and the builder are harmed. In other words, fast action is required to maintain all parties' positions.

If an agency has gone beyond its enabling act, a party can also go directly to court. This matter is more of a challenge to a regulation than it is to the agency's decision, and direct appeal is therefore permitted.

EXHIBIT 6.10   The Roles of Administrative Agencies

ACTIVITY	STEPS	PARTIES	RESULTS
Passing rules	Rule proposed	Agency	New rules
	Comments	Consumers	Modified rules
	Modification, withdrawal, or promulgation	Business Congress Agency	Withdrawn rules
Enforcement	Licensing	Agency Business	
	Inspections	Agency Courts (if warrant is required) Business	Search and inspection
	Complaints	Agency	Fines Penalties Injunctions Consent decrees Hearings

Finally, an agency decision can be appealed directly to court if exhaustion of administrative remedies would be futile, as evidenced by public statements of officials of the agency. When the FTC was trying to develop rules on children's TV advertising, for example, a group of interested parties brought a court action to have then–FTC chairman Michael Pertschuk removed from the rulemaking process because he had indicated strong feelings in the press about his position. It would have been futile to try administrative remedies because the appeal would have been taken to the party they were trying to remove.

A decision of a federal administrative agency is appealed to one of the U.S. courts of appeals (as indicated in Chapter 3). An appellate court can simply affirm an agency action, find that an agency has exceeded its authority, find that an agency has violated the U.S. Constitution, or rule that an agency has acted arbitrarily or that an agency's decision or action is not supported by the evidence. The *State Farm* seatbelt case (see Case 6.2 earlier in the chapter) is an example of a court's reversal of administrative agency action in the area of rulemaking.

Exhibit 6.10 provides a summary of the roles of administrative agencies.

The Role of Administrative Agencies in the International Market

The United States wins the award for having the most administrative agencies and regulations. Some businesses have argued that the amount of regulation hinders them in the international marketplace. For example, the readability level of regulations, as shown in Exhibit 6.11, demands much time and energy as companies attempt to interpret and comply with the laws.

EXHIBIT 6.11 Various Reading Levels of Documents and Populations

DOCUMENTS AND POPULATIONS	GRADE LEVEL
1. *Love Story*	7.64
2. Reading level of U.S. population over age 65	9.71
3. *Playboy*	11.46
4. Reading level of general U.S. population	11.68
5. *Sports Illustrated*	12.82
6. Your Medicare Handbook	14.94
7. ERISA Summary Plan Description	15.29
8. *Wall Street Journal*	16.34
9. *Social Security Handbook*	17.51
10. Reading level of lawyers	19.00
11. *Albemarle* (U.S. Supreme Court ruling)	20.30
12. Occupational Safety and Health Act	30.79
13. Employment Retirement Income Safety Act	32.10
14. Section 18 of the Social Security Act	41.04

Sources: Warren S. Blumenfeld et al., "Readability of an ERISA Summary Plan Description vis-à-vis Intended Readership: An Empirical Test of Local Legal Compliance with a Federal Regulation." Paper presented at the Western American Institute for Decision Science Meeting, Reno, Nevada, March 1979; Warren S. Blumenfeld et al., "Readability of the Real Estate Settlement Procedures Act." Paper presented at the Southeastern Regional Business Law Association Meeting, Chapel Hill, North Carolina, October 1980.

Many regulators, legislators, and businesses have advocated elimination and streamlining of existing regulations, as well as careful consideration before new regulations are promulgated.

Ethical Issues

Some businesses take a backdoor approach to getting around administrative regulations. They go over an agency's head to its source of funding: Congress. After the Association of National Advertisers succeeded in ending Michael Pertschuk's role in the development of regulations for children's television advertising, its attention turned to Congress. As a result of strong lobbying efforts, Congress passed the FTC Improvements Act of 1980. In addition to cutting the FTC budget severely, one of the sections of the act provided that the FTC could not use section 5 (its general power in its enabling act to regulate "deceptive trade practices"; see Chapter 11) to regulate children's television advertising. Shortly after passage, the FTC withdrew all of its rulemaking procedures for children's television advertising. The organizations and businesses lobbying for the FTC Improvements Act contributed money to the political action committees of members of Congress.

Does the ability of businesses to circumvent administrative agencies hinder the agencies' effectiveness? Was the lobbying just an exercise of the businesses' rights? Was the lobbying a way to curtail forever the FTC's power in this area? Is such lobbying an ethical business practice? Does this type of circumvention allow businesses to operate unregulated?

Note: In 1990, the FTC was able to pass some rules on children's television advertising, and Congress held hearings in 1993 to determine whether more regulation of children's television was needed. The industry agreed to self-regulation in the form of clear delineations between programming and commercials. Recently, 13 manufacturers of foods that attract children (cereal, cookies) announced that they would halt ads that targeted children, a voluntary industry move that will find the manufacturers no longer using cartoon characters to sell their products.

Ethical Issues

Some businesses are able to take advantage of one government's regulations. For example, the Energy Policy Act of 1992 requires that toilets installed after the act took effect (1994) use only 1.6 gallons of water rather than the nearly century-old standard of 3.5 gallons. As of 2000, about one-fourth of the nation's toilets were the 1.6-gallon types.

As homeowners have remodeled bathrooms and replaced older toilets, they have learned that the 3.5-gallon toilets are no longer sold in the United States. However, just across the U.S./Canadian border near Detroit, Canadian hardware stores are doing a land-office business selling 3.5-gallon tanks to U.S. citizens.

Those who are remodeling, and even some who are building new homes, generally install a $100 toilet from Home Depot in order to pass inspection. They then purchase a Canadian toilet, which costs in the neighborhood of $500 to $1,000 for a standard fixture because the demand is so high, and install it. Plumbing stores all over Canada report sales are brisk. In a survey conducted in May 2000, owners of Canadian plumbing stores said that they sell, on average, one toilet per day to U.S. citizens via either direct sale or shipment.

Do the citizens break any laws by what they do? Is what they do ethical?

B I O G R A P H Y

Earl Devaney: An Auditor Who Keeps Federal Agencies Clean

Earl Devaney served as the Inspector General (IG) for the Department of Interior (DOI) from 1999 to 2009. Mr. Devaney's reports as Inspector General were known for their forthrightness, insights, and color. When the Denver office of the Minerals Management Service of the DOI received an anonymous complaint from an employee in the Denver office that asked the IG to look into "ethical issues" there, Mr. Devaney responded. He found that agency employees were accepting lodging, gifts, alcohol, and other perks from industry executives in exchange for favorable treatment for the companies. Mr. Devaney also found that agency employees were having affairs with industry executives.[3] The agency employees defended these relationships as "arm's length." Mr. Devaney's report concluded, "Sexual relationships cannot, by definition, be arm's length."

Mr. Devaney spoke truth to power in a way that resulted in reorganization of the DOI. As a result

of his investigation of lobbyist Jack Abramoff on behalf of Indian tribes, DOI secretary Gale Norton resigned. In testimony before Congress on his reports and recommendations, Devaney testified, "Short of a crime, anything goes at the highest level of the Department of Interior. Ethics failures on the part of senior department officials—taking the form of appearances of impropriety, favoritism and bias—have been routinely dismissed with a promise of not to do it again."

Mr. Devaney was appointed by President Obama to oversee the use of $787 billion in federal money under the American Reinvestment and Recovery Act. Mr. Devaney has referred to his new assignment as a challenge because of the significant programs and expenditures but, as a dedicated public servant, he remains committed to maintain public trust in the agencies that promulgate rules and enforce the law.

Summary

What is an administrative agency?

- Administrative agency—statutory entity with the ability to make, interpret, and enforce laws

What laws govern the operation of administrative agencies?

- Administrative Procedure Act—general federal law governing agency process and operations

- Government in the Sunshine Act—federal law requiring public hearings by agencies (with limited exceptions)

- Federal Privacy Act—federal law protecting transfer of information among agencies unless done for enforcement reasons

- Freedom of Information Act—federal law providing individuals with access to information held by administrative agencies (with some exemptions such as for trade secrets)

What do administrative agencies do?

- Rulemaking—process of turning proposed regulations into actual regulations; requires public input

- *Federal Register*—daily publication that updates agency proposals, rules, hearing notices, and so forth

- *Code of Federal Regulations*—federal government publication of all agency rules

- Licensing—role in which an agency screens businesses before permitting operation

- Inspections—administrative agency role of checking businesses and business sites for compliance

How do agencies pass rules?

- Study issue, develop evidence of the need for the rule

- Public comment period—period in rulemaking process when any individual or business can provide input on proposed regulations

- Promulgation—approval of proposed rules by heads of agencies

- Rule must survive challenges based on standards of "arbitrary and capricious," "substantial evidence," "*ultra vires*," and "procedural errors."

How do agencies enforce the law?

- Consent decree—settlement (*nolo contendere* plea) of charges brought by an administrative agency

- Administrative law judge (ALJ)—overseer of hearing on charges brought by administrative agency

Questions and Problems

1. Florida State University (FSU) was under investigation by the NCAA for various types of violations. FSU created a special website where the NCAA and university officials could communicate, send documents, and post transcripts that were part of the investigation. Associated Press (AP) filed a Freedom of Information Act (FOIA) request with FSU for the release of the information on the special website. FSU refused to release the information, maintaining that because the information and documents were posted on a private website, they were not public records and, therefore, not subject to FOIA requests. Applying the principles of law from this chapter as well as what you have learned about precedent and interpretation, decide whether the court granted the FOIA request. [*Associated Press v Florida State University Board of Trustees*, 2009 WL 2762352 (Fla. Cir. 2009)].

2. The use of snowmobiles in Yellowstone and Grand Teton National Parks was first permitted in 1963, and their use has been a topic of ongoing concern because of their impact on park resources. The National Park Service (NPS), part of the Department of the Interior, has been grooming snow-covered roads to allow safe passage by snowmobiles. Snowmobile use has increased dramatically. As many as 1,700 snowmobiles enter the parks on peak days.

Trail grooming and snowmobiling had an effect on the parks' wildlife, especially bison. During the winter of 1996–97, park officials documented that large numbers of bison left the parks, some traveling along the man-made groomed trails created to facilitate snowmobile use. As a consequence of this migration, over 1,000 bison had to be killed to prevent the spread of brucellosis to livestock in areas outside of the parks.

The Fund for Animals and other environmental groups objected to the snowmobile use, and in December 2000, the NPS capped snowmobile use for the winters of 2001–02 and 2002–03 and completely eliminated snowmobile use by the 2003–04 winter season. The NPS received 5,273 comments during the 30-day public comment period; over 4,300 of these comments supported the proposed phase-out rule. On January 22, 2001, the NPS published the final rule ("Snowcoach Rule" or "2001 Rule"), which allowed snowmobile use to continue in 2001–02 but mandated significant reductions in snowmobile use in 2002–03 and a complete elimination of snowmobile use, in favor of snowcoach use ("snowcoach" is the NPS term intended to include all forms of mechanized snow vehicles, including snowmobiles), by the 2003–04 winter season.

The 2001 Rule, promulgated by the Clinton administration, was published the day after President George W. Bush (43) took office and was immediately stayed pending a review by the new administration. Meanwhile, the International Snowmobile Manufacturers Association filed suit, challenging the 2001 Rule as an unsupported decision to ban snowmobiling. The lawsuit called for the NPS to set aside the rules.

In March 2002, the NPS issued another proposed rule. NPS received over 350,000 pieces of correspondence from the public; over 80 percent of the public comments supported the phase-out of snowmobiles. Despite this opposition, on November 18, 2002, one month before the phase-out was scheduled to go into effect, the NPS released a final rule delaying the implementation of the phase-out for an additional year. Snowmobile use was allowed to continue unabated during the 2002–03 winter season.

The Fund for Animals filed suit, challenging the postponement as arbitrary and capricious. Evaluate the action taken under the "arbitrary and capricious" standard. Be sure to note any other procedural issues in this rulemaking process.

3. Because of overcrowded conditions at the nation's airports during the late 1960s, the Federal Aviation Administration (FAA) promulgated a regulation to reduce takeoff and landing delays at airports by limiting the number of landing and takeoff slots at five major airports to 60 slots per hour. The airports were Kennedy, LaGuardia, O'Hare, Newark, and National. At National Airport (Washington), 40 of the 60 slots were given to commercial planes, and the commercial carriers allocated the slots among themselves until October 1980. In 1980, New York Air, a new airline, requested some of the 40 slots, but the existing airlines refused to give up any. The secretary of transportation, in response and "to avoid chaos in the skies" during the upcoming holidays, proposed a rule to allocate the slots at National. The allocation rule was proposed on October 16, 1980, and appeared in the *Federal Register* on October 20, 1980. The comment period was seven days starting from the October 16, 1980, proposal date. The airlines and others submitted a total of 37 comments to the secretary. However, Northwest Airlines filed suit on grounds that the APA required a minimum of 30 days for a public comment period. The secretary argued that the 30-day rule was being suspended for good cause (the holiday season). Who is correct? Should an exception be made, or should the FAA be required to follow the 30-day rule? [*Northwest Airlines, Inc. v Goldschmidt*, 645 F.2d 1309 (8th Cir. 1981)]

4. Richardson-Vicks, Inc. is the manufacturer and seller of Vicks Pediatric Formula 44 (Pediatric 44), a cough medicine for children. In its ads for Pediatric 44, Vicks claims that the syrup contains active ingredients that enable it to begin working instantly. However, Pediatric 44 is considered to have only inactive ingredients, according to FDA regulations on "active" and "inactive"

ingredients. A competitor has alleged that Vicks is "misbranding" its products. Can the FDA take any action? What steps could it take? Will the FDA be required to make an interpretation of the "active"/"inactive" regulation? [*Sandoz Pharmaceuticals v Richardson-Vicks, Inc.*, 902 F.2d 222 (3d Cir. 1990)]

5. Approximately 25 years ago, the Department of the Interior (DOI) implemented regulations that generally prohibited possession of firearms in national parks unless they were "packed, cased or stored in a manner that [would] prevent their ready use." A similar regulation applied to firearms in national wildlife refuges. On December 14, 2007, 47 United States Senators wrote to the Secretary of the Interior asking to have the DOI firearm restrictions lifted.

As a result, the DOI proposed a rule to better respect the rights of states, 48 of which "provide for the possession of concealed firearms by their citizens," a larger number than when the previous regulations were promulgated.

The proposed rule requested public comments until June 30, 2008, a date that was later extended by an additional 30 days. In total, the DOI received approximately 125,000 public comments on the proposed rule. Many of the comments suggested that allowing persons to possess concealed, loaded, and operative firearms in national parks and wildlife refuges would result in the use of those firearms, particularly for self-defense.

On December 10, 2008, the DOI published the final rule, which authorized persons to possess concealed, loaded, and operative firearms if permitted in accordance with the laws of the state in which the national park or wildlife refuge is located.

Prior to issuing the final rule, the Department of the Interior did not prepare an environmental assessment or an environmental impact statement pursuant to the National Environmental Protection Act ("NEPA"), 42 U.S.C. § 4331, *et seq.*

The Brady Campaign to Prevent Gun Violence and the National Parks Conservation Association (Plaintiffs) have brought suit against DOI and other governmental entities and officials (Defendants) for DOI's failure to consider the final rule's environmental impacts in violation of NEPA.

DOI responded that the final rule had no environmental impacts, and that DOI was not required to perform any environmental analysis because the final rule only authorizes persons to possess firearms in national parks and wildlife refuges, and does not authorize persons to discharge, brandish, or otherwise use the concealed, loaded, and operable firearms.

The Brady Campaign brought suit requesting a preliminary injunction to enjoin implementation of the final rule. What would be the basis of the suit? Should the Brady Campaign prevail? [*Brady Campaign to Prevent Gun Violence v Salazar*, 612 F.Supp.2d 1 (D.D.C. 2009)]

6. San Diego Air Sports Center (SDAS) operates a sports parachuting business in Otay Mesa, California. SDAS offers training to beginning parachutists and facilitates recreational jumping for experienced parachutists. The majority of SDAS jumps occur at altitudes in excess of 5,800 feet.

The jump zone used by SDAS overlaps the San Diego Traffic Control Area (TCA). Although the aircraft carrying the parachutists normally operate outside the TCA, the parachutists themselves are dropped through it. Each jump must be approved by the air traffic controllers.

In July 1987, an air traffic controller in San Diego filed an Unsatisfactory Condition Report complaining of the strain that parachuting was putting on the controllers and raising safety concerns. The report led to a staff study of parachute jumping within the San Diego TCA. In October 1987, representatives of the San Diego Terminal Radar Approach Control (TRACON) facility met with SDAS operators. In December 1987, the San Diego TRACON sent to SDAS a draft letter of agreement outlining agreed-upon procedures and coordination requirements. Nonetheless, the San Diego TRACON conducted another study between January 14, 1988, and February 11, 1988, and about two months after the draft letter was sent, the San Diego TRACON withdrew it.

SDAS states that the air traffic manager of the San Diego TRACON assured SDAS that it would be invited to attend all meetings on parachuting in the San Diego TCA. However, SDAS was not informed of or invited to any meetings.

In March 1988, the Federal Aviation Administration (FAA) sent a letter to SDAS informing SDAS that "[e]ffective immediately parachute jumping within or into the San Diego TCA in the Otay Reservoir Jump Zone will not be authorized." The FAA stated that the letter was final and appealable.

SDAS challenged the letter in federal court on grounds that it constituted rulemaking without compliance with required APA procedures. Evaluate SDAS's challenge to the letter by applying administrative law and procedure. [*San Diego Air Sports Center, Inc. v Federal Aviation Administration*, 887 F.2d 966 (9th Cir. 1989)]

7. Hooked on Phonics is a reading program that departs from the current educational reading philosophy of "whole-language learning." The program emphasizes the more traditional reading process of having children sound out letters and combinations of letters. The Federal Trade Commission (FTC) filed a false advertising complaint against Gateway Educational Products, Inc., the owner of the Hooked on Phonics program. The FTC claimed that Gateway's television claims that those with reading disabilities would be helped "quickly and easily" and that Hooked on Phonics could "teach reading in a home setting without additional assistance" were misleading. Gateway does not feel the claims are false, but it does not want to have bad publicity. What advice can you give Gateway on handling the FTC charges?

8. In March 1992, the Federal Communications Commission (FCC) proposed rules that would increase the maximum number of radio stations a company could own from 12 AM stations and 12 FM stations to 30 of each. The FCC proposed the changes because more than half of the nation's 11,000 radio stations are unprofitable and larger ownership blocks would allow some economies of scale. Critics were vocal about domination and monopolization. As a result, the FCC changed the ownership maximums to 18 FM and 18 AM stations and issued its final rules on August 5, 1992. Describe the process the FCC employed to make these changes. Explain what public outcry accomplished.

9. The Food and Drug Administration (FDA) is concerned about laser eye surgery, noting that an industry concerned with correcting vision is spawning joint ventures, holding wine-and-cheese seminars to court potential investors, and creating databases of nearsighted consumers. The corrective laser surgery costs $2,000 per eye and is not covered by insurance. Calls to the available 800 numbers have noted some dissatisfaction among the 700 patients who've had the surgery, including complaints of farsightedness. Further, the only regulation the FDA has in the field covers granting laser manufacturers permission to sell their machines to ophthalmologists. The FDA would like to know more and perhaps control some aspects of patients' care. Describe the steps the FDA must take.

10. Countrywide, the problem mortgage company that was acquired by Bank of America, was once the largest mortgage lender in the country and the biggest supplier of mortgages to Fannie Mae's secondary market program. (Fannie Mae has since collapsed.) Countrywide released information that indicated it made additional loans to Fannie Mae officials at favorable rates. Referred to as the Friends of Angelo group, these officials received favorable rates and expedited service. The following chart shows the officials, their titles at Fannie Mae, and their loan amounts, rates, and terms.

NAME	TITLE	AMOUNT	RATE	TERM
Franklin Raines	Former Chair	$982,253	5.125	10 yrs.
Jamie Gorelick	Former Vice Chair	$960,149	5.000	10 yrs.
Christopher Dodd	Chair, Senate Finance Comm. (Oversight for Fannie Mae)	$506,000	4.250	5 yrs.
James Johnson	Former CEO	$971,650	3.875	5 yrs.
Franklin Raines	Former Chair	$986,340	4.125	10 yrs.
Daniel Mudd	Former CEO	$2,965,000	4.250	7 yrs.

In the last years before the Countrywide problems and Fannie's collapse, the two firms reached an agreement whereby Countrywide would funnel most of its loans to Fannie in exchange for a special rate. At the time they reached the special arrangement, the "Friends of Angelo" program was created. The FOA, as it was known, gave officials an expedited path for processing as well as a one-point reduction in rate. Former Fannie Mae vice chair Jamie Gorelick said, "I don't believe there was any special treatment given."[4] However, an employee at the time said, "I know 100 percent she went through the VIP department."[5] In response, Ms. Gorelick said, "You'd think if somebody was trying to do me a favor, they would tell me they were doing me a favor, and I am unaware of any such treatment. When I did this transaction, I was decidedly a has-been. I had no favor to give."[6]

Apply what you know about conflicts of interest to Ms. Gorelick's responses to the inquiries about her loan. Did former CEO Daniel Mudd have a conflict? What is the relationship of corporate officers to customers? What is the role of regulators? Senators?

Strategy and the Law

The Yamaha Rhino is an off-road vehicle that looks like a golf cart with four-wheel drive. Some have called it an all-terrain cycle (ATC) with a front seat and a steering wheel. With the rise in popularity over two decades ago of the ATC, increasing numbers of accidents (100 deaths and 100,000 injuries) resulted in extensive federal regulation of the design of ATCs, including the requirement of four wheels (rather than three). The Consumer Product Safety Commission (CPSC) also required extensive training, disclosures, warnings, and prohibitions on children driving ATCs. However, the Rhino is not subject to the ATC regulations because it has a steering wheel rather than handlebars. The Rhino is also not subject to federal regulations for cars because it meets neither the size nor the structure thresholds for autos.

In this regulatory no-man's-land, the Rhino has emerged as a popular seller. The vehicle weighs 1,100 pounds, costs $11,000, and has been a popular seller since 2003. The 2008 model was the first of the Rhinos to have doors on the side. Owners say the Rhino offers the comfort of a golf cart but the ability to fit on trails as well as on the back of a pickup truck.

However, there have been 30 deaths caused by Rhino accidents and there are now 200 lawsuits around the country that seek recovery from Yamaha for injuries caused by what the suits claims is the Rhino's defective design. The Rhino is 54.4 inches long, but is narrower than any of its competitors (the design's goal is to allow the Rhino to fit on trails). The cases involve mostly rollover accidents.

Yamaha has always warned its buyers to wear seat belts and helmets when operating the Rhino. In 2006 and 2007, Yamaha sent out stickers to purchasers that read, "Abrupt maneuvers or aggressive driving have caused rollovers—even on flat, open areas." Yamaha also sent out a letter that offered to install doors on doorless Rhinos and extra handholds. The letter also added that drivers should be at least 16 years old.

The death rate for the Rhino (number of deaths in relation to number of vehicles sold per year) is 1 in 10,000.[7] However, the actual death rate for 2006, as provided by Yamaha, was 8 in 10,000. Yamaha said the death rate stat is skewed because you must include the number of hours operated to have the rate mean anything. Yamaha sold 42,000 Rhinos in 2007.

Along with other off-road vehicle manufacturers, Yamaha has formed a voluntary trade association group that has the goal of establishing voluntary safety standards. The Recreational Off-Road Vehicle Association has already proposed changing the generic name of the vehicles to Recreational Off-Highway Vehicle (ROV) from utility terrain vehicle (UTV). Yamaha and other manufacturers say that many accidents are caused by driver error and recklessness.

What are your obligations when you operate in a loophole area of the law? Is Yamaha liable if it complied with any regulations and laws that applied? What is the responsibility of a company to report accidents related to its product?

Notes

1. "Federal Regulation and Aggregate Economic Growth," *Regulation and the Macroeconomy*, (2004), as updated by the authors on their websites, 2008.

2. Since the time of the decision reported here, the emergence of troubling e-mails on the data and the peer review process for climate scientists has raised questions about the validity of the "strong consensus." Patrick J. Michaels, "The Climategate Whitewash," *Wall Street Journal*, July 12, 2010, p. A15.

3. In 2010, the DOI found similar issues of conflicts in the Minerals Management Office, which was responsible for the Deepwater Horizon well off the coast of Louisiana. The problems emerged after the explosion at that deepwater offshore rig and the resulting oil leak that damaged the coasts of all the Gulf states.

4. Glenn R. Simpson, "Countrywide Made Home Loans to Gorelick, Mudd," *Wall Street Journal*, Sept. 25, 2008, p. A10.

5. *Id.*

6. *Id.*

7. Melanie Trottman and Christopher Conkey, "U.S. Probes Off-Road Vehicles After a String of Accidents," *Wall Street Journal*, Nov. 4, 2008, pp. A1 and A16.

Shakespeare was ahead of his time when he wrote that "the world is your oyster." Today's global business environment is the dream of economists, who have fostered the notion of free trade since the publication of Adam Smith's *The Wealth of Nations* nearly 250 years ago. Trade barriers are down, resources are flowing, and even the smallest of businesses are involved in international trade. Trade across borders still involves additional issues and laws and carries risks that do not exist in transactions within nations. Litigation across borders is expensive and complex, so businesses must understand the legal environment of international trade, including contracts, customs and duties, and antibribery provisions, in order to minimize their legal risks. This chapter helps with that understanding of the laws that influence international business. What and whose statutes affect businesses in international trade? What international agreements affect global businesses? What contract issues exist in international business? ■

It's not necessary to use chopsticks. A knife and fork are okay.

Mayor Zhang
Suzhou, China (in encouraging businesspeople to come to his town)

If a foreign country can supply us with a commodity cheaper than we ourselves can make it, better buy it of them with some part of our own industry, employed in a way in which we have some advantage.

Adam Smith
The Wealth of Nations

UPDATE
For up-to-date legal and ethical news, go to
mariannejennings.com

We didn't think of the payments as bribes. We thought of them as useful expenditures.

Reinhard Siekaczek,

former Siemens employee, after Siemens paid the largest fine in U.S. history for violations of the Foreign Corrupt Practices Act

CONSIDER...

American Rice, Inc. (ARI), a Houston-based company, exports rice to foreign countries, including Haiti. Rice Corporation of Haiti, a wholly owned subsidiary of ARI, was incorporated in Haiti to represent ARI's interests and deal with third parties there. Haiti's customs officials assess duties based on the quantity and value of rice imported into the country. Haiti also requires businesses that deliver rice there to remit an advance deposit against Haitian sales taxes, based on the value of that rice. The

businesses are then given a credit for the deposit when they file their Haitian sales tax returns. David Kay and Douglas Murphy, executives of ARI, were charged with violations of the Foreign Corrupt Practices Act (FCPA) for allegedly bribing Haitian officials to accept false bills of lading that reflected total rice imports to be about one-third of actual levels so that ARI would owe less in taxes. Is this type of an arrangement a bribe? Does it violate the FCPA?

Sources of International Law

"When in Rome, do as the Romans do" is advice that can be modified for business: When in Rome, follow Roman law. In each country where a business has operations, it must comply with the laws of that nation. Just as each U.S. business must comply with all the tax, employment, safety, and environmental laws of each state in which it operates, each international business must comply with the laws of the countries in which it operates.

Types of International Law Systems

The various systems of laws can be quite different, and businesses are well advised to obtain local legal counsel for advice on the peculiarities of each nation's laws. Generally, a nation's laws are based on one of three types of systems. The United States, like England, has a **common law** system. Our laws are built on tradition and precedent (see Chapter 1). Not every possible situation is codified; we rely on our courts to interpret and apply our more general statutes and, in many cases, to develop principles of law as cases are presented (as with the common-law doctrine of negligence; see Chapter 9).

Other countries rely on civil law or code law. This form of law is the foundation of legal systems in France, Germany, Spain, and other European countries. Code law systems do not rely on court decisions but rely instead on statutes or codes that are intended to cover all types of circumstances and attempt to spell out the law, leaving little need for interpretation.

A final system of law is Islamic law, which is followed in some form in 27 countries. Islamic legal systems are based on religious tenets and govern all aspects of life, from appropriate dress in public to remedies for contract breaches. Many of the Islamic countries have a combination of civil and Islamic systems that result from the influences of both colonization and Islam.

Before its collapse in the former Soviet Union and Eastern Europe, communism was also classified as a legal system. Now the former communist nations struggle with evolving cultural, market, and governmental systems. Likewise, countries such as Iraq and Afghanistan struggle in their postwar eras to establish constitutions, free elections, and the rule of law.

The Roots of Commerce and Law: Nonstatutory Sources of International Law

Customs and values in a culture often have a controlling effect on negotiations, contracts, and performance in international business. The American Bar Association recommends that businesspeople and their lawyers examine seven cultural factors and do background work in these cultural areas before attempting negotiations and business in a particular country. Referred to as the LESCANT factors, the following issues should be researched as if they were legal background for doing business: language, environment and technology, social organization, contexting, authority, nonverbal behavior, and time concept.

Language

Businesspeople should determine which language is preferred in a particular country for conducting business. Mexico and Latin American countries are accustomed to doing business in English. In Quebec, Canadian government regulations outline the use of French in conducting business. The dominant language for contracts has become English, even for contracts among natives of a country. The trend is attributed by some to the Internet. Those in non–English-speaking countries have become increasingly familiar with English as they have surfed the Net. One French businessman learned English so that he could enjoy the jokes his son sent to him over the Internet. The jokes were in English, and his son was stunned when he visited to find his father so fluent in English following several years of joke exchanges.

Environment and Technology

Communications systems vary in quality and universality in countries around the world. Because U.S. companies are accustomed to rapid communication and verification of offers and acceptances (see Chapter 12 on contract formation), doing business in a country in which technology is less developed and communication is slower and by different means requires advance knowledge and appropriate adjustments and provisions for contract negotiations.

Social Organization

Businesspeople should know the social order in the country: May women negotiate deals? Is it appropriate to discuss business during a meal?

Contexting

Low-context cultures are those that rely on the written word as the controlling factor in their relationship. Little weight is given to the context in which that agreement is reached. Low-context cultures include the North American countries, Switzerland, Germany, and Scandinavian countries (although not Finland). Mid-level-context cultures are France, England, and Italy; high-context cultures are Latin American countries, Arabic nations, and Asian countries, including Japan. In high-context cultures, how and in what setting an agreement is reached are as important as the words in the document itself.

Authority

Who has negotiating authority is important in a business meeting, and who is sent to a meeting sends a signal about importance in high-context cultures. Lawyers are not considered part of the negotiating team in Japan but are considered critical in the United States. Often, in Asian cultures, the negotiators do not have the authority to commit to a deal and must take proposals back to their companies and those who do have authority.

Nonverbal Behavior

In the United States, the tendency is to interpret nonverbal behavior differently from the way it is perceived in other cultures. For example, silence during negotiations in the United States creates a compulsion for businesspeople to fill the awkward silence or interpret the silence as a rejection. In Asian cultures, such silence is simply a method of contemplating and considering and does not indicate a rejection.

Time Concept

The United States is a monochronic nation: Time is everything, and the goal of businesspeople is to get the deal done. Other monochronic nations include Great Britain, Germany, Canada, New Zealand, Australia, the Netherlands, Norway, and Sweden. Countries that operate with great flexibility in time and negotiate within the context of building a relationship as opposed to completing a deal are called polychronic nations. The remainder of the world operates within this flexible form of time culture.

Contracts for the International Sale of Goods (CISG)

Sometimes referred to as the Vienna Convention, the U.N. Convention on Contracts for the International Sale of Goods (CISG) began its development in 1964 as an idea that was later discussed and formulated at the 1980 Vienna Convention. The CISG first became effective in 1988 with its adoption in the United States along with a small group of other countries. Today, CISG has been adopted in 60 countries, with ratification processes under way in many other countries. However, its use is voluntary even in adopting countries. Businesses can opt out of using the CISG to govern their contracts.

The CISG is designed to provide for international contracts the convenience and uniformity that the Uniform Commercial Code provides for contracts across state lines in the United States. Although it includes some differences (see details Chapters 12 and 13), the CISG is a reflection of the Uniform Commercial Code.

For the Manager's Desk

Re: Charting Unknown Legal Territory: Pirates

AARRGGGGGG! Shiver me timbers, and all that other Johnny Depp stuff. We have pirates, savvy? The pirates are from Somalia and they are wreaking havoc on international commerce off the coast of Africa. NATO has sent ships to patrol the African coasts and rescue ships and hostages. However, there are international law issues about what is to be done about—and with—the captured pirates.

In a 1718 trial of pirates, Judge Nicholas Trott ruled, "It is lawful for any one that takes them, if they cannot bring them under some government to be tried, to put them to death." Due process, human rights, and individual country laws require that the pirates receive a trial. However, the questions still remain: How? By whom? And where?

The conduct of pirates violates international norms of behavior, but what specific laws are broken? And who has jurisdiction when the pirates are taking ships in international waters? The principles of autonomy apply here: What country has the right to try a citizen of another country for crimes not committed in either country?

Trials for pirates were generally handled in military tribunals. However, the backlash today against military tribunals because of treatment of prisoners of war, as well as court rulings that have transferred the cases to civil courts, means that the pirates end up being released. Released pirates are free to pirate another day and, perhaps, another sea.

Countries have come up with different solutions. The British Royal Navy has instructed its military not to detain pirates because such detention violates the pirates' human rights. Instructions for the French military are to return the pirates to Somalia. The U.S. policy is to return pirates to their home governments, but only if given assurances that the pirates will be detained and prosecuted. The civil and political unrest in Somalia often means that groups are able to secure the freedom of the pirates through the use of force against the government. In the meantime, companies doing international shipments are vulnerable. There were 300 pirate attacks of shipping vessels in 2009.

Treaties, Trade Organizations, and Controls on International Trade

In international trade, a number of treaties, tariffs, and organizations govern and guide international contracts. This section discusses some of the most important ones.

Whether supported or despised by economists, tariffs and restrictions on trade have existed for as long as trade itself. Duties, quotas, and tariffs have all been used to control the flow of goods over and across national boundaries. For most of history, these limits on trade have been imposed on a nation-by-nation basis. However, new forms of trade agreements are developing, and nations are organizing in larger groups in an attempt to eliminate many of the individually based barriers to trade.

The European Union

As discussed in Chapter 1, the European Union (EU) was established with the goal of removing barriers to the free movement across borders of goods, people, services, and capital. The Treaty on European Union (Maastricht Treaty) established the goals of free trade, a single currency, and uniform laws on commerce and security. Today, for example, the EU handles antitrust violations by companies in any of the EU's 27 member nations.[1]

In addition to the European Commission, the EU created other institutions to assist it in carrying out its goal of unified European commercial operations. The European Council, which consists of the heads of state of the various members, is the policymaking body and establishes the broad directives for the operation of the EU. The next step below the council is the European Commission, the body charged with implementation of Council policies. At the third level is the European

Parliament, an advisory legislative body with some veto powers. Finally, the European Court of Justice (ECJ) is the judicial body created to handle disputes and any violations of regulations and the EU treaty itself. The EU has in place nearly 300 directives that govern everything from health and safety standards in the workplace to the sale of mutual funds across national boundaries.

The WTO

In 1994, the General Agreement on Tariffs and Trade (GATT), a **multilateral treaty** (treaty among more than two nations) (see Chapter 1), was adopted and established the World Trade Organization (WTO). The WTO lists 150 countries as members, including the United States. The WTO is the body charged with the administration and achievement of the GATT objectives. GATT's primary objectives are trade without discrimination and protection through tariffs. Trade without discrimination is achieved through GATT's most-favored-nation clause. The issue of China's membership as a most favored nation was debated extensively, particularly along with the political and social context of human rights issues in that country, prior to its admission in 2001. (*Note:* Russia is currently in the last stages of consideration for MFN status; there are concerns about the stability of its legal system, particularly for enforcement of contract rights.)

Under MFN status, subscribing countries treat each other equally in terms of import and export duties and charges. Subscribing countries do not give more favorable treatment to one country as opposed to another. Domestic production is protected by tariffs and not through any other commercial measures.

Some exceptions under GATT for regional trading arrangements are undertaken through other treaties, such as the North American Free Trade Agreement and the European Union.

The WTO also established a Dispute Settlement Body (DSB), which is an international arbitration body created to bring countries together to resolve trade disputes rather than have those nations resort to trade sanctions. If a WTO panel finds that a country has violated the provisions of GATT, it can impose trade sanctions on that country. The sanctions imposed are generally equal to the amount of economic injury the country caused through its violation of GATT.

The North American Free Trade Agreement (NAFTA)

The North American Free Trade Agreement (NAFTA) is a treaty among Canada, the United States, and Mexico, which took effect in 1994 with a goal of eliminating all tariffs among the three countries over a 15-year period.

Products covered under NAFTA include only those that originate in these countries. All goods traded across the boundaries of these countries must carry a NAFTA certificate of origin, which verifies the original creation of the goods in that country from which they are being exported. NAFTA is unlike the EU in that NAFTA focuses only on free trade and does not create a common labor market, governing body, or currency.

Prohibitions on Trade: Individual Nation Sanctions

In some countries, international tensions have resulted in sanctions being imposed, including trade prohibitions. Countries can impose two types of trade sanctions. With primary trade sanctions, companies based in the United States are prohibited from doing business with certain countries. For example, the United States has prohibited or regulated trade with Iraq since the time of the 1991 Gulf War and lifted those sanctions only over the past few years as the country's new government took hold. Primary boycotts can be limited to certain categories of goods. Other category restrictions can include extreme limitations such as limiting trade to food and medical supplies. In some restrictions, the United States prohibits domestic companies from selling certain types of equipment to certain nations. For example, U.S. firms have severe restrictions on selling certain component parts to Iran. These parts are primarily those that could be used in the development of nuclear weapons and other military capabilities.

The second form of trade prohibition is the secondary boycott, which is a step beyond the primary boycott in that companies from other nations doing business with a sanctioned country will also experience sanctions for such activity. For example, in 1996, the United States passed the Iran and Libya Sanctions Act (ILSA) as a secondary boycott against two nations against which the United States already had imposed trade restrictions. This law was passed because of active lobbying by the families of those killed when Pan Am Flight 103 exploded over Lockerbie, Scotland, as a result of bombs planted on the flight by Libyan terrorists. Under the secondary boycott trade prohibition, the United States will not grant licenses to, permit its financial institutions to loan money to, award government contracts to, or allow imports from any company that finances, supplies, or constructs oil procurement in Iran or Libya. Generally, these types of secondary boycotts do not apply retroactively so that companies already invested need not divest themselves of their holdings in these countries. However, no new business is allowed once the act takes effect if the companies wish to continue trading with the United States.

The International Monetary Fund (IMF) and the World Bank

Created at Bretton Woods, New Hampshire, the International Monetary Fund (IMF) was established following World War II with the goal of expanding international trade through a bank with a lending system designed to bring stability to national currencies. The IMF created the International Bank for Reconstruction and Development (commonly called the World Bank), which allows signing nations to have Special Drawing Rights (SDR) or the ability to draw on a line of credit in order to maintain the stability of their currency.

The idea of the IMF was to enhance and encourage international trade through assurances about monetary stability in various countries. Each time a particular nation, such as Greece or Russia, experiences a difficult economic swing, it generates significant debate about the use of IMF funds to buoy that nation's currency so that international trade with that country is not destroyed.

The Kyoto Treaty

The Kyoto Protocol, often called the Kyoto Treaty or the global-warming treaty, is a 24-page document that focuses on the reduction of greenhouse gas emissions. The treaty requires signatory countries to reduce emissions "by at least 5% below 1990 levels." United States would have been required to reduce its emissions by at least 7 percent had it signed the treaty. China, India, and Mexico are excluded from the treaty's coverage. By the time of the Copenhagen climate summit, late in 2009, the Kyoto Treaty was just a bit of history. The nations in attendance were unwilling to commit to its standards.

The Organization of Petroleum Exporting Countries (OPEC)

The Organization of Petroleum Exporting Countries (OPEC) is a cartel that works together to control oil supplies and production, prices, and taxes. The result of the OPEC cooperation has been increased royalties to those participating countries.

Trust, Corruption, Trade, and Economics

Perhaps the greatest activity in multilateral agreements among countries has been in the area of curbing bribes because of their devastating impact on trust and the chilling of investment, which can stall economic development in a country. In his departure speech as secretary of the U.S. Treasury, Robert Rubin cautioned government employees to never accept any sort of gift as part of their duties for, he noted, "Corruption and bribery benefit a few at the expense of many."

Foreign Corrupt Practices Act (FCPA)

The Requirements of the FCPA

Perhaps the most widely known criminal statute affecting firms that operate internationally is the **Foreign Corrupt Practices Act** (FCPA; 15 U.S.C. §§ 78dd-1). The FCPA applies to business concerns that have their principal offices in the United States. It contains antibribery provisions as well as accounting controls for these firms, and was passed to curb the use of bribery in foreign operations of these companies.

The act prohibits making, authorizing, or promising payments or gifts of money or anything of value to government or NGO officials with the intent to corrupt for the purpose of *obtaining* or *retaining business* for or with, or *directing business*. Under the FCPA, payments designed to influence the official acts of foreign officials, political parties, party officials, candidates for office, any nongovernmental organization (NGO), or any person who will transmit the gift or money to one of the other types of persons are prohibited. Changes in 1998 added the NGO coverage so that foreign officials are now defined to include public international figures, such as officials with the United Nations, the Olympics, or the IMF.

First passed in 1977, the FCPA is the result of an SEC investigation that uncovered questionable foreign payments by large stock issuers who were based in the United States. Approximately 435 U.S. corporations had made improper or questionable payments totaling $300 million in Japan, the Netherlands, and Korea. Under the 1998 amendments to the FCPA, any payment made to those persons listed above, to "secure any improper advantage" in doing business in that country would be a violation. For example, if an American company trying to win a bid on a contract for the construction of highways in a foreign country paid a government official there who was responsible for awarding such construction contracts a "consulting fee" of $25,000, the American company would be in violation of the FCPA. The payment was of money, it was made to a foreign official, and it was made for the purpose of obtaining business within that country. Titan Corporation violated the FCPA when money it paid to an agent in Benin was passed along to the reelection campaign of the president of Benin. The result was an increased management fee for Titan's operation of the telecommunications system in Benin. The payments were uncovered as Lockheed Martin was conducting due diligence for purposes of a merger with Titan. Titan voluntarily disclosed the payment and paid a total fine of $28.5 million as follows: a $13 million criminal penalty, $12.6 million disgorgement of benefits received, and $2.9 million in interest.

BUSINESS PLANNING TIP

Businesses should look at a country's development before doing business there. The following issues are important factors in making that decision:

1. What is the economic climate?

2. What is the government structure?

3. What are the cultural attitudes about economic development? Are there any ill feelings by indigenous people toward other nations?

4. What is the legal structure of the country? What laws exist? How are they made? Are they changed easily?

5. How is the court system? Will it provide an appropriate and fair forum for resolution of disputes?

6. What experiences have other businesses had in dealing with this nation?

Use of Agents and the FCPA

When the FCPA was passed initially, many companies tried to find ways around the bribery prohibitions. Companies would hire foreign agents or consultants to help them gain business in countries and allowed these "third parties" to act independently. However, many of these consultants then paid others who then actually paid bribes to officials. Under the FCPA, even these types of arrangements can constitute a violation if the consulting fees are high, odd payment arrangements occur, or the company has reason to know of a potential or actual violation. Companies must be able to establish that they have performed "due diligence" in investigating those hired as their agents and consultants in foreign countries. For example, if a U.S. company hired a consultant who charged the company $25,000 in fees and $250,000 in expenses, the U.S. company is, under Justice Department guidelines, on notice for excessive expenses that could signal potential bribes being paid. These types of expenses are known as "red flags" for U.S. companies. The Justice Department uses this information as a means of establishing intent even when the company may not know precisely what was done with the funds and what was paid to whom.

The FCPA and "Grease" or Facilitation Payments

Payments to any foreign official for "facilitation," often referred to as "grease payments," are not prohibited under FCPA so long as these payments are made only to get these officials to do their normal jobs that they might not do or would do slowly without some payment. These grease payments can be made for obtaining permits, licenses, or other official documents; processing governmental papers, such as visas and work orders; providing police protection and mail pickup and delivery; providing phone service, power, and water supply; loading and unloading cargo, or protecting perishable products; and scheduling inspections associated with contract performance or transit of goods across the country.

Penalties for Violation of the FCPA

Penalties for violations of the FCPA can run up to $250,000 per violation and five years' imprisonment for individuals. Corporate fines are up to $2 million per violation. Also, under the Alternative Fines Act, the Justice Department can seek to obtain two times the benefit that the bribe attempted to gain, known as disgorgement. The government's methods for computation of the profits on the contracts that involved FCPA violations are often difficult to discern, but the Justice Department has been using disgorgement consistently as a penalty for companies, and these amounts that are recouped have been increasingly steadily.

The Justice Department has stepped up its enforcement of the FCPA. In 2010, there were 150 open cases for FCPA violations, the largest number since the passage of the act. The Department says that the key to its increased enforcement is going after industry sectors. For example, the medical device and pharmaceutical industries have been targeted, and the "Oil for Food" investigations have also yielded a number of corporate defendants. The "Oil for Food" program was established in 1995 by the United Nations and permitted U.S. companies to trade with Iraq, receiving oil in exchange for food, medicine, and other basic supplies. The program was terminated in 2003 but the prosecution of companies involved in the trades continues. *U.S. v Kay* (Case 7.1) answers the chapter's opening "Consider" and deals with a violation of the FCPA.

CASE 7.1

U.S. v Kay
359 F.3d 738 (5th Cir. 2004)

Throwing the Rice Market and Dodging Taxes

FACTS

David Kay (defendant) was an American citizen and a vice president for marketing of American Rice, Inc. (ARI), who was responsible for supervising sales and marketing in the Republic of Haiti. Douglas Murphy (defendant) was an American citizen and president of ARI.

Beginning in 1995 and continuing to about August 1999, Mr. Kay, Mr. Murphy, and other employees and officers of ARI paid bribes and authorized the payment of bribes to induce customs officials in Haiti to accept bills of lading and other documents that intentionally understated the true amount of rice that ARI shipped to Haiti for import, thus reducing the customs duties owed by ARI and RCH to the Haitian government.

In addition, beginning in 1998 and continuing to about August 1999, Mr. Kay and other employees and officers of ARI paid and authorized additional bribes to officials of other Haitian agencies to accept the false import documents that understated the true amount of rice being imported into and sold in Haiti, thereby reducing the amount of sales taxes paid by RCH to the Haitian government.

Mr. Kay directed employees of ARI to prepare two sets of shipping documents for each shipment of rice to Haiti, one that accurately reflected and another that falsely represented the weight and value of the rice being exported to Haiti.

Mr. Kay and Mr. Murphy agreed to pay and authorized the payment of bribes, calculated as a percentage of the value of the rice not reported on the false documents, to Haitian customs and tax officials to induce these officials to accept the false documentation and to assess significantly lower customs duties and sales taxes than ARI would otherwise have been required to pay. ARI reported only approximately 66 percent of the rice it sold in Haiti and saved significant sales taxes.

In 2001, a grand jury charged Mr. Kay and Mr. Murphy with 12 counts of FCPA violations. Both Mr. Kay and Mr. Murphy moved to dismiss the indictment for the failure to state an offense, arguing that obtaining favorable tax treatment did not fall within the FCPA definition of payments made to government officials in order to obtain business. The district court dismissed the indictment, and the United States ("government") (appellant) appealed.

JUDICIAL OPINION

WIENER, Circuit Judge

None contend that the FCPA criminalizes every payment to a foreign official: It criminalizes only those payments that are intended to (1) influence a foreign official to act or make a decision in his official capacity, or (2) induce such an official to perform or refrain from performing some act in violation of his duty, or (3) secure some wrongful advantage to the payor. And even then, the FCPA criminalizes these kinds of payments only if the result they are intended to produce—their *quid pro quo*—will assist (or is intended to assist) the payor in efforts to get or keep some business for or with "any person."

The principal thrust of the defendants' argument is . . . how attenuated can the linkage be between the effects of that which is sought from the foreign official in consideration of a bribe (here, tax minimization) and the briber's goal of finding assistance or obtaining or retaining foreign business with or for some person, and still satisfy the business nexus element of the FCPA?

Invoking basic economic principles, the SEC reasoned in its amicus brief that securing reduced taxes and duties on imports through bribery enables ARI to reduce its cost of doing business, thereby giving it an "improper advantage" over actual or potential competitors, and enabling it to do more business, or remain in a market it might otherwise leave.

For purposes of deciding the instant appeal, the question nevertheless remains whether the Senate, and concomitantly Congress, intended this broader statutory scope to encompass the administration of tax, customs, and other laws and regulations affecting the revenue of foreign states.

Congress was obviously distraught not only about high profile bribes to high-ranking foreign officials, but also by the pervasiveness of foreign bribery by United States businesses and businessmen. Congress thus made the decision to clamp down on bribes intended to prompt foreign officials to misuse their discretionary authority for the benefit of a domestic entity's business in that country.

Obviously, a commercial concern that bribes a foreign government official to award a construction, supply, or services contract violates the statute. Yet, there is little difference between this example and that of a corporation's lawfully obtaining a contract from an honest official or agency by submitting the lowest bid, and—either before

CONTINUED

or after doing so—bribing a different government official to reduce taxes and thereby ensure that the under-bid venture is nevertheless profitable. Avoiding or lowering taxes reduces operating costs and thus increases profit margins, thereby freeing up funds that the business is otherwise legally obligated to expend. And this, in turn, enables it to take any number of actions to the disadvantage of competitors. Bribing foreign officials to lower taxes and customs duties certainly can provide an unfair advantage over competitors and thereby be of assistance to the payor in obtaining or retaining business.

Given the foregoing analysis of the statute's legislative history, we cannot hold as a matter of law that Congress meant to limit the FCPA's applicability to cover only bribes that lead directly to the award or renewal of contracts. Instead, we hold that Congress intended for the FCPA to apply broadly to payments intended to assist the payor, either directly or indirectly, in obtaining or retaining business for some person, and that bribes paid to foreign tax officials to secure illegally reduced customs and tax liability constitute a type of payment that can fall within this broad coverage. In 1977, Congress was motivated to prohibit rampant foreign bribery by domestic business entities, but nevertheless understood the pragmatic need to exclude innocuous grease payments from the scope of its proposals. The FCPA's legislative history instructs that Congress was concerned about both the kind of bribery that leads to discrete contractual arrangements and the kind that more generally helps a domestic payor obtain or retain business for some person in a foreign country; and that Congress was aware that this type includes illicit payments made to officials to obtain favorable but unlawful tax treatment.

Thus, in diametric opposition to the district court, we conclude that bribes paid to foreign officials in consideration for unlawful evasion of customs duties and sales taxes could fall within the purview of the FCPA's proscription. We hasten to add, however, that this conduct does not automatically constitute a violation of the FCPA: It still must be shown that the bribery was intended to produce an effect—here, through tax savings—that would "assist in obtaining or retaining business."

Reversed and remanded.

CASE QUESTIONS

1. What benefit did ARI obtain?
2. Why do Mr. Kay and Mr. Murphy argue that the FCPA does not apply to their conduct?
3. Why does the appellate court conclude differently?
4. What does the court look at in order to reach its conclusion?

CONSIDER...   7.1

A Philip Morris subsidiary, C. A. Tabacalera National, and a B.A.T Industries subsidiary known as C. A. Cigarrera Bigott entered into a contract with La Fundacion del Nino (the Children's Foundation) of Caracas, Venezuela. The agreement was signed on behalf of the foundation by the foundation's president, who also was the wife of the then-president of Venezuela. Under the terms of the agreement, these two tobacco firms were to make periodic donations to the Children's Foundation totaling $12.5 million. In exchange, the two firms would receive price controls on Venezuelan tobacco, elimination of controls on retail cigarette prices in Venezuela, tax deductions for donations, and assurances that the existing tax rates applicable to tobacco companies would not be increased.

Is the donation to the charity a violation of the FCPA?

THINK: The FCPA prohibits payments to government officials for purposes of obtaining contracts/benefits. Third-party payments are also prohibited (i.e., a company cannot get around the FCPA by having someone else make the payment). The *Kay* case indicates that Congress wanted to be as broad as possible to cut back on bribes and corruption.

APPLY: What is different about this situation? The payment here is more indirect and more subtle—the benefit is not to a government official.

ANSWER: If the intent of Congress in passing the FCPA was to stop bribery, both direct and indirect payments should be covered. The *Kay* case covered indirect business benefits, and the statute is clear on the purposes for which payments are made. Here we have an indirect payment with the intent to secure a benefit. The situation is covered under the FCPA. [*Lamb v Philip Morris, Inc.*, 915 F.2d 1024 (6th Cir. 1990; *cert. denied*, 498 U.S. 1086 (1995))]

Ethical Issues

PricewaterhouseCoopers is one of the United States' "Big 4" accounting firms. PwC, as it is known, has had a tax practice in Russia since the time that country changed from Communist rule. One of PwC's clients in Russia was Yukos, a major Russian oil company that is now bankrupt.

Russia's Federal Tax Service, an agency similar to the IRS in the United States, has filed suit against PwC, alleging that it concealed tax evasion by Yukos for the years 2002–2004. The Tax Service also announced a criminal probe of PwC's conduct with regard to its tax services for Yukos. Twenty Tax Service agents searched PwC's offices in Moscow and questioned PwC employees about the Yukos account. Yukos lost its tax case, and has paid $9.2 million in charges for the nonpayment of taxes. However, Yukos and PwC do have the case on appeal.

Many see the battle between PwC and the Tax Service as part of the Russian government's ongoing battle to sell off the assets of Yukos and avoid the surrender of the company's assets to investors and creditors who have filed claims. Those suits are pending in courts in The Hague. Some analysts believe that the Russian government is hoping to press PwC into revealing information that would help it take back the Yukos assets.

If PwC is found to have engaged in evasion, it loses its license to do business in Russia, and if it turns over information is likely to lose its clients in Russia.

What issues should a company consider before doing business in an economically developing country? What are the risks? Did this ethical dilemma begin long before the Russian government's demands of PwC? What international law, culture, and ethical issues should a company consider before deciding to do business in another country?

Source: Neil Buckley and Catherine Belton, "Moscow Raids PwC Ahead of Yukos Case," *Financial Times,* March 11, 2007, p. 1

The FCPA and the OECD

The **Organization for Economic Cooperation and Development** (OECD) is now extremely supportive of the U.S. FCPA and its principles. Member countries have enacted legislation for compliance with its international pact against bribery. The OECD's 38 members[3] now work together to investigate companies' activities across borders. (See the Siemens biography on pp. 237–238.)[4] However, only the United States, Germany, Norway, and Switzerland have active enforcement of their antibribery statutes. The Siemens prosecution (see pp. 237–238) resulted from U.S. and German investigators' cooperation.

When Congress amended the FCPA in order to implement the 1997 OECD Convention on Combating Bribery of Foreign Public Officials in International Business Transactions, the amendments expanded the act's jurisdiction to cover all U.S. citizens acting outside the United States and to all non-U.S. citizens acting inside the United States.

The convention basically adopts the standards of the United States under the FCPA and requires nations signing the agreement to impose criminal penalties, seize profits earned through bribery, and rein in government officials who accept illicit payments by actively prosecuting them along with the companies making the payments. The United States was the first country to pass implementing procedures for the convention in its laws and did so by the end of 1998. Under these amendments to the existing FCPA, all officers, employees, agents, and even foreign nationals working for U.S. companies are covered under the act in order to comply with the OECD requirements.

Ethical Issues

Transnational is an international company that arranges transportation for large cargo items and shipments of large orders. Transnational has a fleet of cargo ships. Each cargo ship has a crew of 25 employees.

Transnational's head of security, Jack Davis, is a retired U.S. Navy officer who, until January 2009, worked for the United States Department of Homeland Security. Since his hiring by Transnational, Davis has alerted senior management to the evolving issue of pirates. Despite an international incident involving a U.S. ship in the spring of 2009, the response of management to Davis's concerns has been one of postponement.

On September 11, 2009, a group of pirates boarded a Transnational ship that was, at the time of the takeover, sailing off the coast of Africa. The pirates have demanded payment of $25 million, or $1,000,000 for each crew member. The pirates have imposed a deadline of five hours for Transnational's decision and promise of payment. The pirates have also indicated that they will begin killing crew members one at a time if their deadline for Transnational's agreement to the payment is not met. Davis has advised Transnational to go ahead and pay the pirates because "Lives of employees are at stake and my job is protecting employees." However, a Transnational senior officer has cautioned in a meeting, "That's a bribe, and Transnational has a long-standing practice of not paying bribes."

The officers, the board, and Davis seek your advice.

BUSINESS STRATEGY

The Costs of Slipping on the FCPA

In companies with 100,000 employees worldwide, supervision of employees with regard to the FCPA can be difficult. Without clear signals from executive management and strong policies, even companies with the best intentions in terms of compliance with the law can fall short. For example, IBM entered into a consent decree with the SEC on charges that it engaged in bribery in violation of the FCPA. The charges filed by the SEC alleged that an IBM subsidiary, IBM Argentina S.A., was awarded a $250 million contract for modernizing the systems of Banco de la Nacion Argentina (BNA), a government-owned commercial bank in Argentina. As part of the arrangement, the IBM subsidiary entered into a $37 million contract to do business with a corporation owned by directors of BNA, with the directors receiving $4.5 million of that $37 million contract as compensation. Those directors then voted to award IBM the contract.

The consent decree requires IBM to pay a $300,000 fine. The fine is minimal because IBM did conduct its own internal investigation to uncover what had happened and fired 13 employees in its subsidiary when the preceding relationships were uncovered.

BNA revoked the contract after paying IBM $80 million, and IBM has agreed to reimburse BNA $34 million of that amount. Other Argentine agencies also revoked their contracts with IBM, with the total amount of business lost in the Argentina market estimated to be $500 million.

IBM has announced a new company policy that prohibits company bids for government projects that are not done in an open bidding process with full public access to documents.

The costs to IBM in this situation, both in terms of its lost contracts and revenues and its reputation, are nearly incalculable. Many companies take the position that they will not even make facilitation payments so that their worldwide staff members understand a clear and definitive line. A Procter & Gamble executive explains that, once a government official knows that a company will pay to get things done or get them done quickly, the price keeps rising and that such payments never serve the shareholders well. Long-term growth in a country is limited when even facilitation payments become part of a company's operations there. Strategically, more than ethically and legally, these types of payments are questionable in their benefits and results.

Source: In the Matter of International Business Machines Corp., Administrative Proceeding File No. 3–13097, Rel. No. 34–43761 (December 21, 2000).

Resolution of International Disputes

As discussed in Chapters 1, 3, and 4, there really is no way to enforce international laws. The International Court of Justice established by the United Nations is a court of voluntary jurisdiction for disputes between nations; it is not a court for the resolution of business disputes between nations. More and more companies and individuals favor arbitration to resolve disputes. The most popular forum chosen for such arbitrations and quasi-trials is London's Commercial Court founded on March 1, 1895, when it heard its first case, which involved a dispute over the quality of cloth sold by a Flemish manufacturer to a London agent. The court was perhaps the first to recognize the role of arbitration in deciding international business disputes; such innovation restored the confidence of business in the settlement of disputes by third parties. The London Commercial Court is viewed as a neutral forum with highly experienced judges who are also experienced commercial litigators.

Principles of International Law

The sources of international law simply serve to govern businesses as they operate in a particular country, and the laws may vary from country to country. However, some principles of international law apply to all countries and people in the international marketplace. The principles of international law do affect the decisions and operations of businesses, regardless of the availability of court resolution of rights.

Act of State Doctrine

The act of state doctrine gives every sovereign state respect from other sovereign states for its laws, actions, decisions, and policies. The act of state doctrine confirms the independence of sovereign nations and their courts. No country will intervene in the judicial and legislative processes of another country, because those actions are inconsistent with that country's standards. Courts of one country will not undertake the responsibility of providing their citizens with remedies against another country, even when that other country has violated the rights of a citizen of the first country. For example, when Union Carbide's plant in Bhopal had a high-fatality accident, Union Carbide's CEO was arrested and taken into custody when he went to Bhopal to ensure appropriate relief efforts. Although his imprisonment would have violated his rights in the United States, the U.S. courts did not intervene in India's criminal processes. Lawyers for the CEO had to work through the courts of India.

Sovereign Immunity

The concept of **sovereign immunity** is based on the notion that each country is a sovereign nation. This status means that each country is an equal with other countries; each country has exclusive jurisdiction over its internal operations, laws, and people; and no country is subject to the jurisdiction of another country's court system unless it so consents. Our court system cannot be used to right injustices in other countries or to subject other countries to penalties. For example, in *Schooner Exchange v McFaddon*, 7 Cr. 116 (1812), a group of American citizens attempted to seize the vessel *Exchange* when it came into port at Philadelphia because the citizens believed that the ship had been taken improperly on the high seas by the French emperor Napoleon and that the ship rightfully belonged to them. The U.S. Supreme Court held that the ship could not be seized because sovereign immunity applied, and France could not involuntarily be subjected to the jurisdiction of U.S. courts.

The Foreign Sovereign Immunities Act of 1976 clarified the U.S. government's position on sovereign immunity and incorporated the *Schooner Exchange* doctrine. Not only are countries immune, but the act also adds a clarification to the concept of sovereign immunity of sovereign nations for illegal acts. For example, in *Argentine Republic v Amerada Hess Shipping Co.*, 488 U.S. 428 (1989), the Supreme Court dismissed a suit brought in a U.S. federal court by a Liberian-chartered commercial ship company against the government of Argentina for its unprovoked and illegal attack on a company ship that was in neutral waters when the war between Great Britain and Argentina broke out over the Falkland Islands. The attack by the Argentine navy was unprovoked and in clear violation of international law. However, the U.S. Supreme Court clarified that under the Sovereign Immunities Act and principles of international law, all sovereign nations are immune from suits in other countries, even for those acts—like that of Argentina—that are clear violations of international law.

There is a distinction, however, under both the Foreign Sovereign Immunities Act and the courts with respect to the commercial transactions of a sovereign nation. For example, the sale of services and goods; loan transactions; and contracts for marketing, public relations, and employment services entered into by a country are, in essence, voluntary agreements that subject that country's government to civil suits in another nation's courts according to the terms of the agreement or according to the basic tenets of judicial jurisdiction (see Chapter 3). The *Riedel v Bancam* (Case 7.2) case deals with an issue of foreign sovereign immunity.

CASE 7.2

Riedel v Bancam
792 F.2d 587 (6th Cir. 1986)

Pesos to Dollars: Exchange Rates Can Kill Investments

FACTS

W. Christian Riedel, a resident of Ohio, had an account with Unibanco, S.A., and asked that it transfer $100,000 to Banca Metropolitana, S.A. (Bamesa) (predecessor to Bancam) for investment in a certificate of deposit (CD). Bamesa merged with another bank to form Bancam, and Mr. Riedel's CD was renewed with the newly merged bank.

Shortly after Mr. Riedel's renewal, the government of Mexico issued new rules governing accounts from foreigners in Mexican banks. The rules required the banks to pay the CDs in pesos at a rate that was substantially below exchange rates. A month after these rules were put into effect, Bancam was nationalized.

When Mr. Riedel's CD came due, the exchange rate was 74.34 pesos to the dollar. He was paid $53,276.23 for his $100,000 investment.

Mr. Riedel brought suit in a U.S. federal district court, alleging that Bancam had violated both federal and Ohio securities laws in selling the CDs in the United States without registration. Bancam filed a motion to dismiss the suit on the ground that the Sovereign Immunities Act of 1976 precluded U.S. courts from taking jurisdiction over the matter. Bancam also claimed protection under the act of state doctrine. Finally, Bancam claimed that the CD was not a security for purposes of U.S. securities laws.

The district court dismissed Mr. Riedel's suit on the grounds that it lacked jurisdiction over the claims under Ohio law and also on grounds of sovereign immunity and the act of state doctrine. Mr. Riedel appealed.

JUDICIAL OPINION

KENNEDY, Circuit Judge

In this appeal, Riedel does not challenge the District Court's conclusion that the certificates of deposit that Bancam issued are not "securities" under federal securities law. Instead, Riedel argues that the "act of state doctrine" does not bar his breach of contract and Ohio securities law claims. The District Court, however, did not refer to the "act of state doctrine" in denying Riedel's motion for a new trial. In addition to holding, as a matter of law, that the certificate of deposit involved in this case was not a "security" under federal securities law, the District Court ruled that it did not have jurisdiction over Riedel's breach of contract and Ohio securities law claims. The District Court concluded that: "Diversity jurisdiction pursuant to 28 U.S.C. Section 1332 does not permit a citizen of this state to sue a foreign government, or agency thereof, in a federal district court."

We agree that the District Court did not have jurisdiction under 28 U.S.C. § 1332 over the breach of contract and Ohio securities law claims. Title 28 U.S.C. § 1332(a)(4) confers original jurisdiction on the district courts over civil actions between a foreign state, as plaintiff, and a citizen of a State. Title 28 U.S.C. § 1332(a)(4), however, does not apply to suits between a citizen of a State and a foreign state, as defendant. A "foreign state," under 28 U.S.C. § 1603(a), "includes a political subdivision of a foreign state or an agency or instrumentality of a foreign state. . . ." Since the Government of Mexico nationalized Bancam on September 1, 1982, Bancam qualifies as an "agency or instrumentality of a foreign state" under 28 U.S.C. § 1603(b)(2). Therefore, this action involves an Ohio citizen and a "foreign state," as a defendant. Consequently, 28 U.S.C. § 1332(a)(4) does not apply. Accordingly, we hold that the District Court properly concluded that it did not have jurisdiction under 28 U.S.C. § 1332 over the breach of contract and Ohio securities law claims.

We conclude, however, that the District Court may have had jurisdiction over the breach of contract and Ohio securities law claims under the [Foreign Sovereign Immunities Act (FSIA) 28 U.S.C. § 1330]. Although the FSIA ordinarily entitles foreign states to immunity from federal jurisdiction, 28 U.S.C. § 1605(a)(2) creates a "commercial activity" exception to this immunity. Title 28 U.S.C. § 1605(a)(2) provides in pertinent part:

> A foreign state shall not be immune from the jurisdiction of courts of the United States or of the States in any case . . . in which the action is based upon commercial activity carried on in the United States by the foreign state; or upon an act performed in the United States in connection with a commercial activity of the foreign state elsewhere or upon an act outside the territory of the United States in connection with a commercial activity of the foreign state elsewhere and that act causes a direct effect in the United States.

Accordingly, 28 U.S.C. § 1605(a)(2) applies only when a foreign state's "commercial activity" has the required jurisdictional nexus with the United States.

We hold that the sale of the certificates of deposit in this case was a "commercial activity." . . . The "act of state doctrine" precludes courts in this country from questioning the validity and effect of a sovereign act of a foreign nation performed in its own territory. . . .

Under the "act of state doctrine," courts exercise jurisdiction but prudentially "decline to decide the merits of the case if in doing so we would need to judge the validity of the public acts of a sovereign state performed within its own territory."

Accordingly, we affirm the portion of the District Court's order denying Riedel's motion for a new trial on the breach of contract claim. The "act of state doctrine," however, does not bar the Ohio securities law claim. Riedel bases that claim on Bancam's failure to register the certificate of deposit with the Ohio Division of Securities and not on Bancam's failure to repay dollars at the certificate's maturity.

Since the District Court may have had the subject matter jurisdiction, we remand the Ohio securities law claim for further proceedings consistent with this opinion. We also note that even if the District Court concludes that it has subject matter jurisdiction, Bancam has also argued that the District Court does not have personal jurisdiction. Assuming that the District Court decides that it has subject matter jurisdiction under the FSIA, the District Court will also have to make findings of fact to determine whether Bancam

CONTINUED

has sufficient "contacts" with the United States to satisfy due process.

Reversed in part.

CASE QUESTIONS

1. Describe Mr. Riedel's investment.

2. What are the bases for his suit against Bancam in Ohio?

3. Does the act of state doctrine apply?

4. Does Mexico have sovereign immunity for its expropriation of the bank?

5. What issues will the court be determining when the case is remanded?

CONSIDER...   7.2

Scott Nelson was employed at the Kingdom of Saudi Arabia, a hospital in Saudi Arabia. He had signed an employment contract to act as a monitoring systems engineer at the hospital. Mr. Nelson responded to an ad run in the United States, was hired, and began work in December 1983.

In the course of his employment, Mr. Nelson discovered numerous safety violations. When he brought them to the attention of hospital officials in March 1984, they told him to ignore it.

On September 27, 1994, Mr. Nelson was summoned to the security office, where agents of the Saudi government arrested him.

He was transported to a jail cell, where he was shackled, tortured, and beaten. He was kept for four days with no food and confined to an overcrowded cell area infested with rats. When food was provided, he had to fight other prisoners for it.

After 39 days and U.S. intervention, Mr. Nelson was released from jail. He refused to return to the hospital and left for the United States.

Mr. Nelson and his wife brought a damages suit against his former employer for their failure to warn him about the government. The Saudi government sought to dismiss the suit under the Foreign Sovereign Immunities Act.

Was the activity commercial? Should the Nelsons be permitted to sue? [*Saudi Arabia v Nelson*, 507 U.S. 349 (1993)]

Protections for U.S. Property and Investment Abroad

Expropriation

The effect of nationalization is that the private property of citizens and businesses operating in that country is taken by the government, an act referred to as expropriation. While courts do not interfere with a sovereign's actions, the effect of expropriation, combined with the act of state doctrine and sovereign immunity, has a chilling effect on U.S. investments in foreign countries. To discourage expropriation, the Foreign Assistance Act of 1962 contained what has been called the Hickenlooper amendment, which requires the president to suspend all forms of assistance to countries that have expropriated the property of U.S. citizens or regulated the property in such a way as to effectively deprive a U.S. citizen of it (through taxation or limits on use).

Minimizing Expropriation   Many trade treaties that have been negotiated or are being negotiated with other countries contain protections against expropriation. Some treaties provide U.S. companies and investors with the same levels of protection as the citizens of those countries. For example, if a country affords its citizens due process before taking over private property, U.S. citizens and companies must be afforded those same protections prior to expropriation.

Finally, Congress has created a federal insurer for U.S. investments abroad. The Overseas Private Investment Corporation (OPIC) is an insurer for U.S. investment in those countries in which the per capita annual income is $250 or less. OPIC will pay damages for expropriation, for inability to convert the currency of the country, or for losses from war or revolution.

Consumer protections in other countries depend on those countries' laws. For example, many U.S. citizens have constructed luxury homes along the coast near Ensenada in Baja California. They did so because the land and construction were so much cheaper than in the United States that they could afford large, luxurious homes. However, the land on which many of the homes were located was the subject of 14 years of litigation and more than 60 court decisions over disputed ownership rights. With the Mexican Supreme Court's decision on land ownership, most of the current U.S. owners have been told that they must vacate their homes and leave everything behind. Despite due process and property rights in the United States, the homeowners in Ensenada have no hope as long as the Mexican Supreme Court has declared the law for its country and land there.

Repatriation

Repatriation is the process of bringing back to your own country profits earned on investments in another country. Some nations establish limits on repatriation; businesses can remove only a certain amount of the profits earned from the operations of a business within a country. Repatriation limits are considered acts of state and are immune from litigation in the United States.

Forum Non Conveniens, or "You Have the Wrong Court"

The doctrine of *forum non conveniens* is a principle of U.S. justice under which cases that are brought to the wrong court are dismissed. The doctrine allows judicial discretion whereby such issues as the location of the evidence, the location of the parties, and the location of the property that will be used to satisfy any judgment are examined. For example, when the Union Carbide disaster occurred at its Bhopal, India, plant, victims and families brought suit against Union Carbide in New York City. A U.S. court of appeals dismissed the case and sent it back to India on the grounds of *forum non conveniens* [*In re Union Carbide Corp. Gas Plant Disaster*, 809 F.2d 195 (2d Cir. 1987); *cert. denied*, 484 U.S. 871 (1987)].

Conflicts of Law

No two countries match in terms of the structure of their legal system or their laws. For example, the law in the United States, codified by the widely adopted Uniform Commercial Code (UCC), is that all contracts and contract relationships are subject to a standard of good faith. In Canada, the good faith exists only if the parties place such a provision in their agreement. Under German law, protections are given not on the basis of good faith but, rather, on the basis of who is the weaker party. Just among these three major commercial powers, laws on contracts are significantly different. The rules on conflicts of law in international transactions are as follows: (1) If the parties choose which law applies, that law will apply, and (2) if no provision is made, the law of the country where the contract is performed will be used. Agreeing to and understanding the set of laws to be applied in a contract is a critical part of international transactions. *Carnival Cruise Lines v Shute* (Case 7.3) is the U.S. Supreme Court's decision on party agreements for resolution of disputes.

| CASE 7.3 | *Carnival Cruise Lines v Shute*
499 U.S. 585 (1991) |

Cruising for Forums: Contracts Clauses on the High Seas

FACTS

Through an Arlington, Washington, travel agent, Eulala and Russel Shute (respondents) purchased passage for a seven-day cruise on the *Tropicale*, a ship owned by Carnival Cruise Lines (petitioner). The Shutes paid the fare to the agent, who forwarded the payment to Carnival's headquarters in Miami, Florida. Carnival then prepared the tickets and sent them to the Shutes in Washington. The face of each ticket, at its left-hand lower corner, contained this admonition:

> SUBJECT TO CONDITIONS OF CONTRACT ON LAST PAGES IMPORTANT! PLEASE READ CONTRACT—ON LAST PAGES 1, 2, 3, App. 15

The following appeared on "contract page 1" of each ticket:

> TERMS AND CONDITIONS OF PASSAGE CONTRACT TICKET...
>
> 3. (a) The acceptance of this ticket by the person or persons named hereon as passengers shall be deemed to be an acceptance and agreement by each of them of all of the terms and conditions of this Passage Contract Ticket. . . .
>
> 8. It is agreed by and between the passenger and the Carrier that all disputes and matters whatsoever arising under, in connection with or incident to this Contract shall be litigated, if at all, in and before a Court located in the State of Florida, U.S.A., to the exclusion of the Courts of any other state or country.

The Shutes boarded the Tropicale in Los Angeles, California. The ship sailed to Puerto Vallarta, Mexico, and then returned to Los Angeles. While the ship was in international waters off the Mexican coast, Eulala Shute was injured when she slipped on a deck mat during a guided tour of the ship's galley. The Shutes filed suit against the petitioner in the U.S. District Court for the Western District of Washington, claiming that Mrs. Shute's injuries had been caused by the negligence of Carnival Cruise Lines and its employees.

Carnival moved for summary judgment, contending that the forum clause in the tickets required the Shutes to bring their suit in a court in the State of Florida. Carnival also contended that the District Court lacked personal jurisdiction over it because its contacts with the State of Washington were insubstantial. The District Court granted the motion, holding that Carnival's contacts

with Washington were constitutionally insufficient to support the exercise of personal jurisdiction.

The Court of Appeals reversed. Reasoning that "but for" Carnival's solicitation of business in Washington, the Shutes would not have taken the cruise and Mrs. Shute would not have been injured, the court concluded that Carnival had sufficient contacts with Washington to justify the District Court's exercise of personal jurisdiction. Carnival appealed.

JUDICIAL OPINION

BLACKMUN, Justice

Turning to the forum-selection clause, the Court of Appeals acknowledged that a court concerned with the enforceability of such a clause must begin its analysis with *The Bremen v Zapata Off-Shore Co.*, 407 U.S. 1, 92 S.Ct. 1907, 32 L.Ed.2d 513 (1972), where this Court held that forum-selection clauses, although not "historically . . . favored," are "prima facie valid." The appellate court concluded that the forum clause should not be enforced because it "was not freely bargained for." As an "independent justification" for refusing to enforce the clause, the Court of Appeals noted that there was evidence in the record to indicate that "the Shutes are physically and financially incapable of pursuing this litigation in Florida" and that the enforcement of the clause would operate to deprive them of their day in court and thereby contravene this Court's holding in *The Bremen*.

In *The Bremen*, this Court addressed the enforceability of a forum-selection clause in a contract between two business corporations. An American corporation, Zapata, made a contract with Unterweser, a German corporation, for the towage of Zapata's oceangoing drilling rig from Louisiana to a point in the Adriatic Sea off the coast of Italy. The agreement provided that any dispute arising under the contract was to be resolved in the London Court of Justice.

After a storm in the Gulf of Mexico seriously damaged the rig, Zapata ordered Unterweser's ship to tow the rig to Tampa, Fla., the nearest point of refuge. Thereafter, Zapata sued Unterweser in admiralty in federal court at Tampa. Citing the forum clause, Unterweser moved to dismiss. The District Court denied Unterweser's motion, and the Court of Appeals for the Fifth Circuit, sitting en banc on rehearing, and by a sharply divided vote, affirmed.

The Court further generalized that "in the light of present-day commercial realities and expanding international trade we conclude that the forum clause should control absent a strong showing that it should be set aside." The Court did not define precisely the circumstances that would make it unreasonable for a court to enforce a forum clause. Instead, the Court discussed a number of factors that made it reasonable to enforce the clause at issue in *The Bremen* and that, presumably, would be pertinent in any determination whether to enforce a similar clause.

The Bremen concerned a "far from routine transaction between companies of two different nations contemplating the tow of an extremely costly piece of equipment from Louisiana across the Gulf of Mexico and the Atlantic Ocean, through the Mediterranean Sea to its final destination in the Adriatic Sea." These facts suggest that, even apart from the evidence of negotiation regarding the forum clause, it was entirely reasonable for the Court in *The Bremen* to have expected Unterweser and Zapata to have negotiated with care in selecting a forum for the resolution of disputes arising from their special towing contract.

In contrast, respondents' passage contract was purely routine and doubtless nearly identical to every commercial passage contract issued by petitioner and most other cruise lines. In this context, it would be entirely unreasonable for us to assume that respondents—or any other cruise passenger—would negotiate with petitioner the terms of a forum-selection clause in an ordinary commercial cruise ticket. Common sense dictates that a ticket of this kind will be a form contract the terms of which are not subject to negotiation, and that an individual purchasing the ticket will not have bargaining parity with the cruise line. But by ignoring the crucial differences in the business contexts in which the respective contracts were executed, the Court of Appeals' analysis seems to us to have distorted somewhat this Court's holding in *The Bremen*.

In evaluating the reasonableness of the forum clause at issue in this case, we must refine the analysis of *The Bremen* to account for the realities of form passage contracts. First, a cruise line has a special interest in limiting the fora in which it potentially could be subject to suit. Because a cruise ship typically carries passengers from many locales, it is not unlikely that a mishap on a cruise could subject the cruise line to litigation in several different fora. Additionally, a clause establishing *ex ante* the forum for dispute resolution has the salutary effect of dispelling any confusion about where suits arising from the contract must be brought and defended, sparing litigants the time and expense of pretrial motions to determine the correct forum and conserving judicial resources that otherwise would be devoted to deciding those motions. Finally, it stands to reason that

passengers who purchase tickets containing a forum clause like that at issue in this case benefit in the form of reduced fares reflecting the savings that the cruise line enjoys by limiting the fora in which it may be sued.

In the present case, Florida is not a "remote alien forum," nor—given the fact that Mrs. Shute's accident occurred off the coast of Mexico—is this dispute an essentially local one inherently more suited to resolution in the State of Washington than in Florida. In light of these distinctions, and because respondents do not claim lack of notice of the forum clause, we conclude that they have not satisfied the "heavy burden of proof" required to set aside the clause on grounds of inconvenience.

It bears emphasis that forum-selection clauses contained in form passage contracts are subject to judicial scrutiny for fundamental fairness. In this case, there is no indication that petitioner set Florida as the forum in which disputes were to be resolved as a means of discouraging cruise passengers from pursuing legitimate claims. Any suggestion of such a bad-faith motive is belied by two facts: Petitioner has its principal place of business in Florida, and many of its cruises depart from and return to Florida ports. Similarly, there is no evidence that petitioner obtained respondents' accession to the forum clause by fraud or overreaching. Finally, respondents have conceded that they were given notice of the forum provision and, therefore, presumably retained the option of rejecting the contract with impunity. In the case before us, therefore, we conclude that the Court of Appeals erred in refusing to enforce the forum-selection clause.

There was no prohibition of a forum-selection clause. Because the clause before us allows for judicial resolution of claims against petitioner and does not purport to limit petitioner's liability for negligence, it does not violate § 183c.

The judgment of the Court of Appeals is reversed.

DISSENTING OPINION

Justice STEVENS, with whom Justice MARSHALL joins, dissenting

I begin my dissent by noting that only the most meticulous passenger is likely to become aware of the forum-selection provision. I have therefore appended to this opinion a facsimile of the relevant text, using the type size that actually appears in the ticket itself. A careful reader will find the forum-selection clause in the 8th of the 25 numbered paragraphs.

The fact that the cruise line can reduce its litigation costs, and therefore its liability insurance premiums, by forcing this choice on its passengers does not, in my opinion, suffice to render the provision reasonable.

Even if passengers received prominent notice of the forum-selection clause before they committed the cost of the cruise, I would remain persuaded that the clause

CONTINUED

was unenforceable under traditional principles of federal admiralty law and is "null and void" under the terms of Limitation of Vessel Owners Liability Act.

Exculpatory clauses in passenger tickets have been around for a long time. These clauses are typically the product of disparate bargaining power between the carrier and the passenger, and they undermine the strong public interest in deterring negligent conduct. For these reasons, courts long before the turn of the century consistently held such clauses unenforceable under federal admiralty law.

The stipulation in the ticket that Carnival Cruise sold to respondents certainly lessens or weakens their ability to recover for the slip and fall incident that occurred off the west coast of Mexico during the cruise that originated and terminated in Los Angeles, California. It is safe to assume that the witnesses—whether other passengers or members of the crew—can be assembled with less expense and inconvenience at a west coast forum than in a Florida court several thousand miles from the scene of the accident.

CASE QUESTIONS

1. Explain where the parties are located and where the accident occurred.

2. What was the nature of the clause at issue, and where was it located?

3. Does it make any difference to the court that this was a business-to-consumer and not a business-to-business contract?

4. What problems do the dissenting justices see in the majority's decision on the clause?

CONSIDER...   7.3

International Ambassador Programs, Inc. is a Washington-based nonprofit organization that arranges tours and informational visits in foreign countries, including Russia. Archpexpo, once a Soviet state enterprise and now a Russian limited partnership, facilitates and expedites tours such as those sponsored by Ambassador to Russia and the other former Soviet republics.

Archpexpo and Ambassador entered into several agreements relating to tours. An April 1989 agreement provided that "all disputes and differences without recourse to courts of law shall be referred to the arbitration tribunal with the USSR Trade and Industry Chamber for resolution, such resolution acknowledged as final by the parties."

A dispute arose between the parties when Archpexpo alleged that it had not been paid certain fees due, and Ambassador claimed it was entitled to an offset of $20,000 for refunds it had to give to travelers who were dissatisfied with Archpexpo's service.

Archpexpo filed for arbitration, and Ambassador brought suit in federal district court in the United States. Does the federal district court have jurisdiction? Must Ambassador submit to arbitration in Russia? What if Ambassador had more than one contract with Archpexpo and some of the contracts contained the arbitration clause and some did not? Would Ambassador be required to submit to arbitration then? [*International Ambassador Programs, Inc. v Archpexpo*, 68 F.3d 337 (9th Cir. 1995)]

Protections in International Competition

Although trade barriers are coming down and a global marketplace seems to be a reality, international competition is still subject to much regulation found in the forms of antitrust laws, protections for intellectual property, and trade treaties.

Antitrust Laws in the International Marketplace

All U.S. firms are subject to the antitrust laws of the United States, regardless of where their operations and anticompetitive behavior may occur. Firms from other countries operating in the United States or engaging in trade that has a substantial impact in the United States are also subject to U.S. antitrust laws. These firms are not covered under the act of state doctrine because they are not governmental entities and are engaging in commercial activity. For example, Go Video, a U.S. firm from Arizona, brought a successful antitrust suit against Japanese manufacturers for their alleged refusal to deal with the company in its attempt to develop a dual-deck VCR. U.S. courts and antitrust laws had jurisdiction because of the substantial impact the actions of the Japanese manufacturers would have on the VCR market in the United States.

The converse is also true. Firms outside the United States may enjoy the protections and benefits of our antitrust laws and bring suit for violations if it can be established that the violations they are alleging had a substantial impact on trade in the United States. Finally, U.S. firms are subject to other countries' antitrust laws. Microsoft and GE have been limited in their acquisitions in the EU because of EU antitrust provisions.

The Export Trading Company Act of 1982 carved an exception to the antitrust laws for U.S. firms that combine to do business in international markets. Large U.S. firms that would otherwise be prohibited from merging for anticompetitive reasons are permitted to form export trading companies (ETCs) for the purpose of participating in international trade. The Justice Department approves applications for ETCs in advance, provided the applicants can demonstrate that the proposed joint venture will not reduce competition in the United States, increase U.S. prices, or cause unfair competition. ETCs such as Mobil and Exxon worked together to explore Siberian oil fields in a combination that would otherwise be prohibited both under the antitrust laws and for purposes of ongoing operations. These combinations allow effective negotiation of large foreign contracts. ExxonMobil is now one firm, a result of its joint drilling ventures.

Tariffs

Tariffs are taxes on goods as they move in and out of countries (import and export tariffs, respectively). Import tariffs are, in effect, a tax on goods coming into a country. Tariffs increase the cost of those goods, particularly in comparison with domestic goods, and therefore limit the competitiveness of foreign goods within a country.

In the United States, the U.S. Customs Service is responsible for developing the tariffs according to a tariff schedule and for enforcing the tariffs on imported

Ethical Issues

When the Taliban was in power in Afghanistan, it banned watching television. The result of the ban was the creation of a substantial market for smuggling television sets into Afghanistan. For example, a Sony TV set smuggled into Pakistan would cost about $400. The legal cost, paying tariffs, would be $440. The same set smuggled into Afghanistan could bring twice as much. Sony gets the same, or $220, for every set sold, regardless of where it is sold and what happens to it in terms of its final destination.

The Taliban decided to impose tariffs and taxes on TV sets even as it held to the ban because the ban resulted in the smuggling market from which they could extract substantial sums.

Do you think Sony had an ethical obligation to not sell to the Taliban? Does it have an ethical obligation to police what happens to its products? What happens when a company profits from a government making money from its own ban?

Source: Daniel Pearl and Steve Stecklow, "Taliban Banned TV but Collected Profits on Smuggled Sonys," *Wall Street Journal,* January 9, 2002, pp. A1, A8. (Note that the source for this ethical issue was an article co-authored by Daniel Pearl, the U.S. journalist who was kidnapped by terrorists and eventually killed by them with graphic coverage of the execution.)

goods. The tariff is based on the computed value of the goods coming into the country. That computed value depends on how the goods are classified under the schedule. For example, if potato chips are classified as bread, they are tariff- or duty-free. If they are classified as snacks, they carry a tariff [*Sabritas v U.S.*, 998 F. Supp. 1123 (Ct. Int'l Trade 1998)]. The federal government has created a specialized court to handle the many disputes that arise over the application of the tariffs and the underlying classification of goods.

Competition may also be controlled by import restrictions, a resulting control on trade balance and prices. By limiting the amounts of certain products or products from certain countries, supply and demand (and, through economic principles, price) are affected. These nontariff regulations also control competition and the flow of goods across borders.

As noted earlier, some countries also limit exports, particularly of technologies to certain countries that could use them to harm others through, for example, the development of nuclear technology.

Exhibit 7.1 provides a summary of international law principles and doctrines.

Protections for Intellectual Property

Protections for intellectual property in the international marketplace are constantly undergoing refinements. Worldwide registration for patents, copyrights, and

EXHIBIT 7.1 The Treaties, Principles, and Statutes of International Law

NAME	PURPOSE
North Atlantic Treaty North Atlantic Treaty Organization (NATO)	Treaty between U.S. and European nations that establishes a deployment of armed forces and security setup in Europe
Foreign Sovereign Immunities Act of 1976	U.S. statute that clarifies the immunity of foreign countries and officials from prosecution for crimes in the United States
Act of state doctrine (expropriation)	Recognition of a foreign government's actions as valid; U.S. courts may not be used to challenge another country's actions, even toward U.S. citizens
Foreign Assistance Act of 1962 (Hickenlooper amendment)	Authorization given to president to cut off aid to countries where U.S. citizens' property has been taken by the government or regulated so as to deprive owner of use
Overseas Private Investment Corporation (OPIC)	Federal insurer for U.S. companies' investments in countries with low per capita income
Expropriation	Act of a sovereign state in taking property from its citizens or businesses operating there
Repatriation	Bringing back to your own country money earned on investments in other countries
Export Trading Company Act of 1982	Antitrust combination exemption for companies joining to compete in international markets
Maastricht Treaty	Agreement that created European Union
General Agreement on Tariffs and Trade (GATT)	Agreement among 150 countries to increase trade by reducing tariffs
North American Free Trade Agreement (NAFTA)	Agreement among United States, Canada, and Mexico with the goal of tariff elimination

trademarks are goals that are within reach as the mechanisms for administration are being put into place. Details on international protections are found in Chapter 15.

Criminal Law Protections

All persons and businesses present within a country are subject to that nation's regulatory scheme for business as well as to the constraints of the country's criminal code. Compliance with the law is a universal principle of international business operations. Expulsion, fines, penalties, and imprisonment are all remedies available to governments when foreign businesses break the law in a particular nation.

Often, the complexities of international operations produce layers of business organizations throughout the world. These layers are often necessary for individual countries and proper business structure under the law. The layers of organizations may provide opportunities for laundering of money, concealment of transactions, and other complex transactions that can escape regulatory detection for a time. However, the activities are eventually discovered, and countries are cooperating more to be certain the complexities of international business do not conceal illicit activities.

B I O G R A P H Y

Siemens: The Company That Paid the Largest Fine Ever for FCPA Violations

Siemens is a German conglomerate that has been in business since 1847. It has three divisions: energy, health care, and industry. Siemens has 428,200 employees and operates in 190 countries. The following chart shows the countries in which Siemens paid bribes for contracts in violation of the FCPA.

COUNTRY	PRODUCT	BRIBES PAID	DATE
Russia	Medical devices	$55 million	2000–2007
Argentina	Identity cards project	$40 million	1998–2004
China	High-voltage transmission lines	$25 million	2002–2003
China	Metro trains	$22 million	2002–2007
Israel	Power plants	$20 million	2002–2005
Bangladesh	Mobile telephone works	$5.3 million	2004–2006
Venezuela	High-speed trains	$16.7 million	2001–2007
Russia	Traffic control systems	$0.75 million	2004–2006
Vietnam	Medical devices	$0.5 million	2005
China	Medical devices	$14.4 million	2003–2007
Nigeria	Telecommunications projects	€4.2 million	2003
Iraq	Power station	$1.7 million	2000
Italy	Power station	€6.0 million	2003
Greece	Telecommunications	€37 million	2006

Both the SEC and the U.S. Department of Justice (DOJ) were investigating Siemens. The two agencies concluded that Siemens had paid more than 4,283 bribes totaling $1.4 billion to government officials to secure contracts. The SEC concluded that the bribes resulted in the company obtaining $1.1 billion in profits.

The DOJ and Siemens AG reached an agreement to settle the company's ongoing violations. As a result of these violations, Siemens agreed to pay $800 million to the United States, a fine 20 times higher than the largest fine ever collected under the FCPA. Siemens also settled charges with 10 other countries and paid total fines of $5.8 billion. The SEC complaint (www.sec.gov/litigation) against Siemens cited the involvement of employees at all levels of the company and a culture that had long been at odds with the FCPA.

The company's cooperation with the U.S. government since 2006, as well as its efforts to correct the violations, caused government officials to reduce the fine from $2.7 billion to $800 million. Siemens' efforts to correct its culture included cooperating with the government, turning over all documents it found, and replacing all but one officer and all board members. Three of the company's former officers are under investigation by German authorities for their role in the ongoing bribery web.

Summary

What laws affect businesses in international trade?

- Foreign Sovereign Immunities Act of 1976
- Foreign Assistance Act of 1962 (Hickenlooper amendment)
- Overseas Private Investment Corporation (OPIC)
- Export Trading Company Act of 1982
- Contracts for the International Sale of Goods (CISG)

What treaties, agreements, practices, and principles affect international business and trade?

- North Atlantic Treaty
- North Atlantic Treaty Organization (NATO)
- Maastricht Treaty
- General Agreement on Tariffs and Trade (GATT)
- North American Free Trade Agreement (NAFTA)
- International Monetary Fund (IMF)
- Duties, quotas, tariffs—controls on prices and quantities of goods by nations with the goal of balancing imports and exports
- Foreign Corrupt Practices Act (FCPA)—controls on means of accessing governments

What principles of international law affect business?

- Sovereign immunity—freedom of one country from being subject to orders from another country
- Expropriation; act of state doctrine—recognition by U.S. courts of the actions of other governments as valid despite noncompliance with traditional U.S. rights and procedures
- Repatriation—returning profits earned in other countries to one's native land
- Conflict of laws—issue as to which country's law applies in international transactions
- Antitrust issues
- *Forum non conveniens*—doctrine requiring dismissal of cases that should be heard in another country's courts

What protections exist in international competition?

- Antitrust laws
- Protections for intellectual property
- Criminal law protections

Questions and Problems

1. Tom Welch and Dave Johnson, two officials of the Salt Lake City Olympic Committee, were charged with bribery and racketeering for their alleged role in paying money to and giving rather large gifts to members of the International Olympic Committee (IOC) in order to win the bid for holding the winter Olympics in Salt Lake City in 2002. Salt Lake City did win the bid, but an anonymous letter to the IOC revealed that these types of payments and gifts had been offered. Following an investigation, nine members of the IOC were removed or resigned and others were sanctioned. The Salt Lake City Olympic Committee removed Mr. Welch and Mr. Johnson and replaced them with Mitt Romney as the head of its committee. Utah declined prosecution under state law, and a federal district court judge dismissed the charges against Mr. Welch and Mr. Johnson. The U.S. Attorney for the case filed an appeal with the tenth circuit federal court of appeals asking that the charges be reinstated. He noted that the Olympics were an "international" event and mandated federal jurisdiction. He also argued in the brief that the payments, accommodations, and gifts were more than goodwill and amounted to bribery in violation of federal law.

Applying the cases and law presented in the discussion on the FCPA, determine whether there was or was not a violation of federal law. What jurisdiction do federal courts have over criminal charges? Describe the appellate process and what an appellate court can do in an appeal such as this. [*U.S. v Welch*, 327 F.3d 1081, at 1085 (10th Cir. 2003)]

2. Suppose that the government of Brazil took possession of the cacao farms of a chocolate factory owned by a U.S. firm. What rights would the U.S. factory have? What limits exist on those rights?

3. Royal Dutch/Shell Group is a network of affiliated but formally independent oil and gas companies, many located in the United States. Royal Dutch/Shell also has extensive financial relationships with banks and other investors and shareholders in New York and other parts of the United States. Among these affiliated companies is Shell Petroleum Development Company of Nigeria, Ltd. ("Shell Nigeria"), a wholly owned Nigerian subsidiary that does extensive oil exploration and development activity in the Ogoni region of Nigeria.

Ken Saro-Wiwa and others were imprisoned, tortured, and killed by the Nigerian government in reprisal for their political opposition to Shell Nigeria's oil exploration activities. Saro-Wiwa and other activists alleged that Shell Nigeria coercively appropriated land for oil development without adequate compensation, and caused substantial pollution of the air and water in the homeland of the Ogoni people. A protest movement arose among the Ogoni. Ken Saro-Wiwa was an opposition leader and president of the Movement for the Survival of the Ogoni People.

According to a suit filed in New York by surviving activists and their families, and Royal Dutch/Shell investors, Shell Nigeria recruited the Nigerian police and military to attack local villages and suppress the organized opposition to its development activity. Saro-Wiwa and others were repeatedly arrested, detained, and tortured by the Nigerian government because of their leadership roles in the protest movement. In 1995, Saro-Wiwa and others were hanged, along with other Ogoni leaders, after being convicted of murder by a special military tribunal. The suit alleges that they were convicted on fabricated evidence solely to silence political criticism and were not afforded the legal protections required by international law. Plaintiffs also alleged that Saro-Wiwa's family—including Ken Saro-Wiwa's 74-year-old mother—was beaten by Nigerian officials while attending his trial. The suit maintains that these abuses were carried out by the Nigerian government and military, but were instigated, orchestrated, planned, and facilitated by Shell Nigeria with the Royal Dutch/Shell Group who allegedly provided money, weapons, and logistical support to the Nigerian military, including the vehicles and ammunition used in the raids on the villages, procured at least some of these attacks, participated in the fabrication of murder charges against Saro-Wiwa, and bribed witnesses to give false testimony against them. The trial court dismissed the case for *forum non conveniens*. The investors and others appealed. What should the appellate court do and why? [*Wiwa v Royal Dutch Petroleum Co.*, 226 F.3d 88 (C.A. 2 2000)]

4. Between January 1983 and June 1987, Richard H. Liebo was vice president in charge of the Aerospace Division of NAPCO International, Inc., of Hopkins, Minnesota. NAPCO's primary business consisted of selling military equipment and supplies throughout the world.

In early 1983, the Niger government contracted with a West German company, Dornier Reparaturwerft, to service two Lockheed C-130 cargo planes. After the Niger Ministry of Defense ran into financial troubles, Dornier sought an American parts supplier in order to qualify the Ministry of Defense for financing through the U.S. Foreign Military Sales program. The Foreign Military Sales program is supervised by the Defense Security Assistance Agency of the U.S. Department of Defense. Under the program, loans are provided to foreign governments for the purchase of military equipment and supplies from U.S. contractors.

In June 1983, representatives from Dornier met with officials of NAPCO and agreed that NAPCO would become the prime contractor on the C-130 maintenance contracts. Under this arrangement, NAPCO would supply parts to Niger and Dornier, and Dornier would perform the required maintenance at its facilities in Munich.

Once NAPCO and Dornier agreed to these terms, Mr. Liebo and Axel Kurth, a Dornier sales representative, flew to Niger to get the president of Niger's approval of the contract. In Niger, they met with Captain Ali Tiemogo, chief of maintenance for the Niger Air Force. Captain Tiemogo testified that during the trip, Mr. Liebo and Mr. Kurth told him that they would make "some gestures" to him if he helped get the contract approved. When asked whether this promise played a role in deciding to recommend approval of the contract, Captain Tiemogo stated, "I can't say 'no,' I cannot say 'yes,' at that time," but "it encouraged me." Following

Captain Tiemogo's recommendation that the contract be approved, the president of Niger signed the contract.

Tahirou Barke, Captain Tiemogo's cousin and close friend, was the first consular for the Niger Embassy in Washington, D.C. Mr. Barke testified that he met Mr. Liebo in Washington sometime in 1983 or 1984. Mr. Barke stated that Mr. Liebo told him he wanted to make a "gesture" to Captain Tiemogo and asked Mr. Barke to set up a bank account in the United States. With Mr. Barke's assistance, Mr. Liebo opened a bank account in Minnesota in the name of "E. Dave," a variation of the name of Mr. Barke's then-girlfriend, Shirley Elaine Dave. NAPCO deposited about $30,000 in the account, and Mr. Barke used the money to pay bills and purchase personal items and also gave a portion of the money to Captain Tiemogo.

In August 1985, Mr. Barke returned to Niger to be married. After the wedding, he and his wife honeymooned in Paris, Stockholm, and London. Before leaving for Niger, he informed Mr. Liebo of his honeymoon plans, and Mr. Liebo offered to buy, as a gift, Mr. Barke's airline tickets for both Mr. Barke's return to Niger and his honeymoon trip. Mr. Liebo made the flight arrangements and paid for the tickets, which cost $2,028, by charging them to NAPCO's Diners Club account. Mr. Barke considered the tickets a personal "gift" from Mr. Liebo.

Over a two-and-a-half-year period beginning in May 1984, NAPCO made payments totaling $130,000 to three "commission agents." The practice of using agents and paying them commissions on international contracts was acknowledged as a proper, legal, and accepted business practice in third-world countries. NAPCO issued commission checks to three "agents" identified as Amadou Mailele, Captain Tiemogo's brother-in-law; Fatouma Boube, Captain Tiemogo's sister-in-law; and Miss E. Dave, Mr. Barke's girlfriend. At Captain Tiemogo's request, both Mr. Mailele and Ms. Boube set up bank accounts in Paris. Neither Mr. Mailele, Ms. Boube, nor Miss Dave, however, received the commission checks or acted as NAPCO's agent. These individuals were merely intermediaries through whom NAPCO made payments to Captain Tiemogo and Mr. Barke. NAPCO's corporate president, Henri Jacob, or another superior of Mr. Liebo's, approved these "commission payments." No one approved the payment for the honeymoon trip. Are there any violations of the FCPA? [*U.S. v Liebo*, 923 F.2d 1308 (8th Cir. 1991)]

5. United Arab Shipping Company (UASC) is a corporation formed under the laws of Kuwait. Its capital stock is wholly owned by the governments of Kuwait, Saudi Arabia, the United Arab Emirates, Qatar, Iraq, and Bahrain. No single government owned more than 19.33 percent of UASC's shares, and the corporation was created by a treaty among the owner nations.

Three seamen who were injured while working for UASC brought suit against it in federal district court in the United States. UASC maintains it enjoys sovereign immunity. The seamen claim it is a commercial enterprise and not entitled to immunity. Who is correct? [*Mangattu v M/V IBN Hayyan*, 35 F.3d 205 (5th Cir. 1994)]

6. Smith & Smith, a U.S. computer firm, contracted to install a computer system for Volkswagen in the company's headquarters in Berlin, Germany. Smith's contract included the following liability limitation: "We are only liable for loss of data which is due to a deliberate action on our part. We are not responsible for lost profits in any event." The contract had no provisions on choice of law. A crash in the Smith & Smith system caused a loss of 92 days' worth of financial data. Volkswagen was required to use its auditors to restructure the database at a substantial cost. Smith & Smith says it did nothing deliberate and, therefore, is not liable. Volkswagen cites German law that mandates protection by sellers against such losses and permits recovery of lost profits. U.S. law would honor the Smith & Smith clause. Which law applies? Why?

7. The Western oil firms once were the dominant players in Kazakhstan, a Central Asian country that is rich in oil resources. However, the Justice Department indicted U.S. citizen James Giffen for allegedly making $80 million in payments to government officials in Kazakhstan on behalf of Mobil and other companies in order that the companies could obtain drilling rights from the government. Giffen had the touch when it came to getting the oil companies access for drilling. Once Giffen was indicted, the Western oil firms' drilling rights diminished substantially and the presence of Chinese oil firms increased. Many have pointed to this example, with direct causal connection between the elimination of U.S. firms and the increased presence of Chinese firms, as evidence that the FCPA puts U.S. firms and the U.S. economy at a distinct disadvantage to those countries that do no take enforcement action against bribery. How would you respond to this argument? Discuss the reasons behind the bribery statutes. (Nathan Wardi, "The Bribery Law Bracket," *Forbes*, May 24, 2010, p. 70.)

8. The European Union has developed a directive on privacy and e-mail. Nations within the EU are permitted to use e-mail for commercial transactions and can exchange information via e-mail. However, businesses from countries outside the EU will not be permitted access to EU business information and EDI systems for contracting purposes unless they can guarantee adequate privacy protections are in place for the data transmitted via e-mail. Most legal experts believe the EU privacy directive applies to all forms of transmissions in business, including commercial contracts and ordering information.

What would happen if a business tapped into an EU business and began entering into transactions without an adequate privacy guarantee? Would there be criminal sanctions? Trade sanctions? How does this directive affect international trade with the EU? The EU has provided that trading privileges can be withdrawn from countries with businesses that violate the privacy standards on e-mail information and data transmission. What happens when trading privileges are withdrawn? Is the EU directive a commercial control of trade?

9. Walid Azab Al-Uneizi was an employee of the Ministry of Defense of Kuwait. Liticia Guzel was an employee of the Willard Inter-Continental Hotel in Washington, D.C. One of her duties was restocking minibars in guest rooms. Al-Uneizi approached Miss Guzel outside Rooms 610 and 612 and conferred with her about restocking Room 612. After Miss Guzel had finished restocking Room 612, Al-Uneizi assaulted and raped her. After the rape, Al-Uneizi gave her a Kuwaiti flag pin.

Miss Guzel has brought suit against both Al-Uneizi and the Kuwaiti government, who seek a dismissal under the act of state doctrine. Should the case be dismissed against both? [*Guzel v State of Kuwait*, 818 F. Supp. 6 (1993)]

10. When the Barings Bank bankruptcy occurred in 1995, Nick Leeson, the trader responsible for the immense losses the bank experienced after heavy derivative investments, fled to Germany. He was brought back to Hong Kong, the site of his trades, for trial. He is a British citizen who was arrested in Germany. Describe all the principles and issues of international law involved in his arrest, return to, and eventual trial in Hong Kong. (Note: Mr. Leeson has been released from prison.)

Strategy, Ethics, and the Law

The SEC complaint in the Siemens case (see pp. 237–238) notes how many "red flags" the board ignored in the years during which the bribery was occurring. Since 1999, when Germany signed on to the antibribery provisions of the OECD, Siemens executives had been concerned about the company's involvement in bribery around the world. The CEO at the time of the OECD adoption voiced concern to the board about the number of executives who were under investigation by the German government for bribery activities. He asked the board to take protective measures because its members could be held responsible for inaction. Despite his plea, the bribes continued, with support from some board members.

In 2001, the general counsel for the NYSE board notified its board members that in order for the company to meet U.S. standards for its new NYSE listing, it needed to end its practice of having off-the-books accounts for the payment of the bribes. The company took no steps to investigate or end its practices. The SEC noted there was a stunning lack of internal controls as well as a tone at the top that did not take the FCPA seriously.

What should Siemens have done? Explain the following quote from a Justice Department official, "Crimes of official corruption threaten the integrity of the global marketplace and undermine the rule of law in host countries."[5] What does she mean?

Siemens' new CEO has said that it will take time for the company to recover because it was so dependent upon such a facile business model. He explains that the company lost the skill sets of negotiating contracts, competing for projects, and submitting effective proposals. What lessons should companies learn from this observation about reliance on bribery?

For more information, the full Siemens complaint can be found at www.sec.gov/litigation.

Notes

1. The members (in the order in which they joined) are Belgium, France, West Germany, Italy, Luxembourg, the Netherlands, Denmark, Ireland, Great Britain, Greece, Spain, Portugal, Austria, Sweden, Finland, Cyprus, the Czech Republic, Estonia, Hungary, Latvia, Lithuania, Malta, Poland, Slovakia, Slovenia, Bulgaria, and Romania. Croatia, Iceland, Macedonia, and Turkey are expected to join the EU in the coming years.

2. Kevin McCoy, "Over 14,700 Take Up IRS on Leniency," *USA Today*, November 18, 2009, p. 1B.

3. The OECD member countries include Australia, Austria, Belgium, Canada, the Czech Republic, Denmark, Finland,

France, Germany, Greece, Hungary, Iceland, Ireland, Italy, Japan, Korea, Luxembourg, Mexico, the Netherlands, New Zealand, Norway, Poland, Portugal, the Slovak Republic, Spain, Sweden, Switzerland, Turkey, the United Kingdom, and the United States.

4. OECD also has relationships with 70 countries and NGOs.

5. Siri Schubert and T. Christian Miller, "Where Bribery Was Just a Line Item," *New York Times*, Dec. 21, 2008, pp. SB1, SB 6–7.

Business Crime

Business and crime have jointly occupied the headlines of newspapers for much of the past decade. In 2009, the Corporate Fraud Task Force of the U.S. Justice Department prosecuted 22 percent more white-collar crime cases than in 2008. In 2009, the Justice Department brought criminal charges against 276 companies and entered into deferred prosecution agreements or non-prosecution agreements in 47 cases. The FBI had 2,800 mortgage fraud cases under investigation as of December 2009. White-collar crime, corporate fraud, and public corruption are three of the FBI's eight priorities on criminal investigations and prosecutions.

Every businessperson is expected to know and understand the types and nature of business crimes. This chapter offers that background by answering the following questions: Why does business crime occur? Who is liable for crimes committed by businesses? What penalties are imposed for business crimes? What are the rights of corporate and individual defendants in the criminal justice system? ■

I'm standing here to say that from the early 1990s until December 2008, I helped Bernie Madoff and other people carry out a fraud. I knew no trades were happening. I knew what I was doing was criminal. But I did it anyway.

Frank DiPascali,
former executive at Madoff Securities, where an 18-year, $50 billion Ponzi scheme was perpetrated

UPDATE ↖
For up-to-date legal and ethical news, go to
mariannejennings.com

> **Embezzlement cannot be condoned in any manner. [N]ot only did he steal from the stockholders . . . but he breached the fiduciary duty placed in him. Wrongdoing of this nature against society is considered a grave matter. . . . [h]e should receive the maximum sentence.**
>
> Dennis Kozlowski,
>
> *former CEO of Tyco, convicted of embezzlement, in a letter, circa 1995, on sentencing of a former Tyco employee who had embezzled (employee did get the maximum sentence)*

CONSIDER...

John Park is the president of Acme Markets, a national retail food chain. Acme operated 16 warehouses that were subject to inspection by the Food and Drug Administration (FDA). During 1970 and 1971, FDA inspectors found rodents in Acme's Philadelphia and Baltimore warehouses. The FDA's chief of compliance wrote to Mr. Park and asked that he direct his attention to cleaning up the warehouses. Mr. Park

told a subordinate officer to take care of the problems. When the FDA inspected the warehouses again, rodent infestation was still evident. The FDA charged Acme and Mr. Park with criminal violations of the Federal Food, Drug, and Cosmetic Act. Mr. Park says he tried to clean up the warehouses but his subordinates failed and that he should not be liable. Is Mr. Park correct?

What Is Business Crime?
The Crimes within a Corporation

Financial Fraud: Employees Manipulating Earnings Numbers

Many business crimes are committed because companies apply pressure to managers and employees to produce results. Economic pressure often leads managers to cross ethical and legal lines. Managers feel compelled to meet earnings goals or to reach incentive bonus plan figures, and then they pass along the pressure they feel to employees. The drive to succeed or present a good earnings record can lead many managers and employees into crimes on behalf of the corporation. These crimes may not directly line employee pockets. The business benefits, and then employees benefit indirectly through profit sharing, salary increases, bonuses, or through just being able to keep their jobs.

For example, in January 2004, Andrew Fastow, the former CFO of the collapsed and bankrupt energy company Enron, entered a guilty plea to two counts of conspiracy to commit securities and wire fraud. His wife, Lea Fastow, pleaded guilty to filing a false joint tax return. Mr. Fastow was the mastermind behind the creation of off-the-books partnerships to which Enron's substantial debt was transferred. The result was that Enron's financial reports made the company seem healthy because, under accounting rules that existed at that time, the debt in the entities, which included Mr. and Mrs. Fastow as principals and officers, did not have to be reported on Enron's financial statements. The Fastows and other officers, including 26 executives who were indicted, have all explained that they were simply trying to meet projected earnings statements so that they could preserve shareholder value and share price on the market. As he testified against his former boss, former Enron CEO Jeffrey Skilling, Mr. Fastow said, "I thought I was being a hero for Enron. At the time, I thought I was helping myself and helping Enron to make its numbers."

Friendly Fire: Employee Theft

In addition to pressure to meet company goals, some individual employees feel personal financial pressure and resort to embezzlement as a means of remedying their own bleak financial positions. The Association of Certified Fraud Examiners estimates that 1 of every 28 employees is caught stealing from his or her employer each year. The FBI estimates that the amount lost in financial institution fraud is 100 times the amount taken by bank robbers. The FBI also estimates that the losses attributable to business crimes are 40 times greater than losses from crimes committed on the street. These losses from business crimes do not include the indirect costs businesses now have because of the amount of crime—the costs of security or insurance against internal thefts. The additional emphasis on internal controls because of Sarbanes-Oxley requirements (see p. 249 and Chapter 20) also add to the costs of preventing and detecting embezzlement. Forensic accounting has been labeled "the most secure job in America," because these individuals are trained to detect fraudulent conduct within companies, whether perpetrated by a management team driven to achieve goals or by individual employees in need of extra funds.

Small businesses have higher employee theft costs because they cannot afford the sophisticated monitoring measures larger corporations adopt. Most employee theft is systematic: For example, Aramark, a company that specializes in vending machine sales, reported that employees had skimmed millions in revenue by underreporting sales, ever so slightly over a period of time, in its cash/coin business. Employee theft has the hallmark of small amounts taken over a period of time with well-planned and executed schemes. For example, employees of an aircraft plant filled their pockets with nuts and bolts each day at the end of the shift. Over time, the employees had accumulated enough hardware to fill kegs, which were then sold. Garment workers for apparel manufacturers have gone home with jeans in their purses. Nine out of every ten purchasing agents take kickbacks. All of these acts constitute crimes that can be prosecuted under federal and state statutes.

These crimes committed for and against a business are often referred to as **white-collar crime.** Exhibit 8.1 provides a partial list of the companies and business executives that have had encounters with laws, regulators, and courts.

Internet Crime

CYBERLAW

In 2008, various agencies in the federal government received 275,884 Internet crime complaints, a 33 percent increase from 2007. The total losses from Internet fraud topped $264.6 million in 2008, with most of the complaints generated by nondelivery of goods and merchandise (33 percent), followed by auction fraud (25 percent), then confidence fraud, which includes Ponzi schemes, check fraud, and computer fraud (in total about 20 percent), and, finally, the notorious Nigerian letter frauds (about 14 percent).

EXHIBIT 8.1 A Roster of Wrongdoing

COMPANY/PERSON	ISSUE	STATUS
Adelphia Communications (2002)	Company guaranteed loans to another entity controlled by the Rigas family (John Rigas and his sons held the top executive spots at Adephia); result was $2.7 billion in guarantees and $1 billion in off-the-balance-sheet debt; overstatement of number of customers and cash	Annual report delayed; shares lost 70% of value from March 2002 to April 2002; Chapter 11 bankruptcy; members of the Rigas family indicted and arrested on charges of "looting" the company of more than $1 billion in one of the largest corporate frauds ever; John Rigas and one son convicted; Sentenced to 15 and 20 years
Boeing (2003)	Charges of illicit use of competitor's proprietary documents; charges of recruiting government official	Loss of 7 government contracts worth $250 million; $615 million fine; guilty plea by official who was wooed; 9-month sentence
Coca-Cola (2003)	Pending investigations over Coke's admissions that product marketing tests for Frozen Coke in Burger King were rigged	Coke settled issue with Burger King, with payments rumored to be $21 million; settled suit with whistle-blower
Computer Associates (2004)	Securities fraud and obstruction	Top officers indicted for securities fraud; former CEO Sanjay Kumar enters guilty plea; 12 years
Enron (2001)	Earnings overstated through mark-to-market accounting; off-the-book/share-special-purpose entities (SPEs) carried significant amounts of Enron debt not reflected in the financial statements; significant offshore SPEs (881 of 3,000 SPEs were offshore, primarily in Cayman Islands)	Third-largest bankruptcy in U.S. history; shareholder litigation settled; Congressional hearings held; 17 criminal convictions or pleas
Andrew Fastow, former CFO of Enron (2004)	Multimillion-dollar earnings from serving as principal in SPEs of Enron created to keep debts off the company books; significant sales of shares during the time frame preceding company collapse	Resigned as CFO; lost a multimillion-dollar home that was under construction in Houston; appeared before Congress and took the Fifth Amendment; entered guilty plea to securities and wire fraud; 6 years; helping plaintiffs in shareholder suits
Lea Fastow (2004)	Filing false income tax return	Guilty plea; 5 months prison; 5 months house arrest
Kenneth Lay, former chairman of Enron (2002)	Significant sales of shares during the time frame preceding Enron collapse; warning memo from one financial executive about possible implosion of company due to accounting improprieties	Resigned as CEO and chairman; appeared before Congress and took the Fifth Amendment; indicted for securities fraud, wire fraud; convicted; died of a massive coronary prior to appeal and sentence; conviction removed
Jeffrey Skilling, former CEO of Enron (2004)	Questions about his role in the Enron fraud; resigned just prior to company's collapse	Testified before Congress; offered assurances that he did not understand what was happening at Enron and that he resigned when he became aware; indicted for securities and wire fraud; found guilty of securities fraud and sentenced to 24.4 years; U.S. Supreme Court partially reversed his conviction on honest services fraud; sentence will be reduced
HealthSouth (2003)	$2.7 billion accounting fraud; overstatement of revenues	16 former executives indicted; 5 guilty pleas

CONTINUED

EXHIBIT 8.1 A Roster of Wrongdoing *(continued)*

COMPANY/PERSON	ISSUE	STATUS
Richard Scrushy, CEO of HealthSouth (2003)	85 federal felony counts, including violations of Sarbanes-Oxley financial certification provisions	Acquitted of financial fraud charges; found guilty of bribery and sentenced to 7 years; honest services fraud issue will find his sentence reduced
ImClone (2002)	Questions surrounding the timing of disclosure of FDA action relating to the company's anticancer drug, Erbitux, and its less-than-touted effectiveness	SEC civil suit; shares dropped significantly after announcement of FDA action on December 28, 2001; shares dropped again on revelations of possible insider trading
Dr. Samuel Waksal, former CEO of ImClone (2002)	Sold $50 million in ImClone shares prior to releasing to public information that FDA had rejected marketing for Erbitux	Charged with insider trading; arrested by FBI at his SoHo residence; took the Fifth Amendment before Congress; investigations of others pending; guilty plea entered; 7 years and $3 million in fines
KMPG (2006)	Tax shelter fraud	Settled with federal regulators by payment of $456 million penalty
Marsh McLennan (2005)	Price-fixing	$850 million in restitution
Joseph P. Nacchio, former CEO of Qwest (2003)	Allocation of IPO shares; friends and family conflicts	Settled with New York attorney general for $400,000; indicted and found guilty of insider trading or, as the blogger Motley Fool says, "guilty of being a moron"
Sotheby's (2003)	Price-fixing	Chairman given 1 year and 1 day in prison and a $7.5 million fine; CEO placed under house arrest for 1 year
Tyco International (2003)	Questions about accounting practices, particularly with regard to the booking of mergers and acquisitions; clandestine deals between CEO and board members for closing deals (one commission to board member was $20 million)	Stock dropped from almost $60 per share to around $20 on announcement of accounting issues; lost 27% value in one day following announcements about CEO; shareholder suits settled; top lawyer for company fired for allegedly impeding probe on board payments
L. Dennis Kozlowski, former CEO of Tyco (2003)	Accused of improper use of company funds	Indicted in New York for failure to pay sales tax on transactions in fine art; found guilty of other charges of larceny; sentenced to 15–25 years
WorldCom (2003)	Accounting issues centered on swaps—selling to other telecommunications companies and hiding expenses, thereby overstating revenue	Workforce cut by 17,000 employees; revenues reversed for 2 years to reflect losses and not profits; CEO Bernard Ebbers resigned with $366 million in loan forgiveness; share price dropped from over $60 per share in 1999 to less than $10 in 2002; WorldCom emerged from bankruptcy as MCI; four officers and managers entered guilty pleas; Ebbers convicted and sentenced to 25 years
Bernie Madoff (2009)	$50 billion Ponzi scheme	Entered guilty plea to all charges; sentenced to 150 years (was 71 years old at time of sentencing)
Galleon Hedge Fund (2009)	Insider trading charges	5 executives, including fund head, charged; Galleon's $3.7 billion fund liquidated
BP (2009)	Violation of Clean Air Act; willful failure to correct OSHA violations	$50 million fine to EPA; $58 million fine to OSHA (largest in U.S. history); all prior to explosion in Gulf in 2010

What Is Business Crime?
The Crimes Against a Corporation

Interbusiness crime occurs among competitors and results in one business gaining a competitive advantage over others. The list of companies and misdeeds in Exhibit 8.1 provides examples of the wide variety of business crimes committed, from kickbacks to antitrust violations to securities fraud to obstruction.

Once again, competitive pressure led to these types of crimes. Employees within one company postponed necessary safety fixes so as to correct OSHA violations in order to contain costs and remain competitive. However, as the remainder of the chapter shows, any competitive advantage gained through criminal activity is only temporary.

Who Is Liable for Business Crime?

One of the major differences between nonbusiness and business crimes is that more people can be convicted of business crimes. For nonbusiness crimes, only those actually involved in the planning or execution of the crime or assistance after it is committed can be convicted. In other words, those who were somehow involved in the criminal act or aftermath are criminally responsible. For business crimes, on the other hand, those in the management of firms whose employees actually commit criminal acts can be held liable if they authorized the conduct, knew about the conduct but did nothing, or failed to act reasonably in their supervisory positions. Liability for crimes also extends to employees who participate with the company and its management in illegal acts. For example, employees who help their employers establish fraudulent tax shelters for customers can be held liable along with the company and its officers. The key to establishing criminal liability is showing personal knowledge of wrongdoing.

U.S. v Park (Case 8.1), a landmark case, discusses the liability standards for those who are in charge but may not themselves commit a criminal act. It also provides an answer to the chapter's opening "Consider."

CASE 8.1

United States v Park
421 U.S. 658 (1975)

Is Chasing Rats from the Warehouse in My Job Description?

FACTS

Acme Markets, Inc., was a national food retail chain headquartered in Philadelphia, Pennsylvania. At the time of the government action, John R. Park (respondent) was president of Acme, which employed 36,000 people and operated 16 warehouses.

In 1970, the Food and Drug Administration (FDA) forwarded a letter to Mr. Park describing, in detail, problems with rodent infestation in Acme's Philadelphia warehouse facility. In December 1971, the FDA found the same types of conditions in Acme's Baltimore warehouse facility. In January 1972, the FDA's chief of compliance for its Baltimore office wrote to Mr. Park about the inspection. The letter included the following language:

> We note with much concern that the old and new warehouse areas used for food storage were actively and extensively inhabited by live rodents. Of even more concern was the observation that such reprehensible conditions

CONTINUED

obviously existed for a prolonged period of time without any detection, or were completely ignored.

We trust this letter will serve to direct your attention to the seriousness of the problem and formally advise you of the urgent need to initiate whatever measures are necessary to prevent recurrence and ensure compliance with the law.

After Mr. Park received the letter, he met with the vice president for legal affairs for Acme and was assured that he was "investigating the situation immediately and would be taking corrective action."

When the FDA inspected the Baltimore warehouse in March 1972, there was some improvement in the facility, but there was still rodent infestation. Acme and Mr. Park were both charged with violations of the Federal Food, Drug, and Cosmetic Act. Acme pleaded guilty. Mr. Park was convicted and fined $500; he appealed based on error in the judge's instruction, given as follows:

The individual is or could be liable under the statute even if he did not consciously do wrong. However, the fact that the Defendant is president and chief executive officer of the Acme Markets does not require a finding of guilt. Though he need not have personally participated in the situation, he must have had a responsible relationship to the issue. The issue is, in this case, whether the Defendant, John R. Park, by virtue of his position in the company, had a position of authority and responsibility in the situation out of which these charges arose.

The court of appeals reversed Mr. Park's conviction, and the government appealed.

JUDICIAL OPINION

BURGER, Chief Justice

Central to the Court's conclusion [in *United States v Dotterweich*], 320 U.S. 277 (1943), that individuals other than proprietors are subject to the criminal provisions of the Act was the reality that "the only way in which a corporation can act is through the individuals who act on its behalf."

At the same time, however, the Court was aware of the concern . . . that literal enforcement "might operate too harshly by sweeping within its condemnation any person however remotely entangled in the proscribed shipment." A limiting principle, in the form of "settled doctrines of criminal law" defining those who "are responsible for the commission of a misdemeanor," was available. In this context, the Court concluded, those doctrines dictated that the offense was committed "by all who have . . . a responsible share in the furtherance of the transaction which the statute outlaws."

The Act does not, as we observed in *Dotterweich*, make criminal liability turn on "awareness of some wrongdoing" or "conscious fraud." The duty imposed by Congress on responsible corporate agents is, we emphasize, one that requires the highest standard of

foresight and vigilance, but the Act, in its criminal aspect, does not require that which is objectively impossible. The theory upon which responsible corporate agents are held criminally accountable for "causing" violations of the Act permits a claim that a defendant was "powerless" to prevent or correct the violation to "be raised defensively at a trial on the merits." *U.S. v Wiesenfield Warehouse Co.*, 376 U.S. 86 (1964). If such a claim is made, the defendant has the burden of coming forward with evidence, but this does not alter the Government's ultimate burden of proving beyond a reasonable doubt the defendant's guilt, including his power, in light of the duty imposed by the Act, to prevent or correct the prohibited condition.

Turning to the jury charge in this case, it is of course arguable that isolated parts can be read as intimating that a finding of guilt could be predicated solely on respondent's corporate position. . . . Viewed as a whole, the charge did not permit the jury to find guilt solely on the basis of respondent's position in the corporation; rather, it fairly advised the jury that to find guilt it must find respondent "had a responsible relation to the situation," and "by virtue of his position . . . had authority and responsibility" to deal with the situation. The situation referred to could only be "food . . . held in unsanitary conditions in a warehouse with the result that it consisted, in part, of filth or . . . may have been contaminated with filth."

Park testified in his defense that he had employed a system in which he relied upon his subordinates, and that he was ultimately responsible for this system. He testified further that he had found these subordinates to be "dependable" and had "great confidence" in them.

[The rebuttal] evidence was not offered to show that respondent had a propensity to commit criminal acts, that the crime charged had been committed; its purpose was to demonstrate that respondent was on notice that he could not rely on his system of delegation to subordinates to prevent or correct unsanitary conditions at Acme's warehouses, and that he must have been aware of the deficiencies of this system before the Baltimore violations were discovered. The evidence was therefore relevant since it served to rebut Park's defense that he had justifiably relied upon subordinates to handle sanitation matters.

Reversed.

CASE QUESTIONS

1. What problems did the FDA find in the Acme warehouses, and over what period?

2. Was Mr. Park warned about the problem? What action did he take?

3. What standard of liability did the instruction given by the judge impose?

4. Explain whether Mr. Park is guilty of a criminal violation.

CONSIDER... 8.1

Rooney Enterprises, Inc., operated a cemetery in Franklin County, Virginia. A state law requires companies that receive advance payments for funeral expenses and burial plots to put those funds into a special trust account. Instead of doing so, Rooney used such funds for operating expenses. It later became insolvent, so all those customers who had prepaid for their burial plots and expenses lost both their money and their plots. The Virginia Attorney General brought criminal charges against Patrick Rooney, as president, for his failure to follow the requirements for trust fund deposits. Mr. Rooney said he was unaware of the requirement, that the requirement was not in effect when his company purchased the cemetery, and that only the company could be prosecuted for the failure to follow trust-fund requirements. Decide whether Mr. Rooney should be convicted. [*Rooney v Com.*, 500 S.E.2d 830 (Va. App. 1998)]

Federal Laws Targeting Officers and Directors for Criminal Accountability

White-Collar Crime's Origins and History

With each wave of accounting and fraud scandals, new legislation at the federal level has increased penalties for those who are the masterminds of white-collar crimes. In 1988, following the Michael Milken junk-bond era and the Ivan Boesky insider trading scandal, Congress passed additional laws against and sanctions covering insider trading in the Insider Trading and Securities Fraud Enforcement Act of 1988 (ITSFEA) (see Chapter 21 for more information). Criminal and civil penalties increased at least tenfold under the law. In 1990, Congress enacted what has been called the "white-collar kingpin" law. A response to the 1980s and 1990s savings and loan scandals, the law imposes minimum mandatory sentences (10 years in most instances) for corporate officers who mastermind financial crimes such as bank and securities fraud.

Sarbanes-Oxley (SOX)

Following the collapses of Enron, WorldCom, Adelphia, and others in the period from 2001 to 2002, Congress passed Sarbanes-Oxley, also known as the White-Collar Criminal Penalty Enhancement Act of 2002. Under SOX, as it is known among businesspeople, penalties for mail and wire fraud increased from their former maximums of 5 years to 20 years in prison. (Refer to Exhibit 8.1 to see the number of wire and fraud charges that have been brought against executives.) Penalties for violation of the trust, reporting, and fiduciary duties under pension laws increased from one year to ten years, with fines increased from $5,000 to $100,000. SOX also provides for the specific crime of false financial statement certification, a crime directed at CEOs and CFOs, who are now required to certify the financial statements issued by their companies. Top officers who certify financial statements that they know contain false information now face a specific federal crime because of SOX reforms. Richard Scrushy, the former CEO of HealthSouth, became the first CEO charged with a violation of these new provisions. Mr. Scrushy was acquitted of all financial fraud charges, but was later convicted of bribery in connection with payments he made to the ad campaign funds of the governor of Alabama's campaign. Mr. Scrushy is currently serving a seven-year sentence.

Honest Services Fraud

Following the Boesky and Milken scandals, part of the 1988 federal reforms included a 28-word addition to the federal mail and wire fraud statutes that provided, "For the purposes of this chapter, the term, *scheme or artifice to defraud* includes a scheme or artifice to deprive another of the intangible right of honest services." 18 U.S.C. §1346. The provision lay fallow for some time until the Enron era of company failures attributable to accounting fraud by officers. Prosecutors began adding so-called "honest services fraud" charges to mail and wire fraud as a way of obtaining harsher sentences for the white-collar criminals. Conviction on this charge requires proof that the activities of the officers deprived the shareholders of the corporation of the honest services they were entitled to as beneficiaries of the officers' fiduciary duties. Conrad Black, Richard Scrushy, and Jeffrey Skilling all received longer sentences because they were convicted of honest services fraud. However, in 2010, the U.S. Supreme Court held in *Skilling v U.S.*, 130 S.Ct.2896 (2010) that this portion of the mail and wire fraud statute was void for vagueness in the way prosecutors were using it for convictions and pleas (see substantive due process in Chapter 5). The court held that company officers would not know when and how they had violated the law because this portion of the statute was being applied when anything went wrong in the company. In other words, it was difficult to know what conduct deprived shareholders of officers' "honest services." The court held that the statute could be applied to the conduct of officers only in those situations in which officers accepted bribes or kickbacks so that they breached their fiduciary duties to shareholders and deprived them of the honest services officers are required to provide. There must be an underlying conflict created by a bribe or a kickback for the statute to apply. This significant decision curbed the government's flexibility in prosecuting white-collar crime and will result in a reduction in sentences for Mr. Black, Mr. Scrushy, Mr. Skilling, and other white-collar criminals serving their sentences at the time of the decision.

Financial Services Reforms

Following the collapses and near-collapses of so many investment firms, banks, insurers, and mortgage lenders, Congress passed the Financial Services Reform Act, also known as the Dodd–Frank Wall Street Reform and Consumer Protection Act. The act creates a Bureau of Consumer Financial Services (CFSB) (see Chapter 14 for more information) that can impose civil penalties and also refer cases to the Department of Justice for criminal prosecution. The act covers brokers, insurers, mortgage lenders, investment firms, banks, and any company that provides consumer financial services.

The Penalties for Business Crime

Statutes specify penalties for crimes. Some statutes have both business and individual penalties. Exhibit 8.2 provides a summary of the penalties under the major federal statutes.

EXHIBIT 8.2 Penalties for Business Crime under Federal Law

ACT	PENALTIES
Internal Revenue Code 26 U.S.C. §7201	$100,000 ($500,000 for corporations) and/or 5 years For evasion (plus costs of prosecution as well as penalties and assessments: 5–50%) $350,000 and/or 3 years
Sherman Act (antitrust) 15 U.S.C. §1	$10,000,000 for corporations Injunctions Divestiture
Sarbanes-Oxley 15 U.S.C. §1341 (document destruction, concealment, alteration, mutilation during pending civil or criminal investigation)	20 years plus fines (25 years for perjury)
Sarbanes-Oxley (certification of financial statements)	$1,000,000 and/or 10 years If willful: $5,000,000 and 20 years Officers who earn bonuses based on falsified financial statements must forfeit them
1933 Securities Act 15 U.S.C. §77x (as amended by Sarbanes-Oxley)	$100,000 and/or 10 years
Securities and Exchange Act of 1934 15 U.S.C. §78ff	$5,000,000 and/or 20 years $25,000,000 for corporations Civil penalties in addition of up to three times profit made or $1,000,000, whichever is greater
Clean Air Act 42 U.S.C. §7413	$1,000,000 and/or 5 years
Clean Water Act 33 U.S.C. §1319	For negligent violations: $25,000 per day and/or 1 year For knowing violations: $50,000 per day and/or 3 years For second violations: $100,000 per day and/or 6 years For false statements in reports, plans, or records: $10,000 per day and/or 2 years
Occupational Health Safety Act 29 U.S.C. §666	Willful violation causing death: $70,000 and/or 1 year; minimum of $5,000 per willful violation Giving advance notice of inspection: $1,000 and/or 6 months False statements or representations: $10,000 and/or 6 months
Consumer Product Safety Act 15 U.S.C. §2070	$50,000 and/or 1 year Tampering: up to $500,000 and/or 10 years

Reforming Criminal Penalties

Some regulators and legislators argue that the difficulty with most criminal law penalties is that they were instituted with "natural" persons in mind, as opposed to "artificial" corporate persons. Fines may be significant to individuals, but a $10,000 fine to a corporation with billions in assets and millions in income is simply a cost of doing business.

A recommendation advanced for the reformation of criminal penalties is that the penalties must cost the corporation as much as a bad business decision would cost. For example, if a company develops a bad product line, net earnings could decline 10 to 20 percent. Penalties expressed in terms of net earnings, as opposed to set dollar amounts, are more likely to have a deterrent effect on business criminal behavior.

Monitors

A new type of sentence for corporations has emerged over the past five years. Judges are increasingly assigning monitors to corporations to follow up on corporate activity. For example, as its sentence in an environmental case, ConEd was assigned a Natural Resources Defense Council lawyer as a monitor for its asbestos activity. Although their cases were not criminal in nature, both Coca-Cola and Mitsubishi agreed to a panel of monitors as part of their settlements in discrimination cases.

Criminal Indictments of Corporations on Common Law Crimes

Another recommendation for reforming criminal penalties requires corporations to stand criminally responsible under traditional criminal statutes for corporate wrongs. For example, when Ford Motor Company manufactured the Pinto automobile with a design flaw involving the gas tank location, many civil suits were brought for deaths and injuries caused by the exploding gas tank. However, Ford was also indicted for a criminal charge of homicide. In 1999, the state of Florida charged ValuJet, Inc., with murder and manslaughter for carelessly handling deadly materials for shipment after an investigation showed that company procedural omissions resulted in an airplane crash and the deaths of 110 passengers and the crew. A traditional common-law crime was applied to corporations for the wrongful deaths of their customers. The owner of Imperial Foods Company in North Carolina pled guilty to workplace hazards that resulted in the burn deaths of 25 employees at his chicken-processing plant and received a 19-year prison sentence. Even though the crimes he was charged with were violations of business laws, the sentence was traditional in the sense that an individual within a company was held personally and criminally responsible for the crimes.

Shame Punishment

"Shame punishment" has been on the increase in corporate criminal cases. Shame punishment involves public disclosure of an offense. For example, a Delaware federal judge ordered Bachetti Brothers Market to take out an ad for three weeks confessing to its crime of violating federal law by selling meat consisting "in whole or in part of filthy, putrid and contaminated substances." Another federal judge, Ricardo Urbina, sentenced a former Bristol-Myers Squibb executive to write a book about his criminal misdeeds in reaching an agreement with a competitor to keep its generic drug off the market. The executive had to write, publish, and distribute the book to other pharmaceutical executives at his own expense. The executive was also sentenced to two years probation and a $5,000 fine. The book was completed, as required, by the end of his probation.

U.S. v Allegheny Bottling Co. (Case 8.2) involves a creative sentence imposed by a judge on a corporation.

| CASE 8.2 | *United States v Allegheny Bottling Co.*
695 F.Supp. 856 (E.D. Va. 1988) *cert. denied*, 493 U.S. 817 (1989) |

Coke and Pepsi Wars Turn Criminal: Imprisonment for Price-Fixing

FACTS

Mid-Atlantic Coca-Cola Bottling Company and Allegheny Pepsi-Cola Bottling Company were charged with conspiracy to fix prices on Coke and Pepsi in order to avoid the ruinous competition that price wars were causing. Several officers pleaded guilty to the charges, and some were found guilty by a jury.

The trial evidence showed that in the Baltimore market, Coke sold from 6,200,000 to 7,000,000 cases of soft drinks a year. Prior to the price-fixing agreement, the price per case was $6.00 to $6.40. After the price-fixing agreement in 1982, the price was $6.80 per case, and it remained there for a full year. This additional 40 cents per case allowed the companies to earn over $1 million more. In pronouncing sentence on the corporate defendants, the judge used a creative solution (later affirmed by the appellate court).

JUDICIAL OPINION

DOUMAR, District Judge

The Lord Chancellor of England said some two hundred years ago, "Did you ever expect a corporation to have a conscience when it has no soul to be damned, and no body to be kicked?" Two hundred years have passed since the Lord Chancellor espoused this view, and the whole area of what is and is not permitted or what is or is not prohibited, has changed both in design and application. Certainly, this Court does not expect a corporation to have a conscience, but it does expect it to be ethical and abide by the law. This Court will deal with this company no less severely than it will deal with any individual who similarly disregards the law.

... Allegheny Bottling Company [parent of Allegheny Pepsi] is sentenced to three (3) years imprisonment and a fine of One Million Dollars ($1,000,000). Execution of the sentence of imprisonment is suspended and all but $950,000 of said fine is suspended, and the defendant is placed on probation for a period of three years.

As special conditions of the probation, in addition to the normal terms of probation, the defendant, Allegheny Bottling Company, shall provide:

(a) An officer or employee of Allegheny of comparable salary and stature to Jerry Polino (former vice president of sales who pled guilty to the conspiracy charges) to perform forty (40) hours of community service per week in the Baltimore, Maryland area for a two (2) year period without

compensation to the defendant. [The court required 40 hours of community service from someone of equal stature for each of the four officers of Allegheny who had been convicted or pleaded guilty to the price-fixing conspiracy charges.]

Corporate imprisonment requires only that the Court restrain or immobilize the corporation. Such restraint of individuals is accomplished by, for example, placing them in the custody of the United States Marshal. The United States Marshal would restrain the corporation by seizing the corporation's physical assets or part of the assets or restricting its actions or liberties in a particular manner.

Cases in the past have *assumed* that corporations cannot be imprisoned, without any cited authority for that proposition. This Court, however, has been unable to find any case which actually held that corporate imprisonment is illegal, unconstitutional, or impossible. Considerable confusion regarding the ability of courts to order a corporation imprisoned has been caused by courts mistakenly thinking that imprisonment necessarily involves incarceration in jail. But since imprisonment of a corporation does not necessarily involve incarceration, there is no reason to continue the assumption, which has lingered in the legal system unexamined and without support, that a corporation cannot be imprisoned. Since the Marshal can restrain the corporation's liberty and has done so in bankruptcy cases, there is no reason he cannot do so in this case as he himself has so stated prior to the imposition of this sentence.

Corporate imprisonment not only promotes the purposes of the Sherman Act, but also promotes the purposes of sentencing. The purposes of sentencing, according to the United States Sentencing Commission, include incapacitating the offender, deterring crime, rehabilitating the offender, and providing just punishment. The corporate imprisonment imposed today is specifically tailored to meet each of these purposes.

CASE QUESTIONS

1. Is corporate imprisonment illegal?
2. How will the corporation be imprisoned?
3. Is community service a sufficient punishment for the corporation?
4. Can the corporation's assets be imprisoned?

Ethical Issues

In 1994, Congress passed a law that permitted nonviolent convicts to cut up to 12 months from their sentences if they complete a drug rehab/counseling program. When the program was first created, there were 3,755 inmates who entered the program. In 2008, there were 18,000 federal prisoners in the program, and there remains a waiting list of 7,000 inmates.

The program has had some big names. For example, Dr. Sam Waksal, the former CEO of ImClone, will serve nine fewer months than his original seven-year sentence because he participated in a prison rehab program for inmates who have a problem with substance abuse. When Dr. Waksal was interviewed for the presentencing report he told the probation officer that he was a "social drinker" and had perhaps five glasses of wine per week. One month after the interview with the probation officer, Waksal's lawyers informed a federal judge that Waksal now had a "dependence on alcohol" and requested approval for Waksal's entry into a prison rehab program.

The former mayor of Atlanta, Bill Campbell, was admitted into a federal rehab program and got a 9-month reduction on his 30-month sentence for tax evasion. He was admitted to rehab despite that fact that his lawyers argued at his sentencing hearing that he had no substance abuse problem and that he hated the taste of alcohol and therefore urged the judge to conclude that Campbell's imprisonment was not necessary.

There are consulting firms that advise white-collar criminals on submitting their applications for the program. The firms also advise their clients (for a $5,000 fee) on how to maximize the sentence write-down for completing the rehab program.

The Bureau of Prisons indicates that it is cracking down on admissions to the program, looking more closely at doctors' letters and past histories of the inmates.

Evaluate the ethics of the inmates who feign addiction. Evaluate the ethics of the consulting firms that help them get into the program.

Source: Kai Falkenberg, "Time Off for Bad Behavior," *Forbes*, January 12, 2009, pp. 64–65

Corporate Sentencing Guidelines: An Ounce of Prevention Means a Reduced Sentence

The U.S. Sentencing Commission, established by Congress in 1984, has developed both federal sentencing guidelines and a carrot-and-stick approach to fighting white-collar crime. Under the commission's guidelines, companies that take substantial steps to prevent, investigate, and punish wrongdoing and cooperate with federal investigators can be treated less harshly in sentencing. The goal of the commission was to ensure that companies would establish internal crime prevention programs. The guidelines were revamped following the Boesky/Milken issues and again following the Enron era.

The sentencing guidelines permit judges to place guilty companies on probation for a period of up to five years if their offense or offenses occurred during a time when they had no crime prevention programs in place. In addition, the Justice Department has the option of agreeing to a deferred prosecution agreement (DPA) or non-prosecution agreement (NPA). The guidelines are a form of mandatory sentencing. If certain factors are present, the judge must order prison times. Corporate officers who are proven to have masterminded criminal activity must be sentenced to some prison time. However, the U.S. Supreme Court has placed some limits on the authority of judges to mete out sentences. In *U.S. v Booker*, 543 U.S. 220 (2005), the court held that when judges are determining sentences for defendants under the guidelines any facts, other than the defendant's prior conviction, must be established by a jury beyond a reasonable doubt. In the case, Booker had been convicted of possession of 50 grams of crack cocaine. The sentencing judge considered additional evidence in the sentencing hearing that Booker had 566 additional grams of crack that was not used as evidence at the trial. The result was that Booker was not eligible under the sentencing guidelines for a lesser sentence of 21 years and 10 months, and the judge imposed a sentence of 30 years. The Supreme Court reversed the sentencing portion of the case, remanded the case for resentencing and held that if the judge was going to consider additional facts that affected the length of sentence, such as the additional crack, those additional facts must be proved in the same way as the crime—before a jury and beyond a reasonable doubt. The impact of the *Booker* case has been widespread and many defendants are now in the process of being resentenced, including many of the business executives convicted and sentenced as a result of the Enron-era scandals.

The federal sentencing guidelines provide for a score that determines the extent of the sentence of the company and individual officers, managers, and employees. The guidelines use a formula that takes into account the seriousness of the offense, the company's history of violations, its cooperation in the investigation, the effectiveness of its compliance program, and the role of senior management in the wrongdoing. A company's "culpability multiplier" can range from 0.05 to 4.00, which is then used to convert a business's culpability score (a number that ranges from 0 to 10 or above). Every company begins with a score of 5, which can be added to or subtracted from depending on various factors in the guidelines. The larger the organization, the greater the number of points added. Involvement of top officers in criminal conduct also adds to the score. Prior violations increase a company's score, as do attempts to cover up the conduct (obstruction of justice).

A company's score is decreased by the presence of effective compliance programs designed to prevent and detect violations. If a company comes forward and reports the violations voluntarily, the score is decreased. Cooperation with investigators and acceptance of responsibility also reduce the score.

These multipliers are also used in the computation of fines for a business and its employees and officers. Restitution made by a company before sentencing reduces penalties and fines. For example, a fine of $1 million to $2 million could be reduced to as low as $50,000 for a company with the following: (1) a code of

BUSINESS STRATEGY

Much More Than Compliance

Businesses should follow these basic principles of the sentencing guidelines.

1. Have a code of ethics in place.
2. Conduct training on the code of ethics.
3. Have a company hotline and ombudsperson for employees to use anonymously to report violations.
4. Protect employees who report violations.
5. Investigate all allegations regardless of their source.
6. Report all violations immediately and voluntarily.
7. Offer restitution to affected parties.
8. Cooperate and negotiate with regulators.
9. Admit your mistakes and shortcomings.
10. Be forthright and public with your code of ethics. Discuss ethics with employees via website examples or illustrations of good ethical choices in the news among companies and employees.

conduct, (2) an ombudsperson, (3) a hotline, and (4) mandatory training for executives. The sentencing guidelines have been referred to as a "quiet revolution" in changing corporate conduct.

Corporate Board Criminal Responsibility

In *In re Caremark International, Inc.*, 698 A.2d 959 (Del. Ch. 1996), a court concluded that corporate boards could be held liable for their failure to institute and monitor adequate internal controls to prevent fraud in the company. This landmark case dealt with a company indicted for its physician referrals fees that were paid in violation of federal laws under the Medicare and Medicaid programs. The court noted that it is the responsibility of the board of directors to ensure that the company's compliance program is in place and functioning effectively. Since the time of this case, directors have been held personally liable for fraud and resulting shareholder losses committed while they were board members. For example, several board members from WorldCom, a company that had an $11 billion overstatement of revenues due to accounting fraud, were required to pay personally in order to settle civil cases brought against them by both the SEC and shareholders.

For the Manager's Desk

Re: Who Really Ends Up Going to Jail for Corporate Crime?

For the most part, those who were sentenced in federal court in the pre-Enron era for white-collar crimes tended to come from the middle classes rather than the upper classes. From 1988 to June 30, 1995, the federal government, through the Office of the Special Counsel of the Justice Department, was given the charge of investigating the collapse of the country's savings and loans "to find and prosecute those who looted our financial institutions." The Office of Special Counsel finished with the following results:

Number of defendants charged: 6,405

Convictions: 5,506 defendants convicted (96.5% conviction rate)

Types of persons convicted: Officers, directors, or CEOs: 29%; accountants, attorneys, and consultants: 71%

Types of persons charged: Directors and officers: 1,268 (97.5%) convicted; presidents or CEOs: 484 (95.1%) convicted

Prison time: Of the 5,506 defendants convicted: 75.5% sentenced to prison

Criminal violations committed by *Fortune* 500 corporations over a two-year period in the post-S&L scandal showed that executives were convicted in only 1.5 percent of the cases. However, managers were more likely than not to be sentenced in such cases. And employees, particularly in securities fraud cases, were more likely to be sentenced to prison than the executives for whom they worked. However,

executives are far more likely than both groups to be given civil sanctions.

Since the time when this data was gathered, there has been a dramatic shift in sentencing for the top executives, as the following list reflects.

Bernie Madoff	150 years
Enron CEO Jeffrey Skilling	24.6 years
WorldCom CEO Bernie Ebbers	25 years
WorldCom CFO Scott Sullivan	5 years

On the other hand, the employees who were simply following orders were given far lesser sentences.

WorldCom Controller David Myers	1 year and 1 day
WorldCom Accounting Director Buford Yates	1 year and 1 day
WorldCom Director of Management Reporting Betty Vinson	5 months
WorldCom Director of Legal Entity Accounting Troy Normand	3 years probation

Prosecutors now take a bottom-up approach. That is, they work their plea deals with employees in order to build their cases carefully against those at the top.

Source: Jane Sasseen, "White-Collar Crime: Who Does Time?" *BusinessWeek,* February 6, 2006, pp. 60–61.

Elements of Business Crime

The **elements,** or requirements for proof, of a business crime vary according to type. Crimes are violations of written laws, such as statutes or ordinances. But all crimes' specific elements can be classified into two general elements: *mens rea* (or *scienter*) and *actus reus.*

Mens Rea

A **crime** implies some voluntary action, which is to say that a criminal wrong is calculated or intentional; this element of criminal intent is the *mens rea* of a crime. *Mens rea* is the required state of mind for a crime—the intent to commit the act that is a crime. A criminal wrong is not based on an accident unless a person was forewarned about the accident or the accident arose from criminal conduct. Driving while intoxicated is a crime, and an accident that happens while a driver is intoxicated is also a criminal wrong. Concealing income is intentional conduct calculated to avoid paying taxes; it is willful and criminal conduct. An oversight in reporting income is not a crime. *U.S. v Ahmad* (Case 8.3) discusses the issue of intent in an environmental case.

**CASE
8.3**

United States v Ahmad
101 F.3d 386 (5th Cir. 1996)

Gasoline, Drains, and Knowledge of the Two Together: A Crime?

FACTS

Mr. Ahmad owns a Spin-N-Market located in Conroe, Texas. Shortly after he purchased the combination gas and convenience store in 1992, he discovered a leak in one of the high-octane gasoline tanks at the location. The leak was at the top of the tank and did not present problems with gasoline seeping out. However, the leak did allow water to get into the tank and contaminate the gas. Because water is heavier than gas, the water sank to the bottom of the tank, and because the tank was pumped from the bottom, Mr. Ahmad was unable to sell gas from it.

In October 1993, Mr. Ahmad hired CTT Environmental Services, a tank-testing company, to examine the tank. CTT determined that the tank contained 800 gallons of water and the rest was mostly gasoline. Jewel McCoy, a CTT employee, told Mr. Ahmad that the leak could not be repaired until the tank was completely empty, which CTT offered to do for 65 cents per gallon plus $65 per hour of labor. After Ms. McCoy gave Mr. Ahmad this CIT estimate, he asked whether he could empty the tank himself. Ms. McCoy told him that it would be dangerous and illegal for him to do so.

Mr. Ahmad then responded, "Well, if I don't get caught, what then?"

On January 25, 1994, Mr. Ahmad rented a handheld motorized water pump from a local hardware store, telling a hardware store employee that he was planning to use it to remove water from his backyard. Mr. Ahmad hooked the pump up to his tank at the Spin-N-Market and pumped 5,220 gallons of fluid into a manhole near the store and into Lewis Street alongside the store. Of the fluid pumped, 4,690 gallons were gasoline.

The gasoline from Lewis Street made its way to a storm drain and the storm sewer system and eventually into Possum Creek. When city officials discovered the gasoline in Possum Creek, several vacuum trucks were required to decontaminate it.

The gasoline from the manhole made its way to the city sewage treatment center. The gasoline was diverted into a different storage pool in order to avoid shutting down the plant altogether, but the plant had to evacuate all but essential personnel, and firefighters and hazardous materials crews from the city had to be called to restore the plant to a safe condition. While the crews worked, two area schools had to be evacuated for safety reasons.

CONTINUED

Mr. Ahmad was indicted for three violations of the Clean Water Act (CWA), of knowingly discharging a pollutant into navigable waters without a permit, knowingly placing others in imminent danger through a pollutant, and knowingly operating a source in violation of pretreatment requirements. Mr. Ahmad did not dispute the conduct; he said he did not meet the "knowingly" requirements because he believed he was discharging water.

The jury found Mr. Ahmad guilty on two of the three charges and deadlocked on the charge of imminent danger. Mr. Ahmad appealed.

JUDICIAL OPINION

SMITH, Circuit Judge

Ahmad contends that the jury should have been instructed that the statutory *mens rea*—knowledge—was required as to each element of the offenses, rather than only with regard to discharge or the operation of a source.

The language of the CWA is less than pellucid. Title 33 U.S.C. § 1319(c)(2)(A) says that "any person who knowingly violates" any of a number of other sections of the CWA commits a felony. The principal issue is to which elements of the offense the modifier "knowingly" applies. The matter is complicated somewhat by the fact that the phrase "knowingly violates" appears in a different section of the CWA from the language defining the elements of the offenses. Ahmad argues that within this context, "knowingly violates" should be read to require him knowingly to have acted with regard to each element of the offenses. The government, in contrast, contends that "knowingly violates" requires it to prove only that Ahmad knew the nature of his acts and that he performed them intentionally. Particularly at issue is whether "knowingly" applies to the element of the discharge's being a pollutant, for Ahmad's main theory at trial was that he thought he was discharging water, not gasoline.

The Supreme Court has spoken to this issue in broad terms. . . . "[T]he presumption in favor of a *scienter* requirement should apply to each of the statutory elements which criminalize otherwise innocent conduct."

Indeed, we find it eminently sensible that the phrase "knowingly violates" in § 1319(c)(2)(A), when referring to other provisions that define the elements of the offenses § 1319 creates, should uniformly require knowledge as to each of those elements rather than only one or two. To hold otherwise would require an explanation as to why some elements should be treated differently from others, which neither the parties nor the case law seems able to provide.

The government also protests that CWA violations fall into the judicially created exception for "public welfare offenses," under which some regulatory crimes

have been held not to require a showing of *mens rea*. On its face, the CWA certainly does appear to implicate public welfare.

The fact that violations of § 1319(c)(2)(A) are felonies punishable by years in federal prison confirms our view that they do not fall within the public welfare offense exception. . . . [P]ublic welfare offenses have virtually always been crimes punishable by relatively light penalties such as fines or short jail sentences, rather than substantial terms of imprisonment. Serious felonies, in contrast, should not fall within the exception "absent a clear statement from Congress that *mens rea* is not required". . . . [W]e hold that the offenses charged in counts one and two are not public welfare offenses and that the usual presumption of a *mens rea* requirement applies. With the exception of purely jurisdictional elements, the *mens rea* of knowledge applies to each element of the crimes.

At best, the jury charge made it uncertain to which elements "knowingly" applied. At worst, and considerably more likely, it indicated that only the element of discharge need be knowingly. The instructions listed each element on a separate line, with the word "knowingly" present only in the line corresponding to the element that something was discharged. That the district court included a one-sentence summary of each count in which "knowingly" was present did not cure the error.

The obvious inference for the jury was that knowledge was required only as to the fact that something was discharged, and not as to any other fact. In effect, with regard to the other elements of the crimes, the instructions implied that the requisite *mens rea* was strict liability rather than knowledge.

There was at least a reasonable likelihood that the jury applied the instructions in this way, so we conclude that the instructions misled the jury as to the elements of the offense. Because the charge effectively withdrew from the jury's consideration facts that it should have been permitted to find or not find, this error requires reversal.

Most of Ahmad's defense, after all, was built around the idea that he thought water, rather than gasoline, was being discharged. A rational jury could so have found, and at the same time could have found that he did not actually know that he was pumping gas.

Reversed and remanded.

CASE QUESTIONS

1. What was wrong with Mr. Ahmad's tank?
2. Of what significance is Jewel McCoy's testimony? Mr. Ahmad's testimony?
3. What is the difference between knowledge of the law and knowledge of conduct?
4. What does the court explain is required for the state of mind under the Clean Water Act?

CONSIDER...   8.2

Consider the following situation and discuss whether the appropriate *mens rea* is present.

Matthew M. Tannin and Ralph Cioffi were indicted for securities, mail, and wire fraud following the collapse of several hedge funds they were managing at their employer, Bear Stearns, which were primarily based on investments in the subprime mortgage markets. The law does not hold fund managers criminally responsible when a market takes a downturn. However, the charges against the two focus on whether they continued to sell interests in the funds when they knew there were problems. The following e-mail is one listed in the indictment:

> "[T]he subprime market looks pretty damn ugly. . . . If we believe [our internal modeling] is ANYWHERE CLOSE to accurate I think we should close the funds now. The reason for this is that if [our internal modeling] is correct then the entire subprime market is toast. . . . If AAA bonds are systematically downgraded then there is simply no way for us to make money— ever." (Emphasis appears in original text.)

This e-mail, from Matthew M. Tannin to Ralph Cioffi (sent using his private e-mail account to Mr. Cioffi's wife's e-mail account), was sent on a Sunday morning in 2006. A meeting later that day between the two found Mr. Tannin convinced he was overreacting to statistics indicative of coming declines in home values. Several days later the two would still recommend Bear funds to investors.

Mr. Tannin then wrote in follow-up e-mails about the fund and his selling it despite his misgivings:

> "Believe it or not I've been able to convince more people to add more money."

In their trial, the lawyers for the two men focused on the difference between optimistic, good old-fashioned sales puffery and misrepresentation, and argued that prosecutors were trying to hold the two responsible for the collapse of the subprime markets. However, one of the federal prosecutors has noted,

> "The question is whether these managers crossed the line from permissible spin to willful misrepresentation."

After the two were indicted, they found themselves together in a holding cell in a Brooklyn jail asking each other, "How did we end up in this spot?" Sadly, Bear Stearns clients lost 100 percent of their investments in the subprime hedge funds. The indictment alleges that the men did withdraw their own funds from the hedge funds even as they continued to sell others on investing more.

However, the jurors could not be convinced, and they acquitted the two men. Jurors who spoke about the case said that the two men's comments to investors were consistent with their private e-mail communications. The jurors also concluded the prosecutors did not present enough evidence to give them the standard of "beyond a reasonable doubt."

What does it take to prove criminal intent? What kinds of statements would be necessary? Was it just a matter of the two being wrong on their risk assessment? Is that a crime?

Do you see any ethical breaches despite the lack of criminal conviction?

THINK: From the Ahmad case, you learned that for someone to be convicted of an environmental crime that involves unlawful discharges, they must be aware that they are actually discharging the substances into the water. From the *Park* case, you learned that executives are liable for the conduct of others in running the company if they are aware of violations and continue to allow those violations to occur without taking action.

CONTINUED

APPLY: What is different here? The employees in this case were worried about their computer models, the risk, where the market was going, and what would happen to the subprime mortgage investments. However, they were not manipulating the numbers and they were selling investments in which risk was disclosed. There were no "smoking gun" documents or actions that tied them to an actual state of mind that showed an intent to defraud.

ANSWER: The jurors correctly concluded that Tannin and Cioffi could not be held criminally liable for fraud when they were unsure but did not cross the line into manipulation or misrepresentation. The e-mails and their sales of their own funds could be tied to uncertainty and a change in their own level of risk, but could not be used to show criminal intent because of these other explanations.

Mens Rea, Conscious Avoidance, and Corporate Officers

Criminal intent has been a particularly significant issue in business crimes. The intent element is significant because two intents are actually involved when a corporation is prosecuted for a crime: the intent of the corporation to commit the crime and the intent of those in charge of the corporation, officers, and directors to direct the corporation to commit the wrong. Officers may have intent, but the company may not be aware of these pockets of deceit and malfeasance. However, courts have also developed the doctrine of **conscious avoidance** as a means of establishing *mens rea* for officers as well as a pattern of behavior that established an unwillingness to curb deception. Under this theory, executives cannot "consciously try to avoid knowledge" about the actions and activities of those within the company. For example, under the criminal portions of SOX that apply to CEOs and CFOs for certification of a company's financial statements, an executive cannot isolate himself from information that the financial reports were inaccurate by not attending meetings or not reading the reports that are disclosed to the public [*U.S. v Ebbers*, 458 F.3d 110 (2d Cir. 2006)]. The *U.S. v Park* case has modern application in that these top executives are fully accountable for the information in their companies' financial statements even when they do not actually prepare those statements. Richard Scrushy's statement, "I certainly had no knowledge of anything they were doing in terms of moving numbers around in the company," is not a defense for a CEO.[1] Bernie Ebbers, the former CEO of WorldCom, denied knowing that information in the company's financial statements was false. In fact, he indicated he did not always read the 10-Ks and 10-Qs. However, testimony of witnesses at his trial showed that he attended the "Close the Gap" meetings in which managers discussed how to have actual numbers meet projections. Mr. Ebbers could not avoid criminal culpability by avoiding the final reports when he was aware of trouble brewing.

Actus Reus

All crimes include, in addition to the mental intent, a requirement of some specific action or conduct, which is the *actus reus* of the crime. For example, in embezzlement the *actus reus* is the taking of an employer's money. Various types of criminal conduct, or *actus reus* examples, are found in subsequent sections on specific crimes.

Examples of Business Crimes

Theft and Embezzlement

The action of employees who take their employers' property is **theft** or **embezzlement.** For theft, the following elements are necessary: (1) intent to take the property, (2) an actual taking of the property for permanent use, and (3) no authorization to take the property. These three elements are the *actus reus* of the crime. The *mens rea* is the taking of the property with the intent of permanently depriving the owner of use and possession.

For embezzlement, the elements are the same as for theft, with the addition of one more element: The person commits the crime while in the employ or position of trust of the property owner. In other words, embezzlement is theft from a specific type of person—an employer. Although it is usually limited to funds, embezzlement can cover such items as inventory and equipment of a business.

CONSIDER...   8.3

Dennis Kozlowski and Mark Swartz, the former CEO and CFO, respectively, of Tyco International, initially had a hung jury in their trial for larceny.

Mr. Kozlowski and Mr. Swartz, who were eventually convicted of embezzlement, enjoyed extensive personal benefits from Tyco, an embarrassment of personal acquisition at company expense. Prosecutors must show *mens rea*, criminal intent. The defense that both men raised to counter intent, and apparently successfully enough to flummox some jurors in their first trial, was that none of what they obtained through the various company agreements and programs was done secretly. Both men produced evidence related to board knowledge of their perks and approvals through the established and proper company procedures for personal loans and the use of company funds for refurbishing and furnishing their homes. Along the lines of a "Why would I be such an idiot?" defense, the two approached their case as one in which the blatancy of their conduct would work in their favor in mitigating intent, or *mens rea*.

None of the loans was made to the men without some form of authorization, however perfunctory. Many in the executive ranks and perhaps even some board members were aware of the loans, the officer loan policy, and the processes used for booking and forgiving the loans. The issue of board approval on the loans remains a question, but compensation committee minutes from February 21, 2002, show that the committee was given a list of loans to officers and also approved all compensation packages. There was no public disclosure of these developments or the committee's review.

Do you believe these facts supported the jury's finding of *mens rea* in the retrial of the cases against Mr. Kozlowski and Mr. Swartz? Was their conduct ethical?

Sources: Adapted from Andrew Ross Sorkin, "Judge Ends Trial When Tyco Juror Reports Threat," *New York Times*, April 3, 2004, pp. A1, B4; Andrew Ross Sorkin, "After a Mistrial, Choices to Make," *New York Times*, April 5, 2004, pp. C1, C6; Jonathan D. Glater, "Prosecutors See More Time in Another Tyco Case," *New York Times*, April 8, 2004, p. C4; Mark Maremont, "Kozlowski's Defense Strategy: Big Spending Was No Secret," *Wall Street Journal*, February 9, 2004, pp. A1, A23; Andrew Ross Sorkin and Jonathan D. Glater, "Some Tyco Board Members Knew of Pay Packages, Records Show," *New York Times*, September 23, 2002, p. A1; Laurie P. Cohen, "Tyco Ex-Counsel Claims Auditors Knew of Loans," *Wall Street Journal*, October 22, 2002, p. A6.

Obstruction of Justice

Because of the cases involving the destruction of documents, SOX amended the federal law on obstruction of justice to make document destruction a specific crime and to increase its penalties. The new obstruction section makes it a felony for anyone, including company employees, auditors, attorneys, and consultants, *to alter, destroy, mutilate, conceal, cover up, falsify, or make a false entry with the "intent to impede, obstruct, or influence the investigation or proper administration of any matter within the jurisdiction of any department or agency of the United States."*[2] Obstruction can be committed by destroying or altering documents that are subject to a subpoena, or that are related to a pending investigation, and also by encouraging others to alter or destroy those types of documents. Encouraging or giving false testimony is also a form of obstruction of justice. Martha Stewart was convicted of obstruction of justice for her alteration of phone logs, backdating of an order to her broker, and encouraging a broker's assistant to lie to support her backdating story.

The SOX provisions on obstruction also cover audit records and require auditors to retain their work papers related to a client's audit for at least five years. Any destruction of these documents prior to the expiration of that period would constitute a felony and carries a penalty of up to 10 years.

 ## Ethical Issues

As the financial performance of the infamous energy company Enron dipped, its audit firm, Arthur Andersen, worried that Enron's accounting and financial statements were doubtful. On October 16, 2001, Enron refused to change its earnings release in response to Andersen's concerns. Andersen was preparing a statement about the release. Nancy Temple, legal counsel for Arthur Andersen, e-mailed back and forth with David Duncan, the audit partner for the Enron account in Houston, about the content of the Andersen statement on Enron.

Later that same day, Temple also sent an e-mail to Andersen's internal team of accounting experts and attached a copy of the company's document policy. On October 20, the Enron crisis-response team held a conference call, during which Temple instructed everyone to "[m]ake sure to follow the [document] policy." On October 23, 2001, then–Enron CEO Kenneth Lay declined to answer questions during a call with analysts because of "potential lawsuits, as well as the SEC inquiry." After the call, Duncan met with other Andersen partners and told them that they should ensure that team members were complying with the company's document policy. Another meeting for all team members followed, during which Duncan distributed the policy and told everyone to comply. These, and other smaller meetings, were followed by considerable shredding and destruction of both paper and electronic documents.

On October 26, 2001, one of Andersen's senior partners circulated a *New York Times* article discussing the SEC's response to Enron. His e-mail commented, "the problems are just beginning and we will be in the cross hairs. The marketplace is going to keep the pressure on this and is going to force the SEC to be tough." On October 30, the SEC opened a formal investigation and sent Enron a letter that requested accounting documents. The document destruction continued despite reservations by some of Andersen's managers. On November 8, 2001, Enron announced that it would issue a comprehensive restatement of its earnings and assets. Also on November 8, the SEC served Enron and Andersen with subpoenas for records. On November 9, Duncan's secretary sent an e-mail that stated, "Per Dave—No more shredding . . . We have been officially served for our documents." Enron filed for bankruptcy less than a month later. Duncan was fired and later pleaded guilty to witness tampering, a plea he later withdrew.[3]

Applying the *Park* case, who is criminally liable for the document shredding? The employees who actually did it? The managers who ordered it to begin? The company itself? Were they technically not in violation of the law during the document destruction because there was no formal notice until November 8? [*Arthur Andersen LLP v U.S.*, 544 U.S. 696 (2005)]

Computer Crime

What Is a Computer Crime?

The term **computer crime** is used as though it were a completely separate body of law from criminal law. Although certain crimes can only be committed using a computer, the nature of crime, with both *mens rea* and *actus reus,* does not change. Specific statutes addressing the unique means by which property is taken and covering the unique type of property found in computer software and hardware make establishing computer crimes easier than reliance on traditional crimes such as larceny and embezzlement.

Some computer crimes may involve a computer without making direct use of one. Ordinary criminal statutes can apply to these types of crimes. For example, a person who mails flyers that falsely advertise a service as computerized is guilty of committing the federal crime of using the mail to defraud.

For more serious and costly computer-related wrongs that do not fit the ordinary definitions of crime, the trend is toward adopting statutes that define specific computer crimes. The following sections give some examples of types of computer crimes.

Theft of Software. When someone takes software, whether in the form of a program written on paper or a program on a disk or tape, something is taken but the common-law crime of larceny covers only tangible property. Virtually every state has amended its definition of larceny or theft so that stealing software is a crime. In some states, the unauthorized taking of information may constitute a crime under a trade secrets protection statute.

Intentional Damage. The computer may be the victim of a crime when it is intentionally destroyed or harmed. Physical destruction is only one small part of the harm. The intent may actually be to cause the destruction of the information stored in the computer, a result with far greater financial implications and consequences for the computer owner.

If the purpose of the physical destruction of a computer is the destruction of software or the stored information on the computer, the *actus reus* for this computer crime of intentional damage is met. Also, physical destruction can be accomplished without physical contact. For example, interfering with the air-conditioning needs for effective computer operation could result in computer malfunction, the loss of files, and perhaps even the future ability of the computer to process. Intentionally planting a bug or virus in software, causing the program to malfunction, give incorrect output, or affect the hard drive and its content, is also conduct that fits under this intentional damage crime. The Melissa virus and the ILUVYOU virus that spread worldwide in just a day caused an estimated $3 billion in damage to businesses. Those who created and spread the bug committed intentional damage, a crime now updated to cover computers, programs, information, and software.

Using Computers to Commit Economic Espionage

The Economic Espionage Act (EEA) is a federal law[4] passed in response to several cases in which high-level executives were taking downloaded proprietary information from their computers to their new employers. In one case, an executive was accused of taking General Motors' full plan for supply chain management in Europe. The EEA makes it a felony to steal, appropriate, or take a trade secret and also makes it a felony to copy, duplicate, sketch, draw, photograph, download, upload, alter, destroy, replicate, transmit, deliver, send, mail, or communicate a trade secret. The penalties for EEA violations are up to $500,000 and 15 years in prison for individuals and $10 million for organizations. When employees take new positions with another company, their former employers are permitted to check the departing employees' computer e-mails and hard drives to determine whether the employees have engaged in computer espionage.

Using Computers to Commit Electronic Fund Transfer Crimes

The Electronic Fund Transfers Act (EFTA)[5] makes it a crime to use any counterfeit, stolen, or fraudulently obtained card, code, or other device to obtain money or goods in excess of a specified amount through an electronic fund transfer system. The EFTA also makes it a crime to ship in interstate commerce devices or goods so obtained or to knowingly receive goods that have been obtained by means of the fraudulent use of the transfer system.

Using Computers to Circumvent Copyright Protection Devices

CYBERLAW

The Digital Millennium Copyright Act (DMCA) makes it a federal offense to circumvent or create programs to circumvent encryption devices that copyright holders place on copyrighted material to prevent unauthorized copying. For example, circumventing the encryption devices on software or CDs would be a violation of the DMCA. Dmitry Sklyarov, a Russian computer programmer, became the first person charged with a violation of DMCA. Mr. Sklyarov was arrested in early 2002 at a computer show after giving a speech on the product he developed that permits the circumvention of security devices on copyrighted materials. Specifically, his program unlocks password-protected e-books and PDF files. He gave his speech in Las Vegas at the Defcon convention, a convention billed as "the largest hacker convention on the planet." He was returned to Russia in exchange for his agreement to testify in a case that will determine the constitutionality of the DMCA. The issues tried in the case included the determination that the development and use of devices and programs to circumvent encryption devices was prohibited under DMCA and could result in criminal liability for those who develop and/or distribute the programs. [*U.S. v Elcom Ltd.*, 203 F.Supp.2d 1111 (N.D. Cal. 2002).]

In addition, the No Electronic Theft Act was passed at the end of 1997, making it a federal criminal offense to willfully infringe copyrighted material worth more than $1,000 using the Internet or other electronic devices even when the infringer does not profit from the use of the material. For example, many Internet users clip articles from subscriber services on the Internet and then send them along via e-mail to nonsubscriber friends. Even though no transaction for profit occurs, the transfer of such copyrighted material still violates this federal law.

Using Computer Access for Unauthorized Advertising: Spamming

CYBERLAW

Spamming, or the practice of sending out thousands of e-mails at once to many different computer users, is an ever-increasing problem. The issues involved include First Amendment rights, privacy, and theft of property. Congress passed the **Controlling the Assault of Non-Solicited Pornography and Marketing (CAN-SPAM)** Act, which allows private companies to bring suit against spammers for their unauthorized use of ISPs. Microsoft was one of the first companies to use CAN-SPAM when it filed suit against eight spammers under CAN-SPAM in January 2004.

An industry group called the Anti-Spam Technical Alliance has been formed and has endorsed several e-mail authentication technologies. Under CAN-SPAM, the FTC is also authorized to bring suit against spammers. Some states have made it a misdemeanor to send out e-mails with a misleading title line; Virginia was the first state to make spamming a criminal act. Under the Virginia statute, spamming becomes a felony when the volume of spam e-mails sent exceeds 10,000 in 24 hours, 100,000 in 30 days, or 1 million in one year.

Using Computers for Crimes in International Markets

The Berne (copyright) and Paris Conventions have provisions that permit businesses in member countries to obtain international copyright protection for their software products. Fifty-nine nations are members of one or more of the conventions (see Chapter 15).

Using Computers to Commit Fraud

The Counterfeit Access Device and Computer Fraud and Abuse Act (CADCFA) makes it a federal crime to use or access federal or private computers without authorization in several types of situations. The CADCFA was amended in 1994 to cover additional new technologies, such as scanners, handheld computers, and laptops.

CADCFA prohibits unauthorized access to U.S. military or foreign policy information, FDIC financial institutions' data, or any government agency computer. For example, in *Sawyer v Department of the Air Force*, 31 MPSR 193 (1986), a federal employee was terminated from his position for tampering with Air Force invoices and payments. Penalties under CADCFA range from 5 to 21 years' imprisonment.

CYBERLAW

The federal Computer Fraud and Abuse Act (CFAA) classifies unauthorized access to a government computer as a felony and trespass into a federal government computer as a misdemeanor. CFAA covers "intentional" and "knowing" acts and includes a section that makes it a felony to cause more than $1,000 damage to a computer or its data through a virus program.

Using Computers for Cyberbullying

In 2008, a federal jury convicted Lori Drew, a 49-year-old Missouri mother of three, on misdemeanor charges of computer fraud for her actions in creating a phony MySpace account in order to trick 13-year-old Megan Meier into believing she had a secret admirer, Josh. Megan was apparently Ms. Drew's daughter's archrival and Ms. Drew plotted revenge via the MySpace medium.[6] Megan committed suicide following Josh's posting of a rejection and devastating personal comments at the site, such as "The world would be a better place without you."

While the prosecutors used the Computer Fraud and Abuse Act as the basis for the charges against Ms. Drew, there was not a good fit. As a result, many states now have anti-cyberbullying criminal statutes that define the crime in detail and provide specific penalties. The statutes are basically anti-harassment statutes that prohibit harassment that involves the medium of computer communication.

Criminal Fraud

Business crimes against individuals usually result from sales transactions. **Criminal fraud** is an example of this type of crime, the elements of which are the same as those the person defrauded would use to establish a contract defense: A false statement was made; the statement was material—that is, it was the type of information that would affect the buying decision; and the person relied on the statement. The only differences between contract fraud and criminal fraud is that criminal fraud requires proof of intent that the seller intended to mislead the buyer for the purpose of effecting the transaction and making money. In the mortgage fraud cases brought against borrowers during 2008–2010, the basis for the fraud is that documents and appraisals were forged or falsified. Forgery always provides proof of the level of intent needed for criminal fraud.

Commercial Bribery

Most states have provisions that govern both the giving and receiving of gifts or funds in exchange for a contract or favor. A supplier offering a purchasing agent of a company $25,000 in cash as an incentive or reward for choosing that supplier has committed commercial bribery. The purchasing agent has betrayed his employer's interest and compromised his judgment by accepting benefits for himself. This condemnation of bribery in commercial transactions dates back to the first eras of business activity because of concerns that quality and pricing would suffer if corruption was introduced into the bargaining process.

 # Ethical Issues

Jim G. Locklear was a purchasing agent. His spectacular career as a buyer began in 1977 with Federated Stores in Dallas, Texas. Federated officers described him as a man with an eye for fashion and a keen ability to negotiate. In 1987, Mr. Locklear was offered a position with Jordan Marsh, a retailer in the Boston area, with an annual salary of $96,000.

Citing a desire to return to Dallas, Mr. Locklear left the Jordan Marsh position after only three months. He returned to Dallas as a buyer for JCPenney at an annual salary of $56,000. Mr. Locklear did a phenomenal job as the buyer for the JCPenney Home Collection. JCPenney was the first department store to feature coordinated lines of dinnerware, flatware, and glasses. During Mr. Locklear's tenure as a purchasing agent, Penney's annual sales for his area of its tabletop line went from $25 million to $45 million.

After receiving an anonymous tip, JCPenney hired an investigator to look into Mr. Locklear's conduct. The investigator found and reported that Mr. Locklear had personal financial difficulties. He had a $500,000 mortgage on his home and child support payments of $900 a month for four children from four previous marriages. Mr. Locklear also had a country club membership, luxury vehicles, and large securities accounts, and he was known to take vacations at posh resorts. Despite the puzzling lifestyle revealed by the investigator, JCPenney took no action.

In 1992, JCPenney received an anonymous letter disclosing a kickback situation between Mr. Locklear and a manufacturer's representative. JCPenney investigated a second time, referred the case for criminal prosecution, and filed a civil suit against Mr. Locklear.

The investigation conducted by authorities found that Mr. Locklear received payments from vendors through several corporations he had established. During the five-year period from 1987 to 1992, Mr. Locklear had received $1.5 million from vendors, manufacturers' representatives, and others.

Mr. Locklear was charged with commercial bribery and entered into a plea agreement. Mr. Locklear also served as a witness for the prosecution at the trials of those who paid him the bribes. A vendor described his payment of a $25,000 fee to Mr. Locklear as follows: "It was either pay it or go out of business." Mr. Locklear was sentenced to 18 months in federal prison, less than the five-year maximum, due to his cooperation.

Should JCPenney have known of the difficulties earlier? Was Mr. Locklear's personal life responsible for his poor value choices at work? Is anyone really harmed by Mr. Locklear's activity? Wasn't he a good buyer?

Racketeer Influenced and Corrupt Organizations (RICO) Act

The RICO Act (18 U.S.C. §§ 1961–1968), a complex federal statute, was passed with the intent of curbing organized crime activity. The ease of proof and severity of penalties for RICO violations have made it a popular charge in criminal cases in which organized crime may not actually be involved.

For RICO to apply, a "pattern of racketeering activity" must be established. That pattern is defined as the commission of at least two racketeering acts within a 10-year period. Racketeering acts are defined under the federal statute to include murder; kidnapping; gambling; arson; robbery; bribery; extortion; dealing in pornography or narcotics; counterfeiting; embezzlement of pension, union, or welfare funds; mail fraud; wire fraud; obstruction of justice or criminal investigation; interstate transportation of stolen goods; white slavery; fraud in the sale of securities; and other acts relating to the Currency and Foreign Transactions Reporting Act (an act passed to prevent money laundering).

RICO provides for both criminal penalties and civil remedies. In a RICO civil suit, injured parties can recover treble damages, the cost of their suit, and reasonable attorney fees. According to the *Journal of Accountancy*, 91 percent of all RICO civil actions have been based on the listed pattern crimes of mail fraud, wire fraud, or fraud in the sale of securities. The statute has been used frequently against corporations. For example, Northwestern Bell Telephone Company lobbyists, who took public utility commissioners to dinner and hired two of them as consultants after they left their commission jobs, were sued under RICO. A lawyer representing phone company customers brought a RICO civil suit based on an alleged pattern of bribing the utility regulators [*H. J., Inc. v Northwestern Bell Telephone Co.*, 492 U.S. 229 (1989)].

Another portion of the RICO statute permits prosecutors to freeze defendants' assets to prevent further crimes. When RICO charges are brought against corporations, the seizure of corporate assets can mean the termination of the business. The Justice Department has issued guidelines requiring prosecutors to seek a forfeiture of assets in proportion to the crime rather than seize all of the business assets. A growing number of states have enacted their own versions of the RICO statute for application at the state level. Some state RICO laws are specifically directed at narcotics, but more than 20 include securities fraud as one of the covered acts.

RICO violations have become added charges in many criminal cases. For example, if someone is charged with ongoing bribery of a state or local official, RICO charges can be added because of the pattern of corruption. Only one U.S. Supreme Court case has restricted RICO's application. In *Reves v Ernst & Young*, 507 U.S. 170 (1993), the accounting firm of Arthur Young (later merged into Ernst & Young) was hired to conduct audits for the Farmer's Cooperative of Arkansas and Oklahoma. An investment by the co-op in a gasohol plant proved to be a financial disaster, and the farmers who held co-op notes that had served as the organization's means of financing over the years lost their investment when the co-op filed for bankruptcy. The investors filed suit against Arthur Young for violations of federal securities laws (see Chapter 21) and RICO. However, the Supreme Court exempted the accounting firm from RICO charges because it found that the firm did not participate in the management of the co-op. The auditor's participation was not that of directing the co-op's affairs, only that of offering its opinions on the financial statements of the firm. The case represents one of the few restrictions on RICO application.

Over the years, businesses have lobbied heavily for reforms to the broad civil and criminal liabilities created by RICO. It seems unlikely that Congress will change the rights of plaintiffs to bring treble damage suits under the act's protective and deterrent mechanisms.

Business Crime and the USA Patriot Act

Prior to September 11, 2001, the federal government had the Money Laundering Control Act, 42 U.S.C. § 5301, that prohibited the knowing and willful participation in any type of financial transaction that was set up in order to conceal or disguise the source of funds. However, investigations into the backgrounds of those who had flown the planes that destroyed the World Trade Center and a portion of the Pentagon revealed intricate financial networks in which the sources of their funds were concealed through various business transactions in different types of industries. As a result, provisions of the USA Patriot Act, passed less than two months after the September 11 destruction, include substantial expansion of the Money Laundering Control Act as well as the Bank Secrecy Act.

Regulation of Money Laundering

Under these changes, title and escrow companies; brokerage firms; travel agents; check-cashing firms; auto, plane, and boat dealers; branches of foreign banks located in the United States; and many other businesses are subject to disclosure and reporting requirements for transactions involving cash or transactions of more than $10,000. In addition, the types of accounts covered under the disclosure requirements include not just savings accounts but also money market savings and brokerage accounts. With these changes, few financial institutions are exempt from reporting and disclosure requirements for cash transactions.

Businesses affected by these amendments developed new policies and procedures for preventing and detecting money laundering. Under the Federal Sentencing Guidelines, businesses subject to these anti–money laundering provisions must have a "Know Thy Customer" program that trains employees in how to spot money laundering and suspicious activities by customers.

Funneling Money to Terrorist Groups

Another portion of the Patriot Act makes it a crime for companies to pay monies to terrorist groups in other countries. For example, a company that pays a mercenary group for protection for its employees or facilities would violate this provision of the act. Under federal law, once an organization is designated by the U.S. government as a terrorist organization, companies cannot continue to do business with them because the purpose of the law is to curb funding to and money laundering by terrorist groups. The list of terrorist groups is available from a website the government provides to businesses via subscription.

CONSIDER...   8.4

Between 1997 and 2004, executives in Chiquita operations in Colombia paid $1.7 million to the United Self-Defense Forces of Colombia (known as AUC, its initials in Spanish). The AUC, according to the U.S. Justice Department, "has been responsible for some of the worst massacres in Colombia's civil conflict and for a sizable percentage of the country's cocaine exports. The U.S. government designated the right-wing militia a terrorist organization in September 2001."[7] The payments were made through a Chiquita wholly owned subsidiary known as Banadex, the company's most profitable unit by 2003.

The payments began in 1997 following a meeting between the then–leader of the AUC, Carlos Castaño, and a senior executive of Banadex. No one disputes that during that meeting, Castaño implied that Chiquita's failure to make the payments could result in physical harm to Banadex employees and property. No one disputes either that the AUC was known for such violence and had been successful in obtaining payments from other companies, either following Castaño's meetings with company officials or, when the companies declined, by carrying out the threat of harm as a form of warning. By September 2000, Chiquita's senior executives were aware that the payments were being made and were also aware that the AUC was a violent paramilitary organization. Chiquita officers, directors, and employees were aware of the Banadex payments to the AUC. Chiquita recorded these payments in its financial reports and other records as "security payments" or payments for "security" or "security services."

Beginning in June 2002, Chiquita began paying the AUC in cash according to new procedures established by senior executives of Chiquita. These new procedures concealed direct cash payments to the AUC. From September 10, 2001, through February 4, 2004, Chiquita made 50 payments to the AUC totaling over $825,000, part of the $1.7 million paid from 1997 through 2004.

On February 20, 2003, a Chiquita employee, aware of the payments to the AUC, told a senior Chiquita officer that he had discovered that the AUC had been designated by the U.S. government as a foreign terrorist organization (FTO). The Justice Department discovered the following sequence of events in response to the employee having raised the issue:

> *Shortly thereafter, these Chiquita officials spoke with attorneys in the District of Columbia office of a national law firm ("outside counsel") about Chiquita's ongoing payments to the AUC. Beginning on Feb. 21, 2003, outside counsel emphatically advised Chiquita that the payments were illegal under United States law and that Chiquita should immediately stop paying the AUC directly or indirectly. Outside counsel advised Chiquita:*
>
> *"Must stop payments."*
> *"Bottom Line: CANNOT MAKE THE PAYMENT [.]"*
> *"Advised NOT TO MAKE ALTERNATIVE PAYMENT through CONVIVIR [.]"*
> *"General Rule: Cannot do indirectly what you cannot do directly [.]"*
> *Concluded with: "CANNOT MAKE THE PAYMENT [.]"*
> *"You voluntarily put yourself in this position. Duress defense can wear out through repetition. Buz [business] decision to stay in harm's way. Chiquita should leave Colombia."*
> *"[T]he company should not continue to make the Santa Marta payments, given the AUC's designation as a foreign terrorist organization[.]"*
> *"[T]he company should not make the payment."*
>
> *On April 3, 2003, a senior Chiquita officer and a member of Chiquita's Board of Directors first reported to the full Board that Chiquita was making payments to a designated FTO. A Board member objected to the payments and recommended that Chiquita consider taking immediate corrective action, including withdrawing from Colombia. The Board did not follow that recommendation, but instead agreed to disclose promptly to the Department of Justice the fact that Chiquita had been making payments to the AUC. Meanwhile, Banadex personnel were instructed to continue making the payments.*[8]

On April 24, 2003, Roderick M. Hills, a member of Chiquita's board and head of its audit committee, Chiquita general counsel Robert Olson, and, some reports indicate, the company's outside counsel met with members of the Justice Department to disclose the payments and explain that they had been made under duress. Mr. Hills, a former chairman of the Securities Exchange Commission, and the Chiquita officer were told that the payments were illegal and had to stop. The payments did not stop, and the company's outside counsel wrote to the board on September 8, 2003, advising that "[Department of Justice] officials have been unwilling to give assurances or guarantees of

CONTINUED

non-prosecution; in fact, officials have repeatedly stated that they view the circumstances presented as a technical violation and cannot endorse current or future payments."[9]

Nonetheless, the payments continued. From April 24, 2003, through February 4, 2004, Chiquita made 20 payments to the AUC totaling $300,000. On February 4, 2004, Chiquita sold the Banadex operations to a Colombian-owned company.

Chiquita then cooperated with the government by making its records available. In March 2007, Chiquita entered a guilty plea and agreed to pay a $25 million fine. Chiquita will be on probation for five years and has agreed to create and maintain an effective ethics program. As of August 2007, Mr. Hills and four former Chiquita officers, including Mr. Olson, were under investigation by the Justice Department for their failure to stop the payments. A Justice Department official said of the investigation, "If the only way that a company can conduct business in a particular location is to do so illegally, then the company shouldn't be doing business there."[10]

Is there the *actus reus* for violation of the Patriot Act? The *mens rea*? What lessons on ethics in international business should companies take from the Chiquita experience?

Additional Federal Crimes

Many of the statutes on business crimes are found at the federal level. Violations of the Securities Exchange Acts (Chapter 21), the Sherman Act (Chapter 16), the Internal Revenue Act, the Pure Food and Drug Act, the environmental statutes (Chapter 11), the Occupational Safety and Health Act (Chapter 18), and Consumer Product Safety statutes (Chapter 10) carry criminal penalties.

State Crimes

Similar criminal statutes at the state level cover such areas as criminal fraud and securities. In addition, states have particular regulations and laws for certain industries. The sale of liquor in most states is strictly regulated. The result is an increase in bribes and kickbacks in these highly regulated industries as businesses try to work around the regulatory restrictions. Since 2002, the state attorneys general have been especially active in white-collar financial crimes. State attorneys general have taken the lead on the financial market collapses in 2007–2008.

Procedural Rights for Business Criminals

Business criminals are treated procedurally in the same manner as other criminals. They have the same rights under the criminal justice system. The U.S. Constitution guarantees protection of certain rights. The **Fourth Amendment** protects the individual's privacy and is the basis for requiring warrants for searches of private property. The **Fifth Amendment** provides the protection against self-incrimination and is also the "due process" amendment, which guarantees that an accused individual has the right to be heard. The **Sixth Amendment** is meant to ensure a speedy trial; it is the basis for the requirement that criminal proceedings and trials proceed in a timely fashion. These constitutional rights are discussed in the following sections.

Fourth Amendment Rights for Businesses

The Fourth Amendment to the U.S. Constitution provides that "the right of the people to be secure in their persons, houses, papers, and effects, against unreasonable searches and seizures, shall not be violated." This amendment protects individual privacy by preventing unreasonable searches and seizures. Before a government agency can seize the property of individuals or businesses, it must obtain a valid **search warrant**—or have an applicable exception to the warrant requirement—which must be issued by a judge or magistrate and be based on probable cause. In other words, authorities must have good reason to believe that instruments or evidence of a crime are present at the business location to be searched. The Fourth Amendment applies equally to individuals and corporations. In an unauthorized search, a corporation's property is given the same protection. If an improper search is conducted (without a warrant and without meeting an exception, see p. 274), any evidence recovered is inadmissible at trial for the purposes of proving the crime.

The courts are continually reviewing cases to determine whether evidence obtained was done so in a way that protects the accused's Fourth Amendment rights. These decisions focus on balancing the privacy rights of the accused with the need to preserve evidence. In *Arizona v Gant,* 129 S.Ct. 1710 (2009), the U.S. Supreme Court limited the use of evidence that is obtained from a driver's vehicle when that driver has been handcuffed and locked in the rear of the squad car. Most officers were in the habit of routinely searching the driver's vehicle on site at the time of the detention/arrest. In the case of Rodney Gant, who was arrested for driving with a suspended license, the officers searched Mr. Gant's car while he was handcuffed in the back seat of the squad car and found cocaine in the pocket of a jacket lying on the back seat of Gant's vehicle. Mr. Gant was charged with possession (as well as the driving with a suspended license).

Mr. Gant's lawyer challenged the search of his client's vehicle on the grounds that there were not exigent circumstances. That is, locked in and handcuffed as he was, there was no emergency or reason to believe that Mr. Gant would spring into action and hide, destroy, or swallow the cocaine. The court held that the officers needed to impound the vehicle and obtain a warrant to search it. Without a warrant, the cocaine was not admissible for purposes of prosecuting Mr. Gant on the cocaine charges. Without the cocaine evidence, unless Mr. Gant confesses, that charge had to be dropped.

This decision is new territory for officers who routinely search cars pursuant to a detention of a driver. They can now search only with permission of the driver or pursuant to a warrant unless the detained individual remains uncuffed and is permitted to amble about, thus posing a risk to the evidence. Warrants also require probable cause. So officers must be able to provide a reason to search a vehicle other than finding a person with a suspended license is driving around.

Warrants and Technology: Texts, E-Mails, and ISPs

CYBERLAW

One of the technological areas that is still evolving deals with the rights of anonymous posters in chat rooms and the identity of those sending e-mails to others. Must the ISP turn over to law enforcement officials the identity of those who are behind their Internet activities? With a warrant, the answer is clearly yes. And warrants are relatively easy to obtain, because law enforcement agencies simply need to furnish the magistrate or judge with the content the poster or e-mailer posted on the Internet. If those postings involve criminal activities or conspiracies, the court can find probable cause. Without a warrant, law enforcement officials' behavior will need to fit into an applicable exception (see p. 274) such as an emergency because of a posted threat. In civil cases, the ISP can require a subpoena before disclosing the identity of its customers. Some ISPs have customers sign agreements that provide that the ISP will keep their identity private except with regard to law enforcement officials. The reason for this agreement is so that the ISP is not held responsible for the conduct of its customers. With this agreement, the ISP can reveal the customer's identity without a warrant. Case 8.4, *City of Ontario v Quon*, deals with another Fourth Amendment issue that involves the technology of text messages and employer access to those of employees.

| **CASE 8.4** | *City of Ontario v Quon*
130 S.Ct. 2619 (2010) |

Text Me, If You Dare

FACTS

Jeff Quon, a sergeant and member of the city of Ontario's SWAT team, sent text messages to Sergeant Steve Trujillo, dispatcher April Florio, and his wife Jerilyn Quon (Respondents) using Arch Wireless text-messaging services that were provided for Quon through the city of Ontario's contract with Arch.

Ontario Police Department (The city) (OPD) (Petitioners) had no official policy directly addressing the use of text messaging. However, the city did have a general "Computer Usage, Internet, and E-mail Policy" applicable to all employees. The policy provided that all software, programs, networks, Internet, e-mail, and other systems were to be used only for city of Ontario–related business. The policy also said, "Users should have no expectation of privacy or confidentiality when using these resources," and indicated that usages were monitored and recorded. Quon attended a meeting during which SWAT team members and others were told that text messages would fall under the city's policy as public information, and be therefore eligible for auditing.

Under the city's contract with Arch Wireless, each pager was allotted 25,000 characters, after which the city was required to pay overage charges. Quon's supervisor told him that he was over by more than 15,000 characters and that he should reimburse the city for the overage charges so that he (the supervisor) would not have to audit the transmission and see how many messages were non–work related. Quon refused to pay and was told to cut down on his transmissions.

When Quon and another officer again exceeded the 25,000-character limit, his supervisor told the officers that he was "tired of being a bill collector with guys going over the allotted amount of characters on their text pagers." Ontario's chief of police, Chief Scharf, then requested an audit of the text messages.

Because city officials were not able to access the text messages themselves, they requested and obtained the messages from Arch Wireless. The audit of the messages revealed abuse of on-the-clock time through sheer numbers of personal texts and their sexually explicit content. The officers were disciplined, and subsequently challenged the discipline by claiming violation of their Fourth Amendment rights. The trial court found that there was a Fourth Amendment violation, but granted Arch Wireless a summary judgment on Quon's claims of invasion of privacy. The Ninth Circuit held that the search was unreasonable and the city appealed.

JUDICIAL OPINION

KENNEDY, Justice

The record does establish that OPD, at the outset, made it clear that pager messages were not considered private. The City's Computer Policy stated that "[u]sers should have no expectation of privacy or confidentiality when using" City computers. Chief Scharf's memo and Duke's statements made clear that this official policy extended to text messaging. The disagreement, at least as respondents see the case, is over whether Duke's later statements overrode the official policy. Respondents contend that because Duke told Quon that an audit would be unnecessary if Quon paid for the overage, Quon reasonably could expect that the contents of his messages would remain private.

Cell phone and text message communications are so pervasive that some persons may consider them to be essential means or necessary instruments for self-expression, even self-identification. That might strengthen the case for an expectation of privacy. On the other hand, the ubiquity of those devices has made them generally affordable, so one could counter that employees who need cell phones or similar devices for personal matters can purchase and pay for their own. And employer policies concerning communications will of course shape the reasonable expectations of their employees, especially to the extent that such policies are clearly communicated.

Even if Quon had a reasonable expectation of privacy in his text messages, petitioners did not necessarily violate the Fourth Amendment by obtaining and reviewing the transcripts. Although as a general matter, warrantless searches "are *per se* unreasonable under the Fourth Amendment," there are "a few specifically established and well-delineated exceptions" to that general rule. The Court has held that the "'special needs'" of the workplace justify one such exception.

The search here was reasonable under that approach. The search was justified at its inception because there were "reasonable grounds for suspecting that the search [was] necessary for a non investigatory work-related purpose." As a jury found, Chief Scharf ordered the search in order to determine whether the character limit on the City's contract with Arch Wireless was sufficient to meet the City's needs. This was, as the Ninth Circuit noted, a "legitimate work-related rationale."

The City and OPD had a legitimate interest in ensuring that employees were not being forced to pay out of their own pockets for work-related expenses, or on the other hand that the City was not paying for extensive personal communications.

As for the scope of the search, reviewing the transcripts was reasonable because it was an efficient and expedient way to determine whether Quon's overages were the result of work-related messaging or personal use. The review was also not "'excessively intrusive.'" Although Quon had gone over his monthly allotment a number of times, OPD requested transcripts for only the months of August and September 2002. While it may have been reasonable as well for OPD to review transcripts of all the months in which Quon exceeded his allowance, it was certainly reasonable for OPD to review messages for just two months in order to obtain a large enough sample to decide whether the character limits were efficacious. And it is worth noting that during his internal affairs investigation, McMahon redacted all messages Quon sent while off duty, a measure which reduced the intrusiveness of any further review of the transcripts.

Even if he could assume some level of privacy would inhere in his messages, it would not have been reasonable for Quon to conclude that his messages were in all circumstances immune from scrutiny. Quon was told that his messages were subject to auditing. As a law enforcement officer, he would or should have known that his actions were likely to come under legal scrutiny, and that this might entail an analysis of his on-the-job communications. Under the circumstances, a reasonable employee would be aware that sound management principles might require the audit of messages to determine whether the pager was being appropriately used. Given that the City issued the pagers to Quon and other SWAT Team members in order to help them more quickly respond to crises—and given that Quon had received no assurances of privacy—Quon could have anticipated that it might be necessary for the City to audit pager messages to assess the SWAT Team's performance in particular emergency situations.

From OPD's perspective, the fact that Quon likely had only a limited privacy expectation, with boundaries that we need not here explore, lessened the risk that the review would intrude on highly private details of Quon's life. OPD's audit of messages on Quon's employer-provided pager was not nearly as intrusive as a search of his personal e-mail account or pager, or a wiretap on his home phone line, would have been. That the search did reveal intimate details of Quon's life does not make it unreasonable, for under the circumstances a reasonable employer would not expect that such a review would intrude on such matters.

The Court of Appeals erred in finding the search unreasonable. It pointed to a "host of simple ways to verify the efficacy of the 25,000 character limit . . . without intruding on [respondents'] Fourth Amendment rights." The panel suggested that Scharf "could have warned Quon that for the month of September he was forbidden from using his pager for personal communications, and that the contents of all his messages would be reviewed to ensure the pager was used only for work related purposes during that time frame. Alternatively, if [OPD] wanted to review past usage, it could have asked Quon to count the characters himself, or asked him to redact personal messages and grant permission to [OPD] to review the redacted transcript."

This approach was inconsistent with controlling precedents. This Court has "repeatedly refused to declare that only the 'least intrusive' search practicable can be reasonable under the Fourth Amendment." That rationale "could raise insuperable barriers to the exercise of virtually all search-and-seizure powers," because "judges engaged in *post hoc* evaluations of government conduct can almost always imagine some alternative means by which the objectives of the government might

CONTINUED

have been accomplished." Even assuming there were ways that OPD could have performed the search that would have been less intrusive, it does not follow that the search as conducted was unreasonable.

Finally, the Court must consider whether the search violated the Fourth Amendment rights of Jerilyn Quon, Florio, and Trujillo, the respondents who sent text messages to Jeff Quon. Petitioners and respondents disagree whether a sender of a text message can have a reasonable expectation of privacy in a message he knowingly sends to someone's employer-provided pager. It is not necessary to resolve this question in order to dispose of the case, however. Respondents argue that because "the search was unreasonable as to Sergeant Quon, it was also unreasonable as to his correspondents." They make no corollary argument that the search, if reasonable as to Quon, could nonetheless be unreasonable

as to Quon's correspondents. In light of this litigating position and the Court's conclusion that the search was reasonable as to Jeff Quon, it necessarily follows that these other respondents cannot prevail.

The judgment of the Court of Appeals for the Ninth Circuit is reversed.

CASE QUESTIONS

1. What general advice could you give a business about its access to employees' text messages based on the decision in this case?

2. Why are alternative methods for searching the text messages not relevant?

3. How does the court deal with the issue of expectation of privacy on the part of the officer's family and friends?

Warrants and Exceptions

Exceptions to the warrant requirement are based on emergency grounds. For example, if an office building with relevant records is burning, government agents could enter the property without a warrant to recover the papers. Similarly, if the records are being destroyed, the government need not wait for a warrant. Another exception to the warrant requirement is the "plain view" exception. This exception allows police officers to seize evidence that is within their view. No privacy rights are violated when evidence is exposed to the view of others. The *Dow Chemical Co. v U.S.* (Case 8.5) deals with a business issue and one of the Fourth Amendment exceptions.

| CASE 8.5 | *Dow Chemical Co. v United States*
476 U.S. 227 (1986) |

Low-Flying Federal Agents: Photographic Searches

FACTS

Dow Chemical (petitioner) operates a two-thousand-acre chemical plant at Midland, Michigan. The facility, with numerous buildings, conduits, and pipes, is visible from the air. Dow has maintained ground security at the facility and has investigated flyovers by other, unauthorized aircraft. However, none of the buildings or manufacturing equipment is concealed.

In 1978, the Environmental Protection Agency (EPA) conducted an inspection of Dow. EPA requested a second inspection, but Dow denied the request. The EPA then employed a commercial aerial photographer to take photos of the plant from 12,000, 3,000, and 1,200 feet. The EPA had no warrant, but the plane was always within navigable air space when the photos were taken.

When Dow became aware of the EPA photographer, it brought suit in federal district court and challenged the action as a violation of its Fourth Amendment rights. The district court found that the EPA had violated Dow's rights and issued an injunction prohibiting the further use of the aircraft. The court of appeals reversed, and Dow appealed.

JUDICIAL OPINION

BURGER, Chief Justice

The photographs at issue in this case are essentially like those used in map-making. Any person with an airplane and an aerial camera could readily duplicate them. In common with much else, the technology of photography has changed in this century. These developments have enhanced industrial processes, and indeed all areas of life; they have also enhanced enforcement techniques. Whether they may be employed by competitors to penetrate trade secrets is not a question presented in this case. Governments do not generally seek to appropriate trade secrets of the private sector, and the right to be free of appropriation of trade secrets is protected by law.

That such photography might be barred by state law with regard to competitors, however, is irrelevant to the questions presented here. State tort law governing unfair competition does not define the limits of the Fourth Amendment. The Government is seeking these photographs in order to regulate, not compete with, Dow.

Dow claims first that the EPA has no authority to use aerial photography to implement its statutory authority of "site inspection" under the Clean Air Act.

Congress has vested in EPA certain investigatory and enforcement authority, without spelling out precisely how this authority was to be exercised in all the myriad circumstances that might arise in monitoring matters relating to clean air and water standards.

Regulatory or enforcement authority generally carries with it all the modes of inquiry and investigation traditionally employed or useful to execute the authority granted. Environmental standards cannot be enforced only in libraries and laboratories, helpful as those institutions may be.

The EPA, as a regulatory and enforcement agency, needs no explicit statutory provisions to employ methods of observation commonly available to the public at large; we hold that the use of aerial photography is within the EPA's statutory authority.

DISSENTING OPINION

POWELL, MARSHALL, BRENNAN, and BLACKMUN, Justices

The Fourth Amendment protects private citizens from arbitrary surveillance by their Government. Today, in the context of administrative aerial photography of commercial premises, the Court retreats from that standard. It holds that the photography was not a Fourth Amendment "search" because it was not accompanied by a physical trespass and because the equipment used was not the most highly sophisticated form of technology available to the Government. Under this holding the existence of an asserted privacy interest apparently will be decided solely by reference to the manner of surveillance used to intrude on that interest. Such an inquiry will not protect Fourth Amendment rights, but rather will permit their gradual decay as technology advances.

EPA's aerial photography penetrated into a private commercial enclave, an area in which society has recognized that privacy interests may legitimately be claimed. The photographs captured highly confidential information that Dow had taken reasonable and objective steps to preserve as private.

CASE QUESTIONS

1. Of what significance is the fact that Dow's plant could be seen from the air?

2. Did Dow take any steps to protect its privacy?

3. Is the EPA specifically given aerial surveillance authority?

4. What objections do the dissenting judges raise to the decision?

CONSIDER... 8.5

The IRS attached levies to the property and other assets of G.M. Leasing Corp. for non-payment of taxes. To satisfy the levy, the IRS seized several automobiles from the street in front of G.M.'s offices. Also, without a warrant, the IRS entered G.M.'s offices and seized business books and records. Has the Fourth Amendment been violated with the seizure of the cars? Of the books and records? [*G.M. Leasing Corp. v United States*, 429 U.S. 338 (1977)]

In many business crimes, the records used to prosecute the defendant are not in the possession of the defendant. The records are, instead, in the hands of a third party, such as an accountant or a bank. Does the Fourth Amendment afford the defendant protection in documents that discuss the defendant or reflect the defendant's finances and transactions when those documents are in the hands of another? In some cases, a privilege exists between the third party and the defendants, and certain documents are protected and need not be turned over. Notes on trial strategy, audit procedures, and other plans and thoughts are not discoverable because such communications are privileged between lawyers and clients. Some states recognize an accountant–client privilege. The priest–parishioner privilege generally exists; however, under certain exceptions, such as in cases of abuse, reporting is required.

Fifth Amendment Rights for Businesses

The Fifth Amendment provides several protections for those facing criminal charges.

Self-Incrimination

The statement "I take the Fifth" is used so often that it has made the Fifth Amendment well known for its protection against self-incrimination. For example, former MLB player Mark McGwire took the Fifth Amendment before a congressional committee investigating MLB's policies on testing players for steroids and suspensions for their use. We cannot be compelled to be witnesses against ourselves. However, this protection applies only to natural persons; corporations are not given this privilege. A corporation cannot prevent the required disclosure of corporate books and records on grounds that they are incriminating.

Corporate officers cannot assert Fifth Amendment protection to prevent compulsory production of corporate records. Nor can corporate officers use the Fifth Amendment to prevent the production of corporate records on grounds that those records incriminate them personally. The rules applicable to corporate officers have been extended to apply to those involved in labor unions, close corporations, and even unincorporated associations. The same rule is applicable to sole shareholders of small corporations as well.

For the Manager's Desk

Re: Knowing When to Hold and When to Fold: What to Do When Your Company Is in BIG Trouble

The *Wall Street Journal* grappled with a question that affects many business professionals in today's economy: What do you do when a scandal at your former employer has caused you to lose your job? How do you handle such a situation on your résumé?

Investment advisers from Stanford Financial Group, Madoff Securities, and a host of Wall Street firms such as Lehman Brothers and Bear Stearns find themselves looking for employment because of their defunct employers. Some executive search firms will not consider former employees from scandal-rocked companies, even if the executives worked at subsidiaries or were not involved in the fraud, even remotely. Most agree there is a long path back from such an employment history, but there are some tips:

- Leave when the indictments and/or arrests occur—don't hang on.

- Don't lie on your résumé.

- Describe your work at the company and others without naming names and wait until the interview to disclose whom you worked for.

- Don't badmouth your former employer in your interview—this is often taken as a sign of guilt; rather, explain how difficult it is to be blindsided, something that most managers can identify with because it happens to the best.

Source: JoAnn S. Lublin, "When Scandal Rocks a Résumé," *Wall Street Journal*, August 4, 2009, p. D1.

Miranda *Rights*

The famous *Miranda* doctrine resulted from an interpretation of the Fifth Amendment by the U.S. Supreme Court in *Miranda v Arizona*, 384 U.S. 436 (1966). *Miranda* **warnings** must be given to all people who are subjected to custodial interrogation. Custody does not necessarily mean "locked in jail," but it is generally based on an individual's perceptions of a situation. If a person feels he is without freedom to leave a place by choice, the level of custody at which *Miranda* rights must be issued has been reached. However, in *Missouri v Seibert*, 542 U.S. 600 (2004), the U.S. Supreme Court provided further clarification on when *Miranda* warnings must be given. A law enforcement official cannot coax a confession from an individual and then provide the warnings. If the individual then refuses to answer questions or offer the same information after the warnings are given, the law enforcement officials cannot use the prior confession, given before the warnings, as evidence in court. The warnings tell those in custody of their Fifth Amendment right to say nothing, as well as their right to an attorney. The failure to give *Miranda* warnings is not fatal to a case as long as the crime can be proved through evidence other than the statement of the defendant; the prosecution can still proceed based on other evidence.

Due Process Rights

The Fifth Amendment also contains due process language. The same language is found in the Fourteenth Amendment and made applicable to the states. **Due process,** as Chapters 5 and 6 discuss, means that no one can be convicted of a crime without the opportunity to be heard, to question witnesses, and to present evidence.

Due process in criminal proceedings guarantees certain procedural protections as a case is investigated, charged, and taken to trial. The Sixth Amendment complements due process rights by requiring that all these procedures be completed in a timely fashion. The following subsections discuss the basic steps in a criminal proceeding as diagrammed in Exhibit 8.3.

Warrant and/or Arrest. A criminal proceeding can begin when a crime is witnessed, as when a police officer attempts to apprehend a person who has just robbed a convenience store. When the convenience store is robbed but the robber escapes, and if the police can establish that a certain individual was probably responsible for the robbery, a **warrant** can be issued and the individual then arrested. Whether with or without a warrant, the due process steps begin with the arrest.

Initial Appearance. Once an arrest has been made, the defendant must have an opportunity to appear before a judicial figure within a short time period (usually 24 hours) to be informed of his charges, rights, and so on. This proceeding is generally referred to as an **initial appearance.** Dates for other proceedings are set at this time and, if the individual can be released, the terms of the release are also established. The individual may be required to post a bond to be released; others are held without release terms (release terms generally depend on the nature of the crime and the defendant). The terms *released on his own recognizance* and *released OR* mean the defendant is released without having to post a bond.

Preliminary Hearing or Grand Jury. Up to this step in the criminal proceedings, the defendant's charges are based on the word of a police officer; there has not yet been any proof brought forth linking the crime and the defendant. The purpose of a preliminary hearing or grand jury proceeding is to require the prosecution to establish that there is some evidence that the defendant committed the crime.

EXHIBIT 8.3   Steps in Criminal Proceedings

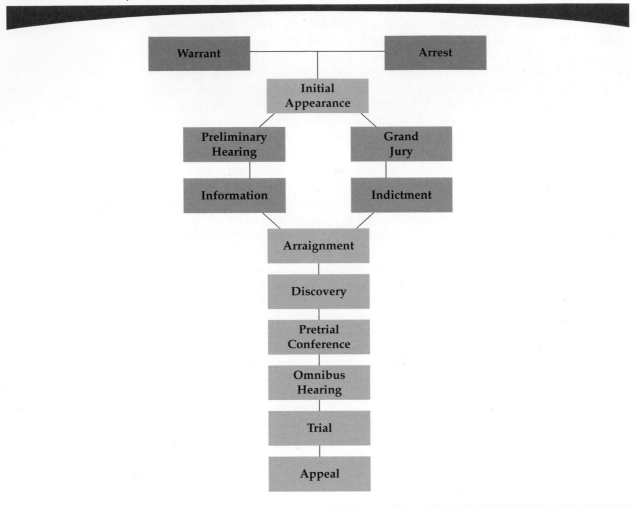

In a **preliminary hearing,** the prosecution presents evidence to a judge to indicate that the accused committed the crime. The prosecution presents witnesses, and the defendant and the defendant's attorney are present for cross-examination of those witnesses. The defense does not present its case at this time but might make an offer of proof to show that the defendant could not have committed the crime. If the judge finds sufficient proof, an **information** is issued. The information is to a criminal proceeding what a complaint is to a civil proceeding: It establishes what the defendant did and when and what crimes were committed.

In some crimes, the evidence of the crime is presented to a **grand jury,** which is a panel of citizens who serve for a designated period of time (usually six months) and act as the body responsible for the review of evidence of crimes. If the grand jury finds sufficient evidence that a crime was committed, it issues an **indictment,** which is similar to an information and serves the same function.

Grand jury proceedings are conducted secretly, whereas preliminary hearings are public. Grand juries also have the authority to conduct investigations to determine whether crimes were committed and who did so. Perhaps one of the most famous grand juries was the San Francisco grand jury investigating steroid use in baseball. The grand jury heard testimony from some of baseball's biggest stars. However, the content of their testimony remains sealed and secret unless and until it is used at a trial.

Arraignment.   An **arraignment** is the proceeding at which the defendant enters a plea of guilty, not guilty, or no contest (*nolo contendere*). If a not guilty plea is entered, a date for trial is set. If the defendant enters a guilty or no contest plea, chances are the plea is the result of a **plea bargain,** which is the term used in criminal proceedings for a settlement. The defendant may plead guilty to a lesser offense in exchange for the prosecution's promise to support a lesser sentence, such as probation or minimum jail time.

Discovery.   If the case is going to trial, the parties then enter a **discovery** period. Many states have mandatory criminal discovery laws that require each side to turn over certain types of information to the other side, including lists of witnesses they will call and lists of exhibits that will be used at trial. Exhibits include documents, murder weapons, and pictures.

Omnibus Hearing.   In some cases, the defense attorney wishes to challenge the prosecution evidence on grounds that it was obtained in violation of any of the constitutional protections discussed earlier. Some documents, for example, may have been seized without a warrant. The **omnibus hearing** is the forum wherein all of these challenges can be presented for the judge's ruling as to the admissibility of evidence. This hearing is held before the trial so the jury is not exposed to evidence that should not have been admitted. In the O. J. Simpson double-homicide trial, an omnibus hearing was held on the admissibility of evidence gathered at Mr. Simpson's estate without a warrant.

Trial.   If no plea agreement is reached before trial, the case then proceeds to **trial.**

B I O G R A P H Y

Amanda Knox: Instruction on International Criminal Justice

Amanda Knox, 22, a student at the University of Washington, was doing a semester of study abroad in Italy. Her roommate in her small Italian rental house, Meredith Kercher, 21, of England, was found dead from a slashed throat. Amanda and her Italian boyfriend, Raffaele Sollecito, 25, were tried and convicted for her murder. Prosecutors in the case were seeking a life sentence for both, but Amanda was sentenced to 26 years and Raffaele to 25. Rudy Guede, a third defendant, was sentenced to 30 years for the sexual assault and murder of Ms. Kercher. The heavily publicized trial, which captured the

attention of everyone in Italy, from the person on the street to playwrights, has shown some stark differences between the Italian and U.S. criminal court processes. Here are some of those differences:

- Amanda spent one year in jail in Italy before she was charged with a crime.

- The trial began in January 2009 and was not completed until December 4, 2009 because the court meets only two days per week, and because Raffaele's lawyer is a member of Parliament and had to be in Rome for meetings. (The jury

CONTINUED

deliberated for 11 hours after the year-long trial before it reached its guilty verdict.)

- The case consists entirely of circumstantial evidence, such as cell phone records that show Amanda and Raffaele halting use of their phones at the time of the murder and then using them again in the early morning at the same time.

- Amanda and Raffaele were permitted to present declarations to the jury at the end of their trial without being subject to cross-examination.

- The Italian system offers no guilty plea or plea-bargaining options.

- Juries in Italy, which in Amanda and Raffaele's trial included six civilians and two judges, are not sequestered during the trial and juries are permitted to have access to media coverage of the case.

- The standard of proof in Italy is beyond a reasonable doubt but not absolute truth.

- Rudy Guede was convicted first because he chose what is known as a fast-track trial, which can result in a lesser sentence.

- The jury also has required Amanda to pay $7.4 million to the Kercher family and $60,000 to a person she falsely accused of the murder.

Explain what differs about this trial and process from the criminal procedures and rights you have studied in this chapter.

Source: Rachel Donadio, "U.S. Student Delivers Appeal at End of Italian Trial," *New York Times*, December 4, 2009, p. A12.

Summary

Who is liable for business crimes?

- Vicarious liability—holding companies accountable for criminal conduct of their officers

- Elements—requirements of proof for crimes

- *Mens rea*—requisite mental state for committing a crime

- *Actus reus*—physical act of committing a crime

What penalties exist for business crimes?

- Penalties—punishments for commission of crimes; include fines and imprisonment

- Corporate sentencing guidelines—federal rules used to determine level of penalties for companies and officers; a system that decreases penalties for effort toward prevention of wrongdoing and cooperation with investigations and increases penalties for lack of effort and other problems in company operations

What is the nature of business crime?

- Obstruction—under Sarbanes-Oxley, prohibits destruction of documents when civil or criminal investigations are pending

- Computer crime—crimes committed while using computer technology

- Counterfeit Access Device and Computer Fraud and Abuse Act (CADCFA)—federal law making it a crime to access computers without authorization

- Controlling the Assault of Non-Solicited Pornography and Marketing (CAN-SPAM) law to control unsolicited pornographic and ad materials

- Electronic Espionage Act (EEA)—makes it a crime to take employer's proprietary information

- Cyberbullying—crime of harassment via Internet communication

- Criminal fraud—misrepresentation with the intent to take something from another without that person's knowledge; to mislead to obtain funds or property

- Racketeer Influenced and Corrupt Organizations (RICO) Act—federal law designed to prevent racketeering by intensifying the punishments for engaging in certain criminal activities more than once

- USA Patriot Act—federal law that deals with due process rights as well as substantive issues such as money laundering prohibitions and mandatory disclosures by those involved in financial transactions, including banks, escrow, and title companies and other financial institutions

What are the rights of corporate and individual defendants in the criminal justice system?

- Fourth Amendment—provision in U.S. Constitution that protects against invasions of privacy; the search warrant amendment

- Fifth Amendment—the self-incrimination protection of the U.S. Constitution

- Sixth Amendment—the right-to-trial protection of the U.S. Constitution

- Search warrant—judicially issued right to examine home, business, and papers in any area in which there is an expectation of privacy

- *Miranda* warnings—advice required to be given to those taken into custody; details the right to remain silent and the right to have counsel

- Due process—right to trial before conviction

- Warrant—public document authorizing detention of an individual for criminal charges; for searches, a judicial authorization

- Initial appearance—defendant's first appearance in court to have charges explained, bail set, lawyer appointed, and future dates set

- Preliminary hearing—presentation of abbreviated case by prosecution to establish sufficient basis to bind defendant over for trial

- Information—document issued after preliminary hearing requiring defendant to stand trial

- Grand jury—secret body that hears evidence to determine whether charges should be brought and whether defendant should be held for trial

- Indictment—document issued by grand jury requiring defendant to stand trial

- Arraignment—hearing at which trial date is set and plea is entered

- Plea bargain—settlement of criminal charges

- Omnibus hearing—evidentiary hearing outside the presence of the jury

- Trial—presentation of case by each side

Questions and Problems

1. The Peanut Corporation of America was a supplier of processed peanuts to some of the largest food production companies in the United States. The company was founded by Hugh Parnell, Sr. when he was selling ice cream vending machines in the 1960s. When he was restocking a machine, he noticed that the peanuts on the Nutty Buddy ice cream cones came from a plant in the North. He decided to begin a company that processed peanuts in the South, where they were grown. The company grew and had plants in Virginia, Georgia, and Texas. Hugh's son Stewart Parnell entered the business in the 1970s after complaining to his father that graduates in his major, oceanography, often ended up working on oil rigs. His father offered him a job, and Stewart left college to begin work in the Virginia facilities.

The major food producers were customers of Peanut Corp. ConAgra, a major peanut butter producer, was a large customer of Peanut Corp. Peanut Corp.'s peanut product base was used in peanut butter, ice cream, cookies, and crackers. Peanut Corporation was known for its cost cutting. When a customer came back with a bid from another peanut product base that was lower, Stewart Parnell, who became the CEO of Peanut Corp., would always cut the price by a few cents in order to win over the potential customer.

E-mails reflect Parnell's concerns about costs. When a salmonella test at the factory was positive, Peanut Corp. was required to hold off shipment for a retest. Parnell wrote in an e-mail, "We need to discuss this. Beside the cost, this time lapse is costing us $$$$ and causing us obviously a huge lapse from the time when we pick up the peanuts until the time we can invoice."[11] He also wrote, about products he was informed had tested positive for salmonella, "Turn them loose."[12] When the FDA made the connection between Peanut Corp. and salmonella poisonings that sickened 644 people in 44 states, which resulted in eight deaths. Mr. Parnell wrote to his managers, "Obviously we are not shipping any peanut butter products affected by the recall but desperately at least need to turn the raw peanuts on the floor into money."[13]

Congress held hearings into Peanut Corp.'s operations. Stewart Parnell took the Fifth Amendment when members of the Commerce Committee in the House of Representatives asked him questions about his company.

The company declared Chapter 7 bankruptcy on February 13, 2009.

   a. Discuss whether Mr. Parnell could be held criminally liable.

   b. Are Mr. Parnell's e-mails admissible as evidence?

   c. Mr. Parnell's father said, "He's being railroaded. Why would anybody send something out that would ruin his own company? It's like an auto dealer sending a car out with no brakes."[14] What defense is he raising for his son?

2. Borland International, Inc., and Symantec Corporation are software manufacturers based in Silicon Valley in California. A Borland executive, Eugene Wang, was planning to depart Borland to work for Symantec, considered Borland's archrival. Other Borland executives and its board uncovered evidence, on the evening of Mr. Wang's departure, that Mr. Wang had communicated trade secrets to Gordon Eubanks, Symantec's chief executive. Those secrets included future product specifications, marketing plans through 1993, a confidential proposal for a business transaction, and a memo labeled "attorney/client confidential" summarizing questions asked by the Federal Trade Commission (FTC) in its probe of restraint of trade allegations by Microsoft Corporation.

Mr. Wang allegedly used his computer to communicate the information to Mr. Eubanks. The local police and Borland executives worked through the night, using Symantec's own software that reconstructs computer files after they have been destroyed.

When Mr. Wang reported for his exit interview, he was detained and questioned by investigators. Searches authorized by warrant of Mr. Eubanks's two homes and his office uncovered evidence that he had received Mr. Wang's information. Borland filed a civil suit against the two men.

Later during the day of the exit interview, Mr. Wang's secretary, who was transferring with him to Symantec, returned to copy from her computer what she called "personal files." A personnel official watched as she copied the files from her computer but became suspicious and notified plainclothes officers in the Borland parking lot. The secretary, Lynn Georganes, was stopped, and the two disks onto which she had copied materials were taken. The disks contained scores of confidential Borland documents, including marketing plans and business forecasts.

Do the actions of Mr. Wang and Mr. Eubanks fit any computer crime statutes? Was theft involved in their actions? Were Ms. Georganes's actions ethical? Can't a competitor always hire an executive away, and wouldn't Mr. Wang have had most of the information in his head anyway? Can Mr. Eubanks be certain Mr. Wang will not do the same thing to him?

3. Emma Mary Ellen Holley and David Holley, an interracial couple, tried to buy a house in Twenty-Nine Palms, California. A real estate corporation, Triad, Inc., had listed the house for sale. Grove Crank, a Triad salesman, prevented the Holleys from obtaining the house for racially discriminatory reasons.

The Holleys brought a lawsuit in federal court against Mr. Crank and Triad. They claimed, among other things, that both were responsible for a fair housing law violation. The Holleys later filed a separate suit against David Meyer, the sole shareholder of Triad and its president and CEO. They claimed that Mr. Meyer was vicariously liable in one or more of these capacities for Mr. Crank's unlawful actions, which were a violation of the Fair Housing Act. Are the Holleys correct? [*Meyer v Holley*, 537 U.S. 280 (2003)]

4. In 1991, Agent William Elliott of the United States Department of the Interior came to suspect that marijuana was being grown in a home belonging to Danny Kyllo, part of a triplex on Rhododendron Drive in Florence, Oregon. Indoor marijuana growth typically requires high-intensity lamps. In order to determine whether an amount of heat was emanating from the petitioner's home consistent with the use of such lamps, at 3:20 A.M. on January 16, 1992, Agents Elliott and Dan Haas used an Agema Thermovision 210 thermal imager to scan the triplex.

Thermal imagers detect infrared radiation, which virtually all objects emit but which is not visible to the naked eye. The imager converts radiation into images based on relative warmth—black is cool, white is hot, shades of gray connote relative differences; in that respect, it operates somewhat like a video camera showing heat images.

The scan of Mr. Kyllo's home took only a few minutes and was performed from the passenger seat of Agent Elliott's vehicle across the street from the front of the house, and also from the street in back of the house. The scan showed that the roof over the garage and a side wall of Mr. Kyllo's home were relatively hot compared to the rest of the home and substantially warmer than neighboring homes in the triplex. Agent Elliott concluded that Mr. Kyllo was using halide lights to grow marijuana in his house, which indeed he was. Based on tips from informants, utility bills, and the thermal imaging, a federal magistrate judge issued a warrant authorizing a search of Mr. Kyllo's home, and the agents found an indoor growing operation involving more than 100 plants. Mr. Kyllo was indicted on one count of manufacturing marijuana. Mr. Kyllo unsuccessfully moved to suppress the evidence seized from his home and then entered a conditional guilty plea. Should the evidence be suppressed? [*Kyllo v U.S.*, 533 U.S. 27 (2001)]

5. The owner of a construction firm in New York City, William Lattarulo, has been charged with manslaughter in the death of one of his workers. Lauro Ortega suffocated when the foundation of a building next to where he was digging at a Lattarulo site collapsed on him. Mr. Ortega's head was all that was uncovered when the foundation collapsed, but the pressure of the dirt and debris that rendered him immobile constricted his chest and made him unable to breathe. He suffocated to death as his coworkers tried to dig him out from the debris.

Mr. Ortega's coworkers as well as a safety consultant had warned Mr. Lattarulo that the trench was unsafe and needed to have some supports placed in it to prevent a collapse. When he was warned a second time by his workers Mr. Lattarulo said, "Don't worry about it."

In addition, digging operations require that a contractor hire a consultant to oversee site safety. While Mr. Lattarulo listed a company as a consultant for the safety job, he did not actually have or pay a consultant, something that saved him $90,000 on the job. On the day of the collapse, a building inspector for the city visited the site following the fatality and said there were "shoddy work conditions." She also found eight violations of city construction codes at the site.

The Lattarulo site involved digging a foundation next to another building, but the Lattarulo building required a deeper dig. The result was that the foundation of the building next to the site was weakened and required support until the Lattarulo concrete was poured to provide a substitute for the former ground support. A consultant working nearby did warn Mr. Lattarulo about the foundation's risk of collapse once the digging went deeper.

When the criminal manslaughter charges were brought, contractors had questions about their criminal liability when there are accidents on job sites. How would you advise these contractors? When is an owner criminally liable for actions and work conducted by employees? (Michael Wilson, "Manslaughter Charge for Builder in Brooklyn Collapse," *New York Times*, October 12, 2008, A24.)

6. Bernard Saul was a salesperson for A. P. Walter Company, a wholesale auto parts business, assigned to the D&S Auto Parts account. Mr. Saul took inventory at D&S each week and phoned in an order to Walter to cover the needed inventory replacements. Between 1976 and 1982, Mr. Saul ordered parts from Walter and invoiced D&S, but he actually kept a portion of the parts for himself, sold them to other dealers, and pocketed the money. Through an audit, D&S discovered that it had paid $155,445.20 for parts that were not received. Can Mr. Saul be charged with any crimes? Can Walter be charged with any crimes? [*D&S Auto Parts, Inc. v Schwartz*, 838 F.2d 965 (7th Cir. 1988)]

7. Odessa Mae French operated the Pines Motel as a house of prostitution for seven years. During that time, Ms. French avoided any local law enforcement action by allowing the sheriff to have free services at the Pines. Eventually, the federal government brought charges against the operation for tax evasion and RICO violations. Would the services to the sheriff constitute a form of bribe that would support a RICO charge? [*United States v Tunnell*, 667 F.2d 1182 (5th Cir. 1982)]

8. The New York City Department of Health is responsible for the inspection of Manhattan restaurants to determine whether they comply with the city's health code. Forty-six of the department's inspectors were inducing restaurateurs to pay money to them for permit approval or for a favorable inspection.

Is this activity a basis for a crime? What crime? What would a prosecutor be required to prove? Are the officers and the restaurateurs equally criminally liable? [*U.S. v Tillem*, 906 F.2d 814 (2d Cir. 1990)]

9. Jason Jones, a 19-year-old U.S. Naval Academy midshipman, killed John and Carole Hall when he collided with the rear of their car, which was on the shoulder of the road. Mr. Jones was driving 80–105 mph and talking on a cell phone when he struck the Halls' car.

He was prosecuted for manslaughter and negligent driving. Negligent driving is a misdemeanor and carries a $500 fine. Manslaughter requires proof that the defendant knew the conduct was likely to cause death or severe bodily harm.

Testimony by experts for the prosecution indicated that cell phone use while driving is an enormous distraction. The increased accident rate during cell phone use while driving is placed at between 34 and 300 percent by various experts.

It is not illegal in Maryland to use a cell phone while driving. Can someone be convicted for crimes related to conduct that is not illegal? Was the *mens rea* present here?

10. Harlan Nolte and others invested in IFC Leasing Company, a master music recording leasing program. The company was created to acquire and lease master music recordings. Jerry Denby, the executive vice president of IFC, contacted Stephen Weiss, a partner in the law firm of Rosenbaum, Wise, Lerman, Katz & Weiss, to draft the prospectus for investors. Mr. Weiss drafted four documents used in the recruitment of investors for IFC. The complex structure of the investments, according to the documents, would have substantial tax consequences (to their benefit) for the investors.

After Mr. Nolte and others had made their investments, the IRS issued an opinion that the deductions explained in the prospectus and other documents would not be allowed. Criminal fraud actions were brought against IFC and its officers, as well as Mr. Weiss. The Justice Department also indicted both Mr. Weiss's law firm and his partners. Mr. Weiss's partners and the firm, through its management committee, maintain they cannot be held criminally liable for the actions of one partner. The Justice Department maintains that the firm and the partners were negligent in their supervision of Mr. Weiss and should, therefore, be held criminally liable. Do you agree with the Justice Department's position? Why or why not? [*Nolte v Pearson*, 994 F.2d 1311 (8th Cir. 1993)]

Ethics, Strategy, and the Law

Particularly When a Company Faces Criminal Charges

In what was called the largest criminal tax fraud case in the history of the United States, 16 former partners and employees of the accounting firm KPMG were charged with criminal tax fraud. The case was so complex that the government alone had produced in discovery, in electronic or paper form, at least 5 million to 6 million pages of documents *plus* transcripts of 335 depositions and 195 income tax returns.

KPMG, following a dismal performance by its partners at a congressional hearing, began negotiations with the Justice Department for the settlement of the case against the firm itself. As a result of those negotiations, KPMG agreed to stop paying the legal fees for the 16 former partners and employees, to waive indictment, to be charged in a one-count information, to admit extensive wrongdoing, to pay a $456 million fine, and to accept restrictions on its practice. In turn, the Justice Department agreed that the information against KPMG would be dismissed if KPMG met all of its obligations under the agreement. Those negotiating on behalf of KPMG had stated to the Justice Department attorneys that their goal was to avoid the fate of Arthur Andersen and save the firm. With KPMG saved, however, the 16 former partners and employees were left without means for paying what had been and would be an expensive defense to the tax shelter fraud accusations.

The 16 argued that the failure of KPMG to pay those fees, as it had done in the past, deprived them of their constitutional rights under the Fifth and Sixth Amendments on self-incrimination as well as the right to a speedy trial. They challenged the agreement in federal court.

The court found that in obtaining the agreement from KPMG, federal prosecutors, acting under Justice Department policy established in the so-called Thompson memo, indicated to KPMG that the firm's continuing to pay the legal fees of the 16 would be considered evidence of the firm's guilt. Federal District Court Judge Lewis Kaplan found that the prosecutors had acted improperly in pressuring KPMG to throw its employees under the bus in order to preserve the firm. Judge Kaplan wrote:

> *An employer often must reimburse an employee for legal expenses when the employee is sued, or even charged with a crime, as a result of doing his or her job. Indeed, the employer often must advance legal expenses to an employee up front, although the employee sometimes must pay the employer back if the employee has been guilty of wrongdoing.*

This principle is not the stuff of television and movie drama. It does not remotely approach Miranda warnings in popular culture. But it is very much a part of American life. Persons in jobs big and small, private and public, rely on it every day. Bus drivers sued for accidents, cops sued for allegedly wrongful arrests, nurses named in malpractice cases, news reporters sued in libel cases, and corporate chieftains embroiled in securities litigation generally have similar rights to have their employers pay their legal expenses if they are sued as a result of their doing their jobs. This right is as much a part of the bargain between employer and employee as salary or wages.

The Thompson memo, written by U.S. Deputy Attorney General Larry D. Thompson, was called *Principles of Federal Prosecution of Business Organizations* and was written to give prosecutors guidelines and policies on the decision to prosecute or not to prosecute companies. Two of the principles in the memo provided as follows:

(1) [I]n gauging the extent of the corporation's cooperation, the prosecutor may consider the corporation's willingness to identify the culprits within the corporation, including senior executives, to make witnesses available, to disclose the complete results of its internal investigation, and to waive attorney-client and work-product privileges.

(2) Another factor to be weighed by the prosecutor is whether the corporation appears to be protecting its culpable employees and agents. Thus, while cases will differ depending upon the circumstances, a corporation's promise of support to culpable employees and agents, either through the advancing of attorneys fees, through retaining the employees without sanction for their misconduct, or through providing information to the employees about the government's investigation pursuant to a joint defense agreement, may be considered by the prosecutor in weighing the extent and value of a corporation's cooperation.

Mr. Thompson defended the use of pressure to have companies cut off payment of defense costs for their employees on the ground that "they [the employees] don't need fancy legal representation" if they do not believe that they acted with criminal intent. (The Thompson Memo was later replaced by the McNulty Memo, but its provisions on fee payment remained intact.)

However, Judge Kaplan ruled that the pressure the Justice Department had placed on KPMG was improper, that there were either explicit or implicit agreements to pay the attorneys' fees for the former partners and employees, and that, as a result, they had been deprived of the constitutional rights they were entitled to in criminal proceedings. Judge Kaplan found that KPMG had a conflict of interest in representing to the government that it did not have an obligation to pay the attorneys' fees and that KPMG was so anxious to "curry favor" with the government that the government should not have relied on KPMG's representations about its obligations.

Once Judge Kaplan made the attorneys' fees ruling, the case developed other issues and problems, and the government dismissed most of the charges against the 16 former partners and employees.

Make a list of the lessons employees and companies can learn from this experience.

Source: Laurie P. Cohen, "In the Crossfire: Prosecutors' Tough New Tactics Turn Firms Against Employees," *Wall Street Journal*, June 4, 2004, A1.

Notes

1. Valerie Bauerlin, "Scrushy Denies Role in HealthSouth Fraud," *Wall Street Journal*, May 21, 2009, p. B4.

2. 15 U.S.C. § 1512.

3. Mr. Duncan withdrew his plea when the Andersen case was decided by the U.S. Supreme Court in Andersen's favor. The government has not pursued prosecution against him.

4. 18 U.S.C. §§ 1831–1839.

5. 41 U.S.C. § 1693.

6. Interestingly, Sarah Drew, the daughter, testified against her mother in the case in exchange for immunity from prosecution. Jennifer Steinhauer, "Woman Guilty in Web Fraud Tied to Suicide," *New York Times*, Nov. 27, 2008, p. A1, A25.

7. U.S. Department of Justice, press release, March 19, 2007, http://www.doj.gov.

8. U.S. Department of Justice, press release #07-161:03, http://www.doj.gov.

9. *Id.*

10. Neil A. Lewis, "Inquiry Threatens Ex-Leader of Security Agency," *New York Times*, August 16, 2007, p. A18.

11. Jane Zhang and Julie Jargon, "Peanut Corp. Emails Cast Harsh Light on Executive," *Wall Street Journal*, February 12, 2009, p. A3.

12. *Id.*

13. *Id.*

14. Ilan Bray and Julie Jargon, "Career in Peanuts Began as a Detour from Oceanography," *Wall Street Journal*, Feb. 19, 2009, p. A6.

Business Torts

Criminal wrongs require guilty parties to pay a debt to society through a fine, imprisonment, and/or community service. However, criminal wrongs also have victims who have suffered financial losses, injuries, and, sometimes, permanent disabilities. Those who are harmed by the conduct of others are the victims of torts. Torts are civil wrongs that provide remedies. This chapter answers these questions: What are the different types of torts? What must you prove to recover for these torts? What are the business and public policy issues in torts and product liability? ■

"Personal sins should not require press releases, and problems within a family shouldn't have to mean public confessions."

Tiger Woods

"One does not seriously attack the expertise of a scientist using the undefined phrase 'Butt-head.'"

Judge Lourdes G. Baird
In dismissing the late Carl Sagan's lawsuit against Apple Computer for its code name change from "Carl Sagan" to "Butt-Head Astronomer"

UPDATE
For up-to-date law and ethics news, go to
mariannejennings.com

CONSIDER...

Alexandra Van Horn, Jonelle Freed, and Lisa Torti smoked and inhaled marijuana together at Ms. Torti's home. They were joined there by Anthony Glen Watson and Dion Ofoegbu, who also joined in on the marijuana. At 10:00 PM, they all headed to a local bar where they drank until 1:30 AM. At 1:30 AM, Ms. Van Horn and Ms. Freed left with Mr. Watson, leaving Ms. Torti to ride with Mr. Ofoegbu. Mr. Watson

struck a curb and then a light pole whilst going 45 mph. After Mr. Watson crashed, both Mr. Ofoegbu and Ms. Torti stopped and got out of their car to render aid. Ms. Torti pulled Ms. Van Horn from the car. Ms. Van Horn had a lacerated liver and damaged vertebrae that rendered Ms. Van Horn paraplegic. She filed suit against Ms. Torti for her negligence in trying to help. Is Ms. Torti liable?

What Is a Tort? Roots of Law and Commerce

Tort comes from the Latin term *tortus,* which means "crooked, dubious, twisted." A **tort** is some type of interference with someone or with someone's property that results in injury to persons or property. For example, using someone else's land without permission is interference with that person's property rights and is the tort of trespass. If you held a concert on someone else's land and the concert crowds destroyed the property's vegetation or left litter that had to be removed, then you have committed the tort of trespass. Tort law provides the basis for recovering the costs of restoring the property damaged by the concertgoers.

Tort Versus Crime

A tort is a private wrong. When a tort is committed, the party who was injured is entitled to collect compensation for damages from the wrongdoer for the private wrong. A crime, on the other hand, is a public wrong and requires the wrongdoer to pay a debt to society through a fine or by going to prison. For example, the crime of assault results in imprisonment, probation, and/or a fine. However, the assault victim could bring suit against the charged assailant to recover damages, such as medical bills, lost wages, and pain and suffering. The suit would be for the tort of assault.

Types of Torts

The three types of tort liability include intentional torts, negligence, and strict tort liability. **Intentional torts** are those that involve deliberate actions. For example, a battery, or hitting another person, is an intentional tort. Hitting someone in the nose deliberately is the tort of battery. Suppose that you stretch your arms in a crowd and you hit a man in the nose and hurt him. You have not committed the tort of battery, but you may have committed the tort of **negligence.** You were carelessly swinging your arms in a crowd of people. Such careless conduct, or actions done without thinking through the consequences, is the tort of negligence. We are still responsible for damages to the nose because when we fail to act cautiously and thoughtfully, we are negligent. **Strict tort liability** does not turn on state of mind or knowledge of possible harm. For example, when contractors use dynamite to raze a building, they have strict liability because the incendiary devices are so risky and consequences so great that we hold them responsible regardless of the precautions they take. Product liability, discussed in Chapter 10, is a form of strict liability. You will see that a company can be held liable for injuries when a customer has misused its product because even the failure to provide enough warnings results in strict liability.

The Intentional Torts

Defamation

Defamation is an untrue statement made by one party to another about a third party. It consists of either slander or libel; slander is oral or spoken defamation, and libel is written (or, in some cases, broadcast) defamation. The elements of defamation are

1. A statement about a person's reputation, honesty, or integrity that is untrue
2. Publication
3. A statement that is directed at a particular person
4. Damages
5. In some cases, proof of malice

Publication

Defamation requires that whatever is said or written be communicated to a third party. An accountant who addresses a group of lawyers at a luncheon meeting and untruthfully states that another accounting firm has been involved in a securities fraud has met the publication element. So has a supplier who notifies other suppliers that a business is insolvent when it is not. The more folks who hear the statement, the greater the defamation damages will be.

CYBERLAW

Internet messages and blog postings meet the publication requirement. They provide instantaneous and international communication, so damages can be substantial.

CONSIDER... 9.1

The law firm of Lavely & Singer has become the law firm that celebrities turn to when they are concerned about a pending story in anything from the *National Enquirer* to the *Wall Street Journal*. Lavely & Singer represented Britney Spears against *US Weekly* in a suit for libel for its publication of a story it ran on a sexually explicit home video that she and her ex-husband made. A California court dismissed the suit, explaining, basically, that given Ms. Spears's reputation it was difficult to defame her. The court said that because Ms. Spears has "put her modern sexuality squarely, and profitably, before the public eye," the publication of such information could not be considered harmful to her reputation, thereby meaning that one of the elements of defamation could not be established. Is the court correct on the Britney Spears decision?

Source: Peter Lattman, "When Celebrities Fear Sting of Publicity, Who Do They Call?" *Wall Street Journal*, December 9, 2006, pp. A1, A6.

Statement about a Particular Person

To qualify as defamation, the statement made must be about an individual or a small enough group that all in the group are affected. For example, the general statement "All accountants are frauds" is too broad to be defamatory. But the statement "All the Andersen audit partners who worked on the Enron accounts were dishonest" is specific enough to meet this requirement.

Product disparagement is defamation of a product. For example, a *Consumer Reports* evaluation of a product that is not truthful about its qualities or abilities would be product disparagement. In *Bose Corporation v. Consumers Union of United States, Inc.*, 466 U.S. 485 (1984), the U.S. Supreme Court dealt with whether product disparagement of the Bose speaker system actually occurred when *Consumer Reports* described individual sounds from the speakers, such as those of violins, as growing to gigantic proportions. The court held that even though Consumers Union had not given the Bose speakers a favorable review, it also did not say anything false about them in its negative review. There was, as a result, no disparagement (see Chapter 15).

Damages

The person who is defamed must be able to establish damages, such as lost business, lost profits, lost advertising, lost reputation, or some economic effect that has resulted from the defamatory statements.

Malice

Malice must be proved in defamation cases that involve public figures. Public figures are those voluntarily in the public eye, such as elected officials, recording artists, actors, sports figures, and media magnets (think Lindsay Lohan). However, someone who is injured by Paris Hilton's driving and experiences the resulting extensive media coverage is not a public figure simply because Paris-watchers brought him or her into the limelight. Such individuals would become public figures only if they used their newfound fame to launch their own careers in the spotlight. Kato Kaelin, for example, was a media hot-spot witness in the O. J. Simpson double-murder trial, but not a public figure. He became a public figure when he followed up his trial testimony with voluntary and paid appearances and interviews. An example of someone who was not a voluntary public figure is the late Richard Jewell, the man who was labeled by several news sources as being a suspect or focus of the investigation into the blast that resulted in two deaths and hundreds of injuries at Olympic Park in Atlanta during the 1996 Summer Olympics. Mr. Jewell settled a defamation case with NBC without having to prove malice on its part because he was not a public figure, only a person with notoriety. As a result of the Jewell case, you will note that media sources and law enforcement officials no longer refer to individuals as "suspects." The term that allows them to escape defamation liability is "person of interest." That label is used until the individual is charged or law enforcement agents clear the individual. In addition, even after charges are brought, media sources phrase their descriptions carefully by stating, "He is alleged to have embezzled $5 million from his employer over three years," or "He is charged with the crime of embezzlement."

Malice provides the balance between personal rights and the protections the First Amendment provides for the media. Malice requires proof that the information was published or broadcast knowing that it was false or with reckless disregard for whether it was true or false.

CONSIDER...   9.2

The basis for Richard Jewell's suit against NBC was the following sentences from a broadcast by Tom Brokaw: "Look, they probably got enough to arrest him. They probably have got enough to try him." Mr. Brokaw finished his on-air commentary by adding, "Everyone, please understand absolutely he is only the focus of this investigation—he is not even a suspect yet."

Decide whether Jewell was defamed by the remarks. Sadly, Mr. Jewell passed away in 2007 at the age of 44 from a heart attack.

The Defenses to Defamation

Truth.   A statement may be damaging, but, if it is the truth, it is not defamation. For example, you could publicly disclose that your boss took LSD during the late 1960s when he was in college. The remark might hurt your employer's reputation, but if it is the truth, it is not the tort of defamation despite the harm it may do to him.

Opinion and Analysis.   One of the current issues in defamation cases is whether the statements made are protected when they are a columnist's analysis of a situation. Courts are trying to determine what level of protection is given for viewpoints when someone objects to the conclusions drawn rather than the statements of fact. A fine line is often all that separates statements of fact from expressions of opinion. In business publications, those opinions can be devastating to companies and their stock performance. In *Wilkow v Forbes, Inc.,* 241 F.3d 552 (7th Cir. 2001), the court dealt with an opinion column in *Forbes* magazine. According to the article, a partnership led by Marc Wilkow "stiffed" the bank, paying only $55 million on a $93 million loan while retaining ownership of the building.

The court held that if it is plain that the columnist "is expressing a subjective view, an interpretation, a theory, conjecture, or surmise, rather than claiming to be in possession of objectively verifiable facts, the statement is not actionable." "Stiffing," as the court noted, may "drip of disapproval," but it is an interpretation of values and is not defamation.

Privileged Speech.   Some speech is privileged; that is, strong public interest supports protecting the speech regardless of whether it is true. For example, members of Congress enjoy an **absolute privilege** when they are speaking on the floor of the Senate or House because of a strong public policy to encourage free debate of issues. The same is true of judicial proceedings; in order to encourage people to come forward with the truth, witnesses enjoy an absolute privilege when testifying about the matters at hand.

There are also some **qualified privileges,** or privileges that provide limited liability for defamation. In nearly all states, there is a qualified privilege for those who have a moral obligation to speak. These types of privilege statutes provide protection for whistle-blowers (see Chapter 17), in that a controlled (limited) disclosure of information made in good faith will not subject a businessperson to liability for defamation. However, verification of the truth of such statements is critical.

Another qualified privilege exists for former employers when discussing former employees. (See For the Manager's Desk on p. 291.)

For the Manager's Desk

Re: Those Glowing Letters of Recommendation vs. Truth vs. Defamation

One area of legal complexity is the intersection of letters of recommendation, the duty to disclose dangerous conduct by former employees, and defamation. Most employers follow a practice of simply disclosing for new employers whether a former employee in fact worked at their company, and for how long. In order to avoid liability for disclosing negative information in a defamation action by the former employee, employers are hesitant to offer any additional information beyond these perfunctory facts.

However, such an approach is not without risk. *In Randi W. v Muroc Joint Unified School District,* 929 P.2d 582 (Cal. 1997), a California court grappled with the problems that arose from glowing letters of recommendation from a former employer. In the case, Randi W., a 13-year-old minor who attended the Livingston Middle School, was molested and sexually touched on February 1, 1992, by Robert Gadams, who served as vice principal at the school. When her parents filed suit against the school district, they uncovered some disturbing facts.

Mr. Gadams had previously been employed at three other school districts:

- Mendota Unified School District (1985–1988). During his time of employment there, Mr. Gadams had been investigated and reprimanded for improper conduct with female junior high students, including giving them back massages, making sexual remarks to them, and being involved in "sexual situations" with them. Gilbert Rossette, an official with Mendota, provided a letter of recommendation for Mr. Gadams in May 1990. The recommendation was extensive and referred to Mr. Gadams's "genuine concern" for students, his "outstanding rapport" with everyone, and concluded, "I wouldn't hesitate to recommend Mr. Gadams for any position."

- Mr. Gadams had also previously been employed at the Tranquility High School District and Golden Plains Unified District (1987–1990). Richard Cole, an administrator at Golden Plains, also provided a letter of recommendation that listed Mr. Gadams's "favorable" qualities and concluded that he "would recommend him for almost any administrative position he wishes to pursue." At that school, Mr. Gadams had been the subject of various parents' complaints, including that he "led a panty raid, made sexual overtures to students, sexual remarks to students." Mr. Cole also knew that Mr. Gadams had resigned under pressure because of these sexual misconduct charges.

- Mr. Gadams's last place of employment (1990–1991) before Livingston was Muroc Unified School District, where disciplinary actions were taken against him for sexual harassment. When allegations of "sexual touching" of female students were made, Mr. Gadams was forced to resign from Muroc. Nonetheless, Gary Rice and David Malcolm, officials at Muroc, provided a letter of recommendation for Mr. Gadams that described him as "an upbeat, enthusiastic administrator who relates well to the students," and who was responsible "in large part," for making Boron Junior High School (located in Muroc) "a safe, orderly and clean environment for students and staff." The letter concluded that they recommended Mr. Gadams "for an assistant principalship or equivalent position without reservation."

The court held the districts liable to Randi W. and her guardians for their glowing letters, which withheld information important for the safety of children at the schools where Mr. Gadams had worked. The districts' issuance of glowing recommendations when there was troubling information resulted in liability.

Nearly all states provide a qualified privilege for letters of recommendation. A survey indicates that without such protection, disclosures about violent tendencies will not be made and the risk to employees at a new firm is high.

Under this privilege, employers are not liable for defamation if the information they disclose about a former employee is provided in "good faith" or "absence of bad faith." The statutes vary in their language from state to state but they do provide immunity for factual statements. For example, a letter on Gadams that said, "The man is a child molester," would not enjoy immunity. However, a letter from a principal that said, "Several parents complained about Mr. Gadams's inappropriate touching of their children," would enjoy the statutory protection. Also adding to the complexity of the reference issue is a U.S. Supreme Court decision in which the court held that giving a negative reference on a former employee who has sued the company for discrimination can be considered retaliatory and a violation of Title VII (see Chapter 19) [*Robinson v Shell Oil Co.,* 519 U.S. 337 (1997)].

Most employers do not rely on the immunity, and opt to disclose nothing other than the time of employment. Fifty-four percent of all employers indicate they would not disclose violent behavior when asked for a reference. However, keep the *Gadams* case in mind, because there can be liability for misleading other employers into hiring those who ultimately cause harm that was predictable based on the facts the previous employer knew. In 2010, Dr. Amy Bishop, a professor at the University of Alabama, was accused of killing three of her colleagues in a dispute over her being denied tenure. As the case was investigated, law enforcement agencies discovered a history of queries about Dr. Bishop over everything from alleged threats to others at work to questions surrounding what was then called the "accidental" shooting of her brother. None of this sordid past had been disclosed when she applied for the position at the University of Alabama. The risks of nondisclosure are often life and death matters.

CONSIDER...   9.3

Paul Calden, a 33-year-old, low-level manager, was fired from his job at Allstate Insurance Company in St. Petersburg, Florida, for carrying a gun to his job. His supervisors at Allstate would later describe him as a "total lunatic."

Mr. Calden applied for a job with Fireman's Fund Insurance in Tampa, Florida. Fireman's Fund contacted the Allstate offices for a reference. Allstate sent a letter signed by a vice president that was neutral in its description of Mr. Calden and did not disclose the true reasons for his termination. Mr. Calden had threatened litigation, there was some fear among the employees about him, and Allstate had agreed to a four-month severance package despite his having worked at Allstate for only nine months. Allstate also agreed to draft and send the neutral letter.

After Mr. Calden was terminated by Fireman's Fund, he shot and killed three executives of the company while they were having lunch at a café. One of the executives' wives filed suit against Fireman's Fund and Allstate. The suit against Allstate was based on its failure to disclose Mr. Calden's bizarre behavior and the risk that he was in the workplace.

Allstate defended its actions on the grounds that the average verdict in a defamation suit by a former employee against his former employer for a job reference was $57,000. In one Florida case, a former employee was awarded $25 million in damages. Allstate argued that the cost to businesses would be too high. Is Allstate liable? Be sure to discuss the privilege, defamation, and reference issues involved.

Another qualified privilege applies when public figures are involved in the defamation. For public figures, the media also have a qualified privilege. If the news organization prints a retraction of a published statement, it has a defense to defamation. Perhaps one of the most famous libel cases addressing the defense of the media privilege involved Carol Burnett and a story about her printed by the *National Enquirer*. The case decision on this incident follows in *Burnett v National Enquirer* (Case 9.1).

CASE 9.1   *Burnett v National Enquirer, Inc.*
144 Cal. App. 3d 991 (1983)

Only the *Enquirer* Didn't Know for Sure:
Carol Burnett, Henry Kissinger, and Defamation

FACTS

On March 2, 1976, the *National Enquirer* (appellant) published in its weekly publication a "gossip column" headlined "Carol Burnett and Henry K. in Row" that included the following four-sentence item:

> *In a Washington restaurant, a boisterous Carol Burnett had a loud argument with another diner, Henry Kissinger. Then she traipsed around the place offering everyone a bite of her dessert. But Carol really raised eyebrows when she accidentally knocked a glass of wine over one diner and started giggling instead of apologizing. The guy wasn't amused and "accidentally" spilled a glass of water over Carol's dress.*

Ms. Burnett (respondent) filed suit against the *Enquirer* alleging that the item was entirely false

and libelous after the *Enquirer* printed the following retraction:

> *An item in this column on March 2 erroneously reported that Carol Burnett had an argument with Henry Kissinger at a Washington restaurant and became boisterous, disturbing other guests. We understand these events did not occur and we are sorry for any embarrassment our report may have caused Miss Burnett.*

After a jury trial, Ms. Burnett was awarded $300,000 compensatory damages and $1,300,000 punitive damages. The trial court reduced the amounts to $50,000 compensatory and $750,000 punitive damages. The *Enquirer* appealed.

JUDICIAL OPINION

ROTH, Presiding Justice

Prior to addressing the merits of appellant's contentions and in aid of our disposition, we set out the following further facts pertaining to the publication complained of. . . .

On the occasion giving rise to the gossip column item hereinabove quoted, respondent, her husband and three friends were having dinner at the Rive Gauche restaurant in the Georgetown section of Washington, D.C. The date was January 29, 1976. Respondent was in the area as a result of being invited to be a performing guest at the White House. In the course of the dinner, respondent had two or three glasses of wine. She was not inebriated. She engaged in banter with a young couple seated at a table next to hers, who had just become engaged or were otherwise celebrating. When curiosity was expressed about respondent's dessert, apparently a chocolate souffle, respondent saw to it the couple were provided with small amounts of it on plates they had passed to her table for the purpose. Perhaps from having witnessed the gesture, a family behind respondent then offered to exchange some of their baked Alaska for a portion of the souffle, and they, too, were similarly accommodated. As respondent was later leaving the restaurant, she was introduced by a friend to Henry Kissinger, who was dining at another table, and after a brief conversation, respondent left with her party.

There was no "row" with Mr. Kissinger, nor any argument between the two, and what conversation they had was not loud or boisterous. Respondent never "traipsed around the place offering everyone a bite of her dessert," nor was she otherwise boisterous, nor did she spill wine on anyone, nor did anyone spill water on her and there was no factual basis for the comment she ". . . started giggling instead of apologizing."

The impetus for what was printed about the dinner was provided to the writer of the item, Brian Walker, by Couri Hays, a freelance tipster paid by the National Enquirer on an ad hoc basis for information supplied by him which was ultimately published by it, who advised Walker he had been informed respondent had taken her Grand Marnier souffle around the restaurant in a boisterous or flamboyant manner and given bites of it to various other people; that he had further but unverified information respondent had been involved in the wine–water spilling incident; but that, according to his sources, respondent was "specifically, emphatically" not drunk. No mention was made by Hays of anything involving respondent and Henry Kissinger.

Having received this report, Walker spoke with Steve Tinney, whose name appears at the top of the National Enquirer gossip column, expressing doubts whether Hays could be trusted. Tinney voiced his accord with those doubts. Walker then asked Gregory Lyon, a National Enquirer reporter, to verify what Walker had been told by Hays. Lyon's inquiry resulted only in his verifying respondent had shared dessert with other patrons and that she and Kissinger had carried on a good-natured conversation at the restaurant.

In spite of the fact no one had told him respondent and Henry Kissinger had engaged in an argument, that the wine-water spilling story remained as totally unverified hearsay, that the dessert sharing incident was only partially bolstered, and that respondent was not under any view of the question inebriated, Walker composed the quoted item and approved the "row" headline.

The National Enquirer is a publication whose masthead claims the "Largest Circulation of Any Paper in America." It is a member of the American Newspaper Publishers Association. It subscribes to the Reuters News Service. Its staff calls themselves newspaper reporters.

By the same token the National Enquirer is designated as a magazine or periodical in eight mass media directories and upon the request and written representation of its general manager in 1960 that "In view of the feature content and general appearance [of the publication], which differ markedly from those of a newspaper . . ." its classification as a newspaper was changed to that of magazine by the Audit Bureau of Circulation. It does not subscribe to the Associated Press or United Press International news services. According to a statement by its Senior Editor it is not a newspaper and its content is based on a consistent formula of "how to" stories, celebrity or medical or personal improvement stories, gossip items, and TV column items, together with material from certain other subjects. It provides little or no current coverage of subjects such as politics, sports, or crime, does not attribute content to wire services, and in general does not make reference to time. Normal "lead time" for its subject matter is one to three weeks. Its owner allowed it did not generate stories "day to day as a daily newspaper does."

At appellant's request, the trial court herein made its determination after hearing and based on extensive evidence that the National Enquirer was not a newspaper for purposes of the application of Civil Code section 48a.

Seen in this light, the essential question is not then whether any publication is properly denominated a magazine or by some other designation, but simply whether it ought to be characterized as a newspaper or not.

Having so decided, we are also satisfied to conclude without extensive recitation of the evidence that

CONTINUED

the trial court consistently with the foregoing rationale correctly determined the *National Enquirer* should not be deemed a newspaper for the purposes of the instant litigation.

Nearly twenty years ago, it was announced in *New York Times Co. v Sullivan*, 376 U.S. 254 (1964) that:

> The constitutional guarantees [relating to protected speech] require, we think, a federal rule that prohibits a public official from recovering damages for a defamatory falsehood relating to his official conduct unless he proves that the statement was made with "actual malice"—that is, with knowledge that it was false or with reckless disregard of whether it was false or not.

[W]e are of the opinion the award to respondent of $750,000 in order to punish and deter appellant was not justified.

In so concluding, we are persuaded the evidence fairly showed that while appellant's representatives knew that part of the publication complained of was probably false and that the remainder of it in substance might very well be, appellant was nevertheless determined to present to a vast national audience in printed form statements which in their precise import and clear implication were defamatory, thereby exposing respondent to contempt, ridicule and obloquy, and tending to injure her in her occupation. We are also satisfied that even when it was thought necessary to alleviate the wrong resulting from the false statements it had placed before the public, the retraction proffered was evasive, incomplete and by any standard, legally insufficient. In other words, we have no doubt the conduct of appellant respecting the libel was reprehensible and was undertaken with the kind of improper motive which supports the imposition of punitive damages.

Nevertheless, evidence on the point of appellant's wealth adequately established appellant's net worth to be some $2.6 million and its net income for the period under consideration to be about $1.56 million, such that the penalty award, even when substantially reduced by the trial court based on its conclusion the jury's compensatory verdict was "clearly excessive and . . . not supported by substantial evidence," continued to constitute about 35% of the former and nearly half the latter.

The judgment is affirmed except that the punitive damage award herein is vacated and the matter is remanded for a new trial on that issue only, provided that if respondent shall, within 30 days from the date of our remittitur, file with the clerk of this court and serve upon appellant a written consent to a reduction of the punitive damage award to the sum of $150,000, the judgment will be modified to award respondent punitive damages in that amount, and so as modified affirmed in its entirety. . . .

CASE QUESTIONS

1. Was malice established in the case? Why was it necessary to establish malice?

2. Is the *National Enquirer* a newspaper for purposes of the protection of the privilege?

3. Were the damages reduced? To what? Why?

4. Should tabloids like the *National Enquirer* enjoy the protection of the privilege?

CONSIDER...   9.4

The *National Enquirer* published a supposed interview with actor Clint Eastwood. The interview had never taken place, and Mr. Eastwood said the publication of such an interview in a sensationalist newspaper made it seem as if he was "washed up as a movie star." Could Mr. Eastwood recover for the publication of the fake interview? What tort has occurred, if any?

THINK: Recall the elements for defamation: a false statement that impugns the integrity of a specific person.

APPLY: We don't have the content of the interview, but it is false that the interview occurred, and Mr. Eastwood argues that just the suggestion that he would be interviewed by the *National Enquirer* harms his career.

ANSWER: Mr. Eastwood took the case to trial and won, precisely because no interview ever took place and the content and even the suggestion of him granting an interview were false.

Contract Interference

The tort of **contract interference** or **tortious interference with contracts** or tortious interference occurs when parties are not allowed the freedom to contract without interference from third parties.

A basic definition for tortious interference is that someone intentionally persuades another to break a contract already in existence. Bryan A. Garner, the author of *Tortious Interference*, offers the following examples: "Say you had a contract with Joe Blow, and I for some reason tried to get you to break that contract. Or say that Pepsi has an exclusive contract with a hotel chain to carry Pepsi products, and Coke tries to get the hotel to carry Coke despite that contract. That's tortious interference."

One of the most famous cases involving the question of tortious interference actually relates to interference with an inheritance. A former Playmate of the Year, the late Anna Nicole Smith (a.k.a. Vicki Lynn Marshall), married 90-year-old J. Howard Marshall II, a wealthy oil company owner. Mr. Marshall died shortly after, leaving a $1.6 billion estate. Ms. Smith was given $90 million by Mr. Marshall's son for what Ms. Smith proved was his interference with the execution of a will by the late Mr. Marshall that would have allowed her to be an heir [*In re Marshall*, 253 B.R. 550, 553 (Bankr. C.D. Cal. 2000), and certain issues in the case made it to the U.S. Supreme Court, where Ms. Smith was in the courtroom for the oral argument of the case. *Marshall v Marshall*, 545 U.S. 1165 (2005)]. Following this decision, Ms. Smith's estate (she died before the final lower court decision following a remand from the U.S. Supreme Court) received nothing from her husband's estate. The case is again on appeal.

False Imprisonment

False imprisonment is often referred to as "the shopkeeper's tort" because it generally occurs as a result of a shoplifting accusation in a store. **False imprisonment** is the detention of a person for any period of time (even a few minutes) against his will. No physical harm need result; the imprisoned party can collect minimal damages simply for being imprisoned without consent. Because shopkeepers need the opportunity to investigate matters when someone is suspected of shoplifting, the tort of false imprisonment does carry the defense of the **shopkeeper's privilege.** This privilege allows a shopkeeper to detain a suspected shoplifter for a reasonable period of time while the matter or incident is investigated. In most states, the shopkeeper must have a reasonable basis for keeping the person; that is, the shopkeeper must have reason to suspect the individual even if it turns out later that the individual has an explanation or did not do what the shopkeeper suspected.

CONSIDER...   9.5

Apply the following Florida statutes to the facts that then follow.
   Section 812.015(5), Florida Statutes (1989), provides:

A merchant, merchant's employee, or farmer who takes a person into custody, as provided in subsection (3) . . . shall not be criminally or civilly liable for false arrest or false imprisonment when the merchant, merchant's employee, or farmer has probable cause to believe that the person committed retail theft or farm theft.

CONTINUED

Subsection (3)(a) provides:

A law enforcement officer, a merchant, a merchant's employee, or a farmer who has probable cause to believe that retail or farm theft has been committed by a person and that he can recover the property by taking the person into custody may, for the purpose of attempting to effect such recovery or for prosecution, take the person into custody and detain him in a reasonable manner for a reasonable length of time. . . . In the event the merchant, merchant's employee, or farmer takes the person into custody, a law enforcement officer shall be called to the scene immediately after the person has been taken into custody.

Lyndon Silva was stopped by Kevin Rivera, an off-duty Houston police officer working as a security officer for Dillard's department store. Mr. Silva was leaving Dillard's at the time. However, before questioning him, Mr. Rivera placed Mr. Silva on the floor, handcuffed him, and then dumped three shirts from his bag onto the floor. He had no receipts in the bag, but Mr. Silva asked Mr. Rivera to check his car for the receipts because he was returning the shirts. Mr. Rivera refused. Mr. Rivera then took Mr. Silva to the offices upstairs and detained him while they waited for the police. Mr. Silva was again placed on the floor while Mr. Rivera switched his handcuffs for those of the police. Mr. Silva was later able to produce a receipt.

Is Dillard's protected by the shopkeeper's privilege? [*Dillard Department Stores, Inc. v Silva*, 106 S.W.3d 789 (Tex. App. 2003).]

Intentional Infliction of Emotional Distress

This tort imposes liability for conduct that goes beyond all bounds of decency and results in emotional distress in the harmed individual. One of the difficulties with this tort is that the only damage the plaintiff is required to prove is that of emotional distress. Although "pain and suffering" damages have been awarded for some time in negligence actions in which the plaintiff recovers damages for physical and property injuries, the awarding of damages for mental distress alone is a relatively new phenomenon. However, the tort of **intentional infliction of emotional distress** has been used quite often by debtors who are harassed by creditors and collection agencies in their attempts to collect funds.

Invasion of Privacy

The intentional tort of *invasion of privacy* is actually three different torts.

1. Intrusion into the Plaintiff's Private Affairs. This tort occurs when photographers or others stalk individuals, such as in *Galella v Onassis*, 353 F. Supp. 196 (S.D.N.Y. 1972). In the case, the late Mrs. Jacqueline Kennedy Onassis brought suit against Ron Galella, a photojournalist, for invasion of her privacy. As a result of the case, Mr. Galella was ordered to remain at least 50 yards from Mrs. Onassis and 100 yards from her children.

2. Public Disclosure of Private Facts. This tort occurs when a company makes information about an employee public, such as disclosing that a CEO used LSD during college or the details of an affair between employees. The information disclosed is not defamation because it is true, but it may well be the tort of invasion of privacy. Public disclosure protections are now a statutory issue because of evolving technologies such as e-mail and Internet access. Computer-stored information also carries ease of access. But ease of access does not mean that privacy rights are lost. Statutes now control use of and rights related to computer-stored information One such statute is the **Health Insurance Portability and Accountability Act of 1996 (HIPAA) (42 U.S.C. 1320d-1320d-8)**. HIPAA controls how medical information is collected, used, and conveyed. For example, doctors must be careful that computer screens of their office personnel are not visible by other patients. HIPAA has resulted in the complex paperwork we sign when we receive medical care that discloses our rights to access our records. It also led to the marked lines at pharmacies behind which we must stand so that we cannot overhear the pharmacy worker's discussions with other customers.

HIPAA has made privacy front and center and introduced some new complexity. One patient services director explained HIPAA's impact as follows: "In the old days, a social workers could pick up the phone and ask Meals on Wheels to deliver lunch to Mrs. Jones five days a week. Under the federal rules, we'll now have to get a release from Mrs. Jones so we can tell Meals on Wheels that, as a diabetic with cardiac problems, she has special dietary needs."[2]

3. Appropriation of Another's Name, Likeness, or Image for Commercial Advantage. This final form of the privacy tort involves using someone's name, likeness, or voice for commercial advantage without his or her permission constitutes the tort of **unauthorized appropriation.** For example, if a gas station used your picture in its window to show you as a satisfied customer, you might not be harmed greatly but your privacy is invaded because you have the right to decide when, how, and where your name, face, image, or voice will be used. *Midler v Ford Motor Co.* (Case 9.2) addresses the unauthorized appropriation of a singer's voice.

CASE 9.2	*Midler v Ford Motor Co.* 849 F.2d 460 (9th Cir. 1988)

Ford to Bette, "Do You Wanna Dance?"; Bette to Ford, "Not Really!"

FACTS

In 1985, Ford Motor Company and its advertising agency, Young & Rubicam, Inc., advertised the Ford Lincoln Mercury with a series of nineteen 30- or 60-second television commercials in its "The Yuppie Campaign." The aim was to make an emotional connection with Yuppies, bringing back memories of when they were in college. The agency tried to get the "original people," that is, the singers who had popularized the songs, to sing them. When those efforts failed, the agency decided to go with "sound-alikes."

When Young & Rubicam was preparing the Yuppie Campaign, it presented the commercial to its client by playing an edited version of Bette Midler (plaintiff/appellant) singing "Do You Want to Dance?" taken from the 1973 Midler album, *The Divine Miss M.*

CONTINUED

After Ford accepted the idea and the commercial, Young & Rubicam contacted Ms. Midler's manager, Jerry Edelstein. The conversation went as follows: "Hello, I am Craig Hazen from Young & Rubicam. I am calling you to find out if Bette Midler would be interested in doing . . . ?" Mr. Edelstein: "Is it a commercial?" "Yes." "We are not interested."

Undeterred, Young & Rubicam sought out Ula Hedwig, who had been one of the "Harlettes," the backup singers for Midler for ten years. Ms. Hedwig was told by Young & Rubicam that "they wanted someone who could sound like Bette Midler's recording of ['Do You Want to Dance?']." She was asked to make a demo tape. She made an a cappella demo and got the job. At the direction of Young & Rubicam, Ms. Hedwig made a record for the commercial. She first had to listen to Ms. Midler's recording of it and was then told to "sound as much as possible like the Bette Midler record."

After the commercial aired, Ms. Midler was told by a number of people that it sounded exactly like her. Ms. Hedwig was told by friends that they thought it was Ms. Midler.

Ms. Midler, a nationally known actress and singer, won a Grammy in 1973 as Best New Artist of the Year. She has had both gold and platinum records. She was nominated in 1979 for an Academy Award for Best Female Actress in *The Rose,* in which she portrayed a pop singer. *Newsweek* described her as an "outrageously original singer/comedienne." *Time* hailed her as "a legend" and "the most dynamic and poignant singer-actress of her time."

Ms. Midler filed suit against Ford and Young & Rubicam for appropriation. Young & Rubicam had a license from the song's copyright holder to use it. Neither the name nor the picture of Ms. Midler was used in the commercial. The district court entered judgment for Ford and Young & Rubicam, and Ms. Midler appealed.

JUDICIAL OPINION

NOONAN, Circuit Judge

At issue in this case is only the protection of Midler's voice. The district court described the defendant's conduct as that "of the average thief." They decided, "If we can't buy it, we'll take it." The court nonetheless believed there was no legal principle preventing imitation of Midler's voice and so gave summary judgment for the defendants.

The First Amendment protects much of what the media do in the reproduction of likenesses or sounds. A primary value is freedom of speech and press. The purpose of the media's use of a person's identity is central. If the purpose is "informative or cultural" the use is immune; "if it serves no such function but merely exploits the individual portrayed, immunity will not be granted." It is in the context of these First Amendment and federal copyright distinctions that we address the present appeal.

Nancy Sinatra once sued Goodyear Tire and Rubber Company on the basis of an advertising campaign by Young & Rubicam featuring "These Boots Are Made for Walkin'," a song closely identified with her; the female singers of the commercial were alleged to have imitated her voice and style and to have dressed and looked like her. The basis of Nancy Sinatra's complaint was unfair competition; she claimed that the song and the arrangement had acquired "a secondary meaning" which, under California law, was protectible. This court noted that the defendants "had paid a very substantial sum to the copyright proprietor to obtain the license for the use of the song and all of its arrangements." To give Sinatra damages for their use of the song would clash with federal copyright law. Summary judgment for the defendants was affirmed. If Midler were claiming a secondary meaning to "Do You Want to Dance" or seeking to prevent the defendants from using that song, she would fail like Sinatra. But that is not this case. Midler does not seek damages for Ford's use of "Do You Want to Dance," and thus her claim is not preempted by federal copyright law. What is put forward as protectible here is more personal than any work of authorship.

Bert Lahr once sued Adell Chemical Co. for selling Lestoil by means of a commercial in which an imitation of Lahr's voice accompanied a cartoon of a duck. Lahr alleged that his style of vocal delivery was distinctive in pitch, accent, inflection, and sounds. The First Circuit held that Lahr had stated a cause of action for unfair competition, that it could be found "that defendant's conduct saturated plaintiff's audience, curtailing his market." That case is more like this one.

A voice is as distinctive and personal as a face. The human voice is one of the most palpable ways identity is manifested. We are all aware that a friend is at once known by a few words on the phone. At a philosophical level it has been observed that with the sound of a voice, "the other stands before me." *A fortiori,* these observations hold true of singing, especially singing by a singer of renown. The singer manifests herself in the song. To impersonate her voice is to pirate her identity.

We need not and do not go so far as to hold that every imitation of a voice to advertise merchandise is actionable. We hold only that when a distinctive voice of a professional singer that is widely known is deliberately imitated in order to sell a product, the sellers have appropriated what is not theirs and have committed a tort in California. Midler has made a showing, sufficient to defeat summary judgment, that the defendants here for their own profit in selling their products did appropriate part of her identity.

CASE QUESTIONS

1. In what context was Ms. Midler's voice sought?

2. Was there some confusion about who was singing in the commercial?

3. What is the difference between this case and the Nancy Sinatra case? Between this case and the Bert Lahr case?

4. Was the use of Ms. Midler's voice unfair competition? Was it appropriation?

Outcome: Ms. Midler's case was tried, and she recovered $400,000 from the defendants in October 1989.

CONSIDER... 9.6

Ads on Times Square that feature well-known personalities clad in brands are not unusual. However, the building-size photo of President Obama in a Weatherproof Garment Company jacket in an ad touting the company's apparel was out of the ordinary. The ad caught the attention of more than the millions filing through the public square. The office of White House Counsel also took note. "The White House has a longstanding policy disapproving of the use of the president's name and likeness for commercial purposes."[3] Mr. Obama had not granted permission for use of his photo.

The photo used in the ad was one taken while the president was at the Great Wall of China in November. Freddie Stollmack, president of Weatherproof Garment Company, spotted the photo in the news and, using a magnifying glass, was able to identify the company's logo and zipper. The company did pay the licensing fees for use of the photo, one taken by the Associated Press (AP). AP, however, noted that it is the user's responsibility to obtain permission and clearances for how the photo is used. The *New York Times*, the *New York Post*, and *Women's Wear Daily* turned down the presidential ads Weatherproof had tried to place with them.

Weatherproof is known for its publicity-grabbing advertising techniques. In 2008 it issued a press release touting its unique approach of running the shortest ads on the Super Bowl—2 seconds. A later press release confirmed that no ad would be run because 2-second ads are not available during the Super Bowl. In 2006, Weatherproof photographed company representatives putting a coat on the Naked Cowboy, a well-known street performer in New York City.

The White House legal counsel had its hands full with ads because during the week prior to the jacket hoopla People for the Ethical Treatment of Animals (PETA) ran an anti-fur ad that featured Michelle Obama on billboards in the Washington, D.C., area. Mrs. Obama had also not given permission. The White House did contact PETA about the ad but did not discuss whether the parties had reached a resolution.

What are the rights of those whose images or likenesses are used for commercial purposes without their permission? Is there something different about public figures? What about First Amendment issues? Could Weatherproof argue that it was simply revealing what type of coat the president was wearing, just as newspapers reveal which designers the First Lady uses for her wardrobe? Evaluate the ethics of PETA and Weatherproof in their use of the First Family's images.

Negligence

The tort of **negligence** is one that applies in a variety of circumstances, but it is always used when the conduct of one party did not live up to a certain minimal standard of care we are all expected to use in driving, in our work, and in the care of our property. Negligence imposes liability on us when we are careless. The elements of and defenses to negligence are covered next.

Element One: The Duty

Each of us has the duty to act like an **ordinary and reasonably prudent person** in all circumstances. We do not always live up to the standard of the ordinary and reasonably prudent person; when we do not, we are negligent. The standard of the ordinary and reasonably prudent person is not always what everyone else does or what the law provides. For example, suppose you are driving on a curvy highway late at night and it is raining quite heavily. The posted speed limit is 45 mph. However, the ordinary and reasonably prudent person will not drive 45 mph because the road and the weather conditions dictate that slower driving is more appropriate. The level of care imposed on us by the ordinary and reasonably prudent person standard is one that requires an examination of all conditions and circumstances surrounding an event that leads to an injury. Many negligence cases struggle with the difficult task of determining whether a duty exists.

Duties, for purposes of negligence actions, can arise because of an underlying statute. Every traffic law carries a criminal penalty (fine and/or imprisonment) for violations of it. However, that law imposes a duty of obedience. A violation of that law is also a breach of duty for purposes of a civil or negligence action. When you run a red light, you have not only committed a crime; you have also breached a duty and are liable for injuries and damages resulting from that breach.

Professionals such as doctors, lawyers, and dentists have the duty of practicing their professions at the level of a reasonable professional. Failure to do so is a breach of duty and a basis for malpractice (negligence by professionals) lawsuits.

Landowners owe duties to people who enter their property. For example, the duty to trespassers, such as thieves, is not to intentionally injure them. Placing mantraps would be a breach of this duty.

There are also the duties we owe each other as fellow journeymen in society. However, those duties that are not defined by statute are becoming more difficult to define and impose. There is a difficult balance courts deal with as they define duty, and what constitutes negligence is fulfilling those duties. There are only a few states that impose a duty to stop and help, but all states provide some form of immunity for those who stop to help but make mistakes in offering their assistance. The *Van Horn v Watson* case deals with these complex issues of duty and provides the answer for the opening "Consider."

CASE 9.3

Van Horn v Watson
197 P.3d 164 (Cal. 2008)

Tugging on the Injured While Loaded

FACTS

On October 31, 2004, Alexandra Van Horn (plaintiff), Jonelle Freed, and Lisa Torti smoked and inhaled marijuana together at Ms. Torti's home. They were joined

there by Anthony Glen Watson and Dion Ofoegbu, who also joined in on the marijuana. At 10:00 PM, they all headed to a local bar where they drank until 1:30 AM. At 1:30 AM, Ms. Van Horn and Ms. Freed left with Mr. Watson, leaving Ms. Torti to ride with Mr. Ofoegbu. Mr. Watson struck a curb and then a light pole whilst going 45 mph. After Mr. Watson crashed, both Mr. Ofoegbu and Ms. Torti stopped and got out of their car to render aid. Mr. Watson got out of the car by himself, Mr. Ofoegbu helped Ms. Freed out by opening a door for her, and Ms. Torti pulled Ms. Van Horn from the car. Ms. Van Horn said Ms. Torti pulled on her arm and dragged her from the car like a "rag doll."

Ms. Torti testified that the crashed car was smoking and that she felt she should save Ms. Van Horn before flames ensued. Emergency personnel arrived moments later. Ms. Van Horn had a lacerated liver and damaged vertebrae that rendered her paraplegic. Ms. Van Horn filed suit claiming that Ms. Torti's pulling her from the wreck contributed to her paralysis. Ms. Van Horn also filed suit against all other party animals riding along in the two vehicles for their negligence. Ms. Torti claimed immunity under California's Good Samaritan statute.

Ms. Van Horn alleged that Ms. Torti was negligent in pulling her from the car and not waiting for trained personnel. There were differing accounts on whether the car was smoking and if there were flames. In other words, the danger to Van Horn was not clear. In fact, given the evening's activities, not one of them was operating in anything less than a fog at the time of the accident.

The trial court granted summary judgment for Ms. Torti on the grounds that she enjoyed immunity from suit for negligence under the California Good Samaritan law. The Court of Appeal reversed, holding that the Good Samaritan law applied only to those rendering medical care, and that Torti had not provided medical care. Ms. Torti and the others appealed.

JUDICIAL OPINION

MORENO, Justice

Section 1799.102 provides, "No person who in good faith, and not for compensation, renders emergency care at the scene of an emergency shall be liable for any civil damages resulting from any act or omission. The scene of an emergency shall not include emergency departments and other places where medical care is usually offered." The parties identify two possible constructions of this provision: Torti urges us to conclude that it broadly applies to both nonmedical and medical care rendered at the scene of any emergency; plaintiff, on the other hand, argues that section 1799.102 applies only to the rendering of emergency medical care at the scene of a medical emergency.

Although the phrase "emergency care" is not separately defined, section 1797.70's definition of "emergency" certainly supports the conclusion that the Legislature intended for "emergency care" to be construed as meaning emergency medical care. After all, if the "scene of an emergency" (§ 1799.102) means a scene where "an individual has a need for immediate medical attention" (§ 1797.70), it logically follows that the Legislature intended for the phrase "emergency care" in section 1799.102 to refer to the medical attention given to the individual who needs it.

This construction also comports with the second sentence of section 1799.102, which reads: "The scene of an emergency shall not include emergency departments and other places where medical care is usually offered." While this sentence does not directly shed light on the intended meaning of the phrase "emergency care" in the previous sentence of section 1799.102, the fact that the Legislature excluded "emergency departments and other places where medical care is usually offered" from section 1799.102's immunity supports construing "emergency care" as meaning emergency medical care-the exclusion suggests that "emergency departments and other places where medical care is usually offered" are locations where the Legislature did not need (or want) to encourage ordinary citizens to provide emergency medical care because trained medical personnel are available to better render such care.

Torti's expansive interpretation of section 1799.102 would undermine long-standing common law principles. As we previously noted, the general rule is that "one has no duty to come to the aid of another." "The origin of the rule lay in the early common law distinction between action and inaction, or 'misfeasance' and 'non-feasance.'" (Rest.2d Torts, § 314, com. c, p. 116.) Courts were more concerned with affirmative acts of misbehavior than they were with an individual "who merely did nothing, even though another might suffer serious harm because of his omission to act."

While there is no general duty to help, a good Samaritan who nonetheless "undertakes to come to the aid of another . . . is under a duty to exercise due care in performance . . ." "'[I]t is ancient learning that one who assumes to act, even though gratuitously, may thereby become subject to a duty of acting carefully, if he acts at all.'"

The broad construction urged by Torti-that *section 1799.102* immunizes any person who provides any emergency care at the scene of any emergency-would largely gut this well-established common law rule. As we recently noted, "'[w]e do not presume that the Legislature intends, when it enacts a statute, to overthrow long-established principles of law unless such intention is clearly expressed or necessarily implied.'" Torti does not identify anything that would overcome the presumption that the Legislature did not intend to work such a radical departure.

As the Court of Appeal points out, Torti's sweeping construction of section 1799.102 would render other

CONTINUED

"Good Samaritan" statutes superfluous. For example, Government Code section 50086 immunizes anyone with first aid training who is asked by authorities to assist in a search and rescue operation and who renders emergency services to a victim. The statute defines "emergency services" to include "first aid and medical services, rescue procedures, and transportation or other related activities." It is difficult to see what conduct Government Code section 50086 immunizes that would not already be protected under section 1799.102 as it is interpreted by Torti.

In light of the foregoing reasons, we conclude that the Legislature intended for section 1799.102 to immunize from liability for civil damages only those persons who in good faith render emergency medical care at the scene of a medical emergency. We accordingly affirm the judgment of the Court of Appeal.

CASE QUESTIONS

1. What is the relationship between statutory immunity and common-law duty here?

2. Would it have been better for Ms. Torti to argue that she was providing medical treatment and have the court deal with the issue of what constitutes medical care, rather than the issue of immunity?

3. What are the implications of this decision for people who are trying to offer assistance at the scene of an accident?

Element Two: Breach of Duty

Once the standard of care and the duty are established under element one, there must be a determination that the defendant fell short of that standard or breached that duty for the plaintiff to recover on the basis of negligence. For example, an accountant owes a duty to his client to perform an audit in a competent and professional manner and to conform the audit to the standards and rules established by the American Institute of Certified Public Accounts (AICPA). Failure to comply with these standards would be a breach of duty and would satisfy this second element of negligence.

In many cases, courts try to determine whether the duty was breached to determine whether the defendant's action satisfied the standard of care established in element one.

Barton v Whataburger, Inc. (Case 9.4) focuses on the issues of safety and the liability of businesses and property owners for injuries that result from the acts of third parties.

CASE 9.4 *Barton v Whataburger, Inc*
276 S.W.3d 456 (Tex. App. 2008)

What a Robbery at Whataburger: A Foreseeable Fatality?

FACTS

On a night in May 2003, Gregory Love was working as a night manager at a Whataburger restaurant in northwest Houston. Love arrived early for his shift that evening, allowing Arthur Murray, another manager, to leave. Murray and Love agreed that Love would count the cash accumulated during Murray's shift and place it in the store safe. Also on duty that night was Christopher Dean, a mentally impaired employee who had worked for Whataburger for 14 years.

Shortly after Murray left the Whataburger, Love called Murray and told him that he also needed to leave work. Love asked Murray if he could leave Dean in charge of the restaurant. Murray responded that Dean was capable of running the restaurant, but he could not authorize Love to delegate his managerial power to Dean.

Love did not ask Murray to return, and instead disregarded Murray's warnings, left the restaurant, and put Dean in charge. Love did not count the money in the cash registers or deposit any money in the safe before he left. When Dean discovered that Love had not counted the money in the registers, he counted it and deposited the excess in the safe. Love never returned to the restaurant that night.

At around 4:00 A.M., three men, later identified as Gerald Marshall, Ronald Worthy, and Kenny Calliham, attempted to rob the Whataburger. Marshall climbed through the drive-through window and chased Dean, eventually into the back of the restaurant, where he demanded that Dean give him the key to the safe. Marshall told Dean that if Dean did not give him the key to the safe, Marshall would shoot him. When Dean, who did not have the key, failed to produce it, Marshall shot him in the face and fled the scene with Worthy and Calliham. Dean died immediately. The robbers left with nothing, but afterward robbed a Shipley Doughnut store equipped with video surveillance.

Police later connected Love to the robbery, and the State charged him with capital felony murder. A jury found Love guilty, and the trial court assessed punishment of life in prison. The court affirmed the conviction.

Rose Barton, individually and on behalf of the estate of her son, filed suit against Whataburger, Inc. The trial court granted summary judgment for Whataburger, holding that the shooting death of Dean was not a foreseeable event. Barton appealed.

JUDICIAL OPINION

BLAND, Justice

A negligence cause of action has four elements: (1) a legal duty owed by one person to another, (2) a breach of that duty, and (3) damages (4) proximately caused by the breach. In the context of the employer-employee relationship, a company has a duty (1) to provide rules for the safety of employees, and to warn them of reasonably foreseeable hazards; (2) to furnish reasonably safe machinery and equipment; (3) to furnish a reasonably safe place to work; and (4) to exercise ordinary care to select careful and competent fellow employees.

Whataburger does not dispute that it owed a duty to Dean, as its employee, but observes that its duty is to protect its employees from foreseeable harms. The issue in this case, whether analyzed as a part of the duty element of negligence or the causation element, is the foreseeability of the criminal conduct that led to Dean's murder. As the Texas cases that discuss the foreseeability of intervening criminal conduct do so, in the main, in the context of the element of duty, we do so as well.

The threshold inquiry in a negligence case is duty. As a general rule, "a person has no legal duty to protect another from the criminal acts of a third person." However, if a criminal's conduct is a foreseeable result of the prior negligence of a party, the criminal act may not excuse that party's liability. To impose liability on a defendant for negligence in failing to prevent the criminal conduct of another, the facts must show more than conduct that creates an opportunity to commit crime—they must show both that the defendant committed negligent acts and that it knew or should have known that, because of its acts, the crime (or one like it) might occur.

Thus, to impose a legal duty to prevent the criminal conduct of another, the crime must have been reasonably foreseeable at the time the defendant engaged in negligent conduct. Foreseeability exists if the actor, as a person of ordinary intelligence, should have anticipated the dangers his negligent act creates for others. Importantly, "[f]oreseeability requires more than someone, viewing the facts in retrospect, theorizing an extraordinary sequence of events whereby the defendant's conduct brings about the injury."

Negligent Hiring

Barton first contends that Whataburger's negligence in hiring Love as a restaurant manager caused the aggravated robbery that led to Dean's murder. Barton produced evidence of an investigative report that revealed Love was convicted of a felony offense of "dealing cocaine" in Indiana in September 1993, and served one year in jail. Love was convicted of felony nonpayment of child support in Texas, in November 2002, the week before he applied for a managerial position at Whataburger. Whataburger performed a background check on Love before hiring him, but only searched for criminal convictions in Harris County that occurred between November 1995 and November 2002. The search did not reveal either of the two felony convictions. Barton alleges that Whataburger's failure to conduct an adequate background check ultimately caused the aggravated robbery that led to Dean's murder.

While Love's convictions, if discovered, should have raised Whataburger's suspicions about his fitness to manage a restaurant, under Texas law, they did not make his eventual participation in an aggravated robbery leading to murder reasonably foreseeable. Even assuming that information about Love's prior convictions, if known, would have torpedoed Love's employment with Whataburger, his criminal acts of selling cocaine and failing to pay child support are different from an aggravated robbery—neither crime inherently requires violence or theft, the two essential ingredients of an aggravated robbery. The record contains no

CONTINUED

evidence that the events underlying either of Love's convictions involved violence or theft, or that Love engaged in any conduct during the seven months he was employed at Whataburger that would have made his participation in an aggravated robbery foreseeable. Even viewed in hindsight, Love's convictions for selling cocaine and nonpayment of child support do not indicate a propensity for violent criminal conduct, like aggravated robbery and murder.

Barton calls our attention to criminal cases that note the connection between drugs and violence. We acknowledge that courts, including ours, have recognized a street-level connection between drugs, weapons, and violence. This connection provides police officers with the constitutionally required reasonable suspicion to conduct a *Terry* stop, or a legislature with a justification for imposing harsher sentences on drug offenders.

A stereotypical connection, however, is insufficient to raise more than a scintilla of evidence that a person convicted of selling cocaine, without any accompanying evidence of violence, will foreseeably commit aggravated robbery leading to murder in the future. While the smell of marijuana or the suspicion that a defendant possesses narcotics might provide a police officer sufficient justification to frisk a suspect for weapons under Terry, a seven-year-old conviction for "dealing" cocaine, standing alone, does not make it foreseeable that a defendant will commit a violent crime in the future.

Failure to Provide a Safe Workplace

Barton further contends that, even if it was not legally foreseeable that Love would engineer the crime that resulted in Dean's murder, Whataburger generally knows of an increased risk of a violent crime occurring at restaurants open late at night and should have taken reasonable security measures to prevent it.

Employees are the invitees of their employer. "[w]hen general danger to invitees is the risk of injury from criminal activity by third parties, the evidence must reveal specific previous crimes on or near the premises in order to establish foreseeability of harm."

The incidence of violent crime, the foreseeability of violent crime on Whataburger's premises, and the preventative measures that Whataburger could or did implement in view of the risk of such crime were the same for Whataburger in its capacity as employer as they were for Whataburger in its capacity as premises occupier.

Barton produced some evidence of criminal activity at the Whataburger in the years preceding Dean's murder: in July 1997, six years before the incident, a customer was shot in the parking lot, and another customer in the drive-through lane was robbed and shot in the thigh; in July 1998, a customer was robbed in the drive-through lane; in June 1999, a customer's purse was stolen; in July 2000, a customer reported an assault (without injury); in April 2001, a woman sought help in the Whataburger, reporting that she had been shot; in August 2001, a woman reported an assault (without injury); in February 2002, a woman reported that her car was stolen from her in the parking lot; in April 2002, one customer intentionally hit another customer's vehicle in the drive-through lane (with property damage but not injury); and, in February 2003, police arrested a person who refused to leave the premises.

In contrast . . . no crime similar to this one had ever occurred: no one had ever robbed the restaurant before, nor had it ever been the scene of any workplace violence, nor had anyone ever committed any sort of crime against a Whataburger employee, nor had anyone ever been murdered.

. . . the evidence does not show the rampant, violent criminal activity sufficient to raise a fact issue about the foreseeability of the aggravated robbery that resulted in Dean's murder.

. . . general evidence of crime rates and of robberies in other locales cannot create "an industry standard of foreseeability" sufficient to impose a duty to prevent crime.

Finally, Barton's contention that Whataburger's earlier employment of a security guard on the weekends proves the foreseeability of the robbery is unavailing. "The mere act of taking preventative measures to protect against the possibility of future crime is not the same as foreseeing that criminal activity." If we equated preventative measures to foreseeability, we would "virtually eliminate the foreseeability requirement for a negligence claim against a person who installs a security system or takes other preventative measures to guard against crime."

We hold that the trial court properly granted summary judgment because the diabolic conduct of others—men who committed aggravated robbery and murder—was a superseding cause of Dean's death that was not reasonably foreseeable to Whataburger. Affirmed.

CASE QUESTIONS

1. After reading the court opinion, list the type of evidence that Dean's mother would have to offer to establish foreseeability.

2. What policies should employers establish based on what happened in this case?

3. What lessons do you learn about employee screening from this case?

CONSIDER... 9.7

Dorothy McClung went shopping at the Walmart in the Delta Square Shopping Center in Memphis, Tennessee, around noon. After she had completed her shopping and was returning to her car, she was abducted at gunpoint and forced into her car. She was later found dead in the trunk of her car after it was spotted by some hunters in a remote area in Arkansas. Roger McClung, her husband, filed suit against Walmart and the owner of the shopping center, Delta Square. Are these companies liable for the criminal acts of another when those acts occurred in their parking lot? [*McClung v Delta Square Limited Partnership*, 937 S.W.2d 891 (Tenn. 1996)]

Element Three: Causation

After establishing a duty and breach of duty, the plaintiff in a negligence suit must also establish that the breach of the duty was the cause of the damages. A test often used to determine **causation** is the **"but for" test**—"but for the action or lack of action of the defendant, the plaintiff would not have been injured." For example, suppose that a guest is enjoying a scenic view of the ocean from a cliff near his hotel. At the edge of the cliff, the hotel had installed a fence, but the hotel does not keep it in good repair. When the guest leans against the fence to take a picture, the fence breaks and the guest falls over the cliff. The hotel breached its duty to keep its premises in reasonably safe condition, and its failure to do so caused the guest's injury. The "but for" test is limited by the so-called zone of danger rule, which requires that the plaintiff be in the zone of danger when the injury occurs. The zone of danger includes all those people who could foreseeably be injured if a duty is breached. For example, the hotel would also be liable to those injured by the guest as he fell through the weak fence because they are in the zone of danger.

For the Manager's Desk

Re: Hooters and Causation

A jury in San Diego returned a verdict that reflects an understanding of duty, breach of duty, and causation in negligence. The case involved a fight that began at an employee party for employees of Hooters. Robert Womack, a guest of one of the employees at the party, had been drinking and became disruptive. Evan Johnson, a security guard at the hotel where the party was held, asked Mr. Womack to leave. Mr. Womack then head-butted Mr. Johnson, and a fight began. Mr. Johnson suffered permanent neurological impairment as a result of the injuries he sustained in the fight.

Mr. Johnson sued both Mr. Womack and Hooters. The jury returned a verdict of $860,000, but only against Mr. Womack. The jury found that Hooters had done nothing to cause the altercation, that it did not know that Mr. Womack was causing trouble, and that it had no advance knowledge of any such tendencies on the part of Mr. Womack. The attorney for Hooters said, "We got by on causation."

Explain what the attorney meant with his statement.

Source: Randy Stewart, "Party fight leads to $860,000 award," *National Law Journal,* January 6, 2003, p. B1.

BUSINESS PLANNING TIP

All businesses should help create a safe environment for their customers and discourage criminal acts with the following:

1. Good lighting

2. Access to public phones

3. Security patrols

4. Locked gates to parking lots; gate or security access

5. Escorts for customers and employees to their vehicles after closing hours

6. Camera security

7. Assigned parking spaces for tenants and employees

8. Warning signs to use caution and be alert

Many hotels change key access codes with each guest and post security personnel near guest elevators at night in order to limit access to the elevators unless you can show your room key. Some hotels have floors for women who are traveling alone, and extra security is provided on those floors.

Element Four: Proximate Cause

Some cutoff line must be drawn between the "but for" causation and events that contribute to the injury of the plaintiff—an element of a negligence case called **proximate cause.** Suppose that you have a tire replaced at a tire store and the technician fails to tighten the wheel sufficiently. As you drive down the street, the tire comes loose, rolls off, and strikes another car. Did the tire store cause the damage to the other car? Yes. Any accidents caused by that car? Yes. Suppose the tire comes off, rolls onto the sidewalk, and strikes a pedestrian. Did the tire store cause that injury? Yes. Suppose the pedestrian sees the tire coming and jumps out of the way but, in so doing, injures another pedestrian. Did the tire store cause that injury? Yes. In all of these accidents, the following statement can be made: "But for the failure to tighten the wheel, the accident would not have occurred." Suppose that the tire injures a pedestrian, although not fatally, but a doctor treating the pedestrian, through malpractice, causes the pedestrian's death. Did the tire store cause the death? No; another's negligence intervened.

Case 9.5, *Palsgraf v Long Island Ry. Co.,* is a landmark case on the element of proximate cause.

CASE 9.5	*Palsgraf v Long Island Ry. Co.* 162 N.E. 99 (N.Y. 1928)

Fireworks in the Passenger's Package and Negligence in the Air

FACTS

Helen Palsgraf (plaintiff) had purchased a ticket to travel to Rockaway Beach on the Long Island Railway (defendant). While she was standing on a platform at the defendant's station waiting for the train, another train stopped at the station. Two men ran to catch the train, which began moving as they were running. One of the men made it onto the train without difficulty, but the other man, who was carrying a package, was unsteady as he tried to jump aboard. Employees of the defendant helped pull the man in and push him onto the train car, but in the process the package was dropped. The package contained fireworks, and when dropped, it exploded. The vibrations from the explosion caused some scales (located at the end of the platform on which Ms. Palsgraf was standing) to fall. As they fell,

they hit and injured Ms. Palsgraf. She filed suit against the railroad for negligence.

JUDICIAL OPINION

CARDOZO, Chief Justice

Negligence is not actionable unless it involves the invasion of a legally protected interest, the violation of a right. "Proof of negligence in the air, so to speak, will not do." The plaintiff, as she stood upon the platform of the station, might claim to be protected against intentional invasion of her bodily security. Such invasion is not charged. She might claim to be protected against unintentional invasion by conduct involving in the thought of reasonable men an unreasonable hazard that such invasion would ensue. These, from the point of view of the law, were the bounds of her immunity, with perhaps some rare exceptions, survivals for the most part of ancient forms of liability, where conduct is held to be at the peril of the actor. If no hazard was apparent to the eye of ordinary vigilance, an act innocent and harmless, at least to outward seeming, with reference to her, did not take to itself the quality of a tort because it happened to be a wrong, though apparently not one involving the risk of bodily insecurity, with reference to some one else.

A different conclusion will involve us, and swiftly too, in a maze of contradictions. A guard stumbles over a package which has been left upon a platform. It seems to be a bundle of newspapers. It turns out to be a can of dynamite. To the eye of ordinary vigilance, the bundle is abandoned waste, which may be kicked or trod on with impunity. Is a passenger at the other end of the platform protected by the law against the unsuspected hazard concealed beneath the waste? If not, is the result to be any different, so far as the distant passenger is concerned, when the guard stumbles over a valise which a truckman or a porter has left upon the walk? The passenger far away, if the victim of a wrong at all, has a cause of action, not derivative, but original and primary. His claim to be protected against invasion of his bodily security is neither greater nor less because the act resulting in the invasion is a wrong to another far removed. In this case, the rights that are said to have been violated, the interests said to have been invaded, are not even of the same order. The man was not injured in his person or even put in danger. The purpose of the act, as well as its effect, was to make his person safe. If there was a wrong to him at all, which may very well be doubted, it was a wrong to a property interest only, the safety of his package. Out of this wrong to property, which threatened injury to nothing else, there has passed, we are told, to the plaintiff by derivation or succession a right of action for the invasion of an interest of another order, the right to bodily security. The diversity of interests emphasizes the futility of the effort to build the plaintiff's right upon the basis of a wrong to some one else. The gain is one of emphasis, for a like result would follow if the interests were the same. Even then, the orbit of the danger as disclosed to the eye of reasonable vigilance would be the orbit of the duty. One who jostles one's neighbor in a crowd does not invade the rights of others standing at the outer fringe when the unintended contact casts a bomb upon the ground. The wrongdoer as to them is the man who carries the bomb, not the one who explodes it without suspicion of the danger. Life will have to be made over, and human nature transformed, before prevision so extravagant can be accepted as the norm of conduct, the customary standard to which behavior must conform.

Here, by concession, there was nothing in the situation to suggest to the most cautious mind that the parcel wrapped in newspaper would spread wreckage through the station. If the guard had thrown it down knowingly and willfully, he would not have threatened the plaintiff's safety, so far as appearances could warn him. His conduct would not have involved, even then, an unreasonable probability of invasion of her bodily security. Liability can be no greater where the act is inadvertent.

DISSENTING OPINION

ANDREWS, Justice

Assisting a passenger to board a train, the defendant's servant negligently knocked a package from his arms. It fell between the platform and the cars. Of its contents the servant knew and could know nothing. A violent explosion followed. The concussion broke some scales standing a considerable distance away. In falling, they injured the plaintiff, an intending passenger.

Upon these facts, may she recover the damages she has suffered in an action brought against the master? The result we shall reach depends upon our theory as to the nature of negligence. Is it a relative concept—the breach of some duty owing to a particular person or to particular persons?

Or, where there is an act which unreasonably threatens the safety of others, is the doer liable for all its proximate consequences, even where they result in injury to one who would generally be thought to be outside the radius of danger? This is not a mere dispute as to words. We might not believe that to the average mind the dropping of the bundle would seem to involve the probability of harm to the plaintiff standing many feet away whatever might be the case as to the owner or to one so near as to be likely to be struck by its fall. If, however, we adopt the second hypothesis, we have to inquire only as to the relation between cause and effect. We deal in terms of proximate cause, not of negligence.

Negligence may be defined roughly as an act or omission which unreasonably does or may affect the rights of others, or which unreasonably fails to protect one's self from the dangers resulting from such acts.

Where there is the unreasonable act, and some right that may be affected there is negligence whether damage does or does not result. That is immaterial. Should we drive down Broadway at a reckless speed, we are negligent whether we strike an approaching car or miss it by an inch. The act itself is wrongful. It is a wrong not only to those who happen to be within the radius of danger, but to all who might have been there—a wrong to the public at large.

Negligence does involve a relationship between man and his fellows, but not merely a relationship between

CONTINUED

man and those whom he might reasonably expect his act would injure; rather, a relationship between him and those whom he does in fact injure. If his act has a tendency to harm someone, it harms him a mile away as surely as it does those on the scene.

The proposition is this: Every one owes to the world at large the duty of refraining from those acts that may unreasonably threaten the safety of others. Such an act occurs. Not only is he wronged to whom harm might reasonably be expected to result, but he also who is in fact injured, even if he be outside what would generally be thought the danger zone.

As we have said, we cannot trace the effect of an act to the end, if end there is. Again, however, we may trace it part of the way. An overturned lantern may burn all Chicago. We may follow the fire from the shed to the last building. We rightly say the fire started by the lantern caused its destruction. A cause, but not the proximate cause. What we do mean by the word "proximate" is that, because of convenience, of public policy, of a rough sense of justice, the law arbitrarily declines to trace a series of events beyond a certain point. This is not logic. It is practical politics.

This last suggestion is the factor which must determine the case before us. The act upon which defendant's liability rests is knocking an apparently harmless package onto the platform. The act was negligent. For its proximate consequences the defendant is liable. If its contents were broken, to the owner; if it fell upon and crushed a passenger's foot, then to him; if it exploded and injured one in the immediate vicinity, to him. Mrs. Palsgraf was standing some distance away. How far cannot be told from the record—apparently 25 to 30 feet, perhaps less. Except for the explosion, she would not have been injured. . . . The only intervening cause was that, instead of blowing her to the ground, the concussion smashed the weighing machine which in turn fell upon her. There was no remoteness in time, little in space. And surely, given such an explosion as here, it needed no great foresight to predict that the natural result would be to injure one on the platform at no greater distance from its scene than was the plaintiff. Just how no one might be able to predict. Whether by flying fragments, by broken glass, by wreckage of machines or structures no one could say. But injury in some form was most probable.

Under these circumstances I cannot say as a matter of law that the plaintiff's injuries were not the proximate result of the negligence.

CASE QUESTIONS

1. Who was carrying the package?
2. How far away from the incident was Ms. Palsgraf, and why is this significant?
3. What does Justice Cardozo find?
4. What point does the dissenting judge make?

Element Five: Damages

The plaintiff in a negligence case must be able to establish damages that resulted from the defendant's negligence. Such damages could include medical bills, lost wages, and pain and suffering, as well as any property damages. In many of the cases in this chapter, plaintiffs have also recovered punitive damages. Often referred to as "smart money," punitive damages are similar to civil penalties that are paid to plaintiffs because of the high level of carelessness involved on the defendant's part.

Defenses to Negligence

Contributory Negligence

In some cases, an accident results from the combined negligence of two or more people. A plaintiff who is also negligent gives the defendant the opportunity to raise the defense of **contributory negligence.** Contributory negligence is simply negligence by the plaintiff that is part of the cause of an accident. For example, suppose that a boat owner is operating his boat late at night on a lake in which the water is choppy and when he is intoxicated. An intoxicated friend is sitting at the bow of the boat trying to put her feet into the water when the owner takes the boat up to high speed. She falls in and is injured. The issue of causation becomes complicated here because there were breaches of duties by both parties. Did he cause the accident by driving at high speed late at night on a choppy lake while intoxicated? Or did she cause the accident by sitting without protection or restraint on the bow of the boat when the boat was being driven like that? The effect of the defense of contributory negligence is a complete bar to both from recovery.

Comparative Negligence

Many states, in order to eliminate the harsh effect of contributory negligence, have adopted a defense of **comparative negligence.** Under this defense, the jury simply determines the level of fault for both the plaintiff and the defendant and, based on this assessment of fault, determines how much each of the parties will be awarded. Using our boat example, the jury could find that the boat owner was 75 percent at fault and the passenger was 25 percent at fault. Under comparative negligence, the passenger could recover for her injuries, but the amount recovered would be 25 percent less because of her fault in causing the accident.

The defense of comparative negligence was developed largely because of the perceived unfairness of contributory negligence, which was a complete bar to recovery. The concept of comparative negligence has resulted in more litigation and more verdicts for plaintiffs permitted to use the defense.

Assumption of Risk

The **assumption of risk** defense requires the defendant to prove that the plaintiff knew of potential risk of injury in the conduct he or she undertook but decided to go forward with it anyway. For example, some dangers are inherent in activities such as skydiving, skiing, and roller-skating. You assume the inherent risks in these activities, but you do not assume the risks caused by the owners of the premises or equipment. For example, when you ski, you assume the natural risks that exist in skiing, but you do not assume the risk of faulty equipment you rent. If the failure of that equipment causes your injuries, the rental company would be responsible for that injury. To assume the risk, you must be completely aware of the risk and you must assume the risk voluntarily. *Mosca v Lichtenwalter* (Case 9.6) deals with the issue of assumption of risk.

**CASE
9.6**

Mosca v Lichtenwalter
68 Cal. Rptr. 2d 58 (Cal. App. 1997)

Hooked while Fishing

FACTS

Joseph Mosca and 23 others boarded a sportfishing boat for a day of fishing off San Clemente Island. David Lichtenwalter, one of the fishermen, was fishing off the stern near Mr. Mosca. Mr. Lichtenwalter's line became entangled in kelp and he was unable to get it released. A deckhand approached Mr. Lichtenwalter to help him. Mr. Lichtenwalter backed up and handed the pole to the deckhand just as the line "slingshotted" over the rail toward Mr. Mosca, who was struck in the eye with the sinker, which caused a partial vision loss.

Mr. Mosca filed suit against Mr. Lichtenwalter and others. The trial court, using the defense of assumption of risk, dismissed the case, and Mr. Mosca appealed.

JUDICIAL OPINION

WALEN, Acting Presiding Justice

The declaration of David Wilhite, a sportfishing expert, was submitted in opposition to the motion for summary judgment. He opined injury from hooks or sinkers when fishing lines slingshot may occur when an improper technique of freeing a stuck line is used. He indicated

CONTINUED

the danger of injury when extricating a line caught on an underwater object can be minimized by reaching down near the waterline, wrapping the line around a hand, and pulling it at a low angle. Lichtenwalter apparently used that approach when he first tried to release it. When he stepped back for the dockhand to intervene, he allegedly pulled the line in a higher, upward direction.

Mosca contends the trial court erred in granting summary judgment based on assumption of risk.

In *Knight v Jewett* (1992) 3 Cal.4th 296, 11 Cal. Rptr.2d 2, 834 P.2d 696, the Supreme Court discussed the difference between "primary" and "secondary" assumption of risk. Primary assumption of risk is a policy-driven legal concept where the courts declare there is no duty at all.

Primary assumption of risk has often been imposed where the plaintiff and defendant are engaged in a sport. "In the sports setting . . . conditions or conduct that otherwise might be viewed as dangerous often are an integral part of the sport itself."

To decide whether a duty will be imposed on a participant in a sporting activity, the court must determine whether the injury suffered arises from an inherent risk in the activity, and whether imposing a duty "might chill vigorous participation in the implicated activity and thereby alter its fundamental nature."

The trial court, at least implicitly, determined the danger of injury from a hook or sinker flying toward a participant is an inherent risk in sportfishing, and imposing the specter of liability regarding the danger would chill or alter the sport. That determination was reasonable. Hooking and catching fish requires a great deal of knowledge, physical skill, and attention. A participant who worries whether he is hooked on a fish or kelp, and what method should be used to deal with the line in either instance, will not be an effective fisherman, and may be inclined to give up the sport.

Mosca argues that getting hit in the eye by a sinker is not an inherent danger in sportfishing because there was evidence none of the parties, witnesses or the expert had ever heard of this type of injury. The inquiry is not that narrow. The question involved is a broader inquiry: whether injury from flying hooks and sinkers is inherent in the sport.

Relying on expert witness Wilhite's declaration, Mosca also asserts the danger of being hit by a recoiling line which is stuck on an underwater object is not inherent in the sport if care is used to release it, by properly pulling it or even by cutting the line. He begs the question by making this argument. The question whether the sport can be made safer if certain techniques are used bears on the standard of care, and is a question that is reached only if the threshold question of duty is resolved against the defendant. Wilhite

admits flying hooks and sinkers are risks in the sport. He merely indicated the danger can be minimized if care is taken and specific techniques to free a line are used.

Courts have recognized these principles in cases dealing with other sports activities. In *Regents of University of California v Superior Court,* 41 Cal.App.4th 1040, 48 Cal.Rptr.2d 922, the court held rock climbers assume the risk climbing anchors may give way, even though it was a standard procedure to double check the anchors to maximize safety. "Falling, whether because of one's own slip, a co-climber's stumble, or an anchor system giving way, is the very risk inherent in the sport of mountain climbing and cannot be completely eliminated without destroying the sport itself." The court found an inherent risk of harm despite the presence of safety measures.

Mosca points out that *Knight v Jewett,* Cal.4th 296, 11 Cal.Rptr.2d 2, 834 P.2d 696, and other cases where primary assumption of risk has been found involved contact sports or other sports where the defendant was an opponent. But there is no such limitation on the doctrine. In *Staten v Superior Court,* 45 Cal.App. 4th at p.1634, 53 Cal.Rptr.2d 657, the court applied the doctrine to figure skating, a "teamless" sport where one participates in close proximity with others so engaged. Sportfishing is the same type of close-proximity endeavor.

Cases declining to find primary assumption of the risk are distinguishable. In *Yancey v Superior Court* (1994), 28 Cal.App.4th 558, 33 Cal.Rptr.2d 777, the court held a participant throwing a discus owes a duty of due care to check the field before throwing because "[n]othing about the inherent nature of the sport requires that one participant who has completed a throw and is retrieving his or her discus should expect the next participant to throw without looking toward the landing area." (See also *Lowe v California League of Professional Baseball* (1997) 56 Cal.App. 4th 112, 123, 65 Cal.Rptr.2d 105 [antics of team mascot that distracted plaintiff who was struck by foul ball were not integral to the sport].) But Lichtenwalter, in attempting to free his line, was engaged in a typical adjunct of fishing.

In *Morgan v Fuji Country USA, Inc.* (1995) 34 Cal. App.4th 127, 40 Cal.Rptr.2d 249, the court found assumption of the risk was not available to the defendants as grounds for summary judgment because their golf course design could be held by a trier of fact to have affirmatively increased the inherent risk of being struck by errant golf balls. Mosca neither claims, nor did he show, the fishing boat design or anything about the boat owners' fishing policy affirmatively increased the risk of harm. At most he alleges a deckhand was guilty of failing to ensure

Lichtenwalter engaged in a preferred line retrieval technique.

Mosca notes that assumption of risk cannot be invoked in hunting accidents, but that is "because of the special danger to others posed by the sport of hunting." Indeed, that concept has been codified by the Legislature. Mosca makes no showing sportfishing has attained a similar status. Although fishing carries with it certain dangers, it does not involve the potentially mortal danger involved in hunting.

The judgment is affirmed.

CASE QUESTIONS

1. What happened on the boat, and how was Mr. Mosca injured?
2. Is the risk of being struck by a line inherent in the sport of fishing?
3. Was Mr. Mosca's injury typical?
4. What is the difference between assumption of risk in day-to-day activities and assumption of risk in sports?

CONSIDER... 9.8

Lisa Winters signed up to take a Latino dance class at the Santa Monica Family YMCA, sort of a dancing-with-the-neighbors experience. However, when she arrived for class on April 17, 2002, the Latino dance instructor was ill and the jazz instructor had agreed to fill in so that the class would proceed. The jazz instructor, however, taught jazz. No one was wearing the appropriate shoes for jazz dance, the floor was made of wood, and the instructor asked the students to perform a pivoting spin maneuver. After Ms. Winters attempted the maneuver, the jazz instructor asked her to put more effort into the move. Ms. Winters first performed the maneuver with no difficulty. During her second attempt, she performed four leaps (e.g., running-type steps with both feet off the ground). As she attempted to perform the pivoting half-spin maneuver, her left foot stuck to the floor. She fell to the floor and sustained personal injuries. She filed suit against the YMCA for her injuries. The YMCA's defense is assumption of risk. Will the defense fly (as it were)? Be sure to explain why all of the facts stated are important in reaching your conclusion. [*Winter v Santa Monica Family YMCA*, 2005 WL 1713936 (Cal. App. 2 Dist)]

New Verdicts on Tort Reform

Over the past decade, a number of reforms have been proposed, particularly with respect to tort litigation, to limit recovery or place other limitations on the amount of increasing tort litigation. For example, some reform proposals would limit damages. Although nearly all states have adopted some form of limitations in tort recovery, these reforms are a maze of laws differing from state to state, have been subject to judicial challenges (in many cases successful).

In *BMW of North America, Inc. v Gore* [517 U.S. 559 (1996)], the U.S. Supreme Court addressed the issue of large recoveries and concluded that $4,000,000 in damages (reduced to $2 million by the judge on a judgment NOV) for the dealer's failure to disclose to a buyer that his BMW had been refinished was excessive. The actual damages were $4,000, and the court ruled, "In most cases, the ratio will be within a constitutionally acceptable range, and remittitur will not be justified on this basis. When the ratio is a breathtaking 500 to 1, however, the award must surely 'raise a suspicious judicial eyebrow.'" However, the dissent pointed out the problem that tort reform still faces: how much is too much?

CONSIDER...   9.9

The Mathiases checked into a Motel 6 and were bitten extensively by bedbugs. Upon investigation, they learned that the managers and owners of the motel had been warned by guests, employees, and exterminators alike that there were bedbugs in the rooms. The exterminator offered to spray the motel each year for $600, but the motel refused. As a result, the bugs remained and propagated. The Mathiases filed suit, seeking punitive damages. The trial court awarded them $5,000 compensatory damages and $186,000 punitive damages. The motel appealed the punitive damage award as excessive. Is the award excessive? Should the punitive damages award be reversed? Why do you think the hotel wants to have a court decision on this suit? [*Mathias v ACCR Economy Lodging, Inc.,* 347 F.3d 672 (7th Cir. 2003)]

Since the time of the *BMW v Gore* case, a number of significant decisions have been rendered on how much is too much in terms of damages awarded to plaintiffs. In *Cooper Industries, Inc. v Leatherman Tool Group,* 532 U.S. 424 (2001), the U.S. Supreme Court held that the Eighth Amendment's prohibition on excessive fines and cruel and unusual punishment requires appellate courts to apply a *de novo* review standard (see Chapter 3) when determining the constitutionality of punitive damages awards made at the trial court level. Several cases that followed the *Leatherman* decision ordered a reduction of punitive damages. In *State Farm Mutual Auto Insurance Co. v Campbell,* 538 U.S. 408 (2003) (originally a Utah case), the U.S. Supreme Court held that a punitive damage award of $145 million in punitive damages and $1 million in compensatory damages against an insurance company for its wrongful refusal to pay a claim violated the due process clause.

Because the highest criminal penalty available for fraud in Utah was $10,000, the court could not find a justification for the large punitive damage award. In addition, the court noted that including out-of-state activities of a company when determining damage awards for plaintiffs for conduct within the state was not proper.

In *Exxon Shipping Co. v Baker,* 128 S.Ct. 2605 (2008) the U.S. Supreme Court that the maximum amount for punitive damages in that case (which had peculiar maritime underpinnings) was an amount equal to the compensatory damages. This line of decisions has provided some limitations on and restraints on trial court punitive damages awards, but the tort reform battle continues in the courts, through legislation, and through continuing studies on the types and levels of verdicts.

Strict Liability

Sometimes the law imposes strict liability on parties for their conduct. **Strict liability** is absolute liability for conduct with few, if any, defenses available. Strict liability can result from violation of a statute. For example, any violation of federal laws on disposal of biomedical waste would result in strict liability. Strict liability can also result because of public policy issues. For example, strict liability is available as a theory for recovery of injury and damages resulting from a defective product (see Chapter 10). There is also strict liability for inherently dangerous activities such as razing buildings through the use of explosives. The activity itself, while sometimes necessary, imposes strict liability on the contractor undertaking the project.

BIOGRAPHY

The Kitty Genovese Story and Duty

Richmond, California, is a suburb of San Francisco and is an industrial area that was ranked the ninth most dangerous city in the United States in 2008. Richmond has received national attention and scorn because of the alleged gang rape of a high school student at the homecoming dance at Richmond High School, which occurred as 20 people watched the horrific conduct of the young men.

No one witnessing the brutality notified the police of the ongoing rape until a woman overheard two people discussing it and called 911.

The Richmond witnesses were overcome by what is known as the "bystander effect," the label given to the apartment dwellers who witnessed the attack

and eventual murder of Kitty Genovese in Queens, New York in 1964. Those living in the complex did nothing as they heard the screams of Miss Genovese as she was being beaten and stabbed because of their fear of getting involved, their assumptions that someone else would take care of it, or perhaps callous disregard.

There is no statutory duty in California (yet) to report an ongoing crime and no statutory duty in most states to help another who is in danger. Indeed, many who do help have had liability imposed on them for not helping in a crackerjack fashion (see the *Van Horn v Watson* case on pp. 300–302). What are our ethical responsibilities to render aid?

Summary

What types of civil wrongs create a right of recovery for harm?

- Tort—a civil wrong; action by another that results in damages that are recoverable
- Intentional tort—civilly wrong conduct that is done deliberately
- Negligence—conduct of omission or neglect that results in damages
- Strict tort liability—imposition of liability because harm results

What are the types and elements of torts?

- Defamation—publication of untrue and damaging statements about an individual or company
- Product disparagement—the tort of defamation of products
- Malice—publication of information knowing it is false or with reckless disregard for whether it is false
- Privilege—a defense to defamation that protects certain statements because of a public interest in having information such as testimony in a trial or media coverage protected from suit
- Interference—the wrong of asking a party to breach a contract with a third party

- False imprisonment—wrongful detention of an individual; shopkeepers have a privilege to reasonably detain those they have good cause to believe have taken merchandise
- Shopkeeper's privilege—defense to torts of defamation, invasion of privacy, and false imprisonment for merchants who detain shoppers when shopkeepers have reasonable cause to believe merchandise has been taken without payment
- Intentional infliction of emotional distress—bizarre and outrageous conduct that inflicts mental and possible physical harm on another
- Invasion of privacy—disclosing private information, intruding upon another's affairs, or appropriating someone's image or likeness
- Appropriation—the use, without permission, of another's likeness, image, voice, or trademark for commercial gain

What are the elements and defenses in negligence?

- Reasonable and prudent person—the standard by which the conduct of others is measured; a hypothetical person who behaves with full knowledge and alertness
- Causation—the "but for" reason for an accident

- Proximate cause—the foreseeability requirement of causation

- Contributory negligence—negligence on the part of a plaintiff that was partially responsible for causing injuries

- Comparative negligence—newer negligence defense that assigns liability and damages in accidents on a percentage basis and thus reduces a plaintiff's recovery by the amount his negligence contributed to the cause of the accident

- Assumption of risk—plaintiff's voluntary subjection to a risk that caused injuries

What are the public policy and business issues in tort recovery?

- Tort reform—political and legislative process of limiting damages and changing methods of recovery for civil wrongs

- Amount of punitive damages

Questions and Problems

1. In the May 31, 2004, issue of *The Weekly Standard*, editor Fred Barnes wrote the following commentary:

A FEW YEARS AGO Michael Moore, who's now promoting an anti-President Bush movie entitled Fahrenheit 9/11, *announced he'd gotten the goods on me, indeed hung me out to dry on my own words. It was in his first bestselling book,* Stupid White Men. *Moore wrote he'd once been "forced" to listen to my comments on a TV chat show,* The McLaughlin Group. *I had whined "on and on about the sorry state of American education," Moore said, and wound up by bellowing: "These kids don't even know what* The Iliad *and* The Odyssey *are!"*

Moore's interest was piqued, so the next day he said he called me. "Fred," he quoted himself as saying, "tell me what The Iliad *and* The Odyssey *are." I started "hemming and hawing," Moore wrote. And then I said, according to Moore: "Well, they're . . . uh . . . you know . . . uh . . . okay, fine, you got me—I don't know what they're about. Happy now?" He'd smoked me out as a fraud, or maybe worse.*

The only problem is none of this is true. It never happened. Moore is a liar. He made it up. It's a fabrication on two levels. One, I've never met Moore or even talked to him on the phone. And, two, I read both The Iliad *and* The Odyssey *in my first year at the University of Virginia. Just for the record, I learned what they were about even before college. Like everyone else my age, I got my classical education from the big screen. I saw the Iliad movie called* Helen of Troy *and while I forget the name of the* Odyssey *film, I think it starred Kirk Douglas as Odysseus.*

So why didn't I scream bloody murder when the book came out in 2001? I didn't learn about the phony anecdote until it was brought to my attention

by Alan Wolfe, who was reviewing Moore's book for the New Republic. *He asked, by email, if the story were true. I said no, not a word of it, and Wolfe quoted me as saying that. That was enough, I thought. After all, who would take a shrill, lying lefty like Moore seriously?*

Was Mr. Barnes defamed? Could he bring suit now?

2. Douglas Margreiter was severely injured in New Orleans on the night of April 6, 1976. He was the chief of the pharmacy section of the Colorado Department of Social Services and was in New Orleans to attend the annual meeting of the American Pharmaceutical Association.

On Tuesday evening, April 6, Mr. Margreiter had dinner at the Royal Sonesta Hotel with two associates from Colorado who were attending the meeting and were staying in rooms adjacent to Mr. Margreiter's in the New Hotel Monteleone. Mr. Margreiter returned to his room between 10:30 P.M. and 11:00 P.M.; one of his friends returned to his adjoining room at the same time. Another friend was to come by Mr. Margreiter's room later to discuss what sessions of the meetings each would attend the next day.

About three hours later, Mr. Margreiter was found severely beaten and unconscious in a parking lot three blocks from the Monteleone. The police who found him said they thought he was highly intoxicated, and they took him to Charity Hospital. His friends later had him moved to the Hotel Dieu.

Mr. Margreiter said two men had unlocked his hotel room door and entered his room. He was beaten about the head and shoulders and had only the recollection of being carried to a dark alley. He required a craniotomy and other medical treatment and suffered permanent effects from the incident.

Mr. Margreiter sued the hotel on grounds that the hotel was negligent in not controlling access to elevators and hence to the guests' rooms. The hotel says Mr. Margreiter was intoxicated and met his fate outside the hotel. Is the hotel liable? [*Margreiter v New Hotel Monteleone,* 640 F.2d 508 (5th Cir. 1981)]

3. The A & N Food Market in Flushing, New York has adopted the following procedures when its security cameras observe shoppers stealing store merchandise:

- The alleged thief's identification is taken.
- The alleged thief is photographed holding the items they are alleged to have taken.
- The store security guards tell the alleged thieves that their pictures (with them holding the merchandise) will be displayed publicly in the store unless they pay for the items and pay a fine of $400.
- If they do not have $400 to pay the fine, the store holds their identification until they return with the $400.

This store, almost all of whose customers are Chinese, is using the same system to curb shoplifting that is used in China. There is a slogan posted at most retailers in China that warns of the store's fine policy, "Steal one, fine 10." The owners of the A & N Food Market maintain that their policies and procedures are legal because they are covered under the shopkeeper's privilege. Are they correct? Are their actions covered under the privilege?[4]

4. The CBS news show "60 Minutes" pulled from a scheduled airing an interview with a Jeffrey S. Wigand, a former tobacco executive, when threats of both libel and tortious interference with contract suits arose. Brown & Williamson lawyers notified CBS News that Wigand had signed a confidentiality agreement and that the company would sue CBS News for interference with that contract if the interview were run. "60 Minutes" ran a story on tobacco companies without the interview. CBS correspondents Mike Wallace and Morley Safer protested the decision of CBS News executives. However, the *Wall Street Journal* ran a story describing CBS News's unusual arrangements with Wigand, including the payment of a consulting fee of $12,000 and the promise of full indemnification. Did CBS commit tortious interference of contract?

5. Two disc jockeys at WPYX-FM radio in Albany, New York, were sued for intentional infliction of emotional distress by Annette Esposito-Hilder, who was identified on the air by the two disc jockeys as the "winner" of the "ugliest bride" contest. The two disc jockeys sponsored an ugliest bride contest based on the wedding pictures in the daily newspaper. Viewers were invited to call in with their guesses as to which bride had been chosen. Generally, the disc jockeys did not reveal last names of the brides. However, in Ms. Esposito-Hilder's case, they broke with past practice and revealed her name.

On appeal of the case from an earlier dismissal, the court held that no defamation was involved in their statements because they were "pure, subjective opinion." The court did hold, however, that a suit for intentional infliction of emotional distress could go forward. The court held, "Comedic expression does not receive absolute First Amendment protection."

Is this defamation? Is opinion protected by the First Amendment? Does it make any difference that Ms. Esposito-Hilder was employed by a competing radio station in the area at the time she "won" the contest? [*Esposito-Hilder v SFX Broadcasting, Inc.,* 665 N.Y.S.2d 697 (1997)]

6. In 2005, Timothy L. O'Brien's book, *Trump Nation: The Art of Being the Donald,* was published. In the book, Mr. O'Brien, who is now the editor of the Sunday Business section of the *New York Times,* estimated the Donald's wealth to be at $150–$250 million. Mr. Trump said that his wealth was actually in the billions and he filed a $5 billion defamation suit against Mr. O'Brien and his publisher, Hachette Book Group. Mr. Trump said his net worth at that time was $5 billion and as of July 2009 was $6 billion. Is this defamation?

7. On the day after Thanksgiving, November 28, 2008, Walmart held a nationwide sale of a limited number of sharply discounted televisions, computers, and video game sets. The "blitz sale" had been advertised heavily in newspapers and on television. At the Valley Stream Walmart store in Long Island, New York, 2,000 shoppers lined up hours before the scheduled 6 A.M. store opening, forming a line at a place marked by a handwritten sign, "Blitz Line Starts Here." The crowd became unruly at one point and the store manager called the police. However, the police left after concluding that things were under control. Shortly afterwards, at 5 A.M., the crowd broke through the glass doors of the store in a stampede. Jdimytai Damour, a Walmart maintenance worker, was trampled by the crowd and died from asphyxiation. OSHA has imposed a $7,000 fine on Walmart for its failure to take appropriate steps to control the crowd. Walmart is fighting the fine because it maintains the stampede and the trampling were not foreseeable simply because Walmart held a post–Thanksgiving day blitz sale. Walmart has argued that OSHA is asking it to predict events and that there were, at that time, no laws or rules on crowd control or so-called "blitz sales" (sales in which there are a limited number of items at a reduced price). Walmart's lawyers argued, "If this was a foreseeable event, why did the police feel comfortable in leaving the scene?"

Walmart has already entered into an agreement with the Nassau County, New York, district attorney to adopt crowd control policies at its 92 stores in New York, create a $400,000 fund to compensate trampling victims, and donate $1.5 million to various community organizations in Nassau County. Walmart also implemented crowd-control policies at its stores nationwide. Evaluate the duty, breach of duty, and foreseeability issues in the Long Island stampede. Be sure to discuss whether Walmart breached any duty to the maintenance worker and why Walmart would push back against the small fine.[5]

8.   E*Trade Financial Corporation ran a memorable ad during the 2010 NFL Super Bowl in which a baby boy and a baby girl are chatting online via the use of a web camera. The dialogue between the two babies, who have the voices of adults, is as follows:

Baby boy: "So, yea, sorry about last night."

Baby girl: "I just don't understand why you didn't call last night."

Baby boy: "I was on E*Trade, you know, diversifying my portfolio, taking control like a wolf."

Baby girl: "Right."

Baby boy: "That volatility in the market, taken care of, wolf-style . . . (howls)."

Baby girl: "And that milkaholic Lindsay wasn't over?"

Baby boy: "Lindsay?"

Second baby girl pops in front of the web camera: "Milkawhat?"

Lindsay Lohan, a 23-year-old actress who has been required to attend drug rehabilitation programs and has served time in jail for various drug charges, has filed a $100 million suit against E*Trade for appropriation of her likeness and image. Ms. Lohan's lawyers have statements from friends and others who indicate that Ms. Lohan was the first person who came to mind when they saw the ad. Is this appropriation?

9.   KSL Recreation Corp. and Boca Partnership signed an agreement on February 23, 1994, to form a joint venture to renovate and expand the 356-acre Boca Raton Hotel & Club resort in Palm Beach County, Florida. The joint venture did not go through because KSL demanded an additional $3.5 million in expenses and fees. Boca then negotiated a loan with Olympus Real Estate Corporation. Boca was about to close on the financing of the renovation with Olympus when KSL faxed a copy of a lawsuit against Boca to Olympus. The lawsuit was not yet filed. Boca had a litigation clause in its agreement with Olympus, and it was required to pay more fees and a higher interest rate. Did KSL interfere with Boca's contract with Olympus?

10.   Lawrence Hardesty, a long-haul tractor-trailer driver, picked up a load of stadium seating equipment for delivery to an NFL stadium under construction in Baltimore. While workers were loading the seats and equipment, Mr. Hardesty stayed in the cab of his truck completing the necessary paperwork for the transport. There was a great deal of unused space in the trailer after the seats and equipment were loaded, but Mr. Hardesty did not check the load. When Mr. Hardesty arrived in Baltimore, he opened the truck doors and the shifted boxes fell on him and injured him. Mr. Hardesty filed suit against American Seating for the negligence of its workers in loading the seats and boxes. American Seating defended on the grounds that its workers were not experts in shipping and hauling and that Mr. Hardesty was contributorily negligent for not checking the load before he left. Discuss the issues and decide who should prevail. [*Hardesty v American Seating Co.*, 194 F.Supp. 447 (D. Md. 2002)]

Management and the Law

If you are assigned the task of developing a new reference policy for your company, remember the following guidelines.

1. Stick with factual disclosures: Use "There was an accusation of embezzlement and he resigned," not "He is an embezzler."

2. Stick with easily defined terms: Use "Angers easily," not "He is a lunatic."

3. Report what happened, not your view: Use "Other staff members complained about her conduct and work," not "She was a constant pain in the neck."

4. Implement an exit interview policy in which you disclose the information you have on file that will be given when references are requested.

5. Verify the protections afforded under your state law, if any.

Notes

1. "Quotation of the Week," *New York Times*, March 21, 2010, p. SB2.

2. Robert Pear, "Health System Warily Prepares for Privacy Rules," *New York Times*, April 6, 2003, pp. A1, A19.

3. Stephanie Clifford, "A Coat Endorsed by the President? The White House Says No," *New York Times*, January 7, 2009, p. B3.

4. Corey Kilgannon and Jeffrey E. Singer, "Shoplifting Suspects' Choice: Pay or Be Shamed," New York Times, June 22, 2010, p. A1.

5. Ann Zimmerman, "Walmart Fights Safety Fine, Worried About Precedent," Wall Street Journal, July 9, 2010, p. B3. Steven Greenhouse, "Wal-Mart Displays Its Legal Might Fighting $7,000 Fine in Trampling Case," New York Times, July 7, 2010, p. B1.

Product Advertising and Liability

The first jury verdict over $1 million in a product liability suit occurred in 1962. Today, the top five verdicts in 2009 in the United States exceeded the top five for 2008 by 52 percent, with the top five verdicts all topping $100 million each.[1]

Product liability is a unique area of law. It has social roots in that it attempts to lessen the burden of losses by requiring a manufacturer or manufacturer's insurer to pay for a defective product. It also has contract roots in that if a product does not do what it is supposed to do, a breach of contract has occurred. Finally, it also has roots in tort law insofar as an injury results from someone else's carelessness. In these senses, product liability is a combination of contract law, tort law, and social responsibility.

This chapter answers the following questions: How did product liability law develop? What are the contract theories for recovery? What is required for a tort-based recovery on a defective product? How does advertising create liability for a business? What is strict tort liability for products? What reforms are proposed for cutting back liability? Are international product liability standards different? ■

Advertising may be described as the science of arresting human intelligence long enough to get money out of it.

Stephen Leacock

Caution: Cape does not enable user to fly.

Instructions on Kenner Products' Batman costume

UPDATE ↖
For up-to-date legal and ethical news, go to
mariannejennings.com

If you do not understand, or cannot read, all directions, cautions and warnings, do not use this product.

Warning on drain cleaner; winner of Lawsuit Abuse Watch's annual "Wacky Label Contest," 2004

Warning: May contain nuts.

Warning on can of Planter's mixed nuts, 2009

Fireplace log may cause fire.

Warning on a fireplace log and winner, 2001

Do not adjust blade while running.

Warning on Craftsman lawn mower

Remove child before folding.

On a stroller

ISTOCKPHOTO.COM/GALINA BARSKAYA

CONSIDER...

Ginger Smith was a passenger on Ronald Smith's boat on West Point Lake, Alabama. Ronald Smith was operating the boat, which was towing Ms. Smith's son, Shane McClellan, on an inflatable inner tube behind the boat. The inner tube was tied to the boat by a 50-foot Model 51650 polypropylene line that was manufactured by The Coleman Company and was purchased at a

nearby Walmart store. While Shane McClellan was being towed on the inner tube, the line snapped, and the end connected to the boat flew back toward the boat and hit Ms. Smith in the eye, causing the loss of that eye. Ms. Smith filed suit against Coleman, Walmart, and Ronald Smith. Coleman says that its package warned against using the line for towing. Who is liable? Why or why not?

Development of Product Liability

For some time, courts followed the principle of *caveat emptor*—"Let the buyer beware." This theory meant that sellers were not liable for defects in their products and that it was the buyer's responsibility to be on the alert for defects and take the appropriate precautions.

Following a series of court decisions in which buyers were allowed recovery and courts questioned the public policy wisdom of *caveat emptor*, the *Restatement (Second) of Torts* adopted its now famous Section 402A on strict tort liability (discussed later in this chapter). With this adoption, the area of product liability had gone full swing from no liability (*caveat emptor*) to an almost *per se* standard of liability for defective products.

Advertising as a Contract Basis for Product Liability

Express Warranties

An **express warranty** as provided in the Uniform Commercial Code (UCC) is an express promise (oral or written) by the seller as to the quality, abilities, or

319

EXHIBIT 10.1 Statements of Fact Versus Opinion

STATEMENT	FACT OR OPINION?
This car gets 20 miles per gallon.	Fact
This car gets great gas mileage.	Opinion
These goods are 100% wool.	Fact
This is the finest wool around.	Opinion
This truck has never been in an accident.	Fact
This truck is solid.	Opinion
This mace stops assailants in their tracks.	Fact (promise of performance)
This mace is very effective.	Opinion
This makeup is hypoallergenic.	Fact
This makeup is good for your skin.	Opinion
This ink will not stain clothes.	Fact
This ink is safe to use.	Opinion
This computer is IBM-compatible.	Fact
This computer is as good as any IBM.	Opinion
This watch is waterproof.	Fact
This watch is durable.	Opinion

performance of a product (UCC § 2–313). The seller need not use the words *promise* or *guarantee* to make an express warranty. A seller makes a warranty by displaying a sample or model or giving a description of the goods. Promises of how the goods will perform are also express warranties. "These goods are 100% wool," "This tire cannot be punctured," and "These jeans will not shrink," are examples of express warranties.

Ads are but one form of express warranties. The negotiation process can find the seller making express warranties to the buyer. For example, if a seller tells the buyer that a dog is a purebred, that a painting is a "painting by Francis Bacon," or that a horse is "disease-free," the seller has made an express warranty. Statements made by the seller to the buyer before the sale that are part of the basis of the sale or bargain are express warranties. Information included on the product packaging is an express warranty if that information includes statements of fact or promises of performance.

Opinions, however, are not considered a basis for transactions and are therefore not express warranties. For example, the statement "This glassware is as good as anyone else's" is sales puffing and not an express warranty. Exhibit 10.1 gives some examples of statements of fact versus opinion.

Castro v QVC Network, Inc. (Case 10.1), deals with an issue of liability for representations via ad statements.

CASE 10.1

Castro v QVC Network, Inc.
139 F.3d 114 (2d Cir. 1998)

A Turkey of a Pan: Liability on Thanksgiving Day

FACTS

In November 1993, QVC Network (appellee), an operator of a cable television home-shopping channel, advertised, as part of a one-day Thanksgiving promotion, the "T-Fal Jumbo Resistal Roaster." The roaster was manufactured by U.S.A. T-Fal Corporation. The QVC ad described the roaster as suitable for roasting a 25-pound turkey. At the time that T-Fal and QVC entered into an agreement for the sale of the roasting pan, T-Fal did not have a pan in its line large enough to roast a 25-pound turkey. T-Fal asked its parent company in France to provide a suitable roasting pan as soon as possible. The parent company provided a larger pan to which it added two small handles.

Loyda Castro (appellant) ordered the roasting pan and used it for roasting her turkey on Thanksgiving Day, 1993. Mrs. Castro was injured when she tried to remove the turkey from the oven. Using two large insulated oven mitts, Mrs. Castro tried to lift the pan from the oven, placing two fingers on each handle. Two fingers were the maximum grip permitted by the small handles. As the turkey tipped toward her, she lost control of the pan, spilling the hot drippings and fat that had accumulated in the pan during the cooking and basting process. Mrs. Castro suffered second- and third-degree burns to her foot and ankle, which have led to scarring, paresthesia, and swelling.

Mrs. Castro filed suit for strict liability and breach of warranty. The warranty charge was dismissed, and the jury returned a verdict for QVC and T-Fal. Mrs. Castro appealed.

JUDICIAL OPINION

CALABRESI, Circuit Judge

Products liability law has long been bedeviled by the search for an appropriate definition of "defective" product design. Over the years, both in the cases and in the literature, two approaches have come to predominate. The first is the risk/utility theory, which focuses on whether the benefits of a product outweigh the dangers of its design. The second is the consumer expectations theory, which focuses on what a buyer/user of a product would properly expect that the product would be suited for.

Not all states accept both of these approaches. Some define design defect only according to the risk/utility approach.

One of the first states to accept both approaches was California, which in *Barker v Lull Engineering Co.*, 20 Cal.3d 413, 143 Cal.Rptr. 225, 573 P.2d 443 (1978), held that "a product may be found defective in design, so as to subject a manufacturer to strict liability for resulting injuries, under either of two alternative tests"— consumer expectations and risk/utility. Several states have followed suit and have adopted both theories.

Prior to the recent case of *Denny v Ford Motor Co.*, 87 N.Y.2d 248, 639 N.Y.S.2d 250, 662 N.E.2d 730 (1995), it was not clear whether New York recognized both tests. In *Denny*, the plaintiff was injured when her Ford Bronco II sports utility vehicle rolled over when she slammed on the brakes to avoid hitting a deer in the vehicle's path. The plaintiff asserted claims for strict products liability and for breach of implied warranty, and the district judge—over the objection of defendant Ford—submitted both causes of action to the jury. The jury ruled in favor of Ford on the strict liability claim, but found for the plaintiff on the implied warranty claim. On appeal, Ford argued that the jury's verdicts on the strict products liability claim and the breach of warranty claim were inconsistent because the causes of action were identical.

This court certified the *Denny* case to the New York Court of Appeals to answer the following questions: (1) "whether, under New York law, the strict products liability and implied warranty claims are identical"; and (2) "whether, if the claims are different, the strict products liability claim is broader than the implied warranty claim and encompasses the latter."

In response to the certified questions, the Court of Appeals held that in a products liability case a cause of action for strict liability is not identical to a claim for breach of warranty.

Moreover, the court held that a strict liability claim is not per se broader than a breach of warranty claim such that the former encompasses the latter. Thus, while claims of strict products liability and breach of warranty are often used interchangeably, under New York law the two causes of action are definitively different. The imposition of strict liability for an alleged design "defect" is determined by a risk/utility standard. The notion of "defect" in a U.C.C.-based breach of warranty claim focuses, instead, on consumer expectations.

Since *Denny*, then, it has been settled that the risk/utility and consumer expectations theories of design defect can, in New York, be the bases of distinct causes of action: one for strict products liability and one for breach of warranty. This fact, however, does not settle the question of

CONTINUED

when a jury must be charged separately on each cause of action and when, instead, the two causes are, on the facts of the specific case, sufficiently similar to each other so that one charge to the jury is enough.

While eminent jurists have at times been troubled by this issue, the New York Court of Appeals in *Denny* was quite clear on when the two causes of action might meld and when, instead, they are to be treated as separate. It did this by adding its own twist to the distinction—namely, what can aptly be called the "dual purpose" requirement. Thus in *Denny*, the Court of Appeals pointed out that the fact that a product's overall benefits might outweigh its overall risks does not preclude the possibility that consumers may have been misled into using the product in a context in which it was dangerously unsafe. And this, the New York court emphasized, could be so even though the benefits in other uses might make the product sufficiently reasonable so that it passed the risk/utility test.

In *Denny*, the Ford Bronco II was not designed as a conventional passenger automobile. Instead, it was designed as an off-road, dual purpose vehicle. But in its marketing of the Bronco II, Ford stressed its suitability for commuting and for suburban and city driving. Under the circumstances, the Court of Appeals explained that a rational fact-finder could conclude that the Bronco's utility as an off-road vehicle outweighed the risk of injury resulting from roll-over accidents (thus passing the risk/utility test), but at the same time find that the vehicle was not safe for the "ordinary purpose" of daily driving for which it was also marketed and sold (thus flunking the consumer expectations test).

That is precisely the situation before us. The jury had before it evidence that the product was designed, marketed, and sold as a multiple-use product. The pan was originally manufactured and sold in France as an all-purpose cooking dish without handles. And at trial, the jury saw a videotape of a QVC representative demonstrating to the television audience that the pan, in addition to serving as a suitable roaster for a twenty-five pound turkey, could also be used to cook casseroles, cutlets, cookies, and other low-volume foods. The court charged the jury that "[a] product is defective if it is not reasonably safe[,] [t]hat is, if the product is so likely to

be harmful to persons that a reasonable person who had actual knowledge of its potential for producing injury would conclude that it should not have been marketed in that condition." And, so instructed, the jury presumably found that the pan, because it had many advantages in a variety of uses, did not fail the risk/utility test.

But it was also the case that the pan was advertised as suitable for a particular use—cooking a twenty-five pound turkey. Indeed, T-Fal added handles to the pan in order to fill QVC's request for a roasting pan that it could use in its Thanksgiving promotion. The product was, therefore, sold as appropriately used for roasting a twenty-five pound turkey. And it was in that use that allegedly the product failed and injured the appellant.

In such circumstances, New York law is clear that a general charge on strict products liability based on the risk/utility approach does not suffice. The jury could have found that the roasting pan's overall utility for cooking low-volume foods outweighed the risk of injury when cooking heavier foods, but that the product was nonetheless unsafe for the purpose for which it was marketed and sold—roasting a twenty-five pound turkey—and, as such, was defective under the consumer expectations test. That being so, the appellants were entitled to a separate breach of warranty charge.

In light of the evidence presented by appellants of the multi-purpose nature of the product at issue, the district court, applying New York law, should have granted appellants' request for a separate jury charge on the breach of warranty claim in addition to the charge on the strict liability claim.

Reversed.

CASE QUESTIONS

1. How was the turkey pan purchased? Does the method and location of purchase make a difference in the case?

2. Was the pan represented as suitable for roasting a turkey?

3. What is the relationship between tort liability and warranty liability?

4. What is the risk/utility test?

CONSIDER...   10.1

John R. Klages was employed as a night auditor at Conley's Motel on Route 8 in Hampton Township. He worked from 11 P.M. until 7 A.M., five days a week. On March 30, 1968, at approximately 1:30 A.M., two individuals entered the motel and announced, "This is a stickup. Open the safe." Mr. Klages indicated that he was unable to open the safe because he did not know the combination. One of the individuals then pointed a gun at his head and pulled the trigger. Fortunately for Mr. Klages, the gun was a starter pistol, and he was not seriously injured.

The next day, Mr. Klages and a fellow employee, Bob McVay, decided that they needed something to protect themselves against the possibility of future holdups. After reading an article concerning the effects of mace, Mr. McVay suggested that they consider using mace for their protection.

After reading and discussing the literature from the Markl Supply Company with their employer, Mr. McVay purchased an MK-II mace weapon, which described the mace as follows.

Rapidly vaporizes on face of assailant effecting instantaneous incapacitation. . . . *It will* instantly stop and subdue *entire groups.* . . instantly stops assailants in their tracks. . . . *[A]n attacker is* subdued instantly, *for a period of 15 to 20 minutes.* . . . Time Magazine *stated the Chemical Mace is "for police the first, if not the final, answer to a nationwide need—a weapon that* disables as effectively *as a gun and yet does no permanent injury."* . . . *The effectiveness is the result of a unique,* incapacitating formulation (*patent pending*), *projected in a shotgun-like pattern of heavy liquid droplets that, upon contact with the face, cause extreme tearing, and a stunned, winded condition, often accompanied by dizziness and apathy.*

At approximately 1:40 A.M. on September 22, 1968, while Mr. Klages was on duty, two unknown individuals entered the motel office, requested a room, and announced a stickup. One of the intruders took out a gun and directed Mr. Klages to open the safe. Using the cash register as a shield, Mr. Klages squirted the mace, hitting the intruder "right beside the nose." Mr. Klages immediately ducked below the register, but the intruder followed him down and shot him in the head. The intruders immediately departed, and Mr. Klages called the police. The bullet wound caused complete loss of sight in Mr. Klages's right eye. He claims a breach of an express warranty. Is he right?

THINK: The requirements for an express warranty are a statement of fact or a promise of performance.

APPLY: What statements of fact or promises of performance are made in the ad or on the product packaging?

"[I]nstantly stops assailants in their tracks" is a promise of performance; "subdued instantly, for a period of 15 to 20 minutes" is also a promise of performance.

ANSWER: The product failed to live up to those promises, so there was a breach of express warranty, and the company is liable for the injury Mr. Klages sustained after using the mace against his attackers. [*Klages v General Ordnance Equipment Corp.*, 19 UCC Rep. Serv. (Callaghan) 22 (Pa. 1976)]

Federal Regulation of Warranties and Advertising

Express warranties are advertisements for goods. Accurate advertising is a basis for full information, and full information is a cornerstone for competitive markets.

In 1914, Congress passed the **Federal Trade Commission Act,** which authorized the **Federal Trade Commission** (FTC) to prevent "unfair and deceptive trade practices." Congress passed the **Wheeler-Lea Act of 1938,** clarifying and expanding the FTC's power by authorizing it to regulate "unfair and deceptive acts or practices" whenever the public is being deceived, regardless of any effects on competition. The FTC has challenged unsubstantiated or ambiguous advertising claims and has reviewed and eliminated deceptive techniques in television ads.

Content Control and Accuracy

The FTC has regulated the accuracy of ads in several ways. First, the FTC challenged certain types of price claims. If an ad announces "50% off," the prices must actually be half the original prices charged for the products or services prior to the sale; that price cannot be inflated to cover the markdown. If an ad quotes a "normal" price, that price must reflect what most sellers in the area are charging.

The FTC has also challenged the accuracy of ads. Claims that goods are "100% wool" are not only the basis for express warranty recovery but also the basis for an FTC challenge. Also, the FTC challenges advertising methods. For example, using "marbles" in soup to make it look thicker as it pours is deceptive. The FTC has used its powers to ensure that ads accurately depict the product as it exists. The regulations also apply to the terms of the contract and the time for performance. For example, the FTC, through its Mail or Telephone Order Merchandise Rule, requires that catalog merchants disclose delays in delivering ordered goods to consumers and that consumers be informed up front about custom product delays, special order delays, and direct-from-the-manufacturer delays. The ads, pamphlets, catalogs, and mailings must disclose delays known up front, and the consumer must be notified after an order is placed if the delay will exceed the maximum amount of time allowed under the rules for delivery. The FTC has enforced those disclosure requirements against Internet merchants as well. In *In the Matter of Macys.com, KBkids.com, and CDnow, Inc.,* the FTC settled charges with these three e-retailers who were alleged to have violated the Mail or Telephone Order Merchandise Rule by failing to provide buyers with adequate notice of shipping delays or had continued to promise specific delivery dates when they were aware that they were unlikely to meet those deadlines.

CYBERLAW

FTC Control of Performance Claims

Any claims of the ability or efficacy of a product must be supportable. If a sunburn-relief product claims to "anesthetize nerves," the advertiser must be able to prove that claim.

Where an advertising claim cannot be substantiated, the FTC has used **corrective advertising** as a remedy. Corrective advertising requires a seller to correct the unsubstantiated claims made in previous ads. The landmark case *Warner-Lambert Co. v FTC* (Case 10.2) involves an issue of corrective advertising.

CASE 10.2   *Warner-Lambert Co. v FTC*
562 F.2d 749 (D.C. Cir. 1977), *cert. den.* 435 U.S. 950 (1978)

Does Listerine Prevent Colds?

FACTS

Listerine, a product of the Warner-Lambert Company (petitioner), has been on the market since 1879 and has been represented through advertising to be beneficial for colds, cold symptoms, and sore throats. After a 1972 complaint about Warner-Lambert advertising for Listerine,

the FTC held four months of hearings on the ad issues and then ordered Warner-Lambert to do the following:

1. Cease and desist representing that Listerine will cure colds or sore throats, that it will prevent colds or sore throats, or that users of Listerine will have fewer colds than nonusers.

2. Cease and desist representing that Listerine is a treatment for, or will lessen the severity of, colds or sore throats; that it will have any significant beneficial effect on the symptoms of sore throats or any beneficial effect on symptoms of colds; or that the ability of Listerine to kill germs is of medical significance in the treatment of colds or sore throats or their symptoms.

3. Cease and desist disseminating any advertisement for Listerine unless it is clearly and conspicuously disclosed in each advertisement, in this exact language, that "Contrary to prior advertising, Listerine will not help prevent colds or sore throats or lessen their severity." This requirement extended only to the next $10 million Listerine would spend on advertising after the order.

Warner-Lambert appealed the order.

JUDICIAL OPINION

WRIGHT, Circuit Judge

The first issue on appeal is whether the Commission's conclusion that Listerine is not beneficial for colds or sore throats is supported by the evidence.

First, the Commission found that the ingredients of Listerine are not present in sufficient quantities to have any therapeutic effect.

Second, the Commission found that in the process of gargling it is impossible for Listerine to reach critical areas of the body in medically significant concentration.

Third, the Commission found that even if significant quantities of the active ingredients of Listerine were to reach critical sites where cold viruses enter and infect the body, they could not interfere with the activities of the virus because they could not penetrate the tissue cells.

... [T]he Commission found that the ability of Listerine to kill germs by millions on contact is of no medical significance in the treatment of colds or sore throats.

... [T]he Commission found that Listerine has no significant beneficial effect on the symptoms of sore throat. The Commission recognized that gargling with Listerine could provide temporary relief from a sore throat by removing accumulated debris irritating the throat. But this type of relief can also be obtained by gargling with salt water or even warm water.

Petitioner contends that even if its advertising claims in the past were false, the portion of the Commission's order requiring "corrective advertising" exceeds the Commission's statutory power. The Commission's position is that the affirmative disclosure that Listerine will not prevent colds or lessen their severity is absolutely necessary to give effect to the prospective cease and desist order; a hundred years of false cold claims have built up a large reservoir of erroneous consumer belief that would persist, unless corrected, long after petitioner ceased making the claims.

If the Commission is to attain the objectives Congress envisioned, it cannot be required to confine its road block to the narrow lane the transgressor has traveled; it must be allowed effectively to close all roads to the prohibited goal, so that its order may not be bypassed with impunity.

We turn next to the specific disclosure required: "Contrary to prior advertising, Listerine will not help prevent colds or sore throats or lessen their severity." Petitioner is ordered to include this statement in every future advertisement for Listerine for a defined period. In printed advertisements it must be displayed in type size at least as large as that in which the principal portion of the text of the advertisement appears and it must be separated from the text so that it can be readily noticed. In television commercials the disclosure must be presented simultaneously in both audio and visual portions. During the audio portion of the disclosure in television and radio advertisements, no other sounds, including music, may occur.

These specifications are well calculated to assure that the disclosure will reach the public. It will necessarily attract the notice of readers, viewers and listeners, and be plainly conveyed. Given these safeguards, we believe the preamble "Contrary to prior advertising" is not necessary. It can serve only two purposes: either to attract attention that a correction follows or to humiliate the advertiser. The Commission claims only the first purpose for it, and this we think is obviated by other terms of the order. The second purpose, if it were intended, might be called for in an egregious case of deliberate deception, but this is not one. While we do not decide whether petitioner proffered its cold claims in good faith or bad, the record compiled could support a finding of good faith. On these facts, the confessional preamble to the disclosure is not warranted.

Accordingly, the order, as modified, is affirmed.

CASE QUESTIONS

1. What claims does the FTC question in the Listerine ads, and why?

2. What proposals for corrective advertising are made in the order?

3. What happens to the preamble, "Contrary to prior advertising"?

4. What standard does the case establish for corrective ads once the FTC finds a company's ads have deceived the public?

CONSIDER... 10.2

Philip Morris Inc. marketed and promoted its low-tar brands to smokers—who were concerned about the health hazards of smoking or considering quitting—as less harmful than full-flavor cigarettes. Internal industry documents revealed that by the late 1960s and early 1970s, Philip Morris and other tobacco companies were aware that lower-tar cigarettes are unlikely to provide health benefits because they do not actually deliver the low levels of tar and nicotine advertised. Smokers of low-tar cigarettes, in order to satisfy their addiction to nicotine, modify their smoking behavior to compensate for the reduced nicotine yields by "taking more frequent puffs, inhaling smoke more deeply, holding smoke in their lungs longer, covering cigarette ventilation holes with fingers or lips, and/or smoking more cigarettes." As a result of this nicotine-driven behavior, smokers of low-tar cigarettes boost their intake of tar, so that lower-tar cigarettes do not result in lower tar intake and therefore do not yield the touted health benefits or serve as a step toward quitting smoking. The FTC and other government agencies brought suit to halt the ads and require corrective advertising by the companies. Discuss whether, based on the *Listerine* case, the government would have the authority to halt the ads and require corrective advertisements. [*U.S. v Philip Morris USA Inc.*, 566 F.3d 1095 (C.A.D.C. 2009), *cert. denied*, 130 S.Ct. 3501 (2010).]

FTC Control of Celebrity Endorsements

During the 1980s, the FTC entered a new aspect of ad content control—namely, the use of **celebrity endorsements** for products. At the time the FTC became involved, its director of consumer protection stated:

> The effectiveness of having a product touted by a well-known movie star or sports figure is apparent from the increasing use of celebrity endorsements in advertising. A sales pitch by a celebrity may be more believable than the same message delivered by an unknown spokesperson. The endorsement can be an important part of sales strategy, and is often quite handsomely rewarded. The endorser may profit from a false advertisement just as much as the manufacturer, and thus it is not unreasonable to obligate him to ascertain the truthfulness of the claims he is being paid to make.[2]

BUSINESS PLANNING TIP

Always review the language used in ads for products. Determine whether express warranties are being made. Make sure that warranties, statements of fact, and promises of performance are accurate.

With a celebrity endorsement, the FTC requires several steps. First, as the quote indicates, the celebrity must ascertain the truth of the ad claims. Second, the celebrity cannot make any claims about product use unless the celebrity has actually used and experienced the product. Finally, if any claims are being made that are not the celebrity's, the source of the information must be disclosed as part of the ad.

FTC Control of Bait and Switch

One of the better-known FTC ad regulations prohibits the use of **bait and switch,** a sales tactic in which a cheaper product than the one in stock is advertised to get customers into a store. The seller has no intention of selling the product and in some cases might not even have the product in stock; but the ad is used as "bait" to get the customers in order to present them with a "better," more expensive product. Such ad tactics are considered deceptive and subject to FTC remedy.

FTC Control of Product Comparisons

Another aspect of active enforcement by the FTC is in the area of product comparisons. The FTC permits and even welcomes comparisons of products, but such comparisons must be accurate. Results of surveys must be supportable, and product preference tests must be done fairly. In the past few years, the FTC has taken a *laissez-faire* approach in ad regulation. Other agencies, such as the offices of state attorneys general, the Better Business Bureau, and private companies and individuals, have undertaken public and private enforcement of deceptive ad claims.

The bulk of litigation over comparative ads is now conducted by and against competitors. The FTC generally focuses on deception by companies about their own products. However, federal trademark law permits competitors to recover from companies for ads that include such misrepresentations. Companies can also be held liable for misrepresentations regarding other companies' products. Litigation over comparative ads is somewhat lucrative because plaintiffs can recover treble damages, the defendant company's profits, and, in some cases, attorney fees. Case 10.3 presents a competitor's litigation over misrepresentation.

CASE 10.3

McNeil-PPC, Inc. v Pfizer Inc.
351 F.Supp.2d 226 (S.D.N.Y. 2005)

Stringing Them Along on No Floss

FACTS

In June 2004, Pfizer Inc. ("Pfizer") launched a consumer advertising campaign for its mouthwash, Listerine Antiseptic Mouthrinse. Print ads and hangtags on the bottles in the stores featured an image of a Listerine bottle balanced on a scale against a white container of dental floss.

The campaign also featured a television commercial that announced, "Listerine's as effective as floss at fighting plaque and gingivitis. Clinical studies prove it." Although the commercial cautions that "[t]here's no replacement for flossing," the commercial repeats two more times the message that Listerine is "as effective as flossing against plaque and gingivitis." The commercial also shows a narrow stream of blue liquid flowing out of a Cool Mint Listerine bottle, then tracking a piece of dental floss being pulled from a white floss container, and then swirling around and between teeth—bringing to mind an image of liquid floss.

McNeil-PPC, Inc. ("PPC") (a division of Johnson & Johnson), the market leader in sales of string dental floss and other interdental cleaning products, brought suit alleging that Pfizer engaged in false advertising and unfair competition in violation of § 43(a) of the Lanham Act, 15 U.S.C. § 1125(a). PPC contends that Pfizer's

advertisements are false and misleading because the ads implicitly claim that Listerine is a replacement for floss—that all the benefits of flossing may be obtained by rinsing with Listerine.

PPC filed a motion for an injunction to stop Pfizer from running the ads.

JUDICIAL OPINION

CHIN, District Judge

Traditionally, the "most widely recommended" mechanical device for removing interproximal plaque (the deposits located in the hard-to-reach areas between the teeth) is dental floss. The ADA recommends "brushing twice a day and cleaning between the teeth with floss or interdental cleaners once each day to remove plaque from all tooth surfaces." Flossing provides a number of benefits. It removes food debris and plaque interdentally and it also removes plaque subgingivally. As part of a regular oral hygiene program, flossing helps reduce and prevent not only gingivitis but also periodontitis and caries.

Some 87% of consumers, however, floss either infrequently or not at all. Although dentists and dental hygienists regularly tell their patients to floss, many consumers do not floss or rarely floss because it is a difficult and time-consuming process.

CONTINUED

As a consequence, a large consumer market exists to be tapped. If the 87% of consumers who never or rarely floss can be persuaded to floss more regularly, sales of floss would increase dramatically. PPC has endeavored, with products such as the RADF and the Power Flosser, to reach these consumers by trying to make flossing easier.

In the context of this case, therefore, Pfizer and PPC are competitors.

Pfizer sponsored two clinical studies involving Listerine and floss: the "Sharma Study" and the "Bauroth Study." These studies purported to compare the efficacy of Listerine against dental floss in controlling plaque and gingivitis in subjects with mild to moderate gingivitis.

The authors of the Sharma Study concluded that the study provided "additional support for the use of the essential oil mouthrinse as an adjunct to mechanical oral hygiene regimens." They cautioned that "[p]rofessional recommendations to floss daily should continue to be reinforced."

The Bauroth Study authors concluded: "[W]e do not wish to suggest that the mouthrinse should be used instead of dental floss or any other interproximal cleaning device."

The ADA reported on the Pfizer studies in its own website. The ADA wrote that "[w]hile some study results [referencing the Sharma and Bauroth Studies] indicate the use of a mouth rinse can be as effective as flossing for reducing plaque between the teeth," it continued to recommend "brushing twice a day and cleaning between the teeth with floss or interdental cleaners once each day."

A number of individual dentists and hygienists complained directly to Pfizer that consumers would get the wrong message.

From the time Pfizer launched its advertising campaign, sales of both the RADF and the Power Flosser have taken a steep decline. Consumers who use the RADF and Power Flosser . . . are predominantly "folks who don't like to floss," who "would love to have a replacement for flossing." These consumers "would be more susceptible to a message like the Listerine advertising campaign."

To prevail on a Lanham Act false advertising claim, a plaintiff must demonstrate the falsity of the challenged advertisement, by proving that it is either (1) literally false, as a factual matter; or (2) implicitly false, *i.e.,* although literally true, still likely to mislead or confuse consumers. The false or misleading statement must be material.

The two studies included in their samples only individuals with mild to moderate gingivitis. They excluded individuals with severe gingivitis or with any degree of periodontitis, and they did not purport to draw any conclusions with respect to these individuals. Hence, the literal claim in Pfizer's advertisements is overly broad, for the studies did not purport to prove that Listerine is as effective as floss "against plaque and gingivitis," but only against plaque and gingivitis in individuals with mild to moderate gingivitis. Consequently, consumers who suffer from severe gingivitis or periodontitis (including mild periodontitis) may be misled by the ads into believing that Listerine is just as effective as floss in helping them fight plaque and gingivitis, when the studies simply do not stand for that proposition.

Pfizer and its experts argue that the two studies are reliable, notwithstanding the indications that the participants in the flossing group did not floss properly, because these conditions reflect "real-world settings." But the ads do not say that "in the real world," where most people floss rarely or not at all, and even those who do floss have difficulty flossing properly, Listerine is "as effective as floss." Rather, the ads make the blanket assertion that Listerine works just as well as floss, an assertion the two studies simply do not prove. Although it is important to determine how a product works in the real world, it is probably more important to first determine how a product will work when it is used properly.

I find that Pfizer's false and misleading advertising also poses a public health risk, as the advertisements present a danger of undermining the efforts of dental professionals—and the ADA—to convince consumers to floss on a daily basis.

Injunction granted.

CASE QUESTIONS

1. What are the limitations of the studies on which Pfizer relied?

2. Why are mouthwash and floss competitors?

3. Describe the standards the court uses for stopping a misleading or false ad.

4. Evaluate Pfizer's use of the studies, the ads, and comment on the company's social responsibility posture. Comment on its competitive strategies.

FTC Remedies

As noted in the previous sections, the FTC has a wide range of remedies available in the event of deceptive advertising, including corrective ads, injunctions to prevent deceptive ads from being run, and reimbursement by companies and endorsers for purchasers who were misled by ads.

More often than not, these remedies come about through a consent decree. A **consent decree** is a negotiated settlement between the FTC and the advertiser. It is the equivalent of a *nolo contendere* or no contest plea. The FTC and the advertiser, endorser, and/or agency or Web site designer agree to remedies, and the case is disposed of through the decree without further action.

The FTC has focused increasingly on companies that, like Pfizer, are making health claims about their products. For example, Kellogg's agreed twice in one year to change the packaging of its cereals that made health claims. It agreed to change its boxes for Frosted Mini-Wheats, which claimed to "increase your child's attentiveness by 20%," and also agreed to change its Rice Krispies packaging, which claimed, "Now helps support your child's immunity."

Ad Regulation by the FDA

The Food and Drug Administration (FDA) also has authority over some forms of advertising. For example, the FDA has control over direct advertising to the public of prescription medications. Products such as Retin-A have had direct ads and news releases subject to FDA regulation. For example, in the case of Retin-A, the FDA warned Ortho, its manufacturer, that Retin-A had been approved as an anti-acne cream, not as an anti-aging cream, and that it could not be advertised to the public as such. The FDA also required General Mills to change its Cheerios cereal boxes to eliminate the claim that the cereal could reduce cholesterol.

Professional Ads

Most states have limitations on the types of ads professionals (such as doctors, lawyers, dentists, and accountants) can use in reaching the public. At one time, states had complete bans on ads by professionals. However, the U.S. Supreme Court held such bans to be too restrictive and violative of First Amendment protections on commercial speech (see Chapter 5). Restrictions may include requirements on fee disclosures or caveats on distinctions in individual cases and needs. The extent and validity of the restrictions continue to be refined through judicial application of First Amendment rights.

Contract Product Liability Theories: Implied Warranties

The UCC's Article 2 governs contracts for the sale of goods and includes several provisions for implied warranties. The following sections cover the requirements for each of the implied warranties.

The Implied Warranty of Merchantability

The **implied warranty of merchantability** (UCC § 2–314) is given in every sale of goods by a merchant seller. The warranty is not given by all sellers, only by merchant sellers. Briefly defined, merchants are those sellers who are engaged in the business of selling the good(s) that are the subject of the contract. The revisions to the UCC changed the wording of this warranty slightly so that it now provides that goods sold by a merchant "(c) are fit for the ordinary purposes for which goods of that description are used." The warranty means the goods are of fair or average quality and are fit for ordinary purposes. Under this warranty, basketballs must bounce, book bindings must hold together, and food items must be free of foreign objects.

For example, in *Metty v Shurfine Central Corp.*, 736 S.W.2d 527 (Mo. 1987), the court found that a breach of the implied warranty of merchantability occurred because part of a grasshopper in a can of green beans was eaten by a pregnant woman who purchased the beans. Shurfine was liable to the woman for resulting complications in her pregnancy. But what happens if there is something naturally present, such as a cherry pit in a cherry pie, that harms someone? Is there still a breach of warranty? *Mitchell v T.G.I. Friday's* (Case 10.4) provides an answer to these questions.

CASE 10.4

Mitchell v T.G.I. Friday's
748 N.E.2d 89 (Ohio App. 2000)

Clamming Up Because of Shell-Shock

FACTS

On April 11, 1996, Sandra Mitchell (appellant) was having dinner at Friday's restaurant (appellee). Ms. Mitchell was eating a fried clam strip when she bit into a hard substance that she believed to be a piece of a clam shell. She experienced immediate pain and later sought dental treatment. Some time later, the crown of a tooth came loose. The crown could not be reattached, and an oral surgeon removed the remaining root of the tooth.

Ms. Mitchell filed a product liability action against Friday's, which had served her the meal, and Pro Source Distributing (also appellee), the supplier of the fried clams. Both Friday's and Pro Source filed motions for summary judgment, which the trial court granted without explanation. Ms. Mitchell appealed.

JUDICIAL OPINION

WAITE, Judge

Appellant asserts that there is a reasonable expectation that clams are completely cleaned of their shells and free of foreign materials.

In the present case, Friday's set forth in its motion for summary judgment appellant's deposition testimony to the effect that while eating a clam strip, she bit down on "a hard, foreign substance." Appellant stated that she assumed it was a piece of a clam shell. Appellant described the size of the object as about a quarter of the size of a small fingernail or about a quarter of an inch or smaller and irregular in shape. Moreover, Friday's

attached an affidavit from its manager, Eric Hicks, who immediately responded to appellant's report of the incident. In that affidavit, Hicks confirmed that the object appellant presented to him was indeed a piece of clam shell and that it was approximately one-quarter inch in length and irregularly shaped.

Both Friday's and Pro Source presented essentially the same argument, that regardless of whether the foreign-natural test or reasonable-expectation test was applied, appellant has no claim against appellees.

The basis of appellant's argument for application of the reasonable-expectation test is found in R.C. 2307.75, which provides that a product is defective if it is more dangerous than an ordinary consumer would reasonably suspect. However, appellant has not set forth any case law or analysis that would suggest that food products fall under the purview of the statute. We can find no case that has analyzed a food item in that context. Indeed, the weight of product liability cases deal with synthetic products, for example, a cargo door hinge, a glass bottle, or a prosthetic hip joint. Thus, we see no compelling reason to abandon any established test due to the enactment of Ohio's product liability legislation.

However, it does not appear necessary to determine which test applies to the present case. Save for reference to the product liability statute, a similar argument was addressed in *Mathews v Maysville Seafoods, Inc.* (1991), 76 Ohio App.3d 624, 602 N.E.2d 764. In *Mathews*, the plaintiff suffered a bowel injury when he swallowed a fish bone while eating a fish fillet served by the defendant.

The trial court granted the defendant's motion for summary judgment. On appeal, the defendant argued for the adoption of the reasonable-expectation test as opposed to the foreign-natural test.

The *Mathews* court set forth both tests. Under the foreign-natural test:

> Bones which are natural to the type of meat served cannot legitimately be called a foreign substance, and a consumer who eats meat dishes ought to anticipate and be on his guard against the presence of such bones.

[Q]uoting *Mix v Ingersoll Candy Co.* (1936), 6 Cal.2d 674, 682, 59 P.2d 144, 148.

The reasonable-expectation test states:

> The test should be what is "reasonably expected" by the consumer in the food as served, not what might be natural to the ingredients of that food prior to preparation. . . . As applied to the action for common-law negligence, the test is related to the foreseeability of harm on the part of the defendant. The defendant is not an insurer but has the duty of ordinary care to eliminate or remove in the preparation of the food he serves such harmful substances as the consumer of the food, as served, would not ordinarily anticipate and guard against.

Mathews, 602 N.E.2d at 765.

The *Mathews* court looked to *Allen v Grafton* (1960), 164 N.E.2d 167, where the plaintiff was injured after swallowing a piece of oyster shell contained in a serving of fried oysters. The Supreme Court held:

> The presence in one of a serving of six fried oysters of a piece of oyster shell approximately 3 × 2 centimeters (about 11/5 inches by 4/5 of an inch) in diameter will not justify a legal conclusion either (a) that that serving of fried oysters constituted "food" that was "adulterated" within the meaning of Section 3715.59, Revised Code, or (b) that that serving constituted food not "reasonably fit for" eating.

The *Mathews* court further noted:

> In the instant case, it is not necessary to hold . . . that, because an oyster shell is natural to an oyster and thus not a substance "foreign" to an oyster, no liability can be predicated upon the sale of a fried oyster containing a piece of oyster shell. However, the fact, that something that is served with food and that will cause harm if eaten is natural to that food and so not a "foreign substance," will usually be an important factor in determining whether a consumer can reasonably anticipate and guard against it.

> In our opinion, the possible presence of a piece of oyster shell in or attached to an oyster is so well known to anyone who eats oysters that we can say as a matter of law that one who eats oysters can reasonably anticipate and guard against eating such a piece of shell, especially where it is as big a piece as the one described in plaintiff's petition.

Despite the opposing interpretations of *Allen*, the *Mathews* court stated that "it is not necessary to decide whether the 'reasonable expectation' test or the 'foreign-natural' test holds sway in Ohio." The court stated that it must be reasonably expected that even a fish fillet may contain fish bones, citing *Polite v Carey Hilliards Restaurants, Inc.* (1985). The *Mathews* court noted that in *Polite*, the court applied the foreign-natural test in affirming a summary judgment for the defendant where the plaintiff swallowed an obviously naturally occurring one-inch fish bone concealed in a fish fillet.

> An occasional piece of clam shell in a bowl of clam chowder is so well known to a consumer that we can say the consumer can reasonably anticipate and guard against it.

> Courts cannot and must not ignore the common experience of life and allow rules to develop that would make sellers of food or other consumer goods insurers of the products they sell.

In the present case, it cannot be disputed that the piece of clam shell that caused appellant's injury was natural to the clam strip she consumed. Turning to the question of whether appellant should have reasonably anticipated the presence of the clam shell, we are reminded of the Ohio Supreme Court's holding in *Allen*, *supra*, that "the possible presence of a piece of oyster shell in or attached to an oyster is so well known to anyone who eats oysters that we can say as a matter of law that one who eats oysters can reasonably anticipate and guard against eating such a piece of shell." The facts of the present case are virtually indistinguishable from *Allen* except for the type of injury and that, here, appellant was eating fried clams rather than fried oysters. We therefore hold that, as a matter of law, one who eats clams can reasonably anticipate and guard against eating a piece of shell.

As appellant's claim fails under both tests, we overrule her assignment of error and affirm the judgment of the trial court.

Judgment affirmed.

CASE QUESTIONS

1. What did Ms. Mitchell eat, and what were her resulting injuries?
2. What did the lower court do in the case that caused an admonition from the appellate court?
3. What test does Ohio follow—the foreign-natural or the reasonable-expectation test?
4. Does the court think the Ohio test makes a difference in this case?
5. Is the reasonable-expectation test one that makes the food producer or provider an insurer?

CONSIDER...   10.3

On November 11, 1994, Loretta Jones was injured when she bit into a meatball at an Olive Garden Restaurant owned by GMRI, Inc. in Pineville, North Carolina. When Ms. Jones attempted to take her first bite of the meatball, she bit down into an unidentified metal object. At that time, she experienced an "incredible stabbing pain in [her] tooth and [her] jaw," caused by a broken tooth. Because she was startled, she "sucked in and immediately sucked down the food" and the object. Ms. Jones said that she cut the meatball into eight pieces prior to taking the bite and that she did not detect any foreign object in the meatball at that time.

She filed suit against GMRI and Rich Products Corporation, which allegedly supplied or manufactured the meatball, asserting claims of negligence, breach of implied warranty, and loss of consortium. GMRI asserted as a defense to the implied warranty claim that it did not have a reasonable opportunity to inspect the meatball in a way that would have discovered the defect.

GMRI said that most of the restaurant's meatballs come into the store frozen and in sealed bags. The restaurant does a visual inspection of the sealed bags of meatballs and sends back those that do not meet the inspection. The meatballs are put into the freezer at the restaurant until needed, then put into a plastic holding container and placed in a refrigerator. The meatballs, which are slightly larger than a golf ball, are then mixed with a tomato sauce, heated, and served whole. Restaurant personnel indicated that they do not poke or slice the meatballs, other than to check the temperature with a probe.

Is GMRI liable to Ms. Jones? [*Jones v GMRI, Inc.*, 551 S.E.2d 867 (N.C. App. 2001)]

The Implied Warranty of Fitness for a Particular Purpose

The **implied warranty of fitness for a particular purpose** (UCC § 2-315) arises when the seller promises a buyer that the goods will be suitable for a use the buyer has proposed. For example, the owner of a nursery makes an implied warranty for a particular purpose when telling a buyer that a weed killer will work in the buyer's rose garden without harming the roses. An exercise enthusiast is given this warranty when the seller recommends a particular shoe as appropriate for aerobics.

The requirements for this warranty are:

1. The seller has skill or judgment in use of the goods.
2. The buyer is relying on that skill or judgment.
3. The seller knew or had reason to know of the buyer's reliance.
4. The seller makes a recommendation for the buyer's use and purpose.

For example, if you went to a pet store and asked for two male hamsters and one cage, the salesperson who picks out the two hamsters for you is making an implied warranty of fitness for a particular purpose: that the hamsters can cohabitate without reproducing. Should your hamsters reproduce, the pet store would be responsible for whatever damage you experience, including taking the baby hamsters from the misidentified hamster couple.

CONSIDER... 10.4

Cynthia Rubin went to Marshall Field's department store on April 5, 1986. While browsing, she got into a conversation with Julianna Reiner, a salesclerk, and told Ms. Reiner that she used Vaseline to remove her eye makeup. Ms. Reiner said Vaseline could clog her eye ducts and cause cataracts or other permanent eye damage, and she recommended Princess Marcella Borghese Instant Eye Make-Up Remover, manufactured by Princess Marcella Borghese, Inc. Ms. Rubin asked if the product was safe. Ms. Reiner showed her the box, which said, "Recommended for all skin types." Ms. Reiner said, "If it wouldn't be safe for you, it wouldn't say this on the box." Relying on Ms. Reiner's representations, Ms. Rubin purchased the product.

That night she used the product to remove her eye makeup. Her eyelids and the skin around her eyes turned red, became taut and rough, and started to sting. She washed her skin repeatedly and kept a cold washrag on her eyes all night. Two days later, when the burning did not subside, she called an ophthalmologist and went to see him the next day. He told her that she had contact dermatitis and prescribed an ointment.

A few weeks later, because the burning and roughness of her eyelids persisted, Ms. Rubin decided to see Dr. Katherine Wier, a dermatologist. Dr. Wier prescribed a similar ointment and told Ms. Rubin that the chemical causing the burning would remain in her system for three or four months. The stinging subsided, but Ms. Rubin could not wear eye makeup again regularly until summer 1987. When she tried to wear makeup again before that, her eyelids turned bright red and began swelling upon removal of the makeup.

Ms. Rubin filed suit for breach of implied warranty of fitness for a particular purpose. Should she recover? [*Rubin v Marshall Field & Co.*, 597 N.E.2d 688 (Ill. 1992)]

Eliminating Warranty Liability by Disclaimers

Warranties can be eliminated by the use of **disclaimers.** The proper method for disclaiming a warranty depends on the type of warranty. Express warranties, however, cannot be given and then taken back. Basically, an express warranty cannot be disclaimed. Exhibit 10.2 includes a summary of the means for disclaiming warranties.

The implied warranty of merchantability and the implied warranty of fitness for a particular purpose can be disclaimed by using a phrase such as "WITH ALL FAULTS," or "AS IS." Either warranty alone can be disclaimed by using the name of the warranty: "There is no warranty of merchantability given" or "There is no implied warranty of fitness for a particular purpose." Under Revised Article 2, the disclaimer for the implied warranty of merchantability must include the following language: "The seller undertakes no responsibility for the quality of the goods except as otherwise provided in this contract." Also under the Revised Article 2 provisions, a warranty can be disclaimed in a record. *"Record"* is new to the Revised UCC and expands the definition of writing to include electronic communications such as e-mails and faxes. For those warranty disclaimers required to be in writing, their presence in a record satisfies the writing requirements (see Chapters 12 and 13 for more information).

Even though the UCC is clear on the language to be used for warranty disclaimers and the process seems to be easy, the warranty disclaimers are still

BUSINESS PLANNING TIP

To disclaim a warranty, follow these guidelines.

1. Use LARGE type.

2. Use a different color for the disclaimer text.

3. Place the disclaimer on the front of the contract.

4. Use proper statutory language.

5. Have buyers initial the disclaimer.

6. On electronic records, get verification of receipt of e-mail or fax with disclaimer.

EXHIBIT 10.2 UCC Warranties: Creation, Restrictions, and Disclaimers

TYPE	CREATION	RESTRICTION	DISCLAIMER
Express	Affirmation of fact or promise of performance (samples, models, descriptions)	Must be part of the basis of the bargain	Cannot make a disclaimer inconsistent with an express
Implied Warranty of Merchantability	Given in every sale of goods by a merchant ("fit for ordinary purposes")	Only given by merchants	(1) Must use disclaimer of quality or use "merchant-ability" or general disclaimer "as is" or "with all faults" (2) If written—(record) must be conspicuous
Implied Warranty of Fitness for a Particular Purpose	Seller knows of buyer's reliance for a particular use (buyer is ignorant)	Seller must have knowledge—buyer must rely	(1) Must be in writing (record) (2) Must be conspicuous (3) Must be clear there are no warranties (using specific language) or (4) Also disclaimed with "as is" or "with all faults"
Title	Given in every sale	Does not apply in circumstances where apparent warranty is not given	Must state "There is no warranty of title"

subject to the general UCC constraint of good faith. **Unconscionable** disclaimers of warranties or waiver of warranties when one party has no bargaining power may not be valid. For example, a disclaimer of liability for personal injury resulting from a breach of the warranty of merchantability for a consumer good would be unconscionable. Consider 10.5 deals with a warranty disclaimer and whether it is valid.

CONSIDER...   10.5

Richard W. La Trace attended an auction at B & B Antiques, Auction & Realty. La Trace purchased five lamps that were identified at the auction as "Tiffany" lamps and one lampshade that was also identified at the auction as a "Tiffany" product. La Trace spent a total of $56,200 on the lamps. La Trace contacted Fontaine's Auction Gallery in Pittsfield, Massachusetts, to inquire about selling the lamps in an auction. Fontaine's sent Dean Lowry, an expert in Tiffany products, to examine La Trace's lamps and Lowry determined that the lamps were not authentic Tiffany products but were, in fact, reproductions. La Trace filed suit against the Websters and B & B for breach of warranty. The "Conditions of Auction" document contained the following disclaimer:

1. All property is sold AS IS WHERE IS, and we make NO guarantees, warranties or representations, expressed or implied, with respect to the property or the correctness of the catalog or other description of authenticity of authorship, physical condition, size, quality, rarity, importance, provenance, exhibitions, literature or historical relevance of the property or otherwise. No statement anywhere, whether oral or written, shall be deemed such a guarantee, warranty or representation.

Could LaTrace recover, or was the warranty disclaimed?
[*La Trace v Webster*, 17 So.3d 1210 (Ala. App. 2008)]

Privity Standards for UCC Recovery

If you have a contract to buy a car and the seller breaches the contract by refusing to deliver, you can bring suit for breach of contract based on the **privity** between you and the seller. The people in your carpool, however, could not recover from the seller for breach because you no longer have a car to use (even though they are affected). They have no privity of contract with the seller. Traditionally, a recovery for a breach of contract requires privity of contract. A breach of warranty is a breach of contract, and until the time of the UCC, privity was required to be able to recover on a breach of warranty theory.

Section 2–318 of the UCC establishes three alternatives that states can adopt, each of which provides warranty protections for *more* persons than the buyer. For example, Alternative A extends warranty protection to "any natural person who is in the family or household . . . of the remote purchaser or who is a guest in the home [of the remote purchaser]." Alternative B extends coverage to "any natural person who is reasonably expected to use, consume, or be affected by the goods" or who is "injured in person" by the goods. Alternative C extends the warranty protection to "any person that may be reasonably expected to use, consume, or be affected by the goods" and is injured by them or their use. Alternative C also prohibits the disclaimer of liability for personal injury to those covered by the warranty.

Exhibit 10.2 summarizes the UCC warranty protections and disclaimers.

CONSIDER...   10.6

Refer to the *Smith v Coleman* case (Case 10.5) that appears on p. 337 in relation to another issue. Was there privity between Coleman and Ms. Smith or Coleman and Mr. Smith?

Strict Tort Liability: Product Liability Under Section 402A

The discussion to this point has focused on the statutory and contract theories of product liability. Liability for making false statements about products is addressed under UCC warranty provisions or under federal and state advertising and consumer protection statutes. But these theories are grounded in contract relationships and limited statutory authority. A broader focus to product liability is grounded in tort law. Section 402A provides a remedy for those who are harmed by defective products through either a theory of strict liability or one of negligence.

The first tort theory for recovery for defective products is **strict liability** in tort. This tort was created and defined by Section 402A of the *Restatement (Second) of Torts*. Restatements of the law are developed by the American Law Institute, a group of professors and practicing attorneys. Restatements are not the law, even though they are adopted and recognized in many states as the controlling statement of law in that state. The adoption of a Restatement generally comes in the form of judicial acceptance of the doctrines provided.

> *Restatement § 402A:*
> *402A. Special Liability of Seller of Product for Physical Harm to User or Consumer*
>
> (1) *One who sells any product in a defective condition unreasonably dangerous to the user or consumer or to his property is subject to liability for physical harm thereby caused to the ultimate user or consumer, or to his property if*
>
> (a) *the seller is engaged in the business of selling such a product, and*
> (b) *it is expected to and does reach the user or consumer without substantial change in the condition in which it is sold.*
>
> (2) *The rule stated in Subsection (1) applies although*
>
> (a) *the seller has exercised all possible care in the preparation and sale of his product, and*
> (b) *the user or consumer has not bought the product from or entered into any contractual relations with the seller.*

Part 2 of 402A spells out the distinction between negligence and strict tort liability. Liability results for physical harm even when sellers have exercised all possible care in developing, producing, and selling the product. The fact that the seller is in the business of making and/or selling the product and someone is injured results in the liability. No negligent error or omission is required as an element of proof for recovery. Section 402A applies to defective conditions regardless of the precautions taken by the manufacturer. Manufacturers or food processors that take great precautions in their procedures could overcome a charge of negligence; however, strict liability focuses on the fact that a defect exists, not whether the manufacturer could or could not have prevented the problem. The *Restatement (Third) of Product Liability* has been proposed and would clarify the definition of "defective" with regard to knowledge requirements and recovery.

Section 402A has no privity requirements and is not subject to the disclaimers that can eliminate warranty liability.

The Requirement of Unreasonably Dangerous Defective Condition

The requirement of proof of an unreasonable defective condition can be produced in many different ways. Unreasonable defects can come from everything from the materials used to the manufacturing processes. Every product liability suit finds a different type of defect. A product can be unreasonably dangerous because it contains a foreign substance. Most product liability cases relating to food are based on this tenet. Rats in pop bottles, moldy bananas in cereal, parts of a snake in frozen vegetables, and stones in soup are all factual circumstances that have been recognized as Section 402A defective conditions.

The most common types of product liability cases are based on the following types of defects:

1. Design defects
2. Dangers of use due to lack of warnings or unclear use instructions
3. Errors in manufacturing, handling, or packaging of the product

Design Defects
A product with a faulty design exposes its users to unnecessary risks. Products must be designed with all foreseeable uses in mind. Cars must be designed in view of the

Ethical Issues

In early 2010, Toyota issued a recall for over 8,000,000 vehicles because there were increasing complaints about a sudden unintended acceleration (SUA) issue. There had been 24,000 consumer complaints about the SUA issue to dealers, to the Consumer Product Safety Commission, and via lawsuits filed against the company between 2001 through 2009. Initially, Toyota responded by claiming that the acceleration was caused by faulty floor mats and/or driver error. Causes then shifted to worn pedals, overheated pedals, condensation, and even software

issues. However, the full recall was not made until January of 2010 following increasingly vocal Toyota owner complaints and a series of fatal accidents. Discuss the possible product liability theories that would apply. If the floor mats were getting in the way of the brake pedal or pressing on the accelerator, would Toyota have liability? Evaluate the ethics of Toyota in holding off on the recalls. What if drivers made a mistake, or were just confused, stepped on the wrong pedal? Is there product liability then?

probability of accidents. A design that creates an otherwise unnecessary explosion upon a rear-end collision is a faulty design. A car that suddenly accelerates because of a flaw in the auto's computer system or accelerator has a design defect.

To make the best possible case in the event of a product liability suit, it is helpful for the manufacturer to have complied with all federal and state regulations on the product. It is also helpful if the manufacturer has used the latest technology and designs available within the industry and has met industry standards in designing its product.

Improper Warnings and Instructions

Manufacturers have a duty to warn buyers of a foreseeably dangerous use of a product that the buyers are not likely to realize is dangerous. They also have a duty to supplement the warnings. For example, as defects are discovered in autos, the manufacturers send recall notices to buyers. Similarly, manufacturers of airplanes have sent warnings on problems and proper repair procedures to airlines throughout the life of a particular plane design's use.

Manufacturers must also give adequate instructions to buyers on the proper use of the product. Over-the-counter drugs carry instructions about proper dosages and the limitations on dosages. The quotes in the chapter opening give an indication of the levels of warnings required on products. Case 10.5 involves an issue of whether a warning was required, provides an answer to the chapter opening "Consider," and involves an integrated discussion of the various types of warranties in the sale of products.

CASE 10.5	*Smith v Coleman Co.,* 71 UCC Rep.Serv.2d 131 (M.D. Ala. 2010)

"Towing" the Line with an Eye on Warnings

FACTS

Ginger Smith (Plaintiff) was a passenger on Ronald Smith's boat on West Point Lake, Alabama. Ronald Smith (no relation to Ginger) was operating the boat, which was towing Ms. Smith's son, Shane McClellan,

on an inflatable inner tube behind the boat. Shane McClellan weighed 150 pounds at the time and the tube itself weighed 5 to 10 pounds. The inner tube was tied to the boat by a 50-foot Model 51650 polypropylene line that was manufactured by Lehigh Consumer Products,

CONTINUED

LLC, but carried the label of The Coleman Company (Defendants) pursuant to a licensing arrangement, and was purchased at a nearby Wal-Mart store. While Shane McClellan was being towed on the inner tube, the line snapped, and the end connected to the boat flew back toward the boat and hit Ms. Smith in the eye, causing the loss of that eye.

The packaging of the line contained several statements. A paper insert identifies it as a "50 ft × 5/16 in UTILITY LINE." Just below that appears the phrase "Ideal for use on boat or dock." Still farther down the insert, and in an all-caps font smaller than that used in the first statement, appears, divided over two lines, "175 LBS WORKING LOAD LIMIT/STAYS AFLOAT." A longer cautionary message appears at the bottom of the insert. It states:

> *Avoid using a knot, splicing is preferable. Knots reduce the strength of the rope up to 40%. Do not use this product where personal safety could be endangered. Never stand in line with a rope under tension. Such a rope, particularly nylon rope, may recoil (snap back). Misuse can result in serious injury or death.*

There was a warning label printed on the inner tube itself, a portion of which advised boaters to "[u]se a tow rope of at least 1500 lbs average tensile strength for pulling a single person. . . ." The overall size of this warning label is 8" × 9", and its text complies with the warning label recommended by the Water Sports Industry Association for use on inflatable tubes.

Ms. Smith filed suit against Coleman, Wal-Mart, and Ronald Smith. (Wal-Mart and Smith were dismissed from the case). Coleman argued that its package warned against using the line for towing and moved for summary judgment.

JUDICIAL OPINION

WATKINS, District Judge

A manufacturer has a duty "to warn users of the dangerous propensities of a product only when such products are dangerous when put to their intended use." "[A] manufacturer is under no duty to warn a user of every danger which may exist during the use of the product, especially when such danger is open and obvious." ". . . the warning need only be one that is reasonable under the circumstances and it need not be the best possible warning."

It is a defense to a negligent failure to warn claim that there is no evidence "that the allegedly inadequate warning would have been read and heeded and would have kept the accident from occurring." In this case, Defendants point to the deposition testimony of Ronald Smith, who purchased the line and attached it to the boat and inner tube. Mr. Smith's testimony was that he did not recall reading "any other part of the warnings on

the package other than the poundage." He specifically answered a question in the negative about whether he had read the warning against tying knots in the line. According to Defendants, Mr. Smith's use of the line violated three parts of the warnings given on the package insert, which he confessed having not read: (1) the warning against tying knots in the line; (2) the warning against using the line where personal safety could be endangered; and (3) the warning against standing in line "with a rope under tension."

The court pauses to contemplate an issue not discussed by either party, but which seems so fundamental to the cause of action asserted by Ms. Smith that it is difficult to adequately address the failure-to-warn claim without touching on it. That issue is how a negligent failure-to-warn claim is affected by the plaintiff not having been the purchaser, or even the "user," of the item at issue. Both parties proceed as if the relevant inquiry is whether Mr. Smith, or perhaps either Mr. or Ms. Smith, read and followed the warnings on the package. It is undisputed that Mr. Smith purchased the rope and is the person who tied it to the boat and inner tube. Given the disposable nature of the package on which the warnings appeared, it is unclear whether Ms. Smith even had the opportunity to read the warnings—and so, in the summary judgment posture, this court must assume that she did not, if that factual question is relevant to the outcome.

Conceding that Mr. Smith did not recall reading the relevant warnings, Plaintiff's argument seems to be that the phrase "warning" has a particular, technical meaning, such that the statements on the package here were not "warnings" for the purposes of the Alabama case law. The contours of this view are not very well fleshed out, but the argument is perhaps that because the statements on the packaging did not actually contain the word "WARNING," with accompanying symbols such as an exclamation mark within a triangle, they were not actually warnings at all, but merely "safety information."

The only basis for this distinction is a statement made by one of Defendants' experts that "warnings can change behavior, but it is difficult to change behavior with safety information." Perhaps there is a technical distinction, recognized by experts in product labeling or in regulations, between the two concepts, and perhaps, under that distinction, the package insert here is "safety information" rather than a "warning," although it is far from clear from the deposition excerpts before the court that this is what the expert meant. Regardless, the argument misses the point that the court must apply the word "warning" as it has been used in the Alabama case law, which governs this diversity case. The cases cited give no indication of limiting the word "warning" to a narrow, technical meaning. Certainly, the common use of the word "warning" does not limit the concept to statements appearing under the word "WARNING," accompanied by particular symbols, or colored in bright orange. The statements appearing on the utility line's package are cautionary in nature, designed to *warn*, in the ordinary sense of the term, users of the product about potential dangers of usage.

Thus, the court concludes that the statements on the package were warnings for purposes of Alabama law. As stated above, it is conceded that Mr. Smith did not read the warnings, except for the weight limitation. The only remaining question is whether failure to heed the warnings caused the accident. The court is reluctant to conclude that the warning against uses "where personal safety could be endangered" can suffice for this purpose; it is so vague as to be essentially meaningless. Any use, no matter how seemingly safe or appropriate, that actually resulted in injury could be said after the fact to have endangered personal safety. The other two warnings, however, are quite specific, and both were violated by Mr. Smith. Mr. Smith tied knots in the rope in order to attach it to the boat and the inner tube. Both Mr. Smith and Plaintiff were on board the open boat towing the inner tube behind it; in the ordinary use of language, they were both standing "in line with a rope under tension."

Indeed, it is difficult to conceive how the rope could ever be used for towing someone behind an open boat without both the person being towed and persons on board the boat violating the warning against standing in line with a rope under tension. While Plaintiff's expert prevaricates somewhat over whether Plaintiff was herself "in line" with the rope at the time it broke, heeding this warning still would have prevented the accident altogether, as there would have been no way to tow Plaintiff's son on the inner tube without putting him in line with the rope under tension.

Finally, the court does not base its ruling on Defendants' argument that towing a 150-pound child (plus a five to ten pound inner tube) would have produced a dynamic load far in excess of the 175-pound limitation on the rope, so Plaintiff's argument that there was no way for Mr. Smith or Plaintiff to be aware of the difference between static and dynamic loads is irrelevant. The court also does not base its decision on arguments concerning the warning label on the inner tube itself. Because there is no evidence that the allegedly inadequate warning was read and heeded, or that, if it had been read and heeded, the accident would have occurred anyway, the motion for summary judgment on the negligent-failure-to-warn claim is due to be granted.

With respect to the express warranty claim, Plaintiff's claim is that the statement that the line was "ideal for use on boat or dock" constitutes an express warranty. Statements "that are mere sales talk or 'puffery' do not give rise to express warranties," while "representations of fact" may give rise to such warranties. While the word "ideal" seems closer to the description of an item as "in good shape" that Alabama courts have found to constitute "puffery," *Scoggin v Listerhill Employees Credit Union,* 658 So.2d 376, 377 (Ala.1995), arguably the reference to use on a boat or dock could constitute a more specific assurance in some circumstances. Regardless, the phrase "ideal for use on boat or dock" is not the equivalent of "ideal for towing behind a boat," especially when, as explained in the previous section, the specific warnings on the package make it essentially impossible to use the utility line for towing in compliance with the packaging. There is no evidence that any express warranty was breached, and summary judgment is due to be granted on this claim.

To the extent that Plaintiff makes a claim for breach of an implied warranty of merchantability, she does not explain how that claim fits the requirements of the statute, and the claim fails for essentially the same reason as the express warranty claim. A use excluded by warning labels cannot be an "ordinary purpose [ ] for which such goods are used."

The final warranty claim is for breach of an implied warranty of fitness for a particular purpose. Plaintiff has done no more than assert that Defendants had "reason to know" that the line would be used to tow persons behind a boat; regardless, Plaintiff clearly did not "rely on the seller's skill or judgment to select or furnish suitable goods." Rather, Mr. Smith selected and purchased the utility line for himself at a Wal-Mart store. Summary judgment is due to be granted on the warranty claims.

The court need not reach Defendants' argument that Coleman is entitled to summary judgment because its only role in producing the utility line was to license its name to Lehigh.

Summary judgment for Defendants.

CASE QUESTIONS

1. What is the law with regard to product users who do not read package warnings?

2. What point does the court make about Ms. Smith not actually being the purchaser of the line?

3. What lessons should Coleman take from its experience of being a defendant along with its licensee for the line?

BUSINESS STRATEGY

Nestlé and the Infant Formula and Product Marketing

While the merits and problems of breast-feeding versus using infant formula are debated in the United States and other developed countries, the issue is not so balanced in Third World nations. Studies have demonstrated the difficulties and risks of bottle-feeding babies in such places.

First, refrigeration is not generally available, so the formula, once it is mixed or opened (in the case of premixed types), cannot be stored properly. Second, the lack of purified water for mixing with the formula powder results in diarrhea or other diseases in formula-fed infants. Third, inadequate education and income, along with cultural differences, often lead to the dilution of formula and thus greatly reduced nutrition.

Medical studies also suggest that regardless of the mother's nourishment, sanitation, and income level, an infant can be adequately nourished through breast-feeding.

In spite of medical concerns about using their products in these countries, some infant formula manufacturers heavily promoted bottle-feeding.

These promotions, which went largely unchecked through 1970, included billboards, radio jingles, and posters of healthy, happy infants, as well as baby books and formula samples distributed through the health care systems of various countries.

Also, some firms used "milk nurses" as part of their promotions. Dressed in nurse uniforms, "milk nurses" were assigned to maternity wards by their companies and paid commissions to get new mothers to feed their babies formula. Mothers who did so soon discovered that lactation could not be achieved and the commitment to bottle-feeding was irreversible.

In the early 1970s, physicians working in nations where milk nurses were used began vocalizing their concerns. For example, Dr. Derrick Jelliffe, the then director of the Caribbean Food and Nutrition Institute, had the Protein-Calorie Advisory Group of the United Nations place infant formula promotion methods on its agenda for several of its meetings.

Journalist Mike Muller first brought the issue to public awareness with a series of articles in the *New Internationalist* in the 1970s. He also wrote a pamphlet on the promotion of infant formulas called "The Baby Killer," which was published by a British charity, War on Want. The same pamphlet was published in Switzerland, the headquarters of Nestlé, a major formula maker, under the title "Nestlé Kills Babies." Nestlé sued in 1975, which resulted in extensive media coverage.

In response to the bad publicity, manufacturers of infant formula representing about 75% of the market formed the International Council of Infant Food Industries to establish standards for infant formula marketing. The new code banned the milk nurse commissions and required the milk nurses to have identification that would eliminate confusion about their "nurse" status.

The code failed to curb advertising of formulas. In fact, distribution of samples increased. By 1977, groups in the United States began a boycott against formula makers over what Jelliffe called "comerciogenic malnutrition."

One U.S. group, Infant Formula Action Coalition (INFACT), worked with the staff of Senator Edward Kennedy of Massachusetts to have hearings on the issue by the Senate Subcommittee on Health and Human Resources, which Kennedy chaired. The hearings produced evidence that 40% of the worldwide market for infant formula, which totaled $1.5 billion at the time, was in Third World countries. No regulations resulted, but Congress did tie certain forms of foreign aid to the development by recipient countries of programs to encourage breast-feeding.

Boycotts against Nestlé products began in Switzerland in 1975 and in the United States in 1977. The boycotts and Senator Kennedy's involvement heightened media interest in the issue and led to the World Health Organization (WHO) debating the issue of infant formula marketing in 1979 and agreeing to draft a code to govern it.

After four drafts, and two presidential administrations (Carter and Reagan), the 118 member nations of WHO finally voted on a code for infant formula marketing. The United States was the only nation to vote against it; the Reagan administration opposed the code being mandatory. In the end, WHO made the code a recommendation only, but the United States still refused to support it.

The publicity on the vote fueled the boycott of Nestlé, which continued until the formula maker announced it would meet the WHO standards for infant formula marketing. Nestlé created the Nestlé Infant Formula Audit Commission (NIFAC) to demonstrate its commitment to and ensure its implementation of the WHO code.

In 1988, Nestlé introduced a new infant formula, Good Start, through its subsidiary, Carnation. The industry leader, Abbott Laboratories, which held 54% of the market with its Similac brand, revealed

Carnation's affiliation: "They are Nestlé," said Robert A. Schoellhorn, Abbott's chairman and CEO. Schoellhorn also disclosed that Nestlé was the owner of Beech-Nut Nutrition Corporation, officers of which had been indicted and convicted (following one reversal) for selling adulterated apple juice for babies.

Carnation advertised Good Start in magazines and on television. The American Academy of Pediatrics (AAP) objected to this direct advertising, and grocers feared boycotts.

The letters "H.A." came after the name "Good Start," indicating the formula was hypoallergenic. Touted as a medical breakthrough by Carnation, the formula was made from whey and advertised as ideal for babies who were colicky or could not tolerate milk-based formulas.

Within four months of Good Start's introduction in November 1988, the FDA was investigating the formula because of six reported cases of vomiting due to the formula. Carnation then agreed not to label the formula hypoallergenic and to include a warning that milk-allergic babies should be given Good Start only with a doctor's approval and supervision.

In 1990, with its infant formula market share at 2.8%, Carnation's president, Timm F. Crull, called on the AAP to "examine all marketing practices that might hinder breast-feeding." Crull specifically cited manufacturers' practices of giving hospitals education and research grants, as well as free bottles, in exchange for having exclusive rights to supply the hospital with formula and to give free samples to mothers. He also called for scrutiny of the practice of paying pediatricians' expenses to attend conferences on infant formulas.

The AAP looked into prohibiting direct marketing of formula to mothers and physicians' accepting cash awards from formula manufacturers for research.

The distribution of samples in Third World countries continued during this time. Studies by the United Nations Children's Fund found that a million infants were dying every year because they were not breast-fed adequately. In many cases, the infant starved because the mother used free formula samples and could not buy more, while her own milk dried up. In 1991, the International Association of Infant Food Manufacturers agreed to stop distributing infant formula samples by the end of 1992.

In the United States in 1980, the surgeon general established a goal that the nation's breast-feeding rate be 75% by 1990. The rate remains below 60%, however, despite overwhelming evidence that breast milk reduces susceptibility to illness, especially ear infections and gastrointestinal illnesses. The AAP took a strong position that infant formula makers should not advertise to the public, but as a result, new entrants into the market (such as Nestlé with its Carnation Good Start) were disadvantaged because long-time formula makers Abbott and Mead Johnson were well established through physicians. In 1993, Nestlé filed an antitrust suit alleging a conspiracy among AAP, Abbott, and Mead Johnson.

Some 200 U.S. hospitals have voluntarily stopped distributing discharge packs from formula makers to their maternity patients because they felt it "important not to appear to be endorsing any products or acting as commercial agents." A study at Boston City Hospital showed that mothers who receive discharge packs are less likely to continue nursing, if they nurse at all. UNICEF and WHO offer "Baby Friendly" certification to maternity wards that take steps to eliminate discharge packs and formula samples.

Discussion Questions

1. If you had been an executive with Nestlé, would you have changed your marketing approach after the boycotts began? Didn't the first mover approach make sense?

2. Did Nestlé suffer long-term damage because of its Third World marketing techniques?

3. How could a marketing plan address the concerns of the AAP and WHO?

4. Is the moratorium on distributing free formula samples voluntary? Would your company comply? If you were a hospital administrator, what policy would you adopt regarding discharge packs?

5. Should formula makers advertise directly to the public? What if their ads read, "Remember, breast is best"?

6. Nestlé recently turned down a merger offer from PepsiCo because it felt that PepsiCo had too many snack foods. Has Nestlé shifted its standards since the time of the infant formula crisis?

Reprinted with permission from Marianne M. Jennings, *Case Studies in Business Ethics*, 7th ed., 2010.

Sources: "Breast Milk for the World's Babies," *New York Times*, 12 March 1992, A18; Burton, Thomas B. "Methods of Marketing Infant Formula Land Abbott in Hot Water," *Wall Street Journal*, 25 May 1993, A1, A6; Freedman, Alix M. "Nestlé's Bid to Crash Baby-Formula Market in the U.S. Stirs a Row," *Wall Street Journal*, 6 February 1989, A1, A10; Garland, Susan B. "Are Formula Makers Putting the Squeeze on the States?" *Business Week*, 18 June 1990, 31; Gerlin, Andrea. "Hospitals Wean from Formula Makers' Freebies," *Wall Street Journal*, 29 December 1994, B1; Meier, Barry. "Battle over the Market for Baby Formula," *New York Times*, 15 June 1993, C1, C15; "Nestlé Unit Sues Baby Formula Firms, Alleging Conspiracy with Pediatricians," *Wall Street Journal*, 1 June 1993, B4; Post, James E. "Assessing the Nestlé Boycott: Corporate Accountability and Human Rights," *California Management Review* 27 (1985): 113–31; Star, Marlene G. "Breast Is Best," *Vegetarian Times*, June 1991, 25–26.

Errors in Manufacturing, Handling, or Packaging

This breach of duty is the most difficult form of negligence to prove. The large number of handlers in the process of manufacturing and packaging a product typically makes it difficult to prove when and how the manufacturer was negligent. One of the issues in drug manufacturing cases is whether the packaging for the materials is sufficient. Does it protect against tampering? Is it childproof? These types of dangers are foreseeable and require special duties with regard to packaging drugs.

CONSIDER...   10.7

Classify the following as design, manufacture, or warning defects:

- Failure to disclose changes in fuel and operations for a helicopter in hot weather and higher altitudes
- A polio vaccine that produces not immunity but polio in a child
- Teflon-induced autoimmune system disease caused by Teflon used in the manufacture of an implanted TMJ jaw device
- Diamond represented as a grade VVS that is actually a lower grade
- Infant swing that causes infants to fall out backward if they fall asleep and their weight shifts
- Tobacco that causes lung cancer
- Fondue pot tipping over and burning a two-year-old child
- Bleeding of pizza-box ink onto pizza

Reaching the Buyer in the Same Condition

The requirement that a product reach the buyer without "substantial change" is a protection for the seller. A seller will not be liable for a product that has been modified or changed. The reason for this requirement is that once a product is modified or changed, it becomes unclear whether the original product or the modifications caused the unreasonably dangerous condition. Volkswagen would not be held liable for a dune buggy accident just because the builder and owner of the dune buggy happened to use a Volkswagen engine in building the vehicle. Because Volkswagen's product has been taken apart and modified, its liability has ended. One issue that arises in airplane crash cases is whether the air carrier followed the manufacturer's repair procedures. The failure to follow these procedures could eliminate the manufacturer's liability because the aircraft may have been altered.

The Requirement of a Seller Engaged in a Business

Section 402A requires the seller to be "engaged in the business of selling the product." This requirement sounds like the merchant requirement for the UCC warranty of merchantability. However, the meaning of "selling the product" is slightly broader under Section 402A than the UCC meaning of merchant. For example, a baseball club is not a merchant of beer, but if the club sells beer at its games, it is a seller for purposes of Section 402A. Section 402A covers manufacturers, wholesalers, retailers, food sellers, and even those who sell products out of their homes.

In recent years, some courts have allowed recovery from groups of sellers. For example, in the controversy over diethylstilbestrol (DES, a drug taken by pregnant women), the plaintiffs could show that their harms resulted from DES but could not show exactly who manufactured the drug their mothers took. The courts permitted recovery against the group of manufacturers of DES during that time period [*Sindell v Abbott Lab.*, 607 P.2d 924 (Cal. 1980)].

Negligence: A Second Tort for Product Liability

A suit for product defects can also be based in negligence. The elements for establishing a negligence case are the same as those for a Section 402A case with one addition: establishing that the product seller or manufacturer either knew of the defect before the product was sold or allowed sales to continue with the knowledge that the product had a defect. Establishing this knowledge is difficult in an evidentiary sense in court, but a plaintiff in a product liability suit who shows that the defendant-seller knew of the problem and sold or continued to sell the product can collect punitive damages in addition to damages for personal injury and property damage. Establishing knowledge in a product liability case usually produces a multimillion-dollar verdict because punitive damages are awarded in addition to compensatory ones.

Examples of cases in which establishing knowledge has been an issue include the Ford Pinto exploding gas tank cases (in which the plaintiffs used internal memos from engineers to establish the company's knowledge of defects) and the Dow Corning breast implant suits (in which an engineer, Thomas Talcott, who worked for Dow Corning in 1976, testified for the plaintiffs regarding his feelings during the product's development that leakage was possible).

Exhibit 10.3 compares product liability theories, and Exhibit 10.4 details the basis for product liability.

EXHIBIT 10.3   Comparison of Product Liability Theories

TYPE	PRIVITY REQUIRED	KNOWLEDGE OF PROBLEM REQUIRED?	WARRANTY PROMISE REQUIRED?
Negligence	No	Yes	No
Section 402A/strict tort liability	No	No	No
Express warranty	Yes	No	Yes
Implied warranty of merchantability	Yes	No	No
Implied warranty of fitness for a particular purpose	Yes	No	Yes

EXHIBIT 10.4 Legal Basis for Product Liability

CONTRACT	TORT
Express warranty	402A—Strict Tort Liability
Implied warranty of merchantability	Elements
Implied warranty of fitness for particular purpose	(1) Defective condition unreasonably dangerous: design; manufacturing defect; or inadequate warning
	(2) Defendant in business of using, selling, or manufacturing product
	(3) Condition of product is the same
	Negligence
	Same; and add
	(4) Knowledge of defect

Privity Issues in Tort Theories of Product Liability

Privity is not the standard for recovery in negligence actions. The standard for recovery in negligence actions is whether the injury that resulted was foreseeable and foreseeable to that particular party. For example, a manufacturer of toasters can foresee use by children and would have a duty to warn that they should not use the equipment unless supervised by adults. A manufacturer of a weed killer could foresee the presence of dogs, cats, and other pets in a yard sprayed with the killer and should either make the product not harmful to them or warn of the need to keep them away from the sprayed area for a certain period of time. Children and pets certainly have no privity with the manufacturers, but they can recover from the manufacturer (or their parents and owners can) on the basis of the foreseeability of the children's and pets' presence and the foreseeability of the danger causing their injuries.

Likewise, parties other than the product manufacturer may be responsible for defective conditions in the products and can be held liable for their participation. For example, parts manufacturers may be held liable if it can be shown that defects in their parts resulted in a product's defect and the injury to the plaintiff.

Defenses to Product Liability Torts

Three defenses are available to a defendant in a product liability tort:

1. Misuse or abnormal use of a product
2. Contributory negligence
3. Assumption of risk

Misuse or Abnormal Use of a Product

Any use of a product that the manufacturer has specifically warned against in its instructions is a **misuse.** Using a forklift to lift 25,000 pounds when the instructions limit its capacity to 15,000 pounds is a misuse of the product, and any injuries resulting from such misuse will not be the liability of the manufacturer. Product misuse also occurs when a plaintiff has used the product in a manner that the defendant could not anticipate and warn against.

Contributory Negligence

Contributory negligence is traditionally a complete defense to a product liability suit in negligence. For example, although a front loader might have a design failure of no protective netting around the driver, a driver who is injured while using the front loader for recreational purposes is contributorily negligent. Contributory negligence overlaps greatly with product misuse.

Some states, as discussed in Chapter 9, have adopted a standard of **comparative negligence,** under which the plaintiff's negligence is not a complete defense: The negligence of the plaintiff merely serves to reduce the amount the plaintiff is entitled to recover. For example, a jury might find that the defendant is 60 percent at fault and the plaintiff is 40 percent at fault. The plaintiff recovers, but the amount of that recovery is reduced by 40 percent.

Assumption of Risk

When a plaintiff is aware of a danger in the product but goes ahead and uses it anyway, **assumption of risk** occurs. If a car manufacturer recalled your car for repair and you failed to have the repair done, despite full opportunity to do so, you have assumed the risk of driving with that problem.

Derienzo v Trek Bicycle Corp. (Case 10.6) involves issues of assumption of risk and also brings together many of the issues in product liability that you have studied in this chapter.

CASE 10.6	*Derienzo v Trek Bicycle Corp.*
	376 F.Supp.2d 537 (S.D.N.Y. 2005)

Jumping on a Trek: Framing Assumption of Risk

FACTS

David DeRienzo (plaintiff) was part of a group of four men who regularly participated in "extreme" sports. The Group would videotape themselves riding mountain bikes and watch each other "hit jumps." Mr. DeRienzo maintained a Web site, www.roadgap.com, which, at one time, described and showed the Group's sports adventures. Mr. DeRienzo was the first of the Group to do "lake jumping," in which the goal is to ride one's bike off a jump into a lake. Mr. DeRienzo had done lake jumping 25–30 times.

Mr. DeRienzo bought a used 1998 Trek (defendant) Y5 model (the Bike), which is a "full-suspension" mountain bike. The Y5 is also called a "cross-country"

mountain bike. Jeremy Ball of Spokane, Washington, was the original purchaser of the bike and the person who sold the bike to Mr. DeRienzo over the Internet sometime in the fall of 1999. Mr. Ball told Mr. DeRienzo that the bike was "a great bike," but he said that there were "cosmetic blemishes" on the frame. Ball had modified the bike, replacing the original front fork with a used "Rock Shox Triple Clamp" fork. The Rock Shox fork is designed to handle a heavier load from the rider, including loads created by jumps and drop-offs. A Trek catalog includes a section entitled "Off Road," listing the different Y model bikes (the Y5 among them) and their features, showing that the Rock Shox fork is available on certain models. Mr. DeRienzo had worked

CONTINUED

on the frame when, after purchasing it, it arrived unassembled and wrapped in towels. The 1999 Trek manual for the Y5 contained the following language:

Jumping your bicycle, performing bicycle stunts, severe off road riding, downhill riding, or any abnormal bike riding can be very dangerous. These activities increase the stress on your frame and components and can lead to premature or sudden failure of your bicycle frame or components. Such failure could cause a loss of control resulting in serious injury or death. Industry pictures and videos of these kinds of activities depict very experienced or professional riders. If you choose to jump your bicycle, use it for stunts, or use it in a severe offroad [sic] or downhill environment, carefully inspect your frame and components for signs of fatigue before and after each ride.

Remember; it is much easier to have an accident resulting in serious personal injury in these situations even if your bicycle performs as intended. Use suitable protective gear, including a certified bicycle helmet.

The following was in the 1997 Manual at the very bottom of page 10, in regular text (with no text box, Warning Sign or other graphic) and takes up approximately 1/10 of the page:

"Avoid jumping. Bicycles are not made for jumping. Doing so may cause your frame to fail. Never ride your bicycle in such a manner as to propel your bicycle airborn [sic], including riding over steps and curbs."

This "Avoid jumping" text is the last of five text segments on page 10, the other four being (in order, from top to bottom): *"Wear a helmet," "Know and observe your local bicycle riding laws," "Use special care when off-road riding,"* and *"Use good shifting techniques."* On the opposite (facing) page, there is a text box with the word "CAUTION" and two segments (including bold text) about the dangers of riding at night and in wet conditions.

Mr. DeRienzo did not read the warnings. Mr. DeRienzo used the bike for mountain biking or "off-road" riding, estimating that he took the bike over approximately 200 jumps and drop-offs before the accident, with the highest being 10 feet off the ground. The day before the crash at issue here, Mr. DeRienzo was involved in an incident in which the front wheel of the bike hit the ground at an angle of between 50 and 70 degrees, causing Plaintiff to go flying over the handlebars. He says he was not injured until the next day when the bike frame fell apart after he jumped five to eight feet off a ledge created by a rock sticking out of the side of a hill. Mr. DeRienzo filed suit against Trek for its defective bike frame as well as its failure to warn him about the dangers of a mountain bike and mountain biking. Trek moved for summary judgment.

JUDICIAL OPINION

MCMAHON, District Judge

Under New York law, a manufacturer who places a defective product on the market that causes injury may be held strictly liable for the ensuing injuries if the product is not accompanied by adequate warnings for the use of the product. The failure to warn must be a proximate cause of plaintiff's injuries. The elements of a failure to warn claim are: (i) a danger existed to a significant portion of defendant's consumers requiring additional warning; (ii) the alleged danger was known or reasonably foreseeable; and (iii) a proposed alternative warning would have prevented Plaintiff's accident.

Some courts in this Circuit have held that a manufacturer may be held liable for injuries caused by its failure to warn of the dangers arising from the foreseeable misuse or modification of the product as well. Under this line of cases, evidence that a manufacturer might reasonably have foreseen a particular type of misuse raises an issue of fact that precludes the granting of summary judgment. . . . [T]here is "no material distinction between foreseeable misuse and foreseeable alteration of a product," and that, "in certain circumstances, a manufacturer may have a duty to warn of dangers associated with the use of its product even after it has been sold." This is a fact-specific inquiry. In addition, "A manufacturer's superior position to garner information and its corresponding duty to warn is no less with its ability to learn of modifications made to or misuse of a product."

Other courts have held that strict liability cannot attach unless a product is being used in a "normal" manner.

An expert opinion accompanied by submissions showing industry-wide advertisements encouraging a particular use of a product is probative on the issue of whether defendant knew its product was being used in a certain manner. This duty is not open-ended, however, and a manufacturer is not required to insure that subsequent owners and users will not adapt the product to their unique uses.

The adequacy of a warning is generally a question of fact for the jury. A warning that is inconspicuously located and written in small print may be deficient.

One issue that typically precludes summary judgment on a failure to warn claim is whether the information contained in any issued warning was "commensurate with the manufacturer's knowledge of the nature and extent of the dangers from foreseeable use of its product."

Finally, failure to read a warning is not dispositive. While it is true that, in many cases, a plaintiff who admits that he failed to read a warning that was issued with the product will have failed to show that any deficiency in that warning was the proximate cause of his injuries, plaintiff's failure to read an insufficiently conspicuous or prominent warning will not necessarily defeat the causation element of a failure to warn claim.

Plaintiff asserts that his use of the Bike for jumping was typical of aggressive mountain bikers—so, normal and not a misuse—and that Trek was aware that riders such as he would purchase a Trek Y5 bike for jumping. Plaintiff asserts that Trek did not warn of the dangers of jumping at all, and that its buried admonitions in an Owner's Manual to check the frame for damage were inadequate because they were inconspicuous and also because a visual inspection of the frame would not lead to the discovery of the type of damage that caused the frame to fail—namely, fatigue cracks in the head tube/down tube weld.

Defendant counters that jumping was not a normal use of a Y5 bike, that Plaintiff misused the Bike causing damage to the frame, that Trek did adequately warn of the dangers of jumping a Y5 Bike, and, as above, that any possible failure to warn was not the proximate cause of the accident in any case. Specifically, Defendant claims Plaintiff cannot recover for failure to warn because (i) Plaintiff admits he never saw an Owner's Manual; and (ii) the accident was caused by his misuse of the Bike and his poor jumping technique.

[The expert witness's] testimony that jumping is an "entirely foreseeable" and "expected" use of a mountain bike is admissible, I find that Plaintiff withstands summary judgment on that issue. Further, [the expert witness] opines that it was foreseeable that a user would modify a bike the way Plaintiff modified this Bike, i.e., by replacing (among other components), the standard fork with a Rock Shox fork, which the parties agree is designed for jumping. This could lead to an inference that Trek knew users would modify Y5 bikes to make them more suitable for jumping.

Further, Exhibits B, C, and D are copies of pages from mountain biking books, all of which include references to jumping and some of which show pictures of mountain bikers airborne on their bikes. In addition, Plaintiff's Exh. 18 shows pages of a 1998 Trek Catalog that includes at least one picture of an airborne mountain biker (the page shows Y model bikes, but not the Y5 model, which appears on the next page, where there is no picture of a rider). Based on this evidence, a jury would be entitled to find that it is both common for mountain bikers to jump their bikes and common for Trek consumers to modify Y5 model bikes to make them more suitable for jumping. If a jury so concluded, it could also conclude that Trek knew or should have known it had a duty to warn explicitly of the dangers of using a Y5 model for jumping.

As for the Owner's Manual, the fact that the parties submitted two different versions with substantially different warnings and graphics is enough to raise triable issues of fact on the failure to warn claim. Moreover, both Manuals contain warnings on almost half of their pages, which could lead a jury to conclude that any warning against jumping was inconspicuous—in either Manual. Thus, it is far from clear whether Trek warned Y5 users not to jump or of the dangers of jumping, and if it did, whether those warnings were conspicuous and/or adequate. Plaintiff's claims withstand summary judgment. There is also a dispute about whether Trek pasted a warning on the Bike itself—and, if so, to which version of the Owner's Manual it referred—which precludes summary judgment.

A plaintiff injured by a defective product may recover for breach of warranty under New York law. This remedy, grounded in various provisions of the New York Uniform Commercial Code, has not been subsumed by the tort cause of action for strict products liability. *Castro v QVC Network, Inc.*, 139 F.3d 114, 117–18 (2nd Cir. 1998).

A product must be "fit for the ordinary purposes for which such goods are used" to be considered merchantable under New York's version of the Uniform Commercial Code. Thus, liability for breach of warranty depends on "the expectations for the performance of the product when used in the customary, usual and reasonably foreseeable manners." Accordingly, a plaintiff must show that the product "was being used for the purpose and in the manner intended." Privity of contract is not required in a personal injury action for breach of warranty.

Where there are questions about whether a product was being used in a reasonably foreseeable manner, summary judgment is not appropriate. Thus, Plaintiff's breach of warranty claim requires proof that the Bike did not meet expectations for performance because it failed during his jump or landing, which was a reasonably foreseeable use of the Bike. As noted above, Plaintiff has supplied admissible evidence sufficient to raise a genuine issue of fact on the question of whether the Y5 was marketed for use in jumping. Accordingly, Defendant's motion for summary judgment on breach of warranty also must be denied.

CASE QUESTIONS

1. List all the conduct of Mr. DeRienzo that would work against his winning a product liability suit.

2. What does the court say about not reading the warnings?

3. What is the relevance of Trek being aware of the use of its bikes?

Ethical Issues

In 1994, a group of Chrysler engineers met to review proposals and recommendations for improving their Chrysler Minivan lines in order to make them more competitive. Paul Sheridan, one of the engineers on Chrysler's Minivan Safety Team, raised the number one issue on the lists of proposals and recommendations: The latches on the minivan rear doors appeared to be popping open even in low-speed crashes. The Chrysler Minivan latches did not appear to have the strength of either the Ford Windstar minivan or the Chevy minivan rear door latches. Mr. Sheridan proposed that Chrysler make the latches stronger and use that strength as a marketing tool.

After Mr. Sheridan made his proposal, and according to testimony in a subsequent product liability suit, a top production engineer told Mr. Sheridan, "That ship has sailed. We told you that last time. Next subject."

In *Jimenez v Chrysler Corporation*, 269 F.3d 439 (4th Cir. 2001), the jury deliberated only 2.5 hours before returning a verdict for the Jimenez family of $262.5 million, $250 million of which was punitive damages.

Chrysler replaced the latches on 4.3 million minivans manufactured since 1984. Chrysler spent $115 million for that replacement program on everything from notification to installation and estimates that about 61 percent of the van latches have now been replaced.

The number of deaths from ejection through the rear minivan doors is 37, which is 11 more than the fatalities from the Ford Pinto exploding gas tank defect but well short of GM's 168 fatalities in side-saddle gas tank collisions in that company's pickups.

The following evidence came out in the *Jimenez* case:

- Chrysler initially used a latch in its vans that the rest of the industry had abandoned.

- When it switched to a better latch, still not meeting federal standards for passenger vehicles, it did not notify the owners of existing vans of the change and safety issues.

- Chrysler destroyed documentation on minivan crash tests, including films and computer records. (The company says that such destruction was part of its routine document destruction program; however, a juror noted, following the trial, that only the documentation on the collisions in which the rear door was affected was destroyed. Chrysler still had the documentation on the vans' front-end collision tests.)

- Engineers proposed adding a latch strengthener for a cost of about $0.25 per vehicle in 1990, but the plan was vetoed by Chrysler executives because it was believed such an addition would be tantamount to an admission to regulators that the latches were not safe, and Chrysler had been taking the position that the latches were indeed safe.

- Chrysler used political clout to prevent a 1994 recall by NHTSA of the vehicles for latch replacement; a letter from Chrysler Vice Chairman Tom Denomme to Chairman Robert Eaton and President Robert Lutz read, "If we want to use political pressure to try to quash a recall letter, we need to go now." Chrysler officials helped staff members for Representative John Dingell of Michigan (the ranking Democrat on the House Commerce Committee, which supervises the NHTSA) draft a letter objecting to the recall. NHTSA postponed the recall. When the recall was made in 1995, there was no acknowledgment that the latches were defective or that there was any safety issue.

Following the verdict, one juror said the evidence painted a picture of corporate indifference and added, "We want people to understand why we made the decision we did. We knew what we were doing. When you speak to a company as big as Chrysler, you've got to speak on terms they understand." Another juror noted that executives answered, "I don't know. I don't remember. I can't recall," too often to have much credibility.

Chrysler had been the first mover in the minivan market. Its product filled a niche in the family auto market, and it occupied a unique position in terms of federal regulation in that there were no applicable federal standards for the lifting rear door on the van. Chrysler used latch designs and parts that had been banned in passenger vehicles for years precisely because of the risk of ejection and associated high fatality rates. However, the lack of federal regulations on the minivan meant that Chrysler violated no law in using the outmoded systems and parts.

When Chrysler began to receive notice of accidents and began holding design and marketing meetings in 1993, lawyers ordered that no notes be taken at meetings, and minutes of meetings were collected and destroyed.

Why were punitive damages appropriate in this case? Are they too high? What message do the punitive damages send to businesses? What should Chrysler do internally to be certain such a series of events does not happen again?

Product Liability Reform

"Our product liability system discourages innovation because of unforeseeable potential liability," says Robert Malcott, CEO of FMC Corporation. Mr. Malcott issued this statement as the chair of the Business Roundtable's task force on product liability. This task force and others have proposed several changes, including limiting punitive damages; meeting government standards as a defense; instituting liability shields for drugs, medical devices, and aircraft; and requiring higher standards of proof for recovery of punitive damages.

The American Law Institute (ALI) has proposed the *Restatement (Third) of Torts,* which would change the current strict liability standard to a negligence standard for defective design and informational defect cases. In other words, plaintiffs who bring product liability cases based on defective design and instruction would have to establish negligence to recover. The strict liability standard would be eliminated under this new proposal. Strict liability would still be the standard for manufacturing defects.

Federal Standards for Product Liability

Consumer Product Safety Commission

The federal level of government generally is not involved in product liability issues. However, the **Consumer Product Safety Commission** (CPSC) is a regulatory agency set up under the Consumer Product Safety Act to regulate safety standards for consumer products. The commission has several responsibilities in carrying out its purposes.

1. *To protect the public against unreasonable risks of injury from consumer products*—To perform this function, the CPSC has been given the authority to recall products and order their repair or correction. The commission also has the power to ban products completely. This ban can apply only if a product cannot be made less dangerous. In 1994, the CPSC recalled nearly all types of metal bunk beds. In 2007, the CPSC worked with Mattel on its recall of 19 million toys that had been made in China using lead-based paint, something banned in the United States. In 2008, the CPSC's authority was expanded by the **Consumer Product Safety Improvement Act (CPSIA)** to cover second-hand sales because of the lead paint issue that affects so many used toys. (See "For the Manager's Desk" on p. 350.)

2. *To develop standards for consumer product safety*—These standards take the form of regulations and minimum requirements for certain products.

3. *To help consumers become more informed about evaluating safety*—Certain regulations require disclosure of the limits of performance and hazards associated with using a particular product.

For the Manager's Desk

Re: The Consumer Product Safety Commission and Garage Sales

Garage sale listings on Craigslist have increased 60 percent during 2009 over 2008.[3] However, after the CPSIA became law in 2008 (see p. 349), second-hand sales came under the CPSC's authority. The CPSC has published a *Handbook for Resale Stores and Product Resellers*. The handbook was published after CPSC discovered that recalled products do find their way into garage sales and buyers may not be aware that the goods are no longer legal to sell. The CPSC indicates that it does not have the resources to police garage sales but is encouraging sellers to be safe and do their research on the goods they are selling.

You can find the handbook online if you search by its title. An excerpt from the pamphlet appears as follows. What you cannot sell or offer for sale:

Products that have been **recalled** by CPSC.

Toys and other articles intended for use by children, and any furniture, with **paint or other surface coatings containing lead** over specified amounts.

Products primarily intended for children age 12 or younger with **lead content** over a specific amount.

Certain toys or child care articles that contain any one of six prohibited chemicals known as **phthalates,** which are primarily used as plasticizers.

Other resellers affected would include antique sellers and nonprofit organizations engaging in second-hand sales. The nonprofits must now screen their donations prior to resale and second-hand sellers will need to verify that the products they are buying for resale are still legal.

4. To fund research in matters of product safety design and in product-caused injuries and illnesses

The act carries civil penalties of up to a maximum of $1,500,000. Knowing or willful violations carry a criminal fine of up to $100,000 and/or one year's imprisonment, and willful repeat violations carry penalties of up to $500,000 and 10 years. In addition, consumers have a right to sue in federal district court for any damages they sustain because of a violation of a regulation or law.

International Issues in Product Liability

The EU directive on product liability limits liability to "producers"; it is not as inclusive as U.S. law, which holds all sellers liable. A 10-year limit on liability and the "state-of-the-art" defense apply to most member countries: If a product upon its release was as good as any available, it is not subject to product liability.

In addition to the council's guidelines are the International Standards Organization's 9000 Guidelines for Quality Assurance and Quality Management. These directives require products to carry a stamp of compliance with standards and procedures as a means of limiting product defects.

The CISG (see Chapter 7 for more details) contains similar provisions to the UCC warranty protections for goods sold in international transactions. However, disclaimers are made more easily under the CISG and the notions of consequential damages are limited because the United States' level of damages in product liability cases far exceeds the levels for any other country in the world. Further, the notion of strict liability for products is unique to the United States, and under EU guidelines the notion of knowledge is used as a standard for imposing liability.

Ethical Issues

In some cases, products outlawed in the United States are sold outside the United States. In a practice referred to as dumping, the products are sold without mention of the U.S. recall or any litigation pending. What can be done about firms that sell defective products in third-world countries? For example, the original type of IUD and non–flame-retardant pajamas were dumped after problems developed in the United States. Discuss the ethical issues.

B I O G R A P H Y

The Space Shuttle, NASA, and O-Rings

On January 28, 1986, NASA launched the space shuttle *Challenger* in 30° F weather. Seventy-four seconds into the launch, the low temperature caused the O-ring seals on the *Challenger*'s booster rockets to fail. The *Challenger* exploded, killing all seven persons aboard (six astronauts and Christa McAuliffe, a schoolteacher chosen and trained for the mission).

Morton Thiokol was the NASA subcontractor responsible for the booster rocket assembly. Roger Boisjoly was an engineer at Morton Thiokol who had raised concerns about the O-rings. Boisjoly had given a presentation on the O-ring issue at a conference, but Thiokol took no action. Boisjoly noted the problems in his activity report and finally, in July 1985, wrote a confidential memo to R. K. Lund, Thiokol's vice president for engineering. Excerpts appear below:

> This letter is written to insure that management is fully aware of the seriousness of the current O-ring erosion problem . . . The mistakenly accepted position on the joint problem was to fly without fear of failure. . . . [This position] is now drastically changed as a result of the SRM [shuttle recovery mission] 16A nozzle joint erosion which eroded a secondary O-ring with the primary O-ring never sealing. If the same scenario should occur in a field joint (and it could), then it is a jump ball as to the success or failure of the joint. . . . The result would be a catastrophe of the highest order—loss of human life. . . .
>
> It is my honest and real fear that if we do not take immediate action to dedicate a team to solve the problem, with the field joint having the number one priority, then we stand in jeopardy of losing a flight along with all the launch pad facilities.

In October 1985, Boisjoly presented the O-ring issue at a conference of the Society of Automotive Engineers and requested suggestions for resolution.

On January 27, 1986, the day before the launch, Boisjoly attempted to halt the launch. However, four Thiokol managers, including Lund, voted unanimously to recommend the launch. One manager urged Lund to "take off his engineering hat and put on his management hat." The managers then developed the following revised recommendations. Engineers were excluded from the development of these findings and the final launch decision.

- Calculations show that SRM-25 [the designation for the *Challenger*'s January 28 flight] O-rings will be 20° colder than SRM-15 O-rings

- Temperature data not conclusive on predicting primary O-ring blow-by

- Engineering assessment is that:

  - Colder O-rings will have increased effective durometer [that is, they will be harder]

  - "Harder" O-rings will take longer to seat

  - More gas may pass primary [SRM-25] O-ring before the primary seal seats (relative to SRM-15)

  - If the primary seal does not seat, the secondary seal will seat

  - Pressure will get to secondary seal before the metal parts rotate

  - O-ring pressure leak check places secondary seal in outboard position, which minimizes sealing time

  - MTI recommends STS-51L launch proceed on 28 January 1986—SRM-25 will not be significantly different from SRM-15

CONTINUED

After the decision was made, Boisjoly returned to his office and wrote in his journal:

I sincerely hope this launch does not result in a catastrophe. I personally do not agree with some of the statements made in Joe Kilminster's [Kilminster was one of the four Thiokol managers who voted to recommend the launch] written summary stating that SRM-25 is okay to fly.

The subsequent investigation by the presidential commission placed the blame for the faulty O-rings squarely with Thiokol. Charles S. Locke, Thiokol's CEO, maintained, "I take the position that we never agreed to the launch at the temperature at the time of the launch. The *Challenger* incident resulted more from human error than mechanical error. The decision to launch should have been referred to headquarters. If we'd been consulted here, we'd never have given clearance, because the temperature was not within the contracted specs."

Boisjoly testified before the presidential panel regarding his opposition to the launch and the decision of his managers (who were also engineers) to override his recommendation. Boisjoly, who took medical leave for post-traumatic stress disorder, has left Thiokol, but he does receive disability pay from the company. Currently, Mr. Boisjoly operates a consulting firm in Mesa, Arizona. He speaks frequently on business ethics to professional organizations and companies.

In May 1986, then-CEO Locke stated, in an interview with the *Wall Street Journal*, "This shuttle thing will cost us this year 10¢ a share." Locke later protested that his statement was taken out of context.

Roger Boisjoly offers the following advice on whistle-blowing:

- You owe your organization an opportunity to respond. Speak to them first verbally. Memos are not appropriate for the first step.
- Gather collegial support for your position. If you cannot get the support, then make sure you are correct.
- Then spell out the problem in a letter.

Summary

How does advertising create liability for a business?

- Express warranty—contractual promise about nature or potential of product that gives right of recovery if product falls short of a promise that was a basis of the bargain
- Bait and switch—using cheaper, unavailable product to lure customers to store with a more expensive one then substituted or offered instead
- Federal Trade Commission (FTC)—federal agency responsible for regulating deceptive ads
- Wheeler-Lea Act—federal law that allows FTC to regulate "unfair and deceptive acts or practices"
- Celebrity endorsements—FTC area of regulation wherein products are touted by easily recognized public figures
- Consent decree—voluntary settlement of FTC complaint

What are the contract theories of product liability?

- Implied warranty of merchantability—warranty of average quality, purity, and adequate packaging given in every sale by a merchant
- Implied warranty of fitness for a particular purpose—warranty given in circumstances in which the buyer relies on the seller's expertise and acts to purchase according to that advice
- Disclaimer—act of negating warranty coverage
- Privity—direct contractual relationship between parties

What is required for tort-based recovery on a defective product? What is strict tort liability for products?

- Strict liability—standard of liability that requires compensation for an injury regardless of fault or prior knowledge
- Restatement (Second) § 402A—American Law Institute's standards for imposing strict liability for defective products
- Negligence—standard of liability that requires compensation for an injury only if the party responsible knew or should have known of its potential to cause such injury
- Punitive damages—damages beyond compensation for knowledge that conduct was wrongful

What defenses exist in product liability?

- Misuse—product liability defense for plaintiff using a product incorrectly

- Contributory negligence—conduct by plaintiff that contributed to plaintiff's injury; serves as a bar to recovery

- Comparative negligence—negligent conduct by plaintiff serves as a partial defense by reducing liability by percentage of fault

- Assumption of risk—defense to negligence available when plaintiff is told of product risk and voluntarily uses the product

What reforms have occurred and are proposed in product liability?

- Consumer Product Safety Commission—federal agency that regulates product safety and has recall power

- Consumer Product Safety Improvement Act of 2008—expands authority to second-hand sales

Questions and Problems

1. A 30-minute infomercial for the DeLonghi America Caffe Sienna espresso/cappuccino machine included this statement from the host/announcer:

Brew cappuccino just like the pros do right at home. Up until now, the home machines, they just didn't work.

The FTC ad division approached Jim McCrusker, the president of the U.S. unit of DeLonghi, on the grounds that the ad was misleading. The ad division, reacting to complaints from competitors, wanted Mr. McCrusker to add language that indicated it wasn't that other machines didn't work. The machines worked, but their frothing processes were not good.

Mr. McCrusker brought in other machines and consumers to talk with the ad division. The presentation of competitors' machines, along with testimonials from consumers about the problems with other machines, convinced the ad council that the statement "They didn't work" was indeed accurate for more than just the frothing process.

What lessons are learned from Mr. McCrusker's experience? Is documentation for ad claims important? Is it appropriate for competitors to complain to a regulatory body about ad content? [*Sunbeam Products, Inc. v DeLonghi America, Inc.*, Not Reported in F.Supp.2d, 2007 WL 1321134 (D.N.J.)]

2. Joyce Payne got a permanent wave from a beautician, Ms. Thrower. Ms. Thrower used a permanent wave product called Soft Sheen, and she carefully read and followed all instructions on the wave kit. While Ms. Thrower applied one step ("rearranger") in the process, Ms. Payne complained of a burning sensation in her back. The wave was completed, but two days later Ms. Payne was diagnosed in a hospital emergency room as having second-degree burns on her back. She brought suit against the manufacturer of the wave and Ms. Thrower. Ms. Thrower says there were no warnings about the rearranger possibly burning skin. Who is liable? [*Payne v Soft Sheen Products, Inc.*, 486 A.2d 712 (D.C. 1985)]

3. Michael Sanders was a 40-year-old man who made his living as a member of various music bands throughout Fresno. Mr. Sanders graduated from Fresno State University in May 2004 and planned to teach music. On August 20, 2004, Fresno police officers responded to a call made at the Sanders's home. When the police entered, they found Mr. Sanders, who appeared disoriented, standing unclothed behind his wife, Lavette Sanders. The officers decided to subdue Mr. Sanders by firing Tasers at his naked body, although Fresno Police Department rules and other instructions require that Tasers not come in contact with human skin. The officers fired numerous Taser darts into Mr. Sanders's body. The officers then handcuffed Sanders, placed him face down on a gurney, which suffocated him, and then placed him in an ambulance. Sanders stopped breathing. One of the officers attempted CPR, but Michael Sanders was pronounced dead at 4:30 A.M.

Mrs. Sanders filed suit against the city of Fresno as well as Taser. She based her suit against Taser on, among other things, that Taser expressly warranted that the product was "safe" and "would not cause injuries to police officers or individuals arrested by police officers." Is this the language of an express warranty? [*Sanders v City of Fresno*, 2006 WL 1883394 (E.D. Cal. 2006), 59 UCC Rep.Serv.2d 1209]

4. Wade Lederman, 31, was at a Fourth of July pool party at a relative's house in 1991. At about 10:30 P.M., Mr. Lederman, his brother, and two others decided to go swimming. They jumped from the sides of the pool into the water and also dove from the pool's diving board. At about midnight, Mr. Lederman dove into the pool from the side and struck his head on the bottom, sustaining permanent physical and neurological injuries.

The pool in which Mr. Lederman was injured is a residential swimming pool that is in-ground and oval-shaped, with a shallow end and a deep end. The pool has three steps at the shallow end by which swimmers can enter the pool. A white line one foot wide is painted on the bottom of the pool between the shallow end and the deep end. At the start of that line, the depth increases to 7 feet and then slowly descends to a depth of 10 feet at the diving-board end of the pool.

Mr. Lederman filed suit against Pacific Industries, Inc., the pool manufacturer, for its failure to display water depths in and around the pool; failure to warn as to which areas were not appropriate for diving; failure to warn that at night, with pool lights on, the depth of the pool was deceptive; and failure to warn that the white line was just the start of the deep end and not a line for diving versus nondiving areas of the pool.

Should Mr. Lederman recover from Pacific? [*Lederman v Pacific Industries Inc.*, 119 F.3d 551 (7th Cir. 1997)]

5. On August 6, 1998, Mr. Ruvolo purchased two chicken gordita sandwiches from Taco Bell. While eating the second sandwich, he felt a sharp pain in his throat and dislodged a chicken bone. The bone caused a scrape in his throat, and, as a result, he was treated at an emergency room. The following day, Mr. Ruvolo was diagnosed with acute tonsillitis, pharyngitis, sinusitis, and gastritis.

Mr. Ruvolo sued Taco Bell and its food distributors, alleging that the infections were due to the chicken bone's scratching his throat and causing an opening where germs and bacteria could enter. He further alleged that Taco Bell and its food distributors were liable because of their failure to properly inspect the chicken. Discuss the theories Mr. Ruvolo might use for recovery and who the defendants might be. [*Ruvolo v Homovich*, 778 N.E.2d 661 (Ohio App. 2002)]

6. On September 6, 1986, Floyd Simeon, 63, and his son, Edward Simeon, 38, went to the Sweet Pepper Grill, a restaurant at the River Walk in New Orleans. They ordered a dozen and a half raw oysters. Floyd ate 6 oysters, and Edward ate 9 or 10. The men had eaten raw oysters before, and these looked and smelled "good."

Two days later, Mr. Floyd Simeon began running a fever and complained of pain in his ankle. Several physicians were consulted, and it was determined that Mr. Simeon was suffering from *vibrio vulnificus* septicemia, an infection resulting from eating raw oysters with *vibrio vulnificus* bacteria. As the disease progressed, Mr. Simeon developed severe blisters on his legs and began to lose subcutaneous tissue. Plastic surgeons and other physicians tried to stop the spread of the disease, but they were unsuccessful, and Mr. Simeon died on September 23, 1986.

Mrs. Simeon brought a suit against Sweet Pepper Grill for breach of the warranty of merchantability. Should the restaurant be held liable? [*Simeon v Doe*, 618 So. 2d 848 (La. 1993)]

7. Roy E. Farrar Produce Co. ordered a shipment of boxes from International Paper Company that were to be suitable for the packing and storage of tomatoes. The dimensions of the two sizes of boxes were to be such that either 20 or 30 pounds of tomatoes could be packed without the necessity of weighing each box. Mr. Farrar requested that the boxes be the same type as those supplied to Florida packers for shipping

tomatoes. Mr. Farrar told Mr. Wilson, an agent for International, to obtain the correct specifications for the Florida-type box.

International shipped Mr. Farrar 21,500 unassembled boxes at a unit price of 64 cents per box. The boxes were not tomato boxes, were not Florida boxes, did not have adequate stacking strength, and would not hold up during shipping. Mr. Farrar had to repack 3,624 boxes (at a cost of $1.92 per box). Substitute boxes were purchased for 10 cents above the International price. The replacement boxes were Florida boxes and did not collapse. Mr. Farrar was also forced to pay growers $6 a box for tomatoes damaged during shipping. He could not use 6,100 boxes, and his sales dropped off, resulting in financial deficiencies in his operation. Can Mr. Farrar recover for his damages? Why or why not? [*International Paper Co. v Farrar*, 700 P.2d 642 (N.M. 1985)]

8. Ms. Hubbs, 80, suffered from arthritis and osteoporosis. She purchased the Clapper, a device designed to turn electrical appliances on by responding to sound, namely, the clapping of hands.

Ms. Hubbs did not follow the instructions in the product to adjust its sensitivity. As a result of continual hard clapping, Ms. Hubbs broke her wrists. Ms. Hubbs also did not follow the product instructions to use (buy) a clicker available for the product if clapping is a chore. She sued the Clapper's manufacturer for breach of the warranty of merchantability. Should she recover? [*Hubbs v Joseph Enterprises*, 604 N.Y.S.2d 292 (1993)]

9. On February 14, 1999, Garry O. Hickman opened a pack of Big Red gum, which is manufactured by Wrigley. Mr. Hickman purchased the gum at a grocery store on the evening of February 13, 1999. Mr. Hickman unwrapped the package, which was still sealed, and put two pieces of the gum into his mouth. Mr. Hickman provided the following description of the events that occurred after he began to chew the gum:

> [A]fter I started chewing the gum I bit down on it, uh, when I bit down on it the tooth exploded in my mouth. I begin to get all of this stuff out of my mouth, tooth fragments all over my mouth and everything. The screw turned up and stuck up in the top of my gum. I had to pull it out which caused me a lot of pain and all and everything and it was very uncomfortable there for a while.

Mr. Hickman sought treatment from Dr. Conly on February 18, 1999. One of Mr. Hickman's bottom teeth was fragmented. Those fragments chipped his top front teeth. Dr. Conly recommended that Mr. Hickman have surgery, which would total approximately $905, to remove the fractured tooth. However, Mr. Hickman had been unable to do so because he could not afford the surgery. His gums stayed sore for several weeks.

Mr. Hickman filed suit against Wrigley. Can he recover? What theories might he try? [*Hickman v Wm. Wrigley, Jr. Co., Inc.*, 768 So.2d 812 (La. App. 2000)]

10. Review the following hypotheticals as well as the cited case and develop a policy for your chain of restaurants on serving coffee, including coffee temperatures, types of cups, and any related issues. Write a memo discussing your new policies and explain why you are implementing them.

Stella Liebeck, 81, suffered third-degree burns when coffee spilled on her lap inside her car after she went through a McDonald's drive-through in Albuquerque, New Mexico. The temperature of the coffee, according to corporate guidelines, is 180 to 190 degrees Fahrenheit. Ms. Liebeck has sued McDonald's to recover for her injuries resulting from the coffee spill. Should Ms. Liebeck be allowed to recover? What theories could she use to recover?

George Morgan, 58, purchased coffee at a Burger King drive-through. He suffered third-degree burns when the bottom of his coffee cup collapsed, spilling hot coffee over his legs and groin. What about Mr. Morgan's accident is different from Ms. Liebeck's accident? Are there different liability issues?

For some insight, read *Austin v W. H. Braum, Inc.*, 249 F.3d 805 (8th Cir. 2001).

Public Policy, Economics, and the Law

One of the evolving product liability issues is whether sellers and manufacturers can be held liable for the dangers inherent in their products, placed there not by design but by nature. For example, eggs that contain a harmful disease or that were injected with a virus would be unreasonably dangerous and subject to product liability recovery claims. However, could there be recovery from egg producers because of the effects of eggs on body cholesterol levels? And is McDonald's liable because its high-calorie, high-fat foods have resulted in weight gains and obesity in those who frequent this restaurant chain? Or can gun and bullet manufacturers be held liable for the crimes, deaths, and injuries that result from the inherently dangerous nature and uses of their products? The courts have been fairly consistent in ruling that the use of a nondefective product with adequate warnings does not result in liability for the manufacturer because such a result would hold manufacturers liable for the criminal conduct of others, for example, in the case of guns, a result that would be a shift in public policy.[4]

In *Greif v Anheuser-Busch Companies, Inc.*, 114 F. Supp. 2d 100 (D. Conn. 2000), a court dealt with the issues of alcohol consumption that result in injuries to others and the liability of the alcohol producer. The court held that beer producers could not be held liable for accidents caused by those who become drunk from imbibing the product. Misuse of the product and its use in combination with other activities can result in dangerous conditions, but the product itself was neither defective nor inherently dangerous.

However, there is a case pending against McDonald's brought by the parents of obese teens who suffer from diabetes and high blood pressure that they claim resulted from their frequenting McDonald's restaurants.[5] The case, which is proceeding through the courts, raises questions about the unintended costs and consequences of imposing liability on a restaurant, not for defective food, but for the harms resulting from overindulgence in that product. The implications of a finding of liability would be tremendously costly for the restaurant industry. Further, there would be limits on the types of foods that would be available in restaurants. Currently, New York and a few other cities have regulations requiring restaurants to disclose trans fats in menu items.

Notes

1. Bloomberg News 2009 Product Liability Report.

2. *FTC News Summary*, May 19, 1978, pp. 1–2.

3. Anjali Athavaley, "Seller, Beware: The New Yard-Sale Rules," *Wall Street Journal*, July 8, 2009, p. D1.

4. See *McCarthy v Olin*, 119 F.3d 148 (2d Cir. 1997). A series of cases dealt with negligent distribution of guns. Those cases too have been dismissed as issues of public policy to be handled by legislatures. See *Hamilton v Beretta U.S.A. Corp.*, 727 N.Y.S.2d 7 (N.Y. App. 2001); *Hamilton v Beretta U.S.A. Corp.*, 264 F.3d 21 (2d Cir. 2001). A new line of cases focuses on public nuisance as a theory for recovery from gun manufacturers. Courts are divided on these cases, with one procedural dismissal for standing, *N.A.A.C.P. v AcuSport, Inc.*, 271 F.Supp.2d 435 (E.D.N.Y.), and one certification for trial, *City of New York v Beretta U.S.A. Corp.*, 315 F.Supp.2d 256 (E.D.N.Y. 2004).

5. The full history of the McDonald's case is as follows: *Pelman v McDonald's Corp.* (*Pelman III*), 396 F.3d 508, 510 (2nd Cir. 2005); *Pelman* was initially dismissed. *Pelman I*, An amended complaint was refiled and dismissed. *Pelman v McDonald's Corp.* (*Pelman II*), No. 02 Civ. 7821(RWS), 2003 WL 22052778 (S.D.N.Y. Sep. 3, 2003. The U.S. Court of Appeals vacated the court's dismissal and remanded the case, see *Pelman III*, 396 F.3d 508, which is pending. *Pelman v McDonald's Corp.* (*Pelman IV*), 396 F. Supp. 2d 439, 446 (S.D.N.Y. 2005); *Pelman v McDonald's Corp.* (*Pelman V*), 452 F. Supp. 2d 320, 328 (S.D.N.Y. 2006).

11 Environmental Regulation and Sustainability

Apart from the damage claims and penalties that can result from unlawful pollution of the environment, social responsibility emerges again as a business concern. Sustainability, or keeping a clean environment, is a long-range goal for society and companies, as citizens benefit from a healthy environment. As the author explained in a conference on the social responsibility of business, "It is not a matter of business profits vs. preserving the environment. You can't keep the first going without taking responsibility for the second. We are all in this together and what each of us does affects the rest." This chapter answers the following questions: What are the public and private environmental laws? What are the protections and requirements in environmental laws? Who enforces environmental laws? What are the penalties for violations? ■

By the shores of Gitche Gumee,
By the shining Big-Sea-Water . . .
How they built their nests in summer,
Where they hid themselves in winter,
How the beavers built their lodges,
Where the squirrels hid their acorns,
How the reindeer ran so swiftly,
Why the rabbit was so timid . . .

Henry Wadsworth Longfellow
"Hiawatha's Childhood"

UPDATE ⬉
For up-to-date legal news, go to
mariannejennings.com

CONSIDER...

Shell Oil sold products to Brown & Bryant, Inc. (B & B), an agricultural chemical distribution business. B & B was what many characterized as a "sloppy" operator. Shell provided guidelines to its distributors, including B & B, for handling its products. Shell also inspected one of B & B's facilities and requested that the company make operational changes. B & B promised to make the changes but did not

follow through. B & B went bankrupt, and state and federal authorities found contaminated soil on B & B's largest site. Both the EPA and state agencies sought to recover the cost of cleanup for the B & B site from Shell. Shell maintains that it did not spill the chemicals, could not control the behavior of B & B, and therefore could not be held liable. Is Shell correct?

Common Law Remedies and the Environment

From earliest times, landowners have enjoyed the protections of the courts and various doctrines to prevent bad smells, noises, and emissions.

Nuisances

The common law doctrine of nuisance provides relief to adjoining landowners and communities when activities of one landowner interfere with the use and enjoyment of others' properties. Bad smells, ongoing damage to paint on buildings, excessive noise, polluted air, and the operation of facilities that present health problems can all be enjoined as nuisances. In many environmental problems, landowners and members of the communities who are affected do not want money for damages as much as they want the harmful activity halted. The courts have the power to issue **injunctions** against those who are causing the harm to land, individuals, communities, or the environment. Courts grant injunctions in those cases in which those who request the injunctive relief can establish ongoing harm as a result of the activities. In *Spur Industries, Inc. v Del E. Webb Dev. Co.* (Case 11.1), the Arizona Supreme Court was faced with issues of property, smells, and the issue of a developer's new project reaching a preexisting nuisance.

CASE 11.1

Spur Industries, Inc. v Del E. Webb Dev. Co.
494 P.2d 700 (Ariz. 1972)

Cattle and Flies and Retirees, Oh, My!

FACTS

Spur Industries operated a cattle feedlot near Youngtown and Sun City, Arizona (communities 14 to 15 miles west of Phoenix). Spur had been operating the feedlot since 1956, and the area had been agricultural since 1911.

In 1959 Del E. Webb began development of the Sun City area, a retirement community. Webb purchased the 20,000 acres of land for about $750 per acre.

In 1960 Spur began an expansion program in which it grew from an operation of five acres to 115 acres. At the time of the suit, Spur was feeding between 20,000 and 30,000 head of cattle, which produced 35 to 40 pounds of wet manure per head per day, or over one million pounds per day, and despite the admittedly good feedlot management and good housekeeping practices by Spur, the resulting odor and flies produced an annoying if not unhealthy situation as far as the senior citizens of southern Sun City were concerned. There is no doubt that some of the citizens of Sun City were unable to enjoy the outdoor living which Del Webb had advertised. Del Webb was faced with sales resistance from prospective purchasers as well as strong and persistent complaints from the people who had purchased homes in that area. Nearly 1,300 lots could not be sold. Webb then filed suit alleging Spur's operation was a nuisance because of flies and odors constantly drifting over Sun City. The trial court enjoined Spur's operations and Spur appealed.

JUDICIAL OPINION

CAMERON, Vice Chief Justice

It is clear that as to the citizens of Sun City, the operation of Spur's feedlot was both a public and a private nuisance. They could have successfully maintained an action to abate the nuisance. Del Webb, having shown a special injury in the loss of sales, had standing to bring suit to enjoin the nuisance. The judgment of the trial court permanently enjoining the operation of the feedlot is affirmed.

In addition to protecting the public interest, however, courts of equity are concerned with protecting the operator of a lawfully, albeit noxious, business from the result of a knowing and willful encroachment by others near his business.

In the so-called "coming to the nuisance" cases, the courts have held that the residential landowner may not have relief if he knowingly came into a neighborhood reserved for industrial or agricultural endeavors and has been damaged thereby:

"Plaintiffs chose to live in an area uncontrolled by zoning laws or restrictive covenants and remote from urban development. In such an area plaintiffs cannot complain that legitimate agricultural pursuits are being carried on in the vicinity, nor can plaintiffs, having chosen to build in an agricultural area, complain that the agricultural pursuits carried on in the area depreciate the value of their homes. The area being primarily agricultural, any opinion reflecting the value of such property must take this factor into account. The standards affecting the value of residence property in an urban setting, subject to zoning controls and controlled planning techniques, cannot be the standards by which agricultural properties are judged.

"People employed in a city who build their homes in suburban areas of the county beyond the limits of a city and zoning regulations do so for a reason. Some do so to avoid the high taxation rate imposed by cities, or to avoid special assessments for street, sewer and water projects. They usually build on improved or hard surface highways, which have been built either at state or county expense and thereby avoid special assessments for these improvements. It may be that they desire to get away from the congestion of traffic, smoke, noise, foul air and the many other annoyances of city life. But with all these advantages in going beyond the area which is zoned and restricted to protect them in their homes, they must be prepared to take the disadvantages."

And:

". . . a party cannot justly call upon the law to make that place suitable for his residence which was not so when he selected it. . . . "

Were Webb the only party injured, we would feel justified in holding that the doctrine of "coming to the nuisance" would have been a bar to the relief asked by Webb, and, on the other hand, had Spur located the feedlot near the outskirts of a city and had the city grown toward the feedlot, Spur would have to suffer the cost of abating the nuisance as to those people locating within the growth pattern of the expanding city.

"The case affords, perhaps, an example where a business established at a place remote from population is gradually surrounded and becomes part of a populous center, so that a business which formerly was not an interference with the rights of others has become so by the encroachment of the population. . . . "

"The law of nuisance affords no rigid rule to be applied in all instances. It is elastic. It undertakes to require only that which is fair and reasonable under all the circumstances. In a commonwealth like this, which depends for its material prosperity so largely on the continued growth and enlargement of manufacturing of diverse varieties, 'extreme rights' cannot be enforced. . . ."

There was no indication in the instant case at the time Spur and its predecessors located in western Maricopa County that a new city would spring up, full-blown, alongside the feeding operation and that the developer of that city would ask the court to order Spur to move because of the new city. Spur is required to move not because of any wrongdoing on the part of Spur, but because of a proper and legitimate regard of the courts for the rights and interests of the public.

Del Webb, on the other hand, is entitled to the relief prayed for (a permanent injunction), not because Webb is blameless, but because of the damage to the people who have been encouraged to purchase homes in Sun City. It does not equitable or legally follow, however, that Webb, being entitled to the injunction, is then free of any liability to Spur if Webb has in fact been the cause of the damage Spur has sustained. It does not seem harsh to require a developer, who has taken advantage of the lesser land values in a rural area as well as the availability of large tracts of land on which to build and develop a new town or city in the area, to indemnify those who are forced to leave as a result.

Having brought people to the nuisance to the foreseeable detriment of Spur, Webb must indemnify Spur for a reasonable amount of the cost of moving or shutting down. It should be noted that this relief to Spur is limited to a case wherein a developer has, with foreseeability, brought into a previously agricultural or industrial area the population which makes necessary the granting of an injunction against a lawful business and for which the business has no adequate relief.

It is therefore the decision of this court that the matter be remanded to the trial court for a hearing upon the damages sustained by the defendant Spur as a reasonable and direct result of the granting of the permanent injunction. Since the result of the appeal may appear novel and both sides have obtained a measure of relief, it is ordered that each side will bear its own costs.

Affirmed in part, reversed in part, and remanded for further proceedings consistent with this opinion.

CASE QUESTIONS

1. What were the factors that made Spur's activities a nuisance?

2. Should it make any difference that Spur was there first?

3. How does the court balance retirement communities and beef production, two of Arizona's biggest industries? (Note: The case was settled when Del Webb agreed to pay Spur $11 million.)

EMF and Nuisances

CYBERLAW

Because any electrical current sets up a magnetic field, computers and wire transmissions to and from computers set up electromagnetic fields (EMF) that might affect electrical equipment in buildings on neighboring land; the stronger the current, the greater the magnetic field. The greater the magnetic field, the greater the interference with neighbors' electronic devices. EMF interference that rises to an unreasonable level may constitute a nuisance and be enjoined or have requirements imposed for mitigation of the field. Adjoining landowners could also recover damages for the resulting harm from the EMF problems, such as the decrease in the value of the property. The issue of EMF has resulted in litigation against electric utilities by adjoining landowners for the placement of overhead wires, transformers, and power plants that result in diminution of value of those landowners' properties. The litigation has used the legal theories of trespass and nuisance.

For example, the Meridian Data Processing Center was an independent contractor that performed all the data processing for a large number of banks and stockbrokers located in California. Because of the large number of computers and direct wire lines to its customers, the center's operation set up a substantial magnetic field that interfered with some of the electronic display equipment in several neighboring stores. The stores sued the data processing center to obtain an injunction against it for nuisance.

Because of the social utility of the activity, and the need for balancing interests in nuisance cases, it is unlikely a court would enjoin the operation of a data processing center. It might, however, impose some limitations on hours of operation or require investment in technology to find a means around the problem.[1]

NIMBYs and Nuisances

Environmental activists that rely on nuisance theories and local zoning laws have emerged as powerful forces in community development. Groups sometimes referred to as NIMBYs (Not In My Back Yard) challenge the placement of everything from power plants to refineries to cell phone towers to Walmarts as nuisances, backing their protests with data on traffic, crime, health and safety, and risk. Another group of activists, called the BANANAs (Build Absolutely Nothing Anywhere Near Anything), deals with the more generic issues of preventing urban sprawl and encouraging urban redevelopment.

Statutory Environmental Laws

At the federal level, most environmental laws can be placed in one of three categories: those regulating air pollution, those regulating water pollution, and those regulating solid waste disposal on land. There are also some specialized areas of regulation covered in this subsection.

Air Pollution Regulation

Early Legislation

The first legislation dealing with the problem of air pollution, the Air Pollution Control Act, was passed in 1955, but it lacked teeth for enforcement. Federal regulation in this area continued to be ineffective in the 1960s. However, under the Air Quality Act of 1967, the federal government was given the authority to oversee the states' adoption of air quality standards and the implementation of those plans. Still, by 1970, because of little enforcement power, no state had adopted a comprehensive plan.

1970 Amendments to the Clean Air Act: New Standards

Because the states did not take action concerning air pollution, Congress passed the 1970 amendments to the original but ineffective 1963 **Clean Air Act** (42 U.S.C. § 7401); these amendments constituted the first federal legislation with any real authority for enforcement. The act created the **Environmental Protection Agency** (EPA), a federal agency authorized to establish air quality standards. Once those standards were developed, states were required to adopt implementation plans to achieve the federally developed standards. These **state implementation plans** (SIPs) had to be approved by the EPA, and adoption and enforcement of the plans were no longer discretionary but mandatory. To obtain EPA approval, the SIPs had to meet deadlines for compliance with the EPA air quality standards.

The EPA air quality standards specify limits for particular substances in the air such as sulfur dioxide, carbon monoxide, and hydrocarbons. Each state must then devise methods for meeting those standards. The EPA required that those state standards also mandate the development of air pollution devices. Lack of technology could no longer be used as a defense to air pollution or as a justification for state delays. Thus, the 1970 amendments were technology forcing.

1977 and 1990 Amendments

The 1977 Clean Air Act amendments gave the EPA the authority to regulate business growth in order achieve air quality standards. The EPA developed two categories for determining areas for business growth. **Nonattainment areas** included those areas with existing, significant air quality problems, the so-called dirty areas. Today, the EPA has reduced the number of nonattainment areas and now refines nonattainment area classifications according to categories of pollutants. Some areas, such as Los Angeles, have achieved air quality for certain pollutants, but are classified as nonattainment areas for others. The second classification, called **prevention of significant deterioration (PSD) areas,** provides the EPA with a means for monitoring these areas to stop increased pollution.

New Forms of Control: EPA Advance Approvals

For nonattainment areas, the EPA developed its **emissions offset policy,** which requires three elements before a new facility can begin operation in an area: (1) The new plant must have the greatest possible emissions controls; (2) the proposed plant operator must have all its other operations in compliance with standards; and (3) the new plant's emissions must be offset by reductions from other facilities in the area.

In applying these elements, the EPA follows the **bubble concept,** which examines all the air pollutants in the area as if they came from a single source. If a new plant will have no net effect on the air in the area (after offsets from other plants), the EPA allows the new facility to operate. This bubble concept approach also now applies in PSD areas. PSD regulations give the EPA the right to review proposed plant constructions and modifications before they can be started. In their submissions for EPA review, the plant operators must establish that air quality will not experience any significant effects and that emissions will be controlled with appropriate devices. In *Environmental Defense v Duke Energy,* 549 U.S. 561 (2007), the U.S. Supreme Court supported the EPA's PSD role in plant modifications, even when those modifications are not major ones. Duke Energy had begun implementing modifications to one of its coal-fired electricity plants without first seeking EPA approval. Duke was relying on past EPA procedures that had required approval for major modifications only. An environmental group brought suit against the company to require EPA approval and the agency agreed. The EPA explained to the Court that its policy shift was due to the increased need for controlling carbon emissions. The Court held, as explained in Chapter 6, that the EPA was acting within the authority granted to it by Congress and that requiring permits for all modifications was not beyond the agency's authority under the Clean Air Act. The Court also held that the EPA could step up its standard for permit requirements to one that goes beyond best available technology (BAT) to **maximum achievable control technology (MACT),** a standard that is not controlled by cost alone.

New Forms of Control: EPA and Global Warming

In *Massachusetts v EPA,* 549 US 497 (2007), the Court held that the Clean Air Act mandated EPA action on greenhouse gases and global warming: "Under the clear terms of the Clean Air Act, EPA can avoid taking further action only if it determines that greenhouse gases do not contribute to climate change or if it provides some reasonable explanation." In a dissent written by Chief Justice Roberts, three justices maintained that responsibility for redress of the EPA inaction on global warming is with Congress and the president, not the federal courts. The justices added that their position was one of jurisdiction and authority and "involves no judgment on whether global warming exists, what causes it, or the extent of the problem." With these decisions and the change of administration in 2009, the EPA has begun developing new regulations under the Clean Air Act. In addition, proposed legislation, known as "cap-and-trade," would create even more limited bubble standards.

New Forms of Control: EPA and Small Businesses

The impact of the 1990 Clean Air Act amendments was more substantial on smaller businesses, such as dry cleaners, paint shops, and bakeries, because the definition of a major source of pollution was changed from those businesses emitting 100 tons or more a year to those emitting 50 tons or more per year. Many dry cleaners impose an environmental surcharge on their customers to cover the cost of emissions compliance.

New Forms of Control: EPA and Economic Forces

The Clean Air Act Amendments of 1990 also resulted in an exchange for the buying and selling of EPA permits for sulfur dioxide emissions. If, for example, a utility has an EPA permit to discharge one ton of sulfur dioxide per year, but its equipment permits it to run "cleaner" so that it discharges less than the one ton, the utility can sell the emissions savings portion of its permit to another utility. The proposed cap-and-trade legislation would sell off all available existing permits annually for an estimated $80 billion per year.

For the Manager's Desk

Re: The Emissions Permit Market

The market for emissions permits continues to expand. Under EPA guidelines, more than 200 utilities are permitted to sell and buy on an open market. The market has created an incentive for utilities to reduce their sulfur dioxide emissions, which the EPA capped with the 1990 statute. No one can gain additional rights to emit sulfur dioxide, substantial penalties are imposed on utilities that do not meet their maximums, and the opportunity to sell any emissions reductions achieved. The result has been that sulfur dioxide emissions have fallen faster than even the EPA anticipated; they are now at one-half their 1980 levels. Even though the cost has been $1 billion in lost production, most experts see it as a net gain because of the sales and also because of the reduced health costs.

As in all free markets, the system of buying and selling emissions permits encouraged creativity. Environmentalist groups that purchase permits retire them so that the air is permanently cleaner—these permits will not go back into the market. In fact, the Chicago Board of Trade conducts a national auction for the sale of such permits. The price for a permit for one ton of sulfur dioxide ranges from $122 to $450. The first day of trading these permits—March 30, 1993—produced sales of 150,000 permits worth $21.4 million; 1 percent of the bids were from environmental groups seeking to prevent use of the permits.

The emissions trading system exists in other countries as well. The EU has the most extensive and active market. Canada has a market for sulfur dioxide, nitrogen oxides, and volatile organic compounds. The Chinese market is for sulfur dioxide. Chile's market is for suspended particulates.

Source: Cait Murphy, "Hog Wild for Pollution Trading," *Forbes,* September 2, 2002, p. 137.

CONSIDER...   11.1

Union Electric Company is an electric utility serving St. Louis and large portions of Illinois and Iowa. It operates three coal-fired generating plants in metropolitan St. Louis that are subject to sulfur dioxide restrictions under Missouri's SIP. Union Electric did not seek review of the implementation plan but applied for and obtained variances from the emissions limitations. When an extension for the variances was denied, Union Electric challenged the implementation plan on the grounds that it was technologically and economically infeasible and should therefore be amended. Will Union Electric succeed in having the plan amended? [*Union Electric Co. v EPA*, 427 U.S. 246 (1976)]

Water Pollution Regulation

Early Legislation

In 1965, the first federal legislation on water quality standards was passed—the **Water Quality Act.** The act established a separate enforcement agency—the **Federal Water Pollution Control Administration** (FWPCA)—and required states to establish quality levels for the waters within their boundaries. Once again, the absence of enforcement procedures resulted in only about one-half of the states developing zones and standards by 1970. None of the states were engaged in active enforcement of those standards with their implementation plans.

The **Rivers and Harbors Act of 1899,** which prohibits the discharge into navigable rivers and harbors of refuse that causes interference with navigation, was used for a time to enforce water standards because state action was minimal. Specifically, the act prohibited the release of "any refuse matter of any kind or description" into navigable waters in the United States without a permit from the Army Corps of Engineers.

Present Legislation

Not until 1972 was meaningful and enforceable federal legislation enacted. With the passage of the **Federal Water Pollution Control Act of 1972** (33 U.S.C. § 1401), Congress set two goals: (1) swimmable and fishable waters by 1983 and (2) zero discharge of pollutants by 1985. The act was amended in 1977 to allow extensions and flexibility in meeting the goals and was renamed the **Clean Water Act.** This amendment transferred water pollution regulation from local to federal control. The EPA established federal standards for water discharges on an industry-wide basis, and all industries, regardless of state location, are required to comply.

The EPA, with the FWPCA merged into it, establishes ranges of discharge allowed for each industrial group. The ranges for pulp mills, for example, differ from those for textile manufacturers, but all plants in the same industry must comply with the same ranges.

The ranges of discharges permitted per industrial group are referred to as **effluent guidelines.** In addition, the EPA has established within each industrial group a specific amount of discharge for each plant, which is the effluent limitation. Generally, the standards set depend on the type of substance to be released. For setting standards, the EPA has developed three categories of pollutants: **conventional, nonconventional,** and **toxic pollutants.**

Finally, for a plant to be able to discharge wastes into waterways, it must obtain a National Pollution Discharge Elimination System (NPDES) permit from the EPA.

This type of permit is required only for direct dischargers, or *point sources,* and is not required of plants that discharge into sewer systems (although these secondary dischargers may still be required to pretreat their discharges). Obtaining a permit is a complicated process that requires not only EPA approval but also state approval, public hearings, and an opportunity for the proposed plant owners to obtain judicial review of a permit decision.

In issuing permits, the EPA prescribes standards for release. If a discharger is going to release a conventional pollutant, the EPA can require it to pretreat the substance with the **best conventional treatment** (BCT). The EPA can also require the **best available treatment** (BAT) prior to discharge, which is the highest standard imposed. Until 2009, the standard for requiring BAT was solely one of considering environmental effects and not the economic effects on the applicant discharger. However, in *Entergy Corporation v Riverkeeper, Inc.,* 129 S.Ct. 1498 (2009), the U.S. Supreme Court held that the EPA can use cost-benefit analysis in setting national performance standards, and can use cost-benefit analysis to allow variances from those standards. The court held that while the Clean Water Act mandates use of the best technology available for minimizing adverse environmental impact, the phrase "best technology available" does not preclude cost-benefit analysis. In the case, Entergy's cost of bringing cooling water intake structures to the higher level the EPA requires for new structures would be nine times current costs. The court held that the additional benefit achieved with new processes and equipment was too small to justify the cost of bringing the cooling water facilities to current standards.

CONSIDER... 11.2

Inland Steel Company applied for a permit from the EPA under the Federal Water Pollution Control Act of 1972. Although Inland was granted the permit, the EPA made the permit modifiable, as new standards for toxic releases and treatment were being developed. Inland filed suit, claiming the modification restriction on the permit was invalid because the EPA did not have such authority and also because Inland would be subject to every technological change or discovery made during the course of the permit. Was the restriction invalid? [*Inland Steel Co. v EPA,* 574 F.2d 367 (7th Cir. 1978)]

Other Water Legislation

In 1986, Congress passed the **Safe Drinking Water Act** (42 U.S.C. §300f), which requires the EPA to establish national standards for contaminant levels in drinking water. The states are primarily responsible for enforcement and can have higher standards than the federal standards, but they must at least enforce the federal standards for their drinking water systems.

In 1990, Congress passed the **Oil Pollution Act** (OPA; 33 U.S.C. §1251). The act was passed in response to large oil tanker spills, such as the one resulting from the grounding of the *Exxon Valdez* in Prince William Sound, Alaska, that resulted in a spill of 11 million gallons of crude oil that coated 1,000 miles of Alaskan coastline. The OPA applies to all navigable waters up to 200 miles offshore and places the federal government in charge of all oil spills. The Oil Spill Liability Trust Fund, established by a five-cent-per-barrel tax, covers cleanup costs when the party responsible is financially unable to do the cleanup. By the summer of 2010, the *Exxon Valdez* oil spill seemed to be a relatively small environmental disaster, despite its scope, in light of the April 2010 explosion and subsequent 90-day leak from BP's Deepwater Horizon rig in the Gulf Coast, which resulted in 200 million gallons of oil flowing into the Gulf before the well was capped on August 3, 2010.

For the Manager's Desk

Re: BP's Deepwater Horizon Well and Oil Spill: Lessons for Leaders

Before the April 20, 2010, explosion of the BP Deepwater Horizon rig in the Gulf Coast, BP was in the midst of a culture change undertaken in response to three previous incidents that injured employees and damaged the environment. BP's Prudhoe Bay pipeline burst in March 2006 and resulted in a spill of 267,000 gallons of oil. Industry standards require smart pigging of pipelines every five years. However, BP had not done smart pigging on the Prudhoe Bay line since 1998. BP had a request from a board member to look into maintenance issues at Prudhoe Bay; he indicated that he was concerned about serious corrosion issues. A 2004 internal report written by an external consultant warned the company about accelerated corrosion on the Prudhoe pipeline but BP did not undertake maintenance, nor did it develop a plant for testing the pipeline.

In addition, BP's Texas City Refinery operated on the edge. In 2005, BP had entered into an agreement with OSHA to fix the safety violations at the plant. At that time, OSHA had found 271 violations at the refinery. The Chemical Safety Board (CSB) report on the refinery concluded that cost cutting played a role in BP's failure to address the ongoing OSHA violations. Beginning in 2002, BP commissioned a series of audits and studies that revealed serious safety problems at the Texas City refinery, including a lack of necessary preventive maintenance and training. These audits and studies were shared with BP executives in London, and were provided to at least one member of the executive board. Some additional investments were made, but they did not address the core problems in Texas City. In addition, in 2004, BP executives challenged their refineries to cut yet another 25 percent from their budgets for the following year."[i]

Tragically, the inattention and cost-cutting was a direct contributor to the explosion at BP's Texas City Refinery that resulted in a loss of 15 lives and injuries to 500 workers. The CSB investigation into the refinery tragedy was headed by James Baker, former U.S. secretary of state, who found "instances of a lack of operating discipline, toleration of serious deviations from safe operating practices and apparent complacency toward serious process safety risks at each refinery." The OSHA investigation of the refinery found a total of 439 "willful and egregious" violations, a finding that resulted in the largest fine in OSHA's history, $87 million.

The Texas City tragedy and the Prudhoe Bay spill were so public and resulted in such negative publicity that the BP board made a change in the company's leadership. CEO Lord Browne was removed and Mr. Tony Hayward, a reserved geologist, was expected to help the company turn the corner on its safety and prudence issues. However, Mr. Hayward was not able to make the cultural corrections the board hoped would happen. A 2007 internal report, issued one year into Mr. Hayward's tenure, concluded that there had been "unprecedented levels of issues and accidents at BP and that there was a culture of pervasive unwillingness to stop work when something was clearly wrong."[ii]

All employees were reminded of Mr. Hayward's singular message, "Safety is our first priority."[iii] But as the safety program was continued in earnest, there were increasing problems with both the decisions about, and the conduct on, BP's offshore rigs.

There was also a precursor event to the Deepwater Horizon explosion and spill. Almost two years after Texas City and Prudhoe Bay, and nearly two years before the Deepwater Horizon spill, was the June 5, 2008, 193-barrel oil spill at BP's Atlantis rig (also in the Gulf of Mexico). The internal report included the following information:

> "[Managers] put off repairing the pump in the context of a tight cost budget."

> "Leadership did not clearly question the safety impact of the delay in repair."

> A BP safety officer told company investigators, "You only ever got questioned on why you couldn't spend less."[iv]

During this period of ongoing safety lapses and resulting casualties, BP continued its stellar financial performance. In 2007, BP's shares were at $77. Its debt/equity ratio was .31, its dividend rate 15 percent, a 20 percent ROE, with gross margins of 27 percent and net margins of 7.47 percent. EPS growth in 2008 was at 64 percent.

The Deepwater Horizon explosion resulted in the deaths of 11 BP workers on the rig. The evidence that has emerged so far reveals decision-making that followed the patterns in place at the refinery and other rigs. A whistle-blower allegation that had emerged early in 2010 has resurfaced, as it were, through the

CONTINUED

release of e-mails related to government investigations. The e-mails express concern about whether crucial engineering drawings and paperwork necessary prior to operation of offshore rigs had been completed. The e-mails also reveal that engineers who asked for an additional 10 hours in the critical path to address their concerns about the well by installing 21 centralizers instead of just 6 were dismissed by the lead engineer with an "I do not like this."[iv]

At hearings before the House of Representatives, other oil company CEOs testified that BP did not follow appropriate design standards in drilling the well.[vi] A *Wall Street Journal* study found that BP used a risky design that was cheaper for one out of three of its deep-water wells. The so-called "long string" design is one that uses a single pipe for bringing the oil to the surface. Experts indicate that the result of using one long pipe is that natural gas accumulates around the pipe and can rise unchecked. Most experts recommend its use only in low-pressure wells, not wells such as Deepwater Horizon. They also note that long-string drilling would not be appropriate when a company does not know the area, something that was true about this well for BP.

The Costs

There are financial risks that accompany poor decisions in any company and at any level. Following the spill, which is the largest in history, BP lost $30 billion, or 16 percent, of its market value.[vii] Prior to the Deepwater Horizon explosion and spill, BP's share price was at $62. By July, the share price was $38, a loss of 33 percent. The reputational damage will last for years. BP certainly has displaced Exxon and its Valdez as the bad poster child for oil companies. Retail sales at BP stations are down 8 to 10 percent since the time of the spill.[viii]

The costs, in terms of cash outlays, continue for BP. From April through July, BP spent $7 million per day trying to contain the spill. BP was given an ultimatum by the Obama administration, and shortly after a White House meeting placed $20 billion in an escrow account for the United States government to distribute to those in the Gulf-area states who have been harmed by the spill. BP sold off $7 billion in assets to cover the expenses and the $20 billion. BP took a $32 billion charge in July 2010 for the Gulf oil spill costs and added the following about its losses to its July 27, 2010, SEC filing:

> "The costs and charges involved in meeting our commitments in responding to the Gulf of Mexico oil spill are very significant and this $17 billion reported loss reflects that. However outside the Gulf it is very encouraging that BP's global business has delivered another strong underlying performance, which means that the company is in robust shape to meet its responsibilities in dealing with the human tragedy and oil spill in the Gulf of Mexico."

What are the management lessons from this brief history of BP? Discuss the relationship between short-term cost savings and long-term performance.

[i]Sheila McNulty, "BP Safety Culture under Attack," *Financial Times*, March 20, 2007, p. 15. The report recommended that BP comply with 29 CFR 1910.119, Process Safety Management of Highly Hazardous Chemicals and implement an effective means of process safety management.

[ii]Guy Chazan, Benoit Faucon, and Ben Casselman, "Safety and Cost Drives Clashed as CEO Hayward Remade BP," *Wall Street Journal*, June 30, 2010, p. A1.

[iii]Sarah Lyall, Clifford Kraus, and Jad Mouawad, "In BP's Record, a History of Boldness and Blunders," *New York Times*, July 13, 2010, p. A1.

[iv]Guy Chazan, Benoit Faucon, and Ben Casselman, "Safety and Cost Drives Clashed as CEO Hayward Remade BP," *Wall Street Journal*, June 30, 2010, p. A1.

[v]Neil King Jr. and Russell Gold, "BP Crew Focused on Costs: Congress," *Wall Street Journal*, June 15, 2010, p. A1, A5.

[vi]Julie Schmit, "Oil Execs: BP Didn't Meet Standards," *USA Today*, June 16, 2010, p. 1B.

[vii]Peter Coy and Stanley Reed, "Lessons of the Spill," *Bloomberg BusinessWeek*, May 10–May 16, 2010, p. 48.

[viii]Naureen S. Malik, "Protests Target BP But Hit Independents," *Wall Street Journal*, June 16, 2010, p. A4.

Ethical Issues

Questions about oil spills and clean-ups have arisen following both the Exxon and BP spills. Companies, including BP, have been using the usual methods for clean-up, such as straw foam, but have discovered that the treatment seems to make the spill worse, gumming the oil and causing more damage to the water, fowl, flora, and fauna. Many experts are now wondering whether the best approach may not be one advocated by Exxon at the time of the *Valdez* spill, which was to let Mother Nature take its course by absorbing the oil and performing its natural cleansing process. By the time BP brought Deepwater Horizon under control, experts noted that much of the oil had disappeared except in areas where it had become concentrated near the shore.

The experts believe that there is some benefit to initial cleanup but that there comes a point when the cleanup efforts actually make things worse. The demand for immediate cleanup, particularly by fishers in the area, is great but may not be in the best interests of long-term recovery. What should oil companies do when there is a spill? Should the fishers consider other stakeholders?

Solid Waste Disposal Regulation

Early Regulation

During the 1970s, two major toxic waste debacles resulted in a new federal regulatory scheme of toxic waste disposal. In 1978, "Love Canal," as it came to be called, made national news as 80,000 tons of hazardous waste were found in the ground in an area that was primarily residential and included an elementary school. Epidemiological studies of cancer and illness rates in the area led to the discovery and eventual cleanup. Also, in Sheppardsville, Kentucky, an area that came to be called "Valley of the Drums," 17,000 drums of hazardous waste leaked tons of chemicals into the ground and water supply before their removal.

The emotional reaction to these two problem areas and the public outcry resulted in the passage of legislation that provided the federal government with some enforcement power for improper solid waste disposal. The **Toxic Substances Control Act** (TOSCA; 15 U.S.C. § 601), passed in 1976, authorized the EPA to control the manufacture, use, and disposal of toxic substances. Under the act, the EPA can stop the manufacture of dangerous substances that the agency concludes are dangerous.

In reaction to dangerous dumping practices, Congress passed the **Resource Conservation and Recovery Act of 1976** (RCRA; 42 U.S.C. § 6901). The two goals of the act are to control the disposal of potentially harmful substances and to encourage resource conservation and recovery. A critical part of the act is a permit system that requires manufacturers to obtain a permit for the storage or transfer of hazardous wastes so that the location of such wastes can be traced through a federal permit system.

CERCLA and the Superfund

In 1980, Congress passed the **Comprehensive Environmental Response, Compensation, and Liability Act** (CERCLA; 42 U.S.C. § 9601), which authorized the president to issue funds for the cleanup of areas that were once disposal sites for hazardous wastes. CERCLA established a **Hazardous Substance Response Trust Fund** to provide funding for cleanup. If federal funds are used for cleanup, the company responsible for the disposal of the hazardous wastes can be sued and required to repay the amounts expended from the trust fund. Often called the **Superfund,** the funds are available for governmental use but cannot be obtained through suit by private citizens affected by the hazardous disposals. Under the **Superfund Amendment and Reauthorization Act,** the EPA can recover cleanup funds from those responsible for the release of hazardous substances. Approximately 700 hazardous substances are now covered. (They are listed at 40 C.F.R. § 302.)

CERCLA Lender Liability.   One of the more intriguing issues under CERCLA liability is whether a lender has the responsibility of cleanup because it took back the property and was in possession of the property as the result of a foreclosure sale or a deed in lieu of foreclosure. The **Asset Conservation, Lender Liability, and Deposit Insurance Protection Act of 1996** provides a specific exclusion for lenders. This provision has been called the "secured lender exemption" from CERCLA liability. However, these lender amendments also provide that lenders can lose their status if they "actually participate[s] in the management or operational affairs of a vessel or facility." A lender can do the following and still not be subject to environmental liability:

- Monitor or enforce terms of the security agreement.
- Monitor or inspect the premises or facility.
- Mandate that the debtor take action on hazardous materials.
- Provide financial advice or counseling.
- Restructure or renegotiate the loan terms.
- Exercise any remedies available at law.
- Foreclose on the property.
- Sell the property.
- Lease the property.

CERCLA—Four Classes of Liability Rules.   Four classes of parties can be held liable under CERCLA. The present owners and operators of a contaminated piece of property comprise one group. While *owner* is self-explanatory, *operator* includes those who lease property and then contaminate it, such as those who lease factories, operate storage facilities, and so forth. The owners and operators at the time the property was contaminated form the second group. This group brings under CERCLA jurisdiction those who were responsible for the property contamination, as opposed to present owners who had the problem deeded to them. For example, many gas stations have been converted to other businesses. Suppose that one of the underground gas tanks once used by the gas station has been leaking hazardous materials into the surrounding soil. Not only would the present owners be liable; so also would be all those who owned the gasoline station previously.

The final two groups consist of those who transport hazardous materials and those who arrange for the transportation of hazardous materials. Virtually no liability exemptions are available to those who fit into these four groups. Case 11.2 deals with a corporation's CERCLA liability and provides the answer to the chapter opening "Consider."

| **CASE 11.2** | *Burlington Northern Railway/Shell Oil Co. v U.S.* 129 S.Ct. 1870 (2009) |

Am I My Customer's Keeper? I'm Only the Arranger

FACTS

In 1960, Brown & Bryant, Inc. (B & B) began operating an agricultural chemical distribution business (the Arvin facility). B & B applied its products to customers' farms. B & B opened its business on a 3.8-acre parcel of former farmland, and then expanded operations onto an adjacent 0.9-acre parcel of land owned jointly by the Atchison, Topeka & Santa Fe Railway Company and the Southern Pacific Transportation Company (Railroads). Wastewater and chemical runoff from the facility were allowed to seep into the groundwater below.

B & B purchased chemicals from Shell. Shell would arrange for delivery by common carrier, f.o.b. destination. When the product arrived, it was transferred from tanker trucks to a bulk storage tank located on B & B's primary parcel. During each of these transfers leaks and spills could—and often did—occur.

In the late 1970s Shell took several steps to encourage the safe handling of its products. Shell provided distributors with detailed safety manuals and instituted a voluntary discount program for distributors that made improvements to their bulk handling and safety facilities. Later, Shell required distributors to obtain an inspection by a qualified engineer and provide self-certification of compliance with applicable laws and regulations. B & B's Arvin facility was inspected twice, and B & B told Shell that it had made a number of recommended improvements to its facilities. Despite these improvements, B & B remained a "'[s]loppy' [o]perator."

The EPA discovered significant contamination of soil and groundwater, and in 1989, B & B's land was designated as a Superfund site. However, B & B went bankrupt that year. By 1998, the governments had spent more than $8 million in cleanup costs.

In 1991, the EPA (referred to in the case as "Governments") ordered the Railroads to conduct certain cleanup processes. The Railroads did so, incurring expenses of more than $3 million in the process. The parties ended up in court seeking a determination of their share of cleanup liability. The U.S. District Court held that both the Railroads and Shell were potentially responsible parties (PRPs) under CERCLA: the Railroads because they were owners of a portion of the facility, and Shell because it had "arranged for" the disposal of hazardous substances through its sale and delivery of chemicals. The court did not impose joint and several liability on Shell and the Railroads for the entire response cost incurred by the Governments. The court apportioned the Railroads' liability as 9 percent of the Governments' total response cost. Based on estimations of chemicals spills of Shell products, the court held Shell liable for 6 percent of the total site response cost.

The state and local governments appealed the District Court's apportionment, and Shell cross-appealed the court's finding of liability. Applying a theory of arranger liability, the Ninth Circuit held that Shell had arranged for the disposal of a hazardous substance and held Shell and the Railroads jointly and severally liable for the Governments' costs.

The Railroads and Shell appealed.

JUDICIAL OPINION

STEVENS, Justice

. . . [A]n entity could not be held liable as an arranger merely for selling a new and useful product if the purchaser of that product later, and unbeknownst to the seller, disposed of the product in a way that led to contamination. Less clear is the liability attaching to the many permutations of "arrangements" that fall between these two extremes—cases in which the seller has some knowledge of the buyers' planned disposal or whose motives for the "sale" of a hazardous substance are less than clear.

The Governments assert that by including unintentional acts such as "spilling" and "leaking" in the definition of disposal, Congress intended to impose liability on entities not only when they directly dispose of waste products but also when they engage in legitimate sales of hazardous substances knowing that some disposal may occur as a collateral consequence of the sale itself. The Governments contend that Shell arranged for the disposal by shipping to B & B under conditions it knew would result in spilling by the purchaser. Because these spills resulted in waste, a result Shell anticipated, the Governments insist that Shell was properly found to have arranged for the disposal. Shell was aware that minor, accidental spills occurred during transfer. . . .

[t]he evidence does not support an inference that Shell intended such spills to occur. To the contrary, the evidence revealed that Shell took numerous steps to encourage its distributors to reduce the likelihood of such spills, providing them with detailed safety manuals, requiring them to maintain adequate storage facilities, and providing discounts for those that took safety precautions.

Although Shell's efforts were less than wholly successful, given these facts, Shell's mere knowledge that spills and leaks continued to occur is insufficient grounds for concluding that Shell "arranged for" the disposal. Accordingly, we conclude that Shell was not liable.

The District Court calculated the Railroads' liability based on three figures. First, the court noted that the Railroad parcel constituted only 19% of the surface area of the Arvin site. Second, the court observed that the Railroads had leased their parcel to B & B for 13 years, which was only 45% of the time B & B operated the Arvin facility. Finally, the court found that the volume of hazardous-substance-releasing activities on the B & B property was at least 10 times greater than the releases that occurred on the Railroad parcel. The District Court's detailed findings make it abundantly clear that the primary pollution at the Arvin facility was contained in an unlined sump and an unlined pond in the southeastern portion of the facility most distant from the Railroads' parcel and that the spills of hazardous chemicals that occurred on the Railroad parcel contributed to no more than 10% of the total site contamination, some of which did not require remediation. With those background facts in mind, we are persuaded that it was reasonable for the court to use the size of the leased parcel and the duration of the lease as the starting point for its analysis.

Although the Court of Appeals faulted the District Court for relying on the "simplest of considerations: percentages of land area, time of ownership, and types of hazardous products," these were the same factors the court had earlier acknowledged were relevant to the apportionment analysis.

CONTINUED

Although the evidence adduced by the parties did not allow the court to calculate precisely the amount of hazardous chemicals contributed by the Railroad parcel to the total site contamination or the exact percentage of harm caused by each chemical, the evidence did show that fewer spills occurred on the Railroad parcel and that of those spills that occurred, not all were carried across the Railroad parcel to the B & B sump and pond from which most of the contamination originated. The fact that no spills on the Railroad parcel required remediation lends strength to the District Court's conclusion . . . any miscalculation on that point is harmless.

Because the District Court's ultimate allocation of liability is supported by the evidence and comports with the apportionment principles, we reverse the Court of Appeals' conclusion that the Railroads are subject to joint and several liability for all response costs arising out of the contamination of the Arvin facility.

For the foregoing reasons, we conclude that the Court of Appeals erred by holding Shell liable as an arranger under CERCLA. Furthermore, we conclude that the District Court reasonably apportioned the Railroads' share of the site remediation costs at 9%. The judgment is reversed.

CASE QUESTIONS

1. Where do you think the term "arranger" fits in the categories of those who are responsible for cleanup costs under CERCLA?

2. What do you think the practical effect of this decision will be on companies who own Superfund sites? Does the complexity of analysis for liability help companies in clean-up cases?

3. What do you think will happen to government agencies in their efforts to seek reimbursement for their cleanup efforts?

CONSIDER...   11.3

Grand Auto Parts Stores receives used automotive batteries from customers as trade-ins. Grand Auto drives a screwdriver through spent batteries and then sells them to Morris Kirk & Sons, a battery-cracking plant that extracts and smelts lead. Tons of crushed battery casings were found on Kirk's land. The EPA sought to hold Grand Auto liable for cleanup. Can Grand Auto be held liable? [*Catellus Dev. Corp. v United States,* 34 E3d 748 (9th Cir. 1994)]

CERCLA and Corporate Liability. CERCLA liability has also extended to corporate board members and corporate successors and officers in cases where a company is purchased by another firm. Those who merge or buy corporations also buy into CERCLA liability—liability under CERCLA continues after a transfer of ownership. The U.S. Supreme Court ruled in *United States v Bestfoods,* 528 U.S. 810 (1999), that a parent corporation is not automatically liable under CERCLA for a subsidiary corporation's conduct, but may be responsible if the subsidiary is simply a shell. In other words, CERCLA liability of parent corporations for the actions of their subsidiaries is governed by corporate law on piercing the corporate veil. Under the *Bestfoods* case (see Chapter 20, p. 702 for full case), liability of the parent corporation for actions of a subsidiary results if

a. the parent corporation operates the facility, is a joint venturer in the operation of the facility, or works side-by-side with the subsidiary in operations;

b. the parent and subsidiary corporations share officers and directors such that it becomes impossible to separate out the decision-making processes; or

c. an officer of the parent corporation (or other designated or authorized employee) operates the facility of the subsidiary[2]

CERCLA and Buying Land. The best safeguard against stepping into CERCLA liability is screening the property carefully before buying it or, in the case of lenders, accepting it as collateral. When lenders sell foreclosed property to a third party, the lender is in the position of trying to sell property with a CERCLA problem. The value of the collateral is reduced substantially. Lenders and any purchasers of a piece of property should conduct a *due diligence review* of the property. A due diligence review consists of three phases. Phase 1 consists of a search to determine whether evidence of past or current environmental problems is present on the property. The EPA has established the "all appropriate inquiries" rule for Phase I, which requires the use of experts and documentation. A Phase 1 search must examine private and public records and include a site inspection. If Phase 1 reveals some concerns, the parties proceed to Phase 2, which consists of chemical analysis of soil, structures, and water from the property. If Phase 2 finds the presence of contaminants, the report for Phase 2 estimates the cost of cleanup. Phase 3 is the actual cleanup plan.

New Developments under CERCLA

Judicial Developments. Courts have begun to examine the issue of causation between the contaminants present on a piece of property and its relation to any injury as a means of a cost-benefit analysis. For example, in *Licciardi v Murphy Oil U.S.A.*, Ill F.3d 396 (5th Cir. 1997), one federal circuit court held that some causation must be established between the cleanup and what the owner or operator is alleged to have dumped at the site. However, not all the federal circuit courts have followed that line of reasoning in their decisions [*Johnson v James Langley Operation Co., Inc.*, 226 F.3d 957 (8th Cir. 2000)].

Another basis for CERCLA judicial challenges has been one grounded in the basic administrative law principle of an arbitrary and capricious challenge to an EPA demand for cleanup of a site when the demand for cleanup is not linked to any danger. [*U.S. v Broderick Investment Co.*, 200 F.3d 679 (10th Cir. 1999)] These types of challenges to CERCLA, including allocation issues, continue their advancement through the judicial system.

The Self-Audit. Companies have been responding to CERCLA liability with voluntary disclosures through the EPA's self-audit procedures. The EPA encourages companies to self-identify problem lands and areas in exchange for reduced fines. Companies have hired executive-level managers such as vice presidents for environment or vice presidents for health, safety, and environment to manage a staff of in-house professionals who do everything from supervising a company's current activities to investigating past activities to determine environmental problems. These problems are then reported to the EPA, and the company and agency work together to solve the problem and be certain cleanup is done where warranted. These self-audits and disclosures also help the companies be more accurate in their disclosures to shareholders and analysts.

The EPA has established a program called Incentives for Self-Policing, Disclosure, Correction, and Prevention of Violations. Under the program, those companies that come forward voluntarily, having met certain conditions, will have their penalties reduced for any violations uncovered. The conditions for reduced penalties are

1. The violations were uncovered as part of a self-audit or due diligence done on property.
2. The violations were uncovered voluntarily.
3. The violations were reported to the EPA within 10 days.
4. The violations were discovered independently and disclosed independently, not because someone else was reporting or threatening to report.
5. There is correction of the violation within 60 days.
6. There is a written agreement that the conduct will not recur.
7. There can be no repeat violations or patterns of violations.
8. There is no serious harm to anyone as a result of the violation.
9. The company cooperates completely with the EPA.

The EPA will reduce fines and penalties by 75 percent if substantially all the conditions are met. If a company falls into the 75 percent mitigation category, the EPA will not recommend criminal prosecution to the Department of Justice. The documents related to the audit can be protected by the attorney–client privilege, even those that are disclosed to the EPA. The clarification of the privilege has resulted in most companies taking advantage of the EPA's self-reporting protections.

CERCLA and Brownfields

CERCLA has been so effective that designated Superfund sites that remained undeveloped as of 2010 totaled 425,000. Called "brownfields," these sites are defined by the EPA as "real property, the expansion, redevelopment, or reuse of which may be complicated by the presence or potential presence of a hazardous substance, pollutant, or contaminant." Brownfields often contribute to urban blight and present barriers to economic development and revitalization.[3]

As a result, the Small Business Liability Relief and Brownfields Revitalization Act was passed to allow 75 federal agencies to work together through the *Federal Partnership Action Agenda.* This agency provides funding for proposals to clean up and use these brownfields (42 U.S.C.A. § 9601). EPA rules promulgated under the act now provide a process for application to become an "innocent landowner," or someone who seeks to develop the brownfield but wants an exemption from CERCLA exposure. That designation then allows the applicant to obtain federal funding for purposes of cleaning up and developing the brownfield.

Insurers and CERCLA

An issue that continues to evolve is whether property insurance can be used to cover CERCLA liability. Environmental exposure is a risk that contractors and owners try to manage, but most insurers now include an exclusion clause on CERCLA exposure. Courts are left with interpretation issues on these policies, and on what is excluded as CERCLA liability and what constitutes a hazard or risk on the property. Ambiguities in the meaning of the term "pollution" in a policy are construed against the insurer and in favor of coverage for the property owner. One court has held that there is no other way to interpret "pollution" other than to include CERCLA liability. [*Sulphuric Acid Trading Co., Inc. v Greenwich Ins. Co.,* 211 S.W.3d 243 (Tenn. App. 2006)]. CERCLA coverage is available, but it is a policy rider and requires additional premiums.

Environmental Quality Regulation

Environmental controls of air, water, and waste are directed at private parties in the use of their land. However, as part of the environmental control scheme, Congress also passed an act that regulates what governmental entities can do in the use of their properties. The **National Environmental Policy Act** (NEPA) of 1969 (42 U.S.C. § 4321) was passed to require federal agencies to take into account the environmental impact of their proposed actions and to prepare an **environmental impact statement** (EIS) before taking any proposed action.

An EIS must be prepared and filed with the EPA whenever an agency sends a proposed law to Congress and whenever an agency will take major federal action significantly affecting the quality of the environment. The information required in an EIS is as follows:

1. The proposed action's environmental impact
2. Adverse environmental effects (if any)
3. Alternative methods
4. Short-term effects versus long-term maintenance, enhancement, and productivity
5. Irreversible and irretrievable resource use

Examples of federal agency actions that have required the preparation of an EIS include the Alaskan oil pipeline, the extermination of wild horses on federal lands, the construction of government buildings such as post offices, and any highway construction paid for with federal funds. Even the North American Free Trade Agreement (NAFTA) was challenged on the basis that an EIS was required.

In 2008, the U.S. Supreme Court held there was an exigency exception to the EIS requirements in a case in which Navy training that was necessary for national defense would have been unduly delayed and the resulting harm from the Navy's use of sonar was not irreparable. *Winter v National Resources Defense Council*, 129 S.Ct. 365 (2008). The case introduces some cost/benefit analysis into the EIS process.

Sierra Club v United States Dep't of Transportation (Case 11.3) involves the question of whether an EIS was needed.

CASE 11.3 *Sierra Club v United States Dep't of Transportation*
753 F.2d 120 (D.C. 1985)

Skiing and Landing at Jackson Hole

FACTS

In 1983, the Federal Aviation Administration (FAA) issued two orders amending the operations specifications for Frontier Airlines, Inc., and Western Airlines, Inc. These amendments gave the airlines permanent authorizations to operate Boeing 737 jet airplanes (B-737s) out of Jackson Hole Airport, which is located within the Grand Teton National Park in Wyoming.

These two airlines are the only major commercial carriers that schedule flights to and from Jackson Hole.

Private jets have flown into the airport since 1960, and Western Airlines has been flying into Jackson Hole since 1941. The airport is the only one in the country located in a national park, and Congress has continually funded expansions and improvements of the once single-dirt-runway airport.

CONTINUED

In 1978, Frontier applied for permission to fly B-737s into the Jackson Hole Airport. The FAA released its EIS on the application in 1980, which found that B-737s were comparable with C-580 propeller aircraft (the type then being used by Western and Frontier) for noise intrusion but were substantially quieter than the private jets using the airport. The study also showed that fewer flights would be necessary because the B-737 could carry more passengers and that different flight paths could reduce noise. Based on this EIS, Frontier was given the right to use B-737s for two years. When Frontier applied for permanent approval, the FAA used the 1980 EIS and found that with flight time restrictions, the impact would not harm the environment.

Following FAA orders allowing the runway expansion, the Sierra Club (petitioner), a national conservation organization, brought suit for the FAA's failure to file an EIS for the 1983 amendments and for the use of national park facilities for commercial air traffic without considering alternatives. (Because this is an appeal of an administrative agency's order, the case goes directly to the federal appellate level.)

JUDICIAL OPINION

BORK, Circuit Judge

We do not think the FAA violated NEPA by failing to prepare an additional EIS. Under NEPA, an EIS must be prepared before approval of any major federal action that will "significantly affect the quality of the human environment." The purpose of the Act is to require agencies to consider environmental issues before taking any major action. Under the statute, agencies have the initial and primary responsibility to determine the extent of the impact and whether it is significant enough to warrant preparation of an EIS. This is accomplished by preparing an Environmental Assessment (EA). An EA allows the agency to consider environmental concerns, while reserving agency resources to prepare full EIS's for appropriate cases. If a finding of no significant impact is made after analyzing the EA, then preparation of an EIS is unnecessary. An agency has broad discretion in making this determination, and the decision is reviewable only if it was arbitrary, capricious or an abuse of discretion.

This court has established four criteria for reviewing an agency's decision to forego preparation of an EIS. First, the agency must have accurately identified the relevant environmental concern. Second, once the agency has identified the problem, it must take a "hard look" at the problem in preparing the EA. Third, if a finding of no significant impact is made, the agency must be able to make a convincing case for its finding. Last, if the agency does find an impact of true significance, preparation of an EIS can be avoided only if the agency finds

that changes or safeguards in the project sufficiently reduce the impact to a minimum.

The first test is not at issue here. Both the FAA and Sierra Club have identified the relevant environmental concern as noise by jet aircraft within Grand Teton National Park. The real issues raised by Sierra Club are whether the FAA took a "hard look" at the problem, and whether the methodology used by the agency in its alleged hard look was proper.

We find that the FAA did take a hard look at the problem. The FAA properly prepared an EA to examine the additional impact on the environment of the plan. The EA went forward from the 1980 EIS. The 1980 EIS, which was based on extensive research by Dr. Hakes of the University of Wyoming, noise testing by the FAA, and data derived from manufacturer information, showed that noise intrusions of B-737 jets over the level caused by C-580 propeller aircraft amounted to only 1 dbl near the Airport and decreased in proportion to the distance from the Airport. The agency, exercising its expertise, has found that an increase this minute is not significant for any environment. In addition, the EIS and Hakes studies were based on a worst-case scenario, and it was determined that if certain precautions were taken the actual noise levels could be diminished greatly.

Petitioner argues that because Jackson Hole Airport is located within national parkland a different standard—i.e., individual event noise level analysis—is mandated. Both individual event and cumulative data were amassed in preparing the 1980 EIS on which the EAs were based. The fact that the agency in exercising its expertise relied on the cumulative impact levels as being more indicative of the actual environmental disturbance is well within the area of discretion given to the agency. We agree with petitioner that although noise is a problem in any setting, "airplane noise is fundamentally inconsistent with the type of recreational experience Park visitors are seeking" and should be minimized. Here the FAA found that a cumulative noise increase of 1 dbl or less is not significant—even for the pristine environment in which Jackson Hole Airport is located.

Given all of these facts, we think the FAA was not required to prepare yet another EIS before granting permanent authorizations for the use of B-737s.

The orders of the FAA are hereby affirmed.

CASE QUESTIONS

1. What airport noise is at issue, and who was concerned about the issue?

2. What is the basis for the appeal?

3. What has the FAA allowed? Will the authorizations stand?

Other Federal Environmental Regulations

In addition to the previously discussed major environmental laws, many other specific federal statutes protect the environment.

Surface Mining

The **Surface Mining and Reclamation Act of 1977** (42 U.S.C. § 6907) requires those mining coal to restore land surfaces to their original conditions and prohibits surface coal mining without a permit.

Noise Control

Under the **Noise Control Act of 1972** (42 U.S.C. § 4901), the EPA, along with the FAA, can control the amount of noise emissions from low-flying aircraft for the protection of landowners in flight paths.

Pesticide Control

Under the **Federal Environmental Pesticide Control Act,** the use of pesticides is controlled. All pesticides must be registered with the EPA before they can be sold, shipped, distributed, or received. Also under the act, the EPA administrator is given the authority to classify pesticides according to their effects and dangers.

OSHA

The **Occupational Safety and Health Administration** (OSHA) is responsible for workers' environments. OSHA controls the levels of exposure to toxic substances and requires safety precautions for exposure to such dangerous substances as asbestos, benzene, and chloride.

Asbestos

Buildings that contain asbestos materials remain a problem for buyers, sellers, and occupants. The **Asbestos Hazard Emergency Response Act** (AHERA), passed in 1986, required all public and private schools to arrange for the inspection of their facilities to determine whether their buildings had asbestos-containing materials. Schools are required to develop plans for containment, but other buildings are not regulated. The Clean Air Act does, however, define airborne asbestos as a toxic pollutant, and liability may result from the release of fibers from this known carcinogen. Further, an amendment to the Superfund Act classified asbestos as a **community-right-to-know substance,** which means a probable duty to disclose the presence of asbestos to buyers, tenants, and employees. Numerous ethical questions arise about the presence of asbestos and the obligations of landowners to replace the asbestos given that the phase-out of its use did not end until 1997. Questions such as the impact of the release of asbestos from the walls when tenants, employees, and others hang photos and other objects by nailing them into the walls remain. The issues of the degree of harm and the cost of replacement continue to be debated among property owners.

Endangered Species

In 1973, Congress passed the **Endangered Species Act** (ESA), a law that has been a powerful tool for environmentalists in protecting certain species through their advocacy of restrictions on commercial use and development when the habitats of certain species are interfered with. Under the act, the secretary of the interior is responsible for identifying endangered terrestrial species, and the secretary of commerce identifies endangered marine species. In addition, these cabinet members must designate habitats considered crucial for these species if they are to thrive. In many instances, litigation results over questions about which species should or should not be on the list. Once a species is on the list, its critical habitat cannot be disturbed by development, noise, or destruction. *Babbitt v Sweet Home Chapter of Communities for a Great Oregon* (Case 11.4) has given federal agencies broad authority in protecting endangered species.

CASE 11.4   *Babbitt v Sweet Home Chapter of Communities for a Great Oregon*
515 U.S. 687 (1995)

Jobs Versus Owls: Lumber Versus Endangered Species

FACTS

Two U.S. agencies halted logging in the Pacific Northwest because it endangered the habitat of the northern spotted owl and the red-cockaded woodpecker, both endangered species. Sweet Home Chapter (respondents) is a group of landowners, logging companies, and families dependent on the forest products industries in the Pacific Northwest. They brought suit, seeking clarification of the authority of the secretary of the interior and the director of the Fish and Wildlife Service (petitioners) to include habitation modification as a harm covered by the ESA.

The federal district court found for the secretary and director and held that they had the authority to protect the northern spotted owl through a halt to logging. The court of appeals reversed. Bruce Babbitt, the secretary of the interior, appealed.

JUDICIAL OPINION

STEVENS, Justice

Section 9(a)(1) of the Endangered Species Act provides the following protection for endangered species:

Except as provided in sections 1535(g)(2) and 1539 of this title, with respect to any endangered species of fish or wildlife listed pursuant to section 1533 of this title it is unlawful for any person subject to the jurisdiction of the United States to—(B) take any such species within the United States or the territorial sea of the United States. [16 U.S.C. § 1538(a)(1)]

Section 3(19) of the Act defines the statutory term "take":

The term "take" means to harass, harm, pursue, hunt, shoot, wound, kill, trap, capture, or collect, or to attempt to engage in any such conduct. [16 U.S.C. § 1532(19)]

The Act does not further define the terms it uses to define "take." The Interior Department regulations that implement the statute, however, define the statutory term "harm":

Harm in the definition of "take" in the Act means an act which actually kills or injures wildlife. Such act may include significant habitat modification or degradation where it actually kills or injures wildlife by significantly impairing essential behavioral patterns, including breeding, feeding, or sheltering. [50 CFR § 17.3 (1994)]

We assume respondents have no desire to harm either the red-cockaded woodpecker or the spotted owl; they merely wish to continue logging activities that would be entirely proper if not prohibited by the ESA. On the other hand, we must assume *arguendo* that those activities will have the effect, even though unintended, of detrimentally changing the natural habitat of both listed species and that, as a consequence, members of those species will be killed or injured. Under respondents' view of the law, the Secretary's only means of forestalling that grave result—even when the actor knows it is certain to occur—is to use his § 5 authority to purchase the lands on which the survival of the species depends. The Secretary, on the other hand, submits that the § 9 prohibition on takings, which Congress defined to include "harm," places on respondents a duty to avoid harm that habitat alteration will cause the birds unless respondents first obtain a permit pursuant to § 10.

The text of the Act provides three reasons for concluding that the Secretary's interpretation is reasonable. First, an ordinary understanding of the word "harm" supports it. The dictionary definition of the verb form of "harm" is "to cause hurt or damage to: injure." *Webster's Third New International Dictionary* 1034 (1966). In the context of the ESA, that definition naturally encompasses habitat modification that results in actual injury or death to members of an endangered or threatened species.

Respondents argue that the Secretary should have limited the purview of "harm" to direct applications of force against protected species, but the dictionary definition does not include the word "directly" or suggest in any way that only direct or willful action that leads to injury constitutes "harm." Moreover, unless the statutory term "harm" encompasses indirect as well as direct injuries, the word has no meaning that does not duplicate the meaning of other words that § 3 uses to define "take." A reluctance to treat statutory terms as surplusage supports the reasonableness of the Secretary's interpretation.

Second, the broad purpose of the ESA supports the Secretary's decision to extend protection against activities that cause the precise harms Congress enacted the statute to avoid. As stated in § 2 of the Act, among its central purposes is "to provide a means whereby the ecosystems upon which endangered species and threatened species depend may be conserved."

Third, the fact that Congress in 1982 authorized the Secretary to issue permits for takings that § 9(a) (1)(B) would otherwise prohibit, "if such taking is incidental to, and not the purpose of, the carrying out of an otherwise lawful activity," 16 U.S.C. § 1539(a) (1)(B), strongly suggests that Congress understood § 9(a) (1) (B) to prohibit indirect as well as deliberate takings. The permit process requires the applicant to prepare a "conservation plan" that specifies how he intends to "minimize and mitigate" the "impact" of his activity on endangered and threatened species, 16 U.S.C. § 1539(a)(2)(A), making clear that Congress had in mind foreseeable rather than merely accidental effects on listed species.

The Court of Appeals made three errors in asserting that "harm" must refer to a direct application of force because the words around it do. First, the court's premise was flawed. Several of the words that accompany "harm" in the § 3 definition of "take," especially "harass," "pursue," "wound," and "kill," refer to actions or effects that do not require direct applications of force. Second, to the extent the court read a requirement of intent or purpose into the words used to define "take," it ignored § 9's express provision that a "knowing" action is enough to violate the Act. Third, the court employed *noscitur a sociis* to give "harm" essentially the same function as other words in the definition, thereby denying it independent meaning. The canon, to the contrary, counsels that a word "gathers meaning from the words around it." The statutory context of "harm" suggests that Congress meant that term to serve a particular function in the ESA, consistent with but distinct from the functions of the other verbs used to define "take." The Secretary's interpretation of "harm" to include indirectly injuring endangered animals through habitat modification permissibly interprets "harm" to have "a character of its own not to be submerged by its association."

When it enacted the ESA, Congress delegated broad administrative and interpretive power to the Secretary. See 16 U.S.C. §§ 1533, 1540(f). The task of defining and listing endangered and threatened species requires an expertise and attention to detail that exceeds the normal province of Congress. Fashioning appropriate standards for issuing permits under § 10 for takings that would otherwise violate § 9 necessarily requires the exercise of broad discretion. The proper interpretation of a term such as "harm" involves a complex policy choice. When Congress has entrusted the Secretary with broad discretion, we are especially reluctant to substitute our views of wise policy for his. In this case, that reluctance accords with our conclusion, based on the text, structure, and legislative history of the ESA, that the Secretary reasonably construed the intent of Congress when he defined "harm" to include "significant habitat modification or degradation that actually kills or injures wildlife."

In the elaboration and enforcement of the ESA, the Secretary and all persons who must comply with the law will confront difficult questions of proximity and degree; for, as all recognize, the Act encompasses a vast range of economic and social enterprises and endeavors. These questions must be addressed in the usual course of the law, through case-by-case resolution and adjudication.

The judgment of the Court of Appeals is reversed.

CASE QUESTIONS

1. Is habitat modification harming endangered species?

2. Does the Court's interpretation mean no intent is required to violate ESA?

3. Did Congress intend to give the secretary authority to shut down an industry?

4. What ethical issues arise from this case?

Aftermath: In August 1995, Congress passed, as a rider to a budget-reduction bill, a provision that suspended environmental laws in some national forest areas in Washington and Oregon through 1996.

BUSINESS STRATEGY

Cooperation as an Alternative Strategy to Litigation

Since the time of these head-on confrontations, the logging and paper industries have adopted a "Sustainable Forestry Initiative." The Initiative, adopted by 200 members of the American Forest and Paper Association, supports eco-friendly logging. The Nature Conservancy supports the Initiative, which

has had the effect of negotiated solutions to the issue of logging versus environmental prohibitions. No further legislation has been needed at the federal level because of the cooperation between and among these groups.

 Ethical Issues

Asia Pacific Resources International Holdings, Ltd. (called April) signed a landmark agreement with the World Wildlife Fund, an environmental activist group. April agreed to curb timber-cutting areas in Sumatra, Indonesia, to preserve a natural rainforest with great biodiversity. Over the past 20 years, more than half of the forest has been cut down for lumber.

April's customers, such as Procter & Gamble (makers of Charmin toilet paper and Bounty paper towels), were shunning April as a supplier because of its damage in Indonesia. While April complied with Indonesian law (leaving 20 percent of the forest untouched), it left long ribbon strips that could not support the local wildlife. Terms of the deal include the following:

- April will not allow other loggers to use its transportation system (barges and roads).

- April will verify the source of all logs it purchases.

- April will plant tree plantations and expects to be able to sell only plantation-grown wood by 2009.

Local residents resent these agreements with environmental groups because their livelihoods have been blocked as April closes its road and prohibits use by illegal loggers. What advantages do you see in these private contract promises on environmental policy? What disadvantages do you see? What ethical issues prompted April's voluntary actions?

Source: Steve Stecklow, "Environmentalists, Loggers Near Deal on Asian Rainforest," *Wall Street Journal,* February 23, 2006, pp. A1, A14.

In *Bennett v Spear,* 520 U.S. 154 (1997), the U.S. Supreme Court held that the ESA also permits lawsuits by landowners affected by the statute's application. Landowners have equal rights along with environmental groups to challenge ESA applications and restrictions. However, in a 2009 decision, the U.S. Supreme Court limited somewhat the ability of individuals and groups to bring suit under the ESA. In *Summers v Earthland Institute,* 129 S.Ct. 1142 (2009), the U.S. Supreme Court held that the claim that the plaintiffs would be using various national parks around the country at some point in the future was not sufficient standing to bring suit to halt the U.S. Forest Service's policies and regulation on forest clearing. The decision means that those who bring such challenges must have an "active, ongoing dispute" that is specific to the activity.

CONSIDER... 11.4

Arizona Cattle Growers' Association and Jeff Menges, a rancher seeking a grazing permit on the lands at issue (together called "ACGA"), sued the Fish and Wildlife Service and the Bureau of Land Management to challenge Incidental Take Statements (ITSs) issued by the Fish and Wildlife Service in a biological opinion for certain grazing lands. Mr. Menges sought livestock grazing permits for land within the area supervised by the Bureau of Land Management's Saffold and Tucson, Arizona, field offices, and the Association represented members who claimed to be harmed by the government action. The Bureau of Land Management's livestock grazing program for this area affects 288 separate grazing allotments that in total comprise nearly 1.6 million acres of land. The Fish and Wildlife Service's biological opinion, issued on September 26, 1997, analyzed 20 species of plants and animals and concluded that the livestock grazing program was not likely to jeopardize the continued existence of the species affected, nor was it likely to result in destruction or adverse modification of the designated or proposed critical habitat. The Fish and Wildlife Service did, however, issue ITSs for various species of fish and wildlife listed or proposed as endangered.

ACGA's suit challenged both the ITSs and their terms and conditions. The challenge was based on the fact that the razorback sucker and the cactus ferruginous pygmy owl were in abundance and not endangered. The environmental groups challenged ACGA's right to challenge the conclusions of the agency. Who is correct?

THINK: The conclusion in the *Bennett* case was that those who sought to protect the species as well as those who were harmed by the protection had the right to challenge the agency's determination. Chapter 6 described the basis for challenging administrative agency actions, including that the action taken was not based on study and information but was arbitrary and capricious.

APPLY: The cattle growers here are the equivalent of Mr. Bennett in that case and therefore have standing to challenge the determination of endangered species status and the resulting impact on grazing lands. If the ACGA can show that the species are not endangered and challenge the factual findings of the agency, the rule can be set aside.

ANSWER: The federal district court found that the Fish and Wildlife Service's issuance of an ITS for both the razorback sucker and the pygmy owl was arbitrary and capricious, reasoning that the Fish and Wildlife Service "failed to provide sufficient reason to believe that listed species exist in the allotments in question." [*Arizona Cattle Growers' Ass'n v U.S. Fish and Wildlife, Bureau of Land Management*, 273 F3d 1229 (9th Cir. 2001)].

State Environmental Laws

In addition to federal enactments, all the states have enacted some form of environmental law and have established their own environmental policies and agencies. Some states may require new industrial businesses to obtain a state permit along with the required federal permits for the operation of their plants. Some states regulate the types of fuels that can be used in vehicles and offer incentives for carpooling.

All states have some form of regulation on hazardous waste, a sort of CERCLA statute at the state level. Some states require sellers of real estate to furnish property disclosure statements to buyers prior to the closing of a sale. All states have some system of fines for environmental violations.

Enforcement of Environmental Laws

Federal environmental laws can be enforced through criminal sanctions, penalties, injunctions, and suits by private citizens. In addition to federal enforcement rights, certain common-law remedies, such as nuisance or trespass, exist for the protection of property rights. This portion of the chapter discusses the various remedies available for environmental violations.

Parties Responsible for Enforcement

Although many federal agencies are involved with environmental issues, the EPA is responsible for the promulgation of specific standards and the enforcement of those standards with the use of the remedies discussed in the following subsections. The federal EPA may work in conjunction with state EPAs in the development and enforcement of state programs.

The **Council on Environmental Quality** (CEQ) was established in 1966 under the National Environment Act and is part of the executive branch of government. Its role in the environment regulatory scheme is that of policymaker. The CEQ is responsible for formulating national policies on the quality of the environment and then making recommendations to lawmakers regarding its policy statements.

In addition to these major environmental agencies, other federal agencies are involved in enforcement of environmental issues, such as the Atomic Energy Commission, the Federal Power Commission, the Department of Housing and Urban Development, the Department of the Interior, the Forest Service, the Bureau of Land Management, and the Department of Commerce. Basically, all federal agencies that deal with the use of land, water, and air are involved in compliance with and enforcement of environmental laws.

Criminal Sanctions and Penalties for Violations

Nearly all of the federal statutes previously discussed carry some form of sanctions, including criminal penalties for violations.

Penalties for Clean Air Act Violations

Under the Clean Air Act, the EPA can issue field citations and assess civil penalties of up to $25,000 a day in general fines. A $5,000-per-day penalty applies to even minor violations, including those related to record keeping. The EPA is also authorized to pay $10,000 rewards to people who provide information leading to criminal convictions or civil penalties. Criminal penalties include up to two years' imprisonment for false statements or failures to report violations. Willful violations carry penalties of up to 15 years and $1 million in fines. The act specifically holds corporate officers involved in the polluting activities criminally responsible.

Exhibit 11.1 summarizes the various penalties. In exercising its enforcement power, the EPA may require businesses to maintain records or to install equipment necessary for monitoring the amounts of pollutants being released into the air or water.

Penalties for Water Violations

The Clean Water Act carries criminal penalties of up to $25,000 per day and one year's imprisonment. For violations that are willful, the penalties increase to $50,000 and/ or three years, with repeat violation carrying penalties of $100,000 and/or six years.

Those responsible for oil spills are liable for penalties of $25,000 per day or $1,000 per barrel spilled. If the spill is the result of negligence or willful

EXHIBIT 11.1   Penalties for Violation of Federal Environmental Laws

ACT	PENALTIES	PRIVATE SUIT
Clean Air Act	$25,000 per day, up to one year imprisonment; 15 years for willful or repeat violations; $10,000 rewards	Citizen suits; authorized EPA suit for injunctive relief
Clean Water Act	$25,000 per day, up to one year imprisonment, or both; $50,000/three years for violations with knowledge; $100,000/six years for subsequent violations	Citizen suits; authorized EPA suit for injunctive relief
Resource Conservation and Recovery Act (Solid Waste Disposal Act)	$250,000 and/or 15 years for intentional; $1,000,000 for corporations; $50,000 and/or 5 years for others	Citizen and negligence suits after EPA refuses to handle
Oil Pollution Act	$25,000 per day, or $1,000 per barrel; $3,000 per barrel if willful or negligent; $250,000 and/or 5 years for failure to report	Hazardous Substance/Response Trust Fund for cleanup; EPA suit for injunctive relief and reimbursement of trust funds; private actions in negligence

misconduct, the penalties are $3,000 per barrel spilled. Failure to report a spill can bring a $250,000 fine for an individual (sole proprietor or officer, according to agency and criminal liability principles) and up to five years imprisonment or $1 million for a corporation. Civil penalties run higher and include the full cost of cleanup (up to $50 million) should those responsible not clean up the oil spill.

United States v Johnson & Towers, Inc. (Case 11.5) deals with the issue of criminal liability for environmental law violations.

CASE 11.5   *United States v Johnson & Towers, Inc.*
741 F.2d 662 (3d Cir. 1984)

Changing Your Oil: It Can Be Criminal

FACTS

Johnson & Towers (Johnson) repairs and overhauls large motor vehicles. In its operations, Johnson uses degreasers and other industrial chemicals that contain methylene chloride and trichlorethylene, classified as "hazardous wastes" under the Resource Conservation and Recovery Act (RCRA) and as pollutants under the Clean Water Act.

The waste chemicals from Johnson's cleaning operations were drained into a holding tank and, when the tank was full, pumped into a trench. The trench flowed from the plant's property into Parker's Creek, a tributary of the Delaware River. Under RCRA, generators of such wastes must obtain a permit from the EPA, but Johnson had not received or even applied for such a permit.

Jack Hopkins, a foreman, and Peter Angel (defendants) the service manager for Johnson, were charged with criminal violations of the RCRA and the Clean Water Act. Johnson was also charged and pled guilty. Mr. Hopkins and Mr. Angel pled not guilty on grounds that they were not "owners" or "operators" as required for RCRA violations. The trial court agreed and dismissed all charges against the two men except for the criminal conspiracy charges.

The government appealed the dismissal.

JUDICIAL OPINION

SLOVITER, Circuit Judge

The single issue in this appeal is whether the individual defendants are subject to prosecution under RCRA's criminal provision, which applies to

CONTINUED

any person who— . . . (2) knowingly treats, stores, or disposes of any hazardous waste identified or listed under this subchapter either—(A) without having obtained a permit under Section 6925 of this title . . . or (B) in knowing violation of any material condition or requirement of such permit.

If we view the statutory language in its totality, the congressional plan becomes . . . apparent. First, "person" is defined in the statute as "an individual, trust, firm, joint stock company, corporation (including a government corporation), partnership, association, State, municipality, commission, political subdivision of a State, or any interstate body." Had Congress meant to take aim more narrowly, it could have used more narrow language. Second, under the plain language of the statute, the only explicit basis for exoneration is the existence of a permit covering the action. Nothing in the language of the statute suggests that we should infer another provision exonerating persons who knowingly treat, store or dispose of hazardous waste but are not owners or operators.

Finally, though the result may appear harsh, it is well established that criminal penalties attached to regulatory statutes intended to protect public health, in contrast to statutes based on common law crimes, are to be construed to effectuate the regulatory purpose.

In summary, we conclude that the individual defendants are "persons" within the RCRA, that all elements of that offense must be shown to have been knowing, but that such knowledge, including that of the permit requirement, may be inferred by the jury as to those individuals who hold the requisite responsible positions with the corporate defendant. For the foregoing reasons, we will reverse the district court's dismissal and we will remand for further proceedings consistent with this opinion.

CASE QUESTIONS

1. Who is charged with criminal violations, and what are those violations?

2. What violations did the lower court dismiss?

3. Did Congress intend to prosecute corporate employees?

4. What proof is required to show violations by the "persons"?

Group Suits: The Effect of Environmentalists

In many circumstances, private suits have had the most effect either in terms of obtaining compliance with environmental regulations or in terms of abating existing nuisances affecting environmental quality. The reason for the success of these suits may be the ultimate outcome of the litigation—possible business shutdowns and, at the least, the payment of tremendous amounts of damages and costs.

Private suits have been brought by environmental groups that have both the organizational structure and sufficient funding to initiate and complete such suits. In some cases, environmental groups are formed to protest one specific action, as is the case of Citizens Against the Squaw Peak Parkway; other groups are national organizations that take on environmental issues and litigation in all parts of the country. Examples of these national groups include the Sierra Club, the Environmental Defense Fund, Inc., the National Resources Defense Council, and the League of Conservation Voters. Some environmental groups represent business interests in environmental issues, as does the Mountain States Legal Foundation, which becomes involved in presenting business issues when private organizations and individuals bring environmental suits.

These environmental groups have been successful not only in bringing private damage and injunctive relief suits, but also in forcing agencies to promulgate regulations and to enjoin projects when EISs should have been filed but were not.

International Environmental Issues

The EU and Environmentalism

The European Union (EU) has passed more than 200 environmental directives that focus on noise restrictions; protection of endangered species; energy efficiency; recycling; and air, land, and water quality. The view of the EU is that environmental planning is to be conducted by member states as part of their economic development plans and processes. The EU's European Environment Agency serves as a clearinghouse for environmental information; eventually the agency will operate for members in a manner similar to the EPA.

Many EU directives are designed to eliminate the need for regulation by encouraging different business choices and educating consumers. One directive requires manufacturers to make 90 percent of all packaging materials recyclable. Another directive awards companies the use of an "eco-audit" sticker on their labels and stationery if they comply with an annual environmental audit of their manufacturing, waste management, materials use, and energy choices. An innovative directive of the EU created an EU-wide "eco-label" to be placed on all consumer goods to provide information about the environmental impact of a product's production, distribution, life, and disposal.

ISO 14000

The International Organization for Standardization (ISO) has developed its ISO 14000 series of international environmental standards.

Under ISO 14000, companies can become ISO certified, which will permit them to place special insignias on their materials, correspondence, and products to indicate their ISO standing. ISO standards emphasize not only compliance but also self-audits and self-correction. Genuine dedication to improvement is a key standard for this environmental certification.

The Kyoto Protocol

At the Kyoto meeting of the United Nations Framework Convention for Climate Change (UNFCCC), the delegates adopted the *Kyoto Protocol*, a plan for reducing six greenhouse gases, primarily in the United States and other industrial nations. Under the Protocol, signatory countries will reduce their carbon dioxide levels to less than their 1990 levels, a reduction that will require transfer of industries to other countries. The Protocol took effect in 2005 and as of July 2006 had 164 signatory countries, but by the time of the Copenhagen Climate Summit in 2009, the Protocol had stalled within the United States and other major economic powers that declined to adopt it.

The Precautionary Principle

The **precautionary principle** has become a dominant force in environmental regulation in Canada, Australia, and Europe. The precautionary principle requires those who propose change to demonstrate that their proposed actions will not cause serious or irreversible harm to the environment. The standard is used, for example, in Australia as the burden of proof for anyone who seeks to obtain a permit to dump hazardous waste. The government will not issue the permit unless and until the applicant demonstrates that the action will not cause serious or irreversible harm. It has been used in applications for logging permits and building construction.

B I O G R A P H Y

The EPA Administrators

1971–1973: William D. Ruckelshaus

Served as the first EPA administrator, appointed by Richard Nixon. Continued to serve under Gerald Ford and was responsible for the implementation of both the Clean Water Act and the Clean Air Act. By the time of his departure, the EPA had 9,077 employees.

1973–1977: Russell E. Train

Established close congressional relationships. Agency size ranged from 9,200 to 10,200 employees during his tenure.

1977–1981: Douglas M. Costle

The first EPA administrator under a Democratic president; appointed by Jimmy Carter. Saw the role of the EPA as that of a health agency. Often credited for the beginning of environmental activism. Responsible for the Superfund Amendments being passed in Congress. Agency grew to 11,000 employees. Budget of EPA went from $1 billion in 1971 to $5.4 billion in 1981.

1981–1983: Anne Burford Gorsuch

Appointed by Ronald Reagan. Questions arose about how effective the EPA had been in Superfund cleanup. Constitutional confrontation with Congress on executive privilege regarding documents relating to Superfund cleanups. Agency was reduced from 13,000 employees to 12,000.

1983–1985: William D. Ruckelshaus

Appointed by Ronald Reagan. His seasoned experience was required in order to restore the EPA's reputation following the Burford years. Pursued an asbestos-removal program in schools. Began global environmental relations and meetings. Agency grew to 13,000 employees.

1989–1993: William K. Reilly

Key figure in getting the Clean Air Act of 1990 through Congress. Issues with contractors and subcontractors in Superfund cleanups plagued his administration. Pushed for the 1992 Earth Summit in Rio de Janeiro. Agency grew to 17,000 employees during his tenure.

1993–2001: Carol M. Browner

Formerly head of Florida's environmental agency. Pushed "environmental justice." Implemented strictest air quality standards to date. Agency budget was increased to $7.5 billion and employees to 18,375 during her tenure.

2001–2003: Christine Todd Whitman

Appointed by George W. Bush in early 2001; formerly the governor of New Jersey. Her first EPA budget was for $7.2 billion. EPA employees at the end of 2001 were 18,050. Indicating that she had no one to talk to in Washington except her plants, Mrs. Whitman resigned as EPA director to return to her family and native New Jersey in 2003.

2003–2009: Michael Leavitt

Sworn in on November 6, 2003; formerly the governor of Utah. Achieved zero emissions during the Salt Lake City Winter 2002 Olympics as the environmental administrator for that event. The budget for the EPA for 2005 is $7.76 billion, and as of July 2004, the agency had 17,094 employees.

2009—present: Lisa P. Jackson

Formerly chief of staff for former New Jersey governor Jon Corzine. First African American to serve as head of the EPA. A staff of 17,000 operates with a budget of $10.02 billion.

Summary

What are the public and private environmental laws? What protections and requirements are present in environmental laws?

- Nuisance—bad smells, noises, or dirt from one property that interferes with another's use and enjoyment of their own property

- Nonattainment areas—areas with significant air pollution problems

- Emissions offset policy—new plants not built until new emissions are offset by reductions elsewhere

- Bubble concept—EPA policy of maximum air emissions in one area

- Clean Air Act—federal law that controls air emissions

- Maximum Achievable Control Technology (MACT)—best means for controlling emissions

- Clean Water Act—federal law that regulates emissions in various water sources

- Effluent guidelines—EPA maximum allowances for discharges into water

- Safe Drinking Water Act—federal law establishing standards for contaminants

- Oil Pollution Act (OPA)—federal law imposing civil and criminal liability for oil spills

- Resource Conservation and Recovery Act (RCRA)—federal law controlling disposal of hazardous waste through a permit system

- Superfund—funds available for government to use to clean up toxic waste sites

- Comprehensive Environmental Response, Compensation, and Liability Act (CERCLA)—federal law providing funds and authority for hazardous waste site cleanups

- Endangered Species Act (ESA)—powerful federal law that can curb economic activity if it presents harm to endangered species or their habitat

Who enforces environmental laws?

- Environmental Protection Agency (EPA)—federal agency responsible for enforcement of environmental laws at the federal level

- National Environmental Policy Act (NEPA)—federal law that requires federal agencies to assess environmental issues before taking actions

- Environmental impact statement (EIS)—report by federal agency on study of proposed action's effect on the environment

What are the penalties for violations?

- Injunction—judicial order halting an activity

- Fines and criminal penalties

Questions and Problems

1. American Rivers, a national river conservation organization, the Environmental Defense, and a number of national and local environmental organizations brought suit against the U.S. Army Corps of Engineers, the Secretary of the Army, and the Secretary of the Interior, seeking to protect the endangered least tern, the endangered pallid sturgeon, and the threatened Great Plains piping plover, all of which are protected by the ESA.

The groups allege that the manner in which the Corps has operated the extensive dam and reservoir system on the Missouri River have adversely affected the three species. Do the groups have the right to assert the claim? What response can the government agencies offer? What should the court do? [*American Rivers v U.S. Army Corps of Engineers*, 271 F.Supp.2d 230 (D.D.C. 2003)]

2. Philip Carey Company owned a tract of land in Plymouth Township, Pennsylvania, on which it deposited a large pile of manufacturing waste containing asbestos. Carey sold the land to Celotex, and Celotex sold the land to Smith Land & Improvement Corporation. The EPA notified Smith in July 1984 that unless Smith took steps to eliminate the asbestos hazard, the EPA would do the work and pursue reimbursement. Smith proceeded with the cleanup to the EPA's satisfaction at a total cost of $218,945.44. Smith then turned to Celotex and Carey, as previous owners of the property, for reimbursement. These firms say they have no liability under CERCLA. Which firms are liable? [*Smith Land & Improvement Corp. v Celotex*, 851 F.2d 86 (3rd Cir. 1988)]

3. A group of landowners situated near the Sanders Lead Company brought suit to recover for damages to their agricultural property from accumulations of lead particulates and sulfur oxide deposits released in Sanders' production process. The landowners' property had increased in value because of its commercial potential in being close to the plant. Sanders employs most of the town's residents in its operations. What common-law and statutory rights do the landowners have, and what relief can be obtained? [*Borland v Sanders Lead Co., Inc.*, 369 So. 2d 523 (Ala. 1979)]

4. In 1985, Manufacturers National Bank of Detroit issued a letter of credit for Z&Z Leasing, Inc., an industrial firm, in order to enable Z&Z to obtain bond financing from Canton Township, Michigan.

After six years of operation, Z&Z was not doing well and had defaulted on its bond obligations. A consultant for the bank found underground storage tanks on Z&Z's site. The tanks contained a yellowish liquid that was found to be a solvent and a hazardous substance. The bank paid off the Canton township bond obligation and foreclosed on the Z&Z property. By 1993, Z&Z had still not sold the property, and the EPA sought to hold the bank liable as an operator for the costs of cleaning up the tanks.

Can the bank be held liable? [*Z&Z Leasing, Inc. v Graying Reel, Inc.*, 873 F. Supp. 51 (E.D. Mich. 1995)]

5. Reynolds Metal has been held to the same technological standards in its pollution control for can-manufacturing plants as those applied to aluminum manufacturers. Reynolds claims the processes are different and that the technology for pollution control in can manufacturing is not yet available. Does Reynolds have a point? [*Reynolds Metals Co. v EPA*, 760 F.2d 549 (D.C. 1985)]

6. Kelley Technical Coatings is an industrial paint manufacturing company that operates two plants in Louisville, Kentucky. Arthur Sumner was the vice president in charge of manufacturing operations for Kelley. Sumner oversaw the manufacturing process at both plants, including the storage and disposal of hazardous wastes. He was also responsible for environmental regulatory compliance, and submitted the necessary paper-

work to the state environmental authorities to register Kelley as a generator of hazardous waste.

In July 1992 when the Kentucky Department of Environmental Protection inspected the Kelley plants, they found between 600 and 1,000 drums behind one of the plants. The drums had been stored on-site for more than 90 days, and in some cases for many years. Some of the drums had rusted and were leaking on the ground.

Between 1986 and 1989, Sumner had arranged for a licensed hazardous waste disposal company to remove and dispose of some of the drums containing hazardous wastes. From late 1989 to July 1992, however, no drums of hazardous waste were shipped off-site. Instead, in an effort to save money, Kelley contracted with a hazardous waste disposal company to come on site and drain the liquids from the drums. Both Kelley and Sumner were convicted under the RCRA. They appealed their convictions on the grounds that they did not have the *mens rea* required for conviction under the RCRA statute. Are they correct? Are they criminally responsible? [*U.S. v Kelley Technical Coatings, Inc.*, 157 F.3d 432 (C.A. 6th 1998)]

7. The Natural Resources Defense Council, Inc., the Humane Society of the United States, Cetacean Society International, League for Coastal Protection, Ocean Futures Society, and Jean-Michel Cousteau filed suit in federal district court to obtain a preliminary injunction against federal officials to prevent the U.S. Navy's peacetime use of a low-frequency sonar system for training, testing, and routine operations. This new technology, Low Frequency Active Sonar (LFA), sends out intense sonar pulses at low frequencies that travel hundreds of miles in order to timely detect increasingly quiet enemy submarines. Their complaint alleges that the use of LFA is a violation of the Marine Mammal Protection Act, the Endangered Species Act, the National Environmental Policy Act, and the Administrative Procedures Act. The complaint claims that these violations will cause irreparable injury to sea creatures, many of them rare and endangered, including whales, dolphins, seals, sea turtles, and salmon.

The Navy argues that enjoining the peacetime use of LFA sonar would harm national security, even though the Navy would still be free to use it during wartime or periods of heightened threat, because training and testing are necessary for military readiness.

Do the groups and Mr. Cousteau have standing to challenge the Navy's work? Can the Navy's work be enjoined? What should the court decide and why? [*Natural Resources Defense Council, Inc. v Evans*, 232 F.Supp.2d 1003 (N.D. Cal. 2002)]

8. The Nuclear Regulatory Commission (NRC) was responsible for the decision to allow the once-crippled Three Mile Island Unit I nuclear plant to resume operation. Pursuant to the NEPA, the NRC considered the impact on the surrounding community and determined that there would be no adverse impact. A group, People Against Nuclear Energy (PANE), intervened in the action by the NRC and asked that the court require the NRC to consider whether the risk of a nuclear accident (as had been experienced with the original shutdown of the plant) might harm the community in a psychological sense. The NRC says the risk of an accident is not an effect on the environment. Is psychological health a factor in EIS evaluations? [*Metropolitan Edison Co. v People Against Nuclear Energy*, 460 U.S. 766 (1983)]

9. The Tennessee Valley Authority (TVA) proposed the construction of Tellico Dam. If the dam is constructed, the known population of snail darters will be eradicated. A snail darter is a three-inch-long fish protected by the Endangered Species Act, which requires all federal agencies (such as the TVA) not to fund, authorize, or carry out projects that would jeopardize the continued existence of an endangered species. At the time an environmental group brought the issue to light, the TVA had already expended $100 million in the construction of the dam, which would bring great economic benefits to the area. What factors are important in resolving such a dispute? Is it a matter of the significance of the species? Should an EIS have discussed this problem? [*Tennessee Valley Authority v Hill*, 437 U.S. 153 (1978)]

10. Albert J. Hubenthal operated a 55-acre worm-farming operation in Winona County, Minnesota. Mr. Hubenthal maintained that large amounts of scrap materials, such as tires, wood, metal, leather, and solid waste, were necessary for a successful worm operation. The 55 acres were "messy, smelly, and germy," as described by the neighbors. The county attorney called the farm a nuisance and warned Mr. Hubenthal that he had 30 days to clean up the farm. He refused, and the county removed all materials from the worm farm. Could the county take this action? Was the farm a nuisance? [*Hubenthal v County of Winona*, 751 F.2d 243 (8th Cir. 1984)]

Sustainability and the Law

Sustainability requires us to think beyond environmental law to consequences and impact. Review the following two situations and develop an analysis that addresses consequences and impact.

People for the Ethical Treatment of Animals (PETA) has been a powerful force in demanding changes in corporate behavior. Its latest target has been Burger King for its treatment of chickens—the group wants the company to stop removing the beaks of laying hens and also to enlarge the animals' cages. Also, PETA would like Burger King to ensure that its animals are stunned before they are slaughtered. PETA has developed a new logo and name for the company, MURDER KING. Burger King is suffering from flat sales and does not welcome the negative publicity. How would you respond to PETA's concerns? Visit the websites of both PETA and Burger King for more information on these issues: http://www.bk.com and http://www.peta.org.

A federal regulation promulgated by the EPA restricts the amount of water than can flow from showerheads to a rate of 2.5 gallons per minute. When the regulation took effect, many hotel chains had complaints from their guests about the slow water flow and the difficulty they had in bathing. Westin Hotels and Resorts announced that it would install two showerheads in the baths and showers of its hotel rooms to accommodate its guests. Each showerhead will meet federal requirements, but if the two are both turned on, the guests will have water at a rate of five gallons per minute. Westin maintains that it is in compliance with the law. A federal employee responded, "But we didn't anticipate the loophole of two shower heads per shower."[4] Discuss the Westin approach to compliance with the law.

Notes

1. E-commerce selection reprinted with permission from David Twomey and Marianne Jennings, *Anderson's Business Law and the Legal Environment* (Mason, OH: South-Western, Cengage Learning, 2010), p. 1203.

2. The work of Professors Cindy A. Schipani and Lynda J. Oswald is an excellent resource for discussions on parent liability for CERCLA violations as well as a history of the development and scope of CERCLA. See, for example, Oswald and Schipani, "CERCLA and the 'Erosion' of Traditional Corporate Law Doctrine," 86 *Northwestern Law Review* 259 (1990). Their work was referred to in the *Bestfoods* case.

3. For more information, about brownfields, go to http://www.epa.gov/brownfields/about.htm.

4. Chris Woodyard, "Dual Shower Heads Land Hotel in Hot Water," *USA Today,* May 22, 2001, p. 1B.

Part 3

Business Competition and Sales

This section of the book covers the laws and regulations on what a business sells, how it sells its product, and how the sales are set up and financed. Do you have the right to sell a product, or have you appropriated someone else's idea? What can you say and write in your advertising? What is fair and legal in competition? When do you have a contract, and what kinds of terms do you need to have in it? In this era of electronic commerce, what exactly is a contract, and when is it formed? When has a contract been performed, and what is a breach? Can you be compensated if the other side fails to perform? How are transactions financed, and what forms do you need? What are a seller's rights for collecting payments due from buyers?

This portion of the text covers all the preliminary aspects of contracts, contract performance, and collection. The materials walk through the heart of business operations: sales, competition, property rights, advertising, contract formation and performance, and receivables collection.

Contracts allow businesses to count on money, supplies, and services. Contracts are the private law of business; the parties develop their own private set of laws through their contracts. These private laws can be enforced by the courts in all states. This chapter covers contract basics: What is a contract? What laws govern contracts? What are the types of contracts? How are contracts formed? What contracts must be in writing? ■

A verbal contract isn't worth the paper it's written on.

Samuel Goldwyn

UPDATE
For up-to-date legal and ethical news, go to
mariannejennings.com

CONSIDER...

In the summer of 1996, PepsiCo, Inc. ran a marketing campaign involving Pepsi Points. The Pepsi Points, obtained by drinking Pepsi, could be redeemed for prizes. One television ad promoting Pepsi Points shows a Harrier jet outside a schoolyard with the campaign's slogan beneath it: DRINK PEPSI GET STUFF. The jet pictured in the ad was generated by computer. The ad said the jet could be yours for 7 million Pepsi Points. PepsiCo maintains the ad was a spoof. John Leonard, then a 21-year-old business student, saw the ad and delivered to Pepsi 15 original Pepsi Points plus a check for $700,008.50—sufficient for the cost of a Harrier jet, plus shipping and handling.

Pepsi refused to deliver the jet. Pentagon spokesman Kenneth Bacon (famous now for the release of Linda Tripp's personnel records from the Pentagon) indicated that no Harrier jets were available at that time because the jets must be demilitarized before a member of the public can buy one.

Pepsi also said that because the ad was a joke, it was not an offer. Mr. Leonard said that the ad induced conduct on his part, as would all Pepsi Points ads, and that Pepsi was required to deliver to him a Harrier jet. Who was correct? Was the ad an offer?

What Is a Contract?

Businesses cannot expand and grow without being able to rely on commitments; resources are wasted if promises are not fulfilled. For example, suppose that Aunt Hattie's Bread Company constructs a new wing and buys new equipment to expand production, but when the wing is ready to operate, the wheat supplier backs out of the supply contract with Aunt Hattie's. Aunt Hattie's has relied on that promise, spent money counting on delivery on that promise, and now cannot expand because that promise was broken. The failure to honor a promise is more than just a breach of contract; economic ripple effects occur when businesses cannot rely on contractual promises.

"A **contract** is a promise or set of promises for breach of which the law gives a remedy, or the performance of which the law in some way recognizes as a duty." This definition comes from the *Restatement (Second) of Contracts*, a statement of contract law by the American Law Institute (ALI), which recognizes a contract as a set of voluntary promises that the law will enforce for private parties. The remainder of this chapter focuses on the creation, performance, and enforcement of those promises.

Sources of Contract Law

The three general sources of contract law for contracts entered into in the United States include common law, the Uniform Commercial Code, and the new sources of law evolving in response to e-commerce—the Uniform Electronic Transactions Act, the Uniform Computer Information Transactions Act, and the Electronic Signatures in Global and National Commerce Act of 2000 (ESIGN).

Common Law

Common law was the first law of contracts. As discussed in Chapter 1, common law consists today of those traditional notions of law and that body of law developed by judicial decisions dealing with contract issues. Although it is not statutory law, the traditional English common law of contracts has been modified by statute in some states. Certain types of contracts have unique and specific content requirements—for example, listing agreements for real estate agents, insurance policies, and consumer credit contracts (see Chapter 14 for a more complete discussion of the statutory requirements in consumer credit contracts); but, whatever specific language and statutory requirements these contracts have, their formation and enforcement are still governed by common law. Common law applies to contracts that have land or services as their subject matter. Contracts for the construction of a home and employment contracts are governed by common law. A rental agreement for an apartment may be covered by specific landlord–tenant statutes in addition to common law.

A general treatment of the common law for contracts can be found in the *Restatement (Second) of Contracts*. A group of legal scholars wrote the *Restatement*, and similar groups work together to consider market changes and dynamics and modify contract law as necessary.

The Uniform Commercial Code

One of the problems with common law is its lack of uniformity. The states do not follow the same case decisions on contract law, and some states do not follow the *Restatement;* the result is that different rules apply to contracts in different states.

Consequently, businesses experienced great difficulty and expense when they contracted across state lines because of differences in state contract common law. To address the need for uniformity, the National Conference of Commissioners on Uniform State Laws and the American Law Institute worked to draft a set of commercial laws appropriate for businesspeople, lawyers, and lawmakers. The result of their efforts was the **Uniform Commercial Code** (UCC). The final draft of the UCC first appeared in the 1940s. With several revisions and much time and effort, the Code was adopted, at least in part, in all the states.

Article 2 of the UCC governs contracts for the sale of goods and has been adopted in all states except Louisiana. Although sections of Article 2 may have various forms throughout the states, the basic requirements for contracts remain consistent. Under Article 2 contracts can be formed more easily, the standards for performance are more readily defined, and the remedies are more easily determined. The remaining sections of the chapter cover specific differences. (Excerpts of Article 2 are reproduced in Appendix G.) Determining which contracts are UCC contracts and which are common law contracts is often difficult. With the rise in electronic commerce and computer transactions, the issue has become the focus of an intense debate. The questions applied in the determination of UCC versus common law include the cost of the goods versus the cost of services in the contract, the parties' intent, and even some public policy issues. *Wall Street Network, Ltd. v New York Times Company* (Case 12.1) addresses an interesting factual issue involving a question of goods and the application of UCC Article 2.

CASE 12.1

Wall Street Network, Ltd. v New York Times Company
164 Cal. App. 4th 1171, 80 Cal Rptr. 3d 6, 66 UCC Rep Serv. 2d 261 (2008)

When the Question of Common Law v UCC Pops Up

FACTS

Click2Boost, Inc. (C2B) entered into an Internet marketing agreement with the *New York Times* (NYT) (respondents) on May 10, 2002 for C2B to solicit subscribers for home delivery of the *New York Times* newspaper through "pop-up ads" on websites with which C2B maintained "[m]arketing [a]lliances." The agreement required NYT to pay C2B a fee or commission for each home delivery subscription C2B submitted to NYT.

NYT paid C2B more than $1.5 million in subscription submission fees from May 2002 to September 2003, but most of the subscriptions were ended, so NYT terminated the C2B agreement on September 16, 2003.

In October 2003, Wall Street Network (WSN) took over C2B and filed suit for breach of contract against NYT. WSN said that NYT had breached the agreement by terminating it before September 30, 2003 because the contract was one for goods and C2B had furnished those goods. WSN wanted damages under the UCC for breach of contract because the pop-up ads were sold independently as goods. NYT argued that the contract was one for services—for furnishing subscribers—something C2B did not do successfully.

WSN countered that the customers generated from the pop-up ads were what was being sold, and that this was just like selling a list of names, something that would be considered a good. The trial court granted the NYT summary judgment and WSN appealed.

JUDICIAL OPINION

MANILLA, Judge

WSN contends that C2B's submissions constitute "goods" under California's version of the Uniform Commercial Code (UCC), and that C2B's performance must therefore be assessed under the principles applicable to contracts for the sale of goods under the UCC. As explained below, the agreement before us involves the provision of services, not the sale of goods. In determining whether the agreement was for the sale of goods or the provision of services, "we must look to the 'essence' of the agreement. When service predominates, the incidental sale of items of personal property does not alter the basic transaction." [T]he agreement stated that NYT and C2B "intend[ed] to form a business relationship whereby [NYT] advertises and promotes its products and services on C2B's POPS cross-selling system in return for a fee from [NYT] to C2B." Under the agreement, C2B was obliged to place pop up ads at the web sites of its marketing partners, and then relay information from customers who responded to the ads to NYT.

Although no California court has confronted the issue presented here, other state courts have concluded that contracts for the placement of advertising do not involve the sale of goods under the UCC. In a case similar to this one, *Pichey v Ameritech Interactive Media Services* (W.D. Mich. 2006) 421 F.Supp.2d 1038, an internet web site designer agreed to create a web site for a furniture retailer that would advertise the retailer's products, and permit interested parties to contact the retailer by e-mail. The court concluded that the contract was for services, and thus fell outside the scope of the UCC. We reach the same conclusion here.

Pointing to *Big Farmer, Inc. v Agridata Resources, Inc.* (Ill. App.Ct.1991) 221 Ill.App.3d 244, 163 Ill. Dec. 629, 581 N.E.2d 783 (Big Farmer), WSN contends that C2B provided goods to NYT because it identified potential subscribers to the New York Times, and was paid a fee for each potential subscriber. In *Big Farmer*, the publisher of a farming magazine bought a list of farmers within an income group from a business that sold demographic information and mailing lists, and used the list to solicit potential subscribers.

The parties subsequently fell into a dispute about whether the purchase agreement obliged the publisher to pay a fee for each name on the list, or each new subscriber. The court concluded that the names and addresses sold constituted "goods" because they were "moveable." Here, C2B did not sell NYT names and addresses of persons to whom NYT intended—by its own efforts—to send solicitations for subscriptions; rather, C2B agreed to solicit subscribers for NYT by placing subscription advertisements for NYT in designated locations, and to forward responses to the advertisements. Whereas the provider in *Big Farmer* sold personal information it had compiled, C2B merely promised to transmit information from customers of C2B's marketing partners who choose to provide the information through the pop up ads. In our view, C2B thus agreed to provide a service for NYT. That NYT

CONTINUED

paid a fee for each submission does not establish that the submissions constituted "goods."

WSN contends that NYT's failure to warn C2B that its submissions were defective interfered with C2B's ability to perform under the agreement. Here, there is no evidence that respondents prevented C2B from performing in accordance with the agreement, that is, from deriving the submitted information from customers of C2B's marketing partners.

WSN also argues that NYT did not terminate the agreement in accordance with its terms, which permitted either party to terminate the agreement "for good cause upon 60 days written notice to the other party." Here, the dispositive question on summary judgment is whether C2B performed under the agreement. Because WSN provided no evidence that C2B performed under the

agreement—a necessary predicate for recovery on WSN's breach of contract claim—any triable issue whether NYT properly terminated the agreement does not preclude summary judgment in respondents' favor. Affirmed.

CASE QUESTIONS

1. Why does the court distinguish between the sale of a list of names and the gathering of names from pop-ups?

2. Why is the failure of NYT to warn C2B about defective submissions not relevant for determining whether the UCC applied?

3. List some other types of contracts that would be similar to this one and whether they would be governed by the UCC or common law.

CONSIDER...   12.1

In September of 1988, Jane Pittsley contracted with Hilton Contract Carpet Co. for the installation of carpet in her home. The total contract price was $4,402. Hilton paid the installers $700 to put the carpet in Ms. Pittsley's home. Following installation, Ms. Pittsley complained to Hilton that some seams were visible, that gaps appeared, that the carpet did not lie flat in all areas, and that it failed to reach the wall in certain locations. Although Hilton tried several times to fix the installation by stretching the carpet and other methods, Ms. Pittsley was not satisfied with the work. Eventually, Ms. Pittsley refused to allow Hilton to try to fix the carpet. Ms. Pittsley had paid Hilton $3,500, but she refused to pay the remaining balance of $902.

Ms. Pittsley filed suit, seeking rescission of the contract, return of her $3,500, and incidental damages. Hilton answered and counterclaimed for the balance remaining on the contract. Hilton also defended on the grounds that the only issue was the installation and that the damages were minimal. Ms. Pittsley argued that the contract was under the UCC and that she was entitled to remedies because the carpet was defective. Hilton disagreed on the application of the UCC. Who is correct? Does the UCC apply to the contract for the carpet sale and installation? Is Ms. Pittsley entitled to the warranty protection of the UCC? [*Pittsley v Houser*, 875 P.2d 232 (Idaho 1994)]

THINK: The discussion of UCC versus common law has us examine the following:

- The cost of goods versus the cost of service in the contract
- The role of the seller in performing the contract
- The nature of the service component

APPLY: In this case, the cost of the carpet is clearly the largest part of the contract price. Even though the buyer wanted the carpet installed (rather than just delivered to her home), the installation is incidental to the purchase itself. The contract was made for the purchase of the carpet, a good, and the agreement to install the carpet was then tacked onto the contract. Goods such as carpet were intended as part of the UCC to have full warranty protection.

ANSWER: The contract is covered by the UCC.

Now apply these reasoning skills to determine whether the following subject matters would be governed by the UCC or by common law.

- Electricity [*Gordonsville Energy, L.P. v Virginia Electric & Power Co.*, 29 U.C.C. Rep. Serv. 2d 849 (Va. Cir. 1996)]
- Boats [*Standing v Midgett*, 22 U.C.C. Rep. Serv. 2d 472, 850 F. Supp. 396 (E.D.N.C. 1993)]
- Software to provide voice messaging, described as a "turnkey" system, that is, it operates without additional work [*Pentagram Software Corp. v Voicetek Corp.*, 22 U.C.C. Rep. Serv. 2d 646 (Mass. Super. 1993)]
- Golf irrigation systems [*Champion Turf, Inc. v Rice, Papuchis Const. Co.*, 21 U.C.C. Rep. Serv. 2d 519, 853 S.W.2d 323 (Mo. App. 1993)]
- Wheat [*Mogan v Cargill, Inc.*, 21 U.C.C. Rep. Serv. 2d 661, 259 Mont. 400, 856 P.2d 973 (1993)]
- Standing timber [*Bohle v Thompson*, 8 U.C.C. Rep. Serv. 2d 897, 78 Md. App. 614, 554 A.2d 818 (1989)]
- Mobile homes [*Aslakson v Home Sav. Ass'n*, 6 U.C.C. Rep. Serv. 2d 35, 416 N.W.2d 786 (Minn. App. 1987)]
- High frequency on-board battery chargers for electric golf carts and the installation and service of the system that charges them [*TK Power, Inc. v Textron, Inc.* 433 F.Supp.2d 1058 (N.D. Cal. 2006)]
- Diamonds [*Wixon Jewelers, Inc. v Di-Star, Ltd.*, 218 F.3d 913, 42 U.C.C. Rep. Serv. 2d 94 (8th Cir. 2000)]
- Livestock [*Flanagan v Consolidated Nutrition, L.C.*, 627 N.W.2d 573 (Iowa Ct. App. 2001)]
- Degas painting [*Weil v Murray*, 161 F. Supp. 2d 250, 44 U.C.C. Rep. Serv. 2d 482 (S.D. N.Y. 2001)]
- Ticket to an amusement park ride [*Dantzler v S.P. Parks, Inc.*, 40 U.C.C. Rep. Serv. 2d 955, 1988 WL 131428 (E.D. Pa. 1988)]
- Concert tickets [*State v Cardwell*, 38 U.C.C. Rep. Serv. 2d 1158, 246 Conn. 721, 718 A.2d 954 (1998)]

Article 2A—Leases

The UCC has added a section called Article 2A Leases, which applies to leases of goods. Over the past 10 years, many new forms of goods transactions have developed, such as the long-term auto lease, which appears to be more of a sale than a lease. Because of the nature of these agreements, leases did not fit well under common law or traditional Article 2. The Leases section, drafted for these types of contracts, covers such issues as the statute of frauds (leases in which payments exceed $1,000, for example, must be in writing), contract formation, and warranties associated with a lease. The Article 2A Leases section of the UCC has been adopted in most states.

Evolving E-Commerce Contract Laws

Uniform Electronic Transactions Act (UETA)

The **Uniform Electronic Transactions Act** (UETA) is a uniform law drafted in 1999. As of mid-2010 it has been adopted in 48 states and the District of Columbia and remains on the agenda of state legislatures in the remaining states.

The UETA was promulgated in response to contracts being formed over the Internet and includes provisions on issues such as electronic signatures. However, state adoptions of the UETA are not nearly as uniform as those of the UCC, and the issues of what constitutes a valid signature and the effect of electronic verification continue to evolve.

Electronic Signatures in Global and National Commerce Act of 2000

CYBERLAW

The UETA is state recognition of the **Electronic Signatures in Global and National Commerce Act of 2000** (ESIGN), 15 U.S.C. § 7001, the federal law that mandates the recognition of electronic signatures for the formation of contracts (see p. 412 for more information). Although states may vary in their specifics under the UETA, they cannot deny legal effect to contracts that are entered into electronically and that bear electronic signatures. ESIGN means that faxes, PDFs, and online clicks on a tab that reads, "I accept" can all be used to form a valid contract.

Uniform Computer Information Transactions Act (UCITA)

The **Uniform Computer Information Transactions Act** (UCITA) was promulgated in 1999 and has been adopted in two states (Virginia and Maryland) and proposed in others.[1] The UCITA would govern all contracts involving the sale, licensing, maintenance, and support of computer software. Those contracts not involving software that are contracts for the sale of other goods would still be governed by the UCC along with the UETA, if adopted in the state.

The UCITA allows terms that are not revealed to the buyer until after payment and delivery to become part of the contract. Typically, these terms are presented in what are often called "shrinkwrap" or "clickwrap" contracts. Once you open the shrinkwrap on the product, you have agreed to the terms, or, once you click "OK" in an electronic transaction, you have agreed to the terms. The UCITA also treats software and digital content contracts as "licenses" rather than sales of goods or sales of copies of software. This classification and treatment creates some questions about these types of contracts and whether they are governed by UCC or common law.

Types of Contracts

The following sections cover the various types of contracts and offer an introduction to contract terminology.

Bilateral Versus Unilateral Contracts

A contract can result from two parties exchanging promises to perform or from one party exchanging a promise for the other party's actions. A **bilateral contract** is one in which both parties promise to perform certain things. For example, if you sign a contract to buy a used red Mini Cooper for $2,000, you have entered into a bilateral contract with the seller. The seller has promised not to sell the car to anyone else and will give you the title to the car when you pay the $2,000. You have promised to buy that red Mini Cooper and will turn over the $2,000 to the seller in exchange for the title. The contract consists of two promises: your promise to buy and the seller's promise to sell.

Some contracts have one party issuing a promise and the other party simply performing. This type of contract is called a **unilateral contract.** For example, suppose that your uncle said, "I will pay you $500 if you will drive my new Mercedes to San Francisco for me within the next five days." Your uncle has promised to pay, but you have not promised to do anything. Nonetheless, you can hold your uncle to his promise if you drive his car to San Francisco. Your agreement is a promise in exchange for performance. If you drive the car to San Francisco, your uncle's promise will be enforceable as a unilateral contract.

For the Manager's Desk

Re: A Unilateral Tattoo

In a case bound to leave an imprint in the halls of justice, David Winkleman and Richard Goddard filed suit against the owner of a Davenport, Iowa, radio station (KORB-FM), Cumulus Broadcasting, because they allege that they had "93 Rock" tattooed on their foreheads in response to a disc jockey's promise. According to the permanently tattooed men, they heard disc jockey Ben Stone say on November 29, 2000, that the radio station would pay anyone who got "93 Rock" tattooed on their foreheads $30,000 per year for five years plus concert tickets, backstage passes, and a TV satellite dish.

Mr. Winkleman and Mr. Goddard say that when they called to confirm the offer, someone at the station referred them to a tattoo parlor. The station refused to pay the men, asserting that the statements by Mr. Stone were simply a joke and no one would assume otherwise.

The two men also say that they have been unable to get jobs since the tattoos and that they have been "publicly scorned and ridiculed for their greed and lack of common good sense."

The case was dismissed in 2003 because the court found no evidence that such an offer had been made. The audiotapes from the interchange indicated that the disc jockey actually said the men could go ahead and tattoo all they wanted, but that there "wasn't even a free CD in it for you." Subsequently, the two tattooed men were involved in dramatic incidents at their trailer park homes, including attempted murder of one by a neighbor wielding a ball peen hammer. Another incident dealt with accusations of arson involving his mobile home because the fire that destroyed the home followed on the heels of his garage sale of all of his personal items that were in the mobile home.

Source: Annie Hsia, "Here's my tattoo. Where's the cash?" *National Law Journal*, June 24–July 1, 2002, p. A4.

Express Versus Implied Contracts (Quasi Contracts)

Some contracts are written, signed (even notarized), and very formal in appearance. Others are simply verbal agreements between the parties (see p. 416 for a discussion of the types of contracts that can be oral). Still others are electronic contracts entered into via e-mail and the Internet. A contract that is written or orally agreed to is an **express contract.** In still other situations, the parties do not discuss the terms of the contract but nonetheless understand that they have some form of contractual relationship. A contract that arises from circumstances and not from the express agreement of the parties is called an **implied contract,** as when you go to a doctor for treatment of an illness. You and the doctor do not sit down and negotiate the terms of treatment, the manner in which the doctor will conduct the examination, or how much you will pay. You understand that the doctor will do whatever examinations are appropriate to determine the cause of your illness and that a fee is associated with the doctor's work. The payment and treatment terms are implied from general professional customs. You have an **implied-in-fact contract.**

CYBERLAW

A second type of implied or enforceable agreement is called an **implied-in-law contract** or a **quasi contract.** The term *quasi* means "as if" and describes the action of a court when it treats parties who do not have a contract "as if" they did. The courts enforce a quasi contract right if one party has conferred a benefit on another, both are aware of the benefit, and the retention of the benefit would be an enrichment of one party at the unjust expense of the other.

The theory of quasi contracts is not used to help "the officious meddler." The officious meddler is someone who performs unrequested work or services and then, based on a quasi contract theory, seeks recovery. For example, you could not be required to compensate a painting contractor who came by and painted your house without your permission because the contractor acted both without your knowledge and without your consent. However, if you are aware the painting is going on and you do nothing to stop it, you would be held liable in quasi contract.

Void and Voidable Contracts

A **void contract** is an agreement to do something that is illegal or against public policy, or one that lacks legal elements (see Chapter 13). For example, a contract to sell weapons to a country under a weapons ban is a void contract. Neither side can enforce the contract, even if the weapons have already been delivered, because allowing the seller to collect payment would encourage further violations of the law banning the weapons sales.

A contract may be partially void; that is, only a portion of the contract violates a statute or public policy and is therefore unenforceable. For example, in many states, it is illegal to charge excessive rates of interest (known as usury; see Chapter 14 for more discussion). In a usurious loan contract, the loan repayment would be enforceable, but the interest terms would not be. As another example, suppose that an owner has sold her business and in the contract has agreed never to start another similar business. Although the buyer deserves some protection for the payment of goodwill, the complete elimination of the seller's right to start a business is an excessive restraint of trade that is against public policy and would not be enforced, even though the actual sale of the business would be enforced.

A **voidable contract** is a contract that can be unenforceable at the election of one of the parties. For example, a minor who signs a contract can choose to be bound by the agreement or can choose to disaffirm the contract. Voidable contracts give one party the option of disaffirming the contract.

Unenforceable Contracts

An **unenforceable contract** is a contract that cannot be honored judicially because of some procedural problem. A contract that should be in writing to comply with the statute of frauds but is not written is unenforceable. Another example of an unenforceable contract is when a party who wishes to enforce a contract does not bring suit within the time limits of the statute of limitations. Filing suit too late means the contract is unenforceable.

Executed Versus Executory Contracts

Contracts are **executed contracts** when the parties have performed according to their promises or required actions (under unilateral agreements). Contracts are **executory contracts** when the promise to perform is made but the actual performance has not been done. If you sign a contract to buy a house but have not obtained a loan or deposited monies in escrow, you have an executory contract. A contract may be wholly executed, wholly executory, or partially executed. For example, when a business files for bankruptcy, some of its contracts are executory and some are partially executed, such as those contracts in which the business has paid for goods but the goods have not been delivered. The bankruptcy trustee has the option of canceling executory contracts, but will generally complete or require other parties to complete partially executed contracts. Courts often distinguish between executed and executory contracts in determining both the rights of the parties (particularly with respect to issues of public policy and capacity) and the remedies available to the parties.

Formation of Contracts

A contract is formed when two parties with the correct mental intent, under the correct circumstances, within the boundaries of the law, and with some detriment to each of them agree to do certain acts in exchange for the other's acts. Formation elements are like ingredients in a recipe: If you leave one ingredient out of the recipe, the final result will be off in some way. So it is with the elements of a contract. You can have all the elements of formation, but if the subject matter is illegal, it will invalidate the contract. Exhibit 12.1 illustrates all elements necessary for the formation of a valid contract.

Offer

The **offer** is the first part of a contract. The person who makes the offer is called the **offeror,** and the person to whom the offer is made is called the **offeree.** The following sections cover the requirements for a valid offer.

Intent to Contract Versus Negotiation

The offeror must have the proper intent (mental state) to contract. Intent is gleaned from the language the offeror uses. This intent requirement distinguishes offers from negotiations. For example, a letter from a businessperson may contain the following: "I am interested in investing in a franchise. I have heard about your opportunities. Please send me all necessary information." The letter expresses an

EXHIBIT 12.1   Overview of Contracts

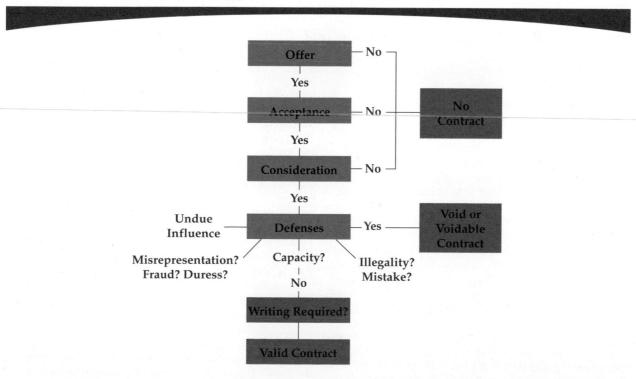

interest in possibly contracting in the future, but it does not express present intent to enter into a contract. But suppose this letter of inquiry was followed by another letter with the following language: "I have decided to invest in one of your franchises. Enclosed are the necessary documents, signatures, and a deposit check." Here the parties have passed the negotiation stage and entered into part one of the contract—an offer.

Courts use an objective standard in determining the intent of the parties, which means that courts look at how a reasonable person would perceive the language, the surrounding circumstances, and the actions of the parties in determining whether a contract was formed. For example, a businessperson who is exasperated with the poor financial performance of her firm may say jokingly to someone over lunch, "I'd sell this company to anyone willing to take it." If that statement is made in the context of a series of complaints about the firm and the workload, it would not be an offer. That same language used in a luncheon meeting with a prospective buyer would create a different result.

In many situations, one party has simply requested bids or is inviting offers. The frustrated business owner could say, "I am interested in selling my firm. If you run into anyone who is interested, have them call me." The owner has not made an offer to sell but, rather, has made an invitation for an offer.

Ads are simply invitations for offers. *Leonard v PepsiCo* (Case 12.2) provides the answer for the chapter's opening "Consider," as it deals with an issue of the role of an ad in contract formation.

CASE 12.2

Leonard v PepsiCo
210 F.3d 88 (2d Cir. 2000)*

Does "Pepsi Stuff" Include a Harrier Jet?

FACTS

PepsiCo (defendant/appellee) ran a promotion titled "Pepsi Stuff," which encouraged consumers to collect Pepsi Points from specially marked packages of Pepsi or Diet Pepsi and redeem these points for merchandise featuring the Pepsi logo. John Leonard (plaintiff/appellant) is a resident of Seattle, Washington, who saw the Pepsi Stuff commercial that he contends constituted an offer for obtaining a Harrier Jet as part of the Pepsi Stuff. The commercial opens on an idyllic, suburban morning, showing a conventional two-story house, and the subtitle, "MONDAY 7:58 AM." The ad shows a well-coiffed teenager preparing to leave for school, dressed in a shirt emblazoned with the Pepsi logo, a red-white-and-blue ball. While the teenager confidently preens, a military drumroll sounds as the subtitle "T-SHIRT 75 PEPSI POINTS" scrolls across the screen. Bursting from his room, the teenager strides down the hallway wearing a leather jacket. The drumroll sounds again, as the subtitle "LEATHER JACKET 1450 PEPSI POINTS" appears. The teenager opens the door of his house and,

unfazed by the glare of the early morning sunshine, puts on a pair of sunglasses. The drumroll then accompanies the subtitle "SHADES 175 PEPSI POINTS." A voiceover then intones, "Introducing the new Pepsi Stuff catalog," as the camera focuses on the cover of the catalog.

The scene then shifts to three young boys sitting in front of a high school building. The three boys gaze in awe at an object rushing overhead as the military march builds to a crescendo. Finally, a Harrier Jet swings into view and lands by the side of the school building, next to a bicycle rack. Several students run for cover, and the velocity of the wind strips one hapless faculty member down to his underwear. While the faculty member is being deprived of his dignity, the voiceover announces, "Now, the more Pepsi you drink, the more great stuff you're gonna get."

The teenager opens the cockpit of the fighter and can be seen, helmetless, holding a Pepsi. Looking very pleased with himself, the teenager exclaims, "Sure beats the bus!" The military drumroll sounds a final time, as the following words appear: "HARRIER FIGHTER 7,000,000 PEPSI POINTS." A few seconds later, the following appears in more stylized script: "Drink Pepsi—Get Stuff."

Inspired by this commercial, Mr. Leonard set out to obtain a Harrier Jet. The Pepsi Points Catalog includes an order form that lists, on one side, 53 items of Pepsi Stuff merchandise redeemable for Pepsi Points. Conspicuously absent from the order form is any entry or description of a Harrier Jet.

The catalog notes that in the event that a consumer lacks enough Pepsi Points to obtain a desired item, additional Pepsi Points may be purchased for 10 cents each; however, at least 15 original Pepsi Points must accompany each order.

Mr. Leonard could not collect 7,000,000 Pepsi Points by consuming Pepsi products fast enough, so through acquaintances, Mr. Leonard raised about $700,000. On March 27, 1996, Mr. Leonard submitted an order form, 15 original Pepsi Points, and a check for $700,008.50. At the bottom of the order form, Mr. Leonard wrote in "1 Harrier Jet" in the "Item" column and "7,000,000" in the "Total Points" column. In a letter accompanying his submission, Mr. Leonard stated that the check was to purchase additional Pepsi Points "expressly for obtaining a new Harrier jet as advertised in your Pepsi Stuff commercial." On May 7, 1996, PepsiCo rejected Mr. Leonard's submission and returned the check, explaining that

The item that you have requested is not part of the Pepsi Stuff collection. It is not included in the catalogue or on the order form, and only catalogue merchandise can be redeemed under this program.

The Harrier jet in the Pepsi commercial is fanciful and is simply included to create a humorous and entertaining ad. We apologize for any misunderstanding or confusion that you may have experienced and are enclosing some free product coupons for your use.

Mr. Leonard responded via his lawyer:

Your letter of May 7, 1996 is totally unacceptable. We have reviewed the video tape of the Pepsi Stuff commercial . . . and it clearly offers the new Harrier jet for 7,000,000 Pepsi Points. Our client followed your rules explicitly . . .

This is a formal demand that you honor your commitment and make immediate arrangements to transfer the new Harrier jet to our client. If we do not receive transfer instructions within ten (10) business days of the date of this letter, you will leave us no choice but to file an appropriate action against Pepsi . . .

Mr. Leonard filed suit, and PepsiCo moved for summary judgment. The court granted summary judgment, and Mr. Leonard appealed.

JUDICIAL OPINION

PER CURIAM

The United States District Court for the Southern District of New York (Wood, J.) [granted] PepsiCo's motion for summary judgment on the grounds (1) that the commercial did not amount to an offer of goods; (2) that no objective person could reasonably have concluded that the commercial actually offered consumers a Harrier Jet; and (3) that the alleged contract could not satisfy the New York statute of frauds.

We affirm for substantially the reasons stated in Judge Wood's opinion. See 88 F.Supp.2d 116 (S.D.N.Y.1999). [To help you understand the issues in the case, portions of Judge Wood's opinion follow.]

WOOD, District Judge

The general rule is that an advertisement does not constitute an offer.

An advertisement is not transformed into an enforceable offer merely by a potential offeree's expression of willingness to accept the offer through, among other means, completion of an order form.

Under these principles, plaintiff's letter of March 27, 1996, with the Order Form and the appropriate number of Pepsi Points, constituted the offer. There would be no enforceable contract until defendant accepted the Order Form and cashed the check.

The exception to the rule that advertisements do not create any power of acceptance in potential offerees is where the advertisement is "clear, definite, and explicit, and leaves nothing open for negotiation," in that circumstance, "it constitutes an offer, acceptance of which will complete the contract." *Lefkowitz v Great Minneapolis Surplus Store*, 251 Minn. 188, 86 N.W.2d 689, 691 (1957). In *Lefkowitz*, defendant had published a newspaper announcement stating: "Saturday 9 AM Sharp, 3 Brand New Fur Coats, Worth to $100.00, First Come First Served $1 Each." Mr. Morris Lefkowitz arrived at the store, dollar in hand, but was informed that under defendant's "house rules," the offer was open to ladies, but not gentlemen. The court ruled that because plaintiff had fulfilled all of the terms of the advertisement and the advertisement was specific and left nothing open for negotiation, a contract had been formed.

The present case is distinguishable from *Lefkowitz*. First, the commercial cannot be regarded in itself as sufficiently definite, because it specifically reserved the details of the offer to a separate writing, the Catalog. The commercial itself made no mention of the steps a potential offeree would be required to take to accept the alleged offer of a Harrier Jet. The advertisement in *Lefkowitz*, in contrast, "identified the person who could accept." Second, even if the Catalog had included a

CONTINUED

Harrier Jet among the items that could be obtained by redemption of Pepsi Points, the advertisement of a Harrier Jet by both television commercial and catalog would still not constitute an offer.

The Court finds, in sum, that the Harrier Jet commercial was merely an advertisement.

[P]laintiff largely relies on a different species of unilateral offer, involving public offers of a reward for performance of a specified act. Because these cases generally involve public declarations regarding the efficacy or trustworthiness of specific products, one court has aptly characterized these authorities as "prove me wrong" cases. The most venerable of these precedents is the case of *Carlill v Carbolic Smoke Ball Co.*, 1 Q.B. 256 (Court of Appeal, 1892), a quote from which heads plaintiff's memorandum of law: "[I]f a person chooses to make extravagant promises . . . he probably does so because it pays him to make them, and, if he has made them, the extravagance of the promises is no reason in law why he should not be bound by them."

The case arose during the London influenza epidemic of the 1890s. Among other advertisements of the time, for Clarke's World Famous Blood Mixture, Towle's Pennyroyal and Steel Pills for Females, Sequah's Prairie Flower, and Epp's Glycerine Jube-Jubes, appeared solicitations for the Carbolic Smoke Ball. The specific advertisement that Mrs. Carlill saw, and relied upon, read as follows:

> *£100 reward will be paid by the Carbolic Smoke Ball Company to any person who contracts the increasing epidemic influenza, colds, or any diseases caused by taking cold, after having used the ball three times daily for two weeks according to the printed directions supplied with each ball. £1000 is deposited with the Alliance Bank, Regent Street, shewing our sincerity in the matter.*

During the last epidemic of influenza many thousand carbolic smoke balls were sold as preventives against this disease, and in no ascertained case was the disease contracted by those using the carbolic smoke ball.

Mrs. Carlill purchased the smoke ball and used it as directed, but contracted influenza nevertheless. The advertisement was construed as offering a reward because it sought to induce performance, unlike an invitation to negotiate, which seeks a reciprocal promise. As Lord Justice Lindley explained, "advertisements offering rewards . . . are offers to anybody who performs the conditions named in the advertisement, and anybody who does perform the condition accepts the offer." Because Mrs. Carlill had complied with the terms of the offer, yet contracted influenza, she was entitled to £100.

In the present case, the Harrier Jet commercial did not direct that anyone who appeared at Pepsi headquarters with 7,000,000 Pepsi Points on the Fourth of July would receive a Harrier Jet. Instead, the commercial urged consumers to accumulate Pepsi Points and to refer to the Catalog to determine how they could redeem their Pepsi Points. The commercial sought a reciprocal promise, expressed through acceptance of, and compliance with, the terms of the Order Form. As noted previously, the Catalog contains no mention of the Harrier Jet. Plaintiff states that he "noted that the Harrier Jet was not among the items described in the catalog, but this did not affect [his] understanding of the offer."

In evaluating the commercial, the Court must not consider defendant's subjective intent in making the commercial, or plaintiff's subjective view of what the commercial offered, but what an objective, reasonable person would have understood the commercial to convey.

Plaintiff's insistence that the commercial appears to be a serious offer requires the Court to explain why the commercial is funny. Explaining why a joke is funny is a daunting task; as the essayist E. B. White has remarked, "Humor can be dissected, as a frog can, but the thing dies in the process . . ." The commercial is the embodiment of what defendant appropriately characterizes as "zany humor."

First, [the commercial] makes the exaggerated claims similar to those of many television advertisements: that by consuming the featured clothing, car, beer, or potato chips, one will become attractive, stylish, desirable, and admired by all. A reasonable viewer would understand such advertisements as mere puffery, not as statements of fact. Second, the callow youth featured in the commercial is a highly improbable pilot, one who could barely be trusted with the keys to his parents' car, much less the prize aircraft of the United States Marine Corps. Rather than checking the fuel gauges on his aircraft, the teenager spends his precious preflight minutes preening. The youth's concern for his coiffure appears to extend to his flying without a helmet. Finally, the teenager's comment that flying a Harrier Jet to school "sure beats the bus" evinces an improbably insouciant attitude toward the relative difficulty and danger of piloting a fighter plane in a residential area, as opposed to taking public transportation.

Third, the notion of traveling to school in a Harrier Jet is an exaggerated adolescent fantasy. As if to emphasize the fantastic quality of having a Harrier Jet arrive at school, the Jet lands next to a plebeian bike rack. This fantasy is, of course, extremely unrealistic. No school would provide landing space for a student's fighter jet, or condone the disruption the jet's use would cause.

Fourth, the primary mission of a Harrier Jet, according to the United States Marine Corps, is to "attack and destroy surface targets under day and night visual conditions." [D]epiction of such a jet as a way to get to school in the morning is clearly not serious even if, as plaintiff contends, the jet is capable of being acquired "in a form that eliminates [its] potential for military use."

Fifth, the number of Pepsi Points the commercial mentions as required to "purchase" the jet is 7,000,000. To amass that number of points, one would have to drink 7,000,000 Pepsis (or roughly 190 Pepsis a day for the next hundred years—an unlikely possibility), or one would have to purchase approximately $700,000 worth of Pepsi Points. The cost of a Harrier Jet is roughly $23 million dollars, a fact of which plaintiff was aware when he set out to gather the amount he believed necessary to accept the alleged offer.

In light of the obvious absurdity of the commercial, the Court rejects plaintiff's argument that the commercial was not clearly in jest.

The absence of any writing setting forth the alleged contract in this case provides an entirely separate reason for granting summary judgment. Under the New York Statute of Frauds, a contract for the sale of goods for the price of $500 or more is not enforceable by way of action or defense unless there is some writing sufficient to indicate that a contract for sale has been made between the parties and signed by the party against whom enforcement is sought or by his authorized agent or broker.

There is simply no writing between the parties that evidences any transaction. Plaintiff argues that the commercial, plaintiff's completed Order Form, and perhaps other agreements signed by defendant which plaintiff has not yet seen, should suffice for Statute of Frauds purposes, either singly or taken together.

The commercial is not a writing; plaintiff's completed order form does not bear the signature of defendant, or an agent thereof.

For the reasons stated above, the Court grants defendant's motion for summary judgment. Summary judgment granted and affirmed.

CASE QUESTIONS

1. When does the court think an offer was made?
2. Why is whether the ad is funny an important issue?
3. Does the commercial satisfy the statute of frauds?
4. Will Mr. Leonard get his Harrier jet? Why or why not?

*The appellate court affirmed the federal district court opinion in a brief affirmation. The bulk of the facts and discussion presented here are taken from the lower court's decision, 88 F. Supp.2d 116 (S.D.N.Y. 1999).

CONSIDER...   12.2

Review the following language and determine whether an offer has been made.

> **TO:**   Brit Ripley
> **FROM:** Yachts International
> **RE:**   Sailing Vessel *Infinity*
>
> We are prepared to make an offer to purchase the U.S. Coast Guard Documented Vessel *Infinity* for the price of $600,000 on the following terms and conditions:
> Price: $600,000
>
> Terms: Cash $300,000 at close of escrow
> Note: $300,000 (unsecured) due in one year
> Interest: 0.5% per month on unpaid balance versus 100,000 shares of stock of a public company
>
> Will guarantee $3.00 per share in one year. Buyer reserves the right to repurchase shares at $3.00 in one year if guarantee given.
> Escrow: ASAP
> Conditions:
>
> 1. All insurance to remain in effect until close.
>
> 2. Seller to deliver to Port of San Francisco in seaworthy and sailable condition.
>
> /s./ J. P. Morgan
> Yachts International

Certain and Definite Terms

One of the ways to determine whether the contract is based on intent is also the second requirement for a valid offer. The offer must contain certain and definite language and cover all the terms necessary for a valid contract, which include the following:

- Parties
- Subject matter of the contract
- Price
- Payment terms
- Delivery terms
- Performance times

Under the UCC, the requirements for an offer are not as stringent as the requirements under common law. So long as the offer identifies the parties and the subject matter, the Code sections can cover the details of price, payment, delivery, and performance (see § 2–204 in Appendix G).

Also under the UCC, courts give great weight to industry custom and the previous dealings of the parties in determining whether the terms are certain and definite enough to constitute an offer (see § 2–208 in Appendix G). For example, the parties may have done business with each other for 10 years and their agreement simply contains a quantity and a price. Whatever payment and delivery terms have been used in their relationship in the past (their *course of dealing*) will be the terms for their ongoing relationship.

Communication of the Offer

An offer must be communicated to the offeree before it is valid. A letter in which an offer is made is not an offer until the letter reaches the offeree. For example, suppose OfficeMax had prepared an offer letter to be sent to Renco Rental Equipment and other customers. The letter included an offer for a substantial price discount for computers so that Renco and its regular customers might buy computers at that discount. Before the letter is mailed to Renco, OfficeMax decides that because the computers are in such high demand it will not send the offer and will just sell them at their full retail price. The letter to Renco and other OfficeMax customers is never mailed. Renco, realizing the value of the computers and learning of the unmailed letter, cannot accept the discount computer offer because it was never communicated to them.

Some forms of communication are not treated as offers. For example, as the *Leonard v PepsiCo* case indicates, television ads are generally not offers. Mass communications of information about deals and prices are generally treated as invitations for offers.

Termination of an Offer by Revocation

Because an offer is one-sided, it can be revoked anytime before acceptance by the offeree. **Revocation** occurs when the offeror notifies the offeree that the offer is no longer good.

Revocation is subject to some limitations. One such limitation has already been mentioned: Acceptance by the offeree cuts off the right to revoke. Also, under common law, **options** cannot be revoked. An option is a contract in which the offeree pays the offeror for the time needed to consider the offer. For example, suppose that Yolanda's Yogurt is contemplating opening a new restaurant, and Yolanda has a property location in mind but is uncertain about the market potential.

Ethical Issues

Anticipating Morality

When they are at the top of their games, Olympic and professional athletes are able to command multi-million–dollar endorsement contracts. For example, Olympic champion Michael Phelps had endorsement contracts with Kellogg's, Subway, Speedo, Visa, and Omega, among others. Even Mr. Phelps's mother obtained an endorsement deal with Chico's, the woman's clothing store thrown into the spotlight when his mother wore its clothes to his Olympic events in China. Golfer Tiger Woods had endorsement agreements with Accenture, Tag Heuer, Gillette, AT&T, Gatorade, and Nike. Michael Vick, the NFL player, had endorsements with Nike.

However, these three athletes ran into some personal difficulties. Michael Phelps was photographed apparently smoking a bong at a party at the University of South Carolina. When the picture made its way onto the Internet, the companies that carry Mr. Phelps's image for their products were listed on the Internet. Mr. Woods's personal life became tabloid fodder when his sexual addiction became public knowledge. Mr. Vick entered a guilty plea to federal charges related to his running of a dog-fighting operation.

The athletes' falls from grace were for very different reasons, and difficult to anticipate in terms of contract language. Increasingly, however, businesses are demanding morality clauses in contracts—clauses that cover moral missteps. Defining those missteps can be difficult and some contracts resort to nonspecific language such as "conduct that results in a negative response to the product or company" or "conduct that reduces the credibility of the endorser."

Definitions and enforcement of such clauses are difficult. In the Phelps situation, many of the companies terminated Mr. Phelps for a time and then reinstated him (after eight months in his case). These are situations in which the parties clearly wish to contract but the challenge is determining when, if, and for what reasons the contract will end, and how to define that ending.

There are also the ethical issues. The athletes provide name recognition for products, but some parents, for example, will no longer buy the products because of the athletes' conduct. Are morality clauses appropriate in these contracts? Should athletes be role models? Is termination of a contract for personal conduct ethical?

Yolanda does not want the property to be sold to someone else until she can complete a market study. Yolanda could pay the seller (offeror) a sum of money to hold the offer open for 30 days. During that 30-day period, the offeror can neither revoke the offer nor sell to anyone else.

Under the UCC, one form of an option makes an offer irrevocable, even without the offeree's payment. Under a **merchant's firm offer** (see § 2–205 in Appendix G), the offer must be made by a merchant, put in some form of record,[2] and signed by the merchant. If these requirements are met, the merchant must hold the offer open for a definite time period (but no longer than three months). A merchant is someone who is in the business of selling the goods that are the subject matter of the contract or who holds particular skills or expertise in dealing with the goods. A rain check for sale merchandise from a store is an example of this type of offer. The firm offer cannot be revoked if the requirements are met, and money or consideration is not one of those requirements.

Termination of an Offer by Rejection

An offer carries no legally binding obligation for the offeree, who is free to accept or reject the offer. Once the offeree rejects the offer, the offer is ended and cannot later be accepted unless the offeror renews the offer.

Rejection by Counteroffer under Common Law. An offer also ends when the offeree does not fully reject the offer but rejects some portion of the offer or modifies it before acceptance. These changes and rejections are called **counteroffers.**

The effect of a counteroffer is that the original offer is no longer valid, and the offeree now becomes the offeror as the counteroffer becomes the new offer. Consider the following dialogue as an example:

> Alice: I will pay you $500 to paint the trim on my house.
> Brad: I will do it for $750.

Alice made the first offer. Brad's language is a counteroffer and a rejection at the same time. Alice is now free to accept or reject the $750 offer. If Alice declines the $750 counteroffer, Brad cannot then force Alice to contract for the original $500 because the offer ended. Consider 12.3 deals with an issue of offers and counteroffers.

CONSIDER... 12.3

December 30, 1977: John Hancock Insurance Company sent a commitment letter to Houston Dairy offering to loan Houston $800,000 at 9.25 percent interest; the letter provided that acceptance must be in writing within seven days and must be accompanied by a $16,000 letter of credit or cashier's check.

January 17, 1978: The president of Houston Dairy sent a letter of acceptance to Hancock along with a cashier's check.

January 23, 1978: Hancock cashed the check, which went through standard company processing.

Hancock claims there is no contract because the acceptance occurred after the offer had expired. Houston Dairy maintains that its letter of acceptance was a new offer that was accepted by Hancock with the cashing of the check. Who is correct? Is there a contract? [*Houston Dairy v John Hancock Mutual Life Insurance Co.*, 643 F.2d 1185 (5th Cir. 1981)]

Rejection by Counteroffer under the UCC. Under the UCC, modification by offerees was seen as a necessary part of doing business, and § 2–207 (see Appendix G) allows flexibility for such modifications. Under § 2–207 (not Revised UCC Article 2, because no state has adopted this new version), two separate rules apply for modifications: one governs merchants, and the other governs nonmerchant transactions. Exhibit 12.2 shows a chart of the rules.

For nonmerchants, the addition of terms in the counteroffer does not result in a rejection; there will still be a contract if there is a clear intent to contract, but the additional terms will not be a part of the contract.

For example, consider the following dialogue:

> Joe: I will sell you my pinball machine for $250.
> Jan: I'll take it. Include $10 in dimes.

Joe and Jan have a contract, but the $10 in dimes is not a part of the contract. If Jan wanted the dimes, she should have negotiated before formally accepting the offer.

For merchants (both parties must be merchants), § 2–207 has more complicated rules and details on additional terms in acceptance. Section 2-207 covers situations, sometimes called the battle of the forms, in which offerors and offerees send purchase orders and invoices back and forth with the understanding that they have a contract. Under § 2–207, if the parties reach a basic agreement but the offeree has added terms, there will be an enforceable contract; the added terms are not a

EXHIBIT 12.2 UCC Rules for Additional Terms in Acceptance Under Article 2

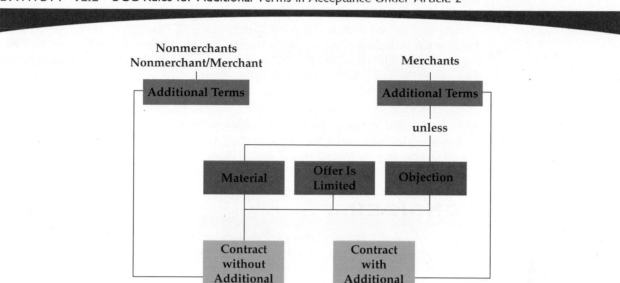

rejection under § 2–207. Whether the added terms will become a part of the contract depends on the following questions:

1. Are the terms material?
2. Was the offer limited?
3. Does one side object?

If the terms the offeree adds to the original offer terms are *material*, they do not become a part of the contract. For example, suppose that Alfie sends a purchase order to Bob for 12 dozen red four-inch balloons at four cents each. Bob sends back an invoice that reflects the quantity and price, but Bob's invoice also has a section that states, "There are no warranties express or implied on these goods." Do Alfie and Bob have a contract with or without warranties? The waiver of warranties is a material change in what Alfie gets: now a contract without warranties. Because it is material, § 2–207 protects Alfie and the warranty waiver is not part of the contract.

Terms that can be added but are not considered material are such payment terms as "30 days same as cash." Shipment terms are generally immaterial unless the method of shipment is unusually costly.

An offeror can avoid the problems of form battles and § 2–207 by simply *limiting* the offer to the terms stated. The following language could be used: "This offer is limited to these terms." If the offeree attempts to add terms in the acceptance, there will be a contract, but the added terms will not be part of the contract. For example, suppose Alfie's offer on the balloons was limited and Bob accepted but added that the payment terms were "30 days same as cash." They would still have a contract but without the additional payment term.

A final portion of § 2–207 allows the parties to take action to eliminate additional terms. They can do so by *objecting* to any added terms within a reasonable time. For example, if Alfie's offer was not limited and Bob accepted the payment terms, Alfie could object to the payment terms and they would then not be a part of the contract. Exhibit 12.2, as already noted, summarizes the UCC's § 2–207 rules. As noted earlier, the most significant changes under Revised Article 2 deal with § 2-207, and these have resulted in the most resistance to the Article's adoption by the states.

Under Revised Article 2 § 2-207, the courts will determine, on a case-by-case basis, what is included as part of the contract, in some cases regardless of what the "record" provides. Revised § 2–207 applies to merchants and nonmerchants alike and regardless of whether the parties use forms. The new UCC § 2–207 is often called the "terms later" provision because it permits parties to go forward with contract performance and decide on terms later or resolve any disputes only if they arise during the course of performance. One writer has referred to "terms later" as bad economics because of the inability of parties to rely on definitive laws in making contracts and then performing under them.[3]

CONSIDER...   12.4

Schulze and Burch Biscuit Company (Schulze) purchased low-moisture 16-mesh dehydrated apple powder from Tree Top, Inc. to use in making strawberry and blueberry "Toastettes," which it sells to Nabisco, Inc.

On April 27, 1984, E. Edward Park, Schulze's director of procurement, telephoned Rudolph Brady, a broker for Tree Top, and ordered 40,000 pounds of Tree Top's apple powder. Mr. Park told Mr. Brady that the purchase was subject to a Schulze purchase order and gave Mr. Brady the number of the purchase order, but Mr. Park did not send the purchase order or a copy of it to Mr. Brady or to Tree Top. On the front of the purchase order was the following clause:

> **Important:** *The fulfillment of this order or any part of it obligates the Seller to abide by the terms, conditions and instructions on both sides of this order. Additional or substitute terms will not become part of this contract unless expressly accepted by Buyer; Seller's acceptance is limited to the terms of this order, and no contract will be formed except on these terms.*

Shortly after the telephone conversation, Mr. Brady sent Schulze a form entitled simply "Confirmation" that listed Mr. Brady as broker, Schulze as buyer, and Tree Top as seller as well as the quantity, price, shipping arrangements, and payment terms. It also showed the purchase order number that Mr. Park had given to Mr. Brady. Several preprinted provisions, including an arbitration clause, stood on the lower portion of the form:

> *Seller guarantees goods to conform to the national pure food laws. All disputes under this transaction shall be arbitrated in the usual manner. This confirmation shall be subordinate to more formal contract, when and if such contract is executed. In the absence of such contract, this confirmation represents the contract of the parties. If incorrect, please advise immediately.*

Mr. Brady had sent a similar confirmation form to Schulze in each of at least 10 previous transactions between Tree Top and Schulze. Schulze had never objected to any of the preprinted provisions. Schulze had sent Mr. Brady a purchase order in two of those transactions; in each of the other transactions, as in the present case, Schulze simply informed Mr. Brady of the number of the appropriate purchase order.

Subsequently, Schulze brought suit seeking damages for breach of contract, alleging that the dehydrated apple powder had been so full of apple stems and wood splinters that it clogged the machinery of Schulze's Toastette assembly line, causing the line to shut down, with various financial losses. Schulze alleged that the powder thus failed to meet Schulze's specifications, which had governed the previous sales of apple powder. Tree Top alleged that the dispute was subject to arbitration because of the arbitration clause in the confirmation sent by Mr. Brady to Schulze. Does the arbitration clause apply? Decide under both old and new UCC § 2–207. [*Schulze and Burch Biscuit Co. v Tree Top, Inc.*, 831 F.2d 709 (7th Cir. 1987)]

For the Manager's Desk

Re: Checklist for Contract Preliminaries

1. Do your contract homework.
   a. Do background checks—check references, complaints at state and private agencies, court dockets.
   b. Learn the nature of the business and industry custom—learn to use the language.
2. Negotiate details.
   a. Agree on terms that help you accomplish your purpose ("apple powder for bakery equipment," not just "apple powder").
   b. Make sure your written agreement is complete.

Re: Checklist for Drafting Contracts

1. Identify both parties clearly. Be certain corporate names are correct. Make sure the parties have the proper authority to enter into the transaction. (Are copies of board resolutions approving the contract available?)
2. Define the terms used in the contract, including industry terms.
3. List all terms: price, subject matter, quantity, delivery, payment terms.
4. Answer "what if" questions. (What if payment is not made? What if deliveries are late?)

CONSIDER... 12.5

In the following three dialogues, determine whether a contract is formed under UCC § 2–207.

1. A: "I'll sell you my Peugeot bicycle for $100."
   B: "I'll take it. Include your tire pump."

2. A: "I'll sell you my white 1974 Ford Torino for $358. This offer is limited to these terms."
   B: "I'll take it. Furnish a history of repairs."

3. A: "I'll sell you my antique Coca-Cola sign."
   B: "I'll take it if you will deliver it."

Termination by Offer Expiration

An offer can end by expiring and, once expired, can no longer be accepted by the offeree. For example, if an offer states that it will remain open until November 1, it automatically terminates on November 1, and no one has the power to accept the offer after that time. The death of the offeror also ends the offer, unless the offeree holds an option. Even offers without time limits expire after a reasonable time has passed. For example, an offer to buy a home is probably only good for one or two weeks because the offeror needs to know whether to try for another house. The offeror's offer terminates naturally if the offeree fails to accept within that time frame.

Acceptance: The Offeree's Response

An **acceptance** is the offeree's positive response to the offeror's proposed contract, and only persons to whom the offer is made have the power of acceptance. That acceptance must be communicated to the offeror using the proper method of communication, which can be controlled by the offeror or left to the offeree. In either case, the method of communication controls the effective time of the acceptance.

EXHIBIT 12.3   Timing Rules for Acceptance

TYPE OF OFFER	METHOD OF ACCEPTANCE	ACCEPTANCE EFFECTIVE?
No means given	Same or reasonable method of communication*	When properly mailed, dispatched (mailbox rule)
No means given	Slower or unreasonable method of communication	When received, if offer still open
Means specified (specified or stipulated means)	Stipulated means used	Mailbox rule
Means stipulated (specified or stipulated means)	Stipulated means not used	Counteroffer and rejection

*Some states still follow the common law rule that requires the same method of communication in order to have the mailbox rule apply, even in UCC transactions.

Acceptance by Stipulated Means

Some offerors give a required means of acceptance called a specified or **stipulated means.** If the offeree uses the stipulated means of acceptance, the acceptance is effective sooner than the offeror's receipt; the acceptance is effective when it is properly sent. For example, if the offeror has required the acceptance to be mailed and the offeree properly mails the letter of acceptance, the acceptance is effective when it is sent. This timing rule for acceptance is called the **mailbox rule,** and it applies in stipulated means offers so long as the offeree uses the stipulated means to communicate acceptance.

Acceptance with No Stipulated Means

If the offeror does not stipulate a means of acceptance, the offeree is free to use any method for communication of the acceptance. If the offeree uses the same method of communication or a reasonable means, the mailbox rule also applies. If the offeree uses a slower method of acceptance, the acceptance is not effective until it is received. Exhibit 12.3 summarizes the timing of acceptance rules. *Cantu v Central Education Agency* (Case 12.3) deals with an issue of timing on offer and acceptance.

CASE 12.3   *Cantu v Central Education Agency*
884 S.W.2d 565 (Tex. App. 1994)

The Teacher's Lesson on Acceptance

FACTS

Ms. Cantu had a teaching contract with the San Benito Consolidated Independent School District. She hand-delivered to her supervisor a written offer to resign. Three days later the superintendent of schools mailed her a letter accepting the offer of resignation. Ms. Cantu then changed her mind and the next day hand-delivered a letter withdrawing her resignation. The superinten-

dent refused to recognize the attempted rescission of the resignation. Ms. Cantu appealed to the state district court. It decided against her, and she again appealed.

JUDICIAL OPINION

SMITH, Justice.

. . . Cantu was hired as a special-education teacher by the San Benito Consolidated Independent School

District under a one-year contract for the 1990–91 school year. On Saturday, August 18, 1990, shortly before the start of the school year, Cantu hand-delivered to her supervisor a letter of resignation, effective August 17, 1990. In this letter, Cantu requested that her final paycheck be forwarded to an address in McAllen, Texas, some fifty miles from the San Benito office where she tendered the resignation. The San Benito superintendent of schools, the only official authorized to accept resignations on behalf of the school district, received Cantu's resignation on Monday, August 20. The superintendent wrote a letter accepting Cantu's resignation the same day and deposited the letter, properly stamped and addressed, in the mail at approximately 5:15 P.M. that afternoon. At about 8:00 A.M. the next morning, August 21, Cantu hand-delivered to the superintendent's office a letter withdrawing her resignation.

This letter contained a San Benito return address. In response, the superintendent hand-delivered that same day a copy of his letter mailed the previous day to inform Cantu that her resignation had been accepted and could not be withdrawn.

The sole legal question presented for our review is the proper scope of the "mail-box rule" under Texas law and whether the rule was correctly applied. . . . Cantu contends . . . that the trial court erred in ruling that the agreement to rescind her contract of employment became effective when the superintendent deposited his letter accepting Cantu's resignation in the mail. Cantu argues that, under Texas law, an acceptance binds the parties in contract on mailing only if the offeror has sent the offer by mail or has expressly authorized acceptance by mail. There was no express authorization for the school district to accept Cantu's offer by mail. The question presented is whether authorization to accept by mail may be implied only when the offer is delivered by mail or also when the existing circumstances make it reasonable for the offeree to so accept.

The aphorism "the offeror is the master of his offer" reflects the power of the offeror to impose conditions on acceptance of an offer, specify the manner of acceptance, or withdraw the offer before the offeree has effectively exercised the power of acceptance. However, more often than not, an offeror does not expressly authorize a particular mode, medium, or manner of acceptance. Consequently, particularly with parties communicating at a distance, a rule of law is needed to establish the point of contract formation and allocate the risk of loss and inconvenience that inevitably falls to one of the parties between the time that the offeree exercises, and the offeror receives, the acceptance. See 1 Arthur L. Corbin, *Contracts*, § 78 (1963).

As Professor Corbin notes, courts could adopt a rule that no acceptance is effective until received, absent express authorization by the offeror; however, the mailbox rule, which makes acceptance effective on dispatch, closes the deal and enables performance more promptly, and places the risk of inconvenience on the party who originally has power to control the manner of acceptance. . . . "Even though the offer was not made by mail and there was no [express] authorization, the existing circumstances may be such as to make it reasonable for the offeree to accept by mail and to give the offeror reason to know that the acceptance will be so made." . . . In short, acceptance by mail is impliedly authorized if reasonable under the circumstances.

The *Restatement* approves and adopts this approach: an acceptance by any medium reasonable under the circumstances is effective on dispatch, absent a contrary indication in the offer. *Restatement (Second) of Contracts* §§ 30(2), 63(a), 65, 66 (1979). In addition, the *Restatement* specifically recognizes that acceptance by mail is ordinarily reasonable if the parties are negotiating at a distance or *even if a written offer is delivered in person to an offeree in the same city.* . . . The same standard, *viz.*, whether the manner of acceptance is reasonable under the circumstances, governs offer and acceptance in commercial transactions under the Texas Business and Commerce Code. (Uniform Commercial Code § 2–206.)

The request or authorization to communicate the acceptance by mail is implied in two cases, namely: (1) Where the post is used to make the offer . . . (2) *Where the circumstances are such that it must have been within the contemplation of the parties that according to the ordinary usages of mankind the post might be used as a means of communicating the acceptance* . . .

Texas courts are directed by statute to consider whether acceptance by mail is reasonable under the circumstances in commercial transactions . . . § 2.206. . . . We hold that it is proper to consider whether acceptance by mail is reasonably implied under the circumstances, whether or not the offer was delivered by mail.

. . . It was reasonable for the superintendent to accept Cantu's offer of resignation by mail. Cantu tendered her resignation shortly before the start of the school year—at a time when both parties could not fail to appreciate the need for immediate action by the district to locate a replacement. In fact, she delivered the letter on a Saturday, when the Superintendent could neither receive nor respond to her offer, further delaying matters by two days. Finally, Cantu's request that her final paycheck be forwarded to an address some fifty miles away

CONTINUED

indicated that she could no longer be reached in San Benito and that she did not intend to return to the school premises or school-district offices. The Commissioner of Education and district court properly considered that it was reasonable for the school district to accept Cantu's offer by mail. . . .

Judgment affirmed.

CASE QUESTIONS

1. Who was the offeror? Does the UCC apply in this case?

2. Why did the court refer to the fact that Ms. Cantu's forwarding address was 50 miles away from the place where she delivered her offer to resign?

E-Commerce and Contract Formation

CYBERLAW

The Internet has provided a means for contracting online. However, the courts have been left to deal with the issue of whether and when a contract has been formed. The new rules that have emerged regarding cyberspace contracts focus on whether the parties knew the terms and whether they voluntarily accepted those terms once aware of them. In other words, the rules on contract formation in cyberspace require that the parties prove that a click was something more than an accidental action and that the click was made after there had been full disclosure of the terms.

A new section of revised Article 2 deals with electronic communication of acceptance, including the timing issues. Section 2–213 provides that "receipt of an electronic communication has a legal effect, it has that effect even though no individual is aware of its receipt," and that acknowledgment of the receipt of an electronic communication is receipt but, "in itself, does not establish that the content sent corresponds to the content received." So, receipt is required for electronic communication and receipt occurs when the e-mail arrives, even if the receiver does not know it has arrived. Also, the parties are left to use other means of proof to establish that all of the message made it from one party to another because acknowledging receipt does not mean that all terms arrived.

Sellers generally accomplish these two goals by establishing on their websites "clickon," "clickthrough," or "clickwrap" agreements. The company or offeror simply lists all the terms of the agreement that the visitor/offeree is about to enter into. The visitor/offeree must click on "I agree" or "I agree to these terms," or he or she cannot proceed to the completion of the contract segments of the site. The terms include cost, payment, warranties, arbitration provisions, and so on, and all applicable terms must be spelled out in advance of the "I agree" click point.

CYBERLAW

Because this type of contract formation is so new, case law is rare, but *Home Basket Co., LLC. v Pampered Chef, Ltd.* (Case 12.4) is one example of a contract-formed-on-the-Internet dispute.

CASE 12.4   *Home Basket Co., LLC. v Pampered Chef, Ltd.*
55 UCC Rep. Serv. 2d 792 (D. Kan 2005)

Making a Basket Case

FACTS

The Greenbrier Basket Company (GBC), a goods distributor (plaintiff) (seller) agreed in October 2003 to sell woven baskets to The Pampered Chef (TPC) (defendant) (buyer). On October 28, 2003, an executive sales agreement was drafted but never signed by the parties. GBC had, however, accepted purchase orders from TPC.

The ordering process would begin with TPC e-mailing GBC regarding an offer to fill an order. GBC would then go to TPC's website and fill out the purchase order using TPC's purchase order management system and would click on the "Accept P.O." button at the end of the terms and conditions field.

Cyndee Pollock (a manager at GBC) would receive offers to purchase goods via e-mail from TPC and would tell an employee, Mark Beal, to accept these purchase orders via TPC's Internet site. GBC denies knowing that there were terms and conditions, including a forum selection clause, on the TPC's Internet acceptance site. TPC provides evidence showing that GBC did have knowledge of the terms and conditions. TPC sent Mark Beal an e-mail with an attachment showing him how to use TPC's purchase order management system. The attachment included instructions regarding the use of the purchase order management system, including, in section 4, three paragraphs under the title "Accepting and Rejecting Purchase Orders," the relevant portion of which states:

> Clicking on the Accept P.O. button will cause the terms and conditions of the purchase order to pop-up. The user should review these terms and conditions and click the Accept P.O. button at the bottom of the pop-up screen. . . . If the purchase order is not acceptable in it's [sic] current form, the user may click on the Reject and Request Changes button. This causes a pop-up window to appear where the user may enter a free-form text describing the reason for rejecting the purchase order and request changes that would make the purchase order acceptable.

Clause 17 of the Terms and Conditions in TPC's purchase management order system states:

> This Purchase Order shall be deemed to have been made in Addison, Illinois USA and shall be governed by and construed in accordance with the laws of State of Illinois [sic]. The sole and exclusive jurisdiction for the purpose of resolving any dispute shall be the United States District Court, Northern District of Illinois, Eastern Division.

When disputes over orders and payments arose, GBC filed suit against TPC in Kansas for breach of contract. TPC moved to dismiss the suit for improper venue (wrong geographic court; see Chapter 3) because the terms of its purchase order called for suits in Illinois. GBC maintains it did not agree to that term because it never signed a contract.

JUDICIAL OPINION

BROWN, Senior J.
Defendant alleges improper venue because of an allegedly agreed upon forum selection clause. Plaintiff does not dispute that the forum selection clause is valid. Plaintiff instead argues that the forum selection clause was never part of the parties' contract.

K.S.A. § 84-2-102. "An offer to make a contract shall be construed as inviting acceptance in any manner and by any medium reasonable in the circumstances." KSA § 84-2-206. The UCC does not define what constitutes an offer so the Court must look to the common law rules. An offer is an expression of a willingness to enter into an agreement and must reasonably lead the offeree to believe that a power to create a contract has been conferred upon him.

TPC's e-mails containing purchase order information constituted an offer to buy baskets. The e-mails consisted of information about the quantity of baskets to be bought, price, shipment information and delivery dates. None of the e-mails had any forum selection clause; however, they did state a specific manner of acceptance:

1. *Upon receipt of order, please acknowledge via Internet at [website]. By acknowledging this P.O. [purchase order], you also acknowledge the terms and conditions of this P.O.*

2. *To accept this P.O. via Internet, visit [website].*

The evidence shows at least nine such e-mail offers. GBC consistently went to the TPC website to accept these offers.

GBC makes several arguments, without supporting case law, that the forum selection clause should not be part of the parties' contract. None of these arguments dispute when acceptance was made.

Plaintiff first argues that the e-mail offers are ambiguous because it did not alert GBC to the forum selection clause that had to be accepted on the website. The TPC e-mails state that the way to acknowledge (i.e. accept) the purchase order was to go to the website. The e-mail is not ambiguous as it also alerted GBC that there were terms and conditions associated with acknowledging the P.O. on the website.

GBC next argues that it should not be held to the terms and conditions accepted on the website because plaintiff thought that the e-mails' terms and conditions were all inclusive.

It is a well-established rule of law that contracting parties have a duty to learn the contents of a written contract before signing it, and such duty includes reading the contract and obtaining an explanation of its terms. The negligent failure of a party to read the written contract entered into will estop the contracting party from voiding the contract on the ground of ignorance of its contents. Therefore, a party who signs a written contract is bound by its provisions regardless of the failure to read or understand the terms, unless the contract was entered into through fraud, undue influence, or mutual mistake.

In determining intent to form a contract, the test is objective, rather than subjective, meaning that the relevant inquiry is the "manifestation of a party's intention, rather than the actual or real intention." Put another way, "the inquiry will focus not on the question of whether the subjective minds of the parties have met, but on whether their outward expression of assent is sufficient to form a contract."

CONTINUED

This was a website that required action on the part of GBC. Plaintiff objectively agreed to the forum selection clause by scrolling through the terms and conditions and clicking on the "Accept P.O." button. Plaintiff's subjective beliefs that it was the e-mail and not the website terms and conditions that governed the contract are both misplaced and irrelevant. Plaintiff was under a duty to read and understand the terms and conditions prior to clicking the "Accept P.O." button as this was the formal acceptance required by TPC's offer to purchase baskets. Failure to read or understand the terms and conditions is not a valid reason to render those provisions nugatory.

Plaintiff next argues that the forum selection clause should not be read into the contract because GBC rejected an Exclusive Sales Agreement containing such a clause. Plaintiff claims that the failure to sign this agreement shows that they did not intend that a forum selection clause be part of the contract. The evidence shows that the Exclusive Sales Agreement was discussed on October 28, 2003. The date of the first e-mail inviting GBC to accept a purchase order was October 7, 2003. Plaintiff's subjective reasons for refusing to sign the Exclusive Sales Agreement are irrelevant as GBC consistently agreed, in an objective manner prior to the Exclusive Sales Agreement, to contracts with the terms and conditions on TPC's website. The Court will not alter the plain terms in the parties' contract because GBC refused to sign the Exclusive Sales Agreement.

Plaintiff also argues that there was no meeting of the minds regarding the forum selection clause on the website. A meeting of the minds requirement is proved when the evidence shows with reasonable definiteness that the minds of the parties met upon the same matter and agreed upon the terms of the contract. Part of clause 17 states "each shipment received by Buyer from Seller shall be deemed to be only upon the terms and conditions as set forth in this Purchase Order . . ." GBC agreed upon these terms and conditions published on TPC's website by clicking the "Accept P.O." button and this satisfied the meeting of the minds standard.

The Court holds that the forum selection clause in the terms and conditions on TPC's website are a part of the parties' contract. GBC must file suit in Illinois.

CASE QUESTIONS

1. Describe the ordering process between the two parties.
2. Does it matter to the court that neither side ever signed a written agreement?
3. What responsibility does the court impose on those who use websites for contracting purposes?

Consideration

Consideration is what distinguishes gifts from contracts and is what each party—offeror and offeree—gives up under the contract; it is sometimes called **bargained-for exchange.** If you sign a contract to buy a 1990 Mercedes for $17,000, your consideration is the $17,000 and is given in exchange for the car. The seller's consideration is giving up the car and is given in exchange for your $17,000. On the other hand, if your grandmother tells you that she will give you her Mercedes, the lack of consideration on your part means your grandmother's promise (unfortunately) is not a contract and is not enforceable.

The courts are not concerned with the amount or nature of consideration as long as it is actually passed from one party to the other. A contract is not unenforceable because a court feels you paid too little under the contract terms. The amount of consideration is left to the discretion of the parties, but one party cannot demand greater consideration once the contract is finalized.

CONSIDER... 12.6

In 1977, George Lucas granted Kenner Toys the exclusive right to produce *Star Wars* toys—the action figures and other replicas from the movie—in perpetuity for $100,000 per year. At the time the contract was negotiated, no one understood how valuable the contract rights were.

In 1991, Hasbro Toys purchased Kenner. By this time, the sales of Princess Leia dolls and R2D2 replicas were nonexistent. Because there was no market for the toys, the toys were no longer produced, and an accountant with Kenner decided to save $100,000 and not send the check to Mr. Lucas.

In 1992, an employee of Mr. Lucas saw a line of Galoob toys at a trade show and asked if Galoob was interested in making the *Star Wars* toy line. Galoob jumped at the chance and did quite well marketing the toys. Some executives believe that the popularity of the toys motivated Mr. Lucas to re-release the movies, which turned out to be a money-maker for Mr. Lucas as well as for the Galoob toy line.

In 1996, Mr. Lucas did grant some rights to Hasbro, but it has lost market share and footing to Galoob. Was the failure to make the payment a failure of consideration? Has Hasbro lost its rights?

Unique Consideration Issues

The concept of consideration and its requirement for contract formation has presented courts with some unique problems. Often an element of fairness and reliance exists in circumstances in which an offer and acceptance are made but no consideration. For example, many nonprofit organizations raise funds through pledges. Such pledges are not supported by consideration, but the nonprofit organizations rely on those pledges. Called **charitable subscriptions,** these agreements are enforced by courts despite the lack of consideration.

The doctrine of **promissory estoppel** is also used as a substitute for consideration in those cases in which someone acts in reliance on a promise that is not supported by consideration. For example, suppose an employer said, "Move to Denver and I'll hire you." There is no detriment on your part until you begin work. The employer has no detriment either. However, if you sold your home in Phoenix and incurred the expense of moving to Denver, it would be unfair to allow the employer to claim the contract did not exist because of no consideration. You have acted in reliance on a promise, and that reliance serves as a consideration substitute.

CONSIDER... 12.7

Alan Fulkins, who owns a construction company that specializes in single-family residences, is constructing a small subdivision with 23 homes. Tretorn Plumbing, owned by Jason Tretorn, was awarded the contract for the plumbing work on the homes at a price of $4,300 per home.

Plumbing contractors complete their residential projects in three phases. Phase 1 consists of digging the lines for the plumbing and installing the pipes that are placed in the foundation of the house. Phase 2 involves the placement of pipes within the walls of the home, and phase 3 handles the surface plumbing, such as sinks and tubs. However, industry practice dictates that the plumbing contractor receive one-half of the contract amount after completion of phase 1.

Mr. Tretorn completed the digs of phase 1 for Mr. Fulkins and received payment of $2,150. Mr. Tretorn then went to Mr. Fulkins and demanded an additional $600 per house for completion of the work. Mr. Fulkins said, "But you already have a contract for $4,300!" Mr. Tretorn responded, "I know, but the costs are killing me. I need the additional $600."

Mr. Fulkins explained the hardship of the demand: "Look, I've already paid you half. If I hire someone else, I'll have to pay them two-thirds for the work not done. It'll cost me $5,000 per house." Mr. Tretorn responded, "Exactly. I'm a bargain because the additional $600 I want only puts you at $4,900. If you don't pay it, I'll just lien the houses and then

CONTINUED

you'll be stuck without a way to close the sales. I've got the contract all drawn up. Just sign it and everything goes smoothly."

Should Mr. Fulkins sign the agreement? Does Mr. Tretorn have the right to the additional $600? Was it ethical for Mr. Tretorn to demand the $600? Is there any legal advice you can offer Mr. Fulkins?

Contract Form: When a Record Is Required

Some contracts can exist just on the basis of an oral promise. Others, however, must be in writing to be enforceable, and these contracts are covered under each state's **statute of frauds.**

Common Law Statute of Frauds

The term *statute of frauds* originated in 1677 when England passed the first rule dealing with written contracts: the Statute for the Prevention of Frauds and Perjuries.

The purpose of the first statute and the descendant statutes today is to have written agreements for the types of contracts that might encourage conflicting claims and possible perjury if oral agreements were allowed. The following is a partial list of the types of contracts required to be in writing under most state laws.

1. Contracts for the sale of real property. This requirement includes sales, certain leases, liens, mortgages, and easements.

2. Contracts that cannot be performed within one year. These contracts run for long periods and require the benefit of written terms.

3. Contracts to pay the debt of another. Cosigners' agreements to pay if a debtor defaults must be in writing. A corporate officer's personal guarantee of a corporate note must be in writing to be enforceable.

UCC Statute of Frauds

Under the UCC, a separate statute of frauds applies to contracts covering the sale of goods. Contracts for the sale of goods costing $500 or more must be evidenced by a record to be enforceable. As noted earlier, a record can be in the form of an electronic communication. Under Revised Article 2, the amount was increased from $500 to $5,000.

CONSIDER... 12.8

Which of the following contracts must be in writing to be enforceable? Answer for both the old and revised UCC for those problems that involve UCC subject matter.

1. A contract for the sale of an acre of land for $400

2. A contract for management consulting for six months for $353,000

3. A contract for the sale of a car for $358

4. A contract for a loan cosigned by a corporation's vice president

5. A contract for the sale of a mobile home for $12,000

EXHIBIT 12.4 Common Law Versus UCC Rules on Formation

AREA	UCC	COMMON LAW
Application	Sales of goods	Services, real estate, employment contracts
Offers	Need subject matter (quantity); code gives details	Need subject matter, price, terms, full details agreed upon
Options	Merchant's firm offer; no consideration needed	Need consideration
Acceptance	Can have additional terms	Mirror image rule followed
	Mailbox rule works for reasonable means of acceptance	Must use same method to get mailbox rule*
Consideration	Required for contracts but not for modification or firm offers	Always required
Writing requirement	Sale of goods for $500 or more	Real estate, contracts, not to be performed in one year, paying the debt of another
Defenses†	Must be free of all defenses for valid contract	Must be free of all defenses for valid contract

* Some courts have adopted the UCC rule for common law contracts.
† See Chapter 13.

Exceptions to the Statute of Frauds

Some exceptions to the UCC and common law statute of frauds provisions were created for situations in which the parties have partially or fully performed their unwritten contract. Under both the UCC and common law, if the parties perform the oral contract, courts will enforce the contract for what has already been done. For example, if Alan agreed to sell land to Bertha under an oral contract and Bertha has paid, has the deed, and has moved in, Alan cannot use the statute of frauds to remove Bertha and get the land back.

What Form of Writing Is Required?

The form of writing required under the statute of frauds is not formal. Evidence of a written agreement can be pieced together from memos and letters. With ESIGN now in place, contracts can be evidenced by electronic communications such as e-mail and website communications. As discussed earlier, electronic communication and forms of contracts in that mode are equal in force and effect with paper contracts. *Rosenfeld v Basquiat* (Case 12.5) deals with the issues of types of writings as well as whether a writing is sufficient to satisfy the statute of frauds requirements. Under the UCC, merchants can meet the statute of frauds by sending confirmation memos (see § 2–201 in Appendix G). These **merchants' confirmation memoranda** summarize the oral agreement and are signed by only one party, but they can be used to satisfy the statute of frauds so long as the memo has been sent to the nonsigning party for review and no objection is raised upon that party's receipt. The confirmation memoranda could be done via e-mail. Exhibit 12.4 provides a summary of provisions for contract formation under UCC and common law.

The Record Requirement in the Electronic Contract

As noted earlier in the chapter, states must provide parity for electronic and paper signatures. That is, electronic contracts and signatures must be recognized as meeting the statute of frauds requirements in the same way that paper contracts and signatures do. However, some documents are exempt from this equal treatment,

CYBERLAW

CASE 12.5   *Rosenfeld v Basquiat*
78 F.3d 84 (2d Cir. 1996)

The Artist, the Crayon, and the Contract

FACTS

Michelle Rosenfeld, an art dealer, alleges she contracted with artist Jean-Michel Basquiat to buy three of his paintings. The works that she claims she contracted to buy were entitled *Separation of the K, Atlas, and Untitled Head.* Ms. Rosenfeld testified that she went to Mr. Basquiat's apartment on October 25, 1982; while she was there, he agreed to sell her three paintings for $4,000 each, and she picked out three. Mr. Basquiat asked for a cash deposit of 10 percent; she left his loft and later returned with $1,000 in cash, which she paid him. When she asked for a receipt, he insisted on drawing up a contract and got down on the floor and wrote it out in crayon on a large piece of paper, remarking that some day this contract would be worth money. The handwritten document listed the three paintings, bore Ms. Rosenfeld's signature and Mr. Basquiat's signature, and stated: "$12,000—$1,000 DEPOSIT—Oct 25 82." Ms. Rosenfeld later returned to Mr. Basquiat's loft to discuss delivery, but Mr. Basquiat convinced her to wait for at least two years so that he could show the paintings at exhibitions.

After Mr. Basquiat's death, the estate argued that there was no contract because the statute of frauds made the agreement unenforceable. The estate contended that a written contract for the sale of goods must include the date of delivery. From a judgment in favor of the estate, Ms. Rosenfeld appealed.

JUDICIAL OPINION

CARDAMONE, J.

. . . Because this case involves an alleged contract for the sale of three paintings, any question regarding the Statute of Frauds is governed by the U.C.C. (applicability to "transactions in goods") (contract for $500 or more is unenforceable "unless there is some writing sufficient to indicate that a contract for sale has been made between the parties and signed by the party [charged]"). Under the U.C.C., the only term that must appear in the writing is the quantity. See N.Y.U.C.C. § 2–201.

Beyond that, "[a]ll that is required is that the writing afford a basis for believing that the offered oral evidence rests on a real transaction." The writing supplied by the plaintiff indicated the price, the date, the specific paintings involved, and that Rosenfeld paid a deposit. It also bore the signatures of the buyer and seller. Therefore, the writing satisfied the requirements of § 2–201.

Citing *Berman Stores Co. v Hirsh*, 240 N.Y. 209 (1925), the estate claims that a specific delivery date, if agreed upon, must be in the writing. *Berman Stores* was decided before the enactment of the U.C.C. and was based on the principle that "the note or memorandum . . . should completely evidence the contract which the parties made." 240 N.Y. at 214 (quoting *Poel v Brunswick-Balke-Collender Co.*, 216 N.Y. 310, 314 [1915]). The rule that a specific delivery date is "an essential part of the contract and must be embodied in the memorandum," *Berman Stores*, 240 N.Y. at 215, was rejected by the legislature—at least for sale-of-goods cases—when it enacted the U.C.C. That rule and the statute upon which it was based were repealed to make way for the U.C.C.

. . . Because the writing, allegedly scrawled in crayon by Jean-Michel Basquiat on a large piece of paper, easily satisfied the requirements of § 2–201 of the U.C.C., the estate is not entitled to judgment as a matter of law. It is of no real significance that the jury found Rosenfeld and Basquiat settled on a particular time for delivery and did not commit it to writing . . . As a consequence . . . the alleged contract is not invalid on Statute of Frauds grounds . . .

Judgment reversed.

CASE QUESTIONS

1. Why was the contract required to be in writing?
2. Did the contract comply with the statute of frauds?
3. Does a writing that does not comply with the statute of frauds make the alleged contract void?

including wills, trusts, checks, letters of credit, court documents, and cancellation of health and life insurance policies. States may require paper documentation for protection of legal rights in these transactions.

ESIGN does not deal with the issues of digital signatures and security. Each of the states must grapple with these issues in adopting their legislation giving e-contracts parity in terms of the writing requirement. Some companies are not comfortable without some form of **digital signature.** A digital signature can be accomplished in different ways. Encryption is used to encode messages so that they cannot be read without the code. This process allows a form of electronic or digital signature that can have the same authenticity and verification of source as a notarized document. However, the use of such systems also creates concerns from the law enforcement perspective because the FBI and national security agencies are unable to monitor secured messages obtained through a warrant. Commercial signature security has been displaced by national security concerns and the need for government access to electronic communications.

The Effect of the Written Contract: Parol Evidence

Once a contract is reduced to its final written form and is complete and unambiguous, the parties to the contract are not permitted to contradict the contract terms with evidence of their negotiations or verbal agreements at the time the contract was executed. This prohibition on extrinsic evidence for fully integrated contracts is called the **parol evidence** rule and is a means for stopping ongoing contradictions to contracts that have been entered into and finalized. It is a protection for the application of the document to the parties' rights as well as a reminder of the need to put the true nature of the agreement into the contract.

Some exceptions apply to the parol evidence rule. If a contract is incomplete or the terms are ambiguous, extrinsic evidence can be used to clarify or complete the contract, as in the case of UCC contracts in which price, delivery, and payment terms can be added (see § 2–202 in Appendix G). Also, if one of the parties to the contract is alleging a defense to the contract's formation, details on the circumstances creating that defense can be used as evidence. Evidence of lack of capacity or fraud does not violate the parol evidence rule.

Ethical Issues

Based on a tip from an employee, Bank of America investigated its senior executive at its student-loan operation, Ms. Kathy Cannon, and uncovered that she had exchanged gifts with Daniel M. Meyers, the CEO and chairman of First Marblehead, a company that provides services for 15 of the top 20 student loan originators. Bank of America is one of the top 20 of those lenders. The exchange of the gifts would be a violation of both Bank of America's and First Marblehead's gift policies. Prior to Bank of America's own revelation about its executive, First Marblehead announced Mr. Meyers's resignation following its disclosure that Mr. Meyers had used personal funds to buy $32,000 in gifts for "a major client." Marblehead did not reveal who the client was, but Bank of America acknowledged that it was the client when it announced Ms. Cannon's departure the following day.

First Marblehead was founded in 1991 and issued an IPO in 2003. It had been a NYSE darling until recently when smaller student loan service companies began entering the business and competing with better services. First Marblehead's stock had lost one-half of its value over 2005. The announcement of the gift scandal and Meyers's departure caused a 17 percent drop in First Marblehead's stock by the end of the day of the announcement.

Why do we worry about gifts between vendors and customers? Isn't this common business practice? Isn't it important that Meyers used his own funds for the gifts and not First Marblehead funds?

Sources: http://www.sec.gov; Bank of America and First Marblehead filed 8-K disclosures; John Hechinger and Anne Marie Chaker, "First Marblehead Chief's Exit Tied to Bank of America Official," *Wall Street Journal,* September 29, 2005, p. A11.

Issues in Formation of International Contracts

International business contracts are similar to domestic contracts. However, the unique aspect of international contracts is that additional risks and questions arise over the choice of currency, the impact of culture on contract interpretation and performance, and the stability of the governments of the parties involved in the contract. In other words, international contracts carry certain risks that are not part of contracts between businesses in the same country. Over the past few years, the increased number of international transactions has resulted in recognition of the need for a more uniform law on international contract formation and performance.

CISG – UCC for the World

The United Nations has developed such a set of laws, called the **United Nations Convention on Contracts for the International Sale of Goods** (CISG) (see Chapter 7).

The CISG, which applies to those contracts in which buyer and seller have their businesses in different countries (unless the parties agree otherwise), has four parts: Part I: Application; Part II: Formation; Part III: Sale of Goods; and Part IV: Final Provisions. Part II includes provisions for the requirements for offers and acceptance, including a merchant's firm offer provision. Acceptance is effective only upon receipt; and, whenever forms do not match, there is no contract unless the nonmatching terms are immaterial. See Exhibit 12.5.

Party autonomy continues to remain a priority. The parties can always choose the applicable law, the nation for the location of courts for resolving disputes, and remedies. You can find details on global contracts in Chapter 7.

EXHIBIT 12.5 Avoiding Legal Pitfalls in International Transactions

1. Use short, simple contracts. The tendency to place all possibilities in a contract is a U.S. tradition. In Germany, for example, the parties have a one-page agreement that references and incorporates terms and conditions of one of the parties.

2. Watch unconscionability protections. The United States focuses its unfairness protections on consumers, but other countries afford these same protections to commercial transactions.

3. Some disclaimers are void in other countries. For example, the clause, "We are only liable for loss of data which is due to a deliberate act on our part. We are not responsible for lost profits in any event," would be valid in the United States but void in Germany. In Germany, sellers of software must assume liability for at least gross negligence.

4. One party's attempt to limit liability would be void in Germany. Any liability limitation must be specifically addressed and negotiated for such a clause to be valid.

5. Unusually long periods for performance are typical in the United States but void in Germany.

6. Price increase limitations are typical in non-U.S. contracts.

7. In other countries, parties can refuse to pay on a current contract if performance on an earlier contract was less than satisfactory and damages are owed.

Several significant differences distinguish the UCC from the CISG. For example, the CISG follows the common law mirror image rule and not the more liberal UCC "battle of the forms" modification exception. The CISG also requires the presence of a price for an offer to be definite enough to be valid. Merchants' firm offers exist under the CISG, but their validity is not subject to time limitations, as with the UCC three-month limit. Parties in international trade need to be familiar with the hybrid nature of the CISG in order to protect their contract rights.

Those firms and countries not relying on the CISG should be familiar with the nuances of commercial law in the countries in which they are doing business. The tendency of many U.S. businesses is to draft a form contract using the home country legal concepts and carry them over to other countries. As Exhibit 12.5 indicates, such a practice and reliance on form contracts can be dangerous.

The Terms and Risks of International Contracts

In negotiating an international contract, parties should determine which country's laws will govern the transaction. Courts will not interfere with this decision as long as the law chosen has some relation to the transaction. The parties should also agree to submit to the jurisdiction of a particular court so that litigation does not begin with the issue of whether jurisdiction resides with a particular court. If the parties wish to submit to arbitration prior to litigation, the terms and nature of arbitration should be delineated in the contract.

The Payment Issues in International Contracts

One of the content and interpretation issues in international contracts focuses on the method of payment. Currently, many contracts specify that payment is to be made in Japanese yen or euros. The increase in the number of international transactions will make negotiating the terms of payment under various contracts more of an issue. Some parties are negotiating now to put substitutes for payment and delivery into their contracts in order to provide more flexibility and a greater likelihood of performance despite changes in the political, geographic, or monetary environments, and all parties working on new agreements are covering the issue in their negotiations.

In addition to the risks of political changes, international contracts have the risks of changing currency exchange rates, long distances in transportation, and difficulties with collection of payments. Most international contracts have built-in performance guarantees. For example, a seller ships goods with a **bill of lading** (a document of title that the carrier will have). To be able to pick up the goods from the carrier, the buyer must have a copy of the bill of lading. The seller can have a bank release the bill of lading to the buyer when the buyer has paid or when the buyer's bank issues a letter of credit (which is the bank's commitment to pay) to the seller for the amount due for the goods. The effect of these two documents is that the seller or carrier does not release the goods until the payment is made or assured. The flow of goods is controlled across borders through documents that travel with the goods and through banks that issue the payment for them. At the same time, the buyer is assured that the goods are there before payment is made or authorized.

In *Intershoe, Inc. v Bankers Trust* (Case 12.6), confusion on payment issues proved expensive for one party.

CASE 12.6 *Intershoe, Inc. v Bankers Trust*
571 N.E.2d 641 (N.Y. 1991)

Lira, Shoes, and Exchange Rates

FACTS

Intershoe, Inc. (plaintiff) is a shoe importer that uses various foreign currencies, including Italian lira, in its business.

On March 3, 1985, Intershoe phoned Bankers Trust (defendant) and entered into several foreign currency transactions, one being a futures transaction involving lira. On March 13, Bankers Trust sent Intershoe a confirmation slip with the following terms: "WE [Bankers] HAVE BOUGHT FROM YOU [Intershoe] ITL 537,750,000" and "WE HAVE SOLD TO YOU USD 250,000.00."

The confirmation slip specified a rate of 2,151 lira per dollar and called for delivery of the lira approximately seven and a half months later, between October 1 and October 31, 1985. Intershoe's treasurer signed the slip and returned it to Bankers Trust on March 18, 1985.

By letter dated October 11, 1985, Bankers Trust notified Intershoe that it was awaiting instructions as to Intershoe's delivery of the lira. Intershoe responded in a letter dated October 25, 1985, that the transaction was a mistake and that it would not go through with it. To cover commitments in other currency transactions, Bankers Trust was forced to purchase lira on the open market at a higher price than that on March 13, 1985, resulting in a loss of $55,014.85. Intershoe filed suit claiming that it had purchased, not sold, lira and that it had sustained damages of $59,336.40. Bankers Trust counterclaimed for its damages.

The trial court held that there were issues of fact. Bankers Trust maintained that the case should be decided in its favor by summary judgment because of the parol evidence rule and appealed.

JUDICIAL OPINION

HANCOCK, Jr., Justice

We turn to defendant's argument that UCC § 2–202 bars the parol evidence submitted in opposition to its motion.

There seems to be no question that the UCC applies to foreign currency transactions. Plaintiff does not dispute this point. Instead, plaintiff simply asserts that UCC § 2–202 has no application because defendant has not made a sufficient showing that the confirmation slip was "intended by the parties as a final expression of their agreement with respect to such terms as are included therein." Something more is required, plaintiff says, either language in the confirmation slip indicating that it was intended to be the final expression of the parties' agreement or uncontroverted evidence that the writing was so intended. Otherwise, according to plaintiff, there are factual issues as to the effect the parties intended the confirmation slip to have and summary judgment must be denied. We disagree.

Here, the essential terms of the transaction are plainly set forth in the confirmation slip: that plaintiff had sold lira to defendant, the amount of the lira it sold, the exchange rate, the amount of dollars to be paid by defendant for the lira, and the maturity date of the transaction. The signature of plaintiff's agent who signed and returned the confirmation slip five days later on March 18, 1985, signifies plaintiff's acceptance of these terms. Nothing in the confirmation slip suggests that it was to be a memorandum of some preliminary or tentative understanding with respect to these terms. On the contrary, it is difficult to imagine words which could more clearly demonstrate the final expression of the parties' agreement than "WE HAVE BOUGHT FROM YOU ITL 537,750,000" and "WE HAVE SOLD TO YOU USD 250,000.00."

The confirmation is not of some bargain to be made in the future but expresses the parties' meeting of the minds as to a completed bargain's essential terms—a sale of 537,750 lira at a rate of 2151 for 250,000 dollars—made in a telephone conversation on March 13, 1985. The only evidence plaintiff has tendered does no more than contradict the stated terms of the confirmation slip—the very evidence which UCC § 2–202 precludes. It does not address the critical question of whether the terms in the confirmation slip were intended to represent the parties' final agreement on those matters. We conclude that where, as here, the form and content of the confirmation slip suggest nothing other than that it was intended to be the final expression of the parties' agreement as to the terms set forth and where there is no evidence indicating that this was not so, UCC § 2–202 bars parol evidence of contradictory terms.

We reject plaintiff's contentions that UCC § 2–202 requires that there be some express indication in the writing itself or some other evidence that the parties intended it to be the final expression of their agreement. . . . To require that the record include specific extraneous evidence that the writing constitutes the parties' final agreement as to its stated terms would in many instances impose a virtually insurmountable obstacle for parties seeking to invoke UCC § 2–202, particularly in cases involving large commercial banks and other financial institutions, which typically close hundreds of transactions over the telephone during a business day. As a practical matter, a confirmation slip or similar writing is usually the only reliable evidence of such transactions, given the unlikely prospect that one who makes scores of similar deals each day will remember the details of any one particular agreement. Indeed, this case is illustrative inasmuch as neither of the participants had a specific recollection of the March 13, 1985, telephone conversation.

Plaintiff also argues that UCC § 2–202 does not bar the parol evidence submitted in opposition to defendant's motion because it is offered to show that there was never a contract between the parties. This argument is unavailing. Plaintiff does not dispute that it entered into a foreign currency transaction with defendant; its only contention is that the transaction called for it to pur-

chase and not sell lira. Hence, the parol evidence is being used to contradict a term of the contract, not to show that there was no contract, and UCC § 2–202 applies.

Reversed.

CASE QUESTIONS

1. Describe the transaction, the parties, and who sold what to whom.

2. Is the memo a final writing?

3. What dangers would the court introduce if orders such as this were contradicted by oral testimony?

4. Did someone fail to read a document carefully before signing? Does the parol evidence rule allow "failure to read" as a defense?

Risk in International Contract Performance: *Force Majeure*

International contracts carry peculiar and additional risks. One of the lessons of the wars in the Middle East, for example, is that international contracts should have provisions for war, interruption of shipping lines, and other political acts. Often referred to as *force majeure* clauses, these provisions in international contracts allow the parties to agree what will happen in the event of sudden changes in government or in the global political climate rather than rely on a court to determine after the fact what rights, if any, the parties had. (See Chapter 13 for more details on contract issues.)

CONSIDER...   12.9

Terrorist acts, such as the September 11, 2001, destruction of the World Trade Center towers in New York City, have become more frequent over the past few years. What happens when substantial interruption in a business's operations occurs because a bombing destroys or damages its leased facilities? Would you add provisions and protections to your lease? What terms would you want if you were the landlord?

B I O G R A P H Y

The Story of Television Contracts

In 1996, the six stars of the cast of the NBC-TV situation comedy *Friends* (Jennifer Aniston, Courteney Cox, Lisa Kudrow, Matt LeBlanc, Matthew Perry, and David Schwimmer) each demanded a salary increase from $40,000 per episode to $100,000 per episode, which was more than double their contract salaries. Further, the six stars threatened to walk out on the beginning of the fall season if their salary demands were not met.

Friends was one of a handful of highly successful programs on NBC, indeed, on any network. The

six actors had examined the ad revenues for their show and concluded that with their short-lived careers and fame, they needed to negotiate as much salary as possible. The six stars were successful in renegotiating their contracts, but they also created a new phenomenon in the television industry whereby stars can command high salaries when nervous executives feel their departure is imminent.

CONTINUED

Some sample salaries are as follows.

Tim Allen	*Home Improvement*	$1.25 million per episode
Paul Reiser	*Mad about You*	$1 million per episode
Helen Hunt	*Mad about You*	$1 million per episode

(Note: Both Mr. Reiser and Ms. Hunt received an increase from $750,000 to $1 million per episode following the end of the *Seinfeld* series, which was the heart of NBC's successful Thursday night lineup. Mr. Seinfeld had been the first and only television actor to receive $1 million per episode—Mr. Allen's contract was negotiated at about the same time as Mr. Reiser and Ms. Hunt's, and Mr. Allen's show was with ABC Television.)

In 2004, the actors who work two days each week to do the voices of the characters for *The Simpsons* received an increase from $15,000–$25,000 per episode to $50,000 per episode. These voice actors work only two days each week, whereas actors in television series work five days per week. Julie Kavner, the voice of Marge Simpson, has a separate deal and did not participate in the threatened walkout by the voice talents for the show.

The trend continued through 2009, when *American Idol* judge Paula Adbul threatened to leave her critical role on the show unless she was given a salary of $20 million. The Fox Network refused to meet her demands. Ms. Abdul left the show following the announcement that the show's host, Ryan Seacrest, had signed a three-year contract for $45 million.

Ethical Issues

Are the actors justified in threatening to walk out if they do not receive pay increases? Is there a legal basis for their walkouts? Some of the actors point to the earnings for the shows as justification for the walkouts. The net profits for the eight-year run of *The Simpsons* were $500 million. Is it ethical to just get what you can while you can? What does the response of Fox show about trends in these types of negotiations?

Summary

What are contracts?

- Contract—promise or set of promises for breach of which the law gives a remedy, or the performance of which the law in some way recognizes as a duty

What laws govern contracts?

- Common law—traditional notions of law and the body of law developed in judicial decisions
- *Restatement (Second) of Contracts*—general summary of the common law of contracts
- Uniform Commercial Code (UCC)—set of uniform laws (49 states) governing commercial transactions

What are the types of contracts?

- Bilateral contract—contract of two promises; one from each party
- Unilateral contract—contract made up of a promise for performance
- Express contract—written or verbally agreed-to contract

- Implied contract—contract that arises from parties' voluntary conduct
- Quasi contract—theory for enforcing a contract even though there is no formal contract because the parties behaved as if there were a contract
- Implied-in-fact contract—contract that arises from factual circumstances, professional circumstances, or custom
- Implied-in-law contract—legally implied contract to prevent unjust enrichment
- Void contract—contract with illegal subject matter or against public policy
- Voidable contract—contract that can be avoided legally by one side
- Unenforceable contract—agreement for which the law affords no remedy
- Executed contract—contract that has been performed
- Executory contract—contract not yet performed

How are contracts formed?

- Offer—preliminary to contract; first step in formation
- Offeror—person making the offer
- Offeree—recipient of offer
- Course of dealing—UCC provision that examines the way parties have behaved in the past to determine present performance standards
- Revocation—offeror canceling offer
- Options—offers with considerations; promises to keep offer open
- Merchant's firm offer—written offer signed by a merchant that states it will be kept open
- Counteroffer—counterproposal to offer
- Battle of the forms—UCC description of merchants' tendency to exchange purchase orders, invoices, confirmations, and so on; under Revised UCC, the court determines terms after the fact looking at intent, forms used, and the UCC terms
- Acceptance—offeree's positive response to offer
- Mailbox rule—timing rule for acceptance

- Consideration—something of value exchanged by the parties that distinguishes gifts from contracts
- Charitable subscriptions—enforceable promises to make gifts
- Promissory estoppel—reliance element used to enforce otherwise unenforceable contracts

When must contracts be in writing?

- Statute of frauds—state statutes governing the types of contracts that must be in writing to be enforceable
- Merchants' confirmation memorandum—UCC provision that allows one merchant to bind another based on an oral agreement with one signature
- Parol evidence—extrinsic evidence that is not admissible to dispute an integrated unambiguous contract

What issues for contracting exist in international business?

- CISG—Contracts for the International Sale of Goods; a uniform law for international commercial transactions that countries can choose to adopt and contracting parties can choose to use

Questions and Problems

1. L. A. Becker Co., Inc., sent D. A. Clardy a $100 down payment along with a merchandise order. Clardy deposited the check, as was its usual daily practice for payments. After examining the offer, Clardy sent a rejection letter along with a check for $100 to Becker, which claims Clardy accepted by cashing the check. Is Becker correct? [*L. A. Becker Co v Clardy*, 51 So. 211 (Miss. 1910)]

2. Consider the following proposal description:

   Attached are an original and two (2) carbon copies of our Proposal No. 620-M-86R covering the subject as agreed upon in your office last Friday, June 20, 1986. Please sign the original and one (1) copy on the lower left corner of page 9 and return to us for our execution. We will return one (1) executed copy for your files.

   Again we thank you for selecting us for this project. We assure you it is receiving our best attention. Our Engineering Department is proceeding with the designs, fabrication drawings, and material orders.

   We look forward to your receiving the necessary permits.

   The "proposal" consists of five pages of typewritten terms, setting forth specifications for the manufacture, assembly, and erection of a television tower and related items, and four pages of preprinted "Terms and Conditions of Sale." The printed portion includes the following relevant terms:

   Acceptance of Proposal

   This proposal is for immediate acceptance and prior to such acceptance is subject to modification or withdrawal without notice.

   Acceptance of this proposal will evidence Buyer's intent that the sale be governed solely by the terms and conditions of this proposal.

   Any modifying, inconsistent or additional terms and conditions of Buyer's acceptance shall not become a part of any contract resulting from this proposal unless agreed to in writing by Kline.

   Any order or offer by Buyer as a result of this proposal shall not be binding upon Kline until accepted by Kline in writing by an officer of Kline. If accepted by Kline, this proposal shall constitute the agreement between the Buyer and Kline.

   At the bottom of the final page are the following signature spaces:

   KLINE IRON & STEEL CO., INC.
   By _____
   Its   (Seller)

   GRAY COMMUNICATIONS, INC.
   By _____
   Its   (Buyer)

   Is there an offer? When would the earliest acceptance be? [*Kline Iron & Steel Co., Inc. v Gray Communications*

Consultants, Inc., 715 F. Supp. 135 (D.S.C. 1989)]

3. Dr. Cook is a licensed dentist who devotes less than 50 percent of his practice to the work of fitting and making dentures. Mrs. Downing is a patient of Dr. Cook who was fitted for dentures. Mrs. Downing filed suit against Dr. Cook after she took delivery of her dentures because she said they were ill fitting and produced sore spots in her mouth. Dr. Cook's expert witness testified that Mrs. Downing's problems were probably due to candidiasis, an autoimmune reaction, or an allergy to the dental material. No expert testified that her problems were due to ill-fitting dentures.

The trial court awarded damages to Mrs. Downing on the basis of a breach of UCC Article 2, implied warranty of fitness for a particular purpose. Dr. Cook appealed, maintaining that the dentures were not a sale of goods. Explain who is correct about UCC vs. common law. [*Cook v Downing,* 891 P.2D 611 (Ok. Ct. App. 1995)]

4. Mace Industries, Inc. sent a quotation to Paddock Pools for water treatment equipment. Paddock responded with a purchase order that had the following written on its reverse side:

"THE SELLER AGREES TO ALL OF THE FOLLOWING TERMS AND CONDITIONS."

The clause was then followed by language stating that acceptance was expressly conditional upon Mace's acceptance of the terms.

Problems between the parties developed. Paddock says there is no contract because of its conditional acceptance. Mace maintains that § 2-207 applies and that there was a contract, with the only issues being the additional terms Paddock wrote on its purchase order and whether they are part of the contract. Who is correct? [*Mace Industries, Inc. v Paddock Pool Equipment Co., Inc.,* 339 S.E.2d 527 (S.C. 1986)]

5. Consider the following sequences of offers and acceptances and determine whether in each case there would be a contract.

a. September 1, 2010: A mails an offer to B.
   September 2, 2010: B receives the offer.
   September 3, 2010: A mails a revocation.
   September 4, 2010: B mails an acceptance.
   September 5, 2010: B receives the revocation.
   September 6, 2010: A receives the acceptance.
   RESULT: _____

b. September 1, 2010: A mails an offer to B.
   September 2, 2010: B receives the offer.
   September 3, 2010: B wires an acceptance.
   September 4, 2010: B wires a rejection.
   September 4, 2010
      (later):   A receives the acceptance.
   September 5, 2010: A receives the rejection.
   RESULT: _____

c. September 1, 2010: A mails an offer to B.
   September 2, 2010: B receives the offer.
   September 3, 2010: A wires a revocation.
   September 3, 2010: B wires an acceptance.
   September 4, 2010: B receives the revocation.
   September 5, 2010: A receives the acceptance.
   RESULT: _____

Would your answers be different under the UCC from those under common law?

6. On March 23, 1994, Northern Distributing Company made two offers to purchase two brands of beer carried by Keis Distributors, Inc.: 683,136 cases of Genesee beer at $1.75 per case and 95,632 cases of Labatt/Rolling Rock beer at $2 per case. The offer contained a termination date of April 11, 1994, and directed Keis to "accept this offer by signing below." Keis countersigned as requested and sent the offer back to Northern with a cover letter that stated both sides should retain counsel to work out "the wording of the final details." A proposed "closing and consulting agreement" was drafted but never signed, and Keis then withdrew from these distribution areas. Northern did purchase some of Keis's inventory after the distributorship termination, and a dispute arose as to the price due on that inventory. Northern claimed the contract price, and Keis said they had no contract, so the price was higher. Who is correct? Read the case and decide. [*Keis Distributors, Inc. v Northern Distributing Co.,* 641 N.Y.S. 2d 417 (App. Div. 1996)]

7. Hillcrest Country Club contacted N. D. Judds Company about replacement of the roof on its clubhouse. Rick Langill served as Judds's representative in negotiating the contract. Hillcrest managers had a brochure that described the RS-18 roofing manufactured by Roof Systems made of galvanized steel laminated with acrylic film called Korad.

Judds maintains Hillcrest received the brochure by calling Roof Systems. Hillcrest managers maintain Mr. Langill gave them the brochures. Mr. Langill generally stamps brochures and attaches a cover letter before mailing them out, but Hillcrest's brochure was not stamped, although it was used as a basis for Hillcrest's specification sheet. The brochure touted a 20-year warranty and promised no chalking, fading, chipping, peeling, or other forms of coating deterioration.

Judds submitted a bid with language that waived all warranties once final payment was made. Hillcrest accepted Judds's bid, and the roof was installed in July 1982.

By September 1984, the roof panels on the Hillcrest clubhouse were flaking and required replacement. Judds cited the warranty waiver. Hillcrest replaced the roof at a cost of $80,000 and filed suit against Judds and Roof Systems.

Did Roof Systems' warranty extend to Hillcrest? Was there privity of contract? Is this a UCC § 2-207 problem?

Was a contract formed? Does Hillcrest have a warranty? [*Hillcrest Country Club v N. D. Judds Co.*, 12 U.C.C.2d Rep. Serv. (Callaghan) 990, 236 Neb. 233 (1990)]

8. Procter & Gamble (P&G) began a Pampers catalog promotional offer in 1981. A statement on each box of Pampers explained that by saving the teddy bear proof-of-purchase symbols (Teddy Bears points) on packages of Pampers diapers, a customer could order various baby items from the Pampers Softouches Baby Catalog at a reduced cost. The catalog would be sent free to consumers upon request. Included in the catalog were pictures of the items for sale and the designated amount of Teddy Bears points and cash necessary for purchase. All sale terms, including the dates during which the offer was in effect, were described in each catalog. The only method for ordering merchandise was the use of the specific order form included in each catalog.

About April 1989, P&G sent out its final catalog. On the front of the catalog was a statement that it was the final catalog and that the offer would expire on February 28, 1990.

Ms. Alligood and others had cut out and saved the teddy bear symbols. The diaper purchasers claim that each package of Pampers contained an offer to enter into a unilateral contract, which they accepted by purchasing Pampers and saving the teddy bear proof-of-purchase symbols.

The precise language of the advertisement printed on packages of Pampers states:

Save these Teddy Bears points and use them to save money on toys, clothes, furniture, and lots of other baby things when you shop the Pampers Baby Catalog.

For your free copy of the Catalog, send your name, complete address and youngest baby's date of birth to:

> *Pampers Baby Catalog*
> *P.O. Box 8634,*
> *Clinton, Iowa 52736.*

If P&G refused to redeem the Teddy Bears points, would the purchasers have any contract rights to force P&G to deliver the catalog merchandise? [*Alligood v Procter & Gamble Co.*, 594 N.E.2d 668 (Ohio App. 1991)]

9. Thomas Koenen signed a car-purchase order form to buy a limited edition Buick Regal. GM would manufacture only 500 of these Regals. The order form was also signed by the car dealer's salesman and sales manager. Mr. Koenen gave Royal Buick Company (the dealer) a check for $500. No price is mentioned on the order form. Is there a contract? [*Koenen v Royal Buick Co.*, 783 P.2d 822 (Ariz. 1989)]

10. Nation Enterprises, Inc. purchased a large (36 by 3 feet) gas-fired convection oven from Enersyst, Inc., to make its pizza crusts. The oven had problems that the parties were working to resolve, but Nation needed a second oven. It was going to purchase one from someone else, but Enersyst orally promised to fix the first oven if Nation bought the second oven from it. (Oven 1 was beyond its 60-day warranty.) Nation bought the second oven, but Enersyst did not fix the first one. Nation sued, but Enersyst claims its promise on the first oven is inadmissible under the parol evidence rule. Is this correct? [*Nation Enterprises, Inc. v Enersyst, Inc.*, 749 F. Supp. 1506 (N.D. Ill. 1990)]

Contracts, Ethics, Economics, and the Law

Donald Trump described his contract negotiation methods and pricing as follows, *"When I build something for somebody, I always add $50 million or $60 million onto the price. My guys come in, they say it's going to cost $75 million. I say it's going to cost $125 million and I build it for $100 million. Basically, I did a lousy job. But they think I did a great job."*

Evaluate this quote, thinking through the economic implications of this pricing. Who is affected by the Trump approach? Is he simply managing expectations? Is he misleading the other party? Is he taking unfair advantage? What happens if pricing does not reflect cost? What would happen if all contractors did this?

Notes

1. UCITA was formerly Article 2B of the Uniform Commercial Code. It was separated out because reforms for the UCC on Article 2 were pending and the controversy related to Article 2B (now UCITA) was isolated with its separate promulgation as a uniform law. UCITA remains controversial. See Americans for Fair Electronic Commerce at http://www.ucita.com for a summary of the concerns and issues.

2. With the UCC modifications and ESIGN, a writing is no longer required. However, there must be some type of record, which could come in the form of an electronic submission.

3. Roger C. Bern, "'Terms Later' Contracting: Bad Economics, Bad Morals, and a Bad Idea for a Uniform Law, Judge Easterbrook Not Withstanding," 12 *Journal of Law and Policy* 641 (2004).

Contracts and Sales:
Performance and Remedies

O nce the parties have formed a contract with an offer, acceptance, and consideration (as discussed in Chapter 12), it would seem that their troubles are over and that all they need to do is carry through with performance. However, sometimes new information arises and one party challenges the formation as invalid; or perhaps what one party believes is performance is just not enough for the other party, or is not what was contemplated when they formed the contract. This chapter focuses on contract problems and answers the following questions: What if the assumptions made in formation turn out to be untrue? Must the parties go through with the contract? If one party does not perform, is the other excused? When is performance required, and when is it sufficient? What remedies exist? Do third parties have rights in a contract? ■

For want of a nail the shoe was lost;

For want of a shoe the horse was lost;

And for want of a horse the rider was lost;

For the want of a rider the battle was lost;

For the want of the battle the kingdom was lost

And all for the want of a horseshoe-nail.

Poor Richard's Almanac (1758)

UPDATE ⬉
For up-to-date legal news, go to
mariannejennings.com

CONSIDER...

Several students from a high school in Fairfax County, Virginia, and another in Tucson, Arizona, filed suit against iParadigms for copyright infringement. iParadigms is the company that owns and operates Turnitin, a software program that allows educational institutions to check student term papers against previous students' papers to detect plagiarism. The students wanted their papers removed from Turnitin  because no contract was ever formed to allow their papers to be posted to Turnitin, that there was duress involved when they clicked to submit their papers because they had no choice but to post them in order to turn in their papers, and that they were minors and could not make valid contracts. Are the students correct? Or was there a valid contract?

Defenses in Contract Formation

Even though a contract may have been formed with the three elements of offer, acceptance, and consideration, one of the elements may be flawed. The result is a contract that may be void, voidable, or unenforceable. When one of the required elements of formation is flawed, the contract is subject to a defense. A **contract defense** is a situation, term, or event that makes an otherwise valid contract invalid. These defenses ensure that the parties enter into contracts voluntarily and on the basis of accurate information. The defenses are displayed in Exhibit 13.1 and are discussed in the following sections.

Capacity

Both parties to a valid contract must have **capacity,** which includes both age and mental capacity.

EXHIBIT 13.1   Defenses in Contract Formation

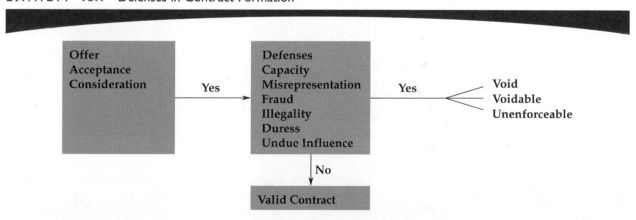

Age Capacity

Age capacity requires that both parties be at least the age of majority. In most states, that age is 18. Contracts entered into by **minors** (sometimes called **infants**) are voidable. A **voidable contract** of a minor allows the minor to choose not to honor the contract, in which case the other party to the contract will have no remedy. But some exceptions apply to the minors' contracts rules. Some statutes make certain contracts of minors enforceable; for example, student loan agreements are enforceable against minors, as are agreements to enter the military. Minors' contracts for such necessities as food and clothing are still voidable, but courts do hold minors liable for the reasonable value of those necessities.

Case 13.1 deals with an issue of a minor's liability under a contract.

CASE 13.1

Yale Diagnostic Radiology v Estate of Fountain
838 A.2d 179 (Conn. 2003)

Shooting for Payment from a Minor

FACTS

In March 1996, Harun Fountain was shot in the back of the head at point-blank range by a playmate. As a result of his injuries, including the loss of his right eye, Fountain required extensive lifesaving medical services from a variety of medical services providers, including Yale Diagnostic Radiology (plaintiff). The expenses at Yale totaled $17,694. Yale billed Vernetta Turner-Tucker (Tucker), Fountain's mother, but the bill went unpaid and, in 1999, Yale obtained a judgment against her. In January 2001, all of Tucker's debts were discharged in bankruptcy, including the Yale judgment. There was no reference to Fountain's father throughout the cases.

Tucker filed suit against the boy who had shot Fountain. However, Fountain succumbed to his injuries, passing away before the case was settled. The settlement on the tort case was placed into probate court as part of Fountain's estate. Tucker was the administrator of Fountain's estate. When the settlement was deposited, Yale asked the probate court for payment of its $17,694 judgment from the estate. The probate court denied the motion, reasoning that parents are liable for medical services rendered to their minor children, and that a parent's refusal or inability to pay for those services does not render the minor child liable. The probate court held that Yale could not get payment from the estate. Yale appealed to the trial court, and the trial court held for Yale. Tucker and the estate (defendants) appealed.

JUDICIAL OPINION

BORDEN, Justice

Connecticut has long recognized the common-law rule that a minor child's contracts are voidable. Under this rule, a minor may, upon reaching majority, choose either to ratify or to avoid contractual obligations entered into during his minority. The traditional reasoning behind this rule is based on the well-established common-law principles that the law should protect children from the detrimental consequences of their youthful and improvident acts, and that children should be able to emerge into adulthood unencumbered by financial obligations incurred during the course of their minority. The rule is further supported by a policy of protecting children from unscrupulous individuals seeking to profit from their youth and inexperience.

The rule that a minor's contracts are voidable, however, is not absolute. An exception to this rule, eponymously known as the doctrine of necessaries, is that a minor may not avoid a contract for goods or services necessary for his health and sustenance. Such contracts are binding even if entered into during minority, and a minor, upon reaching majority, may not, as a matter of law, disaffirm them.

The parties do not dispute the fact that the medical services rendered to Fountain were necessaries; rather, their dispute centers on whether Connecticut recognizes the doctrine of necessaries.

. . . [W]e conclude that Connecticut recognizes the doctrine of necessaries. We further conclude that, pursuant to the doctrine, the defendants are liable for payment to the plaintiff for the services rendered to Fountain.

Courts in other jurisdictions that have held that minors may be liable pursuant to the doctrine of necessaries for medical services have done so by applying varying legal theories. For example, some courts have held minors liable only if the creditor can show that the minor was not living with or being supported by his or her parents at the time the contract arose or the services were rendered. Still other courts have held minors liable after determining that the goods or services rendered were necessaries, and the minor's parent or guardian was unwilling or unable to pay for them. See *Schmidt v Prince George's Hospital*, 366 Md. 535, 555, 784 A.2d 1112 (2001) (minor's father's use of insurance proceeds to buy minor car sufficient for finding that father was unwilling to pay minor's medical expenses). Still other courts have reasoned that the minor's ever present secondary liability for payment for medical services rendered to him gives rise to an implied-in-law contract.

. . . when a medical service provider renders necessary medical care to an injured minor, two contracts arise: the primary contract between the provider and the minor's parents; and an implied-in-law contract between the provider and the minor himself. The primary contract between the provider and the parents is based on the parents' duty to pay for their children's necessary expenses, under both common law and statute. Such contracts, where not express, may be implied in fact and generally arise both from the parties' conduct and their reasonable expectations. The primacy of this contract means that the provider of necessaries must make all reasonable efforts to collect from the parents before resorting to the secondary, implied-in-law contract with the minor.

The present case illustrates the inequity that would arise if no implied in law contract arose between Fountain and the plaintiff. Fountain was shot in the head at close range and required emergency medical care. Under such circumstances, a medical services provider cannot stop to consider how the bills will be paid or by whom. Although the plaintiff undoubtedly presumed that Fountain's parent would pay for his care and was obligated to make reasonable efforts to collect from Tucker before seeking payment from Fountain, the direct benefit of the services, nonetheless, was conferred upon Fountain. Having received the benefit of

necessary services, Fountain should be liable for payment for those necessaries in the event that his parents do not pay.

Fountain received, through a settlement with the boy who caused his injuries, funds that were calculated, at least in part, on the costs of the medical services provided to him by the plaintiff in the wake of those injuries. This fact further supports a determination of an implied-in-law contract under the circumstances of the case.

Nothing in either the language or the purpose of [Connecticut's statutes on minors] indicates an intent on the part of the legislature to absolve minors of their secondary common-law liability for necessaries.

To the contrary, the purposes behind the statutory rule that parents are primarily liable and the common-law rule, pursuant to the doctrine of necessaries, that a minor is secondarily liable, when read together, serve to encourage payment on contracts for necessaries. Those purposes are (1) to reinforce parents' obligation to support their children, and (2) to provide a mechanism for collection by creditors when, nonetheless, the parents either refuse or are unable to discharge that obligation.

The undisputed facts show that Tucker had four years to pay the plaintiff's bill for the services rendered to Fountain. She did not pay that bill even when the plaintiff pursued a collection action against her. These facts are sufficient to show that Tucker was unwilling or unable to pay for Fountain's necessary medical services.

The fact that Tucker may be supplying other necessaries, such as food and shelter, does not undermine the claim that she has not made payment for this necessary medical service, which was already provided by the plaintiff to Fountain.

The judgment is affirmed.

CASE QUESTIONS

1. Describe the series of events that led to Yale requesting that the minor pay for the medical services.

2. What public policy issues and concerns result from this decision?

3. What benefits does the decision provide?

Ethical Issues

LeAnn Rimes, a country western singer, signed a contract at age 12 with Curb Records. Curb Records is owned by Mike Curb, a long-standing presence in the music industry who began his career with a group known as The Mike Curb Congregation. Ms. Rimes will be 35 before she has delivered the 21 albums required under the terms of the agreement. "At 12, I didn't understand everything in my contract. All I know is that I really wanted to sing." Ms. Rimes testified at a hearing of the California Senate Select Committee on the Entertainment Industry looking into the labor issues surrounding long-term album requirements contracts.

Other artists testified about their lack of health insurance benefits under these contracts. Singer Courtney Love testified, in reference to her minimal insurance coverage, "I can maybe get six days in rehab."

Don Henley, a solo artist formerly with The Eagles, testified, "The deck is stacked and has been stacked for 60 years in the recording companies' favor."

Record industry executives testified that the long-term contracts are necessary because of the time, money, and effort required to build young artists. One executive said, "There is one thing that all labels have in common and that's risk."

The Dixie Chicks sued their label, Sony, and Ms. Love sued her label, Vivendi Universal, for what they say are questionable accounting practices in arriving at the artists' share of the profits. Both companies responded with countersuits alleging that the artists did not produce the albums required under their contracts. The suits were settled.

Does Ms. Rimes have a possible defense? Are the recording contracts binding, or are they unconscionable? Are the long-term contracts and their requirements ethical?

Mental Capacity

Contracting parties must also have *mental capacity*, which is the ability to understand that contracts are enforceable, that legal documents have significance, and that contracts involve costs and obligations. Contracts of those lacking mental capacity are voidable. Moreover, if a party to a contract has been declared legally incompetent, that person's contracts are void. A **void contract** is one the courts will not honor, and neither party is obligated to perform under that agreement.

Misrepresentation

When one party to a contract is not given full or accurate information by the other party about the contract subject matter, there is **misrepresentation.** In the case of misrepresentation in the formation of a contract, the law allows a **rescission** of the contract. Rescission means the contract is set aside. Misrepresentation occurs when a seller makes inaccurate statements about its product or fails to disclose pertinent information about its product that would affect someone's decision to enter into the contract. For example, failure to disclose that a deluxe model car has a standard car engine is misrepresentation. The elements required for innocent misrepresentation are as follows:

1. Misstatement of a material fact (or the failure to disclose a material fact)
2. Reliance by the buyer on that material misstatement or omission
3. Resulting damages to the buyer

To be a basis for rescission, the misrepresentation must have been one regarding a **material fact.** A material fact is the type of information that would affect someone's decision to enter into the contract. For example, if a buyer for your stock in XYZ Corporation failed to disclose that a takeover was pending, it would be considered misrepresentation of a material fact. A takeover affects the price of stock, and the price of stock in the future affects your decision to buy and sell presently.

Misrepresentation cannot be based on sales **puffing,** which is opinion about the subject matter of a contract. For example, suppose that a real estate agent told you a house you were considering buying was located in the "best area in town." Such a statement is an opinion and cannot be a basis for misrepresentation.

CONSIDER...   13.1

Analyze the following statements. Are they opinion, or could they be the basis for a misrepresentation claim?

This lightbulb will last 200 hours.

THINK: Misrepresentation requires a statement of fact or a promise of performance that is a basis for entering into a contract.

APPLY: This statement about the lightbulb is a promise of performance. It is the type of information someone relies on when making a buying decision.

ANSWER: The statement is a basis for claiming misrepresentation if it turns out to be false.

These suits are 100 percent wool.

THINK: Misstatement of a material fact that the buyer relies on when making decisions can be the basis for a claim of misrepresentation.

APPLY: Saying that the suits are 100 percent wool is a statement of fact about the goods.

ANSWER: If the goods are not 100 percent wool, the statement is a basis for claiming misrepresentation.

Now use this approach to analyze the following statements.

This fabric is the finest money can buy.

This sweater is 50 percent cashmere.

This toothpaste reduces cavities by 20 percent.

This car gets 22 miles to the gallon.

This stock has never decreased in value.

This house has no easements running through the backyard.

This car has not been in an accident.

These bicycle locks are theft-proof.

This carpet-cleaning machine will remove every type of spot on your rugs.

The buyer must rely on or attach some importance to the statement that was made. A buyer who is buying cars only to take them apart for their used parts does not rely on a misrepresentation that the car has not been in an accident. Whatever information is given must be part of the reason the buyer has agreed to enter into the contract.

Ethical Issues

Yelp.com is a website that has postings from average folks about their experiences with local businesses. "Yelpers," as they are called, write their own reviews of these businesses. So familiar is the website and its power that some local businesses have begun posting signs such as "No Yelpers."

Business owners have complained because they are not permitted to respond to the reviews unless they advertise on the site. However, the Yelp founders respond that the Yellow Pages have always been "pay-to-play," and that Yelp provides the "little guys" a chance to participate in the evaluation of a business. Also, they point out that small businesses that cannot afford the Yellow Pages spread have an opportunity to attract customers when they provide good products and services.

Yelp does offer the various ad services:

- Companies can pay to have their companies featured prominently.

- The ad can link to a business page on Yelp.

- The company can pay to have more favorable reviews moved to the top of its business page.

- Banner ads are available.

What are the ethical issues in the relationship between the site and the businesses? What is the effect of the statement "Well, the Yellow Pages have always done it this way"? Do you see opportunities for misrepresentation here? Or does the site prevent misrepresentation? What are the issues related to libel with the site? Are there any conflict-of-interest issues?

For more information

Dan Post, "'The Coffee Was Lousy. The Wait Was Long,'" *New York Times*, May 21, 2008, p. NY 6.

BUSINESS PLANNING TIP

When employees and agents are working for commissions as well as salary (or are on commission alone), they are subject to great temptation to engage in misrepresentation. For example, in the Sears Roebuck & Company controversy over the allegations that its auto repair centers overcharged customers, Sears's then–CEO Edward Brennan issued a statement indicating that the presence of incentives for selling parts and services may have contributed to poor decisions by employees in handling customers. Incentive-based pay systems must also have ethical guidelines.

Fraud or Fraudulent Misrepresentation

Although misrepresentation can result simply because of inaccurate information, **fraud** is the knowing and intentional disclosure of false information or the knowing failure to disclose relevant information. Fraud has the same elements of proof as misrepresentation, with the added element of *scienter*, or knowledge that the information given is false. An example of the distinction is a situation in which the seller of a home obtains an exterminator's report that says the house is clear of termites and passes the report along to the buyer. If the house actually has termites, it is a case of misrepresentation but not fraud because the seller was simply passing along the information without knowledge of its accuracy. If, however, that same seller received a report from an exterminator that indicated there were termites and then found another exterminator to report there were no termites, and the seller passed only that second report along to the buyer, there would be fraud because there was knowledge of the false report and the intent to defraud the buyer. The failure to disclose material information about the subject matter of a contract can also constitute fraud. For example, a car dealership that fails to disclose to a customer that the car he is buying was in an accident is engaging in misrepresentation. If the car dealership performed the body work on the car in its own body shop, the failure to disclose the accident and repairs would be fraud.

Reed v King (Case 13.2) includes a discussion of the elements of misrepresentation and of when misrepresentation becomes fraud.

CASE 13.2   *Reed v King*
193 Cal. Rptr. 130 (1983)

Buying Property from the Addams Family: How Scary Must It Be?

FACTS

Dorris Reed (plaintiff) purchased a home from Robert King for $76,000. Mr. King and his real estate agents did not disclose to Mrs. Reed that 10 years before, the house had been the site of the murders of a mother and her four children. After Mrs. Reed moved into the home, neighbors disclosed to her the story of the murders and the fact that the house carried a stigma. Because of its history, appraisers evaluated the true worth of the house to be $65,000. Mrs. Reed filed suit on the basis of misrepresentation and sought rescission and damages. Her complaint was dismissed by the trial court, and she appealed.

JUDICIAL OPINION

BLEASE, Associate Justice

In the sale of a house, must the seller disclose it was the site of a multiple murder?

Concealed within this question is the nettlesome problem of the duty of disclosure of blemishes on real property which are not physical defects or legal impairments to use.

Reed seeks to state a cause of action sounding in contract, i.e., rescission, or in tort, i.e., deceit. In either event her allegations must reveal a fraud. "The elements of actual fraud, whether as the basis of the remedy in contract or tort, may be stated as follows: There must be (1) a *false representation* or concealment of a material fact (or, in some cases, an opinion) susceptible of knowledge, (2) made with *knowledge* of its falsity or without sufficient knowledge on the subject to warrant a representation, (3) with the *intent* to induce the person to whom it is made to act upon it; and such person must (4) act in *reliance* upon the representation (5) to his *damage*."

The trial court perceived the defect in Reed's complaint to be a failure to allege concealment of a material fact. "Concealment" and "material" are legal conclusions concerning the effect of the issuable facts pled. As appears, the analytic pathways to these conclusions are intertwined.

Reed's complaint reveals only nondisclosure despite the allegation King asked a neighbor to hold his peace. There is no allegation the attempt at suppression was a cause in fact of Reed's ignorance. Accordingly, the critical question is: does the seller have duty to disclose here? Resolution of this question depends on the materiality of the fact of the murders.

In general, a seller of real property has a duty to disclose: "where the seller knows of facts *materially* affecting the value or desirability of the property which are known or accessible only to him and also knows that such facts are not known to, or within the reach of . . . the buyer."

Materiality "is a question of law, and is part of the concept of right to rely or justifiable reliance." Accordingly, the term is essentially a label affixed to a normative conclusion.

Numerous cases have found nondisclosure of physical defects and legal impediments to use of real property are material. However, to our knowledge, no prior real estate sale case has faced an issue of nondisclosure of the kind presented here. Should this variety of ill repute be required to be disclosed?

The paramount argument against an affirmative conclusion is it permits the camel's nose of unrestrained irrationality admission to the tent. If such an "irrational" consideration is permitted as a basis of rescission the stability of all conveyances will be seriously undermined. Any fact that might disquiet the enjoyment of some segment of the buying public may be seized upon by a disgruntled purchaser to void a bargain. In our view, keeping this genie in the bottle is not as difficult a task as these arguments assume. We do not view a decision allowing Reed to survive a demurrer in these unusual circumstances as endorsing the materiality of facts predicating peripheral, insubstantial, or fancied harms.

The murder of innocents is highly unusual in its potential for so disturbing buyers they may be unable to reside in a home where it has occurred. This fact may foreseeably deprive a buyer of the intended use of the purchase. Murder is not such a common occurrence that *buyers* should be charged with anticipating and discovering this disquieting possibility. Accordingly, the fact is not one for which a duty of inquiry and discovery can sensibly be imposed upon the buyer.

Reed alleges the fact of the murders has a quantifiable effect on the market value of the premises. Reputation and history can have a significant effect on the value of realty. "George Washington slept here" is

CONTINUED

worth something, however physically inconsequential that consideration may be. Ill-repute or "bad will" conversely may depress the value of property. Failure to disclose such a negative fact where it will have a foreseeably depressing effect on income expected to be generated by a business is tortious. Some cases have held that *unreasonable* fears of the potential buying public that a gas or oil pipeline may rupture may depress the market value of land and entitle the owner to incremental compensation in eminent domain.

Whether Reed will be able to prove her allegation, the decade-old multiple murder has a significant effect on market value we cannot determine. If she is able to do so by competent evidence she is entitled to a favorable ruling on the issues of materiality and duty to disclose. Her demonstration of objective tangible

harm would still the concern that permitting her to go forward will open the floodgates to rescission on subjective and idiosyncratic grounds.

CASE QUESTIONS

1. What information did Mrs. Reed discover about her home, and when?

2. Is this the kind of information that is material? What evidence could be used to show materiality?

3. Is Mrs. Reed's case dismissed, or will she be permitted to go forward with the suit?

4. Should Mr. King and the real estate agents have disclosed the information to Mrs. Reed? Was there an ethical obligation to do so?

Most states have passed some form of disclosure statutes for real estate transactions. In some states, the history of criminal activity on a property must be disclosed. In other states, there are prohibitions on disclosure. Some of these states prohibit disclosure of information, such as whether an occupant of the property died of AIDS. However, even in states with protections and immunity from disclosure, the buyer must be told the truth if the buyer asks specifically about the occupants and their health.

CONSIDER... 13.2

Barry Hinesley negotiated with Oakshade Town Center during the spring of 1998 for a lease to a suite within a shopping center being developed by Oakshade in Davis, California. Hinesley said that during the negotiations, Oakshade's agent and representative, Paul Petrovich, told Hinesley the regional restaurant chain Dos Coyotes, the international coffee shop chain Starbucks, and the international ice cream and yogurt chain Baskin-Robbins would be leasing and occupying suites near the suite Hinesley was to lease. All three chains, according to Petrovich, would commence operations by the end of 1998. Hinesley leased 1,200 square feet for five years. Starbucks and Baskin-Robbins never leased space from Oakshade. However, Marble Slab Creamery (an ice cream store) and Common Grounds (a coffee house) did become tenants. Dos Coyotes did become a tenant of Oakshade, but its lease did not commence until December 2000. Was there misrepresentation by Petrovich? Is tenant composition of a shopping center a material issue for tenants entering into a lease agreement for that center? Is reliance on an agent's representations a basis for an action for misrepresentation? [*Hinesley v Oakshade Towne Center*, 135 Cal. App. 4th 289 (2005)]

Duress

Duress occurs when a party is physically forced into a contract or deprived of a meaningful choice when deciding whether to enter into a contract. Requiring employees to sell company stock holdings in order to keep their jobs is an example of duress because of a lack of choice. If duress has occurred, the contract is voidable. The party who experienced the duress has the right to rescind the agreement, but rescission is a choice; the law does not make the contract illegal or unenforceable because duress was present. The choice of enforcement or rescission is left to the party who experienced the duress. Case 13.3 deals with an issue of duress as well as several other contract defenses and provides the answer to the chapter's opening "Consider."

| CASE 13.3 | *A.V. ex rel. Vanderhye v iParadigms, LLC*
544 F.Supp.2d 473, reversed on other grounds, 562 F.3d 630 (4th Cir. 2009) |

Turn It In, Then Turn It Over to the Courts

FACTS

iParadigms (Defendant) owns and operates Turnitin, a proprietary technology system that evaluates the originality of written works in order to prevent plagiarism. Educational institutions contract with iParadigms and require their students to submit their written works via Turnitin. When the student work is submitted to Turnitin, the system compares the work electronically to content available on the Internet, student works previously submitted to Turnitin, and commercial databases of journal articles and periodicals. Turnitin then produces an Originality Report. The teacher evaluates the Originality Report and decides whether to address any issues with the student.

Turnitin can archive a student's work, which allows Turnitin's database to grow with each student work submitted. However, this feature must be specifically authorized by the school district.

In order to submit a paper to Turnitin, a student must click "I Agree" to the terms of the "user agreement" (also referred to as the "Clickwrap Agreement") which is displayed directly above the "I agree" link that the student must click. The Clickwrap Agreement states: "Turnitin and its services are maintained by iParadigms, LLC ['Licensor'], and are offered to you, the user ['User'], conditioned on your acceptance without modification of the terms, conditions, and notices contained herein." The Clickwrap Agreement also contains a limitation of liability clause:

In no event shall iParadigms, LLC and/or its suppliers be liable for any direct, indirect, punitive, incidental, special, or consequential damages arising out of or in any way connected with the use of this web site or with the delay or inability to use this web site, or for any information, software, products, and services obtained through this web site, or otherwise arising out of the use of this web site, whether based in contract, tort, strict liability or otherwise, even if iParadigms, inc. or any of its suppliers has been advised of the possibility of damages.

A.V., a minor, and three other students (Plaintiffs) attended high school in Virginia, in the Fairfax County Public Schools system, and in Arizona, in the Tucson Unified School District. Both school systems contracted with iParadigms to utilize iParadigms's Turnitin technology system and both authorized archiving of student-submitted work. Both school districts required their students to use Turnitin to submit their written works. If a student chose not to submit his or her work via Turnitin, that student would receive a zero on the assignment.

Each of the students read and clicked "I agree" to the terms of the Clickwrap Agreement. However, in an attempt to prevent Turnitin from archiving their written works, the students included a disclaimer on the face of their works indicating that they did not consent to the archiving of their works by Turnitin. iParadigms archived the works submitted by the four students. The students allege there was no contract entered into, that if there was a contract it was void because they were minors, and that the requirement of using Turnitin was unconscionable because it involved duress. iParadigms moved for summary judgment.

JUDICIAL OPINION

HILTON, District Judge

. . . iParadigms first contends that Turnitin's Clickwrap Agreement constitutes a valid contract entered into between Plaintiffs and iParadigms and that the limitation of liability clause precludes any liability in this action. In Virginia, the essential elements of a contract are offer, acceptance and consideration. As one court has stated, "[a] contract is no less a contract simply

CONTINUED

because it is entered into via a computer." In fact, many courts have found clickwrap agreements to be enforceable. Additionally, "waivers and limitation of liability clauses are enforceable."

The Court finds that the parties entered into a valid contractual agreement when Plaintiffs clicked "I Agree" to acknowledge their acceptance of the terms of the Clickwrap Agreement. The first line of the Clickwrap Agreement, which appears directly above the "I Agree" link, states: "Turnitin and its services . . . are offered to you, the user ['User'], conditioned on your acceptance without modification of the terms, conditions, and notices contained herein." Also, the Clickwrap Agreement provides that iParadigms will not be liable for any damages "arising out of the use of this web site." By clicking "I Agree," Plaintiffs accepted iParadigms' offer and a contract was formed based on the terms of the Clickwrap Agreement. Because a limitation of liability clause was among the terms of the Agreement, the Court finds that iParadigms cannot be held liable for any damages arising out of Plaintiffs' use of the Turnitin web site.

The existence of disclaimers on the written works indicating that Plaintiffs did not consent to the archiving of their works does not modify the Agreement or render it unenforceable. The Clickwrap Agreement itself provides that the terms of the Agreement are not modifiable. Plaintiffs had the option to "Agree" or "Disagree"; no third option was available to allow Plaintiffs to modify the Agreement. By clicking "I Agree," Plaintiffs agreed to the terms of the contract as described in the Clickwrap Agreement. Any attempted disclaimers written onto papers submitted after clicking "I Agree" did not change the terms of the Agreement.

Plaintiffs assert the defense of infancy in an attempt to void the terms of the Clickwrap Agreement. In Virginia, a contract with an infant is voidable by the infant upon attaining the age of majority. However, the infancy defense cannot function as "a sword to be used to the injury of others, although the law intends it simply as a shield to protect the infant from injustice and wrong." In other words, "[i]f an infant enters into any contract subject to conditions or stipulations, he cannot take the benefit of the contract without the burden of the conditions or stipulations."

Plaintiffs received benefits from entering into the Agreement with iParadigms. They received a grade from their teachers, allowing them the opportunity to maintain good standing in the classes in which they were enrolled. Plaintiffs cannot use the infancy defense to void their contractual obligations while retaining the benefits of the contract. Thus, Plaintiffs' infancy defense fails.

Plaintiffs also seek to invalidate the contract on the grounds of duress. In Virginia, duress is defined as the "overbearing of a person's free will by an unlawful or wrongful act or by threat such that the party's consent to a contractual agreement is involuntary."

Though Plaintiffs plead duress, there is no evidence that anyone was coerced in any fashion by Turnitin or iParadigms. Insofar as Plaintiffs' duress defense is asserted against Plaintiffs' respective schools, rather than Defendant iParadigms, there is no support for the proposition that a contract can be invalidated on the basis of third party duress. Nevertheless, even if there was evidence of coercion by iParadigms, or even if a claim of third party duress by the school systems was viable, such coercion would not rise to the level of "an unlawful or wrongful act." Schools have a right to decide how to monitor and address plagiarism in their schools and may employ companies like iParadigms to help do so. If Plaintiffs' objection is that their schools' policies requiring students to use Turnitin are wrongful, Plaintiffs' proper redress is with the school systems. Thus, Plaintiffs' duress defense fails.

CASE QUESTIONS

1. Why did the minor/infancy defense not work in this case?
2. Why did the duress defense fail?
3. Why was the students' disclaimer ineffective?

Undue Influence

Undue influence occurs when one party uses a close personal relationship with another party to gain contractual benefits. Before undue influence can be established, a **confidential relationship** of trust and reliance must exist between the parties. Attorneys and clients have a confidential relationship. Elderly parents who rely on a child or children for their care have a confidential relationship with those children. To establish undue influence, abuse of this confidential relationship must occur. For example, conditioning an elderly parent's care upon the signing over of his land to a child is an abuse of the relationship. An attorney who offers advice on property disposition to his benefit is abusing the confidential relationship. Again, contracts subject to undue influence defenses are voidable. They can be honored if the party who experienced the influence desires to honor the contract.

Illegality and Public Policy

A contract that violates a statute or the general standards of public policy is void and cannot be enforced by either party. To enforce contracts that violate statutes or public conscience would encourage the commission of these illegal acts, so contract law is controlled by the statutory prohibitions and public policy concerns of other areas of law.

Contracts in Violation of Criminal Statutes

Contracts that are agreements to commit criminal wrongs are void. For example, the old saying that "there is a contract out on his life" may be descriptive, but it is not accurate in the legal sense. There could never be a valid contract to kill someone because the agreement is one to commit a criminal wrong and is therefore void. No one is permitted to benefit from contracts to commit illegal acts. For example, a beneficiary for a life insurance policy will not collect the proceeds from the insured's policy if the beneficiary arranged for the death of the insured (contract for murder). Consider 13.3 deals with the issue of benefits from an illegal contract.

CONSIDER...   13.3

Janet Peterson signed a contract with Sunrider Corporation in 1976 that provided for her payment arrangements as a participant in Sunrider's sales program. Sunrider was a Utah corporation that sold herbs, dietary supplements, skin care products, and beauty aids through a multilevel marketing plan. The plan includes several "levels of achievement" through which participants may receive compensation based both on their own sales of company products and on the sales of those whom participants have "sponsored," that is, those whom participants have brought into the company.

Peterson received commissions from Sunrider Corporation from 1976 through 1994 for sales that were made by Sunrider distributors who had been recruited by Peterson. Her payments averaged $3,500 per month. In 1994, after Sunrider had been acquired by another company, the payments ended. The new CEO stopped the payments because he claimed they were illegal. The Utah Pyramid Scheme Act (UPSA) provides that "A person may not organize, establish, promote, or administer any pyramid scheme." Part of the UPSA provides:

> receiving bonuses in a multi-level marketing business is illegal when the bonuses are based only upon sponsorship of an organization, rather than promoting a product, selling a product, or training and supervising down-line distributors.

Peterson says that her commissions from the lower levels are based on sales of products, and not just on her having recruited the people and companies to sell Sunrider. The new corporation argues that Peterson still did not make the sales herself and the payments are illegal. Peterson argues that it would be unfair not to pay the commissions. What should the court do and why? Be sure to consider the purpose of the antipyramid statute. Think also about her reliance on the representations of the previous company's officials. Finally, think through the public policy issues in paying or not paying Peterson according to her original contract. [*Peterson v The Sunrider Corp.*, 48 P.3d 918 (Utah 2002)]

Contracts in Violation of Licensing Statutes

In some cases, contracts are not contracts to commit illegal acts but are simply contracts for a legal act to be done by one not authorized to perform such services. Every state requires some types of professionals and technicians to be licensed before they can perform work for the public. For example, a lawyer must be admitted to the bar before representing clients. A lawyer who contracts to represent a client before having been admitted to the practice of law has entered into a void contract. Even if the lawyer successfully represents the client, no fee could be collected because the agreement violated the licensing statute, and to allow the lawyer to collect the fee, even in a quasi contract, would encourage others to violate the licensing requirements.

In some cases, licensing requirements are in place, not for competency reasons, but to raise revenues. For example, an architect may be required to pass a competency screening to be initially licensed in a state, and after that the license may be renewed simply by paying an annual fee. Suppose that the architect forgot to pay the annual renewal fee and, after the license had lapsed, entered into a $300,000 contract with a developer. The developer discovers the renewal problems after the work is completed and wants to get out of paying the architect. In this case, the issue is not one of competency screening but of financial oversight, and the architect would be permitted to collect the fee.

Contracts in Violation of Usury Laws

These contracts are credit or loan contracts that charge interest in excess of the state's limits for interest or finance charges. These statutes are discussed in detail in Chapter 14.

Contracts in Violation of Public Policy

Some contracts do not violate any criminal laws or statutory provisions but do violate certain standards of fairness or encourage conduct in violation of public policy. For example, many firms include **exculpatory clauses** in their contracts that purport to hold the firms completely blameless for any accidents occurring on their premises. Most courts consider a firm's trying to hold itself completely blameless for all accidents, regardless of the degree of care or level of fault, against public policy and will not, therefore, enforce such clauses.

Also grouped into the public policy prohibition are contracts that restrict trade or employment. For example, when a business is sold, part of the purchase price is paid for the business's goodwill. The benefit of that payment is lost if the seller moves down the street and starts another similar business. Hence, the courts have permitted **covenants not to compete** to be included in these contracts as long as they are reasonable in time and geographic scope. These covenants and their legality are discussed in detail in Chapter 16.

Some contracts are not actually contracts for criminal or illegal activities, but the terms of the contract are grossly unfair to one party. A contract that gives all the benefits to one side and all the burdens to the other is an **unconscionable** contract. The standards for determining whether a contract is unconscionable are the public policy standards for fairness that cover all types of contract provisions and negotiations. Many consumer rental contracts have been declared unconscionable because the consumers were paying more in rent than it would cost to buy the rented appliance outright.

The standards for unconscionability are set on a case-by-case basis. The courts have not given a firm definition of unconscionability. Even the UCC does not specifically define unconscionability, although one section (2–302) prohibits the enforcement of unconscionable contracts. The *Waters v Min. Ltd.* case (Case 13.4) provides insights on unconscionability.

CASE 13.4	*Waters v Min Ltd.* 587 N.E.2d 231 (Mass. 1992)

Young, Drugged, and Wealthy: Capable of Contracting?

FACTS

Gail A. Waters (plaintiff) was injured in an accident when she was 12 years old. At age 18, she settled a negligence claim with Commercial Union Insurance Company and purchased an annuity contract, the income from which was her support.

At age 21, Ms. Waters became romantically involved with Thomas Beauchemin (defendant), an ex-convict who introduced her to drugs and to Min Ltd., a partnership consisting of David and Robert DeVito and Michael D. Steamer (defendants), and suggested that she sell her annuity contract to them.

Ms. Waters signed a contract to sell her policy, with a cash value of $189,000, to the defendants for $50,000. The contract was signed on the hood of a car in the parking lot of a restaurant. The guaranteed return to the owner of the policy over its 25-year life was $694,000.

Ms. Waters filed suit to rescind the contract. The trial court found, among other things, that the contract was unconscionable. The DeVitos, Mr. Steamer, and Mr. Beauchemin appealed.

JUDICIAL OPINION

LYNCH, Justice

The defendants contend that the judge erred by (1) finding the contract unconscionable (and by concluding the defendants assumed no risks and therefore finding the contract oppressive); (2) refusing them specific performance; and (3) failing to require the plaintiff to return all the funds received from them.

Unconscionability. The defendants argue that the evidence does not support the finding that the contract was unconscionable or that they assumed no risks and therefore that the contract was oppressive.

The doctrine of unconscionability has long been recognized by common law courts in this country and in England. "Historically, a [contract] was considered unconscionable if it was 'such as no man in his senses and not under delusion would make on the one hand, and as no honest and fair man would accept on the other.' Later, a contract was determined unenforceable because unconscionable when 'the sum total of its provisions drives too hard a bargain for a court of conscience to assist.'"

The doctrine of unconscionability has also been codified in the Uniform Commercial Code (code), G.L.C. 106, § 2-302 (1990 ed.), and, by analogy, it has been applied in situations outside the ambit of the code.

Unconscionability must be determined on a case-by-case basis, with particular attention to whether the challenged provision could result in oppression and unfair surprise to the disadvantaged party and not to allocation of risk because of "superior bargaining power." Courts have identified other elements of the unconscionable contract. For example, gross disparity in the consideration alone "may be sufficient to sustain [a finding that the contract is unconscionable]," since the disparity "itself leads inevitably to the felt conclusion that knowing advantage was taken of [one party]." High-pressure sales tactics and misrepresentation have been recognized as factors rendering a contract unconscionable. If the sum total of the provisions of a contract drive too hard a bargain, a court of conscience will not assist its enforcement.

The judge found that Beauchemin introduced the plaintiff to drugs, exhausted her credit card accounts to the sum of $6,000, unduly influenced her, suggested that the plaintiff sell her annuity contract, initiated the contract negotiations, was the agent of the defendants, and benefited from the contract between the plaintiff and the defendants. The defendants were represented by legal counsel; the plaintiff was not. The cash value of the annuity policy at the time the contract was executed was approximately four times greater than the price to be paid by the defendants. For payment of not more than $50,000 the defendants were to receive an asset that could be immediately exchanged for $189,000, or they could elect to hold it for its guaranteed term and receive $694,000. In these circumstances the judge could correctly conclude the contract was unconscionable.

The defendants assumed no risk and the plaintiff gained no advantage. Gross disparity in the values exchanged is an important factor to be considered in determining whether a contract is unconscionable. "[C]ourts [may] avoid enforcement of a bargain that is shown to be unconscionable by reason of gross inadequacy of consideration accompanied by other relevant factors."

We are satisfied that the disparity of interests in this contract is "so gross that the court cannot resist the inference that it was improperly obtained and is unconscionable."

Amount of repayment order. The defendants also argue that the judge erred in failing to require the plaintiff to return the full amount paid by them for the annuity.

The defendants paid $18,000 cash after deducting $7,000 for a debt which was owed to them by

CONTINUED

Beauchemin. The remaining $25,000 due on the contract was never paid.

The judge's order was consistent with his findings that Beauchemin was the agent of the defendants, and that the plaintiff only received $18,000 for her interest in the annuity.

Judgment affirmed.

Contract Performance

Once parties have contracted, they have the obligation of performance. The following subsections cover when performance is due, what constitutes performance, and when performance is excused.

When Performance Is Due

Performance is due according to the times provided in the contract. In some contracts, however, prescribed events must occur before performance is required. These events are called **conditions. Conditions precedent** are events that give rise to performance. Suppose that Zelda has agreed to buy Scott's house, and their contract provides that Zelda does not have to pay until she is able to obtain a reasonable loan to finance the purchase. This financing clause is a condition precedent to contract performance. If Zelda is denied financing, she is not required to perform under the contract. Another example of a condition precedent is in a contract for construction of jackets out of a material to be furnished by the seller. Unless the seller gives the manufacturer the fabric to work with, the manufacturer has no obligation to perform. **Conditions concurrent,** or **conditions contemporaneous,** exist in every contract; benefits are exchanged at the same time. One is willing to perform because the other side does.

BUSINESS STRATEGY

Dealing with High-Powered Talent

Sometimes, there are no criminal charges, but the conduct raises customer eyebrows and influences buying behaviors. In 2005, international model Kate Moss appeared in a grainy videotape showing her using cocaine. On the tape she is heard to say that she doesn't do drugs more than anyone else.[a]

Following the release of the confession and the pictures from the video in London's *Daily Mirror*, the "super model" apologized. However, Burberry and Chanel, two of the companies who used Ms. Moss as their representative, indicated that they would not be renewing her contract. H&M, Europe's largest clothing retailer (with 78 stores), which carries designers such as Stella McCartney, listened to Ms. Moss's side of the

story and initially agreed to give her a second chance. However, public reaction in London was so negative that the company withdrew the contract.[b] Customers inundated the stores with calls complaining that allowing such a role model for teen-type clothes was unacceptable. The public relations representative for the store said, "If someone is going to be the face of H&M, it is important they be healthy, wholesome and sound."[c]

In 2006, Paramount Pictures ended its multibillion-dollar relationship with superstar Tom Cruise. Mr. Cruise had had a 14-year relationship with Paramount Studios, a division of Viacom. However, Sumner Redstone, the chair of Viacom announced (to the surprise of many) the termination. The Cruise/Paramount partnership earned $2.5 billion in box-office sales since its inception. Citing Mr. Cruise's personal behavior, Mr. Redstone indicated that "As much as we like him personally, we thought it was wrong to renew his deal. His recent conduct has not been acceptable to Paramount."[d] He also added, "It's nothing to do with his acting ability, he's a terrific actor. But we don't think that someone who effectuates creative suicide and costs the company revenue should be on the lot."[e] He also added, in reference to Mr. Cruise jumping on a chair during an interview on the Oprah Winfrey show, "He had never behaved this way before, he really went over the top."[f] The other conduct Mr. Redstone was referring to was Mr. Cruise's public disputes over depression, psychiatry, and treatment (grounded in his Scientology faith), and his public romance with much younger actress Katie Holmes (the couple was then expecting their daughter, Suri, prior to being married).

However, an insider said the issue was the cost of the contract—the overhead as well as the cost of Mr. Cruise's executive team. Mr. Redstone also estimated that Mr. Cruise's behavior prior to the release of *Mission Impossible III* resulted in lost sales of about $100 to $150 million. Mr. Redstone added, "I feel badly. Essentially he's a decent guy and a great actor."[g]

In 2007, Verizon withdrew its sponsorship of the Gwen Stefani tour when a raunchy video of her opening act, Akon, appeared online. The video shows Akon engaged in questionable on-stage behavior with a fan under the age of 18. The video resulted in considerable coverage and outrage from parents and commentators.

Akon indicated that the club where the video was made was supposed to be checking IDs and he assumed that the young woman (a pastor's daughter) was 18. He issued the following apology, "I want to sincerely apologize for the embarrassment and any pain I've caused to the young woman who joined me on stage, her family, and the Trinidad community for the events at my concert."[h]

Akon's album, *Konvicted*, has sold 2.2 million copies and was number 11 on the *Billboard* charts in May 2007. Ms. Stefani's album had sold 1.2 million copies.

Under the terms of its sponsorship contracts, Verizon has the right to end its relationships with singers for criminal charges or other misconduct. Ms. Stefani's manager said, "This kid is not getting a fair shake (referring to Akon). I strongly disagree with their take on it. How this has anything to do with Gwen Stefani I have no idea."[i]

Verizon will still be required to pay Ms. Stefani the cash due under the contract (estimated at $2 million), but it will no longer have advertisements or other promotional materials as part of the tour. Verizon issued the following statement, "We made a

decision, based on what we saw and, in this case, how our own customers, who we listen to, were reacting."[j]

In 2009–2010, golfer Tiger Woods lost endorsement contracts with Accenture, AT&T, and Gatorade following a car crash and resulting revelations about his marital infidelity. Gatorade did continue its relationship with the Tiger Woods Foundation. Nike continued its sponsorship of Woods, with Nike chairman and co-founder Phil Knight explaining that these problems with athletes are just "part of the game" when you sign them. Knight went on to add, "I think he's been really great. When his career is over, you'll look back on these indiscretions as a minor blip, but the media is making a big deal out of it right now."[k]

Tag Heuer did not drop its sponsorship because, as a spokesperson explained, "He's the best in his domain. We respect his performance in the sport. Woods's personal life is not our business."[l] Tag Heuer did, however, stop running its ads featuring Mr. Woods. Gillette also stopped running Woods ads but did not terminate the relationship, stating only that it would limit his role in the company's marketing program.

Do you think highly visible contracts and employees must be handled differently from regular employee contracts? Do you think the high visibility affords fewer rights under the contract? Do the issues of the fairness of contracts and public visibility make contract enforcement more difficult? What do you learn about celebrity contracts from these examples? Is it possible to rein in the stars' behaviors through contracts? How are Nike's and Tag Heuer's postures different and why? What about Gillette and its decision?

[a]César G. Soriano and Karen Thomas, "Moss Issues Apology," *USA Today*, September 23, 2005, p. 3E.

[b]Guy Trebay and Eric Wilson, "Kate Moss Is Dismissed by H & M After a Furor Over Cocaine," *New York Times*, September 21, 2005, pp. C1, C17.

[c]*Id.*

[d]David M. Halbfinger and Geraldine Fabrikant, "Fire or Quit, Tom Cruise Parts Ways with Studio," *New York Times*, August 23, 2006, pp. C1, C2.

[e]Merissa Marr, "Sumner Redstone Gives Tom Cruise His Walking Papers," *Wall Street Journal*, August 23, 2006, pp. A1, A7.

[f]*Id.*

[g]*Id.*

[h]Jeff Leeds, "Verizon Drops Pop Singer from Ads," *New York Times*, May 10, 2007, pp. B1, B6.

[i]*Id.*

[j]*Id.*

[k]John Berman, "Tiger Woods Loses Sponsor," *ESPN News*, December 14, 2009. http://espn.go.com/blog/sportscenter/post/_/id/10567/tiger-woods-loses-sponsor. Last visited August 12, 2010.

[l]*Id.*

Standards for Performance

The contract details what the parties are required to do for complete performance. In some contracts, performance is easily determined. Performance for a contract between an employment agency and a potential employee to find work for the employee is complete once the work is found.

But in some contracts, performance is complicated, and errors may occur in its execution. For example, construction contracts are long-term, complicated agreements. During the construction of a building, it is possible that some mistakes might be made. Is an owner allowed to not pay a contractor because of a mistake or two? The doctrine of **substantial performance** applies in construction contracts, and it means that the constructed building is, for practical purposes, just as good as the one contracted for. For example, a builder might have substituted a type of pipe when the brand name specified in the contract was not available. The substitution is a technical breach of contract, but it is a substitute that is just as good. The builder will be paid for the construction, but the owner will be entitled to damages.

E-Commerce: Payment Performance Has Changed

One aspect of contract performance is payment. Internet transactions have changed dramatically how we pay for goods and services. The most common methods for electronic payment include credit cards, digital cash, and person-to-person payment, or PayPal.

When Performance Is Excused

Sometimes, all conditions of a valid contract are met but performance of the contract is excused. Under common law, the parties are excused from performance if performance has become impossible. **Impossibility** means that the contract cannot be performed by the parties or anyone else. For example, performance under a contract for the purchase and sale of land that has been washed away into a lake is impossible. Completing a year of dance lessons is impossible for someone who has had a paralyzing accident.

Under the UCC (and under the *Restatement*), performance can be excused in cases of commercial impracticability. **Commercial impracticability** (see § 2–615 in Appendix G) excuses performance if the basic assumptions the parties made when they entered into the contract have changed. Although this definition makes it seem that the UCC excuses performance when wars, embargoes, and unusually high price increases occur, courts have been reluctant to apply the excuse of commercial impracticability. The standard of commercial impracticability has been interpreted to mean nothing more or less than the common law standard of impossibility.

Parties can protect themselves from unusual events by putting in their contracts *force majeure* clauses, which excuse the parties from performance in the event of such problems as wars, economic depression, or embargoes. Following the attack on the World Trade Center in New York City, performance under many contracts was excused for impossibility. For example, because air traffic was halted, all overnight shipping contract performances were excused.

For the Manager's Desk

Re: Killer Performance Requirements in Retail

It's called "the Squeeze." The Squeeze refers to the increasingly onerous logistical demands retailers place on clothing suppliers. The logistical demands add tremendous costs to suppliers, they are rigid, they are complex (some retailers' rules run 50 pages), and they carry penalties. Noncompliance with logistical requirements allows the retailer to take a "charge-back," or a deduction from its payment.

Here are some sample logistical requirements:

Shipping and Packing Guidelines from Retailers to Vendors
Packing Hanging Garments

You must have written authorization from Federated to ship GOH. All ready-to-wear merchandise should be shipped in conveyable cartons in order to maximize the use of UCC-128 shipping container label. . . .

Lazarus

Routing Instructions

Determine your RPS Zone number on the Zone Chart. . . . Determine your LTL [less than truckload] Zone number from the Zone Chart and follow the LTL Routing for that zone.

Kaufmann's

Paperwork Documentation

Provide a separate packing list for each store and for each purchase order, detailed as to purchase order #, department #, store # and two letter code, style #, color (when ordered by color), size (when ordered by size), number of cartons, and total units shipped.

Hecht's

Charges include $300 for incorrect labels, $500 for incorrect packing materials, and a 5 percent penalty if a shipment arrives late.

Schwab Co., the manufacturer of "Little Me" infant clothes, was charged $400 for late delivery of a $500 shipment.

A buyer for Federated Department Stores says, ". . . [I]t's not our responsibility to keep vendors afloat. We have a separate philanthropy program." Small vendors complain they must hire extra people to handle special boxing and that retailers' chargebacks are reversed if they offer proof of compliance.

Smaller vendors are taking their products to specialty stores and boutiques. Large retailers say, "This is all still negotiable." Some vendors say that retailers are wrong on their charges about 25–50 percent of the time, but "They throw it up to see what will stick." Vendors note that their cash flow is affected and that, until the disputes are resolved, it often takes a year for them to be paid on their invoices.

(*Lazarus, Kaufmann's, and Hecht's were regional chains that have been acquired by other national chains.*)

Discussion Questions

1. Is there a problem with unconscionability?
2. Is this kind of behavior anticompetitive?
3. Do you feel the guidelines and chargeback fees are truly negotiable?
4. Are the chargeback levels of fees ethical?

CONSIDER...   13.4

Trans World Airlines (TWA) had a sales/leaseback arrangement on 10 aircraft with Connecticut National Bank. TWA was experiencing difficulty making payments, attributing the difficulties to the Gulf War, which resulted in decreased air travel because of terrorism and decreased oil flow. Is this situation an example of commercial impracticability? [*Connecticut Nat'l. Bank v Trans World Airlines, Inc.*, 762 F. Supp. 76 (S.D.N.Y. 1991)]

Sons of Thunder, Inc. v Borden, Inc. (Case 13.5) deals with the issue of business needs changing and whether performance can be excused. It is a case that some experts have labeled a landmark one in terms of imposing a duty of good faith in performance, contains issues of performance and termination of a contract.

CASE 13.5 · Sons of Thunder, Inc. v Borden, Inc.
690 A.2d 575 (N.J. 1997)

Ships and Liability Passing in the Night?

FACTS

Borden, Inc. owned Snow Food Products Division, a leading producer of clam products. Borden had its own four-vessel fleet as well as independent boats for obtaining clams. Boats delivered the clams to Borden's Cape May plant, where the shell stock was processed into clam meat.

In 1978, Borden hired Donald DeMusz to be the captain of the *Arlene Snow*, one of Borden's four boats. Eventually, Mr. DeMusz was hired as an independent contractor to manage Borden's boats, and Mr. DeMusz formed Sea Labor, Inc., to be the company responsible for the management of those boats. Sea Labor received five cents per bushel of clams harvested by the four boats.

At about the same time Mr. DeMusz was hired, Borden began its "Shuck-at-Sea" program, which enabled the fishermen to shuck the clams on the boat, thus allowing the boats to bring back larger amounts of clams, thereby reducing costs and eliminating the need for more plant and facilities. However, the existing boats were not large enough for the shucking equipment.

Wayne Booker, a manager for Borden, asked Mr. DeMusz to undertake the Shuck-at-Sea program. Mr. DeMusz submitted a proposal that Mr. Booker and other executives approved. Along with two partners, Mr. DeMusz formed Sea Works, Inc., and for $750,000 purchased the *Jessica Lori*, a clam-fishing boat with shucking equipment. Mr. DeMusz financed the purchase through a bank loan.

An internal company memo from Mr. Booker included the following paragraph along with a description of how Mr. DeMusz's purchase of a boat would save money:

> [W]e still have a significant mutual interest with DeMuse [sic]. His principal business will still be in chartering the Snow fleet and in captaining Arlene. He needs a dependable customer for the clams that he catches, either shell stock or meat. If we terminate our agreement with him, he would have a hard time making the payments on his boat.

Mr. DeMusz drafted a one-page contract, and Mr. Booker approved it with one small change. Mr. DeMusz then formed Sons of Thunder, Inc. with Bill Gifford and Bob Dempsey in order to purchase the second boat. The final contract was entered into on January 15, 1985, and included the following provision:

> IT IS understood and Agreed to by the parties hereto that Snow Food Products shall purchase shell stock from Sons of Thunder Corp. for a period of one (1) year, at the market rate that is standardized throughout the industry. The term of this contract shall be for a period of one (1) year, after which this contract shall automatically be renewed for a period up to five years. Either party may cancel this contract by giving prior notice of said cancellation in writing Ninety (90) days prior to the effective cancellation date.

> Sons of Thunder Corp. will offer for sale all shell stock that is landed to Snow Food.

In March 1985, Sons of Thunder bought a boat, the *Sons of Thunder*. The cost to rig and purchase the boat was $588,420.26. Sons of Thunder sought financing from First Jersey National Bank but was unable to obtain a loan until Mr. Booker told the bank representative that Mr. DeMusz had a solid relationship with Borden and that although the contract could be terminated within one year, Borden expected the contract to run for five years. Mr. Booker explained to the representative that the five-year term of the contract would be sufficient to pay back the loan. Ultimately, Mr. DeMusz obtained a $515,000 loan, which he, Mr. Gifford, Mr. Dempsey, and their spouses personally guaranteed. Mr. DeMusz used a personal note to cover the remaining balance.

After some preliminary testing, the *Sons of Thunder* started to operate and to fulfill its contract with Borden. For most weeks, the records show that Borden did not buy the minimum amount specified in the contract. Problems continued and the relationship between Mr. DeMusz and his companies and Borden began to deteriorate. When Borden discovered that a $500,000 accounting error had actually overstated the benefits of the Shuck-at-Sea program, Borden exercised its termination rights under the contracts and notified Mr. DeMusz of termination.

Mr. DeMusz and his companies experienced substantial losses as a result of the termination of contracts. Mr. DeMusz filed suit. Borden moved for summary judgment on the grounds that it had properly exercised its termination rights. The jury found for Mr. DeMusz, the court of appeals affirmed, and Borden appealed.

JUDICIAL OPINION

GARIBALDI, Justice

The question whether Borden performed its obligations in good faith appears before the Court. . . .

The obligation to perform in good faith exists in every contract, including those contracts that contain express and unambiguous provisions permitting either party to terminate the contract without cause. See *United Roasters, Inc. v Colgate-Palmolive Co.*, 649 F2d 985 (4th Cir.), cert. denied, 454 U.S. 1054, 102 S.Ct. 599, 70 L.Ed.2d 590 (1981). In *United Roasters*, United Roasters gave Colgate the right to manufacture and distribute Bambeanos, its roasted soybean snack. The contract governing the relationship allowed Colgate to terminate its performance at any time during the test-marketing period so long as it gave United Roasters thirty days' notice. After two years of testing Bambeanos, Colgate announced plans to merge with Riviana Foods, Inc., and in the next five months, it ceased producing Bambeanos, stopped advertising them, sold its entire inventory of raw soybeans and Bambeanos, and transferred its product manager to another project. Eventually, Colgate terminated the contract.

Interpreting North Carolina law in the diversity action, the Fourth Circuit concluded that North Carolina had not decided whether there was a good faith limitation on an unconditional right to terminate a contract. The Fourth Circuit did, however, evaluate United Roasters' claim that Colgate violated the covenant of good faith and fair dealing. The panel stated

> *What is wrong with Colgate's conduct in this case is not its failure to communicate a decision to terminate . . . , but its cessation of performance. Clearly it had an obligation of good faith performance up until its right of termination was actually effective. The contract expressly obliged it to use its best efforts in the promotion of Bambeanos. Instead of doing that, it simply ceased performance. . . . Quite simply, it broke its contract when it terminated its performance, which was United Roasters' contractual due.*

In *Bak-A-Lum Corp.*, supra, 69 N.J. 123 (1976), this Court reached a similar conclusion even though the contract was oral and the parties had not discussed how the contract could be terminated. In that case, Bak-A-Lum and Alcoa made an oral agreement, which gave Bak-A-Lum an exclusive distributorship of aluminum siding and related products manufactured by Alcoa. Alcoa eventually terminated the exclusive part of the agreement by appointing four additional distributors. Even though Alcoa planned on terminating the distributorship, it encouraged Bak-A-Lum to expand its warehouse facilities, which substantially increased its operating costs.

Despite acknowledging Alcoa's unconditional right to terminate the contract, the Court upheld the verdict for Bak-A-Lum because it found that Alcoa had breached the implied covenant of good faith and fair dealing by withholding its plans to terminate the contract while encouraging the plaintiff to expand its facilities. As the Court explained: "While the contractual relation of manufacturer and exclusive territorial distributor continued between the parties an obligation of reciprocal good-

faith dealing persisted between them." The Court found that the implied covenant of good faith and fair dealing required the defendant to give the plaintiff reasonable notice of its termination. Ultimately, the Court concluded that "a reasonable period of notice of termination of the distributorship . . . would have been twenty months."

The case most heavily relied on by Borden and the majority at the Appellate Division, *Karl's Sales & Service, Inc. v Gimbel Brothers Inc.*, 249 N.J. Super. 487 (App. Div.), cert. den. 127 N.J. 548 (1991), is distinguishable from this matter. In that case, the Appellate Division stated that where the contractual right to terminate is express and unambiguous, the motive of the terminating party is irrelevant. As stated previously, we agree with that view of the law. However, in *Karl's Sales*, unlike this case and *Bak-A-Lum*, there were no allegations of bad faith or dishonesty on the part of the terminating party. Accordingly, *Karl's Sales* did not address the issue we are concerned with here.

Borden knew that Sons of Thunder depended on the income from its contract with Borden to pay back the loan. Yet, Borden continuously breached that contract by never buying the required amount of clams from the Sons of Thunder. Furthermore, after Gallant took Booker's place, he told DeMusz that he would not honor the contract with Sons of Thunder. Nicholson also told DeMusz that he did not plan to honor that contract. Borden's failure to honor the contract left Sons of Thunder with insufficient revenue to support its financing for the Sons of Thunder.

Borden was also aware that Sons of Thunder was guaranteeing every loan that Sea Work had taken to finance the rerigging and purchasing costs for the [boat]. Thus, Borden knew that the corporations were dependent on each other, and that if one company failed, the other would most likely fail. Borden, however, fulfilled its obligations to Sea Work only for a short time before it began to breach that agreement. Eventually, Borden terminated its contract with Sea Work even though it knew that terminating the contract would leave Sea Work with no market to fish the *Jessica Lori*.

The final issue is whether the jury's assessment of $412,000, approximately one year's worth of additional profits, for the breach of the implied covenant of good faith and fair dealing was a reasonable verdict. Specifically, can a plaintiff recover lost profits for a breach of the implied covenant of good faith and fair dealing? We agree with Judge Humphreys that the jury's award of one year's additional profits "is a reasonable and fair estimate of 'expectation damages.'" Moreover, we agree with the trial court that lost profits are an appropriate remedy when a buyer breaches the implied covenant of good faith and fair dealing.

> *In order to recover for lost profits under [Section 2-708(2)], the plaintiffs must prove the amount of damages with a*

CONTINUED

reasonable degree of certainty, that the wrongful acts of the defendant caused the loss of profit, and that the profits were reasonably within the contemplation of the parties at the time the contract was entered into.

The jury's award of $412,000, approximately one year's profit, for the breach of the implied covenant of good faith and fair dealing is reasonable and fair.

CASE QUESTIONS

1. Explain the nature of the relationships between Mr. DeMusz and Borden.

2. Were all the DeMusz corporations completely dependent on Borden?

3. What impact does "good faith" have on termination of a contract?

4. What are the damages when there is a lack of good faith in the termination of a contract?

5. What provisions would you suggest be added to a contract such as this in which the relationship is one of contract but also one of dependence?

Often the obligation to perform is discharged by agreement of the parties. In some cases, the parties substitute someone else for the obligation in an agreement called a **novation.** For example, suppose that before forming a corporation, a business owner had signed a lease for store premises and then incorporates the business. The landlord agrees to substitute the new corporation as the tenant. All three parties (landlord, owner, and corporation) sign a novation. The owner is excused from individual liability and performance, and the corporation is substituted. Note that the landlord must agree; the owner cannot discharge his performance obligations by unilaterally substituting the corporation.

In other situations, the parties reach an agreement for payment in full on a contract; such an agreement is called an **accord and satisfaction.** The amount they agree to pay may be less than the original contract amount, but disputes over warranties, repairs, and other issues change the value of the contract. The accord and satisfaction serves to discharge the performance of both parties.

Contract Remedies

If performance is not excused and there is a valid contract, the nonbreaching party can recover for damages from the nonperforming party. The purpose of such **compensatory damages** is to put the nonbreaching party in the same position he or she would have been in had no breach occurred. The law has formulas to calculate the amount of compensatory damages for breach of every type of contract. For example, if a seller has agreed to sell a buyer a car for $5,000 and the seller breaches, the buyer could collect the extra $1,000 it would cost to buy a substitute car priced at $6,000.

In addition to compensatory damages, nonbreaching parties are entitled to collect the extra damages or **incidental damages** involved because of the breach. If a seller must run an ad in a newspaper to sell a car a buyer has refused to buy, the costs of the ad are incidental damages.

Some parties agree in their contracts on the amounts they will pay in the case of nonperformance. Damages agreed upon in advance are **liquidated damages,** and the contractual clauses containing them are enforceable as long as they are not excessive and compensatory damages are not awarded in addition to the liquidated damages.

In some cases, the nonbreaching party may be able to collect **consequential damages.** Consequential damages are damages that result because of the breach and generally involve lost business, lost profit, or late penalties. For example, if a contractor must pay a penalty of $200 for each day a building is late after the completion date stipulated in the contract and the contractor is late because the steel supplier did not meet its deadline, the $200-per-day penalty would be a consequential damage that the steel supplier would be required to pay. Whether a party will be able to collect consequential damages depends on whether the breaching party knew or should have known what the consequences of the breach would be.

CONSIDER... 13.5

Fingerlakes Aquaculture, LLC, an indoor fish hatchery, entered into a contract for Progas Welding Supply to build and deliver a 13,000-gallon oxygen storage tank. The contract required that the tank be delivered during the week of June 21, 1999, with a $400 per day liquidated damages provision, denoted a "fine." Throughout the year, Progas delivered smaller tanks, but was never able to deliver the 13,000-gallon tank. In June 2001, Fingerlakes Aquaculture bought a tank from another supplier and filed suit seeking the $400-per-day liquidated damages. Progas says that because of the other tanks, Fingerlakes Aquaculture had no damages and the total of $292,000 (the $400 per day for the 210 days of delay) was void as a penalty. Who is correct? Why? [*Fingerlakes Aquaculture LLC v Progas Welding Supply, Inc.*, 825 N.Y.S.2d 559 (2006)]

Third-Party Rights in Contracts

Generally, a contract is a relationship between or among the contracting parties and is not enforceable by others who happen to benefit. For example, suppose a landowner and a commercial developer enter into an agreement for the construction of a shopping mall. Such a project means jobs for the area and additional business for restaurants, hotels, and transportation companies, but these businesses would not have the right to enforce the contract or collect damages for breach if the developer pulled out of the project. However, certain groups of people do have rights in contracts even though they may not have been parties to the contracts. A good example is a beneficiary of a life insurance policy. The beneficiary does not contract with the insurance company and does not pay the premiums, but the beneficiary, called a third party beneficiary, has contract rights because the purchaser of the policy directed so.

In other types of third-party contract rights, the third parties are not part of the original contract, as is the life insurance beneficiary, but are brought in after the fact. For example, suppose that a homebuilder owes a plumbing contractor $5,000 for work done on homes in the builder's subdivision. In the sales contracts for the homes, the homebuilder is the seller, and the buyer's purchase monies will go to the homebuilder. However, the homebuilder could assign payment rights to the plumber as a means of satisfying the debt. This process, called **assignment,** gives the plumber the right to collect the contract amount from the buyer. The plumber takes the place of the homebuilder in terms of contract rights.

In some cases, the duty or obligation to perform under a contract is transferred to another party. The transfer of contractual duties and obligation is called a **delegation.** Generally, a delegation of duties carries with it an assignment of benefits. For example, suppose that Neptune Fisheries, Inc. has a contract with Tom Tuna, Inc., to sell 30 fresh lobsters each day. Neptune is stopping its lobster line and delegates its duties under the Tom Tuna contract to Louie's Lobsters, Inc. Louie's takes over Neptune's obligation to furnish the 30 lobsters and is assigned the right to benefits (payment for the lobsters) under the contract. Both Louie's and Neptune are liable to Tom Tuna for performance. A delegation, unlike a novation, does not release the original contracting party.

International Issues in Contract Performance

Assuring Payment

International contract transactions for goods involve extensive shipment requirements. To control access to the goods and payment for them, many sellers use a **bill of lading** for transacting business. The bill of lading is a receipt for shipment issued by the carrier to the seller. It is also a contract for the shipment of the goods and provides evidence of who has title to the goods. If a bill of lading is used, the buyer will not gain access to the goods unless and until the seller provides the necessary documents for release of the goods. Once the seller has the bill of lading, the seller can choose to transfer title to the goods by transferring the bill of lading. The seller could also pledge the bill of lading as security for the payment of a debt. A bill of lading can be made directly to the buyer, or it can be a negotiable bill of lading that can be transferred to anyone.

The bill of lading is often used in conjunction with a line of credit in international transactions because the two together offer the seller assurance of payment and the buyer assurance of arrival of the goods. In international transactions, in which resolution of disputes over great distances can be difficult, this means of controlling access to goods and payment is helpful.

In this type of transaction, the seller delivers goods to a carrier for transportation and receives a bill of lading. The seller then sends the bill of lading through its bank to the buyer's bank to give the buyer's bank title to the goods, which will be turned over to the buyer once the funds are deducted from the line of credit established by the bank for the buyer.

The buyer may also arrange for a **letter of credit** to be used in conjunction with the bill of lading. The letter of credit is issued by the buyer's bank and is sent to a corresponding bank where the seller is located. The letter of credit lists the terms and conditions under which the seller can draw on the letter of credit or be paid. For example, turning the bill of lading over to the corresponding bank may be the condition of drawing on the letter of credit; the bill of lading is then used by the corresponding bank and the buyer's bank to allow the buyer to take possession of the goods. Because banks are involved in these transactions through credit assurances, the seller enjoys more of an assurance of payment prior to shipment because a letter of credit is actually a confirmation of payment.

Assuring Performance: International Peculiarities

International contracts have a particular need for a *force majeure* clause. Wars, revolutions, and coups are often included in international contracts as justification for noncompletion. The *force majeure* clauses are summaries of potential international events that could hamper production or trade.[1]

One other risk of international contracts is the stability of various currencies and their possible devaluation. The method and means of payment should be specified in the contract, and a clause covering devaluation may also be included so that full payment is ensured.

Lakeway Co. v Bravo (Case 13.6) illustrates what can happen between the negotiation of an international contract and the time for contract payment.

CASE 13.6   *Lakeway Co. v Bravo*
576 S.W.2d 926 (Tex. 1979)

Falling Pesos: Negotiating an Exchange Rate

FACTS

Lakeway and Bravo (in a contract drawn and executed in both English and Spanish) agreed that Bravo would buy a certain Lakeway lot in Travis County, Texas. The purchase price was $25,820, with payment by Bravo to be in pesos. The agreement was executed July 31, 1976.

By the time the check was presented for final payment, it was August 30, 1976. The Mexican government devalued the peso on August 31, 1976, and the result was that Lakeway received $8,188.45 less than it would have had the transaction not been subject to an interim devaluation. Lakeway brought suit. The court granted summary judgment for Bravo, and Lakeway appealed.

JUDICIAL OPINION

SUMMERS, Chief Justice

Appellant (Lakeway) contends that the intention of the parties, as set forth in the contract, was for a total purchase price of $25,820.00; that how it was paid, whether in dollars or in pesos, was immaterial so long as the result to the seller was the required number of dollars; and that the peso figure in parenthesis was simply for the convenience of the buyer to let him know how many pesos would be required to buy the property. It urges that this intention is supported by the fact that the contract provides that "Seller agrees to notify Buyers in writing of the total amount due in Mexican pesos if a change in the official exchange rate occurs prior to such payment." We agree with these contentions.

However, in the instant case a check payable in the correct amount of pesos for final payment under the contract was delivered to Lakeway by the Bravos on August 18, 1976; such check was received by Lakeway without objection; said check was honored and cleared appellees' bank account on August 30, 1976, prior to the devaluation of the peso, which occurred on August 31, 1976; and when honored and paid in due course, the payment became absolute and related back to the date of delivery of the check on August 18, 1976; and as of said date of delivery it produced the specified value in dollars and satisfied the terms of the contract.

The judgment of the trial court is affirmed.

CASE QUESTIONS

1. What was the land purchase price?
2. How much did Lakeway lose once there was devaluation?
3. Will Lakeway get more money?
4. How did the contract address the issue of devaluation?

BIOGRAPHY

The NFL: A Third Party in Every Athlete's Contract

Former Atlanta Falcons quarterback Michael Vick served an 18-month sentence in federal prison after pleading guilty to dogfighting and conspiracy charges. The dogs were kept on one of Mr. Vick's properties. Nike pulled, swiftly, Mr. Vick's endorsement deal on its fifth shoe with the swift quarterback. Adidas suspended sales of Vick shirts. Coca-Cola and Kraft indicated that there would be no more Vick endorsements for their products. Provisions in contracts on indictments for criminal conduct provide the companies and franchises with the authority to end the relationship.

The NFL Commissioner prohibited Mr. Vick from playing in the NFL without prior approval. Following negotiations with the Philadelphia Eagles, Mr. Vick received an offer from the team for a two-year contract, with $1.6 million for the first year and an option on the second year for $5.2 million.

However, the NFL controls performance of the contract for Mr. Vick's probationary period with the league. The NFL decided that the Eagles could contract with Mr. Vick but limited the terms of performance for 2009. Under those terms, Mr. Vick could practice with the team, but was not permitted to play until the third preseason game. Also, both Mr. Vick's NFL approval for play and his contract with the Eagles have a so-called morals clause. That is, if Mr. Vick violates any of the terms of his probation, which would include any arrests or charges, he would be suspended again and he would also be in breach of contract. This morals clause is more stringent and well defined than those in other contracts because of the ongoing probation supervision. Violations of his probation could include possession of a weapon, the failure to meet his probation officer as required, the failure to meet the terms of community service requirements, and travel outside the country without prior approval.

Vick's 30th birthday celebration in Virginia Beach, Virginia, in July 2010 created a bit of a problem for the NFL, the Eagles, and contract clauses. Keeping company with one of the co-defendants in his dog-fighting case, Mr. Vick was enjoying the festivities when somehow the celebration reached a point of gunfire. Vick's role remains unclear, but as *Sports Illustrated* noted, the video and Vick's side of the tale of birthday parties gone bad do not match. The NFL and the Eagles did not suspend Mr. Vick.

In another situation, the NFL commissioner banished Pittsburgh Steelers quarterback Ben Roethlisberger from playing for that team for six games. A prosecutor in Georgia declined to prosecute Mr. Roethlisberger for allegedly raping a 20-year-old. The young woman did not want to see Mr. Roethlisberger prosecuted. Mr. Roethlisberger is the first NFL player who has been disciplined even though no criminal charges were brought. Commissioner Roger Goodell indicated the six-game suspension could be longer if Mr. Roethlisberger did not improve his off-the-field behavior, "It's my responsibility to protect our reputation and our integrity. That's what the personal conduct policy is; we all have to be held to a higher standard. It specifically states you don't have to violate the law if there is a pattern of behavior. We go back through all the incidents and try to understand is there is any kind of pattern and we have enough information to believe he's not making sound judgments at critical points."

Summary

What if the assumptions made and the information given turn out to be untrue? Must the parties still go forward with the contract?

- Contract defense—situation, term, or event that excuses performance

- Capacity—mental and age thresholds for valid contracts

- Voidable contract—one party can choose not to honor the contract

- Puffing—statements of opinion

- Material fact—basis of the bargain
- Void contract—contract that courts will not honor
- Misrepresentation—incomplete or inaccurate information prior to contract execution
- Rescission—setting aside of contract as a remedy
- Fraud—intentional misrepresentation
- *Scienter*—knowledge that information given is false
- Duress—physical or mental force that deprives party of a meaningful choice with respect to a proposed contract
- Undue influence—exerting control over another party for purposes of gain
- Confidential relationship—trust, confidence, reliance in a relationship
- Public policy—standards of decency
- Exculpatory clauses—attempt to hold oneself harmless for one's own conduct
- Unconscionable contract—contract that is grossly unfair

If one party does not perform, is the other side excused? When is performance required and when is it excused?

- Conditions precedent—advance events that must occur before performance is due, for example, obtaining financing
- Substantial performance—performance that, for practical purposes, is just as good as full-performance

- Commercial impracticability—defense to performance of sales contract based on objective impracticability
- Novation—agreement to change contract among all affected, for example, agreement to substitute parties
- Accord and satisfaction—agreement entered into as settlement of a disputed debt
- Obligation of good faith—must perform in a reasonable fashion; performance must meet commercial standards

What remedies exist?

- Compensatory damages—amount required to place party in as good a position as before breach
- Incidental damages—costs of collecting compensatory damages
- Liquidated damages—agreement clause in contract that preestablishes and limits damages
- Consequential damages—damages owed to third parties from a breach

What are the contract performance issues in international business?

- Bill of lading—title document used to control transfer of goods
- Letter of credit—pledge by bank of availability of funds for a transaction
- Exchange rate and risk issues in contracts

Questions and Problems

1. On December 5, 1997, Michael Dekofsky and Christopher Vrakelos sold Brea Range, Inc., an indoor shooting range, to Michael J. and Kimberly A. Hansen for $140,000. The Hansens paid $70,000 cash and assumed two promissory notes due and owing from the corporation to Mr. Dekofsky and Mr. Vrakelos. After escrow closed, the Hansens discovered that two patrons committed suicide at Brea Range, in 1995 and March 1997.

The Hansens made interest payments on the promissory notes until January 1, 1999, defaulted on the first principal payment, and ceased making payments on June 1, 1999. Mr. Dekofsky and Mr. Vrakelos sued for the balance due. The Hansens defended on the theory that the sellers had unclean hands and breached a duty to disclose material facts. In a cross-complaint, the Hansens sued for conspiracy, fraud, misrepresentation, and rescission. Do the Hansens have a valid defense to the contract's formation? Was there misrepresentation?

Was there fraud? [*Dekofsky v Brea Range, Inc.*, 2001 WL 1613509, (Cal. App. 2 Dist.) (not printed in Cal. Rptr.—unpublished opinion)]

2. The late Tony Curtis, a respected actor, entered into a contract to write a novel for Doubleday & Company, publishers. Because of complex divorce proceedings and other personal factors, Mr. Curtis was unable to submit a satisfactory manuscript. Doubleday demanded a return of the $50,000 advance Mr. Curtis had received. Is Doubleday entitled to it? [*Doubleday & Co. v Curtis*, 763 F.2d 495 (2d Cir. 1985)]

3. Bernina Sewing Machines imports sewing machines and parts for U.S. distribution. Its contract prices are in francs. Because of the devaluation of the U.S. dollar, Bernina wants to be excused from its contracts. Can it be excused under any contract doctrine? [*Bernina Distributors, Inc. v Bernina Sewing Machines*, 646 F.2d 434 (10th Cir. 1981)]

4. Would failure to disclose a delinquency on your mortgage on a loan application be a misrepresentation? What about not disclosing that your company was about to impose a 20 percent salary reduction on all employees? [*Barrer v Women's National Bank*, 761 F.2d 752 (D.C. 1985)]

5. Dan O'Connor paid $125 to have the University of Notre Dame's leprechaun mascot tattooed on his upper arm with the words "Fighting Irish" inscribed above the little gnome. The tattoo parlor inscribed the chosen leprechaun and "Fighing Irish."

Mr. O'Connor's girlfriend pointed out the spelling error, and Mr. O'Connor filed suit against the Tattoo Shoppe in Carlstadt, New Jersey, seeking unspecified damages.

Mr. O'Connor noted, "I was irate, and for a minute or two after I cooled down I kind of giggled. But I can't just live with this. You're not talking about a dented car where you can get another one . . . you're talking about flesh."

What damages should Mr. O'Connor receive? Would a refund of $125 be enough? What if the Tattoo Shoppe had a clause in its contract limiting damages to a refund? Would it be valid?

6. Northland Ford Dealers sponsored a hole-in-one contest at the Moccasin Creek Country Club in South Dakota. The contest winner would receive a new Ford Explorer. Jennifer Harms registered for the contest. She stood at the women's marker for teeing off and hit a hole-in-one. She was denied her car because the dealers' insurance policy for the event indicated the following, "ALL AMATEUR MEN AND WOMEN SHALL UTILIZE THE SAME TEE." That tee was established in the policy as 170 yards. However, the men and women participating in the contest were not told of this rule or restriction. Must the dealers give Ms. Harms her Ford Explorer, or will she remain "teed off"? [*Harms v Northland Ford Dealers*, 602 N.W. 2d 58 (S.D. 1999)]

7. Robert Hackett became a substitute fireman for the city of New Britain, Connecticut, in 1949. In 1950, he was made a full-time fireman and in 1968 became a lieutenant. After earning the highest mark on the captain's examination, he was promoted to captain in 1974. He then scored the highest score on the deputy chief exam and was promoted to that rank in 1977.

Mr. Hackett had paid an employee in the city department responsible for administering the exams to ensure that he earned the highest grades (which he did). He had, in effect, purchased his last two promotions. When these acts were discovered (after Mr. Hackett had retired), criminal charges were brought against him and the city employee. Both were convicted of felonies.

The pension board of New Britain then met and voted to reduce Mr. Hackett's pension by $5,483.97 a year because that reduction placed his pension at the level it would have been without the last two promotions. The board said the reduction was necessary because the last two promotions were obtained through illegal conduct. Mr. Hackett filed suit. Is illegality a defense to Hackett's suit for his full pension? [*Hackett v City of New Britain*, 477 A.2d 148 (Conn. 1984)]

8. On February 21, 1990, Robert Barto and his wife signed an agreement with Estate Motors, Ltd., of Birmingham, Michigan, to purchase a Mercedes Benz 500 SL automobile. Doug MacFarlane, their salesperson, told the Bartos that because of high demand, their car might not be delivered for 18 months.

In mid-August 1991, Mr. MacFarlane telephoned Mr. Barto and informed him that his Mercedes would be at the dealership and ready for pickup on August 30. Mr. MacFarlane also informed Mr. Barto in that telephone conversation for the first time that he would have to pay a luxury tax on his new car (in addition to the purchase price, state sales tax, and license/title fees) when he came to pick it up.

Mr. Barto was angry about having to pay the luxury tax because he believed that his car fell within the scope of the preexisting binding contract exception, as his order for the car had been placed before September 30, 1990. During the ensuing weeks before his car arrived at Estate Motors, Mr. Barto telephoned the Mercedes-Benz district sales representatives and legal counsel and was informed that Mercedes-Benz was advising their dealers that the new luxury tax was not to be assessed on cars ordered before September 30, 1990. Mr. Barto also learned that of the 114 Mercedes-Benz dealers within the Midwest region, only Estate Motors was assessing the tax on cars ordered before September 30, 1990.

Mr. Barto attempted to negotiate a manner of payment of the tax with Estate Motors. He first proposed that he bring with him two checks when he picked up his car—one check payable to Estate Motors for everything but the amount of the luxury tax, and one check for the luxury tax payable to the IRS. The dealer refused this arrangement. Mr. Barto then suggested that he pay the luxury tax into an escrow account. Again the dealer refused. Because Mr. Barto wanted his new car, he ultimately agreed to pay Estate Motors the full purchase price, including the luxury tax assessment.

On August 30, 1991, when Mr. Barto went to Estate Motors to pick up his Mercedes-Benz, he tendered to the dealer his check for $111,446 to cover the $99,950 purchase price of the car, the sales tax/license/title fees of $4,501, and the 10 percent luxury tax amounting to $6,995. Mr. Barto and the dealer also executed on August 30 Estate Motors' "Statement of Vehicle Sale," which reflected the breakdown of his $111,946 total purchase price, license/title transfer and proof of insurance information, and the odometer disclosure.

Mr. Barto continued to protest having to pay the $6,995 luxury tax on his new Mercedes after picking up the car. The dealer provided Mr. Barto with a blank IRS 843 form for a tax refund. When the IRS denied Mr. Barto's claim a refund, he filed suit against Estate.

Mr. Barto wished to rescind the agreement. He wanted his money back. Is Mr. Barto entitled to it? Is there a contract at all? [*Barto v United States*, 823 F. Supp. 1369 (E.D. Mich. 1993)]

9. Betty Lobianco had a burglar alarm system installed in her home by Property Protection, Inc. The contract for installing the system provided:

> *Alarm system equipment installed by Property Protection, Inc. is guaranteed against improper function due to manufacturing defects or workmanship for a period of 12 months. The installation of the above equipment carries a 90-day warranty. The liability of Property Protection, Inc. is limited to repair or replacement of security alarm equipment and does not include loss or damage to possessions, persons, or property.*

On November 22, 1975, Ms. Lobianco's home was burglarized and $35,815 in jewelry was taken. The alarm system, which had been installed less than ninety days earlier, included a standby source of power in case the regular source of power failed. On the day of the fateful burglary, the alarm did not go off because the batteries installed in the system had no power.

Ms. Lobianco brought suit to recover the $35,815. She claimed that the liability limitation was unconscionable and unenforceable under the UCC. Property Protection claimed that the UCC did not apply to the installation of a burglar alarm system. Who is correct? [*Lobianco v Property Protection, Inc.*, 437 A.2d 417 (Pa. 1981)]

10. Boeing Company was scheduled to deliver several of its 747-400 jumbo jetliners to Northwest Airlines by December 31, 1988. Northwest set that deadline because it needed the $16 million in investment tax credits the planes would bring. Boeing missed the December 31 deadline, and Northwest wants to recover compensation from Boeing for the lost tax credits. Could Northwest recover for these lost credits?

Organizational Behavior, Economics, Ethics, and the Law

Marty Ummel, a homebuyer, brought suit against her real estate agent for his failure to disclose that homes in the area in which she bought her home had declined substantially in value. Mrs. Ummel said that she and her retired husband decided to move from the San Francisco area to the San Diego area in order to be near their grown children. They did market research and had already used one broker and cancelled two deals before settling on ReMax agent Mike Little, who signed the Ummels to a contract for the purchase of a home (owned by another real estate agent) for $1.2 million. Little acted as the mortgage broker for the Ummels as well.

Mrs. Ummel said that Mr. Little told them several times that the house was a good value, but Mr. Little did not disclose that there were listings down the street from her home for $105,000 less that were larger properties.

Experts say brokers aren't appraisers and can't opine on value, and that buyers should do their due diligence. However, Mrs. Ummel says that she trusted Mr. Little and that he breached that trust. Other experts note the pressure the broker feels: "Agents have a lot of fiduciary duties, but they don't make money unless they close the sale."[2] Other experts say that the Ummels just didn't do what responsible and sophisticated buyers should do in researching a property, and now seek to blame someone else for their loss.

Was there misrepresentation? Is it a defense that the agent simply cannot predict when the market has shifted? How does the real estate firm deal with the drive for commissions among their agents? What happens if you shift responsibility for market research to agents?

Notes

1. International history has played a role in the development of *force majeure* clauses because wars, trade, and international relations influence contract rights and performance. For more information, see the course website.

2. David Streitfeld, "Feeling Misled on Home Prices, Buyers Are Suing Their Agent," *New York Times*, Jan. 22, 2008, pp. A1, A14.

CHAPTER 14

Financing of Sales and Leases: *Credit and Disclosure Requirements*

The English refer to credit sales as "buying on the never never" because you never really pay for everything; there is always some outstanding credit. Credit sales are a way of life in the United States. Nearly all sellers advertise not only their products but also the availability of credit terms for buyers. Congress and state legislatures have both enacted statutes regulating credit contracts. This chapter covers those regulations and credit contracts. How is a credit contract set up? What are the requirements? What statutes affect the credit contract? How are credit contracts enforced? ■

Neither a borrower nor a lender be, For a loan oft loses both itself and friend And borrowing dulls the edge of husbandry.

Hamlet, Act 1, Scene 3

Consumer Credit Outstanding (per Federal Reserve Bank) (includes revolving and nonrevolving)

	$ billions
2005	$2291.7
2006	$2385.7
2007	$2522.8
2008	$2561.1
2009	$2448.8
2010	$2447.9

UPDATE
For up-to-date legal news, go to
mariannejennings.com

Delinquency Rate of Consumer Loans

Year	Percent of Loans Outstanding
2001	2.41%
2003	3.93%
2004	3.52%
2005	3.75%
2006	1.94%
2007	3.06%
2008	6.01%
2009	9.38%

Subprime mortgage delinquency rate (2009)   41%
Mortgage delinquency rate (2009)   9.4%

Upon first exposure to the subject of credit regulation, the impression of the average attorney might be that the field is a maze, if not a mess, and probably both.

Christopher L. Peterson

In "Truth, Understanding, and High-Cost Consumer Credit: The Historical Context of the Truth in Lending Act," 55 Fla. L. Rev. 807 (2003)

CONSIDER...

In February 1995, A.B. & S., an auto repair shop owned by Jerry I. Bonner, an African American, applied for a $230,000 business loan from the South Shore Bank. Mr. Bonner submitted the required Small Business Administration Loan Form 912 on December 27, 1994. In response to the question about arrests and convictions, Mr. Bonner noted the following:

1. Domestic matter between 1982 and 1984
2. Conviction for aggravated battery and assault in 1983 (claims self-defense)
3. Possession of a controlled substance in 1985
4. Disorderly conduct between 1985 and 1990
5. Possession of a controlled substance in 1990
6. Possession of a stolen car in September 1994

The bank denied the loan.

Mr. Bonner filed suit under the Equal Credit Opportunity Act, alleging that the bank's practice of considering criminal records has an unlawful disparate impact on African American men. Can the bank consider Mr. Bonner's criminal record in making a loan decision?

Establishing a Credit Contract

A credit contract not only needs the usual elements of a contract (as covered in Chapter 12), including offer, acceptance, and consideration, but also requires additional information for the credit agreement to be valid. The following list covers the extra details needed in a credit contract:

1. How much the buyer/debtor is actually carrying on credit or financing
2. The rate of interest the buyer/debtor will pay
3. How many payments will be made, when they will be made, and for how long
4. Penalties and actions for late payments
5. Whether the creditor will have collateral
6. The necessary statutory disclosures on credit transactions

Statutory Requirements for Credit Contracts

The following statutes affect and, in some cases, control the terms in a credit contract. Exhibit 14.1 summarizes the federal statutes.

State Usury Laws

Usury is charging an interest rate higher than the maximum permitted by law. If the maximum rate of interest permitted by statute is 36 percent, a creditor charging 38 percent has violated a statute and created a void contract.

The usury rate varies from state to state, and many states have different usury rates for the various types of transactions. For example, the usury rate for real estate loans may be lower than the usury rate for credit cards or installment credit transactions. Some states' usury rates are just a percentage figure, whereas other states include loan origination charges, finders' fees, service charges, and other fees paid by the debtor in determining the actual rate of interest charged.

Penalties for charging a usurious rate also vary. Some states treat the usurious agreement as completely void, and the penalty for the creditor is forfeiture of interest and principal. Other states allow the creditor to recoup the principal but deny any interest. Some states simply require the creditor to forfeit any interest above the maximum; others also impose a penalty on the creditor by allowing the debtor to collect two or three times the amount of excess interest charged as damages.

The Subprime Lending Market

From 2004 through 2006, there was a significant increase in the number of high-interest loans. These high-interest loans have often been "do-or-die" loans secured by titles to cars and homes, or loans secured by paychecks (sometimes called

EXHIBIT 14.1 Summary of Federal Laws on Consumer Credit

CREDIT STATUTE (FEDERAL)	PURPOSE AND SCOPE
Equal Credit Opportunity Act 15 U.S.C. § 1691 (1974)	Prohibits discrimination on the basis of sex, race, age, or national origin in credit extension decision
Consumer Credit Protection Act (CCPA) 15 U.S.C. § 1601 (1968)	Umbrella statute passed to deal with fairness of consumer credit transactions
Truth in Lending Act 15 U.S.C. § 1601 (1968)	Part of CCPA that governs disclosure of credit terms
Amendments (1995) 15 U.S.C. § 1605	Closes loopholes for avoiding loan repayments based on clerical errors in loan documents
Fair Credit and Charge Card Disclosure Act 15 U.S.C. § 1646 (1988)	Provides for disclosure requirements in the solicitation of credit cards
Regulation Z 12 C.F.R. § 226 (1981)	Federal Reserve Board regulations providing details for all disclosure statutes
Home Equity Loan Consumer Protection Act 15 U.S.C. § 1647 (1988)	Disclosure requirements for home equity loans and a rescission period
Home Ownership and Equity Protection Act (HOEPA) 15 U.S.C. § 1637 (1994)	Disclosure requirements on payment amounts for home equity loans and cancellation rights
Fair Credit Billing Act 15 U.S.C. § 1637 (1974)	Rights of debtors on open-end credit billing disputes
Fair Credit Reporting Act 15 U.S.C. § 1681 (1970)	Rights of debtors with respect to reports of their credit histories
Consumer Leasing Act 15 U.S.C. § 1667 (1976)	Disclosure requirements for leases of goods by consumers
Fair Debt Collections Practices Act 15 U.S.C. § 1692 (1977)	Regulation of conduct of third-party bill collectors and attorneys
Credit Repair Organization Act (1996) 15 U.S.C. § 1679b	Prohibits misrepresentations by credit repair organizations to consumers seeking help with credit issues
Service Members Civil Relief Act (2003) 50 U.S.C. §§ 501 *et seq.*	Prevents foreclosure while debtor is on active military duty
Defense Authorization Act of 2007 50 U.S.C. §§ 501 *et seq.*	Caps interest on credit to members of military at 36% APR; additional disclosure requirements; administered by Department of Defense
Credit Card Accountability, Responsibility, and Disclosure Act (CARD) 15 U.S.C. § 1666 *et seq.*	New regulations on billing cycle, late fees, disclosures, gift cards, and pay-offs
Dodd–Frank Wall Street Reform and Consumer Financial Protection Act (DFCFPA) also known as The Consumer Financial Protection Act of 2010 (CFPA) Amends various sections of 12 U.S.C. and 15 U.S.C.	Creates the Bureau of Consumer Financial Protection to consolidate regulation of consumer credit and the Federal Insurance Office to increase access of moderate-income individuals to insurance products; imposes additional rules on checking accounts, credit cards, and bank charges and fees

payday loans). In the subprime mortgage market, because of the demand from the secondary market for mortgages to purchase, many borrowers made no down payment on their homes or were qualified without verification of income. The loans were made instantly, and at terms that seemed affordable for borrowers at the time but that then added interest, deferred payments, and/or rate increases. The *subprime lending market*, and other forms of lending to high-risk borrowers, including title and payday (*predatory lending)* loans are now targeted by state and local regulators.

The **Dodd–Frank Consumer Financial Protection Act (DFCFPA), also known as the Wall Street Reform and Consumer Financial Protection Act or the Consumer Financial Protection Act (CFPA),** imposes new requirements on lenders for disclosures to borrowers about loan terms and also controls mortgage lenders' compensation relationships with mortgage brokers. The CFPA prohibits brokers and lenders from steering borrowers into higher-rate loans through the use of incentive systems. Compensation arrangements before the real estate and subprime mortgage markets collapsed centered on yield spread premiums (YSPs), which tied mortgage broker compensation to the amount the borrower's interest rates exceeded the mortgage lender's cost. The higher the mortgage rate, the greater the commission the brokers earned on the loans, despite the fact that the borrower might not be able to repay once those higher rates took effect. The penalty for lenders who use such incentive systems is up to three years of interest payments on the loan. CFPA establishes a Housing Counseling Office within the Department of Housing and Urban Development (HUD) to help consumers understand the nature of their loans and payments.

DFCPA also regulates mortgage lending standards. Mortgage lending and credit practices have become more rigorous and loans and credit are more difficult to obtain. In addition, a new field of lending in response to the high rate of subprime defaults, known as *mortgage rescue lending*, has emerged. The federal government has created several programs for assisting borrowers who mortgages are "under water," which means that they owe more on their homes than they are worth. The Federal Loan Assistance Program (FLAP) is for borrowers with Fannie Mae and Freddie Mac mortgages and includes loan refinancing and loan modification/restructuring programs. Credit extension, credit terms, and defaults are now matters of daily discussion among consumers, legislators, and regulators.

Ethical Issues

Michael McKinney bought a five-bedroom home near Baltimore, Maryland, for $1,000,000 in October 2007. Mr. McKinney put 30 percent down and financed the remaining $700,000. He is current on his $4,400 payments, which are one-half of his monthly income. The value of his property has dropped $130,000. Mr. McKinney says, "People like me are cut out of the process. Why are people in some parts of the country being penalized by a limit that doesn't reflect reality in many areas?"[1] Evaluate Mr. McKinney's mortgage commitment and whether the government programs should be used to help him. Would you accept an approved mortgage loan that you knew was stretching your budget? What are the moral hazards here? Does it matter that re-default rates are 55 percent six months after restructuring?

The Equal Credit Opportunity Act

The **Equal Credit Opportunity Act** (ECOA) was passed to ensure that credit was denied or awarded on the applicant's merits—the ability to pay—and not on such extraneous factors as sex, race, color, religion, national origin, or age. (See Exhibit 14.1 on p. 459.)

Standards for Credit Evaluation Under the ECOA

Creditors may ask about these subject areas for record-keeping purposes, but the decision to extend or deny credit must be based on other factors. The following sections discuss other types of information that cannot be considered in making the credit decision:

1. Marital status of the applicant
2. Applicant's receipt of public assistance income
3. Applicant's receipt of alimony or child support payments
4. Applicant's plans for having children

The ECOA also provides married persons the right to have individual credit applications, lines, and ratings. Credit applications must specify that a spouse's income need not be disclosed unless the applicant is relying on that income to qualify for credit. Further, even on joint accounts, debtors can require creditors to report credit ratings individually for the spouses.

BUSINESS STRATEGY

How to Evaluate Credit Risk

Lawrence B. Lindsey, then 41, who at the time earned $123,100 a year, applied for a Toys "R" Us credit card through the Delaware division of the Bank of New York. He had paid his mortgage on time each month and had a clean credit record and job security. Mr. Lindsey's application was rejected; the letter from the bank explained as follows: "We have received your new account application. We regret that we are not able to approve it at this time."

The bank used a computerized scoring system to evaluate credit applications, and Mr. Lindsey's was rejected, according to his letter, because "Multiple companies requested your credit report in the past six months."

Mr. Lindsey was, at the time, a member of the Federal Reserve Board, the federal agency that sets interest rates and regulates banks. (From 2001 to 2003, he was an economic advisor in the Bush administration and is now CEO of his own consulting firm as well as a scholar at the American Enterprise Institute.) He has expressed concerns about computerized credit scoring and has said, "I would expect credit-scoring type procedures to be overwhelmingly dominant by the end of the decade. We will obtain the fairness of the machine but lose the judgments, talents, and sense of justice that only humans can bring to decision making."

Discussion Questions

1. How is computer scoring of credit applications more fair? Are there advantages to computer scoring?
2. What problems does computer scoring create?
3. Do you foresee a time when computer scoring will be regulated?

A.B. & S. Auto Service, Inc. v South Shore Bank of Chicago (Case 14.1) involves an issue of an ECOA violation and also provides the answer to the chapter's opening "Consider."

CASE 14.1	A.B. & S. Auto Service, Inc. v South Shore Bank of Chicago
	962 F.Supp. 1056 (N.D. Ill. 1997)

Do the Crime, Forget the Loan

FACTS

A.B. & S. Auto Service, Inc. (AB&S) is an automobile repair shop located in Chicago, Illinois. Jerry L. Bonner is AB&S's president, and he is an African American. South Shore is a commercial bank that maintains three branches on Chicago's South Side and a loan office in the Austin neighborhood on Chicago's West Side. South Shore participates in the Small Business Administration's (SBA) loan guarantee program.

The SBA requires all applicants for the loan guarantee program to fill out an SBA Form 912 Statement of Personal History. SBA Form 912 asks applicants if they have ever been charged with or arrested or convicted for any criminal offense other than a minor motor vehicle violation and, if so, asks applicants to provide details. Form 912 also provides:

The fact that you have an arrest or conviction record will not necessarily disqualify you.

Before submitting a loan package for SBA approval, the bank is expected to make an independent determination regarding the criminal record in evaluating the applicant's character.

In February 1995, AB&S applied for a $230,000 business loan from the bank after having a similar SBA request denied by La Salle Bank Lakeview. Mr. Bonner submitted a Form 912 on December 27, 1994. In response to the question about arrests and convictions, Mr. Bonner noted the following:

1. Domestic matters between 1982 and 1984
2. Conviction for aggravated battery and assault (1983) (claims self-defense)
3. Possession of a controlled substance in 1985
4. Disorderly conduct between 1985 and 1990
5. Possession of a controlled substance in 1990
6. Possession of a stolen car in September 1994

Leslie Davis, an African-American vice president at South Shore Bank, recommended approval of Mr. Bonner's application. However, the loan committee agreed that because of Mr. Bonner's criminal record, the application should be denied. The bank then decided to deny the loan.

During the last 15 years, the South Shore Bank had made at least three business loans to applicants with criminal records. One of these three applicants was an African American. South Shore evaluates each application on an individual basis and examines criminal record and other information for purposes of determining character.

Mr. Bonner and his company (plaintiffs) filed suit under the ECOA, alleging that the bank's practice of considering criminal record has an unlawful disparate impact on African-American men. South Shore Bank (defendants) moved for summary judgment because Mr. Bonner did not establish a case of discrimination. Mr. Bonner also moved for summary judgment on the grounds that consideration of criminal record without tying it to creditworthiness violated the ECOA.

JUDICIAL OPINION

WILLIAMS, Anne Claire, District Judge

A credit applicant can prove discrimination under the ECOA by using any one of the following three different approaches used in the employment discrimination context: 1) direct evidence of discrimination; 2) disparate impact analysis, also called the "effects" test; or 3) disparate treatment analysis.

In order to prove discrimination under the disparate impact analysis or "effects" test, an applicant must show how "a policy, procedure, or practice specifically identified by the [applicant] has a significantly greater discriminatory impact on members of a protected class." Plaintiffs traditionally establish this prima facie case by making "a statistical comparison of the representation of the protected class in the applicant pool with representation in the group actually accepted from the pool. . . . If the statistical disparity is significant, then plaintiff is deemed to have made out a prima facie case."

Once the plaintiff has made the prima facie case, the defendant-lender must demonstrate that any policy, procedure, or practice has a manifest relationship to the creditworthiness of the applicant. In other words, the onus is on the defendant to show that the particular practice makes defendant's credit evaluation system more predictive than it would be otherwise.

Courts have held that the use of general population statistics is insufficient to make out a prima facie case under the ECOA.

In *Saldana v Citibank*, 1996 WL 332451 (N.D. Ill. 1996), the plaintiff loan-applicant sued Citibank claiming it denied her loan based on its policy of redlining. Saldana tried to make her case under the disparate impact theory. Specifically, she claimed that Citibank had an unwritten policy that set the minimum amount for a rehab loan at $100,000. This policy, she claims, disproportionately impacted the African-American community because few African-Americans could meet this financial test based on their income and net worth. Saldana offered statistical evidence regarding 1) the bank's loan approval rate for loans over $100,000 in the Austin area; 2) the bank's loan rejection rate for white and African-American applicants in comparison with their representation in the greater Chicago community; and 3) the bank's average refinancing approval and average rejection rate in Austin in comparison to the City of Chicago's average approval and rejection rates. While the court found that this last set of statistics successfully presented some statistical evidence comparing the Austin community to the greater Chicago community, the court still found that "these statistics are of a very general nature and do not relate specifically to the policy identified as having a discriminatory impact."

Similarly, in *Cherry v Amoco Oil Co.*, 490 F.Supp. 1026 (N.D. Ga. 1980), the credit-card applicant sued Amoco Oil Company, alleging that Amoco's use of zip code ratings in Atlanta, which assigned low-ratings to those zip code areas where Amoco had unfavorable delinquency experience, adversely effected [*sic*] black applicants disproportionately.

Plaintiffs claim that South Shore Bank's practice of considering an applicant's criminal record in making commercial lending decisions has a disparate impact on African-Americans. To make the prima facie case plaintiffs offer the testimony of Dr. Jaslin U. Salmon. Dr. Salmon testified that any decision that is based on arrest records would militate against people of color. He suggests that, based on his research, there are many cases in which the black applicant is qualified, credit worthy, but was not given the loan for other reasons and among those reasons, arrest records had been taken into consideration. However, the bank disputes this point because Dr. Salmon was unable to identify a single study showing that consideration of arrest records has a disproportionate impact on African-American applicants for any type of credit, much less any study addressing the impact on business loan applicants.

In addition to Dr. Salmon's testimony, plaintiffs offer the general population statistics of arrest by race in 1990. Considering these general population statistics, the court finds that these statistics are insufficient to make out a prima facie case under the ECOA. The court recognizes that the ECOA prohibits creditors from inquiring into the race, sex, or marital status of an applicant. This in turn places plaintiffs in a difficult position of trying to prove disproportionate impact without any access to a creditor's statistical lending profile. Plaintiffs can refer to the general population as long as plaintiffs clearly demonstrate that the applicant pool would possess approximately the same characteristics. Considering the statistical proof and the testimony of Dr. Salmon, the court finds that plaintiffs have not made this showing that the applicant pool possesses approximately the same characteristics as the general population.

Both the statistics and Dr. Salmon's supporting testimony do not answer the following questions: 1) how many African-Americans with convictions or arrests are otherwise qualified for the loan; and 2) how many African-Americans are deterred from applying because of the bank's practice. Plaintiffs' evidence is further undermined, as it was in *Hill*, by the fact that the bank's practice of considering an applicant's criminal record was not consistently applied to disqualify applicants with criminal records. Rather, the bank has made at least three business loans to applicants with criminal records. One of these three applicants with criminal records is African-American.

South Shore Bank's practice of inquiring into a credit applicant's criminal history is legitimately related to its extension of credit for two reasons. First, the regulations require the SBA, in evaluating a loan guarantee application, to consider "the character, reputation, and credit history of the applicant, its associates, and guarantors." 13 C.F.R. § 120.150. As a participant in the SBA loan guarantee program, South Shore Bank is obligated to consider an applicant's criminal record provided on SBA Form 912 in its evaluation of a loan applicant's character.

Secondly, the bank's inquiry into an applicant's criminal record provides relevant information about an applicant's creditworthiness, particularly his judgment and character. Plaintiff Bonner admits that several of the incidents described in his completed SBA Form 912: possession of a controlled substance, domestic abuse, and disorderly conduct, reflected negatively on his judgment and character. Specifically, Bonner admits that these incidents involved an exercise of bad judgment. Therefore, because an applicant's judgment and character may legitimately be considered in making commercial lending decisions, South Shore Bank's practice of considering criminal history as it relates to

CONTINUED

character and judgment bears a legitimate and manifest relationship to the extension of credit. Therefore, the court finds that the bank has successfully demonstrated that its practice of inquiring into a credit applicant's criminal record is legitimately related to the extension of credit.

For the foregoing reasons, the court grants defendant South Shore Bank's motion for summary judgment and denies plaintiff Bonner and AB&S's motion for summary judgment.

CASE QUESTIONS

1. Who asked for the information about the loan applicant's criminal record?
2. What, according to Mr. Bonner's expert, is the impact of considering criminal records of applicants?
3. Is the use of the criminal record in making a decision to extend credit a violation of the ECOA?
4. Do you think a criminal record is an indication of character?

CONSIDER... 14.1

Lucas Rosa, a biological male, went to Park West Bank & Trust dressed in traditionally feminine attire. He requested a loan application from Norma Brunelle, a bank employee. Ms. Brunelle asked Mr. Rosa for identification. Mr. Rosa produced three forms of photo identification: (1) a Massachusetts Department of Public Welfare Card; (2) a Massachusetts Identification Card; and (3) a Money Stop Check Cashing ID Card. Ms. Brunelle looked at the identification cards and told Mr. Rosa that she would not provide him with a loan application until he "went home and changed." She said that he had to be dressed like one of the identification cards in which he appeared in more traditionally male attire before she would provide him with a loan application and process his loan request. Rosa sued the Bank for violations of the ECOA. The bank moved for summary judgment and the court granted judgment for the bank, finding that there could be no possible theory under the ECOA for discrimination. Did the bank violate ECOA? Be sure to explain your answer.

THINK: The ECOA requires that the decision to not extend credit be related to creditworthiness and not factors such as race, marital status, age, gender, and so on.

APPLY: In this case, the applicant (Mr. Rosa) applied for credit dressed as a woman but his forms of ID showed him to be a man. There may not be enough evidence in the case. The issue is the basis for the request that he go home and change clothes. If the request for changed clothes was based on the need for proper ID, there was no discrimination. If the request was based on discrimination against gay or transgendered individuals, there was no discrimination under the ECOA because those are not categories. If the request to change was because the bank only wished to make loans to male customers, then there was discrimination.

ANSWER: The bank was not entitled to summary judgment until the court determined the reason for the request that Mr. Rosa change clothes. Some of the reasons for requesting the change could be discriminatory and some are not. The ECOA has specific categories and the action of the bank employee does not meet those categories under some reasons for requesting the change of clothes, but it would do on the basis of other reasons. Determining the reason for the request is key to determining whether there was discrimination. [*Rosa v Park West Bank & Trust Co.*, 214 F.3d 213 (1st Cir. 2000)]

Enforcement of the ECOA

Violations of the ECOA carry statutory penalties. The ECOA was enforced by the Federal Trade Commission (FTC), but with the passage of the CFPA will now be enforced by the Bureau of Consumer Financial Protection (BCFP) and the U.S.

attorney general, and through private actions by debtors. Debtors can recover their actual damages for embarrassment and emotional distress and also punitive damages of up to $10,000. If a group of debtors brings a class action against a creditor, it can collect punitive damages of up to the lesser of $500,000 or 1 percent of the creditor's net worth. Punitive damages are recoverable even when no actual damages occur. In addition, the CFPA provides for the creation of the federal Office of Fair Lending and Equal Opportunity to provide a single resource for enforcement.

The Truth in Lending Act

The **Truth in Lending Act** (TILA) is actually part of the **Consumer Credit Protection Act** passed in 1968 by Congress (15 U.S.C. § 1601), which was the first federal statute to deal with credit issues. Its purpose was to make sure debtors were treated fairly through adequate disclosure of credit terms. While the Federal Reserve Board was originally delegated the responsibility for enforcing the TILA, the new BCFP, created under the CFPA will now assume that enforcement role. The BCFP will be funded by the Federal Reserve but it will be independent, with its director appointed by the president of the United States. **Regulation Z** (12 C.F.R. § 226), which was promulgated to carry out the provisions of the TILA, is perhaps better known than the statute that gave rise to it.

TILA Applications

The TILA does not apply to all credit transactions; it is limited to consumer credit transactions, which are contracts for goods or services for personal or home use. A computer purchased for use in a law office is not covered by TILA, but a computer purchased for personal use at home is.

Wherever consumer credit is extended, the TILA applies regardless of the type of credit transaction. **Open-end credit transactions,** like the use of a credit card, are covered under the TILA. **Closed-end transactions,** also covered under the TILA, are those in which the debtor is buying a certain amount and repaying it. A loan to buy a car that will be paid back over a fixed time, such as four years, is a closed-end transaction.

Open-End Disclosure Requirements

In charge card credit arrangements, the creditor has several responsibilities at different stages in the transaction. When a debtor is first sent the credit card, the creditor must include the following information: what the interest (finance) charges and annual percentage rate are for charges on the credit card; when bills will be sent; what to do about questions on the bills; and when payments are due.

Under the Credit Card Accountability, Responsibility, and Disclosure Act (CARD), credit terms must last for at least a period of one year. The disclosures of the terms of the credit card must be in what the act calls "Plain Sight and Plain Language." The terms, in addition to being on paper and sent to customers, must also be posted on the Internet.

BUSINESS STRATEGY

Credit Cards and Privacy

The Federal Trade Commission (FTC) found through an investigation that credit card companies were selling lists of their credit card holders, including their purchasing patterns, to marketing firms so they could engage in targeted marketing. As a result, all credit card companies are now required to send opt-out disclosure and election forms to all customers. The disclosure form explains how the company might use information about the credit card holder and purchasing patterns. The election form permits credit card holders to choose options on disclosure, ranging from full disclosure to anyone to complete removal of the customer's name from all mailing lists used for promotional materials.

In its annual report for 1999, Yahoo! Inc. included a disclosure notice to say the company was cooperating with the FTC in its inquiry into how Internet sites gather personal information about users. By 2003, Yahoo! and the FTC had closed the investigation, and Yahoo! disclosed in its annual report that its privacy policies and practices were in compliance with the FTC rules that resulted from its investigation of Yahoo! and others. Analyze the strategic choices of Yahoo! and others in waiting for the FTC to take action as opposed to taking voluntary action themselves.

CYBERLAW

The monthly bill that the creditor is required to send has been changed substantially by CARD. The bill due date cannot be any sooner than 21 days from the time of mailing and there cannot be any late fee traps such as weekend due dates, changing due dates each month, or due dates that fall in the middle of the day (the time is now 5:00 P.M.). In showing balances and computation of interest, CARD prohibits a previously confusing and unfair practice in which the credit card companies used the balance in a previous month to calculate interest charges on the current month, which was called "double-cycle" billing. In addition, the credit card companies must apply payments in excess of the minimum payment due to those parts of the balance due with the highest interest rates.

Other required information on credit card bills includes the following: the dates of the billing period; the free-ride period, which is the time the debtor has to pay the balance to avoid any finance charges; and where to inquire about billing errors. Any changes in credit terms, billing, or charges must be sent to the debtor at least one month in advance of the change. Under CARD, any promotional interest rates must last for at least six months.

Closed-End Disclosure Requirements

In a closed-end contract, in which the amount to be paid is definite from the beginning, the creditor must include in the credit contract the following terms:

1. The amount the debtor is financing
2. The finance charges, that is, the rate of interest charged for repayment
3. The annual percentage rate (APR), which is the finance charge reflected in a percentage figure
4. The number and amount of payments and when they are due
5. The total cost of financing (a total of the actual price of the goods or services along with all interest charges that will be paid over the scheduled repayment time)

6. Whether any additional penalties such as prepayment penalties or late payment penalties apply

7. Any security interest (lien or collateral) the creditor has in the goods sold by credit

8. The cost of credit insurance if the debtor is paying for credit insurance

The CFPA requires the BCFP to establish new standards of disclosure for consumer loans, with a better readability level and more disclosures about the consequences of loan clauses, such as the effect of variable interest rate changes on their payments. The case *Andrews v Chevy Chase Bank* (Case 14.2) deals with the level of detailed and precise disclosure required in closed-end credit contracts.

| CASE 14.2 | *Andrews v Chevy Chase Bank*[2] 240 F.R.D. 612 (E.D. Wis. 2007) |

Chasing the Truth About the Cost of a Loan Down from Chevy's Bank

FACTS

Susan and Bryan Andrews (plaintiffs) obtained a loan from Chevy Chase Bank (defendant) to refinance their home in Cedarburg, Wisconsin. In April 2004, the bank provided the Andrews with preliminary disclosures about the loan, including a consumer handbook on adjustable rate mortgages, an adjustable rate mortgage ("ARM") disclosure and a preliminary Truth in Lending Disclosure Statement. At the closing, the Andrews received additional disclosures, including an Adjustable Rate Note ("ARN"), a Truth in Lending Disclosure Statement ("TILDS") and an Adjustable Rate Rider ("ARR").

When they obtained the loan, the Andrews believed that the payments and the interest rate were fixed for five years and became variable thereafter. However, although the minimum monthly payment was fixed for five years, the interest rate was not. The loan carried a discounted or "teaser" interest rate of 1.950 percent, but that rate applied only to the first monthly payment, after which the interest rate increased every month according to a formula. As the interest rate increased, an ever-increasing portion of the minimum monthly payment of $701.21 was needed to cover interest, and the minimum payment itself soon became insufficient to cover accrued interest.

JUDICIAL OPINION

ADELMAN, District Judge

Plaintiffs first allege that defendant failed to disclose information concerning the loan's payment schedule as required by TILA.

Defendant properly disclosed that plaintiffs had to make sixty payments of $701.21, followed by three hundred payments at an adjusted level of $983.49.

Defendant also properly based the adjusted level of payments on the initial interest rate.

With respect to payment periods, however, defendant disclosed the due dates of the first and last payments in a column in a box (known as the "federal box") on its TILDS but did not disclose the payment periods, i.e., that payments were due monthly, in either the column or the box. Thus, it would appear that defendant failed to disclose the period of payments as required by TILA. Defendant argues that its disclosures satisfy TILA because it included a sentence on its TILDS stating that "[t]his loan program allows you to select the type of payment you may make each month, in accordance with disclosures provided to you earlier," and because it provided plaintiffs with other documents indicating that they had to make monthly payments.

First, the sentence on which defendant relies does not focus on payment periods but on a borrower's right to select a type of payment. The words "each month" modify the borrower's right to select. Thus, an ordinary consumer would not conclude that the sentence established an obligation to make monthly payments. An ordinary consumer would interpret the sentence's authorization to "select the type of payment you make each month" as permission to decide for herself whether to make a payment each month and in what amount. Thus, the sentence does not clearly require a borrower to pay monthly.

The sentence does not satisfy the clear and conspicuous requirement for other reasons as well. Defendant printed it in very small print and sandwiched it between the bottom of the federal box and information regarding the loan's lack of a demand feature, which defendant printed in larger print. Thus, the sentence would not draw the attention of an ordinary consumer. For this reason also, it is not conspicuous.

CONTINUED

In addition, because defendant located the sentence in a different place than the information concerning the number and amounts of payments, it did not group and segregate the disclosure as TILA requires.

Similarly, defendant's statements in other documents that plaintiffs had to make monthly payments do not satisfy the segregation requirement. This is so because the statements would not draw the ordinary consumer's attention and because defendant did not group them with information regarding the number and amounts of payments, did not segregate the information concerning the payment schedule from the other terms of the loan and obscured the relationship of the terms regarding payment to each other.

For the foregoing reasons, defendant's disclosure of the period of payments portion of the payment schedule does not comply with TILA.

On its TILDS, defendant stated that the APR was 4.047 percent and explained that this figure reflected the cost of the loan "as a yearly rate." Plaintiffs contend that defendant provided other information in its TILDS and other disclosures that strongly implied that the cost of the loan expressed as a yearly rate was 1.950 percent and that therefore defendant's APR disclosure is unclear. I agree. An ordinary consumer reading defendant's disclosures would be confused about the cost of the loan, expressed as an annual percentage rate.

I note first that "a misleading disclosure is as much a violation of TILA as a failure to disclose at all." Defendant made several statements that conflicted with its disclosure that the cost of the loan as an annual percentage rate was 4.047 percent. Defendant stated on its TILDS and in other disclosures, including its preliminary disclosures and documents that it provided at the closing that the loan carried an interest rate of 1.950 percent. In no disclosure did defendant mention any other interest rate. Further, defendant stated that the 1.950 percent rate was a "yearly rate," the identical phrase that it used to define the APR. Thus, in addition to stating that the cost of the loan as a yearly rate was 4.047 percent, defendant suggested that the cost of the loan as a yearly rate was 1.950 percent. As previously indicated, however, the 1.950 percent rate was, in fact, a discounted or teaser rate, which applied only to the first monthly payment. However, defendant also muddied up this fact by failing to disclose that the rate was discounted, stating instead in its ARM only that the rate "may" have been discounted. Defendant's repeated references in its disclosures to the 1.950 percent rate, its characterization of such rate as a yearly rate and its lack of forthrightness about the discounted nature of the rate would both confuse and mislead an ordinary consumer about the cost of the loan as an annual percentage rate.

Finally, on the back of its TILDS, Defendant stated, "if interest was the only Finance Charge, then the interest rate and the Annual Percentage Rate would be the same."

In fact, even if interest were the only finance charge, the annual percentage rate would not be 1.950 percent. Rather, the annual percentage rate was based on a composite of the discounted interest rate (1.950 percent) for as long as it was applied (one month) and the interest rate without the discount feature, which was much higher.

For the foregoing reasons, defendant's disclosure of the cost of the loan as an annual percentage rate was unclear.

Plaintiffs also allege that defendant did not clearly disclose that the loan had a variable interest rate feature. [D]efendant included information on its TILDS from which an ordinary consumer could easily infer that the interest rate on the loan was fixed for five years and became variable thereafter. Specifically, defendant stated on its TILDS that plaintiffs' loan was a "5-year fixed" loan. This statement was confusing because although it is true that the payments on the loan were fixed for five years, the interest rate was not. Defendant could easily have indicated this by including the word "payments" after the word "fixed" on its TILDS, but it did not do so. Rather than narrowing the application of "fixed," defendant used the word to describe the general nature of the loan. Further, defendant placed the "5-year fixed" language immediately above its statement that the interest rate was 1.950 percent and thus strengthened the implication that the five-year fixed language applied to the interest rate. An ordinary consumer reading defendant's TILDS could easily conclude that the interest rate was fixed for five years and variable in the last twenty-five. Further, defendant misleadingly stated that in August 2004 the interest rate "may" change not that, as defendant well knew, it would change.

Defendant responds that it stated in other disclosures as well as the TILDS that the loan had a variable rate feature. However, to be unclear, TILA requires only that a disclosure be capable of being plausibly interpreted in more than one way. An ordinary consumer reading defendant's TILDS could plausibly conclude that the loan had a variable interest rate feature which took effect after the first five years of the loan. Therefore, defendant's disclosure violated TILA.

TILA bars a lender from adding information to its TILDS that is not "directly related" to required information. Plaintiffs argue that defendant's statement on its TILDS that the loan's interest rate was 1.950 percent violated this prohibition. Yet the 1.950 percent figure had virtually no relation to any information required to be disclosed on the TILDS, much less a direct relation. The 1.950 percent rate had no significant connection to the cost of the loan. Moreover, a reference to the 1.950 percent rate would not be useful to an ordinary borrower because it would cause the loan to appear more attractive than it actually was and serve no useful purpose. Thus, by adding information to its TILDS that was not directly related to that required, defendant violated TILA.

A TILA plaintiff may recover statutory damages "only" if the defendant fails "to comply with the requirements of section 1635 . . . or of paragraph (2) (insofar as it requires a disclosure of the 'amount financed').

As previously discussed, defendant violated §§ 1632 and 1638(b) by failing to clearly and conspicuously disclose and segregate information relating to the payment schedule, by failing to clearly disclose the APR and the existence of a variable interest rate feature, and by adding to its TILDS information not directly related to required information. Neither violations of § 1632 or § 1638(b) are among the TILA violations enumerated in § 1640(a) for which statutory damages are available. Therefore, plaintiffs are not entitled to statutory damages.

Under some circumstances, a TILA plaintiff may rescind a loan. Generally, a borrower has three days to rescind after the closing or receipt of notice of the right to rescind along with all material disclosures. If a lender fails to provide a borrower with notice of the right to rescind or if the lender fails to make a material disclosure, the period in which a plaintiff may exercise the right to rescind is extended. "Material disclosures"

are "the required disclosures of the annual percentage rate, the finance charge, the amount financed, the total payments, [and] the payment schedule." Defendant's failures to clearly and conspicuously disclose the payment period, the annual percentage rate and the variable interest rate feature all involve material disclosures for purposes of the right of rescission. Thus, plaintiffs may avail themselves of the remedy of rescission.

A TILA plaintiff may obtain attorneys' fees and costs if she is "determined to have a right of rescission under section 1635." Because I have determined that plaintiffs have a right of rescission, they are entitled to attorneys' fees.

CASE QUESTIONS

1. List the violations of the TILA that Chevy Chase Bank made.

2. Explain the remedies the Andrews are entitled to and which they are not.

3. What advice would you give a lender based on this case regarding "teaser" interest rates on loans?

Special Disclosures and Protections for Service Members

Under the Servicemembers Relief Act of 2005 and the National Defense Act of 2007, Congress updated the credit protections afforded active service members of the military under the 1940 Soldiers and Sailors Relief Act. The protections now apply to reservists who are called up for active duty and include the following:

- A 6 percent interest limit on ARMs while service members are on active duty

- A maximum of 36 percent interest APR on all debt to all service members (this provision preempts any state law that exceeds 36 percent)

- No delinquency reports on service members to credit agencies while they are on active duty

- No repossession of cars during active duty without a court order

- Continuing protection that prevents foreclosure during active duty

BUSINESS PLANNING TIP

When any question arises as to whether a consumer credit transaction is involved or whether a protective statute applies, the question is resolved in favor of the credit applicant. Many businesses treat all credit applications as consumer credit applications and apply the statutes (even though they are not required to do so) so that they can avoid any issues and questions on consumer credit.

Advertising and Disclosure

In addition to ensuring adequate disclosures in credit contracts, Regulation Z covers advertising that includes credit terms. If any part of the credit arrangement is mentioned in an advertisement, all terms must be disclosed. For example, if a creditor advertises payments "as low as $15 per month," the ad must also disclose the APR, the down payment required, and the number of payments.

State v Terry Buick, Inc. (Case 14.3) deals with credit advertising.

CASE 14.3 *State v Terry Buick, Inc.*
520 N.Y.S.2d 497 (1987)

$99 per Month plus Fine Print

FACTS

Terry Buick, Inc. (defendant) is an automobile retailer that displayed across the street-side of its building large yellow signs in block letters that read:

NO MONEY DOWN INSTANT CREDIT! $99/MO.

Terry Buick was located on Route 9, a very busy public highway in Poughkeepsie, New York. The actual credit terms of the sales were printed on $2\frac{1}{4}" \times \frac{3}{8}"$ stickers, which could be read only by close inspection and were attached to the windshields of cars that were for sale. These small stickers showed the price of the car, the down payment, the term in months, and the average interest rate applied to installment payments. The state of New York brought suit for violation of the credit advertisement regulations of TILA.

JUDICIAL OPINION

BENSON, Justice

This action for an injunction under 15 U.S.C. § 1664 (Truth in Lending Act), General Business Law Article 22-A and CPLR § 6301 enjoining Terry Buick, Inc. from continuing to advertise the terms for credit on vehicles it is selling in an illegal, false and deceptive manner is determined as follows:

The Court viewed the defendant's place of business with the attorneys and examined a number of the windshield stickers. They were legible only upon inspection from a distance of a few feet and set forth the financial details of each offer. Examination of the stickers showed that almost every offering required a down payment to obtain $99 per month financing. Other used cars had only "99/MO" painted on their windshields. According to the testimony of one witness, the salesman did not know the price of several of such cars. He testified that no cars were offered for sale for $2,000 down and $99 per month.

The plaintiff relied heavily upon the testimony of an undercover agent, a woman in the employ of the Attorney General who went to the defendant's place of business in the guise of a prospective purchaser and engaged a salesman in conversation about the cars. She recorded the conversation secretly and offered the tape, which the Court admitted into evidence. The plaintiff emphasized in argument a statement which the salesman made to the plaintiff's agent in which he admitted that the purpose of the advertising was to capture

people's attention as they drove by and get them into the dealership.

The Truth in Lending statutes which govern the defendant's conduct are 15 U.S.C. § 1664(d) and New York General Business Laws §§ 350 and 350-a. The Federal statute is amplified by Regulation Z, 12 C.F.R. § 226.24. State courts have concurrent jurisdiction to enforce the Federal statute.

§ 1664(d) reads as follows:

If any advertisement . . . states the amount of the downpayment, if any, the amount of any installment payment, the dollar amount of any finance charge, or the number of installments or the period of repayment, then the advertisement shall state all of the following items . . .

1. the downpayment, if any;
2. the terms of repayment;
3. the rate of the finance charge, expressed as an annual percentage rate.

The regulation adopted pursuant to the statute requires that "The creditor shall make the disclosures required by this subpart clearly and conspicuously."

The Court's inspection of the defendant's place of business and its advertising material showed beyond question that the announcement signs were a "come on" designed to lure the eager seeker of a good deal. It also showed that "what you see is not what you get." We have not given the testimony of the undercover agent much weight. It was a contrived tactic practiced upon a relatively guileless salesman by a young woman who pretended to be a purchaser. Her testimony is not necessary, however, to convince the Court that defendant's public announcement of its deals fell far short of the candid display which the law requires. The law requires full disclosure described in the plain language of the statute. A look at the defendant's advertising scheme leads directly to the conclusion that it was designed to attract customers by half truths or falsity. No customer could buy a car on the terms boldly announced on the face of the building. The defendant's intentions did not have to be explained by testimony. No undercover agent was needed to obtain admissions. The message spoke for itself and could not be misread. It was "misleading in a material respect."

Truth in lending laws were not adopted for the canny shopper. They were made for the gullible and those easily led. . . . "In weighing a statement's capacity, tendency or effect in deceiving or misleading customers, we do not look to the average customer but to the vast multitude which the statutes were enacted to safeguard, including the ignorant, the unthinking and the credulous who, in making purchases, do not stop to analyze but are governed by appearances and general impressions." The plaintiff was not required to show that anyone had been deceived or that the advertising had injured anyone. It met its burden by showing its misleading effect.

The defendant's violation of Federal and New York State truth in lending laws has been demonstrated.

The motion for an order granting a preliminary injunction enjoining the defendant Terry Buick, Inc.

from continuing to advertise the terms for credit on vehicles it is selling in an illegal, false and deceptive manner is granted.

CASE QUESTIONS

1. Describe the location of the large signs about the credit terms.

2. Did the court need the testimony concerning the salesman's words?

3. Did it matter that no one was deceived by the ads?

Credit Card Liabilities

Regulation Z provides protection for credit card holders in addition to the required open-end disclosures. These additional protections are designed to limit the liability of a debtor for unauthorized use of a credit card.

Credit Card Solicitation

The Fair Credit and Charge Card Disclosure Act of 1988 regulates the solicitation of credit card customers. The CFPA also gives the BCFP authority to change and improve the disclosure requirements for credit card terms. Those changes had not yet been promulgated as of October 2010. However, under existing requirements a creditor cannot send an unsolicited credit card to a debtor. The debtor must have applied for the card or consented to have one sent. This protection is necessary so that debtors will be aware of what cards are coming and will know when to report losses or thefts.

Second, even if a credit card is stolen, Regulation Z provides dollar limitations for debtor liability. The maximum amount of liability a debtor can have for the misuse of a credit card, including in cases of identity theft, is $50; this liability limitation applies only if the debtor takes the appropriate steps for notifying the creditor of the theft or loss. The procedures for notification are given when the credit card is first sent to the debtor.

Lenders and credit card companies are discovering that credit cards are often not stolen physically, but through electronic surveillance. Whether the credit card is taken physically or the information lifted through cyber space, consumers have the same liability limitations.

CYBERLAW

The rules that implement the law require up-front disclosure of items such as the fees for issuing the card, the annual percentage rate for the card, any finance or transaction charges, and whether a grace period for payment exists. In addition, the solicitation must include how the average daily balance is computed, when payments are due, whether there is a late payment fee, and whether there are charges for going over the credit limit.

CARD places additional restrictions on credit card solicitations for those under the age of 21. Credit card companies must have a written application in hand from those under 21 and those applications must carry the signature of a parent, guardian, or someone over the age of 21 who has the means to repay debt. The line of credit on a co-signed card for someone under the age of 21 cannot be increased without the co-signer's permission. Colleges and universities are now restricted in their partnering with credit card companies in order to raise funds through the solicitation of their students. The CARD act limits locations for college student credit card solicitations, requires colleges and universities to disclose their financial relationships with such credit card companies, and also requires colleges and universities to provide debt counseling for their students.

Canceling Credit Contracts: Regulation Z Protections

In addition to all the usual disclosures for a closed-end contract, certain types of credit contracts must include a **three-day cooling-off period** for the debtor, which is a buyer's protection for "cold feet." The buyer has the right to rescind certain types of credit contracts anytime during the seventy-two hours immediately following execution of a credit contract.

The types of credit contracts covered by the cooling-off period are those in which the creditor takes a security interest in the debtor's home. For example, if Alfie is installing a solar hot water system in his home, has purchased it on credit, and is giving the solar company a lien on his house, the three-day period applies; Alfie has three days to change his mind after he signs the contract. The three-day period also applies to **home solicitation sales,** in which sellers/creditors first approach consumers in the buyers' homes. The protection here allows buyers to recoup from any sales pressure that might have been used.

Where the three-day rescission period applies, the creditor must include both a description of the rights in the contract and a full explanation of the procedures the debtor should follow to rescind the contract during the three-day period.

Under the **Home Equity Loan Consumer Protection Act of 1988** and the **Home Ownership and Equity Protection Act (HOEPA) of 1994,** additional disclosures are required for those transactions in which consumers use their homes as security for the credit. The CFPA increases the disclosure requirements and grants the BCFP broad authority to promulgate regulations to prevent hidden fees, deceptive terms, and abusive practices in this area. Existing regulations on mortgage and equity loans mandate that additional disclosures explain that consumers who do not pay these debts could lose their dwellings, which could be sold to pay the debts. The three-day rescission period also applies to home equity credit lines. If notice of this three-day rescission right is not given to the homeowner/debtor, the right of rescission will continue for three years. Variable rate loans require specific disclosures on maximum increases in interest rates and the impact on payments. Most experts agree that the types of disclosures required through CFPA will increase and that lenders will need to include sample computations for consumers so that they can evaluate the total costs, potential and otherwise, of their credit transactions. One such disclosure is likely to be an analysis for the borrower of the impact the mortgage loan would have on the borrower's budget and discretionary spending. In other words, the disclosures will be personalized enough for the borrower to see how that percentage of income changes as the mortgage interest rate increases. In addition, CFPA requires the lender to establish its basis for approving the loan, making a determination that the borrower is likely and able to repay the mortgage.

Congress has provided additional rescission rights for home mortgage refinancings. The three-day rescission right applies. However, additional protections are afforded to consumers who are refinancing. If the lender has not made the correct disclosures on the right of rescission, the consumers then have a three-year right of rescission. That right exists even when the consumers have gone on to refinance with another lender. Their remedy would be a refund of any interest paid on the loan as well as the elimination of any security the lender had in the home [*Barrett v JP Morgan Chase Bank, N.A.*, 445 F.3d 874 (C.A. 6 2006)].

Under the CFPA, the BCFP has the authority to promulgate rules and obtain administrative relief related to mortgage loans. Such relief may include

(A) rescission or reformation of contracts

(B) refund of moneys or return of real property

(C) restitution

(D) disgorgement or compensation for unjust enrichment

(E) payment of damages or other monetary relief

(F) public notification regarding the violation, including the costs of notification

(G) limits on the activities or functions of the person

(H) civil money penalties

As a result of these expanded remedies and additional authority, lenders' disclosure forms for borrowers could change substantially.

Exhibit 14.2 is an example of a three-day cancellation provision.

EXHIBIT 14.2 Sample Three-Day Cancellation Notice

H-9 RESCISSION MODEL FORM (REFINANCING)

NOTICE OF RIGHT TO CANCEL

Your Right to Cancel

You are entering into a new transaction to increase the amount of credit provided to you. We acquired a [mortgage/lien/security interest] [on/in] your home under the original transaction and will retain that [mortgage/lien/security interest] in the new transaction. You have a legal right under federal law to cancel the new transaction, without cost, within three business days from whichever of the following events occurs last:

(1) the date of the new transaction, which is _____; or

(2) the date you received your new Truth-in-Lending disclosures; or

(3) the date you received this notice of your right to cancel.

If you cancel the new transaction, your cancellation will apply only to the increase in the amount of credit. It will not affect the amount that you presently owe or the [mortgage/lien/security interest] we already have [on/in] your home. If you cancel, the [mortgage/lien/security interest] as it applies to the increased amount is also cancelled. Within 20 calendar days after we receive your notice of cancellation of the new transaction, we must take the steps necessary to reflect the fact that our [mortgage/lien/security interest] [on/in] your home no longer applies to the increase of credit. We must also return any money you have given to us or any one else in connection with the new transaction.

You may keep any money we have given you in the new transaction until we have done the things mentioned above, but you must then offer to return the money at the address below. If we do not take possession of the money within 20 calendar days of your offer, you may keep it without further obligation.

How to Cancel

If you decide to cancel the new transaction, you may do so by notifying us in writing, at (creditor's name and business address).

You may use any written statement that is signed and dated by you and states your intention to cancel, or you may use this notice by dating and signing below. Keep one copy of this notice because it contains important information about your rights. If you cancel by mail or telegram, you must send the notice no later than midnight of (date) (or midnight of the third business day following the latest of the three events listed above). If you send or deliver your written notice to cancel some other way, it must be delivered to the above address no later than that time.

I WISH TO CANCEL

_____   _____
Consumer's Signature   Date

TILA Penalties

The TILA provides specific penalties for violations of disclosure provisions. A creditor is liable to an individual for twice the amount of finance charges and for the debtor's attorney fees. The minimum recovery for an individual is $100 and the maximum, $1,000. A group of debtors bringing a class action against a creditor can collect the lesser of $500,000 or 1 percent of the creditor's net worth as damages. As noted earlier, penalties under the CFPA have been increased and expanded for various types of violations.

Fair Credit Billing Act

The **Fair Credit Billing Act** affords debtors the opportunity to challenge the figures on an open-end transaction monthly statement. Errors on credit card accounts are covered by this act and, to a lesser degree, by Regulation Z. Creditors are required to supply on the monthly statement an address or phone number to write or call in the event a debtor has questions or challenges regarding the bill. The language must read: "IN CASE OF ERRORS, CALL OR WRITE . . ."

Under the act, debtors can collect damages if they comply with all the act's procedural requirements. First, a debtor must notify the creditor of any errors within 60 days of the receipt of the statement. The notification must be in writing for the damage sections to apply. If a creditor supplies a phone number for inquiries, the notice must explain that oral protests do not preserve all Regulation Z rights. The written protest of the debtor must include the debtor's name, the account number, and a brief explanation of the claimed error.

The creditor has 30 days from the time of receipt of the written protest to acknowledge to the debtor receipt of the protest. The creditor has ninety days from receipt of the protest to take final action, either giving the debtor's account a credit or reaffirming that the charges are valid.

During the time the creditor is considering the debtor's protest, the debtor is not required to pay the questioned amount or any finance charges on that amount. If the charges are in fact accurate, the debtor will be charged for the finance charges during this time period. If the creditor fails to comply with any of the requirements or deadlines on bill protests, the debtor can be excused from payment even if the charges disputed were actually accurate.

For the Manager's Desk

Re: ESIGN and Credit

ESIGN allows e-retailers and creditors to rely on Internet transactions and signatures. However, ESIGN's requirements also mean that creditors must have consumers point and click their ways through the detailed information of TILA, the ECOA, and any state disclosure laws. Consumers must give electronic consent or confirmation. Once this digital interchange of consent is given, the creditor can send the consumer the required credit disclosures. If the consumer remains online at this point, goods can be purchased on credit, or an e-loan can be executed, through a credit agreement or promissory note, electronically.

Source: Adapted from Robert A. Cook and Nicole F. Munro, "Giving Consumer Disclosures On-Line: Is ESIGN the Path to the Paperless Loan?" 57 *Bus. Law.* 1187, (2002).

CYBERLA

Fair Credit Reporting Act

The **Fair Credit Reporting Act** (FCRA) is designed to provide debtors some rights and protections regarding the credit information held by third parties about them. Before the passage of the FCRA, many debtors were denied the right to see their credit reports and were often victims of inaccurate reports. The FCRA brought credit reports out in the open. The enforcement of this law has been assigned to the new BCFP.

When the FCRA Applies

The FCRA applies to consumer reporting agencies, which are third parties (not creditors or debtors) that compile, evaluate, and sell credit information about consumer debt and debtors. Commercial credit reporting agencies and commercial debtors are not subject to FCRA standards.

Limitations on FCRA Disclosures

Under the FCRA, consumer reporting agencies can disclose information only to the following:

1. A debtor who asks for his own report
2. A creditor who has the debtor's signed application for credit
3. A potential employer
4. A court pursuant to a subpoena

Phillips v Grendahl (Case 14.4) deals with an issue of disclosure of credit information.

CASE 14.4   *Phillips v Grendahl*
312 F.3d 357 (8th Cir. 2002)

Credit and In-Law Trouble

FACTS

Mary Grendahl's daughter Sarah became engaged to marry Lavon Phillips and moved in with him. Mary Grendahl became suspicious that Mr. Phillips was not telling the truth about his past, particularly about whether he was an attorney and whether he had done legal work in Washington, D.C. She also was confused about who his ex-wives and girlfriends were and where they lived. She contacted Kevin Fitzgerald, a family friend who worked for McDowell Agency, a private investigation agency. She asked Mr. Fitzgerald to do a "background check" on Mr. Phillips, and she also gave him the name of the woman Mr. Phillips had lived with before Sarah Grendahl.

Mr. Fitzgerald began his search by obtaining Mr. Phillips's Social Security number from a computer database. He also searched public records in

Minnesota and Alabama, where Mr. Phillips had lived earlier. He discovered one suit against Mr. Phillips for delinquent child support in Alabama, a suit to establish child support for two children in Minnesota, and one misdemeanor conviction for writing dishonored checks.

Mr. Fitzgerald then supplied the Social Security information to Econ Control and asked for "Finder's Reports" on Mr. Phillips and his former girlfriend. Robert McDowell, on behalf of McDowell Agency, had signed an Econ Control registration agreement, titled "Agreement for Consumer Credit Services." One clause of the registration agreement stated:

> *3. I certify that I will order consumer reports, as defined by the Fair Credit Reporting Act, only when they are intended to be used as a factor in establishing a consumer's eligibility for new or continued credit, collections of*

CONTINUED

an account, insurance, licensing, employment purposes, or otherwise in connection with a legitimate business transaction involving the consumer. Such reports will be used for no other purpose. Each time I request a report I intend to use for employment purposes, I will specifically identify it to [Econ Control] at the time I request the report.

Econ Control did not ask why McDowell wanted the report, and McDowell did not disclose his purpose in requesting it. Econ Control obtained a report from Computer Science Corporation on Mr. Phillips and passed it on to McDowell and Mr. Fitzgerald.

Mr. Fitzgerald gave Mary Grendahl the results of his investigation, including the Finder's Report.

Mr. Phillips eventually found out about the background check and became angry, as did Sarah. Mary Grendahl then telephoned and left the following voicemail for Sarah: "Sarah, this is mom. I didn't directly do a credit report. I hired a PI and they have every right to do that."

Mr. Phillips brought suit against Mary Grendahl, McDowell Agency, and Econ Control, alleging violations of the Fair Credit Reporting Act. Mr. Phillips appealed the lower court's summary judgment for Mary Grendahl and the others.

JUDICIAL OPINION

GIBSON, Circuit Judge

The Fair Credit Reporting Act, 15 U.S.C. §§ 1681b–1681u (2000), prohibits the disclosure of consumer credit reports by consumer credit reporting agencies, except in response to the following kinds of requests: (1) court order or subpoena; (2) request by governmental agencies involved in setting or enforcing child support awards; (3) request authorized in writing by the consumer about whom the report is made; or (4) request by a person whom the reporting agency has reason to believe intends to use the consumer report for permissible business reasons.

In this case, there is no dispute that the Finder's Report was (1) a written communication (2) by a consumer reporting agency, Computer Science Corporation. The two issues in dispute pertaining to whether the Finder's Report is a consumer report are (3) whether it contained the sort of personal information that would bring it within the definition and (4) whether anyone "expected" the Finder's Report or the information in it to be used for one of the purposes listed in the definition or "collected" the information in it for that purpose.

A consumer report must contain information "bearing on a consumer's credit worthiness, credit standing, credit capacity, character, general reputation, personal characteristics, or mode of living." The Finder's Report listed the names of several creditors with whom

Phillips had credit accounts and the existence of a child support obligation, with dates for "last activity," but no other details such as amount of obligation or payment history. The Finder's Report also lists Phillips's former employers, which also would bear on his mode of living by showing that he has been employed . . . the Finder's Report contains the kind of personal information required by the definition of consumer report.

The second question, whether the putative consumer report or the information in it was "used or expected to be used" or "collected for" one of the listed purposes is more difficult. Three statutory ambiguities in this clause could affect what communications are covered by the clause: the statutory language does not specify who must do the using, collecting or expecting; whether those verbs describe a specific or habitual action; or whether those actions must be done with regard to "information" or with regard to the consumer report itself.

We need not choose among the competing interpretations of the clause urged by the parties, because we conclude that the Finder's Report fell within the "used, expected to be used, or collected" clause even under the interpretation urged by McDowell Agency. The record demonstrates that the Finder's Report, not just the information in it, was actually intended by the credit reporting agency that prepared it to be used for a statutory purpose. The sample Finder's Report supplied by Econ Control to McDowell Agency states [so].

We next determine whether each of the defendants "obtained or used" the consumer report. There is no dispute that McDowell Agency and Econ Control obtained a consumer report, for each of them requested a Finder's Report.

Mary Grendahl, on the other hand, testified that she did not request the release of any credit information on Phillips. Mere passive receipt of the report would not be enough to satisfy the statutory element that she "use or obtain" a consumer report. However, Phillips argues that the phone machine message Grendahl left for Sarah is evidence that she asked Fitzgerald to obtain credit information: "Sarah, this is mom. I didn't directly do a credit report. I hired a PI and they have every right to do that." This evidence is ambiguous. On the one hand, it could mean that Grendahl hired a private investigator because she thought he was entitled to do a credit report. On the other hand, it could mean that she simply hired a private investigator who ordered a credit report on his own initiative, which she now understood he was entitled to do. Because this case was disposed of on summary judgment, we must resolve any ambiguities in the evidence in favor of Phillips. In this procedural posture, the ambiguous telephone message is sufficient to create a genuine issue of fact as to whether Mary Grendahl asked Fitzgerald to obtain a consumer report on Phillips.

The next inquiry is whether any of the defendants had a permissible statutory purpose for obtaining the consumer report. The only purpose for obtaining the report was to obtain information on Mary Grendahl's prospective son-in-law. Investigating a person because he wants to marry one's daughter is not a statutory consumer purpose under section 1681b(a). Even if getting married can be characterized as a consumer transaction under section 1681b(a)(3), it was not Mary Grendahl, but her daughter, whom Phillips was engaged to marry. He had no business transaction pending with Mary Grendahl. There was no permissible purpose for obtaining or using a consumer report.

Section 1681n(a) provides civil liability for willful noncompliance with any requirement of the Fair Credit Reporting Act.

The statute's use of the word "willfully" imports the requirement that the defendant know his or her conduct is unlawful.

Here, there is evidence that none of the three defendants believed their conduct to be covered by the Fair Credit Reporting Act. Kevin Fitzgerald of McDowell Agency knew of Econ Control from the Minnesota Private Investigators Association meeting, where Porter had told the attendees that they could obtain Finder's Reports without the authorization of the subject.

Fitzgerald testified, "To the best of my knowledge, a finder's report is not considered a credit history." He also testified: "I did not do anything that I know to be illegal, unethical, or outside the standard practice of private investigators." Mary Grendahl testified that she only asked Fitzgerald to look into Phillips's background and that she gave him no instructions on how to do the investigation. She stated: "At no time did I ask Mr. Fitzgerald to try to obtain credit information or a 'credit report,' and it is my understanding that he did not do so."

On the other hand, there is also evidence that each defendant had some experience in dealing with credit reports and either knew of the Fair Credit Reporting Act or at least knew that such reports can only be obtained legally under certain circumstances. This kind of experience can support an inference that the defendants knew that their actions were impermissible. These facts are sufficient to create a genuine issue of material fact as to whether defendants acted knowingly and with conscious disregard for Phillips's legal rights.

We reverse the entry of summary judgment and remand for further proceedings.

CASE QUESTIONS

1. Who sought the credit report? Does it matter that a mother was trying to help her child by finding out relevant information about her future spouse?

2. Does the report qualify for protection under the FCRA?

3. Is there enough factual basis for the case to go forward?

When consumers file applications for credit with lenders, they have the right to know where a credit report came from. However, the creditor cannot show the report to the debtor, who must get the report through a credit reporting agency.

Consumer agencies are limited not only as to whom disclosures can be made but also as to what can be disclosed. The following are the general limitations on debtor disclosures:

1. No disclosure of bankruptcies that occurred more than 10 years ago

2. No disclosure of lawsuits concluded more than seven years ago

3. No disclosure of criminal convictions and arrests that were disposed of more than seven years ago

When a debtor applies for a loan of more than $50,000 or a job that pays more than $20,000, these limitations on disclosures do not apply.

Under the FCRA, debtors have not only the right to see reports but also the right to make corrections of inaccurate information included in those reports. A debtor simply notifies the reporting agency of the alleged error. If the agency acknowledges the error, the debtor's report must be corrected, and anyone who has received a report on that debtor during the previous two years must be notified.

If the agency still stands by the information challenged by the debtor, the debtor has the right to have included in the credit report a 100-word statement explaining his position on the matter. This statement is then included with the actual credit report in all future reports sent to third parties.

Morris v Trans Union LLC (Case 14.5) deals with a problem of an inaccurate credit report.

| CASE 14.5 | *Morris v Trans Union LLC.*
 987 F.2d 288 (5th Cir. 1993) |

The Ex-Husband with the Wife's Target Credit Rating

FACTS

In 1997, Kenneth Morris's then-wife applied for and opened a revolving credit account at Target—the "RNB-Target" account—as a joint account. Morris did not know of the account and did not sign the application. In 2002, over a year after Morris and his wife divorced, she charged $129.91 to the account. The statement was mailed to Morris's home address, the address shown on the application. Morris forwarded the bill to his former wife, who had moved to Louisiana. Morris received a second statement showing the bill as unpaid and handled it the same way. Morris's former wife only paid $20 on the account. When Morris received another statement, he contacted RNB-Target and told them to deal with his former wife. RNB-Target nonetheless continued to send the statements to Morris, who threw them away. In May 2003, RNB Target notified Morris that it had closed the account and charged off the unpaid amount of $253.10, including late fees and interest. RNB-Target passed the information to national credit bureaus.

In July 2003, Morris's automobile insurance quote was high because of poor credit. He downloaded a credit report that listed Morris as jointly responsible for the RNB-Target account and showed the unpaid balance charged off as a bad debt.

Morris notified Trans Union in writing that the information in the credit report about the RNB-Target account was incorrect. Morris explained that despite his request, Target had not provided any information showing that the account was in fact "ever a 'joint' account." Morris explained that the unpaid amount was charged by his former wife after their divorce. Morris asked Trans Union to correct the item and show it as disputed until then.

On July 30, 2003, Trans Union notified Target that "Consumer not liable for acct (i.e., ex-spouse, business)." Trans Union provided further explanation with the message: "ACCT NEVER JOINT." Target responded and said that the account was indeed a joint one. Morris

wrote a letter of dispute, and Trans Union wrote to Target again and received the same response. Morris filed suit against Trans Union in January 2004 for violation of the Fair Credit Reporting Act. Target then instructed Trans Union to remove the account from Morris's credit report. Trans Union moved for summary judgment.

JUDICIAL OPINION

ROSENTHAL, District Judge

. . . Trans Union violated the FCRA only with regard to the requirement that it notify the creditor of a dispute within five days, but that the violation caused Morris no harm. Morris is correct that an inaccurate report can cause damage to a consumer in addition to the denial of credit. Each element of damage must be linked to the consumer-reporting agency's failure to comply with its FCRA obligations. With respect to Trans Union's conceded failure to comply with the five-day rule, the evidence shows no ill effects or harm to Morris as a result. Despite the initial delay, Trans Union provided Morris a timely report of its investigation. The undisputed evidence demonstrates that the information contained within Morris's credit report after his complaint was the same as it would have been had Trans Union initially given RNB-Target notice of Morris's dispute within the five-day statutory period.

On the issue of a heightened duty, this court agrees with Morris that a reporting agency may have a duty to go beyond a creditor's response. Such a heightened duty arises only when the evidence demonstrates that the agency has a basis for questioning the reliability of the creditor's information. Morris's invective-laced railing against RNB-Target is not in itself sufficient to raise a fact issue as to whether Trans Union had a basis for questioning RNB-Target's reliability. The record shows that Trans Union had worked with RNB-Target for at least eleven years and had received no report that RNB-Target had provided unreliable information. Morris simply failed to raise a fact question as to whether Trans Union's knowledge of RNB-Target's reliability required Trans Union to conduct a different kind of investigation.

Willfulness is an element of proof necessary both to show entitlement to punitive damages under the FCRA and to overcome statutory qualified immunity from state-law defamation claims. Morris asserts that Trans Union had the obligation to develop specific formal policies and procedures to measure or evaluate creditor reliability and to perform a cost-benefit analysis comparing in a given situation the cost of verifying the accuracy of the source of the credit information against the possible harm inaccurately reported information may cause the consumer. [T]he absence of formal policies and procedures to evaluate a creditor's reliability does not show that a consumer-reporting agency acted in conscious disregard for a consumer's rights in a specific case. In this case, the record contains no evidence of material misrepresentations or concealment by Trans Unio.

Trans Union's motion for summary judgment is granted.

CASE QUESTIONS

1. What types of violations of the FCRA by Trans Union does Morris allege?

2. What would you recommend Trans Union and Target do as they go forward in dealing with FCRA challenges?

3. What action would you recommend to couples who obtain a divorce and still have credit accounts that were opened during the course of their marriages?

CONSIDER... 14.2

Jennifer Cushman has a permanent residence in Pennsylvania but attended college in Vermont. In the summer of 1993, an unknown person, possibly a member of her household in Philadelphia, applied under Ms. Cushman's name for credit cards from three credit grantors: American Express (Amex), Citibank Visa, and Chase Manhattan Bank. The person provided the credit grantors with Ms. Cushman's Social Security number, address, and other identifying information. Credit cards were issued to that person in Ms. Cushman's name, and that person accumulated balances totaling approximately $2,400 on the cards between June 1993 and April 1994. All this occurred without Ms. Cushman's knowledge.

In August 1994, an unidentified bill collector informed Ms. Cushman that Trans Union (TUC) was publishing a consumer credit report indicating that she was delinquent on payments to these three credit grantors. Ms. Cushman notified TUC that she had not applied for or used the three credit cards in question and suggested that a third party had fraudulently applied for and obtained the cards. In response, a TUC clerk called American Express (Amex) and Chase to inquire whether the verifying information (such as Ms. Cushman's name, Social Security number, and address) in Amex's and Chase's records matched the information in the TUC report. The TUC clerk also asked if Ms. Cushman had opened a fraud investigation with the credit grantors. Because the information matched, and because Ms. Cushman had not opened a fraud investigation, the information remained in the TUC report. TUC was unable to contact Citibank, so TUC deleted the Citibank entry from the report. TUC's investigations are performed by clerks who are paid $7.50 per hour and are expected to perform 10 investigations per hour.

TUC did not obtain records to perform a handwriting comparison. Ms. Cushman was denied credit because of the report. She filed suit under the FCRA. Did TUC violate the law? [*Cushman v Trans Union Corp.*, 115 F.3d 220 (3d Cir. 1997)]

Consumer Leasing Act

The **Consumer Leasing Act** is an amendment to TILA that provides disclosure protection for consumers who lease goods. Under this act, the lessor must disclose how much will be paid over the life of the lease, whether any money will be owed at the end of the lease, and whether the lease can be terminated.

The Federal Trade Commission (FTC) and the Federal Reserve Board jointly developed a disclosure form for consumer leases. The form requires disclosure of the following:

1. The amount due at the lease signing (must be itemized, too)
2. Total of payments
3. Monthly payments and other charges
4. Capitalized cost (shows the actual price of the goods—was previously missing from most lease agreements so as to discourage consumer shopping, especially for cars)
5. Residual value (value at the end of the lease, which helps determine the monthly payments)
6. Rent charge (which really is the interest rate)
7. Trade-ins, rebates, and other credits given at signing
8. Early termination conditions and terms
9. Excessive wear, use, and mileage provisions

Enforcement of Credit Transactions

Although a debtor has the benefit of paying over time, a creditor has the worry of trying to ensure payment. A creditor may be able to increase sales by extending credit, but risks of nonpayment also increase with each extension of credit. Fortunately, the law affords creditors some additional protections that can be used to guarantee repayment.

The Use of Collateral: The Security Interest

One way a creditor can have additional assurances of repayment is to obtain a pledge of collateral from the debtor. For goods, this collateral pledge is called a **security interest.** The creation of security interests is governed by Article 9 of the Uniform Commercial Code.

A security interest is created by a written agreement called a **security agreement.** Once a security interest is created, the creditor is given the right to repossess the pledged goods in the event the debtor defaults on repayment. When a debtor purchases a car on credit, there is nearly always a security interest in that car that allows the lender the right to repossess the car and sell it to satisfy the loan in the event the debtor defaults. This right to sell gives the creditor some additional assurances that the debt will be repaid.

Collection Rights of the Creditor

If a debtor falls behind on payments, the creditor has the right to proceed with collection tactics. Many creditors refer or sell their delinquent credit accounts to collection agencies. At one time, some of these agencies engaged in questionable conduct in the collection of debts, including harassing debtors with phone calls and embarrassing them by contacting their friends and relatives. Enacted to control abuses in the collection process, the **Fair Debt Collections Practices Act** (FDCPA) controls a great deal of debt collection. Most of the states have adopted some form of debt collection statute. If state law, relative to the federal act, provides the same or greater protection for debtors in the collection process, the state law governs. In states without a collection law, the FDCPA applies.

When the FDCPA Applies

The FDCPA applies to consumer debts and debt collectors. Consumer debts are defined here as they are under the TILA: debts for personal, home, or family purposes. Debt collectors are third-party collectors. The FDCPA does not apply to original creditors collecting their own debts; for example, Sears collecting Sears's debts is not governed by the FDCPA. However, if Sears referred its collection accounts to Central Credit Collection Agency, Central Credit would be under the FDCPA. If Sears created its own collection agency with a name other than Sears, the FDCPA would apply to that agency as well.

CONSIDER... 14.3

Telecredit Service Corporation's business is the collection of dishonored checks. Telecredit purchases these checks and then contacts the drawers to collect the funds. Stanley Holmes wrote a $315 check to Union Park Pontiac that was dishonored. Union Park sold the check to Telecredit, and Telecredit sent letters and made contacts to collect the check. Some contacts would be violations of FDCPA, but Telecredit says it is not covered by FDCPA because it is not collecting the debts of another. Is this correct? [*Holmes v Telecredit Service Corp.*, 736 F. Supp. 1289 (D. Del. 1990)]

The FDCPA does not apply to the collection of commercial accounts or to banks and the Internal Revenue Service. In a rule revision, attorneys collecting debts for clients were made subject to coverage of the FDCPA.

Collector Requirements under the FDCPA

One of the requirements for collectors under the FDCPA is written verification of debt. A collector must provide such verification if a debtor asks. The collector must also automatically provide written verification within five days after contacting the debtor. Written verifications must include the following information:

1. The amount of the debt
2. The name of the creditor
3. The debtor's right to dispute the debt and the procedures for doing so

If a debtor disputes a debt, the collector has 30 days to verify the debt and its amount before any collection contact can continue.

Collector Restrictions under the FDCPA

In addition to affirmative disclosure requirements, the FDCPA prohibits certain conduct by collectors, covered in the next sections.

Debtor Contact. One of the most frequent abuses by collectors prior to the FDCPA was constant debtor contact and harassment. The FDCPA curbs the amount of contact: Debtors cannot be contacted before 8:00 A.M. or after 9:00 P.M., and debtors who work night shifts cannot be disturbed during their sleeping hours in the daytime.

The place of contact is also controlled by the FDCPA: Collectors must avoid contact at inconvenient places. Home contact is permitted, but contact in club, church, or school meetings is prohibited. Collectors can approach debtors at their places of employment unless employers object or have a policy against such contact.

To prevent harassment, the FDCPA gives debtors a chance to "call off" a collector. If a debtor tells the collector that he wants no more contact, the collector must stop and take other steps, such as legal action, to collect the debt. If the debtor is represented by an attorney and gives the name of the attorney to the collector, the collector can contact only the attorney from that point.

Third-Party Contact.   The FDCPA also prohibits notifying other parties of the debtor's debts and collection problems. However, the debtor's spouse and parents can be contacted regarding the debt. Other parties can be contacted for information, but the collector cannot disclose the reason for the contact. Further, the only information that can be obtained from these third parties is the address, phone number, and place of employment of the debtor.

These third parties cannot be told about the debt, the amount, delinquencies, or any other information about the debtor. The collector must even be careful to use appropriate stationery when writing for information so that the letterhead does not disclose the nature of the collector's business. Postcard contact with the debtor or third parties is prohibited because of the likelihood that others will see the information about the debtor.

Prohibited Acts.   Collectors have certain other restrictions on their conduct under the FDCPA. The general prohibition in the FDCPA is that collectors cannot "harass, oppress, or abuse" the debtor. Continuing to make calls without identifying themselves as collectors is also a FDCPA violation. Using abusive language or physical force is prohibited. Misrepresenting the authority of a collector is also prohibited, as is posing as a law enforcement official or producing false legal documents. Debtors cannot be threatened with prison or other actions not authorized by law.

Gryzbowski v I.C. System, Inc. (Case 14.6) involves an issue of FDCPA violations.

CASE 14.6   *Gryzbowski v I.C. System, Inc.*
691 F.Supp.2d 618 (M.D. Pa. 2010)

Cell Phones, Debts, and Anonymous Callers

FACTS

I.C. Systems, Inc. (Defendant) is a debt collection company located in Minnesota that collects nationwide, particularly in Pennsylvania. Donna Gryzbowski (Plaintiff) was a resident of Archibald, Pennsylvania, and was a debtor who owed money to one of I.C. Systems's clients, Washington Mutual. IC Systems employees called Ms. Gryzbowski's cell phone 11 times and requested that she return the call to I.C. Only one employee identified herself as a collector. On only four of the calls did the employees give their names with the request for the

returned call. I.C. employees said they did not identify themselves because they thought they were calling Ms. Gryzbowski's employer. However, the greeting on the cell phone provided:

Hi, you have reached Donna. Please leave your name, your number, and a brief message and a good time to call and I'll get back to you just as soon as I can. I appreciate your call, so I'll talk to you when I can. Thank you. Bye.

Ms. Gryzbowski filed suit alleging violations of the FDCPA for excessive contact and the failure of I.C.

workers to identify themselves as debt collectors. She filed a motion for summary judgment.

JUDICIAL OPINION

VANASKIE, District Judge

The FDCPA provides that a violation occurs when the debt collector fails to disclose in the initial written communication with the consumer and, in addition, if the initial communication with the consumer is oral, in the initial oral communication, that the debt collector is attempting to collect a debt and that any information obtained will be used for that purpose, and the failure to disclose in subsequent communications that the communication is from a debt collector . . . 15 U.S.C.A. § 1692e(11).

With regard to communication with third parties, the FDCPA provides:

[W]ithout the prior consent of the consumer given directly to the debt collector, or the express permission of a court of competent jurisdiction, or as reasonably necessary to effectuate a postjudgment judicial remedy, a debt collector may not communicate, in connection with the collection of any debt, with any person other than the consumer, his attorney, a consumer reporting agency if otherwise permitted by law, the creditor, the attorney of the creditor, or the attorney of the debt collector.

It is Defendant's position that based on the FDCPA's blanket prohibition regarding disclosure of debt information to third parties, Defendant does not state that it is a debt collector calling to collect a debt when it contacts a consumer at their place of employment because they want to avoid the "inadvertent or unintentional disclosure of this information" to the debtor's employer. Accordingly, the essence of Defendant's argument is that in order to guard against the potential violation of section 1692c(b), Defendant violates section 1692c(11) by failing to identify itself as a debt collector.

Just as it is not reasonable to destroy a village in order to save it, neither is it reasonable to violate an Act in order to comply with it. It was not reasonable for [the Defendant] to violate § 1692e(11) of the Fair Debt Collection Practices Act with every message it left in order to avoid the possibility that some of those messages might lead to a violation of § 1692c(b).

The defendant complained that leaving messages on answering machines would result in potential violation of § 1692c(b), therefore resulting in a rule of law forcing it not to leave any messages on answering machines. We have not decided that issue, but even if [the Defendant's] assumption is correct, the answer is that the Act does not guarantee a debt collector the right to leave answering machine messages.

[Defendant argues that] when leaving a voicemail or answering machine message, there is a concern that someone other than the consumer will hear the message. Thus, debt collectors are faced with a "Hobson's choice" of, on the one hand, leaving a "short, non-offensive message" that fails to make the necessary disclosures and thereby exposes the debt collector to claimed violations of § 1692d and § 1692e or, alternatively, leaving a message that makes the necessary disclosures but in so doing runs the risk that a third party will hear the message, thus exposing the debt collector to claimed violations of the prohibition in 15 U.S.C. § 1692c(b) on third party disclosures.

First, the calls were not placed to Plaintiff at her place of employment; they were calls to her personal cellular telephone. Although Defendant believed that the number was that of her employer, its subjective belief is irrelevant as the FDCPA is a strict liability statute. Second, Defendant has failed to cite persuasive authority that a debt collector's identification duty changes when it leaves voicemail messages on a person's cellular telephone as opposed to a home or work voicemail. As found by other courts, "leaving the recorded messages on the consumer's home telephone number [does] not cure the dilemma because the possibility still existed that a spouse, relative, or roommate would listen to the message." Accordingly, Defendant finds itself in its current "predicament" only because of the specific way that was selected to collect debts.

A message left with a co-worker, identifying the caller as a debt collector, would be a clear violation of section 1692c(b), as the co-worker is clearly a third party. A voicemail or answering machine, however, is not a third party. The potential violation of the statute does not occur when the message is left, but instead, if or when a third party overhears the debt collector's message.

Defendant does not dispute that the voicemail messages were left in connection with the collection of a debt. Accordingly, Defendant has admitted to leaving messages on Plaintiff's voicemail that, though in connection with the collection of a debt, did not disclose Defendant's identity as a debt collector, excepting the October 1, 2008 call, in violation of the FDCPA.

Although Defendant does not specifically proffer the bona fide error defense, it is clear that the defense would also be without merit. "To prevail on this defense, the debt collector must establish by a preponderance of the evidence that the FDCPA violation was unintentional and resulted from a bona fide error notwithstanding procedures reasonably adapted to avoid error." Defendant admits that it called Plaintiff, left messages on her voice mail, and did not identify itself as a debt collector. As Defendant admits that its violation was intentional, in order to guard against a potential violation of section 1692c(b), Defendant does not present a valid bona fide error defense. Moreover,

CONTINUED

its subjective belief that it was calling a place of employment where the messages may be heard by someone other than Plaintiff was unreasonable in light of the message that it received when it called Plaintiff's number, which gave no indication that messages left for her number were heard by anyone else.

As the FDCPA imposes strict liability, and Defendant admits to leaving messages on Plaintiff's voicemail without identifying itself as a debt collector, Defendant violated section 1692e(11) of the FDCPA. Defendant is not entitled to a bona fide error defense as it admits that the failure to identify itself as debt collector was intentional. Accordingly, Plaintiff's Motion for Summary Judgment based on Defendant's violation of section 1692e(11) of the FDCPA will be granted.

The FDCPA provides that "the placement of telephone calls without meaningful disclosure of the caller's identity" is conduct that a debt collector may not engage in and is a violation of the statute. 15 U.S.C.A. § 1692d(6). Plaintiff argues that Defendant's voicemail messages also violated section 1692d(6) of the FDCPA. Defendant again contends that the violation occurred in order to guard against potential disclosure pursuant to section 1692c(b).

The statute requires that debt collectors give meaningful disclosure to the debtor, except when the communication is with a third party. Meaningful disclosure has been held to require the debt collector "to disclose the caller's name, the debt collection company's name, and the nature of the debt collector's business."

As already discussed, Defendant does not contend that it provided meaningful disclosure of its identity when it called, but instead argues that to do so would potentially violate section 1692c(d). Accordingly, Plaintiff is entitled to summary judgment as to her claim pursuant to section 1692d(6) of the FDCPA.

Plaintiff's Motion for Summary Judgment will be granted.

CASE QUESTIONS

1. What does the court mean when it uses the term "Hobson's choice"?

2. What would you advise debt collectors to do in light of this case?

3. Are the rules for cell phones the same as those for landlines under the FDCPA?

Penalties for FDCPA Violations

Under the CFPA, much of the FDCPA enforcement has been transferred to the BCFP. The Federal Trade Commission (FTC) still has some authority but the goal of the CFPA was to consolidate consumer protection into one bureau and have one source for consumer relief. The BCFP will have the same enforcement authority that the FTC did, in addition to any expanded powers it promulgates under the authority it has been given under the CFPA. At present, those remedies include cease-and-desist orders to stop collectors from violating the FDCPA and penalties for violations. However, the greatest power of enforcement under the FDCPA lies with individual debtors. Debtors who can prove collector violations can collect for actual injuries and mental distress. Debtors can also collect up to $1,000 in addition to actual damages for actions by collectors that are extreme, outrageous, malicious, or repeated. Attorney fees incurred by debtors in bringing their suits are also recoverable.

Suits for Enforcement of Debts

Occasionally, collection is ineffective and there is no collateral to repossess. The creditor has few options left but to bring suit to enforce collection of the debt. In bringing a successful suit, the creditor will obtain a **judgment,** which is the court's official document stating that the debtor owes the money and the collector is entitled to that money. However, in debt cases, the judgment is only the beginning. Once the creditor has the judgment, it must be executed to obtain funds.

A judgment is executed by having it attach to various forms of the debtor's property. For example, a judgment can attach to real property. A judgment can also attach to funds by **garnishment,** which is the attachment of a judgment to an account, paycheck, or receivables. Once there is attachment, the creditor is entitled to those funds. The third party holding the funds must comply with the terms of the garnishment and release the appropriate amount of funds to the creditor.

Employees are given some protection under the Consumer Credit Protection Act with respect to garnishments. One such protection is the limitation on the employer's ability to fire employees who have their wages garnisheed by a single creditor.

Under the Consumer Credit Protection Act, the amount that consumer creditors can garnish on debtor wages is limited to 25 percent of the net wages. Garnishment for past-due child support is limited to 50 percent of net wages.

The End of the Line on Enforcement of Debts: Bankruptcy

Federal laws afford debtors shelter when their obligations cannot be paid. *Bankruptcy* is the legal process of having a debtor—individual, partnership, corporation, LLC (see Chapter 20)—turn over all nonexempt assets in exchange for a release from debts following the distribution of those assets to creditors. In October 2005, the **Bankruptcy Abuse Prevention and Consumer Protection Act of 2005** (BAPCPA) took effect. One purpose of BAPCPA was to curb a 15-year trend of increases in the number of bankruptcies. The data indicated that bankruptcy was being used as a strategic tool by consumers and businesses alike, rather than as a relief mechanism for those who had experienced a loss of income through illness, accident, or loss of employment. Changes in the law require consumers who wish to declare bankruptcy to show through a prescribed statutory formula that they do not have the means for repaying debts. The ability to declare bankruptcy hinges on disposable income, a figure obtained after the court allows for housing, food, and other necessary expenses. If the consumer has disposable income, then a debt adjustment plan, rather than a bankruptcy, is required.

Bankruptcy takes one of three forms. *Chapter 7* bankruptcy is the liquidation form, in which the entity is dissolved or the individual's debts are discharged. *Chapter 11* is the reorganization form, in which a business enjoys protection from collection and creditors until a new plan for satisfying the business obligations is approved. *Chapter 13* is the consumer debt adjustment plan, under which consumers can be given a new repayment plan for their debts. Before consumers can declare Chapter 7 (liquidation) bankruptcy, they must go through Chapter 13. In fact, if consumers who file directly for Chapter 7 bankruptcy do not meet the means test, the courts classify their filing as an abuse of the bankruptcy process and require Chapter 13 proceedings.

Credit repair organizations, counseling and debt service organizations that, for a fee, help consumers work through debt crises, are subject to additional disclosure requirements under the CFPA. These CROs, as they are known, must disclose fully their role, their fees, and that bankruptcy may be a result or recommendation from their efforts on behalf of the consumer debtor. CROs are regulated under the Credit Repair Organizations Act (15 U.S.C. §§ 1679–1679j) and are subject to private suit by consumer debtors for misrepresentations and failures to disclose information about fees, payments, and bankruptcy. In addition, CROs must disclose any affiliations with creditors or credit organizations. The BCFP has been given expanded authority to regulate credit counseling organizations as well.

Individuals and businesses can file a petition for bankruptcy themselves or they can be petitioned into bankruptcy through an involuntary petition. In a voluntary case, the court now must make the disposable income determination. In an involuntary case, the debtor must have a chance to present evidence against being placed into bankruptcy.

Debtors do have certain property exemptions in bankruptcy—property they do not lose to the bankruptcy estate. Those exemptions have been cut back substantially. For example, the homestead exemptions in many states protected all homes, regardless of costs. The reforms limit the amount of equity the debtor can retain following the bankruptcy and how long the protection applies.

Not all debts are discharged in bankruptcy. Alimony, child support, student loans, and taxes are examples of debts that survive bankruptcy.

International Credit Issues

With the problems in the world economy, bankruptcies are increasing substantially.[3] However, significant differences distinguish a declaration of bankruptcy in the United States from one in another country. In Japan, for example:

- Individual debtors can keep only kitchen utensils and $1,500 in cash.
- A meeting, called *dogeza*, is held wherein a company owner sits on the floor among creditors and begs for forgiveness while the creditors are permitted to yell abusive epithets at the debtor.

Other aspects of Japanese law make a company's failure and the impact on individual businesspeople very different. Japanese creditors routinely require guarantors, even on business debts, and most businesspeople rely on family for such guarantors. As a result, many in-laws find themselves responsible for debt when the business of their son-in-law fails. The divorce rate for executives of bankrupt Japanese businesses is twice the national average.

The suicide rate for failed Japanese businesspeople is 50 percent greater than in the general population. Under Japanese law, insurance companies do pay benefits even when death results from suicide, as long as the policy has been in effect for at least one year. And the suicide rate for people with insurance policies is 50 percent higher than in the general population.

B I O G R A P H Y

The Brokes: A Case Study on Bankruptcy

The Brokes, a married couple in their early 40s, have two children in private schools. They are residents of Memphis, Shelby County, Tennessee; their annual gross income is $86,496. Like many debtors, the Brokes lost their home following an unsuccessful Chapter 13 case three years ago. They now rent a house for $2,000 a month. They owe back federal taxes in the amount of $9,000. They have secured debt on two cars with remaining balances of $10,000 and $6,000, respectively, and unsecured consumer debt totaling $28,000. They desire to seek relief under Chapter 7 of the Bankruptcy Code. The Brokes' gross monthly income is $7,208. After deducting taxes and other mandatory payroll deductions of $1,509, the couple has $5,699 in monthly income. The means test requires several additional deductions from the Brokes' gross monthly income. Section 707(b)(A)(2)(ii) provides a deduction for living and housing expenses using National Standards and Local Standards and additional Internal Revenue Service (IRS) figures. Allowable living expenses for a family of four in Ura and Ima Brokes' income bracket, based on national standards, total $1,564, and housing and utility figures for Shelby County, Tennessee, allow $1,354. In addition, there are allowable expenses for transportation. Based on IRS figures, the Brokes can subtract national ownership costs of $475 for the first car and $338 for the second, as well as regional $336, respectively. They are also permitted to deduct vehicle operating and public transportation costs of $242. They can also deduct their reasonably necessary health insurance costs, here $600, and $250 a month for private school tuition. Subtracting all of these figures from the Brokes' monthly income leaves $540. Under § 707(b)(2)(A)(iii), the Brokes can subtract payments on secured debt. The amount contractually due on

their two automobiles over the next 60 months is $16,000. After dividing this total by 60 and rounding to the nearest dollar, the monthly allowable deduction for secured debt is $267. Subtracting this amount from $540 leaves $273. Next come priority claim deductions. The Brokes are not subject to any child support or alimony claims, but they do owe $9,000 in back taxes. Again, dividing this amount by 60 yields a deductible amount of $150. Subtracting this from $273 leaves $123 in disposable monthly income. This figure would be multiplied by 60, amounting to a total of $7,380 in disposable income over the five-year period. Abuse is thus statutorily presumed because the debtors' current monthly income reduced by allowable amounts is not less than either $7,000 (25 percent of their non-priority unsecured claims of $28,000) or $6,000. The Brokes' Chapter 7 case will therefore be dismissed (or they will be allowed voluntarily to convert their Chapter 7 case to a case under Chapter 13). Does the means test make it more difficult for debtors to declare bankruptcy?*

*Robert J. Landry III and Nancy Hisey Mardis, "Consumer Bankruptcy Reform: Debtors' Prison without Bars or 'Just Desserts' for Deadbeats?" 36 *Golden Gate UL Rev* 91 (2006).

Summary

What statutes affect credit contracts?

- Usury—charging interest in excess of the statutory maximum
- Equal Credit Opportunity Act (ECOA)—federal law prohibiting denial of credit on the basis of sex, race, color, religion, national origin, age, marital status, public assistance income, alimony, or child support income and plans for additional family
- Truth in Lending Act (TILA)—federal law governing disclosures in credit contracts
- Consumer Credit Protection Act (CCPA)—first federal statute on credit disclosure requirements
- Credit Card Accountability, Responsibility, and Disclosure Act (CARD)—recent federal law that expands rights of consumers in solicitation, billing, and payment in open-end credit transactions
- Open-end transactions—credit card transactions

- Closed-end transactions—finance contracts for preestablished amounts, such as the financing of a television purchase
- Bureau of Consumer Financial Protection (BCFP)—new federal agency created to enforce consumer credit laws
- Home Ownership and Equity Protection Act (HOEPA)—a credit disclosure and consumer rights statutes directed at second mortgages and home equity lines of credit
- Fair Credit and Charge Card Disclosure Act of 1988—federal law governing solicitation of credit card customers
- Regulation Z—federal regulation governing credit disclosures
- Three-day cooling-off period—right of rescission on credit contracts initiated in the home

- Home Equity Loan Consumer Protection Act of 1988—federal law requiring disclosures for home equity consumer loans
- Fair Credit Billing Act—federal law governing rights of debtors to dispute credit card charge
- Fair Credit Reporting Act (FCRA)—federal law regulating disclosure of credit information to and by third parties
- Consumer Leasing Act—federal law governing consumer lease transactions
- Credit Repair Organizations Act—federal law that provides consumer debtors with disclosures regarding counseling and payment arrangement services
- Bankruptcy Abuse Prevention and Consumer Protection Act of 2005 (BAPCPA)—new bankruptcy law that sets higher requirements for consumer declaration of Chapter 7 bankruptcy
- Dodd–Frank Consumer Financial Protection Act, also called Wall Street Reform and Consumer Financial Protection Act of 2010 (DFCFPA); expands

consumer protection in mortgage credit transactions and creates one agency, the Bureau of Consumer Financial Protection, to consolidate interpretation, promulgation, and enforcement of all consumer credit laws

How are credit contracts enforced?

- Security interest—pledge of collateral for credit
- Fair Debt Collections Practices Act (FDCPA)—federal law regulating collection of consumer debt by third parties
- Judgment—court order authorizing collection of money from party
- Garnishment—attachment of account, paycheck, or receivables to collect judgment
- Bankruptcy—federal process of collecting assets to pay creditors and discharge debts
- Chapter 7—liquidation bankruptcy
- Chapter 11—reorganization bankruptcy
- Chapter 13—consumer debt adjustment plan

Questions and Problems

1. In May 1976, TRW (a credit reporting agency) issued a consumer report on Bennie E. Bryant in connection with his application for a federally insured home loan under the Veterans Administration. The consumer report had several inaccuracies, and Mr. Bryant went to TRW to point out the matters needing correction. For unrelated reasons, the mortgage did not close.

In August 1976, Mr. Bryant applied for another mortgage. On September 28, TRW called the mortgage company to let them know his credit report would be unfavorable. When the mortgage company notified Mr. Bryant, he again went to TRW offices and explained that the September report contained new inaccuracies in addition to those that were part of the May report. After this meeting, a memo about possible inaccuracies was placed in Mr. Bryant's file. However, the credit report without corrections was issued to the mortgage company on September 30. No follow-through had been done on the file memo.

Mr. Bryant's August mortgage application was originally denied. After personal efforts on his part, however, the credit report was corrected and the mortgage was eventually given.

Does Mr. Bryant have any rights and protections? [*Bryant v TRW, Inc.*, 689 F.2d 72 (6th Cir. 1982)]

2. Clarence J. Ellis was employed by Glover & Gardner as a laborer and carpenter from August 1979 until June 18, 1980. On June 18, 1980, Charles Gardner, the president and owner of Glover & Gardner, received a notice of garnishment of Mr. Ellis's wages and fired Mr. Ellis that day. It was Mr. Ellis's first garnishment. Mr. Gardner said he fired Mr. Ellis because of alcoholism, poor job performance, insubordination, and dishonesty. However, Mr. Ellis's separation notice, which was sent to the Tennessee Department of Employment Security, gave as the reason for termination the garnishment. Did Mr. Gardner violate the law? [*Ellis v Glover & Gardner Construction Co.*, 562 F. Supp. 1054 (M.D. Tenn. 1983)]

3. Maurice Miller obtained an American Express credit card in 1966, and his wife, Virginia, was given a supplementary card. Her card had a different number, was issued in her name, and had a separate annual fee. When Mr. Miller died in 1979, American Express canceled both credit cards. Mrs. Miller sued for violation of the ECOA. Has there been a violation?

[*Miller v American Express Co.*, 688 F.2d 1235 (9th Cir. 1982)]

4. The city administration of Columbus, Ohio, was frustrated because of problems with water bills and tenants. If the city set up a direct billing relationship with the tenants, their landlord was unaware that there were delinquent water bills. Tenants would then move out and leave the landlord with the water bills, bills the landlord refused to pay because they were not on the landlord's account. The city developed a process whereby it would contract directly with the tenant, but through a joint agreement would notify the landlord when the tenant was delinquent. The city could then refuse to turn the water on for any property where there was a delinquency from a previous tenant because the landlord was jointly liable. Hazel Golden, a tenant, tried to get direct billing for a home she rented but was denied because the city required the landlord's joint signature. Golden filed suit alleging a violation of the ECOA because the city's policy has the effect of rejecting a higher proportion of female and minority applicants for water service than other applicants. Golden's expert witness testified that women and minorities are underrepresented in the population of homeowners in the city. Because the policy permits only homeowners to directly contract for water service, the policy has a disparate impact on anyone who is underrepresented among homeowners. Is the city's policy a violation of the ECOA? [*Golden v City of Columbus*, 404 F.3d 950 (6th Cir. 2005)]

5. Would the collection by a collection agency of a dishonored check for $23.15 written by a consumer to a Circle K store be covered under the FDCPA? [*Wade v Regional Credit Association*, 87 F.3d 1098 (9th Cir. 1996)]

6. James A. Swanson received a letter from a collection agency, the Southern Oregon Credit Service, indicating that if payment in full or definite arrangements for payment of his account were not made within 48 hours, the agency would begin a complete investigation into his employment and assets. Is the agency's threat a violation of the FDCPA? [*Swanson v Southern Oregon Credit Service, Inc.*, 869 F.2d 1222 (9th Cir. 1988)]

7. Nash Cooley is a 66-year-old African American male who lives in Montgomery, Alabama. Since the mid-1980s, Mr. Cooley had earned a living from his ownership of residential rental properties in the Montgomery area. Mr. Cooley owns approximately 15 apartment units and 24 houses.

In order to have the financial flexibility to invest in new real estate ventures, Mr. Cooley maintained active lines of credit with various financial institutions. By the summer of 2000, Mr. Cooley had $100,000 in unsecured lines of credit at two separate banks. He ultimately hoped to establish five $100,000 lines of credit in order to complete a real estate project that he began in 1992. To meet his financial goals, Mr. Cooley approached Sterling Bank in September 2000 about another $100,000 unsecured line of credit. He chose Sterling because he had a prior business relationship with Kenny Hill, who had worked at another bank where Mr. Cooley had a line of credit. In early 2000, Mr. Hill had spoken with Mr. Cooley about bringing some of his business to Sterling. Mr. Cooley opened a checking account with Sterling and maintained a balance of approximately $15,000 in the account, then deposited a $100,000 insurance settlement several months before applying for his credit line.

In September 2000, Mr. Cooley met with Mr. Hill to apply for a $100,000 unsecured line of credit with Sterling. He submitted a credit application and provided Mr. Hill with all of his relevant financial information, including tax returns and a personal financial statement. On September 15, 2000, Mr. Hill conducted a credit check on Mr. Cooley that revealed a "Beacon Score" of 749. Although this score was commensurate with an "excellent credit rating," Mr. Hill became concerned about Mr. Cooley's income level after reviewing the remainder of Mr. Cooley's financial information. His most recent tax return indicated that Mr. Cooley and his wife had a joint pretax income of $106,214. Of this amount, Mr. Hill calculated that the income attributable to Mr. Cooley was $51,483. Because Mr. Cooley was applying for an unsecured line of credit in his name only, Mr. Hill was worried that the income level was insufficient for him to obtain a $100,000 line of credit. Additionally, Mr. Hill was apprehensive about approving Mr. Cooley's request knowing that Mr. Cooley had two existing $100,000 lines of credit.

After Mr. Hill compiled Mr. Cooley's loan materials, he presented them to Bob Ramsey, Sterling's executive vice president in charge of lending. Because Mr. Hill did not have the authority to approve a loan in excess of $50,000, he met with Mr. Ramsey to discuss the Cooley loan application. During this meeting Mr. Ramsey reviewed Mr. Cooley's financial statement and tax return. Mr. Hill expressed his concerns about Mr. Cooley's financial situation, and Mr. Ramsey concurred. In short, Mr. Ramsey concluded that Mr. Cooley's "individual income of $51,464 simply did not justify adding another $100,000 unsecured debt on top of the two existing lines of credit at other banks totaling $200,000." Instead of denying Mr. Cooley's request outright, Mr. Ramsey suggested making either a secured loan in the same amount or an unsecured loan for $25,000. After Mr. Ramsey and Mr. Hill agreed that a counteroffer was the best solution, Mr. Hill informed Mr. Ramsey that Mr. Cooley was "African American and might claim racism." In response,

Mr. Ramsey suggested discussing the matter with Alan Worrell, Sterling's chief executive officer. Mr. Worrell agreed with Mr. Hill and Mr. Ramsey's assessment of Mr. Cooley's financial situation and indicated his preference to find an alternative way to establish a credit relationship with Mr. Cooley.

On September 18, 2000, Mr. Hill informed Mr. Cooley of Sterling's decision and gave him a document entitled "Notice of Action Taken." The document explained that Sterling could not provide Mr. Cooley with a $100,000 unsecured line of credit but was willing to offer "a $25,000 unsecured line of credit or a larger secured line." In response, Mr. Cooley immediately requested a list of the individuals on Sterling's Board of Directors so he could contact them about his loan denial. Mr. Cooley also expressed his belief that Sterling was discriminating against him on the basis of race.

Mr. Worrell met with Mr. Cooley and told him that he had "good credit" but expressed concerns about his income level and existing lines of credit. At the conclusion of the meeting, Mr. Worrell emphasized that he wanted to do business with Mr. Cooley.

During Sterling's Board of Directors meeting on September 20, 2000, and, according to Greg Calhoun, an African-American member of Sterling's Board of Directors, individual Board members began discussing Mr. Cooley's application during the meeting. Mr. Calhoun stated in his deposition that the Board "didn't think [Mr. Cooley] could qualify for a hundred thousand dollar line of credit being . . . that he was a retired school teacher." Moreover, Board members "jok[ed] about [Mr. Cooley's application]" and "laughed about Cooley." In response, Mr. Calhoun told the other Board members that he believed they were putting Mr. Cooley down. Mr. Calhoun then "told them they was [*sic*] all Republicans, and they're all members of the Montgomery Country Club. And there's no way that a black man can come in here and get money from the bank." Following this statement, Mr. Calhoun informed the Board that he was resigning. In Mr. Calhoun's opinion, Sterling denied the loan application "because of [Mr. Cooley's] skin color."

Mr. Cooley filed suit for violation of the ECOA. Should he prevail in the suit? [*Cooley v Sterling Bank*, 280 F.Supp.2d 1331 (M.D. Ala. 2003)]

8. American Future Systems, Inc. (AFS), sells china, cookware, crystal, and tableware, and extends credit to its customers for such purchases. Sales on a credit basis amount to over 95 percent of AFS sales. First National Acceptance Corporation (FNAC) is AFS's credit company and is wholly owned by AFS. AFS affords young people and minorities a chance to obtain credit in spite of their lack of prior credit histories.

Its general standards for credit are (1) a telephone in the residence, (2) positive credit experience of at least $100, and (3) employment with regular income. AFS has three specific marketing programs: a summer program; a winter program for single white females; and a winter program for minorities, married persons, and males.

Under the summer program, target customers are single white females living at home with a parent who could cosign for the credit. AFS does not always require the parent's signature and might ship goods to this group without checking credit histories. This market is reached by salespeople who are sent only to white neighborhoods and instructed to avoid neighborhoods where there might be a racial mix.

If salespeople encounter a minority customer in their presentations, AFS will sell the goods and extend credit to them, but a credit check is done on both the applicant and cosigner before goods are shipped. About 20 percent of the applications of minority applicants are denied.

The winter program has two parts. The preferred part of the winter program consists of sales to single white women who are sophomores, juniors, or seniors in four-year colleges or nursing schools. The other part of the program focuses on minorities, males, and married persons attending college or vocational schools. Shipment to preferred customers is immediate, with automatic credit approval. Shipment to the nonpreferred winter group is deferred until the applicant makes three timely monthly payments.

AFS presented evidence that minority customers are, as a group, less creditworthy than their white counterparts. However, the statistics presented did not account for AFS's failure to solicit in minority neighborhoods.

The U.S. government brought suit for violation of the ECOA. Is the AFS program a violation of ECOA? [*United States v American Future Systems, Inc.*, 743, F2d 169 (3d Cir. 1984)]

9. In 1984, Jean Mayes purchased Albert L. Silva, d/b/a Rainbow Motors, a Nantucket car dealership. In May 1985, Mr. Mayes entered into financing arrangements with Chrysler Credit Corporation to finance his car inventory. The borrower was Rainbow Motors, with Mr. Mayes as president and sole shareholder.

Chrysler demanded that Mr. Mayes and his wife, Michele Mayes, sign a "continuing guaranty" before it would extend credit. Mrs. Mayes, a well-compensated corporate attorney, was listed as a director and officer of Rainbow, but she did not participate in managing it. Rainbow defaulted, and Chrysler brought suit against Mrs. Mayes, seeking $750,126.41. Mrs. Mayes said Chrysler was stopped from collecting the debt because of the ECOA. Is she correct? [*Mayes v Chrysler Credit Corp.*, 37 F.3d 9 (1st Cir. 1994)]

10. In late 1999, Paula Rossman received a "Pre-Qualified Invitation" to obtain a credit card from defendant Fleet Bank. The solicitation was for a "Fleet Platinum MasterCard" with a low annual percentage rate and "no annual fee." If interested, the recipient of this offer was to check a box next to which was written, "YES! I want the top card for genuine value and superior savings, the no-annual-fee Platinum MasterCard." An asterisk directed the recipient to a note that stated, "See the TERMS OF PREQUALIFIED OFFER and CONSUMER INFORMATION for detailed rate and other information."

The enclosure entitled "Consumer Information" contained the Schumer Box, the table of basic credit card information required under the Truth in Lending Act, 15 U.S.C. § 1601 et seq., as amended by the Fair Credit and Charge Card Disclosure Act of 1988. Within the Schumer Box was a column with the heading "Annual Fee"; the box beneath that heading contained only the word "None." On the "Consumer Information" enclosure, but outside the Schumer Box, Fleet listed other fees. Also in that location was the statement, "We reserve the right to change the benefit features associated with your Card at any time."

Ms. Rossman responded to Fleet's offer, and soon thereafter received her "no-annual-fee Platinum MasterCard." Along with the card, Ms. Rossman was sent Fleet's "Cardholder Agreement," which contained the following provision concerning annual fees: "No annual membership fee will be charged to your Account."

The agreement provided for various applicable annual percentage rates charged on outstanding balances, including the standard rate for purchases (7.99%) and several higher rates that could be triggered by certain acts or omissions on the part of the cardholder. Among these was a rate of 24.99 percent that Fleet was entitled to impose "upon any closure of [the] Account." The Agreement also contained a change-in-terms provision, which stated:

> We have the right to change any of the terms of this Agreement at any time. You will be given notice of a change as required by applicable law. Any change in terms governs your Account as of the effective date, and will, as permitted by law and at our option, apply both to transactions made on or after such date and to any outstanding Account balance.

In May 2000, Fleet sent a letter to Ms. Rossman announcing its intention to change the terms of the agreement.

Soon thereafter, Fleet notified Ms. Rossman that the annual fee would be imposed almost immediately:

> We are modifying the terms of your Fleet Cardholder Agreement only to correct the timing of the annual membership fee previously disclosed. That fee will first be charged to your Account in your billing cycle that closes in July, 2000, and will be charged in that billing cycle each year thereafter.

A $35 fee was charged to Ms. Rossman's account by July 6, 2000, in accordance with the second letter. Ms. Rossman filed a class action suit against Fleet for violations of the TILA. The District Court dismissed the case. Ms. Rossman appealed. Should the case have been dismissed? [*Rossman v Fleet Bank Nat. Ass'n*, 280 F.3d 384 (3d Cir., 2002)]

Economics and the Law

The Moral Hazard of Walking Away from Debt

Ask folks who's responsible for this economic recession, malaise, recovery . . . (substitute your own ideological bent word here), and you will get a barrage of "B" words: Bush, Bernanke, Barack, and bums, those of the Wall Street type. However, to continue the "B" alliteration, before you blame the bums, a little introspection on mortgage walk-aways.

Those collateralized debt obligations (CDOs) that felled Lehman, Bear Stearns, and quite nearly AIG, were securities based on pools of mortgages. Wall Streeters sold and analyzed those CDOs based on the usual notions of risk about home mortgages: banks screened for deadbeats, those with home mortgages put in a fairly good chunk of change as a down payment, and monthly mortgage payments were not consuming net income.

Their assumptions about mortgage risks were wrong. During the real estate boom, bubble, etc., mortgages down payments ranged from 0–3%. Pick-a-Pay mortgages allowed borrowers to choose their monthly payments for the first three years of their loan. Of course, there was interest

CONTINUED

and plenty of hell to pay at that three-year mark. These creative mortgages financed granite countertops, 3500 square feet, and shattered normal lending standards. Once the boom busted, mortgage risks emerged with a vengeance. Wall Street nearly collapsed. We clicked our tongues and blamed greed. Yet, where would we be if creative mortgages hadn't happened? Better yet, where would we be if there had been responsible mortgage borrowers?

Ethical analysis looks at this question: How did you get in this situation in the first place? In the words of the not-so-great Bob Dylan, "When you got nothin', you got nothin' to lose." In the words of the great UT Austin economics Professor Stan Liebowitz, "skin in the game" is the single most important factor in determining default, think walk-away. If you had a little down payment and no equity to speak of, as creative borrowers do, you walk when your mortgage is more than your property value—underwater. Some walked away with arms full—taking everything that moves (or doesn't) from their homes, including copper plumbing.

USA Today headlines read as if innocents are robbed of their under-water homes by Bush, Bernanke, Barack *et al.* Facts reveal otherwise. One under-water fellow, who was but one year from retirement, confessed that he took a second mortgage of $100,000 on his $642,000 home to put in a theater, fitness room, and bathroom in his basement and expand his living room. He now faces foreclosure because his payments are going up (he signed at a 3.25% rate that goes to 5.85%) and his house value has dropped to $590,000. He cannot get another second mortgage to pay off the first second mortgage for the remodeling lollapalooza. One borrower, grinching about his ineligibility for government foreclosure aid, bought a $1,000,000 home with $4,400 monthly payments, over 50% of the net income of this single-wage earner family.

If the anecdotes don't dispel the myths about hardship, the data are irrefutable. Of the foreclosures in the second half of 2008, only 183,447 resulted from the loss of employment. Other foreclosures? Negative net equity: 283,305; a 3% or less down payment: 130,014; low initial interest rate going higher: 60,942; and poor FICO score: 148,697. So, 624,958 foreclosures for financial folly vs. 183,447 for loss of employment. The 12% of the homes with negative equity are responsible for 47% of the foreclosures. Pick-a-Pay re-default rates are 55%. If you refinance the mortgage challenged, the default rate is 55% on their refinance.

Yet there are economists, largely those who still believe Keynes reigns, who say the walk-away is the smart thing to do because business does it all the time. This trite advice is rationalization. "Everybody does it" is not ethical analysis; it is shortsighted comfort language designed to salve that conscience that pricks, "You have not fulfilled your promise to pay for your not-so-humble abode."

Ethical analysis also looks at the impact our choices and conduct have on others, including neighborhoods, communities, and the economic system. In lieu of, "Hey, I'm just getting what I can, just like everyone else," ponder, "What would the world look like if everyone behaved as you are?" What would things look like if everyone just walked away? Well, dear readers, you are living through what happens. The market is glutted and prices, even for the above-water mortgage folks, fall further. The drop is about 50% in Phoenix, Atlanta, and even Chula Vista. Detroit has homes for sale for $7,000. Short sales reduce the value of every home in a neighborhood. The presence of so many abandoned properties finds city workers, paid by tax dollars, mowing lawns and doing upkeep on abandoned properties. Vandalized vacant properties attract criminal activity. Baltimore and Detroit are bulldozing areas with high concentrations of walk-away properties.

If you've raised a child you know that consequences for poor choices modify behavior. Keep buying a new bike for your kids each time they leave it outside and it is stolen will find you mortgaging your home to buy replacement bikes. Make them earn the money to pay for their own new bike and that bike will be inside and securely locked, probably to their wrists and beds. Moral hazard does result in economic sensibility and produces long-term prosperity.

So, howl about Wall Street and the failure of executives who walked away unscathed from their companies' collapses. Apply the same standard to those who took out mortgages that put them in over the heads in even the best of economies. They have left messes in neighborhoods, cities, and lenders with their abandoned homes and unpaid mortgages. Accountability and responsibility apply on Main Street, too.

For a look at the American Bankruptcy Institute: http://www.abiworld.org.

Reprinted from *The Arizona Republic*, by Marianne M. Jennings, April 25, 2010.

Notes

1. Nick Timiraos, "Homeowners Size Up Housing-Aid Plan," *Wall Street Journal*, March 5, 2009, p. A4.

2. The case has a complex procedural history. This decision concluded that there was no class action but that a violation of TILA did occur. However, Chevy Chase Bank appealed and earned a stay on the case until the class action made its way through the court system, *Andrews v Chevy Chase Bank, FSB*, 2007 WL 419507 (E.D. Wis. 2007), until the class action issue was resolved. *Andrews v Chevy Chase Bank, FSB*, 474 F.Supp.2d 1006 (E.D. Wis. 2007). The judgment of that court was reversed and remanded by the federal appellate court. *Andrews v Chevy Chase Bank*, 545 F.3d 570 (7th Cir. (Wis.) 2008). Certiorari denied, *Andrews v Chevy Chase Bank*, 129 S.Ct. 2864 (2009). The case then went back to the lower court for damage computation for the Andrews (not a class action), 2010 WL 959996 (E.D. Wis.)

3. Bankruptcy is a universal process that has a deep history. See the course website and *Instructor's Manual* for more background.

15

Business Intellectual Property

T

he Vatican Library. The House of Windsor. The estates of Princess Diana and Albert Einstein. Louis Vuitton. NASCAR. Octomom. The common thread? They all have lucrative arrangements for the licensing of their images and symbols. The law affords protection for these images and symbols even though the property right is a bundle of images and feelings about a person, business, or logo. This chapter covers the rights of businesses and their intellectual property. Property comes in different forms, and this chapter focuses on one form of personal property: intellectual property rights. What types of intellectual property does a business own? What are the rights and issues in this property owned by a business? What statutory protections exist for intellectual property? What issues of property protection exist in international business operations? In marketing, we learn the importance of "brand." This chapter gives the legal backdrop for ensuring a brand's exclusivity. Protecting the goodwill, symbols, names, and motifs that give a business its identity is an important part of the ongoing success of a business.[1] ■

Possession is nine points of the law. No, it's not. Paperwork is.

Harvard Business Review, September/October 1995

We must take care to guard against two extremes equally prejudicial: the one, that men of ability, who have employed their time for the service of the community, may not be deprived of their just merits, and the reward for their ingenuity and labour; the other, that the world may not be deprived of improvements, nor the progress of the arts retarded.

Sayre v Moore,
102 Eng. Rep. 138, 140 (1785)

UPDATE ⬉
For up-to-date legal news, go to
mariannejennings.com

CONSIDER...

Victor and Cathy Moseley owned and operated an adult toy, gag gift, and lingerie shop near Elizabethtown, Kentucky that they called Victor's Little Secret. The store advertised its grand opening in a publication for the Fort Knox army base, and an army colonel notified Victoria's Secret of the shop's name and merchandise. Victoria's Secret owns 750 stores around the country and distributes 400 million catalogs each year via U.S.

mail. Two of Victoria's Secret's stores were located in Louisville, Kentucky, a short drive from Elizabethtown and Fort Knox.

Legal counsel for Victoria's Secret asked the Moseleys to stop using the name Victor's Secret because of possible confusion over the trademark and resulting dilution. Is Victoria's Secret correct? Are the Moseleys infringing the trademark, image, and name of Victoria's Secret?

What Can a Business Own? Intangible Property Rights

When we see a Dreyer's or Edy's Ice Cream truck driving along beside us, we understand that Dreyer's or Edy's Ice Cream owns that truck; it is a part of the Dreyer/Edy fleet and is carried as business equipment on the books of the Dreyer/Edy corporation. If someone took that truck, it would be theft, and Dreyer's or Edy's would be entitled to compensation if the truck were damaged or destroyed by the theft. Dreyer's or Edy's would also be entitled to compensation if someone hit the truck in an accident and damaged it. Because the truck is Dreyer or Edy's property, these companies enjoy certain rights of ownership. If someone stole or damaged the truck, the business could recover for the damages. However, the business also owns the distinctive label, colors, and stripes that are part of the Dreyer's or Edy's packaging and labels. If someone uses those symbols of their quality ice cream, the business can recover for the resulting damages.

Painted on to ice cream trucks, you see the signature brown and white stripes that are part of the ice cream's packaging. You recognize the writing, "Dreyer's (or Edy's) Grand Ice Cream." You know the truck from its distinctive paint and writing, probably before you even read the name "Dreyer's" or "Edy's." That distinctive color scheme, name, and writing are also business property. The recognition and goodwill that come from those brown stripes and the name are forms of **intangible property** that enjoy statutory protections. These protections include Dreyer's/Edy's right to prevent others from using their distinctive names and colors, which represent the goodwill and reputation of the company. The name, colors, stripes, and symbols represent a bundle of valuable rights for the business.

Forms of intangible property include patents, copyrights, trademarks, trade names, trade dress, and trade secrets. The protections for these types of property rights come from federal laws, international treaties, and common law rights of action for the damage to or taking of these forms of intangible property.

Patents

Patents are a type of legal monopoly obtained by filing certain information and forms with the U.S. Patent Office. So fundamental is the protection of new products and processes that the founding fathers placed protection for inventors in Article 1, Section 8, of the U.S. Constitution.

The Types and Length of Patents

There are three forms of patents. *Utility* or *function patents* cover machines, processes, and improvements to existing devices. For example, a computerized method for tracking a dry cleaner's inventory of clothing is protected by a patent. Prior to 1995, such a patent was valid for 17 years. However, in order to bring the U.S. laws into compliance with GATT provisions (see Chapter 7 for more information on this treaty), the protection was extended to 20 years. All WTO members follow the 20-year period for protection.

Design patents are those that protect the features of a product. The lace configuration on Eve of Milady bridal gowns and Procter & Gamble's method for putting elasticized legs on its disposable diapers are examples of product designs protected by patent. Design patents are granted for 14 years.

Finally, *plant patents* are obtained by those who develop new forms of plants and hybrids. Plants patents also carry a 20-year protection.

What You Can Patent: Patentability

Because protection is so extensive, an idea is patentable only if it is nonobvious, novel, and useful; and the idea must be reduced to some tangible form. The categories for patent eligibility include processes and machines as well as production of new matter. Whatever the category, the invention or process must be something that is new and nonobvious. New discoveries of existing matter are not patentable, but developing a process to extract that new matter for other use would be. For example, a discovery of a reproductive hormone in the male body is not patentable, but a product to stop production of that hormone for birth control purposes can be patented. A microbiologist who developed a bacterium that would break down crude oil, a valuable tool for cleaning up oil spills, was initially denied a patent because he was not manufacturing something, but just using something that was living. However, the U.S. Supreme Court held that developing a method for creating something that exists in nature is protected by the patent laws [*Diamond v Chakrabarty*, 447 U.S. 303 (1980)].

Business methods patents have been an area of judicial controversy. For example, patent number 4,022,227, called Method of Concealing Baldness, is a step-by-step process for combing hair so as to create the classic "comb-over," to attempt to conceal baldness. These types of patents, often called *junk patents*, are distinguishable from those patents that are granted for a business method tied to a machine or step-by-step process for recycling or physical production. The courts have been restricting patents on marketing methods or structuring relationships that do not involve machines and production. In *Bilski v Kappos*, 130 S.Ct. 3218 (2010), the U.S. Supreme Court further restricted the requirements for the patent of a process. In the case, the court held that two individuals' claimed invention for helping buyers and sellers of commodities in the energy market protect, or hedge, against the risk of price changes in the form of a mathematical formula was an "abstract idea" and not a patentable "process."

What a Patent Does

During these exclusive rights periods of 14 and 20 years, the patent holder has the sole rights to profits on sales.

Anyone who sells or uses a patented product or process without the consent of the patent holder has committed patent infringement. Infringement entitles the patent holder to a statutory action for damages. The patent holder (the plaintiff) in such a case need only show patent ownership and infringement of that patent. A Patent Office registration for a product or process, however, is not a guarantee of recovery. A court must still agree with the Patent Office determination that the product or process is nonobvious, useful, and novel. That is, an issue in every infringement case is whether the patent was properly granted.

Amazon.com had a battle with Barnes & Noble over the "One-Click" shopping method. Amazon.com obtained a patent for its buyers' shopping method that permits shoppers to place items in a virtual shopping cart and then click just one button when they are ready to purchase. The buyers need not go through the process of filling in shipping, billing, and credit information for each purchase.

Barnes & Noble created a similar "One-Click" shopping experience for its online customers, and Amazon.com sued for patent infringement. On appeal, a court held that Barnes & Noble could continue to use the "One-Click" method while the parties proceeded to trial on the issue of whether the "One-Click" patent was a valid one or simply an obvious convenience for online shoppers. The parties then settled the case [*Amazon.com, Inc. v Barnes & Noble.com*, 239 F.3d 1343 (Fed. Cir. 2001)].

CYBERLAW

On the other hand, the peculiar shading and look of Oakley sunglasses survived judicial review and the court ordered an injunction against Sunglass Hut and others from selling sunglasses that had the same green or blue lens tinting for which Oakley held a patent [*Oakley, Inc. v Sunglass Hut Intern.*, 2001 WL 1683252, 61 U.S.P.Q.2d 1658 (C.D. Cal., Dec. 7, 2001)].

CONSIDER...   15.1

Procter & Gamble (P&G) was issued patent #4,455,333 on June 19, 1984, for an invention entitled "Doughs and Cookies Providing Storage-Stable Texture Variety." The patent covers a method of manufacturing ready-to-serve cookies that remain crispy on the outside and chewy on the inside for an extended shelf life. P&G markets these cookies under the Duncan Hines label.

P&G brought a patent infringement action against Nabisco Brands, Inc., which markets its own lines of dual-textured cookies called "Almost Home" and "Chewy Chips Ahoy." P&G also sued Keebler Company for its dual-textured cookie called "Soft Batch" and Frito-Lay, Inc. for its "Grandma's Rich and Chewy." Each of the defendants denies infringement. They have moved for dismissal of the case on grounds that the patent is invalid because baking cookies is not patentable. Do you agree? Would you protect P&G's process? [*Procter & Gamble Co. v Nabisco Brands, Inc.*, 604 F. Supp. 1485 (D.C. Del. 1985)]

The Remedies for Patent Infringement

There are two types of remedies available for patent infringement: monetary damages and injunctions. Injunctions can be temporary, as when the court orders a halt to production or use whilst it determines whether a patent is valid. However, there is also the possibility of a permanent injunction, one that stops the other party from using the process or product for the life of the patent because the injury to the patent holder is so great that money damages are insufficient compensation. In *eBay, Inc. v MercExchange, LLC*, the U.S. Supreme Court set forth the criteria for granting a permanent injunction in a patent case.

| CASE 15.1 | *eBay, Inc. v MercExchange, LLC*
547 U.S. 388 (2006) |

Whether "Buy It Now" Is Halted for 20 Years

FACTS

eBay and its subsidiary, half.com, operate popular websites that allow private sellers to list goods they wish to sell at either an auction or a fixed price (its "Buy it Now" feature). MercExchange, LLC, sought to license its business-method patent to eBay, but the two companies could not reach an agreement. eBay still used the "Buy It Now" process. MercExchange filed suit for patent infringement and a jury found that eBay had infringed a valid patent and awarded MercExchange $29.5 million in damages. MercExchange requested a permanent injunction against eBay for use of its process, but the trial court denied the motion. The Court of Appeals reversed and the U.S. Supreme Court granted *certiorari*.

JUDICIAL OPINION

THOMAS, Justice

According to well-established principles of equity, a plaintiff seeking a permanent injunction must satisfy a four-factor test before a court may grant such relief. A plaintiff must demonstrate: (1) that it has suffered an irreparable injury; (2) that remedies available at law, such as monetary damages, are inadequate to compensate for that injury; (3) that, considering the balance of hardships between the plaintiff and defendant, a remedy in equity is warranted; and (4) that the public interest would not be disserved by a permanent injunction. . . . The decision to grant or deny permanent injunctive relief is an act of equitable discretion by the district court.

The Patent Act . . . declares that "patents shall have the attributes of personal property," § 261, including "the right to exclude others from making, using, offering for sale, or selling the invention," § 154(a)(1).

According to the Court of Appeals, this statutory right to exclude alone justifies its general rule in favor of permanent injunctive relief. But the creation of a right is distinct from the provision of remedies for violations of that right. Indeed, the Patent Act itself indicates that patents shall have the attributes of personal property "[s]ubject to the provisions of this title," 35 U.S.C. § 261, including, presumably, the provision that injunctive relief "may" issue only "in accordance with the principles of equity," . . . Because we conclude that neither court below correctly applied the traditional four-factor framework that governs the award of injunctive relief, we vacate the judgment of the Court of Appeals, so that the District Court may apply that framework in the first instance. In doing so, we take no position on whether permanent injunctive relief should or should not issue in this particular case, or indeed in any number of other disputes arising under the Patent Act . . .

[Reversed and Remanded]

Justice Kennedy, with whom Justice Stevens, Justice Souter, and Justice Breyer join, concurring . . .

To the extent earlier cases establish a pattern of granting an injunction against patent infringers almost as a matter of course, this pattern simply illustrates the result of the four-factor test in the contexts then prevalent. The lesson of the historical practice, therefore, is most helpful and instructive when the circumstances of a case bear substantial parallels to litigation the courts have confronted before.

In cases now arising trial courts should bear in mind that in many instances the nature of the patent being enforced and the economic function of the patent holder present considerations quite unlike earlier cases. An industry has developed in which firms use patents not as a basis for producing and selling goods but, instead, primarily for obtaining licensing fees.

For these firms, an injunction, and the potentially serious sanctions arising from its violation, can be employed as a bargaining tool to charge exorbitant fees to companies that seek to buy licenses to practice the patent.

When the patented invention is but a small component of the product the companies seek to produce and the threat of an injunction is employed simply for undue leverage in negotiations, legal damages may well be sufficient to compensate for the infringement and an injunction may not serve the public interest. In addition injunctive relief may have different consequences for

the burgeoning number of patents over business methods, which were not of much economic and legal significance in earlier times. The potential vagueness and suspect validity of some of these patents may affect the calculus under the four-factor test. . . .

CASE QUESTIONS

1. Why is this type of patent different from the traditional product patents?

2. What are the risks in granting a permanent injunction in cases such as these?

3. Why are the concurring judges raising the issue of undue leverage?

Copyrights

What Is a Copyright and What Does It Protect?

Patents protect inventors. **Copyrights** protect authors of books, magazine articles, plays, movies, songs, dances, recordings, architectural designs, broadcasts, photographs, computer programs, and so on. Ideas cannot be copyrighted, but the way an idea is expressed can be. Under the **Computer Software Copyright Act of 1980,** all software can be copyrighted, whether it is written in ordinary language (source code) or machine language (object code). Although software copyrights do not cover methods of operation (such as menus), they do cover the underlying programs themselves.

A copyright gives the holder of the copyright the exclusive right to sell, control, or license the copyrighted work. A copyright exists automatically for works created after 1989. Although the placement of the traditional C or copyright symbol (©) is not required, it is recommended. Further, the existence of a copyright in the United States is recognized in all nations that have signed the Berne Convention. For example, the transmission of NFL games by satellite to Canada is a violation of U.S. copyright laws because Canada is a signatory to the Berne Convention. Under the terms of the Berne Convention and U.S. law, copyright registration is not required, but it is recommended. Registration is a means of preventing someone violating the copyright from claiming a lack of knowledge about the work's protection. In order to register a copyright, the creator need only file two copies of the work with the Copyright Office in Washington, D.C. Without copyright registration, the owner cannot bring a suit for copyright infringement.

The Rights of Copyright Holders Against Third-Party Infringers

As you learned in Chapter 1 in reading and discussing the *Grokster* case, copyright holders also have the right to enforce their copyright against those who are vicariously allowing infringement. Those who develop programs or facilitate infringement can be liable for infringement vicariously, and copyright holders have the right to obtain injunctions to stop their facilitation of infringement by others. Those who distribute software that facilitates peer-to-peer file sharing can be liable for infringement by the file sharers.

Ethical Issues

In the summer of 1996, the dance song "Macarena" hit the pop music scene and charts in the United States. The line-type dance inspired by the song is called the Macarena. At camps around the country, the song was played and children were taught the dance.

The American Society of Composers, Authors, and Publishers (ASCAP) serves as a clearinghouse for fee payments for use of copyrighted materials belonging to its members. ASCAP sent a letter to the directors of camps and nonprofit organizations sponsoring camps (Girl Scouts, Boy Scouts, Camp Fire Girls, American Cancer Association, and so forth) that warned them that licensed songs should not be used without paying ASCAP the licensing fees and that violators would be pursued. ASCAP's prices for songs are, for example, $591 for the camp season for "Edelweiss" (from *The Sound of Music*) or "This Land Is Your Land."

Some of the nonprofit-sponsored camps charge only $44 per week per camper. The directors could not afford the fees, and the camps eliminated their oldies dances and dance classes. ASCAP declined to offer discounted licensing fees for the camps.

Why did ASCAP work so diligently to protect its rights? What ethical and social responsibility issues do you see with respect to the nonprofit camps? Some of these camps are summer retreats for children who suffer from cancer, AIDS, and other terminal illnesses. Does this information change your feelings about ASCAP's fees?

Irving Berlin (now his estate), the author of "God Bless America," earns royalties each time the song is played or performed. The song became a standard at memorial services for the September 11, 2001, victims. Mr. Berlin's estate always gave the royalties from the song to the Boy Scouts of America. What would you do if you were an ASCAP member and owned the rights to a song a camp wished to use?

How Long Does a Copyright Run?

Like patents, copyrights are so important that they are found in Article I, Section 8 of the U.S. Constitution, which provides that Congress can secure "for limited times to Authors and Inventors the exclusive Right to their respective Writings and Discoveries." The initial period of protection for copyrights (established in 1790), one that covered books, maps, and charts was for 14 years, with the right of renewal for another 14 years. In 1831, the protection period increased to 28 years with renewal rights for another 14. In 1909, the time expanded to 28 years with a 28-year renewal. In 1976, the time was increased to 50 years with no renewal. Under the Sonny Bono Copyright Extension Act of 1998, passed as the copyright on Mickey Mouse was about to expire, copyrights were increased to run for the life of the creator plus 70 years. If the work produced was done by an employee of a business, the business then registers the copyright. These types of business copyrights run for 120 years from the time of creation or 95 years from publication of the work, whichever is shorter. The late Representative Bono led the charge for the increased protection period concerned because copyrights he and many others held were about to expire. Even though the Constitution prohibits granting copyrights in perpetuity, a clear trend in congressional actions favors extending the protection period.

Rights of a Copyright Holder

A copyright holder has control over the use of the created work. That control includes control over reproduction, distribution, public performances, derivative works, and public displays. Some copyright holders assign or license these rights to others in exchange for royalties. For example, most songwriters assign their rights for public performances of their songs to the American Society of Composers, Authors, and Publishers (ASCAP) and Broadcast Music, Inc. (BMI), who then pay the writers each time their song is used, according to a previously determined schedule of fees. An international fee schedule for payment for tapes, CDs, and records is also in place; it could be a flat fee, a per-minute fee, a per-record fee, or a per-song fee. The rates of the Copyright Royalty Tribunal are the greater of 9.1 cents or 1.75 cents per minute. Iron Butterfly's "In-a-Gadda-Da-Vida" will cost you $38 to play, but the Box Tops' "The Letter," at two minutes, will run you the 9.1 cents.

Damages for copyright infringement include the profits made by the infringer, actual costs, attorney fees, and any other expenses associated with the infringement action. A court can order all illegal copies destroyed and issue an injunction that halts distribution of the illegal copies. In addition to civil recovery for the damages from infringement, federal criminal penalties for copyright infringement can be imposed when the infringement was willful and for "commercial advantage or private financial gain."

Rights of Copyright Holders and the Internet

Technology has created new issues in copyright infringement, particularly in the areas of copyrighted software and music, with the availability of digital technology. For example, an MIT student uploaded and downloaded copyrighted software programs and then gave fellow students passwords for access. The result was that students at MIT enjoyed free access to the Internet at a cost of $1 million to the system's owners. However, the student did not charge for the access and thus realized no personal financial gain from the project. Technically, no violation of the copyright laws occurred.

As a result of this case, music producers and software developers added protection technology to their copyrighted products and lobbied for a change in copyright law, which came with the **Digital Millennium Copyright Act** (DMCA) in 1998. This act criminalizes the circumvention of protection technology in order to make copies of copyrighted materials. Assisting others, providing expertise, or manufacturing products to circumvent protection technology are also criminal activities under the DMCA. Circumvention and facilitating circumvention are now violations of copyright laws. The liability has also been extended to those who facilitate the infringement via downloading programs. Individuals who maneuver around encryption devices and those who hire them to avoid those devices, as in the case of industrial espionage, may face criminal sanctions.

However, thanks largely to the lobbying efforts of colleges and universities, the DMCA has a safe harbor provision. Internet service providers (ISPs) do not have vicarious liability for copyright infringement by their users (such as for downloading copyright music and films without payment) if the ISPs can establish that they did not know of the infringement, that they are not benefiting from the infringement, that they take action when they know of the infringement, and that they have policies and procedures in place to warn of and prevent infringement. For example, Google's YouTube has a number of clips from copyrighted television shows and movies. However, Google is not responsible for the posting of the clips; individuals post the clips. In *Viacom International, Inc. v YouTube, Inc.*, 2010 WL 2532404 (S.D.N.Y. 2010), a federal district court held that Google had not violated the DMCA by continuing to allow copyrighted clips to post on its site as long as it had the clips removed upon request by the owner. The key to infringement liability immunity is prompt removal upon request as well as advance warning. When you obtained access to the college or university's website, you agreed to abide by its standards as well as U.S. copyright laws. In fact, you agreed that your access rights could be terminated if you violated their rules or U.S. law.

Ethical Issues

Google has been copying and posting portions of books, and, in some cases, full books, for access via the Google search system. Google refers to many of the excerpts as "snippets." However, authors have filed a class-action suit against Google for infringement. Evaluate the legal issues in the use of snippets. Evaluate the ethical issues in Google's mass reproduction of the books.

Fair Use and Copyrights

When the copyright laws were amended in 1976, one change permitted "fair use" of copyrighted materials. **Fair use** is occasional and spontaneous use of copyrighted materials for limited purposes—for example, a short quote from a copyrighted work. Fair use also allows instructors to reproduce a page or chart from a copyrighted work to use in the classroom; and copies of book pages can be made for research purposes. The three key questions to ask on fair use are:

1. Is the use for commercial or nonprofit/educational use?

2. Is the work large or small, song, poem, or book? Using a sentence from a book is different from using a sentence from a poem.

3. What is the effect of the use on the copyrighted work? If you copy a book, the author and publisher lose sales. If you use a clip from a film, folks may rent or buy the film and you may actually increase sales.

The photocopying of articles for use in the classroom or workplace is a common practice, but one that does not always comply with the protections afforded the copyright owners of that article. For example, in *American Geophysical Union v Texaco Inc.*, 60 F.3d 913 (2nd Cir. 1995), the court held that Texaco scientists' copying of articles from journals for use by fellow scientists at the company was not fair use but infringement because it deprived the journals of subscription revenues or revenues from licenses for reproduction of the articles. Likewise, in *Princeton University Press v Michigan Document Services, Inc.*, 99 F.3d 1381 (6th Cir. 1996) the court held that the reproduction of coursepacks by the University of Michigan for sale to its students was not a fair use by a nonprofit educational institution. The failure to pay royalties to copyright holders not only deprived the holders of their rights but also placed the for-profit copy shops at a competitive disadvantage because they were required to pay such royalties. Because of that case, the reproduction of course materials is now outsourced to professional copying services that also handle the permissions rights for the materials.

One interesting question that has arisen is the relationship between the notion of fair use and the prohibitions under the Digital Millennium Copyright Act. Can a professor circumvent protection technology for fair use in the classroom? Some feel the professor can do so if he has purchased the work. In other words, the professor can use an excerpt from the Beatles' *White Album* if the professor owns that album.

Another matter in fair use involves First Amendment issues. For example, satirical works use the lyrics and speech of others as a form of social commentary such as that found in *Mad Magazine* and *Saturday Night Live*. The First Amendment protects social commentary, and the copyright laws protect original work. *Campbell v Acuff-Rose Music, Inc.* (Case 15.2), involves an issue of a parody of copyrighted material being used for commercial gain, dealing with the balancing of First Amendment rights and copyright protection.

CASE 15.2

Campbell v Acuff-Rose Music, Inc.
510 U.S. 569 (1994)

Justice Souter Does the Pretty Woman Rap

FACTS

2 Live Crew, a popular rap musical group, recorded and performed "Pretty Woman," a rap music version of Roy Orbison's famed 1964 "Oh, Pretty Woman" rock ballad. The song was written by Mr. Orbison and William Dees, and the rights to the song were assigned to Acuff-Rose Music, Inc. (respondent). 2 Live Crew's manager had written to Acuff-Rose to request permission to do the parody and offered to pay for rights to do so. Acuff-Rose's response: "I am aware of the success enjoyed by the '2 Live Crew,' but I must inform you that we cannot permit the use of a parody of 'Oh, Pretty Woman.'"

2 Live Crew recorded the parody anyway and named Mr. Orbison and Mr. Dees as the songwriters and Acuff-Rose as the publisher on the CD cover. After over 250,000 copies of the CD had been sold and over one year later, Acuff-Rose filed suit against Luther Campbell (also known as Luke Skywalker), Christopher Wongwon, Mark Ross, and David Hobbs, members of the 2 Live Crew group, for infringement. 2 Live Crew maintained that its song was a parody and fell into a fair use exception of the copyright laws. The district court granted summary judgment for 2 Live Crew. The court of appeals held that the commercial nature of the parody rendered it presumptively unfair. 2 Live Crew (petitioners) appealed.

JUDICIAL OPINION

SOUTER, Justice

We are called upon to decide whether 2 Live Crew's commercial parody of Roy Orbison's song, "Oh, Pretty Woman," may be a fair use within the meaning of the Copyright Act of 1976, 17 U.S.C. § 107 (1988 ed. and Supp. IV).

It is uncontested here that 2 Live Crew's song would be an infringement of Acuff-Rose's rights in "Oh, Pretty Woman," under the Copyright Act of 1976, 17 U.S.C. § 106 (1988 ed. and Supp. IV), but for a finding of fair use through parody.

The first factor in a fair use enquiry is "the purpose and character of the use, including whether such use is of a commercial nature or is for nonprofit educational purposes." The central purpose of this investigation is to see whether the new work merely "supersede[s] the objects" of the original creation, or instead adds something new, with a further purpose or different character, altering the first with new expression, meaning, or message; it asks, in other words, whether and to what extent the new work is "transformative." Although such transformative use is not absolutely necessary for a finding of fair use, *Sony Corp. of America v Universal City Studios, Inc.*, 464 U.S. 417 (1984), the goal of copyright, to promote science and the arts, is generally furthered by the creation of transformative works. Such works thus lie at the heart of the fair use doctrine's guarantee of breathing space within the confines of copyright and the more transformative the new work, the less will be the significance of other factors, like commercialism, that may weigh against a finding of fair use.

Suffice it to say now that parody has an obvious claim to transformative value, as Acuff-Rose itself does not deny. Like less ostensibly humorous forms of criticism, it can provide social benefit, by shedding light on an earlier work, and, in the process, creating a new one. We thus line up with the courts that have held that parody, like other comment or criticism, may claim fair use under § 107.

Parody needs to mimic an original to make its point, and so has some claim to use the creation of its victim's (or collective victims') imagination, whereas satire can stand on its own two feet and so requires justification for the very act of borrowing.

The fact that parody can claim legitimacy for some appropriation does not, of course, tell either parodist or judge much about where to draw the line. Like a book review quoting the copyrighted material criticized, parody may or may not be fair use, and petitioner's suggestion that any periodic use is presumptively fair has no more justification in law or fact than the equally hopeful claim that any use for news reporting should be presumed fair.

As the District Court remarked, the words of 2 Live Crew's song copy the original's first line, but then "quickly degenerate[e] into a play on words, substituting predictable lyrics with shocking ones . . . [that] derisively demonstrate[e] how bland and banal the Orbison song seems to them." Although the majority below had difficulty discerning any criticism of the original in 2 Live Crew's song, it assumed for purposes of its opinion that there was some.

CONTINUED

We have less difficulty in finding that critical element in 2 Live Crew's song than the Court of Appeals did, although having found it we will not take the further step of evaluating its quality. The threshold question when fair use is raised in defense of parody is whether a periodic character may reasonably be perceived. Whether, going beyond that, parody is in good taste or bad does not and should not matter to fair use. As Justice Holmes explained, "[i]t would be a dangerous undertaking for persons trained only to the law to constitute themselves final judges of the worth of [a work]."

While we might not assign a high rank to the periodic element here, we think it fair to say that 2 Live Crew's song reasonably could be perceived as commenting on the original or criticizing it, to some degree. 2 Live Crew juxtaposes the romantic musings of a man whose fantasy comes true, with degrading taunts, a bawdy demand for sex, and a sigh of relief from paternal responsibility. The later words can be taken as a comment on the naïveté of the original of an earlier day, as a rejection of its sentiment that ignores the ugliness of street life and the debasement that it signifies. It is this joinder of reference and ridicule that marks off the author's choice of parody from the other types of comment and criticism that traditionally have had a claim to fair use protection as transformative works.

The use, for example, of a copyrighted work to advertise a product, even in a parody, will be entitled to less indulgence under the first factor of the fair use enquiry, than the sale of a parody for its own sake, let alone one performed a single time by students in school. . . .

It is true, of course, that 2 Live Crew copied the characteristic opening bass riff (or musical phrase) of the original, and true that the words of the first line copy the Orbison lyrics. But if quotation of the opening riff and the first line may be said to go to the "heart" of the original, the heart is also what most readily conjures up the song for parody, and it is the heart at which parody takes aim. Copying does not become excessive in relation to parodic purpose merely because the portion taken was the original's heart. If 2 Live Crew had copied a significantly less memorable part of the original, it is difficult to see how its parodic character would have come through.

This is not, of course, to say that anyone who calls himself a parodist can skim the cream and get away scot-free. In parody, as in news reporting, context is everything, and the question of fairness asks what else the parodist did besides go to the heart of the original. It is significant that 2 Live Crew not only copied the first line of the original, but thereafter departed markedly from the Orbison lyrics for its own ends. 2 Live Crew not only copied the bass riff and repeated it, but

also produced otherwise distinctive sounds, interposing "scraper" noise, overlaying the music with solos in different keys, and altering the drum beat. This is not a case, then, where "a substantial portion" of the parody itself is composed of a "verbatim" copying of the original. It is not, that is, a case where the parody is so insubstantial, as compared to the copying, that the third factor must be resolved as a matter of law against the parodists.

It was error for the Court of Appeals to conclude that the commercial nature of 2 Live Crew's parody of "Oh, Pretty Woman" rendered it presumptively unfair. The court also erred in holding that 2 Live Crew had necessarily copied excessively from the Orbison original, considering the parodic purpose of the use. We therefore reverse the judgment of the Court of Appeals.

The case was remanded for trial.

Appendix A
"Oh, Pretty Woman," by Roy Orbison and William Dees

Pretty Woman, walking down the street,
Pretty Woman, the kind I like to meet,
Pretty Woman, I don't believe you,
you're not the truth,
No one could look as good as you
Mercy
Pretty Woman, won't you pardon me,
Pretty Woman, I couldn't help but see,
Pretty Woman, that you look lovely as can be
Are you lonely just like me?
Pretty Woman, stop a while,
Pretty Woman, talk a while,
Pretty Woman give your smile to me
Pretty Woman, yeah, yeah, yeah
Pretty Woman, look my way,
Pretty Woman, say you'll stay with me
'Cause I need you, I'll treat you right
Come to me baby, Be mine tonight
Pretty Woman, don't walk on by,
Pretty Woman, don't make me cry,
Pretty Woman, don't walk away,
Hey, O.K.
If that's the way it must be, O.K.
I guess I'll go on home, it's late
There'll be tomorrow night, but wait!
What do I see
Is she walking back to me!
Oh, Pretty Woman.

Appendix B
"Pretty Woman," as recorded by 2 Live Crew

Pretty woman walkin' down the street
Pretty woman girl you look so sweet
Pretty woman you bring me down to that knee

Pretty woman you make me wanna beg please
Oh, pretty woman
Big hairy woman you need to shave that stuff
Big hairy woman you know I bet it's tough
Big hairy woman all that hair it ain't legit
'Cause you look like "Cousin It"
Big hairy woman
Bald headed woman girl your hair won't grow
Bald headed woman you got a teeny-weeny afro
Bald headed woman you know your hair could look nice
Bald headed woman first you got to roll it with rice
Bald headed woman here, let me get this hunk of biz for ya
Ya know what I'm saying you look better than Rice-a-Roni
Oh bald headed woman
Big hairy woman come on in
And don't forget your bald headed friend
Hey pretty woman let the boys
Jump in
Two timin' woman girl you know you ain't right
Two timin' woman you's out with my boy last night
Two timin' woman that takes a load off my mind
Two timin' woman now I know the baby ain't mine
Oh, two timin' woman
Oh pretty woman

CASE QUESTIONS

1. What is the significance of 2 Live Crew's commercial gain from the parody?

2. Why is the *Sony* case cited?

3. Why did 2 Live Crew's manager seek permission first?

4. Do you agree with the court's decision? Was it a fair use? Should the owner of the rights be allowed to decide how a song will be parodied for commercial gain?

5. Does the court comment on bad taste and parody quality? Why?

Aftermath: The 2 Live Crew case began a trend in the music parody industry, based on what has become known as "Footnote 10." In Footnote 10 in the Supreme Court opinion, the Court noted its concern about the use of injunctions in parody cases. The footnote indicates that automatic injunctive relief when the parody goes beyond fair use is wrong because there may be a strong public interest in the publication of the secondary work, as in the 2 Live Crew parody, in which social commentary is present.

CONSIDER... 15.2

John David California has written a sequel to J.D. Salinger's *The Catcher in the Rye.* Salinger and the Salinger Literary Trust brought suit, *J.D. Salinger v John Doe,* 607 F.3d 68 (2nd Cir. 2010), seeking an injunction to halt the reproduction, publication, advertisement, distribution or other dissemination of the book, which is entitled *60 Years Later: Coming Through the Rye,* to be published by Windupbird and Nicotext. Salinger (and subsequently his estate) alleged in the suit that the book is an unauthorized sequel of the acclaimed copyrighted novel that Salinger wrote. Salinger's estate based its suit for infringement on the use of the character Holden Caulfield of *Catcher,* who is the narrator and the very essence of the novel. At the time of the suit, the sequel was available in Britain and at Amazon.com, but had not yet been distributed in bookstores.

Catcher in the Rye is one of the all-time classic American novels, named one of the 100 best novels by both *Time* magazine and The Modern Library, and is taught in schools across the country. It has been described in reviews as "a crucial American novel . . . ," an "unusually brilliant novel" and "a cult book, a rite of passage for the brainy and disaffected" (*The New York Times*)

The sequel begins, as does *Catcher,* with Holden Caulfield's departure from an institution (prep school in *Catcher;* a nursing home in the sequel) and ends with Holden and his sister Phoebe at the carousel in Central Park. In between, Holden hangs out aimlessly in New York for a few days, encountering many of the same people, visiting many of the same settings, and ruminating. The sequel is not a parody and it does not comment upon or criticize the original.

Mr. Salinger never allowed any derivative works to be made using either *The Catcher in the Rye* or his Holden Caulfield character. Indeed, in 1980 Salinger stated to the press, "There's no more to Holden Caulfield. Read the book again. It's all there. Holden Caulfield is only a frozen moment in time."[2] Is the sequel infringement? Would the court be justified in issuing a temporary and/or permanent injunction against its publication and distribution? Why or why not?

Trademarks

What Are Trademarks?

Trademarks are words, names, symbols, designs, or devices that businesses use to identify their products or services. To be protected, a trademark must have some distinctiveness. There are categories for distinctiveness including fanciful (M&Ms or Xerox), descriptive (*Sports Illustrated* or the *Wall Street Journal*), arbitrary (such as the use of the word "Apple" for computers), or acquired distinctiveness (such as the Mercedes-Benz triangle coming to represent the car and the company). Generic terms cannot be trademarks and the failure to enforce the use of a trademark can cause it to fall into generic use. Some other examples of trademarks include Owens Corning's use of the color pink for its insulation (fanciful and distinctive). No other insulation company can have pink insulation, and the use of the Pink Panther reminds us of the company's unique product. If the symbol is one for a service, such as the symbol for "Martinizing" at the dry cleaners, it is a service mark.

What Are the Legal Protections for Trademarks?

The **Lanham Act of 1946** is a federal law passed to afford businesses protection of their trademarks. This law is really a protection of a company's goodwill. A trademark becomes associated with that company and is used as a means of identifying that company's goods or services. The Lanham Act assures the right to retain that unique identification.

To obtain the federal protection, which lasts in perpetuity as long as the owner enforces the rights, the trademark must be registered with the Patent and Trademark Office. To be a valid trademark, the mark must serve to distinguish the company's goods or services from others. The Principal Register at the PTO is the official recording of the trademark rights. From the time of the registration, others have five years to contest the grant of a trademark. If, after five years, there has been no contest, the trademark belongs to the registered owner and is incontestable. Trademarks can also be reserved in advance of beginning a business; but the business must be started within 36 months of the time the trademark is reserved.

Trademarks are also protected internationally through the Madrid System of International Registration of Marks, known as the Madrid Protocol. The United States became a signatory to that agreement in 2003. Once a U.S. company has registered its trademark in the United States, it can then do the same in the other 60 countries that have adopted the Madrid Protocol and obtain protection in those countries as well.

BUSINESS STRATEGY

The Best Defense to Infringement Is a Good Offense of Disparagement

Gucci brought suit against Duty Free America (DFA) for trademark infringement. Gucci alleges that DFA sells knock-off goods such as purses, wallets, and shirts with the Gucci logo but that the goods are not authentic. Gucci discovered the sales when DFA customers came to Gucci stores to return or exchange their Gucci items without a receipt. When Gucci filed suit against DFA for infringement, DFA filed a counterclaim for disparagement. DFA alleges that its Gucci goods are indeed authentic, and that it has been damaged because its customers are told by Gucci personnel that anything purchased at DFA is not authentic Gucci.

What will Gucci need to establish for infringement? What will DFA need to establish for disparagement? To show that its goods are authentic?

[*Gucci America, Inc. v Duty Free Apparel, Ltd.*, 315 F.Supp.2d 511 (S.D.N.Y. 2004) and 277 F.Supp.2d 269 (S.D.N.Y. 2003)]

CONSIDER...   15.3

Nadya Suleman, the divorced and unemployed California mother of octuplets (as well as six other children), has filed two applications with the U.S. Patent and Trademark Office for a trademark for her media-originated name, "Octomom." Ms. Suleman wishes to use the term for a television program, clothing, and both cloth and disposable diapers.

There is, however, a competing application, one filed by G & S Computer, a company headquartered in Austin, Texas, which was filed almost one month prior to Ms. Suleman's April 2009 application. G & S seeks to use the term for computer games. Evaluate the type of trademark/tradename proposal and decide whether each applicant is entitled to protection. As you consider this situation, recall that Orenthal James Simpson applied for trademark registration for his widely used nicknames, O.J. and Juice. Joseph J. Gleason, vice president and general counsel of Florida Citrus Mutual, a trade group, responded, "I'd question if he could copyright something that generic." The trade names and trademarks were used for the merchandising of Simpson products. Ms. Suleman wants to use her nickname for marketing baby products. G & S wants to use the name for a game. Could the two rights to the trademark coexist?

Enforcing Trademarks and the Risk of Going Generic

Once a trademark is registered, the holder must self-enforce the unique nature of that trademark. The owner must take care so that the trademark does not fall into common use by the public as a descriptive or generic term. For example, there are "Band-Aid brand adhesive strips" instead of "Band-Aids." There is "Jell-O brand gelatin dessert" instead of "Jell-O." There are "Formica brand kitchen countertops" instead of "Formica" ones and "Rollerblade in-line skates" instead of "Rollerblades." Parker Brothers lost its "Monopoly" trademark because there is no generic term for the type of board game it was. Other examples of generics are "aspirin" and "cellophane."

Harley-Davidson, Inc. v Grottanelli (Case 15.3) deals with an issue of generic or protectable use.

CASE 15.3   *Harley-Davidson, Inc. v Grottanelli*
164 F.3d 806 (2d Cir. 1999) *cert. denied* 531 U.S. 1103 (2001)

When Is a Hog Generic?

FACTS

Harley-Davidson (Harley-Davidson, Harley, or the company), a corporation based in Milwaukee, Wisconsin, manufactures and sells motorcycles, motorcycle parts and accessories, apparel, and other motorcycle-related merchandise. It brought suit against The Hog Farm, owned by Ronald Grottanelli (Grottanelli), for its use of the word "hog" in its business name and in reference to other products. Harley maintains that "hog" is a trademark associated with its motorcycles.

The lower court enjoined Mr. Grottanelli from using the term "hog" in his store except as to his store's name, which he could keep so long as confined to a narrow geographic area. Mr. Grottanelli appealed, as did Harley-Davidson (the latter to request a more narrow geographic scope for use of "The Hog Farm" name by Mr. Grottanelli).

JUDICIAL OPINION

NEWMAN, Circuit Judge

This appeal primarily involves trademark issues as to whether the mark "HOG" as applied to large motorcycles is generic. [We] conclude that the word "hog" had become generic as applied to large motorcycles before Harley-Davidson began to make trademark use of "HOG" and that Harley-Davidson's attempt to withdraw this use of the word from the public domain cannot succeed.

In the late 1960s and early 1970s, the word "hog" was used by motorcycle enthusiasts to refer to motorcycles generally and to large motorcycles in particular. The word was used that way in the press at least as early as 1965, and frequently thereafter, prior to the 1980s when Harley first attempted to make trademark use of the term. Several dictionaries include a definition of "hog" as a motorcycle, especially a large one. The October 1975 issue of *Street Chopper* contained an article entitled "Honda Hog," indicating that the word "hog" was generic as to motorcycles and needed a trade name adjective.

See *The Oxford Dictionary of Modern Slang* (1992) ("hog noun U.S. A large, often old, car or motorcycle. 1967-."); *American Heritage Dictionary* (3d ed. 1992) ("hog . . . 4. Slang. A big, heavy motorcycle"); Eric Partridge, *A Dictionary of Slang and Unconventional English* (8th ed. 1984) ("hog n . . . 8. a homebuilt motorcycle . . ."); see also Glossary of Sportscycle Terms,

Bike and Rider, Aug. 1992, at 84 ("HOG Old fashioned, heavyweight sportscycle").

A likely etymology of "hog" to mean a motorcycle is suggested in the entry for "road-hog" in Eric Partridge, *A Dictionary of Slang and Unconventional English* (6th ed. 1996), which reports that in the United States as early as 1891 "road-hog" was applied to an "inconsiderate" cyclist and somewhat later to motorists.

Beginning around the early 1970s and into the early 1980s, motorcyclists increasingly came to use the word "hog" when referring to Harley-Davidson motorcycles. However, for several years, as Harley-Davidson's Manager of Trademark Enforcement acknowledged, the company attempted to disassociate itself from the word "hog." The Magistrate Judge drew the reasonable inference that the company wished to distance itself from the connection between "hog" as applied to motorcycles and unsavory elements of the population, such as Hell's Angels, who were among those applying the term to Harley-Davidson motorcycles.

In 1981, Harley-Davidson's new owners recognized that the term "hog" had financial value and began using the term in connection with its merchandise, accessories, advertising, and promotions. In 1983, it formed the Harley Owners' Group, pointedly using the acronym "H.O.G." In 1987, it registered the acronym in conjunction with various logos. It subsequently registered the mark "HOG" for motorcycles. That registration lists Harley-Davidson's first use as occurring in 1990.

Grottanelli opened a motorcycle repair shop under the name "The Hog Farm" in 1969. Since that time his shop has been located at various sites in western New York. At some point after 1981, Grottanelli also began using the word "hog" in connection with events and merchandise. He has sponsored an event alternatively known as "Hog Holidays" and "Hog Farm Holidays," and sold products such as "Hog Wash" engine degreaser and a "Hog Trivia" board game. . . .

In this case, one dictionary cites a generic use of "hog" to mean a large motorcycle as early as 1967, long before Harley's first trademark use of the word, and the recent dictionary editions continuing to define the word to mean a large motorcycle indicate that the word has not lost its generic meaning. We have observed that newspaper and magazine use of a word in a generic sense is "a strong indication of the general public's perception" that the word is generic.

Supporting the generic nature of "hog" as applied to motorcycles is Harley-Davidson's aversion to linking the word with its products until the early 1980s, long after the word was generic. Harley's Manager of Trademark Enforcement acknowledged that in the past Harley had attempted to disassociate itself from the term "hog." As the Magistrate Judge noted, Harley's own history of the company, "The Big Book of Harley-Davidson," makes no reference to "hog" as relating to its products before the early 1980s. Though Harley-Davidson was not shown to have used the word "hog" in a generic sense, its deliberate resistance to linking the word to its products is nonetheless probative. . . .

"Dual usage" in trademark law refers to a mark that starts out as proprietary and gradually become [*sic*] generic as to some segments of the public. If such a mark "retains" trademark significance, injunctive relief must be carefully tailored to protect only the limited trademark use and not to bar the generic use. Our case, however, concerns a mark that starts out generic and is sought to be given trademark significance by a manufacturer.

Harley-Davidson suggests, albeit in a footnote, that it is entitled to trademark use of "HOG" as applied to motorcycles because a substantial segment of the relevant consumers began to use the term specifically to refer to Harley-Davidson motorcycles before the company made trademark use of the term. . . . "[H]og"

was a generic term in the language as applied to large motorcycles before the public (or at least some segments of it) began using the word to refer to Harley-Davidson motorcycles. The public has no more right than a manufacturer to withdraw from the language a generic term, already applicable to the relevant category of products, and accord it trademark significance, at least as long as the term retains some generic meaning.

The public may also take a trademark and give it a generic meaning that is new. See *Lucasfilm, Ltd. v High Frontier*, 622 F. Supp. 931 (D.D.C.1985) ("Strategic Defense Initiative" referred to as "Star Wars Program" without infringing movie trademark STAR WARS).

For all of these reasons, Harley-Davidson may not prohibit Grottanelli from using "hog" to identify his motorcycle products and services. Like any other manufacturer with a product identified by a word that is generic, Harley-Davidson will have to rely on all or a portion of its trade name (or other protectable marks) to identify its brand of motorcycles, e.g., "Harley Hogs."

Reversed.

CASE QUESTIONS

1. Which of the two parties used the term *hog* first?
2. Did Harley-Davidson reclaim the term *hog* from its generic standing?
3. Is the term *hog* generic now?

CONSIDER...   15.4

Wordspy.com is a site that specializes in noting newly coined words. The site noted that the popularity of the search engine Google has netted a verb, such as when someone says, "I went in and googled it." A lawyer from Google has asked that the new term be deleted from Wordspy's site. Why does Google want to stop its use as a verb?

Trade Names

Not all commonly used terms, however, are generic because they may be trade names. In *San Francisco Arts & Athletics, Inc. v United States Olympic Committee*, 483 U.S. 522 (1987), the Supreme Court held that the term *Olympic* belongs to the U.S. Olympic Committee and could not be used by San Francisco Arts & Athletics, Inc. (SFAA) in promoting its "Gay Olympic Games."

The SFAA did not have permission to use the term *Olympic*. Use of a **trade name** without the registered owner's permission is infringement. The owner of the trade name can seek injunctive relief to stop the use of the trade name. The plaintiff owner can also recover all damages and attorney's fees. If the plaintiff can show a willful infringement, the Lanham Act allows the plaintiff to recover treble damages. Relief by a suit seeking an injunction is also available for using a trademark without authorization in advertising. Recent changes in the law allow a competitor to seek treble damages when its product is used deceptively in a comparative ad.

What Are the Rights When a Trademark or Tradename is Misused?

In 1995, Congress passed the **Federal Trademark Dilution Act,** a statute that permits recovery and injunctions for "dilution" of distinctive trademarks. The purpose of the law was to prevent others from capitalizing on the recognition, familiarity, and reputation of a distinctive trademark. This statute protects the trademark owner who can establish confusion, that is, that buyers assumed they were purchasing goods or services with the trademark and from the company who owns that trademark. The act covers the problem of blurring or creating confusion among consumers about the source of a product and tarnishing or portraying a product in an unsavory manner.

Moseley, dba Victor's Little Secret, v V Secret Catalogue, Inc. (Case 15.4) deals with a trademark dilution issue and also provides the answer to the chapter's opening "Consider."

CASE 15.4   *Moseley, dba Victor's Little Secret, v V Secret Catalogue, Inc.*
537 U.S. 418 (2003)

The Bare Essentials on Trademark Law: Victor or Victoria's Secret?

FACTS

Victor and Cathy Moseley (petitioners) owned and operated an adult toy, gag gift, and lingerie shop that they called Victor's Little Secret near Elizabethtown, Kentucky. In the February 12, 1998, edition of a weekly publication distributed to residents of the military installation at Fort Knox, Kentucky, the Moseleys advertised the "GRAND OPENING Just in time for Valentine's Day!" of their store "VICTOR'S SECRET" in Elizabethtown. The ad featured "Intimate Lingerie for every woman," "Romantic Lighting," "Lycra Dresses," "Pagers," and "Adult Novelties/Gifts."

An army colonel, who saw the ad and was offended by what he perceived to be an attempt to use a reputable company's trademark to promote the sale of "unwhole-some, tawdry merchandise," sent a copy to Victoria's Secret, Inc. (respondents).

Victoria's Secret owns 750 stores around the country and distributes 400 million catalogs each year via U.S. mail. Victoria's Secret spends $55 million annually on advertising "the VICTORIA'S SECRET brand—one of moderately priced, high quality, attractively designed lingerie sold in a store setting designed to look like a wom[a]n's bedroom." Two of Victoria's Secret's stores were located In Louisville, Kentucky, a short drive from Elizabethtown and Fort Knox.

Legal counsel for Victoria's Secret asked the Moseleys to stop using the name Victor's Secret because of possible confusion over the trademark and resulting dilution. The Moseleys changed the name of their store to Victor's Little Secret. Not satisfied, Victoria's Secret filed suit for dilution of its trademark under the Federal Trademark Dilution Act (FTDA).

The District Court granted summary judgment for Victoria's Secret under the FTDA, and the Sixth Circuit affirmed, finding that the respondents' mark was "distinctive" and that the evidence established "dilution" even though no actual harm had been proved. The Moseleys appealed.

JUDICIAL OPINION

STEVENS, Justice

The record contained uncontradicted affidavits and deposition testimony describing the vast size of respondents' business, the value of the VICTORIA'S SECRET name, and descriptions of the items sold in the respective parties' stores. Respondents sell a "complete line of lingerie" and related items, each of which bears a VICTORIA'S SECRET label or tag. Respondents described their business as follows: "Victoria's Secret stores sell a complete line of lingerie, women's undergarments and nightwear, robes, caftans and kimonos, slippers, sachets, lingerie bags, hanging bags, candles, soaps, cosmetic brushes, atomizers, bath products and fragrances." Petitioners sell a wide variety of items, including adult videos, "adult novelties," and lingerie. In answer to an interrogatory, petitioners stated that they "sell novelty action clocks, patches, temporary tattoos, stuffed animals, coffee mugs, leather biker wallets, zippo lighters, diet formula, diet supplements, jigsaw puzzles, whyss, handcufs [*sic*], hosiery, bubble machines, greeting cards, calendars, incense burners, car air fresheners, sunglasses, ball caps, jewelry, candles, lava lamps, blacklights, fiber optic lights, rock and roll prints, lingerie, pagers, candy, adult video tapes, adult novelties, t-shirts, etc."

Victor Moseley stated in an affidavit that women's lingerie represented only about five percent of their sales. In support of their motion for summary judgment, respondents submitted an affidavit by an expert in marketing who explained "the enormous value" of respondents' mark. Neither he, nor any other witness, expressed any opinion concerning the impact, if any, of petitioners' use of the name "Victor's Little Secret" on that value.

However, the Sixth Circuit held, "While no consumer is likely to go to the Moseleys' store expecting to find Victoria's Secret's famed Miracle Bra, consumers who hear the name 'Victor's Little Secret' are likely automatically to think of the more famous store and link it to the Moseleys' adult toy, gag gift, and lingerie shop. This, then, is a classic instance of dilution by tarnishing (associating the Victoria's Secret name with sex toys and lewd coffee mugs) and by blurring (linking the chain with a single, unauthorized establishment). Given this conclusion, it follows that Victoria's Secret would prevail in a dilution analysis."

In reaching that conclusion the Court of Appeals expressly rejected the holding of the Fourth Circuit in *Ringling Bros.-Barnum & Bailey Combined Shows, Inc. v Utah Div. of Travel Development*, 170 F.3d 449 (1999). In that case, which involved a claim that Utah's use on its license plates of the phrase "greatest snow on earth" was causing dilution of the "greatest show on earth," the court had concluded "that to establish dilution of a famous mark under the federal Act requires proof that (1) a defendant has made use of a junior mark sufficiently similar to the famous mark to evoke in a relevant universe of consumers a mental association of the two that (2) has caused (3) actual economic harm to the famous mark's economic value by lessening its former selling power as an advertising agent for its goods or services." Because other Circuits have also expressed differing views about the "actual harm" issue, we granted certiorari to resolve the conflict.

Infringement law protects consumers from being misled by the use of infringing marks and also protects producers from unfair practices by an "imitating competitor."

. . . [w]e decide the case on the assumption that the Moseleys' use of the name "Victor's Little Secret" neither confused any consumers or potential consumers, nor was likely to do so. Neither the absence of any likelihood of confusion nor the absence of competition, however, provides a defense to the statutory dilution claim alleged. . . .

"The term 'dilution' means the lessening of the capacity of a famous mark to identify and distinguish goods or services, regardless of the presence or absence of—

"(1) competition between the owner of the famous mark and other parties, or

"(2) likelihood of confusion, mistake, or deception." § 1127.

The contrast between the initial reference to an actual "lessening of the capacity" of the mark, and the later reference to a "likelihood of confusion, mistake, or deception" in the second caveat confirms the conclusion that actual dilution must be established.

Of course, that does not mean that the consequences of dilution, such as an actual loss of sales or profits, must also be proved. We do agree, however, at least where the marks at issue are not identical, the mere fact that consumers mentally associate the junior user's mark with a famous mark is not sufficient to establish actionable dilution. As the facts of that case demonstrate, such mental association will not necessarily reduce the capacity of the famous mark to identify the goods of its owner, the statutory requirement for dilution under the FTDA. For even though Utah drivers may be reminded of the circus when they see a license plate referring to the "greatest snow on earth," it by no means follows that they will associate "the greatest show on earth" with skiing or snow sports, or associate it less strongly or exclusively with the circus. "Blurring" is not a necessary consequence of mental association. (Nor, for that matter, is "tarnishing.")

The record in this case establishes that an army officer who saw the advertisement of the opening of a store named "Victor's Secret" did make the mental association with "Victoria's Secret," but it also shows that he did not therefore form any different impression of the store that his wife and daughter had patronized. There is a complete absence of evidence of any lessening of the capacity of the VICTORIA'S SECRET mark to identify and distinguish goods or services sold in Victoria's Secret stores or advertised in its catalogs. The officer was offended by the ad, but it did not change his conception of Victoria's Secret. His offense was directed

CONTINUED

entirely at petitioners, not at respondents. Moreover, the expert retained by respondents had nothing to say about the impact of petitioners' name on the strength of respondents' mark.

Noting that consumer surveys and other means of demonstrating actual dilution are expensive and often unreliable, respondents and their *amici* argue that evidence of an actual "lessening of the capacity of a famous mark to identify and distinguish goods or services" may be difficult to obtain. It may well be, however, that direct evidence of dilution such as consumer surveys will not be necessary if actual dilution can reliably be proved through circumstantial evidence— the obvious case is one where the junior and senior marks are identical. Whatever difficulties of proof may be entailed, they are not an acceptable reason

for dispensing with proof of an essential element of a statutory violation. The evidence in the present record is not sufficient to support the summary judgment on the dilution count. The judgment is therefore reversed, and the case is remanded for further proceedings consistent with this opinion.

CASE QUESTIONS

1. Describe the connection between the two companies.
2. What is Victoria's Secret concerned about?
3. What do they have to prove to get an injunction under the FTDA?
4. Why does Victoria's Secret argue against that burden of proof?

For the Manager's Desk

Re: Surveys and Trademark Confusion

Consumer surveys have become a critical part of infringement trials. Where the issue is whether the public has been misled by a trademark infringement, the responses of a representative sample are critical evidence in a case. One such case involved a survey of consumers in 24 shopping malls nationwide. The

Baltimore Colts had become the Indianapolis Colts, and the Canadian Football League proposed calling one of its teams the Baltimore CFL Colts. The survey showed consumers were confused, and the data carried the case for the former Baltimore Colts' owners.

CONSIDER...   15.5

Nautilus and ICON are direct competitors in the market for home exercise equipment. Both produce resistance-training systems that use bendable rods. In Nautilus's product, the Bowflex exerciser, the rods are arranged vertically; when a user pulls on a cable connected to the upper ends of the rods, the rods curve or "bow" outward. The rods are structured to resist this outward movement, requiring exertion by the user.

Nautilus has continuously produced the Bowflex exerciser since 1984 and holds two patents on related technology. Nautilus registered the trademark for the Bowflex brand in 1986. Since 1993, when Nautilus began to market its Bowflex exerciser directly to consumers, the company has invested in excess of $233 million in promotion efforts. Nautilus's advertising has focused on infomercials, the Internet, and print publications. As a result, over 780,000 machines have been sold, with total revenues to Nautilus of $900 million.

In 2002, ICON introduced a competing rod-based resistance training system it called CrossBow. In the CrossBow exerciser, the bendable rods are arranged horizontally so that they bend downward, in an inverted U-shape, rather than outward, as in Bowflex's vertical rod configuration. According to ICON, the product's resemblance to the medieval crossbow weapon inspired the brand name. In ICON's two-line logo for the machine, the "o" in "Cross" is replaced by a circular crosshairs. Beneath the mark, in smaller type, appears an additional line, "by Weider," signaling the machine's source. Since it introduced the CrossBow exerciser, ICON has spent $13 million on marketing in many of the same advertising channels as Nautilus, including infomercials and the Internet.

Nautilus commenced a suit for patent infringement against ICON. Is there infringement? What must Nautilus establish? [*Nautilus Group, Inc. v ICON Health and Fitness, Inc.*, 372 F.3d 1330 (Fed. Cir. 2004)]

Trade Dress

A more recent and critical aspect of the Lanham Act is the concept of **trade dress.** Trade dress consists of the colors, designs, and shapes associated with a product. If someone copies the color schemes and shapes, they are likely to benefit from the goodwill of the owner and developer of the trade dress. The subtle copying of trade dress dilutes the value of the company's goodwill and reputation. In *Two Pesos, Inc. v Taco Cabana, Inc.,* 505 U.S. 763 (1992), the U.S. Supreme Court resolved issues related to trade dress infringement. In the case, Taco Cabana, Inc., which operated a chain of fast-food restaurants in Texas that serve Mexican food, had opened in San Antonio and had distinctive trade dress that Two Pesos used as its motif when it opened its restaurants in Houston. With expansion around Texas, the two chains ended up in head-to-head competition in Dallas, and a trade dress infringement suit resulted. The U.S. Supreme Court held that a claim of trade dress infringement requires proof of the same elements as trademark infringement. That is, a company must show that its trade dress is distinctive and that consumers are likely to be confused by the similarity.

In *Wal-Mart v Samara,* 529 U.S. 205 (2000), the U.S. Supreme Court limited its ruling in *Two Pesos* to product packaging and held that no trade dress protection is available for product design absent some form of registration under federal law such as trademark or patent or the product design having achieved some level of distinctiveness. In the case, Samara designed, produced, and sold a line of seersucker children's clothes with bold appliqués and large collars. Wal-Mart had introduced its own line of clothing that was similar. Product design trade dress enjoys no inherent protection. Product packaging, which the court noted was involved in *Two Pesos*, does enjoy protection, as in the shape of a Coca-Cola bottle. However, absent some other statutory protection, product design, with the exception of famous designers such as Tommy Hilfiger, Ralph Lauren, and Izod, requires legislative change for protection.

Cyber Infringement

What are the rights of search engines such as Google to use the symbols and trademarks of companies to direct Internet users to sites that are not affiliated with the trademark owners? Playboy Enterprises filed suit against Netscape to stop that search engine's use of the Playboy Bunny symbol in ads that directed Internet users to sites oriented toward sexual content. Netscape benefits when users click onto those sites. However, the use of the Playboy symbol allows Netscape and the sites to capitalize on Playboy's name, advertising, and goodwill. In *Playboy Enterprise, Inc. v Netscape Communications,* 354 F.3d 1020 (9th Cir. 2004), a unanimous Ninth Circuit ruled that such use was an infringement.

CYBERLAW

Companies also have the right to stop Internet sales that are not by authorized distributors. For example, in *Australian Gold, Inc. v Hatfield*, 436 F.3d 1228 (10th Cir. 2006), ETS Inc., like most beauty supply companies, sold its tanning products primarily through tanning salons. ETS, like most beauty suppliers, has distribution contracts that limit sales to beauty and tanning salons. ETS does not want its products available in stores because of the need for in-person consultation on their use and application. The Hatfields used a series of fictitious names to purchase ETS products through distributors and then made the products available on the Internet through seven different websites. The seven websites used the ETS trademark, product pictures, and metatags. ETS recovered $3.7 million for infringement because of the unauthorized use of the trademark and the resulting diversion of Internet traffic and sales to the Hatfields. Use of a trademark on the Internet without permission brings the resulting profits back to the owner.

Cybersquatting

CYBERLAW

Cybersquatting is registering sites and domain names that are deceptively or confusingly similar to existing trademarks that belong to others. Although the Federal Trademark Dilution Act had been used to halt cybersquatting, Congress enacted the Federal Anticybersquatting Consumer Protection Act (ACPA) in 1999 to prohibit cybersquatting and to offer clear standards of proof as well as remedies for this activity. The remedies available include injunctions to stop use of the name, forfeiture of the name, and recovery of money damages and costs of litigation. Although a defense of good faith can be used, cybersquatters may not use the intent to compete in good faith as a defense to using a deceptively similar name. For example, in *Victoria's Secret Stores Inc. v Artco*, 194 F. Supp.2d 704 (S.D. Ohio 2002), the court held that the use of the name www.victoriassecrets.net was too confusing with www.victoriassecret.com, and the cybersquatter must halt its use even though his stated intention was simply to get people to come to his site and look at competitive lingerie.

The **Internet Corporation for Assigned Names and Numbers** (ICANN) has been the provider of arbitration services for disputes between trademark owners and Internet sites.

CONSIDER... 15.6

They can be spotted from a distance. The classic Ferrari design with its lined side panels and hidden headlights is unique. Although the Ferrari name is a registered trademark, the design of the Ferrari is not. Roberts Motor Company designed a car with a look similar to the Ferrari, but the Roberts car would sell for a much lower price. Ferrari brought suit against Roberts, alleging infringement. Is Ferrari correct? Can a nonpatented, noncopyrighted design belong exclusively to Ferrari?

THINK: The protections for design require proof that consumers would be confused about the product, that they would likely think the Roberts car was a Ferrari. Also, where the products are the same and one company seeks to draw upon the advertising and goodwill of the other, the confusion and damages are more easily established.

APPLY: If Ferrari is able to show confusion, it can halt the design and seek damages. But proof of that confusion is necessary to seek a remedy for design infringement. Would your answer be the same if Avanti Motor Corporation designed and built a new vehicle that looks like General Motors' Hummer?

ANSWER: The court held that (1) the automobile designs had acquired secondary meaning; (2) there was likelihood of confusion between plaintiff's cars and defendant's replicas; and that (3) injunction granted by district court was proper. [*Ferrari v Roberts Motor Co.*, 944 F.2d 1235 (6th Cir. 1991), **cert. denied**, 505 U.S. 1219 (1992)]

Trade Secrets

A business often has worked to develop information that is not known by the public or its competitors. However, the information the business has developed may not fit into any of the federally protected categories covered earlier in the chapter. In fact, sometimes the business does not even want to make the information public in a filing for the federal protections. Therefore, the business protects its rights by keeping the information as a trade secret.

What Are Trade Secrets?

Trade secrets are lists of information, formulas, and even data that businesses compile for use in the marketplace, with customers, or in securing contracts. A trade secret is anything that gives the business a competitive edge and that is not known generally or by competitors.

How Are Trade Secrets Protected?

Trade secrets are protected by the business keeping them secret. The information should have controlled access and should be available only to those within the business who have reason to know or need to use the information.

Most companies have employees sign nondisclosure agreements so that should they leave their employment they would be subject to suit for breach of contract if they took the information with them.

Forty-five states have adopted the Uniform Trade Secrets Act (UTSA), an act that was drafted and passed to eliminate the common-law remedies that relate to the appropriation of trade secrets by current and former employees. The law was intended to make it easier for employers to recover when employees take trade secrets and use them, either while employed or postemployment (by turning them over to another employer or using the information themselves). However, the application of UTSA has proven to be a challenge for employers because of differing interpretations and applications.

If what the employee has done fits within the definition of a trade secret under the UTSA, then all is well. That is, the employer can recover the remedies afforded under UTSA. Trade secrets have been defined to include everything from processes and procedures to customer lists and customer preferences. (The last two items are not protected under common-law theories for trade secret appropriation.) However, there are those situations in which the employee uses something that is not considered a trade secret but by doing so is disloyal to the employer. Some courts have held that UTSA preempts such claims and that there is no recovery unless the actions of the employee fit within the UTSA.

For example, in *Huong Que Inc. v Luu*, 58 Cal. Rptr. 3d 527 (Cal. 6th Ct. App. 2007), a California appellate court held that the customer list for a calendar company was not a trade secret and so the USTA did not apply. Mui Luu and Cu Tu Nyguyen founded a Vietnamese calendar company that was the number-one calendar company in the United States. In 2003, the husband and wife team sold their company to Huong Que, Inc., but remained as employees of the new company. Subsequently Huong discovered an e-mail message entitled "address list" in the electronic mailbox of Mui Luu. The e-mail message was an apparent response by one Huan Nguyen to an earlier message from Luu in which she had written, "Please remember to email address list to me." His reply stated, "Attached are customers' addresses and meeting's report on 5/22/05. Please forward to other procalendar's members." Attached to the e-mail was a text file in Vietnamese, which plaintiffs later translated into English. Entitled "Minutes of meeting regard [sic] creation of PROCALENDAR," it called for the formation of a company using capitalization of $100,000 in five equal shares, of which two ($40,000) would be distributed to one Amy Khuu "c/o Mr. & Mrs. Nguyen Tu Cu, Mr. Phan Don." The minutes set forth, among other things, the "responsibilities of each partner. . . ." As relevant here, they stated, "Mrs. Luu Mui will be responsible for bookkeeping, tax, contact with Taiwan for calendar/book printing for customer, and distributing calendar for customer-no direct contact with customer, and no salary. Mr. Cu will be responsible for direct sales with Mr. Xanh, no salary."

Since list did not qualify as a trade secret, the court held the UTSA did not apply. However, the court clarified that there was a right of recovery—an independent action for breach of the duty of loyalty, which is the right of an employer to recover from an employee for what amounts to "biting the hand that feeds you." Because the two were using the information of an employer to start their own calendar company there was a cause of action. The loyalty breach claims are based on competitive use. However, USTA does not require competitive use; rather, the employer need only prove that the information was taken by the employee.

Criminal Penalties for Theft of Trade Secrets

The Industrial Espionage Act of 1996 makes it a felony to copy, download, upload, fax, or otherwise communicate trade secrets of U.S. companies to benefit anyone other than the owner of that information. Trade secrets are defined under the IEA very similarly to how they are defined under the UTSA. Again, the IEA does not apply unless the information has been treated as a trade secret.

Fines for violations by individuals are up to $500,000, and imprisonment can be for up to 15 years. For corporations that violate the IEA, the fine is the greater of up to $10,000,000 or twice the value of the secret that was communicated.

Exhibit 15.1 provides a summary of intellectual property rights and protections.

International Intellectual Property Issues

Patent Protection

The period for patent protection varies from country to country. The United States does not permit patent protection for products until the patent is granted, whereas other countries afford protection from the time application is made. Procedures for obtaining patents also vary significantly from country to country. For example, many countries hold **opposition proceedings** as part of the patent process. Much

EXHIBIT 15.1   Summary of Intellectual Property Rights

TYPE OF INTELLECTUAL PROPERTY	TRADEMARKS	COPYRIGHTS	PATENTS	TRADE SECRETS
Protection	Words, names, symbols, or devices used to identify a product or service	Original creative works of authorship, such as writings, movies, records, and computer software	Utility, design, and plant patents	Advantageous formulas, devices, or compilation of information
Applicable standard	Identifies and distinguishes a product or service	Original creative works in writing or in another format	New and non-obvious advances in the art	Not readily ascertainable, not disclosed to the public
Where to apply	Patent and Trademark Office	Register of Copyrights	Patent and Trademark Office	No public registration necessary
Duration	Indefinite so long as it continues to be used	Life of author plus 70 years; corporate is 120 years from creation or 95 years from publication of the work	Utility and plant patents, 20 years from date of application; design patents, 14 years	Indefinite so long as secret is not disclosed to public

Source: Adapted from Anderson's Business Law, © 2010 by David Twomey and Marianne Jennings.

like the federal regulatory promulgation steps (see Chapter 6), the process includes publishing the description of the patent, and inviting the public to study the description and possibly oppose the granting of a patent.

Many countries impose working requirements on the patent holder's use of the patent, which means that the idea or product must be produced commercially within a certain period of time or the patent protection is revoked.

Trademark Protection

As noted earlier in the discussion of trademarks, the 1891 **Madrid Agreement** (updated in 1989) provides for the Madrid Protocol, which is central registration through the International Bureau, which is part of the World Intellectual Property Organization (WIPO) in Geneva, Switzerland. Registrations with the bureau are effective for five years in all member countries unless one of the members objects to the trademark registration, in which case the registration is not effective in that country.

In 1996, the European Union began its one-stop trademark registration, known as Community Trademark (CTM). Under the provisions of this program, U.S. companies register their trademarks once and enjoy protection in all countries that are part of the European Union. The trademark and backup materials are filed with the Office of Harmonization of the Internal Market (OHIM). The OHIM will then notify the trademark offices in each of the member states of the European Union.

Many countries have permitted the unauthorized use of trademarks in an effort to develop local economies. These countries permit the production of **knock-off goods,** which are goods that carry the trademark or trade name of a firm's product but are not actually produced by that firm. A costly problem for trademark holders is the **gray market.** Manufacturers in foreign countries are authorized to produce a certain amount of goods, but many foreign manufacturers exceed their licensed quota and dump the goods into the market at a much lower price and thereby reduce the trademark owner's market. Both knock-off and gray market goods are forms of infringement.

CONSIDER... 15.7

Illia Lekach and Simon Falic are brothers-in-law who founded Perfumania, Inc. Perfumania is a chain of no-frills stores that sells 170 brands of upscale perfumes, such as Estée Lauder, Calvin Klein, and Chanel, at prices 20–70 percent below department store prices. Mr. Lekach referred to the company as the Toys "R" Us of perfume sales.

Manufacturers of expensive perfumes like to sell only to their full-price department store customers. Perfumania must get its supplies from the gray market—unauthorized and authorized distributors in other countries where manufacturers charge less than in the United States.

Givenchy, Boucheron, and Cosmair have sued Perfumania for copyright infringement and patent violations. The manufacturers maintain that they must pay the promotion fees on the perfumes and Perfumania enjoys the benefits of the expensive promotions without paying costs. One manufacturer notes, "I don't want to sell to the gray market. It's not a strategy. You kill your name."

Evaluate the legalities and ethics of Perfumania's gray-market purchases and discount sales.

Copyrights in International Business

The purpose of the Berne Convention, mentioned earlier and called the Convention for the Protection of Literary and Artistic Works, was to establish international uniformity in copyright protection. The convention was signed on September 9, 1986, and became effective in the United States on March 1, 1989. The convention is administered by WIPO and covers member countries. However, the Berne Convention gives backdoor copyright protection to works originating in non–Berne member countries if the work is simultaneously published in a Berne member country.

Differing International Standards

The protection of intellectual property in other countries is a difficult task, particularly when the standards of those countries do not recognize computer software as a property right.

 Ethical Issues

The United States is the world's largest personal computer software market. The rate of software piracy in the United States in 2000 was 20 percent. In Asia, the average piracy rate is 70 percent; that is, 70 percent of all users of software have pirated copies. China and Thailand have become known as "one copy" countries; a joke that circulates among software producers is that there is only one legitimate copy of the personal computer software in the country, and all remaining copies are pirated. Evaluate the costs and who is harmed by such widespread pirating.

China has led the world with software piracy. In 1994, the U.S. Trade Representative placed China on its Special 301 Priority Watch List. By February 1995, the United States had threatened to impose more than $1 billion in trade sanctions if China did not take action to curb software pirating. In August 1995, the United States and China reached an agreement to prevent the sanctions. China agreed to take immediate action against known software pirates and to confiscate software packages without the seals that U.S. companies place on their software packages and materials. China remains on the trade watch list as the cultural change for appreciation of ownership rights with respect to computer programs takes place.

Enforcing Business Property Rights

Product Disparagement

When an untrue statement is made about a business product or service, the defamation is referred to as **disparagement** and is either **trade libel** (written) or **slander of title** (oral). These business torts occur when one business makes untrue statements about another business, its product, or its abilities. The elements for disparagement follow:

1. False statement about a business product or about its reputation, honesty, or integrity

2. Publication

3. Statement that is directed at a business (in many cases, businesses are considered public figures, and the statement must be made with malice and the intent to injure that business)

4. Damages

These elements are the same as those discussed in Chapter 9 for the personal tort of defamation (see p. 288). *Bose Corporation v Consumers Union of United States, Inc.* (Case 15.5) deals with the tort of disparagement.

| CASE 15.5 | *Bose Corporation v Consumers Union of United States, Inc.*
466 U.S. 485 (1984) |

Woofers, Tweeters, and Disparagement

FACTS

Bose Corporation manufactures the Bose 901, a stereo loudspeaker. In May 1970, the Consumers Union publication *Consumer Reports* analyzed and evaluated the middle-range price group of loudspeaker systems, including the Bose 901. It was described in a two-page boxed-off section as "unique and unconventional," but the description also pointed out that a listener could "pinpoint the location of various instruments much more easily with a standard speaker than with the Bose system." The following is an excerpt from the boxed description:

> *Worse, individual instruments heard through the Bose system seemed to grow to gigantic proportions and tended to wander about the room. For instance, a violin appeared to be ten feet wide and a piano stretched from wall to wall. With orchestral music, such effects seemed inconsequential. But we think they might become annoying when listening to soloists. . . .*

CONTINUED

We think the Bose system is so unusual that a prospective buyer must listen to it and judge it for himself. We would suggest delaying so big an investment until you were sure the system would please you after the novelty value had worn off.

The article was not written by the same people who made the observation of the speakers. The observers described the sound as moving around the room and the article described the sounds as wandering back and forth.

Bose Corporation took exception to many of the statements made and asked *Consumer Reports* to publish a retraction. *Consumer Reports* would not retract the statements, and Bose sued for disparagement. The district court found that Bose was a public figure and, as such, was required to prove that the statements were made with knowledge they were false (malice). However, the court did find that some of the remarks constituted disparagement and held for Bose (petitioner). The court of appeals reversed on the grounds that the statements were not made with malice, and that the article did not accurately reflect what evaluators heard, but was written for a mass audience and not with reckless disregard for the truth. Bose appealed.

JUDICIAL OPINION

STEVENS, Justice

. . . There are categories of communication and certain special utterances to which the majestic protection of the First Amendment does not extend because they "are no essential part of any exposition of ideas, and are of such slight social value as a step to truth that any benefit that may be derived from them is clearly outweighed by the social interest in order and morality." Libelous speech has been held to constitute one such category. . . .

We agree with the Court of Appeals that the difference between hearing violin sounds move around the room and hearing them wander back and forth fits easily within the breathing space that gives life to the First Amendment. We may accept all of the purely factual findings of the District Court and nevertheless hold as a matter of law that the record does not contain clear and convincing evidence that [Consumers Union] prepared the loudspeaker article with knowledge that it contained a false statement, or with reckless disregard for the truth.

The judgment of the Court of Appeals is affirmed.

CASE QUESTIONS

1. Who prepared the *Consumer Reports* article?
2. Why is malice an important part of the case?
3. What classes of speech are exceptions to First Amendment protection?
4. Is disparagement a difficult tort to prove?

Palming Off

Palming off, one of the oldest unfair methods of competition, occurs when one company sells its product by leading buyers to believe it is really another company's product. For example, many cases of palming off took place during the 1980s, when Cabbage Patch dolls were popular, in demand, and scarce. Many replicas were made and called "Cabbage Patch dolls" even though they were not manufactured by Coleco, the original creator.

Establishing that someone is palming off requires proof that consumer confusion is likely because of the appearance or name of the competing product. For example, labeling a diamond DeBiers instead of DeBeers is likely to cause confusion. Competitors' packaging with the same colors and design as an original product creates confusion. Potential buyers are likely to be confused as to who actually made the product and who has what market and quality reputation.

Misappropriation

The tort of **misappropriation** is a form of protection for a business whose trade secrets are taken without authorization. Misappropriation is conversion of a trade secret for self-benefit or the benefit of a new employer. For example, an employee who takes proprietary information such as a customer list from her employer and uses it to start a competing business is guilty of misappropriation. Most companies put noncompete clauses that address the issue of taking trade secrets to a new company or forming a competing company in their employment contracts. Those clauses are covered in Chapter 16.

CONSIDER... 15.8

Ross Klein and Amar Lalvani, two former employees of Starwood Hotels & Resorts Worldwide, were hired by Hilton Hotels Corporation in the summer of 2008. A suit filed by Starwood alleges that its two former executives took with them more than 100,000 electronic documents that contained proprietary information that Hilton then used in creating its new Denizen hotel chain.

In developing a concept for a new chain (Denizen is geared at the high-end market), companies spend years and millions on studying consumer needs and preferences, social trends, lighting, costs, food choices, and even fabrics and designs. The suit alleges that all of Starwood's preliminary work on its developmental plans was taken by the executives to Hilton and that its concepts made their way into the Denizen brand. The suit maintains that the two executives sent the documents to Hilton via e-mail and through document shipments.

Starwood uncovered the alleged theft via serendipity. Starwood had begun an arbitration proceeding against Hilton for its recruitment of eight Starwood employees. While Hilton's in-house legal counsel was preparing for that arbitration, he discovered bundles of Starwood documents in the files of Mr. Klein and other Hilton employees. Hilton then sent the electronic files and documents back to Starwood. Eight boxes of materials were mailed to Starwood in February 2009. Hilton's general counsel said in a cover letter that he did not think the information was proprietary or confidential but that he was sending them back as a precaution.

However, Starwood noted that its files included its development plans for its "zen den" which it was going to put in its upscale "W" hotels. Hilton's development plans for Denizen referred to it as their "den of zen."

The Starwood complaint also alleges that the two men took along Starwood's strategic marketing plans and that Starwood has heard from existing customers that Hilton has been approaching them using the same tools and marketing techniques that Starwood has used with them.

What are the rights of companies on proprietary information? What are the rights of companies in terms of enforcing covenants not to compete against employees? Be sure to apply all the enforcement and legal tools you have covered in this chapter. Evaluate the ethics of Hilton in hiring the two men from Starwood.

B I O G R A P H Y

Pepsi Is Honest with Coke

A former executive administrative assistant to Coca-Cola's global brand director, Joya Williams (42), was sentenced to eight years in prison for her role in an attempt to sell confidential materials to Pepsi. Together with Ibrahim Dimson (31) and Edmund Duhaney (43), Williams hatched a plan to make money by selling the materials. A man named "Dirk" sent a letter to Pepsi

headquarters in May 2006 offering secrets for sale, including recipes, details of future promotions, and the formula for a new beverage, for $100,000.

When a Pepsi employee got the letter, the employee took it immediately to corporate counsel, who then called the FBI. The FBI set up a sting operation that included videotaping Ms. Williams. Ms. Williams was

CONTINUED

observed on the videotape putting the confidential materials into her personal handbag. An undercover FBI agent also met the infamous "Dirk," who turned out to be Dimson. Dimson handed over a beverage sample and some of the documents, which Coke later confirmed to be valid and highly confidential trade secrets. The undercover agent gave Dimson $30,000 in cash as a down payment, with the remainder to come after the items were authenticated. The two then agreed that there would be more secrets coming for a total price of $1.5 million. According to FBI press releases, Dimson later e-mailed the undercover agent the following:

> I must see some type of seriousness on there [sic] part, if I'm to maintain the faith to continue with you guys. . . . I can even provide actual products and packaging of certain products, that no eye has seen, outside of maybe 5 top execs. I need to know today, if I have a serious partner or not. If the good faith moneys is in my account by Monday, that will be an indication of your seriousness.

After leaving, Dimson met in a rental car with Duhaney and they drove to Duhaney's home. Call records showed that Duhaney was in contact with Dimson and Williams on that day. Following these events, the undercover agent arranged for a July 5, 2006 meeting to transfer documents and $1.5 million. Following that meeting, the three were arrested.

When news of the arrests were made public, Pepsi released a statement that included the following, "Competition can be fierce, but must also be fair and legal."[a]

At the trial, Ms. Williams testified that Dimson and Duhaney took the information from her home without her knowledge. However, the videotape of her at the company contradicted her testimony. There was also a recorded tape of her accomplices deciding how to divvy up the money among the three of them. And the day after the June 2006 exchange between Dimson and the undercover agent, Ms. Williams deposited $4,000 cash into her checking account. Both Dimson and Duhaney entered guilty pleas, and Duhaney testified against Williams at her trial. Dimson was sentenced to five years in prison, and both Dimson and Williams were ordered to pay $40,000 in restitution. Duhaney's sentence was postponed.

Williams' sentence of 8 years in prison is 2 years longer than prosecutors recommended (although 2 years shorter than the possible 10 years) because of Williams's attempts to obstruct justice and because Judge Forrester felt the sentencing guidelines as written did not begin to approach the seriousness of the case.[b]

At her sentencing hearing, Ms. Williams offered the following, "Your honor, I have expanded my consciousness through this devastating experience. This has been a very defining moment in my life. I have become infamous when I never wanted to become famous. . . . I am sorry to Coke and I'm sorry to my boss and to you and to my family as well."[c] She also added, "Punishment is the memories and the moments that I'm going to miss. Punishment is never having a family of my own."[d]

Following the Dimson and Williams sentencings, the U.S. attorney issued the following statement:

> As the market becomes more global, the need to protect intellectual property becomes even more vital to protecting American companies and our economic growth. This case is an example of good corporate citizenship leading to a successful prosecution, and that unlawfully gaining a competitive advantage by stealing another's trade secrets can lead straight to federal prison.[e]

[a] From FBI press release, http://www.fbi.gov.

[b] Kathleen Kingsbury, "You Can't Beat the Real Thing," TIME, July 9, 2006, http://www.time.com; "Ex-Secretary Gets 8-Year Term in Coca-Cola Secrets Case," *New York Times*, May 24, 2007, p. C3.

[c] *Id.*

[d] *Id.*

[e] From FBI press release, http://www.fbi.gov.

Summary

What are the types of intellectual property businesses own?

- Patents—for products, processes, discoveries
- Copyrights—for books, designs, dramatic works, photographs, films, etc.
- Trademarks—the brand protections for product symbols

- Trade names—the brand protections for product names
- Trade dress—the brand protection for those easily recognizable shapes and colors of a company and its product
- Trade secrets—the knowledge a business develops that provide its competitive edge

What are the legal protections for intellectual property?

- Patents—statutory protection of exclusivity for products and processes

- Copyrights—statutory protection of exclusivity for words, thoughts, ideas, music

- Trademarks—statutory protection of exclusivity for product symbols

- Trade names—statutory protection of exclusivity for unique product labels and names

- Trade dress—statutory protection of exclusivity for product colors and motifs

- Trade secrets—criminal sanctions for unauthorized transfer or use and violation of employer nondisclosure agreements

What issues of intellectual property protection exist in international operations?

- The Berne Convention—copyright recognition and protection across borders

- OPTH—European Community Trademark registration

- WIPO—World Intellectual Property Organization

What private remedies exist for property protections?

- Product disparagement—false and damaging statements

- Misappropriation—use of another's ideas or trade secrets

- Palming off—causing deception about the maker or source of a product

Questions and Problems

1. The San Diego Chicken, a mascot at professional baseball games, has a portion of his act in which he grabs a purple dinosaur and stomps it, stamps it, pounds it, and pummels it. Lyons Partnership, L.P., produces the *Barney the Dinosaur* television show, which features a purple dinosaur, and holds all its product licenses. Lyons filed suit against Ted Giannoulas (the man beneath the San Diego Chicken costume) for copyright infringement.

A Texas court classified the portion of Mr. Giannoulas's act that involved a purple dinosaur as a form of parody or satire that was thereby protected by the First Amendment. Kenneth Fitzgerald, the lawyer for Mr. Giannoulas, said Mr. Giannoulas will seek to recover his attorney's fees in the case.

Mr. Fitzgerald noted during the case that Barney has been spoofed by Jay Leno as well as on the television show "Saturday Night Live," but Lyons chose only to pursue Mr. Giannoulas.

What is wrong with selective enforcement of one's copyright protections? Is Barney the Dinosaur something that can be copyrighted? [*Lyons Partnership v Giannoulas,* 179 F.3d 384 (5th Cir. 1999)]

2. Yankee Candle Company, a leading manufacturer of scented candles, sued competitor Bridgewater Candle Company for trade name and trade dress infringement. Yankee alleged that Bridgewater's labels were the same size, had the same border, and featured similar photographs to depict the scents of the candles. For example, the Bridgewater "French Vanilla" photograph has ice cream cones filled with vanilla ice cream and the Yankee "French Vanilla" only features empty cones, with no ice cream. Both the Bridgewater fragrance "Cinnamon Rolls" and the Yankee "Cinnamon" display photographs of cinnamon rolls. However, the Yankee photograph also includes cinnamon sticks, while the Bridgewater rolls highlight the sugary frosting found on a cinnamon roll. Both the Bridgewater "Apple Pie" and the Yankee "Spiced Apple" contain photographs of apple pies. However, the Yankee photograph also features a basket and several apple slices. The Bridgewater photograph contains several whole apples. In addition, in the Bridgewater photographs, the darkish filling is oozing out of the pies, while the Yankee pies are lighter in color and not leaking apple filling.

Yankee also claimed that Bridgewater had infringed its trade dress: (i) by copying Yankee's method of shelving and displaying candles in its stores, called the "Vertical Display System", (ii) by copying the overall "look and feel" of Yankee's Housewarmer line of candles; and (iii) by copying the design of Yankee's merchandise catalog, specifically its one-fragrance-per-page layout.

Is there enough here to support any intellectual property claims by Yankee? Specify what types and the elements required to establish any possible claims. [*Yankee Candle Co., Inc. v Bridgewater Candle Co., LLC,* 259 F.3d 25 (1st Cir. 2001)]

3. GM developed an ad for its Terrain utility vehicle that featured a tattooed, shirtless image of Albert Einstein with "his underpants on display." The body featured in the ad with Dr. Einstein's head was that of one of *People* magazine's "sexiest men alive." The ad carries the caption, "Ideas are sexy too."

The Hebrew University of Jerusalem has filed suit against GM to enforce the name and intellectual property rights that Dr. Einstein willed to the university. GM has responded that it purchased the image of Dr. Einstein for use from a licensing firm. Does the university have a basis for its claim for $75,000? Could it stop the use of Dr. Einstein's head on another body in an ad? Discuss what intellectual property rights are at issue here.

4. Robert Conroy invented and holds the patent for "inflatable bladders used in athletic footgear." The patent is called "Athletic Armor and Inflatable Bag Assembly." The "Bladders" can be inflated with air to cushion and protect the feet of athletic shoe wearers.

Reebok International, Ltd. manufactures a basketball shoe with inflatable bladders that it sells under the name of "the PUMP." Mr. Conroy brought suit, claiming Reebok infringed his patent. Reebok says the design and method of inflation are different from Mr. Conroy's patented system. Mr. Conroy says the idea of an inflatable shoe is his and he is entitled to royalties from Reebok. Is Mr. Conroy correct? [*Conroy v Reebok International, Ltd.*, 29 U.S. P. Q.2d 1373 (Mass. 1994)]

5. Rich Leivenberg and Jane Wyler, founders of the company, Reuseniks, developed a new product called reusable dry-cleaning bags. Ms. Wyler met another couple in 2008 and explained to them her plan to develop the reusable dry-cleaning bags. The couple was "blown away" by the idea and developed their own, "The Green Garmento." What are the rights of Reuseniks founders? What do you need to know to be able to answer their questions about their rights?

6. LVM has registered trademarks for "LOUIS VUITTON" in connection with luggage and ladies' handbags (the "LOUIS VUITTON mark"), and for a stylized monogram of "LV," used in connection with traveling bags and other goods (the "LV mark"). In 2005, LVM adopted other designs consisting of canvas with repetitions of the LV mark (in multiple colors of red, green, and blue) and smiling cherries on a brown background (the "Cherry design").

The Multicolor design and the Cherry design attracted immediate and extraordinary media attention and publicity in magazines such as *Vogue, W, Elle, Harper's Bazaar, Us Weekly, Life and Style, Travel & Leisure, People, In Style*, and *Jane*. The press published photographs showing celebrities carrying these handbags, including Jennifer Lopez, Madonna, Eve, Elizabeth Hurley, Carmen Electra, and Anna Kournikova, among others. *People* magazine said, "the wait list is in the thousands." The handbags retailed in the range of $995 for a medium handbag to $4500 for a large travel bag.

Haute Diggity Dog, LLC, which is a relatively small and relatively new business located in Nevada, manufactures and sells nationally—primarily through pet stores—a line of pet chew toys and beds whose names parody elegant high-end brands of products such as perfume, cars, shoes, sparkling wine, and handbags. These include—in addition to Chewy Vuiton (LOUIS VUITTON)—Chewnel No. 5 (Chanel No. 5), Furcedes (Mercedes), Jimmy Chew (Jimmy Choo), Dog Perignonn (Dom Perignon), Sniffany & Co. (Tiffany & Co.), and Dogior (Dior). The chew toys and pet beds are plush, made of polyester, and have a shape and design that loosely imitate the signature product of the targeted brand. They are mostly distributed and sold through pet stores, although one or two Macy's stores carry Haute Diggity Dog's products. The dog toys are generally sold for less than $20, although larger versions of some of Haute Diggity Dog's plush dog beds sell for more than $100.

Haute Diggity Dog's "Chewy Vuiton" dog toys, in particular, loosely resemble miniature handbags and undisputedly evoke LVM handbags of similar shape, design, and color. In lieu of the LOUIS VUITTON mark, the dog toy uses "Chewy Vuiton"; in lieu of the LV mark, it uses "CV"; the other symbols and colors employed are imitations, but not exact ones, of those used in the LVM Multicolor and Cherry designs. LVM brought suit against Haute Diggity alleging trademark infringement, trademark dilution, copyright infringement, and common law violations. Can it recover? Why or why not? And what basis would LVM argue for its allegations? [*Louis Vuitton Malletier S.A. v Haute Diggity Dog, LLC,* 507 F.3d 252 (4th Cir. 2007)]

7. Charles Atlas has been in the business of selling bodybuilding courses for more than 70 years. Advertisements for Atlas's bodybuilding courses, which have appeared in DC Comic books, have included a one-page comic strip story titled "The Insult that Made a Man out of Mac." In the storyline: (1) a bully kicks sand in Mac's face at the beach; (2) after taking the Atlas course, the skinny Mac develops a muscular physique; (3) Mac finds the bully, again on the beach, and punches him, for which he receives newfound respect, particularly from his female companion; (4) in the final panel, the phrase "HERO OF THE BEACH" appears as a halo-like formation hovering over Mac's head. Mr. Atlas registered Mac with the Principal Register as the before and after characters of "Skinny" and "Joe." "Joe" is Mac in his muscular form with the leopard-skin trunks.

DC Comics created a character known as Flex Mentallo, who like Mac, came to be imbued with extraordinary strength. Flex Mentallo, once a scrawny weakling who has sand kicked in his face by a bully, returns to the beach with his muscular physique, and like Mac in the Atlas comic ad, he beats up the bully and becomes "the Hero of the beach."

However, after Flex Mentallo acquires his powers, the Charles Atlas tale changes a bit and Flex beats up the woman he had been with by smashing her in the face and proclaims, "I don't need a tramp like you anymore!" Mr. Atlas sued for infringement, saying that the depiction tarnished the image of Mac and, thus, the Atlas product line. DC defends its new character and storyline as parody. Determine what the court should do with the Atlas infringement suit. [*Charles Atlas, Ltd. v DC Comics, Inc.* 112 F.Supp.2d 330 (S.D.N.Y. 2000)]

8. Freddie Fuddruckers, Inc. used glass-enclosed bakeries and butcher areas exposed to the public to emphasize its freshness as a decor theme in all its Fuddruckers restaurants. Fuddruckers floors are checkered, walls tiled, and lighting bright to communicate cleanliness and quality. Ridgeline opened its restaurants with nearly identical decor. Does Fuddruckers have any rights? [*Freddie Fuddruckers, Inc. v Ridgeline, Inc.*, 589 F. Supp. 72 (1984)]

9. Do the following slogans constitute protectable business properties?
    a. MetLife: "Get Met, It Pays"
    b. General Electric: "GE Brings Good Things to Life"
    c. Nike: "Just Do It"
    d. Toys "R" Us: "R Us"

10. Starbucks, Inc., the international coffee house, is an aggressive defender of its name as well as the names for its coffees. It has ongoing litigation for infringement.

- A & D Café of Brooklyn, New York, uses the name "Warbucks" for its coffee, and Starbucks has filed suit against the café for dilution of its trade name.

- Sambuck's Coffee House of Astoria, Oregon, has been sued by Starbucks for dilution. However, the owner of the café is Samantha Buck-Lundberg, and she explains that the name of the café is a play on her name.

- Black Bear Monster Roastery in New Hampshire uses the name "Charbucks Blend" for one of its coffees, and Starbucks has filed suit for disparagement.

- Backwash.com had a link to Starbucks on its website. Starbucks filed suit to have the link removed, which Backwash did, citing "unappreciative" reasons.

- Coffee Bean & Tea Leaf Co. of Los Angeles has sued Starbucks for trademark infringement for the company's use of the term "ice blended," a term that the LA company claims it coined.[3]

What protections exist for trade names? For trademarks? Do you think there is infringement in these cases?

Economics, Business Strategy, and the Law

Derivative Works and Earnings Rights

In 1946, director Frank Capra produced *It's a Wonderful Life*, a movie based on a short story by Philip Van Doren Stern called "The Greatest Gift." The movie, starring Jimmy Stewart, did not perform well at the box office, and, although it received five Academy Award nominations, it won no awards. The movie's copyright was allowed to lapse. Television stations showed the classic without paying fees since the copyright had lapsed.

However, the U.S. Supreme Court decision in *Stewart v Abend*, 495 U.S. 207 (1990), offering an extension of the copyright protection of the underlying story to the movie, affected Jimmy Stewart's life once again. The original story owner, Mr. Stern, held the rights to the story since the movie rights had lapsed. With his story copyright in place, royalties for

its use in the movie had to be paid once again. The owners of *It's a Wonderful Life* began charging fees to cover their fees to Mr. Stern, and the result was costly access. *It's a Wonderful Life* was seen on television day and night during the holiday season when the copyright on the movie had lapsed. Now, with the copyright clarification, the movie rights have been reprotected. The story's continuing protection and the high royalty fees make *It's a Wonderful Life* a singular holiday event.

What is the relationship between movie copyrights and the rights to the underlying story? Who owns what between story authors and movie producers? What should businesses negotiating movie rights and royalties be certain about before signing an agreement?

Notes

1. The protection of intellectual property has been important to commercial development both here and in other countries for centuries. See the course website and the *Instructor's Manual* for more information.

2. From the Salinger complaint filed with the court.

3. Emily Lambert, "The Buck Stops Here," *Forbes*, January 6, 2003, p. 52.

Economic power is an inevitable result of the free enterprise system. Building a better mousetrap should result in attracting more customers and developing-economic power. But gaining economic power through means other than "superior skill, foresight, and industry" destroys the free enterprise system and often means that buyers don't get a better mousetrap. They are stuck with a mediocre mousetrap built by a firm with ill-gained economic power and resulting market control.

Antitrust law exists to prevent the growth of economic or market power through means other than superior skill, foresight, and industry. Making sure that the free enterprise system has its necessary fuel of competition is the purpose of antitrust laws. This chapter answers the following questions: What interferes with competition? Or, in other words, what are restraints of trade? What forms do they take? What antitrust laws apply when concerns about competition arise? What penalties can be imposed for violations of these laws? ■

People of the same trade seldom meet together, even for merriment and diversion, but the conversation ends in some contrivance to raise prices. It is impossible indeed to prevent such meetings, by any law which would be consistent with liberty and justice. But though the law cannot hinder people of the same trade from sometimes assembling together, it ought to do nothing to facilitate such assemblies.

Adam Smith
The Wealth of Nations

UPDATE ↖
For up-to-date legal news, go to
mariannejennings.com

> **While the law of competition may be sometimes hard for the individual, it is best for the race, because it ensures the survival of the fittest in every department.**
>
> Andrew Carnegie

CONSIDER...

Leegin Creative Leather Products, Inc., designs, manufactures, and distributes leather goods and accessories under the brand name "Brighton." The Brighton brand, often known as the brand with the silver heart, has now expanded into a full line of women's fashion accessories and is sold across the United States in more than 5,000 retail stores. In 1997, Leegin notified its retailers that it was going to continue focusing on its strong customer service, so readily available in its

smaller outlets, but not in places such as Walmart or Costco. To prevent the Brighton brand from being sold at warehouses and over the Internet, Leegin required its retailers to follow a minimum price policy or be terminated as a Brighton retailer. Kay's Kloset was terminated for holding sales on Brighton items in order to compete with local retailers. Kay's Kloset wants to know, "Can Leegin do that because we sold at a cheaper price? Isn't this anticompetitive?"

What Interferes with Competition? Covenants Not to Compete

As early as the 16th century, businesspeople developed agreements or covenants not to compete. The initial reaction to those agreements was not positive, with the courts issuing a resounding "No!" to those who came seeking to keep others from competing. However, by the 17th and 18th centuries, the courts began to see that some circumstances required trade restraint if competition was to flourish. As odd as it may sound, covenants not to compete can ensure competition. Through careful review of the covenants that resulted in judicial disputes, the courts began to carve out permissible types of restraints, such as protections for the buyer of a business. In these purchase agreements, the seller agreed not to open a competing business. This trade restraint, called a **covenant not to compete,** was necessary to preserve competition. A buyer purchasing a business meant someone else was entering the market. If the seller dropped down a few doors and opened the same business again, the seller would take customers and put the new buyer out of business.

So, covenants that were part of business purchase agreements are valid as long as they are reasonable in length and scope. For example, in *Mitchell v Reynolds,* 24 Eng. Rep. 347 (1711), a baker who sold his bakery agreed not to compete in the immediate area for five years, and a court held the covenant valid because it was limited in time and geographic scope.

Contracts and covenants that restrain trade are not illegal *per se*, meaning prohibited all the time no matter what. Courts continue to examine the scope of covenants and contracts that restrain trade to make sure that they are necessary for protection and not too broad in scope. For example, a covenant in a contract for the sale of a dry cleaning business that prohibits the seller from opening another dry cleaning business anywhere in the state is unreasonably broad, but a similar covenant limited to the town where the business is located is probably reasonable. The goodwill of the business must be preserved if competition is to take hold. The extent of the protection for the goodwill is determined by the economic base of the area: How many dry cleaners can the area support?

Partners' and employees' restrictions that prevent them from competing for a certain time period after they leave a partnership or corporation are also reasonable as long as they are not excessive. More details are provided in Chapter 17, but these covenants protect the investment the employers or partnerships make in recruiting and training the employees or new partners.

Competition restraints in leases for commercial property are another example of covenants not to compete that are generally valid. For example, a restriction in a shopping center lease that prohibits a lessee from operating a business that competes with other tenants is valid as long as the purpose of the restriction is to obtain a proper mix in the shopping center with the idea of attracting more business. In *Child World, Inc. v South Towne Centre, Ltd.* (Case 16.1), the court addresses the issue of a shopping center lease covenant and its reasonableness under common law standards.

BUSINESS PLANNING TIP

When negotiating valid covenants not to compete, follow these guidelines.

1. Be certain the covenant is necessary.

2. Be certain the covenant is reasonable.

   a. It covers only the geographic scope necessary. (A five-mile radius for the sale of a dry cleaning business is reasonable; a worldwide prohibition is not.)

   b. It covers only the time necessary. (Five years is reasonable; a lifetime prohibition is not.)

3. Make the covenant part of the agreement of sale, lease, or employment. Separate agreements arouse suspicions.

4. Be certain both parties initial the non-compete clause or paragraph.

5. Legal representation helps ensure validity by assumed understanding.

CASE 16.1

Child World, Inc. v South Towne Centre, Ltd.
634 F.Supp. 1121 (S.D. Ohio 1986)

Toys "R" Us Only

FACTS

Child World, Inc. (plaintiff) operates large retail toy stores throughout Ohio and other states called Children's Palace. South Towne Centre, Ltd. (defendant) is a limited partnership in Ohio that leases space in its South Towne Centre shopping complex to a Children's Palace store. Section 43(A) of the lease, executed in February 1976, provided as follows:

Except insofar as the following shall be unlawful, the parties mutually agree as follows:

A. Landlord shall not use or permit or suffer any other person, firm, corporation or other entity to use any portion of the Shopping Center or any other property located within six (6) miles from the Shopping Center and owned, leased, or otherwise controlled by the landlord (meaning thereby the real property or parties in interest and not a "straw" person or entity) or any person or entity having a substantial identity of interest, for the operation of a toys and games store principally for the sale at retail of toys and games, juvenile furniture and sporting goods such as is exemplified by the Child World and Children's Palace stores operated by Tenant's parent company, Child World, Inc. at the demised premises and elsewhere.

The lease was for 20 years and was signed by Barbara Beerman Weprin, the sole general partner of South Towne. Mad River, Ltd. is another limited partnership in which Ms. Weprin is the sole general partner. Mad River owns another parcel of land approximately one-half mile from the South Towne Centre. On December 24, 1985, Mad River entered into an agreement to sell the parcel of land to Toys "R" Us, Inc. Toys "R" Us intends to construct a retail facility similar to the description in the above-noted lease clause. When Children's Palace was informed of the sale, they brought suit, seeking to enforce the covenant not to lease or sell to a competitor of Children's Palace.

JUDICIAL OPINION

RICE, Circuit Judge

The consensus of the federal courts which have considered covenants in shopping center leases is one with which this Court can agree; namely, that the varying terms, conditions, and economic justifications for such restrictions render them inappropriate subjects for application of the *per se* rule. Defendants have not alleged nor proven anything about Section 43(A) of the lease which would indicate that it has only anticompetitive consequences. Indeed, in Finding of Fact #9, Defendants agree that Section 43(A) was negotiated as an inducement for Plaintiff to erect a Children's Palace store on Defendants' premises and to enter into a 20-year lease. This economic justification for exclusivity clauses is among the primary reasons that clauses such as Section 43(A) have not been found to be *per se* illegal, but rather have been found consistent with the public interest in economic development. Such laws can induce tenants to establish stores and to enter into a particular marketplace, often then encouraging the entry of other, often smaller, merchants.

A number of factors have been considered by the courts which have excluded restrictive covenants in shopping center leases: (1) the relevant product and geographic markets, together with the showing of unreasonable impact upon competition in these markets, due to the restrictive covenant; (2) the availability of alternate sites for the entity excluded by the operation of such a covenant; (3) the significance of the competition eliminated by the exclusivity clause, and whether present or future competitors were the parties excluded; (4) the scope of the restrictive covenant and whether it varied depending on particular circumstances; and (5) the economic justifications for the inclusion of the restrictive covenant in the lease.

Due to the particular facts of this case, however, the Court needs not, and specifically does not, reach the validity of the six-mile limitation contained in Section 43(A). Regardless of possible overbreadth, a restrictive covenant challenged as unreasonable . . . will be upheld to the extent that a breach of the covenant has occurred or is threatened to occur within a reasonable geographic area and time period. The parties have agreed, in Finding of Fact #12, that the parcel which Defendants seek to convey to Toys "R" Us is approximately one-half mile from the Children's Palace store covered by the Lease. The Court finds that Section 43(A) is lawful and enforceable to the extent of one-half mile, as required by the facts of this case.

Turning to the impact which enforcement of Section 43(A), as applied in this case, would have upon the Defendants, the burdens of enforcement are not unduly great. As noted *supra,* Section 43(A) does not appear to preclude rental or sale, even within a one-half mile radius, to any number of stores which can compete with a Children's Palace toy and game store but which are not "copycat" stores. On the financial level, there is testimony from a representative of Defendants in the record to the effect that the value of the parcel in question increases almost daily. Moreover, Defendants believe that they will have no difficulty in finding another purchaser, should Section 43(A) preclude their sale of the parcel to Toys "R" Us.

Enforcement of Section 43(A) to the extent of one-half mile would also not appear to foreclose the entry of Toys "R" Us into competition with Plaintiff's store in the environs of the South Towne Centre shopping center. In his deposition, J. Tim Logan indicated that, even were Section 43(A) upheld, presumably in its entirety, Toys "R" Us would still establish a store in the vicinity of Plaintiff's store.

Other courts have believed that restrictive covenants of a scope of one-half mile or more, albeit less than six miles, are legitimate lures by landlords in order for shopping center tenants to enter particular marketplaces and to thereby enhance the economic development of the community. The public has surely benefited from the development of South Towne Centre. As a restriction of six miles appeared reasonable to Defendants' predecessors at the time of bargaining, enforcement of Section 43(A) of the Lease to the extent of one-half mile is consistent with that original calculation of value, and certainly reasonable.

CASE QUESTIONS

1. Who leased what from whom? And what was the scope of the restrictions?

2. How did Toys "R" Us become involved?

3. Is the sale a violation of the anticompetition clause? Why or why not?

What Interferes with Competition? An Overview of the Federal Statutory Scheme on Restraint of Trade

During the last half of the 19th century, the United States experienced a tremendous change in its economy. A primarily agricultural economy changed to an industrial economy. Law on business combinations was largely undeveloped and unsuitable for the types of predatory business practices this new industrial age brought. Using the common-law standards discussed in the first section resulted in nonuniform standards for anticompetitive behavior. Congress addressed anticompetitive behavior with a series of antitrust statutes passed in the late 19th and early 20th centuries. With some amendments and changes, this scheme still exists and applies today. Exhibit 16.1 summarizes the general federal statutory antitrust statutes.

Federal antitrust laws apply to business conduct in interstate commerce. Even if an activity is purely intrastate, it is subject to federal laws if the activity has

EXHIBIT 16.1   Federal Antitrust Statutes

STATUTE	ORIGINAL DATE	JURISDICTION	COVERAGE	PENALTIES
Sherman Act 15 U.S.C. § 1	1890	Commerce clause	Monopolies; attempts to monopolize; boycotts; refusals to deal; price fixing; resale price maintenance; division of markets	Criminal; $100,000,000 if a corporation, or, individual, $1,000,000, or by imprisonment not exceeding 10 years, $10,000,000, for individuals if intentional or by both private suits
Clayton Act 1914 15 U.S.C. § 12	1914	Persons engaged in commerce	Tying; treble damages; mergers; interlocking directorates	Private suits
Federal Trade Commission Act 15 U.S.C. § 41	1914	Commerce clause	Unfair methods of FTC competition	
Robinson–Patman Act 15 U.S.C. § 13	1936	Persons engaged in commerce and selling	Price discrimination	Private suits and criminal for international acts goods across state lines
Celler–Kefauver (part of Clayton Act) 15 U.S.C. § 18	1950		Asset acquisitions	
Hart–Scott–Rodino Antitrust Improvements Act 15 U.S.C. § 1311	1976 amended 1980, 1994	Gives greater authority to Justice Department for prosecution; requires premerger notification to Justice Department		
Antitrust Modernization Commission	2002	Gave authority to study antitrust laws and the 2007 report recommended no changes in the laws		

a substantial economic effect on interstate commerce. In only a few instances is interstate commerce not found. In *McClain v Real Estate Board of New Orleans*, 441 U.S. 942 (1980), for example, an antitrust action against real estate brokers who worked only in the New Orleans area was permitted under the Sherman Act because the U.S. Supreme Court found that the brokers facilitated the loans and insurance for the properties they sold. The loans and insurance were provided by national firms, and funding came from outside the state. This involvement of interstate commerce, even in an indirect fashion, is sufficient for **Sherman Act** jurisdiction.

The **Clayton Act** and the **Robinson–Patman Act** have more stringent requirements for federal application, such as having sales across state lines or two businesses involved in interstate commerce.

Even if the federal laws do not apply to a particular transaction, states will also have their own laws on anticompetitive behavior, with some states regulating different sorts of activities, such as price-gouging, which is charging a price that produces a gross or net profit above a certain percentage determined by the statute or regulation. These statutes go into effect in situations such as post-hurricane areas when clean water is not readily available but willing sellers are offering it at prices up to five times higher than normal.

What Types of Activities Do the Federal Laws Regulate?

The federal antitrust laws can be broken down into a chart overview that will help you to understand what anticompetitive behavior is and where the federal antitrust laws apply. Exhibit 16.2 is a diagram of the types of activities and what laws apply.

Anticompetitive behavior breaks down first into two large chunks: horizontal and vertical. Horizontal behaviors are those between and among competitors, and federal law takes any activities here seriously. In these types of behaviors, the statutes and courts find ***per se* illegal** behavior, which means that courts do not analyze what the competitors did; their behavior is just plain illegal. Fixing prices and monopolizing are *per se* illegal. Vertical behaviors are those along the supply

EXHIBIT 16.2   A Look at Markets, Competition, and Antitrust Laws

HORIZONTAL MARKETS	VERTICAL MARKETS
Monopolization	Tying
(Sherman Act)	Monopsony
	(Sherman Act)
Price fixing	Price discrimination
(Sherman Act)	(Robinson–Patman Act)
Refusals to deal	Resale price maintenance
Group boycotts	Exclusive dealing, sole outlets, customer and territory restrictions
Mergers among competitors	Mergers along the supply chain
Interlocking directorates	Interlocking directorates
(Clayton Act)	(Clayton Act)

chain, between manufacturer and distributor, or between manufacturer and retailer. Because other manufacturers and retailers are competing with the parties in the supply chain for the same customers, arrangements that these parties make could actually help competition. Although some vertical behaviors are *per se* illegal, the courts have been chipping away to make more of the vertical activities subject to a **rule of reason** standard, which means that the courts examine whether the activities help or hinder competition.[1]

Horizontal Restraints of Trade

Horizontal restraints of trade are designed to lessen competition among a firm's competitors. For example, the collusion on fuel surcharges discovered between Virgin and British Airways would be a horizontal restraint. The Sherman Act covers the horizontal restraints of **price fixing,** market division, **group boycotts** and refusals to deal, and monopolization. The Clayton Act also covers the problem of anticompetitive horizontal mergers or mergers with competitors.

Monopolization

Section 2 of the Sherman Act prohibits the act of **monopolizing.** A Sherman Act monopolization charge requires proof of (1) market power in the relevant market, and (2) some intentional or willful abuse of that power.

Market power is the power to control prices or exclude competition in a relevant market. **Market power** is an economic term that means the firm has a relatively inelastic demand curve. An elastic demand curve means that the firm's products have competition from other firms or from firms with substitute products. For example, cosmetic firms have an elastic demand; buyers can switch to other products when prices increase in one line or they can even give up the use of cosmetics. On the other hand, the demand curve for gasoline is less elastic. Although substitute means of transportation are available, most drivers need to use their cars and hence need gasoline.

The factors that courts look at to determine market power include the firm's market share. No set percentage figure translates into a final determination of market power. However, most monopolization cases were directed at firms with market shares greater than 50 percent.

Market share is measured after we determine the **relevant market;** including a look at the relevant **geographic market.** For example, a beer producer may have 50 percent of all nationwide beer sales, but, in a suit involving a local competitor, the producer's share might be only 20 percent because of the local beer's popularity. This local or **submarket** could be used as the relevant geographic market. A product may have an international market but may have only 10 percent market share in a particular area.

Each firm also has its own relevant **product market,** which is determined by consumers' preferences and their willingness to substitute other products for the product at issue. For example, a market could be defined as plastic wrapping materials, or it could be defined as food storage materials and include such wraps as wax paper, aluminum foil, and plastic storage bags. A company may have 90 percent of the plastic wrap market, but if buyers use plastic wrap interchangeably with foil, storage bags, plastic containers, and Press-n-Seal, then that share may only be 20 percent. The product market is determined by the **cross-elasticity** of demand, explained earlier.

However, the Sherman Act does not prohibit market power or even all monopolies—certain types of monopolies are recognized as lawful exceptions. For example, a small town usually only has an economic base large enough to support one newspaper; such an operation is a lawful monopoly. Some businesses are monopolies because they make a product or provide a service that is superior or unique. When a business has obtained a large market share by **superior skill, foresight, and industry,** it has simply put its product in the market in a superior way and is entitled to its market share. However, a firm that acquired or is maintaining monopoly power by some purposeful or deliberate act that is not "superior skill, foresight, and industry" (which, in short, is the ability to build a better mousetrap) may be violating the Sherman Act. Monopolization charges require some proof of conspiratorial or nefarious activity, and not just market power. In *Bell Atlantic v Twombly*, 550 U.S. 544 (2007), the U.S. Supreme Court held that companies can't be required to figure out on their own, as defendants in an antitrust suit, what exactly they did that was monopolistic. An antitrust suit must allege enough facts to give the alleged monopolist notice of what they are defending against. In *Bell Atlantic*, the plaintiffs alleged that phone companies were engaging in parallel behaviors. However, that companies in the same industry might have similar practices is not enough to put the companies on notice of monopolistic behaviors.

Some examples of prohibited purposeful conduct are **predatory pricing** and **exclusionary conduct.** Predatory pricing is pricing below actual cost for a temporary period to drive a potential competitor out of business. Exclusionary conduct is conduct that prevents a potential competitor from entering the market. For example, interfering with the purchase of a factory by a competitor would be improper exclusionary conduct. The landmark case *U.S. v Microsoft* (Case 16.2) deals both judicially and economically with the conduct requirement of a monopolization case.

CASE 16.2	*U.S. v Microsoft* 253 F.3d 34 (D.C. Cir. 2001)

You Have Performed an Illegal Operation

FACTS

Microsoft Corporation, a company based in Washington that does business in all 50 states and around the world, is the leading supplier of operating systems for personal computers (PCs). Although Microsoft licenses its software programs directly to consumers, the largest part of its sales consists of licensing the products to manufacturers of personal computers.

Microsoft was concerned about its strategic position with respect to the Internet and whether it would be able to maintain a dominant market position there similar to the one it enjoyed in software and operating systems.

The United States Justice Department had an ongoing inquiry into the market shares and practices of Microsoft, and 23 state attorneys general were also looking into the company's practices. The concerns of the Justice Department and attorneys general (plaintiffs) include the following:

1. Microsoft's position in the market as a monopolist (90 percent market share for operating systems).

2. Microsoft's barriers to entry for operating systems and Web browsers. Microsoft has refused to sell its software operating system to computer companies that installed the competitive browser, Netscape, which was gaining popularity as Microsoft's Internet Explorer (IE) struggled.

3. Microsoft worked to inhibit the efforts of Netscape with its browser by first trying to acquire Netscape and then working to "cut off [its] air supply"

CONTINUED

by retarding Sun Corporation's development and implementation of the Java program. When Microsoft altered the portions of Sun's Java program that allowed it to work without Windows, Sun notified Microsoft that such was a violation of its licensing agreement. Microsoft's response was, "Sue us." Sun sued Microsoft one week before the Justice Department brought its suit against Microsoft. Sun's suit then ran parallel with the Justice Department's.

In issuing a three-part opinion, Judge Thomas Penfield Jackson of the district court found that Microsoft had violated the antitrust laws and ordered a remedy of breaking up the company. Microsoft appealed the decision.

JUDICIAL OPINION

PER CURIAM
We decide this case against a backdrop of significant debate amongst academics and practitioners over the extent to which "old economy" § 2 monopolization doctrines should apply to firms competing in dynamic technological markets characterized by network effects. In technologically dynamic markets, however, such entrenchment may be temporary, because innovation may alter the field altogether. Rapid technological change leads to markets in which "firms compete through innovation for temporary market dominance, from which they may be displaced by the next wave of product advancements." Microsoft argues that the operating system market is just such a market. . . .

II. Monopolization
A. Monopoly Power
While merely possessing monopoly power is not itself an antitrust violation, it is a necessary element of a monopolization charge. Because direct proof is only rarely available, courts more typically examine market structure in search of circumstantial evidence of monopoly power.

The District Court considered these structural factors and concluded that Microsoft possesses monopoly power in a relevant market. Defining the market as Intel-compatible PC operating systems, the District Court found that Microsoft has a greater than 95% share. It also found the company's market position protected by a substantial entry barrier.

Microsoft argues that the District Court incorrectly defined the relevant market. It also claims that there is no barrier to entry in that market. . . . [W]e uphold the District Court's finding of monopoly power in its entirety.

1. Market Structure
a. Market definition
In this case, the District Court defined the market as "the licensing of all Intel-compatible PC operating systems worldwide," finding that there are "currently no products—and . . . there are not likely to be any

in the near future—that a significant percentage of computer users worldwide could substitute for [these operating systems] without incurring substantial costs."

The District Court found that consumers would not switch from Windows to Mac OS in response to a substantial price increase because of the costs of acquiring the new hardware needed to run Mac OS (an Apple computer and peripherals) and compatible software applications, as well as because of the effort involved in learning the new system and transferring files to its format. The court also found the Apple system less appealing to consumers because it costs considerably more and supports fewer applications.

. . . the District Court found that because information appliances fall far short of performing all of the functions of a PC, most consumers will buy them only as a supplement to their PCs.

Operating systems also function as platforms for software applications. They do this by "exposing"—i.e., making available to software developers—routines or protocols that perform certain widely—used functions. These are known as Application Programming Interfaces, or "APIs."

Every operating system has different APIs. Ultimately, if developers could write applications relying exclusively on APIs exposed by middleware, their applications would run on any operating system on which the middleware was also present. Netscape Navigator and Java—both at issue in this case—are middleware products written for multiple operating systems.

Microsoft argues that, because middleware could usurp the operating system's platform function and might eventually take over other operating system functions (for instance, by controlling peripherals), the District Court erred in excluding Navigator and Java from the relevant market. The District Court found, however, that neither Navigator, Java, nor any other middleware product could now, or would soon, expose enough APIs to serve as a platform for popular applications, much less take over all operating system functions. . . .

Considering the possibility of new rivals, the court focused not only on Microsoft's present market share, but also on the structural barrier that protects the company's future position. That barrier—the "applications barrier to entry"—stems from two characteristics of the software market: (1) most consumers prefer operating systems for which a large number of applications have already been written; and (2) most developers prefer to write for operating systems that already have a substantial consumer base. This "chicken-and-egg" situation ensures that applications will continue to be written for the already dominant Windows, which in turn ensures that consumers will continue to prefer it over other operating systems.

The consumer wants an operating system that runs not only types of applications that he knows he will want to use, but also those types in which he might develop an interest later. . . . The fact that a vastly larger number of applications are written for Windows than for other PC operating systems attracts consumers to Windows, because it reassures them that their interests will be met as long as they use Microsoft's product.

2. Direct Proof

. . . [W]e turn to Microsoft's alternative argument that it does not behave like a monopolist. Claiming that software competition is uniquely "dynamic," the company suggests a new rule: that monopoly power in the software industry should be proven directly, that is, by examining a company's actual behavior to determine if it reveals the existence of monopoly power. . . .

Even if we were to require direct proof, moreover, Microsoft's behavior may well be sufficient to show the existence of monopoly power. Certainly, none of the conduct Microsoft points to—its investment in R&D and the relatively low price of Windows—is inconsistent with the possession of such power. The R&D expenditures Microsoft points to are not simply for Windows, but for its entire company, which most likely does not possess a monopoly for all of its products. Moreover, because innovation can increase an already dominant market share and further delay the emergence of competition, even monopolists have reason to invest in R&D. Microsoft's pricing behavior is similarly equivocal. The company claims only that it never charged the short-term profit-maximizing price for Windows. . . .

More telling, the District Court found that some aspects of Microsoft's behavior are difficult to explain unless Windows is a monopoly product. For instance, the company set the price of Windows without considering rivals' prices, something a firm without a monopoly would have been unable to do. Microsoft's pattern of exclusionary conduct could only be rational "if the firm knew that it possessed monopoly power."

B. Anticompetitive Conduct

The challenge for an antitrust court lies in stating a general rule for distinguishing between exclusionary acts, which reduce social welfare, and competitive acts, which increase it.

1. Licenses Issued to Original Equipment Manufacturers [OEMs]

Microsoft's efforts to gain market share in one market (browsers) served to meet the threat to Microsoft's monopoly in another market (operating systems) by keeping rival browsers from gaining the critical mass of users necessary to attract developer attention away from Windows as the platform for software development. . . .

[T]he District Court condemned the license provisions prohibiting the OEMs from: (1) removing any desktop icons, folders, or "Start" menu entries; (2) altering the initial boot sequence; and (3) otherwise altering the appearance of the Windows desktop.

The District Court concluded that the first license restriction—the prohibition upon the removal of desktop icons, folders, and Start menu entries—thwarts the distribution of a rival browser by preventing OEMs from removing visible means of user access to IE. The OEMs cannot practically install a second browser in addition to IE, the court found, in part because "[p]re-installing more than one product in a given category . . . can significantly increase an OEM's support costs, for the redundancy can lead to confusion among novice users."

The second license provision at issue prohibits OEMs from modifying the initial boot sequence—the process that occurs the first time a consumer turns on the computer. Upon learning of OEM practices including boot sequence modification, Microsoft's Chairman, Bill Gates, wrote: "Apparently a lot of OEMs are bundling non-Microsoft browsers and coming up with offerings together with [Internet access providers, IAPs] that get displayed on their machines in a FAR more prominent way than MSN or our Internet browser." Because this prohibition has a substantial effect in protecting Microsoft's market power, and does so through a means other than competition on the merits, it is anticompetitive.

b. Microsoft's justifications for the license restrictions

Microsoft argues that the license restrictions are legally justified because, in imposing them, Microsoft is simply "exercising its rights as the holder of valid copyrights." Microsoft's primary copyright argument borders upon the frivolous. The company claims an absolute and unfettered right to use its intellectual property as it wishes: "[I]f intellectual property rights have been lawfully acquired," it says, then "their subsequent exercise cannot give rise to antitrust liability." That is no more correct than the proposition that use of one's personal property, such as a baseball bat, cannot give rise to tort liability. As the Federal Circuit succinctly stated: "Intellectual property rights do not confer a privilege to violate the antitrust laws." . . .

3. Agreements with Internet Access Providers

The District Court also condemned as exclusionary Microsoft's agreements with various IAPs. The IAPs include both Internet Service Providers, which offer consumers internet access, and Online Services ("OLSs") such as America Online ("AOL"), which offer proprietary content in addition to internet access and other services. The District Court deemed Microsoft's agreements with the IAPs unlawful because Microsoft licensed [IE] and the [IE] Access Kit to hundreds of IAPs for no charge. Then, Microsoft extended valuable promotional treatment to the ten most important IAPs in exchange for their commitment to promote and distribute [IE] and to exile Navigator from the desktop. Finally, in exchange for efforts to upgrade existing subscribers to client software that came bundled with [IE] instead of Navigator,

CONTINUED

Microsoft granted rebates—and in some cases made outright payments—to those same IAPs.

Although offering a customer an attractive deal is the hallmark of competition, the Supreme Court has indicated that in very rare circumstances a price may be unlawfully low, or "predatory." The rare case of price predation aside, the antitrust laws do not condemn even a monopolist for offering its product at an attractive price, and we therefore have no warrant to condemn Microsoft for offering either IE or the IEAK [IE Access Kit] free of charge or even at a negative price. Likewise, as we said above, a monopolist does not violate the Sherman Act simply by developing an attractive product.

4. Dealings with Internet Content Providers [ICPs], Independent Software Vendors [ISVs], and Apple Computer

. . . In dozens of "First Wave" agreements signed between the fall of 1997 and the spring of 1998, Microsoft has promised to give preferential support, in the form of early Windows 98 and Windows NT betas, other technical information, and the right to use certain Microsoft seals of approval, to important ISVs that agree to certain conditions. One of these conditions is that the ISVs use Internet Explorer as the default browsing software for any software they develop with a hypertext-based user interface.

[T]he effect of these deals is to "ensure . . . that many of the most popular Web-centric applications will rely on browsing technologies found only in Windows," and that Microsoft's deals with ISVs therefore "increase [ ] the likelihood that the millions of consumers using [applications designed by ISVs that entered into agreements with Microsoft] will use Internet Explorer rather than Navigator."

When Microsoft entered into the First Wave agreements, there were 40 million new users of the internet. Because, by keeping rival browsers from gaining widespread distribution (and potentially attracting the attention of developers away from the APIs in Windows), the deals have a substantial effect in preserving Microsoft's monopoly, we hold that plaintiffs have made a *prima facie* showing that the deals have an anticompetitive effect . . .

5. Java

Java, a set of technologies developed by Sun Microsystems, is another type of middleware posing a potential threat to Windows' position as the ubiquitous platform for software development.

In May 1995 Netscape agreed with Sun to-distribute a copy of the Java runtime environment with every copy of Navigator, and "Navigator quickly became the principal vehicle by which Sun placed copies of its Java runtime environment on the PC systems of Windows users." Microsoft, too, agreed to promote the Java technologies—or so it seemed.

When specifically accused by a *PC Week* reporter of fragmenting Java standards so as to prevent cross-platform uses, Microsoft denied the accusation and indicated it was only "adding rich platform support" to what remained a cross-platform implementation. An e-mail message internal to Microsoft, written shortly after the conversation with the reporter, shows otherwise:

> [O]k, i just did a followup call . . . [The reporter] liked that i kept pointing customers to w3c standards [(commonly observed internet protocols)] . . . [but] he accused us of being schizo with this vs. our java approach, i said he misunderstood [—] that [with Java] we are merely trying to add rich platform support to an interop layer . . . this plays well . . . at this point its [sic] not good to create MORE noise around our win32 java classes. instead we should just quietly grow j++ [(Microsoft's development tools)] share and assume that people will take more advantage of our classes without ever realizing they are building win32-only java apps.

. . . Microsoft's ultimate objective was to thwart Java's threat to Microsoft's monopoly in the market for operating systems. One Microsoft document, for example, states as a strategic goal: "Kill cross-platform Java by grow[ing] the polluted Java market."

Microsoft's conduct related to its Java developer tools served to protect its monopoly of the operating system in a manner not attributable either to the superiority of the operating system or to the acumen of its makers, and therefore was anticompetitive. Accordingly, we conclude this conduct is exclusionary, in violation of § 2 of the Sherman Act.

d. The threat to Intel

In 1995 Intel was in the process of developing a high-performance, Windows-compatible JVM. Microsoft wanted Intel to abandon that effort because a fast, cross-platform JVM would threaten Microsoft's monopoly in the operating system market. At an August 1995 meeting, Microsoft's Gates told Intel that its "cooperation with Sun and Netscape to develop a Java runtime environment . . . was one of the issues threatening to undermine cooperation between Intel and Microsoft." Three months later, "Microsoft's Paul Maritz told a senior Intel executive that Intel's [adaptation of its multimedia software to comply with] Sun's Java standards was as inimical to Microsoft as Microsoft's support for non-Intel microprocessors would be to Intel."

And Microsoft threatened Intel that if it did not stop aiding Sun on the multimedia front, then Microsoft would refuse to distribute Intel technologies bundled with Windows.

Intel finally capitulated in 1997.

. . . Microsoft's "advice" to Intel to stop aiding cross-platform Java was backed by the threat of retaliation, and this conclusion is supported by the evidence cited above. Therefore we affirm the conclusion that Microsoft's threats to Intel were exclusionary, in violation of § 2 of the Sherman Act.

REMEDIES

The District Court's remedies-phase proceedings are a different matter.

The reason the court declined to conduct an evidentiary hearing [on remedies] was not because of the absence of disputed facts, but because it believed that those disputes could be resolved only through "actual experience," not further proceedings. But a prediction about future events is not, as a prediction, any less a factual issue. . . . Trial courts are not excused from their obligation to resolve such matters through evidentiary hearings simply because they consider the bedrock procedures of our justice system to be "of little use."

. . . we vacate the District Court's remedies decree for [failure] . . . to hold an evidentiary hearing despite the presence of remedies-specific factual disputes.

Affirmed in part, reversed in part, remanded in part. We remand the case to the District Court for reassignment to a different trial judge for further proceedings consistent with this opinion.

CASE QUESTIONS

1. Make a list of the conduct Microsoft engaged in that the court finds indicated it was a monopoly.

2. What is the relevant market? What does Microsoft say the relevant market is?

3. What intellectual property argument does Microsoft make as a defense to the antitrust charges?

4. Why was the case remanded?

Aftermath: The Justice Department reached a settlement of the case with Microsoft near the end of 2001. No breakup of Microsoft was required as part of the remedies for the antitrust violation. Microsoft agreed to pay penalties, the majority of which ($180 million) would be in software donations to schools.

For the Manager's Desk

Re: E-Commerce, E-Mail, and Technology

E-mail is redefining the way cases are tried. In the U.S. Justice Department's case against Microsoft, a lawyer commented, "The Government does not need to put Mr. Gates on the stand because we have his e-mail and memoranda." The lawyer's comment reflects the tendency of e-mail to speak for itself. Witnesses can shrug and assert they cannot remember, but an e-mail from them is always available for recollection purposes as well as admission as evidence. At Microsoft, e-mail supplanted the telephone as the primary means of communication, and the government was able to tap into the entire e-mail system. There are 30 million pages of e-mail used as evidence in the Microsoft trial.

CYBERLAW

E-mail provides what is known as a contemporaneous record of events and has the added bonus that, for whatever psychological reason, those communicating with e-mail tend to be more frank and informal than they would be in a memo. E-mail can also contradict a witness's testimony and serve to undermine credibility. For example, when asked whether he recalled discussions with a subordinate about whether Microsoft should offer to invest in Netscape, Mr. Gates responded in his deposition, "I didn't see that as something that made sense." But Mr. Gates's e-mail included an urging to his subordinates to consider a Netscape alliance: "We could even pay them money as part of the deal, buying a piece of them or something."

E-mail is discoverable, it is admissible as evidence, and it is definitely not private. Employees should follow the admonition of one executive whose e-mail was used to fuel a million-dollar settlement by his company with a former employee: "If you wouldn't want anyone to read it, don't send it in e-mail." The impact of e-mail in the Microsoft antitrust case on companies and their e-mail policies was widespread. For example, Amazon.com launched a company-wide program called "Sweep and Keep," under which employees are instructed to purge e-mail messages no longer needed for conducting business. Amazon.com is offering employees who purge immediately free lattes in the company cafeteria.

The company had a two-part program. The first portion included instructions on document retention and deletion. The second part of the program was on document creation and included the following warning for employees: "Quite simply put, there are some communications that should not be expressed in written form. Sorry, no lattes this time."

Eliot Spitzer, New York's then-attorney general, used e-mails as critical parts of his cases against analysts and investment bankers. When asked to speak at an analyst's meeting he began by saying, "It's nice to be able to put faces with so many of your e-mails that I have read." Employees around the country report that they are now holding back on their e-mail communications and being careful about their choices of words.

Sources: Steve Lohr, "Antitrust Case Is Highlighting Role of E-Mail," *New York Times,* November 2, 1998, pp. C1, C4; John R. Wilke, "Old E-Mail Dogs Microsoft in Fighting Antitrust Suits," *Wall Street Journal,* August 27, 1998, p. B1.

Ethical Issues

The Running Fox is a small running-shoe manufacturer well known among professional runners for its high-quality, highly protective shoes. Athletic Feet is a manufacturer of a full line of running shoes, from track to long-distance running. Athletic Feet also publishes *Runner's Monthly,* a top magazine in the field of running with a circulation almost exclusively composed of runners. For the past three years, *Runner's Monthly* has published its "annual shoe survey" in which all the running shoes on the market are rated. Athletic Feet's shoes have been ranked as the top three in every category. Running Fox did not perform well in the ratings and has brought a monopolization suit against Athletic Feet. Athletic Feet says the relevant market is athletic footwear because it not only manufactures running shoes but also tennis, basketball, baseball, and other types of sport shoes. In the athletic shoe market, Athletic Feet holds a 20 percent share of the market; but in the running-shoe market, it holds an 80 percent share. Obviously, Running Fox wants to argue that running shoes are the relevant market. Who is correct? What is the relevant market? Does *Runner's Monthly* have a conflict of interest?

CONSIDER... 16.1

Penny Stafford, the owner of a coffee shop, Belvi Coffee and Tea Exchange, located in Bellevue, Washington, has brought an antitrust suit against Starbucks. She alleges that through its exclusive leases, Starbucks bans other coffee shops from competing.

Starbucks currently has a 73 percent market share, $8.4 billion in annual sales in the United States, and owns 7,551 of the 21,400 coffeehouses located in the United States. However, if Dunkin' Donuts, Krispy Kreme and Tim Hortons are included in the gourmet coffee market, then Starbucks holds only 43 percent of the coffee market. Starbucks purchased Seattle's Best Coffee (SBC) in 2003 and Torrefazione Italia in the same year. Starbucks then closed one-half of all the SBC stores and all of the Torrefazione outlets. Starbucks runs 59 stores within a two-mile radius of downtown Seattle.

Safford alleges that Starbucks has exclusive leases with landlords, that the landlords cannot lease space in the same building to another coffee shop. Does such an exclusive lease violate any antitrust laws or are such clauses permitted under the law?

Source: Edward Iwata, "Owner of small coffee shop takes on java titan Starbucks," *USA Today,* December 20, 2006, p. 1B.

Price Fixing

Any agreement or collaboration among competitors "for the purpose and with the effect of raising, depressing, fixing, pegging, or stabilizing the price of a commodity" is price fixing, a *per se* violation of Section 1 of the Sherman Act.

Price fixing can take many forms, but all of them are illegal. A minimum fee or price schedule discourages competition, puts an artificial restriction on the market, and provides a shield from market forces. Even proof that the minimum price is a reasonable price is irrelevant once there is proof of an agreement. Although establishing maximum prices sounds like an excellent benefit for consumers, the effect is to stabilize prices, which translates into a restriction on free-market forces.

Some competitors have tried to use list prices as a guideline, but such lists are still a violation even though the list prices are not mandatory. Just the exchange of price information has an effect on the market and interferes with competition.

Often price can be controlled through competitors' actions that affect supply. An agreement among competitors to limit production is an agreement to fix prices because the parties are controlling the supply, which in turn controls the right to demand the resulting price. Likewise, an agreement to limit or eliminate bidding, a form of a group boycott, has an effect on price because the supply is constrained. In *National Soc'y of Professional Engineers v United States*, 435 U.S. 679 (1978), a professional society agreed that there should not be bidding on engineering projects because the bidding process encouraged cost cutting and posed possible safety risks in the construction of the projects bid. Although its motives were well intentioned, it was still price fixing and a *per se* violation of the Sherman Act.

For the Manager's Desk

Re: How Does Price Fixing Happen? The Story of Sotheby's and Christie's

Christie's International and Sotheby's, international auction houses for art and estate items, are known for their handling of the estates and property of the rich and famous, such as the estate of Jacqueline Kennedy Onassis; the gowns of Diana, Princess of Wales; and the effects of Marilyn Monroe. Together, the two firms controlled 95 percent of the international auction market.

Sotheby's CEO of more than 20 years, Diana (Dede) Brooks, and Christopher M. Davidge, the CEO of Christie's, testified that at the direction of their bosses, Sotheby's chairman, A. Alfred Taubman, and Christie's chairman, Sir Anthony Tennant, they met to discuss their commissions. Sir Alfred and Sir Anthony had met and agreed that they were "killing" each other with their competition. Both then directed Brooks and Davidge to reach agreements that ensured their firms' survivals.

Ms. Brooks and Mr. Davidge then began a series of meetings, many of which were in the back seat of Ms. Brooks's car as she picked Mr. Davidge up from the airport, in which they discussed the following:

- Their commission rates

- An agreement to publish nonnegotiable commission rates

- An agreement as to who would publish rates first

- Exchange of customer information so that they could monitor each other's commission rates

- Eliminate interest-free loans to their seller/customers on consignment arrangements

- Eliminating charitable deductions as part of their pricing to sellers

The agreements reached in the town-car meetings worked. In March 1995, Christie's announced that it was increasing sellers' fees from a flat commission rate to a sliding scale that ranged from 2 to 20 percent. In April 1995, Sotheby's announced the same change. Their rates would change in this pattern until Mr. Davidge was fired in December 1999. Upset about a "paltry" severance package he turned documents over to the Justice Department. When Christie's learned that the documents had been turned over, it announced that it was increasing its buyer's commission from 15.5 to 18 percent and charging its sellers less. Seller commissions would drop to between 1 and 5 percent. Sotheby's did not follow the change, the first time in the nearly five year period that there was any difference in the two houses' commission rates.

The price fixing charges against the two auction houses involve "conscious parallelism." That is, two federal agencies

CONTINUED

were investigating why the two auction houses raised their commissions in lockstep over the years with virtually no price competition in auction commissions.

The records Mr. Davidge turned over to the Justice Department have been described as establishing "classic cartel behavior—price fixing pure and simple" between Christie's and Sotheby's. The correspondence in his files was between him and Ms. Brooks. The correspondence reflects a pattern of the two auction houses matching their commission rates.

Mr. Taubman denied any involvement in the price fixing and offered a lie detector test conducted by a former FBI agent to establish that he did not know of the arrangements and communications between Ms. Brooks and Mr. Davidge. The two key questions in the polygraph exam, which Mr. Taubman passed, were:

Did you tell Dede Brooks to try and reach an agreement with Davidge regarding amounts to be charged to buyers or sellers?

Did Dede Brooks ever tell you that she had reached an agreement with Davidge about amounts to be charged to buyers and sellers?

Mr. Taubman's answers of "no" to each of these questions were found to be truthful by the polygraph examiner. The test was conducted without any current law enforcement agents present.

Christie's and Sotheby's were not charged criminally for the price fixing because of their cooperation and agreements to pay fines. Christie's agreed to pay $256 million (one-half of $512 million requested in a civil suit brought against the company), and settled a shareholder lawsuit for $30 million. Sotheby's also agreed to pay its $256 million of the suit amount

to settle civil claims. Mr. Taubman agreed to be responsible for paying $156 million of that corporate obligation.

Mr. Davidge got immunity in exchange for his cooperation. Ms. Brooks entered a guilty plea on October 5, 2000, and declined all of her stock options. In exchange for favorable sentencing, Ms. Brooks, Mr. Taubman's one-time protégée, turned state's evidence and cooperated with the Justice Department in its investigation.

In May 2001, four years after the investigation began, the Justice Department announced the indictment of Mr. Taubman as well as his counterpart at Christie's, Sir Anthony Tennant. The indictment charged price fixing over a six-year period involving more than 13,000 customers. The criminal case proceeded to trial near the end of 2001. Ms. Brooks testified against Mr. Taubman. Mr. Taubman was found guilty of price fixing and related charges.

Sotheby's stock suffered during the time of the daily disclosures about the investigations, the evidence, and the resulting litigation. At the beginning of the investigation, in March 1999, Sotheby's stock was trading at $42 per share. By March 2000, it was down to $15 per share.

There are many lessons beyond price fixing in this story. Never trust the people you cheat with; they will throw you under the bus. The companies offered their executives as the sacrificial lambs to the Justice Department. Humans fix prices, and they are held accountable even when their companies have benefited.

Sources: Alexandria Peers and Ann Davis, "Christie's Overhauls Commissions," *Wall Street Journal,* February 8, 2000, pp. A3, A10; Douglas Frantz, with Carol Vogel and Ralph Blumenthal, "Files of Ex-Christie's Chief Fuel Inquiry into Art Auction," *New York Times,* October 8, 2000, pp. A1, A28.

CONSIDER... 16.2

General Electric, through its GES (General Electric Superabrasives) subsidiary, and DeBeers are both diamond processors and sellers. In 1991, both GES and DeBeers announced a price increase for their diamonds.

Edward Russell was a former GES employee who, in 1986, was promoted to the position of vice president in charge of GES. During this period Mr. Russell exchanged notes and held meetings with the managing director of a customer who also served as a board member for DeBeers. Following the meetings, both companies announced a 1991 price increase. There was some evidence that the customer indicated to GES that DeBeers would be increasing its prices. However, the customer who offered the information about the forthcoming price increase was not authorized to negotiate contracts or agreements on behalf of DeBeers.

Mr. Russell held his position as vice president of GES until November 11, 1991, when General Electric terminated his employment. In early 1992, Mr. Russell contacted the government, alleging that General Electric employees had committed various acts of wrongdoing, including antitrust violations.

Soon after contacting the government, Mr. Russell filed a civil wrongful termination action against General Electric. He alleged that General Electric fired him because he was a whistle-blower. Mr. Russell settled his wrongful termination suit against General Electric on February 16, 1994, one day before the grand jury handed down an indictment against General Electric (GE) for price fixing in violation of the Sherman Act. Mr. Russell was a key witness for the government. His testimony was that there was advance contact between GES and DeBeers before the announcement of the price increases. GE and DeBeers do not deny the advance contact but assert that there was no agreement to increase prices.

THINK: The elements for price fixing are that competitors act together to keep prices at a certain level or agree to charge a certain price. The statute does require an agreement between the parties.

APPLY: There must be evidence of an agreement to fix prices.

ANSWER: The court held that the fact that the managing director of the customer was also the director of a company that manufactured industrial diamonds did not establish that the managing director was acting on behalf of the competitor and that the industrial diamond manufacturer knew this when the managing director and the manufacturer exchanged advance list pricing information, for purposes of establishing that the manufacturer and the competitor conspired to raise list prices of industrial diamonds, where no evidence showed that the managing director's corporate links were used by the director or the competitor to form or facilitate an agreement with the manufacturer to fix prices.

ANSWER: Just because a managing director of the customer, who was also director of company that manufactured industrial diamonds under a joint venture between the customer and a competitor, supported an industrial diamond price increase did not establish that the managing director was acting on behalf of the competitor. Any exchange of information took place with both parties aware that the managing director had no authority to act on behalf of the competitor. [*U.S. v General Elec. Co.*, 869 F.Supp. 1285 (1994)]

Divvying Up the Markets

Any agreement between competitors to divide up an available market is a *per se* violation under the Sherman Act. The result of such an agreement is to give the participants monopolies in their particular area. Such a market division introduces an unnatural force into the competitive market. For example, office product supply companies agreeing to operate only in certain cities throughout a state would be a division of markets and a *per se* violation.

CONSIDER...   16.3

BRG of Georgia, Inc. (BRG), and Harcourt Brace Jovanovich Legal and Professional Publications (HBJ) are the nation's two largest providers of bar review materials and lectures. HBJ began offering a Georgia bar review course on a limited basis in 1976 and was in direct, often intense competition with BRG from 1977 to 1979. BRG and HBJ were the two main providers of bar review courses in Georgia during this period. In early

1980, they entered into an agreement that gave BRG an exclusive license to market HBJ's materials in Georgia and to use its trade name "BAR/BRI." The parties agreed that HBJ would not compete with BRG in Georgia and that BRG would not compete with HBJ outside of Georgia.

Under the agreement, HBJ received $100 per student enrolled by BRG and 40 percent of all revenues over $350. Immediately after the 1980 agreement, the price of BRG's course was increased from $150 to over $400.

Is this an illegal division of markets? Discuss any perceived economic efficiencies in the arrangement? [*Palmer v BRG of Georgia, Inc.*, 498 U.S. 46 (1990)]

Group Boycotts and Refusals to Deal

A group of competitors that agrees not to deal with buyers unless those buyers agree to standard credit or arbitration clauses has committed a *per se* violation.

Some group boycotts appear to have the best intentions. Many garment manufacturers once agreed not to sell to buyers who sold discount or pirated designer clothing. Certainly their intentions were good, but the result still has the anticompetitive effect of controlling the marketplace. Competitors cannot enforce the law through boycotts; other avenues of relief are available. The American Medical Association's rules that prohibited salaried medical practices and prepaid medical plans are illegal boycotts in spite of the protection motivations behind the restrictions. In *FTC v Superior Court Trial Lawyers Ass'n*, 493 U.S. 411 (1990), the U.S. Supreme Court held that the action of a group of well-intentioned defense lawyers who went on strike to get a higher hourly rate for public defenders was noble and perhaps in the interest of justice, but it was still an illegal boycott by horizontal market participants.

Free Speech and Anticompetitive Behavior

Some activities by competitors are protected even though the competitors act as a group and even though the effect may be to reduce competition. One such exception is the **Noerr–Pennington doctrine,** under which competitors are permitted to work together for the purpose of governmental lobbying and other political action.[2] Their activity enjoys the protection of the First Amendment. For example, competitors can make appearances at new licensee hearings and oppose the granting of a license. The resulting reduction in competition enjoys First Amendment protection, which trumps the Sherman Act. In *City of Columbia v Omni Outdoor Advertising*, 499 U.S. 365 (1991), a company that was controlling the outdoor advertising market in one city attempted to use its lobbying First Amendment rights to protect its market control. An objection and suit by a competitor still resulted in the protection of *Noerr–Pennington* and First Amendment rights.

CONSIDER...   16.4

In Arizona, fees for title insurance searches and policies were established by rating bureaus established by the title companies. The bureaus recommended rates to the state, and the state adopted those rates unless some specific objection was made. The result was that title search and insurance fees were the same for all companies within the state. The FTC filed a complaint against the title companies, alleging that they were engaged in price fixing. The companies responded that government regulation of prices is not price fixing. Do you agree? [*FTC v Ticor Title Ins. Co.,* 504 U.S. 621 (1992)]

Subtle Anticompetitive Behavior: Interlocking Directorates

If officers of competing companies serve on each other's boards of directors, it opens the door to an exchange of information about everything from price to supply chain systems to new products. Certain types of these **interlocking directorates** are prohibited under Section 8 of the Clayton Act. A director of a firm with $10 million or more in capital cannot be a director of a competing company. The risk of anticompetitive results from just the exchange of information is too great. This antitrust concern has percolated in the past several years as directors in high-tech companies have realized their overlapping business conflicts. For example, Eric Schmidt, the CEO of Google, Inc., resigned from Apple's board. Immediately following Mr. Schmidt's resignation from Apple, Arthur Levinson, the CEO of Genentech, Inc., who had served on the boards of both Google and Apple, resigned from the Google board. The two companies were increasingly competing with each other because of, among other things, Google's announcement of its own phone. The two companies were facing increased scrutiny from regulators as a result of their increasingly overlapping business areas. John Doer, a director at both Google and Amazon.com, resigned

Ethical Issues

The Federal Trade Commission (FTC) has charged AOL Time Warner, Inc., and its subsidiaries, Warner Music Group and Vivendi Universal SA, with price fixing in connection with the sales of the Three Tenors' audio and video CDs and tapes. (The Three Tenors are the late Luciano Pavarotti, Placido Domingo, and Jose Carreras.)

When all were alive, the Three Tenors made a recording of their live performances together—done once every four years. The first two CDs and videos in the series sold millions, with both becoming two of the highest–sales volume opera recordings in history. However, by the third live performance and its CD and video, the public demand was not as great. The FTC charges that Warner felt the first two releases would cannibalize the sales for the third. As a result, all parties involved in the sales of these CDs and tapes had to agree not to discount the first two performance tapes so

that the third would have an opportunity to sell. The FTC also alleges that there were agreements on when advertisements could run for the third series' sales and availability.

The FTC stumbled across a memo on the marketing plan and advertising constraints as it was reviewing documents in connection with the Warner/EMI Music merger proposal, a merger that fell through after European officials balked at the idea. The FTC pursued the case, and Warner settled the charges by agreeing not to restrain competition or set prices in the future.

Is it permissible for an agency investigating one issue to use evidence it comes across related to another issue? What lessons does this situation offer on the percolating nature of the truth? Is establishing a minimum price a violation of the Sherman Act? Is restricting advertising a violation of the Sherman Act?

from the Amazon.com board under pressure from regulators over that interlocking directorship. Google and Amazon had become direct competitors in the electronic book markets.

Merging Competitors and the Effect on Competition

To determine the legality of mergers among horizontal competitors, courts have applied a test of "presumptive illegality": Any merger that produces an undue percentage share of the market or significantly increases market concentration is a violation. Courts examine market share and the relevant markets to determine whether undue concentration is a factor.

Not all horizontal mergers are prohibited. The **failing-company doctrine** allows the acquisition of a competitor that is teetering on insolvency, shut down, or bankruptcy if it is an asset or inventory acquisition. Under the **small-company doctrine,** two small companies are permitted to merge because the hope is that they will be better able to compete with the larger businesses in that market.

The trend in mergers has been to approve larger and larger combinations. In *United States v Von's Grocery Co.,* 384 U.S. 270 (1966), the Supreme Court held that a merger between Von's Grocery Company and Shopping Bag Food Stores, which would have given the two companies together a 7.5 percent share of the retail grocery market in Los Angeles, was an anticompetitive violation of the Clayton Act. However, by 1988, the Justice Department approved the merger of Von's and Safeway in southern California. The merger made the new Von's the largest competitor in terms of market percentage as well as in the number of stores. Justice Department attitudes and guidelines on mergers have changed and geographic markets are now defined in light of international trade.

Vertical Trade Restraints

Various steps are involved in getting a product from its creation to its ultimate consumer. For example, producing packaged sandwich meats requires the manufacturer to obtain bulk-butchered meat (originally from a ranch) through a distributor and turn it into packaged sandwich meat that is sold to another distributor. This distributor sells to a grocery wholesaler, who sells to grocery stores, where consumers buy the packaged meat. This entire process has different levels of production and distribution, but it consists of one vertical chain from start to finish.

The types of vertical restraints, discussed in the following subsections, are

- Resale price maintenance
- Monopsony
- Sole outlets and exclusive distributorships
- Customer and territorial restrictions
- Tying arrangements
- Price discrimination

Resale Price Maintenance

Resale price maintenance is an attempt by a manufacturer to control the price that retailers charge for the manufacturer's product. Resale price maintenance is a rule-of-reason violation of Section 1 of the Sherman Act (see *State Oil v Khan*, Case 16.3). Resale price maintenance includes either minimum or maximum prices, or both. A minimum price encourages a retailer to carry a certain product because its profit margin will be higher. One explanation offered to justify minimum prices is that, without them, dealers who advertise and offer service may be used by consumers for information only, after which these consumers actually buy at discount houses.

State Oil v Khan (Case 16.3) deals with the issue of resale price maintenance and its change from a *per se* violation to a rule-of-reason standard.

CASE 16.3	*State Oil v Khan*
	522 U.S. 3 (1997)

Fill It Up, but Only at My Price

FACTS

Barkat U. Khan and his corporation (respondents) entered into an agreement with State Oil (petitioner) to lease and operate a gas station and convenience store owned by State Oil. The agreement provided that Mr. Khan would obtain the gasoline supply for the station from State Oil at a suggested retail price set by State Oil, less a margin of 3.25 cents per gallon. Mr. Khan could charge any price he wanted, but if he charged more than State Oil's suggested retail price, the excess was rebated to State Oil. Mr. Khan could sell the gasoline for less than State Oil's suggested retail price, but the difference came out of his allowed margin.

After a year, Mr. Khan fell behind on his lease payments, and State Oil began proceedings for eviction. The court had Mr. Khan removed and appointed a receiver to operate the station. The receiver operated the gas station without the price constraints and received an overall profit margin above the 3.25 cents imposed on Mr. Khan.

Mr. Khan filed suit, alleging that the State Oil agreement was a violation of Section 1 of the Sherman Act because State Oil was controlling prices. The district court held that there was no *per se* violation and that Mr. Khan had failed to demonstrate antitrust injury. The Court of Appeals reversed, and State Oil appealed.

JUDICIAL OPINION

O'CONNOR, Justice

In *Albrecht v Herald Co.*, 390 U.S. 145, 88 S.Ct. 869, 19 L.Ed.2d 998 (1968), this Court held that vertical maximum price fixing is a per se violation of that statute.

In this case, we are asked to reconsider that decision in light of subsequent decisions of this Court. We conclude that *Albrecht* should be overruled.

Although the Sherman Act, by its terms, prohibits every agreement "in restraint of trade," this Court has long recognized that Congress intended to outlaw only unreasonable restraints.

As a consequence, most antitrust claims are analyzed under a "rule of reason," according to which the finder of fact must decide whether the questioned practice imposes an unreasonable restraint on competition, taking into account a variety of factors, including specific information about the relevant business, its condition before and after the restraint was imposed, and the restraint's history, nature, and effect.

Some types of restraints, however, have such predictable and pernicious anticompetitive effect, and such limited potential for procompetitive benefit, that they are deemed unlawful per se. . . .

In *White Motor Co. v United States*, 372 U.S. 253, 83 S.Ct. 696, 9 L.Ed.2d 738 (1963), the Court considered the validity of a manufacturer's assignment of exclusive territories to its distributors and dealers. The Court determined that too little was known about the competitive impact of such vertical limitations to warrant treating them as per se unlawful.

Four years later, in *United States v Arnold, Schwinn & Co.*, 388 U.S. 365, 87 S.Ct. 1856, 18 L.Ed. 2d 1249 (1967), the Court reconsidered the status of exclusive dealer territories and held that, upon the transfer of title to goods to a distributor, a supplier's imposition of territorial restrictions on the distributor was "so obviously destructive of competition" as to constitute a per se violation of the Sherman Act. In *Schwinn*, the Court

CONTINUED

acknowledged that some vertical restrictions, such as the conferral of territorial rights or franchises, could have procompetitive benefits by allowing smaller enterprises to compete, and that such restrictions might avert vertical integration in the distribution process. The Court drew the line, however, at permitting manufacturers to control product marketing once dominion over the goods had passed to dealers.

Albrecht, decided the following Term, involved a newspaper publisher who had granted exclusive territories to independent carriers subject to their adherence to a maximum price on resale of the newspapers to the public. . . .

Albrecht was animated in part by the fear that vertical maximum price fixing could allow suppliers to discriminate against certain dealers, restrict the services that dealers could afford to offer customers, or disguise minimum price fixing schemes. The Court rejected the notion (both on the record of that case and in the abstract) that, because the newspaper publisher "granted exclusive territories, a price ceiling was necessary to protect the public from price gouging by dealers who had monopoly power in their own territories."

Nine years later, in *Continental T.V., Inc. v GTE Sylvania, Inc.*, 433 U.S. 36, 97 S.Ct. 2549, 53 L.Ed.2d 568 (1977), the Court overruled *Schwinn*, thereby rejecting application of a per se rule in the context of vertical nonprice restrictions. The Court acknowledged the principle of *stare decisis*, but explained that the need for clarification in the law justified reconsideration of *Schwinn*:

> Since its announcement, Schwinn *has been the subject of continuing controversy and confusion, both in the scholarly journals and in the federal courts. The great weight of scholarly opinion has been critical of the decision, and a number of the federal courts confronted with analogous vertical restrictions have sought to limit its reach.*

Thus, our reconsideration of *Albrecht*'s continuing validity is informed by several of our decisions, as well as a considerable body of scholarship discussing the effects of vertical restraints. Our analysis is also guided by our general view that the primary purpose of the antitrust laws is to protect interbrand competition. See, e.g., *Business Electronics Corp. v Sharp Electronics Corp.*, 485 U.S. 717, 726, 108 S.Ct. 1515, 1520–1521, 99 L.Ed.2d 808 (1988). "Low prices," we have explained, "benefit consumers regardless of how those prices are set, and so long as they are above predatory levels, they do not threaten competition." Our interpretation of the Sherman Act also incorporates the notion that condemnation of practices resulting in lower prices to consumers is "especially costly" because "cutting prices in order to increase business often is the very essence of competition." *Matsushita Elec. Industrial Co. v Zenith Radio Corp.*, 475 U.S. 574, 594, 106 S.Ct. 1348, 1360, 89 L.Ed.2d 538 (1986).

So informed, we find it difficult to maintain that vertically imposed maximum prices could harm consumers or competition to the extent necessary to justify their per se invalidation. As Chief Judge Posner wrote for the Court of Appeals in this case:

> *As for maximum resale price fixing, unless the supplier is a monopsonist he cannot squeeze his dealers' margins below a competitive level; the attempt to do so would just drive the dealers into the arms of a competing supplier. A supplier might, however, fix a maximum resale price in order to prevent his dealers from exploiting a monopoly position. . . . [S]uppose that State Oil, perhaps to encourage . . . dealer services . . . has spaced its dealers sufficiently far apart to limit competition among them (or even given each of them an exclusive territory); and suppose further that Union 76 is a sufficiently distinctive and popular brand to give the dealers in it at least a modicum of monopoly power. Then State Oil might want to place a ceiling on the dealers' resale prices in order to prevent them from exploiting that monopoly powerfully. It would do this not out of disinterested malice, but in its commercial self-interest. The higher the price at which gasoline is resold, the smaller the volume sold, and so the lower the profit to the supplier if the higher profit per gallon at the higher price is being snared by the dealer.* 93 F.3d at 1362.

Further, although vertical maximum price fixing might limit the viability of inefficient dealers, that consequence is not necessarily harmful to competition and consumers.

After reconsidering *Albrecht*'s rationale and the substantial criticism the decision has received, however, we conclude that there is insufficient economic justification for per se invalidation of vertical maximum price fixing. That is so not only because it is difficult to accept the assumptions underlying *Albrecht*, but also because *Albrecht* has little or no relevance to ongoing enforcement of the Sherman Act. . . .

We approach the reconsideration of decisions of this Court with the utmost caution. *Stare decisis* reflects "a policy judgment that 'in most matters it is more important that the applicable rule of law be settled than that it be settled right.'"

But "[s]tare decisis is not an inexorable command." In the area of antitrust law, there is a competing interest, well represented in this Court's decisions, in recognizing and adapting to changed circumstances and the lessons of accumulated experience. Thus, the general presumption that legislative changes should be left to Congress has less force with respect to the Sherman Act in light of the accepted view that Congress "expected the courts to give shape to the statute's broad mandate by drawing on common-law tradition."

In overruling *Albrecht*, we of course do not hold that all vertical maximum price fixing is per se lawful.

Instead, vertical maximum price fixing, like the majority of commercial arrangements subject to the antitrust laws, should be evaluated under the rule of reason. In our view, rule-of-reason analysis will effectively identify those situations in which vertical maximum price fixing amounts to anticompetitive conduct. . . .

We therefore vacate the judgment of the Court of Appeals and remand the case for further proceedings consistent with this opinion.

Remanded.

CASE QUESTIONS

1. What were the terms of Mr. Khan's lease? Include a discussion of the price terms.

2. Is vertical price fixing a *per se* violation?

3. What does the court say about inefficient retailers and vertical price controls?

4. What does the court say about a long-standing precedent and *stare decisis?*

The "suggested retail price" has been tolerated under the rule-of-reason standard as long as manufacturers and distributors did not enforce that suggested price through refusals to sell. In fact, a 1975 federal law eliminated state laws that protected these enforcement arrangements, often called **fair trade contracts.** However, in 2007, the U.S. Supreme Court reversed a long-standing precedent with the *Leegin* case (Case 16.4) that has changed the nature of distribution agreements by allowing enforcement of the suggested prices. This case also provides the answer for the chapter's opening "Consider" problem.

| CASE 16.4 | *Leegin Creative Leather Products, Inc. v PSKS, Inc.* 551 U.S. 877 (2007) |

It's Not in the Bag; It's in the Service*

FACTS

Leegin Creative Leather Products, Inc. (Leegin) (petitioner), designs, manufactures, and distributes leather goods and accessories under the brand name "Brighton." The Brighton brand has now expanded into a full line of women's fashion accessories and is sold across the United States in over 5,000 retail stores. PSKS, Inc. (PSKS) (respondent) runs Kay's Kloset, a Brighton retailer in Lewisville, Texas, that carried about 75 different product lines, but was known as the place in that area to go for Brighton. Kay's ran Brighton ads and had Brighton days in its store.

Leegin's president, Jerry Kohl, who also has an interest in about 70 stores that sell Brighton products, believes that small retailers treat customers better, provide customers more services, and make their shopping experience more satisfactory than do larger, often impersonal retailers. In 1997, Kohl released a new strategic refocus for Brighton by explaining: "[W]e want the

consumers to get a different experience than they get in Sam's Club or in Wal-Mart. And you can't get that kind of experience or support or customer service from a store like Wal-Mart." As a result, Leegin instituted the "Brighton Retail Pricing and Promotion Policy," which banished retailers that discounted Brighton goods below suggested prices. The policy had an exception for products not selling well that the retailer did not plan on reordering. The established prices gave its retailers sufficient margins to provide customers with the quality service central to Brighton's strategy.

In December 2002, Leegin discovered Kay's Kloset had been marking down Brighton's entire line by 20 percent. Kay's Kloset said it did so to compete with nearby retailers who also were undercutting Leegin's suggested prices. Leegin, nonetheless, requested that Kay's Kloset cease discounting. Its request refused, Leegin stopped selling to the store. The loss of the Brighton brand had a considerable negative impact on

CONTINUED

the store's revenue from sales (about 40–50 percent of its profits were from Brighton).

PSKS sued Leegin for violation of the antitrust laws. Leegin asked to introduce expert testimony describing the procompetitive effects of its pricing policy. The District Court excluded the testimony, relying Leegin's conduct to be a *per se* violation of federal antitrust laws. The jury awarded PSKS $1.2 million in damages and the judge trebled the damages and reimbursed PSKS for its attorney's fees and costs, for a judgment against Leegin of $3,975,000.80. The Court of Appeals affirmed. Leegin appealed. The U.S. Supreme Court granted certiorari.

JUDICIAL OPINION

KENNEDY, Justice

In *Dr. Miles Medical Co. v John D. Park & Sons Co.*, 220 U.S. 373, 31 S.Ct. 376, 55 L.Ed. 502 (1911), the Court established the rule that it is per se illegal under § 1 of the Sherman Act, 15 U.S.C. § 1, for a manufacturer to agree with its distributor to set the minimum price the distributor can charge for the manufacturer's goods. The question presented by the instant case is whether the Court should overrule the per se rule and allow resale price maintenance agreements to be judged by the rule of reason, the usual standard applied to determine if there is a violation of § 1. The Court has abandoned the rule of per se illegality for other vertical restraints a manufacturer imposes on its distributors. Respected economic analysts, furthermore, conclude that vertical price restraints can have procompetitive effects. We now hold that *Dr. Miles* should be overruled and that vertical price restraints are to be judged by the rule of reason Section 1 of the Sherman Act prohibits "[e]very contract, combination in the form of trust or otherwise, or conspiracy, in restraint of trade or commerce among the several States." The rule of reason is the accepted standard for testing whether a practice restrains trade in violation of § 1. The rule of reason does not govern all restraints. Some types "are deemed unlawful *per se.*" The *per se* rule, treating categories of restraints as necessarily illegal, eliminates the need to study the reasonableness of an individual restraint in light of the real market forces at work, and, it must be acknowledged, the *per se* rule can give clear guidance for certain conduct. Restraints that are *per se* unlawful include horizontal agreements among competitors to fix prices, or to divide markets.

. . . [T]he *per se* rule is appropriate only after courts have had considerable experience with the type of restraint at issue, and only if courts can predict with confidence that it would be invalidated in all or almost all instances under the rule of reason.

Dr. Miles treated vertical agreements a manufacturer makes with its distributors as analogous to a horizontal combination among competing distributors. . . . [I]t is necessary to examine, in the first instance, the economic effects of vertical agreements to fix minimum resale prices, and to determine whether the per se rule is nonetheless appropriate.

Though each side of the debate can find sources to support its position, it suffices to say here that economics literature is replete with procompetitive justifications for a manufacturer's use of resale price maintenance.

The justifications for vertical price restraints are similar to those for other vertical restraints. Minimum resale price maintenance can stimulate interbrand competition—the competition among manufacturers selling different brands of the same type of product—by reducing intrabrand competition—the competition among retailers selling the same brand. The promotion of interbrand competition is important because "the primary purpose of the antitrust laws is to protect [this type of] competition." A single manufacturer's use of vertical price restraints tends to eliminate intrabrand price competition; this in turn encourages retailers to invest in tangible or intangible services or promotional efforts that aid the manufacturer's position as against rival manufacturers. Resale price maintenance also has the potential to give consumers more options so that they can choose among low-price, low-service brands; high-price, high-service brands; and brands that fall in between.

Absent vertical price restraints, the retail services that enhance interbrand competition might be underprovided. This is because discounting retailers can free ride on retailers who furnish services and then capture some of the increased demand those services generate. Consumers might learn, for example, about the benefits of a manufacturer's product from a retailer that invests in fine showrooms, offers product demonstrations, or hires and trains knowledgeable employees. Or consumers might decide to buy the product because they see it in a retail establishment that has a reputation for selling high-quality merchandise. If the consumer can then buy the product from a retailer that discounts because it has not spent capital providing services or developing a quality reputation, the high-service retailer will lose sales to the discounter, forcing it to cut back its services to a level lower than consumers would otherwise prefer. Minimum resale price maintenance alleviates the problem because it prevents the discounter from undercutting the service provider. With price competition decreased, the manufacturer's retailers compete among themselves over services.

Resale price maintenance, in addition, can increase interbrand competition by facilitating market entry for new firms and brands. "[N]ew manufacturers and manufacturers entering new markets can use the restrictions in order to induce competent and aggressive retailers to make the kind of investment of capital and labor that is often required in the distribution of products unknown to the consumer."

Resale price maintenance can also increase interbrand competition by encouraging retailer services that would not be provided even absent free riding. It may be difficult and inefficient for a manufacturer to make and enforce a contract with a retailer specifying the different services the retailer must perform. Offering the retailer a guaranteed margin and threatening termination if it does not live up to expectations may be the most efficient way to expand the manufacturer's market share by inducing the retailer's performance and allowing it to use its own initiative and experience in providing valuable services While vertical agreements setting minimum resale prices can have procompetitive justifications, they may have anticompetitive effects in other circumstances. Vertical price restraints also "might be used to organize cartels at the retailer level." A group of retailers might collude to fix prices to consumers and then compel a manufacturer to aid the unlawful arrangement with resale price maintenance. In that instance, the manufacturer does not establish the practice to stimulate services or to promote its brand but to give inefficient retailers higher profits. Retailers with better distribution systems and lower cost structures would be prevented from charging lower prices by the agreement.

Resale price maintenance, furthermore, can be abused by a powerful manufacturer or retailer. A dominant retailer, for example, might request resale price maintenance to forestall innovation in distribution that decreases costs. A manufacturer might consider it has little choice but to accommodate the retailer's demands for vertical price restraints if the manufacturer believes it needs access to the retailer's distribution network.

Vertical agreements establishing minimum resale prices can have either procompetitive or anticompetitive effects, depending upon the circumstances in which they are formed.

Respondent's argument, furthermore, overlooks that, in general, the interests of manufacturers and consumers are aligned with respect to retailer profit margins. The difference between the price a manufacturer charges retailers and the price retailers charge consumers represents part of the manufacturer's cost of distribution, which, like any other cost, the manufacturer usually desires to minimize. The retailers, not the manufacturer, gain from higher retail prices. The manufacturer often loses; interbrand competition reduces its competitiveness and market share because consumers will "substitute a different brand of the same product."

Resale price maintenance, it is true, does have economic dangers. If the rule of reason were to apply to vertical price restraints, courts would have to be diligent in eliminating their anticompetitive uses from the market.

Reversed.

DISCUSSION QUESTIONS

1. What reasons did Leegin give for wanting the minimum price established for its retailers?

2. What points does the court make about not having minimum prices in terms of reducing competition?

3. What risks are there in allowing minimum price requirements?

CONSIDER... 16.5

The Federal Trade Commission is conducting an investigation into the informal agreements reached between Toys "R" Us and toy manufacturers. Toys "R" Us holds a 19.4 percent share of the U.S. toy market and has informal agreements with Mattel and Hasbro with respect to the sale of their toys to discount warehouse clubs such as Costco and Sam's Club. The clubs are sold toys only in more expensive packaging arrangements. For example, Hollywood Hair Barbie can be purchased at Toys "R" Us for $10.95 but at warehouse clubs can be purchased only in a package with a dress for $15.95. Some of the most popular toy items are never sold to the warehouse clubs. For example, Hasbro has not sold its Hall of Fame GI Joe action figures to warehouse clubs, and Mattel will not sell its Fisher Price pool table to the clubs.

The FTC commissioners voted 5 to 3 to begin the investigation because toy manufacturers are put into a situation of choosing between selling to Toys "R" Us and other retailers. Toys "R" Us maintains that the warehouse clubs do not have the overhead of advertising the toys and simply choose those items that sell the best at very low margins. The low margins can be maintained because, for example, Costco took in more in membership fees over the last 10 years than its total net profit.

Apply the *Leegin* rule-of-reason standard. Have the antitrust laws been violated?

Monopsony

A **monopsony** exists when the buyer, rather than the seller, has the ability to control market prices. In *Weyerhaeuser v Ross-Simons*, 549 U.S. 312 (2007), the U.S. Supreme Court held that antitrust laws apply to both predatory pricing and **predatory bidding.** In the case, Ross-Simons Hardware Lumber alleged that Weyerhaeuser tried to drive it out of business by bidding up the price of sawlogs to a level that prevented Ross-Simons from being profitable. Although the lower courts found for Ross-Simons, the U.S. Supreme Court held that a plaintiff in a predatory bidding case must be able to show what a plaintiff in a predatory pricing case must show—that the bids were at such a level that below-cost pricing resulted.

In the case, Weyerhaeuser was able to show that its investment in equipment and advanced processes allowed it to process more timber and that its huge demand was driving up the price. Ross-Simons was not able to establish that the price increases were actually sought by Weyerhaeuser. The demand drove up the price, but the demand came through Weyerhaeuser's superior processing, not through nefarious means.

Sole Outlets and Exclusive Distributorships

A **sole outlet** or **exclusive distributorship** agreement is one in which a manufacturer appoints a distributor or retailer as the sole or exclusive outlet for the manufacturer's product. This type of arrangement can be a violation of Section 1 but is subject to a rule of reason analysis. In a rule of reason analysis of sole outlets or exclusive distributorships, courts examine a manufacturer's freedom to pick and choose outlets or distributors. However, the extent of the **interbrand competition,** which is the competition available for the manufacturer's product, is critical. For example, in the case of the sandwich-meat manufacturer, as long as other manufacturers are selling their products in the area, the manufacturer could agree to sell to only one chain of grocery stores. But without interbrand competition, the antitrust laws require more **intrabrand competition.** If a manufacturer were the only one distributing sandwich meats in the area, dealing with only one grocery chain might not survive an antitrust challenge under the rule of reason.

Customer and Territorial Restrictions

Sole outlets allow manufacturers to decide (within limitations) to whom they will sell goods. However, manufacturers are not given the right to control what the buyer does with goods and how those goods are sold. The restrictions are subject to the rule of reason because interbrand competition may be increased even though intrabrand competition is reduced. For **customer and territorial restrictions** to be valid, enough interbrand competition must balance out decreased intrabrand competition. Also, the more market power the manufacturer has, the fewer substitute goods consumers have, resulting in less interbrand competition. Vertical restrictions are likely to be reasonable when the manufacturer is new to the market or is having financial or sales difficulties. If the restrictions will help the manufacturer get started or keep going, the positive impact on interbrand competition allows the limit on intrabrand competition.

Ethical Issues

Department 56 is a company that manufactures and sells collectible Christmas village houses and other replica items to allow collectors to create the whimsical "Snow Village" town or "Dickens Christmas." Department 56 has only authorized dealers. Sam's Club, a division of Walmart Stores, Inc., began selling Department 56 pieces from The Heritage Village Collection.

Susan Engel, president and CEO of Department 56, attempted to contact Walmart because it is not an authorized Department 56 dealer. Walmart did not respond, and Ms. Engel sent by FedEx to National Collector clubs a letter that contained the following language:

> Sam's Club should not have any Department 56 merchandise. In a marketing environment where most companies are fighting to get their merchandise into the Wal-Marts of the world, we are fighting to get our merchandise out. While we recognize there is surely a place for mass market and warehouse stores, Department 56 Villages enjoy a strong heritage of dealer sales and service support. Our products simply do not fit the warehouse-style selling environment of Sam's Club.

> Of strong importance to us—and we hope to you too—is the tradition of selling our villages through an exclusive dealer network made up almost entirely of independent retailers. Wal-Mart Stores, Inc., and its subsidiaries are predators on these hard-working individuals. Sales of our products mean virtually nothing to the bottom line of a company the size of Wal-Mart. But to many of our loyal dealers, healthy Department 56 product sales mean survival.

> Do you really need to shop at Sam's Club or Wal-Mart? Let's refuse to purchase villages or any other products from local Wal-Mart owned stores.

The letter asked collector club members to write Walmart executives and local store managers. Names, mailing addresses, and telephone and fax numbers were offered.

Has Ms. Engel violated any laws? How does this situation relate to the *Leegin* case? How do you think Sam's Club obtained the Department 56 products? Evaluate Ms. Engel's conduct in sending out the letter. Were her statements about Walmart and calls to action fair? Ethical? Should Walmart respond? How?

Tying Arrangements

Tying sales require buyers to take an additional product in order to buy a needed product. For example, requiring the buyer of a copier machine to buy the seller's paper when other brands of paper are equally suitable for use in the machine is a tying arrangement. The copier machine is the tying product or the desired product, and the paper is the tied product or the required product. Tying is usually an illegal *per se* violation of Section 3 of the Clayton Act (for goods contracts) and Section 1 of the Sherman Act (for services, real property, and intangibles). The presence of market power is the key to whether tying is a violation. For example, requiring the purchase of inferior films in order to buy copyrighted quality films is an example of the presence of market power. Because the seller is the only one with the copyrighted films, market power is being used to sell another unnecessary, low-demand product.

Two defenses have been recognized in tying cases. The first is the *new industry defense*. Under this defense, the manufacturer of the tying product is permitted to have a tied product to protect initially the quality control in the start-up of a business. For example, a cable television antenna manufacturer required purchasers to take a service contract also. The tying was upheld during the outset of the business so that the system could begin functioning properly and this new cable television industry could catch hold.

A second defense is *quality control for the protection of goodwill*. This defense is rarely supportable. This defense applies if the specifications for the tied goods were so detailed that they could not possibly be supplied by anyone other than the manufacturer of the tying product.

Jefferson Parish Hosp. Dist. No. 2 v Hyde (Case 16.5) involves an issue of whether a tying arrangement was valid.

CASE 16.5   *Jefferson Parish Hosp. Dist. No. 2 v Hyde*
466 U.S. 2 (1984)

B.Y.O. Anesthesiologist: Tying Hospital Arrangements

FACTS

Dr. Edwin G. Hyde, a board-certified anesthesiologist, applied for permission to practice at East Jefferson Hospital (petitioners) in Louisiana. An approval was recommended for his hiring, but the hospital's board denied him employment on grounds that the hospital had a contract with Roux & Associates for Roux to provide all anesthesiological services required by the hospital's patients. Dr. Hyde filed suit, which the district court dismissed. The court of appeals reversed that decision and held that the contract for the services with Roux was illegal *per se*. The hospital appealed.

JUDICIAL OPINION

STEVENS, Justice

The exclusive contract had an impact on two different segments of the economy: consumers of medical services, and providers of anesthesiological services. Any consumer of medical services who elects to have an operation performed at East Jefferson Hospital may not employ any anesthesiologist not associated with Roux. No anesthesiologists except those employed by Roux may practice at East Jefferson.

There are at least twenty hospitals in the New Orleans metropolitan area and about 70 percent of the patients living in Jefferson Parish go to hospitals other than East Jefferson. Because it regarded the entire New Orleans metropolitan area as the relevant geographic market in which hospitals compete, this evidence convinced the District Court that East Jefferson does not

possess any significant "market power"; therefore it concluded that petitioners could not use the Roux contract to anticompetitive ends. The same evidence led the Court of Appeals to draw a different conclusion. Noting that 30 percent of the residents of the Parish go to East Jefferson Hospital, and that, in fact, "patients tend to choose hospitals by location rather than price or quality," the Court of Appeals concluded that the relevant market was the East Bank of Jefferson Parish. The conclusion that East Jefferson Hospital possessed market power in that area was buttressed by the facts that the prevalence of health insurance eliminates a patient's incentive to compare costs, that the patient is not sufficiently informed to compare quality, and that family convenience tends to magnify the importance of location.

The Court of Appeals held that the case involves a "tying arrangement" because the "users of the hospital's operating rooms (the tying product) are also compelled to purchase the hospital's chosen anesthesia service (the tied product)."

It is clear, however, that every refusal to sell two products separately cannot be said to restrain competition. For example, we have written that "if one of a dozen food stores in a community were to refuse to sell flour unless the buyer also took sugar it would hardly tend to restrain competition if its competitors were ready and able to sell flour by itself." Buyers often find package sales attractive; a seller's decision to offer such packages can merely be an attempt to compete effectively—conduct that is entirely consistent with the Sherman Act.

Accordingly, we have condemned tying arrangements when the seller has some special ability—usually called "market power"—to force a purchaser to do something that he would not do in a competitive market. When "forcing" occurs, our cases have found the tying arrangement to be unlawful.

The hospital has provided its patients with a package that includes a range of facilities and services required for a variety of surgical operations. At East Jefferson Hospital the package includes the services of the anesthesiologist. Petitioners argue that the package does not involve a tying arrangement at all—that they are merely providing a functionally integrated package of services.

Unquestionably, the anesthesiological component of the package offered by the hospital could be provided separately and could be selected either by the individual patient or by one of the patient's doctors if the hospital did not insist on including anesthesiological services in the package it offers to its customers. As a matter of actual practice, anesthesiological services are billed separately from the hospital services petitioners provide. There was ample and uncontroverted testimony that patients or surgeons often request specific anesthesiologists to come to a hospital and provide anesthesia, and that the choice of a hospital is particularly frequent in respondent's specialty, obstetric anesthesiology.

Thus, the hospital's requirement that its patients obtain necessary anesthesiological services from Roux combined the purchase of two distinguishable services in a single transaction. As noted above, there is nothing inherently anticompetitive about packaged sales. Only if patients are forced to purchase Roux's services as a result of the hospital's market power would the arrangement have anticompetitive consequences.

It is safe to assume that every patient undergoing a surgical operation needs the services of an anesthesiologist; at least this record contains no evidence that the hospital "forced" any such services on unwilling patients. The record therefore does not provide a basis for applying the *per se* rule against tying to this arrangement.

In order to prevail in the absence of *per se* liability, respondent has the burden of proving that the Roux contract violated the Sherman Act because it unreasonably restrained competition.

All the record establishes is that the choice of anesthesiologists at East Jefferson has been limited to one of the four doctors who are associated with Roux and therefore have staff privileges. Even if Roux did not have an exclusive contract, the range of alternatives open to the patient would be severely limited by the nature of the transaction and the hospital's unquestioned right to exercise some control over the identity and number of doctors to whom it accords staff privileges.

Petitioner's closed policy may raise questions of medical ethics, and may have inconvenienced some patients who would prefer to have their anesthesia administered by someone other than a member of Roux & Associates, but it does not have the obviously unreasonable impact on purchasers that has characterized the tying arrangements that this Court has branded unlawful.

Reversed.

CASE QUESTIONS

1. What is East Jefferson's share of the medical care market?

2. Do patients ever indicate any choice or knowledge regarding anesthesiologists?

3. Is the arrangement illegal *per se*? Does it violate the antitrust laws?

4. Why was the issue of "force" important?

CONSIDER...   16.6

David Ungar holds a Dunkin' Donuts franchise. The terms of his franchise agreement require him to use only those ingredients furnished by Dunkin' Donuts. He is also required to buy their napkins, cups, and so on with the Dunkin' Donuts trademark on them. Is this an illegal tying arrangement? What if Dunkin' Donuts maintains that it needs these requirements to maintain its quality levels on a nationwide basis? [*Ungar v Dunkin' Donuts of Am., Inc.*, 531 F.2d 1211 (3d Cir. 1976)]

Price Discrimination

The Robinson–Patman Act prohibits **price discrimination,** which is selling goods at prices that have different ratios to the marginal cost of producing them. If two goods have the same marginal cost and are sold to different people at different prices, it is a case of price discrimination. Price discrimination is an example of the use of vertical restraints to lessen horizontal competition. Predatory pricing or pricing below cost is an example of conduct that will injure or destroy competition. Price discrimination has four elements:

1. A seller engaged in commerce
2. Discrimination in price among purchasers
3. Commodities sold that are of like grade or quality
4. A substantial lessening of competition in any line of commerce or a tendency to create a monopoly; or competition is injured, destroyed, or prevented

If all the elements are established, both the buyer and the seller have violated the Robinson–Patman Act.

Price discrimination can come in the form of the actual price charged but can also come from indirect charges. For example, offering different credit terms to equally qualified buyers can constitute price discrimination. The products sold must be of **like grade or quality,** which means no physical differences in the product. Label differences do not make the products different. For example, the sandwich-meat manufacturer that makes a private label meat cannot discriminate in price for the sale of that meat if the contents are the same as the manufacturer's advertised label meat and only the label is different. However, if the private-label meat has lower-quality meat in it, a price difference can be justified because the products are not the same. In *Utah Pie Co. v Continental Baking Co.* 386 U.S. 685, the U.S. Supreme Court held that a company that prices differently in different markets to eliminate competition, particularly when that pricing is below cost, has engaged in price discrimination. In the case, an out-of-state pie manufacturer priced its pies below cost in Utah so that it could eliminate competition from a local pie manufacturer. The mark of price discrimination is that once the competition is eliminated, prices return to a much higher level. The larger out-of-state company sustains the losses on the sales until the competitor is driven out of business. The result is less competition.

CONSIDER...   16.7

A&P Grocery Stores decided to sell its own brand of canned milk (referred to as "private-label" milk). A&P asked its longtime supplier, Borden, to submit an offer to produce the private-label milk. Bowman Dairy also submitted a bid, which was lower than Borden's. A&P's Chicago buyer then contacted Borden and said, "I have a bid in my pocket. You people are so far out of line it is not even funny. You are not even in the ballpark." The Borden representative asked for more details but was told only that a $50,000 improvement in Borden's bid "would not be a drop in the bucket."

A&P was one of Borden's largest customers in the Chicago area. Furthermore, Borden had just invested more than $5 million in a new dairy facility in Illinois. The loss of the A&P account would result in underutilization of the plant. Borden lowered its bid by more than $400,000. The Federal Trade Commission has charged Borden with price discrimination, but Borden maintains it was simply meeting the competition. Has Borden violated the Robinson–Patman Act? Does it matter that the milk was private-label milk and not its normal trade-named Borden milk? Are the ethics of the A&P representative troublesome? [*Great A&P Tea Co., Inc. v FTC*, 440 U.S. 69 (1979)]

Defenses to Price Discrimination

Legitimate cost differences in the manufacture or handling of a product mean price discrimination is not the issue. Additional costs of delivery or of adding specifications to a product can increase the price without violating the Robinson–Patman Act. For example, if a sandwich-meat manufacturer produces a special low-fat bologna, the price for that product can be different. If the manufacturer uses different shipping companies for its customers, a price differential may be acceptable.

Quantity discounts are permitted as long as the seller can show actual cost savings are realized in the sale of increased quantities and not just an assumption that larger sales are more economical. The law on price discrimination is based on marginal cost differences. Limiting the number of buyers who qualify for quantity discounts is some proof that the actual cost savings are not present.

Prices for products also can change according to market, inflation, material costs, and other variable factors. The seller must simply establish that a price change was initiated in response to one of these factors.

Another defense to a charge of price discrimination is **meeting the competition.** This defense must establish that a price change was made in a certain market to meet the competition there. Also, the seller must charge the same as its competitors and not a lower price. Finally, the price differences must be limited to an area or individuals. For example, a national firm may have a different price in one state because of more competition within that particular state.

Vertical Mergers

Vertical mergers are between firms that have a buyer-seller relationship. For example, if a sandwich-meat manufacturer merged with its meat supplier, it would be a vertical merger. In determining whether a vertical merger violates the Clayton Act, the courts determine the relevant geographic and product markets and then determine whether the effect of the merger will be to foreclose or lessen competition.

What Are the Penalties and Remedies for Anticompetitive Behavior?

The federal antitrust laws have powerful incentives for compliance that include substantial penalties and remedies. The penalties and remedies are summarized in the following text and in Exhibit 16.3.

Criminal Penalties

The Sherman Act carries felony criminal penalties. For individuals, the penalties are fines of up to $10 million and/or up to 10 years in prison. Corporations may

EXHIBIT 16.3 Antitrust Remedies

	SHERMAN ACT	CLAYTON ACT	ROBINSON-PATMAN ACT	FTC ACT
Criminal	$350,000 and/or three years in prison for individuals; $10 million for corporations; directors and officers also liable as to intent and knowledge	None	Section 4 for intentional price discrimination	None
Civil	Treble damages plus costs and attorney fees	Same	Same	None
Equitable	Injunctions, divestitures, asset distributions, sales	Same	Same	Same
Enforcers	Justice Department; U.S. attorney; state attorneys general; private persons	Same	Same	FTC

be assessed fines of up to $100 million. These criminal penalties require proof that the violator intended the anticompetitive conduct and realized the consequences of the action taken.

The FTC and Clayton Acts do not carry criminal penalties. However, Section 4 of the Robinson–Patman Act makes criminal certain forms of intentional price discrimination. Officers and directors of violating corporations can also be held criminally liable for antitrust violations, depending upon their level of knowledge and involvement. For example, in the Archer Daniels Midland price fixing case, officers were held responsible for the violations because of their direct knowledge of the price fixing activities. The Antitrust Division of the Department of Justice or the local U.S. attorney's office is responsible for bringing criminal actions under the antitrust laws.

Equitable Remedies

Equitable remedies consist of court orders that restrain or prevent anticompetitive conduct. Equitable remedies are available in both private and government enforcement actions. An **injunction** is a frequent form of antitrust relief; it is a court order prohibiting a violating party from engaging in anticompetitive conduct. For example, a firm can be ordered to divest itself of an acquired firm or, in an unlawful asset acquisition, a court order can require that the assets be divided with a competing firm. Contracts whose terms violate the antitrust laws can be canceled by court order. Equitable remedies give the courts discretion to fashion remedies that will eliminate the results of anticompetitive behavior.

Private Actions for Damages

Section 4 of the Clayton Act allows any person whose business or property is injured as a result of an antitrust violation to recover "threefold the damages by him sustained"—commonly referred to as **treble damages**—along with the costs of the suit and reasonable attorney fees. This section, with its substantial recovery provisions, is strong incentive for private enforcement of antitrust laws. Consumers, businesses, and state attorneys general can all bring private damage actions under

Section 4. These treble damages have found plaintiffs looking for ways to tap into the antitrust statutes, but the U.S. Supreme Court has been cautious in extending the remedies. In *Credit Suisse Securities (USA) LLC v Billing*, 551 U.S. 264 (2007), the Court held that securities investors who were bringing suit for IPO (initial primary offerings, see Chapter 21) pricing and allocation needed to turn to the securities laws for their remedies, not the antitrust laws and their treble damages. The court held that securities regulation is so extensive and investor protections so readily available that the antitrust laws did not apply to the conduct of investment bankers and brokers for purposes of investor relief.

Types of damages include lost profits, increased costs, and decreased value in property. These damage suits have a four-year statute of limitations; that is, suit must be brought within four years of the alleged violation. Those who bring private damage suits enjoy a proof benefit: If the government has brought suit and a violation is found, that judgment can be used in a private suit as *prima facie* evidence against the violating defendant. A *prima facie* case allows a plaintiff to survive a directed verdict and entitles the plaintiff to a judgment if the defendant offers no contradictory evidence (see Chapter 4 for more discussion).

What Lies Ahead in Anticompetitive Behavior: The Antitrust Modernization Commission

The Antitrust Modernization Commission (AMC), created in 2002, finished its work and completed its report on May 31, 2007. The AMC had the following general findings and recommendations:

1. Courts have been taking the correct approach in their reasoning and analyses of cases involving antitrust issues by carefully examining markets, economic systems, and individual companies and products. That approach should continue.

2. Congress does not need to change either Section 2 of the Sherman Act or Section 7 of the Clayton Act. Although some individuals and particular companies may not be happy with outcomes on monopolization and merger cases, the case law has evolved in a consistent and understandable manner.

3. The AMC also noted that change in the antitrust laws was unnecessary because, as many argued, the reality is now a "new economy" of technology-driven business rather than an old economy of traditional businesses. The AMC noted that the laws of economics are the same and if applied to cases with consistency, the issues of the "new economy" were resolved correctly through judicial interpretation and application.

4. The Justice Department and the FTC could help with the application of the Clayton Act if they would issue reports and findings when they make decisions with regard to mergers. These reports or findings could then serve to provide businesses with guidance for future proposed deals, mergers, and acquisitions.

5. The AMC did find some issues with regard to the interaction of patent protections with competition and that certain provisions and protections in the patent laws may actually be serving as blockades for competition. Also, the AMC noted that holding a patent does not automatically translate into

monopolistic behavior. The AMC felt that Congress should address the patent law issues but not the antitrust laws.

What lies ahead is now up to Congress and its response to the findings.

Antitrust Issues in International Competition

As the level of international trade has increased, so also has the number of competitors. For example, three domestic manufacturers produce cars in the United States. However, the availability of international trade markets has resulted in the importing of cars from Japan, Great Britain, Germany, Sweden, and Yugoslavia; and international competition changes the market perspective because the relevant market is not the United States, but the world. In fact, in 2007, Toyota became the number one seller of autos in the United States because of open international competition.

As a result of increased levels of international competition, more joint ventures of competitors and large companies that once would have seemed unthinkable under antitrust protections will be permitted. For example, American Telephone and Telegraph (AT&T) has entered into a joint venture agreement with the Economic Ministry of Taiwan to improve that nation's telecommunications systems. General Mills, Inc. was permitted to acquire RJR Nabisco's cold-cereal business in both the United Kingdom and the United States so that it could compete more effectively in the large North American and European markets.

The EU has developed its own antitrust guidelines and has challenged a number of proposed U.S. firm mergers in the EU. As these large mergers are proposed, the EU and other countries are taking a closer look at their anticompetitive effects. In 2001, General Electric was handed one of the few management setbacks legendary and then-CEO Jack Welch ever experienced. The proposed acquisition of Honeywell International by General Electric was opposed by EU antitrust enforcers. The EU's Merger Task Force recommended that the $41 billion proposed merger not be permitted.

The U.S. Supreme Court has held that companies from other countries that engage in commerce in the United States will be subject to U.S. antitrust laws. Foreign corporations doing business here are subject to the same rules of competition required of U.S. corporations.

B I O G R A P H Y

Intel and AMD: The Never-Ending Antitrust Story

Intel announced that it would pay its small competitor, Advanced Micro Devices (AMD), $1.25 billion to settle what has been a decade-long antitrust battle that has seen Intel sanctioned by the European Union and facing investigations by authorities in Asia and the United States. Intel's market share for microprocessors, the heart of PCs and laptops, is 80 percent worldwide.

AMD has alleged that Intel has been using large rebates and co-marketing arrangements to persuade computer makers to use its chips instead of those made by AMD. During the course of the 10-year battle, the discovery process has unearthed some interesting e-mails from Intel executives, including one from current CEO Paul Otellini in which he said that Dell, Inc., which, at the time was using only Intel chips, was "the best friend money could buy."[3] At that time Intel is alleged to have given massive discounts and cash rebates to customers who agreed to use Intel chips exclusively. Other customers indicate that Intel threatened not to deal with them if they did business with AMD.

There is plenty of bad blood between the two companies. A brief history appears below:

- The two companies actually began battling in 1990 when Intel filed suit against AMD for copyright infringement.
- In 1991, AMD filed its first antitrust complaint.
- In 1993, the Justice Department cleared Intel of any antitrust charges.
- In 1995, the two companies settled their infringement and antitrust case.
- In 1997, the Justice Department opened its second antitrust investigation of Intel's practices.
- In 1999, the FTC filed antitrust charges against Intel for withholding information about its chips from computer manufacturers who were dealing with Intel's competitors even as it did not withhold that same information from manufacturers who were using Intel chips. Shortly afterwards, and in that same year, Intel and the FTC reached a settlement.
- In 2000, the EU began an antitrust investigation into Intel's sales tactics.

- In 2004, Japanese regulators raided Intel offices as part of an antitrust investigation it was conducting of Intel.
- In 2005, AMD filed antitrust actions against Intel in the United States and Japan. The allegations in the complaint centered on conversations AMD had had with its customers. One customer told AMD sales folks that Intel's financial inducements were like "cocaine," and that they were "hooked." This is the suit the parties just settled. At the time AMD's market share was growing in Japan, to 22 percent, Intel began a program there that offered millions to its customers in discounts and promotional fee-sharing arrangements for product promotion. Gateway Corporation said it had paid a high price for doing business with AMD and that Intel had "beaten them into guacamole."
- In 2007, the EU charged Intel with antitrust violations, charges that resulted in a $1.45 billion fine against Intel.
- During this 20-year period, Intel's sales have continued to grow.

Intel has hired Douglas Melamed as its general counsel. Mr. Melamed worked in the U.S. Justice Department for five years and was part of the team that prosecuted the Microsoft monopolization case.

ADDITIONAL RESOURCES

Steve Lohr and James Kanter, "AMD–Intel Settlement Won't End Their Woes," *New York Times*, November 13, 2009, at B1, B2.

Summary

What restraints of trade are permissible?

- Covenant not to compete—clause in employment or business sale contracts that restricts competition by one of the parties; must be reasonable in scope and time

What antitrust laws exist?

- Sherman Act—first federal antitrust law; prohibits monopolization and horizontal trade restraints such as price fixing, boycotts, and refusals to deal
- Clayton Act—federal antitrust statute that prohibits tying and interlocking directorates; controls mergers
- Federal Trade Commission Act—federal law that allows the FTC to regulate unfair competition

- Robinson–Patman Act—anti–price discrimination federal statute
- Celler–Kefauver Act—regulates asset acquisitions
- Hart–Scott–Rodino Antitrust Improvements Act—antitrust law that broadened Justice Department authority and provided new merger guidelines

What penalties can be imposed for restraints of trade?

- Equitable remedies—nonmonetary remedies such as injunctions
- Treble damages—three times actual damages available in antitrust cases

What are the forms of horizontal trade restraint and defenses?

- Horizontal restraints of trade—anticompetitive behavior among a firm's competitors
- Price fixing—controlling price of goods through agreement, limiting supply, controlling credit
- Group boycotts—agreement among competitors to exclude competition
- Joint ventures—temporary combinations that may restrain trade
- *Per se* violation—violation of antitrust laws that has no defense or justification
- Monopolization—possession of monopoly power in the relevant market by willful acquisition
- Monopsony—control of a market through the control of market supply
- Market power—power to control prices or exclude competition

- Relevant market—geographic and product market used to determine market power
- Predatory pricing—pricing below actual cost to monopolize
- *Noerr–Pennington* doctrine—protection of First Amendment activities from antitrust laws

What are the forms of vertical trade restraints and defenses?

- Resale price maintenance—requiring prices be set in vertical distribution
- Exclusive distributorship—limited dealership rights; not an antitrust violation as long as horizontal competition exists
- Tying—requiring buyers to take an additional product in order to purchase the product they wish
- Price discrimination—selling goods across state lines at prices that have different ratios to marginal costs

Questions and Problems

1. Harold Vogel, an experienced gem appraiser, is a member of the American Society of Appraisers. Mr. Vogel's fee for his work is based on a percentage of the value of the appraised item. The society expelled him under the authority of a bylaw that provides: "It is unprofessional and unethical for the appraiser to do work for a fixed percentage of the amount of value." Mr. Vogel brought suit under Section 1 of the Sherman Act, alleging that his expulsion was a boycott and that he no longer had referrals from the society. Mr. Vogel also claims the bylaw is a means of fixing prices. Is he right? [*Harold Vogel v American Society of Appraisers*, 744 F.2d 598 (7th Cir. 1984)]

2. Booklocker, Inc. is a print-on-demand (POD) book company that specializes in handling the printing of a run of books when there is an online order for those books. Amazon.com facilitated such orders by having customers pay up front for a print run and then placing the order with a POD company. Amazon is the dominant channel for those who wish to order books that are not available for immediate purchase but must be done through a POD. In April 2005, Amazon acquired BookSurge, another POD company. BookSurge's prices are generally higher than those of other POD companies. On February 10, 2008, Amazon began notifying publishers that Amazon would only continue to sell POD books through the Direct Amazon Sales Channel if the publisher agreed to print its books through BookSurge. If publishers and authors wanted to have the POD sales, they had

to use Amazon's printing company. (Brick-and-mortar retailers such as Borders and Barnes & Noble do not handle PODs.) Are there any antitrust issues with this requirement? [*BookLocker.com, Inc. v Amazon.com, Inc.* 650 F.Supp.2d 89 (D. Me. 2009)]

3. Amanda Reiss had completed her residency in ophthalmology in Portland, Oregon, and was moving to Phoenix, Arizona, to start her practice. She began looking for office space and met with a leasing agent who showed her several complexes of medical suites. Dr. Reiss was ready to sign for one of them when the leasing agent turned to her and said, "Oh, by the way, you're not one of those advertising doctors, are you? Because they don't want that kind in any of my complexes." Has there been a violation of the antitrust laws?

4. Budget Rent-a-Car and Aloha Airlines have developed a "fly-drive" program. Under their agreement, customers of Aloha receive a $7 first-day rental rate for car rentals (the usual rate is $14). Robert's Waikiki U-Drive has brought suit, challenging the agreement as a tying arrangement and unlawful. Is Robert's correct? [*Robert's Waikiki U-Drive v Budget Rent-a-Car*, 732 F.2d 1403 (9th Cir. 1984)]

5. In April 1965, Berkeley Heights Shopping Center leased 11,514 square feet of space to A&P Supermarkets. Under the terms of the lease, Berkeley agreed not to lease any other shopping center space to another grocery store. On April 16, 1977, A&P informed Berkeley that it was ceasing operations and subleasing the premises to Drug Fair, a modern drug store chain that sells food-stuffs. In 1985, Berkeley sought to lease other space in the center to another grocery store, and Drug Fair objected on the grounds of the covenant not to compete. Berkeley maintains the covenant only applies when the premises Drug Fair occupies are used as a grocery store operation. Who is correct? [*Berkeley Dev. Co. v Great Atlantic & Pacific Tea Co.*, 518 A.2d 790 (N.J. 1986)]

6.   Gardner-Denver, the largest manufacturer of ratchet wrenches and their replacement parts in the United States, has a dual pricing system for wrench parts and components. Its blue list had parts that, if purchased in quantities of five or more, were available for substantially less than its white list prices. Has Gardner-Denver engaged in price discrimination with its two price lists? [*D. E. Rogers Assoc., Inc. v Gardner-Denver Co.*, 718 F.2d 1431 (6th Cir. 1983)]

7.   Russell Stover is a candy manufacturer that ships its products to 18,000 retailers nationwide. Stover designates resale prices for its dealers but does not request assurances from them that they are honoring the prices. It has, however, refused to sell to those retailers it believes will sell below the prices suggested. Is there an antitrust violation in this conduct? [*Russell Stover Candies, Inc. v FTC*, 718 F.2d 256 (8th Cir. 1982)]

8.   William Inglis & Sons is a family-owned wholesale bakery with production facilities in Stockton, California, that manufactured and distributed bread and rolls in northern California. ITT Continental is one of the nation's largest wholesale bakeries and was a competitor of Inglis in the northern California market. Both Inglis and Continental sold their bread under a private label and an advertised label. Continental's advertised bread was "Wonder" bread, whereas Inglis's advertised bread was "Sunbeam." The private label bread is sold at a lower price than the advertised brand, but the principal difference between the two is the profit. Inglis filed a complaint stating that Continental was selling its private label bread at below-cost prices in a predatory price scheme designed to drive Inglis out of the market.

Inglis also says the lower price on private bread earned Continental more grocery-shelf space for its "Wonder" bread. Is such conduct illegal under the Sherman Act? Is predatory pricing a *per se* violation? [*William Inglis v ITT Continental Baking Co.*, 668 F.2d 1014 (9th Cir. 1980)]

9.   Systems and Software, Inc. (SAS), located in Colchester, Vermont, designs, develops, sells, and services software that allows utility providers to organize their data, including customer information, billing, work management, asset management, and finance and accounting. In August 2002, SAS hired Randy Barnes as an at-will employee to become a regional vice president of sales. At the time he commenced work for SAS, Barnes signed a noncompetition agreement that, among other things, prohibited him—during his employment and for six months thereafter—from becoming associated with any business that competes with SAS. In April 2004, Barnes voluntarily left his position with SAS and started a partnership with his wife called Spirit Technologies Consulting Group. Spirit Technologies' only customer was Utility Solutions, Inc., which, like SAS, services municipalities and utilities nationwide with respect to customer-information-systems software. Shortly after Barnes left SAS, he represented Utility Solutions at a trade fair in a booth near SAS's booth and identified himself as Utility Solution's sales director.

SAS filed suit requesting injunctive relief and enforcement of the noncompetition agreement. Barnes says that the effect of enforcement of the clause is to prevent him from working for six months and stopping competition in Vermont. Who is correct on the noncompetition agreement? Is it valid? Why or why not? [*Systems and Software, Inc. v Barnes*, 886 A.2d 762, (Vt. 2005)]

10.   British Airways and Virgin Atlantic Airlines discussed fuel surcharges at least six times during an 18-month period from 2005 through 2006. As a result, the two companies' fuel surcharges rose in tandem from 5 pounds (about $10) to 60 pounds (about $120). Would Britain's Office of Fair Trading be able to establish an antitrust violation?

Economics, Strategy, and the Law

Reverse Payments and Competition

The Justice Department and the FTC are seeking to end "reverse-payment settlements." These are payments made by the manufacturers of brand-name drugs to generic drug manufacturers that are wrapped up in patent litigation; they are used as a way to keep generics off the market for a longer period of time.

The process works like this:

1.   A generic drug manufacturer is permitted to seek FDA approval for its generic version of a branded drug based on the clinical trials of the brand manufacturer. The Hatch–Waxman Act permits this use of the brand manufacturer's clinical trials

CONTINUEDCONTINUED

with the goal of getting generics to the market faster.

2. However, by seeking approval using the clinical trials, the generic manufacturer opens the door for patent litigation by the brand manufacturer because such a filing is an admission that the generic is the same as the branded drug.

3. The brand manufacturer then brings a patent suit against the generic manufacturer for infringement.

4. The brand manufacturer is willing to settle the case. The settlement, however, does not involve the defendant generic manufacturer paying the plaintiff brand manufacturer. Rather, the brand manufacturer pays the generic manufacturer money to agree to not market or sell its generic version. The reverse payment makes economic sense because the generic is then kept off the market for a longer period of time and the brand manufacturer is allowed to continue its exclusive market control. For example, Bayer AG paid $398.1 million to various generic drug manufacturers for them to keep their versions of Cipro off the market.

Reverse-payment settlements have been the subject of several antitrust suits. [*In re Tamoxifen Citrate Antitrust Litigation,* 466 F.3d 187 (2nd Cir. 2006) and *In re Ciprofloxacin Hydrochloride Antitrust Litigation,* 544 F.3d 1323 (Fed. Cir. 2008).] These courts have found antitrust violations in the reverse-payment agreements. However, other courts have upheld such agreements as long as they do not cover time frames beyond the patent period.

The FTC is doing what is known as "forum shopping," or filing antitrust cases in circuits to get a split in the circuits on whether reverse-payment settlements violate antitrust laws. With a split in the circuits in the law, the U.S. Supreme Court would likely take jurisdiction to resolve the issue of whether the agreements violate antitrust laws. The FTC has some discretion in where it files an action. Companies must decide whether to pursue these cases or allow the uncertainty to continue. In many cases, continuing without a definitive decision is to their benefit.

Explain why the payments to keep a product off the market would be an antitrust violation. What benefits are there for the companies on reverse-payment settlements? Who is harmed by these agreements? Are they anticompetitive?

[*Ark. Carpenters Health & Welfare Fund v Bayer A.G.,* 544 F.3d 1323 (Fed. Cir. 2008).]

Notes

1. The author is grateful for the work and insights of Professor Sue Mota, Associate Dean, College of Business Administration, Bowling Green State University, Ohio. More on her work can be found at Sue Mota, "Antitrust Limited: The Supreme Court Reins in Antitrust Enforcement in 2007," 7 *Fla. St. U. Bus. Rev.* 1 (2007).

2. The doctrine is named after the two U.S. Supreme Court cases in which it was developed: *Eastern R.R. President's Conference v Noerr Motor Freight, Inc.,* 365 U.S. 127 (1961), and *United Mine Workers v Pennington,* 381 U.S. 657 (1965).

3. Don Clark and Jerry A. DiColo, "Intel, AMD Reach Truce in Long War," *Wall Street Journal,* November 13, 2009, p. A1.

Part 4

Business and Its Employees

This portion of the book covers the rights and duties of employers and employees as they work together to operate a business. What are the regulations and restrictions related to the hiring and firing of employees? How much authority do employees have to make decisions and take actions with respect to their work? How are safety regulations enforced in the workplace? What legal limits exist with respect to work hours? What role do unions play in employee and employer relations? What do federal and state antidiscrimination statutes provide? What are their effects on hiring, firing, promoting, and rewarding?

Management of Employee Conduct:
Agency

All businesses have a common thread: employees. They need them, rely on them, pay them, and give them authority to perform certain business tasks. This chapter focuses on that delegation of authority and these questions: When does an employee act on behalf of an employer? How much authority does an employee have? What duties and obligations do employees owe employers? When is a business liable for an employee's acts? ■

How to Fire Someone Without Being Sued

1. Do not fire anyone.
2. Fire everyone.
3. Fire everyone in the same division.
4. Fire only those employees with well-documented and written performance problems.
5. Fire only those employees for whom managers can articulate a legitimate business justification.
6. Do not violate any internal company procedures when selecting employees for termination.
7. Offer terminated employees a severance package in exchange for signing a release not to sue the company.
8. Do not threaten the employee.
9. Give the employee a brief but specific reason for the termination.
10. Be kind.

From Cameron Stracher,
"How to Fire Someone Without Being Sued," *New York Times Magazine*, April 8, 2001, p. 54

UPDATE ⬉
For up-to-date legal news, go to
mariannejennings.com

CONSIDER...

Jerome Lange was the manager of a small grocery store that carried Nabisco products. Ronnell Lynch had been hired by Nabisco as a cookie salesman–trainee in October 1968. On March 1, 1969, Mr. Lynch was assigned his own territory, which included Mr. Lange's store.

On May 1, 1969, Mr. Lynch came to Mr. Lange's store to place previously delivered merchandise on the shelves. An argument developed between the two over Mr. Lynch's

service to the store. Mr. Lynch became very angry and started swearing. Mr. Lange told him to either stop swearing or leave the store because children were present. Mr. Lynch then became uncontrollably angry and said, "I ought to break your neck." He then went behind the counter and dared Mr. Lange to fight. When Mr. Lange refused, Mr. Lynch viciously assaulted him, after which he threw merchandise around the store and left.

Is Nabisco liable for Mr. Lynch's actions?

Names and Roles: Agency Terminology

A principal–agent relationship is one in which one party acts on behalf of another. A clerk who helps you to the dressing room and takes your payment in a department store is an agent. LeBron James has an agent who negotiates his basketball contracts for him. A **power of attorney** is a form of agency relationship that grants another authority to enter into transactions. A special power of attorney is one limited in time or scope, as when a landowner gives another the authority to close a particular land transaction. A general power of attorney is one in which an individual gives another the rights to manage his financial affairs in everything from handling checking accounts to entering into contracts. The common thread in all of these relationships is that one party acts on behalf of another.

Although some terms are used interchangeably, the parties in an agency relationship are known by exact labels and definitions. This section outlines and defines the agency relationship.

Agency

In an agency relationship, one party agrees to act on behalf of another party according to directions. The principal grants authority to an agent. Agency is a consensual relationship—both sides agree to it—and also a fiduciary relationship with duties and responsibilities on both sides. The general term *agency* can be used to refer to many different types of relationships. A real estate agent who is hired to help market your house is an agent of yours; talent agents are agents for many actors at the same time.

Principals

In the employer–employee relationship, the employers are referred to as the **principals.** The term *principal* is used because some agents are not truly employees. A literary agent, for example, represents many authors who are the agent's principals, but the principals are not "employers," in the usual sense, of the agent.

Agents

Agents are those who do a task on behalf of the principal. The agent represents the principal in such a way that if the agent negotiates a contract, the principal, but not the agent, is bound by and a party to the contract. A president of a corporation is an agent of the corporation. When the president negotiates a contract with proper authority, the corporation, not the president, is bound to perform that contract.

All employees are agents of the principal (employer), but not all agents are employees. A corporation might hire an architect to design a new office building and obtain bids for the construction of the building. The architect would be an agent for limited purposes but not an employee of the company.

Employers and Employees: Master–Servant Relationships

A master–servant relationship is one in which the principal (master) exercises a great deal of control over the agent (servant).[1] An employer–employee relationship for a production line worker is an example of a master–servant relationship. Among the various factors considered are whether an employee works regular hours, is paid a regular wage, and is subject to complete supervision and control by the employer during work hours. The factors used to determine whether a master–servant relationship exists are as follows:

- Level of supervision and control of the agent (most important)
- Nature of the agent's work
- Regularity of hours and pay
- Length of employment

The presence of a master-servant relationship also determines whether the principal must pay wage taxes such as FICA and FUTA and withhold income taxes. (See Chapter 18 for more details.)

Independent Contractors

An **independent contractor** acts on behalf of another to perform a task but is not under the direct control of the other person. For example, a corporation's attorney is an agent of the corporation only for purposes of legal representation and court appearances. The attorney is not a corporate employee, and the corporation has no control over the attorney's office operations. The attorney is an independent contractor. A subcontractor hired to perform partial work on a construction site is also an example of an independent contractor.

Principals have less responsibility for independent contractors than for servants because they have little control over a contractor's conduct. The distinction between master–servant relationships and independent contractor relationships is important because a principal's liability for an agent's actions varies depending on the agent's status as servant or contractor.

Agency Law

In general, agency relationships are not governed by statutory law; rather, these relationships are governed by common law. The common law of agency that the majority of states follow is found in a compilation called the *Restatement of Agency*. which is followed by many courts in deciding cases that involve agency law disputes.

Studying agency law actually involves examining three different areas. The first area deals with the creation of the agency relationship. The second area involves the relationship between principals and agents. The final area examines the relationship of the agents and principals to third parties.

Creation of the Agency Relationship

Agency relationships can be created in different ways, and the requirements vary.

Express Authority

An employee who is hired by agreement (oral or written) is an agent and has been given **express authority** to act on behalf of the business. Express authority is limited to what is spoken or written. A driver employee, for example, may only have the authority to deliver packages; a sales employee may have the authority to represent the company but may be required to obtain another employee's signature to finalize sales contracts. An **express contract** specifies the limitations of an employee/agent's authority.

The Record

An agency relationship is created by agreement, which need not be evidenced by a writing or record, although it is best for both employer and employee if it is. Some form of a record, electronic or written, that specifies the agent's authority is required only if the agent will enter into contracts required to have a record or if a state statute requires an agent's authority to be in some record form. For example, most states require that real estate agents' commission contracts be evidenced by a record. That record could be a written, faxed, or PDF document that is signed by the principal.

Capacity

Because agents will enter into contracts for their principals, the principals must have the **capacity** to contract. *Capacity* here means capacity in the traditional contract sense: age and mental capacity (as covered in Chapter 13). In addition, the principal must be in existence for an agent to have authority. If a company has not been incorporated, those who sign for the nonexistent corporation as agents have liability.

One agency capacity issue that comes up frequently in sole proprietorships, general partnerships, and other smaller businesses that are dependent on individual personalities is the stalemate that results when mental incapacity (through accident or illness frequently) in one of these key individuals becomes a factor. For example, if one of two general partners is injured in an accident and unconscious, the remaining partner has his or her hands tied for certain types of business transactions. Under the **Uniform Durable Power of Attorney Act** (UDPAA) (a uniform law that has been adopted in most states), these key individuals can execute a type of power of attorney that comes into existence in the event of disability or incapacity of the principal. This authority then "kicks in" when needed. The UDPAA has also been helpful for children who are trying to manage their parents' financial affairs when their parents become mentally or physically disabled. The durable power of attorney allows the child or children to manage payments, accounts, and assets, depending on the scope of authority given. In many cases, the child or children need the authority just to be able to manage the medical bills and insurance claims for the parent's illness.

The contractual capacity of the agent is not an issue in the agency relationship for purposes of the agent's authority to enter into contracts. However, the capacity of the agent to drive, operate equipment, or work with the public is an issue that affects the employer's liability to third parties. Because of this liability, many employers conduct background checks, polygraph and psychological tests, and drug screening as a precondition to hiring employees. Many firms also have ongoing drug-testing programs to ensure that employees are not reporting for work—or working—under the influence of drugs or alcohol.

One of the most controversial issues in agency law concerns the **unincorporated association,** which is a group that acts as an entity but has no legal existence. Some charitable organizations—churches, for example—have an ongoing existence and have probably built buildings, had fund-raising drives, and entered into many contracts. However, because these organizations are not incorporated and do not have any legal existence, those who sign contracts for these groups are not agents. Moreover, they are liable under these contracts because the organizations are not principals with capacity. For example, suppose that a Little League coach signs a credit contract for the purchase of Little League equipment. The Little League organization is nonprofit and is not incorporated. In the event the league does not raise enough money to pay for the sporting equipment, the signing coach is liable because the league is not a principal with capacity.

The National Conference of Commissioners on Uniform State Laws proposed the *Uniform Unincorporated Nonprofit Association Act* (UUNAA) in 1996 and revised it in 2008, and it has been adopted in 12 states. Under the UUNAA, the contract and tort liability of individual members of a nonprofit association would be eliminated if they were acting on behalf of their nonprofit unincorporated association. The UUNAA also gives unincorporated nonprofits the right to bring suits and be sued in their names and to own property in similar fashion.

Implied Authority

An agent under contract not only has the authority given expressly but also has certain **implied authority.** Implied authority is the extension of express authority by custom. For example, a person who is hired as president of a corporation probably does not have his or her exact duties specified in the contract. However, this president will likely have the same type of authority customarily held by corporate presidents: to sign contracts, to authorize personnel changes, to conduct salary reviews and changes, and to institute operational changes. The law gives the president customary authority unless the president's contract specifies otherwise. This implied authority can be limited by agreement between the parties if they do not want custom and practice to control their relationship.

Together, express and implied authority are called **actual authority.** The type of authority an agent has determines the liability of the principal to third parties for contracts and torts.

Apparent Authority

In many cases, an agency relationship arises not by express or implied contracts but because of the way a principal presents himself to third parties. This theory of agency law, called **apparent authority** or **agency by estoppel,** holds a principal liable if the principal makes someone else think he or she has an agent.

Apparent authority exists by appearance. A third party is led to believe that an agent, although not actually holding express and accompanying implied authority, had the proper authority to deal with the third party. The third party is led to believe that certain promises will be fulfilled. For example, a mobile home dealer who has brochures, note pads, and other materials from a mobile home manufacturer has the appearance of having the authority to sell those homes even no actual authority exists. *Montoya v Grease Monkey Holding Corp.* (Case 17.1) is a landmark case in agency and corporation law that deals with issues of apparent authority.

CASE 17.1

Montoya v Grease Monkey Holding Corp.
904 P.2d 468 (Colo. 1995)

A Grease Monkey's Uncle, er, Agent

FACTS

Grease Monkey Holding Corporation is a Utah corporation, and Grease Monkey International is a wholly owned subsidiary of Grease Monkey Holding Company. From 1983 through 1991, Arthur Sensenig was Grease Monkey's President, COO (chief operating officer), and Chairman of the Board. During that time, Mr. Sensenig ran Grease Monkey and had broad authority to act as general officer and agent for Grease Monkey. Mr. Sensenig had authority to raise capital from banks and other lenders . . . Mr. Sensenig did not need board approval to obtain loans unless they exceeded $500,000.

Nick and Aver Montoya (respondents) were married for over 50 years. The trial court found Nick Montoya to be a person of "average investor sophistication." Aver Montoya was a factory worker for approximately 17 years, and she left financial matters primarily to her husband.

Nick Montoya met Mr. Sensenig in the mid-1960s when Mr. Sensenig was a teller at a bank where Mr. Montoya was a customer. During the 1960s and 1970s, Mr. Sensenig gave Mr. Montoya investment advice. Mr. Montoya was impressed by Mr. Sensenig, who ultimately became vice-president of the bank before leaving. Mr. Montoya also knew Mr. Sensenig through a church connection.

From 1983 through 1991, Mr. Sensenig got payments from the Montoyas under the guise that the payments were investments in Grease Monkey. Mr. Sensenig told the Montoyas that because Grease Monkey was a new company, it did not have its own account, and that as President and Chairman of the Board, Mr. Sensenig used his personal account as the corporate account. Mr. Sensenig took Mr. Montoya to the Grease Monkey offices and showed him a promotional slide show presentation used by Grease Monkey to solicit franchise business. However, none of the payments was invested in Grease Monkey, and Grease Monkey did not receive any of the funds. Rather, Mr. Sensenig used the Montoyas' money for his own personal benefit.

Generally, about a week after writing an investment check, the Montoyas received a promissory note as evidence of their investment. When Mr. Sensenig delivered interest payments to the Montoyas, he brought charts showing the growth and success of Grease Monkey. Mailings to the Montoyas concerning their investments were on Grease Monkey letterhead, and calls regarding the investments were made to Mr. Sensenig at Grease Monkey Mr. Sensenig gave the Montoyas many Grease Monkey promotional items, such as pens, hats, and sweatshirts.

Dreams turned to dust, and the Montoyas sought to put the monkey on the back of the corporation and filed suit against Grease Monkey, as Mr. Sensenig's

CONTINUED

employer, for breach of contract, fraud, misrepresentation, breach of duty of good faith and fair dealing, promissory estoppel, extreme and outrageous conduct, and negligent hiring and supervision.

After a trial to the court, the Montoyas prevailed on their fraud and misrepresentation claims, and their other claims were dismissed. The trial court entered judgment against Grease Monkey for the outstanding balance due on the promissory notes. The court of appeals affirmed the trial court's "judgment . . . because, Mr. Sensenig, as its [P]resident, acting within the scope of his apparent authority as an agent of the corporations, engaged in conduct which was customary for an individual employed in Sensenig's position, and was placed in that position by Grease Monkey." Grease Monkey appealed.

JUDICIAL OPINION

ERICKSON, Justice

Section 261 of the Restatement (Second) of Agency provides that "[a] principal who puts a servant or other agent in a position which enables the agent, while apparently acting within his authority, to commit a fraud upon third persons is subject to liability to such third persons for the fraud." The application of section 261 is not limited to principals and agents but extends also to masters and servants. . . .

Under the doctrine of respondeat superior, "a master is liable for the unauthorized torts of his servant if committed while the servant is acting within the scope of his employment." Because "the master's peculiar liability is based on the physical activities of servants, including their batteries, . . . he is liable only if the servant's conduct was in some way caused by an intent to serve his employer's interests and connected with his authorized acts."

A master may also be liable for tortious conduct by a servant, as he would be for the conduct of any agent, whether servant or not. Acts that are apparently authorized or committed within an agent's inherent powers or where the agent's position enables him to commit a tort exemplify the situations where a principal may be liable for the torts of servants and non-servant agents. . . .

Apparent authority liability is not based upon the rules of respondeat superior, and it is not "essential to find that the agent was motivated by an intent to act for his master's purposes." Actions for misrepresentations and fraud generally fit into the category of torts which do not lie within the scope and principles of respondeat superior. In many of these situations, the agent's position enables him to perpetrate the fraud, and the agent acted for his own purposes. However, "[t]he fact that the agent is acting from purely personal motives is immaterial unless this is known to the other party."

A principal is subject to liability for physical harm to the person or the tangible things of another caused by the negligence of a servant or a non-servant agent. . . .

The application of section 261 to the present case squares with the misrepresentation or fraud analysis of the principal-agent doctrine. Respondeat superior and master-servant principles constitute an aspect of agency law distinct from fraud based on the apparent authority.

In the present case, Grease Monkey did not possess the right to control the physical movements or activities of Sensenig, who was the Chief Operating Officer of Grease Monkey. Sensenig was expected to perform certain tasks for Grease Monkey. Grease Monkey did not monitor Sensenig's physical activities, but was only concerned with the results achieved.

Generally, "[a] principal is not bound by the false representations of his agent made without his knowledge, consent, or authority. However, if an agent acts with apparent authority, a principal may be liable even though the agent acts solely for his own purposes." Applying an apparent authority theory, "'[l]iability is based upon the fact that the agent's position facilitates the consummation of the fraud, in that from the point of view of the third person the transaction seems regular on its face and the agent appears to be acting in the ordinary course of the business confided to him.'" In both state and federal misrepresentation cases, "[c]ourts have commonly imposed liability based on 'apparent authority' . . . particularly when the person making the misrepresentation is an important corporate official." . . .

Under section 261, a plaintiff must establish that the servant or other agent was put in a position which enabled the agent to commit fraud, the agent acted within his apparent authority, and the agent committed fraud. First, the trial court found that Sensenig was the highest authority at Grease Monkey. He had authority to raise up to $500,000 without Board approval, and as general officer and agent for Grease Monkey, he had broad authority to act without corporate restrictions. The findings of the trial court support a conclusion that Grease Monkey put Sensenig in a position where he could commit fraud if he had a mind to.

Second, the trial court found that Sensenig acted within his apparent authority when he raised capital from individuals such as respondents. We also note that "[u]nder section 261 and the theory of apparent authority . . . the agent's conduct is seen through the eyes of the third party. . . ."

Third, the trial court found that Sensenig made false representations to respondents. Sensenig made these representations with the awareness they were false and with intent to induce respondents to rely on the representations. The representations were material, and respondents reasonably relied on the representations to their detriment. The trial court found for respondents on their claim of fraud and misrepresentation, and we are unwilling to disturb that finding on review.

Grease Monkey contends that the use of section 261 amounts to strict liability for the principal. However, "'few doctrines of the law are more firmly established or more in harmony with accepted notions of social policy than that of the liability of the principal without fault of his own.'" Our decision recognizes the legal principle that "when one of two innocent persons must suffer from the acts of a third, he must suffer who put it in the power of the wrongdoer to inflict the injury." This policy motivates organizations to see that their agents abide by the law.

Affirmed.

CASE QUESTIONS

1. What did the CEO of the corporation do to a third party? Is Grease Monkey liable to the Montoyas?

2. What is the purpose of the apparent authority doctrine?

3. What duties does apparent authority impose on principals?

CONSIDER... 17.1

Suppose that a bar owner has employed a bouncer and the bouncer injures someone while removing him from the premises. Is the employer liable for the conduct of the bouncer?

THINK: The *Grease Monkey* case held that a principal is liable for the acts of an agent that a third party would perceive are within the scope of the authority of the agent.

APPLY: When an agent is hired as a bouncer, battery and assault could be within the agent's apparent scope of authority.

ANSWER: The bar owner is liable for the bouncer's conduct. [*Byrd v Faber*, 57 Ohio St.3d 56, 565 N.E.2d 584, 587 (1991)]

CONSIDER... 17.2

On September 20, 1973, a Beech Model 18 Aircraft carrying singer Jim Croce and his entourage crashed shortly after takeoff from Natchitoches, Louisiana. All were killed.

At the time of the crash, the plane was being flown by Robert N. Elliott, an employee of Roberts Airways. Roberts had been asked by Mustang Aviation to fly the entourage according to a prepared itinerary. Mustang originally had entered into a contract with Lloyd St. Martin of Variety Artists International, a booking agent for popular singers, to fly the group itself. The agreement was entered into on September 18, 1973. Later that same day, Mustang learned that its aircraft was disabled, so Mustang's director of operations called Roberts and asked it to substitute.

Relatives of Mr. Croce and the others killed in the crash brought suit against Mustang for the crash. What, if any, agency relationships existed in this case? How did they arise? Is Mustang liable for the crash? [*Croce v Bromley Corp.*, 623 F2d 1084 (5th Cir. 1980)]

Ratification

On occasion, an agent without proper authority enters into a contract that the principal later ratifies. **Ratification** occurs when the principal reviews a contract and voluntarily decides that, even though the agent did not have proper authority, the contract will be honored as if the agent had full authority. Once a contract is ratified, it is effective from the time the agent entered into it even though the agent had no authority until after the fact. Ratification is a way for a principal to give an agent authority retroactively.

For example, suppose that an apartment manager does not have the authority to contract for any type of construction work except routine maintenance. Because the fence around the apartment complex is deteriorated, the manager contracts for the construction of a completely new fence at a cost that exceeds by six times any maintenance work he has had done in the past. The contractor begins work on the fence, and the apartment owner drives by, sees the work, and says nothing. By her inaction in allowing the contractor to continue building the fence, the apartment complex owner ratifies the contract.

CONSIDER... 17.3

Benjamin Chavez served as executive director of the National Association for the Advancement of Colored People (NAACP). Mary Stansee, a former employee of the NAACP executive offices, charged Mr. Chavez with sexual harassment, and he settled the claim for $332,400. The NAACP was financially troubled at the time of the settlement, with a deficit of $2.7 million in 1993, and Mr. Chavez did not disclose the settlement to the board until after it was completed. Did Mr. Chavez have implied authority to make the settlement? Did he have apparent authority?

The Principal–Agent Relationship

The discussion to this point, the focus has been on the relationship between the agent and the principal on the one hand and third parties on the other. However, it is important to realize that a contractual relationship exists between the agent and the principal, so that each has certain obligations and rights. This section of the chapter covers that relationship.

The Agent's Rights and Responsibilities

Principals and agents have a fiduciary relationship, which is characterized by loyalty, trust, care, and obedience. An agent in the role of fiduciary must act in the principal's best interests.

Duty of Loyalty: General

An agent is required to act only for the benefit of the principal, and an agent cannot represent both parties in a transaction unless each knows about and consents to the agent's representation of the other. Further, an agent cannot use the information gained or the offers available to or by the principal to profit personally. For example, an agent hired to find a buyer for a new invention cannot interfere with the principal's possible sale by demonstrating his own product. Neither can an agent hired to find a piece of property buy the property and then sell it (secretly of course) to the principal. *Lucini Italia Co. v Grappolini* (Case 17.2) involves an issue of an agent's fiduciary duty in a sale transaction.

CASE 17.2

Lucini Italia Co. v Grappolini
2003 WL 1989605 (N.D. Ill. 2003)

A Slick Deal by the Olive Oil Agent

FACTS

Lucini Italia imports and sells premium extra-virgin olive oil of Italy. Lucini was formed by Arthur Frigo, a Chicago entrepreneur and adjunct professor of management and strategy at Northwestern University's Kellogg Graduate School of Management. Giuseppe Grappolini, from Loro Ciuffenna, Italy, served as a consultant to Lucini. Under the terms of his consulting contract, Mr. Grappolini was to develop Lucini Premium Select extra-virgin olive oil as well other flavored olive oil products. Mr. Frigo had discovered a market niche in the United States for high-end olive oil ($10 to $12 per bottle).

Mr. Grappolini is also the sole owner of the Grappolini Company, an Italian limited liability company. The Grappolini Company distributes small volumes of extra-virgin olive oil in Chicago and other markets throughout the United States, but has much larger sales volume in Europe. Between December 1997 (the date of the Grappolini consulting contract with Lucini) and June 2000, the Grappolini Company was Lucini's supplier of extra-virgin olive oil. The two companies had signed a supply agreement for this arrangement, also in December 1997.

Mr. Frigo instructed Mr. Grappolini to try to negotiate an exclusive supply contract for Lucini with Vegetal, an Italian company with a unique olive oil that Mr. Frigo needed to develop another premium brand of olive oil that would have flavors such as lemon and garlic added (called the LEO project). Vegetal was the only company that could supply the type of olive oil Mr. Frigo needed for the blending process with the extra flavors. Mr. Grappolini led Mr. Frigo along with promises of a deal with the Vegetal company for nearly a year, through reports of meetings as well as with faxes and memos appearing to detail terms, conditions, and dates for delivery. At the same time, Mr. Grappolini was meeting with Mr. Frigo almost daily as they discussed the plans for the new Lucini olive oil. In the meetings, Mr. Frigo discussed the formulas, the marketing, consumer profiles, and marketing strategies for the LEO project. Apparently, Mr. Grappolini was impressed by the plans and entered into his own exclusive supply contract with Vegetal. Mr. Grappolini did not tell Mr. Frigo of the contract and continued to work as a consultant. Mr. Grappolini also assured Mr. Frigo that Lucini had a supply contract with Vegetal.

Mr. Frigo proceeded with all the contracts, ads, and plans for the LEO product launch based on assurances from Mr. Grappolini that it had the supply contract with Vegetal. However, when pressed, Mr. Grappolini could not deliver the paperwork. When Mr. Frigo requested a meeting with the CEO of Vegetal, Mr. Grappolini arranged for the meeting but cautioned Mr. Frigo not to mention the supply arrangement because such a discussion in a first-time meeting would be considered rude in the Italian culture.

With the LEO product launch approaching, and no copy of the alleged Vegetal supply contract available, Mr. Frigo had Lucini's lawyer in Italy contact Vegetal directly for a copy. The lawyer learned that Vegetal had a supply contract, but the contract was with Mr. Grappolini's company and that it was not transferable to Lucini. Mr. Frigo then confronted the officers of Vegetal they acknowledged that they had negotiated with Mr. Grappolini for his company, not for Lucini and were not aware of Lucini's needs or Mr. Grappolini's representation of Lucini. The officers at Vegetal said that Grappolini had been a "bad boy" in negotiating the contract for himself. Vegetal agreed to supply Lucini with olive oil in the future, but could not deliver it in time for the launch of Lucini's new line. The soonest it could deliver would be after the next harvest, a time that meant the marketing and sales plans of Lucini for its new product had been wasted.

Mr. Frigo and Lucini filed suit against Mr. Grappolini and his company (defendants) for breach of fiduciary duty.

JUDICIAL OPINION

DENLOW, Magistrate

As agents, Defendants owed Lucini general duties of good faith, loyalty, and trust. In addition, Defendants owed Lucini "full disclosure of all relevant facts relating to the transaction or affecting the subject matter of the agency."

Defendants were Lucini's agents and owed Lucini a fiduciary duty to advance Lucini's interests, not their own. When Defendants obtained an exclusive supply agreement with Vegetal for the Grappolini Company instead of for Lucini, they were disloyal and breached their fiduciary duties. Lucini suffered substantial damages as a result of this breach.

Punitive damages are appropriate where the defendant has intentionally breached a fiduciary duty.

CONTINUED

Defendants' breach of their fiduciary duties was flagrant and intentional. Defendants deliberately usurped a corporate opportunity sought by Lucini, which Lucini had entrusted Defendants to secure on Lucini's behalf. Although Defendants explicitly accepted this trust and ensured Lucini that Mr. Grappolini and his company would do as Lucini requested, Defendants failed to do so and hid this fact from Lucini.

Defendants misappropriated Lucini's valuable trade secrets. Defendants acquired Lucini's trade secrets under circumstances giving rise to a duty to maintain their secrecy. Defendants' assistant Marco Milandri testified that he understood that Lucini's Premium Select and LEO product formulations were company secrets. Likewise, Grappolini testified that he understood the secrecy of trade secret information communicated to him. Indeed, his various contracts specified that he would maintain the confidentiality of Lucini's research conclusions. After Defendants had secretly secured their own exclusive supply contract with Vegetal, they hid this fact from Lucini in order to induce Lucini to continue sharing its trade secret research, strategies, and plans with Grappolini.

Lucini's decision to focus its LEO project around essential oils from Vegetal Progress was a closely guarded trade secret. When Mr. Grappolini used this information on behalf of the Grappolini Company to allow it unfettered access to negotiate its own exclusive arrangement with Vegetal, it is necessary to conclude that the Grappolini Company "acquired" the information with full knowledge that: (i) Lucini had not consented to the use of the information by a competitor, and (ii) Mr. Grappolini had no right to transmit or use the information for his own purposes or on behalf of the Grappolini Company.

As a proximate result of Defendants' breach of their fiduciary duties, Lucini suffered lost profits damages of at least $4.17 million from selling its grocery line of LEO products from 2000 through 2003. The Court will award Lucini its lost profits of $4,170,000, together with its $800,000 of development costs for LEO project. Defendants engaged in willful and malicious misappropriation as evidenced by their use of the information for directly competitive purposes and their efforts to hide the misappropriation and, accordingly, the Court will award $1,000,000 in exemplary damages. Such an award is necessary to discourage Defendants from engaging in such conduct in the future.

CASE QUESTIONS

1. Explain how Mr. Grappolini breached his fiduciary duty.

2. What lessons can you learn about contracts, suppliers, and product launches from the case?

3. Explain why the court decided to award both lost profits and punitive damages.

4. Evaluate the ethics of Mr. Grappolini's conduct. Why did Vegetal's officers refer to Mr. Grappolini as a "bad boy"?

Ethical Issues

Ausaf Umar Siddiqui, a computer salesman at Fry's Electronics who worked his way up to vice president of merchandising and operations at Fry's, has been charged with receiving $65 million in kickbacks from vendors. The indictment alleges that vendors agreed to pay as much as 31 percent commission to Siddiqui in exchange for his promise to buy merchandise from them at inflated prices. The commissions he received were then paid to a company called PC International LLC. According to the IRS, the money was used to pay off gambling debts Siddiqui owed to Las Vegas casinos. Fry's has fired Siddiqui, and his co-workers at Fry's were stunned when he was arrested at work. He was released on $300,000 bond with the stipulation that he not travel to Las Vegas.

The charges came when the IRS received an anonymous tip from an upper-level manager at Fry's whose tip included copies of spreadsheets showing the payments from vendors. The anonymous tipper said that he had stumbled across the documents when he made an unannounced visit to Siddiqui's office. Vendors included U.S. Media Technology, Elitegroup Company Computer Services, Inc., Phoebe Micro, and Lead Data International Inc. The commissions paid were 10 times the normal amounts and were sent to Siddiqui's home in Palo Alto. The IRS review of Siddiqui's bank account set up for the commissions shows that $167 million was deposited in the account during the past three years, something that leads investigators to believe that they have not uncovered all the vendors or payments. What are the duties of an agent with respect to commissions earned? What ethical issue exists here? Is this commercial bribery? Could the vendors be charged? Why do we worry about this type of conduct by an agent?

Source: Miguel Bustillo, "Fry's Official Faces Fraud Charges," *Wall Street Journal*, Dec. 24, 2008, p. B3.

Duty of Loyalty: Postemployment and Noncompete Agreements

Many companies have their employees sign contracts that include covenants not to compete or covenants not to disclose information about their former employers should the employees leave their jobs or be terminated from their employment.

Downsizings in the high-tech industry have brought back the issue of noncompete and confidentiality agreements. When employees were recruited by upstart firms and lured with stock options, it was difficult for them to imagine a time when the company would need to downsize or would no longer exist. As a result, most of them signed fairly restrictive covenants not to compete.

In dealing with these covenants, courts are striking a balance between employees' right to work and an employer's right to protect the trade secrets, training, etc. that the former employee has and then transfers to another company or to herself for purposes of starting a business.

Requirements for Noncompete Agreements

1. The Need for Protection

The laws on noncompete agreements vary from state to state, with California's being the most protective of employees. California's statute in essence prohibits employers from enforcing agreements that prohibit employees from working in their chosen fields. However, across all states, courts are clear in their positions that there must first be an underlying need or reason for the noncompete agreement. That is, the employee must have had access to trade secrets or be starting his or her own business in competition with the principal/employer.

2. Reasonableness in Scope

The covenant must also be reasonable in geographic scope and time. These factors depend upon the economic base and the nature of the business. For example, a noncompete in a high-tech employee's contract could be geographically global but must be shorter in duration because technology changes so rapidly. A noncompete for a collection agency could not be global but might be longer in duration because the nature of that business is one of relationships.

3. Valid Formation

Noncompete agreements are also subject to the basics of contract law (see Chapters 12 and 13). There must be consideration and there cannot be duress. For example, one dot-com company agreed to give its employees stock options if they would sign a noncompete agreement. Amazon.com offered downsized employees an additional 10 weeks' pay plus $500, in addition to the normal severance package, if they would sign a three-page "separation agreement and general release" in which they promised not to sue Amazon over the layoff or disparage it in any way. Amazon, as a longstanding practice, has had employees sign a confidentiality agreement at the beginning of their employment that restricts their use of information and systems knowledge they gained whilst working at Amazon.

California has provided protection for employees who refuse to sign noncompete agreements, punishing employers with punitive damages in wrongful termination cases brought by employees terminated following their refusals to sign.

4. Other Theories for Noncompete Enforcement

Some employers have begun to use the tort of tortious interference with contracts as a means of preventing former employees from working for competitors or beginning their own competing businesses. In those states in which noncompete clauses are unenforceable, the tort avenue has been used as a means of enjoining the former employee's business activities. For example in *TruGreen Companies, LLC v Mower Brothers, Inc.*, 199 P.3d 929 (Utah 2008), the Utah Supreme Court held that a company whose former employer had gone to work for a competing company and recruited other employees to join him was liable for tortious interference and allowed recovery of lost profits.

Coady v Harpo, Inc. (Case 17.3) deals with an interesting type of covenant in an employment contract that covers postemployment activities of departed employees.

CASE 17.3	*Coady v Harpo, Inc.* 719 N.E.2D 244 (III. App. 1999)

O! Oprah! Do Tell!

FACTS

Elizabeth Coady (plaintiff) was employed by Harpo, Inc. (defendant), a company owned by Oprah Winfrey, as a senior associate producer for "The Oprah Winfrey Show" from November 1993 until March 1998. Ms. Coady alleged that for some time prior to March 26, 1998, those working at Harpo engaged in conduct so intolerable as to amount to constructive termination. On March 26, 1998, Ms. Coady notified Harpo by letter from her attorney that she resigned effectively immediately.

Ms. Coady, a trained journalist, indicated her intent to write or otherwise report about her experiences as an employee of Harpo. She asserted that she would write about her experiences as an exercise of her rights of free speech and free press and was not prohibited from doing so by a confidentiality policy, entitled "Business Ethics, Objectivity, and Confidentiality Policy," which was contained in Harpo's September 1996 employee manual.

In a letter dated April 24, 1998, Harpo "reminded" Ms. Coady that she had signed a document entitled "Business Ethics, Objectivity, and Confidentiality Policy" on March 12, 1995, and provided a copy of the agreement in the letter. The letter further stated that in the March 12, 1995, agreement, Ms. Coady "agreed (among other things) to keep confidential, during her employment and thereafter, all information about the Company, Ms. Winfrey, her private life, and Harpo's business activities which she acquired during or by virtue of her employment with Harpo." Harpo representatives indicated in the letter their intentions to enforce and ensure compliance with the confidentiality agreement.

Ms. Coady filed suit seeking, among other things, a declaration that the covenant was unenforceable.

The trial court dismissed the claim, and Ms. Coady appealed.

JUDICIAL OPINION

GREIMAN, Justice

Both the independent document entitled "Business Ethics, Objectivity, and Confidentiality Policy" (hereinafter the 1995 agreement) and the portion of the employee manual with the same title (hereinafter the 1996 employee manual) include a section entitled "Confidentiality Assurances," which provides in pertinent part as follows:

> 1. During your employment or business relationship with Harpo, and thereafter, to the fullest extent permitted by law, you are obligated to keep confidential and never disclose, use, misappropriate, or confirm or deny the veracity of, any statement or comment concerning Oprah Winfrey, Harpo (which, as used herein, included all entities related to Harpo, Inc., including Harpo Productions, Inc., Harpo Films, Inc.) or any of her/its Confidential Information. The phrase 'Confidential Information' as used in this policy, includes but is not limited to, any and all information which is not generally known to the public, related to or concerning: (a) Ms. Winfrey and/ or her business or private life; (b) the business activities, dealings or interests of Harpo and/or its officers, directors, affiliates, employees or contractors; and/or (c) Harpo's employment practices or policies applicable to its employees and/or contractors.

> 2. During your employment or business relationship with Harpo, and thereafter, you are obligated to refrain from giving or participating in any interview(s) regarding or related to Ms. Winfrey, Harpo, your employment or business relationship with Harpo and/or amy [sic] matter which concerns, relates to or involves any Confidential Information.

The relevant documents also provide that commitment to the stated policies is required as a condition of employment: "Your commitment to the guidelines set forth in this policy is a condition of your employment or business relationship with Harpo."

In addition, defendant's motion to dismiss attached a copy of plaintiff's acknowledgment of the employee manual, which she signed upon the commencement of her employment at defendant in 1993. The acknowledgment signed by plaintiff states in relevant part:

> I acknowledge and understand that I may not use any confidential or proprietary information of HARPO for my own purposes either during or after my employment with HARPO, and I understand that I am prohibited from removing, disclosing or otherwise misappropriating any of HARPO's confidential or proprietary information for any reason.

"A postemployment restrictive covenant will be enforced if its terms are reasonable." To determine the reasonableness of a restrictive covenant, "it is necessary to consider whether enforcement of the covenant will injure the public, whether enforcement will cause undue hardship to the promisor and whether the restraint imposed by the covenant is greater than is necessary to protect the interests of the employer."

The reasonableness of some types of restrictive covenants, such as nonsolicitation agreements, also is evaluated by the time limitation and geographical scope stated in the covenant. However, a confidentiality agreement will not be deemed unenforceable for lack of durational or geographic limitations where trade secrets and confidential information are involved. . . .

Although restraint of trade is a significant concern, "[a]n equally important public policy in Illinois is the freedom to contract." Furthermore, postemployment restrictive covenants "have a social utility in that they protect an employer from the unwarranted erosion of confidential information."

. . . Defendant does not seek to restrain plaintiff's future career. Plaintiff is free to choose her future occupation, the locale in which she may choose to work, and the time when she can commence her new career. Defendant does not object to plaintiff becoming a journalist, competing with defendant in the same venue and in any locale, including Chicago, and in beginning her new venture immediately. The confidentiality agreement does not restrict commerce and does not restrict plaintiff's ability to work in any chosen career field, at any time. Instead, the 1995 confidentiality agreement restricts plaintiff's ability to disseminate confidential information that she obtained or learned while in defendant's employ. Most certainly, plaintiff had no problem with keeping confidences as long as she was a senior associate producer and continued her work with defendant.

Moreover, we find unpersuasive plaintiff's argument that the confidentiality agreement is too broad because it remains effective for all time and with no geographical boundaries. Whether for better or for worse, interest in a celebrity figure and his or her attendant business and personal ventures somehow seems to continue endlessly, even long after death, and often, as in the present case, extends over an international domain.

Under the facts of this case and the terms of the restrictive covenant at issue, we find that the 1995 confidentiality agreement is reasonable and enforceable. Accordingly, we affirm the trial court's order dismissing plaintiff's cause of action as stated in count 1 of her complaint.

Affirmed.

CASE QUESTIONS

1. What did Ms. Coady agree to when she became a Harpo employee?

2. Does it matter whether the covenant was part of the employee manual or part of a contract?

3. Is there a difference between a confidentiality agreement and a covenant not to compete?

4. Does this restrictive covenant prevent Ms. Coady from working as a journalist?

CONSIDER...   17.4

Eric Rush (a.k.a. Eric Romero in the dance world) was a dance instructor at a Plano, Texas, Arthur Murray dance studio. Mr. Rush says he was fired but the attorney for the Arthur Murray studio indicates he resigned. Under the terms of his employment contract, which included a noncompete clause, Mr. Rush was prohibited from teaching dance lessons within a 25-mile radius of the Plano Arthur Murray studio. However, Mr. Rush created a Craigslist notice offering dance lessons and also contacted former students from Arthur

Murray to offer dance lessons. He also taught a cha-cha lesson at Tango and Cha-Cha's Dance Studio in Dallas (to the tune of "I Left My Heart in San Francisco").

A Texas judge ordered Mr. Rush to take down the Craigslist notices and stop teaching dance through the end of 2009 within the 25-mile radius. Mr. Rush was also ordered to spend 30 days in jail for contempt of court, which consisted of his ongoing refusals to comply with the court's orders for his violations of the noncompete clause. The jail sentence represents the latest in a 10-month legal battle between Rush and his former employer. Rush's lawyer called the sentence excessive and said that the judge was "killing a fly with a bazooka."

As for Mr. Rush, he is dismayed at his clipped wings, er, silenced taps. He says that the noncompete clause "is like asking a doctor not to practice medicine."[2] He also says that if he did stop dancing "it would be, like, blasphemous."[3] Rush also adds that dancing is his calling in life and, "I just want to make a living." Mr. Rush's lawyer acknowledges that Mr. Rush could teach in cities such as Arlington and Fort Worth and not be in violation of the court order enforcing the covenant. However, Mr. Rush says that with the price of gas and the poor economy, the travel distance is prohibitive.

Mr. Rush says he is teaching dancing to his fellow inmates. From prison, Mr. Rush described dancing: "It means healing. It means grace, serenity, elegance, sex appeal. It means ambition and drive and achievement and confidence."[4]

Discuss whether the covenant is enforceable, whether it is too broad, and how a jail sentence resulted from a contract matter.

Duty of Obedience

An agent has the duty to obey reasonable instructions from the principal. The agent is not required to do anything criminally wrong or commit torts, of course; but agents are required to operate according to the principal's standards and instructions. Failure to do so could mean the agent has gone beyond the authority given and is personally liable for the conduct.

Duty of Care

Agents have a duty to use as much care and to act as prudently as they would if managing their own affairs. Agents must take the time and effort to perform their principals' assigned tasks. For example, officers of corporations must base their decisions on information, not guesses, and must ensure that their decisions are carried out by employees.

An agent who does not use reasonable care is liable to the principal for any damages resulting from a lack of care. When an agent does not make adequate travel arrangements for a speaker, the agent is liable to the speaker for damages that result from the speaker's nonappearance at an engagement.

The Principal's Rights and Responsibilities

Just like the agent on the other side of the agreement, the principal also has certain duties and obligations.

Duty of Compensation

The first obligation is that of compensation, which can take various forms that range from salary to commission to combinations of both. Some agents work for a fee on a contingency basis. A real estate agent, for example, may have an arrangement in which she receives compensation only if a buyer for the property is found. However, compensation is not required for a valid agency if the agent and principal agree that there will be no compensation.

In an agency relationship in which there will be no compensation—a **gratuitous agency**—the agent has all the same authority to act for the principal but will not be compensated. For example, some charitable organizations have agents who act in fund-raising capacities, but who do not expect compensation.

Duty of Indemnification

Principals also have an obligation to indemnify agents for expenses the agents incur in carrying out the principal's orders. Corporate officers, for example, are entitled to travel compensation; sales agents are entitled to compensation for placing ads to sell goods, realty, or services.

Liability of Principals for Agents' Conduct: The Relationship with Third Parties

Contract Liability

Although the types of authority an agent has and the terms of the agency agreement define the authority of the agent, the contract liability of a principal is not determined by either intent or by the limitations agreed to privately by the agent and the principal. In other words, third parties have certain contract enforcement rights depending on the nature of the agent's work and the authority given by the principal. The liability of the principal for contracts made by an agent is controlled by the perceptions created for and observed by the third party to the contract. Those perceptions vary, so the liability of the principal varies depending on the way in which the agent does business. For example, an officer of a corporation has the authority to bind the corporation, but what if the officer does not disclose that there is a principal corporation? This section deals with those issues.

The Disclosed Principal

In a situation in which a third party is aware a principal is involved and also knows who the principal is, the principal is liable to the third party, but the agent is not, regardless of whether the agent has express, implied, or apparent authority. If the agent has no authority, however, then the agent, not the principal, is liable. For example, suppose that Paula Abbaduhla is the vice president of Video Television, Inc., and she signs for a line of credit for the corporation at First Bank. As long as she signed the documents "Video Television, Inc., by Paula Abbaduhla, VP," Video would be solely responsible for the line of credit. If, however, she signed that same way but had no authority, she would be liable to Video if it had to honor the agreement. As another example, most title insurers and escrow companies require corporations selling or buying real property to have board authorization in the form of a resolution. If Paula signed to buy land and did not have a resolution, she would have no express authority, and without implied or apparent authority, she would be liable for the land contract. (See Chapter 20 for a more thorough discussion of board resolutions and officers' authority.)

The Partially Disclosed Principal

In this situation, the third party knows that the agent is acting for someone else, but the identity of the principal is not disclosed. For example, an agent might be used to purchase land for development purposes when the developer does not want to be disclosed because disclosure of a major developer's involvement might drive up land prices. In this situation, the third-party seller of the land can hold either the principal or the agent liable on the contract. The agent assumes some risk of personal liability by not disclosing the identity of the principal.

The Undisclosed Principal

In this situation, an agent acts without disclosing either the existence of a principal or the principal's identity. Again, such an arrangement might be undertaken to avoid speculation, or it could be intended simply to protect someone's privacy, such as when a famous person purchases a home and does not want any advance disclosure of the purchase or its location. Here, the agent is directly liable to the third party. If the third party discovers the identity of the principal, the third party could hold either the principal or the agent liable. Exhibits 17.1 and 17.2 provide summaries of the liability of agents and principals under the three forms of disclosure of the relationship.

EXHIBIT 17.1   Contract Liability of Disclosed Principal

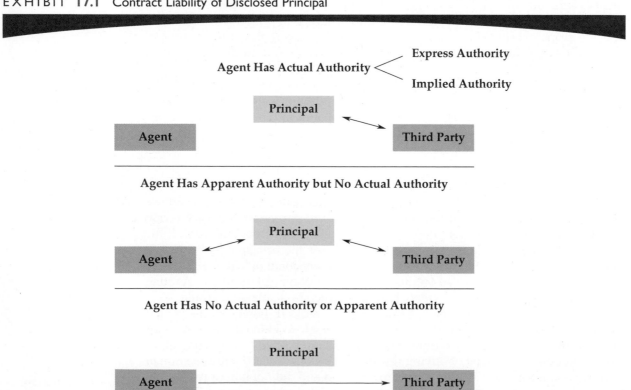

EXHIBIT 17.2   Contract Liability of Undisclosed or Partially Disclosed Principal

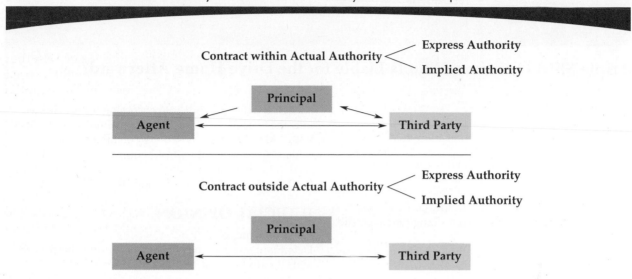

Liability of Principals for Agents' Torts

The liability of principals for torts committed by agents is controlled is by the type of agency relationship—master–servant or independent contractor and by the type of conduct.

Master–Servant Relationship

As discussed earlier in the chapter, the liability of a principal for the acts of a servant differs from that for the acts of an independent contractor. The principal is liable for the torts of the servant—an agent whose work, assignments, and time are controlled by the principal.

Scope of Employment

Employers (principals) are liable for the conduct of employees (agents/servants) while those employees are acting in the **scope of employment.** Scope of employment means that an employee is doing work for an employer at the time a tort occurs. Suppose a florist delivery driver, while delivering flowers, has an auto accident that is the delivery driver's fault. In addition to the driver's responsibility for the negligence in the accident, the florist is also liable to injured parties under the doctrine of *respondent superior.*

Scope of employment has been defined broadly by the courts. Negligent torts committed while an employee is driving to a sales call or delivery are clearly within the scope of employment.

An employee who takes the afternoon off is not within the scope of employment, and the principal is not liable if an accident occurs during that time. When an employee begins acting on personal business, the scope of employment ends. An employee who uses the lunch hour to shop is not within the scope of employment. Likewise, an employer who requires an employee to use his lunch hour to run errands for the company has changed personal time into scope-of-employment time. *Faverty v McDonald's Restaurants of Oregon, Inc.* (Case 17.4) deals with an issue of when the scope of employment ends, in a timing sense.

CASE 17.4

Faverty v McDonald's Restaurants of Oregon, Inc.
892 P.2d 703 (Ct. App. Or. 1995)

Triple Shift Overtime: Who Is Liable for the Drive Home Afterward?

FACTS

Matt Theurer was an 18-year-old high school senior with many extracurricular activities, including being a member of the National Guard. Mr. Theurer was employed by a McDonald's restaurant (defendant) in Portland, Oregon, on a part-time basis. While his employer called Mr. Theurer an enthusiastic worker, his friends and family felt that he was doing too much and getting too little sleep.

McDonald's employed many high school students on a part-time basis, and their restaurants closed at 11:00 P.M., with clean-up and other procedures taking up another hour until midnight. McDonald's informal policy did not permit high school students to work more than one midnight shift per week or allow split shifts. Split shifts forced the students to work in the morning and then evening. McDonald's felt the commuting time between the shifts prevented "people from getting their rest." Despite these policies, high school employees frequently complained about being tired, and at least two of McDonald's employees had accidents while driving home after working the closing shift until midnight.

A few times each year, McDonald's scheduled special cleanup projects at the restaurant that required employees to work after the midnight closing until 5 A.M. Student workers were to be used for cleanup shifts only on weekends or during spring break. However, for one scheduled cleanup project, there were not enough regular employees, and the manager asked for volunteers for a midnight to 5 A.M. cleanup shift. Mr. Theurer volunteered; the manager knew that Mr. Theurer had to drive about 20 minutes to and from work.

During the week of the scheduled special cleanup, Mr. Theurer had worked five nights. One night he worked until midnight, another until 11:30 P.M., two until 9 P.M., and another until 11 P.M. On Monday, April 4, 1988, Mr. Theurer worked his regular shift from 3:30 until 7:30 P.M., followed by a cleanup shift beginning at midnight until 5 A.M. on April 5, and then worked another shift from 5 A.M. until 8:21 A.M. During that shift, Mr. Theurer told his manager that he was tired and asked to be excused from his next regular shift. The manager excused him, and Mr. Theurer began his drive home.

Mr. Theurer was driving 45 miles per hour on a two-lane road when he became drowsy or fell asleep, crossed the dividing line into oncoming traffic, crashed into the van of Frederic Faverty (plaintiff), and was killed. Mr. Faverty was seriously injured. Mr. Faverty settled his claims with Mr. Theurer's estate and then filed suit against McDonald's. The jury found for Mr. Faverty, and McDonald's appealed.

JUDICIAL OPINION

LANDAU, Judge

Defendant argues that it was Theurer's employer and, because of that relationship, it was subject to a limited duty to both Theurer and plaintiff, as a matter of law.

According to defendant, there is no evidence that it knew or should have known that Theurer was so exhausted or fatigued that it should have foreseen that working him three shifts in one 24-hour period would create a foreseeable risk of harm to motorists such as plaintiff. Plaintiff argues that defendant failed to preserve that argument and that, in any event, the evidence is sufficient to support the trial court's ruling.

There is evidence that defendant controlled all work assignments. Therefore, defendant knew or had reason to know of the number of hours Theurer had been working. There also is evidence that defendant ordinarily did not use high school students to work after midnight, and when it did, it tried to limit that late shift to once a week. Defendant also had a policy of not working its employees two shifts in one day. According to at least one of the defendant's managers, those policies were adopted and enforced out of concern that employees not become overly tired on the job. In fact, defendant was aware that at least two of its employees had recently had automobile accidents as a result of falling asleep while driving home after working late shifts. There is evidence that, during and after his late-night shift, Theurer was visibly fatigued, and that defendant's managers were on site and saw Theurer throughout that shift. It is undisputed that defendant knew that Theurer was a high school student, and that most of the high school students who worked there drove to work in their own cars. On the basis of that evidence, a reasonable jury could conclude that defendant knew or should have known that working Theurer so many hours would impair his ability to drive home safely.

Defendant and the dissent insist that, because Theurer "volunteered" to work so many hours, the evidence simply is insufficient to establish defendant's negligence, as a matter of law. The evidence shows that defendant—not its employees—generally controlled all work assignments and that defendant penalized its employees for not working as assigned.

Second, even indulging the assumption that Theurer volunteered for his all-night shift, the evidence still is sufficient to support the jury's verdict. Defendant's managers knew that Theurer already had been scheduled to work more than its own policies permitted. Moreover, they saw him in a visibly fatigued state and continued to work him as scheduled. In that regard, defendant was much like a bartender who served alcoholic beverages to a visibly intoxicated person who then caused an automobile accident that harmed another. No one required the intoxicated person to have the extra drink. He or she asked for the drink and "volunteered" to pay for it. Nevertheless, the courts have held that, because the bartender saw the driver in a visibly intoxicated state, and it is reasonably foreseeable that the customer will drive when he or she leaves, the bartender is liable for the consequences of the automobile accident.

Finally, defendant itself conceded at trial that, if it had allowed Theurer to "volunteer" to work around the clock three full days, the "court can almost say as a matter of law, allowing someone to work that long without any rest or sleep might very well constitute affirmative misconduct by an employer, but [it] may be a matter of degrees. . . ."

Defendant, the dissent and the *amid curiae* the National Council of Chain Restaurants and the Defense Research Institute, Inc., implore us to reverse the trial court's judgment on the public policy ground that the result is "patently unreasonable," "shocking," "far-fetched" and "goes beyond the commonsense application of tort law." However, that argument was not made to the trial court, and we will not consider it for the first time on appeal.

Affirmed.

DISSENTING OPINION

EDMUNDS, Judge

The majority need have gone no further than defendant's motion for a directed verdict in deciding this case. Defendant is entitled to a directed verdict as a matter of law because of certain uncontroverted facts. First, Theurer was not a minor, but an adult at the time of the accident. He was 18 years old and serving in the National Guard. Defendant did not owe any special responsibility to him because he also attended high school. The fact that he was a student working part time and had over-extended himself physically is of no import to defendant's liability. No rule of negligence requires an employer to inquire into the private lives of its adult employees to determine if, on a given occasion, the employee is not getting enough sleep.

Second, Theurer volunteered to work the cleanup shift. He was not sought out by defendant and "required" to work on April 5, 1988.

Third, Theurer never asked to be relieved from working the shift either before the shift started or during it; nor is there any evidence that defendant refused such a request.

Fourth, Theurer was not on defendant's business premises and was on his own time when he drove home from work that morning. Theurer was not acting on defendant's behalf, nor did defendant have actual control of or the right to control Theurer's driving conduct or where he went after he got off work. Moreover, no omission or affirmative act by defendant prevented Theurer from choosing to have someone pick him up after work, or to take a nap in his car before driving home, or some other preventive measure. . . .

In effect, the opinion says to Oregon employers, "Do not schedule your employees in a manner that will cause fatigue, because if you do, you risk liability for negligence in the event that your employee acts in a negligent manner off-premises and after work." That is not the law of this state and it cannot be unreasonable conduct for an employer to accept an offer from an adult employee, made days in advance of the shift, to work overtime, insofar as the safety of motorists is concerned after the employee gets off work. Because the majority opinion extends the duty of care owed to the general public by employers in the scheduling of their employees' work shifts to beyond any reasonable boundary, I dissent.

CASE QUESTIONS

1. Of what significance is the fact that Mr. Theurer volunteered for the all-night shift?

2. Why would a restaurant association have an interest in the outcome of the case?

3. Did McDonald's violate any Oregon statute?

4. Was Mr. Theurer acting within the scope of employment?

5. Is McDonald's liable to Mr. Faverty?

6. What counterpoints does the dissenting judge make?

Aftermath: Some courts have declined to follow the decision in this case. In *Behrens v Harrah's Illinois Corp.* 852 N.E.2d 553 (Ill. 2006), the court did not allow the family of an employee to recover from the employer when she experienced catastrophic

CONTINUED

injuries following a rollover accident that occurred when she was driving home from work after being required to work overtime at the casino. A hospital is not liable for injuries caused by a sleep-deprived doctor working extra hours at the hospital [*Brewster v Rush-Presbyterian-St. Luke's Medical Center*, 836 N.E.2d 635 (111. App. 2005)]. However, other courts have followed the decision, In *Bussard v Minimed, Inc.*, 105 Cal.App.4th 798,129 Cal.Rptr.2d 675 (2003), an employer was held liable to a third party under a *respondeat superior* theory where the employee became dizzy and light-headed after being exposed to pesticides at work and, while driving home, struck a car driven by the third party.

Generally, intentional acts not authorized by employers do not result in liability. However, under the theories of the **negligent failure to supervise** and **negligent hiring,** an employer may have liability for inaction when it has notice of the violent tendencies of an employee. The 1973 *Lange v National Biscuit Co.* case (Case 17.5) opened the door for recovery from employers for the intentional acts of employees in certain well-defined circumstances. This case also provides the answer for the chapter's opening "Consider."

CASE 17.5

Lange v National Biscuit Co.
211 N.W.2d 783 (Minn. 1973)

Shelf Space Is My Life: Flipping Out over Oreos

FACTS

Jerome Lange (plaintiff) was the manager of a small grocery store in Minnesota that carried Nabisco (defendant) products. Ronnell Lynch had been hired by Nabisco as a cookie salesman–trainee in October 1968. On March 1, 1969, Mr. Lynch was assigned his own territory, which included Mr. Lange's store.

Between March 1 and May 1, 1969, Nabisco received numerous complaints from grocers about Mr. Lynch being overly aggressive and taking shelf space in the stores reserved for competing cookie companies.

On May 1, 1969, Mr. Lynch came to Mr. Lange's store to place Nabisco merchandise on the shelves. An argument developed between the two over Mr. Lynch's service to the store. Mr. Lynch became very angry and started swearing. Mr. Lange told him to either stop swearing or leave the store because children were present. Mr. Lynch then became uncontrollably angry and said, "I ought to break your neck." He then went behind the counter and dared Mr. Lange to fight. When Mr. Lange refused, Mr. Lynch viciously assaulted him, after which he threw cookies around the store and left.

Mr. Lange filed suit against Nabisco and was awarded damages based on the jury's finding that although the acts of Mr. Lynch were outside the scope of employment, Nabisco was negligent in hiring and retaining him. The judge granted Nabisco's motion for judgment notwithstanding the verdict, and Mr. Lange appealed.

JUDICIAL OPINION

TODD, Justice

There is no dispute with the general principle that in order to impose liability on the employer under the doctrine of *respondeat superior* it is necessary to show that the employee was acting within the scope of his employment. Unfortunately, there is a wide disparity in the case law in the application of the "scope of employment" test to those factual situations involving intentional torts. The majority rule as set out in Annotation, 34 A.L.R.2d 372, 402, includes a twofold test: (a) Whether the assault was motivated by business or personal considerations; or (b) whether the assault was contemplated by the employer or incident to the employment.

Under the present Minnesota rule, liability is imposed where it is shown that the employee's acts were motivated by a desire to further the employer's business. Therefore, a master could only be held liable for an employee's assault in those rare instances where the master actually requested the servant to so perform, or the servant's duties were such that that motivation was implied in law.

The fallacy of this reasoning was that it made a certain mental condition of the servant the test by which to determine whether he was acting about his master's business or not. Moreover, with respect of all intentional acts done by a servant in the supposed furtherance of his master's business, it clothed the master with immunity if the act was right, because it was right, and, if it was wrong, it clothed him with a like immunity, because it was wrong. He thus got the benefit of all his servant's acts done for him, whether right or wrong, and escaped the burden of all intentional acts done for him which were wrong. Under the operation of such a rule, it would always be more safe and profitable for a man to conduct his business vicariously than in his own person. He would escape liability for the consequences of many acts connected with his business springing from the imperfection of human nature, because done by another, for which he would be responsible if done by himself. Meanwhile, the public, obliged to deal or come in contact with his agents, for intentional injuries done by them, might be left wholly without redress. . . . A doctrine so fruitful of mischief could not long stand unshaken in an enlightened system of jurisprudence.

In developing a test for the application of *respondent superior* when an employee assaults a third person, we believe that the focus should be on the basis of the assault rather than the motivation of the employee. We reject as the basis for imposing liability the arbitrary determination of when, and at what point, the argument and assault leave the sphere of the employer's business and become motivated by personal animosity. Rather, we believe the better approach is to view both the argument and assault as an indistinguishable event for purposes of vicarious liability.

We hold that an employer is liable for an assault by his employee when the source of the attack is related to the duties of the employee and the assault occurs within work-related limits of time and place. The assault in this case obviously occurred within work-related limits of time and place, since it took place on authorized premises during working hours. The precipitating cause of the initial argument concerned the employee's conduct of his work. In addition, the employee originally was motivated to become argumentative in furtherance of his employer's business. Consequently, under the facts of this case we hold as a matter of law that the employee was acting within the scope of employment at the time of the aggression and that plaintiff's post-trial motion for judgment notwithstanding the verdict on that ground should have been granted under the rule we herein adopt. To the extent that our former decisions are inconsistent with the rule now adopted, they are overruled.

Plaintiff may recover damages under either the theory of *respondeat superior* or negligence. Having disposed of the matter on the former issue, we need not undertake the questions raised by defendant's asserted negligence in the hiring or retention of the employee.

Reversed and remanded.

CASE QUESTIONS

1. What previous indications did Nabisco have that Mr. Lynch might cause some problems?

2. What test does the court give for determining scope of employment?

3. What is the "motivation test," and does this court accept or reject it?

Negligent Hiring and Supervision

The *Lange* case provided the types of circumstances in which employers could be liable for the tort of negligent hiring and/or supervision of employees. Negligent hiring requires proof that the principal/employer hired an agent/ employee whose background made her ill suited for the position. For example, a school district that does not check the background of a bus driver or teacher, particularly for past charges or history of child abuse and molestation, has committed the tort of negligent hiring. Negligent supervision liability results when an employer has been put on notice that an employee has engaged in behavior that is harmful to others but leaves the employee in his position. An example is a college or university leaving a professor in the classroom after having received complaints regarding his inappropriate conduct in class and with students. If the professor then harms one of his students, the college or university would be liable to the student for the failure to make a timely termination, suspension, or other action to remove the professor from student contact or at least provide appropriate monitoring of the professor with the students. *Doe v Norwich Roman Catholic Diocesan Corp.* (Case 17.6) involves a sensitive issue that revolves around the question of negligence in hiring and supervision.

**CASE
17.6**

Doe v Norwich Roman Catholic Diocesan Corp.
268 F.Supp.2d 139 (Conn. 2003)

Confessing Liability

FACTS

Jane Doe (plaintiff) brought suit against the St. Columba Church and the Norwich Diocese (defendants) alleging that while a parishioner at St. Columba Church, she was sexually assaulted and abused by Patrick Sullivan, a Roman Catholic priest assigned to perform various tasks on behalf of the Diocese and St. Columba. From 1968 through 1969, Sullivan allegedly sexually abused the plaintiff, who was 15 to 16 years old at the time. The alleged sexual abuse occurred at various locations, including the St. Columba rectory.

The Diocese moved to dismiss the complaint.

JUDICIAL OPINION

GOETTEL, District Judge

Cases of sexual abuse often represent such a strong deviation from furthering an employer's business. In most cases of alleged sexual abuse by priests, the courts have held that *respondent superior* is not applicable to hold a church or diocese liable, because such acts by the priests are not in furtherance of the church's business. See *Nutt v Norwich Roman Catholic Diocese*, 921 F.Supp. 66, 71 (D.Conn.1995).

In *Nutt*, former altar boys claimed that a priest had shown them pornographic movies and taken them on trips where he engaged in sexual abuse. The court noted that the Roman Catholic Church expressly forbids its priests from engaging in any sexual activity, so any form of sexually abusive acts would demonstrate abandonment of the church's business; thus, the court granted the defendant church's and diocese's motions for summary judgment on all counts relating to *respondeat superior*. . . .

Plaintiff has merely made the conclusory statement that "Sullivan was acting within the scope of his duties as a Roman Catholic priest for the Defendant Diocese and/or the Defendant St. Columba Church and within the scope of his employment with the aforementioned Defendants and in furtherance of their business purpose." As a Roman Catholic priest, Sullivan would have abandoned the business of the Church by engaging in sexual conduct with Plaintiff, which is expressly forbidden, so as a matter of law it could not be shown that his actions were in furtherance of Church business.

Plaintiff urges us to deny the motion because *respondeat superior* has been applied in some cases of sexual abuse by priests, but those cases involved very unique circumstances, which are not present here. See *Martinelli v Bridgeport Roman Catholic Diocesan Corp.*, 989 F.Supp. 110, 118 (D. Conn. 1997). In *Martinelli*, the plaintiff claimed that a priest attempted to teach the sacraments to him and other teenage boys by using sexual contact. The district court denied summary judgment for the diocese, because there was a genuine dispute as to whether the priest's activities represented a "total departure from the [d]iocese's business."

Unlike *Martinelli*, in this case, Plaintiff has not alleged any facts to indicate that the nature of the alleged sexual acts by the priest somehow furthered the Church's business. The allegations of this case are more similar to those cases where the courts have found that as a matter of law *respondeat superior* does not apply. . . .

Here, Plaintiff has broadly alleged negligent hiring and supervision of Sullivan by St. Columba and Diocese. As we construe her claims, they do not involve the entanglement of this Court with the church's religious practices. . . .

At this point, all we are concerned with is whether Plaintiff has alleged enough to state a claim. Even though some of the allegations are quite broad, they do provide sufficient information from which knowledge could be inferred, even if it is not explicitly alleged. . . .

Nevertheless, we again caution both parties that just as this Court will not entangle itself in the Church's religious practices or doctrine, it will not examine the specific employment practices of the Church and Diocese unless they clearly indicate that Defendants knew or should have known that Sullivan was likely to engage in sexual misconduct. It is not the place of this Court to determine the fitness of individuals for the priesthood or the internal policies that are maintained to promote the clergy's morality. We are merely concerned with whether Defendants had knowledge or should have known about Sullivan's alleged misconduct.

Diocese argues that even if it and St. Columba had a duty to Plaintiff, they should not be liable, because the "proximate cause of the plaintiff's alleged injuries must necessarily have been the alleged sexual misconduct of . . . Sullivan and not any breach of duty on the part of the Diocese . . . or St. Columba."

At this point we simply do not have enough facts regarding Defendants' knowledge of Sullivan's alleged misconduct to make a determination regarding whether

Defendants could have proximately caused the harm. A motion to dismiss is often ill-suited for disposing of proximate cause without the benefit of evidence indicating the Defendants' knowledge, and it would be would be premature and inappropriate to dismiss the negligence claim at this stage of the pleadings, even though Plaintiff may have difficulty ultimately proving knowledge, and therefore, proximate cause.

Accordingly, we DENY Defendants' Motion to Dismiss.

CASE QUESTIONS

1. What is the general position of the courts on the liability of churches and dioceses for the sexual misconduct of priests?

2. What must a plaintiff allege to be able to recover from a church or diocese?

3. What must a plaintiff prove to be able to recover from a church or diocese?

4. Is there liability for negligent supervision of priests?

CONSIDER... 17.5

Oklahoma Nursing Homes, Ltd. employed numerous health care professionals at its various nursing homes, including nurse's aides, who assisted occupants of the homes with daily activities such as eating, bathing, and dressing.

Glen Rodebush, a person with Alzheimer's disease, was a resident of one of the company's homes. His condition caused him to be combative sometimes. Mr. Rodebush's wife, Zelda, arrived one day for a visit and discovered large welts and red marks on his face. Mrs. Rodebush called her husband's doctor, who found that the marks were caused by slaps of the human hand and were 6 to 12 hours old. Earlier in the day, Mr. Rodebush had been bathed by a male nurse's aide and, during the course of the bath, Mr. Rodebush had become unruly. Following the bath, a supervisor noted that the aide smelled of liquor and saw from his time card that he had arrived 30 minutes late. The nurse's aide confessed that he had "partied all night." The aide had been hired without a background check. Following the incident and Mrs. Rodebush's complaint about the marks, the company discovered that the aide had a felony conviction for violent assault and battery with intent to kill, escape, and carrying a weapon following conviction of a felony.

The company, which had never given the aide training, had been cited by the State Department of Human Services for violations of reporting requirements as well as the failure to take proper steps against employees who report to work while intoxicated.

Mrs. Rodebush has filed suit against the nursing home on behalf of her husband. The nursing home claims it cannot be held liable for the intentional and unauthorized acts of its employees. Who is correct? Should there be recovery? [*Rodebush v Oklahoma Nursing Homes, Ltd.*, 867 R2d 1241 (Okl. 1993)]

The liability of principals for the torts of agents has become a costly part of doing business. Many firms are undertaking various forms of testing to prevent employees who could cause injuries from driving, operating machinery, or otherwise working in situations in which human safety is an issue. The courts have upheld the employer's right to test for the presence of drugs and alcohol when the firms can show a public safety need established by the employee's contact with the public during the course of employment.

Independent Contractors

Principals are not generally liable for the torts of independent contractors, but three exceptions apply to this general no-liability rule. The first exception covers

inherently dangerous activities, which are those that cannot be made safe. For example, using dynamite to demolish old buildings is an inherently dangerous activity. Without this liability exception, a principal could hire an independent contractor to perform the task and then assume no responsibility for the damages or injuries that might result.

The second exception to the no-liability rule occurs when a principal negligently hires an independent contractor. A landlord who hires a security guard, therefore, must check that guard's background because if a tenant's property is stolen by a guard with a criminal record, the landlord is responsible. Similarly, if a principal hires independent contractors knowing of their past employment history, the principal is liable for the conduct of those independent contractors. A business that hires a collection agency to collect past-due accounts, knowing that agency's reputation for violence, is liable for the agency's torts even though they are independent contractors.

The third exception is the situation in which the principal has provided the specifications for the independent contractor's procedures or process. Because the independent contractor is required to follow the principal's directions, the principal will also have liability.

Termination of the Agency Relationship

An agency relationship can end in several different ways. First, the parties can have a definite duration for the agency relationship. A listing agreement for the sale of real property usually ends after 90 days. An agency can also end because the agent quits or the principal fires the agent. When the principal dies or is incapacitated, an agency ends automatically because the agent no longer has anyone to contract on behalf of.

Although the agency relationship ends easily when an agent is fired or quits, the authority of the agent does not end so abruptly or easily. An agent can still have **lingering apparent authority** that exists beyond the termination of the agency in relation to third parties who are unaware of the agency termination. For example, if the purchasing agent for a corporation retires after 25 years, the agency that consists of actual authority (express and implied authority) between the agent and corporation has ended. However, departure, retirement, and termination do not end apparent authority. Many customers are used to dealing with the agent and may not be aware of the end of the agency. That purchasing agent could still bind the principal corporation even though the agent's actual authority has ended. The principal corporation can end lingering apparent authority by giving public or **constructive notice** or private or **actual notice.** Public notice is publication of the resignation. Many trade magazines and business newspapers publish announcements and personal columns about business associate changes and other personnel news. Even though not everyone dealing with the agent may see the notice, these public notices are deemed to serve as constructive notice. However, the principal must also give private notice to those firms that have dealt with the agent or have been creditors in the past. This notice is accomplished by sending a letter to each firm or individual that has dealt with the agent. Without this notice, the agent's apparent authority lingers with respect to those third parties who have not received notice.

EXHIBIT 17.3 The Do's and Don'ts of Laying People Off

DO	DON'T
Conduct regular reviews of employees, using objective, uniform measures of performance.	Don't make oral promises of job security to employees who might later be laid off. **Danger: breach-of-contract suit.**
Give clear, business-related reasons for any dismissal, backed by written documentation when possible.	Don't put pressure on an employee to resign in order to avoid getting fired. **Danger: coercion suit.**
Seek legal waivers from older workers who agree to leave under an early-retirement plan, and make sure they understand the waiver terms in advance.	Don't make derogatory remarks about any dismissed worker, even if asked for a reference by a prospective employer. **Danger: defamation suit.**
Follow any written company guidelines for termination, or be prepared to show in court why they're not binding in any particular instance.	Don't offer a fired employee a face-saving reason for the dismissal that's unrelated to poor performance. **Danger: wrongful-discharge suit.**

Source: "Layoffs Take Careful Planning to Avoid Losing the Suits That Are Apt to Follow," *Wall Street Journal*, November 2, 1990, p. 131, by Arthur S. Hayes. Copyright © 1990 by Dow Jones & Company, Inc. Reprinted by permission of Dow Jones & Company, Inc. via the Copyright Clearance Center.

Termination of Agents Under Employment at Will

Most employees do not have written contracts that specify the start and duration of their employment. Rather, most employees work at the discretion of their employers, which is to say that they have **employment at will.** Recent cases have placed some restrictions on this employer freedom to hire and fire at will, as courts have been giving employees/agents the benefit of their reliance. Employees have based their protection rights on several theories, including implied contract and public policy. Exhibit 17.3 summarizes the "do's" and "don'ts" of terminating employees.

The Implied Contract

Many courts have implied the existence of a contract because of the presence of promises, procedures, and policies in an employee personnel manual. Personnel manuals have been held to constitute, both expressly and impliedly, employee contracts or to become part of the employee contracts when they are given to employees at the outset. One of the factors that determines whether a personnel manual and its terms constitute a contract is the reliance of an employee on its procedures and terms.

Because the employee manual represents a potential contract for the employer, its nature and content should be considered carefully. Of the two approaches to employee manuals, one takes a detailed approach in which all rules, rights, and expectations are carefully established. Another approach is the simple one, in which overall general policies and rights are established with details to be filled in as individual issues arise. *Dillon v Champion Jogbra, Inc.* (Case 17.7) deals with one state's view on the issue of implied contract.

CASE 17.7 *Dillon v Champion Jogbra, Inc.*
819 A.2d 703 (Vt. 2002)

Letting a Champion Employee Go

FACTS

Linda Dillon began working for Jogbra part-time in January 1997. She was hired as a full-time employee in August 1997 in the position of charge-back analyst. In the summer of 1998, the position of sales administrator was going to become vacant. Ms. Dillon was approached by Jogbra management about applying for the position, which started on July 31. She eventually decided to apply and interviewed for the position. In the course of interviewing, Ms. Dillon recalls that she was told that she would receive "extensive training." The human resources manager told her that she would overlap with her predecessor, who would train her during those days. However, in the course of Ms. Dillon's interview with the vice president of sales, who would be her immediate supervisor, he informed her that her predecessor was actually leaving earlier and would be available for only two days of training before Ms. Dillon started the job. He reassured her, though, that the predecessor would be brought back sometime thereafter for more training. Ms. Dillon also recalls that he told her that "it will take you four to six months to feel comfortable with [the] position" and not to be concerned about it. Ms. Dillon accepted the position and spent most of her predecessor's remaining two days with her. Her predecessor then returned in early September for an additional two days of training. Ms. Dillon stated that she felt that, after the supplemental training, she had received sufficient training for the job.

On September 29, Ms. Dillon was called into her supervisor's office. The human resources manager was also present. They informed Ms. Dillon that things were not working out and that she was going to be reassigned to a temporary position, at the same pay and benefit level, which ended in December. She was told that she should apply for other jobs within the company, but if nothing suitable became available, she would be terminated at the end of December. According to Ms. Dillon, her supervisor stated that he had concluded within 10 days of her starting that "it wasn't going to work out." Prior to the meeting, Ms. Dillon was never told her job was in jeopardy, nor did Jogbra follow the procedures laid out in its employee manual when terminating her.

Ms. Dillon applied for one job that became available in the ensuing months but was not selected for it. She

left Jogbra in December when her temporary position terminated. Ms. Dillon then brought suit against Jogbra for wrongful termination. She asserted claims for breach of contract and promissory estoppel. Jogbra filed a motion for summary judgment, which the trial court granted. Ms. Dillon appealed.

JUDICIAL OPINION

MORSE, Justice

We affirm with respect to Dillon's claim for promissory estoppel, but reverse and remand on her breach of contract claim.

Jogbra has an employee manual that it distributes to all employees at the time of their employment. The first page of the manual states the following in capitalized print:

The policies and procedures contained in this manual constitute guidelines only. They do not constitute part of an employment contract, nor are they intended to make any commitment to any employee concerning how individual employment action can, should, or will be handled.

Champion Jogbra offers no employment contracts nor does it guarantee any minimum length of employment. Champion Jogbra reserves the right to terminate any employee at any time "at will," with or without cause.

During the period from 1996 to 1997, however, Jogbra developed what it termed a "Corrective Action Procedure." This procedure established a progressive discipline system for employees and different categories of disciplinary infractions. It states that it applies to all employees and will be carried out in "a fair and consistent manner." Much of the language in the section is mandatory in tone.

. . . [A]n employer may modify an at-will employment agreement unilaterally. When determining whether an employer has done so, we look to both the employer's written policies and its practices. An employer not only may implicitly bind itself to terminating only for cause through its manual and practices, but may also be bound by a commitment to use only certain procedures in doing so.

When the terms of a manual are ambiguous, however, or send mixed messages regarding an employee's status, the question of whether the presumptive at-will status has been modified is properly left to the jury.

This may be the case even if there is a disclaimer stating employment is at-will, as the presence of such a disclaimer is not dispositive in the determination. Furthermore, an employer's practices can provide context for and help inform the determination. The question of whether a written manual is ambiguous is a determination of law that we review *de novo*. In this case, we cannot agree with the trial court that the terms of Jogbra's manual are unambiguous.

Notwithstanding the disclaimer contained on the first page of the manual quoted above, the manual goes on to establish in Policy No. 720 an elaborate system governing employee discipline and discharge. It states as its purpose: "To establish Champion Jogbra policy for all employees." It states that actions will be carried out "in a fair and consistent manner." It provides that "[t]he Corrective Action Policy requires management to use training and employee counseling to achieve the desired actions of employees." It establishes three categories of violations of company policy and corresponding actions to be generally taken in each case. It delineates progressive steps to be taken for certain types of cases, including "[u]nsatisfactory quality of work," and time periods governing things such as how long a reprimand is considered "active." All of these terms are inconsistent with the disclaimer at the beginning of the manual, in effect sending mixed messages to employees. Furthermore, these terms appear to be inconsistent with an at-will employment relationship, its classic formulation being that an employer can fire an employee "for good cause or for no cause, or even for bad cause."

With respect to the record before the court on Jogbra's employment practices, Dillon herself was aware of at least one employee whose termination was carried out pursuant to the terms set forth in the manual. She also testified in her deposition to conversations with the human resources manager, with whom she was friendly, in which the manager had described certain procedures used for firing employees. She stated that the manager had told her that Jogbra could not "just get rid of" people, but instead had to follow procedures. The human resources manager herself testified that "she could only recall two instances in which the portion of the manual providing for documentation of progressive action was not followed, one of which resulted in a legal claim against the company and the other of which involved an employee stealing from the company. In fact, the manual specifically provides that stealing "will normally result in discharge on the first offense." Thus, it is not clear how that discharge deviated from the provisions of the manual.

In conclusion, the manual itself is at the very least ambiguous regarding employees' status, and Jogbra's

employment practices appear from the record to be both consistent with the manual and inconsistent with an at-will employment arrangement. Therefore, summary judgment was not proper on Dillon's breach of implied contract claim. . . .

We have held that, even if an employee otherwise enjoys only at-will employment status, that employee may still be able to establish a claim for wrongful termination under a theory of promissory estoppel if that employee can demonstrate that the termination was in breach of a specific promise made by the employer that the employer should have reasonably expected to induce detrimental reliance on the part of the employee, and that the employee did in fact detrimentally rely on the promise. We agree with the trial court in this case, however, that essential elements of promissory estoppel are absent with regard to both statements.

With respect to Jogbra's promise to Dillon that she would receive training, Dillon specifically conceded that, upon her predecessor's return in September, she had received adequate training to perform the job. In other words, Jogbra had delivered on its promise. Furthermore, even assuming that Jogbra failed to provide the full extent of promised training, Dillon has failed to explain how, as a matter of law, the promise of training modified her at-will status. In other words, it is not clear from Dillon's brief how the promise of training foreclosed Jogbra from nevertheless terminating her either on an at-will basis or for cause. . . .

With respect to the assurance that it would take four to six months to become comfortable with the position, the statement cannot reasonably be relied upon as a promise of employment in the sales administrator position for a set period of time. Courts have generally required a promise of a specific and definite nature before holding an employer bound by it.

In sum, the trial court properly granted Jogbra summary judgment on Dillon's promissory estoppel claim. The grant of summary judgment on Linda Dillon's claim for promissory estoppel is affirmed; the grant of summary judgment on her breach of contract claim is reversed and remanded.

DISSENTING OPINION

AMESTOY, Chief Justice, dissenting

In support of employee's contention that employer's practices were at odds with an at-will policy, employee cites to her own deposition, wherein she claimed to have known of other employees who received progressive discipline prior to termination. When pressed, however, employee admitted that, of the three employees with whose discharge she was

CONTINUED

familiar, she could state with certainty that only one received progressive discipline. Moreover, employee stated that she was unfamiliar with the manner in which the other two employees' cases were handled prior to their discharge. While her own experience is relevant, it does not by itself suggest a definitive company-wide practice. Hearsay statements about what employee "had heard" is insufficient to raise a genuine issue.

CASE QUESTIONS

1. What is the effect of the disclaimer in the Jogbra employment manual?
2. What is the importance of an ambiguity?
3. Why is there no promissory estoppel claim?
4. What changes the application of the employment-at-will doctrine to Dillon?
5. What is the dissenting justice's concern?

The Public Policy Exception

In a second group of employment-at-will cases, the courts have afforded protection to those employees called **whistleblowers** who report illegal conduct and to those who refuse to participate in conduct that is illegal or that violates public policy. For example, an employee was found to be wrongfully discharged when fired after supplying information to police who were investigating alleged criminal violations by a co-employee [*Palmateer v International Harvester Co.*, 421 N.E.2d 876 (Ill. 1981)]. Other cases in which courts have found a wrongful discharge involve a refusal by an employee to commit perjury, a refusal by an employee to participate in price fixing, and an employee-reported violation of the Food, Drug, and Cosmetic Act. There are significant statutory protections for whistleblowers at the state and federal level that prohibit retaliation against employees who report matters covered by the statute and allow these employees to recover damages for the retaliatory conduct by the employer. (See Chapter 21 for more information about whistleblower protections for employees who report financial fraud.)

In *Gardner v Loomis Armored, Inc.* (Case 17.8), a court deals with the issue of an employer firing an employee who has taken action in an area not directly related to his employment.

| CASE 17.8 | *Gardner v Loomis Armored, Inc.*
913 P.2d 377 (Wash. 1996) |

Termination for Helping During a Knife Attack

FACTS

Kevin Gardner is a driver with Loomis Armored, Inc., which is a company that supplies armored truck delivery services to banks, businesses, and others requiring secure transport of funds and other valuables. Because of the safety and liability issues surrounding armored truck deliveries, Loomis has adopted a policy for all drivers that their trucks cannot be left unattended. The policy is provided in

the employee handbook and the penalty for violation of the rule is stated as follows:

Violations of this rule will be grounds for termination.

While Mr. Gardner was making a scheduled stop at a bank for a pickup of funds, he noticed a woman being threatened with a knife by an obviously agitated man. Mr. Gardner left his truck unattended as he went to the aid of the woman. The woman was saved and her assailant apprehended, and Mr. Gardner was then fired by Loomis for violating the company policy of not leaving the truck unattended. Mr. Gardner filed suit for wrongful termination in violation of public policy.

JUDICIAL OPINION

DOLLIVER, Justice

The narrow public policy encouraging citizens to rescue persons from life threatening situations clearly evinces [demonstrates] a fundamental societal interest. . . . The value attached to such acts of heroism is plainly demonstrated by the fact that society has waived most criminal and tort penalties stemming from conduct necessarily committed in the course of saving a life. If our society has placed the rescue of a life above constitutional rights and above the criminal code, then such conduct clearly rises above a company's work rule. Loomis' work rule does not provide an overriding justification for firing Gardner when his conduct directly served the public policy encouraging citizens to save persons from serious bodily injury or death.

We find that Gardner's discharge for leaving the truck and saving a woman from an imminent life threatening situation violates the public policy encouraging such heroic conduct. This holding does not create an affirmative legal duty requiring citizens to intervene in dangerous life threatening situations.

We simply observe that society values and encourages voluntary rescuers when a life is in danger. Additionally, our adherence to this public policy does nothing to invalidate Loomis' work rule regarding drivers' leaving the trucks. . . . Our holding merely forbids Loomis from firing Gardner when he broke the rule because he saw a woman who faced imminent life threatening harm, and he reasonably believed his intervention was necessary to save her life. Finally, by focusing on the narrow public policy encouraging citizens to save human lives from life threatening situations, we continue to protect employers from frivolous lawsuits.

CASE QUESTIONS

1. Why is this case different from one in which an employee "rescues" a member of the public from fraud in bids or injury from defective products?

2. Did Mr. Gardner do the right thing in leaving his truck unattended? What were his ethical obligations under the circumstances? What would you have done?

3. Does this case create any affirmative legal duty to help those in danger?

4. Can an employee in Washington be fired for assisting a citizen who is a crime victim?

Handling Employee Termination Disputes

The number of suits brought by employees for improper discharge has increased tremendously. Many companies, in the interest of maintaining fairness and saving expenses, have adopted a peer review policy. **Peer review** is a formal grievance procedure for nonunion employees. Employees who feel that they cannot get an adequate response from their supervisors or by following the lines of authority have the opportunity to present their cases to a panel of fellow employees and managers (three employees, two managers is the general configuration). Panel members listen to the presentation, can ask for more information, vote on the issue, and issue a written opinion with an explanation.

Many companies (including Coors and GTE) are avoiding lawsuits through what seems to be a mutually satisfactory resolution of wrongful termination and other grievance cases. Some employers say this process encourages both managers and employees to make better decisions. The peer review process should be in the employee handbook, should be required prior to court action, and should be widely publicized.

BUSINESS PLANNING TIP

Encourage internal whistleblowing. Employees can benefit from following these suggestions.

1. Work within your system and through its chain of command before going public. Go through the various layers of management, even to the board of directors.

2. Voice/write your concerns; don't make accusations.

3. Maintain records of your internal contacts and their objections.

4. Find other employees who also know about this potentially volatile situation.

5. Keep a record of your information and carefully document.

BUSINESS STRATEGY

The Employee Handbook as a Source of Litigation: Taking Precautionary Steps

The employee handbook continues to be a source of litigation. Every appellate court that has heard a case on the issue of employee handbooks has ruled that an implied contract results from the terms in the employee handbook.

This focus on employee handbooks has been combined with the majority of courts finding the right of an employee to recover for wrongful discharge. Only Florida, Georgia, North Carolina, and Rhode Island do not recognize wrongful employment action rights. Indiana, Louisiana, and Texas have not ruled on the issue of wrongful discharge.

The law on employee handbooks is as follows.

1. The offer of employment is made to the employee by the employer, and included in the terms of the offer are the terms in the employee handbook.

2. Those handbooks include grounds for termination as well as the process that must be followed in order for termination to occur.

3. The employee accepts these terms by beginning employment.

Here is some advice from lawyers on employee handbooks.

1. Avoid using general phrases such as "employees may only be terminated for cause."

2. Avoid phrases such as employment continues as long as the employee "does a satisfactory job."

3. Say what you mean and mean what you say.

4. State that the employee relationship is an at-will relationship and can be ended at any time.

5. Make sure supervisors know the terms and procedures in the handbook and follow them.

6. Don't make reference to long-term employment, uninterrupted employment, continuing employment.

7. Don't make promises to employees in the handbook.

8. Update handbooks and review them periodically.

9. Make sure employees receive copies of changes and modified handbooks.

10. Have employees acknowledge receipt of the handbook.

Sources: Mark W. Bennett, *Employment Relationship: Law & Practice* (2000).
Pleva v Norquist, 195 F.3d 905 (7th Cir. 1999).
Knight v Vernon, 214 F.3d 544 (4th Cir. 2000).
Demasse v ITT Corp., 984 R2d 1138 (Ariz. 1999).

The Antiretaliation Statutes: Protections for Whistleblowers

Rather than having employees rely on a case-by-case determination of when they are protected in taking action in the course of employment and when they are not, many states as well as the federal government have passed whistleblower protection statutes, which prevent employers from firing employees who report violations, note safety concerns, or in some way take action that benefits the public but does not help or reflect well on their employers.

Two generic federal statutes afford protection for federal employees: the Civil Service Reform Act of 1978 and the Whistleblower Protection Act of 1989. The statutes protect federal employees who report wrongdoing and permit them to recover both back pay and their attorney's fees in the event they litigate or protest a termination for their disclosure of possible violations of the law. Some federal statutes also have specific provisions for certain categories of federal employees. For example, a portion of the Energy Reorganization Act provides protection for employees of nuclear facilities who report violations of federal laws and regulations at nuclear plants. The False Claims Act permits employees of government contractors whose tips and disclosures to federal investigators and agencies result in fines and penalties to collect 25 percent of those fines and penalties. Whistleblowers who have obtained recovery under the False Claims Act include many employees of the health care providers involved in Medicare/Medicaid fraud cases (an employee in one case recovered $51.5 million after a $550 million fine was paid).

Sarbanes–Oxley (SOX) also provides antiretaliation protections for employees who raise concerns about the financial reports or internal controls of their companies. Under the Dodd-Frank Wall Street Reform Act, these SOX protections were expanded to include financial rewards for whistleblowers of 10–30 percent of any fines the company pays for the reported conduct. The protections apply to employees who help with an audit, employees who join in a shareholder suit against the company, employees who report financial issues to a government agency, and employees who use internal reporting systems to raise a financial concern or compliance issue. The SOX protections are unique because they are the first whistleblower protections that go beyond those for employees who raise public safety concerns. The protections cover not only employees, but also analysts who raise concerns about companies they study. The research firms or investment houses the analysts work for cannot take retaliatory action against the analysts for issuing negative reports on companies that might also be clients of the analyst's employer. Companies that retaliate face criminal penalties or fines as well as imprisonment for those within the company who take action against the whistleblower. The individual penalties for SOX retaliation are up to 10 years. For the employee, damages for retaliation include back pay, actual damages, and a right to reinstatement.

All 50 states plus the District of Columbia have antiretaliation whistleblower protection statutes of some type. About half of the states protect all employees, while the other half provides protection only for government employees. Three states offer monetary rewards for employees who report wrongdoing that results in the collection of fines from a company, as does the federal government. Thirty-two states provide protection for employees who report civil rights violations, and 19 states provide protections for reporting minimum wage violations. Other areas in which the states provide whistleblower protection include reporting violations of environmental laws, child welfare laws, and child-care facility health and safety standards.

Agency Relationships in International Law

One of the complexities that has developed in law because of global business organizations is the liability of various subsidiaries, officers, and owners of multinational organizations when the interrelationships and operations may not be clear or even known to them. Perhaps the best example of the pitfalls of global structure is the multinational bank BCCI, a bank that proved elusive as authorities from several countries investigated it for criminal activity. BCCI was a layered, multinational organization with banks in 70 countries, including the United States (First American Bankshares, headed by the late Clark Clifford and Robert Altman). The banks and businesses in the different countries were staffed by residents of those countries, and the full global network of BCCI was not disclosed to these subsidiaries or to the individuals operating them. Regulations of operations were limited to the entities located in each of the various nations. Jurisdiction over other operations was limited. The layers of the organization made it difficult for anyone, even those in the subsidiaries, to be certain of the roles and activities of the full organization or of other subsidiaries.

BCCI collapsed and surrendered its U.S. assets to U.S. regulators in settlement of various charges. The late Clark Clifford and Robert Altman were indicted for activities involving BCCI, although they were affiliated with U.S. operations only. Mr. Altman was acquitted of the charges, and the court determined that Mr. Clifford was too ill to stand trial.

Following this complex case with its structuring of principal and agent relationships to evade the laws of any country, the United Kingdom, the United States, and other countries now work together to share information about tangled and evasive bank structures in order to prevent collapses and also detect the flow of funds by terrorist organizations. The cooperating nations now require filing and full disclosure of all principal–agent and parent–subsidiary relationships in all countries in which a bank conducts business.

B I O G R A P H Y

The Avant-Garde Ad Exec at Walmart in Arkansas: Julie Roehm

Julie Roehm was known throughout the advertising industry for her cutting-edge approach to advertising. When she worked for Chrysler, Ms. Roehm had agreed to have Chrysler sponsor an alternative halftime show that would feature scantily clad models playing football, which came to be known as the Lingerie Bowl. When consumers and dealers howled, Chrysler dropped its sponsorship. She was the idea person behind the "Grab life by the horns" and "That thang got a hemi?" campaigns for Dodge Ram trucks. She also raised a few advertising eyebrows when she launched a Chrysler campaign for the Durango truck with a television commercial that had two men at a urinal who were also having a double-entendre conversation about size. A Chrysler executive indicated Ms. Roehm was known for going over the marketing edge, but that you don't know where the edge is unless you go over it once in awhile.

Walmart recruited Ms. Roehm, a fit that many of her friends felt was wrong. Ms. Roehm herself worried about moving her East Coast family to Bentonville, Arkansas. Walmart had to pull one of her first ads, one that was referred to as "sexy." The ad showed a couple having an intimate discussion about red lingerie in front of their extended family

at a holiday gathering. Walmart pulled the ad after it aired on "Desperate Housewives" and Walmart received consumer complaints.

Ms. Roehm's tenure at Walmart would last only 10 months. She was hired in 2006, and by 2007, Walmart was in litigation with Ms. Roehm, who filed a wrongful termination suit against Walmart.

Walmart counterclaimed against Ms. Roehm's allegations with its allegations that Ms. Roehm had an affair with Sean Womack (both are married with children), her second-in-command at the company. The filing included e-mails allegedly to Mr. Womack from Ms. Roehm that were provided by Mrs. Womack:

"I hate not being able to call you or write you. I think about us together all the time. Little moments like watching your face when you kiss me."

The filing also accuses the two of seeking employment with Draft FCB. Draft FCB was the company that was awarded the Walmart ad account by Ms. Roehm. Walmart fired Draft FCB after revelations about the conflicts and hired Interpublic Group. Walmart has since reassigned its ad contracts to three different agencies.

The Walmart counterclaim includes the following information about the perks Roehm and Womack enjoyed from Draft FCB:

- $1,100 dinner
- $700 at LuxBar in Chicago
- $440 at the bar in the Peninsula Hotel

Draft FCB has cooperated with Walmart by providing copies of the e-mail communications between its employees and Roehm and Womack. However, Draft FCB also released a statement indicating that the employee communicating with Womack about employment for the two had no authority to negotiate such employment contracts or even had the authority to engage in business development.

Once Walmart counterclaimed, Ms. Roehm fired back with her own allegations, ones that basically argued, "What's sauce for the goose is sauce for the gander," a timeless legal principle in these battles of will. She has alleged Lee Scott, Walmart's CEO, enjoyed favorable prices from Irwin Jacobs, a Walmart supplier, on everything from jewelry to boats and that Mr. Scott's son, Eric, has worked for Mr. Jacobs for years. Her allegation is that Mr. Scott was not fired for these conflicts and, ergo, she was dismissed wrongfully. Walmart's code of ethics states that employees are not to have social relationships with suppliers if those relationships create even the appearance of impropriety.

While Walmart and Mr. Jacobs dismissed the allegations as false and outrageous, Mr. Jacobs and Mr. Scott acknowledged that their families have vacationed together and that Mr. Jacobs attended Mr. Scott's daughter's wedding. Mr. Jacobs has also stated that when the two are out together, Mr. Scott always pays and will not allow Mr. Jacobs to pay for even a lunch or other meal. Mr. Jacobs also says, 'I swear to God Lee never called me about [putting Eric to work].'

Walmart has counterclaimed for its legal fees as well as for the damages (costs) it experienced when it had to re-bid the advertising agency contract Ms. Roehm had awarded. Walmart's counterclaim alleges that because Ms. Roehm had accepted expensive meals and other gifts from the agency she violated Walmart's code of ethics, a strict one when it comes to suppliers, which prohibits employees from accepting anything from those suppliers.

The suit has been dismissed. The parties agreed to walk away from the other suits that related to the situation surrounding Ms. Roehm's termination.

Sources: Louise Story and Michael Barbaro, "Wal-Mart Criticizes 2 in a Filing," *New York Times,* March 20, 2007, pp. C1, C5; Gary McWilliams and James Covert, "Roehm Claims Wal-Mart Brass Defy Ethics Rules," *Wall Street Journal,* May 27, 2007, pp. A1, A5.

Summary

When is an employee acting on behalf of an employer?

- Principal—employer; responsible party
- Agent—party hired to act on another's behalf
- *Restatement of Agency*—common law view of agent-principal relationship
- Unincorporated association—nonlegal entity; no legal existence as natural or fictitious person

How much authority does an employee hold?

- Express authority—written or stated authority
- Implied authority—authority by custom
- Apparent authority—authority by perceptions of third parties

- Lingering apparent authority—authority left with terminated agent because others are not told of termination
- Actual notice—receipt of notice of termination
- Constructive notice—publication of notice of termination
- Ratification—after-the-fact recognition of agent's authority by principal
- Disclosed principal—existence and identity of principal are known
- Partially disclosed principal—existence but not identity of principal is known
- Undisclosed principal—neither existence nor identity of principal is known

- Gratuitous agency—agent works without compensation

When is a business liable for an employee's acts?

- Master–servant relationship—principal–agent relationship in which principal exercises great degree of control over agent
- Independent contractor—principal–agent relationship in which principal exercises little day-to-day control over agent
- Scope of employment—time when agent is doing work for the principal
- Inherently dangerous activities—activities for which, even if performed by independent contractor, principal is liable

What duties and obligations do employees owe employers?

- Fiduciary—one who has utmost duty of trust, care, loyalty, and obedience to another

How is an agency relationship terminated?

- Employment at will—right of employer to terminate noncontract employees at any time
- Protections for employees through express contract (manuals), implied contracts, and public policy
- Whistleblowers protected by antiretaliation statutes

Questions and Problems

1. Dr. Warren Lesch had a leak in his car's gas tank that had been repaired by Malcolm Weeks, an employee of Walker's Chevron, Inc., in Bel Air, Maryland. The tank was not repaired properly, and Dr. Lesch's home and garage were destroyed when the gas tank exploded. Dr. Lesch and his wife were severely burned as a result.

Walker's Chevron is a "branded" station: It displays only Chevron signs and colors and sells only Chevron gas and oil. The Lesches have sued Mr. Weeks, Walker's Chevron, and Chevron USA. Who is liable for the explosion? [*Chevron USA, Inc. v Lesch*, 570 A.2d 840 (Md. 1990)]

2. On September 29, 1984, Wilton Whitlow was taken to Good Samaritan Hospital's emergency room in Montgomery County, Ohio, because he had suffered a seizure and a blackout. He was examined by Dr. Dennis Aumentado, who prescribed the anti-epileptic medication Dilantin. Mr. Whitlow experienced no further seizures and was monitored as an outpatient at Good Samaritan over the next few weeks.

Mr. Whitlow complained to Dr. Aumentado of warm and dry eyes, and his Dilantin dose was reduced. On October 20, 1984, he was again admitted to the emergency room with symptoms that were eventually determined to be from Stevens–Johnson syndrome, a condition believed to be caused by a variety of medications. Mr. Whitlow sued Dr. Aumentado and Good Samaritan for malpractice and Parke-Davis, the manufacturer of Dilantin, for breach of warranty.

The hospital maintains it is not liable because Dr. Aumentado was an independent contractor. Is the hospital correct? [*Whitlow v Good Samaritan Hosp.*, 536 N.E.2d 659 (Ohio 1987)]

3. On March 29, 1983, Barry Mapp was observed in the JCPenney department store in Upper Darby, Pennsylvania, by security personnel, who suspected that he might be a shoplifter. Michael DiDomenico, a security guard employed by JCPenney, followed Mr. Mapp when he left the store and proceeded to Gimbels department store. There, Mr. DiDomenico notified Rosemary Federchok, a Gimbels security guard, about his suspicions. Even though his assistance was not requested, Mr. DiDomenico decided to remain to assist in case Ms. Federchok, a short woman of slight build, required help in dealing with Mr. Mapp if he committed an offense in Gimbels. It came as no surprise when Mr. Mapp was observed taking items from the men's department of the store; when he attempted to escape, he was pursued. Although Ms. Federchok was unable to keep up, Mr. DiDomenico continued to pursue Mr. Mapp and ultimately apprehended him in the lower level of the Gimbels parking lot. When Ms. Federchok arrived with Upper Darby police, merchandise that had been taken from Gimbels was recovered. Mr. Mapp, who had been injured when he jumped from one level of the parking lot to another, was taken to the Delaware County Memorial Hospital, where he was treated for a broken ankle.

Mr. Mapp filed suit against Gimbels for injuries sustained while being chased and apprehended by Mr. DiDomenico. He alleged in his complaint that Mr. DiDomenico, while acting as an agent of Gimbels, had chased him, had struck him with a nightstick, and had beaten him with his fists. Gimbels says it is not liable because Mr. DiDomenico was not its agent. Is Gimbels correct? [*Mapp v Gimbels Dep't Store*, 540 A.2d 941 (Pa. 1988)]

4. Nineteen-year-old Lee J. Norris was employed by Burger Chef Systems as an assistant manager of one of its restaurants. On a day when he was in charge and change was needed, Mr. Norris left to get change but also decided to get Kentucky Fried Chicken at a nearby store for his lunch to take back to Burger Chef. The bank where Mr. Norris usually got change is 1.6 miles from Burger Chef, and the Kentucky Fried Chicken outlet is 2.5 miles from Burger Chef. After Mr. Norris left the bank and was on his way to the Kentucky Fried Chicken restaurant, he negligently injured Lee J. Govro in an accident. Is Burger Chef liable for the accident? [*Burger Chef Systems v Govro*, 407 F.2d 921 (8th Cir. 1969)]

5. CAA is a Hollywood talent agency that represents sports figures. IMG Worldwide is its major competitor. Over the past two years, IMG agents Casey Close and Tom Condon have left their jobs and been hired by CAA. Shortly after their departure, IMG clients Derek Jeter, Tony Gonzalez, and LaDainian Tomlinson left IMG for CAA. In April 2010, Matthew Baldwin, a junior agent at IMG in Ohio, left his $90,000-per-year job and joined CAA. Mr. Baldwin also moved to California. IMG has filed suit against both Mr. Baldwin and CAA for violation of Mr. Baldwin's noncompete clause. The clause, which is part of a contract Mr. Baldwin signed when he was hired by IMG in Ohio, prohibits him from moving to a competing talent firm for a one-year period. IMG's suit also alleges that Mr. Baldwin took 7,000 confidential files from IMG when he left. Mr. Baldwin has denied the allegations, maintaining that his computer contained only personal information he had gathered from public records on coaches, salaries, and teams. CAA has responded to the suit by citing the California statute that makes covenants not to compete unenforceable. IMG has responded by noting that Ohio law, not California law, applies and that California's law does not apply when a former employee has take confidential information from company files to his new employer. Evaluate the enforceability of the covenant not to compete. Be sure to think back to Chapter 3 and discuss which court would have jurisdiction and which law would apply. Why is it important to determine which law applies?

6. Reverend John Fisher is the pastor of St. James Episcopal Church in Ohio. Catherine Davis served there as parish secretary from 1978 until six months after Reverend Fisher arrived at St. James in January 1988. Reverend Fisher fired her after she went to the bishop of the diocese to complain about sexual harassment by Reverend Fisher. The bishop promised an investigation, which was not conducted because Reverend Fisher denied the allegations. Ms. Davis then brought suit against the Episcopal Diocese. The diocese denied liability, claiming it was not in control of Reverend Fisher's actions because he was an independent contractor. Do you agree? [*Davis v Black*, 591 N.E.2d 11 (Ohio 1991)]

7. Lennen & Newell, Inc. (L&N), is an advertising agency hired by Stokely-Van Camp to do its advertising. L&N contracted for the purchase of ad time from CBS, but no Stokely representative's signature is on the contract. If L&N does not pay for the ad time, is Stokely liable? [*CBS, Inc. v Stokely-Van Camp, Inc.*, 456 F Supp. 539 (E.D.N.Y. 1977)]

8. John Guz, 49, first hired in 1971, had worked for Bechtel Corporation for 22 years. In 1986, he was assigned to BNI, a division specializing in engineering, construction, and environmental remediation that focuses on federal government programs, principally for the Departments of Energy and Defense (BNI MI). Mr. Guz worked his way up through Bechtel and BNI both, going from administrative assistant, beginning at a salary of $750 per month, to financial reports supervisor, earning $70,000 per year. During his time with Bechtel and BNI, Mr. Guz had been given generally favorable performance evaluations, steady pay increases, and a continuing series of promotions.

During this time, Bechtel maintained Personnel Policy 1101, dated June 1991, on the subject of termination of employment (Policy 1101). Policy 1101 stated that "Bechtel employees have no employment agreements guaranteeing continuous service and may resign at their option or be terminated at the option of Bechtel."

Between 1986 and 1991, BNI-MI's size was reduced from 13 to 6 persons, and its costs were reduced from $748,000 in 1986 to $400,000 in 1991. Bechtel eventually eliminated Mr. Guz's division. Mr. Guz was discharged, as were all the employees in the division. Mr. Guz brought suit against Bechtel alleging that he had an "implied-in-fact contract" with Bechtel that prevented the company from terminating him as long as the company was performing well financially.

The trial court granted Bechtel's motion for summary judgment and dismissed the action. In a split decision, the Court of Appeal reversed. Bechtel appealed. Who should prevail on appeal? [*Guz v Bechtel*, 8 P3d 1089 (Cal. 2000)]

9. Bernice Bisbee is a real estate broker employed by Midkiff Realty, Inc. In September 1972, she obtained from Richard and Marian Silva an exclusive listing agreement for the sale of their property in Kaleheo, Kauai. The land, which fronted on the Kaumualii highway, consisted of 34,392 square feet, one two-bedroom house, and one four-bedroom house. The Silvas told Ms. Bisbee that they wanted $100,000 for the property.

Some time later, Ms. Bisbee obtained an offer for the property from David Larsen. The down payment was set at $35,000, with payments of $2,000 a month at 8 percent a year, but Mr. Larsen backed out before closing. After that, a joint venture of six members formed the Pacific Equity Associates to buy the property. Ms. Bisbee was to manage the joint venture and would receive 10 percent of the profits for her services. One of the joint venture members, Toshio Morikawa, appeared as the buyer at the July 1973 closing of the property sale. Ms. Bisbee did not tell the Silvas of the venture nor of her pecuniary interest in it.

In August 1973, Ms. Bisbee prepared for the venture a financial statement that listed the market value of the Silva property at $149,424. Several times the venture was late making payments, which Ms. Bisbee covered. Mr. Silva and his wife were emotionally distressed about the late payments and told Ms. Bisbee. Eventually, because of defaults on the payments, the Silvas brought suit to cancel the contract and for damages for fraud by Ms. Bisbee, naming Midkiff Realty in the suit as well.

The jury returned a verdict for $29,000 in general damages for the Silvas and $50,000 in punitive damages. Ms. Bisbee and Midkiff appealed. Was there a breach of fiduciary duty? Should the damage award stand because of Ms. Bisbee's actions? [*Silva v Bisbee*, 628 P2d 214 (Haw. App. 1981)]

10. Recovery Express and Interstate Demolition (IDEC) are two Boston-based companies with the same business address. Albert Arillotta, who claimed to be a partner at IDEC, sent an e-mail to Leo Whitehead of CSX Transportation about purchasing rail cars for scrap purposes. The e-mail came from albert@recoveryexpress.com. The two reached an agreement, and Arillotta went to the CSX yard and disassembled rail cars and hauled them away. Mr. Whitehead sent invoices to IDEC for $115,757.36 because he believed Arillotta to be an agent for IDEC and Recovery Express. IDEC has no assets and CSX seeks to recover the amount due from Recovery Express. Recovery Express's CEO said he just allowed IDEC, a new company, to share office space and the e-mail server. Mr. Whitehead says that he assumed from the e-mail and the same address that Arillotta was an agent for Recovery as well. Who is liable? [*CSX Transportation, Inc. v Recovery Express, Inc.*, 415 F. Supp.2d 6 (D. Mass. 2006)]

Organizational Behavior and the Law

Former Indiana University basketball coach Bobby Knight had a long history of violent temper eruptions both on and off the court. Nonetheless, he had been a successful coach for the team, often taking Indiana to the NCAA Final Four competition. The flamboyant coach had been known to confront officials during games, throw chairs during games, and use colorful language continually. A videotape captured the coach lunging for the throat of an Indiana University student and player during a practice session.

Coach Knight initially denied that it happened, and then the videotape was produced. The trustees of Indiana University placed the coach on probation and wrote in a letter to him that any violation of the terms of the probation—including no striking of students, no temper eruptions, and no foul language—was grounds for termination.

Many fans and alumni were outraged at the agreement and defended keeping the coach in good standing because he never had any NCAA violations (i.e., he ran a "clean" program) and he saw to it that most of his players also graduated from college in addition to playing basketball or being recruited by professional teams.

Write a memo explaining why the trustees took the action they did. Be sure to include discussion of the principles of agency law, potential liability, and the rights of Coach Knight with regard to his employment contract.

Notes

1. The terminology of master and servant has its roots in the historical nature of the employment relationship of indentured servants and slaves. For more information, see the course website and the *Instructor's Manual*.

2. Eric Assen, "Dancer's Misstep Lands Him in Collin County Jail," *Dallas Morning News,* October 18, http://www.dallasnews.com/sharedcontent/dws/news/localnews/stories/DN-chacha_18met.ART.State.Edition2.4a6b315.html.

3. "Dancing Fool," *National Law Journal,* October 27, 2008, p. 16.

4. Assen.

Management of Employee Welfare

The employer–employee relationship has evolved from one of a paternal nature in the 1600s and 1700s to one of a contractual nature.[1] In those earlier periods, employers often assumed responsibility for the well-being of their employees, through personal relationships that were possible because of the less-complex nature of business at the time. With the Industrial Revolution, however, more employees were needed, and personal relationships were no longer possible. The employer–employee relationship became thoroughly contractual.

One effect of the change in the relationship to one of contract was that both parties behaved as parties in contracts and negotiation do: they wanted to maximize their own economic benefits. Employers wanted the most work for the least amount of money. Employees wanted maximum pay, safe working conditions, and some type of insurance for retirement, unemployment, and disability. Because employers had the upper hand—they controlled the jobs—their bargaining positions were stronger than those of employees. To balance the scales of power a bit, workers organized to give themselves more bargaining power through unionization, and the federal government enacted worker protection legislation to provide workers with some of their needs.

This chapter discusses the work and safety standards covered in federal legislation and answers the following questions: What wage and work hour protections exist for employees? Are there restrictions on children's work? What protections exist for safety in the workplace? What happens when an employee is injured in the workplace? Are workers entitled to pensions, and are they regulated? What is the Social Security system, and what benefits does it provide? What rights do unemployed workers have? How are labor unions formed, and what is their relationship with employees? ■

UPDATE
For up-to-date legal news, go to
mariannejennings.com

Fatal Occupational Injuries in 2008: 5,214
Causes
Transportation accidents: 41%
Equipment accidents: 18%
Assaults and violence: 6%
Homicides: 10%
Falls: 13%
Environmental: 8%
Fire and explosions: 3%

Data on Injuries:

Females killed: 7%
Female percentage of workforce: 43%
Highest fatality rates:
Agriculture, forestry, fishing, and hunting
Second-highest fatality rates:
Transportation and warehousing
Third-highest fatality rate:
Mining

Accident rate in the workplace in 1995:
8.1 per 100
Accident rate in the workplace in 2008:
4.2 per 100
U.S. Department of Labor Statistics, 2010

OSHA Violations Found in 2008 in the Workplace: 87,687

Total OSHA inspections 2008: 38,591
Top five violations
1. Scaffolding issues
2. Fall protection
3. Respiratory protection
4. Machine guards
5. Electrical systems

Occupational Safety and Health Administration
http://www.osha.gov

CONSIDER...

Hotel Oasis, Inc. operates a hotel and restaurant in south-western Puerto Rico. Dr. Lionel Lugo-Rodríguez ("Lugo") is the president of the corporation, runs the hotel, and manages its employees. Between October 3, 1990, and June 30, 1993, Oasis employees were paid less than minimum wage, were not paid for training time or meetings held during non-working hours, were paid in cash "off the books," and were  not paid correctly for overtime. Oasis also maintained two sets of payroll records for the same employees, covering the same time periods, one showing fewer hours at a higher rate, and the other showing more hours at a sub-minimum wage rate. The Department of Labor brought charges against Oasis and Dr. Lugo. Dr. Lugo says he is not liable. Is he correct? What are the penalties for violating the wage laws?

Wage and Hours Protection

Exhibit 18.1 summarizes the series of laws affecting employee rights over the past 50 years, which are discussed in this chapter.

EXHIBIT 18.1 Statutory Scheme for Employee Welfare

STATUTE	DATE	PROVISIONS
Worker's Compensation (state laws)	1900	Absolute liability of employers for employee injury; no common-law tort suits by employees against employers
Social Security Act 42 U.S.C. § 301	1935	FICA contributions; unemployment compensation; retirement benefits
Fair Labor Standards Act 29 U.S.C. § 201	1938	Minimum wages; child labor restrictions; overtime pay
Equal Pay Act 29 U.S.C. § 206	1963	Amendment to FLSA; equal pay for equal work
Occupational Safety and Health Act 29 U.S.C. § 651	1970	Safety in the workplace; employee rights; employer reporting; inspections
Employment Retirement Income Security Act 29 U.S.C. § 441	1974	Disclosure of contributions, investments, loans; employee vesting; employee statements
Family and Medical Leave Act 29 U.S.C. § 2601	1993	Protection of job after family leave (for pregnancy, child care, adult illness, elderly care)
Pension Protection Act 29 U.S.C. §§ 302 et. seq.	2006	Amends ERISA to require higher funding levels as well as limits on officer stock sales during blackout periods
Patient Protection & Affordable Care Act 42 U.S.C. §§ 18001 et seq.	2010	Imposes responsibility on employers for health care coverage for employees

The Fair Labor Standards Act

The **Fair Labor Standards Act** (FLSA) is commonly called by workers the "minimum wage law" or the wage and hour law. This act does establish a minimum wage, but it also includes provisions regulating child labor, overtime pay requirements, and equal pay provisions. The FLSA was originally introduced in the Senate by Hugo L. Black when he was a senator from Alabama. His 1937 appointment to the U.S. Supreme Court may have helped it pass the high court's scrutiny. Amended several times, the FLSA is an enabling statute that sets up various administrative agencies to handle the regulations and necessary enforcement.

Coverage of FLSA
The FLSA applies to all businesses that affect interstate commerce. As discussed in Chapter 5, "affecting" interstate commerce is a broad standard.

FLSA Minimum Wage and Overtime Regulations
Under FLSA, all covered employees must be paid a **minimum wage.** The minimum wage is established by Congress and is increased through legislation, with the latest increase taking effect in 2010. Domestic service workers, including full-time babysitters, cooks, and housekeepers must be paid a minimum wage. The minimum wage is determined after the employer deducts any expenses for housing and food.

The FLSA also includes an hours protection for covered employees in the form of time-and-one-half pay for hours worked above 40 hours per week. Regardless of the pay period for covered employees (monthly, weekly, or biweekly), overtime is computed on the basis of 40 hours per week. For example, if a covered employee worked 38, 42, 35, and 47 hours in four consecutive weeks and is paid on a monthly basis, that employee is entitled to 9 hours of **overtime pay.**

The definition of covered employees is provided in the FLSA. Some categories of employees are covered for purposes of minimum wage protections but not for overtime pay. For example, professionals, executives, and others who exercise discretion and judgment in their positions may be covered for purposes of minimum wage protections but not for purposes of overtime protections. The reason for this exemption is that these employees, often referred to as "white-collar" workers, possess sufficient training, knowledge, and experience to counter employer unfairness. The FLSA, under rules promulgated by the Department of Labor, has specific salary and job requirements for employees to be covered under the overtime exemption. The trend has been one of expanding the list of employees who are protected by overtime pay requirements. One issue that has resulted from the impact of downsizing is whether employees can be required to work overtime hours. The FLSA simply provides the right to time-and-one-half pay for overtime worked; it does not include limitations on hours (except in child labor regulations for children under the age of 18), nor does it provide a statutory right to refuse to work overtime. Union collective bargaining agreements can impose restraints, and many employers seek volunteers for overtime. However, employers should exercise caution with overly tired employees because, as *Faverty v McDonald's Restaurants of Oregon, Inc.* (Chapter 17, Case 17.4) held, employers may be liable for accidents of such employees even when employees are on their way home.

FLSA and Child Labor Provisions

The child labor provisions of the FLSA keep children in school for at least a minimum number of years. The provisions of the act govern particular ages and restrict the types of jobs those age groups can hold.

1. *Eighteen years old and older.* This is the cutoff age for the child labor provisions. Anyone 18 or older can work in any type of job.

2. *Sixteen to seventeen years old.* This age group can work in any "nonhazardous" job for unlimited hours. Hazardous jobs include mining, logging, roofing, and excavation.

3. *Fourteen to fifteen years old.* This group can work only in nonhazardous, non-manufacturing, and nonmining jobs, and only during nonschool hours. Work hours are limited on school days and during school weeks. Time-of-day restrictions also apply for work hours.

Among the exemptions to the laws are those for young actors and actresses, for example. However, Screen Actors Guild rules place stringent limits on "set time" for children. But in the film industry, states may require approval of minors' contracts and also require that some of the earnings be put in trust for use by the child actor when he or she becomes an adult. Other exemptions apply to work-study programs and farm work. (For information on child labor in international business, see p. 631.)

Enforcement of FLSA

Enforcement of the FLSA requirements comes about in different ways. Employees can initiate the process by filing a complaint with the U.S. Department of Labor. In some cases, employers make the laws self-enforcing by requesting interpretations from the Labor Department that are then published in the *Code of Federal Regulations*.

In a final type of case, the Labor Department initiates its own investigation of a firm for possible violations. For example, in 1999, the Labor Department focused on the car dealership programs that had high-school-age vocational students working in service departments. Although the mechanical work was permissible, using the under-18 students as car jockeys to bring the customers' cars around to them following service was a violation of the age restrictions in the labor laws on certain types of work.

Penalties for FLSA Violation

The FLSA carries both civil and criminal penalties for violations. Employees have the right to sue civilly to recover from an employer any wages that were not paid or any overtime compensation that was denied, plus reasonable attorney fees required to bring the action to recover. In addition to the employees' rights, the U.S. Department of Labor's Wage and Hour Division has enforcement power for violations. A willful violation of FLSA carries a maximum $10,000 fine and possible imprisonment of up to six months.

To help employees pursue their rights, the FLSA makes it a violation for any employer to fire an employee for filing an FLSA complaint or for participating in any FLSA proceeding.

Liability for FLSA Violation

Officers of a corporation can be held individually liable for the corporation's violations. The FLSA imposes fines on both corporations and officers involved in managing employees. These personal penalties are particularly likely in cases in which the company has not kept accurate records of the wages and hours worked of its employees, a requirement of the FLSA. Case 18.1, *Chao v Hotel Oasis, Inc.*, indicates the new enforcement standards and policies of the Department of Labor and provides the answer for the chapter-opening "Consider."

CASE 18.1

Chao v Hotel Oasis, Inc.
493 F.3d 26 (1st Cir. 2007)

Two Sets of Books, One Big Penalty

FACTS

Hotel Oasis, Inc. operates a hotel and restaurant in southwestern Puerto Rico. Dr. Lionel Lugo-Rodríguez (Defendant-appellant) (Lugo) is the president of the corporation, runs the hotel, and manages its employees. Oasis's records show that between October 3, 1990, and June 30, 1993, employees were paid less than minimum wage, were not paid for training time or meetings held during non-working hours, were paid in cash "off the books," and were not paid correctly for overtime. Oasis also maintained two sets of payroll records for the same employees, covering the same time periods, one showing fewer hours at a higher rate, and the other showing more hours at a sub–minimum wage rate. Lugo maintains that the two sets of books were necessary, one for temporary employees and one for permanent employees.

On April 5, 1994, the Secretary of Labor (the "Secretary") filed a complaint in the United States District Court for the District of Puerto Rico against Oasis and Lugo ("Defendants"), alleging violations of the minimum wage, overtime, and recordkeeping provisions of the Fair Labor Standards Act ("FLSA"). The Secretary also sought liquidated damages.

After years of litigation, the district court ordered Oasis to pay $141,270.64 in back wages and an equal amount in liquidated damages to 282 current and former employees. The court also found Lugo personally liable for the back wages and penalties. Lugo and Oasis appealed.

JUDICIAL OPINION

TORRUELLA, Circuit Judge

"[T]he overwhelming weight of authority is that a corporate officer with operational control of a corporation's covered enterprise is an employer along with the corporation, jointly and severally liable under the FLSA for unpaid wages." Although we found it "difficult to accept . . . that Congress intended that *any* corporate officer or other employee with ultimate operational control over payroll matters be personally liable," we narrowly determined that the FLSA did not preclude personal liability for "corporate officers with a significant ownership interest who had operational control of significant aspects of the corporation's day to day functions, including compensation of employees, and who personally made decisions to continue operations despite financial adversity during the period of nonpayment.". . .

. . . [Because] not every corporate employee who exercised supervisory control should be held personally liable, we identified several factors that were important to the personal liability analysis, including the individual's ownership interest, degree of control over the corporation's financial affairs and compensation practices, and role in "caus[ing] the corporation to compensate (or not to compensate) employees in accordance with the FLSA."

Based on the above considerations, we affirm the district court's judgment holding Lugo personally liable for Oasis's compensation decisions. Lugo was not just any employee with some supervisory control over other employees. He was the president of the corporation, and he had ultimate control over the business's day-to-day operations. In particular, it is undisputed that Lugo was the corporate officer principally in charge of directing employment practices, such as hiring and firing employees, requiring employees to attend meetings unpaid, and setting employees' wages and schedules. He was thus instrumental in "causing" the corporation to violate the FLSA. The FLSA contemplates, at least in certain circumstances, holding officers with such personal responsibility for statutory compliance jointly and severally liable along with the corporation.

Finally, Defendants argue that the district court erred in awarding liquidated damages based on a finding of willfulness. The FLSA authorizes the Secretary of Labor to recover on behalf of employees unpaid wages and overtime compensation plus an equal amount in liquidated damages. The only way an employer can escape liquidated damages is to "show [ ] to the satisfaction of the court" that it acted in good faith and had reasonable grounds for believing that its acts did not violate the FLSA.

Here, the district court found that Defendants failed to show good faith or objective reasonableness, referring back to its findings on willfulness with respect to the applicable statute of limitations. Defendants "intentionally and consistently failed to keep accurate records of the time worked by its employees[,] . . . disguised minimum wage, as well as overtime pay violations, . . . did not record the amounts of cash tips . . . [and] most salient . . . [to] a finding of willfulness . . . [paid] employees 'off the books.'"

Oasis's failure to keep adequate payroll records and its intentional manipulation of the records it did keep are sufficient grounds for concluding that Oasis did not act in good faith or with a reasonable belief that it was in compliance with the FLSA. "[T]he fact that an employer knowingly under-reported its employee's work hours could suggest to a [fact finder] that the employer was attempting to conceal its failure to pay overtime from regulators, or was acting to eliminate evidence that might later be used against it in a suit by one of its employees."

Defendants' primary argument on appeal is that the court had indicated at trial that the willfulness issue was "close" and that the Secretary had offered no evidence that Oasis acted in reckless disregard of its statutory obligations. These arguments are unpersuasive. First, the district court noted its "initial inclination against a determination of willfulness," but explained that it ultimately relied on the employees' testimony and Defendants' own documentary evidence to reach its conclusion regarding willfulness. We have already determined that the willfulness finding is not clearly erroneous. Furthermore, it is the *employer's* burden to show good faith and objective reasonableness, and therefore the Secretary's alleged failure to offer evidence of willfulness is not an impediment to the court's decision to refrain from awarding liquidated damages.

Affirmed.

CASE QUESTIONS

1. What shows willfulness of a violation?
2. What are the standards for holding an officer liable for FLSA violations?
3. Explain what liquidated damages are and when they are available for recovery.

The Equal Pay Act of 1963

The **Equal Pay Act of 1963** is an amendment to the FLSA that makes it illegal to pay different wages based on gender to men and women who are doing substantially the same work. If the jobs involve equal responsibility, training, or skill, men and women must have equal pay. Merit systems and seniority systems instituted in good faith do not violate the Equal Pay Act even though they may result in different pay rates for the same jobs. As long as the disparate pay is based on length of employment or a merit-raise system, the disparity is within the act.

The Equal Pay Act is not an act that requires the application of comparable worth. Comparable worth requires that men and women be paid on the same scale, not just for the same jobs but when they are doing different jobs that require equal skill, effort, and responsibility. This issue came to light in 1983 when Louise Peterson, a licensed practical nurse at Western State Hospital in Tacoma, Washington, brought suit when she discovered that her salary of $1,462 per month for her supervision of the daily care of 60 men convicted of sex crimes was $192 less per month than that of the hospital groundskeeper and $700 less per month than men doing similar jobs at Washington's state prisons. A federal court found no violation of the Equal Pay Act.

Workplace Safety

The Occupational Safety and Health Act

One of the worker welfare concerns of Congress has been safety in the workplace. In the past, the economic concerns of employers often overshadowed their concern for proper safety precautions. To ensure worker safety, Congress passed the **Occupational Safety and Health Act of 1970.** Its application was broad, protecting virtually every employee in the country. It was an enabling statute that created three agencies responsible for worker safety standards: the **Occupational Safety and Health Administration** (OSHA), the Occupational Safety and Health Review Commission (OSHRC), and the National Institute for Occupational Safety and Health (NIOSH). OSHA is the agency responsible for the promulgation and enforcement of workplace safety standards. OSHA's enforcement powers include investigations, record-keeping requirements, and research. The stated purpose of the act is to "assure so far as possible every working man and woman in the nation safe and healthful working conditions and to preserve our human resources."

OSHA Coverage and Duties

OSHA coverage is broad: Every employer that is in a business affecting commerce and has at least one employee is covered by OSHA. Several other federal acts regulate safety for particular industries, including the Coal Mine and Safety Act and the Railway Safety Act.

OSHA Responsibilities

Promulgating Rules and Safety Standards

OSHA is responsible for promulgating rules and regulations for safety standards and procedures. The rules are adopted by the standard administrative process of notice in the *Federal Register*, public input, and final decision (see Chapter 6).

Inspections

OSHA inspections are an enforcement tool. Inspectors can enter the workplace "without delay and at a reasonable time" to inspect. They can check the workplace and the records and can question employees. OSHA's inspection power is limited by numbers, however. Because of OSHA's limited staff, the regulations provide for an order of priority on inspections:

1. Hazards or conditions that could cause death
2. Investigations of fatal accident sites
3. Employee complaints
4. Particularly hazardous industries
5. Random inspections incorporating an emphasis on certain types of industries (roofing, lumbering, meat packing, transportation [car, truck] manufacturing, and longshoring)

Inspection procedures are regulated. An OSHA inspector who appears at a workplace must show identification and ask the employer's permission to conduct an inspection. If the employer allows the inspection, the employer or an agent of the employer can accompany the OSHA inspector. After the inspection, the inspector and employer meet to discuss violations, and the problems are often worked out on the spot and the violations remedied immediately.

Employee Rights, Inspections, and OSHA. If an inspection is the result of an employee complaint, the employer cannot take any retaliatory action against that employee. Because of OSHA's limited staff, the agency relies on those in the workplace to bring violations to its attention. If workers fear retaliation, the violations will remain unreported. An employee who is fired, demoted, or discriminated against for registering an OSHA complaint can file a complaint, and the Department of Labor can pursue the employee's rights in federal district court. In *Whirlpool Corporation v Marshall,* 445 U.S. 1 (1980), the U.S. Supreme Court held that employees could not be sent home from work or docked on their pay if they refused to work because of an unsafe condition or employer practice.

OSHA Search Warrant Requirements

Although most businesses voluntarily permit OSHA inspections, employers do have the right to refuse access. In *Marshall v Barlows, Inc.,* 436 U.S. 307 (1978), the U.S. Supreme Court ruled that OSHA inspectors must obtain warrants if employers refuse access.

OSHA Penalties

There are five types of OSHA violations, and each carries a different range of penalties. Exhibit 18.2 is a summary of OSHA penalties.

State OSHA Programs

Most federal regulatory laws preempt state laws, but state laws addressing occupational safety are not generally preempted, and the states share responsibility for workplace safety with the federal government. Some states do go beyond the federal standards. For example, some states have "right to know" laws for employees—laws that require employers to post the presence of hazardous substances at the office, plant, etc. Also, state criminal laws may be used to prosecute officers and companies already sanctioned by OSHA.

EXHIBIT 18.2 OSHA Penalties

TYPE OF OFFENSE	DESCRIPTION	PENALTY
Willful	Employer aware of danger or a repeat violator	Up to $70,000 (not less than $5,000) and/or six months imprisonment
Serious	Violation is a threat to life or could cause serious injury	$7,000
Nonserious	No threat of serious injury	Up to $7,000
De minimis	Failure to post rights	Up to $7,000 per violation
Failure to correct	Citation not followed	$7,000 per day

For a state to assume responsibility for an OSHA program, the agency must be assured that the state plan will be as effective as federal OSHA would be. Also, OSHA is in charge of the Complaints against State Program Administration, which permits those affected and interested in safety to file complaints with OSHA regarding state performance. OSHA can then investigate and, if necessary, eliminate state approval.

Employee Impairment and Testing Issues

One safety problem in the workplace is the presence of impaired coworkers. An employee operating equipment, whether a drill press or a delivery van, while under the influence of drugs or alcohol presents a substantial safety concern for any business. Current estimates are that between 14 and 20 percent of the U.S. workforce is impaired on the job. Employees who use drugs are almost four times more likely to be involved in workplace accidents. Further, the annual cost in reduced productivity attributable to impaired workers is $100 billion. In 1989, the U.S. Supreme Court issued two decisions—*Skinner v Railway Labor*

For the Manager's Desk

Re: Fix the Violations

OSHA levied the largest fine in its history against BP for its failure to correct safety violations at its Texas City, Texas, refinery, a violation that resulted in a 2005 explosion that killed 15 workers and injured 170 others. The fine is $87 million, one that is four times larger than any fine OSHA has ever issued against a company.

BP had entered into a 2005 agreement with OSHA to fix the safety violations, but BP had failed to do so. OSHA had found 271 violations at the refinery. Following the explosion, the OSHA investigation and report found 439 "willful and egregious" violations, including many of the 271 that had not been fixed as promised.

OSHA attributed many of the violations to overzealous cost-cutting on maintenance and safety, undue production pressures, antiquated equipment, and fatigued employees.

BP had already entered into an agreement with the EPA for a guilty plea to Clean Air Act violations and paid a $50 million fine. BP has also settled civil suits (4,000 in total) and paid them from a fund of $2.1 billion that the company set aside for the litigation.

OSHA will find willful violations when employers are warned but do not fix the violations. Cuts in maintenance budgets when the company has been cited for OSHA violations will also result in extra penalties.

Executives' Association, 489 U.S. 602 (1989), and *National Treasury Employees Union v Von Raab*, 489 U.S. 656 (1984)—that upheld the right of government employers to conduct drug screening of federal employees without a warrant and without probable cause if those employees were in "safety-sensitive" positions. These two particular cases involved railway employees and customs officers, respectively.

In the area of drug and alcohol screening, the interests of employee privacy collide with safety and business issues. Courts at the state and federal levels have adopted a near-uniform position of holding safety concerns above employees' right of privacy. Their decisions have upheld the right of employer testing even in the private sector, especially in work situations where safety is a concern.

Employee Pensions, Retirement, and Social Security

One of the concerns of workers is what happens to them when they retire: Will they have an income? Other concerns are whether they will have a source of income in the event of disability, or whether their survivors will have income in the event of their death. Finally, what if no work is available? What income will they have until they find another job? These issues are the social issues of employment law—providing for those who, because of age, disability, or unemployment, are unable to provide for themselves.

Social Security

The **Social Security Act of 1935** was a key component of the massive reforms in federal government during Franklin Roosevelt's presidency.

The idea of the Social Security system was to have those who could work shoulder the social burden of providing for those who could not. Every employer and employee is required to contribute to the Social Security programs under the **Federal Insurance Contributions Act** (FICA). The amount employees contribute is based on their annual wage. Changes under the Patient Protection and Affordable Care Act, passed in 2010, now make FICA contributions applicable to interest and dividend income as well as capital gains at a rate of nearly 4 percent. FICA contributions are paid one-half by employers and one-half by employees. Independent contractors pay their own FICA contributions. Social Security includes provision of death benefits for spouses and children, as well as disability and retirement benefits.

The benefits paid to retired and disabled people are based on formulas. The amount depends on how long an individual worked and within what salary range. Surviving spouse and children's benefits are likewise tied to the employee's work and salary history.

Private Retirement Plans

For many, Social Security retirement benefits do not provide enough security, and at present there is no assurance that those employed today will be able to collect their Social Security benefits upon retirement. For these reasons, many employees have invested in their own private retirement plans.

For the Manager's Desk

Re: Who Is an Employee and Who Is an Independent Contractor?

For purposes of Social Security taxes, unemployment compensation, workers' compensation, and, of course, principal liability, the definition of an employee versus that of independent contractor is critical. Many businesses apply a label of "independent contractor" to agents doing work for them, but the activities of those independent contractors may, in fact, make them employees. Employers should check the status of those who are doing work so that they are paying wage taxes properly and have adequate coverage for liability.

In a 1987 revenue ruling, the Internal Revenue Service (IRS) listed the following 20 factors for determining whether an employer has sufficient control to label an agent an employee (servant) as opposed to an independent contractor.

1. Instructions on worker's performance of duties versus independent work
2. Training by coworkers versus no training required
3. Integration of worker's services into the business
4. Services benefit the business personally as opposed to a group of employers
5. Worker hires, supervises, and pays his own assistants (more likely to be independent contractor)
6. Continuing relationship as opposed to one-time projects
7. Set hours of work as opposed to flexibility
8. Full time required as opposed to working for others
9. Doing work on the employer's premises as opposed to own facilities
10. Order of tasks established by employer
11. Oral or written reports as opposed to independence
12. Payment by hour, week, or month as opposed to payment by project or task
13. Payment of business or travel expenses as opposed to personal payment as part of fee
14. Furnishing tools and materials versus furnishing own supplies
15. Use of and payment for outside facilities
16. Realization of profit or loss by worker
17. Working for more than one firm at a time
18. Making services available to the general public
19. Employer's right to discharge versus employee processes and procedures
20. Worker's right to terminate without consequences such as breach of contract

These 20 complex and burdensome factors were consolidated by the Ninth Circuit in *Donovan v Sureway Cleaners*, 656 F.2d 1368 (9th Cir. 1981), into six factors:

1. Degree of control over workers
2. Whether the worker has the risk of profit or loss
3. Whether the worker makes an investment
4. Level of skills and training for the work
5. Permanency of worker
6. Integration into economics of the business

One consistent factor not present in any of the evaluation lists is what the employer labels the worker—the label is irrelevant, and courts are consistent in their unwillingness to accept employers' labels of workers.

In 2010, the IRS began a new process of reexamining who is and who is not a federal contractor. Under the Obama administration, the 20-point test is simply background information for the ultimate determination under the guidelines, which are designed to look at the overall relationship of the business with the worker.

Many retirement and pension plans are set up by employers, who enjoy tax benefits from some plans. However, when evidence revealed that employees' funds in plans were being misused, not invested wisely, and in some cases embezzled, Congress enacted the **Employee Retirement Income Security Act of 1974** (ERISA), which was amended in 2006 by the **Pension Protection Act of 2006.**

Coverage of ERISA

ERISA applies to any employer engaged in or affecting interstate commerce and to any organization (such as a union) representing employees in interstate commerce. ERISA covers any medical, retirement, or deferral-of-income plan.

Requirements of ERISA Plans

ERISA does not require employers to have pension plans, but if an employer chooses to have a pension plan, the employer is subject to funding, accounting, and disclosure requirements imposed by federal law, including changes under the Pension Protection Act, enacted because of company and pension funding failures. As part of its 2006 Chapter 11 bankruptcy, United Airlines was relieved of its pension liabilities. Many lawmakers were taken aback when a company was able to renege on pension benefits when so many protections were built into the law under ERISA. Further, many former Enron employees lost their pensions because it was funded with Enron stock. Congressional hearings uncovered that loopholes in the accounting processes for pension fund reporting had permitted United, and many others, to report pension numbers that made the health of the fund look better than it actually was. The loopholes were Enronesque in nature, allowing obligations to be spun off the books so that the existing levels of obligations of the plan looked small and the assets rich.

Under the Pension Protection Act of 2006, these financial reporting accounting loopholes for general financial reports were changed. The changes require companies to fund their pension plans according to the numbers reported to the SEC in their financials. Companies reported their pension obligations and funding accurately to the SEC, but for ERISA purposes, those numbers were inflated. For example, if United had funded its plans when its SEC numbers indicated it needed to (i.e., 1998), United would have had a sufficiently funded plan at the time of its bankruptcy. However, under ERISA guidelines, it was not required to kick in funds until 2002, by which time the fund was so grossly underfunded that the company was unable to salvage the fund or provide the cash for increased levels of funding.

ERISA Employee Rights

Under ERISA, employees are entitled to receive an annual statement showing both their total benefits in any of the covered plans and the amount that is vested or that is nonforfeitable should they leave their jobs. In addition, ERISA sets minimum vesting requirements for employees before they will have rights in their retirement, pension, or annuity plans. The Pension Protection Act of 2006 added another protection for employees that prohibits officers of the company from selling their shares when employees are subject to blackout periods on their pension funds. That is, when employees cannot make changes in their pension fund allocations or deposits, officers likewise cannot trade in the company's stock. This provision was passed to prevent what happened at Enron. Enron officers sold off large blocks of stock even as the employees' pension plan was frozen by a blackout period. All the employees could do was sit and watch the values of their plans decline. They were unable to allocate pension funds to other sources.

Unemployment Compensation

Benefits Provided

State laws provide for the amount of **unemployment compensation** that will be paid. The amount is tied to the average amount earned by an individual during the months preceding employment termination. The benefits are usually paid on a weekly or biweekly basis. Most states also have a minimum and maximum amount that can be collected regardless of average earnings during the base period. Benefit payments have been increasing gradually to up to 99 weeks.

Qualifying for Benefits

Each state has its own standards for payment of benefits. Generally, eligibility requirements demand that an individual be (1) involuntarily terminated from a job, (2) able and available for work, and (3) involved in seeking employment.

The payment of unemployment benefits raises many social issues regarding its effects. For example, many opponents of such benefits maintain that awarding them encourages unemployment. In addition, unemployment compensation has created some conflicts in federal labor legislation. In *Wimberly v Labor and Industrial Relations Comm'n of Missouri* (Case 18.2), the U.S. Supreme Court dealt with the conflicting federal rights for labor, management, and unemployment compensation.

CASE 18.2	*Wimberly v Labor and Indus. Relations Com'n of Missouri*
	479 U.S. 511 (1987)

Post-Partum Employment

FACTS

After the birth of her child on November 5, 1980, Linda Wimberly (petitioner) was on pregnancy leave from her job at JCPenney. Under Penney policy, she could return to work only if a position was available. A position was not available when Mrs. Wimberly tried to return, and she then filed a claim for unemployment benefits with the Missouri Division of Employment Security. She was denied the claim because she had left "work voluntarily without good cause attributable to [her] work or [her] employer," a provision of a Missouri statute.

Mrs. Wimberly filed suit, and the trial court held that the Missouri statute was inconsistent with the Federal Unemployment Tax Act that prohibits denying compensation "solely on the basis of pregnancy or termination of pregnancy." The court of appeals affirmed, but the Missouri Supreme Court reversed. Mrs. Wimberly appealed to the U.S. Supreme Court.

JUDICIAL OPINION

O'CONNOR, Justice

The Federal Unemployment Tax Act (Act), 26 U.S.C. §§ 3301 *et seq.*, enacted originally as Title IX of the Social Security Act in 1935, 49 Stat. 639, envisions a cooperative federal-state program of benefits to unemployed workers. The standard at issue in this case, § 3304(a)(12), mandates that "no person shall be denied compensation under such State law solely on the basis of pregnancy or termination of pregnancy."

Apart from the minimum standards reflected in § 3304(a), the Act leaves to state discretion the rules governing the administration of unemployment compensation programs.

The treatment of pregnancy-related terminations is a matter of considerable disparity among the States. Most States regard leave on account of pregnancy as a voluntary termination for good cause. Some of these States have specific statutory provisions enumerating pregnancy motivated termination as good cause for leaving a job, while others, by judicial or administrative decision, treat pregnancy as encompassed within larger categories of good cause such as illness or compelling personal reasons. A few states, however, like Missouri, have chosen to define "leaving for good cause" narrowly. In these states, all persons who leave their jobs are disqualified from receiving benefits unless they leave for reasons directly attributable to the work or to the employer.

Petitioner does not dispute that the Missouri scheme treats pregnant women the same as all other persons who leave for reasons not causally connected to their work or their employer, including those suffering from other types of temporary disabilities. She contends, however, that § 3304(a)(12) is not simply an antidiscrimination statute, but rather that it mandates preferential treatment for women who leave work because of pregnancy. According to petitioner, § 3304(a)(12) affirmatively requires states to provide unemployment benefits to women who leave work because of pregnancy when they are next available and able to work, regardless of the state's treatment of other similarly situated claimants.

Contrary to petitioner's assertions, the plain import of the language of § 3304(a)(12) is that Congress intended to prohibit states from singling out pregnancy for unfavorable treatment. The text of the statute provides that compensation shall not be denied under state law "solely on the basis of pregnancy." The focus of this language is on the basis of the state's decision, not the claimant's reason for leaving her job. Thus, a state could not decide to deny benefits to pregnant women while at the same time allowing benefits to persons who are in other respects similarly situated: The "sole basis" for such a decision would be on account of pregnancy. On the other hand, if a state adopts a neutral rule that incidentally disqualifies pregnant or formerly pregnant claimants as part of a larger group, the neutral application of that rule cannot readily be characterized as a decision made "solely on the basis of pregnancy."

Even petitioner concedes that § 3304(a)(12) does not prohibit states from denying benefits to pregnant or formerly pregnant women who fail to satisfy neutral eligibility requirements such as ability to work and availability for work. Missouri does not have a "policy" specifically relating to pregnancy: It neutrally disqualifies workers who leave their jobs for reasons unrelated to their employment.

In *Turner v Department of Employment Security*, this Court struck down on due process grounds a Utah statute providing that a woman was disqualified for 12 weeks before the expected date of childbirth and for 6 weeks after childbirth, even if she left work for reasons unrelated to pregnancy.

In short, petitioner can point to nothing in the Committee Reports, or elsewhere in the statute's legislative history, that evidences congressional intent to mandate preferential treatment for women on account of pregnancy. There is no hint that Congress disapproved of, much less intended to prohibit, a neutral rule such as Missouri's. Indeed, the legislative history shows that Congress was focused only on the issue addressed by the plain language of § 3304(a)(12): prohibiting rules that single out pregnant women or formerly pregnant women for disadvantageous treatment.

Because § 3304(a)(12) does not require states to afford preferential treatment to women on account of pregnancy, the judgment of the Missouri Supreme Court is affirmed.

CASE QUESTIONS

1. Why was Mrs. Wimberly denied unemployment compensation?
2. Was the pregnancy given as a reason?
3. What is the difference between the Utah statute mentioned in the Court's opinion and the Missouri statute?
4. Is the Missouri statute valid?
5. What implications does the decision carry for maternity leaves?

CONSIDER... 18.1

Alfred Smith and Galen Black were fired by a private drug rehabilitation center because they ingested peyote for sacramental purposes at a ceremony of the Native American Church, of which both are members. When Mr. Smith and Mr. Black applied for unemployment compensation from the state of Oregon, their requests were denied because they were fired for "misconduct." They challenged the decision as a violation of their religious freedom. Are Mr. Smith and Mr. Black correct? [*Employment Div., Dep't of Human Resources of Oregon v Smith*, 496 U.S. 913 (1990)]

Who Pays for Unemployment Benefits?

Although the idea and mandate for unemployment compensation came from the federal government, the states actually administer their own programs. Employers in each state are taxed based on the number of workers they employ and their wages. Those taxes are collected by the states on a quarterly basis. These funds are deposited with the federal government, which maintains an unemployment insurance program with the funds. Each state has an account in the federal fund on which it can draw. Employers effectively pay the costs of the unemployment compensation system.

Workers' Compensation Laws

The purpose of **workers' compensation** laws is to provide wage benefits and medical care to victims of work-related injuries. Although each state has its own system of workers' compensation, several general principles remain consistent throughout the states:

1. An employee who is injured in the scope of employment is automatically entitled to certain benefits (a discussion of work-related injuries and the scope of employment follows).
2. Fault is immaterial. Employees' contributory negligence does not lessen their right to compensation. Employers' care and precaution do not lessen their responsibility.
3. Coverage is limited to employees and does not extend to independent contractors.
4. Benefits include partial wages, hospital and medical expenses, and death benefits.
5. In exchange for these benefits, employees, their families, and dependents give up their common-law right to sue an employer for damages.
6. If third parties (e.g., equipment manufacturers) are responsible for an accident, recovery from the third party goes first to the employer for reimbursement.
7. Each state has some administrative agency responsible for administration of workers' compensation.
8. Every employer who is subject to workers' compensation regulation is required to provide some security for liability (such as insurance).

Employee Injuries

As they originated, workers' compensation systems were created to provide benefits for accidental workplace injuries. Over the years, however, the term *accident* has been interpreted broadly. Most injuries are those that result suddenly, such as broken arms, injured backs caused by falls, burns, and lacerations. But workers' compensation has been extended to cover injuries that develop over time. For example, workers involved in lifting heavy objects might eventually develop back problems. Even such medical problems as high blood pressure, heart attacks, and nervous breakdowns have in some cases been classified as work related and compensable.

The standard for recovery under the workers' compensation system is that the injury must originate in the workplace, be caused by the workplace, or develop over time in the workplace. Even stress, when shown to be caused or originated by employment, is a compensable injury.

Workers' compensation issues have become more complex, and many of the hearings involve the issue of determining whether a disability originated on the job or would have existed independently of the job. *Gacioch v Stroh Brewery Co.* (Case 18.3) deals with this type of issue.

> ### CASE 18.3
> *Gacioch v Stroh Brewery Co.*
> 396 N.W.2d 1 (Mich. 1990)

Free-Beer Lunches, Alcoholism, and Workers' Comp

FACTS

Casimer Gacioch (plaintiff) began working for Stroh Brewery on February 24, 1947. When he began his work for Stroh, he was predisposed to alcoholism, but he had not yet become an uncontrolled alcoholic.

Beer was provided free at the brewery and was available to all employees on the job at "designated relief areas." This availability had been negotiated through a collective bargaining agreement. Employees could drink beer during their breaks and at lunch with no limit on the amount.

Mr. Gacioch did not drink at home during the week but drank three or four bottles of beer on the weekend. At work he drank 12 bottles a day. He was not a test taster; he ran a machine that fed cases of beer to a soaker.

In 1973, Stroh Brewery noticed Mr. Gacioch's drinking problem and required him to sign an agreement stating that he could no longer drink on the job. He continued to drink, and seven months after the first agreement he signed a second agreement not to drink on the job. He again continued to drink, was intoxicated on the job, and could not perform his work. He was fired on August 30, 1974.

From April 1976 until September 1978, Mr. Gacioch worked part-time as a church custodian. He pursued a workers' compensation claim against Stroh, alleging he was disabled because of alcoholism. He was denied recovery and appealed to the Workers' Compensation Appeal Board (WCAB), which found that alcoholism is a disease, that the free-beer policy accelerated the problem, and that Stroh should pay compensation. Stroh appealed.

JUDICIAL OPINION

ARCHER, Justice

This case involves a claim for workers' compensation benefits for the chronic alcoholism suffered by plaintiff. We must determine whether, under the circumstances extant in this case, chronic alcoholism, suffered by plaintiff who, during breaks drank beer provided free by Stroh Brewery pursuant to a collectively bargained contract provision negotiated by the union, is compensable under the Workers' Disability Compensation Act as a personal injury which arose out of and in the course of plaintiff's employment.

The statute in effect on the last day of plaintiff's employment at Stroh Brewery read:

An employee, who receives a personal injury arising out of and in the course of his employment by an employer who is subject to the provisions of this act, at the time of such injury, shall be paid compensation in the manner and to the extent provided in this act, or in case of his death resulting from such injuries the compensation shall be paid to his dependents as defined in this act.

"Personal injury" shall include a disease or disability which is due to causes and conditions which are characteristic of and peculiar to the business of the employer and which arises out of and in the course of the employment. Ordinary diseases of life to which the public is generally exposed outside of the employment shall not be compensable.

Defendants contend that alcoholism is not a disease, but, rather, a "social aberration." All three experts testifying in this case, Drs. Smith and Tanay, plaintiff's experts, and Dr. Rauch, defendants' expert, referred to alcoholism as a disease. Dr. Smith described alcoholism as a "lifelong metabolic disease, much like diabetes." Dr. Tanay testified that alcoholism is associated with particular personality disorders which begin during a person's childhood. The WCAB treated plaintiff's chronic alcoholism as a disease. Our review of the professional literature on the subject indicates that various organizations representing health care professionals have officially pronounced alcoholism as a disease. Hence, plaintiff's chronic alcoholism is a disease for purposes of the above statute.

Plaintiff asserts that his chronic alcoholism was an occupational disease. We disagree. A review of the record indicates that the WCAB also did not conclude that plaintiff's alcoholic condition was an occupational disease. The board treated plaintiff's alcoholism as an ordinary disease of life. The proper inquiry in this case, therefore, is whether plaintiff's chronic alcoholism was a disease or disability which was due to causes and conditions which are characteristic of and peculiar to the business of Stroh and which arose out of and in the course of employment. In reaching the question concerning whether chronic alcoholism is a disease which is due to causes and conditions which are characteristic of and peculiar to the business of Stroh and which arose

CONTINUED

out of and in the course of plaintiff's employment, we must be careful not to equate "circumstance" of employment with "out of and in the course" of employment. If chronic alcoholism can be categorized as an ordinary disease of life to which the public is generally exposed outside of the employment, plaintiff is not entitled to a workers' compensation award. The pertinent question then is whether the board made specific findings as to whether brewery workers are more prone to develop chronic alcoholism than is the general public.

We are unable to discern from the opinion of the board whether it found as fact that brewery workers are more prone to suffer from chronic alcoholism (an ordinary disease of life) than is the general public. We note that none of the experts testifying in this case stated that plaintiff's alcoholism was due to the inherent characteristics and peculiarities of his employment in the brewery industry as a production worker responsible for running a machine. Dr. Smith, for example, testified that "Mr. Gacioch would have most likely become an alcoholic anyway and his drinking outside of work eventually [was] far greater than during work." Dr. Rauch opined that individuals who are predisposed

to alcoholism, like plaintiff herein, are likely to become an alcoholic no matter where they work.

We are unable to determine from the opinion of the WCAB whether it understood the applicable legal standard and what facts it specifically relied upon in reaching its conclusion that plaintiff's alcoholism was compensable under the Workers' Disability Compensation Act.

We therefore remand this case to the WCAB for its statement of the law and the specific facts relied upon to support its conclusion.

CASE QUESTIONS

1. Why do you believe Stroh's had a free-beer policy?
2. Was Mr. Gacioch predisposed to alcoholism? Is alcoholism a disease?
3. What additional factual information is needed to resolve the case?
4. How do you feel about the free-beer policy? Can you foresee other issues of liability for Stroh beyond workers' compensation?

Fault Is Immaterial

The fact that an injury occurs in the workplace is enough for recovery. Employee negligence, employer precautions, contributory negligence, and assumption of risk are generally not issues in workers' compensation cases.

Employees versus Independent Contractors

Workers' compensation applies to employees but not to independent contractors. Employees are those who are present at the workplace on a regular basis, paid a wage, and supervised. **Independent contractors** are those who work on a job basis, work irregular hours, and are not supervised by the employer. A backhoe operator working daily from 5 A.M. to 1 P.M. for a plumbing company and paid a weekly wage is an employee. A backhoe operator hired and paid on a per-job basis is an independent contractor. A more complete discussion of employee status can be found in Chapter 17.

Benefits

Workers' benefits can be grouped into three different categories: medical, disability, and death. Medical benefits include typical insurance-covered costs such as hospital costs, physician and nursing fees, therapy fees, and rental costs for equipment needed for recovery.

Disability benefits are payments made to compensate employees for wages lost because of a disability injury. The amount of benefits is based on state statutory figures. Most states base disability benefits on an employee's average monthly wage, and they also specify a maximum amount. State statutes also generally have a list of **scheduled injuries,** which will carry a percentage disability figure. For example, loss of a body part is a typical injury. In Arizona, the disability amount for a lost thumb is 55 percent of the average monthly wage for 15 months (Ariz. Rev. Stat. § 23–1044). For a lost foot, the amount is 55 percent of the average monthly wage for 50 months. Total disability is also defined by statute. Workers who have total disability are generally entitled to two-thirds of their average monthly salary for the period of the disability. Total disability usually includes the loss of both eyes or both hands, or complete paralysis.

Some injuries suffered by workers are not listed in statutes. Those not specifically described in statutes are called **unscheduled injuries.** The amount allowed for unscheduled injuries is discretionary and an area of frequent litigation.

Death benefits are paid to the family of a deceased employee and generally include burial expenses. In addition, survivors who were economically dependent on an employee are also paid benefits. The amount of death benefits is generally some percentage of the average monthly salary; for example, a surviving spouse might be entitled to a 35 percent benefit.

Forfeiture of the Right of Suit

The majority of states require employees to forfeit all other lawsuit rights in exchange for workers' compensation benefits. Employees receive automatic benefits but lose the right to sue their employers for covered incidents. Some states even prohibit employees from suing their coworkers under most conditions. In addition, some states allow family members to sue employers for direct injury to themselves. In those states, a spouse could bring a lawsuit against an employer for loss of consortium (marital companionship).

Third-Party Suits

If an employee is injured by a machine malfunction while on the job, the employee is covered by workers' compensation. However, product liability may also be at issue in the accident. If suit is brought against the machine's manufacturer for product liability, any recovery goes first to the employer to compensate for the cost of the employee's benefits. In other words, third-party recovery is first used to reimburse the employer.

Administrative Agency

Every state has some administrative agency responsible for the administration of claims, hearings, and benefits. In most states, this agency holds hearings for claims, and its decision is appealable in the same manner as any other agency decision.

The procedure for compensation requires employees to file claims with the agency along with medical documentation for the claim. Most claims are paid without contest; but if a challenge is made to a decision, a hearing with evidence and testimony is held.

Insurance

All states with workers' compensation systems require employers to be financially responsible for benefits under their systems. Employers can show financial responsibility by (1) maintaining an insurance policy, (2) obtaining a policy through the state agency, or (3) offering evidence of sufficient assets and resources to cover potential claims and benefits.

Problems in Workers' Compensation Systems

Increasingly, states and employers are experimenting with reforms to workers' compensation systems. Concerns focus on fraud that stems from incentives in the system. For example, medical benefits in workers' compensation are better than most medical plans. Because nearly all disability payments are tax-free, employees may be living on close to 90 percent of what they lived on (after taxes) before their disability.

Some doubts exist about the legitimacy of many complaints. For example, in one state, a janitor moonlighting for HGO, Inc., hurt his little finger while on the job. He collected $16,800 in disability payments over the next three years, even though he was able to continue his regular day job as a police officer.

Suggested reforms have included the elimination of certain claims, such as "mental stress," from workers' compensation coverage. Some states impose a maximum number of years for disability payouts. Other states have hired more investigators to detect fraud. Companies are also attempting to cut costs by using staff doctors or by returning employees to other jobs that can be done despite an injury.

Workers' compensation systems were established during the Industrial Revolution, when the injuries sustained were primarily the types of factory and machinery accidents we traditionally associate with workers' compensation claims. However, the majority of jobs in the United States are now in service industries, and the nature of work-related injuries has changed from sudden-accident types to ongoing, progressive problems that are more expensive to treat and correct. For example, the repetitive hand and arm motions of computer keyboard operators can injure word processors, journalists, reservationists, and cashiers. This injury, often called carpal tunnel syndrome, can require expensive surgery and results in many lost workdays, if not new job assignments. Such repetitive stress injuries (RSIs) are the basis of pending lawsuits by workers against keyboard and equipment manufacturers.

The office environment itself is presenting new and difficult-to-control health-related problems for workers. Ergonomics is a rapidly growing field that examines the design of work areas and office equipment to minimize such worker injuries as repetitive motion syndromes and back problems. Architects and engineers are working together to design buildings that eliminate the so-called sick-building syndrome, in which poor air quality or the lack of fresh air circulation increases the incidence of illness and causes other symptoms in office workers.

A final issue in workers' compensation is the relationship between the state systems and the Americans with Disabilities Act (see Chapter 19), which prohibits discrimination against employees with disabilities and requires accommodation of employer facilities to permit disabled persons to work. Traditionally, when an accident caused disability, an employee collected payment in lieu of being rehired. An issue that arises as the systems of laws interact is whether an employer is required to rehire a disabled employee.

Labor Unions

The Norris–LaGuardia Act of 1932

The **Norris–LaGuardia Act** prohibits the use of injunctions as a remedy in labor disputes. Violent strikes can still be enjoined, provided evidence shows that violence did or would have occurred and that public officers could not control the violence and any resulting damage. Injunctions cannot be issued without first holding a hearing.

The Wagner Act

The **Wagner Act,** also known as the **National Labor Relations Act of 1935** (NLRA), gave employees the right to organize and choose representatives to bargain collectively with their employers. Further, it established the **National Labor Relations Board** (NLRB), which had two functions: to conduct union elections and to investigate and remedy unfair labor practices.

The Taft–Hartley Act: The Labor-Management Relations Act of 1947

Over President Truman's veto, Congress passed the **Taft–Hartley Act,** which was a response to the public's concern about too many strikes, secondary boycotts, and the unrestrained power of union officials. Strikes to force employers to discharge nonunion employees, secondary boycotts, and strikes over work assignments are prohibited as unfair labor practices. Employees were also given the right to remove a union they no longer wanted as their representative. The act also contains provisions that allow the president to invoke a **cooling-off period** of bargaining before a strike that threatens to imperil the public health and safety can begin. This power has been used by presidents in transportation and coal strikes.

The Landrum–Griffin Act: The Labor-Management Reporting and Disclosure Act of 1959

The **Landrum–Griffin Act** provides employee protection within union organizations. The act gave union members a bill of rights, required certain procedures for election of officers, prescribed financial reporting requirements for union funds, and established criminal and civil penalties for union misconduct.

Today nearly 450 unions are active in the United States, from the Screen Actors Guild to the Airline Pilots Association. However, more than 75 percent of these unions are affiliated with the AFL-CIO (the American Federation of Labor and Congress of Industrial Organizations), the giant that resulted from the merger of the two original labor unions in 1955. These unions, however, make up only 10.9 percent of today's workforce, compared to 35 percent in 1955.

Union Organizing Efforts

Employees make the decision as to whether a union will represent them and, if so, which will serve as their representative. This process is called selecting a bargaining representative, and the NLRB has strict procedures for such selection. The NLRB carefully chooses how employees will be grouped together so that they share common interests.

The Collective Bargaining Unit

The first step in union organization is the establishment of a collective bargaining unit. The **collective bargaining unit** is a group of employees recognized by the NLRB as appropriate for exclusive representation of all employees in that group. Collective bargaining units are determined by the NLRB. The standard for a collective bargaining unit is that it must consist of homogeneous employees.

Some bargaining units consist of entire plants of workers, whereas others are specialized units within a plant, such as the maintenance staff or the line workers in an assembly plant. For some national companies, the bargaining unit is all employees, whereas for other national firms the bargaining unit is one particular plant or store.

The Petition, Cards, and Vote

Once the collective bargaining unit is set, the union, employees, or employers can file a petition for exclusive representation of employees within a unit. An employer can voluntarily recognize the union. However, if a majority of employees in the bargaining unit do not support the union, the employer can insist on a formal election.

The NLRB monitors closely the conduct of both employer and union as the election approaches. Employers can prohibit oral campaigning during work hours and can restrict literature distribution both during and, to a degree, before and after work hours. Employers cannot make threats about relocation or make speeches to captive audiences (employees on their shifts) in the 24 hours before an election.

Certification

If a majority of employees vote for the union in a secret ballot process administered by the NLRB, the union has completed its **certification.** An employer who refuses to deal with the certified union can be forced to by an injunction obtained by the NLRB.

After a union has been certified, an election for a new union cannot be held for twelve months from the time of certification. If the union signs a collective bargaining agreement, no union certification election can be held until the collective bargaining agreement expires. These limitations on elections and certifications prevent chaos in the workplace that would result from constant changeovers in union representation.

Nonunion Members in the Certified Workplace

Although the NLRA gave unions the right to exist, it also gave workers the right to a choice. Workers are not required to join unions and cannot be coerced into supporting union action. Attempts by a union to force its members to participate in strikes and other union activities are considered unfair labor practices. In *Pattern Makers' League of North America, AFL-CIO v NLRB* 473 U.S. 95 (1985), the U.S. Supreme Court held that a union member could not be fined for his failure to participate in a strike.

Union Contract Negotiations

Once a union is certified as the employees' representative, one of its major roles is to obtain a contract or **collective bargaining agreement** between employer and employees. Both sides must engage in **good-faith bargaining,** which the NLRB defines as a mutual obligation of employer and union to meet at reasonable times, confer in good faith on employment issues, and execute a written agreement reflecting their oral agreement. Both parties must bargain with an open mind and the sincere intent of reaching an agreement.

Two types of subject matters can be discussed during bargaining: (1) mandatory or compulsory subject matter and (2) permissive subject matter. As to the former, the NLRA describes **mandatory bargaining terms** as those dealing with

EXHIBIT 18.3 Usual Topics for a Collective Bargaining Agreement

Recognition of the union	Insurance	Union announcements (bulletin board rights)
Wages	Pension/retirement plans	Definition of terms
Work hours	Employee grievances	Leaves of absence
Vacations	Length of agreement/expiration date	Drug testing
Sick leave	Incentive plans	
Seniority		

"wages, hours, and other terms and conditions of employment." Obviously, the amount to be paid as wages is included but so also are related issues, such as merit pay, vacations, overtime, work hours, leaves, and pay days. Exhibit 18.3 lists the usual topics covered in a collective bargaining agreement.

Permissive subject matters, in contrast to compulsory subject matters, would be those the parties are required to negotiate but on which they need not reach an agreement. A strike vote of employees before a strike starts is an example of a permissive subject. Any topic that does not directly concern employer–employee relations is a permissive subject. A refusal to bargain on a permissive subject is not, however, an unfair labor practice; a refusal to bargain on mandatory subject matter *is* an unfair labor practice.

Some subjects are "unbargainable." Employers and employees cannot bargain to give away statutory rights—for example, the procedures for certifying a union. Nor can they bargain about having a **closed shop,** which requires employees to be union members before they can be hired. Such shops are illegal under the Taft–Hartley Act.

CONSIDER... 18.2

Are insurance plans a mandatory, permissive, or nonbargainable topic?

THINK: The law says that the terms and conditions of employment are mandatory collective bargaining topics.

APPLY: Insurance is a term and condition of employment—it determines the level of employee benefits.

ANSWER: Insurance plans are a mandatory topic.

Now determine whether the following subjects are mandatory, permissive, or nonbargainable:

- Maternity leaves
- Plant rules
- Subcontracting procedures
- Strikes
- Layoffs
- Union bookkeeping procedures
- Meal periods

CONSIDER... 18.3

E. I. DuPont de Nemours & Company is renegotiating its contract with the International Brotherhood of DuPont Workers. Two issues have arisen during the course of bargaining. The union has asked DuPont to release a map that was developed as a result of a DuPont study on its toxic waste locations. The second issue was DuPont's implementation of its business ethics policy and its application to union members without its being a subject of bargaining. Must the map be released? Is this a mandatory subject? Must the application of the ethics policy be negotiated? [*DuPont v International Bhd. of DuPont Workers*, 301 N.L.R.B. No. 14 (1991)]

Failure to bargain on mandatory subject matter is an **unfair labor practice**, which is conduct prohibited by statute or NLRB decision. When employer or union fails to bargain on a mandatory topic, a charge can be brought and the NLRB can proceed with a complaint.

Protected Concerted Activities

Some union activities are protected under the NLRA. Ads and handbills that explain the union's issues and position are permitted and can be an effective tool for obtaining boycotts. Employees' handbills and ads can encourage customers not to deal with their employer until the strike is settled. A union currently recognized as a certified collective bargaining agent can engage in **picketing** an employer, but picketing for recognition of a union is not permitted. The **strike** is the best-known and most widely used economic weapon of unions. A strike is a work stoppage because employees no longer report to work.

In recent years, unions have developed a new economic tool—contacting institutional shareholders and board members to put public pressure on corporate officers to work with unions. These public-attention tactics have been effective.

BUSINESS STRATEGY

Unions, Employees, Employers, and E-Mails

The issue of the use of e-mail continues to be problematic for the NLRB, employers, and union organizers. All recognize the efficiency of e-mail contact because an estimated 70 percent of all Americans have access to a private computer for viewing private e-mail. Both unions and employers would benefit from such direct contact. However, clear statements of the law allow employers to control access of union members to employees while they are on the job so that there is no interference with their work or disruption of facilities. If union organizers cannot enter the plant to distribute pamphlets and buttons, they cannot invade the company e-mail and have employees use company time to read their messages.

However, some scholars have proposed a solution to the dilemma of efficient communication and rights under the law.

CYBERLAW

- Use employees' private e-mail accounts for contact, not their work e-mails. The employer's e-mail system need not be used or taxed as a result.

- If employees reading private e-mails while on the job becomes a problem, employers can issue a generic policy of no private e-mails while at work. With this policy, they will not run into any accusations or issues over singling out unions and union organizers for different treatment.

Unfair Employee Practices

Employees are also prohibited from engaging in some activities that are classified as unfair labor practices. A **slowdown** is an economic tool that interrupts the employer's business but falls short of a stoppage or strike. Slowdowns usually occur when employees refuse to perform work or use certain equipment that is in violation of their collective bargaining agreement with the employer. For example, in early 1999, American Airlines pilots staged a slowdown by calling in sick, known as a sickout. After more than 1,000 flights per day were canceled, a federal court ordered the pilots to halt their slowdown.

Featherbedding is payment for work not actually performed. It is an unfair labor practice for a union to negotiate an agreement that requires an employer to pay for work that was not actually performed. For example, some bricklayers' unions at one time required payment for a minimum number of bricks even though the work might not have actually involved that many bricks.

Employer Rights

Employers have the right to give information to employees about unions and the results of union organization. The speech of employers cannot be controlled by the NLRB unless the speech is accompanied by some unlawful conduct, such as a threat of physical force or a promise of benefit. For example, an employer who threatens the loss of jobs if employees join the union is not protected by the free speech rule. An employer who tells employees that it will not negotiate with a union is also not protected by the free speech rule.

Exhibit 18.4 is a summary of management do's and don'ts when faced with an upcoming union election.

EXHIBIT 18.4 Management Do's and Don'ts in the Unionization Process

DO	DON'T
Tell employees about current wages and benefits and how they compare to other firms.	Promise employees pay increases or promotions if they vote against the union.
Tell employees you will use all legal means to oppose unionization.	Threaten employees with termination or discriminate when disciplining employees.
Tell employees the disadvantages of having a union (especially cost of dues, assessments, and requirements of membership).	Threaten to close down or move the company if a union is voted in.
Show employees articles about unions and negative experiences others have had elsewhere.	Spy or have someone spy on union meetings.
Explain the unionization process to your employees accurately.	Make a speech to employees or groups at work within twenty-four hours of the election (before that, it is allowed).
Forbid distribution of union literature during work hours in work areas.	Ask employees how they plan to vote or if they have signed authorization cards.
Enforce in a consistent and fair manner disciplinary policies and rules.	Urge local employees to persuade others to vote against the union (such a vote must be initiated solely by the employee).

Source: R. L. Mathis and J. H. Jackson, *Human Resource Management*, 8th ed., p. 533. © 1997. Reprinted with permission of South-Western, a part of Cengage Learning.

Ethical Issues

Many employers are ranking employees, or "placing them in buckets" as it is commonly called, as part of their annual performance evaluations. For example, Ford Motor Company, when it used this system, had 18,000 managers who were grouped into sets of 30 to 50. Of each group, 10 percent must be assigned an "A" grade, 80 percent must be assigned a "B" grade, and 10 percent must be given a "C" grade. Those with the bottom grades are then eased out of the company. Those with a "C" grade cannot be given a pay raise, and those with a "C" grade for two years in a row are demoted or terminated. No exceptions are made for any of the groups, but Ford did cut back on the "C" requirement to 5 percent in 2001 and changed the system in 2003.

Other companies with grading systems include Intel and Sun Microsystems.

Cisco Systems has established a goal of getting rid of 1 of every 20 employees, with the purpose of terminating employees who are given substandard performance evaluations.

GE has a 20–70–10 plan for ranking employees. GE follows a carrot approach in that it rewards the top 20 percent so well that few ever leave the company. GE uses the 10 percent group to terminate employees, and it terminates about 8,000 management and professional employees each year. Former GE CEO Jack Welch noted that employees in the 10 percent bottom group would end up leaving the company anyway because they are unhappy in not performing, and GE just makes the inevitable decision for them early.

Workers' rights groups call the systems inhumane. Some say that instead of motivating employees to do better, the result is that they are demoralized and do worse or leave the company.

Do these systems violate any laws? Are they a mandatory collective bargaining issue? Are you comfortable with them from the perspective of business ethics?

Source: Del Jones, "More Firms Cut Workers Ranked at the Bottom to Make Way for Talent," *USA Today,* May 30, 2001, pp. 1B, 2B.

Right-to-Work Laws

Section 14(b) of the Taft–Hartley Act is in some ways a protection for employers as well as for employees. This section outlaws the closed shop, which, as discussed earlier, is a business that requires union membership before an employee can be hired. Based on this section of Taft–Hartley, states can pass **right-to-work laws** that give people the right to work without having to join a union. About half the states have right-to-work statutes.

Economic Weapons of Employers

Employers have economic weapons that can be used in response to employee economic weapons. In response to union certifications and strikes, some employers have opted to close the affected plants. In some cases, employers have abandoned the business altogether. It is clear that these shutdowns and closures are strong economic weapons, and their legality under the federal labor law scheme has some restrictions. In *Textile Workers Union v Darlington Manufacturing Co.,* 380 U.S. 263 (1965), the Supreme Court ruled that employers have the right to terminate their entire business for any reason. Even if the reason for the closing is vindictiveness toward the union, neither the NLRB nor the courts can require an employer to stay in business.

Employers cannot use a temporary closing with a promise of reopening after a union is defeated in an election. Further, employers cannot stage a **runaway shop,** which is when work is transferred to another plant or a new plant is opened to carry the workload of the old plant.

The concern of the NLRB in the closing of one plant is that employees in other plants, fearful that their plants will be closed, will fail to exercise their rights to unionize. For a plant closure to be an unfair labor practice, the evidence must show that the closure was done with the intent of curbing unionization in that and other plants owned by the employer.

Federal plant-closing legislation is called the **Worker Adjustment and Retraining Notification Act of 1988** (WARN). Under this act, employers with 100 or more workers are required to give workers 60 days' advance notice of plant shutdowns that would affect at least 50 workers and of layoffs that would last more than six months and affect one-third of the workers at the site. There are some exceptions to the 60-day notice requirement, such as unforeseeable circumstances and seasonal, agricultural, and construction businesses. Penalties for violations include back pay and benefits for employees for each day of violation and up to $500 per day for each day notice was not given. The closing of Arthur Andersen following Enron resulted in WARN litigation, but the court held the closing was not foreseeable. [*Roquet v Arthur Andersen LLP,* 398 F.3d 585 (7th Cir. 2005)].

One result of the increased globalization of business is the availability of lower-cost labor pools outside the United States. When union demands increase business costs beyond what managers feel will allow a firm to remain competitive, plants are closed and work is transferred to plants outside the United States. The global marketplace provides management with a bargaining tool that becomes difficult for unions to address. Demands for wage increases, more benefits, and better working conditions are often met with a plant closing in the United States and a plant opening in another country where the labor pool is large and the wages low.

A **lockout** is an employer's economic weapon in which the employer refuses to allow employees to work. Lockouts have been recognized by the U.S. Supreme Court as a legitimate measure to help an employer avoid a strike at an economically damaging time. The reason for an employer's lockout must be economic. A lockout to discourage union membership, therefore, is an unfair labor practice.

Employers can use benefits as economic weapons; the only restriction is the timing of those benefits. Offering them too close to an election can be an unfair labor practice. Conferring benefits on a temporary basis to gain an advantage (precluding the union) is also an unfair labor practice.

Bankruptcy has become a solution for many business problems, labor problems among them. When strikes extend for long periods of time, the financial well-being of the firms affected can deteriorate, often to the degree that some firms declare bankruptcy. The type of bankruptcy proceedings initiated will determine the fate of labor contracts. In a reorganization, the contracts remain in force. In a straight bankruptcy, the workers stand in line (although with some priority) to collect any wages due and any contributions made to the firm's retirement plan. Bankruptcy can be an escape for a firm, but the bankruptcy laws themselves limit the availability of this economic weapon. The firm must still meet the tests for declaring bankruptcy, so the weapon is not entirely optional.

Exhibit 18.5 provides a summary of labor weapons, rights, and unfair practices.

EXHIBIT 18.5　Union Disputes: Economic Weapons and Rights of Employers and Employees

ECONOMIC WEAPONS	RIGHTS	UNFAIR LABOR PRACTICES
Employer		
Business closing	Freedom of speech	Refusal to bargain in good faith
Plant closings	Demand election	Refusal to bargain on a mandatory issue
Lockouts		Violation of collective bargaining agreement
Right to confer benefits (timing)		Interference with joining union
		Timing of benefits
		Observation of union activities
		Domination of labor union
		Discrimination in promotion of union members
		Blacklisting
Employee		
Strike	Freedom of speech	Violation of collective bargaining agreement
Ads	Right to union representation upon investigation	Secondary boycotts
Picketing		Payment for union cards
Boycotts	Right to join union	Coercion or discrimination in union membership
Shareholders	Right of members to adequate representation	Causing an employer to pay excessive wages—featherbedding
	Right to union office	

International Issues in Labor

Today's labor market is considerably different from the market that existed at the time of the enactment of federal labor legislation. Both operations within the United States and operations in other countries are affected by a new international labor force. Domestic operations must be certain that all employees from other countries are documented workers. International operations present numerous ethical and public policy issues in the conditions and operations of plants in other countries with different labor standards.

Immigration Laws

The fluidity of commerce across borders has found companies in the United States with employees from around the world. Employers are responsible for ensuring that their employees are properly in the United States. This section deals with immigration laws, documentation for alien employees, and the penalties for employer violations of the compliance requirements.

The **Immigration and Naturalization Act** (INA), the **Immigration Reform and Control Act of 1986** (IRCA), and the **Immigration Act of 1990** (8 U.S.C. § 11101 *et seq.*) are the federal laws that apply to immigrants in the United States and impose requirements on employers in the United States that employ immigrants. The Immigration Act of 1990, or IMMACT 90, increased legal immigration by 35 percent, enabled more family-sponsored immigration, and increased employment-based immigration, while providing a "diversity" program to increase the number of immigrants from countries traditionally underrepresented in the U.S. immigrant mix (e.g., Ireland and some African countries). This program is also known as the "green card visa lottery."

In 1996, two federal statutes changed dramatically the issues of immigration, deportation, and penalties for hiring illegal immigrants: the **Illegal Immigration Reform and Immigrant Responsibility Act of 1996** and the **Antiterrorism and Effective Death Penalty Act** (18 U.S.C. § 1). The statutes served to increase the types and numbers of crimes that rendered illegal immigrants deportable from the United States and denied them entry from other countries. The statutes also decreased the defenses to deportation as well as the procedural protections for opposing deportation. The enforcement of the immigration laws is now under a cabinet-level agency known as the **U.S. Department of Homeland Security** (DHS). DHS has Immigration and Customs Enforcement (ICE) as one of its reporting agencies. The Immigration and Naturalization Service (INS), originally housed within the U.S. Department of Justice, was abolished and INS's responsibilities have been divided among separate bureaus within DHS. This reorganization and the creation and elevation of DHS to a cabinet-level position was the result of the **Uniting and Strengthening America by Providing Appropriate Tools Required to Intercept and Obstruct Terrorism Act** (**USA Patriot Act;** 18 U.S.C. § 1). With the passage of Homeland Security Act of 2002, the nature of immigration enforcement issues changed. The USA Patriot Act toughened security clearances and background checks for nonimmigrant and immigrant admittance into the United States, tightened coordination between immigration-related government agencies, and increased the U.S. government's ability to track foreign nationals in the United States.

Before hiring a new employee, employers must verify that the employee is either a U.S. citizen or is permitted to work in the United States. All non–U.S. citizens must have an I-9 form on file with the employer. Form I-9 provides complete information about noncitizens and requires the employer to verify the information provided through an Alien Registration Card, commonly called a "green card." Verification of U.S. citizenship can be provided by a driver's license from a state in the United States, a Social Security card, or a U.S. passport. If someone with a foreign accent can provide evidence of U.S. citizenship, the employer is not permitted to question further or require additional documentation, for such questioning on the basis of the accent would be an act of discrimination under the immigration laws.

Because of lobbying from the high-tech industries, Congress has passed a series of laws that address immigration exemptions, the latest of which is the **American Competitiveness in the Twenty-First Century Act** of 2000. Under this statute, employers cannot lay off American employees within the 90 days following their submission of an application for entrance and employment of one of these highly skilled workers. Referred to as *H-1B professionals,* their pay scale is also controlled by the act so that their pay is equivalent to what an equally skilled U.S. worker would earn in the same position. This constraint on wages eliminates the incentive for companies to hire all foreign H-1B professionals at much lower salaries. Workers who have H-1 visa classification have "distinguished merit and ability" and are permitted to work in the United States on a temporary basis. These types of aliens include architects, engineers, lawyers, physicians, and teachers. H-1B visas are limited to 65,000 per annum. L-1 visas allow companies to make intracompany transfers of employees who work in other countries on temporary assignment and seek permission from the government through their visas.

For the Manager's Desk

Re: The High Cost of the Failure to Comply with U.S. Immigration Laws

The tale of Agriprocessors, Inc. has nearly come to an end. However, the story of the company's demise is a lesson in the importance of following labor and employment laws. The company had received more than 12 letters in 2005 and 2006 that indicated the Social Security numbers that the company as using for its workers did not match the information that the federal agency had in its files. The 3,000 discrepancies the agency found affected 78 percent of the plant's workers. The letters did not provoke any response from the company and the Social Security Administration stopped sending letters after 2007. The following chart, from the Social Security website, shows the discrepancies pointed out to the company by the agency:

Social Security Administration Correspondence with Agriprocessors

DATE	SS# DISCREPANCIES	TAX YEAR
May 9, 2002	22	2001
May 19, 2005	500	2004
May 19, 2005	500	2003
May 19, 2005	500	2002
May 19, 2005	500	2001
May 19, 2005	461	2000
March 24, 2006	52	2004
March 24, 2006	42	2003
March 24, 2006	37	2002
March 24, 2006	24	2000
April 21, 2006	68	2005
May 5, 2006	500	2005

Elizabeth Billmeyer was the director of HR at the Agriprocessors, Inc. plant in Postville, Iowa, a company that has been called the largest kosher slaughterhouse in the country. Federal authorities conducted a raid at the plant in April 2008 and arrested 900 undocumented workers there.

Ms. Billmeyer was charged with conspiracy to harbor undocumented aliens for profit and knowingly accepting false resident alien cards. Ms. Billmeyer entered two guilty pleas to two counts, one on each charge.

In September 2008, the Iowa attorney general charged the food processor with over 9,000 violations of child labor laws. The charges focused on 32 minors who were working at the company and had been assigned work tasks or worked in areas not permitted for minors under Iowa law. The charges alleged that children under the age of 18 were exposed to poisonous chemicals and that children under 16 were employed in the operation or tending of power-driven machinery, including but not limited to conveyor belts, meat grinders, circular saws, power washers, and power shears.

The Rubashkins had also been charged with fraud and money laundering schemes, and Sholom was convicted of 86 of the 91 charges. The media coverage of the company and the raid and arrests was so extensive that the trial had to be moved to South Dakota. Their trials on the labor charges were scheduled to begin in December 2009. However, following his conviction on the fraud charges, a federal judge dismissed the immigration charges against Sholom. He has remained in prison pending sentencing.

The senior Mr. Rubashkin is proceeding with his trial and recently had a motion to be released from custody, a motion that government opposed on the grounds of his risk of flight. A motion for change of venue was denied because the court held that enough time had elapsed to allow the selection of an impartial jury in Iowa.

The following is a summary of the fates of other Agriprocessors managers and executives.

- Penny Ann Hanson, 41 and a former human resources employee, pleaded guilty to conspiracy to make false statements on immigration documents.

- Karina Pilar Freund, 29 and a former human resources employee, pleaded guilty to one misdemeanor count of aiding and abetting a pattern or practice of hiring undocumented aliens.

- Laura Althouse, 38 and a former human resources employee, pleaded guilty to one count of conspiracy to harbor undocumented aliens and one count of aggravated identity theft.

- Martin De La Rosa-Loera, 43 and a former plant supervisor, pleaded guilty to one count of aiding and abetting the harboring of undocumented aliens.

- Juan Carlos Guerrero-Espinoza, 35 and a former plant supervisor, pleaded guilty to one count of conspiracy to hire illegal aliens and one count of aiding and abetting the hiring of illegal aliens.

- Former plant operations manager Brent Beebe, 51, has been going through procedural issues regarding change of venue and jury *voir dire* in his federal court trial.

- Two additional plant managers, Hosam Amara and Zeev Levi, have been charged with federal violations but have not been found by authorities. Amara is believed to be in Israel. Sholom Rubashkin was not released from prison pending sentencing because he is perceived to be a flight risk, largely because of ongoing communications with Amara.

Agriprocessors filed for bankruptcy in 2008, was purchased by a Canadian company, and is now known as AgriStar.

The company and the Rubashkin family were known for their generosity in the community.

Using your textbook, go through this summary of events and list how many chapter topics you can find that are covered in this scenario. When you are finished, reach some conclusions about what the executives and managers could have done to avoid the company's demise and their criminal prosecution.

Sources: "H.R. Chief Pleads Guilty After Immigration Raid," *National Law Journal,* April 20, 2009, p. B5; Lynda Waddington, "Agriprocessors Ignored Government Warnings For Years," *The Iowa Independent,* May 24, 2008, www.iowaindependent.com; *U.S. v Agriprocessors,* 2009 WL 2255729 (N.D. Iowa).

Working Conditions and International Labor Law

Companies today are using more conciliatory methods to balance the economic interests of management and labor. Labor law is moving from the strike to arbitration in advance of disputes.

Solutions to labor issues have been occurring outside the statutory protections and rights given in the massive union legislation of earlier decades. Employees have turned to an individual posture and have sought the protection of individual rights, such as employment at will (see Chapter 17 for a discussion of these individual rights).

Many employers have reorganized their companies around teams of employees to empower them and use their knowledge and ideas. Motorola and Ford are among "team companies" that let workers make key decisions. A concern raised by unions is that the mixing of labor and management violates the Wagner Act. For example, teams of workers at Electromation, Inc. in Elkhart, Indiana, determined that a wage hike should be skipped because of heavy losses and instead developed programs for absenteeism. Foreign competition has made it difficult for unions to organize and for laborers to command more than minimum wage.

The United Nations Commission on Human Rights has developed the International Covenant on Economic, Social, and Cultural Rights. This covenant includes the right to work; join trade unions; enjoy leisure; earn a decent living; and receive education, medical care, and Social Security. Although this international covenant would carry with it the protections outlined in this chapter for U.S. workers, enforcement of the covenant is difficult. Its real strength comes through documentation and disclosure of its violation.

One of the most successful organs of the United Nations is the International Labour Organization (ILO). This commission, founded in 1920, continues to work to develop such principles as the right to work, to join trade unions, and to have a safe work environment. Member nations submit reports on their nation's status and compliance with the standards of the ILO agreement.

Some nations have individual legislation for their workers. For example, Germany has its own OSHA-like agency for the administration of worker safety issues. Germany's agency has existed longer than OSHA and tends to experience more self-reporting by employers.

The National Labor Committee (NLC), an activist group, periodically releases information on conditions in foreign factories and the companies utilizing those factories.

U.S. companies' investments in foreign manufacturing in major developing nations such as China, Indonesia, and Mexico have tripled in the past 15 years to $56 billion, a figure that does not include the subcontracting work. In Hong Kong, Singapore, South Korea, and Taiwan, where plants make apparel, toys, shoes, and wigs, national incomes have risen from 10 percent to 40 percent of American incomes over the past 10 years. In Indonesia, since the introduction of U.S. plants and subcontractors, the portion of malnourished children in the country has gone from one-half to one-third. As these benefits take hold, new issues about the use of foreign labor and factories are emerging. Mattel, a company that has the majority of its inventory produced by factories in China had to recall 70 percent of its inventory in 2007 because Chinese contractors had used paint on the toys that contained lead at levels prohibited in the United States. The recall of pet food because of another toxic material used in production in Chinese factories has required U.S. companies to rethink the foreign outsourcing process because of the damage to their brands when these massive recalls are forced upon them through substandard conditions and lesser standards in other countries.

In a practice that is widely accepted in other countries, children ages 10 to 14 labor in factories for 50 or more hours per week. Their wages enable their families to survive. School is a luxury, and children attend only until they are able to work in a factory.

In the United States, the issue of sweatshops came to the public's attention when it was revealed that talk-show host Kathie Lee Gifford's line of clothing at Walmart had been manufactured in sweatshops in Guatemala and CBS ran a report on conditions in Nike subcontractor factories in Vietnam and Indonesia. The reports on Nike's factories issued by Vietnam Labor Watch included the following: women required to run laps around the factory for wearing nonregulation shoes to work; payment of subminimum wages; physical beatings, including with shoes, by factory supervisors; and employment mostly of women between the ages of 15 and 28. Philip Knight, CEO of Nike, included the following in a letter to shareholders:

> *Q: Why on earth did Nike pick such a terrible place as Indonesia to have shoes made?*
>
> *A: Effectively the U.S. State Department asked us to. In 1976, when zero percent of Nike's production was in Taiwan and Korea, Secretary of State Cyrus Vance asked Charles Robinson . . . to start the U.S.-ASIAN Business Council to fill the vacuum left by the withdrawal of the American military from that part of the world. . . . Chuck Robinson accepted the challenge, put together the council and served as Chairman of the U.S. side for three years. Mr. Robinson was a Nike Board member at that time as he is today. . . . "Nike's presence in that part of the world," according to a senior state department official at that time, "is American foreign policy in action."*

Nike sent former U.N. Ambassador Andrew Young to its overseas factories in order to issue a report to Mr. Knight, the board, and the shareholders. Mr. Young did tour factories but only with Nike staff and only for a few hours. Mr. Young issued the following findings:

- Factories that produce Nike goods are "clean, organized, adequately ventilated, and well-lit."
- No evidence of a "pattern of widespread or systematic abuse or mistreatment of workers."

- Workers don't know enough about their rights or about Nike's own code of conduct.
- Few factory managers speak the local language, which inhibits workers from lodging complaints or grievances.
- Independent monitoring is needed because factories are controlled by absentee owners and Nike has too few supervisors on site.

On November 8, 1997, an Ernst & Young audit about unsafe conditions in a Nike factory in Vietnam was leaked to the *New York Times* and made front-page news.

Michael Jordan, NBA and Nike's superstar endorser, agreed to tour Nike's factories in July 1998, stating, "The best thing I can do is go to Asia and see for myself. The last thing I want to do is pursue a business with a negative over my head that I don't have an understanding of. If there are issues . . . if it's an issue of slavery or sweatshops, [Nike executives] have to revise the situation."

From June 1997 to January 1998, Nike distributed 100,000 plastic "code of conduct" cards to plant workers. The cards list workers' rights. Nike's performance dropped. Its stock price dropped from a 1996 high of $75.75 per share to a March 1998 low of $43 per share. Retailers canceled orders so that sales decreased 3 percent for 1997. Nike reduced its labor force by 10–15 percent or 2,100–3,100 positions. However, Nike has never quite recovered in a financial or public relations sense from the activism of the last decade. By 2000, Nike, still experiencing campus protests for its overseas plant conditions, began to experience economic impact as the students protested their colleges and universities signing licensing agreements with Nike. For example, Nike ended negotiations with the University of Michigan for a six-year, multimillion-dollar licensing agreement because Michigan joined the consortium. Phil Knight withdrew a pledge to make a $30 million donation to the University of Oregon because the university also joined the consortium. Nike continues to support the Fair Labor Association, an organization backed by the White House, with about 135 colleges and universities as members, but its membership there has not halted the consortium's activities.[2] As noted in Chapter 5, Nike settled a case with regard to this international labor issue. Nike now has policies to help relieve productions pressures in the international plants and holds sessions to train managers in those plants.

Companies have begun to follow various codes and standards. Press for Change and Global Exchange suggest the following steps for companies with factories in other countries.

1. Accept independent monitoring by local human rights groups to ensure that the company's code of conduct is respected by its subcontractors.
2. Settle disputes with workers who have been unfairly dismissed for seeking decent wages and work conditions.
3. Improve the wages paid in line with economic structures in the country.

The American Apparel Manufacturers Association (AAMA), which counts 70 percent of all U.S. garment makers in its membership, has a database for its members to check labor compliance by contractors. The National Retail Federation has established the following statement of Principles on Supplier Legal Compliance (now signed by 250 retailers).

1. We are committed to legal compliance and ethical business practices in all of our operations.
2. We choose suppliers that we believe share that commitment.

3. In our purchase contracts, we require our suppliers to comply with all applicable laws and regulations.

4. If it is found that a factory used by a supplier for the production of our merchandise has committed legal violations, we will take appropriate action, which may include canceling the affected purchase contracts, terminating our relationship with the supplier, commencing legal actions against the supplier, or other actions as warranted.

5. We support law enforcement and cooperate with law enforcement authorities in the proper execution of their responsibilities.

6. We support educational efforts designed to enhance legal compliance on the part of the U.S. apparel manufacturing industry.

The U.S. Department of Labor has recommended the following to improve the current situation.

1. All sectors of the apparel industry, including manufacturers, retailers, buying agents and merchandisers, should consider the adoption of a code of conduct.

2. All parties should consider whether there would be any additional benefits to adopting more standardized codes of conduct [to eliminate confusion resulting from a proliferation of different codes with varying definitions of child labor].

3. U.S. apparel importers should do more to monitor subcontractors and home-workers [the areas where child labor violations occur].

4. U.S. garment importers—particularly retailers—should consider taking a more active and direct role in the monitoring and implementation of their codes of conduct.

5. All parties, particularly workers, should be adequately informed about codes of conduct so that the codes can fully serve their purpose.

B I O G R A P H Y

Aaron Feuerstein: An Odd CEO

Aaron Feuerstein is the chief executive officer and chairman of the board of Malden Mills, a 93-year-old privately held company that manufactures Polartec and is located in Methuen, Massachusetts. Polartec is a fabric made from recycled plastic that stays dry and provides warmth. It is used in everything from ski parkas to blankets by companies such as L.L.Bean, Patagonia, Lands' End, and Eddie Bauer. Malden employs 2,400 locals, and Mr. Feuerstein and his family have steadfastly refused to move production overseas. Their labor costs are the highest in the industry—an average of $12.50 per hour. Malden Mills is the largest employer in one of the poorest towns in Massachusetts.

On December 11, 1995, a boiler explosion at Malden Mills resulted in a fire that injured 27 people and destroyed three of the buildings at Malden Mills' factory site. With only one building left in functioning order, many employees assumed they would be laid off temporarily. Other employees worried that Mr. Feuerstein, then 70 years old, would simply take the insurance money and retire. Mr. Feuerstein could have retired with about $300 million in insurance proceeds from the fire.

Instead, Mr. Feuerstein announced on December 14, 1995, that he would pay the employees their salaries for at least 30 days. He continued that promise for six months, when 90 percent of the employees were back to work. The cost of covering the wages was approximately $25 million to the company. During that time, Malden ran its Polartec through its one working facility as it began and completed the reconstruction of the plant, at a cost of $430 million. Only $300 million of that amount was covered by the insurance on the plant; the remainder was borrowed so that Malden Mills would be a state-of-the-art environmentally friendly plant. Interestingly, production output during this time was nine times what it had been before the fire. One worker noted, "I owe him everything. I'm paying him back." After the fire and Feuerstein's announcement, customers pledged their support, with one customer, Dakotah, sending in $30,000 to help. Within the first month following the fire, $1 million in donations was received.

Malden Mills was rededicated in September 1997 with new buildings and technology. About 10 percent of the 2,400 employees were displaced by the upgraded facilities and equipment, but Feuerstein created a job training and placement center on site in order to ease these employees' transition.

By the end of 2001, six years after the fire, Malden Mills had debts of $140 million and was teetering near bankruptcy. However, Malden Mills has been through bankruptcy before, in the 1980s, and emerged very strongly with its then-new product, Polartec, developed through the company's R&D program.

Some have suggested that Mr. Feuerstein's generosity during that time is responsible for the present financial crisis. However, the fire destroyed the company's furniture upholstery division and customers were impatient at that time. They were not inclined to wait for production to ramp up, and Malden Mills lost most of those customers. It closed the upholstery division in 1996.

Also, there was the threat of inexpensive fleece from the Asian markets that was ignored largely because of the plant rebuilding and the efforts focused there. Finally, in 2000, the company had a shakeup in its marketing team just as it was launching its electric fabrics—fabrics with heatable wires that are powered by batteries embedded in the fleece.

Once again, however, the goodwill from 1995 remains. Residents of the town have been sending in checks to help the company, some as small as $10. An Internet campaign was begun by town residents to "Buy Fleece." The campaign is enjoying some success as Patagonia, Lands' End, and L.L.Bean report increased demand. In addition, the U.S. military placed large orders for fleece jackets for soldiers fighting in Operation Enduring Freedom in Afghanistan.

Senators Ted Kennedy and John Kerry lobbied GE not to involuntarily petition Malden Mills into bankruptcy. GE Capital held one-fourth of Malden Mills' debts. Its other creditors included Finova Capital, SAI Investment, Pilgrim Investment, LaSalle Bank, and PNC Bank. The lobbying was to no avail. By 2002, Malden Mills was in bankruptcy. Feuerstein labored to raise the money to pay off creditors and buy his company back, but he was unable to meet the bankruptcy deadline. Malden Mills emerged from bankruptcy on September 30, 2003, but under management other than Mr. Feuerstein. He still hopes to buy the company back, but the price, originally $93 million, has increased to $120 million. Feuerstein is the president of Malden Mills, serves on its board, and earns a salary of $425,000 per year, but he is no longer in charge and cannot be until the creditors are repaid.

In January 2004, members of the U.S. House and Senate lobbied to convince the Export-Import Bank to loan Mr. Feuerstein the money he needed to buy back his company. The Ex-Im Bank, swayed by Mr. Feuerstein's commitment to keep Malden's production in the United States, increased the loan amount from the $20 million it had originally pledged, to the $35 million Mr. Feuerstein needed.

By the end of January 2004, Malden Mills had three new strategies: Mr. Feuerstein was selling Polarfleece blankets on QVC, the company would be in partnership in China with Shanghai Mills, and the company announced it would expand its military contracts. Mr. Feuerstein remains as president and chairman of the board.

The company's patient union had its patience wearing thin. During the 2002–2003 time frame of the bankruptcy, the union leader said, "We're ready to make sacrifices for a little while. Whatever he asks us to do to keep the place going." However, a threatened strike in December 2004 resulted in negotiations and a new union three-year contract, a more expensive one for the company.

As for Mr. Feuerstein, his view is simple, "There are times in business when you don't think of the financial consequences, but of the human consequences. There is no doubt this company will survive." Mr. Feuerstein appears to have been correct. In 2006, Malden Mills landed a multimillion-dollar contract with the U.S. Department of Defense to be a supplier of the lightweight PolarTec blankets for the U.S. military branches.

Mr. Feuerstein has stated, "I don't deserve credit. Corporate America has made it so that when you behave the way I did, it's abnormal." Is he right? Was he right in continuing the salaries?

CONTINUED

Mr. Feuerstein is a Talmudic scholar who often quotes the following proverbs:

"In a situation where there is no righteous person, try to be a righteous person."

"Not all who increase their wealth are wise."

Sources: From Marianne M. Jennings, *Business Ethics: Selected Cases and Readings, 7th Ed.* (2011); Steve Wulf, "The Glow from a Fire," *Time,* January 8, 1996, p. 49. © 1996 Time, Inc. Reprinted with permission; Rabbi Avi Shafran, "Bankrupt and Wealthy," *Society Today,* July 29, 2007, (as originally accessed for research) http://www.aish.com/societyWork/work/Aaron_Feuerstein_Bankrupt_and_Wealthy.asp.

Summary

What wage and hour protections exist for employees?

- Fair Labor Standards Act (FSLA)—federal law that regulates minimum wage and overtime pay
- Minimum wage—federal hourly rate of pay
- Overtime pay—rate of 1½ times the hourly rate for hours over 40 per week worked
- Equal Pay Act—equal wages for equal work regardless of gender
- Child labor standards—restrictions on hours and types of work for children under the age of 18

What protections exist for safety in the workplace?

- Occupational Safety and Health Act—federal law setting and enforcing workplace safety standards
- Occupational Safety and Health Administration (OSHA)—federal agency responsible for safety in the workplace
- Drug testing—screening of employees for impairment

What happens when a worker is injured in the workplace?

- Workers' compensation—state-by-state system of employer strict liability for injuries of workers on the job; the few exceptions to recovery include self-inflicted injuries

What is the Social Security system, and what benefits does it provide?

- Social Security Act—federal law establishing disability, beneficiary, and retirement benefits
- Federal Insurance Contributions Act (FICA)—statute establishing system for withholding contributions for Social Security benefits

Are workers entitled to pensions, and are they regulated?

- Employment Retirement Income Security Act (ERISA)—federal law regulating employer-sponsored pension plans
- Pension Protection Plan of 2006

What rights do unemployed workers have?

- Unemployment compensation—federal program handled by states to provide temporary support for displaced workers
- Workers' compensation—system of no-fault liability for employees injured on the job

How are labor unions formed, and what is their relationship with employees?

- Norris-LaGuardia Act—federal law prohibiting injunctions to halt strikes
- National Labor Relations Act (Wagner Act)—federal law authorizing employee unionization
- Labor Management Relations Act (Taft–Hartley Act)—federal law limiting union economic weapons
- Labor–Management Reporting and Disclosure Act (Landrum–Griffin Act)—federal law regulating union membership and organizations
- National Labor Relations Board (NLRB)—federal agency responsible for enforcing labor laws
- Collective bargaining unit—group of employees recognized as exclusive bargaining agent
- Certification—recognition of union as exclusive bargaining agent
- Collective bargaining agreement—exclusive rights agreement between employer and employee
- Good-faith bargaining—requirement that parties negotiate terms in earnest
- Unfair labor practice—conduct by labor or management prohibited by statute
- Concerted activities—union-sponsored activities
- Picketing—public appearance of striking union members
- Boycotts—refusal to work for or to buy from or handle products of an employer
- Slowdown—workers report to job but do not operate at full speed

- Right-to-work laws—right to work at a company without being required to join a union
- Worker Adjustment and Retraining Notification Act (WARN)—federal law requiring employers to give 60 days' notice of plant shutdowns
- Lockout—employer closure of plant or business so workers cannot work

What are the laws and procedures related to immigrants and employment?

- Immigration and Naturalization Act (INA)
- Immigration Reform and Control Act of 1986 (IRCA)

- Immigration Act of 1990
- Illegal Immigration Reform and Immigrant Responsibility Act of 1996
- Antiterrorism and Effective Death Penalty Act
- Uniting and Strengthening America by Proving Appropriate Tools Required to Intercept and Obstruct Terrorism Act (USA Patriot Act)
- The Homeland Security Act
- American Competitiveness in the Twenty-First Century Act of 2000

Questions and Problems

1. Whirlpool is a manufacturer of household appliances. In its plant in Marion, Ohio, Whirlpool uses a system of overhead conveyor belts to send a constant stream of parts to employees on the line throughout the plant. Beneath the conveyor belt is a netting or mesh screen to catch any parts or other objects that might fall from the conveyor belt.

Some items did fall to the mesh screen, located some 20 feet above the plant floor. Maintenance employees had the responsibility for removing the parts and other debris from the screen. They usually stood on the iron frames of the mesh screen, but occasionally they found it necessary to go onto the screen itself. While one maintenance employee was standing on the mesh, it broke, and he fell the 20 feet to his death on the floor below. After this fatal accident, maintenance employees were prohibited from standing on the mesh screen or the iron frames. A mobile platform and long hooks were used to remove objects.

Two maintenance employees, Virgil Deemer and Thomas Cornwell, complained about the screen and its safety problems. When the plant foreman refused to make corrections, Mr. Deemer and Mr. Cornwell asked for the name of an OSHA inspector, and Mr. Deemer contacted an OSHA official on July 7, 1974.

On July 8, 1974, Mr. Deemer and Mr. Cornwell reported for work and were told to do their maintenance work on the screen in the usual manner. Both refused on safety grounds, so the plant foreman sent them to the personnel office. They were then forced to punch out and were not paid for the six hours left on their shift.

Explain Mr. Deemer and Mr. Cornwall's rights under OSHA. [*Whirlpool Corporation v Marshall*, 445 U.S. 1 (1980)]

2. Supervisors at Walmart asked employees to work off the clock, erase hours from their time cards, and not take lunch and other breaks. Determine whether there would be any FLSA violations if the employees voluntarily agreed to do what the supervisors requested.

3. Joe Ortiz was discharged from Magma Copper Co. for absenteeism. He missed the last shift of work before he was fired because he was temporarily in custody following an arrest for a criminal offense. He filed for unemployment but was denied. Mr. Ortiz said he notified Magma that he was missing because of being detained in jail. The unemployment compensation agency says Mr. Ortiz is disqualified for benefits because he was fired for misconduct. Who is right? [*Magma Copper v Department of Employment Security*, 625 P.2d 935 (Ariz. 1981)]

4. Donald Thompson worked as a machine operator for Hughes Aircraft for 13 years. During that time, the skin on his hands was exposed to Wynn's 331, a coolant oil. In 1978, while working with machines and using Wynn's 331 oil, Mr. Thompson developed an active scaly eruption. He required medical attention but continued to work. The scaly eruption stopped only when Mr. Thompson was off work for medical treatment. He was certified to return to work but only if he avoided contact with Wynn's 331 oil. Hughes refused to rehire him, and Mr. Thompson filed for a permanent unscheduled disability. Does he qualify? [*Hughes Aircraft v Industrial Comm'n*, 606 P.2d 819 (Ariz. 1981)]

5. Janice W. Craig was employed by Drenberg and Associates, an insurance agency. She had approximately 15 years' experience when she started to work at Drenberg in August 1974 and was initially assigned underwriting duties in the personal and commercial lines of insurance. About the time she started to work, Drenberg began a year of explosive growth. Under normal conditions, an agency with 400,000 accounts could expect to acquire approximately 40,000 new accounts in the period of a year. Drenberg grew from 400,000 to 1,200,000 in just over one year. Craig and the agency's employees worked many overtime hours. Yet, in spite of their best efforts, the agency remained 30 days behind in its accounts.

Mrs. Craig was a conscientious perfectionist. She also took over a part of the commercial desk, handling correspondence, renewals, and changes. She was under constant pressure.

In April 1975, Drenberg purchased another agency, thereby acquiring 500 new accounts and an additional employee. Mrs. Craig was given responsibility for supervising the new employee and merging the books of the two agencies. The additional responsibility and mounting pressure began to affect her. She began to feel frustrated and ineffective. She experienced difficulty relating to her coworkers and on occasions had heated exchanges with customers. On September 25, 1975, she engaged in a particularly emotional telephone conversation with one of the agency's customers, after which she eventually left the office in tears.

In addition to Mrs. Craig's difficulties at the office, she was experiencing domestic disharmony. She and her husband argued frequently concerning his drinking habits. She encountered difficulties in relating to her daughters, and her mother's death caused additional internal pressures. On the evening of September 25, 1975, the Craigs again argued, following which she took an overdose of medication.

The following day she sought help at the Tri-City Mental Hospital and was subsequently admitted to Camelback Hospital, where her condition was diagnosed as neurotic depression, or a mental breakdown.

Mrs. Craig filed a claim with the Industrial Commission wherein she related facts establishing that she was suffering from a disabling mental condition brought on by the gradual buildup of the stress and strain of her employment.

Should Mrs. Craig receive workers' compensation? [*Fireman's Fund Ins. Co. v Industrial Comm'n*, 579 P.2d 555 (Ariz. 1979)]

6. Harry Connelly was an embalmer's helper. When he cut his hand during the preparation of a corpse, germs from the gangrenous corpse got into his cut and caused blood poisoning, and he eventually died. Would Mr. Connelly's survivors be entitled to workers' compensation? [*Connelly v Hunt Furniture*, 147 N.E. 366 (N.Y. 1925)]

7. An employee of Walmart worked at the store on the night restocking crew. For security reasons, the manager of the store implemented a policy of locking all doors leading into and out of the store at the close of the business day. Only management personnel had keys to the store and no one in management worked on the night crew. Consequently, employees on the night crew were locked in the store without a key to exit the building until it opened the following day. While working one night, the employee suffered a stroke and collapsed, unconscious. When the emergency medical personnel arrived, approximately six minutes later, they were unable to enter the store because no one on the night crew had a key to the door. By the time the emergency crew was able to assist the employee, they were unable to revive her. The deceased employee was taken to the hospital where she was declared brain dead, and after 15 hours, the life support systems to which she was connected were discontinued. Subsequently, the executor of her estate and guardian for her child filed suit against Walmart for unlawful false imprisonment. The trial court granted Walmart's motion for summary judgment, and the executor/guardian appealed. How should the appellate court decide the case and why? [*Bryant v Wal-Mart Stores, Inc.*, 417 S.E.2d 688 (Ga. App. 1992)]

8. Michael Kittell was an employee at Vermont Weatherboard. While he was operating a saw at work, a splinter flew into his eye and went into his cranium. Kittell filed suit against his employer because he was an inexperienced employee who was put to work straight away on the saw, without any training. He also said that his employer had removed all the safety devices from the saw thereby causing the injury to his eye and brain. Can Kittell recover from his employer? What about the manufacturer of the saw? [*Kittell v Vermont Weatherboard, Inc.*, 417 A.2d 926 (Vt. 1980)]

9. A group of exotic dancers at several clubs in the San Fernando Valley of California brought a class action suit against their employers, the club owners, for the following violations of labor law:

- The failure to provide meal breaks
- The failure to provide rest breaks
- Club managers taking 50 percent of the dancers' tips, which resulted in some dancers earning less than the minimum wage for hours worked
- The failure to reimburse dancers for the costs of their uniforms

The club owners acknowledge that the dancers worked over 40 hours each week but that they were professionals and not subject to the provisions of the FLSA. The club owners also claim that the dancers work on a type of commission basis and so are not covered by the minimum wage law. Are there labor law violations going on at the clubs? Are you able to respond to the defenses that the club owners raised?

10. Suppose an employer decided to spin off a particular plant or part of its business to avoid either unionization or the recognition of a collective bargaining agreement. Would the spin-off work, or is this an unfair labor practice? [*International Union, UAW v NLRB*, 470 F.2d 422 (D.C. Cir. 1972)]

Public Policy and the Law

Controlling Employee Cell Phone Use

This is the sad tale of the texting engineer. Just seconds before the fatal collision of a Los Angeles commuter train with a freight train, the commuter train's engineer sent a text message. Engineer Robert Sanchez received a text message at 4:21:03. He sent a text message at 4:22:01. The crash occurred 22 seconds later.

The last text was received at the same time the train would have been passing the red warning light that was flashing to indicate the approach of the freight train. Sanchez, who was killed in the crash, had received seven text messages and sent five from the time he began his shift at 3:03 PM. Earlier that day, on his morning shift, Sanchez had received 21 text messages and sent 24 (from 6:44 to 8:53 AM). The railroad, Metrolink, prohibits its employees from receiving or sending text messages when they are on duty.

Discuss the costs for employers of enforcing a no-texting rule. Explain the reasons for a no-texting rule. What is the liability of Metrolink, and why do we hold a company liable when employees violate an on-the-job rule?

Notes

1. For more information on the history of employment law, see the course website and the *Instructor's Manual*.

2. Steven Greenhouse, "Anti-Sweatshop Group Invites Input by Apparel Makers," *New York Times*, April 29, 2000, p. A9.

Employment Discrimination

E mployment discrimination has been one of the fastest-growing legal issues of the past decade. Few employers have remained unaffected by the impact of antidiscrimination laws and cases.

This chapter answers the following questions: What laws governing employment discrimination exist? What types of discrimination exist? Are there any defenses to discrimination? What penalties or damages can be imposed for violations? ■

Nature of Complaint	Number of Complaints
Total	93,277
Race	33,579
Sex	28,028
Disabilities	21,451
Age	22,778
National origin	11,134
Religion	3,386
Equal pay	942

EEOC 2009 Data on Employment Discrimination Cases

I have a dream that one day this nation will rise up and live out the true meaning of its creed: "We hold these truths to be self-evident; that all men are created equal." I have a dream . . . I have a dream that my four little children will one day live in a nation where they will not be judged by the color of their skin but by the content of their character. I have a dream. . . .

Dr. Martin Luther King, Jr.

UPDATE ⬉
For up-to-date legal news, go to
mariannejennings.com

CONSIDER...

The city of New Haven, Connecticut, used objective examinations to identify those firefighters best qualified for promotion to fill vacant lieutenant and captain positions. On the basis of the examinations' results, no black candidates were eligible for immediate promotion. There was a rancorous public debate when the issue became public. The city threw out the results, based on the statistical racial disparity, to avoid potential liability in a lawsuit based on *disparate impact* on the black candidates. White and Hispanic firefighters who passed the exams but were denied a chance for promotion because of the city's refusal to certify the test results sued the city, alleging *disparate treatment*—that is, that discarding the test results discriminated against them based on their race in violation of Title VII. The federal district court found that there was discrimination against the white and Hispanic firefighters, and the City appealed. The appellate court reversed the district court's decision. The firefighters appealed to the U.S. Supreme Court. Should they win?

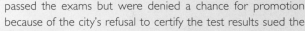

ISTOCKPHOTO.COM/YVONNE CHAMBERLAIN

History of Employment Discrimination Law

Protections against employment discrimination are strictly statutory. Common law afforded employees no protection against discrimination. Indeed, common law viewed the entire employment relationship as a private contractual matter that should be free from judicial interference.[1]

Notwithstanding the **Civil Rights Acts of 1866 and 1870,** the first effective antidiscrimination employment statute was a long time in coming. The first federal legislation to deal directly with the issue of discrimination was the **Equal Pay Act of 1963** (see Chapter 18 for more details). The statutory right to equality was expanded beyond the issue of pay less than a year later by **Title VII** of the **Civil Rights Act of 1964.** Title VII is the basis for discrimination law and judicial decisions in such matters. Although it has been amended many times, its basic purpose is to prohibit discrimination in employment on the basis of race, color, religion, sex, or national origin.

Title VII was first amended by the **Equal Employment Opportunity Act of 1972.** This amendment gave the act's enforcer, the **Equal Employment Opportunity Commission** (EEOC), greater powers—for example, the right to file suits in federal district court. In 1975, Title VII was again amended, with the **Pregnancy Discrimination Act,** which defined "sex" discrimination to include discrimination on the basis of pregnancy and childbirth.

Laws have also been enacted to protect against discrimination because of age or handicap. Discrimination on the basis of age was prohibited by the **Age Discrimination in Employment Act of 1967** (discussed later in this chapter). Under the **Rehabilitation Act of 1973,** federal contractors are prohibited from discriminating against certain employees in performing their contracts. With the **Americans with Disabilities Act,** passed in 1990, employers of 15 or more employees are prohibited from discriminating against employees with disabilities and are required to make reasonable accommodations for qualified employees with disabilities. Although the substance of the existing antidiscrimination laws remains, the **Civil Rights Act of 1991** made significant changes in procedural aspects of Title VII litigation. Exhibit 19.1 provides a summary of federal antidiscrimination legislation to date.

EXHIBIT 19.1   Employment Discrimination Statutory Scheme

STATUTE	DATE	PROVISIONS
Civil Rights Acts of 1866 and 1870 42 U.S.C. § 1981	1866 1870	Prohibited intentional discrimination based on race, color, national origin, or ethnicity; permit lawsuits
Equal Pay Act 29 U.S.C. § 206	1963	Prohibits paying workers of one sex different wages from the other when the jobs involve substantially similar skill, effort, and responsibility; Wage and Hour Division of Department of Labor enforces; private lawsuits permitted; double damage recovery for up to three years' wages plus attorney fees
Civil Rights Act of 1964 42 U.S.C. § 1981	1964	Outlaws all employment discrimination on the basis of race, color, religion, sex, or national origin; applies to hiring, pay, work conditions, promotions, discipline, and discharge; EEOC enforces; private lawsuits permitted; costs and attorney fees recoverable
Age Discrimination in Employment Act 42 U.S.C. § 6101	1967	Prohibits employment discrimination because of age against employees over 40 and mandatory retirement restrictions; EEOC enforces; private lawsuits permitted; attorney fees and costs recoverable
Equal Employment Opportunity Act 42 U.S.C. § 2000	1972	Expanded enforcement power of EEOC
Rehabilitation Act 29 U.S.C. § 701	1973	Prohibits employment discrimination on the basis of handicaps
Pregnancy Discrimination Act 42 U.S.C. § 2000e	1975	Prohibits discrimination on the basis of pregnancy and childbirth
Americans with Disabilities Act 42 U.S.C. § 12101	1990	Prohibits discrimination against those with covered disabilities (plus 2008 amendments)
Civil Rights Act of 1991 42 U.S.C. § 1981	1991	Clarifies disparate impact suit requirements; clarifies the meaning of "business necessity" and "job related"; changes some Supreme Court decisions (*Wards Cove*); punitive damage recovery
Glass Ceiling Act 42 U.S.C. § 2000e	1991	Creates commission to study barriers to women entering management and decision-making positions
Family and Medical Leave Act 29 U.S.C. § 26	1993	Establishes 12 weeks of unpaid leave for medical or family reasons
Title II of the Genetic Information Nondiscrimination Act of 2008 (GINA) 42 U.S.C. §2000ff	2008	Prohibits employment discrimination based on genetic information about an applicant, employee, or former employee
Lilly Ledbetter Fair Pay Act (2009) 42 USC § 2000a	2009	Changes the recovery period for back wages to the EEOC standard that existed prior to the decision in *Ledbetter v Goodyear Tire & Rubber Co., Inc.*, 550 U.S. 618 (2007); each paycheck triggers a new 180-day filing period regardless of when the discrimination began

In addition to this legislation, several executive orders that apply to administrative agencies (see Chapter 6) have been issued. These orders require federal government contractors to institute, among other things, affirmative action programs in their labor forces.

Employment Discrimination: Title VII of the Civil Rights Act

Title VII of the Civil Rights Act of 1964—also known as the **Fair Employment Practices Act**—as amended in 1991, prohibits discrimination in all areas of employment on the basis of race, color, religion, national origin, and sex (including pregnancy, childbirth, or abortion). Other acts prohibit discrimination based on physical disability or age.

Application of Title VII

Groups Covered

Title VII does not apply to all employers but is limited to the following groups:

1. Employers with at least 15 workers during each working day in each of 20 or more calendar weeks in the current or preceding year (state antidiscrimination statutes may apply to employers with fewer than 15 employees)

2. Labor unions that have 15 members or more or operate a hiring hall that refers workers to covered employers

3. Employment agencies that procure workers for an employer who is covered by the law

4. Any labor union or employment agency, provided it has 15 or more employees. Companies should note, however, that even if they do not meet the minimum size requirements for federal laws, state anti-discrimination laws most likely do apply to their operations and employment practices.

Employment Procedures Covered

Every step in the employment process is covered by Title VII. Hiring, compensation, training programs, promotion, demotion, transfer, fringe benefits, employer rules, working conditions, and dismissals are all covered. In the case of an employment agency, the system for the agency's job referrals is also covered.

Theories of Discrimination Under Title VII

Three basic but not mutually exclusive theories of discrimination under Title VII include **disparate treatment, disparate impact,** and **pattern or practice of discrimination.**

Disparate Treatment

The most common form of discrimination at the time Title VII was passed was treating employees of one race or sex differently from employees of another race or sex. This different, or disparate, treatment results in unlawful discrimination when an individual is treated less favorably than other employees because of race, color, religion, national origin, or sex. The U.S. Supreme Court established the elements required to be shown to establish disparate treatment under Title VII in *McDonnell Douglas Corp. v Green*, 411 U.S. 792 (1973). The case involved the rights of a black mechanic who had been laid off during a general workforce reduction and then not rehired. McDonnell claimed Mr. Green was not rehired because of his participation in a lock-in at the plant to protest racial inequality. Mr. Green brought suit for a Title VII violation, and the Supreme Court established the following elements as a *prima facie* case for discrimination.

1. The plaintiff belongs to a racial minority.
2. The plaintiff applied for and was qualified for a job with the employee.
3. The plaintiff, despite job qualifications, was rejected.
4. After the plaintiff's rejection, the job remained open and the employer continued to seek applicants.

These same elements can be applied to other forms of discrimination by just substituting, for example, "The plaintiff belongs to a protected age group," or "The plaintiff has a disability." The employer has the burden of proof to show that the employment decision was made for a nondiscriminatory reason. That burden arises when the employee-plaintiff establishes the four elements set out in *Green*. For example, a company may have retained a male supervisor when it terminated a female supervisor, but if the company can show that, because of reductions in force, it needed managers with broader experience and the male supervisor had that experience, the decision is not discriminatory. *Chescheir v Liberty Mutual Ins. Co.* (Case 19.1) deals with an issue of disparate treatment and proof of discrimination in an employment decision.

| **CASE 19.1** | *Chescheir v Liberty Mutual Ins. Co.*
713 F.2d 1142 (5th Cir. 1983) |

Why Can He Go to Law School But I Can't?
The Case of the Law Student Claims Adjuster

FACTS

Liberty Mutual Insurance Company has a rule prohibiting its adjusters and first-year supervisors from attending law school. This "law school rule" was proposed and implemented on a national basis by Edmund Carr, a vice president and general claims manager, in November 1972.

Joan Chescheir (plaintiff) was hired by Liberty Mutual's Dallas office in March 1973 as a claims adjuster. In January 1975, she voluntarily resigned but in June of that year was hired in Liberty's Houston office as a claims adjuster.

In August 1976, Wyatt Trainer, the claims manager at the Houston office, received an anonymous letter informing him that Ms. Chescheir was attending law school. After consulting with his assistants and superior, Mr. Trainer fired her after she admitted she was attending law school.

Charity O'Connell also worked in the Houston office as a claims adjuster during the same period Ms. Chescheir did. During a coffee break with a new employee, Timothy Schwirtz (also an adjuster), Ms. O'Connell relayed the story of Ms. Chescheir's firing. Mr. Schwirtz then said, "Oh, that's strange, because when I was hired, when Wells [Southwest Division claims manager] interviewed me, he told me that I could go to law school and in fact if I came down to the Houston office, there were law schools in Houston." Ms. O'Connell then went to her supervisor and told him she also was attending law school. She refused to quit law school and was fired.

William McCarthy, Liberty's house counsel in its Houston office, attended law school while working as an adjuster and was retained as house counsel upon his graduation. The trial court found that Mr. McCarthy's supervisors were aware of his contemporaneous law school career. Alvin Dwayne White was employed as an adjuster in Liberty's Fort Worth office and asked for a transfer to Houston so he could attend law school. He was given the transfer and attended law school in Houston. James Ballard worked as an adjuster in Houston, attended law school, and was promoted to supervisor while in law school. Supervisors and employees were aware of his law school attendance, but the law school rule was not enforced against him. In short, none of the male employees known to have been attending law school was fired.

Ms. Chescheir and Ms. O'Connell both filed complaints with the EEOC, were given right of suit letters, and filed suit in federal district court. After a lengthy trial, the court found that Liberty Mutual had violated Title VII. Both women were given back pay. Liberty Mutual appealed.

JUDICIAL OPINION

GOLDBERG, Circuit Judge

Title VII applies . . . not only to the more blatant forms of discrimination, but also to subtler forms, such as discriminatory enforcement of work rules.

The four-part test for demonstrating a *prima facie* case for discriminatory discharge due to unequal imposition of discipline [is]:

1. That plaintiff was a member of a protected group;

2. That there was a company policy or practice concerning the activity for which he or she was discharged;

3. That nonminority employees either were given the benefit of a lenient company practice or were not held to compliance with a strict company policy; and

4. That the minority employee was disciplined either without the application of a lenient policy, or in conformity with the strict one.

Of course, if an employer is unaware that a nonminority employee is in violation of company policy, the absence of discipline does not demonstrate a more lenient policy. It follows from this that if an employer applies a rule differently to people it believes are differently situated, no discriminatory intent has been shown.

"It is clear that the plaintiffs are members of a protected group and that there was a company policy or practice concerning the activity for which the plaintiffs were discharged; thus the first two elements of the test are met. It is also clear that minority employees were disciplined without the application of a lenient policy, and in conformity with a strict policy. All women known to violate the law school rule were immediately discharged. Furthermore, even potential violations of the rule by women were investigated promptly. An anonymous letter was sufficient to trigger an investigation of Chescheir, and the fact that Chescheir was attending law school moved the company to interrogate another woman.

The only remaining element of the *prima facie* case is a finding that male employees either were given the benefit of a lenient company practice or were not held to compliance with a strict company policy. This is the element upon which Liberty Mutual focuses its attack. Recasting Liberty Mutual's argument slightly, it claims that other males were strictly disciplined in accord with the law school rule, and that Liberty Mutual never knew that McCarthy, White, and Ballard were attending law school. Thus, claims Liberty Mutual, the third element was not met.

We are not persuaded. First, our review of the record does not disclose any males in the Southwest Division who were discharged because of the law school rule. Second, even were we to accept Liberty Mutual's contention that it did not actually know McCarthy, White, and Ballard were attending law school, we would still affirm the judgment. The operative question is merely whether Liberty Mutual applied a more liberal standard to male employees. The district court found that there were widespread rumors that McCarthy and Ballard were attending law school. Also, the EEOC notified Liberty Mutual that a male adjuster was attending law school (Ballard) and requested an explanation. Key managerial employees, at a minimum, suspected McCarthy was attending law school but preferred not to ask and confirm their suspicions. One male adjuster was told when he was hired that he could attend law school. In contrast to Liberty Mutual's energetic investigation of women it believed might be attending law school, Liberty Mutual never investigated any of these allegations, suspicions, or rumors about male adjusters. The case of Mr. White is even more dramatic. After he expressed a desire to transfer

CONTINUED

to Houston in order to attend law school, that transfer was granted and he was never told he could not attend law school.

The preceding facts are more than enough to support the third leg [of the test]. Males at Liberty Mutual were subject to lenient enforcement of the law school rule. The district court's ultimate finding of fact that Liberty Mutual applied its law school rule discriminatorily finds firm support in the record; all four elements of the *prima facie* case are present.

Once Chescheir and O'Connell established a *prima facie* case of discrimination, the burden shifted to Liberty Mutual to present a justification. The district court found that Liberty Mutual offered no justification.

Accordingly, the judgment of the district court is affirmed.

CASE QUESTIONS

1. What employer rule is at issue?
2. Had any male employees ever been fired under the rule?
3. Were there examples of disparate use of the rule?
4. Is there a *prima facie* case?
5. Give an example of some facts that would have supported a defense theory that there were nondiscriminatory reasons for the terminations.

CONSIDER... 19.1

White employees at A. J. Gerrard Manufacturing were warned about their excessive absenteeism before they were discharged, but black employees were simply discharged for excessive absenteeism without warning. Is such a policy discriminatory?

THINK: The rulings in *Green* and *Chescheir* are that employers cannot treat those who are members of different groups or protected classes (race, gender, religion) using different standards or rules, with the result being that the members of the nonprotected group are hired or retained, while those in the protected class are not.

APPLY: A. J. Gerrard did not apply the same standard to all employees. White employees were warned; black employees were not. The result was that white employees were retained, and black employees were not.

ANSWER: The treatment was disparate and constituted discrimination. [*Brown v A. J. Gerrard Mfg. Co.*, 643 E2d 273, 25 Fair Empl. Prac. Cas. (BNA) 1089, 25 Empl. Prac. Dec. (CCH) 131758 (5th Cir. 1981)]

Disparate Impact

Many employment hiring, promoting, and firing practices are not intentionally discriminatory. In fact, the basis for such decisions may be quite rational. Even so, the effect or impact of many employment standards is to discriminate against particular races or on the basis of sex.

In one case, the Alabama prison system had a minimum height requirement of 5'2" and a minimum weight requirement of 120 pounds for all of its "correctional counselors" (prison guards). The impact of the rule was to exclude many females and very few males [*Dothard v Rawlinson*, 433 U.S. 321 (1977)]. Although the rule had a purpose other than one of discrimination, namely, making sure guards were large enough to perform their jobs, the effect of the rule was to exclude women from the job position.

Disparate impact cases do not require the four steps of proof outlined in the *Green* case. Rather, the proof required in disparate impact cases is a statistical showing of the impact of an employment practice.

The 1991 amendments to the Civil Rights Act require a plaintiff to establish that a practice or practices have a disparate impact on a protected class. The burden then shifts to the employer to show "business necessity" for the practice. The employer must show that the practice is "job related for the position in question and consistent with business necessity." However, disparate impact cases cannot be based on an analysis of only the demographics of the labor market; the proper comparison is between the skilled labor force (as defined by the position in question) and those actually holding the position.

The *Ricci v DeStefano* case (Case 19.2) is a landmark U.S. Supreme Court decision on the issue of testing and disparate impact. The case provides the answer for the chapter opening and focuses on an area of active litigation in employment discrimination—the validity of employer skill and knowledge tests for hiring and promoting.

CASE 19.2	*Ricci v DeStefano* 129 S.Ct. 2658 (2009)

Fighting Fire with Stats

FACTS

In 2003, 118 firefighters in the city of New Haven, Connecticut, took examinations to qualify for promotion to the rank of lieutenant or captain. Promotion examinations in New Haven (City) were infrequent, so the stakes were high. Exam results determined which firefighters would be considered for promotions during the next two years, and their order for consideration. Many firefighters, including Frank Ricci, studied for months, at considerable personal and financial cost.

The examination results showed that white candidates had outperformed minority candidates. Seventy-seven candidates completed the lieutenant examination—43 whites, 19 blacks, and 15 Hispanics. Of those, 34 candidates passed—25 whites, 6 blacks, and 3 Hispanics. Eight lieutenant positions were vacant at the time of the examination, which meant that the top 10 candidates were eligible for an immediate promotion to lieutenant. All 10 were white. Subsequent vacancies would have allowed at least three black candidates to be considered for promotion to lieutenant.

Forty-one candidates completed the captain examination—25 whites, 8 blacks, and 8 Hispanics. Of those, 22 candidates passed—16 whites, 3 blacks, and 3 Hispanics. Seven captain positions were vacant at the time of the examination. Nine candidates were eligible for an immediate promotion to captain—seven whites and two Hispanics.

Following a briefing on the exam results, the mayor and other local politicians opened a public debate on the results that turned rancorous. The firefighters argued that the test results should be discarded because the results were discriminatory. Some firefighters threatened a discrimination lawsuit if the city made the promotions on the basis of the tests. Other firefighters said the exams were neutral and fair, and they, in turn, threatened a discrimination lawsuit if the city, relying on the statistical racial disparity, ignored the test results and denied promotions to the candidates who had performed well. In the end, the city took the side of those who protested the test results. It threw out the examination results. Mr. Ricci and others filed suit.

The federal district court found that there was discrimination against the white and Hispanic firefighters, and the city (Respondents) appealed. The appellate court reversed the district court's decision.[2] The firefighters (Petitioners) appealed to the U.S. Supreme Court.

JUDICIAL OPINION

KENNEDY, Justice

Twenty years after *Griggs*, the Civil Rights Act of 1991, [which] included a provision codifying the prohibition on disparate-impact discrimination. That provision is now in force along with the disparate-treatment section. Under the disparate-impact statute, a plaintiff establishes a prima facie violation by showing that an employer uses "a particular employment practice that causes a disparate impact on the basis of race,

CONTINUED

color, religion, sex, or national origin." An employer may defend against liability by demonstrating that the practice is "job related for the position in question and consistent with business necessity." Even if the employer meets that burden, however, a plaintiff may still succeed by showing that the employer refuses to adopt an available alternative employment practice that has less disparate impact and serves the employer's legitimate needs.

The City's actions would violate the disparate-treatment prohibition of Title VII absent some valid defense. All the evidence demonstrates that the City chose not to certify the examination results because of the statistical disparity based on race—i.e., how minority candidates had performed when compared to white candidates. As the District Court put it, the City rejected the test results because "too many whites and not enough minorities would be promoted were the lists to be certified." Without some other justification, this express, race-based decision making violates Title VII's command that employers cannot take adverse employment actions because of an individual's race.

Whatever the City's ultimate aim—however well intentioned or benevolent it might have seemed—the City made its employment decision because of race. The City rejected the test results solely because the higher scoring candidates were white. The question is not whether that conduct was discriminatory but whether the City had a lawful justification for its race-based action.

Allowing employers to violate the disparate-treatment prohibition based on a mere good-faith fear of disparate-impact liability would encourage race-based action at the slightest hint of disparate impact. A minimal standard could cause employers to discard the results of lawful and beneficial promotional examinations even where there is little if any evidence of disparate-impact discrimination. That would amount to a de facto quota system, in which a "focus on statistics . . . could put undue pressure on employers to adopt inappropriate prophylactic measures."

Congress has imposed liability on employers for unintentional discrimination in order to rid the workplace of "practices that are fair in form, but discriminatory in operation." But it has also prohibited employers from taking adverse employment actions "because of" race. Applying the strong-basis-in-evidence standard to Title VII gives effect to both the disparate-treatment and disparate-impact provisions, allowing violations of one in the name of compliance with the other only in certain, narrow circumstances. The standard leaves ample room for employers' voluntary compliance efforts, which are essential to the statutory scheme and to Congress's efforts to eradicate workplace discrimination. And the standard appropriately constrains

employers' discretion in making race-based decisions: It limits that discretion to cases in which there is a strong basis in evidence of disparate-impact liability, but it is not so restrictive that it allows employers to act only when there is a provable, actual violation.

Examinations like those administered by the City create legitimate expectations on the part of those who took the tests. As is the case with any promotion exam, some of the firefighters here invested substantial time, money, and personal commitment in preparing for the tests. Employment tests can be an important part of a neutral selection system that safeguards against the very racial animosities Title VII was intended to prevent. Here, however, the firefighters saw their efforts invalidated by the City in sole reliance upon race-based statistics.

If an employer cannot rescore a test based on the candidates' race, then it follows *a fortiori* that it may not take the greater step of discarding the test altogether to achieve a more desirable racial distribution of promotion-eligible candidates—absent a strong basis in evidence that the test was deficient and that discarding the results is necessary to avoid violating the disparate-impact provision. Restricting an employer's ability to discard test results (and thereby discriminate against qualified candidates on the basis of their race) also is in keeping with Title VII's express protection of bona fide promotional examinations.

For the foregoing reasons, we adopt the strong-basis-in-evidence standard as a matter of statutory construction to resolve any conflict between the disparate-treatment and disparate-impact provisions of Title VII.

The City argues that, even under the strong-basis-in-evidence standard, its decision to discard the examination results was permissible under Title VII. That is incorrect. Even if respondents were motivated as a subjective matter by a desire to avoid committing disparate-impact discrimination, the record makes clear there is no support for the conclusion that respondents had an objective, strong basis in evidence to find the tests inadequate, with some consequent disparate-impact liability in violation of Title VII.

On the record before us, there is no genuine dispute that the City lacked a strong basis in evidence to believe it would face disparate-impact liability if it certified the examination results. In other words, there is no evidence—let alone the required strong basis in evidence—that the tests were flawed because they were not job-related or because other, equally valid and less discriminatory tests were available to the City. Fear of litigation alone cannot justify an employer's reliance on race to the detriment of individuals who passed the examinations and qualified for promotions. The City's discarding the test results was impermissible under

Title VII, and summary judgment is appropriate for petitioners on their disparate-treatment claim.

Our statutory holding does not address the constitutionality of the measures taken here in purported compliance with Title VII. We also do not hold that meeting the strong-basis-in-evidence standard would satisfy the Equal Protection Clause in a future case.

Reversed.

CASE QUESTIONS

1. Explain what happened on the exam and why the city decided to toss the exam results.

2. What does the court establish as the law applicable to "tossing" exam results?

3. What is the court trying to balance in interpreting the law?

Pattern or Practice of Discrimination

The "pattern or practice" theory involves discrimination not against one person but, rather, against a group or class of persons (e.g., women or African Americans).

The standards for establishing a pattern or practice of discrimination are affected by the 1991 amendments to the Civil Rights Act; the burdens of proof are those discussed under disparate impact, with a "reasonable justification" defense for employers. The plaintiff must show causation between the practice of the employer and the disparate impact. For example, in one case that immediately preceded the 1991 amendments, the Seventh Circuit found that a company's low percentage of African Americans in its workforce was due to its location in a Hispanic neighborhood and not because of its practice of hiring by word of mouth [*EEOC v Chicago Miniature Lamp Works*, 947 F. 2d 292 (7th Cir. 1991)].

In pattern or practice cases, the initial burden of proof of discrimination is upon the plaintiff or the EEOC.

BUSINESS PLANNING TIP

Tests have become tricky for employers. Those who allege discrimination do not need to prove that there is anything discriminatory about the test. They need only allege that the employer did not choose a test with the least impact on protected classes. Employers that use testing will need to review the results of the tests and use caution in their use of those results as well as in the continuing use of the test for screening.

CONSIDER...   19.2

In *Dukes v Wal-Mart Stores*, 603 F.3d 571 (9th Cir. 2010), the female employees of Walmart filed suit under Title VII of the 1964 Civil Rights Act, 42 U.S.C. § 2000e *et seq.*, alleging that women employed in Walmart stores (1) are paid less than men in comparable positions, despite having higher performance ratings and greater seniority; and (2) receive fewer promotions to in-store management positions than do men, and those who are promoted must wait longer than their male counterparts to advance.

The court allowed the women to use statistical evidence as a basis for certification as a class. The statistical evidence cited was the approximate percentages of women in specific hourly and salaried management positions as follows:

Salaried Positions

- Store manager—14 percent
- Co-manager (only in larger stores)—23 percent
- Assistant manager—36 percent

Hourly Positions

- Management trainee—42 percent
- Support manager—50 percent
- Department manager—78 percent

- Customer service manager—85–90 percent
- Other hourly positions—70 percent

Walmart challenged the case (brought on behalf of 1.5 million women employed at Walmart; the largest employment class-action suit ever filed) on the grounds that mere statistics do not establish a Title VII violation. What do the women have to prove to establish discrimination? Are the statistics enough? What explanation could Walmart offer for the numbers that would evidence no discrimination on its part?

The Ninth Circuit certified another class-action suit against Walmart by women from around the country in *Dukes v Wal-Mart Stores, Inc.*, 603 F.3d 571 (9th Cir. 2010). The case is believed to be the largest class-action suit in the history of the federal antidiscrimination laws.[3] [*Comer v Wal-Mart Stores, Inc.*, 454 F.3d 544 (C.A. 6 2006)]

Specific Applications of Title VII

The various theories of Title VII discrimination apply to specific types of discrimination. The following sections cover these types of discrimination and Title VII's application to them.

Sex Discrimination

Although Title VII included sex discrimination in its prohibitions, its presence and effects were not as obviously in existence as the more blatant racial discrimination. Many of the initial discrimination suits were brought in response to "protective legislation," which consisted of state statutes that prohibited women from working in certain fields and occupations for safety reasons. The reasons for such prohibitions were that the jobs were too strenuous, too dangerous, or too stressful. Because the effect of the statutes was to keep women from certain higher-paying occupations and men from certain female-dominated jobs, the EEOC issued guidelines providing that employers guilty of discrimination could not use these statutory cloaks. The *Dothard v Rawlinson case* discussed earlier [433 U.S. 321 (1977)] is an example of a sex discrimination case.

A *prima facie* case of sex discrimination by an employer requires proof of the same elements established in the *Green* case. The only difference is that the issue of rejection, firing, or demotion is based on sex rather than race.

Other more subtle hints of discrimination have slowly been eliminated from every area of employment. Even job listings in classified ads cannot carry any sexual preference. For example, an employer cannot advertise for just a "waitress," the ad must be for a "waiter/waitress." Further, state laws and company policies that prohibit women from working during certain hours if they have school-age children are violations of Title VII.

Sexual Harassment
Sexual harassment is a violation of Title VII of the Civil Rights Act. Company policies on this issue should attempt to make it clear that an environment of harassment is not appropriate for any employee. Companies should also enforce policies uniformly.

Sexual harassment cases take two forms. In *quid pro quo* cases, an employee is required to submit to sexual advances in order to remain employed, secure a promotion, or obtain a raise. In the other—*atmosphere of harassment* cases—the invitations, language, pictures, or suggestions become so pervasive as to create a hostile work environment.

Quid Pro Quo Harassment   This form of harassment occurs when someone in a position of authority in the workplace has made sexual advances to an employee that carry the threat of employer sanctions if the employee does not accept the advances. While a supervisor may be the individual who initiates the *quid pro quo* advance, the company or employer of the supervisor may also be liable for the supervisor's conduct in certain circumstances. *Burlington Industries, Inc. v Ellerth* (Case 19.3) deals with the issue of when an employer is vicariously liable for the sexual harassment of one of its employees by another employee.

CASE 19.3   *Burlington Industries, Inc. v Ellerth*
524 U.S. 742 (1998)

The Boorish Supervisor Meets Vicarious Liability

FACTS

Kimberly Ellerth (respondent) worked as a salesperson in one of Burlington's divisions from March 1993 to May 1994. During her employment, she reported to a mid-level manager, Ted Slowik. Ms. Ellerth worked in a two-person office in Chicago and was one of Burlington's 22,000 employees. Mr. Slowik was based in New York but was responsible for Ms. Ellerth's office. The following incidents of boorish and offensive behavior occurred during Ms. Ellerth's employment.

Summer 1993	While on a business trip, Ms. Ellerth accepted Mr. Slowik's invitation to the hotel lounge. Mr. Slowik made remarks about Ms. Ellerth's breasts, told her to "loosen up," and said, "You know, Kim, I could make your life very hard or very easy at Burlington."
March 1994	Ms. Ellerth was being considered for a promotion, and Mr. Slowik expressed concern during the interview that she was not "loose enough." Mr. Slowik then reached out and rubbed her knee.
March 1994	Mr. Slowik called Ms. Ellerth to give her the promotion and said, "You're gonna be out there with men who

work in factories, and they certainly like women with pretty butts/legs."

May 1994	Ms. Ellerth called Mr. Slowik for permission to insert a logo into a fabric sample. Mr. Slowik said, "I don't have time for you right now, Kim—unless you want to tell me what you're wearing." Ms. Ellerth ended the call.
May 1994	Ms. Ellerth called again for permission, and Mr. Slowik said, "Are you wearing shorter skirts yet, Kim, because it would make your job a whole heck of a lot easier."

In May 1994, the supervisor in the Chicago office cautioned Ms. Ellerth about returning phone calls. Ms. Ellerth quit and faxed a letter giving reasons for her decision unrelated to the alleged sexual harassment. Three weeks later, however, she sent another letter complaining of Mr. Slowik's behavior.

During her employment at Burlington, Ms. Ellerth did not tell anyone about Mr. Slowik's behavior. She chose not to tell her supervisor in the Chicago office because, "It would be his duty as my supervisor to report any incidents of sexual harassment."

Ms. Ellerth filed suit against Burlington for violation of Title VII in that the sexual harassment forced her constructive discharge.

CONTINUED

The District Court found Mr. Slowik's behavior created a hostile work environment but found that Burlington neither knew nor should have known about the conduct. The Court of Appeals reversed, with eight separate opinions imposing vicarious liability on Burlington. Burlington appealed.

JUDICIAL OPINION

KENNEDY, Justice

The terms quid pro quo and hostile work environment are helpful, perhaps, in making a rough demarcation between cases in which threats are carried out and those where they are not or are absent altogether, but beyond this are of limited utility.

"Quid pro quo" and "hostile work environment" do not appear in the statutory text. The terms appeared first in the academic literature, see C. MacKinnon, *Sexual Harassment of Working Women* (1979); found their way into decisions of the Courts of Appeals, see, e.g., *Henson v Dundee*, 682 F.2d 897, 909 (CA11 1982); and were mentioned in this Court's decision in *Meritor Savings Bank, FSB v Vinson*, 477 U.S. 57 (1986). . . .

We do not suggest the terms quid pro quo and hostile work environment are irrelevant to Title VII litigation. When a plaintiff proves that a tangible employment action resulted from a refusal to submit to a supervisor's sexual demands, he or she establishes that the employment decision itself constitutes a change in the terms and conditions of employment that is actionable under Title VII. Because Ellerth's claim involves only unfulfilled threats, it should be categorized as a hostile work environment claim which requires a showing of severe or pervasive conduct.

We must decide, then, whether an employer has vicarious liability when a supervisor creates a hostile work environment by making explicit threats to alter a subordinate's terms or conditions of employment, based on sex, but does not fulfill the threat. We turn to principles of agency law, for the term "employer" is defined under Title VII to include "agents." We rely "on the general common law of agency, rather than on the law of any particular State, to give meaning to these terms." . . .

The general rule is that sexual harassment by a supervisor is not conduct within the scope of employment.

Scope of employment does not define the only basis for employer liability under agency principles. In limited circumstances, agency principles impose liability on employers even where employees commit torts outside the scope of employment.

In a sense, most workplace tortfeasors are aided in accomplishing their tortious objective by the existence of the agency relation: Proximity and regular contact may afford a captive pool of potential victims.

Tangible employment actions are the means by which the supervisor brings the official power of the enterprise to bear on subordinates.

For these reasons, a tangible employment action taken by the supervisor becomes for Title VII purposes the act of the employer. An employer is subject to vicarious liability to a victimized employee for an actionable hostile environment created by a supervisor with immediate (or successively higher) authority over the employee. When no tangible employment action is taken, a defending employer may raise an affirmative defense to liability or damages, subject to proof by a preponderance of the evidence. The defense comprises two necessary elements: (a) that the employer exercised reasonable care to prevent and correct promptly any sexually harassing behavior, and (b) that the plaintiff employee unreasonably failed to take advantage of any preventive or corrective opportunities provided by the employer or to avoid harm otherwise. While proof that an employer had promulgated an anti-harassment policy with complaint procedure is not necessary in every instance as a matter of law, the need for a stated policy suitable to the employment circumstances may appropriately be addressed in any case when litigating the first element of the defense. And while proof that an employee failed to fulfill the corresponding obligation of reasonable care to avoid harm is not limited to showing any unreasonable failure to use any complaint procedure provided by the employer, a demonstration of such failure will normally suffice to satisfy the employer's burden under the second element of the defense. No affirmative defense is available, however, when the supervisor's harassment culminates in a tangible employment action, such as discharge, demotion, or undesirable reassignment.

Affirmed.

DISSENTING OPINION

Justice THOMAS, with whom Justice SCALIA joins, dissenting

The Court today manufactures a rule that employers are vicariously liable if supervisors create a sexually hostile work environment, subject to an affirmative defense that the Court barely attempts to define. . . .

Sexual harassment is simply not something that employers can wholly prevent without taking extraordinary measures—constant video and audio surveillance, for example—that would revolutionize the workplace in a manner incompatible with a free society. Indeed, such measures could not even detect incidents of harassment such as the comments Slowik allegedly made to respondent in a hotel bar. The most that employers can be charged with, therefore, is a duty to act reasonably under the circumstances.

The Court's holding does guarantee one result: There will be more and more litigation to clarify applicable legal rules in an area in which both practitioners and the courts have long been begging for guidance. . . .

Popular misconceptions notwithstanding, sexual harassment is not a freestanding federal tort, but a form of employment discrimination. As such, it should be treated no differently (and certainly no better) than the other forms of harassment that are illegal under Title VII. I would restore parallel treatment of employer liability for racial and sexual harassment and hold an employer liable for a hostile work environment only if the employer is truly at fault. I therefore respectfully dissent.

CASE QUESTIONS

1. When will an employer be held liable (i.e., vicariously liable) for sexual harassment despite a lack of actual knowledge?

2. What is the liability of a company for harassment of an employee by an immediate supervisor?

3. What defenses exist to vicarious liability?

4. What major issues does the dissenting opinion raise?

Atmosphere of Harassment   Unwanted advances are one type of sexual harassment. However, sexual harassment can also exist when the atmosphere of the workplace becomes one of sexual tone or suggestion. Derogatory, suggestive, and offensive e-mails and electronic bulletin boards on servers sponsored by an employer can be the basis for a hostile environment sexual harassment suit. employers not only have the responsibility to prohibit employees from posting such materials; they also have a responsibility to supervise such bulletin boards and e-mails to be certain that no atmosphere of harassment results from the contents.

CYBERLAW

Further, in litigation over such materials, plaintiffs may rely on printed copies of the materials and messages to use in establishing their cases even though the materials may have already been deleted from the company system.

CONSIDER... 19.3

Determine whether the following would constitute sexual harassment (either *quid pro quo* or atmosphere of harassment) under Title VII.

1 A manager who referred to female customers as "bitchy" or "dumb," flirted with an employee's female relatives, and told of spending a weekend at a nudist camp [*Gleason v Mesirow Financial, Inc.*, 118 R 3d 1134 (7th Cir. 1997)]

2 A manager who told a single, pregnant female employee that he disapproved of premarital sex [*Brill v Lante*, 119 R 3d 1266 (7th Cir. 1997)]

3 Calendar photographs of women in swimwear posted in a co-employee's workstation [*Guidry v Zale Corp.*, 969 R Supp. 988 (M.D. La. 1997)]

4 A supervisor who called his wife "ignorant" and women in his department "dumb" and used the term "gals" for all his female employees [*Penry v Federal Home Loan Bank of Topeka*, 970 F. Supp. 833 (D. Kan. 1997)]

5 A supervisor who referred to the architecture of a shopping mall as looking like "two hooters" and a "bra bazaar," while having dinner with an employee on a business trip [*Penry v Federal Home Loan Bank of Topeka*, 970 R Supp. 833 (D. Kan. 1997)]

6 Two uninvited hugs by a supervisor and notes to employees signed, "Love, Steph" [*Drew v First Sav. of New Hampshire*, 968 F. Supp. 762 (D. N.H. 1997)]

For the Manager's Desk

Re: Office and Contractor Romances: The Lessons of HP

Former Hewlett-Packard (HP) CEO Mark Hurd "resigned" after the HP board conducted an investigation into both his relationship with Jodie Fisher, a marketing contractor for the company, and his expense claims. Ms. Fisher had filed a sexual harassment complaint with the company, Mr. Hurd settled it privately. "Following an investigation by outside legal counsel and the General Counsel's office, overseen by the Board, of the facts and circumstances surrounding a claim of sexual harassment against Hurd and HP by a former contractor to HP" the HP board found ". . . that there was no violation of HP's sexual harassment policy, but did find violations of HP's Standards of Business Conduct."[4]

HP filed its 8-K notice (see Chapter 21 for more information) about the termination with the SEC just seven seconds prior to the SEC's closing time for filing on Friday, August 5, 2010. The company included the following statement from Mr. Hurd: "As the investigation progressed, I realized there were instances in which I did not live up to the standards and principles of trust, respect and integrity that I have espoused at HP and which have guided me throughout my career. After a number of discussions with members of the board, I will move aside and the board will search for new leadership. This is a painful decision for me to make after five years at HP, but I believe it would be difficult for me to continue as an effective leader at HP and I believe this is the only decision the board and I could make at this time."[5]

Office romances and even friendly relationships between co-workers and company executives and contractors are tricky. Here are some tips based on lessons learned from the all-too-typical Hurd/HP experience:

1. When meeting with employees and contractors over lunch or dinner, never meet alone. Have other employees with you.

2. When meeting with employees or contractors over lunch or dinner, think about the purpose of the meeting, the need for the social setting, and the number of times the social-type meetings have occurred. Curbing non-office interaction prevents misunderstandings.

3. Be careful of any physical contact, including kisses on the cheek and hugs. There is often a fine line between romance and sexual harassment.

4. Hold all meetings in a setting in which others are present or doors are open.

5. Misunderstandings about relationships can be curbed by limiting one-on-one interaction and meetings held in social settings.

6. Be sure other employees are aware of meetings and their purpose. Undisclosed meetings and meetings that are not on the calendar create suspicions and fuel speculation. Keeping everything in public prevents inappropriate interaction and relationships.

7. Watch the content of conversations at meetings. Limit discussions to issues related to the business at hand. Even small talk can result in misunderstandings and is often the beginning of the departure from a business purpose.

8. Sexual harassment can occur in employees' relationships with contractors.

9. Sexual harassment can occur even without a physical relationship.

Sex Discrimination and Pensions

Another area of sex discrimination in employment involves the statistical fact that women live longer than men. It costs more for a female employee to have a pension than a male employee because she will likely live longer after retirement. In *City of Los Angeles Department of Water v Manhart*, 435 U.S. 702 (1978), the Supreme Court held that employers could not require female employees to contribute more to their pension plans than males. The additional contributions for the female employees were required by the employer because the pension planner had statistical evidence that longevity of female employees exceeded that of male employees. If the Supreme Court had sanctioned the disparity in pension plan payments, the higher cost of having female employees could have been cited by employers as the reason for their hiring practices.

The Pregnancy Discrimination Act

This act, which revolutionized maternity issues in the employment world, prohibits an employer from forcing someone to resign because of a pregnancy, refusing to allow a mother to return to work after her pregnancy is completed, providing different benefits for sick leaves than for pregnancy, and refusing to hire or promote someone because of pregnancy or family plans.

The landmark case *International Union v Johnson Controls, Inc.* (Case 19.4) focuses on some nuances in sex discrimination issues.

CASE 19.4 *International Union v Johnson Controls, Inc.*
499 U.S. 187 (1991)

The Acid Test for Women: The Right to Choose High-Risk Jobs

FACTS

Johnson Controls, Inc. (respondent) manufactures batteries. In the manufacturing process, the element lead is a primary ingredient. Occupational exposure to lead entails health risks, including the risk of harm to any fetus carried by a female employee.

Before the Civil Rights Act of 1964 became law, Johnson Controls did not employ any woman in a battery-manufacturing job. In June 1977, however, it announced its first official policy concerning its employment of women in jobs with lead exposure risk:

> [P]rotection of the health of the unborn child is the immediate and direct responsibility of the prospective parents. While the medical profession and the company can support them in the exercise of this responsibility, it cannot assume it for them without simultaneously infringing their rights as persons. . . .

> Since not all women who can become mothers wish to become mothers (or will become mothers), it would appear to be illegal discrimination to treat all who are capable of pregnancy as though they will become pregnant.

Consistent with that view, Johnson Controls "stopped short of excluding women capable of bearing children from lead exposure" but emphasized that a woman who expected to have a child should not choose a job in which she would have such exposure. The company also required a woman who wished to be considered for employment to sign a statement indicating that she had been advised of the risk of having a child while she was exposed to lead. The statement informed the woman that although there was

evidence "that women exposed to lead have a higher rate of abortion," this evidence was "not as clear . . . as the relationship between cigarette smoking and cancer," but that it was, "medically speaking, just good sense not to run that risk if you want children and do not want to expose the unborn child to risk, however small. . . ."

In 1982, Johnson Controls shifted from a policy of warning to a policy of exclusion. Between 1979 and 1983, eight employees became pregnant while maintaining lead levels in excess of 30 micrograms per deciliter of blood. The company responded by announcing a broad exclusion of women from jobs that exposed them to lead:

> [I]t is [Johnson Controls'] policy that women who are pregnant or who are capable of bearing children will not be placed into jobs involving lead exposure or which could expose them to lead through the exercise of job bidding, bumping, transfer or promotion rights.

The policy defined "women . . . capable of bearing children" as "[a]ll women except those whose inability to bear children is medically documented."

Several employees (petitioners) and their unions filed suit alleging that Johnson Controls' fetal protection policy violated Title VII of the Civil Rights Act. Included in the group were

- Mary Craig—sterilized to avoid losing her job
- Elsie Nason—50-year-old divorcee who lost compensation when transferred out of lead exposure job
- Donald Penney—denied request for leave of absence to lower his lead level before becoming a father

CONTINUED

The district court entered summary judgment for Johnson Controls. The court of appeals affirmed, and the employees appealed.

JUDICIAL OPINION

BLACKMUN, Justice

The bias in Johnson Controls' policy is obvious. Fertile men, but not fertile women, are given a choice as to whether they wish to risk their reproductive health for a particular job. Section 703(a) of the Civil Rights Act of 1964, 78 Stat. 255, as amended, 42 U.S.C. § 2000e-2(a), prohibits sex-based classifications in terms and conditions of employment, in hiring and discharging decisions, and in other employment decisions that adversely affect an employee's status. Respondent's fetal-protection policy explicitly discriminates against women on the basis of their sex. The policy excludes women with childbearing capacity from lead-exposed jobs and so creates a facial classification based on gender. Respondent assumes as much in its brief before this Court.

Nevertheless, the Court of Appeals assumed, as did the two appellate courts who already had confronted this issue, that sex specific fetal-protection policies do not involve facial discrimination. These courts analyzed the policies as though they were facially neutral, and had only a discriminatory effect upon the employment opportunities of women. Consequently, the courts looked to see if each employer in question had established that its policy was justified as a business necessity. The business necessity standard is more lenient for the employer than the statutory BFOQ [bona fide occupational qualification] defense. The court assumed that because the asserted reason for the sex-based exclusion (protecting women's unconceived offspring) was ostensibly benign, the policy was not sex-based discrimination. That assumption, however, was incorrect.

First, Johnson Controls' policy classifies on the basis of gender and childbearing capacity, rather than fertility alone. Respondent does not seek to protect the unconceived children of all its employees. Despite evidence in the record about the debilitating effect of lead exposure on the male reproductive system, Johnson Controls is concerned only with the harms that may befall the unborn offspring of its female employees. . . .

The Pregnancy Discrimination Act has now made clear that, for all Title VII purposes, discrimination based on a woman's pregnancy is, on its face, discrimination because of her sex. In its use of the words "capable of bearing children" in the 1982 policy statement as the criterion for exclusion, Johnson Controls explicitly classifies on the basis of potential for pregnancy. Under the PDA, such a classification must be regarded, for Title VII purposes, in the same light as explicit sex discrimination. Respondent has chosen to treat all its female employees as potentially pregnant; that choice evinces discrimination on the basis of sex.

We concluded above that Johnson Controls' policy is not neutral because it does not apply to the reproductive capacity of the company's male employees in the same way as it applies to that of the females. Moreover, the absence of a malevolent motive does not convert a facially discriminatory policy into a neutral policy with a discriminatory effect. Whether an employment practice involves disparate treatment through explicit facial discrimination does not depend on why the employer discriminates but rather on the explicit terms of the discrimination.

In sum, Johnson Controls' policy "does not pass the simple test of whether the evidence shows 'treatment of a person in a manner which but for that person's sex would be different.'"

We therefore turn to the question whether Johnson Controls' fetal-protection policy is one of those "certain instances" that come within the BFOQ exception.

Johnson Controls argues that its fetal-protection policy falls within the so-called safety exception to the BFOQ. Our cases have stressed that discrimination on the basis of sex because of safety concerns is allowed only in narrow circumstances. In *Dothard v Rawlinson*, 433 U.S. 321 (1977), this Court indicated that the danger to a woman herself does not justify discrimination. We there allowed the employer to hire only male guards in contact areas of maximum-security male penitentiaries only because more was at stake than the "individual woman's decision to weigh and accept the risks of employment." We found sex to be a BFOQ inasmuch as the employment of a female guard would create real risks of safety to others if violence broke out because the guard was a woman. Sex discrimination was tolerated because sex was related to the guard's ability to do the job—maintaining prison security. We also required in *Dothard* a high correlation between sex and ability to perform job functions and refused to allow employers to use sex as a proxy for strength although it might be a fairly accurate one.

Similarly, some courts have approved airlines' layoffs of pregnant flight attendants at different points during the first five months of pregnancy on the ground that the employer's policy was necessary to ensure the safety of passengers.

The unconceived fetuses of Johnson Controls' female employees, however, are neither customers nor third parties whose safety is essential to the business of battery manufacturing. No one can disregard the possibility of injury to future children; the BFOQ, however, is not so broad that it transforms this deep social concern into an essential aspect of battery making. . . .

A word about tort liability and the increased cost of fertile women in the workplace is perhaps necessary. It is correct to say that Title VII does not prevent the employer from having a conscience. The statute, however, does prevent sex-specific fetal-protection policies. These two aspects of Title VII do not conflict.

More than 40 states currently recognize a right to recover for a prenatal injury based either on negligence or on wrongful death. According to Johnson Controls, however, the company complies with the lead standard developed by OSHA and warns its female employees about the damaging effects of lead. It is worth noting that OSHA gave the problem of lead lengthy consideration and concluded that "there is no basis whatsoever for the claim that women of childbearing age should be excluded from the workplace in order to protect the fetus or the course of pregnancy." Instead, OSHA established a series of mandatory protections which, taken together, "should effectively minimize any risk to the fetus and newborn child." Without negligence, it would be difficult for a court to find liability on the part of the employer. If, under general tort principles, Title VII bans sex-specific fetal-protection policies, the employer fully informs the woman of the risk, and the employer has not acted negligently, the basis for holding an employer liable seems remote at best.

Although the issue is not before us, the concurrence observes that "it is far from clear that compliance with Title VII will preempt state tort liability."

Our holding today that Title VII, as so amended, forbids sex-specific fetal-protection policies is neither remarkable nor unprecedented. Concern for a woman's existing or potential offspring historically has been the excuse for denying women equal employment opportunities.

It is no more appropriate for the courts than it is for individual employers to decide whether a woman's reproductive role is more important to herself and her family than her economic role. Congress has left this choice to the woman as hers to make.

The judgment of the Court of Appeals is reversed and the case is remanded for further proceedings consistent with this opinion.

CASE QUESTIONS

1. Describe Johnson Controls' evolving policy on lead exposure.

2. Describe the plaintiffs who brought suit in the case.

3. Are there circumstances when sex is a BFOQ?

4. What problem is presented by the exclusion of men from the policy?

5. What is the court's position on tort liability of the company with respect to the fetus?

BUSINESS STRATEGY

Dangerous Exposure

The *Johnson Controls* decision has allowed many women to work in jobs that expose them to toxins. The U.S. Supreme Court did acknowledge in its holding that tort liability might result from its decision but that such liability was often used as a guise or cover for gender discrimination. However, nearly 20 years after the decision, women who were protected by Title VII in their right to high-risk jobs are now suing their employers for the birth defects in their children. For example, IBM has several suits from employees and their children against it for defects allegedly tied to production-line toxins. The

position of many of the employers is that even if there were evidence linking the toxins to birth defects, the women took the jobs with knowledge about the risk and agreed to that risk. How can employers, legislators, and public policy specialists reconcile antidiscrimination laws and these risks of exposure?

Source: Stephanie Armour, "Workers Take Employers to Court over Birth Defects," *USA Today,* February 26, 2002, pp. 1A, 2A.

For more information, visit http://www.cdc.gov/niosh.

Religious Discrimination

Employers are required to make reasonable efforts to accommodate an employee's religious practices, holidays, and observances. Not all religious or church activities, however, are protected; for example, the observance of a religion's Sabbath is a protected activity but taking time to prepare for a church bake sale or pageant is an unprotected activity. The 1972 amendments to Title VII defined religion to include "all aspects of religious observance and practice, as well as belief." The accommodation of religion thus defined is required unless an employer is able to establish that allowing the employee such an accommodation would result in "undue hardship on the conduct of the employer's business."

In *Trans World Airlines, Inc. v Hardison,* 432 U.S. 63 (1977), the Supreme Court confirmed the clear language of the 1972 act that requires an employer to demonstrate an ability to accommodate an employee's religious needs. As a member of a church that worshiped on Saturdays, Larry G. Hardison expressed a desire not to work that day. TWA worked through several alternatives to afford Mr. Hardison the opportunity for Saturdays off, including asking the union to waive a seniority rule that limited substitutes for him and looking for an alternative job that would not require Saturday work. The union would not waive its rule, and no managers were available to take the shift. When Mr. Hardison refused to work on Saturdays, he was dismissed and filed suit, but the Court found for TWA because of its extensive efforts and the constraints that prevented shifting of workers without substantial interference in TWA's operations.

Title VII requires only reasonable accommodation. Employees are not necessarily entitled to the accommodation they desire. For example, in *American Postal Workers Union v Postmaster General,* 781 F.2d 772 (9th Cir. 1986), several postal employees refused to work at a window in the post office where draft registration forms were handled. They asked to be able to direct draft registrants to the windows of employees who did not have religious objections to the draft. The Postal Service transferred the employees to nonwindow jobs, which was supported by the court as a reasonable accommodation.

In *TWA v Hardison,* the Court noted, "The statute is not to be construed to require an employer to discriminate against some employees in order for others to observe their Sabbath." The *Cloutier v Costco* case (Case 19.5) deals with the issues of what is protected as a religious tenet and the extent of employer accommodation required.

CASE 19.5	*Cloutier v Costco*
	390 F.3d 126 (1st Cir. 2004)

The Costco Employee Who Worshipped at the Church of Body Modification

FACTS

Kimberly Cloutier was a member of the Church of Body Modification. In 1997, during her job interview for a position at Costco, Ms. Cloutier sported four tattoos and multiple earrings, but she had no facial piercings. She was hired and given a copy of the Costco dress code, which was modified several times between 1997 and 2001. One of the modifications prohibited employees from having facial piercings. As the policy was modified, Ms. Cloutier increased the number of body piercings she had, including an eyebrow ring. Ms. Cloutier maintained that they were part of her adherence to her faith, the Church of Body Modification (CBM), but she did not join the CBM until 2001. The CBM, which anyone can join via electronic application, had approximately 1,000 members at that time. The members participate in piercing, tattooing, branding, cutting, and body manipulation. Among the goals espoused in the CBM's mission statement are for its members to "grow as individuals through body modification and its teachings," to "promote growth in mind, body and spirit," and to be "confident role models in learning, teaching, and displaying body modification." However, the tenets of the faith do not require that body modifications be on display at all times.

She did not object to the dress code or any of the modifications on religious grounds until, in 2001, her supervisors asked to either remove the eyebrow ring whilst she was working or cover it with some form of Band-Aid adhesive bandage. Costco also proposed having her wear a clear plastic ring in the eyebrow piercing whilst she was working so that her body modification could still be seen but would not be conspicuous. Ms. Cloutier refused the proposed accommodations and filed a complaint with the EEOC. The EEOC concluded that Costco had discriminated on the basis of Ms. Cloutier's religion and she then filed suit against Costco for religious discrimination in violation of Title VII. The district court granted summary judgment for Costco and Cloutier appealed.

JUDICIAL OPINION

LIPEZ, Circuit Judge

Cloutier asserts that the CBM mandate to be a confident role model requires her to display all of her facial piercings at all times. In her view, the only reasonable accommodation would be exemption from the no-facial-jewelry policy. Costco maintains that such an exemption would cause it to suffer an undue hardship, and that as a result it had no obligation to accommodate.

An accommodation constitutes an "undue hardship" if it would impose more than a *de minimis* cost on the employer. *Trans World Airlines, Inc. v Hardison*, 432 U.S. 63, 84, 97 S.Ct. 2264, 53 L.Ed.2d 113 (1977). This calculus applies both to economic costs, such as lost business or having to hire additional employees to accommodate a Sabbath observer, and to non-economic costs, such as compromising the integrity of a seniority system.

Cloutier argues that Costco has not met its burden of demonstrating that her requested accommodation would impose an undue hardship. She asserts that she did not receive complaints about her facial piercings and that the piercings did not affect her job performance. Hence, she contends that any hardship Costco posits is merely hypothetical and therefore not sufficient to excuse it from accommodating her religious practice under Title VII.

Courts are "somewhat skeptical of hypothetical hardships that an employer thinks might be caused by an accommodation that never has been put into practice." "Nevertheless, it is possible for an employer to prove undue hardship without actually having undertaken any of the possible accommodations . . . "

The district court acknowledged that "Costco has a legitimate interest in presenting a workforce to its customers that is, at least in Costco's eyes, reasonably professional in appearance." Costco's dress code, included in the handbook distributed to all employees, furthers this interest. The preface to the code explains that, "Appearance and perception play a key role in member service. Our goal is to be dressed in professional attire that is appropriate to our business at all times. . . . All Costco employees must practice good grooming and personal hygiene to convey a neat, clean and professional image."

It is axiomatic that, for better or for worse, employees reflect on their employers. This is particularly true of employees who regularly interact with customers, as Cloutier did in her cashier position. Even if Cloutier did not personally receive any complaints about her appearance, her facial jewelry influenced Costco's public image and, in Costco's calculation, detracted from its professionalism.

Costco is far from unique in adopting personal appearance standards to promote and protect its image. As the D.C. Circuit noted, "Perhaps no facet of business life is more important than a company's place in public estimation. . . . Good grooming regulations reflect a company's policy in our highly competitive business environment. Reasonable requirements in furtherance of that policy are an aspect of managerial responsibility." Courts have long recognized the importance of personal appearance regulations, even in the face of Title VII challenges. Such regulations are often justified with regard to safety concerns. E.g., *Bhatia v Chevron U.S.A., Inc.*, 734 F.2d 1382 (9th Cir.1984) (affirming summary judgment for employer who refused to exempt a Sikh employee from the requirement that all machinists be clean-shaven, where the policy was based on the necessity of being able to wear a respirator with a gas-tight face seal because of potential exposure to toxic gases).

Courts considering Title VII religious discrimination claims have also upheld dress code policies that, like Costco's, are designed to appeal to customer preference or to promote a professional public image.

Costco has made a determination that facial piercings, aside from earrings, detract from the "neat, clean and professional image" that it aims to cultivate. Such a business determination is within its discretion.

Cloutier argues that regardless of the reasons for the dress code, permitting her to display her facial jewelry would not be an undue hardship because Costco already overlooks other violations of its policy. In support of her position, she cites affidavits from two Costco employees identifying co-workers who "were allowed to wear facial piercing[s] . . . and were not disciplined." Costco responds that any employees who displayed facial jewelry did so without its permission or

CONTINUED

knowledge, noting that constant monitoring is impossible in a facility with several hundred employees.

We find Cloutier's contention, and the affidavits underlying it, unpersuasive. To the extent that the ambiguous term "allowed" implies that Costco was aware of the piercings, the affidavits are marred by an evidentiary flaw: the affiants do not appear to have personal knowledge of Costco's awareness.

Costco's offer of accommodation was manifestly reasonable as a matter of law.

The temporary covering of plaintiff's facial piercings during working hours impinges on plaintiff's religious scruples no more than the wearing of a blouse, which covers plaintiff's tattoos. The alternative of a clear plastic retainer does not even require plaintiff to cover her piercings. Neither of these alternative accommodations will compel plaintiff to violate any of the established tenets of the CBM.

Affirmed.

CASE QUESTIONS

1. Why was it important for the court to know the tenets of Ms. Cloutier's faith?

2. What happens if an employer does not enforce the dress code standards?

3. How does this type of reasonable accommodation case differ from those of employees who object to working on certain days?

Racial Discrimination

When Title VII was first enacted, its clear intent was to prevent discrimination against the minority workforce. After Title VII had been in effect for several years, an unanticipated problem arose: Does Title VII's protection extend to all races? Are white employees entitled to the same protection Title VII affords other races?

In 1976, the Supreme Court provided the answer in *McDonald v Santa Fe Trail Transportation Co.*, 427 U.S. 273 (1976). Here, some black employees had been reinstated after committing the same offense as a group of white employees who were not reinstated. The Court held that Title VII prohibited such racial discrimination.

Antidiscrimination Laws and Affirmative Action

Some employers, either voluntarily or through the EEOC, have instituted affirmative action programs. Nothing prohibits such programs under Title VII, and the Supreme Court has sanctioned them as methods for remedying all the past years of discrimination. Although Title VII does not mandate such programs, employers may legally institute them.

What Is Affirmative Action?

Affirmative action is a remedial step taken to ensure that those who have been victims of discrimination in the past are given the opportunity to work in positions they would have attained had there not been discrimination.

Affirmative action programs are used to improve job opportunities for those in the so-called protected classes, including African Americans, Hispanics, Native Americans, Asians, women, persons with disabilities, and Vietnam veterans.

Who Is Required to Have Affirmative Action Programs?

Some federal funding laws, such as those for education and state and local governments, mandate affirmative action programs.

Some employers have an obligation to take steps to equalize the representation of minorities and women in their labor forces. This equalization of representation in the labor force is the process of affirmative action. The following types of employers are obligated to undertake affirmative action programs:

1. Employers who, pursuant to consent decree or court order, must implement plans to compensate for past wrongs
2. State and local agencies, colleges, and universities that receive federal funds
3. Government contractors
4. Businesses that work on federal projects (10 percent of their subcontract work must employ minority businesses)

Affirmative action plans cannot simply be **quotas.** (A quota program is an unlawful infringement of the rights of a majority group of employees.) Rather, affirmative action programs set goals—for example, a certain number of minorities employed by a certain date. If the goal is not met, a business has not violated the law so long as it has made a good-faith effort to recruit and hire minorities. That good-faith effort can be established by a showing of internal and external advertising, monitoring of the program's progress, and changes and improvements in the program's development.

Affirmative Action Backlash: The Theory of Reverse Discrimination

Currently, some legislative movements and grassroots referenda mandate the elimination of affirmative action programs. The University of California system eliminated affirmative action programs in 1995, but the programs were reinstated by a court after the elimination was challenged. A state referendum then passed, eliminating racial preferences by any state agency, including its colleges and universities.

In *Adarand Constructors, Inc. v Vena,* 515 U.S. 200 (1995), the U.S. Supreme Court was faced with the issue of affirmative action programs in a case brought by a contractor that challenged the federal government's program granting socially and economically disadvantaged contractors and subcontractors preferences in the awarding of government contracts. The case was remanded for trial after a ruling by the Court that such programs were subject to a standard of review known as strict scrutiny. The Court held that the government's set-aside program offering preferences to minority-owned businesses was a racial classification. To survive the strict scrutiny test, which is derived from the Equal Protection Clause of the U.S. Constitution (see Chapter 5), the federal government must be able to show, when a case goes to trial, that the contractor preferences serve a compelling government interest. *Adarand II,* heard by the U.S. Supreme Court in 2001, was upheld without opinion.[6]

In *Taxman v Board of Education of Piscataway* [91 F.3d 1547 (3d Cir. 1996), *cert.* granted, 521 U.S. 1117 (1997); *cert.* dismissed, 522 U.S. 1010 (1997)], a school district, when facing the need to reduce the size of its teaching staff, decided to retain an African-American schoolteacher, Debra Williams. Sharon Taxman, a white schoolteacher, challenged the decision as discriminatory, and the school board defended on the grounds of its affirmative action program. On appeal, the circuit court held that the decision was unconstitutional because the school board's program was adopted to promote diversity and not to remedy any past wrongs the school district had committed. The U.S. Supreme Court granted *certiorari* to review the case, but the school board agreed to a settlement, paying Ms. Taxman $433,500, of which $308,500 was paid by national civil rights organizations. The civil rights organizations indicated that they agreed to pay the bulk of the settlement because they were fearful that the court might outlaw affirmative action programs. A few years later, and on the same day, the U.S. Supreme Court issued two landmark decisions on affirmative action in admissions programs: *Gratz v Bollinger* (Case 19.6) and *Grutter v Bollinger* (Case 19.7).

| CASE 19.6 | *Gratz v Bollinger* 539 U.S. 244 (2003) |

Admit It: Affirmative Action Programs Are Difficult to Explain

FACTS

Jennifer Gratz and Patrick Hamacher (petitioners), along with other students in a class action suit, were denied admission to the University of Michigan's College of Literature, Science, and the Arts (LSA). Both Ms. Gratz and Mr. Hamacher are Caucasian. Ms. Gratz, who applied for admission for the fall of 1995, was notified in January of that year that a final decision regarding her admission had been delayed until April. This delay was based on the University's determination that, although Ms. Gratz was "well qualified," she was "less competitive than the students who ha[d] been admitted on first review." Ms. Gratz was notified in April that the LSA was unable to offer her admission. She enrolled in the University of Michigan at Dearborn, from which she graduated in the spring of 1999.

Mr. Hamacher applied for admission to the LSA for the fall of 1997. A final decision as to his application was also postponed because, though his "academic credentials [were] in the qualified range, they [were] not at the level needed for first review admission." Mr. Hamacher's application was subsequently denied in April 1997, and he enrolled at Michigan State University. He has since graduated from Michigan State University.

The University's Office of Undergraduate Admissions (OUA) oversees the LSA admissions process. OUA considers a number of factors in making admissions decisions, including high school grades, standardized test scores, high school quality, curriculum strength, geography, alumni relationships, and leadership. OUA also considers race. During all periods relevant to this litigation, the University considered African-Americans, Hispanics, and Native Americans to be "underrepresented minorities," and it is undisputed that the University admits "virtually every qualified . . . applicant" from these groups. During 1995 and 1996, OUA counselors evaluated applications according to grade point average combined with what were referred to as the "SCUGA" factors. These factors included the quality of an applicant's high school

(S), the strength of an applicant's high school curriculum (C), an applicant's unusual circumstances (U), an applicant's geographical residence (G), and an applicant's alumni relationships (A). After these scores were combined to produce an applicant's "GPA 2" score, the reviewing admissions counselors referenced a set of "Guidelines" tables, which listed GPA 2 ranges on the vertical axis, and American College Test/Scholastic Aptitude Test (ACT/SAT) scores on the horizontal axis. Each table was divided into cells that included one or more courses of action to be taken, including admit, reject, delay for additional information, or postpone for reconsideration.

In both years, applicants with the same GPA 2 scores and ACT/SAT scores were subject to different admissions outcomes based on their racial or ethnic status. For example, as a Caucasian in-state applicant, Ms. Gratz's GPA 2 score and ACT score placed her within a cell calling for a postponed decision on her application. An in-state or out-of-state minority applicant with Ms. Gratz's scores would have fallen within a cell calling for admission.

Under the 1997 procedures, Mr. Hamacher's GPA 2 score and ACT score placed him in a cell on the in-state applicant table calling for postponement of a final admissions decision. An underrepresented minority applicant placed in the same cell would generally have been admitted.

In October 1997, Ms. Gratz and Mr. Hamacher filed a lawsuit in the U.S. District Court for the Eastern District of Michigan against the University of Michigan, the LSA, James Duderstadt, and Lee Bollinger (administrators at the University of Michigan) for discrimination on the basis of their race.

Following complicated proceedings at the district and appellate levels that eventually concluded in a holding in favor of the University, the former students appealed.

JUDICIAL OPINION

REHNQUIST, Chief Justice

As they have throughout the course of this litigation, petitioners contend that the University's consideration of race in its undergraduate admissions decisions violates § 1 of the Equal Protection Clause of the Fourteenth Amendment, Title VI, and 42 U.S.C. § 1981.

It is by now well established that "all racial classifications reviewable under the Equal Protection Clause must be strictly scrutinized." *Adarand Constructors, Inc. v Pena,* 515 U.S. 200, 224, 115 S.Ct. 2097, 132 L.Ed.2d 158 (1995).

We find that the University's policy, which automatically distributes 20 points, or one-fifth of the points needed to guarantee admission, to every single "underrepresented minority" applicant solely because of race, is not narrowly tailored to achieve the interest in educational diversity that respondents claim justifies their program.

The LSA's policy automatically distributes 20 points to every single applicant from an "underrepresented minority" group, as defined by the University. The only consideration that accompanies this distribution of points is a factual review of an application to determine whether an individual is a member of one of these minority groups. Moreover, where the race of a "particular black applicant" could be considered without being decisive, the LSA's automatic distribution of 20 points has the effect of making "the factor of race . . . decisive" for virtually every minimally qualified underrepresented minority applicant.

"The Admissions Committee, with only a few places left to fill, might find itself forced to choose between A, the child of a successful black physician in an academic community with promise of superior academic performance, and B, a black who grew up in an inner-city ghetto of semi-literate parents whose academic achievement was lower but who had demonstrated energy and leadership as well as an apparently abiding interest in black power. If a good number of black students much like A but few like B had already been admitted, the Committee might prefer B; and vice versa. If C, a white student with extraordinary artistic talent, were also seeking one of the remaining places, his unique quality might give him an edge over both A and B. Thus, the critical criteria are often individual qualities or experience not dependent upon race but sometimes associated with it."

This example further demonstrates the problematic nature of the LSA's admissions system. Even if student C's "extraordinary artistic talent" rivaled that of Monet or Picasso, the applicant would receive, at most, five points under the LSA's system. At the same time, every single underrepresented minority applicant, including students A and B, would automatically receive 20 points for submitting an application. Clearly, the LSA's system does not offer applicants the individualized selection process described in Harvard's example. Instead of considering how the differing backgrounds, experiences, and characteristics of students A, B, and C might benefit the University, admissions counselors reviewing LSA applications would simply award both A and B 20 points because their applications indicate that they are African-American, and student C would receive up to 5 points for his "extraordinary talent."

We conclude, therefore, that because the University's use of race in its current freshman admissions policy is not narrowly tailored to achieve respondents' asserted compelling interest in diversity, the admissions policy violates the Equal Protection Clause of the Fourteenth Amendment. We further find that the admissions policy also violates Title VI and 42 U.S.C. § 1981. Accordingly, we reverse.

CASE 19.7   *Grutter v Bollinger*
539 U.S. 306 (2003)

The Law of Admissions and the Admissions of Law

FACTS

The University of Michigan Law School seeks "a mix of students with varying backgrounds and experiences who will respect and learn from each other." In 1992, the dean of the law school charged a faculty committee with crafting a written admissions policy to implement these goals.

In reviewing an applicant's file, admissions officials must consider the applicant's undergraduate grade point average (GPA) and Law School Admissions Test (LSAT) score because they are important (if imperfect) predictors of academic success in law school. The policy stresses that "no applicant should be admitted unless we expect that

CONTINUED

applicant to do well enough to graduate with no serious academic problems."

The policy makes clear, however, that even the highest possible score does not guarantee admission to the law school. Nor does a low score automatically disqualify an applicant. Rather, the policy requires admissions officials to look beyond grades and test scores to other criteria that are important to the Law School's educational objectives. So-called "'soft' variables" such as "the enthusiasm of recommenders, the quality of the undergraduate institution, the quality of the applicant's essay, and the areas and difficulty of undergraduate course selection" are all brought to bear in assessing an "applicant's likely contributions to the intellectual and social life of the institution."

The policy aspires to "achieve that diversity which has the potential to enrich everyone's education and thus make a law school class stronger than the sum of its parts."

The policy does not restrict the types of diversity contributions eligible for "substantial weight" in the admissions process, but instead recognizes "many possible bases for diversity admissions." The policy does, however, reaffirm the Law School's longstanding commitment to "one particular type of diversity," that is, "racial and ethnic diversity with special reference to the inclusion of students from groups which have been historically discriminated against, like African Americans, Hispanics and Native Americans, who without this commitment might not be represented in our student body in meaningful numbers."

Barbara Grutter (petitioner) is a white Michigan resident who applied to the Law School in 1996 with a 3.8 GPA and 161 LSAT score. The Law School initially placed her on a waiting list but subsequently rejected her application. In December 1997, Ms. Grutter filed suit in the U.S. District Court for the Eastern District of Michigan against the Law School, the Regents of the University of Michigan, Lee Bollinger (Dean of the Law School from 1987 to 1994), and others. She alleged that respondents discriminated against her on the basis of race in violation of the Fourteenth Amendment and Title VI of the Civil Rights Act of 1964.

She alleged that her application was rejected because the Law School uses race as a "predominant" factor, giving applicants who belong to certain minority groups "a significantly greater chance of admission than students with similar credentials from disfavored racial groups." Ms. Grutter also alleged that the respondents "had no compelling interest to justify their use of race in the admissions process." After a complicated battle in the lower courts that held for the law school and university, Ms. Grutter appealed.

JUDICIAL OPINION

O'CONNOR, Justice

We last addressed the use of race in public higher education over 25 years ago. In the landmark *Bakke* case, we reviewed a racial set-aside program that reserved 16 out of 100 seats in a medical school class for members of certain minority groups. The decision produced six separate opinions, none of which commanded a majority of the Court.

In the wake of our fractured decision in *Bakke,* courts have struggled to discern whether Justice Powell's diversity rationale, set forth in part of the opinion joined by no other Justice, is nonetheless binding precedent [f]or the reasons set out below, today we endorse Justice Powell's view that student body diversity is a compelling state interest that can justify the use of race in university admissions.

"We apply strict scrutiny to all racial classifications to 'smoke out' illegitimate uses of race by assuring that [government] is pursuing a goal important enough to warrant use of a highly suspect tool." . . .

The Law School asks us to recognize, in the context of higher education, a compelling state interest in student body diversity.

The Law School's educational judgment that such diversity is essential to its educational mission is one to which we defer. The Law School's assessment that diversity will, in fact, yield educational benefits is substantiated by respondents and their amici. . . . The Law School's interest is not simply "to assure within its student body some specified percentage of a particular group merely because of its race or ethnic origin." That would amount to outright racial balancing, which is patently unconstitutional. Rather, the Law School's concept of critical mass is defined by reference to the educational benefits that diversity is designed to produce.

As the District Court emphasized, the Law School's admissions policy promotes "cross-racial understanding," helps to break down racial stereotypes, and "enables [students] to better understand persons of different races." These benefits are "important and laudable," because "classroom discussion is livelier, more spirited, and simply more enlightening and interesting" when the students have "the greatest possible variety of backgrounds."

We have repeatedly acknowledged the overriding importance of preparing students for work and citizenship, describing education as pivotal to "sustaining our political and cultural heritage" with a fundamental role in maintaining the fabric of society. Effective participation by members of all racial and ethnic groups in the civic life of our Nation is essential if the dream of one Nation, indivisible, is to be realized.

Moreover, universities, and in particular, law schools, represent the training ground for a large number of our Nation's leaders. Individuals with law degrees occupy roughly half the state governorships, more than half the seats in the United States Senate, and more than a third of the seats in the United States House of Representatives. The pattern is even more striking when it comes to highly selective law schools. A handful of these schools accounts for 25 of the 100 United States Senators, 74 United States Courts of Appeals judges, and nearly 200 of the more than 600 United States District Court judges. . . .

To be narrowly tailored, a race-conscious admissions program cannot use a quota system—it cannot "insulat[e] each category of applicants with certain desired qualifications from competition with all other applicants." Instead, a university may consider race or ethnicity only as a "'plus' in a particular applicant's file," without "insulat[ing] the individual from comparison with all other candidates for the available seats." In other words, an admissions program must be "flexible enough to consider all pertinent elements of diversity in light of the particular qualifications of each applicant, and to place them on the same footing for consideration, although not necessarily according them the same weight."

We are satisfied that the Law School's admissions program, like the Harvard plan described by Justice Powell, does not operate as a quota. Properly understood, a "quota" is a program in which a certain fixed number or proportion of opportunities is "reserved exclusively for certain minority groups."

Justice Powell's distinction between the medical school's rigid 16-seat quota and Harvard's flexible use of race as a "plus" factor is instructive. Harvard certainly had minimum goals for minority enrollment, even if it had no specific number firmly in mind.

THE CHIEF JUSTICE believes that the Law School's policy conceals an attempt to achieve racial balancing, and cites admissions data to contend that the Law School discriminates among different groups within the critical mass. But, as THE CHIEF JUSTICE concedes, the number of underrepresented minority students who ultimately enroll in the Law School differs substantially from their representation in the applicant pool and varies considerably for each group from year to year.

Here, the Law School engages in a highly individualized, holistic review of each applicant's file, giving serious consideration to all the ways an applicant might contribute to a diverse educational environment. The Law School affords this individualized consideration to applicants of all races. Unlike the program at issue in *Gratz v Bollinger*, the Law School awards no mechanical, predetermined diversity "bonuses" based on race or ethnicity.

What is more, the Law School actually gives substantial weight to diversity factors besides race. The Law School frequently accepts nonminority applicants with grades and test scores lower than underrepresented minority applicants (and other nonminority applicants) who are rejected. This shows that the Law School seriously weighs many other diversity factors besides race that can make a real and dispositive difference for nonminority applicants as well.

We take the Law School at its word that it would "like nothing better than to find a race-neutral admissions formula" and will terminate its race-conscious admissions program as soon as practicable. It has been 25 years since Justice Powell first approved the use of race to further an interest in student body diversity in the context of public higher education. Since that time, the number of minority applicants with high grades and test scores has indeed increased. We expect that 25 years from now, the use of racial preferences will no longer be necessary to further the interest approved today.

The judgment of the Court of Appeals for the Sixth Circuit, accordingly, is affirmed.

CASE QUESTIONS

1. Explain the undergraduate admissions process.

2. Explain the law school admissions process.

3. Which process does the U.S. Supreme Court uphold? Why?

4. What standards could you offer to colleges and universities trying to establish admissions programs that create diversity but do not violate the U.S. Supreme Court's standards for affirmative action programs?

The Defenses to a Title VII Charge

Title VII is not a strict liability statute. The act provides some defenses that employers can use to defend against a charge of discrimination.

Bona Fide Occupational Qualification

A **bona fide occupational qualification** (BFOQ) is a job qualification based on sex, religion, or national origin that is necessary for the operation of business. A

For the Manager's Desk

Re: Screening for Personality and Honesty

Employers are developing and using different types of exams and questions for screening employees. The *Wall Street Journal* reports that retailers are having job applicants take personality tests. The questions on this test include "You have to give up on some things that you start," "You would like a job that is quiet and predictable," and "Any trouble you have is your own fault." The answers are "Strongly agree," "Agree," "Disagree," and "Strongly Disagree." The test and the retailers' preferred answers have made their way onto the Internet where job applicants studied them so that they could perform well on the "test." Wikipedia removed the questions and answers, but they can still be found on YouTube. In addition, some applicants have been taking the tests for their friends to help their friends get in the door and get hired.

Some managers believe there is no correlation between the tests and the performance of those who are hired. The consultants who have developed the tests are trying to have the questions removed from the Internet.

The ethics of taking the test for someone else or posting the questions on the Internet are security problems that the employers must resolve. However, there is also the issue of validating the tests so that they are non-discriminatory in a disparate-impact sense. Without the data to support the tests and their screening ability, employers face a tough climb in the event any of the denied applicants litigates on the basis of disparate impact.

Source: Vanessa O'Connell, "Test for Dwindling Retail Jobs Spawns a Culture of Cheating," *Wall Street Journal*, Jan. 7, 2009, pp. A1, A10.

particular religious belief is a BFOQ for a pastor of a church. Similarly, an actor, to qualify for a role, may need to be a certain sex for purposes of realism and thus sex is a BFOQ for such employment.

The BFOQ exception has been applied narrowly, however. For a discriminatory qualification for employment to fall within the BFOQ exception, the employer must be able to establish that the job qualification is carefully formulated to respond to public safety, privacy, or other public needs; and the formulation of the policy must not be broader than is reasonably necessary to preserve the safety or privacy of individuals involved. For example, a restriction on hiring male employees for work in a nursing home occupied by women is excessive if male employees can work in jobs not involved with the personal care of the residents. Nor is personal preference a justification for a BFOQ; for example, many airlines have argued that there is a customer preference for female as opposed to male flight attendants. But customer preference is not a basis for a BFOQ; it is not a business necessity.

Seniority or Merit Systems

The goals and objectives of Title VII are often inconsistent with labor union rules of operation. Although matters of discrimination and union supervision are both covered by federal law, the two statutory schemes conflict on some points. Which controls the other: the remedial effect of Title VII or the longstanding history of seniority and other union rules?

The following criteria are used to determine whether a seniority or merit system is valid.

1. The system must apply to all employees.
2. Whatever divisions or units used for the system must follow the industry custom or pattern; that is, the divisions cannot be set up so as to discriminate against particular races or groups.

3. The origins of the system cannot lie in racial discrimination.

4. The system must be maintained for seniority and merit purposes and not to perpetuate racial discrimination.

Aptitude and Other Tests

Any employer charged with Title VII discrimination because of employee aptitude testing must be able to show that the tests used are valid. Validity means that the tests are related to successful job performance and that a test does not have the effect of eliminating certain races from the employment market.

An employer can validate a test in any of several different ways. Test scores of applicants can later be compared with the applicants' eventual job performance to validate the test. An employer can also give the test to current employees and use the correlation between their scores and job performance as a means for validating the test. Some tests can be validated by their content. For example, requiring potential police officers to complete a driving course, a physical fitness test, and a marksmanship test is valid because the tests are based on the things police officers actually do. (Refer to p. 646 and the discussion of disparate impact for more information on validation of tests.)

Misconduct

For many years, an absolute defense to discrimination was employee misconduct. If an employee violated company rules, the case did not involve discrimination. The defense was so broad that even evidence the employer acquired *after* the termination and charge of discrimination could be used as a defense. In *McKennon v Nashville Banner Publishing Co.* (Case 19.8), the Supreme Court limited this defense.

| CASE 19.8 | *McKennon v Nashville Banner Publishing Co.* 524 U.S. 742 (1995) |

Lying Is Not a Defense for Discrimination

FACTS

For 30 years, Christine McKennon (petitioner) worked for Nashville Banner Publishing Company (respondent) (Banner), but she was terminated as part of a work reduction plan. She was 62 years old at the time of her termination. Ms. McKennon filed suit, alleging her termination was a violation of the Age Discrimination in Employment Act (ADEA).

During Ms. McKennon's deposition, she testified that during her final year of employment, she had copied several confidential documents bearing upon the company's financial condition. She had access to these records as secretary to Banner's comptroller. Ms. McKennon took the copies home and showed them to her husband. Her motivation, she averred, was apprehension that she was about to be fired because of her age. When she became concerned about her job, she removed and copied the documents for "insurance" and "protection." A few days after these deposition disclosures, Banner sent Ms. McKennon a letter declaring that removal and copying of the records was in violation of her job responsibilities and advised her (again) that she was terminated. Banner's letter also recited that had it known of Ms. McKennon's misconduct, it would have discharged her at once for that reason.

Banner conceded its discrimination in district court, which granted summary judgment for Banner on grounds that Ms. McKennon's misconduct

CONTINUED

was a defense. The court of appeals affirmed, and Ms. McKennon appealed.

JUDICIAL OPINION

KENNEDY, Justice

We shall assume that the sole reason for McKennon's initial discharge was her age, a discharge violative of the ADEA. Our further premise is that the misconduct revealed by the deposition was so grave that McKennon's immediate discharge would have followed its disclosure in any event. We do question the legal conclusion reached by those courts that after-acquired evidence of wrongdoing which would have resulted in discharge bars employees from any relief under the ADEA. That ruling is incorrect.

The ADEA and Title VII share common substantive features and also a common purpose: "the elimination of discrimination in the workplace." Congress designed the remedial measures in these statutes to serve as a "spur or catalyst" to cause employers "to self-examine and to self-evaluate their employment practices and to endeavor to eliminate, so far as possible, the last vestiges" of discrimination. The ADEA, in keeping with these purposes, contains a vital element found in both Title VII and the Fair Labor Standards Act: it grants an injured employee a right of action to obtain the authorized relief.

The objectives of the ADEA are furthered when even a single employee establishes that an employer has discriminated against him or her. The disclosure through litigation of incidents or practices which violate national policies respecting nondiscrimination in the work force is itself important, for the occurrence of violations may disclose patterns of noncompliance resulting from a misappreciation of the Act's operation or entrenched resistance to its commands, either of which can be of industry-wide significance. The efficacy of its enforcement mechanisms becomes one measure of the success of the Act.

As we have said, the case comes to us on the express assumption that an unlawful motive was the sole basis for the firing. McKennon's misconduct was not discovered until after she had been fired. The employer could not have been motivated by knowledge it did not have and it cannot now claim that the employee was fired for the nondiscriminatory reason. Mixed motive cases are inapposite here, except to the important extent they underscore the necessity of determining the employer's motives in ordering the discharge, an essential element in determining whether the employer violated the federal antidiscrimination law. As we have observed, "proving that the same decision would have been justified . . . is not the same as proving that the same decision would have been made."

The ADEA, like Title VII, is not a general regulation of the workplace but a law which prohibits discrimination. The statute does not constrain employers from exercising significant other prerogatives and discretions in the course of the hiring, promoting, and discharging of their employees. In determining appropriate remedial action, the employee's wrongdoing becomes relevant not to punish the employee, or out of concern "for the relative moral worth of the parties," but to take due account of the lawful prerogatives of the employer in the usual course of its business and the corresponding equities that it has arising from the employee's wrongdoing.

The proper boundaries of remedial relief in the general class of cases where, after termination, it is discovered that the employee has engaged in wrongdoing must be addressed by the judicial system in the ordinary course of further decisions, for the factual permutations and the equitable considerations they raise will vary from case to case. We do conclude that here, and as a general rule in cases of this type, neither reinstatement nor front pay is an appropriate remedy. It would be both inequitable and pointless to order the reinstatement of someone the employer would have terminated, and will terminate, in any event and upon lawful grounds.

Where an employer seeks to rely upon after-acquired evidence of wrongdoing, it must first establish that the wrongdoing was of such severity that the employee in fact would have been terminated on those grounds alone if the employer had known of it at the time of the discharge. The concern that employers might as a routine matter undertake extensive discovery into an employee's background or performance on the job to resist claims under the Act is not an insubstantial one, but we think the authority of the courts to award attorney's fees, mandated under the statute, 29 U.S.C. §§ 216(b), 626(b), and in appropriate cases to invoke the provisions of Rule 11 of the Federal Rules of Civil Procedure will deter most abuses.

The judgment is reversed.

CASE QUESTIONS

1. Why is the timing of the misconduct disclosure important?

2. Does Banner deny discriminatory intent?

3. Why are "mixed motive" cases not relevant in this analysis?

4. Is reinstatement a remedy?

Ethical Issues

Consider the following circumstances and decide whether there has been a violation of Title VII. Consider the ethical implications of the conduct along with the legal ones.

1. An employee must be dismissed. Two women, one white and the other black, have been with the company for the same amount of time and have the same rate of absenteeism. Their performance evaluations are about the same. Can the black employee be dismissed without violating Title VII?

2. Company B has had a significant problem with absenteeism, tardiness, and failure to follow through on job assignments among the employees who are of a certain race. The personnel director is concerned about company productivity, the costs of training, and the costs of constant turnover. The personnel director is also aware of the constraints of Title VII. The director instructs those staffing the front office to tell members of that particular race who apply for a job that the company is not accepting applications. The director's theory is that his applicant pool will be prescreened and he will not have to make discriminatory hiring decisions. Is the director correct?

Enforcement of Title VII

Title VII is an enabling act that created the Equal Employment Opportunity Commission for the purpose of administration and enforcement. The EEOC is a five-member commission whose members are appointed by the president with the approval of the Senate. As with all other federal commissions, no more than three members can belong to the same political party.

The EEOC was given broad powers under Title VII. In addition to its rulemaking and charging powers, the EEOC has broad investigatory authority, including the authority to subpoena documents and testimony.

Steps in an EEOC Case

The Complaint

An EEOC complaint can be filed by an employee or by the EEOC. An employee has 180 days (in some cases, up to 300 days) from the time of the alleged violation to file a complaint. In *Ledbetter v Goodyear*, 550 U.S. 618 (2007), the U.S. Supreme Court clarified the 180-day rule for individual suits. Lilly Ledbetter filed suit against Goodyear after her retirement in 1999, following 19 years of employment at the company's plant in Gadsden, Alabama. While she filed suit within 180 days after receiving her last paycheck, the court held that she must have brought her pay discrimination suit within 180 days from when the alleged discrimination in pay occurred. The suit was dismissed, with the high court noting that employers must have current enough allegations so that they can defend the suit with their records, which may not be available after 19 years. The decision required employees to bring suit within 180 days from the time of the discriminatory conduct. In 2009, Congress passed the **Lilly Ledbetter Fair Pay Act,** which provides that each paycheck triggers a new 180-day filing period regardless of when the discriminatory practices that led to pay disparity began.

The complaint may be filed with either the EEOC or the state administrative agency set up for employment discrimination issues. For the state agency to continue handling the complaint, it must be an EEOC-approved program. If it is not, the EEOC handles the complaint. The EEOC has special forms that can be filled out by any employee wishing to file such a complaint.

Notification of the Employer

Once a complaint has been filed, the EEOC has 10 days to notify the employer of the charges. Employers are prohibited from the time of notification from taking any retaliatory action against the charging employee.

EEOC Action

After the complaint is filed, the EEOC has 180 days from that time to take action in the case before the complaining party can file suit on the matter. During this time, the EEOC can use its investigatory powers to explore the merits of the charges. In the case of *University of Pennsylvania v EEOC*, 493 U.S. 182 (1990), the Supreme Court ruled that the EEOC could have access to all information in an employee's file—even evaluation letters in which evaluators were promised confidentiality. During this conciliation period, the EEOC may also try to work out a settlement between the employer and the employee.

The Right-to-Sue Letter

If the EEOC has not settled its complaint within 180 days from the time of its filing, the employee has the right to demand a **right-to-sue letter** from the EEOC, which is a certification that the employee has exhausted available administrative remedies. If a state agency is involved, the time for its settlement of the matter must also expire before the employee can take the matter to court.

The employee has the right to this letter regardless of the EEOC's findings. Even if the EEOC has investigated and determined the charges have no merit, the employee can still pursue the case in court. Under *EEOC v Waffle House*, 534 U.S. 279 (2002), the U.S. Supreme Court held that the EEOC, as an agency, has the right to proceed with its remedies even if the private remedies are dismissed or not available to the affected employee.

Remedies Available under Title VII

Remedies available under Title VII include injunctions, back pay, punitive damages, and attorneys' fees. If a court finds a violation, it may order that corrective or affirmative action be taken to compensate for past wrongs. An injunction usually requires the employer to stop the illegal discrimination and then institute a plan to hire or promote minorities. Back-pay awards are limited to two years under Title VII. Section 706(b) of the act permits successful parties to recover "reasonable attorneys' fees."

An employer cannot take retaliatory action against employees who file charges or who are successful in a suit; Title VII makes such action unlawful.

Title VII originally allowed damages for back pay for all forms of discrimination. Punitive and compensatory damages are now permitted in racial and ethnic discrimination cases. The 1991 amendments extend the recovery of punitive and compensatory damages to cases involving sex, religion, or disability.

Other Antidiscrimination Laws

Age Discrimination in Employment Act of 1967

Title VII does not cover the real problem of age discrimination, which generally involves companies' hiring preference for younger people. To correct this loophole, the Age Discrimination in Employment Act (ADEA) was passed in 1967, and the EEOC was given responsibility for its enforcement. The act covers all employers with 20 or more employees and prohibits age discrimination in the hiring, firing, and compensation of employees. All employment agencies are covered. The act protects workforce members above age 40.

The elements in an age discrimination case are similar to those in other discrimination cases—simply substitute that the terminated employee was replaced with a younger employee. The replacement need not be below the age of 40 [*O'Connor v Consolidated Coin Caterers Corp.*, 517 U.S. 308 (1996)]

CONSIDER... 19.4

On October 29, 1982, Preview Subscription Television, Inc., a subsidiary of Time, Inc., hired Thomas Taggart as a print production manager for Preview's magazine guide. Mr. Taggart was 58 years old at the time and had more than 30 years of experience in the printing industry. In May 1983, Time notified Mr. Taggart that Preview would be dissolved and that Preview employees would receive special consideration for all Time positions.

Mr. Taggart applied for 32 positions in various divisions at Time and its subsidiaries, including *Sports Illustrated, People, Life, Money, HBO,* and *Cinemax Guide.* He was interviewed but never hired. The reason given was that he was "overqualified." Mr. Taggart filed suit, alleging age discrimination. Time responded by saying he performed poorly at interviews, his letters and resumes for jobs contained numerous typographical errors, and he was argumentative with management and counselors.

Time hired less-qualified younger applicants for all the jobs. Has there been age discrimination? [*Taggart v Time, Inc.*, 924 F. 2d 43 (2nd Cir. 1991)]

Equal Pay Act of 1963

The Equal Pay Act of 1963 is an amendment to the Fair Labor Standards Act. (The details of its coverage are outlined in Chapter 18.)

Communicable Diseases in the Workplace

Whether employees can be fired because they may carry a communicable disease has recently become a crucial issue. Court decisions on the treatment of infected employees have varied, but the Supreme Court decision *School Board of Nassau County v Arline*, 480 U.S. 273 (1987), has been touted as a protectionist measure as a result of its finding that a school board could not discriminate against a teacher because she had tuberculosis (a contagious disease). The Americans with Disabilities Act will provide new issues and remedies with regard to communicable diseases (see the following discussion).

Rehabilitation Act of 1973

Congress enacted the Rehabilitation Act to prohibit discrimination in employment against handicapped persons by persons and organizations that receive federal contracts or assistance. The Labor Department is responsible for enforcing the act.

The Rehabilitation Act laid the groundwork for the Americans with Disabilities Act, but is limited in application to employers who have federal contracts and requires the same reasonable accommodation standards now required under ADA.

Americans with Disabilities Act

The intent of the Americans with Disabilities Act (ADA) was to eliminate discrimination against individuals with disabilities. The ADA has been called the "Emancipation Proclamation" for disabled U.S. citizens.

Portions of the ADA apply to employment discrimination issues while other sections ensure that those with disabilities have access to public streets, walkways, buildings, and transportation.

Under the ADA, employers of 15 or more employees cannot discriminate in hiring, promotion, and selection criteria against a "qualified individual with a disability." A disability is defined by the ADA and its 2008 amendments as a physical or mental impairment that substantially limits one or more major life activities such as seeing, hearing, speaking, walking, breathing, learning, or self-care. Pursuant to a U.S. Supreme Court case [*Bragdon v Abbott*, 524 U.S. 624 (1998)], human immunodeficiency virus (HIV) is considered a physical impairment for purposes of the ADA. In that case, a dentist's refusal to treat an HIV-positive patient who needed a cavity filled violated the ADA public accommodation provisions.

Employers must make "reasonable accommodations" for disabled individuals to enable them to perform essential functions. Included in reasonable accommodations are providing employee facilities that are readily accessible to and usable by disabled individuals, job restructuring, allowing part-time or modified work schedules, reassigning disabled individuals to vacant positions, acquiring or modifying equipment, and providing qualified readers or interpreters. Perhaps the accommodation best known to the public is the right golfer Casey Martin won in *PGA Tour, Inc. v Martin* (Case 19.9) to use a cart in PGA tournaments because of his circulatory ailment.

CASE 19.9	*PGA Tour, Inc. v Martin*
	531 U.S. 1049 (2001)

A Stroke of Genius for an ADA in Full Swing

FACTS

Casey Martin (respondent) is a talented golfer. As an amateur, he won 17 Oregon Golf Association junior events before he was 15 and won the state championship as a high school senior. He played on the Stanford University golf team that won the 1994 National Collegiate Athletic Association (NCAA) championship. As a professional, Mr. Martin qualified for the Nike Tour in 1998 and 1999, and based on his 1999 performance, he qualified for the PGA Tour in 2000.

Mr. Martin is also an individual with a disability, as defined in the Americans with Disabilities Act of

1990 (ADA). Since birth he has been afflicted with Klippel-Trenaunay-Weber Syndrome, a degenerative circulatory disorder that obstructs the flow of blood from his right leg back to his heart. The disease is progressive; it causes severe pain and has atrophied his right leg. During the latter part of his college career, the Pacific 10 Conference and the NCAA waived for Mr. Martin their rules requiring players to walk and carry their own clubs.

The PGA Tour, Inc. (petitioner) sponsors and cosponsors professional golf tournaments conducted on three annual tours.

The basic rules of golf apply equally to all players in tour competitions. As one of the petitioner's witnesses explained with reference to "the Masters Tournament, which is golf at its very highest level . . . the key is to have everyone tee off on the first hole under exactly the same conditions and all of them be tested over that 72-hole event under the conditions that exist during those four days of the event." The PGA interpretation of its rules was that Mr. Martin's use of a cart for participation in the four-day, 72-hole event would be an unfair advantage. The PGA would not allow him to use a cart.

The lower court and the court of appeals found that the hard cards (that contain the PGA rule on no carts) violated the ADA and required the PGA to permit Mr. Martin to use a cart pursuant to the act's rules on reasonable accommodation. The PGA appealed.

JUDICIAL OPINION

STEVENS, Justice

This case raises two questions concerning the application of the Americans with Disabilities Act of 1990, to a gifted athlete: first, whether the Act protects access to professional golf tournaments by a qualified entrant with a disability; and second, whether a disabled contestant may be denied the use of a golf cart because it would "fundamentally alter the nature" of the tournaments, § 12182(b)(2)(A)(ii), to allow him to ride when all other contestants must walk. . . .

It seems apparent, from both the general rule and the comprehensive definition of "public accommodation," that petitioner's golf tours and their qualifying rounds fit comfortably within the coverage of Title III, and Martin within its protection.

According to petitioner, . . . petitioner operates not a "golf course" during its tournaments but a "place of exhibition or entertainment," and a professional golfer such as Martin, like an actor in a theater production, is a provider rather than a consumer of the entertainment that petitioner sells to the public. Martin therefore cannot bring a claim under Title III because he is not one of the "'clients or customers of the covered public accommodation.'" Rather, Martin's claim of discrimination

is "job-related" and could only be brought under Title I—but that Title does not apply because he is an independent contractor (as the District Court found) rather than an employee. . . .

Petitioner does not contest that a golf cart is a reasonable modification that is necessary if Martin is to play in its tournaments. Martin's claim thus differs from one that might be asserted by players with less serious afflictions that make walking the course uncomfortable or difficult, but not beyond their capacity. In such cases, an accommodation might be reasonable but not necessary. In this case, however, the narrow dispute is whether allowing Martin to use a golf cart, despite the walking requirement that applies to the PGA TOUR, the NIKE TOUR, and the third stage of the Q-School, is a modification that would "fundamentally alter the nature" of those events.

We are not persuaded that a waiver of the walking rule for Martin would work a fundamental alteration in either sense.

Over the years, there have been many changes in the players' equipment, in golf course design, in the Rules of Golf, and in the method of transporting clubs from hole to hole. Originally, so few clubs were used that each player could carry them without a bag. Then came golf bags, caddies, carts that were pulled by hand, and eventually motorized carts that carried players as well as clubs. . . . The walking rule that is contained in petitioner's hard cards, based on an optional condition buried in an appendix to the Rules of Golf, is not an essential attribute of the game itself.

To be sure, the waiver of an essential rule of competition for anyone would fundamentally alter the nature of petitioner's tournaments. As we have demonstrated, however, the walking rule is at best peripheral to the nature of petitioner's athletic events, and thus it might be waived in individual cases without working a fundamental alteration.

The judgment of the Court of Appeals is affirmed.

DISSENTING OPINION

Justices SCALIA and THOMAS

In my view today's opinion exercises a benevolent compassion that the law does not place it within our power to impose. The judgment distorts the text of Title III, the structure of the ADA, and common sense. I respectfully dissent. . . .

The Court, for its part, pronounces respondent to be a "customer" of the PGA TOUR or of the golf courses on which it is played. That seems to me quite incredible. The PGA TOUR is a professional sporting event, staged for the entertainment of a live and TV audience. The professional golfers on the tour are no more "enjoying" (the statutory term) the entertainment that the tour provides, or the facilities of the golf courses on which it is held, than

CONTINUED

professional baseball players "enjoy" the baseball games in which they play or the facilities of Yankee Stadium. To be sure, professional ballplayers participate in the games, and use the ballfields, but no one in his right mind would think that they are customers of the American League or of Yankee Stadium. They are themselves the entertainment that the customers pay to watch. . . .

It is as irrelevant to the PGA TOUR's compliance with the statute whether walking is essential to the game of golf as it is to the shoe store's compliance whether "pairness" is essential to the nature of shoes. If a shoe store wishes to sell shoes only in pairs it may; and if a golf tour (or a golf course) wishes to provide only walk-around golf, it may. The PGA TOUR cannot deny respondent access to that game because of his disability, but it need not provide him a game different (whether in its essentials or in its details) from that offered to everyone else.

Nowhere is it writ that PGA TOUR golf must be classic "essential" golf. Why cannot the PGA TOUR, if it wishes, promote a new game, with distinctive rules (much as the American League promotes a game of baseball in which the pitcher's turn at the plate can be taken by a "designated hitter")? If members of the public do not like the new rules—if they feel that these rules do not truly test the individual's skill at "real golf" (or the team's skill at "real baseball") they can withdraw their patronage. But the rules are the rules. They are (as in all games) entirely arbitrary, and there is no basis on which anyone—not even the Supreme Court of the United States—can pronounce one or another of them to be "nonessential" if the rulemaker (here the PGA TOUR) deems it to be essential.

. . . It has been rendered the solemn duty of the Supreme Court of the United States, laid upon it by Congress in pursuance of the Federal Government's power "[t]o regulate Commerce with foreign Nations, and among the several States," U.S. Const., Art. I, § 8, cl. 3, to decide What Is Golf. I am sure that the Framers of the Constitution, aware of the 1457 edict of King James II of Scotland prohibiting golf because it interfered with the practice of archery, fully expected that sooner or later the paths of golf and government, the law and the links, would once again cross, and that the judges of this august Court would some day have to wrestle with that age-old jurisprudential question, for which their years of study in the law have so well prepared them: Is someone riding around a golf course from shot to shot really a golfer? The answer, we learn, is yes. The Court ultimately concludes, and it will henceforth be the Law of the Land, that walking is not a "fundamental" aspect of golf.

Either out of humility or out of self-respect (one or the other) the Court should decline to answer this incredibly difficult and incredibly silly question.

CASE QUESTIONS

1. Why does Mr. Martin wish an accommodation?
2. Does use of a cart fundamentally alter the game of golf?
3. Is Mr. Martin seeking a public accommodation or an employee accommodation?
4. Do the dissenting justices believe that the court must define the essential elements of the game of golf?[7]

Preemployment medical examinations are prohibited under the ADA, as are specific questions about a protected individual's disabilities. However, an employer may inquire about the ability of the applicant to perform job-related functions. "Can you carry 50 pounds of mail?" is an appropriate question; "Do you have the use of both arms?" is not.

Employers can refuse employment if an ADA-protected individual cannot perform necessary job functions. Also, employers can refuse to hire individuals who pose a direct threat to the health and safety of others in the workplace (assuming the risk cannot be minimized through accommodation).

The ADA is enforced through the EEOC and carries the same rights and remedies provided under Title VII. Exhibit 19.2 provides a list of items to help employers comply with ADA. Exhibit 19.3 examines proper and improper questions for job interviews under ADA.

The Family and Medical Leave Act

Passed in 1993, the Family and Medical Leave Act (FMLA) requires companies with 50 or more employees to provide 12 weeks' leave each year for medical or

EXHIBIT 19.2 Compliance Tips for ADA

MINIMIZING AN EMPLOYER'S ADA RISKS

1. Post notices describing the provisions of the ADA in your workplace.

2. Review job requirements to ensure that they bear a direct relationship to the ability to perform the essential functions of the job in question.

3. Identify, in writing, the "essential functions" of a job before advertising for or interviewing potential candidates.

4. Before rejecting an otherwise qualified applicant or terminating an employee on the basis of a disability, first determine that (a) the individual cannot perform the essential duties of the position, or (b) the individual cannot perform the essential duties of the position without imminent and substantial risk of injury to self or others, and (c) the employer cannot reasonably accommodate the disability.

5. Articulate factors, other than an individual's disability, that are the basis of an adverse employment decision. Document your findings and the tangible evidence on which a decision to reject or terminate was based; make notes of accommodations considered.

6. Ask the disabled individual for advice on accommodations. This shows the employer's good faith and a willingness to consider such proposals.

7. Institute programs of benefits and consultation to assist disabled employees in effectively managing health, leave, and other benefits.

8. Check with insurance carrier regarding coverage of disabled employees and attempt (within economic reason) to maintain provided coverage or arrange for separate coverage.

9. Keep disabled individuals in mind when making structural alterations or purchasing office furniture and equipment.

10. Document all adverse employment actions, including reasons for the employment action with respect to disabled employees; focus on the employee's inability to do the job effectively rather than any relation to the employee's disability.

Source: EEOC Enforcement Guidance, http://www.eeoc.gov

EXHIBIT 19.3 Legal and Illegal Versions of Similar Job Interview Questions

LEGAL	ILLEGAL
1. Do you have 20/20 corrected vision?	What is your corrected vision?
2. How well can you handle stress?	Does stress ever affect your ability to be productive?
3. Can you perform this function with or without reasonable accommodation?	Would you need reasonable accommodation in this job?
4. How many days were you absent from work last year?	How many days were you sick last year?
5. Are you currently illegally using drugs?	What medications are you currently taking?
6. Do you regularly eat three meals per day?	Do you need to eat a number of small snacks at regular intervals throughout the day in order to maintain your energy level?
7. Do you drink alcohol?	How much alcohol do you drink per week?

Source: EEOC's "Enforcement Guidance on Pre-Employment Disability-Related Inquiries," May 12, 1994.

For the Manager's Desk

Re: The Respect of Rank

Charlene Barshefsky was the former U.S. trade representative. In that role, she was both an ambassador and a cabinet officer during the Clinton administration. With the recent vote to open trade with China, Ms. Barshefsky saw the culmination of years of negotiations with the Chinese.

When interviewed by the *New York Times* about her experience as a woman serving as the United States' chief negotiator, she explained that in China and other countries, gender is not as important as rank:

Because my rank is high, my foreign counterparts treat me with the deference one might expect. Rank is much more important than gender, and rank can tend to overcome any potential

gender bias. To the extent women are thought to be, in general, more perceptive about people, more aware of their surroundings, more sensitive to body language, it is a decided advantage to be a woman in a negotiation, particularly in watching. The body always speaks well before the mouth ever opens.

Are other nations ahead of the United States in treating women as equals? Should rank matter more than gender? What other examples can you point to outside the United States where women have achieved high ranks?

Source: Eric Schmitt, "The Negotiator," *New York Times Magazine,* October 1, 2000, p. 21.

---

family reasons, including the birth or adoption of a child or the serious health condition or illness of a spouse, parent, or child. Although pay is not required during the leave, medical benefits of the employee must continue, and the same or an equivalent job must be available for the employee upon return.

The Global Workforce

Currently 2,000 U.S. companies have 21,000 subsidiary operations in 21 countries throughout the world. With the free trade agreements (see Chapter 7), those numbers will increase, as will the sizes of global operations.

One of the many employment issues that arises with respect to employees in subsidiary operations is whether the protections of Title VII apply to workers in these foreign operations. In *EEOC v Arabian American Oil Co.*, 499 U.S. 244 (1991), the U.S. Supreme Court was faced with the issue of whether U.S. companies could engage in employment discrimination against U.S. citizens when they are working in countries outside the United States. The Court held that the companies are governed by the employment laws of the country of operations and not the provisions of U.S. legislation.

Congress responded to the Supreme Court's ruling in *Arabian American Oil* by adding a section to the Civil Rights Act of 1991 addressing the issue of foreign operations. The statutory provision on foreign operations and civil rights protections is neither universal nor automatic. The amendment provides basically that in a case of conflict between U.S. employment discrimination laws and those of a host country, a company should follow the laws of the host country. An example is a law in the host country that prohibits the employment of women in management. The company would be required to follow that prohibition for operations located in the host country. If the host country has no laws on employment discrimination, the company is then required to follow all U.S. antidiscrimination laws.

Several multilateral treaties govern the rights of workers. In 1948, the United Nations adopted its Universal Declaration of Human Rights. The declaration supports, among other things, equality of pay and nondiscriminatory employment policies. Also, the Helsinki Final Act of 1973 supports nondiscriminatory employment policies. In 1977, the International Labor Office issued its Tripartite Declaration of Principles Concerning Multinational Enterprises, which supports equal pay and nondiscriminatory payment policies. The EU has adopted all of these treaties and policies for their implementation.

B I O G R A P H Y

Ann Hopkins, a Shunned Partner

Ann Hopkins was a senior manager in the Management Advisory Services division of the Price Waterhouse Office of Government Services (OGS) in Washington, D.C. After earning undergraduate and graduate degrees in mathematics, she taught mathematics at her alma mater, Hollins College, and worked for IBM, NASA, Touche Ross, and American Management Systems before beginning her career with Price Waterhouse in 1977. She became the firm's specialist in large-scale computer system design and operations for the federal government. While salaries in the accounting profession are not published, estimates put her salary as a senior manager at about $65,000. Estimates of the increase in salary were that she would earn almost double that, or $125,000 annually, on average (1980 figures).

At that time, Price Waterhouse was known as one of the "Big 8," or one of the top public accounting firms in the United States. A senior manager became a candidate for partnership when the partners in her office submitted her name for partnership status. In August 1982, the partners in Hopkins's office proposed her as a candidate for the partner for the 1983 class of partners. Of the 88 candidates who were submitted for consideration, Hopkins was the only woman. Hopkins was responsible for bringing to Price Waterhouse a two-year, $25 million contract with the Department of State, the largest contract ever obtained by the firm. At that time Price Waterhouse had 662 partners, 7 of whom were women. All of the firm's partners were invited to submit written comments

regarding each candidate, but not every partner did so. Of the 32 partners who submitted comments on Hopkins, one stated that "none of the other partnership candidates at Price Waterhouse that year [has] a comparable record in terms of successfully procuring major contracts for the partnership."

Her billable hours were 2,442 in 1982 and 2,507 in 1981, amounts that none of the other partnership candidates' billable hours even approached.

There were no limits on the number of persons to whom partnership could be awarded and no guidelines for evaluating comments about candidates. Price Waterhouse offered 47 partnerships to the 88 candidates in the 1983 round; another 27 were denied partnerships, and 20, including Ms. Hopkins, were put on hold. Ms. Hopkins had received more "no" votes than any other candidate for partnership, with most of those votes coming from members of the partnership committee outside the firm's government services unit.

Thirteen of the 32 partners who submitted comments on Hopkins supported her; 3 recommended putting her on hold; 8 said they did not have enough information; and 8 recommended denial.

The partners in Hopkins's office praised her character as well as her accomplishments, describing her in their joint statement as "an outstanding professional" who had a "deft touch," a "strong character, independence, and integrity." Clients appear to have agreed with these assessments. One official from the State Department described her

CONTINUED

as "extremely competent, intelligent," "strong and forthright, very productive, energetic, and creative." She "was generally viewed as a highly competent project leader who worked long hours, pushed vigorously to meet deadlines, and demanded much from the multidisciplinary staffs with which she worked."

On too many occasions, however, Hopkins's aggressiveness apparently spilled over into abrasiveness. Staff members seem to have borne the brunt of Hopkins's brusqueness. Long before her bid for partnership, partners evaluating her work had counseled her to improve her relations with staff members. Although later evaluations indicate an improvement, Hopkins's perceived shortcomings in this important area eventually doomed her bid for partnership. Virtually all of the partners' negative remarks about Hopkins—even those of partners who supported her—concerned her "interpersonal skills." Both "[s]upporters and opponents of her candidacy indicated that she was sometimes overly aggressive, unduly harsh, difficult to work with, and impatient with staff."

Another partner testified at trial that he had questioned her billing records and was left with concerns because he found her answers unsatisfying.

One partner's evaluation described her as "macho," while another suggested that she "overcompensated for being a woman"; a third advised her to take "a course at charm school." One partner wrote that Hopkins was "universally disliked." Several partners criticized her use of profanity. In response, one partner suggested that those partners objected to her swearing only "because it[']s a lady using foul language." Another supporter explained that Hopkins "ha[d] matured from a tough-talking, somewhat masculine, hardnosed manager to an authoritative, formidable, but much more appealing lady partner candidate." In order for Hopkins to improve her chances for partnership, Thomas Beyer, a partner who supervised Hopkins at OGS, suggested that she "walk more femininely, talk more femininely, dress more femininely, wear make-up, have her hair styled, and wear jewelry." Ms. Hopkins said she could not apply makeup because that would require removing her trifocals and she would not be able to see. Also, her allergy to cosmetics made it difficult for her to find appropriate makeup. Mr. Beyer also suggested that she should not carry a briefcase, should stop smoking, and should not drink beer at luncheon meetings.

Dr. Susan Fiske, a social psychologist and associate professor of psychology at Carnegie-Mellon University who would testify for Hopkins in her suit against Price Waterhouse, reviewed the Price Waterhouse selection process and concluded that it was likely influenced by sex stereotyping. Dr. Fiske indicated that some of the partners' comments were gender-biased, while others that were gender-neutral were intensely critical and made by partners who barely knew Hopkins. Dr. Fiske concluded that the subjectivity of the evaluations and their sharply critical nature were probably the result of sex stereotyping.

Although Hopkins and 19 others were put on hold for the following year, her future looked dim. Later, two partners withdrew their support for Hopkins, and she was informed that she would not be reconsidered the following year. Hopkins, who maintains that she was told after the second nomination cycle that she would never be a partner, then resigned and filed a discrimination complaint with the EEOC.

At that time, the law was not clear and the assumption was that Title VII did not apply to partnership decisions in companies. With the EEOC refusing to take action, Hopkins filed suit against Price Waterhouse. She has stated she filed the suit to find out why Price Waterhouse made "such a bad business decision." The U.S. Supreme Court found that Ms. Hopkins did indeed have a cause of action for discrimination in the partnership decision. The *Hopkins* case was an important employment discrimination case because the Supreme Court recognized stereotyping as a way of establishing discrimination. However, the case is also known for its clarification of the law on situations in which employers take action against employees for both lawful and unlawful reasons. Known as "mixed-motive" cases, this form of discrimination case shifts the burden of proof to the employer to establish that it would have made the same decision if using only the lawful considerations and in spite of unlawful considerations that entered into the process. The "same-decision" defense requires employers to establish sufficient grounds for termination or other actions taken against employees that are independent of the unlawful considerations.

In 1990, on remand, Ms. Hopkins was awarded her partnership and damages. She was awarded back pay plus interest, and while the exact amount of the award is unclear, Hopkins later verified that she paid $300,000 in taxes on her award that year and also paid her attorneys the $500,000 due and owing them. Ms. Hopkins rejoined Price Waterhouse as a partner in 1991.

Ms. Hopkins retired from Pricewaterhouse-Coopers in 2002, and she has written a book about her experience as a litigant. She also gardens, does carpentry work, and enjoys spending time with her grandchildren. She is still in litigation over the death of her youngest son, who was struck by a drunk driver.

Sources: Adapted from Marianne M. Jennings, *Business Ethics: Cases and Selected Readings,* 7th ed., 2011; and Ann Hopkins, "Price Waterhouse v Hopkins: A Personal Account of a Sexual Discrimination Plaintiff," 22 *Hofstra Lab. & Emp. L.J.* 357 (2005).

Summary

What laws govern employment discrimination?

- Civil Rights Acts of 1866, 1964, 1991—federal statutes prohibiting discrimination in various aspects of life (employment, voting)

- Equal Pay Act—equal pay for the same work regardless of gender

- Equal Employment Opportunity Act—antidiscrimination employment amendment to Civil Rights Act

- Pregnancy Discrimination Act—prohibits refusing to hire, refusing to promote, or firing because of pregnancy

- Age Discrimination in Employment Act (ADEA)—prohibits hiring, firing, promotion, benefits, raises based on age

- Rehabilitation Act of 1973—federal statute prohibiting discrimination on basis of disability by federal agencies and contractors

- Americans with Disabilities Act (ADA)—federal law prohibiting discrimination on basis of disability by certain employees

- Family and Medical Leave Act (FMLA)—federal law providing for 12 weeks of leave for childbirth, adoption, or family illness

- Lilly Ledbetter Fair Pay Act—(federal law that expands the time for filing claims for violations of Title VII for compensation)

What types of discrimination exist?

- Disparate treatment—form of discrimination in which members of different races/sexes are treated differently

- Disparate impact—test or screening device that affects one group more than another

- Pattern or practice of discrimination—theory for establishing discrimination that compares population percentages with workplace percentages

- Sexual harassment—form of discrimination that involves a *quid pro quo* related to sexual favors or an atmosphere of harassment

What are the defenses to discrimination?

- Bona fide occupational qualification (BFOQ)—job qualification of sex, religion, or national origin that is necessary for the operation of a business, such as religious affiliation for the pastor of a church

- Affirmative action—programs created to remedy past wrongs that permit choices on the basis of race, sex, or national origin

Questions and Problems

1. When a white employee refused to perform cleanup work that was not within his job description, he suffered no repercussions. When four black employees refused to perform the same cleanup work for the same reason, they were discharged. Is there discrimination? [*Slack v Havens,* 522 F.2d 1091 (9th Cir. 1975)]

2. Calvin Rhodes began as a salesman with Dresser Industries in 1955. In 1986, the oil industry experienced a severe economic downturn, and Mr. Rhodes was laid off. His severance report said he was discharged as part of a reduction in force. Within two months, Dresser had hired a 42-year-old replacement. Mr. Rhodes sued for violation of ADEA. Will he win? [*Rhodes v Guiberson Oil Tools* (subsidiary of Dresser), 75 F.3d 989 (5th Cir. 1996)]

3.   Vivian Martyszenko was working as a cashier at a Safeway grocery store in Ogallala, Nebraska, when she received a call from the police informing her that her two children might have been molested. Ms. Martyszenko's supervisor gave her two weeks' vacation leave to care for her children.

   The psychiatrist's exam of the children was inconclusive, and Ms. Martyszenko was told it would take time for their recovery. She asked for leave under the FMLA, which Safeway denied. She then filed suit, alleging Safeway had violated FMLA. Was the boys' condition a serious health condition covered under FMLA? [*Martyszenko v Safeway, Inc.*, 120 F.3d 120 (8th Cir. 1997)]

4.   On August 11, 1980, Shelby Memorial Hospital hired Sylvia Hayes, a certified X-ray technician, to work the 3–11 P.M. shift in the hospital's radiology department. Two months later, she was fired after she informed her supervisor that she was pregnant. The supervisor fired Ms. Hayes because Dr. Cecil Eiland, the hospital's radiology director and director of radiation safety, recommended that Ms. Hayes be removed from all areas using ionizing radiation, and the hospital could not find alternative work for her. After her dismissal, Ms. Hayes filed suit for violation of the Pregnancy Discrimination Act and Title VII. Should she recover? [*Hayes v Shelby Memorial Hosp.*, 726 F.2d 1543 (11th Cir. 1984)]

5.   The Masonic nursing home has mostly female occupants and hires fewer male attendants than female ones. Home administrators maintain that the female occupants (for privacy reasons) would not consent to intimate personal care by males and would, in fact, leave the home. A substantial portion of the women at the home are "total care" patients who require assistance in performing virtually all activities, including bathing, dressing, and using toilets, catheters, and bedpans. In a suit brought by a male nurse's aide who was denied employment, who would win? [*Fessel v Masonic Home*, 17 FEP Cases 330 (Del. 1978)]

6.   Between 1985 and 1990, while attending college, Beth Ann Faragher worked part time and during the summers as an ocean lifeguard for the Parks and Recreation Department of the City of Boca Raton. Ms. Faragher worked for three immediate supervisors during this period: Bill Terry, David Silverman, and Robert Gordon. Ms. Faragher resigned in June 1990 and brought a Title VII sexual harassment suit against the City in 1992. She alleged a sexually hostile atmosphere because of "uninvited and offensive touching," lewd remarks, and Mr. Silverman's comment, "Date me or clean the toilets for a year."

Ms. Faragher had not complained to higher management, and the lifeguards had no significant contact with higher city officials. Two months before Ms. Faragher's resignation, a former lifeguard, Nancy E. Wanchew, wrote to the City's personnel director complaining about Mr. Terry and Mr. Silverman's harassment of female lifeguards. Should the City be held liable? Does it matter that Ms. Faragher asked only for nominal damages, attorney's fees, and costs? [*Faragher v City of Boca Raton*, 524 U.S. 775 (1998)]

7.   After working for Ace Drill Bits for nearly 10 years as a production supervisor, Constance Price learns that she is being paid less than the other four production supervisors in her department, who are all men. Immediately after learning about the pay discrepancy, Constance files an EEOC charge alleging sex-based wage discrimination in violation of Title VII. The investigation shows that Constance generally received lower pay raises than her male counterparts as the result of lower performance ratings. These performance ratings and related pay raises all occurred more than 300 days before Constance filed her charge. Discuss whether there has been a Title VII violation. Also discuss whether Constance has filed within the time limits for an EEOC claim.

8.   Would the following actions constitute sexual harassment?

a.   Making sexual comments or innuendoes; telling sexual jokes or stories

b.   Asking questions about social or sexual life

c.   Telling lies or spreading rumors about a person's personal sex life

d.   Making sexual comments about a person's body

e.   Turning work discussions to sexual topics

f.   Looking a person up and down

g.   Staring repeatedly at someone

h.   Blocking a person's path or hindering them

i.   Giving unwanted gifts of a sexual nature

j.   Invading a person's body space

k.   Making sexual gestures or kissing sounds or offering massages

l.   Displaying sexual posters, cartoons, or handouts

9.   American Airlines passed a grooming rule that prohibited "cornrow" hairstyles on all employees. Renee Rogers, a black woman, brought a Title VII suit alleging that the denial of her right to wear the hairstyle intruded upon her rights and discriminated against her. What will be the result? [*Rogers v American Airlines, Inc.*, 527 F. Supp. 229 (S.D.N.Y. 1981)]

10. American Airlines has a policy of not hiring flight officers over the age of 40. The reason for their policy is that it takes 10–15 years for a flight officer to become a copilot and then another 10–15 years for a copilot to become a captain. Because the FAA requires retirement at age 60, service would be limited. Edward L. Murnane, age 43, was denied employment on the basis of age and filed an age discrimination suit. Is age a BFOQ for the job? [*Murnane v American Airlines, Inc.,* 667 F.2d 98 (D.C. 1981)]

Ethics, Organizational Behavior, and the Law

English-only policies in the workplace have become the fastest-growing area of EEOC challenges as well as litigation under Title VII. In 1996, the EEOC had 30 discrimination complaints related to English-only policies of employers. Since 1996, the EEOC has had a 500 percent increase in those complaints.[8] Employers that have implemented English-only policies include the Salvation Army, All-Island Transportation (a Long Island taxi company), a geriatric center in New York, and Oglethorpe University in Atlanta.

One lawyer noted that employers seem more willing to make the policies and risk the legal battles because they think such policies are appropriate and necessary in order to provide adequate customer service, or in the case of health operations such as the geriatric center, correct medical care. Employers are, however, warned by their lawyers that they will have "a target on their backs" if they implement the policies.

A case that an employer lost was *Maldonado v City of Altus,* 433 F.3d 1294 (10th Cir. 2006). In that case, the city of Altus promulgated an English-only policy that affected 29 of the city's employees, who are Hispanic. All 29 of the employees are fluently bilingual. In the spring of 2002, the city's street commissioner issued a rule that employees in his division could speak only English while on the job. The city's HR director told the commissioner that the policy would be upheld only if limited to when the employees were using the radio to communicate for purposes of city business. However, the rule was enforced throughout the workday, even during lunch and breaks. The employees filed suit alleging that the rule created a hostile environment for them. The 10th Circuit agreed with the employees and reversed the summary judgment for the city.

Lawyers offer the following guidelines for enforceable English-only policies:

1. Such policies are permitted if they are needed to promote safe or efficient operations.

2. Such policies are permitted where communication with customers, coworkers, or supervisors who speak only English is also important.

3. Such policies are permitted where there are frequent emergency encounters in which speaking a common language is necessary for purposes of managing such situations.

4. Such policies are necessary in situations in which cooperation and close working relationships demand a common language and some workers speak only English.

Discussion Questions

1. Is there a common thread among the companies mentioned that have English-only policies?

2. Do these language policies create a hostile environment?

3. Give a list of the types of employers you believe could qualify for an English-only policy under the EEOC guidelines.

Notes

1. See the website and the *Instructor's Manual* for additional background on the history of employment discrimination law.

2. Justice Sonia Sotomayor's confirmation to the high court was pending at the time of this decision. She was one of the appellate judges who reversed the lower court decision.

3. Walmart has issued several statements about its programs for women and minorities and offered statistics that indicate significant changes have been made the composition of its management team since the time the suits were filed.

4. www.sec.gov. Click on EDGAR database. Go to Hewlett-Packard and click on 8-k filed on August 6, 2010.

5. *Id.*

6. For updates on affirmative action and other issues in employment discrimination law, be sure to visit the course website.

7. Mr. Martin has retired from the PGA and is now the head golf coach at the University of Oregon, his alma mater. His last PGA play was in 2006 and his total earnings that year were $1,328. He finished 23rd in the U.S. Open in 1998 after a stunning start that found him in the lead early in the tournament.

8. www.eeoc.gov. Click on "litigation statistics."

Part 5

Business Forms and Capitalization

This portion of the book covers legal issues in forming and financing a business. The structure of a business determines its owners' rights and liabilities. Different business forms afford varying levels of flexibility for operations. In addition, the type of business structure creates opportunities for both the initial financing of the business and its expansion.

Some forms of business financing require compliance with state and federal laws for sales of such business interests as securities and bonds. These laws include disclosure requirements for sales; they also provide remedies for investors and impose liabilities on businesses when disclosures made about the nature of the interest and the business are incomplete or inaccurate.

Some businesses combine or merge in order to compete better in the evolving global economy. State and federal laws afford disclosure and protections for merging businesses and their owners and investors.

20 Forms of Doing Business

Creating a sole proprietorship is a popular way to do business, but the most popular forms of business organizations, and the ones producing the most revenues, are those formed by more than one person. Partnerships, limited partnerships, limited liability companies, and corporations are all multi-individual forms of doing business. This chapter answers the following questions: How are various business entities formed? What are the advantages and disadvantages of various entities? What are the rights, responsibilities, and liabilities of the individuals involved?

Each of the forms of doing business is examined by reviewing its formation, sources of funding, the personal liability of owners, tax consequences, management and control, and the ease of transferring interests. Exhibit 20.1 on page 686 presents an overview of the types of business entities. ■

Please accept my resignation. I don't want to belong to any organization that will accept me as a member.

Groucho Marx

Although our form is corporate, our attitude is partnership. We do not view the company itself as the ultimate owner of our business assets but instead view the company as a conduit through which our shareholders own the assets.

Warren Buffett
Chairman, Berkshire Hathaway

UPDATE
For up-to-date legal news, go to
mariannejennings.com

CONSIDER...

Michael Eisner, then–CEO and chairman of Disney, hired Michael Ovitz as his second-in-command at Disney. Mr. Eisner had a history of not working well with powerful seconds-in-command, and Mr. Ovitz was a powerful Hollywood talent agent and producer. In less than one year, Mr. Ovitz and Mr. Eisner were at such odds that Mr. Eisner and the board agreed to pay Mr. Ovitz more than $38

million in cash compensation and three million shares of Disney stock to leave the company. The shareholders brought suit against the Disney board alleging that the board's supervision of Eisner was lax, that the hiring was a poor business decision, and that the amount paid to end the arrangement constituted waste. The board says it just made a mistake. Can the shareholders recover?

Sole Proprietorships

Formation

A **sole proprietorship** is not a true business entity because it consists of only one individual operating a business. According to the U.S. Small Business Association, most small businesses operate as sole proprietorships, with 50 percent operating as home-based businesses. Often, a sole proprietorship is evidenced by the following language: "Homer Lane d/b/a Green Grower's Grocery"; "d/b/a" is an acronym for "doing business as." Because a sole proprietorship is not a separate organization, it has no formal requirements for formation. The individual simply begins doing business. In some states, "d/b/a" businesspeople are required to file their name(s) with a designated state agency and then publish the fictitious names under which they will be doing business.

Sources of Funding

Most sole proprietorships have small business capital needs initially. Their financing usually comes from loans, either direct loans from banks or loans through government agencies such as the Small Business Administration.

Some sole proprietorships are started with financial backing from other people, usually in the form of personal loans. In such cases, the sole proprietor may have the skills or clients for a successful business but not the funds necessary to begin.

Liability

Because financing for a sole proprietorship is based on the sole proprietor's credit rating and assets, the proprietor is personally liable for the business loan, and his or her assets are subject to attachment should a default occur. To get financing, a sole proprietor takes personal financial risk.

EXHIBIT 20.1 Comparison of Forms of Conducting Business

FORM	FORMATION	FUNDING	MANAGEMENT	TRANSFER CONTROL	TAXES	DISSOLUTION	LIABILITY
Sole proprietorship	No formal requirements	Individual provides funds	Individual	No transfer	Individual pays on individual return	Death; voluntary	Individual
Partnership	Articles of partnership	Capital contributions of partner	All partners or delegated to one	Transfer interest but not partners status	Partner takes profits and losses on individual return (flow-through)	Dissolution upon death; withdrawal of partner	Partners are personally liable
Limited partnership	Filing of articles of partnership	Capital contributions of general and limited partners	General partner	More easily transferred	Same as partnership (flow-through)	Death of general partner	General partner is personally liable; limited partners liable to extent of contribution
Corporation	Formal filing of articles of incorporation	Debt (bonds)/equity (shareholders)	Board of directors, officers, and/or executive committee	Shares (with reasonable restrictions) are easily transferred	Corporation pays taxes; shareholders pay taxes on dividends	Dissolved only if limited in duration or shareholders vote to dissolve	No shareholder personal liability unless (1) watered or (2) corporate veil
S corporation* or Subchapter S	Same as above (special IRS filings to create special tax [flow-through] status)	Same as above	Same as above	Restrictions on transfer to comply with S corporation	Shareholders pay taxes on profits; take losses	Same as above	Same as above
C corporation†	Created as normal corporation	Same as above	Same as above	No restrictions	Corporation pays taxes; shareholders pay taxes on dividends	Same as above	Same as above
Limited liability company (LLC)	Formal filing—articles of organization	Capital contributions of members	All members manage or delegate to one member	No admission without consent of majority	Flow-through treatment	Dissolved upon death, bankruptcy	Same as above (except professional negligence)
Limited liability partnership	Filing of articles of limited liability partnership	Capital contributions of partners	All partners or delegated to one	No admission without consent of majority	Flow-through treatment	Dissolved upon death, bankruptcy	Varies by state but liability for acts of partners is limited in some way

*S corporations are formed under state incorporation laws but structured to obtain flow-through or pass-through status for income and losses under IRS regulations.

† "C corporation" is, again, a label for tax purposes.

Tax Consequences

The positive side of a sole proprietor's unlimited personal liability is the right to claim all tax losses associated with the business. The income of the business is the income of the sole proprietor and is reported on the individual's income tax return. The IRS does not require a separate filing for the business itself; the sole proprietor files a Schedule C form with the usual 1040 form. Moreover, although sole proprietors owe all the taxes, they also get the benefit of all business deductions.

Management and Control

The proprietor is the manager of the business. In many businesses, the sole proprietor is both manager and employee. The proprietor makes all decisions. This form of business operation is truly centralized management.

Transferability of Interest

Because the business in many ways is the owner, the business can be transferred only if the owner allows it. When a sole proprietor's business is transferred, the transfer consists of the property, inventory, and goodwill of the business. The sole proprietor is generally required to sign a noncompetition agreement so that the goodwill that has been paid for is preserved (see Chapters 16 and 17 for more details). In addition, upon the owner's death the heirs or devisees of the owner inherit the property involved in the business. They may choose to operate the business, but the business usually ends upon the death of the sole proprietor.

Partnerships

Partnerships are governed by some version of the **Uniform Partnership Act** (UPA), which has been adopted in 49 states. There is the original UPA and also the **Revised Uniform Partnership Act** (RUPA). The states have adopted one or a combination of the UPA and RUPA. The RUPA defines a partnership as "the association of two or more persons to carry on as co-owners of a business for profit forms a partnership, whether or not the persons intend to form a partnership." "Persons" can include corporations, known as "artificial" persons, and natural persons.

Formation

A partnership can be formed voluntarily by direct action of the parties, such as through a partnership agreement or articles of partnership (see Exhibit 20.2 for content of such an agreement), or its formation can be implied by the ongoing conduct of the parties.

Conduct That Forms Partnerships by Implication

A partnership can arise even though no express agreement is made and the parties do not call themselves partners. In certain circumstances, courts infer that a partnership exists even if the persons involved say they are not partners.

Simply owning property together does not result in a **partnership by implication.** A cousin to apparent authority (see Chapter 17), a partnership by implication arises because the behaviors of the principals lead others to believe there is a partnership. Courts examine a number of factors in determining whether a partnership exists by implication. Section 7 of the RUPA provides that if two or more parties

EXHIBIT 20.2 Information Included in Articles of Partnership

MINIMUM REQUIREMENTS	SUGGESTED PROVISIONS
1. Names of the partners	1. Disability issues
2. Name of the partnership	2. Insurance coverage
3. Nature of the partnership's business	3. Sale of interest
4. The time frame of operation	4. Divorce of one of the partners
5. Amount of each partner's capital contribution	5. Indemnity agreements
6. Managerial powers of partners	6. Noncompetition agreements
7. Rights and duties of partners	7. Leaves of absence
8. Accounting procedures for partnership books and records	
9. Methods for sharing profits and losses	
10. Salaries (if any) of the partners	
11. Causes and methods of dissolution	
12. Distribution of property if the partnership is terminated	

share the profits of a business, it is *prima facie* evidence that a partnership exists. (*Prima facie* evidence means the presumption that a partnership exists.) However, the presumption of partnership by profit sharing can be overcome if someone received profits for any of the following reasons:

1. Profits paid to repay debts
2. Profits paid as wages or rent
3. Profits paid to a widow or estate representative
4. Profits paid for the sale of business goodwill

Many shopping center leases, for example, provide for the payment of both a fixed amount of rent and a percentage of net profits. The owners of the shopping center profit as the stores do, but they profit as landlords, not as partners with the shopping center businesses.

Byker v Mannes (Case 20.1) addresses the question of whether a partnership is implied by the conduct of two principals.

CASE 20.1 *Byker v Mannes*
641 N.W.2d 210 (Mich. 2002)*

Dumb and Dumbfounded

FACTS

In 1985, David Byker (plaintiff) was doing accounting work for Tom Mannes (defendant). The two talked about going into business together because they had complementary business skills. Mr. Mannes could locate certain properties because of his real estate

background, and Mr. Byker could raise money for their property purchases. Indeed, the parties stipulated the following as part of the litigation process in this case:

> [T]he Plaintiff . . . and Defendant . . . agreed to engage in an ongoing business enterprise, to furnish capital, labor and/or skill to such enterprise, to raise investment funds

and to share equally in the profits, losses and expenses of such enterprise. . . . In order to facilitate investment of limited partners, Byker and Mannes created separate entities wherein they were general partners or shareholders for the purposes of operating each separate entity.

They also stipulated that they had investment interests in five real estate limited partnerships. With regard to these partnerships in which they invested over a nine-year period, they shared equally in the commissions, financing fees, and termination costs. The two also personally guaranteed loans for these investments from several financial institutions.

The business relationship between the parties began to deteriorate after they created Pier 1000 Ltd. in order to own and manage a marina. Shortly after the creation of Pier 1000 Ltd., the marina encountered serious financial difficulties. To address these difficulties, the parties placed their profits from another partnership, the M & B Limited Partnership II, into Pier 1000 Ltd. and borrowed money from several financial institutions.

When Mr. Mannes refused to make any additional monetary contributions, Mr. Byker continued to make loan payments and incurred accounting fees on behalf of Pier 1000 Ltd., as well as on behalf of other business entities. Mr. Byker also entered into several individual loans for the benefit of Pier 1000 Ltd. These business transactions were performed without Mr. Mannes's knowledge.

The marina was returned to its previous owners in exchange for their assumption of Mr. Byker and Mr. Mannes's business obligations. At this point, the business ventures between Mr. Byker and Mr. Mannes ceased.

Mr. Byker then approached Mr. Mannes to obtain his share of the payments required as a result of the losses from the various businesses. Mr. Mannes testified that he was "absolutely dumbfounded" by the request for money.

Mr. Byker then filed suit for the payments, saying that the two had entered into a partnership. Following a bench trial, the court determined that the parties had created a general partnership that included all of the business entities. The Court of Appeals reversed that decision. Mr. Byker appealed.

JUDICIAL OPINION

MARKMAN, Justice

"[T]here is no necessity that the parties attach the label 'partnership' to their relationship as long as they in fact both mutually agree to assume a relationship that falls within the definition of a partnership."

In determining whether a partnership exists, the focus is not on whether individuals subjectively intended to form a partnership, that is, it is unimportant whether the parties would have labeled themselves "partners." Instead, the focus is on whether individuals intended to jointly carry on a business for profit regardless of whether they subjectively intended to form a partnership.

Whether Michigan partnership law, M.C.L. § 449.6(1), requires a subjective intent to form a partnership or merely an intent to carry on as co-owners a business for profit is a question of law.

. . . At present, partnership is defined as "an association of 2 or more persons, which may consist of husband and wife, to carry on as co-owners a business for profit. . . . "

In 1994, however, the UPA definition of partnership was amended by the National Conference of Commissioners. The amended definition stated that "the association of two or more persons to carry on as co-owners a business for profit forms a partnership, whether or not the persons intend to form a partnership.". . .

Although Michigan has not adopted the amended definition of partnership as set forth in § 202 of the Uniform Partnership Act of 1994, we believe nonetheless that M.C.L. § 449.6 is consistent with that amendment.[†]

. . . [I]f the parties associate themselves to "carry on" as co-owners a business for profit, they will be deemed to have formed a partnership relationship regardless of their subjective intent to form such a legal relationship. The statutory language is devoid of any requirement that the individuals have the subjective intent to create a partnership. Stated more plainly, the statute does not require partners to be aware of their status as "partners" in order to have a legal partnership.

Pursuant to this common law, individuals would be found to have formed a partnership if they acted as partners, regardless of their subjective intent to form a partnership.

If parties intend no partnership the courts should give effect to their intent, unless somebody has been deceived by their acting or assuming to act as partners; and any such case must stand upon its peculiar facts, and upon special equities.

It is nevertheless possible for parties to intend no partnership and yet to form one. If they agree upon an arrangement which is a partnership in fact, it is of no importance that they call it something else, or that they even expressly declare that they are not to be partners. The law must declare what is the legal import of their agreements, and names go for nothing when the substance of the arrangement shows them to be inapplicable.

Thus, one analyzes whether the parties acted as partners, not whether they subjectively intended to create, or not to create, a partnership. . . .

CONTINUED

Accordingly, we believe that our prior case law has, consistent with M.C.L. § 449.6(1), properly examined the requirements of a legal partnership by focusing on whether the parties intentionally acted as co-owners of a business for profit, and not on whether they consciously intended to create the legal relationship of "partnership."

With the language of the statute as our focal point, we conclude that the intent to create a partnership is not required if the acts and conduct of the parties otherwise evidence that the parties carried on as co-owners a business for profit. Thus, we believe that, to the extent that the Court of Appeals regarded the absence of subjective intent to create a partnership as dispositive regarding whether the parties carried on as co-owners a business for profit, it incorrectly interpreted the statutory (and the common) law of partnership in Michigan.

Accordingly, we remand this matter to the Court of Appeals for analysis under the proper test for determining the existence of a partnership under the Michigan Uniform Partnership Act.

CASE QUESTIONS

1. What type of relationship did Mr. Byker and Mr. Mannes have?

2. When did the relationship end? When did the parties believe it ended?

3. What does the court say about the intent of the parties?

4. Is Mr. Mannes liable to Mr. Byker for the payments Mr. Byker made with regard to their investments?

*This case created a bit of a tussle between the Michigan Court of Appeals and its Supreme Court. Following this decision and remand, the Court of Appeals found that there was no partnership because the parties had to be aware of it to be liable, thus defying the Michigan Supreme Court. On appeal, the Michigan Supreme Court reversed the Court of Appeals, 668 N.W.2d 909 (Mich. 2003), not offering an opinion but explaining it was reversing for the reasons stated in the dissenting opinion at the Court of Appeals on the second round.

†Note how the court traces the history of the law of partnership. Instructors should refer to the *Instructor's Manual* for more information on the history of business organizations.

CONSIDER...   20.1

Richard Chaiken entered into agreements with both Mr. Strazella and Mr. Spitzer to operate a barbershop. Mr. Chaiken was to provide barber chairs, supplies, and licenses. Mr. Strazella and Mr. Spitzer were to bring their tools, and the agreements included work hours and holidays for them. The Delaware Employment Security Commission determined that Mr. Strazella and Mr. Spitzer are employees, not partners, and seeks to collect unemployment compensation for the two barbers. Mr. Chaiken maintains that they are partners and not employees. Who is correct? [*Chaiken v Employment Security Comm'n*, 274 A.2d 707 (Del. 1971)]

Conduct That Forms a Partnership by Estoppel

At times, someone can be held to be a partner because he or she acted like a partner. Some court decisions have held that those who help a new business obtain a loan are holding themselves out as partners. Section 16 of the UPA provides as follows:

> When a person by words spoken or written or by conduct, represents himself, or consents to another representing him to anyone as a partner in an existing partnership or with one or more persons not actual partners, he is liable to any party to whom such representation has been made.

In other words, if the conduct of two or more parties leads others to believe a partnership exists, that partnership may be found to exist legally under the notion of **partnership by estoppel.** Partnerships by estoppel arise when others are led to believe there is a partnership. Partnership by estoppel is a cousin to agency by estoppel, another ostensible relationship.

Sources of Funding

Funding for a partnership comes from the partners who initially contribute property, cash, or services to the partnership accounts. These contributions are the capital of the partnership. Not only are these contributions put at the risk of the business, but so also are each of the partners' personal assets: Partners are personally liable for the full amount of the partnership's obligations. Partners can also make loans to the partnership.

CONSIDER...   20.2

Triangle Chemical Company supplied $671.10 worth of fertilizer and chemicals to France Mathis to produce a cabbage crop. When Mr. Mathis first asked for credit, he was denied. He then told Triangle that he had a new partner, Emory Pope. The company president called Mr. Pope, who said he was backing Mr. Mathis. Mr. Pope had loaned Mr. Mathis money to produce the crop, and Mr. Mathis said Mr. Pope would pay the bills. Mr. Pope said, "We're growing the crop together and I am more or less handling the money." When Mr. Mathis could not pay, Triangle wanted to hold Mr. Pope personally liable. Mr. Pope said his promise to pay another's debt would have to have been in writing. Triangle claimed Mr. Pope was a partner and personally liable. Is he? [*Pope v Triangle Chemical Co.*, 277 S.E.2d 758 (Ga. 1981)]

Partner Liability

Each partner is both a principal and an agent to the other partners and is liable both for the acts of others and to the others for individual acts. If one partner enters into a contract for partnership business supplies, all the partners are liable. Similarly, if partners have a motor vehicle accident while out doing partnership deliveries, the individual partners are liable for their own negligence, but because they were acting in the scope of partnership business, the partnership itself is also liable. Under the RUPA, partners are jointly and severally liable for all obligations.

If partnership assets are exhausted, each partner is individually liable. Creditors can satisfy their claims by looking to the assets of the individual partners after the partnership assets are exhausted.

Vrabel v Acri (Case 20.2) deals with an issue of partnership liability.

| CASE 20.2 | *Vrabel v Acri*
103 N.E.2d 564 (Ohio 1952) |

Shot Down in a Ma & Pa Cafe: Is Ma Liable When Pa Goes to Jail?

FACTS

On February 17, 1947, Stephen Vrabel and a companion went into the Acri Cafe in Youngstown, Ohio, to buy alcoholic drinks. While Mr. Vrabel and his companion were sitting at the bar drinking, Michael Acri, without provocation, drew a .38-caliber gun, shot and

killed Mr. Vrabel's companion, and shot and seriously injured Mr. Vrabel. Mr. Acri was convicted of murder and sentenced to a life term in the state prison.

Florence and Michael Acri, as partners, had owned and operated the Acri Cafe since 1933. From the time of his marriage to Mrs. Acri in 1931 until 1946, Mr. Acri

CONTINUED

had been in and out of hospitals, clinics, and sanitariums for the treatment of mental disorders and nervousness. Although he beat Mrs. Acri when they had marital difficulties, he had not attacked, abused, or mistreated anyone else. The Acris separated in September 1946, and Mrs. Acri sued her husband for divorce soon afterward. Before their separation, Mrs. Acri had operated and managed the cafe primarily only when Mr. Acri was ill. Following the marital separation and until the time he shot Mr. Vrabel, Mr. Acri was in exclusive control of the management of the cafe.

Mr. Vrabel brought suit against Mrs. Acri to recover damages for his injuries on the grounds that, as Mr. Acri's partner, she was liable for his tort. The trial court ordered her to pay Mr. Vrabel damages of $7,500. Mrs. Acri appealed.

JUDICIAL OPINION

ZIMMERMAN, Judge

The authorities are in agreement that whether a tort is committed by a partner or a joint adventurer, the principles of law governing the situation are the same. So, where a partnership or a joint enterprise is shown to exist, each member of such project acts both as principal and agent of the others as to those things done within the apparent scope of the business of the project and for its benefit.

Section 13 of the Uniform Partnership Act provides: "Where, by any wrongful act or omission of any partner acting in the ordinary course of business of the partnership or with the authority of his copartners, loss or injury is caused to any person, not being a partner in the partnership, or any penalty is incurred, the partnership is liable therefore to the same extent as the partner so acting or omitting to act."

However, it is equally true that where one member of a partnership or joint enterprise commits a wrongful and malicious tort not within the actual or apparent scope of the agency, or the common business of the particular venture, to which the other members have not assented, and which has not been concurred in or ratified by them, they are not liable for the harm thereby caused.

Because at the time of Vrabel's injuries and for a long time prior thereto Florence had been excluded from the Acri Cafe and had no voice or control in its management, and because Florence did not know or have good reason to know that Michael was a dangerous individual prone to assault cafe patrons, the theory of negligence urged by Vrabel is hardly tenable.

We cannot escape the conclusion, therefore, that the above rules, relating to the nonliability of a partner or joint adventurer for wrongful and malicious torts committed by an associate outside the purposes and scope of the business, must be applied in the instant case. The willful and malicious attack by Michael Acri upon Vrabel in the Acri Cafe cannot reasonably be said to have come within the scope of the business of operating the cafe, so as to have rendered the absent Florence accountable.

Since the liability of a partner for the acts of his associates is founded upon the principles of agency, the statement is in point that an intentional and willful attack committed by an agent or employee, to vent his own spleen or malevolence against the injured person, is a clear departure from his employment and his principal or employer is not responsible therefore.

Judgment reversed.

CASE QUESTIONS

1. What was the nature of the business?
2. What type of injury occurred, and who caused it?
3. Why was Mr. Acri not a defendant?
4. Is Mrs. Acri liable for the injuries?

Tax Consequences in Partnerships

A partnership does not pay taxes. It simply files an informational return. The partners, however, must report their shares of partnership income (or losses) and deductions on their individual tax returns on Schedule C, and must pay taxes on the reported share.

Management and Control

Partnership Authority

Unless agreed otherwise, each partner has a duty to contribute time to manage the partnership. Each partner has an equal management say, and each has a right to use partnership property for partnership purposes. No one partner controls the property, funds, or management of the firm (unless the partners so agree).

The partners may agree to delegate day-to-day management responsibilities to one or more of the partners. However, the agency rules of express, implied, and apparent authority (see Chapter 17) apply to partnerships. Each partner is an agent of the other partners, and each has express authority given by the UPA and any partnership agreement, implied authority relating to those powers, and apparent authority as is customary in their business. Some management matters are simply a matter of a vote; a majority of the partners makes the decision. The unanimous consent of the partners is required for some decisions, however, such as confessing a judgment (settling a lawsuit), transferring all the partnership's assets, or selling its goodwill. Basically, unusual transactions in which no apparent authority could be claimed require all the partners' approval.

The partners are not entitled to compensation for their management of the partnership's business, unless so specified in the partnership agreement. Under the UPA, a partner who winds up a dissolved partnership's business can be compensated.

Partner Fiduciary Duties

Because each partner is an agent for the partnership and the other partners as well, each owes the partnership and the other partners the same fiduciary duties an agent owes a principal. Partners' obligations as fiduciaries are the same as agents' duties to principals.

CONSIDER...   20.3

Silvio Giannetti, his daughter, Anne Marie, and her husband, Jerry Prozinsky, were partners in the Giannetti Investment Company (GIC). GIC owned and operated the Brougham Manor Apartments. Mr. Prozinsky signed a contract with Omnicon to give it the right to install the equipment for and promote cable television in the apartment complex. Mr. Giannetti was most disturbed when he learned that Mr. Prozinsky had signed the agreement. He refused to allow Omnicon further access to the complex. The result was that cable service was interrupted, lines could not be repaired, and Omnicon was forced to discontinue all its cable customers in the apartment complex. Omnicon filed suit against GIC for breach of contract. Mr. Giannetti maintains that GIC is not liable because Mr. Prozinsky did not have the authority to sign such a contract. Is Mr. Giannetti correct? [*Omnicon v Giannetti Investment Company*, 561 N.W.2d 138 (Mich. App. 1997)]

Partnership Property

Partnership property is defined as property contributed to the firm as a capital contribution or purchased with partnership funds. Partners are co-owners of partnership property in a form of ownership called *tenancy in partnership*. Tenants in partnership have equal rights in the use and possession of the property for partnership purposes. On the death of one of the partners, rights in the property are transferred to the surviving partner or partners. The partnership interest in the property remains, and the property or a share of the property is not transferred to the estate of the deceased partner. The estate of the deceased partner simply receives the value of the partner's interest, not the property.

Partner Interests

Partners' interests in the partnership are different from partnership property. A partner's interest is a personal property interest that belongs to the partner. It can be sold (transferred) or pledged as collateral to a creditor. Creditors (personal) can attach a partner's interests to collect a debt.

A transfer of a partner's interest affects the partnership interests in several ways. The transfer does not result in the transferee becoming a new partner because no person can become a partner without the consent of all the existing partners. Further, the transfer does not relieve the transferring partner of personal liability. A transfer of interest will not eliminate individual liability to existing creditors.

Some partnership agreements place restrictions on transfer. For example, a provision may allow the partnership the right to buy out a partner before the partner has the authority to transfer interest.

Transferability of Interests

A partner cannot transfer her partnership status without the unanimous consent of the other partners. However, if that transfer is approved, the departing or outgoing partner and the incoming partner should be aware of their liability. Absent an agreement from creditors, the outgoing partner remains personally liable for all partnership debts up to the time of departure. If the departing partner gives public notice of disassociation, no further personal liability results from contracts and obligations entered into after departure. The incoming partner is liable for all contracts after the date of entry into the firm. Incoming partners are liable for existing debts only to the extent of their capital contribution.

The *Byker* case also illustrates that partnership liabilities do not end when the partners no longer do business together. The debts remain and must be satisfied, even from partners no longer involved in running the business.

Dissolution and Termination of the Partnership

Dissolution is not necessarily termination. The UPA defines dissolution as one partner's ceasing to be associated with carrying on the business. The RUPA refers to "dissociation" of partners, which may or may not lead to dissolution. When a partner leaves, retires, or dies, the partnership is dissolved, though not terminated. Dissolution is basically a change in the structure of the partnership. Dissolution may have no effect on the business: The partnership may be reorganized and continue business without the partner who is leaving.

Dissolution *can* lead, however, to termination of the partnership. Termination means all business stops, the assets of the firm are liquidated, and the proceeds are distributed to creditors and partners to repay capital contributions and distribute profits (if any). The following events are grounds for dissolution.

Dissolution by Agreement

The partnership agreement itself may limit the partnership's time of existence. Once that time expires, the partnership is dissolved. If the agreement does not specify the time or there is no partnership agreement, the partners can (by unanimous consent) agree to dissolve the partnership.

Dissolution by Operation of Law

Another way a partnership is dissolved is by operation of law when certain events require the dissolution of the partnership. When one partner dies, the partnership is automatically dissolved. The business could go on, but the partnership as it once existed ends, and the deceased partner's estate must be paid for his or her interest. Also, if the partnership or an individual partner becomes bankrupt, the partnership is dissolved by law.

Dissolution by Court Order

The third method for dissolution of a partnership is by court order. Sometimes partners just cannot work together any longer. In such circumstances, they can petition a court for dissolution in the interest of preserving their investments.

Limited Partnerships

A **limited partnership** is a partnership with a slight variation in the liability of those involved. The types of partners in a limited partnership include at least one **general partner** and one **limited partner.** General partners have the same obligations as partners in general partnerships—full liability and full responsibility for the management of the business. Limited partners have liability limited to the amount of their contribution to the partnership, and they cannot be involved in the management of the firm. General partners run the limited partnership, and the limited partners are the investors.

The Uniform Limited Partnership Act (ULPA) was drafted in 1916. At that time only few limited partnerships existed, and most of them were quite small. The limited partnership, however, has become a favored type of business structure, particularly over the past 20 years. It has been the predominant form of business organization for oil exploration and real estate development because of the tax advantages available through limited partnerships. The attractiveness of limited liability combined with tax advantages has resulted in an increase in the numbers and sizes of limited partnerships.

In 1976, the National Conference of Commissioners on Uniform State Laws developed the **Revised Uniform Limited Partnership Act** (RULPA). The act was designed to update limited partnership law to address the ways limited partnerships were doing business. The RULPA was revised in 1985 and has been adopted in nearly every state.

Formation

A limited partnership is a statutory creature and requires compliance with certain procedures in order to exist. If these procedures are not followed, it is possible that the limited partners could lose their limited liability protection.

The RULPA requires the following information for filing at the appropriate government agency:

1. Name of the limited partnership (cannot be deceptively similar to another corporation's or partnership's name and must contain the words "limited partnership"; no abbreviations permitted)
2. Address of its principal office
3. Name and address of the statutory agent
4. Business address of the general partner
5. Latest date for dissolution of the partnership

Under the RULPA, the limited partners need not be named in the certificate, nor are they all required to sign the certificate. These changes resulted from recognition of the size of limited partnerships and the tremendous paperwork burden created by the ULPA. If an error is made in formation, the partnership could be deemed a general partnership, and the limited partners could lose the protection of their limited liability. However, under RULPA, limited partners are permitted to file an amendment correcting the problem or withdrawing from the business altogether. A limited partner would still be liable to any third parties for liabilities incurred by the general partnership prior to the time the correction is made.

The certificate of limited partnership is simply public disclosure of the formation and existence of the limited partnership; it does not deal with the many more rights and obligations that the partners may agree on among themselves. Those issues are generally addressed in a much longer document called a **limited partnership agreement** or the **articles of limited partnership.**

Sources of Funding

Capital contributions supply the initial funding for a limited partnership. Both the general and limited partners make contributions upon entering the partnership. Under the RULPA, the contribution can be in the form of cash, property, services already performed, or a promissory note or other obligation to pay money or property. The RULPA requires that limited partners' promises to contribute must be in writing to be enforceable. The limited partners are always personally liable for the difference between what has actually been contributed and the amount promised to be contributed.

Some partners make **advances** or loans to the partnership. The partnership can also borrow money from third parties. However, only the general partner has any personal liability for repayment of the loan to the third party.

Liability

The principal advantage of a limited partnership is the limited personal liability. To ensure personal limited liability, several requirements must be met. First, as already discussed, a certificate of limited partnership must be filed, indicating the limited liability status of the limited partners. Second, at least one general partner is required. The general partner can be a corporation. Third, the limited partners cannot be involved in the management of the business because such involvement would give the appearance of general partner status. Finally, limited partners cannot use their names in the name of the partnership, which would give the wrong impression to outside parties and create an estoppel type of relationship.

Under the RULPA, a limited partner who participates in the management of the firm in the same way the general partner does is liable only to those persons who are led to believe by the limited partner's conduct that the limited partner is a general partner. The RULPA also provides a list of activities that limited partners can engage in without losing their limited liability status, such as

1. Being employed by the general partnership as an employee or a contractor
2. Consulting with or advising the general partner
3. Acting as a surety or guarantor for the limited partnership
4. Voting on amendments, dissolution, sale of property, or assumption of debt

If limited partners comply with the rules for limited liability, their liability is limited to the amount of their capital contribution. If they have pledged to pay a certain amount as capital over a period of time, they are liable for the full amount. For example, some real estate syndications that are limited partnerships allow the limited partners to make their investment in installment payments over two to four years. Limited partners in these arrangements are liable for the full amount pledged whenever an obligation to a creditor is not paid.

Tax Consequences

Limited partnerships are taxed the same way as general partnerships. The general and limited partners report the income and losses on their individual returns and pay the appropriate taxes. A limited partnership files an information return but does not pay any taxes as an entity.

One of the benefits of limited partnership status is the combination of limited liability with direct tax benefits. In this sense, a limited partnership is the best of both worlds. Because of this ideal situation, limited partnership interests are closely scrutinized by the IRS to determine whether they are, in reality, corporations as opposed to true limited partnerships. Some of the factors examined in determining whether an organization is a corporation or a limited partnership are (1) the transferability of the interests, (2) the assets of the general partners, and (3) the net worth of the general partners. From the perspective of the IRS, organization as a limited partnership is no assurance of treatment as such for tax purposes.

Management and Control

Profits and Distributions

A general partner has absolute authority to decide not only when distributions are made, but also whether they will be made; for example, the general partner might decide not to distribute funds but to put them back into the business.

Profits and losses are allocated on the basis of capital contributions. Under the RULPA, the agreement for sharing of profits and losses must be in writing.

Partner Authority

The authority of the general partner in a limited partnership is the same as the authority of the partners in a general partnership. These powers can be restricted by agreement. There are, however, some general activities the general partner cannot perform without the consent of the limited partners, including the following:

1. Admitting a new general partner (also requires consent of other general partners)
2. Admitting a new limited partner unless the partnership agreement allows it
3. Extraordinary transactions, such as selling all the partnership assets

Limited partners can monitor the general partner's activity with the same rights provided to partners in general partnerships: the right to inspect the books and records and the right to an accounting.

Transferability of Interests

Although the assignment of limited partnership interests is not prohibited by the RULPA, a limited partnership agreement may provide for significant restraints on assignment. Transfer restrictions are placed on limited partners' interests for two reasons. First, limited partnership interests may have been sold without registration as exemptions to the federal securities law (see Chapter 21 for more details on securities registrations). If those exempt interests are readily transferable, the exemption could be lost. Second, for the limited partners to enjoy the tax benefits of limited partner status, the ease of transferability is a critical issue. The more easily an interest can be transferred, the more likely the limited partnership will be treated (for tax purposes) as a corporation.

The assignment of a partnership interest does not terminate a limited partnership. The assignee is entitled to receive only the distributions and profits to which the partner is entitled. The assignee does not become a partner without the consent of the other partners. Under the RULPA, a limited partnership can agree that the assigning limited partner will have the authority to make the assignee a limited partner. The effect of the RULPA provision is to simplify transfers and allow limited partners to decide whether they want to transfer their interest or their limited partner status.

Dissolution and Termination of a Limited Partnership

A limited partnership can be dissolved in one of the following ways:

1. Expiration of the time period designated in the agreement or the occurrence of an event causing dissolution, as specified in the agreement
2. Unanimous written consent of all partners
3. Withdrawal of a general partner
4. Court order after application by one of the partners

Upon dissolution, a partnership can continue (assuming a general partner remains); but the partnership can also be terminated after dissolution. If termination occurs, all assets of the partnership are liquidated. The RULPA specifies that the money from the sale of the assets be used to pay partnership obligations in the following order of priority:

1. Creditors (including partners, but not with respect to distributions)
2. Partners and former partners, for distributions owed to them
3. Return of capital contributions
4. Remainder split according to distribution agreement

Corporations

Corporations have the following characteristics: unlimited duration, free transferability of interest, limited liability for shareholders/owners, continuity, and centralized management. Corporations are legal entities in and of themselves. Because they are treated as persons under the law, they can hold title to property, they can sue or be sued in the corporate name, and they are taxed separately. Corporations earn nearly 90 percent of all business profits in the United States.

Types of Corporations

Each of the diverse types of corporations can be described by one or more adjectives. For example, corporations are either **profit corporations** (those seeking to earn a return for investors) or **nonprofit corporations.** In addition, they are either **domestic corporations** or **foreign corporations.** A corporation is a domestic corporation in the state in which it is incorporated and a foreign corporation in every other state. Further, corporations organized by government agencies that exist to achieve a social goal are called **government corporations. Professional corporations** are corporations organized by physicians, dentists, attorneys, and accountants; they exist by statute in most states. Professional corporation shareholders have no personal liability for any corporate debts, as in any other corporation, except for professional malpractice claims. The **corporate veil** or shield (explained later) will not give individuals personal immunity for professional negligence despite their general liability limitation through incorporation. **Close corporations** are the opposite of **publicly held corporations;** that is, the former are corporations with few shareholders. Close corporations and publicly held corporations are created in the same way, but most states then have a separate statute governing the operation of close corporations. Close corporation owners are generally given more discretion in their internal operations, and the degree of formality required for publicly held corporations is not required.

The **S corporation** (sometimes called subchapter S or sub S corporation) is formed no differently from any other corporation, but it must meet the IRS requirements for an S corporation and must file a special election form with the IRS indicating it wishes to be treated as an S corporation. The benefit of an S corporation is that shareholders' income and losses are treated like those of partners, but the shareholders enjoy the protection of limited liability behind a corporate veil. The income earned and losses incurred by an S corporation are reported on the shareholders' individual returns, but the shareholders' personal assets are protected from creditors of the business. For tax purposes, the S corporation is like a partnership in the sense of the flow-through of profits and losses, and the shareholders avoid the double taxation of having the corporation pay tax on its earnings and the shareholders pay tax on the dividends distributed to them.

The Law of Corporations

The **Model Business Corporation Act** (MBCA), as drafted and revised by the Corporate, Banking, and Business Section of the American Bar Association, is the uniform law on corporations. The provisions of the MBCA are quite liberal and give management great latitude in operations. The MBCA tends to follow the principles of corporate law long established in Delaware, a state where many of the country's major companies are incorporated. Delaware boasts a rich body of case law on corporate governance that offers the stability companies want as they incorporate. Despite the ability to draw on the Delaware case law and experience, the MBCA is not adopted as widely as the UPA or the Uniform Commercial Code (UCC). Even those states that have adopted the MBCA have made significant changes in their adopted versions. As a result, each state's law on corporations is quite different. The following sections cover the revised MBCA rules, but each state may have its own variations.

Formation

A corporation is a statutory entity. Formal public filing is required to form a corporation. The following procedures for corporate formation are those of the MBCA.

Where to Incorporate

The following factors should be considered when determining in which state to incorporate:

1. The status of the state's corporation laws (See the preceding discussion about Delaware; also, some states' laws and judicial decisions are oriented more toward management than toward shareholders.)

2. State tax laws

3. The ability to attract employees to the state

4. The incentives that states offer to attract the business (new freeways, office space, attractive urban renewal)

The Formation Document

All states require **articles of incorporation** to be filed in order to create a corporation. These articles give the structure and basic information about the corporation. Under the MBCA, the articles of incorporation must include the following information:

1. The name of the corporation

2. The names and addresses of all incorporators (In addition, each incorporator must sign the articles of incorporation.)

3. The share structure of the corporation: (a) the common and preferred classes, (b) which shares vote, and (c) the rights of shareholders, or preemptive rights

4. The statutory agent (the party who will be served with any lawsuits against the corporation)

Who Is Incorporating

The **incorporators** (required to be listed in the articles of incorporation) are the parties forming the corporation. Under the MBCA, only one incorporator is required, and that person may be a natural person, a corporation, a partnership, a limited partnership, or an association.

Incorporators are personally liable for any contracts entered into or actions taken during the pre-incorporation stage. Until the corporation exists, incorporators are acting as individuals. After incorporation, the corporation could agree to assume liability through a **novation** of the incorporators' acts.

For example, if an incorporator of a lumberyard entered into a contract for the purchase of lumber and the corporate board (after formation) agreed that the contract was a good one, the corporation could ratify it or enter into a novation to assume liability. In novation, the lumberyard agrees to substitute the corporation as the contracting party. In a **ratification,** the corporation assumes primary liability for payment, but the incorporator still remains liable. Incorporators generally are paid for their efforts in shares of the corporation's stock. They may also be the contributors of initial corporate assets and may be paid in shares for their contributions.

Postformation

After the paperwork of incorporating is complete, a corporation must begin its day-to-day operations with an **initial meeting.** At this meeting, the officers of the corporation are elected and **bylaws** are adopted to govern corporate procedures. The bylaws define the authority of each of the officers, prescribe procedures for announcing and conducting meetings (i.e., quorum numbers and voting numbers), and set the terms of officers and directors and who is eligible to serve in such offices. Articles of incorporation give an overview of a corporate entity; the bylaws constitute the operational rules.

Capital and Sources of Corporate Funds

A corporation has a variety of sources of funds. It may use short-term financing, which consists of loans from banks or credit lines. The problems with short-term financing are higher interest rates and shorter payback periods. The other forms of financing used most frequently by corporations are debt and equity.

Debt Financing: The Bond Market

Long-term debt financing is available to corporations when they issue bonds. Bonds are, in effect, long-term promissory notes from a corporation to the bond buyers. The corporation pays the holders interest on the bonds until the maturity date, which is when the bonds are due or must be paid. The interest is fixed and is a fixed payment responsibility regardless of the corporation's profitability. The benefits of debt financing include the tax deductibility of interest as an expense. Further, bondholders have the benefit of first rights in corporate assets in the event of insolvency. However, a corporation cannot maintain a sound financial policy or rating with debt financing only.

Equity Financing: Shareholders

Equity financing comes through the sale of stock in a corporation. It provides a means of raising capital up front with the exchange of proportionate corporate ownership and the promise of proportionate profits. Shareholders are given shares of stock in exchange for their money. To avoid personal liability, the shareholders must pay at least par value for their shares and must honor the terms of their subscription agreement (share purchase agreement). A shareholder who has not paid at least par value is said to hold **watered shares** and is liable to creditors for the amount not paid. For example, if a shareholder paid $500 for shares with a par value of $1,000, the shareholder would be personally liable for the $500 difference. Along with those shares of stock come certain promises of future performance from the corporation. The rights of shareholders depend on the type of stock purchased. A discussion of the various types of stock follows.

Common Stock

Common stock is the typical stock in a corporation and is usually the most voluminous in terms of the number of shares. Common stock generally carries voting rights so that common shareholders have a voice in the election of directors, the amendment of articles and bylaws, and other major corporate matters. Common stock generally does not have a fixed dividend rate and does not carry with it any right to have a dividend declared. Common stock dividends depend on both profitability and decisions of the board of directors. If a corporation is dissolved, the common shareholders have a right to a proportionate share of the assets (after creditors and preferred stockholders have been paid).

Preferred Stock

Preferred stock is appropriately named because its owners enjoy preferred status over holders of a corporation's common stock. For example, preferred stockholders have priority in the payment of dividends. Some preferred dividends are even at a fixed rate, and **cumulative preferred stock** guarantees the payment of a dividend so that if a dividend is not paid one year, the holder's right to be paid carries over until funds are available. Preferred shareholders also have priority over common shareholders in the event the corporation is dissolved and the assets distributed.

Liability Issues

Limited liability for shareholders is one of the advantages of corporate organization. Sometimes, however, individuals—such as shareholders, directors, and officers—can be personally liable for corporate obligations.

Shareholder Liability

Shareholders' personal liability is limited to the amount of their investment in the corporation. The personal assets of shareholders are not subject to the claims of corporate creditors. In some circumstances, however, a shareholder is liable for more than the amount of investment. For example, if a shareholder has not paid for his shares or has paid for them with overvalued property, creditors could turn to the shareholder's personal assets for satisfaction of his debt, but only to the extent of the amount due on the shares.

In other more serious circumstances, shareholders can be held liable for the full amount of corporate debts. A creditor who successfully pierces the corporate veil overcomes the shield of limited liability protecting shareholders from having to accept personal liability for corporate debts. The corporate veil can be pierced for several reasons. One is inadequate capitalization. The owners of a corporation are required to place as much capital at risk in the corporation as is necessary to cover reasonably anticipated expenses of the business. The purpose of this requirement is to ensure that someone does not use the corporation to avoid liability without actually transferring to the corporation some assets for the payment of corporate liabilities.

Another theory a court can use to pierce the corporate veil is the **alter ego theory,** which means that the owners and managers of the corporation have not treated the corporation as a separate entity but have used the structure more as a personal resource. Personal and corporate assets and debts are mixed, no formality is observed with regard to operations and meetings, and transfers of property are made without explanation or authorization.

U.S. v Bestfoods (Case 20.3) deals with an issue of piercing the corporate veil in a situation involving CERCLA liability (see Chapter 11).

| **CASE 20.3** | *U.S. v Bestfoods, Inc.* 524 U.S. 51 (1998) |

Lifting the Veil Is Best for Cleanup, but Not for Shareholders

FACTS

In 1957, Ott Chemical Co. manufactured chemicals at its plant near Muskegon, Michigan, and both intentionally and unintentionally dumped hazardous substances in the soil and groundwater near the plant. Ott sold the plant to CPC International, Inc.

In 1965, CPC incorporated a wholly owned subsidiary (Ott II) to buy Ott's assets. Ott II then continued both the chemical production and dumping. Ott II's officers and directors had positions and duties at both CPC and Ott.

In 1972, CPC (now Bestfoods) sold Ott II to Story Chemical, which operated the plant until its bankruptcy in 1977. Aerojet-General Corp. bought the plant from the bankruptcy trustee and manufactured chemicals there until 1986.

In 1989, the EPA filed suit to recover the costs of cleanup on the plant site and named CPC, Aerojet, and the officers of the now defunct Ott and Ott II.

The District Court held both CPC and Aerojet liable. After a divided panel of the Court of Appeals for the Sixth Circuit reversed in part, the court granted rehearing *en banc* and vacated the panel decision. This time, seven judges to six, the court again reversed the District Court in part. Bestfoods appealed (Ott settled prior to the appeal).

JUDICIAL OPINION

SOUTER, Justice

The issue before us, under the Comprehensive Environmental Response, Compensation, and Liability Act of 1980 (CERCLA), is whether a parent corporation that actively participated in, and exercised control over, the operations of a subsidiary may, without more, be held liable as an operator of a polluting facility owned or operated by the subsidiary. We answer no, unless the corporate veil may be pierced. But a corporate parent that actively participated in, and exercised control over, the operations of the facility itself may be held directly liable in its own right as an operator of the facility.

The District Court said that operator liability may attach to a parent corporation both directly, when the parent itself operates the facility, and indirectly, when the corporate veil can be pierced under state law. The court explained that, while CERCLA imposes direct liability in situations in which the corporate veil cannot be pierced under traditional concepts of corporate law, "the statute and its legislative history do not suggest that CERCLA rejects entirely the crucial limits to liability that are inherent to corporate law."

Applying that test to the facts of this case, the court found it particularly telling that CPC selected Ott II's board of directors and populated its executive ranks with CPC officials, and that a CPC official, G.R.D. Williams, played a significant role in shaping Ott II's environmental compliance policy.

[W]here a parent corporation is sought to be held liable as an operator pursuant to 42 U.S.C. § 9607(a)(2) based upon the extent of its control of its subsidiary which owns the facility, the parent will be liable only when the requirements necessary to pierce the corporate veil [under state law] are met. In other words . . . whether the parent will be liable as an operator depends upon whether the degree to which it controls its subsidiary and the extent and manner of its involvement with the facility, amount to the abuse of the corporate form that will warrant

piercing the corporate veil and disregarding the separate corporate entities of the parent and subsidiary.

It is a general principle of corporate law deeply "ingrained in our economic and legal systems" that a parent corporation (so-called because of control through ownership of another corporation's stock) is not liable for the acts of its subsidiary. . . .

But there is an equally fundamental principle of corporate law, applicable to the parent-subsidiary relationship as well as generally, that the corporate veil may be pierced and the shareholder held liable for the corporation's conduct when, inter alia, the corporate form would otherwise be misused to accomplish certain wrongful purposes, most notably fraud, on the shareholder's behalf.

Nothing in CERCLA purports to rewrite this well-settled rule, either. If a subsidiary that operates, but does not own, a facility is so pervasively controlled by its parent for a sufficiently improper purpose to warrant veil piercing, the parent may be held derivatively liable for the subsidiary's acts as an operator.

The fact that a corporate subsidiary happens to own a polluting facility operated by its parent does nothing, then, to displace the rule that the parent "corporation is [itself] responsible for the wrongs committed by its agents in the course of its business." It is this direct liability that is properly seen as being at issue here.

We are satisfied that the Court of Appeals correctly rejected the District Court's analysis of direct liability. But we also think that the appeals court erred in limiting direct liability under the statute to a parent's sole or joint venture operation, so as to eliminate any possible finding that CPC is liable as an operator on the facts of this case.

In imposing direct liability on these grounds, the District Court failed to recognize that "it is entirely appropriate for directors of a parent corporation to serve as directors of its subsidiary, and that fact alone may not serve to expose the parent corporation to liability for its subsidiary's acts."

The Government would have to show that, despite the general presumption to the contrary, the officers and directors were acting in their capacities as CPC officers and directors, and not as Ott II officers and directors, when they committed those acts. The District Court made no such enquiry here, however, disregarding entirely this time-honored common-law rule. . . .

In sum, the District Court's focus on the relationship between parent and subsidiary (rather than parent and facility), combined with its automatic attribution of the actions of dual officers and directors to the corporate parent, erroneously, even if unintentionally, treated CERCLA as though it displaced or fundamentally altered common-law standards of limited liability. . . .

There is, in fact, some evidence that CPC engaged in just this type and degree of activity at the Muskegon

CONTINUED

plant. The District Court's opinion speaks of an agent of CPC alone who played a conspicuous part in dealing with the toxic risks emanating from the operation of the plant. G.R.D. Williams worked only for CPC; he was not an employee, officer, or director of Ott, and thus, his actions were of necessity taken only on behalf of CPC. The District Court found that "CPC became directly involved in environmental and regulatory matters through the work of . . . Williams, CPC's governmental and environmental affairs director. Williams . . . became heavily involved in environmental issues at Ott II." He "actively participated in and exerted control over a variety of Ott II environmental matters," and he "issued directives regarding Ott II's responses to regulatory inquiries."

We think that these findings are enough to raise an issue of CPC's operation of the facility through Williams's actions, though we would draw no ultimate conclusion from these findings at this point. Prudence thus counsels us to remand, on the theory of direct operation set out here, for reevaluation of Williams's role, and of the role of any other CPC agent who might be said to have had a part in operating the Muskegon facility.

The judgment of the Court of Appeals for the Sixth Circuit is vacated, and the case is remanded.

CASE QUESTIONS

1. Describe the corporate ownership history that surrounds the Muskegon facility.

2. Is there a special CERCLA rule for piercing the corporate veil?

3. What must be shown to hold a parent liable for the actions of the subsidiary?

4. Are joint directors of parent and corporate subsidiaries evidence of a need to pierce the corporate veil?

Corporate Tax Consequences

The Double-Taxation Cost of Limited Liability

Although corporations have the benefit of limited liability, they have the detriment of double taxation. Not only does the corporation pay taxes on its earnings, but shareholders must also report their dividend income on their separate returns and pay individual taxes on their dividend income. However, these shareholders pay taxes only if the dividends are paid. Unlike partnerships in which the partners pay taxes on earnings whether they are distributed or not, shareholders pay taxes on corporate earnings only when they are distributed to them.

Statutory Solutions to Double Taxation

One way to resolve the problem of the cost of double taxation is the S corporation (see p. 699) is one solution.

Corporate Management and Control: Directors and Officers

Election of Directors

A corporation might be owned by a million shareholders, but its operation will be controlled by the hands of a few, the **board of directors.** The shareholders elect these directors, who serve as the corporate policy makers. The directors also have responsibility for management of the corporation. To that end, the directors usually set up an **executive committee** composed of three board members to handle the more routine matters of running the corporation so that board meetings are not required as frequently.

Role of Directors

Directors are the strategic planning and policy makers for the corporation. They are also the outside perspective for the company. They can provide insight on current management practices. They also serve a watchdog role, as with the now mandatory **audit committees** required of all stock exchange companies. Audit committees, made up of independent outside directors and at least one financial expert under Sarbanes–Oxley, none of whom have any contracts or former salary ties with the company, are responsible for assuring that the financial reports the management issues are accurate.

Institutional investors and other groups have been placing increasing pressure on boards for accountability. Some have developed standards for service on boards such as required stock ownership in the company, nominating committees to assure sufficient business background and knowledge, and term limits so that members do not become complacent. Some companies have procedures for the board to evaluate itself and its performance.

One area of director responsibility that receives ongoing attention is that of officers' compensation. Directors not only elect the officers of the corporation; they also decide the salaries for these officers and themselves. Some possible reforms are on the horizon. The issue of officer compensation has long been a contentious one for lawmakers and regulators. During the Clinton administration, Congress limited the deductibility of officer compensation to $1 million annually. Under the **Dodd–Frank Wall Street Reform and Consumer Financial Protection Act,** shareholders will have a "say on pay." At least once every three years shareholders must have the right to cast votes (nonbinding) on executive compensation as well as golden parachutes. In addition, Dodd–Frank requires companies to have "claw-back" provisions giving them the right to take back executive compensation if it was paid as a result of inflated financial reports. The SEC will be promulgating rules on incentive compensation disclosure. In addition to the new Dodd–Frank rights, shareholders can continue to make proposals to limit executive compensation (see Chapter 21 for more information on additional regulation of pay as well as shareholder proposals) and exercise

For the Manager's Desk

Re: CEO Compensation

The highest-paid CEOs (2009) are as follows:

CEO	COMPANY	COMPENSATION ($)
Sanja K. Jha	Motorola	104,000,000
Lawrence J. Ellison	Oracle	84,600,000
Robert A. Iger	Disney	51,100,000
Kenneth I. Chenault	American Express	42,800,000
Vikram S. Pandit	Citigroup	Took no salary because of government bailout
Mark V. Hurd	Hewlett-Packard	33,900,000
Jack Fusco	Calpine	32,600,000
David M. Cote	Honeywell Int'l	28,700,000
Miles D. White	Abbott	25,100,000
John J. Donahoe	eBay	22,400,000
James T. Hackett	Anadarko Petroleum	22,100,000

For more information, go to the companies' 10-K forms at http://www.sec.gov; click on EDGAR.

their rights of director removal if the board is not responsive to their concerns about compensation.

Director Liability

Officers and directors are **fiduciaries** of the corporation, which means they are to act in the best interests of the corporation and not profit at the corporation's expense. They are subject to the **business judgment rule,** a standard of corporate behavior under which it is understood that officers and directors can make mistakes, but they are required to show that their decisions were made after careful study and discussion. In those decisions, they may consult experts, such as attorneys, accountants, and financial analysts; but again, they need to show that these experts were well-chosen and reliable individuals.

Brehm v Eisner (Case 20.4) deals with the business judgment rule and provides the answer for the chapter's opening "Consider."

| CASE 20.4 | *Brehm v Eisner*
746 A.2d 244 (Del. 2000) |

Kind of a Mickey-Mouse Judgment Call

FACTS

On October 1, 1995, Michael Eisner, then CEO and chairman of Disney, hired Michael Ovitz as Disney's president. Mr. Ovitz was a long-time friend of Mr. Eisner. Mr. Ovitz was also an important talent broker in Hollywood. Although he lacked experience managing a diversified public company, other companies with entertainment operations had been interested in hiring him for high-level executive positions. Mr. Ovitz's employment agreement was unilaterally negotiated by Eisner and approved by the board. Since the hiring, there had been shareholder uprisings and director battles that resulted in a shift in the board structure. Eisner had recommended an extraordinarily lucrative contract for Ovitz, with a base salary of $1 million per year, a discretionary bonus, and two sets of stock options (the "A" options and the "B" options) that collectively would enable Ovitz to purchase five million shares of Disney common stock.

Disney needed a strong second-in-command because Mr. Eisner's health, due to major heart surgery, was in question, and there really was no succession plan. Mr. Eisner also had a rugged history when it came to working with important or well-known subordinate executives who wanted to position themselves to succeed him. Over the past five years, Disney executives Jeffrey Katzenberg, Richard Frank, and Stephen Bollenbach had all left after short tenures under Eisner.

Following a tumultuous year that enjoyed intense media coverage about legendary battles between the two, Mr. Ovitz and Mr. Eisner negotiated Mr. Ovitz's departure on December 11, 1996. Mr. Ovitz was given a "Non-Fault Termination" that carried $38,888,230.77 as well as the option to purchase three million Disney shares under the terms of his employment agreement.

The shareholders (plaintiffs) filed suit against the directors for their failure to adequately consider the Ovitz contract initially, for not considering the issues surrounding that hiring as well as the employment package itself, and for committing waste in giving Ovitz what amounted to a $140 million severance package (when the value of the options were included). The Court of Chancery dismissed the suit and the shareholders appealed.

JUDICIAL OPINION

VEASEY, Chief Justice

This is potentially a very troubling case on the merits. On the one hand, it appears from the Complaint that: (a) the compensation and termination payout for Ovitz were exceedingly lucrative, if not luxurious, compared to Ovitz' value to the Company; and (b) the processes of the boards of directors in dealing with the approval and termination of the Ovitz Employment [this is a close case].

This is a case about whether there should be personal liability of the directors of a Delaware corporation to the corporation for lack of due care in the decision-making process and for waste of corporate assets. This case is not about the failure of the directors to establish and carry out ideal corporate governance practices. All good corporate governance practices include compliance with statutory law and case law establishing fiduciary duties. But the law of corporate fiduciary duties and remedies for violation of those duties are distinct from the aspirational goals of ideal corporate governance practices. Aspirational ideals of good corporate governance practices for boards of directors that go beyond the minimal legal requirements of the corporation law are highly desirable, often tend to benefit stockholders, sometimes reduce litigation and can usually help directors avoid liability. But they are not required by the corporation law and do not define standards of liability.

The facts in the Complaint (disregarding conclusory allegations) show that Ovitz' performance as president was disappointing at best, that Eisner admitted it had been a mistake to hire him, that Ovitz lacked commitment to the Company, that he performed services for his old company, and that he negotiated for other jobs (some very lucrative) while being required under the contract to devote his full time and energy to Disney.

All this shows is that the Board had arguable grounds to fire Ovitz for cause. But what is alleged is only an argument—perhaps a good one—that Ovitz' conduct constituted gross negligence or malfeasance.

The Complaint contends that the Board committed waste by agreeing to the very lucrative payout to Ovitz under the non-fault termination provision because it had no obligation to him, thus taking the Board's decision outside the protection of the business judgment rule. Construed most favorably to plaintiffs, the Complaint contends that, by reason of the Board's available arguments of resignation and good cause, it had the leverage to negotiate Ovitz down to a more reasonable payout than that guaranteed by his Employment Agreement. But the Complaint fails on its face to meet the waste test because it does not allege with particularity facts tending to show that no reasonable business person would have made the decision that the Board made under these circumstances.

The Board made a business decision to grant Ovitz a Non-Fault Termination. Plaintiffs may disagree with the Board's judgment as to how this matter should have been handled. But where, as here, there is no reasonable doubt as to the disinterest of or absence of fraud by the Board, mere disagreement cannot serve as grounds for imposing liability based on alleged breaches of fiduciary duty and waste. There is no allegation that the Board did not consider the pertinent issues surrounding Ovitz's termination. Plaintiffs' sole argument appears to be that they do not agree with the course of action taken by the Board regarding Ovitz's separation from Disney. This will not suffice to create a reasonable doubt that the Board's decision to grant Ovitz a Non-Fault Termination was the product of an exercise of business judgment.

One can understand why Disney stockholders would be upset with such an extraordinarily lucrative compensation agreement and termination payout awarded a company president who served for only a little over a year and who underperformed to the extent alleged. That said, there is a very large—though not insurmountable—burden on stockholders who believe they should pursue the remedy of a derivative suit instead of selling their stock or seeking to reform or oust these directors from office.

Affirmed.

CASE QUESTIONS

1. What must the shareholders prove to recover?
2. What does the court say is the relationship between good corporate governance, liability, and business judgment?
3. What alternatives to litigation do shareholders have?

CONSIDER...   20.4

William Shlensky was a minority shareholder of Chicago National League Ball Club, Inc. (the Cubs). In 1966, he brought suit against the directors of the Cubs for violation of the business judgment rule because at the time of the suit the Cubs did not play night games at Wrigley Field, their home field. All of the other 19 teams in the major leagues had some night games, with substantially all of their weekday and nonholiday games scheduled under the lights. Between 1961 and 1965, the Cubs had sustained operating losses. Mr. Shlensky filed a derivative suit (a suit on behalf of shareholders) against the Cubs' directors for negligence and mismanagement.

Mr. Shlensky's suit maintained that the Cubs would continue to lose money unless night games were played. The directors' response was that baseball was a "daytime" sport and that holding night games would have a "deteriorating effect upon the surrounding neighborhood."

Why does Mr. Shlensky believe the directors did not use good judgment? Is there a difference between negligence and differing business opinions? Does the business judgment rule allow directors to make mistakes?

THINK: Under the principles of liability for directors and the protection of the business judgment rule, a director and board can make mistakes. They can make decisions that ultimately prove to be big mistakes, even in judgment. However, courts do not step in and, with hindsight, second-guess the directors. So long as the directors have given their time, thought, and effort to the decision and obtained independent advice, their judgment is protected from liability to shareholders, even if they are proven completely wrong.

APPLY: While the parties disagree over whether to hold day games or night games, the Cubs organization has articulated its reasons, rightly or wrongly.

ANSWER: The reasons show that the Cubs directors have devoted the time, energy, and thought necessary to make the decision and thus enjoy protection from liability under the business judgment rule. [*Shlensky v Wrigley*, 237 N.W. 2d 776 (Ill. 1968)]

Officers and directors are also required to follow the **corporate opportunity doctrine,** under which officers and directors may not take an opportunity for themselves that the corporation might be interested in taking. For example, a director of a lumber company who discovers a deal on timberland would be required to present that opportunity to the corporation before she could take it. If the director does not first present the idea to the corporation, a constructive trust is put on the profits the director makes, and the corporation is the beneficiary of that trust. If, however, the director presents the opportunity and the corporation is unable or unwilling to take it, the director may go ahead with the opportunity without the problem of a constructive trust.

Officer Liability

Recent prosecutions have demonstrated an increased effort to hold corporate officers criminally responsible for the acts of the corporation. In environmental law, changes in the law and aggressive prosecutions have brought about convictions of officers, particularly concerning the disposal of hazardous waste. The issues of officer liability are covered in Chapters 8, 11, 17, and 21.

Officers, Boards, Sarbanes–Oxley, and Dodd–Frank

Sarbanes–Oxley, the legislation passed following the collapse of companies such as Enron and WorldCom, imposed detailed requirements on boards and officers of publicly traded companies (see Chapter 8 for more details). These reforms imposed new duties beyond any statutory requirements imposed by state corporation laws such as the MBCA. In addition, the passage of the Dodd–Frank Wall Street Reform and Consumer Financial Protection Act has resulted in more regulation of board structure and directors' duties and responsibilities to shareholders.

Prohibitions on Loans to Officers. Corporations can no longer make loans to officers and directors. This provision is the result of revelations that companies such as WorldCom, Adelphia, and others had made hundreds of millions of dollars in loans to their CEOs and other executives because they had pledged their shares in the company for their personal investments. When those investments did not perform well, their shares needed to be sold to satisfy the loans. A sell-off of their major holdings would have sent the company's stock into a dive. The result was a vicious circle in which more loans were made in order to prevent the sale of shares, with ever-increasing pressure to keep the share price up in order to satisfy the loans the shares secured. (See "Buoying Bernie.")

Codes of Ethics for Financial Reporting. Companies must now have codes of ethics in place for the financial officers of their companies. Even though 97 percent of publicly held companies now have codes of ethics, this provision requires specific content about the standards for financial reporting and accounting in the company. These financial officers are also subject to greater federal penalties for certifying false financial statements (see Chapter 8 for more information on their criminal liability).

Role of Legal Counsel to the Company. In many of the collapsed companies, two of the questions that arose were "Where were the auditors?" and "Where were the lawyers?"[1] As Congress and the SEC grappled with these questions, they imposed extensive disclosure obligations on auditors and accountants (see Chapter 21 for those requirements), but they also imposed reporting requirements on legal counsel for corporations. Under the new requirements, lawyers have several progressive steps in their duties and disclosure requirements.[2]

- A lawyer who suspects material violations must instigate an investigation to determine whether such violations have occurred.
- The lawyer must inform the CEO of the investigation.
- The lawyer must report material violations of the law to the CEO.
- If no action is taken, the lawyer must go "up the ladder" and report the material violations to the audit committee or a group of independent board members.
- Companies must create a legal compliance committee based on the idea of strength in numbers, in that the committee will be told of investigations and findings and can take the matter "up the ladder."
- Because of concerns and objections from the American Bar Association, the SEC did not adopt the so-called noisy withdrawal rule, a process that would have required a lawyer who has found a material violation that the company will not remedy to resign from the company and report the violation to the SEC.

Role of the Chairman and CEO. Under Dodd–Frank, companies will be required to inform shareholders when the offices of CEO and chairman of the

For the Manager's Desk

Re: Buoying Bernie

Bernie Ebbers, the former CEO of WorldCom, was a flamboyant, charming, 6'4" man. When, because of WorldCom's growth and acquisitions, Mr. Ebbers was a billionaire, he went on a personal buying spree. He purchased the largest private ranch in Canada, his native land, as well as dealerships, lumber companies, and a number of other businesses near Mississippi. In order to make these purchases, Mr. Ebbers obtained loans, some of them secured by his WorldCom stock holdings. Mr. Ebbers had a great idea on how to build a phone company, but he was not known for his ability to execute ideas or even handle the day-to-day management tasks of business. As a result, many of his personal investments were in great financial difficulty.

Low on cash, Mr. Ebbers was able to persuade the WorldCom board to extend loans to him, in excess of $415 million, to rescue his failing businesses. One problem with the loans, among many others, was that the stock Mr. Ebbers used to secure them was also the stock he had pledged to his creditors in order to obtain financing for his ventures. The result was that WorldCom directors had taken a subordinated security interest in stock that had already been pledged, placing the company well at the end of the line in terms of creditors. Worse, everyone was acting on the assumption that the value of the WorldCom stock would remain at equal or higher levels.

While the board's loans to Mr. Ebbers put it at risk of losing $415 million, the control of the company was actually at greater risk because Mr. Ebbers had pledged about $1 billion in WorldCom stock in total to his creditors for loans. By 2001, when WorldCom's stock price began to drop, Mr. Ebbers's net worth had slipped to $295 million,

$286.6 million of which was WorldCom stock. The board had to continue to make loans to cover margin calls on Mr. Ebbers's loans because otherwise Mr. Ebbers would have had to dump his shares onto the market, thus depressing the price of WorldCom's already depressed shares even further as well as jeopardizing the collateral for the loans. The board had climbed into a bottomless pit. The loans continued from 2000 through 2002. The compensation committee, headed by a long-time friend of Mr. Ebbers, approved the loans, but the issue of the loans was not presented to the full board because legal counsel for WorldCom indicated full board approval was not necessary.

Knowing the pressure the board faced with the loans tied to the WorldCom share price, Scott Sullivan—the CFO, a board member, and secretary to the corporation—and other financial officers within the company began capitalizing ordinary expenses to keep earnings numbers high. During the period from 2000 to 2002, the officers, most of whom entered guilty pleas, capitalized $9 billion in ordinary expenses. When the expenses were actually announced and the proper accounting entries made, WorldCom reversed its earnings for those two years and was forced into Chapter 11 bankruptcy. The story of the WorldCom loans to Mr. Ebbers, more so than any of the other failed companies, motivated the prohibition against corporate loans to officers that is now part of Sarbanes–Oxley and federal law.

Sources: Jared Sandberg and Susan Pulliam, "Report by WorldCom Examiner Finds New Fraudulent Activities," *Wall Street Journal,* November 5, 2002, p. A1; Kurt Eichenwald, "Corporate Loans Used Personally, Report Discloses," *New York Times,* November 5, 2002, p. C1.

board are combined or separated and provide an explanation for the decision on the role of the two offices or their combination. Some studies indicate that the separation of these two roles resulted in better governance as well as better financial performance.

Role of the Compensation Committee.   Also under Dodd–Frank, board compensation committees must be composed of independent directors, meaning directors who do not have affiliations or contractual relationships with the company (see p. 711 for more information on the definition of "independent directors.") Board compensation committees that hire consultants (and most publicly traded companies do) must hire those consultants independent of management input, and the consultants must have a direct line of reporting to the compensation committee, not management.

Ethical Issues

Sitting in the Hot Seat for Officers' Loans

Tyco experienced financial setbacks following the indictment and conviction of its CEO, Dennis Kozlowski (best known for his $6,000 shower curtain and Jimmy Buffett birthday party for his wife) and its CFO, Mark Swartz, on state charges of crimes related to larceny and embezzlement. Some of the charges stemmed from Tyco's Key Employee Corporate Loan Program (the KELP), a program established to encourage officers and some employees to own Tyco shares by offering them loans to pay income taxes due when their ownership of shares granted to them under Tyco's restricted share ownership plan vested. This way, instead of selling some of their shares, the officers could pledge their shares in exchange for cash to pay the taxes on this employee benefit.*

The second Tyco loan program was a relocation program established to help employees who had to move from New Hampshire to New York. The idea was to provide low-interest loans for employees who had to relocate from one set of company offices to another in order to lessen the impact on their budgets of the move to a much costlier housing market. One of the requirements of the relocation program was each employee's certification that he or she was indeed moving from New Hampshire to New York, or, in some cases, to Boca Raton, another site for company offices.

Mark Belnick, general counsel for Tyco during the final Kozlowski years, who was indicted and acquitted of all charges, had loans from the relocation program. Mr. Belnick had been a partner in a New York City law firm and had done work for Tyco before he was hired as general counsel for the company. When he took the Tyco position, he received a relocation loan for a difference of 25 miles between his home in Connecticut and Tyco's New York offices, despite the fact that he had never lived in New Hampshire as the relocation program required. Mr. Belnick used the $4 million he borrowed under the program to buy and renovate an apartment in New York City. He later borrowed another $10 million to construct a home in Park City, Utah, because he was moving his

family there and planned to divide his time between the two locations and the extensive international travel his job required. Mr. Belnick got Mr. Kozlowski's approval for both loans.

The issue of board approval on the loans remains a question, but compensation committee minutes from February 21, 2002, show that the committee was given a list of loans to officers and also approved Mr. Belnick's new compensation package. There was no public disclosure of these developments or the committee's review. In grand jury testimony, Patricia Prue, the Tyco employee in charge of administration of the two loan programs, indicated that board member Joshua Berman pressured her in June 2002 to change the minutes from that February compensation committee meeting. Mr. Berman denies the allegation. However, Ms. Prue did send a memo on June 7, 2002, to John Fort (a Tyco board member), Mr. Swartz, and the board's governance committee with the following included: "As a result of the fact that I was recently pressured by Josh Berman to engage in conduct which I regarded as dishonest—and which I have refused to do—I will decline to have any personal contact with him in the future. In addition, I ask that Josh not go to my staff with any requests for information or directions." Both sides acknowledge that Ms. Prue sent the memo.

Do you think Ms. Prue did the right thing? Should she have done more to stop the loans? Is it a crime if the board authorized the loans and all the paperwork is in place? Did Ms. Prue facilitate abuse of the loan programs? Should she have notified someone? Should she have resigned? What would you have done if you had been in her position? Do you think the officers acted ethically in their use of the loan relocation program?

*This information was obtained from the SEC's press release issued when it filed suit against Mark Swartz, Dennis Kozlowski, and Mark Belnick for the return of the loan amounts. See http://www.sec.gov; click on litigation releases. Mr. Belnick has settled those charges with the SEC.

Board Membership. Under Sarbanes–Oxley, boards must consist of a majority of members who are independent. *Independent* is defined as someone who has not been an officer, employee, or manager of the company during any of the past three years; who is not related to anyone who works for the company; who is not under any type of consulting or remuneration arrangement with the company; and who

BUSINESS STRATEGY

Governing Corporate Governance

In addition to incorporating the statutory requirements under Sarbanes–Oxley, many companies are adopting new policies and procedures for corporate governance. Some of those changes, policies, and processes are mentioned here as possible strategies for effective governance.

- Some companies have created the position of a corporate ombudsperson who will create the audit and ethics committees in their boards and will watch for officer share trading.

- Some companies have had the majority of their board resign.

- WorldCom paid Richard Breeden, a former chairman of the SEC, to prepare a 149-page report on "Restoring Trust" and will implement all of his recommended changes. The changes are part of the articles of incorporation and now cannot be changed without shareholder approval.

- Tyco is required to submit annual reports on its board and corporate governance processes.

- At WorldCom, an executive's salary and compensation package cannot exceed $1.5 million without shareholder approval.

- Some companies have agreed to fund university research into effective corporate governance.

Companies are also working to change their board policies and processes beyond the requirements under Sarbanes–Oxley. One company highlighted in the *Wall Street Journal* for its changes is E*TRADE, a company that got a black eye when in 2001 it revealed that its CEO had an $80 million pay package despite significant problems with the company's performance and a plunging share price. The share price had

dropped from more than $60 per share to less than $5 per share when the pay package for then–CEO Christos Cotsakos was announced. (He did return $20 million of the package.)

The following changes have taken place at the E*TRADE board.

- Board meetings are now two days in length (they were four hours or less).

- All directors must have a three-hour orientation session before beginning their service. (Tyco also now requires this training.)

- The CFO was terminated in June when a financial restatement was necessary.

- All pay packages have been revamped and bonuses for executives are limited to three times their annual salaries.

- The $14,000-per-month concierge service for employees has ended.

- As leases expire, the company has moved into less expensive office spaces.

- The board members who allowed the compensation package of $80 million have resigned and been replaced.

- The board has open access to all E*TRADE executives.

Ironically, Mr. Cotsakos just received his PhD from the University of London in corporate governance. His degree was paid for by E*TRADE.

Sources: Susanne Craig, "How One Firm Uses Strict Governance to Fix Its Troubles," *Wall Street Journal,* August 21, 2003, pp. A1, A6; Edward Iwata, "Prosecutors slap new rules on companies," *USA Today,* March 22, 2004, p. 1B.

is not a principal or owner of a company that does business with the board or the company. This independence requirement caused some shake-ups in boards. For example, Kenneth Chenault, the CEO of American Express, was no longer an independent member of IBM's board because IBM does business with American Express. Under Dodd–Frank, independence requirements now apply to compensation committees. Audit committee chairs must be independent directors, and at least one member of the audit committee must meet standards for certification as a financial expert.

Corporate Management and Control: Shareholders

Shareholder Rights: Annual Meetings

Shareholders have the opportunity to express their views at the annual meeting by electing directors who represent their interests. Annual meetings also give shareholders the opportunity to vote on critical corporate issues. Under the MBCA, the failure to hold an annual meeting does not result in dissolution or revocation of corporate status.

Shareholder Rights: Voting

At annual and special meetings, shareholders have the right to vote. Shareholders may vote their own shares or delegate their votes in a variety of ways.

The Proxy.   The most common method of delegating voting authority is the **proxy,** with which shareholders can transfer their right to vote to someone else. This type of vote assignment is temporary. Under the MBCA, a proxy is good only for 11 months, which allows a shareholder to decide to give a different proxy before the next annual meeting. Many shareholder groups solicit proxies to obtain control. Those solicitations are subject to the federal securities laws, and certain disclosures are required (see Chapter 21).

Pooling Agreements.   A method of grouping shareholder votes is the **pooling agreement,** which is a contract among shareholders to vote their shares a certain way or for a certain director. One of the problems with pooling agreements is enforceability: If the agreements are breached, it is really too late to do anything about the breach because the corporation will take the action authorized by the votes or a particular director will take a seat.

Voting Trust.   Another form of shareholder cooperation is the **voting trust.** In this form of group voting, shareholders actually turn their shares over to a trustee and are then issued a trust certificate. The shareholders still have the right to dividends and may sell or pledge the certificate. However, the shares remain in the hands of the trustee, and the trustee votes those shares according to the terms of the trust agreement. The shareholders get their shares back only when the trust ends. Most states have specific requirements for the voting trust: A copy must be filed with the corporate offices, and some states have a maximum duration (such as 10 years) for such trusts.

Shareholder Rights in Combinations

Because shareholders' interests are involved, corporations are not free to combine at will or to merge or consolidate without shareholder input. All states have procedures for obtaining shareholder approval for business combinations.

The Procedure.   All mergers, consolidations, and sales of assets (other than in the ordinary course of business) must have shareholder approval. Further, that approval must be obtained in a manner prescribed by the MBCA.

- Board resolution. The process of obtaining shareholder approval begins with the board of directors. They must adopt and approve a resolution favoring the merger, consolidation, or asset sale.

- Notice to shareholders. Once the resolution is adopted, it must be sent to the shareholders along with a notice of a meeting for the purpose of taking action on the resolution. A notice is sent to all shareholders regardless of whether they are entitled to vote under the corporation's articles.

- Shareholder approval. The shareholders must then vote to approve the resolution at the announced meeting. In the cases of mergers and consolidations, all shareholders are entitled to vote whether they own voting or nonvoting shares because their interests are affected by the results. The number of votes needed to approve a merger under the MBCA is a majority. However, the articles of incorporation or the bylaws may require more, known as a supermajority.

Shareholder approval is not required for a short-form merger, which is one between a subsidiary and a parent that owns at least 90 percent of the stock of the subsidiary. In the absence of these narrow requirements, the long-form merger provisions of resolution and voting must be followed.

Shareholder Rights: The Dissenting Shareholder

Not all shareholders vote in favor of a merger or a consolidation. Under the MBCA and most state statutes, these **dissenting shareholders** are entitled to their appraisal rights. **Appraisal rights** allow shareholders to demand the value of their shares. Under the MBCA, a dissenting shareholder must file a written objection to the merger or consolidation before the meeting to vote on either is held.

If the merger or consolidation is approved, the corporation must notify dissenting shareholders and offer them the fair value of the shares. Fair value is determined as of the *day before* the action is taken on the merger or consolidation because the action taken will affect the value of the shares. If the dissenting shareholders do not believe the corporation's offer is fair, they can bring suit against the corporation for establishing fair value. However, if the value the corporation offered is found to be fair and the dissenting shareholders' rejection arbitrary, they will be required to pay the corporation's costs of the lawsuit.

Shareholders also enjoy some protections during merger activity that are offered under federal securities laws in terms of notice and disclosure (see Chapter 21).

Some corporations have experienced a **freeze-out,** which is a merger undertaken to get rid of the minority shareholders in a corporation. Although these minority shareholders have their dissenting rights, it is expensive to pursue a court action for a determination of fair value. The majority shareholders are able to buy out, at a low price, the minority shareholders, who are left without a remedy and usually with a loss. For this reason, many courts now impose on majority stockholders a fiduciary duty to the minority stockholders and will prevent a merger without a business purpose from freezing out minority shareholders. Courts, and some state laws (corporate constituency statutes), also require a showing that a merger or consolidation is fair to the minority shareholders. These general terms of "business purpose" and "fairness" are defined on a case-by-case basis.

Shareholder Rights: Inspection of Books and Records

The MBCA gives shareholders the absolute right to examine shareholder lists. For other records (minutes, accounting), shareholders must give notice of their request. In addition to this mechanical requirement, some courts also require a **proper purpose,** which means a shareholder has a legitimate interest in reviewing corporate progress, financial status, and fiduciary responsibilities. Improper purposes are those related to use of corporate records to advance the shareholders' moral, religious, or political ideas.

Shareholder Rights: Transfer of Shares

Stock shares can have **transfer restrictions,** which are valid as long as the following requirements are met.

1. The restrictions must be necessary. Valid circumstances include family-owned corporations, employee-owned corporations, and corporations that need restrictions to comply with SEC registration exemptions (see Chapter 21).
2. The restrictions must be reasonable. Requiring that the shares first be offered to the board before they can be sold is reasonable; requiring that the shares be offered to all the other shareholders first may be unreasonable if there are more than 5 to 10 shareholders.
3. The restrictions and/or their existence must be conspicuously noted on the stock shares.

The Dissolution of a Corporation

A corporation can continue indefinitely unless its articles of incorporation limit its duration. Long before perpetuity, however, a corporation can be dissolved voluntarily or involuntarily.

Voluntary Dissolution

Voluntary dissolution occurs when the shareholders agree to dissolve the corporation. This type of dissolution occurs in smaller corporations when the shareholders no longer get along, the business does not do well, or one of the shareholders is ill or dies.

A voluntary dissolution begins with a resolution by the board of directors, which is then put before the shareholders at a special meeting called for that purpose. Under the MBCA, all shareholders (voting and nonvoting alike) vote on the issue of dissolution because all of them will be affected by it. Once the shareholders pass the resolution (a majority or two-thirds vote in most states), the assets of the corporation are liquidated, and debts and shareholders are paid in the order of their priorities. Each state also has filing and publication requirements for dissolution.

Involuntary Dissolution

An involuntary dissolution is forced by some state agency, usually the state attorney's office. A dissolution can be forced because of fraud or failure to follow state law regarding reporting requirements for corporations.

Limited Liability Companies

The **limited liability company** (LLC), first created in 1977, is the newest form of business structure and is now available in 48 states and the District of Columbia. The LLC has actually been in existence for many years in Europe (known as a GMBH) and South America (*limitada*). The LLC is more of an aggregate form of business organization than an entity such as a corporation. Owners of an LLC are called members. An LLC provides limited liability (members lose only up to their capital contributions) and flow-through tax treatment similar to a partnership in that tax liability is assessed only at the member's level of income and not at the business level. An LLC is not a corporation or a partnership. It can be taxed as a partnership, with limited liability for all its owners, unlike a limited partnership, and all personal owners can participate in management without risking liability.

It has been said that the LLC combines the best of all of the business structures: limited liability for the owners, flexibility in management in that all the owners can participate in management, and flow-through of the income directly to personal profits and losses and resulting tax liability. However, this ideal creation, in order to enjoy the flow-through characteristics necessary for the tax break, must be distinguished from a corporation. The result is that LLCs are limited in duration, with most statutes allowing them to run for periods of 30 to 40 years. The point at which LLCs dissolve by statutory limitations has not yet arrived because LLCs did not exist until 1977. However, when those dissolutions come, the restructuring and recreation should create interesting issues among and between the owners of the LLCs.

Formation

An LLC is formed through the filing of a document called the **articles of organization,** which is filed with a centralized state agency. The name of the business formed must contain either "limited liability company," "L.L.C.," or "LLC."

Sources of Funding

Members of an LLC make capital contributions in much the same way as partners make capital contributions.

Liability

Members of an LLC have limited liability; the most they can lose is their capital contributions. Debts belong to the LLC, and creditors' rights lie with the LLC's assets, not the personal assets of the members. However, many states require that the nature of the business organization appear on the business cards and stationery of the company so that members of the public are not misled about the nature of the business as well as the nature of the limited liability of the owners.

CONSIDER... 20.5

Larry Clark and David Lanham formed a limited liability company in Colorado called Preferred Income Investors, LLC (PII). All of the necessary paperwork for the creation of an LLC had been filed with the secretary of state, as required by Colorado statute.

Mr. Clark negotiated with a Westec representative about doing construction work for PII on a Taco Cabana restaurant the LLC was building. Mr. Clark gave the Westec rep his card, which had PII's name above Mr. Clark's name. Westec drew up a contract that was never signed by anyone from PII. However, Mr. Clark gave oral authorization for the work, and Westec completed it. PII did not have the assets to pay the bill for the work, and Westec sued to hold Mr. Clark liable for the contract. Mr. Clark said that as an owner of a limited liability company, he had no personal liability. Westec says it was never made aware that PII was an LLC and that it should have been given that information in advance. Is Mr. Clark personally liable? [*Water, Waste, & Land, Inc., dba Westec v Lanham*, 995 P.2d 997 (Colo. 1998)]

For the Manager's Desk

Re: Enron and Its LLCs and LLPs

Part of Enron's collapse was due to its reliance on extensive creation of LLCs and LLPs across which it could spread its debt without carrying that debt on its balance sheet. At the time of Enron's massive creation of LLCs and LLPs, the GAAP and FASB standards for disclosure of a company's transactions with related entities (FASB 125), or those entities in which the company holds an interest, applied only when the company owns at least 50 percent of the related entity. If a company owned 49 percent or less of an entity, any debt obligations the related entity carried did not have to be carried as debt on the company's balance sheet. Known as SPEs (special purpose entities), these off-the-books creations allowed companies to paint a much brighter financial picture. Consolidation was not required until the company owned 50 percent or more of its subsidiaries and other business ventures.

Enron began creating off-the-book entities in 1997. By the time of Enron's collapse in 2001, it had created 3,000 special purpose entities (SPEs), with 881 of them located in the Cayman Islands. Their offshore status was designed to eliminate the need for the entities and other business ventures to pay U.S. federal income tax.*

The names of these off-the-books LLCs and LLPs provide insight into the nature of Enron's business, its culture, and the hubris that engulfed its senior management. Some were named after Jurassic Park creatures, some were named after Star Wars creatures and characters, and one name was a thumb of the nose at the accounting rule (FASB 125) being capitalized upon to hide the company's true financial picture: Hawaii 125-0.

To satisfy FASB 125, the SPEs were required to have at least 3 percent equity ownership by outsiders. However, Enron often served as guarantor for the SPE as well as the 3 percent investment of the outsiders. And as time went by, the definition of "outsiders" became more flexible the more the labyrinthine web of Enron finances grew. For example, Andrew Fastow, Enron's CFO, proposed using his wife's family as the outside investors. When the accounting firm Arthur Andersen nixed the idea, Mr. Fastow used Michael Kopper, a mid-level manager whose interest in the outside LLCs and LLPs did not have to be disclosed on securities documents. Both Mr. Kopper and Mr. Fastow are in prison, having entered guilty pleas to various federal charges.

It seems that most board members understood the SPEs' overall effect. Notes from Enron's corporate secretary at a meeting of one of Enron's board committees reads, "Does not transfer economic risk, but transfers P&L volatility." ("P&L" is profit and loss.)

Evaluate the director's comment and the board's oversight.

*"The Enron Scandal by the Name Numbers," *USA Today*, January 22, 2002, p. 3B.

Tax Consequences

The LLC enjoys the so-called flow-through treatment: The LLC does not pay taxes; income and losses are passed through to the members to be reported on their individual returns. LLC agreements must be drafted carefully to enjoy flow-through status.

Management and Control

Members of an LLC adopt an operating agreement that specifies the voting rights, withdrawal rights and issues, responsibilities of members, and how the LLC is to be managed. The members can agree to manage collectively, delegate authority to one member, or hire an outsider to manage the business.

Transferability of Interest

A member's LLC interest is personal property and is transferable. However, the transferee does not become a member without approval by the majority of members. Members do not hold title to LLC property; the LLC owns the property, and each member has an interest in the LLC that reflects the property's value. Further, the owners of the LLC should structure their LLC and its operation in order to address their tax status issues.

Dissolution and Termination

Most LLC statutes provide that the LLC dissolves upon the withdrawal, death, or expulsion of a member. Some states permit judicial dissolution, and all states permit voluntary dissolution upon unanimous (usually written) consent of the owners.

LLC agreements can dictate terms, timing, and results of dissolution, as well as the rights of withdrawing partners.

Limited Liability Partnerships

A **limited liability partnership** (LLP) is a partnership with unique statutory protection for all its members.

Formation

Not all states have LLP statutes, but those with such statutes have strict formal requirements for the creation of an LLP. The failure to comply with these requirements results in a general partnership with full personal liability for all the partners. The general requirements for LLP registration are filing (1) the name of the LLP (which must include LLP or Reg LLP); (2) the name of the registered agent; (3) the address; (4) the number of partners; and (5) a description of the business.

Sources of Funding

As in partnerships and limited partnerships, LLP partners make capital contributions.

Liability

In most of the states with LLP statutes, partners are shielded from liability for the negligence, wrongful acts, or misconduct of their partners. Other states provide more extensive protection, such as limited liability even for debts entered into by other partners. In order to attain this liability limitation, some states require, upon registration, evidence of adequate liability insurance. In some states, professional negligence by partners is not covered by the shield from liability.

Tax Consequences

All LLP income is a flow-through or pass-through to partners.

Management and Control

Partners can manage without risking personal liability exposure because the LLP is identified as such and registered with the state.

Transferability

For tax and security regulation reasons, the transferability must be restricted and is generally governed by the same principles of transfer for limited partnerships.

Dissolution and Termination

Causes similar to those for the dissolution of limited partnerships and notification to the state are required.

International Issues in Business Structure

Global trade has resulted in global business structures, with many companies discovering the benefits of **joint ventures.** A joint venture is a partnership of existing businesses for a limited time or a limited purpose. The existing businesses are then partners for that limited transaction or line of business. The Justice Department has relaxed antitrust merger rules to permit joint ventures so that U.S. firms can compete more effectively internationally. For example, Mobil and Exxon are involved in a joint oil exploration venture in the West Siberian Basin in Russia. The joint venture allows the combination of their experience and financing so that Russian negotiators can be persuaded to contract for the exploration rights.

In an attempt to break into the Japanese toy market, Toys "R" Us, Inc., entered into a joint venture with McDonald's Co., Ltd., a Japanese toy company with 20 percent of the market. Nestlé and Coca-Cola formed a joint venture to market ready-to-drink coffees and teas; Nestlé's expertise is in dry goods (instant coffee) and Coca-Cola is a beverage company, so each plans to take advantage of the other's established reputation.

Business structures vary in other countries. In Germany, for example, a public company has both a board of directors and a shareholder advisory committee, which elects the board of directors. It is quite likely, however, that the shareholder advisory committee is composed of shareholders that are large institutional investors (such as banks) or representatives from labor unions.

B I O G R A P H Y

Hank Greenberg: The Disgruntled CEO

Maurice R. "Hank" Greenberg was the formidable CEO of AIG, the largest insurer in the United States, for nearly four decades. Mr. Greenberg was removed from his position when the SEC raised issues regarding the company's accounting practices and the accuracy of its financial statements. Mr. Greenberg settled fraud charges with the SEC for $15 million, but he denied any wrongdoing. In addition, AIG filed suit against Mr. Greenberg for breach of his fiduciary duty as chairman for taking over $4 billion in AIG stock and placing it in another company, known as Starr International, as a means of providing under-the-SEC-radar compensation for top performers in AIG. The suit alleged that Mr. Greenberg had exceeded his authority as CEO and chairman and that the funneling off of the stock required board knowledge and approval. The jury, however, found that Mr. Greenberg had not violated his fiduciary duty and was not required to reimburse AIG for the shares that were siphoned off into the separate company. Mr. Greenberg argued that the shares were all used as a means of compensation for AIG top performers.

The AIG shareholders also brought a derivative action against the board, Mr. Greenberg, and others (*AIG, Inc. v Greenberg,* 965 A.2d 763 (Del. Ch. 2009). While Mr. Greenberg continues to maintain that he did nothing wrong, the allegations in the complaint and the opinion of the judge who heard the shareholders' case tell a different story.

According to the suit, AIG embarked on illegal activities at the direction and under the control of Mr. Greenberg. Mr. Greenberg and a core "Inner Circle" directly oversaw all aspects of AIG's business and kept a close watch on their subordinates. Greenberg's Inner Circle was comprised of a small group of long-time AIG executives whom Greenberg rewarded with very lucrative compensation packages.

Most of the wrongdoing the shareholders have alleged involved action by AIG insiders to misstate AIG's financial performance in order to deceive investors into believing that AIG was more prosperous and secure than it really was. The single largest act of deception alleged involved a fraudulent $500 million reinsurance transaction in which various AIG insiders staged an elaborate artificial transaction with Gen Re Corporation. Four Gen Re executives and one AIG executive either were convicted or entered guilty pleas to criminal charges related to this transaction. Although AIG portrayed the transaction as providing Gen Re with reinsurance, in reality the transaction had no substance and was simply staged to make AIG's balance sheet look better. In other instances, AIG insiders allegedly used secret offshore subsidiaries to mask AIG losses, blatantly misstated accounts with no basis for their adjustments, failed to correct well-documented accounting problems in an AIG subsidiary, and hid AIG's involvement in controversial insurance policies that involved betting on when elderly people would die.

Eventually, all of these schemes were uncovered. As a result, AIG was forced to restate years of financial statements, eventually reducing stockholder equity by $3.5 billion. AIG still faces litigation and regulatory proceedings on a number of fronts, an ongoing process that has already required the corporation to pay over $1.6 billion in fines and other costs necessary to resolve proceedings against it. Further, AIG became a central figure in the financial market collapses in 2008 because it was the insurer for the elaborate mortgage-backed instruments of Goldman Sachs, Bear Stearns, Lehman Brothers, Citigroup, and other investment banks that sought their payments when the real estate market collapsed and those instruments became toxic as. One expert has concluded that AIG's legal saga will never end.

In the center of all the legal controversy and questions about AIG's business strategy and corporate governance is Mr. Greenberg. With each regulatory action and suit, Mr. Greenberg walks away with a relatively small fine and, often, vindication as regulators, prosecutors, and shareholders try to cobble together some violation of the law. A story from his youth offers some insight into his ethical philosophy. When he was stationed in London during World War II, the United States and its military command were concerned about the impression the soldiers left and their conduct. They also recognized the need for the soldiers to have some recreation. The commanding officers gave the soldiers extra leave days if they used them for cultural events. The commanding officers had the theater, the symphony, and the ballet in mind as culture, not the usual activities for leave, such as drinking and chasing women (and, all too often, catching the women). The only requirement for the extra leave day was that the soldiers had to bring back a playbill or program from whatever cultural event they had attended. Mr. Greenberg would buy a ticket to the theater, go in, collect the playbill, and then head out the side exit to spend the time on the types of activities the commanders were trying to have the soldiers avoid, to wit, carousing. Mr. Greenberg had his proof of cultural activities, but he also had his usual fun.

Discussion Questions

1. Did Mr. Greenberg violate any rules as a soldier? As a board chairman and CEO? Isn't the lack of clarity on the part of his commanding officers

what caused the problem? What's wrong with using a loophole in the system?

2. The following is an excerpt from an editorial Mr. Greenberg wrote for the *Wall Street Journal*: "So, in order to stay out of the crosshairs of government regulators, companies are avoiding risks they might otherwise take to innovate or grow their businesses: 'Keep your head down.'" What does Mr. Greenberg believe is the impact of regulation? Is he correct?

Source: Maurice R. Greenberg, "Regulation, Yes. Strangulation, No," *Wall Street Journal*, August 21, 2006, p. A10.

Summary

What are the various forms of business organization?

- Sole proprietorship—individual ownership and operation of a business

- Partnership—voluntary association of two or more persons as co-owners in a business for profit

- Corporation—an entity formed by statute that has the rights of a legal person along with limited liability for its shareholder owners

- Limited liability company—newer form of business organization in which liability is limited except for conduct that is illegal

- Limited liability partnership—newest form of business organization, in which partners' liability is limited

How is a partnership formed and operated?

- Uniform Partnership Act (UPA)—law on partnerships adopted in 49 states

- Revised Uniform Partnership Act (RUPA)—update of partnership law

- Partnership by implication—creation of a partnership by parties' conduct

- Partnership by estoppel—partnership that arises by perception of third parties of its existence

- Dissolution—when partner ceases to be associated with the partnership

- Limited partnership—partnership with two types of partners: general and limited

- General partner—full and personal liability partner

- Limited partner—partner whose personal liability is limited to capital contributions

- Uniform Limited Partnership Act (ULPA)—uniform law adopted in nearly every state

- Revised Uniform Limited Partnership Act (RULPA)—update of limited partnership law

- Advances—partners' loans to partnership

How is a corporation formed and operated?

- Corporation—business organization that is a separate entity with limited liability and full transferability

- Domestic corporation—a corporation is domestic in the state in which its incorporation is filed

- Foreign corporation—category or label for corporation in all states except in state in which it is incorporated

- Professional corporation—entity with limited liability except for malpractice/negligence by its owners

- S corporation—IRS category of corporation with flow-through characteristics

- Model Business Corporation Act (MBCA)—uniform law adopted in approximately one-third of the states

- Articles of incorporation—document filed to organize a corporation

- Common stock—generally most voluminous type of corporate shares and usually allows shareholders to vote

- Preferred stock—ownership interest with priority over common stock

- Corporate veil—liability shield for corporate owners

- Watered shares—failure to pay par value for shares

- Business judgment rule—standard of liability for directors

- Corporate opportunity doctrine—fiduciary responsibility of directors with respect to investments

- Board of directors—policy-setting body of corporations

- Proxy—right to vote for another

- Pooling agreement—shareholder contract to vote a certain way

- Voting trust—separation of legal and equitable title in shares to ensure voting of shares in one way

- Dissenting shareholder—shareholder who objects to merger

- Appraisal rights—value of shares immediately before merger that is paid to dissenting shareholder

How is a limited liability company formed?

- Articles of organization

- Flow-through of income

How is a limited liability partnership formed?

- Register with state

- Flow-through of income

- May need proof of liability insurance

Questions and Problems

1. Gailey, Inc., incorporated in 1980, removed asbestos and mechanical insulation on contract jobs that required union labor. Richard Gailey had been the president, controlling shareholder, and director of Gailey, Inc. from its inception.

Universal Labs, Inc. was incorporated by Mr. Gailey in March 1984 to analyze asbestos samples and air samples and to perform general laboratory work. Mr. Gailey was the sole shareholder of Universal Labs.

As president and director of Gailey, Inc., Mr. Gailey directed Gailey to pay certain debts of Universal Labs. Subsequent to that, $14,500 was provided by Gailey, Inc. to Universal Labs to pay for the latter's start-up expenses and costs.

Gailey, Inc. filed a voluntary petition pursuant to Chapter 11 of the Bankruptcy Code on January 28, 1985. The case was converted to a Chapter 7 proceeding on September 30, 1985.

The trustee in bankruptcy filed suit alleging that Mr. Gailey usurped a corporate business opportunity belonging to Gailey, Inc., when he incorporated Universal Labs. Is the trustee correct? [*In re Gailey, Inc.*, 119 B.R. 504 (Bankr. W.D. Pa. 1990)]

2. Former Governor J. Fife Symington of Arizona was, during the 1980s, a director of Southwest Savings & Loan, a federal thrift headquartered in Phoenix. Mr. Symington was also a developer who constructed two major commercial projects in Phoenix, with Southwest Savings & Loan providing the loans for development. Southwest was a victim of the 1980s downturn and was taken over by the Resolution Trust Corporation (RTC). The RTC brought suit against Mr. Symington, alleging that he took advantage of his board position to obtain the loans. Mr. Symington said he was required to present the projects to the Southwest

Board as part of the corporate opportunity doctrine and Southwest took the investment. Who is correct?

3. Aztec Enterprises, Inc. was incorporated in Washington with a capital contribution of $500. Aztec's incorporator and sole stockholder was H. B. Hunting. Aztec operated a gravel-hauling business and was plagued with persistent working capital problems. Carl Olson, a frequent source of loans for Aztec, eventually acquired the firm. Mr. Olson, who had no corporate minutes or tax returns, personally paid Aztec's lease fees but did not pay when he had Aztec deliver gravel to his personal construction sites. Mr. Olson never had stock certificates issued to him. Despite annual gross sales of more than $800,000, Aztec was unable to pay its debts. Truckweld Equipment Company, a creditor of Aztec, brought suit to pierce the corporate veil and recover its debt from Mr. Olson. Can it pierce the corporate veil? [*Truckweld Equipment Co. v Olson*, 618 P.2d 1017 (Wash. 1980)]

4. The SEC charged HealthSouth with inflating its earnings by $1.4 billion over a three-year period, with total inflated earnings of $2.5 billion over a decade. The case was the first one brought under the new provisions of Sarbanes–Oxley for financial fraud.

In a federal district court hearing the following information emerged.

- Two of the company's CFOs and its current CFO have been indicted for fraud.

- CFO William Owen recorded his conversations with former CEO Richard Scrushy at the request of the FBI.

- Mr. Scrushy said on tape to Mr. Owen, "We just need to get those numbers where we want them to be. You're my guy. You've got the technology and the know-how."

- Mr. Scrushy has sold $175 million in HealthSouth shares since the accounting fraud began.

- The bookkeeper for Mr. Scrushy's personal companies committed suicide in September 2002. His new bookkeeper, Mary Schabacker, indicated that all of Mr. Scrushy's five corporations owe debts to each other, with no intention to repay them.

- HealthSouth stock was delisted from the NYSE for a period of time. It was listed at $15 per share one year ago and is worth pennies today.

- Mr. Owen's wife told him that if he kept signing "phony financial statements" he might go to jail.

- Mr. Scrushy maintains that he knew nothing about the accounting fraud and that Mr. Owens did it all.

- The acting chairman of the HealthSouth board said, "We [directors] really don't know a lot about what has been occurring at the company."

- For seven years, one director was paid a consulting fee of $250,000 per year.

- One director purchased a $395,000 resort property as a partner with Mr. Scrushy.

- One director secured a $5.6 million contract to install glass at a hospital HealthSouth was constructing.

- MedCenterDirect.com had as investors HealthSouth, Mr. Scrushy's private investment company, six of HealthSouth's directors, and the wife of one of the HealthSouth directors.

- HealthSouth directed business to MedCenterDirect.com totaling almost $174 million in 2001.

- The audit committee and compensation committee were joint committees made up of the same directors.

- HealthSouth invested $2 million in Acacia Venture Partners, a venture capital fund founded and run by C. Sage Givens, a director of HealthSouth. When a shareholder questioned Givens's independence as a result, HealthSouth defended her board position.

- Ernst & Young served as HealthSouth's auditor. It earned $1.2 million for financial statement audits and $2.5 million for other services.

Discuss the legal issues that each of these revelations raises. Be sure to cover the changes that Sarbanes–Oxley would impose on the company's governance practices. Also, refer back to Chapter 8 and determine what criminal charges were brought.

5. Allan Jones sold a ski shop franchise to Edward Hamilton. Although Mr. Jones did not contribute equity to the business or share in the profits, he did give Mr. Hamilton advice and share his experience to help him get started. Most of Mr. Hamilton's capital came in the form of a loan from Union Bank. When Mr. Hamilton failed to pay, Union Bank sued Mr. Jones for payment under the theory that Mr. Jones was a partner by implication or estoppel. Was he? [*Union Bank v Jones*, 411 A.2d 1338 (Vt. 1980)]

6. Heritage Hills (a land development firm) was organized on July 2, 1975, as a limited partnership, but the partnership agreement was never properly filed. Heritage Hills went bankrupt, and the bankruptcy trustee has sought to recover the debts owed by the partnership from the limited partners. Can he? [*Heritage Hills v Zion's First Nat'l Bank*, 601 F.2d 1023 (9th Cir. 1979)]

7. In June 1985, Carolyn Boose sought the dental services of Dr. George Blakeslee, who proposed to fill two cavities in her teeth. As part of the procedure, he administered nitrous oxide to Ms. Boose. She was rendered semiconscious by the drug and while she was in this state, Dr. Blakeslee lifted her shirt and fondled one of her breasts. He was subsequently charged with, and pled guilty to, the crime of indecent liberties.

Prior to the incident in question, Dr. Blakeslee had incorporated his dental practice as a professional services corporation. He was the corporation's sole shareholder, officer, and director. The corporation thereafter executed an employment agreement with Dr. Blakeslee, who signed the agreement both as an employee of the corporation and as its president.

At the time of the incident in question, Dr. Blakeslee and the corporation were covered by an insurance policy with Standard Fire Insurance Company that provided general and professional liability coverage. The general liability portion of the policy provided coverage for bodily injury or property damage caused by an "occurrence" arising out of the use of the insured premises. The insurance contract defined "occurrence" as "an accident, including continuous or repeated exposure to conditions, which results in bodily injury or property damage *neither expected nor intended by the insured.*"

The professional liability portion of the policy limited coverage to damages for "injury . . . arising out of the rendering of or failure to render, during the policy period, professional services by the individual insured, or by any person for whom acts or omissions such insured is legally responsible. . . ."

In November 1985, Ms. Boose commenced an action against Dr. Blakeslee and the professional services corporation for the damages she allegedly sustained as a result of his conduct. Standard subsequently commenced a declaratory judgment action against

Ms. Boose and Dr. Blakeslee in order to obtain a declaration of its rights and duties in connection with the lawsuit by Ms. Boose against Dr. Blakeslee and the corporation. All parties moved for summary judgment. The trial court granted judgment to Standard, concluding that it had no duty to defend or indemnify the insured (that is, Dr. Blakeslee and the corporation) against Ms. Boose's claim. Should the corporate veil be pierced to hold Dr. Blakeslee liable? [*Standard Fire Insurance Co. v Blakeslee*, 771 P.2d 1172 (Wash. 1989)]

8. The Orleans Parish School Board hired Johnson & Higgins (J & H) to provide consulting services. J & H provided those services over the next few years but was then acquired by Marsh & McLennan, a larger insurance firm. Marsh continued the work that J & H had been doing and submitted an invoice to the Orleans Parish School Board for reimbursement. The Board said that it had no contractual arrangement with Marsh and, as such, was not liable for the services. Is the Board correct? Describe what happened in the relationships and apply the principles of corporate law to determine whether Marsh can be paid. [*Marsh Advantage America v Orleans School Board*, 995 So.2d 53 (La. App. 2008)]

9. Johnson & Johnson, Procter & Gamble, and Eastman Kodak have joined together to form a joint venture in order to develop security tags for their products sold in drug and grocery stores. Shoplifting thefts of drugstore items are estimated to be $16 billion per year. The manufacturers point to Pampers, Tylenol, and Preparation H as the most frequently stolen items from stores.

The companies will jointly fund the development of security tags designed to set off alarms at store doors, much as the tags on clothing do today.

What is the liability of the companies as joint venturers on this project?

10. A. W. Ham Jr. served on the board of directors for Golden Nugget, Inc., a Nevada corporation. In 1969, while Mr. Ham was a director and legal counsel for Golden Nugget, he obtained a leasehold interest with an option to purchase in the California Club. The California Club is at 101 Fremont Street, Las Vegas, Nevada, and is located next to a series of properties on which Golden Nugget operates its casinos. Mr. Ham leased the property from his former wife. Golden Nugget was looking for property to expand and had, in fact, been expanding onto other lots in the area. Was there a breach of a corporate opportunity? What if Mr. Ham offers to lease the property to Golden Nugget? [*Ham v Golden Nugget, Inc.*, 589 P.2d 173 (Nev. 1979)]

HR and the Law

Who Says What the CEO Makes?

The so-called "say-on-pay" legislation has been kicking around Congress for a number of sessions and now, with the passage of the Dodd–Frank Wall Street Reform and Consumer Financial Protection Act, shareholders will have an advisory vote on executive compensation. Steve Hafner, the CEO of Kayak (a travel search engine), explained, "I wonder if the congressmen backing this legislation would propose similar laws governing their own compensation. I'd love to vote on congressional pay and perks."[3]

There are concerns on both sides about CEO pay. From the investors' perspective, the concerns are

- Increases in pay and bonuses despite poor performance of the company and its stock

- Failure of the board to provide independent oversight on compensation

- The say-on-pay is not binding; directors can take the advice of shareholders or go against it (but they are elected by the same shareholders)

- Say-on-pay takes away shareholder frustration with the process

- In companies that are already allowing shareholders a say on pay, the shareholders appear to be fairly reasonable. For example, at Aflac, 93 percent of the shareholders voted in 2008 in favor of the multimillion-dollar pay package for CEO Dan Amos. His pay approval package rate rose to 97 percent of the shareholders in 2009 after Amos turned down the $2.8 million bonus he was entitled to under the 2008 approval.

From the CEO's perspective,

- There are concerns about shareholders micromanaging the company.

- There are concerns that some shareholders are fairly sophisticated and may, through the say-on-pay approval process, force CEOs into making decisions that carry a very short-term focus for the company that can prove harmful in the long run.

- This type of micro-regulation could result in a talent pool drain in what is now an international marketplace; it would allow CEOs to go to companies not subject to U.S. regulation.

- The say-on-pay rule would be another impetus for companies to go private, where there would be less transparency on true market performance.

- Say-on-pay does not promote a dialogue between management and shareholders that could bring about more meaningful self-reform on pay packages.

How will the advisory vote work? Could companies go further and ask for shareholder ratification as a required step for compensation packages? How would this work from a governance perspective? Are the roles of shareholders and managers blending together? Do you believe the advisory vote that is now law will evolve into something more?

Notes

1. The questions were actually a resurrection of questions asked by Judge Stanley Sporkin when he was dealing with all of the fraud cases from the savings and loan collapses in the early 1990s. [*Lincoln Savings & Loan Ass'n v Wall*, 743 F. Supp. 901, at 920 (D.D.C. 1990)]

2. The final rules can be found at 17 C.F.R. § 205 (2003).

3. Del Jones, "CEOs Openly Pull Against Say-on-Pay," *USA Today*, July 16, 2009, p. 1B.

O ne of the methods for raising the capital needed for a corporation or partnership is to sell interests in it. Corporations sell shares, and partnerships sell limited partnership interests. Investors provide the capital these businesses need to operate. They give the businesses their money to work with and in return are given an interest in the business. The investors' hope is that the business will give them a profit on their investment (dividends on stock and interest income on bonds and other forms of securities) and that the value of their investment will grow as the business in which they have invested increases in value. The investment arrangement in theory is mutually beneficial. However, because people are so eager to have their money grow and because businesses need money for growth, the interests of business and investors are often at odds. Because of this inherent conflict of interest in the investment relationship, laws regulate investments at both state and federal levels. These laws, called securities laws, govern everything from the sale of securities to soliciting proxies from owners of securities. This chapter answers these questions: Why do we have securities laws, and what is their history? What requirements affect primary offerings of securities? How do securities laws regulate the secondary market? How do those laws protect shareholders in share and company acquisitions? ■

UPDATE ↖
For up-to-date legal news, go to
mariannejennings.com

October. This is one of the peculiarly dangerous months to speculate stocks in. The others are July, January, September, April, November, May, March, June, December, August, and February.

Mark Twain
Pudd'nhead Wilson

We are doing God's work.[1]

Jeffrey Skilling
former Enron CEO, circa 2000

Lloyd Blankfein
Goldman Sachs CEO, November 2009

Total Enforcement Actions by the SEC

YEAR	TOTAL ENFORCEMENT ACTIONS INITIATED
1999	525
2000	503
2001	484
2002	598
2003	680
2004	897
2005	1039
2006	760
2007	1169
2008	671
2009	664

The SEC's Annual Reports
http://www.sec.gov

CONSIDER...

James Herman O'Hagan was a partner in the law firm of Dorsey & Whitney in Minneapolis, Minnesota. In July 1988, Grand Metropolitan PLC, a company based in London, retained Dorsey & Whitney as local counsel to represent it regarding a potential tender offer for common stock of Pillsbury Company.

Mr. O'Hagan did not work on the Grand Met matter, but on August 18, 1988, he began purchasing call options for Pillsbury stock. Each option gave him the right to purchase 100 shares of Pillsbury stock. By the end of September,

Mr. O'Hagan owned more than 2,500 Pillsbury options. Also in September, Mr. O'Hagan purchased 5,000 shares of Pillsbury stock at $39 per share.

Grand Met announced its tender offer in October, and Pillsbury stock rose to $60 per share. Mr. O'Hagan sold his call options and made a profit of $4.3 million.

The SEC indicted Mr. O'Hagan on 57 counts of illegal trading on inside information. He says he did nothing wrong. Who is right?

History of Securities Law

Although most people think of the market crash of 1929 as the beginning of securities regulation, regulation actually began nearly 20 years earlier at the state level. In 1911, Kansas passed the first securities law, which regulated the initial sale of securities to members of the public. Some states followed the lead of Kansas, but until 1929 the field of securities was relatively free of regulation.[2]

At that time, investors were engaging in a great deal of speculation in stocks. Investors traded "on margin," which means they borrowed money to invest in a stock and when the stock went up in value, they sold it, paid off the loan, and still made money. On a Friday in 1929, however, stock prices dropped on all the exchanges and continued to drop. Investors defaulted on the margin loans, lenders foreclosed on their properties, and the entire country was thrown into a depression.

Because of the 1929 market crash, Congress perceived a problem with the investment market. As a result, the **Securities Act of 1933** and the **Securities Exchange Act of 1934** were passed, the former to regulate initial sales of stock by businesses and the latter to regulate the secondary trading of stock on the markets. These statutes, as amended, and their accompanying regulations still govern the sale of securities today.

Primary Offering Regulation: The 1933 Securities Act

A **primary offering**—an offering by an issuer, which could be its first, known as an initial public offering (IPO)—is a sale of securities by the business itself. The 1933 act regulates these initial sales of securities.

What Is a Security?

The 1933 act applies only to the sale of **securities.** The language of the act itself is broad in the definition of *securities*, and approximately 20 items are considered securities, including notes; stock; bonds; debentures; warrants; subscriptions; voting trust certificates; rights to oil, gas, and minerals; and limited partnership interests. Every investment contract that gives the owner evidence of indebtedness or business participation is a security.

In interpreting the application of the 1933 act, the courts have been liberal. The landmark case on the definition of a security is *SEC v W. J. Howey Co.*, 328 U.S. 293 (1946). In holding that the sale of interests in Florida citrus groves constituted the sale of securities, the U.S. Supreme Court defined a security as "a contract, transaction, or scheme whereby a person invests his money in a common enterprise and is led to expect profits solely from the efforts of a promoter or a third party." With this even broader definition than the actual 1933 act language, known as the ***Howey* test,** courts have been reluctant to impose restrictions on the definition of a security. In recent years, the only type of arrangement the U.S. Supreme Court has excluded from this definition is an employer pension plan in which employees are not required to make contributions. The exclusion of these plans from securities laws is probably based on the fact that employees are afforded other statutory protections (see Chapter 18 and the discussion of the Employment Retirement Income Security Act and the Pension Protection Act of 2006).

CONSIDER...   21.1

Determine whether general partnership interests would be considered securities for purposes of the 1933 Securities Act.

THINK: The *Howey* definition is that securities are investments in a common enterprise with profits to come from the efforts of others.

APPLY: Even though partnerships are investments in a common enterprise, we learned in Chapter 20 that each partner is required to contribute work and effort to the partnership. General partners, unless otherwise specified, are not paid salaries for their work and effort in making the partnership work. Because of this obligation to work and the full liability exposure, the results from investing in a partnership do not come primarily from the efforts of others but through the partnership itself.

ANSWER: A general partnership interest is not a security for purposes of the 1933 act.

Now determine whether the following are securities under the 1933 Securities Act.

- Limited partnership interests
- Limited liability company interests
- Limited liability partnership interests
- Oil and gas leases
- Limited partnership in an oil field
- An interest in a real estate investment trust
- Options to buy tickets for the World Series if your team makes it to that point

Regulating Primary Offerings: Registration

The **Securities and Exchange Commission** (SEC) is the administrative agency responsible for regulating the sale of securities under both the 1933 and 1934 acts. The SEC is subject to all of the administrative rules covered in Chapter 6 because it was the administrative agency created by Congress in its enabling legislation, the 1934 Securities Exchange Act. The SEC can issue injunctions, institute criminal proceedings, bring civil suits, enter into consent decrees, handle enforcement, and promulgate rules.

The rules promulgated by the SEC provide the requirements for the registration of securities, financial reporting, and stock exchange operations. The SEC has a complete staff of lawyers, accountants, financial analysts, and other experts to assist in both the review of informational filings and the enforcement of the securities laws.

Regulating Primary Offerings: Exemptions

Unless an **exemption** applies, anyone selling securities must complete certain filing requirements before the securities can be sold legally. The two types of exemptions are exempt securities and exempt transactions. These exemptions work only for the 1933 act.

Exempt Securities

Certain investments, called **exempt securities,** have been excluded specifically from coverage of the 1933 act. The following is a list of some of the exemptions:

1. Securities (bonds, etc.) issued by federal, state, county, or municipal governments for public purposes

2. Commercial paper (includes notes, checks, and drafts with a maturity date under nine months)

3. Banks, savings and loans, and religious and charitable organizations

4. Insurance policies

5. Annuities

6. Securities of common carriers (those regulated by the Interstate Commerce Commission)

7. Stock dividends and stock splits

8. Charitable bonds

Exempt Transactions

Exempt transactions are more complicated than exempt securities; more details are required to comply with the exempt transaction standards. The following subsections discuss these transaction exemptions, which are summarized in Exhibit 21.1.

The Intrastate Offering Exemption

This exemption exists because the Commerce Clause prohibits the federal government from regulating purely intrastate matters (see Chapter 5 for a full discussion of Commerce Clause issues). To qualify for the intrastate exemption, the investors (offerees) and issuer must all be residents of the same state. (If there is one out-of-state offeree, the exemption will not apply.) Further, the issuer must meet the following requirements:

1. Eighty percent of its assets must be located in the state.

2. Eighty percent of its income must be earned from operations within the state.

Eighty percent of the proceeds from the sale must be used on operations within the state.

Under the SEC's Rule 147, some restrictions apply to the transfer of exempt intrastate offerings, including a nine-month transfer restriction to state residents only.

Small-Offering Exemption: Regulation A

Although it is not a true exemption, **Regulation A** is a shortcut method of registration. The lengthy, complicated processes of full registration are simplified in that only a short-form registration statement is filed, a sort of fill-in-the-blanks application. Regulation A applies to issues of $5 million or less during any 12-month period.

The SEC groups or "integrates" registration. Three registrations of $2 million each would not qualify for this exemption if issued within one 12-month period. They would qualify, however, if issued over three years.

Small-Offering Exemption: Regulation D

Regulation D is the product of the SEC's evaluation of the impact of its rules on the ability of small businesses to raise capital. It was promulgated to simplify and clarify existing exemptions, expand the availability of exemptions, and achieve uniformity between state and federal exemptions.

Regulation D creates a three-tiered exemption structure that consists of Rules 504, 505, and 506, which permits sales without registration. Sellers are, however, required to file a Form D informational statement about the sale. Rule 501 of Regulation D lists the definitions of various terms used in the three exemptions. One of the key definitions under Regulation D is that of an **accredited investor,**

EXHIBIT 21.1 1933 Securities Act Transaction Exemptions

NAME	SIZE LIMITATION	GENERAL SOLICITATION	OFFEREE/BUYER LIMITATION	RESALE LIMITATION	DISCLOSURE	PUBLIC OFFERING	SEC FILING	TIME
Intrastate exemption, 15 U.S.C. § 77(c)(a)(11)	No	No	Buyers must be residents of state of incorporation; triple 80% requirements	Yes, stock transfer restrictions Rule 147—9 months	No	Yes, in state	No	No restriction
Small-offering exemption, 15 U.S.C. § 77D Regulation A	$5,000,000	Yes	Short-form registration required (offering circular)	No	Offering circular	Yes	Short-form	12-month period
Rule 504, Regulation D	$1,000,000* or less (in 12-month period)	YES	None, unlimited accredited and nonaccredited alike	Yes	No†	Yes	Notice of offering within 15 days of first sale	12-month period
Rule 505, Regulation D	Up to $5,000,000	No	No more than 35, excluding accredited investors	Yes, 2 years†	Yes, to nonaccredited†	No	Notice of offering (15 days)	12-month period
Rule 506, Regulation D	No	No	Unlimited accredited and 35 nonaccredited investors (nonaccredited must be sophisticated)	Yes, stock restrictions	Yes, to nonaccredited†	No	Notice of offering (15 days)	12-month period
Rule 144 (Private placement)								

*In certain circumstances. $2,000,000 if blue-sky registration (504). Up to $7,500,000 if blue-sky registration (505).
†Must verify purchaser is buying for himself must have restrictions on shares.

a term that was changed significantly by the Dodd–Frank Wall Street Reform and Consumer Financial Protection Act that was signed into law in July 2010.[3] Under the most current definition with the Dodd–Frank changes, an accredited investor is any investor who at the time of the sale falls into any of the following categories:

1. Any bank
2. Any private business development company
3. Any director, executive officer, or general partner of the issuer
4. Any person who purchases at least $150,000 of the securities being offered
5. Natural persons whose net worth is greater than $1 million (excluding the value of their primary residence)[4]
6. Any natural person who had an individual income in excess of $200,000 in each of the two most recent years or joint income with that person's spouse in excess of $300,000 in each of those years and has a reasonable expectation of reaching the same income level in the current year

Rule 502 places a number of limitations on the means an issuer can use in offering securities. In order to qualify for these exemptions, securities cannot be sold through general advertising or through seminars initiated through advertising. Further, all of the securities sold must be subject to restrictions to prevent the immediate rollover of the securities involved in these exempt transactions.

The three tiers of Regulation D exemptions are as follows.

- The **Rule 504** exemption applies to offerings of $1 million or less (within any 12-month period). Sales of stock to directors, officers, and employees are not counted in the $1 million limitation. Recent changes permit the use of the Rule 504 exemption in offerings of up to $2 million, provided the offering is registered under a state **blue-sky law.**

- The **Rule 505** exemption covers sales of up to $5 million, provided no more than 35 nonaccredited investors are involved. Again, with state registration, it is possible to take a Rule 505 exemption up to $7.5 million. Issuers qualifying under this exemption cannot engage in public advertising. Also, if the issue is sold to both accredited and nonaccredited investors, the issuer must give all buyers a prospectus.

- The **Rule 506** exemption has no dollar limitation, but the number and type of investors are limited. Any number of accredited investors is allowed, but the number of nonaccredited investors is limited to 35, and these investors must be sophisticated (capable of evaluating the offering and its risk). Under a Rule 506 exemption, the resale of the shares is subject to some restrictions.

- Under Dodd–Frank, the private placement market that comes under Regulation D is likely to undergo significant changes because of mandated studies of this portion of the securities market. One change that is likely is that the SEC will be able to prevent so-called "bad actors" from making private placement offerings. "Bad actors" are those who have a history of failed offerings and investor litigation. These types of offerors would be required to go through the supervised registration process. Another possible change that is to be studied is the creation of a self-regulatory organization to regulate behavior of those firms involved in the private placement market. This organization would be comparable to the Financial Industry Regulatory Authority (FINRA), the self-regulatory body for the publicly traded securities market.

Ethical Issues

When investment banking firm Goldman Sachs's representatives appeared before Congress to testify about their failure to disclose to investors that the firm was shorting securities it was selling to its clients (betting that the securities would drop in value), members of the committee asked whether Goldman had an obligation to disclose its position to those investors. All witnesses testified with an unequivocal "No!" because of Rule 506. Rule 506 is a sale to accredited (sophisticated) investors, investors who understand how markets work, can afford to invest, and/or can afford to have advisers regarding their investments. Goldman maintains that its clients were "qualified accredited" and/or "sophisticated" investors to whom the firm was not required to provide the detailed information that is mandated for general

public offerings. Goldman's position is that the clients who purchased the instruments had enough knowledge of markets to understand and process the risk and realize that all investment bankers are positioned in the market according to their theories on risk.

Did Goldman have a fiduciary duty to its investing clients under the regulations? Evaluate Goldman's position from an ethical perspective. That is, you know Goldman met its legal requirements for disclosure, now determine whether its conduct in nondisclosure was ethical. Discuss what role Goldman's conduct may have had in the Dodd–Frank changes to accredited investor definitions and the private placement securities market. Be sure to think back on the regulatory cycle from Chapter 2 as you provide your answer.

Corporate Reorganizations

If a firm is issuing new shares of stock under a Chapter 11 bankruptcy reorganization supervised by a bankruptcy court, registration is not necessary, provided court approval is obtained for the issue.

What Must Be Filed: Documents and Information for Registration

If none of the exemptions applies, the offeror of the securities must go through the registration process. The offeror (issuer) must file a **registration statement (S-1)** and sample **prospectus** with the SEC. A prospectus here means the formal document the SEC requires all shareholders to have. However, for purposes of disclosure and misrepresentation issues, a prospectus is any ad or written materials the offeror provides or places.

A filing fee is based on the aggregate offering price of the sale. The SEC has 20 days to act on the filing, after which the registration statement automatically becomes effective. The SEC takes some form of action within that time period. The SEC need not actually approve or disapprove the offering within that time limit as long as a **comment letter** or **deficiency letter** is issued. A new registration, for a first-time offeror, generally takes about six months to get through the SEC. In 2000, a high point for the market in terms of both IPOs and securities issuances, the SEC reviewed 3,970 proposed stock offerings, of which 1,350 were IPOs. In 2003, the SEC reviewed only 370 IPOs. By 2009, the number of IPOs was down to 47, which was still an uptick from the 43 IPOs of 2008, which was called the "valley of the shadow of death" for IPOs.

The SEC's guide in reviewing the registration materials is the **full-disclosure standard.** The SEC does not pass on the merits of the offering or the soundness of the investment; rather, it simply requires that certain information be supplied. The SEC does not verify the accuracy of the information, only that it is on file. The following information is required in the registration statement:

1. A description of what is being offered, why it is offered, how the securities will fit into the business's existing capital structure, and how the proceeds will be used

2. An audited financial statement

3. A list of corporate assets

4. The nature of the issuer's business

5. A list of those in management and their shares of ownership in the firm

6. Other relevant and material information, such as pending lawsuits

Before and after the registration statement is filed, the issuer is very much restricted in what can be done to sell the securities. After the registration statement is filed, the issuer can run a **tombstone ad,** as shown in Exhibit 21.2, which simply announces that securities will be sold and who will have information—but clearly indicates that the ad is not an offer. Also, after filing, but before the registration statement becomes effective, the issuer can send out a **red-herring prospectus,** which has printed in red at the top that the registration is not yet effective. These red herrings are a way to get out information while waiting for SEC approval.

During this interval between filing and the effective date, no sales and no general advertising are allowed. Activity is limited until the date the registration gets SEC approval and becomes effective. Exhibit 21.3 is a diagram of federal securities registration and exemptions.

The SEC permits firms to complete *shelf registrations*. Under this process, a firm completes all the registration requirements and is then free to issue the securities any time within a two-year period, generally when market conditions are most favorable. The company's quarterly and annual filings serve to update the shelf registration. This means of filing was permitted to help corporations raise capital.

Violations of the 1933 Act

Section 11 Violations
Section 11 of the 1933 act imposes civil and criminal liability on those who do not comply with the act's requirements regarding the submission of a registration statement. Section 11 is used when full disclosure has not been made in the registration statement or if any of the information in that registration statement is false. Section 11 is a statutory fraud section that applies to security registrations.

What Is Required for a Violation?
For an investor to recover civilly under Section 11, the following elements must be proved.

1. The investor purchased a security that was required to have a registration statement.

2. The registration statement contained a material misstatement or omission.

3. The investor need not show reliance unless the purchase was made over a year after the effective date.

4. The investor experienced a loss.

EXHIBIT 21.2 Sample of a Tombstone Ad

This announcement is neither an offer to sell nor a solicitation of offers to buy any of these securities. The offering is made only by the Prospectus, copies of which may be obtained in any State or jurisdiction in which this announcement is circulated only from such of the underwriters as may legally offer these securities in such State.

NEW ISSUE

January 22, 1999

$50,000,000

< a l l a i r e >

2,500,000 Shares
Common Stock

NASDAQ Symbol: "ALLR"

Price $20 Per Share

Prior to the offering there had been no public market for these securities. Allaire Corporation develops, markets and supports application development and server software for a wide range of Web development, from building static Web pages to developing high volume, interactive Web applications.

Credit Suisse First Boston

Dain Rauscher Wessels
a division of Dain Rauscher Incorporated
NationsBanc Montgomery Securities LLC

Hambrecht & Quist

Invemed Associates, Inc.

Needham & Company, Inc.

Charles Schwab & Co., Inc.

Tucker Anthony
Incorporated
C.E. Unterberg, Towbin

Wedbush Morgan Securities

CREDIT SUISSE | FIRST BOSTON

EXHIBIT 21.3 Federal Securities Registration and Exemptions

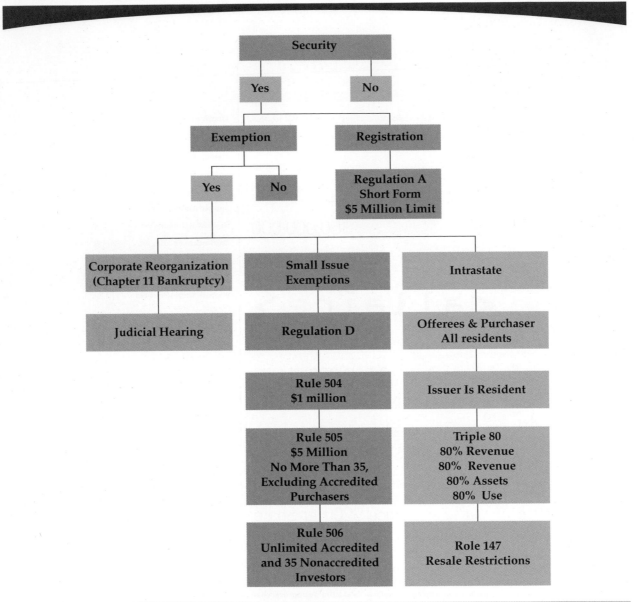

Who Is Liable?

Liability under Section 11 attaches to all individuals who signed the registration statement—each director and officer of the issuing corporation and every accountant, engineer, appraiser, attorney, geologist, or other expert whose input was used in the preparation of the statement. Underwriters are also included as potential defendants. Experts (such as accountants, engineers, appraisers, lawyers) are liable only for the information they provided. Directors and officers are jointly and severally liable under Section 11. Under the Dodd–Frank changes, the SEC will be studying whether to expand Section 11 liability to "aiders and abettors"— those who help offerors continue to hold out a deceptive appearance of financial solvency. (See the full discussion of this issue on p. 750.)

Defenses for Section 11 Violations

Several defenses are available to defendants. The burden of proof for these defenses rests with Section 11 defendants.

1. *Immateriality.* Because proving that a **material misstatement** or omission was made is part of the investor's case, proving that the statement or omission was immaterial is a valid defense. The standards for what is or is not material are basically the same standards used in contract misrepresentation cases.

2. *Investor knowledge.* If the investor knew of the misstatement or omission and purchased the stock anyway, there is no Section 11 liability. Section 11 defendants can offer proof of knowledge of the investor to establish a defense.

3. *Due diligence.* The **due diligence** defense is one that allows defendants (non-issuers) to show that they were acting reasonably in preparing and signing the registration statement. The experts are required to show that they acted within the standards of their profession in preparing their portions of the registration statement. Officers and directors are required to show that they had no reason to suspect or had no knowledge of an omission or misstatement.

This area of due diligence came under fire with the collapses of Enron, WorldCom, and so many dot-com IPOs. The result was an extensive network of regulation under Sarbanes–Oxley, a network explained in next "For the Manager's Desk" on p. 741.

Escott v BarChris Constr. Corp. (Case 21.1) is the leading case on Section 11 liability. It involves a variety of defendants, including an accounting firm and audit partners, and discusses the defense of due diligence. Ironically, although the case is from 1968, it remains the classic example of the type of financial overstatement of a company's performance that SOX was passed to address.

CASE 21.1	*Escott v BarChris Constr. Corp.* 283 F. Supp. 643 (S.D.N.Y. 1968)

Bowling for Fraud: Right Up Our Alley

FACTS

BarChris was a bowling alley company established in 1946. The bowling industry grew rapidly when automatic pin resetters went on the market in the mid-1950s. BarChris began a program of rapid expansion and in 1960 was responsible for the construction of over 3 percent of all bowling alleys in the United States. BarChris used two methods of financing the construction of these alleys, both of which substantially drained the company's cash flow.

In 1959 BarChris sold approximately one-half million shares of common stock. By 1960, its cash flow picture was still troublesome, and it sold debentures. The debenture issue was registered with the SEC, approved, and sold. In spite of the cash boost from the sale, BarChris was still experiencing financial difficulties and declared bankruptcy in October 1962. The debenture holders were not paid their interest; BarChris defaulted.

The purchasers of the BarChris debentures brought suit under Section 11 of the 1933 act. They claimed that the registration statement filed by BarChris contained false information and failed to disclose certain material information. Their suit, which centered on the audited financial statements prepared by a CPA firm, claimed that the statements were inaccurate and full of omissions. The following chart summarizes the problems with the financial statements submitted with the registration statements.

CONTINUED

1. *1960 Earnings*
   (a) *Sales*
Per prospectus	$ 9,165,320
Correct figure	8,511,420
Overstatement	$ 653,900
   (b) *Net Operating Income*
Per prospectus	$ 1,742,801
Correct figure	1,496,196
Overstatement	$ 246,605
   (c) *Earnings per Share*
Per prospectus	$ .75
Correct figure	.65
Overstatement	$ .10

2. *1960 Balance Sheet*
   Current Assets
Per prospectus	$ 4,524,021
Correct figure	3,914,332
Overstatement	$ 609,689

3. *Contingent Liabilities as of December 31, 1960, on Alternative Method of Financing*
Per prospectus	$ 750,000
Correct figure	1,125,795
Understatement	$ 375,795
Capitol Lanes should have been shown as a direct liability	$ 325,000

4. *Contingent Liabilities as of April 30, 1961*
Per prospectus	$ 825,000
Correct figure	1,443,853
Understatement	$ 618,853
Capitol Lanes should have been shown as a direct liability	$ 314,166

5. *Earnings Figures for Quarter Ending March 31, 1961*
   (a) *Sales*
Per prospectus	$ 2,138,455
Correct figure	1,618,645
Overstatement	$ 519,810
   (b) *Gross Profit*
Per prospectus	$ 483,121
Correct figure	252,366
Overstatement	$ 230,755

6. *Backlog as of March 31, 1961*
Per prospectus	$ 6,905,000
Correct figure	2,415,000
Overstatement	$ 4,490,000

7. *Failure to Disclose Officers' Loans Outstanding and Unpaid on May 16, 1961* $ 386,615

8. *Failure to Disclose Use of Proceeds in Manner Not Revealed in Prospectus: Approx.* $1,160,000

9. *Failure to Disclose Customers' Delinquencies in May 1961 and BarChris's Potential Liability with Respect Thereto: Over*$1,350,000

10. *Failure to Disclose the Fact that BarChris Was Already Engaged and Was About to Be More Heavily Engaged in the Operation of Bowling Alleys*

The federal district court reviewed all of the exhibits and statements included in the prospectus and dealt with each defendant individually in issuing its decisions. The defendants consisted of those officers and directors who signed the registration statement, the underwriters of the debenture offering, the auditors (Peat, Marwick, Mitchell & Co.[5]), and BarChris's attorneys and directors.

JUDICIAL OPINION

McLEAN, District Judge

Russo. Russo was, to all intents and purposes, the chief executive officer of BarChris. He was a member of the executive committee. He was familiar with all aspects of the business. He was personally in charge of dealings with the factors. He acted on BarChris's behalf in making the financing agreement with Talcott and he handled the negotiations with Talcott in the spring of 1961. He talked with customers about their delinquencies.

Russo prepared the list of jobs which went into the backlog figure. He knew the status of those jobs.

It was Russo who arranged for the temporary increase in BarChris's cash in banks on December 31, 1960, a transaction which borders on the fraudulent. He was thoroughly aware of BarChris's stringent financial condition in May 1961. He had personally advanced large sums to BarChris of which $175,000 remained unpaid as of May 16.

In short, Russo knew all the relevant facts. He could not have believed that there were no untrue statements or material omissions in the prospectus. Russo has no due diligence defenses.

Vitolo and Pugliese. They were the founders of the business who stuck with it to the end. Vitolo was president and Pugliese was vice president. Despite their titles, their field of responsibility in the administration of BarChris's affairs during the period in question seems to have been less all-embracing than Russo's.

Pugliese in particular appears to have limited his activities to supervising the actual construction work. Vitolo and Pugliese are each men of limited education. It is not hard to believe that for them the prospectus was difficult reading, if indeed they read it at all.

But whether it was or not is irrelevant. The liability of a director who signs a registration statement does not depend upon whether or not he read it or, if he did, whether or not he understood what he was reading.

And in any case, Vitolo and Pugliese were not as naive as they claim to be. They were members of BarChris's executive committee. At meetings of that committee BarChris's affairs were discussed at length. They must have known what was going on. Certainly they knew of the inadequacy of cash in 1961. They knew of their own large advances to the company which remained unpaid. They knew that they had agreed not to deposit their checks until the financing proceeds were received. They knew and intended that part of the proceeds were to be used to pay their own loans.

All in all, the position of Vitolo and Pugliese is not significantly different, for present purposes, from Russo's. They could not have believed that the registration statement was wholly true and that no material facts had been omitted. And in any case, there is nothing to show that they made any investigation of anything which they may not have known about or understood. They have not proved their due diligence defenses.

Kircher. Kircher was treasurer of BarChris and its chief financial officer. He is a certified public accountant and an intelligent man. He was thoroughly familiar with BarChris's financial affairs. He knew the terms of BarChris's agreements with Talcott. He knew of the customers' delinquency problems. He participated actively with Russo in May 1961 in the successful effort to hold Talcott off until the financing proceeds came in. He knew how the financing proceeds were to be applied and he saw to it that they were so applied. He arranged the officers' loans and he knew all the facts concerning them.

Moreover, as a member of the executive committee, Kircher was kept informed as to those branches of the business of which he did not have direct charge. He knew about the operation of alleys, present and prospective. In brief, Kircher knew all the relevant facts.

Knowing the facts, Kircher had reason to believe that the expertised portion of the prospectus, i.e., the 1960 figures, was in part incorrect. He could not shut his eyes to the facts and rely on Peat, Marwick for that portion.

As to the rest of the prospectus, knowing the facts, he did not have a reasonable ground to believe it to be true. On the contrary, he must have known that in part it was untrue. Under these circumstances, he was not entitled to sit back and place the blame on the lawyers for not advising him about it. Kircher has not proved his due diligence defenses.

Trilling. Trilling's position is somewhat different from Kircher's. He was BarChris's controller. He signed the registration statement in that capacity, although he was not a director.

Trilling entered BarChris's employ in October 1960. He was Kircher's subordinate. When Kircher asked him for information, he furnished it. On at least one occasion he got it wrong.

Trilling may well have been unaware of several of the inaccuracies in the prospectus. But he must have known of some of them. As a financial officer, he was familiar with BarChris's finances and with its books of account. He knew that part of the cash on deposit on December 31, 1960, had been procured temporarily by Russo for window dressing purposes. He should have known, although perhaps through carelessness he did not know at the time, that BarChris's contingent liability was greater than the prospectus stated. In the light of these facts, I cannot find that Trilling believed the entire prospectus to be true.

But even if he did, he still did not establish his due diligence defenses. He did not prove that as to the parts of the prospectus expertised by Peat, Marwick he had no reasonable ground to believe that it was untrue. He also failed to prove, as to the parts of the prospectus not expertised by Peat, Marwick, that he made a reasonable investigation which afforded him a reasonable ground to believe that it was true. As far as appears, he made no investigation. As a signer, he could not avoid responsibility by leaving it up to others to make it accurate. Trilling did not sustain the burden of proving his due diligence defenses.

Birnbaum. Birnbaum was a young lawyer, admitted to the bar in 1957, who, after brief periods of employment by two different law firms and an equally brief period of practicing in his own firm, was employed by BarChris as house counsel and assistant secretary in October 1960. Unfortunately for him, he became secretary and director of BarChris on April 17, 1961, after the first version of the registration statement had been filed with the Securities and Exchange Commission. He signed the later amendments, thereby becoming responsible for the accuracy of the prospectus in its final form.

It seems probable that Birnbaum did not know of many of the inaccuracies in the prospectus. He must, however, have appreciated some of them. In any case, he made no investigation and relied on the others to

CONTINUED

get it right. Unlike Trilling, he was entitled to rely upon Peat, Marwick for the 1960 figures, for as far as appears, he had no personal knowledge of the company's books of account or financial transactions. As a lawyer, he should have known his obligations under the statute. He should have known that he was required to make a reasonable investigation of the truth of all the statements in the unexpertised portion of the document which he signed. Having failed to make such an investigation, he did not have reasonable ground to believe that all these statements were true. Birnbaum has not established his due diligence defenses except as to the audited 1960 exhibits.

Auslander. Auslander was an "outside" director, i.e., one who was not an officer of BarChris. He was chairman of the board of Valley Stream National Bank in Valley Stream, Long Island. In February 1961 Vitolo asked him to become a director of BarChris. As an inducement, Vitolo said that when BarChris received the proceeds of a forthcoming issue of securities, it would deposit $1 million in Auslander's bank.

Auslander was elected a director on April 17, 1961. The registration statement in its original form had already been filed, of course without his signature. On May 10, 1961, he signed a signature page for the first amendment to the registration statement which was filed on May 11, 1961. This was a separate sheet without any document attached. Auslander did not know that it was a signature page for a registration statement. He vaguely understood that it was something "for the SEC."

Auslander attended a meeting of BarChris's directors on May 15, 1961. At that meeting he, along with the other directors, signed the signature sheet for the second amendment which constituted the registration statement in its final form. Again, this was only a separate sheet without any document attached.

Auslander never saw a copy of the registration statement in its final form. It is true that Auslander became a director on the eve of the financing. He had little opportunity to familiarize himself with the company's affairs.

Section 11 imposes liability in the first instance upon a director, no matter how new he is.

Peat, Marwick. Peat, Marwick's work was in general charge of a member of the firm, Cummings, and more immediately in charge of Peat, Marwick's manager, Logan. Most of the actual work was performed by a senior accountant, Berardi, who had junior assistants, one of whom was Kennedy.

Berardi was then about thirty years old. He was not yet a CPA. He had had no previous experience with the bowling industry. This was his first job as a senior accountant. He could hardly have been given a more difficult assignment.

After obtaining a little background information on BarChris by talking to Logan and reviewing Peat, Marwick's work papers on its 1959 audit, Berardi examined the results of test checks of BarChris's accounting procedures which one of the junior accountants had made, and he prepared an "internal control questionnaire" and an "audit program." Thereafter, for a few days subsequent to December 30, 1960, he inspected BarChris's inventories and examined certain alley construction. Finally, on January 13, 1961, he began his auditing work which he carried on substantially continuously until it was completed on February 24, 1961. Toward the close of the work, Logan reviewed it and made various comments and suggestions to Berardi.

It is unnecessary to recount everything that Berardi did in the course of the audit. We are concerned only with the evidence relating to what Berardi did or did not do with respect to those items found to have been incorrectly reported in the 1960 figures in the prospectus.

Accountants should not be held to a standard higher than that recognized in their profession. I do not do so here. Berardi's review did not come up to that standard. He did not take some of the steps which Peat, Marwick's written program prescribed. He did not spend an adequate amount of time on a task of this magnitude. Most important of all, he was too easily satisfied with glib answers to his inquiries.

This is not to say that he should have made a complete audit. But there were enough danger signals in the materials which he did examine to require some further investigation on his part. Generally accepted accounting standards required such further investigation under these circumstances. It is not always sufficient merely to ask questions.

CASE QUESTIONS

1. How much time transpired between the sale of the debentures and BarChris's bankruptcy?

2. Give a summary of the types of items that were materially misstated.

3. Who was sued under Section 11? Who was held liable?

For the Manager's Desk

Re: A Primer on Sarbanes–Oxley

The introduction to SOX, as it has come to be known, gives the following purpose: *An Act to protect investors by improving the accuracy and reliability of corporate disclosures made pursuant to the securities laws, and for other purposes.*

The new portions of the law appear at 15 U.S.C. § 7201. However, because many of the provisions amend the Securities Exchange Act of 1934, which begins at 78 U.S.C. § 1 *et seq.*, many of the provisions can be found there.

Part I: The Creation of the Public Company Accounting Oversight Board

This section of SOX established a quasigovernmental entity called the Public Company Accounting Oversight Board (PCAOB, but called "Peek-a-Boo) under the direction of the SEC to (1) oversee the audit of public companies covered by the federal securities laws (the 1933 and 1934 Acts); (2) establish audit report standards and rules; and (3) investigate, inspect, and enforce compliance through both the registration and regulation of public accounting firms.

Under this section of SOX, companies that conduct audits of companies covered under federal securities laws must register with PCAOB. With this registration control, PCAOB is given the power to discipline public accounting firms, including the ability to impose sanctions such as prohibitions on conducting future audits. PCAOB's powers related to intentional conduct or repeated negligent conduct by audit firms when they are doing company audits and financial certifications. PCAOB's power to regulate was upheld in *Free Enterprise Fund v Public Company Accounting Oversight Board,* 130 S.Ct. 3138 (2010). Under the Dodd–Frank changes, PCAOB will also have authority to regulate the auditors of broker/dealer firms.

This part of SOX also makes the SEC responsible for determining what are or are not "generally accepted" accounting principles for purposes of complying with securities laws. The SEC is also directed to study and then adopt a system of principles-based accounting for purposes of compliance with the securities law on registrations and required filings by publicly traded companies.

Part II: Auditor Independence

This portion of SOX is a bit of a statutory code of ethics for public accounting firms. Accounting firms that audit publicly traded companies cannot also perform the following consulting services for the companies for which they conduct audits:

1. Bookkeeping and other services related to the accounting records or financial statements of the audit client

2. Design and implementation of financial information systems

3. Appraisal and valuation services, fairness opinions, and contribution-in-kind reports

4. Actuarial services

5. Internal audit outsourcing services

6. Management functions and human resources

7. Broker or dealer, investment adviser, and investment banking services

8. Legal services and expert services unrelated to the audit

Any other consulting services that are not listed in this section cannot be performed without preapproval by PCAOB.

Another conflicts prohibition is that the audit firm cannot audit, for one year, a company that has one of its former employees as a member of senior management. For example, if a partner from PwC is hired by Xena Corporation as its controller or CFO, PwC cannot be the auditor (for SEC purposes) for Xena for one year. At least one year must elapse between the hire date of the former partner and the start of the audit if PwC is to conduct the audit.

Procedural requirements in this section include rotating the audit partner for the accounting firm every five years. Also, the auditor must report directly to the audit committee of the company.

This section encourages states to develop laws and regulations that are applicable to accounting firms that may not be involved with SEC work.

Part III: Corporate Responsibility

This section of SOX deals with the audit committees of publicly traded companies and makes these committees responsible for the hiring, compensation, and oversight of the public accounting firm responsible for conducting the company's audits and certifying its financial statements. All members of the audit committee must be members of the company's board of directors, and must be independent. *Independent* is defined by the SEC to require that the director be an outside board member (not an officer), not have been an officer for a period of time (if retired from the company), not have close relatives working in management in the company, and not have contractual or consulting ties to the company. The SEC and companies have developed complex checklists to help directors determine whether they meet the standards for independence for purposes of qualifying audit committee membership.

CONTINUED

In addition to these structural changes in audit committees, this portion of SOX is also the officer certification section (more related to the 1934 Securities Exchange Act covered on pp. 744). The company's CEO and CFO are required to certify the financial statements the company files with the SEC as being fair in their representation of the company's financial condition and accurate "in all material respects." CFOs and CEOs forfeit any bonuses and compensation that were received based on financial reports that subsequently had to be restated because they were not materially accurate or fair in their disclosures.

The SEC is given the authority to ban those who violate securities laws from serving as an officer or director of a publicly traded company if the SEC can prove that they are unfit to serve. The standard under the statute is "substantial unfitness." For example, a director who has been involved in insider trading in the company's shares would be banned. Likewise, an officer who backdated stock options could be similarly banned. Since its enactment, the SEC has used this provision to ban officers and directors for life as well as for limited times, such as for five years.

One final section in Part III was passed in response to activity at Enron in the months leading up to its collapse. During the so-called "blackout periods" on pension plans, those times when owners of the plans cannot trade in the company stock, officers of the company are also subject to the blackout periods. The penalty for violating this prohibition on stock dealing is that the officers must return any profits from blackout period trading to the company. This requirement to return the profits exists even when the trading was not intentional. At Enron, the officers were busily selling off their shares during a time when employees were prohibited from selling shares in their pension plans. Officers, such as Jeffrey Skilling and Clifford Baxter walked away with the cash from selling at the stock's high point while employees, because of the blackout period, were left to simply watch as Enron's stock lost virtually all of its value.

Part IV: Enhanced Financial Disclosures

This section of SOX is the accounting section. Congress directed the SEC to do something about accounting practices for off-balance sheet transactions, including special purpose entities and relationships that while immaterial in amount may have a material effect upon the financial status of the company. For example, a spin-off company that concealed $2 million in company debt is not a material amount. But if the spin-off company is involved in leveraged transactions (as was the case with Enron) and the company has agreed to serve as a guarantor to investors in the spin-off for those leveraged amounts, then the spin-off can have a material effect. The SEC changed the rules for off–balance sheet transactions quite substantially to require companies to show the economics of such off–balance sheet transactions in a transparent fashion. Lehman Brothers' bankruptcy revealed another debt spin-off

strategy that company used to hide its obligations and there will be further regulations in this area.

A second portion of Part IV gets right to the heart of pro forma and EBITDA. Companies must use Generally Accepted Accounting Principles (GAAP) and non-GAAP, side by side.

A third segment of Part IV deals again with officers. In direct response to the issues at WorldCom, Adelphia, and others, corporations can no longer make personal loans to corporate executives. The only exception is when the company is in the business of making loans, i.e., GE executives are permitted to use GE Capital as long as they have the same types of loans that are available to the general public. Another officer requirement shortens the time for them to disclose transactions in the company's shares. Prior to SOX, the executives simply had to disclose transactions within 10 days from the end of the month in which the transactions occurred. The disclosure period now is within two business days of the transaction.

Again, in all of the companies that experienced financial collapse and/or restatements, the executives were dealing in company stock at a fast clip, but shareholders, creditors, and other outsiders were not aware of the transactions until weeks after they occurred and well after the drop in value in the shares. As a result of the activities that led to these two major statutory revisions, this portion of SOX also requires companies to develop a separate code of ethics for senior financial officers, one that applies to the principal financial officer, comptroller, and/or principal accounting officer. Interestingly, Enron had just such a separate code of ethics. However, the board waived its provisions to allow former CFO Andrew Fastow to have the off-the-book transactions.

Referred to fondly now as just "404," a final portion of SOX requires companies to include an internal control report and assessment as part of the 10-K annual reports. A public accounting firm that issues the audit report must also certify and report on the state of the company's internal controls.

Although the audit committee provisions are covered in a different section, Part IV does mandate that every audit committee have at least one member who is a financial expert. The SEC has already established rules for who qualifies as a financial expert and companies' annual reports identify the financial expert and give the background.

Title V: Analyst Conflicts of Interest

The issue of analysts and their conflicts was one that contributed to the failure of the markets to heed the warning signals at Enron, WorldCom, and other companies. The SEC now regulates

1. Prepublication clearance or approval of research reports by investment bankers

2. Supervision, compensation, and evaluation of securities analysts by investment bankers

3. Retaliation against a securities analyst by an investment banker because of an unfavorable research report that may adversely affect an investment banker's relationship or a broker's or dealer's relationship with the company that is discussed in the report

4. Separating securities analysts from pressure or oversight by investment bankers in a way that might potentially create bias

5. Developing rules on disclosure by securities analysts and broker/dealers of specified conflicts of interest

Under Dodd–Frank, the SEC has been directed to further study analysts' relationships and roles in financial markets, and is authorized to promulgate additional rules on conflicts.

Title VIII: Corporate and Criminal Fraud Accountability

This section of SOX is the expansion, clean-up, and criminal law portion that created new crimes, increased penalties on existing crimes, and elaborated on the elements required to prove already existing crimes. Also known as the Corporate and Criminal Fraud Accountability Act of 2002, most of this SOX section was covered in Chapter 8.

This section amended federal bankruptcy law to make fines, profits, and penalties that result from violation of federal securities laws a nondischargeable debt in bankruptcy. Also, if common-law fraud is involved in the sale of securities, any

judgment owed as a result of the fraud is also a nondischargeable bankruptcy debt.

This section also extended the time for bringing a civil law suit for securities fraud to not later than the earlier of (1) five years after the date of the alleged violation or (2) two years after its discovery.

Finally, this section prohibits retaliation against employees in publicly traded companies who assist in an investigation of possible federal violations or file or participate in a shareholder suit for fraud against the company (see Chapter 17). The protections for whistleblowers are expanded under Dodd–Frank to provide for their recovery of 10-30% of any fines the company must pay.

Title IX: White-Collar Criminal Penalty Enhancements

Most of this section was covered in Chapter 8, but it also contains some remarkable grants of authority to the SEC. For example, this section gives the SEC the authority to freeze bonus, incentive, and other payoffs to corporate officers during an ongoing investigation. The SEC has the authority to banish violating officers and directors from the securities markets as well as from working at a publicly traded company in the future. Auditors must keep their work papers for five years and the penalties for destruction of documents was increased.

Source: Adapted from Jennings, *Business Ethics: Case Studies and Selected Readings,* 7th ed., 2011.

BUSINESS STRATEGY

Huddles with Analysts or Strategists: Does it Matter?

The SEC prohibits an analyst from issuing reports on securities that run contra to the analyst's personal beliefs about the securities. The SEC also requires an investment firm to engage in "fair dealing with its customers."[6] Whether those two requirements were met at the investment firms continues to be the subject of debate. Goldman Sachs held what were known as "trading huddles." The huddle found analysts and traders meeting to determine short and long investments on particular shares. The conclusions of the huddle were then shared with Goldman's traders and a selected few of Goldman's thousands of clients; those conclusions were often different from the Goldman analysts' reports and recommendations that

were issued publicly. Other firms such as Morgan Stanley also have huddles in addition to their published research recommendations, but their conclusions from the weekly meetings are then sent out in an e-mail blast to all clients.

One distinction between Goldman's huddles and those of other investment firms was that Goldman's huddles did not involve equity research analysts, the analysts who are subject to the SEC rules. Rather, those who participated in the huddle were from Goldman's "Fundamental Strategies Group," a group that would be exempt from the SEC rules.[7]

Was this change of name a good business strategy? Are there risks in this strategy?

Penalties for Violations of Section 11

Violations of Section 11 carry maximum penalties of $10,000 and/or five years' imprisonment. In addition, the SEC has the authority to bring suit seeking an injunction to stop sales based on false or omitted information in the registration statement. Purchasers harmed by the false or omitted statements have a right of civil suit in federal district court for recovery of their losses and other damages.

The Private Securities Litigation Reform Act of 1995 (PSLRA) limits attorneys' fees to a reasonable percentage of the amount recovered or the agreed-upon settlement amount. The problem of "professional plaintiffs" was also addressed through a section in the PSLRA that prevents a plaintiff from being named in more than five class action securities lawsuits in a three-year period.

One final portion of PSLRA is the so-called safe-harbor protection. With certain precautions and qualifications, companies can make forward-looking predictions for company performance in materials given to investors. The company is not held to these statements about its future as long as it makes the required SEC disclosures on forward-looking statements.

Section 12 Violations

Section 12 carries the same criminal penalties as Section 11 and covers the following offenses:

1. Selling securities without registration and without an exemption
2. Selling securities before the effective date of the registration statement
3. Selling securities using false information in the prospectus (In this case, "prospectus" includes not only the formal document but all ads, circulars, and so on used in the sale of securities.)

The SEC also has injunctive remedies here, and buyers also have the right of civil suit. The same defenses that apply to Section 11 apply to Section 12.

The Securities Exchange Act of 1934

The **Securities Exchange Act of 1934** regulates securities and their issuers once they are on the market. Securities sales, brokers, dealers, and exchanges are all regulated under the 1934 act. In addition, the act requires public disclosure of financial information for certain corporations. In effect, the 1934 act is responsible for the regulation of the securities marketplace. The SEC accomplishes its goal of regulating undesirable market practices in several ways, which are discussed in the following sections.

Securities Registration

Under the 1934 act, all securities traded on a national stock exchange must be registered. In addition, any issuer with over $10 million in assets and 500 or more shareholders must register its equity stock (not bonds) under the 1934 act if those shares are traded in interstate commerce. This registration is in addition to all the filing requirements for issuing discussed under the 1933 act.

Periodic Filing Under the 1934 Act: Those Alphabet Reports

In addition to the one-time registration required under the 1934 act, those same companies (national stock exchange companies or those with 500 or more shareholders and $10 million in assets) must comply with the periodic reporting requirements imposed by the SEC. Each quarter, these firms must file a **10-Q form,** which is basically a quarterly financial report. An annual report, the **10-K form,** must be filed by the company at the end of its fiscal year. Any unusual events—bankruptcies, spin-offs, takeovers, and other changes in company control—must be reported on the **8-K form.** The 10-Qs and 10-Ks are the reports the CEO and CFO must certify under SOX. The certification means the CEO and CFO offer the following assurances:

- They have reviewed the report.
- Based on their knowledge, the report contains no untrue statements, has no omissions of fact, and includes nothing misleading.
- Based on their knowledge, the financial statements included with the periodic reports fairly present all material aspects of the company's financial performance.
- They are responsible for establishing, maintaining, and certifying internal controls for the financial operations and reporting of the company.

More detail on the certification process can be found in the Primer on SOX. Chapter 8 covers the increased penalties for the certifying officers, which now run up to 20 years and $10 million.

The 1934 Act Antifraud Provision: 10(b)

In addition to regulating the reporting of information, the 1934 act regulates the propriety of sales in the marketplace. **Section 10(b)** and **Rule 10b-5** (the SEC regulation on 10(b)) are the antifraud provisions of the 1934 act. These sections are statutory versions of common law fraud. If the free market is to work, all buyers and sellers must have access to the same information. To withhold information is to commit fraud and is a violation of Section 10(b).

Application of Section 10(b)

Of all the provisions of the 1934 act, Section 10(b) has the broadest application. It applies to all sales of securities: exempt, stock-exchange-listed, over-the-counter, public, private, small, and large. The only prerequisite for 10(b) application is that interstate commerce be involved in the sales transaction. As Chapter 5 indicates, it is not difficult to find an interstate commerce connection; for example, if mail or phones were used in the transaction, 10(b) applies. The practical effect is that 10(b) applies to all sales of securities.

Proof of Section 10(b) Violation Corporations Running Afoul

The language of 10(b) does not really specify what constitutes an offense of misrepresentation. Determination of 10(b) violations has been left to the SEC and the courts, which have shown that violations of 10(b) can take a variety of forms.

The corporate dissemination violation of 10(b) means that a corporation has not been forthcoming with material information, whether positive or negative, about the company, its performance, and its future. In 2000, the SEC promulgated the **"fair-disclosure rule" (Regulation FD);** now, material information about the company must be made available to everyone at the same time. The Dodd–Frank legislation requires the SEC to perform several additional studies to examine the issues in disclosure, analysts' reports, and conflicts between and among underwriters and offerors.

The application and enforcement of Section 10(b) have become two of the most significant issues affecting Wall Street. Under SOX, as noted in the Primer, sales of shares by officers now require immediate reporting on 8-K forms. The previous standard of reporting by the close of the month in which the transactions occur has been changed to a two-day period.

Corporations have an obligation to disclose material information. To determine whether an item is material, the question to be answered is, "Is this the type of information that would affect the buying or selling decision?" Examples of items that have been held to be material are

1. Pending takeovers
2. Drops in quarterly earnings
3. Pending declaration of a large dividend
4. Possible lawsuit on product line

One of the most famous corporate (and individual) 10(b) cases is *SEC v Texas Gulf Sulphur Co.*, 401 F.2d 833 (2nd Cir. 1968). In that case, Texas Gulf Sulphur was involved in test-drilling operations in Canada. Early tests indicated that the company would make a substantial strike. Press releases did not indicate the richness of the strike. Corporate officers, geologists, and relatives bought stock before the richness of the find was finally disclosed, and the price of the stock soared. The court found that the overly pessimistic press release was misleading under 10(b). The company and the individual purchasers both ran afoul of 10(b).

One issue that resulted in over 250 SEC investigations was that of backdating stock options. The issue is whether shareholders were aware of the full extent of the cost of the options granted to the officers when their strike price was not reported accurately. The options would eventually be an expense for the company but the true cost of granting the options was not always reflected accurately in the company's financial statements because the dates were changed, and as a result, the strike price changed. Backdating by executives to a time when the stock price was lower gave the executives greater gains when they exercised their options when the value of the company's stock increased. But that increase in value to the executives represented a greater expense for the company that was not reflected in the financial statements.

Proof of a Violation: How Individuals Run Afoul of 10(b)

In simplest form, an individual's 10(b) violation occurs when one side to a securities transaction has information not generally available to the public and the transaction proceeds without disclosure. For example, the factual backdrop in the Galleon Hedge Fund insider trading investigation provides examples of what the SEC believes is inside information. Mr. Raj Rajaratnam, founder and CEO of Galleon, had information furnished to him by former Intel employee Roomy Khan. Court documents filed in the case indicate that Intel was conducting its own internal investigation when it realized that Mr. Rajaratnam's earnings predictions were "eerily accurate."[8] Using hidden video cameras, Intel

Ethical Issues

John Mackey, the CEO of Whole Foods, using the name Rahodeb (a scrambled version of his wife's name, Deborah), posted more than 1,000 messages in chat rooms that were dedicated to stock trading. During the period that Mr. Mackey was posting messages, Whole Foods stock quadrupled in value. The messages were flattering to Whole Foods (even to Mackey himself, with one posting reading, "I like Mackey's haircut. I think he looks cute."[a]) The postings were also negative about Wild Oats, a company Whole Foods was trying to acquire, even as the anonymous postings continued. On February 24, 2005, Mackey posted the following about Wild Oats CEO Perry Odak: "Perhaps the OATS Board will wake up and dump Odak and bring in a visionary and highly competent CEO."[b] Mackey was particularly active during that time frame, having posted 17 messages on September 5, 2005, and another 17 on November 11, 2005, with plenty of postings on the days in between.[c] Referred to as "sock-puppeting," it is a common practice for online identities to be concealed in order to praise, defend, garner allies, and a host of other functions accomplished more effectively when identity is concealed.

When his identity was discovered, he apologized and halted the postings. The apology came just six days after the first reports on Rahodeb's identity were reported in the *Wall Street Journal*. The Federal Trade Commission has collected the postings he made to show that to allow the merger with Wild Oats would reduce competition in the marketplace. The identity of Rahodeb became public after the FTC filing.

John Coffee, a securities law and corporate governance expert and professor at Columbia Law School, said, "This evidence raises more doubts about his sanity than his criminality. The merger is a major business strategy, and he's undercut it with reckless, self-destructive behavior. It's a little weird, like catching him as a Peeping Tom."[d] A crisis communication expert said, "It's more of an embarrassment than an issue of profound ethical and legal consequence."[e]

Where do you stand on this issue? Do you think this situation is a case of insider trading? Was this move a fair one on Mackey's part? What about sock-puppeting in general? Is it ethical?

[a] Andrew Martin, "CEO of Whole Foods Extolled His Stock Online," *New York Times*, July 13, 2007, p. C4.
[b] *Id.*
[c] Greg Farrell and Paul Davidson, "Whole Foods' CEO Was Busy Guy Online," *USA Today*, July 13, 2007, p. 4B.
[d] *Id.*
[e] *Id.*

recorded Ms. Khan sending information to Mr. Rajaratnam. Ms. Khan entered a guilty plea and was terminated from Intel. Interestingly, the SEC opted not to bring civil charges against Ms. Khan and, despite extensive debriefings from her on what she was doing, opted not to pursue a case against Galleon or Mr. Rajaratnam. Mr. Rajaratnam and 14 others are now under indictment for what the SEC alleges were years of insider trading in the shares of many companies.

Who Runs Afoul: The Extent of Section 10(b) Liability

Anyone who has access to information not readily available to the public is covered under 10(b). Officers, directors, and large shareholders are included in this group. However, 10(b) also applies to people who get information from these corporate **insiders.** These people are called **tippees.** For example, relatives of officers and directors would be considered tippees if they were given nonpublic information.

Who is covered under Section 10(b) has been a critical question during the past few years. The Supreme Court has made a distinction between true insiders and those who misappropriate information. *United States v O'Hagan* (Case 21.2) is a U.S. Supreme Court ruling on 10(b)'s application. The case answers the chapter's opening "Consider."

CASE 21.2 *United States v O'Hagan*
521 U.S. 657 (1997)

Pillsbury Dough Boy: The Lawyer/Insider Who Cashed In

FACTS

James Herman O'Hagan (respondent) was a partner in the law firm of Dorsey & Whitney in Minneapolis, Minnesota. In July 1988, Grand Metropolitan PLC (Grand Met), a company based in London, retained Dorsey & Whitney as local counsel to represent it regarding a potential tender offer for common stock of Pillsbury Company (based in Minneapolis).

Mr. O'Hagan did no work on the Grand Met matter, so on August 18, 1988, he began purchasing call options for Pillsbury stock. Each option gave him the right to purchase 100 shares of Pillsbury stock. By the end of September, Mr. O'Hagan owned more than 2,500 Pillsbury options. Also in September, Mr. O'Hagan purchased 5,000 shares of Pillsbury stock at $39 per share.

Grand Met announced its tender offer in October, and Pillsbury stock rose to $60 per share. Mr. O'Hagan sold his call options and made a profit of $4.3 million.

The SEC indicted Mr. O'Hagan on 57 counts of illegal trading on inside information, including mail fraud, securities fraud, fraudulent trading, and money laundering. The SEC alleged that Mr. O'Hagan used his profits from the Pillsbury options to conceal his previous embezzlement and conversion of his clients' trust funds. Mr. O'Hagan was convicted by a jury on all 57 counts and sentenced to 41 months in prison. A divided Court of Appeals reversed the conviction, and the SEC appealed.

JUDICIAL OPINION

GINSBURG, Justice

We hold, in accord with several other Courts of Appeals, that criminal liability under § 10(b) may be predicated on the misappropriation theory.

Under the "traditional" or "classical theory" of insider trading liability, § 10(b) and Rule 10b-5 are violated when a corporate insider trades in the securities of his corporation on the basis of material, nonpublic information. Trading on such information qualifies as a "deceptive device" under § 10(b), we have affirmed, because "a relationship of trust and confidence [exists] between the shareholders of a corporation and those insiders who have obtained confidential information by reason of their position with that corporation." *Chiarella v United States*, 445 U.S. 222, 228 (1980). That relationship, we recognized, "gives rise to a duty to disclose [or to abstain from trading] because of the 'necessity of preventing a corporate insider from . . . tak[ing] unfair advantage of . . . uninformed . . . stockholders.'" The classical theory applies not only to officers, directors, and other permanent insiders of a corporation, but also to attorneys, accountants, consultants, and others who temporarily become fiduciaries of a corporation. See *Dirks v SEC*, 463 U.S. 646, 655, n. 14 (1983).

The "misappropriation theory" holds that a person commits fraud "in connection with" a securities transaction, and thereby violates § 10(b) and Rule 10b-5, when he misappropriates confidential information for securities trading purposes, in breach of a duty owed to the source of the information. Under this theory, a fiduciary's undisclosed, self-serving use of a principal's information to purchase or sell securities, in breach of a duty of loyalty and confidentiality, defrauds the principal of the exclusive use of that information. In lieu of premising liability on a fiduciary relationship between company insider and purchaser or seller of the company's stock, the misappropriation theory premises liability on a fiduciary-turned-trader's deception of those who entrusted him with access to confidential information.

The two theories are complementary, each addressing efforts to capitalize on nonpublic information through the purchase or sale of securities. The classical theory targets a corporate insider's breach of duty to shareholders with whom the insider transacts; the misappropriation theory outlaws trading on the basis of nonpublic information by a corporate "outsider" in breach of a duty owed not to a trading party, but to the source of the information. The misappropriation theory is thus designed to "protec[t] the integrity of the securities markets against abuses by 'outsiders' to a corporation who have access to confidential information that will affect th[e] corporation's security price when revealed, but who owe no fiduciary or other duty to that corporation's shareholders."

We agree with the Government that misappropriation, as just defined, satisfies § 10(b)'s requirement that chargeable conduct involve a "deceptive device or contrivance" used "in connection with" the purchase or sale of securities. We observe, first, that misappropriators, as the Government describes them, deal in deception. A fiduciary who "[pretends] loyalty to the principal while secretly converting the principal's information for personal gain" "dupes" or defrauds the principal.

Deception through nondisclosure is central to the theory of liability for which the Government seeks recognition.

The misappropriation theory comports with § 10(b)'s language. The theory is also well tuned to an animating purpose of the Exchange Act: to insure honest securities markets and thereby promote investor confidence. Although informational disparity is inevitable in the securities markets, investors likely would hesitate to venture their capital in a market where trading based on misappropriated nonpublic information is unchecked by law. An investor's informational disadvantage vis-à-vis a misappropriator with material, nonpublic information stems from contrivance, not luck; it is a disadvantage that cannot be overcome with research or skill.

In sum, considering the inhibiting impact on market participation of trading on misappropriated information, and the congressional purposes underlying § 10(b), it makes scant sense to hold a lawyer like O'Hagan a § 10(b) violator if he works for a law firm representing the target of a tender offer, but not if he works for a law firm representing the bidder.

In sum, the misappropriation theory, as we have examined and explained it in this opinion, is both consistent with the statute and with our precedent. Vital to our decision that criminal liability may be sustained under the misappropriation theory, we emphasize, are two sturdy safeguards Congress has provided

regarding scienter. To establish a criminal violation of Rule 10b-5, the Government must prove that a person "willfully" violated the provision. In addition, the statute's "requirement of the presence of culpable intent as a necessary element of the offense does much to destroy any force in the argument that application of the [statute]" in circumstances such as O'Hagan's is unjust.

The Eighth Circuit erred in holding that the misappropriation theory is inconsistent with § 10(b). The Court of Appeals may address on remand O'Hagan's other challenges to his convictions under § 10(b) and Rule 10b-5.
Reversed.

CASE QUESTIONS

1. What did Mr. O'Hagan do with information obtained through his employment?

2. What does the court say the misappropriation theory is?

3. Could others have done research and obtained the same information?

4. What advice would you give to those who are employed in law and equity firms that are working on pending deals?

Running Afoul of 10(b) with Timing: When Disclosure Must Be Made

Once information becomes public knowledge, insiders and tippees are free to buy and sell the shares affected. However, the time of "public knowledge" is not always easy to determine. In *SEC v Texas Gulf Sulphur*, 401 F.2d 833 (2d Cir. 1968), some of the insiders and tippees waited to buy Texas Gulf Sulphur stock until after a press conference announcement had been made regarding a major mineral find. However, the information released at the press conference had not yet made its way out of the press conference room; not enough dissemination had yet occurred for it to be public knowledge. Those who bought by phone immediately following the announcement were found to be in violation of 10(b).

Running Afoul Using the Net: E-Commerce and Insider Trading

One trend that has emerged in stock trading is the practice of "pump and dump." This practice uses the rapid communication of the Internet to disperse information about a company so that the market price is affected. Those who have pumped the stock then sell, or dump, their shares when their efforts on the Internet have caused a sufficient jump in the price.

CYBERLAW

For example, Mark S. Jakob was dealing in call options in Emulex stock. His prediction that Emulex stock would take a dive was wrong, and the stock in fact increased in value. He had a loss of $100,000. In order to cover his losses, the 23-year-old sent an e-mail press release to an Internet wire service. The fake press release indicated that the CEO of Emulex would resign due to the fact that earnings had been overstated. The news release was then distributed to various websites. The overall loss to shareholders in reaction to the negative news was $2.5 billion as the share price plummeted. However, Mr. Jakob made $240,000 on his trades in the stock.

Mr. Jakob was arrested for securities fraud and wire fraud.[9] However, his use of the Internet resulted in significant damage to the company's stock value. The rapid dissemination of information via the Internet and the resulting damage has resulted in significant enforcement efforts against fraud committed online.

Running Afoul of 10(b): Aiders and Abettors

One area of 10(b) liability that remained unclear for almost two decades was whether those who participated with a company in disseminating false information, i.e., those who aided and abetted, could be held liable under 10(b). The U.S. Supreme Court's decision in *Stonebridge Investment Partners, LLC v Scientific-American, Inc.,* 552 U.S.148 (2008) limited the civil liability of third-party aiders and abettors to accounting manipulation and fraud. However, Dodd–Frank will expand the liability of those who participate in helping a company to overstate or understate items in financial reports that result in a rosier picture such as inflating inventory levels and valuations of accounts receivable.

In the *Stonebridge* case, the conduct of third parties helped a company appear to be in better financial condition than it really was. Scientific-Atlanta and Motorola supplied Charter Communications with the digital cable converter boxes that Charter furnished to its customers. Charter arranged to overpay these two suppliers $20 for each set top box it purchased until the end of the year, with the understanding that Scientific-Atlanta and Motorola would return the overpayment by purchasing advertising from Charter. The transactions had no economic substance; but, because Charter would then record the advertising purchases as revenue and capitalize its purchase of the boxes, in violation of generally accepted accounting principles, the transactions would enable Charter to fool its auditor into approving a financial statement that showed Charter had met projected revenue and operating cash flow numbers. So that Arthur Andersen would continue auditing in the dark and not discover or understand the link between Charter's increased payments for the boxes and the advertising purchases by Motorola and Scientific-Atlanta, the companies drafted documents to make it appear the transactions were unrelated and were just business as usual between and among friends, suppliers, and customers (although it was not entirely clear to an outsider that the two roles were being played with the same cash). Charter asked Scientific-Atlanta to send documents to Charter stating that it had increased production costs. It raised the price for boxes for the rest of 2000 by $20 per box. Charter, under a written agreement, would then purchase from Motorola a specific number of boxes and pay liquidated damages of $20 for each unit it did not take. The whole idea of the contract was to set up Charter's failure to purchase all the units and then have Charter ship the cash back by paying Motorola the liquidated damages.

To cloud the transactions for the auditor further, the new box agreements were backdated to have a different start date from the advertising agreements. The backdating was important to convey the impression that the negotiations were unconnected; this is a point auditors get testy about.

The case resulted in outrage from the investors who lost their investments because two companies participated in obfuscation that duped the auditor and resulted in a clean audit opinion that offered investors ongoing reassurance of an investment that was actually going south very quickly. The court held, correctly as the law existed at that time, that the two companies could not be held liable because they did not assist in preparing Charter's financial statements. Aiders and abettors who help create the atmosphere for deceptive financial statements but do not prepare them can now be held liable under the changes Dodd–Frank provides for that expanded liability.

For the Manager's Desk

Re: What's Ethical in Insider Trading?

Insider trading is a tough area. Consider a few examples to test how well you understand the law.

1. You are employed by Marsh, a large insurance underwriter. Marsh has been charged with antitrust violations, and the price of the company's shares has taken a beating. As you and your coworkers worry about your future, you decide to have a happy hour session at a local bar. During the discussion, a coworker says, "The stock is down now, but there's still value in the company. I am buying a bunch of shares now, while the market is down on us. I can make a killing when it all comes back, and it will." You take his words to heart and on Monday buy a large block of your company's shares. Did you violate 10b?

   __Yes __No __ Maybe __Ethical __Unethical

2. On March 6, 1973, Dirks, an investment analyst, received information from Secrist, a former officer of Equity Funding of America, that the assets of Equity Funding were vastly overstated, and that fraud was afoot at the company. After he did some checking, and employees confirmed to Dirks what he had heard, he told a number of clients and investors what he had discovered and they sold their shares. Neither Dirks nor his company had any shares in Equity Funding. Did Dirks and his clients violate 10b?

   __Yes __No __Maybe __Ethical __Unethical

3. Mark Cuban, the wealthy Internet entrepreneur and owner of the Dallas Mavericks, purchased a 6.3 percent interest in Mamma.com, Inc., a Canadian-based company.

In June 2004, Mamma.com, Inc., executives invited Cuban to participate in a private equity placement (private investment in public equity (PIPE)) for Mamma.com. Cuban was told that the offering would be made at a discount and that it would result in dilution for existing shareholders. At the end of the call, Cuban told the CEO, "Well, now I'm screwed. I can't sell."

The CEO called Cuban again and offered to let him speak with the investment adviser (Merriman) handling the private equity placement. Cuban did so and the investment adviser has described Cuban as angry. Within one minute of this conversation and within hours of his conversation with Mamma.com's CEO, Cuban called his broker and instructed him to sell Cuban's entire position in the company. Cuban instructed his broker, "Sell what you can tonight and just get me out the next day." On June 29, 2004, Cuban sold his remaining 590,000 Mamma.com shares during regular trading at an average cost per share of $13.2937. The SEC has charged Cuban with insider trading. When the offering was publicly announced, Mamma.com's stock price opened at $11.89, down $1.215 or 9.3 percent from the prior day's closing price of $13.105. According to the complaint, Cuban avoided losses in excess of $750,000 by selling his stock prior to the public announcement of the offering. Was this insider trading?

   __Yes __No __Maybe __ Ethical __Unethical

Standing to Sue Under Section 10(b)

To be able to recover under Section 10(b), a party suing must have standing. **Standing** in these cases has been defined by the U.S. Supreme Court as the actual sale or purchase of stock in reliance upon the information or lack of information given. For example, persons who would have purchased stock had they known the truth could not recover for damages under 10(b). Likewise, they cannot recover damages because they would have sold their stock had they known the truth. An actual sale or purchase must have occurred for a plaintiff to satisfy the standing requirements of 10(b). In *Blue Chip Stamp v Manor Drug Store*, 421 U.S. 723 (1975), the U.S. Supreme Court held that a pessimistic statement of income and potential was not a 10(b) violation because a potentially interested buyer who did not buy because of the pessimism did not have actual damages and, hence, no standing.

The Requirement of Scienter Under Section 10(b)

A conviction under 10(b) cannot be based on negligence—that is, the failure to discover financial information. Because 10(b) is a criminal statute, violators must have some intent to defraud or knowledge of wrongdoing, or *scienter*. Convictions are only for knowing the financial information but failing to disclose it.

In *Ernst & Ernst v Hochfelder*, 425 U.S. 185 (1978), the Supreme Court held that an accounting firm that had negligently performed an audit of a business based on a fraud could not be held liable under 10(b) because, although the accounting firm made a mistake, it had no intent to defraud.

Penalties for Running Afoul of Section 10(b)

Each time a major scandal breaks, the penalties for insider trading increase. Following Boesky's insider schemes on Wall Street, the **Insider Trading and Securities Fraud Enforcement Act of 1988,** an amendment to the 1934 act, increased substantially the penalties for violations of Section 10(b). SOX changes have more than doubled the penalties of those earlier reforms. Violations of 10(b) carry prison terms of up to 25 years plus penalties. Corporate financial officers also face the penalties already noted with regard to certification of financial statements. In addition, officers who earn bonuses and other compensation based on false financial information will be required to return those funds to the company. Further, the bankruptcy code was amended to prohibit the discharge of these debts in bankruptcy so that repayment becomes a lifetime obligation. In addition to these criminal penalties, the SEC is authorized to bring civil actions against the companies and its officers and collect civil penalties for financial reporting violations, insider trading, and other activities related to 10(b) violations.

To increase the likelihood of corporate employees coming forward with information on fraudulent financial reporting, the SEC can pay bounties in the form of a percentage of the amount recovered to informants who report violations. Sarbanes-Oxley includes protections for company whistleblowers who report violations to the SEC. These protections are similar to many antiretaliation statutes at the federal and state levels and provide the employees with a shield against termination for reporting violations. Dodd–Frank allows the SEC to increase the bounties paid to whistleblowers to up to 30% and also provides employees who are retailiated against for reporting information to the SEC a right of private action against their employers. Officers and legal counsel are also protected under this provision. The American Bar Association (ABA) amended its Model Code of Ethics to allow lawyers, without being considered in violation of their duty of client confidentiality, to report the conduct of clients who are using the lawyer's advice to commit a fraud. As noted in Chapter 20, lawyers are also required to report conduct of company officers "up the ladder" in the corporation to the board and audit committee, and the ABA changed its Model Code of Ethics to allow such reporting.

Dodd–Frank also establishes an Officer of Investor Advocate that will report to Congress and will work with a new Investor Advisory Committee whose role will be to develop protections and remedies for investors.

Insider Trading and Short-Swing Profits

In addition to the application of Section 10(b) and Rule 10b-5 to trading on inside information, the 1934 act also has a form of a strict liability statute for insider trading. Officers, directors, and 10 percent or more shareholders have greater access to inside information. They are involved in setting a corporation's policy and directions in dividend decisions, in product decisions, and in expansion decisions. They will always have access to information that is not yet available to the public. **Section 16** of the 1934 act is a *per se* liability section designed to deal with stock trading by corporate insiders, who are defined as officers, directors, and 10 percent shareholders of those companies and are required to be registered under the 1934 act.

Under 16(a), officers, directors, and 10 percent shareholders (10 percent of any class of stock) are required to file reports declaring their holdings. In addition, they must file updated reports after any change in ownership (purchase, sale, or transfer). Any changes in ownership must be reported within one day.

Under 16(b), officers, directors, and 10 percent shareholders are required to give to the corporation any **short-swing profits**—that is, profits earned on the sale and purchase or purchase and sale of stock during any six-month period. For example, suppose Director Cadigan of a listed New York Stock Exchange company engaged in the following transactions:

April 11, 2010—Ms. Cadigan buys 200 shares of her corporation's stock at $50 each.

April 30, 2010—Ms. Cadigan sells 200 shares at $30 each.

May 15, 2010—Ms. Cadigan buys 200 shares at $20 each.

The SEC will match the highest sale with the lowest purchase. Ms. Cadigan has a profit of $10 per share even though she has a net loss. This profit must be returned to the corporation. It is irrelevant whether the officer, director, or 10 percent shareholder actually used inside information: The presumption under 16(b) for short-swing trades is that the officer, director, or 10 percent shareholder had access to inside information.

These rules also apply to stock options. However, the issue of stock options and compensation has become a sensitive one following their role in the collapse of so many companies. To minimize or eliminate the incentives for making the financial picture brighter for purposes of increasing the value of stock options, some companies, such as GE and Coca-Cola, have changed their compensation plans to eliminate options and offer employees special classes of stock that have predetermined values or that are awarded only after a period of years following the release of earnings.

Regulating Voting Information

At one time, shareholders could give their proxies to the company just by endorsing the backs of their dividend checks; proxies then were obtained easily and without much disclosure. The 1934 act changed the way proxies were solicited. With the same philosophy used for registration, the SEC required full disclosure to be the goal of all **proxy solicitations.** To achieve that goal, the SEC now requires prior filing and adequate representation of shareholder interests.

The Proxy Statement
Under Section 14 of the 1934 act, all companies required to register under the act must file their proxy materials with the SEC at least 10 days before those materials are to be sent. Proxy materials include the proxy statement and all other solicitation materials that will be sent to shareholders. The proxy statement required by the SEC must contain the following details:

1. Who is soliciting the proxy

2. How the materials will be sent

3. Who is paying for the costs of soliciting

4. How much has been spent to date on the solicitation

5. How much is expected to be spent on the solicitation

6. Why the proxy is being solicited—annual meeting elections, special meeting on a merger, and so on

   Exhibit 21.4 shows a sample proxy.

EXHIBIT 21.4 Sample Proxy

P   **ARIZONA PUBLIC SERVICE COMPANY**   **PROXY CARD**
P.O. Box 53999
Phoenix, Arizona 85072-3999

R   **THIS PROXY IS SOLICITED ON BEHALF OF THE BOARD OF DIRECTORS FOR THE ANNUAL MEETING ON MAY 21, 1996.**

O   The undersigned hereby appoints O. Mark DeMichele and Nancy C. Loftin, and each of them, proxies for the undersigned, each with full power of substitution, to attend the annual meeting of shareholders of Arizona Public Service Company to be held May 21, 1996, at 10:00a.m., Phoenix time, and at any adjournment thereof, and to vote as specified in this Proxy all the shares of stock of the company which the undersigned would be entitled to vote if personally present.

X

Y   Voting with respect to the election of directors and the proposals may be indicated on the reverse of this card. Nominees for director are: O. Mark Demichele, Martha O. Hesse, Marianne Moody Jennings, Robert G. Matlock, Jaron B. Norberg, John R. Norton III, William J. Post, Donald M. Riley, Henry B. Sargent, Wilma W. Schwada, Richard Snell, Dianne C. Walker, Ben F. Williams, Jr., and Thomas G. Woods, Jr.

Your vote is important! Please sign, date, and mail promptly in the enclosed postage-paid envelope.

This proxy, when properly executed, will be voted in the manner directed herein. If no direction is made, it will be voted FOR the election of directors and FOR the proposals.

The board of Directors recommends a vote FOR the election of directors.	The board of Directors recommends a vote FOR the proposal to amend Article Sixth of the Company's Articles of Incorporation.	The board of Directors recommends a vote FOR the proposal to amend Article Fifth of the Company's Articles of Incorporation.
1. Election of Directors (see other side)	2. Proposal to amend Article Sixth of the Company's Articles of Incorporation.	3. Proposal to amend article Fifth of the Company's Articles of Incorporation.
FOR* WITHHELD ☐ ☐ *For all nominees, except withhold vote for the following: _____	FOR AGAINST ABSTAIN ☐ ☐ ☐	FOR AGAINST ABSTAIN ☐ ☐ ☐

4.   In their discretion, the proxies are to vote upon such other business as may properly come before the meeting.

_____   _____
Signature   date

_____   _____
Signature   date
Please sign as your name(s) appear to the left. Joint owners should both sign.
Fiduciaries, attorneys, corporate officers, etc., should state their capacities.

Shareholder Proposals

Because the purpose of Section 14 is full disclosure, the representation of views other than those of corporate management is important in proxy solicitations. Shareholders can submit proposals to be included in proxy solicitation materials. If the company does not oppose what is being proposed, the proposition is included as part of the proxy materials. If management is opposed, the proposing shareholder has the right to include a 200-word statement on the proposal in the materials. These proposals are not permitted along with their 200-word statements unless they propose conduct that is legal and related to business operations, as opposed to social, moral, religious, and political views. During the Vietnam era, many shareholders wanted to include proposals in proxy materials for companies that were war suppliers. Their proposals centered on the political opposition to the war and not the business practices of the company. Through 2003, shareholders focused on social issues such as human rights initiatives for companies' international operations. However, as shown in Exhibit 21.5, attention has shifted back to corporate governance proposals.

Under Dodd–Frank, the SEC must issue rules permitting shareholders to use proxy solicitation materials supplied by the company in order to distribute their proposals, something that eliminates a barrier shareholders faced in getting proposals to go forward. With this access, shareholders will be able to nominate individuals for board membership.

The focus of shareholder proposals shows a distinct shift from social and environmental issues to straight procedural and governance issues. Directors and management have also changed their approaches with shareholders, often meeting with the activists and agreeing to make changes without the need for a vote. With almost half of shareholder proposals approaching 50 percent approval, this new strategy seems to be an inevitable one.

EXHIBIT 21.5 The Top Topic Areas for Shareholder Proposals

The top shareholder proposals during the 2009–2010 annual meeting season:

Advisory vote on compensation

Right to call a special meeting

Repeal classification of directors

Review of report on company political spending

Independent board chairman

Require a majority to elect directors

Take action on climate change

End supermajority vote requirement

Retention period for stock awards

Report on sustainability

Adopt sexual orientation anti-bias policy

CONSIDER...   21.2

A shareholder for Cracker Barrel Cheese submitted for SEC approval a proposal that would require the company not to discriminate against employees who are homosexuals. Should the SEC allow the proposal?

Remedies for Violations of Section 14

If proxies are solicited without following the Section 14 guidelines, the proxies are invalid. They must then be resolicited, and if the meeting has been held in which the invalid proxies were used, the action taken at the meeting can be set aside.

Shareholder Rights in Takeovers, Mergers, and Consolidations

Definitions

Mergers.   A **merger** is a combination of two or more corporations, after which only one corporation continues to exist. If Hubbard Company and Inez Corporation decide to merge, then the newly merged corporation must be either Hubbard Company or Inez Corporation. One of the corporations ceases to exist, and the two continue under one name. If Hubbard and Inez decide to merge into Inez Corporation, then Inez will own all of Hubbard's assets and will assume all of Hubbard's liabilities. The three types of mergers are horizontal, vertical, and conglomerate.

Consolidations.   In a **consolidation,** two or more companies combine into one new company and none of the old companies continues to exist. Instead of Hubbard Company and Inez Corporation becoming Inez Corporation, under a consolidation Hubbard and Inez become Jasmine Corporation. Each company involved in the consolidation gives all its rights and liabilities to the new company, which holds all assets of the consolidating companies and assumes all their liabilities.

Tender Offers.   A **tender offer** is not a business combination; it is a method for achieving a business combination. An offer that is publicly advertised to shareholders for the purchase of their stock is a tender offer. The offering price for the stock is usually higher than the market price of the shares, which makes the tender offer attractive to the shareholders.

Originally the tender offer was used as a means for a corporation to reacquire its shares. However, it has become a tool of business combinations of every sort, sometimes friendly and sometimes hostile.

Takeovers.   **Takeovers** are accomplished through the use of tender offers and can be either friendly or hostile. A **friendly takeover** is one the management of a firm favors, whereas a **hostile takeover** is one the management of a firm opposes. Restrictions on the use of tender offers and procedures for accomplishing a takeover are discussed later in the chapter.

Acquisitions. The acquisition of another firm's assets is either a means of expanding or a way to eliminate a creditor; **asset acquisition,** however, is different from the other business combinations. Because the corporate structure does not change, shareholder approval is not required for an asset acquisition. However, asset acquisitions are subject to the constraints of the Clayton Act.

1934 Act Regulation of Takeovers

In all of these business combinations (except asset acquisitions), someone is buying enough stock to own a company. That much buying and selling has long had the attention of the SEC. The **Williams Act** amendment to the Securities Exchange Act of 1934 regulates these offers to buy stock or tender offers. The Williams Act was passed in 1968 to apply to all offers to buy more than 5 percent of a corporation's securities.

Filing Requirements Under the Williams Act. Any offeror subject to the Williams Act is required to file a tender offer statement with both the SEC and the target company. The offeror must also send or publish for shareholders of the target company all the information and details about the offer. If the target company is opposing the takeover (that is, if it is hostile), the target must also file its materials with the SEC.

A registration statement for a tender offer must include the name of the offeror, its source of funding for the offer, its plans for the company if its attempted takeover is successful, and the number of shares now owned.

Shareholders have seven days after a tender offer to withdraw their shares. This seven-day period is to prevent shareholders from being forced into a "now-or-never" transaction. The actual purchase of the shares cannot take place until at least 15 days after the tender offer began. If the offeror changes the tender offer terms, shareholders must be notified; and if a better price is offered, all shareholders must be given 10 days to tender their shares at that price (even those who have already tendered their shares at the lower price).

Williams Act Penalties for Violations. The Williams amendments provide for both civil and criminal penalties for violations of the act's procedures. The penalties are based on the same type of language used for 10(b) violations. Criminal and civil penalties are imposed for "fraudulent, deceptive or manipulative" practices used in making a tender offer. Penalties may also be assessed for omissions or misstatements of material facts in the tender offer materials.

Special Protections for the Hostile Takeover. In a noncontested takeover, the target company must declare to its shareholders one of the following within 10 days after the date the tender offer commenced:

1. That it recommends acceptance or rejection of the offer
2. That it has no opinion and remains neutral
3. That it is unable to take a position

The target company must also justify its position.

In those cases in which the target company does not want to be taken over, both the target company and the offeror develop strategies for stopping the other. Some of the tactics used by a target company to fight takeovers are:

1. Persuading shareholders that the tender offer is not in their best interests
2. Filing legal suits or complaints on the grounds that the takeover violates provisions of the antitrust laws

3. Matching the buyout with a target company offer

4. Soliciting a "white knight" merger or a merger from a friendly party

State Laws Affecting Tender Offers

The U.S. Supreme Court has held that state statutes that change the regulatory process for takeovers are violations of the Supremacy Clause (see Chapter 5). Congress has preempted the field by establishing a full regulatory scheme for takeovers under the Williams Act [*Edgar v MITE Corp.*, 457 U.S. 624 (1982)]. However, following the *MITE* case, the states passed a new type of antitakeover statute that permits shareholders to have some say in whether a corporation should be taken over.

Current shareholder proposal activity focuses on having their companies opt out of these state takeover requirements as a matter of governance so that managers can deal with takeover offers more efficiently.

Proxy Regulations and Tender Offers

Once some shares are acquired, a firm poised for a takeover wages a proxy battle, which means it solicits proxies in order to be able to command the number of votes needed to gain control of the board. Even though these proxy solicitations originate outside the company, the proxy statement and solicitation materials must be filed with the SEC.

Failure to file these materials makes the proxies invalid, and any action taken at a meeting using the proxies can be set aside. Mergers voted on with invalid proxies can be "unwound." The SEC or the shareholders can bring an action to prevent the use or undo the use of invalid proxies. If a shareholder successfully brings an action seeking a remedy for a violation of the SEC proxy solicitation rules outlined in Section 14, the offeror must fully reimburse the shareholder for all costs of the court action.

Proxies obtained by using misleading information or by not disclosing material information are also invalid. Again, either the SEC or individual shareholders can bring suit to stop the use of these proxies or to set aside action taken with them.

Ethical Issues

Joseph Horne Company, a department store in Pennsylvania, entered into an agreement to have Dillard's (a national retail chain) take it over. Dillard's performed its due diligence—the process of getting internal access to computers and records to verify financial statements. During due diligence, Dillard's assumed responsibility for ordering and shipping merchandise. Employees in Horne's management were told that they would no longer have jobs, and nearly 500 employees left Horne. Horne's Christmas merchandise was delayed and was often wrong, and the merger fell through. Horne says that Dillard's went too far. Dillard's says that due diligence is part of a takeover, that Horne's financial statements were inaccurate, and that Horne could have stopped the ordering and shipping at any time. One of the officers at Horne's bank says a Dillard's official told him that Dillard's would just wait until the company was in Chapter 11 bankruptcy and pick it up cheaply. Evaluate the ethics of both parties.

Proxy contests are expensive. Who pays for their costs? If management wins, they can be reimbursed for reasonable costs. However, some courts limit this reimbursement right to battles waged over corporate policy and not over personality conflicts. If the new group wins, they can vote to reimburse for reasonable expenses, but many states require shareholders to ratify such reimbursement.

The Foreign Corrupt Practices Act

The **Foreign Corrupt Practices Act** (FCPA) was passed in 1977 as an amendment to the 1934 Securities Exchange Act. (See Chapter 7 for more details.)

State Securities Laws

Today all states have their own securities laws. In addition to federal laws, all issuers are required to follow state **blue-sky laws** in all states in which their securities are sold. Two types of state securities laws govern registration: those that follow the SEC standards for full disclosure and those that follow a merit review standard. Under SEC standards, a filing is required, and as long as all the required information is there, the offering will be approved for public sale. Under a **merit review** standard, the regulatory agency responsible for securities enforcement can actually examine a filed offering for its merits as to adequate capitalization, excessive stock ownership by the promoters, and penny-stock problems. These agencies apply a general standard that the offering must be "fair, just, and equitable." This general standard gives them great latitude in deciding which issues will be approved.

Many companies do not register their offerings in states that conduct merit review. They sell in the other states to avoid the problems of being denied registration.

As on the federal level, all states have their own exemptions from registration. Most SEC exemptions also work at the state level, the only requirement being that the issuer file a notice of sale with the state agency.

In addition to regulating securities offerings, these state agencies also control the licensing of brokers and agents of securities within the state. The licensing

Ethical Issues

Iroquois Brands, Ltd., is a food company that imports French foie gras, a pâté made from the enlarged livers of force-fed geese. There is a French practice in raising the geese of funneling corn down the geese's throats and gagging them with rubber bands to keep them from regurgitating. A shareholder wishes to include in the proxy materials a proposal that the company study this method of force-feeding as an unethical business practice (cruelty to animals). Should the proposal be included? Does Section 14 require that it be included? [*Lovenheim v Iroquois Brands, Ltd.*, 618 F. Supp. 554 (D.C. 1985)]

EXHIBIT 21.6 State and Federal Securities Law

1933 ACT	1934 ACT	BLUE SKY
S1—Registration statement	*Application*	State securities registration
Financial information	500 or more shareholders with	Merit vs. disclosure standards
Officers/directors	$5 million or more in assets	Federally exempt securities may still
Prospectus 20-day effective date, deficiency letter	or listed on national exchange Sec. 10b—insider trading/fraud	need to register at state level
Section 11—Filing false registration statement	*10K*	
	Annual reports	
Liability: Anyone named in prospectus or offering expert materials for it	*10Q*	
	Quarterly report	
Material, false statement; privity not required unless longer than one year	*Foreign Corrupt Practices Act*	
	Financial reports	
	Internal controls	
Defenses; due diligence; buyer's knowledge	Applies to 1933 and 1934 act registrants	
Section 12—Failure to file; selling before effective date; False prospectus	*Section 14*	
	Proxy registration	
	·Compensation disclosure	
Materials; false statement; privity required	*Section 16A*	
Defenses; due diligence; buyer's knowledge	Officers, directors, 10% shareholders	
Penalties	Sales registration	
$100,000 and/or five years (criminal/civil suit)	*Section 16B—Short-swing profits*	
	Tender offer regulations (Williams Act)	
	Penalties—up to 25 years	
	Separate financial certification penalties under Sarbanes-Oxley	

process consists of an application and a background check conducted by the agency to identify possible criminal problems.

Exhibit 21.6 provides a summary of securities regulation under state and federal law.

International Issues in Securities Laws

The following policy statement from the State Department summarizes the nature of international capital markets today: "The United States Government is committed to an international system which provides for a high degree of freedom in the movement of trade and investment flows."

The United States has 10 stock exchanges; Germany, 8; France, 7; and Switzerland, 7. The United Kingdom, Japan, Canada, the Netherlands, Belgium,

Luxembourg, Norway, Kuwait, Australia, and many other countries have at least one stock exchange each.

A directive from the European Union has developed uniform requirements for disclosure in primary offering. Often called a "listing of particulars" instead of a "prospectus," uniform information is given to shareholders prior to their purchases. One difficulty that must be resolved is that accounting practices outside the United States are not uniform. Insider trading has been prosecuted vigorously in the United States for the past 30 years. European enforcement has been limited. In addition to the lack of enforcement, little regulatory structure for investigation and prosecution is in place.

B I O G R A P H Y

Bernie Madoff: The Largest and Longest Ponzi Scheme in History ($50 Billion and 18 years)

It is a remarkable story, that of Madoff (pronounced MADE-off) Securities. An entrepreneur from his early years, Bernie Madoff, the founder of Madoff Investments, Inc, worked his way through college as a part-time lifeguard who also ran his own lawn sprinkler system company. He installed and repaired lawn sprinkler systems in the mornings and went to class in the afternoons. He graduated from Hofstra University and then went on to Brooklyn Law School, again running his business in the morning and going to classes in the afternoon. Because he was not really interested in practicing law, he left law school after the first year and, using $5,000 he had saved from his business, bought a trader position on Wall Street. He had grown up familiar with stocks, bonds, and trading because his mother had operated a small securities trading firm when Bernie was younger. She had even been investigated by the SEC, but when she withdrew her registration as a trader, the SEC withdrew its investigation.

From the time he began his Wall Street career until his arrest, Bernie was on an upward swing. Over decades he delivered 12–18 percent returns to his investors. He was the investment firm for the rich and famous. Kevin Bacon, Kyra Sedgwick, Steven Spielberg, and others from the wealthiest sets in New York City and Palm Beach were clients of Madoff Securities. He was one of the founders of NASDAQ and served as chairman of its board in its early years. He spent a great deal of time in Washington, D.C., testifying at Congressional hearings and meeting with regulators on markets, regulations, and trading issues.

Madoff and his wife were kind to employees, generous to charities, and active with colleges and universities, donating money to Hofstra, Brooklyn University, and Yeshiva University. They were also known for their wealth and spending.

Some have said the scheme began in the 1980s, but Madoff said in court that he believes it began in the 1990s. Mr. Madoff put clients' money in a Chase Manhattan bank account and then used the money to pay individual investors, trust funds, charitable organizations and others as they requested withdrawals from their accounts. He said he did not promise a specific rate of return, but his clients expected that he would outperform the market, so he concocted a bogus investment strategy that he then used to recruit new clients. Mr. Madoff was adamant in insisting that his other businesses, including a stock trading company with offices in New York and London, which were run by his sons and his brother, were not connected to his Ponzi scheme, "The other businesses my firm engaged in, proprietary trading and market-making, were legitimate, profitable, and successful in all respects. Those businesses were managed by my brother and two sons."[10]

In order to keep the funds flowing, he was dependent upon the classic Ponzi scheme model: getting more investors in with additional money, which is critical to keeping the earlier investors satisfied. However, there comes a point when there are not enough new recruits to satisfy the existing participants and the fund collapses under even just the daily demands for payouts, let alone the draw-downs that can come from fears in a bull market.

CONTINUED

The scheme was uncovered by federal investigators in December 2008, and Mr. Madoff entered a guilty plea to criminal charges of securities fraud, wire fraud, conspiracy, and other crimes and was sentenced to 150 years in prison. When he entered his guilty plea, Mr. Madoff told the packed courtroom,

> *"I am actually grateful for this opportunity to publicly speak about my crimes, for which I am so deeply sorry and ashamed. I knew what I was doing was wrong, indeed, criminal. When I began the Ponzi scheme, I believed it would end shortly and I would be able to extricate myself and my clients. [Finding an exit] proved difficult and ultimately impossible. As the years went by I realized this day, and my arrest, would inevitably come.*

> *I am painfully aware that I have deeply hurt many, many people, including members of my family, my closest friends, business associates and the thousands of clients who gave me their money. I cannot adequately express how sorry I am for what I have done."*[11]

The psychology of Madoff, like that of all diabolical Ponzi schemers, is fascinating. One of his best friends, for whom Mr. Madoff served as best man, was asked to explain why Bernie would engage in such behavior and not understand the consequences of the huge fraud, "There is no way to. I can't make it add up. It doesn't make sense. I cannot take the Bernie I knew and turn him into the Bernie we're hearing about 24/7. It doesn't compute."[12]

Summary

What requirements affect primary offerings?

- Primary offering—sale of securities by the business in which interests are offered
- Security—investment in a common enterprise with profits to come from efforts of others

Why do we have securities laws, and what is their history?

- Securities Act of 1933—federal law regulating initial sales of securities
- Securities Act of 1934—federal law regulating securities and companies in the secondary market
- Amendments include SOX and PSLRA

How do securities laws regulate the primary market?

- Blue-sky laws—state securities registration regulations
- Merit review—regulation of merits of an offering as opposed to disclosure
- *Howey* test—Supreme Court definition of security
- SEC—federal agency responsible for enforcing federal securities laws
- Exemption—security not required to be registered
- Exempt transaction—offering not required to be registered
- Regulation D—small offering exemption rules
- Accredited investor—investor who meets threshold standards for assets and income

- Rules 504, 505, 506—portion of Regulation D affording exemptions for variously structured offerings
- Registration statement—disclosure statement filed by the offeror with the SEC
- Prospectus—formal document explaining offering or any ad or written materials describing offering
- Comment letter—request by SEC for more information
- Deficiency letter—request by SEC for more information
- Full-disclosure standard—review for information, not a review on the merits
- Tombstone ad—ad announcing offering that can be run prior to effective date of registration statement
- Red herring prospectus—redlined prospectus that can be given to potential purchasers prior to effective date of registration statement
- Shelf registrations—SEC approval process that allows approval and then waiting period for market conditions
- Material misstatement—false information that would affect the decision to buy or sell
- Section 11—portion of 1933 act that provides for liability for false statements or omissions in registration statements

- Due diligence—defense of good faith and full effort to Section 11 charges
- Section 12—portion of 1933 act that provides for liability for selling without registration or exemption before effective date or with a false prospectus
- SOX numerous protections on certifications and disclosures

How do securities laws regulate the secondary market?

- 10-Q—periodic reporting forms required of 1934 act companies
- SOX and certification of financial reports by CEO and CFO
- 10-K—periodic reporting forms required of 1934 act companies
- 8-K—periodic reporting forms required of 1934 act companies
- Section 10(b)—antifraud provision of Securities Exchange Act
- Rule 10b-5—SEC regulation on antifraud provision of Securities Exchange Act
- Insider—person with access to nonpublic information about a company

- Tippee—person who gains nonpublic information from an insider
- Fair Disclosure Rule—SEC regulation on disclosure to analysts
- Insider Trading and Securities Fraud Enforcement Act of 1988—federal law increasing penalties for insider trading violations
- Section 16—portion of 1934 act regulating short-swing profits by officers, directors, or 10 percent shareholders
- Short-swing profits—gain on sale and purchase or purchase and sale of securities within a six-month period
- Proxy solicitations—formal paperwork requesting authority to vote on behalf of another

How do securities laws protect shareholders in share and company acquisitions?

- Mergers, consolidations, tender offers, and asset acquisitions are regulated
- Williams Act regulates tender offers
- States have antitakeover statutes

Questions and Problems

1. The Farmer's Cooperative of Arkansas (Co-Op) was an agricultural cooperative that had approximately 23,000 members. In order to raise money to support its general business operations, the Co-Op sold promissory notes payable on demand by the holder. The notes were uncollateralized and uninsured and paid a variable rate of interest that was adjusted to make it higher than the rate paid by local financial institutions. The notes were offered to members and nonmembers and were marketed as an "investment program." Advertisements for the notes, which appeared in the Co-Op newsletter, read in part: "YOUR CO-OP has more than $11,000,000 in assets to stand behind your investments. The Investment is not Federal [*sic*] insured but it is . . . Safe."

Despite the assurance, the Co-Op filed for bankruptcy in 1984. At the time of the bankruptcy filing, over 1,600 people held notes worth a total of $10 million.

After the bankruptcy filing, a class of note holders filed suit against Arthur Young & Co., alleging that Young had failed to follow generally accepted accounting principles in its audit, specifically with respect to the valuation of the Co-Op's major asset, a gasohol plant. The note holders claimed that if Young had properly treated the plant in its audited financials, they would

not have purchased the notes. The petitioners were awarded $6.1 million in damages by the federal district court. Are the notes securities? [*Reves v Ernst & Young*, 494 U.S. 56 (1990)]

2. In August 1994, Mervyn Cooper, a psychotherapist, was providing marriage counseling to a Lockheed executive. The executive had been assigned to conduct the due diligence (review of the accuracy of the books and records) of Martin Marietta, a company with which Lockheed was going to merge.

At his August 22, 1994, session with Mr. Cooper, the executive revealed to him the pending, but nonpublic, merger. Following his session with the executive, Mr. Cooper contacted a friend, Kenneth Rottenberg, and told him about the pending merger. They agreed that Mr. Rottenberg would open a brokerage account so they could buy Lockheed call options and common stocks and then share in the profits.

When Mr. Rottenberg went to some brokerage offices to set up an account, he was warned by a broker about the risks of call options. Mr. Rottenberg told the broker that Lockheed would announce a major business combination shortly and that he would not lose his money.

Did Mr. Rottenberg and Mr. Cooper violate Section 10(b)? What about the broker? [*SEC v Mervyn Cooper and Kenneth E. Rottenberg,* No. 95-8535 (C.D. Cal. 1995)]

3. Rollo Norton II, a.k.a. Rick, a financial planner, worked diligently for a number of years to try to keep a San Diego condo project afloat during a real estate downturn. He has confessed to forging signatures, faking loan applications, kiting checks intended for deposit in escrow accounts, and using credit of buyers to borrow money to keep his project going. He and two associates entered guilty pleas and are cooperating with federal authorities in their ongoing investigation of the project.

Fidelity National Financial, which is the largest title insurance company in the United States, was the title insurer for most of the buyers in the project. The project began to unwind in 2006 when several buyer victims filed suit and the architect for the project entered a guilty plea to fraud. However, Fidelity did not disclose the suits, suits that increased from 2006 until October 2009 when the fraud issues emerged. There is no mention in any of the company's 8-K, 10-Q, or 10-K filings about the developments in the project, the litigation, or the guilty pleas.

When Fidelity shareholders filed suit against the company for violations of 10b, company expert witnesses maintained that disclosure when there is uncertainty can harm the company's share price and result in unnecessary losses.

Should there have been disclosure? Of what, how much, and when?

4. Steve Hindi is an animal rights activist who owns $5,000 in Pepsi stock. He discovered that Pepsi advertises in bull rings in Spain and Mexico, and he has attended annual shareholder meetings and put forward shareholder proposals to have the company halt the practice. His proposal did not pass, but he did not give up easily and started a website to increase pressure on the company. (See http://www.sharkonline.org for an article containing more details regarding this issue.)

Pepsi has withdrawn bullfighting ads in Mexico but continues with them in Spain. Mr. Hindi continues his quest. Should the proposal have been approved? Does Mr. Hindi run any risk with his website activism?

5. Beginning in March 1981, R. Foster Winans was a *Wall Street Journal* reporter and one of the writers of the "Heard on the Street" column (the "Heard" column), a widely read and influential column in the *Journal*. David Carpenter worked as a news clerk at the *Journal* from December 1981 through May 1983. Kenneth Felis, who was a stockbroker at the brokerage house of Kidder Peabody, had been brought to that firm by another Kidder Peabody stockbroker, Peter Brant, Mr. Felis's longtime friend, who later became the government's key witness in this case.

Since February 2, 1981, it had been the practice of Dow Jones, the parent company of the *Wall Street Journal*, to distribute to all new employees "The Insider Story," a 40-page manual with 7 pages devoted to the company's conflicts-of-interest policy. Mr. Winans and Mr. Carpenter knew that company policy deemed all news material gleaned by an employee during the course of employment to be company property and that company policy required employees to treat nonpublic information learned on the job as confidential.

Notwithstanding company policy, Mr. Winans participated in a scheme with Mr. Brant, and later Mr. Felis and Mr. Carpenter, in which he agreed to provide the two stockbrokers (Mr. Brant and Mr. Felis) with securities-related information that was scheduled to appear in "Heard" columns; based on this advance information, the two brokers would buy or sell the subject securities. Mr. Carpenter, who was involved in a private, personal, nonbusiness relationship with Mr. Winans, served primarily as a messenger for the conspirators. Trading accounts were established in the names of Kenneth Felis, David Carpenter, R. Foster Winans, Peter Brant, David Clark, Western Hemisphere, and Stephen Spratt. During 1983 and early 1984, these defendants made prepublication trades on the basis of their advance knowledge of approximately 27 *Wall Street Journal* "Heard" columns, although not all of those columns were written by Mr. Winans. Generally, he would inform Mr. Brant of an article's subject the day before its scheduled publication, usually by calls from a pay phone and often using a fictitious name. The net profits from the scheme approached $690,000. Was this scheme a 10(b) violation? [*United States v Carpenter,* 791 F.2d 1024 (2d Cir. 1986); *affirmed, Carpenter v United States,* 484 U.S. 19 (1987)]

6. Following the collapse of the World Trade Center (WTC) in New York City on September 11, 2001, the stock markets were closed for several days. When the stock markets reopened on Monday, September 17, 2001, there was unusual activity in stocks that were hit the hardest by the attacks and subsequent shut-down of the United States' airline industry: airlines and insurance. Investors based in Europe has purchased puts in airline and insurance companies with the expectation of earning returns based on the fall in these companies' share prices.

Puts work as follows: A company sells 1,000,000 put options on its stock (trading at $100 per share) exercisable at $100 within a month or two months or one year. Investors buy the puts at $10 a share. Company pockets $10,000,000 in cash.

When the put date arrives: If the stock price is $100 or more, the puts expire worthless. Company A has made $10,000,000. If the stock price drops to $50, the investor can buy shares at $50 and exercise the puts. Company A must buy back the shares at $100. The company loses $50 million less its $10 million for a net loss of $40 million.

In the case of the WTC disaster, someone with advance knowledge of the attacks, by buying puts, bet that the stocks of these companies would go down. They were correct, and the SEC placed a hold on the payments to the put holders as investigators looked into trading on inside information and tracing the links of those who bought the puts. Would advance knowledge of the attacks be a form of inside information? Would buying with that advance knowledge be a violation of 10(b)? What about the fact that they were foreign investors?

7. Vincent Chiarella was employed as a printer in a financial printing firm that handled the printing for takeover bids. Although the firm names were left out of the financial materials and inserted at the last moment, Mr. Chiarella was able to deduce who was being taken over and by whom from other information in the reports being printed. Using this information, Mr. Chiarella was able to dabble in the stock market over a 14-month period for a net gain of $30,000. After an SEC investigation, he signed a consent decree that required him to return all of his profits to the sellers he purchased from during that 14-month period. He was then indicted for violation of 10(b) of the 1934 act and the SEC's Rule 10b-5. Did Mr. Chiarella violate 10b-5? [*Chiarella v United States*, 445 U.S. 222 (1980)]

8. The president's letter in Rockwood Computer Corporation's annual report stated that most of its inventory consisted of its old computer series. The letter suggested that its new series would cost more money for all users. However, the letter did not disclose, although evidence had indicated, that the new system might be less expensive for those who needed greater performance and capacity. Walter Beissinger (who sold his shares based on the information) brought suit under 10(b). Rockwood claims the statements were based on opinions of sales and were not statements of fact. Who should win? [*Beissinger v Rockwood Computer Corp.*, 529 F. Supp. 770 (E.D. Pa. 1981)]

9. William H. Sullivan, Jr., gained control of the New England Patriots Football Club (Patriots) by forming a separate corporation (New Patriots) and merging it with the old one. Plaintiffs are a class of stockholders who voted to accept New Patriots' offer of $15 a share for their common stock in the Patriots' corporation. They now claim that they were induced to accept this offer by a misleading proxy statement drafted under the direction of Mr. Sullivan, who owned a controlling share in the voting stock of the Patriots at the time of the merger. The proxy statement, plaintiffs claim, contained various misrepresentations designed to paint a gloomy picture of the financial position and prospects of the Patriots, so that the shareholders undervalued their stock. They seek to rescind the merger or to receive a higher price per share for the stock they sold. Does the court have the authority to rescind under Section 14? [*Pavlidis v New England Patriots Football Club*, 737 F.2d 1227 (1st Cir. 1984)]

10. The National Bank of Yugoslavia placed $71 million with Drexel Burnham Lambert, Inc., for short-term investment just months before Drexel's bankruptcy. In effect, the bank made a time deposit. Would the bank be able to proceed under a theory of securities laws violations? Would these time deposits be considered securities? [*National Bank of Yugoslavia v Drexel Burnham Lambert, Inc.*, 768 F.Supp. 1010 (S.D.N.Y 1991)]

Ethics, Public Policy, and the Law

Goldman Sachs: The Gold (?) Standard of Wall Street

Goldman Sachs was founded in 1869 as an originator and a clearinghouse for commercial paper. Marcus Goldman, a German immigrant, founded the company along with his son-in-law, Samuel Sachs. But the stodgy negotiable instruments market proved insufficient as the firm drifted from its founders' influence and its basic roots in tangible one-on-one business loans to more complex and sophisticated financial instruments.

In 1999, the same year Goldman itself went public, Goldman underwrote 47 companies. The 1990s investors did not know that the standard underwriting practice of requiring that a company show three years of profitability before being taken public was no longer enforced. That profitability standard had been slowly eased back to one year and then to one quarter. In fact, some Internet IPOs that Goldman underwrote had not yet seen any profits and their business plans indicated that profits were not on the immediate horizon.

In addition, Goldman engaged in laddering in the 1990s. Goldman and its best clients arranged for the allocation of a certain portion of an IPO at a pre-established price. However, those clients also had to agree to purchase a certain number of shares later during the IPO rollout at $10–$15 higher. Laddering

CONTINUED

is a trick, a sort of insider scam by the underwriter and its favored clients. The underwriter locks precommitted buyers into a price above the initial price and the shares of the IPO are guaranteed to rise. Goldman knows the fixed hand, but those in the market who are evaluating the IPO do not know that the increase in price is not due to legitimate demand for the company's shares.

For example, in 2000, Goldman was the underwriter for eToys, whose stock was priced for the IPO at $20. Goldman had laddered the shares and the price climbed to $75 per share by the end of the first day. By March 2001, eToys was in bankruptcy. Then–Goldman Chairman Hank Paulson condemned the practice when the firm received its SEC Wells notice for laddering, but denied any charges of securities fraud. Goldman settled the SEC charges of laddering by agreeing to pay a $40 million fine.[13]

In the 2000s, Goldman was a big player in mortgage-backed securities such as collateralized debt obligations (CDOs). Goldman made recommendations to clients to purchase CDOs as it was pushing to have the instruments rated high even as it was positioning itself short on the instruments. Positioning short means that Goldman stood to make money when the value of the CDOs declined. Internal e-mails at Goldman found the investment banker referring to CDO securities as "junk," "s____," or "crappy."[14] When Goldman executives were asked at a congressional hearing about their internal negative characterizations of securities the firm was touting and selling to its clients, Goldman executive David Viniar responded, "I think that's very unfortunate to have on e-mail." When his response elicited laughter in the hearing room, Mr. Viniar changed his answer to, "It's very unfortunate to have said that in any form."[15]

When the real estate market declined rapidly, the value of the CDOs plummeted to junk levels. Goldman received $10 billion from the U.S. government as a bailout. In addition, the government had to bail out AIG, the insurer Goldman had used for its hedges against the CDO market.

Goldman's 2009 annual revenues topped $13 billion, with first-quarter earnings for 2010 of $3.2 billion showing it on track for a repeat. The company has 32,000 employees worldwide and takes no new clients unless they have a minimum of $10 million to invest. The company has several management mantras. One is "long-term greedy," which Goldman executives translate to mean "don't kill the marketplace,"[16] and the other is "filthy rich by 40," a motivator for young people.

The SEC filed a civil action against Goldman for its conduct in ABACUS, a CDO deal. According to the complaint, 31-year-old Goldman employee Fabrice Tourre put together a deal of CDOs with the mortgage pool handpicked by John Paulson, a financial wizard who planned to position himself short on the securities Goldman would sell to its clients. The SEC complaint shows that Paulson chose mortgage pools that were dogs, i.e., "crappy." Those mortgages were chosen because these securities "tanking" was important to Goldman and Paulson due to their positions on the mortgage instrument markets.

Goldman's position is that the clients who purchased the instruments were "qualified" or "sophisticated" investors and had a sufficient level of knowledge of markets to understand and process the risk and realize that all investment bankers are positioned in the market according to their theories on risk.

Goldman's activities have been described as "Heads Goldman wins, tails you lose."[17] And "Every game has a sucker, and in this case, the sucker was not so much AIG as it was the U.S. government and the taxpayer."[18] Goldman CEO Lloyd Blankfein defended his firm's conduct in November 2009 in an interview with the *London Times* by stating that he was just a banker "doing God's work."[19]

Discussion Questions

1. What are the results when companies create a business model based on loopholes and interpretations of the law?

2. Evaluate Goldman's ethics on the role it believed it played with its clients.

Notes

1. John Arlidge, "I'm Doing 'God's Work.' Meet Mr. Goldman Sachs," *London Times* interview, *The Sunday Times*, November 8, 2009, p. 1.

2. "Ahold Ex-Official Sentenced," *New York Times*, May 18, 2007, p. C2.

3. Dodd–Frank requires the SEC to review the definition of an "accredited investor" at least once every four years to be certain that the exemption is not including those who need further disclosures and protections from securities sales not subject to full registration. The Government Accounting Office (GAO) must conduct a study every three years to determine whether the private investment thresholds are appropriate for necessary protections.

4. Under Dodd–Frank, the amount of $1,000,000 must be reviewed by the SEC each year to determine whether the amount provides the necessary protection given economic and market conditions.

5. Peat, Marwick, Mitchell was one of the Big 8 accounting firms that existed during the 1960s and 1970s. These firms did all the audits on publicly traded companies. During the 1980s, the firms merged down to the Big 5. With the demise of Andersen following Enron, the Big 4 accounting firms remain.

6. Susanne Craig, "Goldman's Trading Trips Reward Its Biggest Clients," *Wall Street Journal*, August 24, 2009, p. A1.

7. Andrew Ross Sorkin, "At Goldman, E-Mail Message Lays Bare Conflicts in Trading," *New York Times*, January 13, 2010, p. B1.

8. Ashlee Vance and Zachery Kouwe, "Inquiry of Hedge Fund Halted in '02," *New York Times*, Dec. 5, 2009, p. B3.

9. Alex Berenson, "Man Charged in Stock Fraud Based on Fake News," *New York Times*, September 1, 2000, pp. C1, C2.

10. Joanna Chung and Brooke Masters, "Madoff Says He Acted Alone," *Financial Times*," March 13, 2009, pp. 1 and 7.

11. Diana Henriques and Jack Healy, "Madoff Jailed After Pleading Guilty to Fraud," *New York Times*, March 13, 2009, p. A1; Robert Frank, Amil Efrati, Aaron Luchetti, and Chad Bray, "Madoff Jailed After Admitting Epic Swindle," *Wall Street Journal*, March 13, 2009, p. A1.

12. Julie Creswell and Landon Thomas, Sr., "The Talented Mr. Madoff," *New York Times*, January 25, 2009, pp. SB1.

13. *SEC v Goldman Sachs*, http://www.sec.gov/litigation/complaints/comp19051.pdf. January 25, 2005. Settlement at http://www.sec.gov/litigation/litreleases/lr19051.htm.

14. Michael M. Phillips, "Senators Seek, Fail to Get an 'I'm Sorry,'" *Wall Street Journal*, April 28, 2010, p. A3, A5.

15. *Id.* at A5.

16. *Id.* at A6.

17. Robert Farzad and Paula Dwyer, "Not Guilty, Not One Little Bit," *BusinessWeek*, April 12, 2010, p. 31.

18. *Id.* at 32.

19. John Arlidge, "I'm Doing 'God's Work.' Meet Mr. Goldman Sachs," *London Times* interview, *The Sunday Times*, November 8, 2009, p. 1.

Appendix A

The United States Constitution

We the People of the United States, in Order to form a more perfect Union, establish Justice, insure domestic Tranquility, provide for the common defence, promote the general Welfare, and secure the Blessings of Liberty to ourselves and our Posterity, do ordain and establish this Constitution for the United States of America.

ARTICLE I

Section 1

All legislative Powers herein granted shall be vested in a Congress of the United States, which shall consist of a Senate and House of Representatives.

Section 2

The House of Representatives shall be composed of Members chosen every second Year by the People of the several States, and the Electors in each State shall have the Qualifications requisite for Electors of the most numerous Branch of the State Legislature.

No Person shall be a Representative who shall not have attained to the Age of twenty five Years, and been seven Years a Citizen of the United States, and who shall not, when elected, be an Inhabitant of that State in which he shall be chosen.

Representatives and direct Taxes shall be apportioned among the several States which may be included within this Union, according to their respective Numbers, which shall be determined by adding to the whole Number of free Persons, including those bound to Service for a Term of Years, and excluding Indians not taxed, three fifths of all other Persons. The actual Enumeration shall be made within three Years after the first Meeting of the Congress of the United States, and within every subsequent Term of ten Years, in which Manner as they shall by Law direct. The Number of Representatives shall not exceed one for every thirty Thousand, but each State shall have at Least one Representative; and until such enumeration shall be made, the State of New Hampshire shall be entitled to choose three,

Massachusetts eight, Rhode Island and Providence Plantations one, Connecticut five, New York six, New Jersey four, Pennsylvania eight, Delaware one, Maryland six, Virginia ten, North Carolina five, South Carolina five, and Georgia three.

When vacancies happen in the Representation from any State, the Executive Authority thereof shall issue Writs of Election to fill such Vacancies.

The House of Representatives shall chuse their Speaker and other Officers; and shall have the sole Power of Impeachment.

Section 3

The Senate of the United States shall be composed of two Senators from each State, chosen by the Legislature thereof, for six Years; and each Senator shall have one Vote.

Immediately after they shall be assembled in Consequence of the first Election, they shall be divided as equally as may be into three Classes. The Seats of the Senators of the first Class shall be vacated at the Expiration of the second Year, of the second Class at the Expiration of the fourth Year, and of the third Class at the Expiration of the sixth Year, so that one third may be chosen every second Year; and if Vacancies happen by Resignation, or otherwise, during the Recess of the Legislature of any State, the Executive thereof may make temporary Appointments until the next Meeting of the Legislature, which shall then fill such Vacancies.

No Person shall be a Senator who shall not have attained to the Age of thirty Years, and been nine Years a Citizen of the United States, and who shall not, when elected, be an Inhabitant of that State for which he shall be chosen.

The Vice President of the United States shall be President of the Senate, but shall have no Vote, unless they be equally divided.

The Senate shall chuse their other Officers, and also a President pro tempore, in the Absence of the Vice President, or when he shall exercise the Office of President of the United States.

The Senate shall have the sole Power to try all Impeachments. When sitting for that Purpose, they shall be on Oath or Affirmation. When the President of the United States is tried the Chief Justice shall preside: And no Person shall be convicted without the Concurrence of two thirds of the Members present.

Judgment in Cases of Impeachment shall not extend further than to removal from Office, and disqualification to hold and enjoy any Office of honor, Trust or Profit under the United States: but the Party convicted shall nevertheless be liable and subject to Indictment, Trial, Judgment and Punishment, according to Law.

Section 4

The Times, Places and Manner of holding Elections for Senators and Representatives, shall be prescribed in each State by the Legislature thereof; but the Congress may at any time by Law make or alter such Regulations, except as to the Places of chusing Senators.

The Congress shall assemble at Least once in every Year, and such Meeting shall be on the first Monday in December, unless they shall by Law appoint a different Day.

Section 5

Each House shall be the Judge of the Elections, Returns and Qualifications of its own Members, and a Majority of each shall constitute a Quorum to do Business; but a smaller Number may adjourn from day to day, and may be authorized to compel the Attendance of absent Members, in such Manner, and under such Penalties as each House may provide.

Each House may determine the Rules in its Proceedings, punish its Members for disorderly Behaviour, and, with the Concurrence of two thirds, expel a Member.

Each House shall keep a Journal of its Proceedings, and from time to time publish the same, excepting such Parts as may in their Judgment require Secrecy; and the Yeas and Nays of the Members of either House on any question shall, at the Desire of one fifth of those Present, be entered on the Journal.

Neither House, during the Session of Congress, shall, without the Consent of the other, adjourn for more than three days, nor to any other Place than that in which the two Houses shall be sitting.

Section 6

The Senators and Representatives shall receive a Compensation for their Services, to be ascertained by Law, and paid out of the Treasury of the United States. They shall in all Cases, except Treason, Felony and Breach of the Peace, be privileged from Arrest during their Attendance at the Session of their respective Houses, and in going to and returning from the same; and for any Speech or Debate in either House, they shall not be questioned in any other Place.

No Senator or Representative shall, during the Time for which he was elected, be appointed to any civil Office under the Authority of the United States, which shall have been created, or the Emoluments whereof shall have been encreased during such time; and no Person holding any Office under the United States, shall be a Member of either House during his Continuance in Office.

Section 7

All Bills for raising Revenue shall originate in the House of Representatives; but the Senate may propose or concur with amendments as on other Bills.

Every Bill which shall have passed the House of Representatives and the Senate, shall, before it become a Law, be presented to the President of the United States; If he approve he shall sign it, but if not he shall return it, with his Objections to that House in which it shall have originated, who shall enter the Objections at large on their Journal, and proceed to reconsider it. If after such Reconsideration two thirds of that House shall agree to pass the Bill, it shall be sent, together with the Objections, to the other House, by which it shall like wise be reconsidered, and if approved by two thirds of that House, it shall become a Law. But in all such Cases the Votes of both Houses shall be determined by Yeas and Nays, and the names of the Persons voting for and against the Bill shall be entered on the Journal of each House respectively. If any Bill shall not be returned by the President within ten Days (Sundays excepted) after it shall have been presented to him, the Same shall be a Law, in like Manner as if he had signed it, unless the Congress by their Adjournment prevent its Return, in which Case it shall not be a Law.

Every Order, Resolution, or Vote to which the Concurrence of the Senate and House of Representatives may be necessary (except on a question of Adjournment) shall be presented to the President of the United States; and before the Same shall take

Effect, shall be approved by him, or being disapproved by him, shall be repassed by two thirds of the Senate and House of Representatives, according to the Rules and Limitations prescribed in the Case of a Bill.

Section 8

The Congress shall have Power To lay and collect Taxes, Duties, Imposts and Excises, to pay the Debts and provide for the common Defense and general Welfare of the United States; but all Duties, Imposts and Excises shall be uniform throughout the United States;

To borrow Money on the credit of the United States;

To regulate Commerce with foreign Nations, and among the several States, and with the Indian Tribes;

To establish an uniform Rule of Naturalization, and uniform Laws on the subject of Bankruptcies throughout the United States;

To coin Money, regulate the Value thereof, and of foreign Coin, and fix the Standard of Weights and Measures;

To provide for the Punishment of counterfeiting the Securities and current Coin of the United States;

To establish Post Offices and post Roads;

To promote the Progress of Science and useful Arts, by securing for limited Times to Authors and Inventors the exclusive Right to their respective Writings and Discoveries;

To constitute Tribunals inferior to the supreme Court;

To define and punish Piracies and Felonies committed on the high Seas, and Offenses against the Law of Nations;

To declare War, grant Letters of Marque and Reprisal, and make Rules concerning Captures on Land and Water;

To raise and support Armies, but no Appropriation of Money to that Use shall be for a longer Term than two Years;

To provide and maintain a Navy;

To make Rules for the Government and Regulation of the land and naval Forces;

To provide for calling forth the Militia to execute the Laws of the Union, suppress Insurrections and repel Invasions;

To provide for organizing, arming, and disciplining, the Militia, and for governing such Part of them as may be employed in the Service of the United States, reserving to the States respectively, the Appointment of the Officers, and the Authority of training the Militia according to the discipline prescribed by Congress;

To exercise exclusive Legislation in all Cases whatsoever, over such District (not exceeding ten Miles square) as may, by Cession of particular States, and the Acceptance of Congress, become the Seat of the Government of the United States, and to exercise like Authority over all Places purchased by the Consent of the Legislature of the State in which the Same shall be, for the Erection of Forts, Magazines, Arsenals, dock-Yards, and other needful Buildings;—And

To make all Laws which shall be necessary and proper for carrying into Execution the foregoing Powers, and all other Powers vested by this Constitution in the Government of the United States, or in any Department or Officer thereof.

Section 9

The Migration or Importation of such Persons as any of the States now existing shall think proper to admit, shall not be prohibited by the Congress prior to the Year one thousand eight hundred and eight, but a Tax or duty may be imposed on such Importation, not exceeding ten dollars for each Person.

The Privilege of the Writ of Habeas Corpus shall not be suspended, unless when in Cases of Rebellion or Invasion the public Safety may require it.

No Bill of Attainder or ex post facto Law shall be passed.

No Capitation, or other direct, Tax shall be laid, unless in Proportion to the Census or Enumeration herein before directed to be taken.

No Tax or Duty shall be laid on Articles exported from any State.

No Preference shall be given to any Regulation of Commerce or Revenue to the Ports of one State over those of another; nor shall Vessels bound to, or from, one State, be obliged to enter, clear or pay Duties in another.

No Money shall be drawn from the Treasury, but in Consequence of Appropriations made by Law; and a regular Statement and Account of the Receipts and Expenditures of all public Money shall be published from time to time.

No Title of Nobility shall be granted by the United States: And no Person holding any Office of Profit or Trust under them, shall, without the Consent of the Congress, accept of any present, Emolument, Office, or Title, of any kind whatever, from any King, Prince or foreign State.

Section 10

No State shall enter into any Treaty, Alliance, or Confederation; grant Letters of Marque and Reprisal; coin Money; emit Bills of Credit; make any Thing but gold and silver Coin a Tender in Payment of Debts; pass any Bill of Attainder, ex post facto Law or law impairing the Obligation of Contracts, or grant any Title of Nobility.

No State shall, without the Consent of the Congress, lay any Imposts or Duties on Imports or Exports, except what may be absolutely necessary for executing its inspection Laws: and the net Produce of all Duties and Imposts, laid by any State on Imports or Exports, shall be for the Use of the Treasury of the United States; and all such Laws shall be subject to the Revision and Control of the Congress.

No State shall, without the Consent of Congress, lay any Duty on Tonnage, keep Troops, or Ships of War in time of Peace, enter into any Agreement or Compact with another State, or with a foreign Power, or engage in War, unless actually invaded, or in such imminent Danger as will not admit of delay.

ARTICLE II

Section 1

The executive Power shall be vested in a President of the United States of America. He shall hold his Office during the Term of four Years, and, together with the Vice President, chosen for the same Term, be elected, as follows:

Each State shall appoint, in such Manner as the Legislature thereof may direct, a Number of Electors, equal to the whole Number of Senators and Representatives to which the State may be entitled in the Congress: but no Senator or Representative, or Person holding an Office of Trust or Profit under the United States, shall be appointed an Elector.

The Electors shall meet in their respective States, and vote by Ballot for two Persons, of whom one at least shall not be an Inhabitant of the same State with themselves. And they shall make a List of all the Persons voted for, and of the Number of Votes for each; which List they shall sign and certify, and transmit sealed to the Seat of the Government of the United States, directed to the President of the Senate. The

President of the Senate shall, in the Presence of the Senate and House of Representatives, open all the Certificates, and the Votes shall then be counted. The Person having the greatest Number of Votes shall be the President, if such Number be a Majority of the whole Number of Electors appointed; and if there be more than one who have such Majority, and have an equal Number of Votes, then the House of Representatives shall immediately chuse by Ballot one of them for President; and if no Person have a Majority, then from the five highest on the List the said House shall in like Manner chuse the President. But in chusing the President, the Votes shall be taken by States, the Representation from each State having one Vote; a quorum for this Purpose shall consist of a Member or Members from two thirds of the States, and a Majority of all the States shall be necessary to a Choice. In every Case, after the Choice of the President, the Person having the greatest Number of Votes of the Electors shall be the Vice President. But if there should remain two or more who have equal Votes, the Senate shall chuse from them by Ballot the Vice President.

The Congress may determine the Time of chusing the Electors, and the Day on which they shall give their Votes; which Day shall be the same throughout the United States.

No Person except a natural born Citizen, or a Citizen of the United States, at the time of the Adoption of this Constitution, shall be eligible to the Office of President; neither shall any Person be eligible to that Office who shall not have attained to the Age of thirty-five Years, and been fourteen years a Resident within the United States.

In Case of the Removal of the President from Office, or of his Death, Resignation, or Inability to discharge the Powers and Duties of the said Office, the Same shall devolve on the Vice President, and the Congress may by Law provide for the Case of Removal, Death, Resignation, or Inability, both of the President and Vice President, declaring what Officer shall then act as President, and such Officer shall act accordingly, until the Disability be removed, or a President shall be elected.

The President shall, at stated Times, receive for his Services, a Compensation, which shall neither be increased nor diminished during the Period for which he shall have been elected, and he shall not receive within that Period any other Emolument from the United States, or any of them.

Before he enter on the Execution of his Office, he shall take the following Oath or Affirmation:—"I do solemnly swear (or affirm) that I will faithfully execute the Office of President of the United States, and will to the best of my Ability, preserve, protect, and defend the Constitution of the United States."

Section 2

The President shall be Commander in Chief of the Army and Navy of the United States, and of the Militia of the several States, when called into the actual Service of the United States; he may require the Opinion, in writing, of the principal Officer in each of the executive Departments, upon any Subject relating to the Duties of their respective Offices, and he shall have Power to grant Reprieves and Pardons for Offenses against the United States, except in Cases of Impeachment.

He shall have Power, by and with the Advice and Consent of the Senate, to make Treaties, provided two thirds of the Senators present concur; and he shall nominate, and by and with the Advice and Consent of the Senate, shall appoint Ambassadors, other public Ministers and Consuls, Judges of the supreme Court, and all other Officers of the United States, whose Appointments are not herein otherwise provided for, and which shall be established by Law: but the Congress may by Law vest the Appointment of such inferior Officers, as they think proper, in the President alone, in the Courts of Law, or in the Heads of Departments.

The President shall have Power to fill up all Vacancies that may happen during the Recess of the Senate, by granting Commissions which shall expire at the End of their next Session.

Section 3

He shall from time to time give to the Congress Information of the State of the Union, and recommend to their Consideration such Measures as he shall judge necessary and expedient; he may, on extraordinary Occasions, convene both Houses, or either of them, and in Case of Disagreement between them, with Respect to the Time of Adjournment, he may adjourn them to such Time as he shall think proper; he shall receive Ambassadors and other public Ministers; he shall take Care that the Laws be faithfully executed, and shall Commission all the Officers of the United States.

Section 4

The President, Vice President and all Civil Officers of the United States, shall be removed from Office on Impeachment for, and Conviction of, Treason, Bribery, or other high Crimes and Misdemeanors.

ARTICLE III

Section 1

The judicial Power of the United States, shall be vested in one supreme Court, and in such inferior Courts as the Congress may from time to time ordain and establish. The Judges, both of the supreme and inferior Courts, shall hold their Offices during good Behaviour, and shall, at stated Times, receive for their Services, a Compensation, which shall not be diminished during their Continuance in Office.

Section 2

The judicial Power shall extend to all Cases, in Law and Equity, arising under this Constitution, the Laws of the United States, and Treaties made, or which shall be made, under their Authority;—to all Cases affecting Ambassadors, other public Ministers and Consuls;—to all Cases of admiralty and maritime Jurisdiction;—to Controversies to which the United States shall be a Party;—to Controversies between two or more States;—between a State and Citizens of another State;—between Citizens of different States,—between Citizens of the same State claiming Lands under Grants of different States, and between a State, or the Citizens thereof, and foreign States, Citizens or Subjects.

In all Cases affecting Ambassadors, other public Ministers and Consuls, and those in which a State shall be Party, the Supreme Court shall have original Jurisdiction. In all the other Cases before mentioned, the supreme Court shall have appellate Jurisdiction, both as to Law and Fact, with such Exceptions, and under such Regulations as the Congress shall make.

The Trial of all Crimes, except in Cases of Impeachment, shall be by Jury; and such Trial shall be held in the State where the said Crimes shall have been committed; but when not committed within any State, the Trial shall be at such Place or Places as the Congress may by Law have directed.

Section 3

Treason against the United States, shall consist only in levying War against them, or in adhering to their Enemies, giving them Aid and Comfort. No Person shall be convicted of Treason unless on the Testimony of two Witnesses to the same overt Act, or on Confession in open Court.

The Congress shall have Power to declare the Punishment of Treason, but no Attainder of Treason shall work Corruption of Blood, or Forfeiture except during the Life of the Person attainted.

ARTICLE IV

Section 1

Full Faith and Credit shall be given in each State to the public Arts, Records, and judicial Proceedings of every other State. And the Congress may by general Laws prescribe the Manner in which such Acts, Records and Proceedings shall be proved, and the Effect thereof.

Section 2

The Citizens of each State shall be entitled to all Privileges and Immunities of Citizens in the several States.

A Person charged in any State with Treason, Felony, or other Crime, who shall flee from Justice, and be found in another State, shall on Demand of the executive Authority of the State from which he fled, be delivered up, to be removed to the State having Jurisdiction of the Crime.

No Person held to Service or Labour in one State, under the Laws thereof, escaping into another, shall, in Consequence of any Law or Regulation therein, be discharged from such Service or Labour, but shall be delivered up on Claim of the Party to whom such Service or Labour may be due.

Section 3

New States may be admitted by the Congress into this Union; but no new State shall be formed or erected within the Jurisdiction of any other State; nor any State be formed by the Junction of two or more States, or Parts of States, without the Consent of the Legislatures of the States concerned as well as of the Congress.

The Congress shall have Power to dispose of and make all needful Rules and Regulations respecting the Territory or other Property belonging to the United States; and nothing in this Constitution shall be so construed as to Prejudice any Claims of the United States, or of any particular State.

Section 4

The United States shall guarantee to every State in this Union a Republican Form of Government, and shall protect each of them against Invasion; and on Application of the Legislature, or of the Executive (when the Legislature cannot be convened) against domestic Violence.

ARTICLE V

The Congress, whenever two thirds of both Houses shall deem it necessary, shall propose Amendments to this Constitution, or, on the Application of the Legislatures of two thirds of the several States, shall call a Convention for proposing Amendments, which, in either Case, shall be valid to all Intents and Purposes, as Part of this Constitution, when ratified by the Legislatures of three fourths of the several States, or by Conventions in three fourths thereof, as the one or the other Mode of Ratification may be proposed by the Congress; Provided that no Amendment which may be made prior to the Year One thousand eight hundred and eight shall in any Manner affect the first and fourth Clauses in the Ninth Section of the first Article; and that no State, without its Consent, shall be deprived of its equal Suffrage in the Senate.

ARTICLE VI

All Debts contracted and Engagements entered into, before the Adoption of this Constitution, shall be as valid against the United States under this Constitution, as under the Confederation.

This Constitution, and the Laws of the United States which shall be made in Pursuance thereof; and all Treaties made, or which shall be made, under the Authority of the United States, shall be the supreme Law of the Land; and the judges in every State shall be bound thereby, any Thing in the Constitution or Laws of any State to the Contrary notwithstanding.

The Senators and Representatives before mentioned, and the Members of the several State Legislatures, and all executive and judicial Officers, both of the United States and of the several States, shall be bound by Oath or Affirmation, to support this Constitution; but no religious Test shall ever be required as a Qualification to any Office or public Trust under the United States.

ARTICLE VII

The Ratification of the Conventions of nine States, shall be sufficient for the Establishment of this

Constitution between the States so ratifying the Same.

AMENDMENT I (1791)

Congress shall make no law respecting an establishment of religion, or prohibiting the free exercise thereof; or abridging the freedom of speech, or of the press; or the right of the people peaceably to assemble, and to petition the Government for a redress of grievances.

AMENDMENT II (1791)

A well regulated Militia, being necessary to the security of a free State, the right of the people to keep and bear Arms, shall not be infringed.

AMENDMENT III (1791)

No Soldier shall, in time of peace be quartered in any house, without the consent of the Owner, nor in time of war, but in a manner to be prescribed by law.

AMENDMENT IV (1791)

The right of the people to be secure in their persons, houses, papers, and effects, against unreasonable searches and seizures, shall not be violated, and no Warrants shall issue, but upon probable cause, supported by Oath or affirmation, and particularly describing the place to be searched, and the persons or things to be seized.

AMENDMENT V (1791)

No person shall be held to answer for a capital or otherwise infamous crime, unless on a presentment or indictment of a Grand Jury, except in cases arising in the land or naval forces, or in the Militia, when in actual service in time of War or public danger; nor shall any person be subject for the same offense to be twice put in jeopardy of life or limb; nor shall be compelled in any criminal case to be a witness against himself, nor be deprived of life, liberty, or property, without due process of law; nor shall private property be taken for public use, with out just compensation.

AMENDMENT VI (1791)

In all criminal prosecutions, the accused shall enjoy the right to a speedy and public trial, by an impartial jury of the State and district wherein the crime shall have been committed, which district shall have been previously ascertained by law, and to be informed of the nature and cause of the accusation; to be confronted with the witnesses against him; to have compulsory process for obtaining Witnesses in his favor, and to have the Assistance of Counsel for his defense.

AMENDMENT VII (1791)

In Suits at common law, where the value in controversy shall exceed twenty dollars, the right of trial by jury shall be preserved, and no fact tried by a jury, shall be otherwise reexamined in any Court of the United States, than according to the rules of the common law.

AMENDMENT VIII (1791)

Excessive bail shall not be required nor excessive fines imposed, nor cruel and unusual punishments inflicted.

AMENDMENT IX (1791)

The enumeration in the Constitution, of certain rights, shall not be construed to deny or disparage others retained by the people.

AMENDMENT X (1791)

The powers not delegated to the United States by the Constitution, nor prohibited by it to the States, are reserved to the States respectively, or to the people.

AMENDMENT XI (1798)

The Judicial power of the United States shall not be construed to extend to any suit in law or equity, commenced or prosecuted against one of the United States by Citizens of another State, or by Citizens or Subjects of any Foreign State.

AMENDMENT XII (1804)

The Electors shall meet in their respective states and vote by ballot for President and Vice President, one of whom, at least, shall not be an inhabitant of the same state with themselves; they shall name in their ballots the person voted for as President, and in distinct ballots the person voted for as Vice-President, and they shall make distinct lists of all persons voted for as President, and of all persons voted for as Vice-President, and of the number of votes for each, which lists they shall sign and certify, and transmit sealed to the seat of the government of the United States, directed to the President of the Senate;—The President of the Senate shall, in the presence of the Senate and House of Representatives, open all the certificates and the votes shall then be counted;—The person having the greatest number of votes for President, shall be the President, if such number be a majority of the whole number of Electors appointed; and if no person have such majority, then from the persons having the highest numbers not exceeding three on the list of those voted for as President, the House of Representatives shall choose immediately, by ballot, the President. But in choosing the President, the votes shall be taken by states, the representation from each state having one vote; a quorum for this purpose shall consist of a member or members from two-thirds of the states, and a majority of all the states shall be necessary to a choice. And if the House of Representatives shall not choose a President whenever the right of choice shall devolve upon them, before the fourth day of March next following, then the Vice-President shall act as President, as in the case of the death or other constitutional disability of the President—The person having the greatest number of votes as Vice-President, shall be the Vice-President, if such number be a majority of the whole number of Electors appointed, and if no person have a majority, then from the two highest numbers on the list, the Senate shall choose the Vice-President; a quorum for the purpose shall consist of two-thirds of the whole numbers of Senators, and a majority of the whole number shall be necessary to a choice. But no person constitutionally ineligible to the office of President shall be eligible to that of Vice President of the United States.

AMENDMENT XIII (1865)

Section 1
Neither slavery nor involuntary servitude, except as a punishment for crime whereof the party shall have been duly convicted, shall exist within the United States, or any place subject to their jurisdiction.

Section 2
Congress shall have power to enforce this article by appropriate legislation.

AMENDMENT XIV (1868)

Section 1
All persons born or naturalized in the United States and subject to the jurisdiction thereof, are citizens of the United States and of the State wherein they reside. No State shall make or enforce any law which shall abridge the privileges or immunities of citizens of the United States; nor shall any State deprive any person of life, liberty, or property, without due process of law; nor deny to any person within its jurisdiction the equal protection of the laws.

Section 2
Representatives shall be apportioned among the several States according to their respective numbers, counting the whole number of persons in each State, excluding Indians not taxed. But when the right to vote at any election for the choice of electors for President and Vice President of the United States, Representatives in Congress, the Executive and Judicial officers of a State, or the members of the Legislature thereof, is denied to any of the male inhabitants of such State, being twenty-one years of age, and citizens of the United States, or in any way abridged, except for participation in rebellion, or other crime, the basis of representation therein shall be reduced in the proportion which the number of such male citizens shall bear to the whole number of male citizens twenty-one years of age in such State.

Section 3
No person shall be a Senator or Representative in Congress, or elector of President and Vice President, or hold any office, civil or military, under the United States, or under any State, who, having previously taken an oath, as a member of Congress, or as an officer of the United States, or as a member of any State legislature, or as an executive or judicial officer of any State, to support the Constitution of the United States, shall have engaged in insurrection or rebellion against the same, or given aid or comfort to the enemies thereof. But Congress may by a vote of two-thirds of each House, remove such disability.

Section 4
The validity of the public debt of the United States, authorized by law, including debts incurred for payment of pensions and bounties for services in suppressing insurrection or rebellion, shall not be questioned. But neither the United States nor any State shall assume or pay any debt or obligation

incurred in aid of insurrection or rebellion against the United States, or any claim for the loss or emancipation of any slave; but all such debts, obligations and claims shall be held illegal and void.

Section 5
The Congress shall have power to enforce, by appropriate legislation, the provisions of this article.

AMENDMENT XV (1870)

Section 1
The right of citizens of the United States to vote shall not be denied or abridged by the United States or by any State on account of race, color, or previous condition of servitude.

Section 2
The Congress shall have power to enforce this article by appropriate legislation.

AMENDMENT XVI (1913)

The Congress shall have power to lay and collect taxes on incomes, from whatever source derived, without apportionment among the several States, and without regard to any census or enumeration.

AMENDMENT XVII (1913)

The Senate of the United States shall be composed of two Senators from each State, elected by the people thereof, for six years; and each Senator shall have one vote. The electors in each State shall have the qualifications requisite for electors of the most numerous branch of the State legislatures.

When vacancies happen in the representation of any State in the Senate, the executive authority of such State shall issue writs of election to fill such vacancies: *Provided*, That the legislature of any State may empower the executive thereof to make temporary appointments until the people fill the vacancies by election as the legislature may direct.

This amendment shall not be so construed as to affect the election or term of any Senator chosen before it becomes valid as part of the Constitution.

AMENDMENT XVIII (1919)

Section 1
After one year from the ratification of this article the manufacture, sale, or transportation of intoxicating liquors within, the importation thereof into, or the exportation thereof from the United States and all territory subject to the jurisdiction thereof for beverage purposes is hereby prohibited.

Section 2
The Congress and the several States shall have concurrent power to enforce this article by appropriate legislation.

Section 3
This article shall be inoperative unless it shall have been ratified as an amendment to the Constitution by the legislatures of the several States, as provided in the Constitution, within seven years from the date of the submission hereof to the States by the Congress.

AMENDMENT XIX (1920)

The right of citizens of the United States to vote shall not be denied or abridged by the United States or by any State on account of sex.

Congress shall have power to enforce this article by appropriate legislation.

AMENDMENT XX (1933)

Section 1
The terms of the President and Vice President shall end at noon on the 20th day of January, and the terms of Senators and Representatives at noon on the 3d day of January, of the years in which such terms would have ended if this article had not been ratified; and the terms of their successors shall then begin.

Section 2
The Congress shall assemble at least once in every year, and such meeting shall begin at noon on the 3d day of January, unless they shall by law appoint a different day.

Section 3
If, at the time fixed for the beginning of the term of the President, the President elect shall have died, the Vice President elect shall become President. If a President shall not have been chosen before the time fixed for the beginning of his term, or if the President elect shall have failed to qualify, then the Vice President elect shall act as President until a President shall have qualified; and the Congress may by law provide for the case wherein neither

a President elect nor a Vice President elect shall have qualified, declaring who shall then act as President, or the manner in which one who is to act shall be selected, and such person shall act accordingly until a President or Vice President shall have qualified.

Section 4

The Congress may by law provide for the case of the death of any of the persons from whom the House of Representatives may choose a President whenever the right of choice shall have devolved upon them, and for the case of the death of any of the persons from whom the Senate may choose a Vice President whenever the right of choice shall have devolved upon them.

Section 5

Sections 1 and 2 shall take effect on the 15th day of October following the ratification of this article.

Section 6

This article shall be inoperative unless it shall have been ratified as an amendment to the Constitution by the legislatures of three fourths of the several States within seven years from the date of its submission.

AMENDMENT XXI (1933)

Section 1

The eighteenth article of amendment to the Constitution of the United States is hereby repealed.

Section 2

The transportation or importation into any State, Territory, or possession of the United States for delivery or use therein of intoxicating liquors, in violation of the laws thereof, is hereby prohibited.

Section 3

This article shall be inoperative unless it shall have been ratified as an amendment to the Constitution by conventions in the several States, as provided in the Constitution, within seven years from the date of the submission hereof to the States by the Congress.

AMENDMENT XXII (1951)

Section 1

No person shall be elected to the office of the President more than twice, and no person, who has held

the office of President, or acted as President, for more than two years of a term to which some other person was elected President shall be elected to the Office of the President more than once. But this Article shall not apply to any person holding the office of President when this Article was proposed by the Congress, and shall not prevent any person who may be holding the office of President, or acting as President, during the term within which this Article becomes operative from holding the Office of President or acting as President during the remainder of such term.

Section 2

This article shall be inoperative unless it shall have been ratified as an amendment to the Constitution by the legislatures of three fourths of the several States within seven years from the date of its submission to the States by the Congress.

AMENDMENT XXIII (1961)

Section 1

The District constituting the seat of Government of the United States shall appoint in such manner as the Congress may direct:

A number of electors of President and Vice President equal to the whole number of Senators and Representatives in Congress to which the District would be entitled if it were a State, but in no event more than the least populous State; they shall be in addition to those appointed by the States, but they shall be considered, for the purposes of the election of President and Vice President, to be electors appointed by a State; and they shall meet in the District and perform such duties as provided by the twelfth article of amendment.

Section 2

The Congress shall have power to enforce this article by appropriate legislation.

AMENDMENT XXIV (1964)

Section 1

The right of citizens of the United States to vote in any primary or other election for President or Vice President, for electors for President or Vice President, or for Senator or Representative in Congress, shall not be denied or abridged by the United States or any State by reason of failure to pay any poll tax or other tax.

Section 2

The Congress shall have power to enforce this article by appropriate legislation.

AMENDMENT XXV (1967)

Section 1

In case of the removal of the President from office or of his death or resignation, the Vice President shall become President.

Section 2

Whenever there is a vacancy in the office of the Vice President, the President shall nominate a Vice President who shall take office upon confirmation by a majority vote of both Houses of Congress.

Section 3

Whenever the President transmits to the President pro tempore of the Senate and the Speaker of the House of Representatives his written declaration that he is unable to discharge the powers and duties of his office, and until he transmits to them a written declaration to the contrary, such powers and duties shall be discharged by the Vice President as Acting President.

Section 4

Whenever the Vice President and a majority of either the principal officers of the executive departments or of such other body as Congress may by law provide, transmit to the President pro tempore of the Senate and the Speaker of the House of Representatives their written declaration that the President is unable to discharge the powers and duties of his office, the Vice President shall immediately assume the powers and duties of the office as Acting President.

Thereafter, when the President transmits to the President pro tempore of the Senate and the Speaker of the House of Representatives his written declaration that no inability exists, he shall resume the powers and duties of his Office unless the Vice President and a majority of either the principal officers of the executive department or of such other body as Congress may by law provide, transmit within four days to the President pro tempore of the Senate and the Speaker of the House of Representatives their written declaration that the President is unable to discharge the powers and duties of his office. Thereupon Congress shall decide the issue, assembling within forty-eight hours for that purpose if not in session. If the Congress, within twenty-one days after receipt of the latter written declaration, or, if Congress is not in session, within twenty-one days after Congress is required to assemble, determines by two-thirds vote of both Houses that the President is unable to discharge the powers and duties of his office, the Vice President shall continue to discharge the same as Acting President; otherwise, the President shall resume the powers and duties of his office.

AMENDMENT XXVI (1971)

Section 1

The right of citizens of the United States, who are eighteen years of age or older, to vote shall not be denied or abridged by the United States or by any State on account of age.

Section 2

The Congress shall have power to enforce this article by appropriate legislation.

AMENDMENT XXVII (1992)

No law varying the compensation for services of the Senators and Representatives shall take effect until an election of representatives shall have intervened.

Appendix B

The Freedom of Information Act (FOIA) (Excerpts)

SECTION 552. PUBLIC INFORMATION; AGENCY RULES, OPINIONS, ORDERS, RECORDS, AND PROCEEDINGS (THE FREEDOM OF INFORMATION ACT)

(a) Each agency shall make available to the public information as follows:

(1) Each agency shall separately state and currently publish in the Federal Register for the guidance of the public—

(A) descriptions of its central and field organization and the established places at which, the employees (and in the case of a uniformed service, the members) from whom, and the methods whereby, the public may obtain information, make submittals or requests, or obtain decisions;

(B) statements of the general course and method by which its functions are channeled and determined, including the nature and requirements of all formal and informal procedures available;

(C) rules of procedure, descriptions of forms available or the places at which forms may be obtained, and instructions as to the scope and contents of all papers, reports, or examinations;

(D) substantive rules of general applicability adopted as authorized by law, and statements of general policy or interpretations of general applicability formulated and adopted by the agency; and

(E) each amendment, revision, or repeal of the foregoing.

SECTION 552B. OPEN MEETINGS ("SUNSHINE LAW")

(a) For purposes of this section—

(1) the term "agency" means any agency, as defined in section 552 (e) of this title, headed by a collegial body composed of two or more individual members, a majority of whom are appointed to such position by the President with the advice and consent of the Senate, and any subdivision thereof authorized to act on behalf of the agency;

(2) the term "meeting" means the deliberations of at least the number of individual agency members required to take action on behalf of the agency where such deliberations determine or result in the joint conduct or disposition of official agency business, but does not include deliberations required or permitted by subsection (d) or (e); and

(3) the term "member" means an individual who belongs to a collegial body heading an agency.

(b) Members shall not jointly conduct or dispose of agency business other than in accordance with this section.

SECTION 553. RULE MAKING

(c) After notice required by this section, the agency shall give interested persons an opportunity to participate in the rule making through submission of written data, views, or arguments with or without opportunity for oral presentation. After consideration of the relevant matter presented, the agency shall incorporate in the rules adopted a concise general statement of their basis and purpose. When rules are required by statute to be made on the record after opportunity for an agency hearing, sections 556 and 557 of this title apply instead of this subsection.

(d) The required publication or service of a substantive rule shall be made not less than 30 days before its effective date, except—

(1) a substantive rule which grants or recognizes an exemption or relieves a restriction;

(2) interpretive rules and statements of policy; or

(3) as otherwise provided by the agency for good cause found and published with the rule.

(e) Each agency shall give an interested person the right to petition for the issuance, amendment, or repeal of a rule.

SECTION 603. INITIAL REGULATORY FLEXIBILITY ANALYSIS

(a) Whenever an agency is required by section 553 of this title, or any other law, to publish general notice of proposed rulemaking for any proposed rule, the agency shall prepare and make available for public comment an initial regulatory flexibility analysis. Such analysis shall describe the impact of the proposed rule on small entities. The initial regulatory flexibility analysis or a summary shall be published in the Federal Register at the time of the publication of general notice of proposed rule-making for the rule. The agency shall transmit a copy of the initial regulatory flexibility analysis to the Chief Counsel for Advocacy of the Small Business Administration.

(b) Each initial regulatory flexibility analysis required under this section shall contain—

(1) a description of the reasons why action by the agency is being considered;

(2) a succinct statement of the objectives of, and legal basis for, the proposed rule;

(3) a description of and, where feasible, an estimate of the number of small entities to which the proposed rule will apply;

(4) a description of the projected reporting, recordkeeping and other compliance requirements of the proposed rule, including an estimate of the classes of small entities which will be subject to the requirement and the type of professional skills necessary for preparation of the report or record;

(5) an identification, to the extent practicable, of all relevant Federal rules which may duplicate, overlap or conflict with the proposed rule.

(c) Each initial regulatory flexibility analysis shall also contain a description of any significant alternatives to the proposed rule which accomplish the stated objectives of applicable statutes and which minimize any significant economic impact of the proposed rule on small entities. Consistent with the stated objectives of applicable statutes, the analysis shall discuss significant alternatives such as—

(1) the establishment of differing compliance or reporting requirements or timetables that take into account the resources available to small entities;

(2) the clarification, consolidation, or simplification of compliance and reporting requirements under the rule for such small entities;

(3) the use of performance rather than design standards; and

(4) the exemption from coverage of the rule, or any part thereof, for such small entities.

Appendix C

Title VII of the Civil Rights Act (Employment Provisions) (Excerpts)

SECTION 703. UNLAWFUL EMPLOYMENT PRACTICES

Employer Practices

(a) It shall be an unlawful employment practice for an employer—

(1) to fail or refuse to hire or to discharge any individual, or otherwise to discriminate against any individual with respect to his compensation, terms, conditions, or privileges of employment, because of such individual's race, color, religion, sex, or national origin; or

(2) to limit, segregate, or classify his employees or applicants for employment in any way which would deprive or tend to deprive any individual of employment opportunities or otherwise adversely affect his status as an employee, because of such individual's race, color, religion, sex, or national origin.

Employment Agency Practices

(b) It shall be an unlawful employment practice for an employment agency to fail or refuse to refer for employment, or otherwise to discriminate against, any individual because of his race, color, religion, sex, or national origin, or to classify or refer for employment any individual on the basis of his race, color, religion, sex, or national origin.

Labor Organization Practices

(c) It shall be an unlawful employment practice for a labor organization—

(1) to exclude or to expel from its membership, or otherwise to discriminate against, any individual because of his race, color, religion, sex, or national origin;

(2) to limit, segregate, or classify its membership or applicants for membership, or to classify or fail or refuse to refer to employment any individual, in any way which would deprive or tend to deprive any individual of employment opportunities, or would limit such employment opportunities or otherwise adversely affect his status as an employee

or as an applicant for employment, because of such individual's race, color, religion, sex, or national origin; or

(3) to cause or attempt to cause an employer to discriminate against an individual in violation of this section.

Training Programs

(d) It shall be an unlawful employment practice for any employer, labor organization, or joint labor-management committee, controlling apprenticeship or other training or retraining, including on-the-job training programs to discriminate against any individual because of his race, color, religion, sex, or national origin in admission to, or employment in, any program established to provide apprenticeship or other training.

Businesses or Enterprises with Personnel Qualified on Basis of Religion, Sex, or National Origin; Educational Institutions with Personnel of Particular Religion

(e) Notwithstanding any other provision of this subchapter, (1) it shall not be an unlawful employment practice for an employer to hire and employ employees, for an employment agency to classify or refer for employment any individual, for a labor organization to classify its membership or to classify or refer for employment any individual, or for an employer, labor organization, or joint labor-management committee controlling apprenticeship or other training or retraining programs to admit or employ any individual in any such program, on the basis of his religion, sex, or national origin in those certain instances where religion, sex, or national origin is a bona fide occupational qualification reasonably necessary to the normal operation of that particular business or enterprise, and (2) it shall not be an unlawful employment practice for a school, college, university, or other educational institution or institution of learning to hire and employ employees of a particular religion if such school, college, university, or other educational institution or institution of learning is, in whole or in substantial part, owned, supported, controlled, or managed by a particular religion or by a particular religious corporation, association, or society, or if the curriculum of such school, college, university, or other educational institution or institution of learning is directed toward the propagation of a particular religion.

Seniority or Merit System; Quantity or Quality of Production, Ability Tests; Compensation Based on Sex and Authorized by Minimum Wage Provisions

(h) Notwithstanding any other provisions of this subchapter, it shall not be an unlawful employment practice for an employer to apply different standards of compensation, or different terms, conditions, or privileges of employment pursuant to a bona fide seniority or merit system, or a system which measures earnings by quantity or quality of production or to employees who work in different locations, provided that such differences are not the result of an intention to discriminate because of race, color, religion, sex, or national origin, nor shall it be an unlawful employment practice for an employer to give and to act upon the results of any professionally developed ability test provided that such test, its administration or action upon the results is not designed, intended or used to discriminate because of race, color, religion, sex, or national origin. It shall not be an unlawful employment practice under this subchapter for any employer to differentiate upon the basis of sex in determining the amount of the wages or compensation paid or to be paid to employees of such employer if such differentiation is authorized by the provisions of section 206(d) of Title 29.

SECTION 704. OTHER UNLAWFUL EMPLOYMENT PRACTICES

Discrimination for Making Charges, Testifying, Assisting, or Participating in Enforcement Proceedings

(a) It shall be an unlawful employment practice for an employer to discriminate against any of his employees or applicants for employment, for an employment agency, or joint labor-management committee controlling apprenticeship or other training or retraining, including on-the-job training programs to discriminate against any individual, or for a labor organization to discriminate against any member thereof or applicant for membership, because he has opposed any practice, made an unlawful employment practice by this subchapter, or because he has made a charge, testified, assisted, or participated in any manner in an investigation, proceeding, or hearing under this subchapter.

Printing or Publication of Notices or Advertisements Indicating Prohibited Preference, Limitation, Specification, or Discrimination; Occupational Qualification Exception

(b) It shall be an unlawful employment practice for an employer, labor organization, employment agency, or joint labor-management committee controlling apprenticeship or other training or retraining, including on-the-job training programs, to print or publish or cause to be printed or published any notice or advertisement relating to employment by such an employer or membership in or any classification or referral for employment by such a labor organization, or relating to any classification or referral for employment by such an employment agency, or relating to admission to, or employment in, any program established to provide apprenticeship or other training by such a joint labor-management committee, indicating any preference, limitation, specification, or discrimination, based on race, color, religion, sex, or national origin, except that such a notice or advertisement may indicate a preference, limitation, specification, or discrimination based on religion, sex, or national origin when religion, sex, or national origin is a bona fide occupational qualification for employment.

Appendix D

The Civil Rights Act (Excerpts)

§ 1981. EQUAL RIGHTS UNDER THE LAW

(a) All persons within the jurisdiction of the United States shall have the same right in every State and Territory to make and enforce contracts, to sue, be parties, give evidence, and to the full and equal benefit of all laws and proceedings for the security of persons and property as is enjoyed by white citizens, and shall be subject to like punishment, pains, penalties, taxes, licenses, and exactions of every kind, and to no other.

(b) For purposes of this section, the term "make and enforce contracts" includes the making, performance, modification, and termination of contracts, and the enjoyment of all benefits, privileges, terms, and conditions of the contractual relationship.

(c) The rights protected by this section are protected against impairment by nongovernmental discrimination and impairment under color of State law.

§ 1981A. DAMAGES IN CASES OF INTENTIONAL DISCRIMINATION IN EMPLOYMENT

(a) Right of recovery.

(1) Civil rights. In an action brought by a complaining party under section 706 or 717 of the Civil Rights Act of 1964 (42 U.S.C. § 2000e-5 [or 2000e-16]) against a respondent who engaged in unlawful intentional discrimination (not an employment practice that is unlawful because of its disparate impact) prohibited under section 703, 704, or 717 of the Act (42 U.S.C. § 2000e-2 or 2000e-3 [or 2000e-16]), and provided that the complaining party cannot recover under section 1977 of the Revised Statutes (42 U.S.C. § 1981), the complaining party may recover compensatory and punitive damages as allowed in subsection (b), in addition to any relief authorized by section 706(g) of the Civil Rights Act of 1964 [42 USCS § 2000e-5(g)], from the respondent.

Appendix E

The Americans with Disabilities Act (Excerpts)

TITLE I—EMPLOYMENT

Sec. 101. Definitions.

As used in this title: . . .

(8) Qualified individual with a disability.—The term "qualified individual with a disability" means an individual with a disability who, with or without reasonable accommodation, can perform the essential functions of the employment position that such individual holds or desires. For the purposes of this title, consideration shall be given to the employer's judgment as to what functions of a job are essential, and if an employer has prepared a written description before advertising or interviewing applicants for the job, this description shall be considered evidence of the essential functions of the job.

(9) Reasonable accommodation.—The term "reasonable accommodation" may include—

(A) making existing facilities used by employees readily accessible to and usable by individuals with disabilities; and

(B) job restructuring, part-time or modified work schedules, reassignment to a vacant position, acquisition or modification of equipment or devices, appropriate adjustment or modifications of examinations, training materials or policies, the provision of qualified readers or interpreters, and other similar accommodations for individuals with disabilities.

(10) Undue Hardship.—

(A) In general.—The term "undue hardship" means an action requiring significant difficulty or expense, when considered in light of the factors set forth in subparagraph (B).

(B) Factors to be considered.—In determining whether an accommodation would impose an undue hardship on a covered entity, factors to be considered include—

(i) the nature and cost of accommodation needed under this Act;

(ii) the overall financial resources of the facility or facilities involved in the provision of the reasonable accommodation; the number of persons employed at such facility; the effect on expenses and resources, or the impact otherwise of such accommodation upon the operation of the facility;

(iii) the overall financial resources of the covered entity; the overall size of the business of a covered entity with respect to the number of its employees; the number, type, and location of its facilities; and

(iv) the type of operation or operations of the covered entity, including the composition, structure, and functions of the workforce of such entity; the geographic separateness, administrative, or fiscal relationship of the facility or facilities in question to the covered entity.

Sec. 102. Discrimination.

(a) General Rule.—No covered entity shall discriminate against a qualified individual with a disability because of the disability of such individual in regard to job application procedures, the hiring, advancement, or discharge of employees, employee compensation, job training, and other terms, conditions, and privileges of employment.

(b) Construction.—As used in subsection (a), the term "discriminate" includes—

(1) limiting, segregating, or classifying a job applicant or employee in a way that adversely affects the opportunities or status of such applicant or employee because of the disability of such applicant or employee;

(2) participating in a contractual or other arrangement or relationship that has the effect of subjecting a covered entity's qualified applicant or employee with a disability to the discrimination prohibited by this title (such relationship includes a relationship with an employment or referral agency, labor union, an organization providing fringe benefits to an employee of the covered entity, or an organization providing training and apprenticeship programs);

(3) utilizing standards, criteria, or methods of administration—

(A) that have the effect of discrimination on the basis of disability; or

(B) that perpetuate the discrimination of others who are subject to common administrative control;

(4) excluding or otherwise denying equal jobs or benefits to a qualified individual because of the known disability of an individual with whom the qualified individual is known to have a relationship or association;

(5) (A) not making reasonable accommodations to the known physical or mental limitations of an otherwise qualified individual with a disability who is an applicant or employee, unless such covered entity can demonstrate that the accommodation would impose an undue hardship on the operation of the business of such covered entity; or

(B) denying employment opportunities to a job applicant or employee who is an otherwise qualified individual with a disability, if such denial is based on the need of such covered entity to make reasonable accommodation to the physical or mental impairments of the employee or applicant;

(6) using qualification standards, employment tests or other selection criteria that screen out or tend to screen out an individual with a disability or a class of individuals with disabilities unless the standard, test or other selection criteria, as used by the covered entity, is shown to be job-related for the position in question and is consistent with business necessity; and

(7) failing to select and administer tests concerning employment in the most effective manner to ensure that, when such test is administered to a job applicant or employee who has a disability that impairs sensory, manual, or speaking skills, such test results accurately reflect the skills, aptitude, or whatever other factor of such applicant or employee that such test purports to measure, rather than reflecting the impaired sensory, manual, or speaking skills of such employee or applicant (except where such skills are the factors that the test purports to measure). . . .

Sec. 104. Illegal Use of Drugs and Alcohol. . . .

(b) Rules of Construction.—Nothing in subsection (a) shall be construed to exclude as a qualified individual with a disability an individual who—

(1) has successfully completed a supervised drug rehabilitation program and is no longer engaging in the illegal use of drugs, or has otherwise been rehabilitated successfully and is no longer engaging in such use;

(2) is participating in a supervised rehabilitation program and is no longer engaging in such use; or

(3) is erroneously regarded as engaging in such use, but is not engaging in such use; except that it shall not be a violation of this Act for a covered entity to adopt or administer reasonable policies or procedures, including but not limited to drug testing, designed to ensure that an individual described in paragraph (1) or (2) is no longer engaging in the illegal use of drugs. . . .

The Family and Medical Leave Act (Excerpts)

29 U.S.C. § 2601 ET SEQ. § 2601. FINDINGS AND PURPOSES

(a) Findings

Congress finds that—

(1) the number of single-parent households and two-parent households in which the single parent or both parents work is increasing significantly;

(2) it is important for the development of children and the family unit that fathers and mothers be able to participate in early childrearing and the care of family members who have serious health conditions;

(3) the lack of employment policies to accommodate working parents can force individuals to choose between job security and parenting;

(4) there is inadequate job security for employees who have serious health conditions that prevent them from working for temporary periods;

(5) due to the nature of the roles of men and women in our society, the primary responsibility for family caretaking often falls on women, and such responsibility affects the working lives of women more than it affects the working lives of men; and

(6) employment standards that apply to one gender only have serious potential for encouraging employers to discriminate against employees and applicants for employment who are of that gender.

(b) Purposes

It is the purpose of this Act—

(1) to balance the demands of the workplace with the needs of families, to promote the stability and economic security of families, and to promote national interests in preserving family integrity;

(2) to entitle employees to take reasonable leave for medical reasons, for the birth or adoption of a child, and for the care of a child, spouse, or parent who has a serious health condition;

(3) to accomplish the purposes described in paragraphs (1) and (2) in a manner that accommodates the legitimate interests of employers;

(4) to accomplish the purposes described in paragraphs (1) and (2) in a manner that, consistent with the Equal Protection Clause of the Fourteenth Amendment, minimizes the potential for employment discrimination on the basis of sex by ensuring generally that leave is available for eligible medical reasons (including maternity-related disability) and for compelling family reasons, on a gender-neutral basis; and

(5) to promote the goal of equal employment opportunity for women and men, pursuant to such clause.

§ 2611. DEFINITIONS

(2) Eligible employee

(A) In general

The term "eligible employee" means an employee who has been employed—

(i) for at least 12 months by the employer with respect to whom leave is requested under section 2612 of this title; and

(ii) for at least 1,250 hours of service with such employer during the previous 12-month period.

(B) Exclusions

The term "eligible employee" does not include—

(i) any Federal officer or employee covered under subchapter V of chapter 63 of Title 5; or

(ii) any employee of an employer who is employed at a worksite at which such employer employs less than 50 employees if the total number of employees employed by that employer within 75 miles of that worksite is less than 50.

§ 2612. LEAVE REQUIREMENT

(a) In general

(1) Entitlement to leave

Subject to section 2613 of this title, an eligible employee shall be entitled to a total of 12 workweeks of leave during any 12-month period for one or more of the following:

(A) Because of the birth of a son or daughter of the employee and in order to care for such son or daughter.

(B) Because of the placement of a son or daughter with the employee for adoption or foster care.

(C) In order to care for the spouse, or a son, daughter, or parent, of the employee, if such spouse, son, daughter, or parent has a serious health condition.

(D) Because of a serious health condition that makes the employee unable to perform the functions of the position of such employee.

(2) Expiration of entitlement
The entitlement to leave under subparagraphs (A) and (B) of paragraph (1) for a birth or placement of a son or daughter shall expire at the end of the 12-month period beginning on the date of such birth or placement.

(b) Leave taken intermittently or on a reduced leave schedule

(1) In general
Leave under subparagraph (A) or (B) of subsection (a)(1) of this section shall not be taken by an employee intermittently or on a reduced leave schedule unless the employee and the employer of the employee agree otherwise. Subject to paragraph (2), subsection (e)(2) of this section, and section 2613(b)(5) of this title, leave under subparagraph (C) or (D) of subsection (a)(1) of this section may be taken intermittently or on a reduced leave schedule when medically necessary. The taking of leave intermittently or on a reduced leave schedule pursuant to this paragraph shall not result in a reduction in the total amount of leave to which the employee is entitled under subsection (a) of this section beyond the amount of leave actually taken.

(2) Alternative position
If an employee requests intermittent leave, or leave on a reduced leave schedule, under subparagraph (C) or (D) of subsection (a)(1) of this section, that is foreseeable based on planned medical treatment, the employer may require such employee to transfer temporarily to an available alternative position offered by the employer for which the employee is qualified and that—

(A) has equivalent pay and benefits; and

(B) better accommodates recurring periods of leave than the regular employment position of the employee.

(c) Unpaid leave permitted

Except as provided in subsection (d) of this section, leave granted under subsection (a) of this section may consist of unpaid leave. Where an employee is otherwise exempt under regulations issued by the Secretary pursuant to section 2613(a)(1) of this title, the compliance of an employer with this subchapter by providing unpaid leave shall not affect the exempt status of the employee under such section.

(d) Relationship to paid leave

(1) Unpaid leave
If an employer provides paid leave for fewer than 12 workweeks, the additional weeks of leave necessary to attain the 12 workweeks of leave required under this subchapter may be provided without compensation.

(2) Substitution of paid leave
  (A) In general
    An eligible employee may elect, or an employer may require the employee, to substitute any of the accrued paid vacation leave, personal leave, or family leave of the employee for leave provided under subparagraph (A), (B), or (C) of subsection (a) (1) of this section for any part of the 12-week period of such leave under such subsection.

  (B) Serious health condition
    An eligible employee may elect, or an employer may require the employee, to substitute any of the accrued paid vacation leave, personal leave, or medical or sick leave of the employee for leave provided under subparagraph (C) or (D) of subsection (a)(1) of this section for any part of the 12-week period of such leave under such subsection, except that nothing in this subchapter shall require an employer to provide paid sick leave or paid medical leave in any situation in which such employer would not normally provide any such paid leave.

§ 2614. EMPLOYMENT AND BENEFITS PROTECTION

(a) Restoration to position

(1) In general
Except as provided in subsection (b) of this section, any eligible employee who takes leave under section 2612 of this title for the intended purpose of the leave shall be entitled, on return from such leave—

(A) to be restored by the employer to the position of employment held by the employee when the leave commenced; or

(B) to be restored to an equivalent position with equivalent employment benefits, pay, and other terms and conditions of employment.

(2) Loss of benefits

The taking of leave under section 2612 of this title shall not result in the loss of any employment benefit accrued prior to the date on which the leave commenced.

(3) Limitations

Nothing to this section shall be construed to entitle any restored employee to—

(A) the accrual of any seniority or employment benefits during any period of leave; or

(B) any right, benefit, or position of employment other than any right, benefit, or position to which the employee would have been entitled had the employee not taken the leave.

§ 2617. ENFORCEMENT

(a) Civil action by employees

(1) Liability

Any employer who violates section 2615 of this title shall be liable to any eligible employee affected—

(A) for damages equal to—

(i) the amount of—

(I) any wages, salary, employment benefits, or other compensation denied or lost to such employee by reason of the violation; or

(II) in a case in which wages, salary, employment benefits, or other compensation have not been denied or lost to the employee, any actual monetary losses sustained by the employee as a direct result of the violation, such as the cost of providing care, up to a sum equal to 12 weeks of wages or salary for the employee;

(ii) the interest on the amount described in clause (I) calculated at the prevailing rate; and

(iii) an additional amount as liquidated damages equal to the sum of the amount described in clause (I) and the interest described in clause (ii), except that if an employer who has violated section 2615 of this title proves to the satisfaction of the court that the act or omission which violated section 2615 of this title was in good faith and that the employer had reasonable grounds for believing that the act or omission was not a violation of section 2615 of this title, such court may, in the discretion of the court, reduce the amount of the liability to the amount and interest determined under clauses (i) and (ii), respectively; and

(B) for such equitable relief as may be appropriate, including employment reinstatement, and promotion.

Appendix G

The Uniform Commercial Code (Excerpts)*

ARTICLE I GENERAL PROVISIONS

Part 1 Short Title, Construction, Application and Subject Matter of the Act

[Note: As marked, there are sections of both the Revised UCC and the old UCC. The old UCC sections for the revised sections that have had accompanying controversy are included because as states adopt these revisions, they may opt for variations.]

Section I—203. Obligation of Good Faith

Every contract or duty within this Act imposes an obligation of good faith in its performance or enforcement.

Section 1–303. Course of Performance, Course of Dealing, and Usage of Trade (Revised UCC) (formerly Section 2–208)

(a) A "course of performance" is a sequence of conduct between the parties to a particular transaction that exists if:

(1) the agreement of the parties with respect to the transaction involves repeated occasions for performance by a party; and

(2) the other party, with knowledge of the nature of the performance and opportunity for objection to it, accepts the performance or acquiesces in it without objection.

(b) A "course of dealing" is a sequence of conduct concerning previous transactions between the parties to a particular transaction that is fairly to be regarded as establishing a common basis of understanding for interpreting their expressions and other conduct.

(c) A "usage of trade" is any practice or method of dealing having such regularity of observance in a place, vocation, or trade as to justify an expectation that it will be observed with respect to the transaction in question. The existence and scope of such a usage must be proved as facts. If it is established that such a usage is embodied in a trade code or similar record, the interpretation of the record is a question of law.

(d) A course of performance or course of dealing between the parties or usage of trade in the vocation or trade in which they are engaged or of which they are or should be aware is relevant in ascertaining the meaning of the parties' agreement, may give particular meaning to specific terms of the agreement, and may supplement or qualify the terms of the agreement. A usage of trade applicable in the place in which part of the performance under the agreement is to occur may be so utilized as to that part of the performance.

(e) Except as otherwise provided in subsection (f), the express terms of an agreement and any applicable course of performance, course of dealing, or usage of trade must be construed whenever reasonable as consistent with each other. If such a construction is unreasonable:

(1) express terms prevail over course of performance, course of dealing, and usage of trade;

(2) course of performance prevails over course of dealing and usage of trade; and

(3) course of dealing prevails over usage of trade.

(f) Subject to Section 2–209, a course of performance is relevant to show a waiver or modification of any term inconsistent with the course of performance.

(g) Evidence of a relevant usage of trade offered by one party is not admissible unless that party has given the other party notice that the court finds sufficient to prevent unfair surprise to the other party.

Section 1—206. Statute of Frauds for Kinds of Personal Property Not Otherwise Covered

(1) Except in the cases described in subsection (2) of this section a contract for the sale of personal property is not enforceable by way of action or defense beyond five thousand dollars in amount or value of remedy unless there is some writing which indicates that a contract for sale has been made between the parties at a defined or stated price, reasonably identifies the subject matter, and is signed by the party against whom enforcement is sought or by his authorized agent.

(2) Subsection (1) of this section does not apply to contracts for the sale of goods (Section 2—201) nor of securities (Section 8—319) nor to security agreements (Section 9—203).

ARTICLE II SALES
PART 1 SHORT TITLE, GENERAL CONSTRUCTION AND SUBJECT MATTER*

SECTION 2–102. SCOPE (revised UCC)

(1) Unless the context otherwise requires, and subject to Section 2–108, this article applies to transactions in goods. This Article does not apply to any transaction which although in the form of an unconditional contract to sell or present sale is intended to operate only as a security transaction.

(2) Except as provided in subsection (4), in the case of a transaction involving both goods and non-goods, a court may resolve a dispute by the application of this article to the entire transaction, by the application of other law to the entire transaction, or by the application of this article to part of the transaction and other law to part of the transaction. In making the determination as to the law applicable to the transaction, the court shall take into consideration the nature of the transaction and of the dispute.

(3) This article does not apply to transactions that do not involve goods.

(4) A transaction in a product consisting of computer information and goods that are solely the medium containing the computer information is not a transaction in goods, but a court is not precluded from applying provisions in this article to a dispute concerning whether the goods conform to the contract.

*Underlined portions are the most recent changes to UCC Article 2.

(5) Nothing in this article alters, creates, or diminishes rights in intellectual property.

SECTION 2–103. DEFINITIONS AND INDEX OF DEFINITIONS (Revised UCC)

(1) In this article unless the context otherwise requires

(a) "Buyer" means a person that buys or contracts to buy goods.

(b) "Computer information" means information in electronic form which is obtained from or through the use of a computer or which is in a form capable of being processed by a computer.

(c) "Conspicuous", with reference to a term, means so written, displayed, or presented that a reasonable person against which it is to operate ought to have noticed it. A term in an electronic record intended to evoke a response by an electronic agent is conspicuous if it is presented in a form that would enable a reasonably configured electronic agent to take it into account or react to it without review of the record by an individual. Whether a term is "conspicuous" or not is a decision for the court. Conspicuous terms include the following:

(i) for a person:

(A) a heading in capitals equal to or greater in size than the surrounding text, or in contrasting type, font, or color to the surrounding text of the same or lesser size;

(B) language in the body of a record or display in larger type than the surrounding text, or in contrasting type, font, or color to the surrounding text of the same size, or set off from surrounding text of the same size by symbols or other marks that call attention to the language; and

(ii) for a person or an electronic agent, a term that is so placed in a record or display that the person or electronic agent cannot proceed without taking action with respect to the particular term.

(d) "Consumer" means an individual who buys or contracts to buy goods that, at the time of contracting, are intended by the individual to be used primarily for personal, family, or household purposes.

SECTION 2–104. DEFINITIONS: "MERCHANT"; "BETWEEN MERCHANTS"; "FINANCING AGENCY" (Revised UCC)

(1) "Merchant" means a person who that deals in goods of the kind or otherwise is held out by occupation as having knowledge or skill peculiar to the

practices or goods involved in the transaction or to which the knowledge or skill may be attributed by the person's employment of an agent or broker or other intermediary that is held out by occupation as having such the knowledge or skill.

PART 2 FORM, FORMATION AND READJUSTMENT OF CONTRACT

SECTION 2–201. FORMAL REQUIRE-MENTS; STATUTE OF FRAUDS (Revised UCC)

(1) A contract for the sale of goods for the price of $5,000 or more is not enforceable by way of action or defense unless there is some record sufficient to indicate that a contract for sale has been made between the parties and signed by the party against which enforcement is sought or by his the party's authorized agent or broker. A record is not insufficient because it omits or incorrectly states a term agreed upon but the contract is not enforceable under this subsection beyond the quantity of goods shown in the record.

(2) Between merchants if within a reasonable time a record in confirmation of the contract and sufficient against the sender is received and the party receiving it has reason to know its contents, it satisfies the requirements of subsection (1) against the recipient unless notice of objection to its contents is given in a record within 10 days after it is received.

(3) A contract which does not satisfy the requirements of subsection (1) but which is valid in other respects is enforceable

(a) if the goods are to be specially manufactured for the buyer and are not suitable for sale to others in the ordinary course of the seller's business and the seller, before notice of repudiation is received and under circumstances which reasonably indicate that the goods are for the buyer, has made either a substantial beginning of their manufacture or commitments for their procurement; or

(b) if the party against which enforcement is sought admits in his the party's pleading, or in the party's testimony or otherwise in court under oath that a contract for sale was made, but the contract is not enforceable under this paragraph beyond the quantity of goods admitted; or

(c) with respect to goods for which payment has been made and accepted or which have been received and accepted (Sec. 2–606).

(4) A contract that is enforceable under this section is not rendered unenforceable merely because it is not capable of being performed within one year or any other applicable period after its making.

SECTION 2–202. FINAL EXPRESSION in a record PAROL OR EXTRINSIC EVIDENCE (Revised UCC)

(1) Terms with respect to which the confirmatory records of the parties agree or which are otherwise set forth in a record intended by the parties as a final expression of their agreement with respect to such terms as are included therein may not be contradicted by evidence of any prior agreement or of a contemporaneous oral agreement but may be supplemented by evidence of:

(a) course of performance, course of dealing or usage of trade (Section 1–303); and

(b) consistent additional terms unless the court finds the record to have been intended also as a complete and exclusive statement of the terms of the agreement.

(2) Terms in a record may be explained by evidence of course of performance, course of dealing, or usage of trade without a preliminary determination by the court that the language used is ambiguous.

SECTION 2–204. FORMATION IN GENERAL (Revised UCC)

(1) A contract for sale of goods may be made in any manner sufficient to show agreement, including offer and acceptance, conduct by both parties which recognizes the existence of such a contract, the interaction of electronic agents, or the interaction of an electronic agent and an individual.

(2) An agreement sufficient to constitute a contract for sale may be found even though the moment of its making is undetermined.

(3) Even though one or more terms are left open a contract for sale does not fail for indefiniteness if the parties have intended to make a contract and there is a reasonably certain basis for giving an appropriate remedy.

(4) Except as otherwise provided in Sections 2–211 through 2–213, the following rules apply:

(a) A contract may be formed by the interaction of electronic agents of the parties, even if no individual was aware of or reviewed the electronic agents' actions or the resulting terms and agreements.

(b) A contract may be formed by the interaction of an electronic agent and an individual acting on the individual's own behalf or for another person. A contract is formed if the individual takes actions that the individual is free to refuse to take or makes a statement that the individual has reason to know will:

(i) cause the electronic agent to complete the transaction or performance; or

(ii) indicate acceptance of an offer, regardless of other expressions or actions by the individual to which the electronic agent cannot react.

SECTION 2–205. FIRM OFFERS (Revised UCC)

An offer by a merchant to buy or sell goods in a signed record which by its terms gives assurance that it will be held open is not revocable, for lack of consideration, during the time stated or if no time is stated for a reasonable time, but in no event may such period of irrevocability exceed three months; but any such term of assurance in a form record supplied by the offeree must be separately signed by the offeror.

SECTION 2–206. OFFER AND ACCEPTANCE IN FORMATION OF CONTRACT (Revised UCC)

(1) Unless otherwise unambiguously indicated by the language or circumstances

(a) an offer to make a contract shall be construed as inviting acceptance in any manner and by any medium reasonable in the circumstances;

(b) an order or other offer to buy goods for prompt or current shipment shall be construed as inviting acceptance either by a prompt promise to ship or by the prompt or current shipment of conforming or non-conforming goods, but the shipment of non-conforming goods does not constitute an acceptance if the seller seasonably notifies the buyer that the shipment is offered only as an accommodation to the buyer.

(2) Where the beginning of a requested performance is a reasonable mode of acceptance an offeror that is not notified of acceptance within a reasonable time may treat the offer as having lapsed before acceptance.

(3) A definite and seasonable expression of acceptance in a record operates as an acceptance even if it contains terms additional to or different from the offer.

Section 2—207. Additional Terms in Acceptance or Confirmation (Old UCC)

(1) A definite and seasonable expression of acceptance or a written confirmation which is sent within a reasonable time operates as an acceptance even though it states terms additional to or different from those offered or agreed upon, unless acceptance is expressly made conditional on assent to the additional or different terms.

(2) The additional terms are to be construed as proposals for addition to the contract. Between merchants such terms become part of the contract unless:

(a) the offer expressly limits acceptance to the terms of the offer;

(b) they materially alter it; or

(c) notification of objection to them has already been given or is given within a reasonable time after notice of them is received.

(3) Conduct by both parties which recognizes the existence of a contract is sufficient to establish a contract for sale although the writings of the parties do not otherwise establish a contract. In such case the terms of the particular contract consist of those terms on which the writings of the parties agree, together with any supplementary terms incorporated under any other provisions of this Act.

SECTION 2–207. TERMS OF CONTRACT; EFFECT OF CONFIRMATION (Revised UCC)

If (i) conduct by both parties recognizes the existence of a contract although their records do not otherwise establish a contract, (ii) a contract is formed by an offer and acceptance, or (iii) a contract formed in any manner is confirmed by a record that contains terms additional to or different from those in the contract being confirmed, the terms of the contract, subject to Section 2–202, are:

(a) terms that appear in the records of both parties;

(b) terms, whether in a record or not, to which both parties agree; and

(c) terms supplied or incorporated under any provision of this Act.

Section 2—208. Course of Performance or Practical Construction (Now Article 1, Section 303 under Revised UCC)

SECTION 2–211. LEGAL RECOGNITION OF ELECTRONIC CONTRACTS, RECORDS AND SIGNATURES (Revised UCC) (Completely new section)

(1) A record or signature may not be denied legal effect or enforceability solely because it is in electronic form.

(2) A contract may not be denied legal effect or enforceability solely because an electronic record was used in its formation.

(3) This article does not require a record or signature to be created, generated, sent, communicated, received, stored, or otherwise processed by electronic means or in electronic form.

(4) A contract formed by the interaction of an individual and an electronic agent under Section 2–204(4)(b) does not include terms provided by the individual if the individual had reason to know that the agent could not react to the terms as provided.

SECTION 2–213. ELECTRONIC COMMUNICATION (Revised UCC) (Completely new section)

(1) If the receipt of an electronic communication has a legal effect, it has that effect even though no individual is aware of its receipt.

(2) Receipt of an electronic acknowledgment of an electronic communication establishes that the communication was received but, in itself, does not establish that the content sent corresponds to the content received.

PART 3 GENERAL OBLIGATION AND CONSTRUCTION OF CONTRACT

SECTION 2–302. UNCONSCIONABLE CONTRACT OR TERM (Revised UCC)

(1) If the court as a matter of law finds the contract or any term of the contract to have been unconscionable at the time it was made the court may refuse to enforce the contract, or it may enforce the remainder of the contract without the unconscionable term, or it may so limit the application of any unconscionable term as to avoid any unconscionable result.

(2) When it is claimed or appears to the court that the contract or any ~~clause~~ term thereof may be unconscionable the parties shall be afforded a reasonable opportunity to present evidence as to its commercial setting, purpose and effect to aid the court in making the determination.

SECTION 2–312. WARRANTY OF TITLE AND AGAINST INFRINGEMENT; BUYER'S OBLIGATION AGAINST INFRINGEMENT (Revised UCC)

(1) Subject to subsection (2) there is in a contract for sale a warranty by the seller that

(a) the title conveyed shall be good and its transfer rightful and shall not, because of any colorable claim to or interest in the goods, unreasonably expose the buyer to litigation; and

(b) the goods shall be delivered free from any security interest or other lien or encumbrance of which the buyer at the time of contracting has no knowledge.

(2) Unless otherwise agreed a seller that is a merchant regularly dealing in goods of the kind warrants that the goods shall be delivered free of the rightful claim of any third person by way of infringement or the like but a buyer that furnishes specifications to the seller must hold the seller harmless against any such claim that arises out of compliance with the specifications.

(3) A warranty under this section may be disclaimed or modified only by specific language or by circumstances that give the buyer reason to know that the seller does not claim title, that the seller is purporting to sell only the right or title as the seller or a third person may have, or that the seller is selling subject to any claims of infringement or the like.

SECTION 2–313. EXPRESS WARRANTIES BY AFFIRMATION, PROMISE, DESCRIPTION, SAMPLE; REMEDIAL PROMISE (Revised UCC)

(1) In this section, "immediate buyer" means a buyer that enters into a contract with the seller.

(2) Express warranties by the seller to the immediate buyer are created as follows:

(a) Any affirmation of fact or promise made by the seller which relates to the goods and becomes part of the basis of the bargain creates an express warranty that the goods shall conform to the affirmation or promise.

(b) Any description of the goods which is made part of the basis of the bargain creates an express warranty that the goods shall conform to the description.

(c) Any sample or model which is made part of the basis of the bargain creates an express warranty that the whole of the goods shall conform to the sample or model.

(3) It is not necessary to the creation of an express warranty that the seller use formal words such as "warrant" or "guarantee" or that the seller have a specific intention to make a warranty, but an affirmation merely of the value of the goods or a statement

purporting to be merely the seller's opinion or commendation of the goods does not create a warranty.

(4) Any remedial promise made by the seller to the immediate buyer creates an obligation that the promise will be performed upon the happening of the specified event.

SECTION 2–313A. OBLIGATION TO REMOTE PURCHASER CREATED BY RECORD PACKAGED WITH OR ACCOMPANYING GOODS (Revised UCC)

(1) This section applies only to new goods and goods sold or leased as new goods in a transaction of purchase in the normal chain of distribution. In this section:

(a) "Immediate buyer" means a buyer that enters into a contract with the seller.

(b) "Remote purchaser" means a person that buys or leases goods from an immediate buyer or other person in the normal chain of distribution

SECTION 2–314. IMPLIED WARRANTY: MERCHANTABILITY; USAGE OF TRADE (Revised UCC)

(1) Unless excluded or modified (Section 2–316), a warranty that the goods shall be merchantable is implied in a contract for their sale if the seller is a merchant with respect to goods of that kind. Under this section the serving for value of food or drink to be consumed either on the premises or elsewhere is a sale.

(2) Goods to be merchantable must be at least such as

(a) pass without objection in the trade under the contract description; and

(b) in the case of fungible goods, are of fair average quality within the description; and

(c) are fit for the ordinary purposes for which ~~such~~ goods of that description are used; and

(d) run, within the variations permitted by the agreement, of even kind, quality and quantity within each unit and among all units involved; and

(e) are adequately contained, packaged, and labeled as the agreement may require; and

(f) conform to the promise or affirmations of fact made on the container or label if any.

(3) Unless excluded or modified (Section 2–316) other implied warranties may arise from course of dealing or usage of trade.

Section 2–315. Implied Warranty: Fitness for Particular Purpose (Old and Revised UCC)

Where the seller at the time of contracting has reason to know any particular purpose for which the goods are required and that the buyer is relying on the seller's skill or judgment to select or furnish suitable goods, there is unless excluded or modified under the next section an implied warranty that the goods shall be fit for such purpose.

SECTION 2–316. EXCLUSION OR MODIFICATION OF WARRANTIES (Revised UCC)

(1) Words or conduct relevant to the creation of an express warranty and words or conduct tending to negate or limit warranty shall be construed wherever reasonable as consistent with each other; but subject to the provisions of this Article on parol or extrinsic evidence (Section 2–202) negation or limitation is inoperative to the extent that such construction is unreasonable.

(2) Subject to subsection (3), to exclude or modify the implied warranty of merchantability or any part of it in a consumer contract the language must be in a record, be conspicuous and state "The seller undertakes no responsibility for the quality of the goods except as otherwise provided in this contract," and in any other contract the language must mention merchantability and in case of a record must be conspicuous,—Subject to subsection (3), to exclude or modify the implied warranty of fitness the exclusion must be in a record and be conspicuous. Language to exclude all implied warranties of fitness in a consumer contract must state "The seller assumes no responsibility that the goods will be fit for any particular purpose for which you may be buying these goods, except as otherwise provided in the contract," and in any other contract the language is sufficient if it states, for example, that "There are no warranties which extend beyond the description on the face hereof." Language that satisfies the requirements of this subsection for the exclusion and modification of a warranty in a consumer contract also satisfies the requirements for any other contract.

(3) Notwithstanding subsection (2):

(a) unless the circumstances indicate otherwise, all implied warranties are excluded by expressions like "as is", "with all faults" or other language which in common understanding calls the buyer's attention to the exclusion of warranties ~~and~~, makes plain that there is no implied warranty, and in a consumer contract evidenced by a record is set forth conspicuously in the record; and

(b) when the buyer before entering into the contract has examined the goods or the sample or model as fully as ~~he~~ desired or has refused to examine the goods after a demand by the seller there is no implied warranty with regard to defects which an examination ought in the circumstances to have revealed to ~~him~~ the buyer; and

(c) an implied warranty can also be excluded or modified by course of dealing or course of performance or usage of trade.

(4) Remedies for breach of warranty can be limited in accordance with the provisions of this article on liquidation or limitation of damages and on contractual modification of remedy (Sections 2–718 and 2–719).

SECTION 2–318. THIRD PARTY BENEFICIARIES OF WARRANTIES EXPRESS OR IMPLIED (Revised UCC)

(1) In this section:

(a) "Immediate buyer" means a buyer that enters into a contract with the seller.

(b) "Remote purchaser" means a person that buys or leases goods from an immediate buyer or other person in the normal chain of distribution.

Alternative A to subsection (2)

(2) A seller's warranty whether express or implied to an immediate buyer, a seller's remedial promise to an immediate buyer, or a seller's obligation to a remote purchaser under Section 2–313A or 2–313B extends to any natural person who is in the family or household of the immediate buyer or the remote purchaser or who is a guest in the home of either if it is reasonable to expect that the person may use, consume or be affected by the goods and who is injured in person by breach of the warranty, remedial promise or obligation. A seller may not exclude or limit the operation of this section.

Alternative B to subsection (2)

(2) A seller's warranty whether express or implied to an immediate buyer, a seller's remedial promise to an immediate buyer, or a seller's obligation to a remote purchaser under Section 2–313A or 2–313B extends to any natural person who may reasonably be expected to use, consume or be affected by the goods and who is injured in person by breach of the warranty, remedial promise or obligation. A seller may not exclude or limit the operation of this section.

Alternative C to subsection (2)

(2) A seller's warranty whether express or implied to an immediate buyer, a seller's remedial promise to an immediate buyer, or a seller's obligation to a remote purchaser under Section 2–313A or 2–313B extends to any person that may reasonably be expected to use, consume or be affected by the goods and that is injured by breach of the warranty, remedial promise or obligation. A seller may not exclude or limit the operation of this section with respect to injury to the person of an individual to whom the warranty, remedial promise or obligation extends.

Section 2–318. Third Party Beneficiaries of Warranties Express or Implied (Old UCC)

Note: If this Act is introduced in the Congress of the United States this section should be omitted. (States to select one alternative.)

Alternative A

A seller's warranty whether express or implied extends to any natural person who is in the family or household of his buyer or who is a guest in his home if it is reasonable to expect that such person may use, consume or be affected by the goods and who is injured in person by breach of the warranty. A seller may not exclude or limit the operation of this section.

Alternative B

A seller's warranty whether express or implied extends to any natural person who may reasonably be expected to use, consume or be affected by the goods and who is injured in person by breach of the warranty. A seller may not exclude or limit the operation of this section.

Alternative C

A seller's warranty whether express or implied extends to any person who may reasonably be expected to use, consume or be affected by the goods and who is injured by breach of the warranty. A seller may not exclude or limit the operation of this section with respect to injury to the person of an individual to whom the warranty extends. As amended 1966.

SECTION 2–615. EXCUSE BY FAILURE OF PRESUPPOSED CONDITIONS (Revised UCC)

Except so far as a seller may have assumed a greater obligation and subject to the preceding section on substituted performance:

(a) Delay in performance or non-performance in whole or in part by a seller that complies with paragraphs (b) and (c) is not a breach of the seller's duty under a contract for sale if performance as agreed has been made impracticable by the occurrence of a contingency the non-occurrence of which was a basic assumption on which the contract was made or by compliance in good faith with any applicable foreign or domestic governmental regulation or order whether or not it later proves to be invalid.

(b) Where the causes mentioned in paragraph (a) affect only a part of the seller's capacity to perform, the seller must allocate production and deliveries among his its customers but may at its option include regular customers not then under contract as well as its own requirements for further manufacture. The seller may so allocate in any manner which is fair and reasonable.

(c) The seller must notify the buyer seasonably that there will be delay or non-delivery and, when allocation is required under paragraph (b), of the estimated quota thus made available for the buyer.

Appendix H

The Securities Act of 1933 and the Securities Exchange Act of 1934 (Excerpts)

SECURITIES ACT OF 1933

Civil Liabilities on Account of False Registration Statement

SECTION 11. (a) In case any part of the registration statement, when such part became effective, contained an untrue statement of a material fact or omitted to state a material fact required to be stated therein or necessary to make the statements therein not misleading, any person acquiring such security (unless it is proved that at the time of such acquisition he knew of such untruth or omission) may, either at law or in equity, in any court of competent jurisdiction, sue—

(1) every person who signed the registration statement;

(2) every person who was a director of (or person performing similar functions) or partner in, the issuer at the time of the filing of the part of the registration statement with respect to which his liability is asserted;

(3) every person who, with his consent, is named in the registration statement as being or about to become a director, person performing similar functions, or partner;

(4) every accountant, engineer, or appraiser, or any person whose profession gives authority to a statement made by him, who has with his consent been named as having prepared or certified any part of the registration statement, or as having prepared or certified any report or valuation which is used in connection with the registration statement, with respect to the statement in such registration statement, report, or valuation, which purports to have been prepared or certified by him;

(5) every underwriter with respect to such security.

If such person acquired the security after the issuer has made generally available to its security holders an earning statement covering a period of at least twelve months beginning after the effective date of the registration statement, then the right of recovery under this subsection shall be conditioned on proof that such person acquired the security relying upon such untrue statement in the registration statement or relying upon the registration statement and not knowing of such omission, but such reliance may be established without proof of the reading of the registration statement by such person.

(b) Notwithstanding the provisions of subsection (a) no person, other than the issuer, shall be liable as provided therein who shall sustain the burden of proof—

(1) that before the effective date of the part of the registration statement with respect to which his liability is asserted (A) he had resigned from or had taken such steps as are permitted by law to resign from, or ceased or refused to act in, every office, capacity, or relationship in which he was described in the registration statement as acting or agreeing to act, and (B) he had advised the Commission and the issuer in writing that he had taken such action and that he would not be responsible for such part of the registration statement; or

(2) that if such part of the registration statement became effective without his knowledge, upon becoming aware of such fact he forthwith acted and advised the Commission, in accordance with paragraph (1), and, in addition, gave reasonable public notice that such part of the registration statement had become effective without his knowledge; or

(3) that (A) as regards any part of the registration statement not purporting to be made on the authority of an expert, and not purporting to be a copy of or extract from a report or valuation of an expert, and not purporting to be made on the authority of a public or official document or statement, he had, after reasonable investigation, reasonable ground to believe and did believe, at the time such part of the registration statement became effective, that the

statements therein were true and that there was no omission to state a material fact required to be stated therein or necessary to make the statements therein not misleading; and (B) as regards any part of the registration statement purporting to be made upon his authority as an expert or purporting to be a copy of or extract from a report or valuation of himself as an expert, (i) he had, after reasonable investigation, reasonable ground to believe and did believe, at the time such part of the registration statement became effective, that the statements therein were true and that there was no omission to state a material fact required to be stated therein or necessary to make the statements therein not misleading, or (ii) such part of the registration statement did not fairly represent his statement as an expert or was not a fair copy of or extract from his report or valuation as an expert; and (C) as regards any part of the registration statement purporting to be made on the authority of an expert (other than himself) or purporting to be a copy of or extract from a report or valuation of an expert (other than himself), he had no reasonable ground to believe and did not believe, at the time such part of the registration statement became effective, that the statements therein were untrue or that there was an omission to state a material fact required to be stated therein or necessary to make the statements therein not misleading, or that such part of the registration statement did not fairly represent the statement of the expert or was not a fair copy of or extract from the report or valuation of the expert; and (D) as regards any part of the registration statement purporting to be a statement made by an official person or purporting to be a copy of or extract from a public official document, he had no reasonable ground to believe and did not believe, at the time such part of the registration statement became effective, that the statements therein were untrue, or that there was an omission to state a material fact required to be stated therein or necessary to make the statements therein not misleading, or that such part of the registration statement did not fairly represent the statement made by the official person or was not a fair copy of or extract from the public official document.

(c) In determining, for the purpose of paragraph (3) of subsection (b) of this section, what constitutes reasonable investigation and reasonable ground for belief, the standard of reasonableness shall be that required of a prudent man in the management of his own property.

Civil Liabilities Arising in Connection with Prospectuses and Communications

SECTION 12. Any person who—(1) offers or sells a security in violation of section 5, or

(2) offers or sells a security (whether or not exempted by the provisions of section 3, other than paragraph (2) of subsection (a) thereof), by the use of any means or instruments of transportation or communication in interstate commerce or of the mails, by means of a prospectus or oral communication, which includes an untrue statement of a material fact or omits to state a material fact necessary in order to make the statements, in the light of the circumstances under which they were made, not misleading (the purchaser not knowing of such untruth or omission), and who shall not sustain the burden of proof that he did not know, and in the exercise of reasonable care could not have known, of such untruth or omission, shall be liable to the person purchasing such security from him, who may sue either at law or in equity in any court of competent jurisdiction, to recover the consideration paid for such security with interest thereon, less the amount of any income received thereon, upon the tender of such security, or for damages if he no longer owns the security.

Penalties

SECTION 24. Any person who willfully violates any of the provisions of this title, or the rules and regulations promulgated by the Commission under authority thereof, or any person who willfully, in a registration statement filed under this title, makes any untrue statement of a material fact or omits to state any material fact required to be stated therein or necessary to make the statements therein not misleading, shall upon conviction be fined not more than $10,000 or imprisoned not more than five years, or both.

SECURITIES EXCHANGE ACT OF 1934

Regulation of the Use of Manipulative and Deceptive Devices

SECTION 10. It shall be unlawful for any person, directly or indirectly, by the use of any means or instrumentality of interstate commerce or of the mails, or of any facility of any national securities exchange—

(a) To effect a short sale, or to use or employ any stop-loss order in connection with the purchase or sale, of any security registered on a national securities exchange, in contravention of such rules and regulations as the Commission may prescribe as necessary or appropriate in the public interest or for the protection of investors.

(b) To use or employ, in connection with the purchase or sale of any security registered on a national securities exchange or any security not so registered, any manipulative or deceptive device or contrivance in contravention of such rules and regulations as the Commission may prescribe as necessary or appropriate in the public interest or for the protection of investors.

Proxies

SECTION 14. (a) It shall be unlawful for any person, by the use of the mails or by any means or instrumentality of interstate commerce or of any facility of a national securities exchange or otherwise, in contravention of such rules and regulations as the Commission may prescribe as necessary or appropriate in the public interest or for the protection of investors, to solicit or to permit the use of his name to solicit any proxy or consent or authorization in respect of any security (other than an exempted security) registered pursuant to section 12 of 78(*l*) this title.

Directors, Officers, and Principal Stockholders

SEC. 16. DIRECTORS, OFFICERS, AND PRINCIPAL STOCKHOLDERS.

" (a) DISCLOSURES REQUIRED.—

"(1) DIRECTORS, OFFICERS, AND PRINCIPAL STOCKHOLDERS REQUIRED TO FILE.—Every person who is directly or indirectly the beneficial owner of more than 10% of any class of any equity security (other than an exempted security) which is registered pursuant to section 12, or who is a director or an officer of the issuer of such security, shall file the statements required by this subsection with the Commission (and, if such security is registered on a national securities exchange, also with the exchange).

"(2) TIME OF FILING.—The statements required by this subsection shall be filed—

"(A) at the time of the registration of such security on a national securities exchange or by the effective date of a registration statement filed pursuant to section 12(g);

"(B) within 10 days after he or she becomes such beneficial owner, director, or officer;

Liability for Misleading Statements

SECTION 18. (a) Any person who shall make or cause to be made any statement in any application, report, or document filed pursuant to this title or any rule or regulation thereunder or any undertaking contained in a registration statement as provided in subsection (d) of section 15 of this title, which statement was at the time and in the light of the circumstances under which it was made false or misleading with respect to any material fact, shall be liable to any person (not knowing that such statement was false or misleading) who, in reliance upon such statement, shall have purchased or sold a security at a price which was affected by such statement, for damages caused by such reliance, unless the person sued shall prove that he acted in good faith and had no knowledge that such statement was false or misleading. A person seeking to enforce such liability may sue at law or in equity in any court of competent jurisdiction. In any such suit the court may, in its discretion, require an undertaking for the payment of the costs of such suit, and assess reasonable costs, including reasonable attorneys' fees, against either party litigant.

(b) Every person who becomes liable to make payment under this section may recover contribution as in cases of contract from any person who, if joined in the original suit, would have been liable to make the same payment.

(c) No action shall be maintained to enforce any liability created under this section unless brought within three years after the discovery of the facts constituting the cause of action and within five years after such cause of action accrued.

Appendix I

The Copyright Act (as Amended) (Excerpts)

SECTION 102. SUBJECT MATTER OF COPYRIGHT: IN GENERAL

(a) Copyright protection subsists, in accordance with this title, in original works of authorship fixed in any tangible medium of expression, now known or later developed, from which they can be perceived, reproduced, or otherwise communicated, either directly or with the aid of a machine or device. Works of authorship include the following categories:

(1) literary works;

(2) musical works, including any accompanying words;

(3) dramatic works, including any accompanying music;

(4) pantomimes and choreographic works;

(5) pictorial, graphic, and sculptural works;

(6) motion pictures and other audiovisual works;

(7) sound recordings; and

(8) architectural works.

(b) In no case does copyright protection for an original work of authorship extend to any idea, procedure, process, system, method of operation, concept, principle, or discovery, regardless of the form in which it is described, explained, illustrated, or embodied in such work.

SECTION 106. EXCLUSIVE RIGHTS IN COPYRIGHTED WORKS

Subject to sections 107 through 120, the owner of copyright under this title has the exclusive rights to do and to authorize any of the following:

(1) to reproduce the copyrighted work in copies or phonorecords;

(2) to prepare derivative works based upon the copyrighted work;

(3) to distribute copies or phonorecords of the copyrighted work to the public by sale or other transfer of ownership, or by rental, lease, or lending;

(4) in the case of literary, musical, dramatic, and choreographic works, pantomimes, and motion pictures and other audiovisual works, to perform the copyrighted work publicly; and

(5) in the case of literary, musical, dramatic, and choreographic works, pantomimes, and pictorial, graphic, or sculptural works, including the individual images of a motion picture or other audiovisual work, to display the copyrighted work publicly.

SECTION 107. LIMITATIONS ON EXCLUSIVE RIGHTS: FAIR USE

Notwithstanding the provisions of sections 106 and 106A, the fair use of a copyrighted work, including such use by reproduction in copies or phonorecords or by any other means specified by that section, for purposes such as criticism, comment, news reporting, teaching (including multiple copies for classroom use), scholarship, or research, is not an infringement of copyright. In determining whether the use made of a work in any particular case is a fair use the factors to be considered shall include—

(1) the purpose and character of the use, including whether such use is of a commercial nature or is for nonprofit educational purposes;

(2) the nature of the copyrighted work;

(3) the amount and substantiality of the portion used in relation to the copyrighted work as a whole; and

(4) the effect of the use upon the potential market for or value of the copyrighted work.

SECTION 406. COPYRIGHT REGISTRATION IN GENERAL

(a) Registration Permissive.—At any time during the subsistence of copyright in any published or unpublished work, the owner of copyright or of any exclusive right in the work may obtain registration of the copyright claim by delivering to the Copyright Office the deposit specified by this section, together with the application and fee specified by sections 409 and 708. Such registration is not a condition of copyright protection.

SECTION 591. INFRINGEMENT OF COPYRIGHT

(a) Anyone who violates any of the exclusive rights of the copyright owner as provided by sections 106 through 118 or of the author as provided in section 106A(a), or who imports copies or phonorecords into the United States in violation of section 602, is an infringer of the copyright or right of the author, as the case may be. For purposes of this chapter (other than section 506), any reference to copyright shall be deemed to include the rights conferred by section 106(a). As used in this subsection the term "anyone" includes any State, any instrumentality of a State, and any officer or employee of a State or instrumentality of a State acting in his or her official capacity. Any State, and any such instrumentality, officer, or employee, shall be subject to the provisions of this title in the same manner and to the same extent as any nongovernmental entity.

(b) The legal or beneficial owner of an exclusive right under a copyright is entitled, subject to the requirements of section 411, to institute an action for any infringement of that particular right committed while he or she is the owner of it. The court may require such owner to serve written notice of the action with a copy of the complaint upon any person shown, by the records of the Copyright Office or otherwise, to have or claim an interest in the copyright, and shall require that such notice be served upon any person whose interest is likely to be affected by a decision in the case. The court may require the joinder, and shall permit the intervention, of any person having or claiming an interest in the copyright.

REMEDIES FOR INFRINGEMENT: DAMAGES AND PROFITS

Section 504.

(a) In General. Except as otherwise provided by this title, an infringer of copyright is liable for either—

1. the copyright owner's actual damages and any additional profits of the infringer, as provided by subsection (b); or

2. statutory damages, as provided by subsection (c).

(b) Actual Damages and Profits.—The copyright owner is entitled to recover the actual damages suffered by him or her as a result of the infringement, and any profits of the infringer that are attributable to the infringement and are not taken into account in computing the actual damages. In establishing the infringer's profits, the copyright owner is required to present proof only of the infringer's gross revenue, and the infringer is required to prove his or her deductible expenses and the elements of profit attributable to factors other than the copyrighted work.

(c) Statutory Damages—(1) Except as provided by clause (2) of this subsection, the copyright owner may elect, at any time before final judgment is rendered, to recover, instead of actual damages and profits, an award of statutory damages for all infringements involved in the action, with respect to any one work, for which any one infringer is liable individually, or for which any two or more infringers are liable jointly and severally, in a sum of not less than $500 or more than $20,000 as the court considers just. For the purposes of this subsection, all the parts of a compilation or derivative work constitute one work.

(2) In a case where the copyright owner sustains the burden of proving, and the court finds, that infringement was committed willfully, the court in its discretion may increase the award of statutory damages to a sum of not more than $100,000. In a case where the infringer sustains the burden of proving, and the court finds, that such infringer was not aware and had no reason to believe that his or her acts constituted an infringement of copyright, the court in its discretion may reduce the award of statutory damages to a sum of not less than $200. The court shall remit statutory damages in any case where an infringer believed and had reasonable grounds for believing that his or her use of the copyrighted work was a fair use under section 107, if the infringer was: (i) an employee or agent of a nonprofit educational institution, library, or archives acting within the scope of his or her employment who, or such institution, library, or archives itself, which infringed by reproducing

the work in copies or phonorecords; or (ii) a public broadcasting entity which or a person who, as a regular part of the nonprofit activities of a public broadcasting entity (as defined in subsection (g) of section 118) infringed by performing a published nondramatic literary work or by reproducing a transmission program embodying a performance of such a work.

SECTION 506. CRIMINAL OFFENSES

(a) Criminal infringement—Any person who infringes a copyright willfully and for purposes of commercial advantage or private financial gain shall be punished as provided in section 2319 of title 18.

Appendix J

The Foreign Corrupt Practices Act (Excerpts)

15 U.S.C. § 78dd-1

§ 78dd-1. Prohibited foreign trade practices by issuers

(a) Prohibition

It shall be unlawful for any issuer which has a class of securities registered pursuant to section 78l of this title or which is required to file reports under section 78o(d) of this title, or for any officer, director, employee, or agent of such issuer or any stockholder thereof acting on behalf of such issuer, to make use of the mails or any means or instrumentality of interstate commerce corruptly in furtherance of an offer, payment, promise to pay, or authorization of the payment of any money, or offer, gift, promise to give, or authorization of the giving of anything of value to—

(1) any foreign official for purposes of—

(A)(i) influencing any act or decision of such foreign official in his official capacity, (ii) inducing such foreign official to do or omit to do any act in violation of the lawful duty of such official, or (iii) securing any improper advantage; or

(B) inducing such foreign official to use his influence with a foreign government or instrumentality thereof to affect or influence any act or decision of such government or instrumentality, in order to assist such issuer in obtaining or retaining business for or with, or directing business to, any person;

(2) any foreign political party or official thereof or any candidate for foreign political office for purposes of—

(A)(i) influencing any act or decision of such party, official, or candidate in its or his official capacity, (ii) inducing such party, official, or candidate to do or omit to do an act in violation of the lawful duty of such party, official, or candidate, or (iii) securing any improper advantage; or

(B) inducing such party, official, or candidate to use its or his influence with a foreign government or instrumentality thereof to affect or influence any act or decision of such government or instrumentality, in order to assist such issuer in obtaining or retaining business for or with, or directing business to, any person; or

(3) any person, while knowing that all or a portion of such money or thing of value will be offered, given, or promised, directly or indirectly, to any foreign official, to any foreign political party or official thereof, or to any candidate for foreign political office, for purposes of—

(A)(i) influencing any act or decision of such foreign official, political party, party official, or candidate in his or its official capacity, (ii) inducing such foreign official, political party, party official, or candidate to do or omit to do any act in violation of the lawful duty of such foreign official, political party, party official, or candidate, or (iii) securing any improper advantage; or

(B) inducing such foreign official, political party, party official, or candidate to use his or its influence with a foreign government or instrumentality thereof to affect or influence any act or decision of such government or instrumentality, in order to assist such issuer in obtaining or retaining business for or with, or directing business to, any person.

(b) Exception for routine governmental action

Subsections (a) and (g) of this section shall not apply to any facilitating or expediting payment to a foreign official, political party, or party official the purpose of which is to expedite or to secure the performance of a routine governmental action by a foreign official, political party, or party official.

(c) Affirmative defenses

It shall be an affirmative defense to actions under subsection (a) or (g) of this section that—

(1) the payment, gift, offer, or promise of anything of value that was made, was lawful under the written laws and regulations of the foreign official's, political party's, party official's, or candidate's country; or

(2) the payment, gift, offer, or promise of anything of value that was made, was a reasonable and bona fide expenditure, such as travel and lodging

expenses, incurred by or on behalf of a foreign official, party, party official, or candidate and was directly related to—

(A) the promotion, demonstration, or explanation of products or services; or

(B) the execution or performance of a contract with a foreign government or agency thereof.

15 U.S.C. § 78dd-2

(g) Penalties

(1)(A) Any domestic concern that is not a natural person and that violates subsection (a) or (i) of this section shall be fined not more than $2,000,000.

(B) Any domestic concern that is not a natural person and that violates subsection (a) or (i) of this section shall be subject to a civil penalty of not more than $10,000 imposed in an action brought by the Attorney General.

(2)(A) Any natural person that is an officer, director, employee, or agent of a domestic concern, or stockholder acting on behalf of such domestic concern, who willfully violates subsection (a) or (i) of this section shall be fined not more than $100,000 or imprisoned not more than 5 years, or both.

(B) Any natural person that is an officer, director, employee, or agent of a domestic concern, or stockholder acting on behalf of such domestic concern, who violates subsection (a) or (i) of this section shall be subject to a civil penalty of not more than $10,000 imposed in an action brought by the Attorney General.

(3) Whenever a fine is imposed under paragraph (2) upon any officer, director, employee, agent, or stockholder of a domestic concern, such fine may not be paid, directly or indirectly, by such domestic concern.

(h) Definitions

For purposes of this section:

(1) The term "domestic concern" means—

(A) any individual who is a citizen, national, or resident of the United States; and

(B) any corporation, partnership, association, joint-stock company, business trust, unincorporated organization, or sole proprietorship which has its principal place of business in the United States, or which is organized under the laws of a State of the United States or a territory, possession, or commonwealth of the United States.

(2)(A) The term "foreign official" means any officer or employee of a foreign government or any

department, agency, or instrumentality thereof, or of a public international organization, or any person acting in an official capacity for or on behalf of any such government or department, agency, or instrumentality, or for or on behalf of any such public international organization.

(B) For purposes of subparagraph (A), the term "public international organization" means—

(i) an organization that is designated by Executive order pursuant to section 1 of the International Organizations Immunities Act (22 U.S.C. 288); or

(ii) any other international organization that is designated by the President by Executive order for the purposes of this section, effective as of the date of publication of such order in the Federal Register.

(3)(A) A person's state of mind is "knowing" with respect to conduct, a circumstance, or a result if—

(i) such person is aware that such person is engaging in such conduct, that such circumstance exists, or that such result is substantially certain to occur; or

(ii) such person has a firm belief that such circumstance exists or that such result is substantially certain to occur.

(B) When knowledge of the existence of a particular circumstance is required for an offense, such knowledge is established if a person is aware of a high probability of the existence of such circumstance, unless the person actually believes that such circumstance does not exist.

(4)(A) The term "routine governmental action" means only an action which is ordinarily and commonly performed by a foreign official in—

(i) obtaining permits, licenses, or other official documents to qualify a person to do business in a foreign country;

(ii) processing governmental papers, such as visas and work orders;

(iii) providing police protection, mail pick-up and delivery, or scheduling inspections associated with contract performance or inspections related to transit of goods across country;

(iv) providing phone service, power and water supply, loading and unloading cargo, or protecting perishable products or commodities from deterioration; or

(v) actions of a similar nature.

(B) The term "routine governmental action" does not include any decision by a foreign official whether, or on what terms, to award new business to or to continue business with a particular party, or any action taken by a foreign official involved in the decision-making process to encourage a decision to award new business to or continue business with a particular party.

(5) The term "interstate commerce" means trade, commerce, transportation, or communication among the several States, or between any foreign country and any State or between any State and any place or ship outside thereof, and such term includes the intrastate use of—

(A) a telephone or other interstate means of communication, or

(B) any other interstate instrumentality.

(i) Alternative jurisdiction

(1) It shall also be unlawful for any United States person to corruptly do any act outside the United States in furtherance of an offer, payment, promise to pay, or authorization of the payment of any money, or offer, gift, promise to give, or authorization of the giving of anything of value to any of the persons or entities set forth in paragraphs (1), (2), and (3) of subsection (a), for the purposes set forth therein, irrespective of whether such United States person makes use of the mails or any means or instrumentality of interstate commerce in furtherance of such offer, gift, payment, promise, or authorization.

(2) As used in this subsection, the term "United States person" means a national of the United States (as defined in section 101 of the Immigration and Nationality Act (8 U.S.C. 1101)) or any corporation, partnership, association, joint-stock company, business trust, unincorporated organization, or sole proprietorship organized under the laws of the United States or any State, territory, possession, or commonwealth of the United States, or any political subdivision thereof."

SEC. 201. SERVICES OUTSIDE THE SCOPE OF PRACTICE OF AUDITORS

(a) PROHIBITED ACTIVITIES.—Section 10A of the Securities Exchange Act of 1934 (15 U.S.C. 78j-1) is amended by adding at the end the following:

"(g) PROHIBITED ACTIVITIES.—Except as provided in subsection (h), it shall be unlawful for a registered public accounting firm (and any associated person of that firm, to the extent determined appropriate by the Commission) that performs for any issuer any audit required by this title or the rules of the Commission under this title or, beginning 180 days after the date of commencement of the operations of the Public Company Accounting Oversight Board established under section 101 of the Sarbanes-Oxley Act of 2002 (in this section referred to as the 'Board'), the rules of the Board, to provide to that issuer, contemporaneously with the audit, any non-audit service, including—

"(1) bookkeeping or other services related to the accounting records or financial statements of the audit client;

"(2) financial information systems design and implementation;

"(3) appraisal or valuation services, fairness opinions, or contribution-in-kind reports;

"(4) actuarial services;

"(5) internal audit outsourcing services;

"(6) management functions or human re- sources;

"(7) broker or dealer, investment adviser, or investment banking services;

"(8) legal services and expert services unrelated to the audit; and

"(9) any other service that the Board determines, by regulation, is impermissible.

"(h) PREAPPROVAL REQUIRED FOR NON-AUDIT SERVICES.—A registered public accounting firm may engage in any non-audit service, including tax services, that is not described in any of paragraphs (1) through (9) of subsection (g) for an audit client, only if the activity is approved in advance by the audit committee of the issuer, in accordance with subsection (i)."

SEC. 203. AUDIT PARTNER ROTATION

Section 10A of the Securities Exchange Act of 1934 (15 U.S.C. 78j-1), as amended by this Act, is amended by adding at the end the following:

"(j) AUDIT PARTNER ROTATION.—It shall be unlawful for a registered public accounting firm to provide audit services to an issuer if the lead (or coordinating) audit partner (having primary responsibility for the audit), or the audit partner responsible for reviewing the audit, has performed audit services for that issuer in each of the 5 previous fiscal years of that issuer."

SEC. 302. CORPORATE RESPONSIBILITY FOR FINANCIAL REPORTS

(a) REGULATIONS REQUIRED.—The Commission shall, by rule, require, for each company filing periodic reports under section 13(a) or 15(d) of the Securities Exchange Act of 1934 (15 U.S.C. 78m, 78o(d)), that the principal executive officer or officers and the principal financial officer or officers, or persons performing similar functions, certify in each annual or quarterly report filed or submitted under either such section of such Act that—

(1) the signing officer has reviewed the report;

(2) based on the officer's knowledge, the report does not contain any untrue statement of a material fact or omit to state a material fact necessary in order to make the statements made, in light of the circumstances under which such statements were made, not misleading;

(3) based on such officer's knowledge, the financial statements, and other financial information

included in the report, fairly present in all material respects the financial condition and results of operations of the issuer as of, and for, the periods presented in the report;

(4) the signing officers—

(A) are responsible for establishing and maintaining internal controls;

(B) have designed such internal controls to ensure that material information relating to the issuer and its consolidated subsidiaries is made known to such officers by others within those entities, particularly during the period in which the periodic reports are being prepared;

(C) have evaluated the effectiveness of the issuer's internal controls as of a date within 90 days prior to the report; and

(D) have presented in the report their conclusions about the effectiveness of their internal controls based on their evaluation as of that date;

(5) the signing officers have disclosed to the issuer's auditors and the audit committee of the board of directors (or persons fulfilling the equivalent function)—

(A) all significant deficiencies in the design or operation of internal controls which could adversely affect the issuer's ability to record, process, summarize, and report financial data and have identified for the issuer's auditors any material weaknesses in internal controls; and

(B) any fraud, whether or not material, that involves management or other employees who have a significant role in the issuer's internal controls; and

(6) the signing officers have indicated in the report whether or not there were significant changes in internal controls or in other factors that could significantly affect internal controls subsequent to the date of their evaluation, including any corrective actions with regard to significant deficiencies and material weaknesses.

SEC. 304. FORFEITURE OF CERTAIN BONUSES AND PROFITS

(a) ADDITIONAL COMPENSATION PRIOR TO NONCOMPLIANCE WITH COMMISSION FINANCIAL REPORTING REQUIREMENTS.—If an issuer is required to prepare an accounting restatement due to the material noncompliance of the issuer, as a result of misconduct, with any financial reporting requirement under the securities laws, the chief executive officer and chief financial officer of the issuer shall reimburse the issuer for—

(1) any bonus or other incentive-based or equity-based compensation received by that person from the issuer during the 12-month period following the first public issuance or filing with the Commission (whichever first occurs) of the financial document embodying such financial reporting requirement; and

(2) any profits realized from the sale of securities of the issuer during that 12-month period.

SEC. 404. MANAGEMENT ASSESSMENT OF INTERNAL CONTROLS

(a) RULES REQUIRED.—The Commissions shall prescribe rules requiring each annual report required by section 13(a) or 15(d) of the Securities Exchange Act of 1934 (15 U.S.C. 78m or 78o(d) to contain an internal control report, which shall—

(1) state the responsibility of management for establishing and maintaining an adequate internal control structure and procedures for financial reporting; and

(2) contain an assessment, as of the end of the most recent fiscal year of the issuer, of the effectiveness of the internal control structure and procedures of the issuer for financial reporting.

SEC. 406. CODE OF ETHICS FOR SENIOR FINANCIAL OFFICERS

(a) CODE OF ETHICS DISCLOSURE.—The Commission shall issue rules to require each issuer, together with periodic reports required pursuant to section 13(a) or 15(d) of the Securities Exchange Act of 1934, to disclose whether or not, and if not, the reason therefor, such issuer has adopted a code of ethics for senior financial officers, applicable to its principal financial officer and comptroller or principal accounting officer, or persons performing similar functions.

SEC. 802. CRIMINAL PENALTIES FOR ALTERING DOCUMENTS

(a) IN GENERAL.—Chapter 73 of title 18, United States Code, is amended by adding at the end the following:

§ 1519. Destruction, alteration, or falsification of records in Federal investigations and bankruptcy

Whoever knowingly alters, destroys, mutilates, conceals, covers up, falsifies, or makes a false entry in any record, document, or tangible object with the-intent to impede, obstruct, or influence the investigation or proper administration of any matter within the jurisdiction of any department or agency of the United States or any case filed under title 11, or in relation to or contemplation of any such matter or case, shall be fined under this title, imprisoned not more than 20 years, or both.

§ 1520. Destruction of corporate audit records

(a)(1) Any accountant who conducts an audit of an issuer of securities to which section 10A(a) of the Securities Exchange Act of 1934 (15 U.S.C. 78j-1(a)) applies, shall maintain all audit or review workpapers for a period of 5 years from the end of the fiscal period in which the audit or review was concluded.

(2) The Securities and Exchange Commission shall promulgate, within 180 days, after adequate notice and an opportunity for comment, such rules and regulations, as are reasonably necessary, relating to the retention of relevant records such as workpapers, documents that form the basis of an audit or review, memoranda, correspondence, communications, other documents, and records (including electronic records) which are created, sent, or received in connection with an audit or review and contain conclusions, opinions, analyses, or financial data relating to such an audit or review, which is conducted by any accountant who conducts an audit of an issuer of securities to which section 10A(a) of the Securities Exchange Act of 1934 (15 U.S.C. 78j-1(a)) applies. The Commission may, from time to time, amend or supplement the rules and regulations that it is required to promulgate under this section, after adequate notice and an opportunity for comment, in order to ensure that such rules and regulations adequately comport with the purposes of this section.

(b) Whoever knowingly and willfully violates subsection (a)(1), or any rule or regulation promulgated by the Securities and Exchange Commission under subsection (a)(2), shall be fined under this title, imprisoned not more than 10 years, or both.

SEC. 906. CORPORATE RESPONSIBILITY FOR FINANCIAL REPORTS

(a) IN GENERAL.—Chapter 63 of title 18, United States Code, is amended by inserting after section 1349, as created by this Act, the following:

"§ 1350. Failure of corporate officers to certify financial reports

(a) CERTIFICATION OF PERIODIC FINANCIAL REPORTS.—Each periodic report containing financial statements filed by an issuer with the Securities Exchange Commission pursuant to section 13(a) or 15(d) of the Securities Exchange Act of 1934 (15 U.S.C. 78m(a) or 78o(d)) shall be accompanied by a written statement by the chief executive officer and chief financial officer (or equivalent thereof) of the issuer.

(b) CONTENT.—The statement required under subsection (a) shall certify that the periodic report containing the financial statements fully complies with the requirements of section 13(a) or 15(d) of the Securities Exchange Act pf 1934 (15 U.S.C. 78m or 78o(d)) and that information contained in the periodic report fairly presents, in all material respects, the financial condition and results of operations of the issuer.

(c) CRIMINAL PENALTIES.—Whoever—

"(1) certifies any statement as set forth in subsections (a) and (b) of this section knowing that the periodic report accompanying the statement does not comport with all the requirements set forth in this section shall be fined not more than $1,000,000 or imprisoned not more than 10 years, or both; or

(2) willfully certifies any statement as set forth in subsections (a) and (b) of this section knowing that the periodic report accompanying the statement does not comport with all the requirements set forth in this section shall be fined not more than $5,000,000, or imprisoned not more than 20 years, or both.

SEC. 1102. TAMPERING WITH A RECORD OR OTHERWISE IMPEDING AN OFFICIAL PROCEEDING

Section 1512 of title 18, United States Code, is amended—

(1) by redesignating subsections (c) through (i) as subsections (d) through (j), respectively; and

(2) by inserting after subsection (b) the following new subsection:

(c) Whoever corruptly—

(1) alters, destroys, mutilates, or conceals a record, document, or other object, or attempts to do so, with the intent to impair the object's integrity or availabilityfor use in an official proceeding; or

(2) otherwise obstructs, influences, or impedes any official proceeding, or attempts to do so, shall be fined under this title or imprisoned not more than 20 years, or both."

Appendix L

The Federal Trade Commission Act (Excerpts)

SECTION 5. UNFAIR METHODS OF COMPETITION UNLAW-FUL; PREVENTION BY COM-MISSION—DECLARATION OF UNLAWFULNESS; POWER TO PROHIBIT UNFAIR PRACTICES

(a) (1) Unfair methods of competition in or affecting commerce, and unfair or deceptive acts or practices in or affecting commerce, are declared unlawful.

Penalty for Violation of Order; Injunctions and Other Appropriate Equitable Relief

(1) Any person, partnership, or corporation who violates an order of the Commission after it has become final, and while such order is in effect, shall forfeit and pay to the United States a civil penalty of not more than $10,000 for each violation, which shall accrue to the United States and may be recovered in a civil action brought by the Attorney General of the United States. Each separate violation of such an order shall be a separate offense, except that in the case of a violation through continuing failure to obey or neglect to obey a final order of the Commission, each day of continuance of such failure or neglect shall be deemed a separate offense. In such actions, the United States district courts are empowered to grant mandatory injunctions and such other and further equitable relief as they deem appropriate in the enforcement of such final orders of the Commission.

SECTION 7. ACQUISITION BY ONE CORPORATION OF STOCK OF ANOTHER

No corporation engaged in commerce shall acquire, directly or indirectly, the whole or any part of the stock; or other share capital and no corporation subject to the jurisdiction of the Federal Trade Commission shall acquire the whole or any part of the assets of another corporation in any section of the country, the effect of such acquisition may be substantially to lessen competition, or to tend to create a monopoly.

No corporation shall acquire, directly or indirectly, the whole or any part of the stock or other share capital and no corporation subject to the jurisdiction of the Federal Trade Commission shall acquire the whole or any part of the assets of one or more corporations engaged in commerce, where in any line of commerce in any section of the country, the effect of such acquisition, of such stocks or assets, or of the use of such stock by the voting or granting of proxies or otherwise, may be substantially to lessen competition, or to tend to create a monopoly.

Appendix M

The Clayton Act (Excerpts)

SECTION 8. INTERLOCKING DIRECTORATES AND OFFICERS

No private banker or director, officer, or employee of any member bank of the Federal Reserve System or any branch thereof shall be at the same time a director, officer, or employee of any other bank, banking association, savings bank, or trust company organized under the National Bank Act or organized under the laws of any State or of the District of Columbia, or any branch thereof, except that the Board of Governors of the Federal Reserve System may by regulation permit such service as a director, officer, or employee of not more than one other such institution or branch thereof; . . .

Appendix N

The Sherman Act (Excerpts)

SECTION 1. TRUSTS, ETC., IN RESTRAINT OF TRADE ILLEGAL; PENALTY

Every contract, combination in the form of trust or otherwise, or conspiracy, in restraint of trade or commerce among the several States, or with foreign nations, is declared to be illegal. Every person who shall make any contract or engage in any combination or conspiracy hereby declared to be illegal shall be deemed guilty of a felony, and, on conviction thereof, shall be punished by fine not exceeding one million dollars if a corporation, or, if any other person, one hundred thousand dollars or by imprisonment not exceeding three years, or by both said punishments, in the discretion of the court.

SECTION 2. MONOPOLIZATION; PENALTY

Every person who shall monopolize, or attempt to-monopolize, or combine or conspire with any other person or persons, to monopolize any part of-the trade or commerce among the several States, or with foreign nations, shall be deemed guilty of-a-felony, and, on conviction thereof, shall be punished by fine not exceeding $10,000,000 if a corporation, or, if any other person, $350,000 or by imprisonment not exceeding three years, or by both said punishments, in the discretion of the court.

Appendix O

The Robinson–Patman Act (Excerpts)

SECTION 2. DISCRIMINATION IN PRICE, SERVICES, OR FACILITIES—PRICE; SELECTION OF CUSTOMERS

(a) It shall be unlawful for any person engaged in commerce, in the course of such commerce, either directly or indirectly, to discriminate in price between different purchasers of commodities of like grade and quality, where either or any of the purchases involved in such discrimination are in commerce, where such commodities are sold for use, consumption, or resale within the United States or any Territory thereof or the District of Columbia or any insular possession or other place under the jurisdiction of the United States, and where the effect of such discrimination may be substantially to lessen competition or tend to create a monopoly in any line of commerce, or to injure, destroy, or prevent competition with any person who either grants or knowingly receives the benefit of such discrimination, or with customers of either of them; Provided, That nothing herein contained shall prevent differentials which make only due allowance for differences in the cost of manufacture, sale, or delivery resulting from the differing methods or quantities in which such commodities are to such purchasers sold or delivered: Provided, however, That the Federal Trade Commission may, after due investigation and hearing to all interested parties, fix and establish quantity limits, and revise the same as it finds necessary, as to particular commodities or classes of commodities, where it finds that available purchasers in greater quantities are so few as to render differentials on account thereof unjustly discriminatory or promotive of monopoly in any line of commerce; and the foregoing shall then not be construed to permit differentials based on differences in quantities greater than those so fixed and established: And provided further, That nothing herein contained shall prevent persons engaged in selling goods, wares, or merchandise in commerce from selecting their own customers in bona fide transactions and not in restraint of trade: And provided further, That nothing herein contained shall prevent price changes from time to time where in response to changing conditions affecting the market for or the marketability of the goods concerned, such as but not limited to actual or imminent deterioration of perishable goods, obsolescence of seasonal goods, distress sales under court process, or sales in good faith in discontinuance of business in the goods concerned.

SECTION 3. DISCRIMINATION IN REBATES, DISCOUNTS, OR ADVERTISING SERVICE CHARGES; UNDERSELLING IN PARTICULAR LOCALITIES; PENALTIES

It shall be unlawful for any person engaged in commerce, in the course of such commerce, to be a party to, or assist in, any transaction of sale, or contract to sell, which discriminates to his knowledge against competitors of the purchaser, in that, any discount, rebate, allowance, or advertising service charge is granted to the purchaser over and above any discount, rebate, allowance, or advertising service charge available at the time of such transaction to said competitors in respect of a sale of goods of like grade, quality, and quantity; to sell, or contract to sell, goods in any part of the United States at prices lower than those exacted by said person elsewhere in the United States for the purpose of destroying competition, or eliminating a competitor in such part of the United States; or, to sell, or contract to sell, goods at unreasonably low prices for the purpose of destroying competition or eliminating a competitor.

Any person violating any of the provisions of this section shall, upon conviction thereof, be fined not more than $5,000 or imprisoned not more than one year, or both.

Glossary

A

absolute privilege A defense to defamation; a protection given to legislators and courtroom participants for statements made relating to the proceedings; encourages people to come forward and speak without fear of liability.

acceptance Offeree's positive response to offeror's proposed contract.

accord and satisfaction An agreement (accord) to pay a certain amount, the payment of which constitutes full payment (satisfaction) of that debt.

accredited investor For purposes of Regulation D, an investor with certain financial stability who is not counted in the number of purchaser limitations for Rules 505 and 506.

act of state doctrine In international law, a theory that each country's governmental actions are autonomous and not subject to judicial review by the courts in other countries.

actual authority Authority given from a principal to an agent by express oral or written instructions or contract.

actual notice Private or individual notice sent directly to affected parties; this type of notice is effective only if the party actually receives it, as compared to constructive notice, for which publication is sufficient.

actus reus Latin term for the criminal act or conduct required for proof of a crime.

administrative agency Governmental unit created by a legislative body for the purposes of administering and enforcing the laws.

administrative law judge (ALJ) Special category of judicial official who presides over agency enforcement hearings.

Administrative Procedures Act (APA) Basic federal law governing the creation, operation, and reporting of federal administrative agencies.

advances In partnerships, loans by the partners to the partnership; makes the partner a creditor of the partnership.

affirm Action taken by an appellate court on an appealed case; the effect is that the court upholds the lower court's decision.

affirmative action Label given to employment processes and programs designed to help underrepresented groups obtain jobs and promotions.

Age Discrimination in Employment Act of 1967 (ADEA) Federal law that prohibits job discrimination on the basis of age; prohibits the consideration of age in an employment decision.

agency by estoppel Theory for creation of an agency relationship that holds the principal liable because the principal has allowed the agent to represent him as his principal.

agent One who acts on behalf of and at the direction of another.

alter ego theory Theory used for disregarding the corporate protection of limited liability for shareholders; results when individuals treat the corporation's properties and accounts as their own and fail to follow corporate formalities.

alternative dispute resolution (ADR) Means other than litigation used to resolve disputes and claims; includes arbitration, mediation, and negotiated settlements.

American Competitive and Workforce Investment Act of 1998 Federal law that permits greater numbers of immigrants who are highly skilled.

American Competitiveness in the Twenty-First Century Act of 2000 Federal law that increased the quotas for highly skilled immigrants.

Americans with Disabilities Act (ADA) A 1991 federal law that prohibits discrimination in the workplace against persons with disabilities and requires employers to make reasonable accommodations for employees with disabilities who are otherwise qualified to perform a job.

annual percentage rate (APR) A financing term representing the annual debt cost and a required disclosure under Regulation Z.

answer Pleading filed by the defendant in a lawsuit; contains the defendant's version of the basis of the suit, counterclaims, and denials.

Antiterrorism and Effective Death Penalty Act One of several post 9/11/2001 federal statutes passed to increase grounds for deportation and penalties for criminal conduct for terrorist activities.

apparent authority Authority of an agent to act on behalf of a principal that results from the appearance of the agent's authority to third parties.

appellant The name on appeal for the party who appeals a lower court's decision.

appellate Adjective that describes courts and processes above the trial level; management of the appeals after trial court procedures.

appellate brief Lawyer's summation of issues of law and/or error for appellate court to consider.

appellate court A court of appeals or a court of review; a court whose function is to review the decision and actions of a trial court; does not hear witnesses; only reviews the transcript and studies the arguments and briefs of the parties.

appellee The name on appeal for the party who won a lower court's decision—that is, the party who does not appeal the lower court decision.

appraisal rights Rights of dissenting shareholders after a merger or takeover to be paid the value of their shares before the takeover or merger.

appropriation In international law, the taking of private property by a government; also known as expropriation; in torts, use of the name, likeness, or image of another for commercial purposes.

arbitrary and capricious Standard for challenging administrative agency rules; used to show decisions or rules were not based on sufficient facts.

arbitration Alternative form of dispute resolution in which parties submit evidence to a third party who is a member of the American Arbitration Association and who makes a decision after hearing the case.

arraignment Hearing in criminal procedure held after an indictment or information is returned; trial date is set and plea is entered.

articles of incorporation Organizational papers of a corporation; list the company's structure, capitalization, board structure, and so on.

articles of limited partnership Contract governing the rights and relations of limited partners.

articles of partnership Organizational papers of a partnership; often called the partnership agreement; list rights of partners, profit/loss arrangements, and so on.

Asbestos Hazard Emergency Response Act (AHERA) Federal environmental legislation that requires removal of asbestos from public schools and other facilities where exposure is particularly dangerous (where young children are present).

asset acquisition Form of takeover in which another firm buys all the assets of a firm and gains control through control of the firm's property.

Asset Conservation, Lender Liability, and Deposit Insurance Protection Act of 1996 Federal law that clarified the liability of lenders for CERCLA violations and clean-up upon their foreclosure and repossession of debtor's property.

assignment In contract law, the transfer of the benefits under a contract to a third party; the third party has a right to benefits but is subject to any contract defenses.

assumption of risk Defense in negligence cases that prevents an injured party from recovering if it can be established that the injured party realized the risk and engaged in the conduct anyway.

attorney-client privilege Protection of client's disclosures to her attorney; attorney cannot disclose information client offers (with some exceptions, such as the client telling the attorney of an ongoing or planned crime); the confession of a crime already committed cannot be disclosed by the lawyer.

audit committee Committee of the board responsible for oversight of company financial statements.

authorization cards Cards signed by employees and required to establish the 30 percent support necessary to hold an election for a union as exclusive bargaining agent for the collective bargaining unit.

B

bait and switch Term given to advertising technique in which a low-price product is advertised and then the customer is told that the product is unavailable or is talked into a higher-priced product; prohibited by the FTC.

bankruptcy Federal process of obtaining relief from debts in exchange for the surrender of most assets.

Bankruptcy Abuse Prevention and Consumer Protection Act of 2005 The bankruptcy reform act that changed the requirements for declaring bankruptcy and limited the exemptions for debtor property.

bargain and sale deed A special warranty deed.

bargained-for exchange The mutual exchange of detriment as the consideration element in a contract.

basis of the bargain Information the buyer relies on in making the decision to make a purchase.

battle of the forms Term used to describe the problem of merchants using their purchase orders and invoices with conflicting terms as their contractual understanding; problem is remedied by § 2–207 of the UCC.

Berne Convention Implementation Act of 1988 Federal law that changed U.S. copyright law to comply with international agreement at Berne Convention.

best available treatment (BAT) In environmental law, the most advanced and effective technology for preventing pollution; a higher standard than the best conventional treatment.

best conventional treatment (BCT) Requirement imposed by EPA on point source pollution that requires firms to use the best existing treatments for water pollution.

bilateral contract Contract in which both parties make promises to perform.

bilateral treaty In international law, a treaty between two nations.

bill of lading Receipt for goods issued by a carrier; used as a means of transferring title in exchange for payment or a draw on a line of credit.

Bill of Rights Portion of the U.S. Constitution that consists of the first ten amendments and includes such rights as freedom of speech, right to privacy, the protections afforded in criminal procedures under the Fourth Amendment search and seizure, and the Fifth Amendment protections against self-incrimination.

binding arbitration Arbitration from which there is no judicial appeal.

blackout period Period during which employees of a company cannot trade the company's stock because of pending events or announcements that will affect the company's performance and/or share price.

blue-sky laws State laws regulating the sale of securities.

board of directors Policy-setting governing group of a corporation.

bona fide occupational qualification (BFOQ) A justification for discrimination on the basis of sex if it can be established that gender is a requirement for a job; also applies to discrimination on the basis of religion, national origin, and so on.

brief Document prepared by lawyers on the appeal of a case to provide the appellate court with a summary of the case and the issues involved.

bubble concept Tactic employed by the EPA in determining levels of air pollution that determines appropriate levels of release by assuming that all the pollution in an area comes from one source.

burden of proof The responsibility of the party for proving the facts needed to recover in a lawsuit.

business ethics *See* **ethics.**

business judgment rule Duty of care imposed upon members of corporate boards that requires adequate review of issues and information, devotion of adequate time to deliberations, and hiring of outside consultants as necessary for making decisions; the standard does not require foolproof judgment, only reasonable care in making the judgment.

"but for" test In negligence, the standard used for determining whether the defendant's negligence caused the plaintiff's injury; "but for" the fact that the defendant was negligent, the plaintiff would not have been injured.

bylaws Operating rules of a corporation and its board; usually describe the officers and their roles and authority, along with meeting procedures and notices.

C

capacity Legal term for the ability to enter legally into a contract; for example, age capacity (minors do not have capacity).

causation In negligence, an element that requires the plaintiff to show that the defendant's lack of care caused the plaintiff's injury.

caveat emptor Latin term for "Let the buyer beware"; summarizes an attitude that once prevailed in contract law of a lack of protection for a buyer of defective goods.

celebrity endorsements Public figures advertising products on the basis of their personal use.

Celler-Kefauver Act Act that amended Section 7 of the Clayton Act and closed the loophole of merger through asset acquisition by regulating asset acquisitions.

certification Process of authorizing a union to represent exclusively a group of workers.

certiorari Latin term meaning "to become informed." A court agrees to hear a case when it grants *certiorari.*

charge Complaint to the NLRB brought by a private party.

charitable subscription A promise to make payment to a charitable organization; a pledge; it is enforceable even though the charity gives nothing in exchange.

checks and balances Term describing our tripartite system of government, in which each branch has some check mechanism to control abuses of powers by the other branches.

citation Name given to abbreviated description of a court case or statute; for example, 355 F. Supp. 291.

cite *See* **citation.**

civil law Laws affecting the private rights of individuals.

Civil Rights Act of 1964 Cornerstone of the antidiscrimination statutes; the original statute passed to prevent discrimination in housing, education, and employment.

Civil Rights Act of 1991 Amendments to original civil rights laws that changed damages, burden of proof, and claims standards for private suits for discrimination.

Civil Rights Acts of 1866 and 1870 Initial acts of Congress to help curb discrimination in employment; little was done with them once passed.

class action suit In civil law, a suit by a group of plaintiffs with the same claims; generally used in antitrust and securities lawsuits.

Clayton Act One of the major antitrust laws; governs the control of business through mergers, acquisitions, and interlocking directorates.

Clean Air Act The first effective anti-air-pollution act and the cornerstone of air pollution legislation.

Clean Air Act Amendments of 1990 First major changes to federal environmental laws on air pollution since 1977; impose additional requirements on industrial emissions controls, auto emissions, and other types of chemical emissions that affect the ozone layer.

Clean Water Act The first effective anti-water-pollution act and the cornerstone of water pollution legislation.

close corporation A type of corporation created by statute that allows limited liability with direct tax benefits.

closed-end transaction Term used in Regulation Z to describe credit transactions with definite times for and amounts of repayment that are not ongoing; for example, retail installment contracts.

closed shop A place of employment restricting hirees to union members only.

closing argument The summary attorneys give to the jury before it deliberates and after all the evidence has been presented.

code of ethics A set of rules adopted by a company to establish acceptable behavior standards for its employees.

Code of Federal Regulations (C.F.R.) Series of volumes carrying the enactments of all federal agencies.

collateral Property subject to a lien, security interest, or chattel mortgage.

collective bargaining agreement Contract between management and labor represented by one union for a collective bargaining unit.

collective bargaining unit NLRB term for a group of employees represented by one bargaining agent and agreement; can be a plant, a national group, or a subpart of a plant.

comment letter SEC response to registration filing; requires additional information or clarification on proposed offering.

Commerce Clause Provision in the U.S. Constitution controlling the regulation of intrastate, interstate, and foreign commerce and delineating authority for such regulation.

commercial impracticability Contract defense for nonperformance under the UCC that excuses a party when performance has become impossible or will involve much more than what was anticipated in the contract negotiations.

commercial speech The speech of business in the form of advertising, political endorsements, or comments on social issues.

common law Originally, the law of England made uniform after William the Conqueror; today, the nonstatutory law and the law found in judicial precedent.

common stock Type of shares in a corporation; the voting shares of the corporation and generally the bulk of ownership.

community-right-to-know substance Under federal environmental laws, a toxin used by a business or an operation that must be publicly disclosed; EPA filing is required.

comparative negligence In negligence, a defense that allocates responsibility for an accident between the plaintiff and defendant when both were negligent and determines liability accordingly.

compensatory damages Damages to put nonbreaching party in the same position he would have been in had the breach not occurred.

complaint The first pleading in a lawsuit; the document that outlines the plaintiff's allegations against the defendant and specifies the remedies sought; with respect to federal agencies, can also be a formal change of rules or statutory violations by a company or individual.

Comprehensive Environmental Response, Compensation, and Liability Act (CERCLA) Federal law that authorized federal funds to clean up hazardous waste disposal.

computer crime Theft, espionage, and other illegal activities accomplished through the use of a computer.

Computer Software Copyright Act of 1980 Provides copyright protection for software.

concurrent jurisidiction Authority of more than one court to hear a case.

condition precedent In contracts, an event or action that must take place before a contract is required to be performed; for example, qualifying for financing is a condition precedent for a lender's performance on a mortgage loan.

conditions Events that must occur before contract performance is due.

conditions concurrent (conditions contemporaneous) In contracts, the conditions that must occur simultaneously for contract performance to be required; for example, in an escrow closing in real property, an agent collects title, insurance, funds, and other documents and sees that all the exchanges under the contract occur at the same time; the parties perform their part of the agreement at the same time.

confidential relationship A relationship of trust and reliance; necessary to establish the defense to undue influence.

conglomerate merger A merger between two firms in different lines of business.

congressional enabling act Legislation that creates a new agency for enforcement of legislation or assigns enforcement of a new law to an existing agency; establishes the authority of the agency and scope of enforcement responsibilities.

conscious avoidance Term used to apply to CEO and CFO of a company trying to avoid criminal culpability for financial fraud by choosing to avoid understanding or examining the financial statements prepared by others in their companies.

consent decree For administrative agencies, a type of plea bargain; a settlement document for an administrative agency's charges.

consequential damages Damages resulting from a contract breach, such as penalties or lost profits.

consideration In contracts, what each party gives to the other as part of the contract performance.

consolidation A form of merger in which two firms unite and become known by a new name.

constitution Document that contains the basic rights in a society and the structure of its government; cannot be changed without the approval of the society's members.

constructive notice Notice given in a public place or published notice, as opposed to actual notice.

Consumer Credit Protection Act Act that provides disclosure requirements for lenders and protections for debtors; more commonly referred to as the Truth in Lending Act.

consumer debt Debt entered into for the purpose of purchasing goods or services for personal or household use.

Consumer Financial Protection Act *See* **Dodd-Frank Wall Street Reform and Consumer Financial Protection Act (DFCFPA).**

Consumer Leasing Act Act that provides for disclosure protection for consumers who are leasing goods.

Consumer Product Safety Commission Federal agency that establishes safety standards for consumer goods.

Consumer Product Safety Improvement Act (CPSIA) Federal law that regulates secondary sale of products and requires evaluation of toys and other products for lead paint content.

contentious jurisdiction Consensual jurisdiction of a court that is consented to when the parties have a dispute; for example, UN courts.

contract Binding agreement between two parties for the exchange of goods, real estate, or services.

contract defense Situation, term, or event that makes an otherwise valid contract invalid.

contract interference Tort involving a third party's actions resulting in a valid contract being lost or invalidated; an unfair method of competition.

contributory negligence Negligence defense that results when the injured party acted in a negligent way and contributed to her own injuries.

Controlling the Assault of Non-Solicited Pornography and Marketing (CAN-SPAM) Federal law that deals with those who use unsolicited e-mails for purposes of advertising.

Convention on Combating Bribery of Foreign Public Officials in International Business Transactions Treaty agreed to by OECD nations by which all agreed to make bribery of public officials a criminal act so as to curb corruption in business.

conventional pollutant EPA classification of water pollutant that must be treated prior to its release into waterways.

cooling-off period Under the Taft-Hartley Act, a provision that can be invoked by the president to require laborers threatening to strike in an industry that affects the health and safety of the nation to continue to work during a negotiation period.

copyright Under federal law, a right given to protect the exclusive use of books, music, and other creative works.

corporate opportunity doctrine A business proposition or investment opportunity that a corporation would have an interest in pursuing; precludes directors from taking a profit opportunity when the corporation would have an interest.

corporate political speech *See* **political speech.**

corporate veil The personal liability shield; the corporate protection that entitles shareholders, directors, and officers to limited liability; can be pierced for improper conduct of business or fraud.

corporation Business entity created by statute that provides limited liability for its owners.

corrective advertising Potential FTC remedy required when ads run by a firm have been deceptive; requires company to run ads explaining previous ads or run a new statement in future ads.

Council on Environmental Quality (CEQ) Agency under the executive branch created in 1966 to formulate environmental policy and make recommendations for legislation.

counterclaim Pleading in a lawsuit in which the defendant makes allegations against the plaintiff in response to the plaintiff's complaint.

counteroffer Response by offeree to offer or when offeree changes terms of offer.

county courts Lesser trial courts that hear smaller disputes and misdemeanor cases; like justice of the peace courts in many states.

course of dealing Pattern of a relationship between two parties who have contracted previously.

Court of Justice of European Communities The court of dispute settlement for the nations of the European Community.

courts of chancery Courts that were once separate and administered equitable remedies; now chancery courts are not separate; most courts have the authority to order legal or equitable remedies.

covenants not to compete Promises to protect employers and buyers from loss of goodwill through employee or seller competition.

crime A wrong against society that carries penalties of imprisonment and/or fines.

criminal fraud A crime in which the victim is defrauded by an intentional act of the perpetrator.

criminal law As opposed to civil law, the law on wrongs against society.

cross-elasticity Economic term describing the willingness of customers to substitute various goods; for example, waxed paper for plastic wrap.

cross-examination Questioning by opposing parties of a witness in court; that is, defendant cross-examines plaintiff's witnesses and plaintiff cross-examines defendant's witnesses.

cumulative preferred stock Type of ownership in a corporation that gives the stock owners preference in the distribution of dividends and also guarantees earnings each year; in the event those earnings are not paid, they are carried over or accumulate until they can be paid.

customer and territorial restrictions Manufacturer's restrictions on retail sales locations and customers.

cyber law Collection of laws from various sources that apply to transactions, use and abuse of Internet, and e-mail communications.

cybersquatting Process of registering sites and domain names that are deceptively or confusingly similar to existing names, trade names, and trademarks.

D

defamation Tort of making untrue statements about another that cause damage to his reputation or character.

default Judgment entered when the defendant fails to file an answer in a lawsuit.

defendant The party who is alleged to have committed a wrong in a civil lawsuit; the charged party in a criminal prosecution.

deficiency letter *See* **comment letter.**

del credere **agency** Agent who sells principal's goods to a buyer on credit and agrees to pay the principal if the buyer does not pay for the goods.

delegation Transfer of obligations under a contract; generally accompanied by assignment of benefits.

de minimis Latin term meaning small or minimal.

de novo Latin term for starting over or anew; a trial de novo is a special form of appeal of a trial decision that allows the case to be retried in a different forum.

deposition Form of discovery in which witnesses or parties can be questioned under oath in recorded testimony outside the courtroom.

derivative suit Lawsuit brought on behalf of another through the other's rights; for example, a shareholder suing to enforce corporation's rights.

DFCFPA *See* **Dodd-Frank Wall Street Reform and Consumer Financial Protection Act.**

dicta In a judicial opinion, the explanation for the decision; not the actual rule of law but the reasoning for the ruling.

Digital Millennium Copyright Act (DMCA) 1998 amendment to federal copyright laws that includes use of computer technology to copy music and other copyrighted materials as infringement.

digital signature Authorization for a contract provided via electronic means.

direct examination Term that describes a party's questioning of her own witness.

directed verdict Verdict entered by judge upon motion of a party after the presentation of either side's case; can be entered if the plaintiff has not met his burden of proof or if the defendant fails to rebut the plaintiff's case.

disclaimer A provision in a contract that eliminates liability such as a warranty disclaimer or a disclaimer of tort liability.

discovery Process before trial for investigation of the case; includes collection of evidence, deposing witnesses, posing and answering interrogatories and admissions, and production of documents.

disparagement Form of unfair competition in which a business, its trademark, or its name is maligned; business defamation.

disparate impact Theory for establishing discrimination; involves using statistical analysis to demonstrate that a particular practice or an employer's hiring practices have a greater impact on protected classes.

disparate treatment In discrimination law, the application of different rules or standards to people of different races, genders, or national origins.

dissenting opinion In an appellate court's review of a case, an opinion written by a judge who disagrees with the decision of the majority of the court.

dissenting shareholder Shareholder who has objected to a merger or consolidation and votes against it; is entitled to receive the value of her shares before the merger or consolidation.

dissolution In partnerships, occurs when one partner ceases to be associated with the business; in corporations, the termination of the corporate existence.

diversity of citizenship A term referring to a requirement for federal court jurisdiction that plaintiff and defendant must be citizens of different states.

Dodd-Frank Consumer Financial Protection Act (DFCFPA) *See* **Dodd-Frank Wall Street Reform and Consumer Financial Protection Act (DFCFPA).**

Dodd-Frank Wall Street Reform and Consumer Financial Protection Act (DFCFPA) Federal law over 2000 pages in length the increases and modifies the regulation of financial markets, investment firms, securities analysts, rating agencies, corporate boards, and consumer credit (including mortgage disclosures).

domain registration Public filing for ownership of the name for a Web site.

domestic corporation A term used to describe a corporation in the state in which it is incorporated.

double jeopardy In criminal law, a constitutional prohibition against being tried twice for the same crime.

due diligence Under the Securities Act of 1933, a defense for filing a false registration statement that requires proof that the individuals involved did all they could to uncover the truth and could not have discovered the false statements despite their due diligence.

due process Constitutional protection ensuring notice and a fair trial or hearing in all judicial proceedings.

duress In contract law, a defense that permits nonperformance of a contract if the party can show that physical or mental force was used to obtain the agreement to enter into the contract.

E

early neutral evaluation A third party's assessment of the issues and likely resolution of a dispute prior to any significant judicial process.

EEOC complaint Complaint against an employer filed by either an employee or the EEOC; initiates an investigation by the EEOC.

effluent guidelines In environmental law, the standards for release of nonnatural substances into natural waters.

8-K form A filing required by the SEC under the 1934 Securities Act; an 8-K is filed by a registered company within ten days of a significant or material event affecting the company (e.g., a dividend being suspended).

Electronic Communications Privacy Act of 1986 (ECPA) Federal statute that prohibits the interception of and/or eavesdropping on live conversations; designed to prevent listening device use on phone conversations, the act has reemerged with the Internet to be used against those who intercept or "eavesdrop" on e-mail.

Electronic Signatures in Global and National Commerce Act of 2000 (ESIGN) A federal law that recognizes digital signatures as authentic for purposes of contract formation; E-sign puts electronic signatures on equal footing with paper contracts.

elements The requirements for proof of a crime.

embezzlement Name for the crime of an employee stealing funds, property, or services from his employer.

eminent domain In constitutional law, the taking of private property by a government entity for a public purpose, with compensation paid to the owner.

emissions offset policy EPA procedure for approval of new facilities in nonattainment areas.

employment at will Doctrine that gives the employer the right to fire an employee at any time with or without cause; the doctrine and its protection for employers have been eroded by judicial decisions over recent years.

Employment Retirement Income Security Act of 1974 (ERISA) Congressional act establishing requirements for disclosure and other procedures with relation to employees' retirement plans.

enabling act Act of a legislative body establishing an administrative agency and providing it with guidelines and authority for the enforcement of the law.

en banc French term for the full bench; refers to an appellate hearing in which the full court, as opposed to a panel of three judges, hears a case on review.

Endangered Species Act (ESA) Federal environmental law that requires federal agencies to disclose the impact of proposed projects on species listed as protected under the act.

enlightened self-interest Theory of corporate social responsibility under which managers believe that by serving society they best serve their shareholders.

environmental impact statement (EIS) Report required to be filed when a federal agency is taking action that will affect land, water, or air; an analysis of the effect of a project on the environment.

Environmental Protection Agency (EPA) The main federal agency responsible for the enforcement of all the federal environmental laws.

Equal Credit Opportunity Act (ECOA) Federal law that prohibits discrimination on the basis of race, sex, national origin, marital status, or ethnicity in the decision to extend credit.

Equal Employment Opportunity Act of 1972 Congressional act that established the EEOC and provided strong enforcement powers for Title VII provisions.

Equal Employment Opportunity Commission (EEOC) Federal agency responsible for the enforcement of Title VII and other federal antidiscrimination laws.

Equal Pay Act of 1963 Act prohibiting wage discrimination on the basis of age, race, sex, ethnicity, and so on.

equal protection Constitutional right of all citizens to be treated in the same manner and afforded the same rights under law regardless of sex, race, color, or national origin.

equitable remedy A remedy other than money damages, such as specific performance, injunction, and so on.

equity That portion of the law that originated to afford remedies when money damages were not appropriate; currently, remedies of law and equity have merged and courts can award either or both.

estoppel Doctrine of reliance; prevents parties from backing out of an obligation they have created; for example, a partner by estoppel has allowed others to use her name in connection with a partnership and is estopped from denying liability to third parties who have relied on that representation.

ethical standards Standards of conduct based on ethical principles such as honesty and fairness.

ethics Moral behavior constraints.

European Court of Human Rights A noncommercial court dealing with disputes over the treatment of a country's citizens.

exclusionary conduct Monopolistic behavior that attempts to prevent market entry and exclude competition.

exclusive dealing Antitrust term for contract arrangements in which the seller sells to only one buyer in an area.

exclusive distributorship *See* **sole outlet.**

exclusive jurisdiction Authority granted to only one court for particular types of cases.

exculpatory clause Clause that attempts to hold a party harmless in the event of damage or injury to another's property.

executed contracts Contracts in which performance has been completed.

executive branch That portion of the federal government that consists of the president and the administrative agencies; often referred to as the enforcement branch.

executive committee A working board of directors' committee that usually includes company officers and makes day-to-day decisions between regular board meetings; manages ongoing operations.

executive order Law of the executive branch; sets policies for administrative workers and contracts.

executory contracts Contracts that have been entered into but not yet performed.

exempt securities Securities not required to be registered with the SEC under the 1933 Securities Act.

exempt transactions Under the 1933 Securities Act, sales of securities not required to be registered, such as shares issued under a Chapter 11 bankruptcy court reorganization.

exemptions Under the Securities Act of 1933, the securities and transactions that need not be registered with the SEC.

exhausting administrative remedies Requirement that all procedures internal to an administrative body be exhausted before an individual pursues a remedy in court.

ex parte **contacts** Latin term for contacts with a judicial figure or hearing officer outside the presence of the opposing side.

express authority In agency law, the authority given either in writing or orally to the agent for his conduct.

express contract Contract agreed to orally or in writing.

express warranty Expressed promise by seller as to the quality, abilities, or performance of a product.

expropriation The taking of private property by a government for government use, also known as appropriation.

F

failing-company doctrine Under the Clayton Act, a justification for a generally illegal merger on the basis that the firm being merged is in financial difficulty and would not survive alone.

Fair Credit Billing Act Federal law governing credit card bills and requiring monthly statements, disclosure of dispute rights, and so on.

Fair Credit and Charge Card Disclosure Act of 1988 Amendment to the Truth in Lending Act that requires disclosure of terms in credit card solicitations.

Fair Credit Reporting Act (FCRA) Federal law governing the disclosure of credit information to consumers and the content of those credit reports.

Fair Debt Collections Practices Act (FDCPA) Federal law controlling the methods debt collectors may use in collecting consumer debts and also requiring disclosures to consumers when the debt collection process begins.

"fair-disclosure rule" (Regulation FD) Federal securities regulation that requires publicly traded companies to distribute information to the market as a whole and not to selected investment firms, analysts, or investors; responsible for the birth of the webcast by companies as a means of distributing to the market in a fair and open fashion the financial reports and pending and evolving issues of a publicly traded company.

Fair Employment Practices Act The Civil Rights Act of 1964.

Fair Labor Standards Act (FLSA) Federal law on minimum wages, maximum hours, overtime, and compensatory time.

fair trade contracts Agreements requiring retailers not to sell products below a certain price; permitted in some states.

fair use One of the exceptions to copyright protection; permits limited use of copyright material; for example, an excerpt from a poem.

false imprisonment The intentional tort of retaining someone against that person's will.

Family and Medical Leave Act (FMLA) Federal law that permits unpaid leave up to twelve weeks with a job guarantee upon return; allowed for birth or adoption of child or illness of parent, spouse, or child.

featherbedding Union unfair labor practice of requiring payment for work not actually performed; for example, requiring payment for a minimum number of bricks even though the job does not involve that many bricks.

federal circuits Geographic groupings of the federal district courts for purposes of appellate jurisdiction.

Federal Consumer Product Warranty Law of 1975 The Magnuson-Moss Act; governs the definitions of limited and full warranties; requires disclosure of warranty terms.

federal district court The trial court of the federal system.

Federal Environmental Pesticide Control Act Federal law that requires registration of all pesticides with the EPA.

federal implementation plan (FIP) Under the Clean Air Act Amendments of 1990, requirements established by the EPA (in the absence of state action) regarding the control of emissions by plants and autos.

Federal Insurance Contributions Act (FICA) Federal law that requires the joint contribution by employers and employees of the funds used for the Social Security system.

Federal Privacy Act Federal law that prohibits exchange of information about individuals among agencies without request and notification, unless for law enforcement purposes.

Federal Register A daily federal publication that reports the day-to-day actions of administrative agencies.

Federal Register Act Federal law that establishes all the publications and reporting mechanisms for federal administrative law, such as the *Federal Register* and the *Code of Federal Regulations*.

Federal Register System Part of the federal government responsible for the publication of government notices and rules.

Federal Reporter Series of volumes reporting the decisions of the U.S. Court of Appeals.

Federal Supplement Series of volumes reporting the decisions of the federal district courts.

Federal Trade Commission (FTC) Federal agency responsible for regulation of unfair and deceptive trade practices, including deceptive advertisements.

Federal Trade Commission Act Federal law establishing the FTC and its regulatory role.

Federal Trademark Dilution Act Federal law that permits litigation to halt the use of a trademark that results in the loss of unique appeal for its owner.

Federal Water Pollution Control Act of 1972 Federal law that set goals of swimmable and fishable waters by 1983 and zero pollution discharge by 1985.

Federal Water Pollution Control Administration (FWPCA) Separate federal agency established to monitor water quality standards.

fiduciary Position of trust and confidence.

Fifth Amendment Portion of the Bill of Rights of the U.S. Constitution providing protection against self-incrimination and ensuring due process.

finance charges For credit cards, the interest paid each month on outstanding balances.

First Amendment Portion of the Bill of Rights of the U.S. Constitution providing protection for freedom of speech and religious freedom.

FOIA request Request to a government agency for information retained in that agency's files.

force majeure Clause in a contract that excuses performance in the event of war, embargo, or other generally unforeseeable event.

foreclosure Process of creditor acquiring mortgaged land for resale.

foreign corporation A corporation in any state except the state in which it is incorporated.

Foreign Corrupt Practices Act (FCPA) Federal law prohibiting bribes in foreign countries and requiring the maintenance of internal controls on accounting for firms registered under the Securities Exchange Act of 1934.

formal rulemaking Process for developing rules in an administrative agency; involves hearings and public comment period.

Fourteenth Amendment Provision of the U.S. Constitution that provides for equal protection and due process.

Fourth Amendment Part of the Bill of Rights of the U.S. Constitution that provides protection and assurance of privacy; the search and seizure amendment.

fraud Term for deception or intentional misrepresentation in contract negotiation.

Freedom of Information Act (FOIA) Federal law that permits access to information held by federal administrative agencies.

freeze-out Merger undertaken with the objective of eliminating minority shareholders.

friendly takeover A takeover of one firm by another firm when the target firm solicits or agrees to the takeover.

FTC Improvements Act of 1980 Federal act that provided change in the role of the FTC and placed some limitations on its authority after the FTC's attempt to regulate children's television advertising.

full-disclosure standard SEC standard for registration; materiality disclosure requirements; not a merit standard.

G

garnishment Judicial process of taking funds or wages for satisfaction of a judgment.

GATT Multilateral trade treaty to which the U.S. is a signatory.

general partner Partner in a general or limited partnership whose personal assets are subject to partnership creditors in the event of nonpayment of partnership debts.

geographic market Relevant geographic location for a firm's market; used as a basis for determining monopoly power and market share.

good-faith bargaining Mutual obligation of employer and union to meet at reasonable times, confer in good faith on employment issues, and execute a written agreement.

government corporation Corporation created by a government agency to achieve a social goal.

Government in the Sunshine Act Federal law that requires advance notice and open meetings of agency heads.

grand jury Special group of jurors established as a review board for potential criminal prosecutions; generally established for a year to eighteen months.

gratuitous agency Agency relationship in which the agent has the authority to act for the principal but will not be compensated.

gray market Market in which trade name goods are sold through unauthorized dealers or without authorization from the owner of the trade name.

group boycotts A practice, prohibited by federal antitrust laws, in which several firms agree not to sell or buy from one or several other firms.

H

Hart-Scott-Rodino Antitrust Improvements Act Act passed in 1976 that gave the Justice Department greater investigative authority in antitrust violations and established premerger notification requirements.

Hazardous Substance Response Trust Fund Fund set up by CERCLA for waste site cleanup that is funded by the responsible company.

Health Insurance Portability and Accountability Act of 1996 (HIPAA) Federal law that provides protections and procedures for patient privacy.

hearing examiner *or* **hearing officer** Quasi-judicial figure for agency hearings.

hearsay Testimony about the statements of another; often inadmissible evidence in a trial.

Home Equity Loan Consumer Protection Act of 1988 Amendment to the Truth in Lending Act that requires disclosures in home equity loan documents, including the possibility of foreclosure, and allows three-day rescission period for home equity loans.

Home Ownership and Equity Protection Act (HOEPA) of 1994 Federal law that increased disclosure requirements on home mortgages and home equity loans.

home solicitation sales Sales originated in the home of the buyer.

Homeland Security Act of 2002 Federal law that created the Department of Homeland Security and added additional funds and processes for security and antiterrorism tools.

horizontal merger A merger between two competitors.

horizontal restraint of trade Anticompetitive activity among competitors; for example, price fixing among competitors.

hostile takeover A takeover not solicited or approved by the target's management.

Howey test U.S. Supreme Court definition of a security; investment in a common enterprise with profits to come from the efforts of others.

hung jury Term used to describe a jury unable to come to a verdict.

hybrid rulemaking Process by which agency promulgates rules with some hearings but relies mostly on public comments.

I

Illegal Immigration Reform and Immigrant Responsibility Act of 1996 Federal statute that increased employer responsibility for use of illegal immigrants in their workforces.

Immigration Act of 1990 Federal law that requires an I-9 form for every employee who is an immigrant.

Immigration and Naturalization Act (INA) Original federal act governing employer obligations on employing immigrants.

Immigration Reform and Control Act of 1986 (IRCA) Federal law imposing additional requirements on employers for lawful employment of immigrants.

implied authority Authority of an agent that exists because of business custom in the principal's operation and in industry.

implied contract A contract that arises from circumstances and is not expressed by the parties.

implied warranty of fitness for a particular purpose Warranty given by seller to buyer that promises goods will meet the buyer's specified needs.

implied warranty of merchantability Under the Uniform Commercial Code, Article 2, Sales, a warranty that the goods are of average quality; given in every sale of goods by a merchant.

implied-in-fact contract A contract deemed to exist because of the way the parties have interacted (e.g., accepting treatment at a doctor's office).

implied-in-law contract *See* quasi-contract.

impossibility Contract defense that excuses performance when there is no objective way to complete the contract.

in personam **jurisdiction** Jurisdiction over the person; type of jurisdiction court must have to require a party to appear before it.

in rem **jurisdiction** Jurisdiction over the thing; a method whereby a court obtains jurisdiction by having property or money located within its geographic jurisdiction.

inadequate capitalization In corporation law, the lack of sufficient funds to cover the anticipated debts and obligations of a corporation.

incidental damages Damages suffered by the nonbreaching party to a contract as a result of the breach; for example, late performance fees on a buyer's contract because the seller failed to deliver on time.

incorporators Individuals who sign the incorporation papers for a newly formed corporation.

independent contractor Person who works for another but is not controlled in her day-to-day conduct.

indictment Formal criminal charges issued by the grand jury.

infant A minor; a person below the age of majority, in most states below the age of 18.

informal rulemaking Process by which an agency promulgates rules without formal public hearings.

information Formal criminal charges issued by a judge after a preliminary hearing.

infringement The use of a copyright, patent, trademark, or trade name without permission.

inherence Theory of corporate social responsibility under which managers serve shareholders only.

inherently dangerous activities In agency law, those activities that carry a high risk and for which the party hiring an independent contractor cannot disclaim liability; for example, dynamiting a building to demolish it.

initial appearance In criminal procedure, the first appearance of the accused before a judicial figure; must take place shortly after arrest.

initial meeting First meeting of a corporation's organizers after the state provides certification that the corporation exists.

initial public offering (IPO) The first public offering of securities by a corporation.

injunction Equitable remedy in which courts order or enjoin a particular activity.

insider A corporate officer or director or other executive with access to corporate information not available to the public.

Insider Trading and Securities Fraud Enforcement Act of 1988 Act increasing the Securities Exchange Act of 1934 penalties for insider trading.

instructions Explanation of the law applicable in a case given to the jury at the end of the evidence and arguments.

intangible property Intellectual property, such as patents and copyrights.

intentional infliction of emotional distress Intentional tort in which the defendant engages in outrageous conduct that is psychologically damaging to the plaintiff.

intentional torts Civil wrongs against individuals that are committed with a requisite state of mind and intent to harm; includes defamation, false imprisonment, battery, assault, and intentional infliction of emotional distress.

Inter-American Court of Human Rights In international law, the court for resolution of noncommercial issues or the violation of human rights by a particular nation in North or South America.

interbrand competition Competition among like products; for example, competition between Pepsi and Coke.

interlocking directorates In antitrust law, the presence of the same directors on the boards of various companies that occupy positions in the same chain of distribution or are competitors; the concern is the concentration of power.

International Chamber of Commerce (ICC) Voluntary body with uniform rules on commerce and contracts.

International Court of Justice (ICJ) Voluntary court in the international system of law; nonbinding decisions.

Internet Corporation for Assigned Names and Numbers (ICANN) Organization that registers domain names for purposes of protection of those names as intellectual property.

interrogatories Method of discovery in which parties send written questions to each other, with responses required to be given under oath.

intervenors Interested parties who are permitted to participate in agency hearings even though they are not parties to the case.

intrabrand competition Competition among products made by the same manufacturer; for example, competition between Coke Zero and Diet Coke.

invisible hand Theory of corporate social responsibility under which managers believe they serve society but do so in the best way by being accountable to shareholders.

J

joint venture A partnership for one activity or business venture.

judge Elected or appointed government official responsible for supervising trials, hearing appeals, and ruling on motions.

judgment The final decision of a court; formal entry of the decision or verdict.

judgment NOV Judgment *non obstante veredicto;* a judgment notwithstanding the verdict; a judgment issued by the judge after the jury has rendered a verdict; a trial court's reversal of a jury's decision on the grounds that the verdict was against the weight of the evidence.

judgment on the pleadings A dismissal of a suit by a court for the failure of the plaintiff to state a case in the complaint.

judicial branch The one (of three) branches of the federal government that consists of all levels of federal courts.

judicial review Review by appellate court of decisions and actions of a lower court to determine whether reversible errors in procedure or law were made.

jurisdiction The concept of authority of a court to settle disputes.

jurisprudence The philosophy of law.

jury instructions Explanation to the jury of the law applicable in the case.

just compensation Principle in eminent domain that requires the government entity taking private property to pay the owner a fair amount.

justice of the peace courts Lower courts generally handling traffic citations and other lesser civil matters.

K

knock-off goods Goods manufactured by someone other than the trademark or trade name holder without authorization and not according to the standards of the owner.

L

Labor Management Cooperation Act Federal law providing funding for the study of alternative solutions to labor disputes.

Labor-Management Relations Act The Taft-Hartley Act; governs management conduct in its relationships with unions.

Landrum-Griffin Act Labor-Management Reporting and Disclosure Act; legislation passed to regulate unions and their governance.

Lanham Act of 1996 Federal law dealing with trademark and trade name protection.

lawyer Licensed professional who serves as a representative for another in private negotiations and in judicial and other types of legal proceedings.

Lawyer's Edition Private publisher's series of volumes reporting U.S. Supreme Court decisions; contains summaries of the cases and the briefs of counsel.

lease Temporary possession and use of real property, or right of use and possession of personal property.

legal remedy In common law, a legal remedy consisted of money damages versus equitable remedies of injunctions and specific performance; different courts afforded different remedies in common law England, but the distinction has disappeared today, and all courts have authority to award legal and equitable remedies.

legislative branch One of the three branches of government; at the federal level, consists of the Congress (the Senate and the House of Representatives) and is the branch responsible for making laws.

letter of credit Generally used in international transactions; an assurance by a bank of the seller's right to draw on a line of credit established for the buyer.

libel Written defamation; defamation in a newspaper or magazine or, in some states, on television.

license Right of access; generally oral; personal right that is not transferrable.

lien An interest in property used to secure repayment of a debt; entitles creditor to foreclosure rights in the event the debt is not repaid; creditor's right in property to secure debt.

like grade or quality Under Robinson-Patman Act, this means that there are no differences in the physical product.

Lilly Ledbetter Fair Pay Act Federal law that extended the statute of limitations for employees to bring discrimination suits against employers for pay discrimination; time is now measured from each paycheck and not limited to 180 days from the act of discrimination.

limited jurisdiction Specialty courts that have only limited authority over certain types of cases with distinct subject matter; probate courts have limited jurisdiction over probate matters only.

limited liability company (LLC) A business entity with limited liability but management participation permitted by all; statutory creature.

limited liability partnership (LLP) Partnership in which all partners have limited liability; statutory creature with strict formation requirements.

limited partner Partner in a limited partnership who has no personal liability and can only lose his investment in the partnership; must be formed according to statutory requirements; cannot use name in partnership name and cannot participate in the firm's management.

limited partnership Type of partnership in which some partners have unlimited liability (general partners) and other partners have only their investments at risk in the business (limited partners); must follow statutory procedures to properly create a limited partnership.

limited partnership agreement Contract governing the rights and relations of limited partners.

line of commerce Area of business; determination used by the Justice Department in evaluating mergers.

lingering apparent authority Type of authority an agent has when the principal fails to announce that the agent is no longer associated with her.

liquidated damages Damages agreed to in advance and provided for in the contract; usually appropriate when it is difficult to know how much the damages will be.

lockout Economic weapon of employer in which employees are not permitted to work; shop is closed down to avoid a strike.

long-arm statutes Statutes in each state that allow the state courts to bring in defendants from outside the state so long as they have some "minimum contact" with the state.

M

Madrid Agreement Concerning the International Registration of Trademarks In international law, 1891 multilateral treaty for protection of trademarks that permits registration and protection through a centralized registrar in Geneva.

mailbox rule Timing rule in contract acceptances that provides that acceptance is effective upon mailing if properly done.

mandatory bargaining terms In collective bargaining, the terms both sides are required to discuss, such as wages, hours, and so on.

market power The ability of a firm to control prices and the nature of product demand.

master-servant relationship Type of agency relationship in which the principal directly controls the agent; for example, principal controls hours and supervises work directly.

material fact (*or* material misstatement) A statement of fact that would influence an individual's decision to buy or sell.

maximum achievable control technology (MACT) Under the 1990 Clean Air Act, the standard required for factories in controlling air emissions; replaced the old, less-stringent standard of best available technology (BAT).

mediation Alternative dispute resolution mechanism in which a third party is brought in to find a common ground between two disputing parties.

meeting the competition Defense to price discrimination that allows the defense of price reduction when competition in the area dictates that price.

mens rea Mental intent or state of mind necessary for the commission of a crime.

merchant's confirmation memoranda Memos between merchants, signed by one of them, that will satisfy the statute of frauds requirements and create an enforceable contract against both parties.

merchant's firm offer Under § 2–205 of the UCC, an offer required to be held open if made in writing by a merchant, even though no consideration is given.

merger Process of combining firms so that one firm becomes a part of the other and only one firm's name is retained.

merit review Process at the state level of reviewing securities registrations for their merit, as opposed to the federal review for full disclosure.

minimum contacts Standard used for determining *in personam* jurisdiction over residents outside the state of the court of litigation; nonresident defendants must have some contact with the state to justify a court taking jurisdiction.

minimum wage Part of the FLSA that requires all employees to be paid a minimum wage.

minitrial Alternative dispute resolution method in which the officers of two firms in a dispute listen to the key evidence in a case to see if a settlement can be determined.

minor An infant; an individual under the age of majority; generally someone under the age of 18.

Miranda **warnings** Statement required to be given to individuals when taken into custody to alert them to their right to remain silent, the fact that statements can be used against them, their right to an attorney, and the right to an appointed attorney if they cannot afford one.

misappropriation Intentional tort of using someone's name, likeness, voice, or image without permission.

misrepresentation In contract formation, misstatements of materials facts.

misuse In product liability, a defense based on the plaintiff's failure to follow instructions or use of a product for improper purposes.

Model Business Corporation Act (MBCA) Uniform law on corporations.

modify An option for an appellate court in its review of a lower court case; an action that is something less than reversing a decision but something more than simply affirming it; for example, an appellate court could agree with the verdict but modify the judgment amount or the remedy.

monopolizing Controlling a product or geographic market.

monopoly power The ability to control prices and exclude competition.

monopsony The ability to control the market through the control of a supplier and/or supplier's prices.

moral relativism Ethical theory holding that there is no absolute right and wrong and that right and wrong vary according to circumstances, often referred to as "situational ethics."

mortgage Lien on real property.

motion A party's request to the court for action.

motion for judgment on the pleadings A motion made to dismiss a suit for failure by the plaintiff to establish a cause of action in the pleadings.

motion for summary judgment A motion made for final disposition of a case in which there is no dispute of facts and only a dispute of law and its application.

motion to dismiss A motion made after the presentation of the plaintiff's case or the defendant's case for failure to establish a *prima facie* case (in the case of the plaintiff) or failure to rebut the presumption (in the case of the defendant).

multilateral treaty A treaty agreed to by several nations.

N

National Environmental Policy Act (NEPA) The federal legislation on environmental impact statements.

National Labor Relations Act (Wagner Act 1935) (NLRA) First universal federal legislation that gave employees the right to organize and choose representatives for collective bargaining.

National Labor Relations Board (NLRB) Federal agency charged with supervising union elections and handling unfair labor practice complaints.

National Pollution Discharge Elimination System (NPDES) A system established by the EPA that requires those who discharge pollutants to obtain a permit, the granting of which is based on limits and pretreatments.

nationalization The taking of private property by a government for governmental use.

natural law Law or principles of behavior that exist without being written; supreme laws that cannot be circumvented.

necessaries With regard to minors, items for which minors can be held responsible.

negligence Tort of accidental wrong committed by oversight or failure to take precautions or corrective action.

negligent failure to supervise Tort that imposes liability on a principal/employer for the failure to take steps to curb employee behavior that has resulted in or could result in injury to third parties.

negligent hiring Tort that imposes liability on a principals/employers for injuries to third parties that result from their failure to perform adequate screening and background check on employees prior to hiring.

nexus Connection; a term used in constitutional analysis of the authority to tax; there must be a sufficient connection between the business and the taxing state.

NLRB National Labor Relations Board.

Noerr-Pennington **doctrine** An exception to the antitrust laws that allows business to lobby against competitors before legislative and administrative bodies, even though the effect may be anticompetitive.

Noise Control Act of 1972 Federal statute controlling noise levels and requiring product labels.

nolo contendere A "no contest" plea; the charges are neither denied nor admitted.

nonattainment area In federal air pollution regulation, an area unable to meet federal clean air goals and guidelines.

nonbinding arbitration Arbitration in which the decision is not final, that is, the parties can still take the matter to court.

nonconventional pollutant EPA classification of pollutant that requires the highest level of treatment prior to release into waterways.

nonprofit corporations Those corporations performing a function that covers cost but does not provide a return on investment.

Norris-LaGuardia Act The anti-injunction act; one of the first federal labor acts passed to prevent courts from issuing injunctions to stop labor strikes except in dangerous or emergency situations.

novation Process of reworking a contract to substitute parties or terms, so that the old contract is abandoned and the new contract becomes the only valid contract.

nuisance Civil wrong of creating a situation (noise, dust, smell) that interferes with others' ability to enjoy the use of their properties.

O

Occupational Safety and Health Act Worker safety statute passed by Congress in 1970 that established OSHA and directs the development of safety standards in the workplace as well as systems for record keeping and compliance.

Occupational Safety and Health Administration (OSHA) Federal agency responsible for the enforcement of federal health and safety standards in business and industry.

offer Indication of present intent to contract; the first step in making a contract.

offeree In contract negotiations, the person to whom the offer is made.

offeror In contract negotiations, the person who makes the offer.

Oil Pollution Act (OPA) Federal law providing penalties for oil spills and authorizing federal cleanup when private companies' cleanup efforts fail; also authorizes federal government to collect for costs of cleanup when firm or firms responsible for the spill fail to do so.

omnibus hearing In criminal procedure, a hearing held before the trial to determine the admissibility of evidence.

open-end credit transaction Under Regulation Z, credit transactions without a definite beginning and ending balance; for example, credit cards.

open meeting law Law (at either state or federal level) requiring that notice be given of meetings of agency heads and that they be open to the public.

opening statement In a trial, each side's overview of the case and the evidence that will be presented.

opposition proceedings In non-U.S. countries, the patent process that allows third parties to appear and object to a patent application.

option A contract for time on an offer; an agreement to hold an offer open for a period of time in exchange for consideration.

oral argument Upon appeal of a case, the attorneys' presentation of their points on appeal to the panel of appellate judges.

ordinances Laws at the city, town, or country level.

ordinary and reasonably prudent person In negligence, standard used for determining the level of care required in any given situation.

Organization for Economic Cooperation and Development (OECD) International organization of countries committed to developing trade, initially through the elimination of corruption.

original jurisdiction Jurisdiction of trial courts; jurisdiction of courts where a case begins.

overtime pay Pay rate required for work beyond the maximum forty-hour work week.

P

palming off Unfair trade practice of passing off mock goods as the goods of another.

parol evidence Extrinsic evidence regarding a contract.

partnership Voluntary association of two or more persons, co-owners in a business for profit.

partnership by estoppel *See* **estoppel.**

partnership by implication A partnership that exists because of the conduct of the parties rather than by agreement.

party autonomy The right of parties to determine privately their choice of law.

patent Government license or protection for a process, product, or service.

pattern or practice of discrimination In employment discrimination, a theory for establishing discrimination based on a pattern of dealing with minorities, women, and certain ethnic groups.

peer review Method of dispute resolution in which peers of the party making a claim decide on its merits; for example, employee peer review of claims against the employer.

Pension Protection Act of 2006 Federal law that imposes additional funding and disclosure requirements on employers who have employee pension plans.

per curiam A judicial opinion of the full court with no judge or justice claiming authorship.

peremptory challenge Right to strike jurors with or without cause; lawyer's discretionary tool in selecting a jury; number of peremptory challenges is usually limited.

per se "On its face"; "without further proof."

petition Often the first document in a case.

petitioner Party filing a petition; or in the case of an appeal, the party filing the appeal of a lower court decision.

picketing Economic weapon of labor unions; right to demonstrate in front of employer's place of business to display grievances publicly.

plain view exception Under the Fourth Amendment, an exception to the warrant requirement that applies when what is seen is in the "plain view" of the law enforcement official.

plaintiff Party filing suit, who is alleging a wrong committed by the defendant.

plea bargain A negotiated settlement of a criminal case prior to trial.

pleadings The complaint, answer, and counterclaim filed in a lawsuit.

point and click The process of using the Internet and a computer to form a contract—pointing to a box that indicates affirmation and clicking the mouse.

point sources In environmental law, direct discharges of effluents.

police power Constitutional term describing the authority given to the states to regulate the health, safety, and welfare of their citizens.

political speech Term given to speech of businesses related to political candidates or issues; given First Amendment protection.

pooling agreement Agreement among shareholders to vote their stock a certain way.

positive law Codified law; law created and enforced by governmental entities.

power of attorney A lay term for granting another the right to act on your behalf; a general power of attorney grants full contractual and financial authority; a special power of attorney is one that is limited by function or time.

precautionary principle A principle used to guide regulations in the area of the environment and product liability; the principle mandates regulation as a prevention measure even when data are not clear as to whether harm results from product or practice (in environmental context).

precedent Prior judicial decisions; the law as it exists; *see also* *stare decisis.*

predatory bidding Company with market power using high-bid pricing to drive its competitors from the market place by inflating the cost of supplies.

predatory pricing Discount pricing below cost for a short period of time in an attempt to drive new competition out of the market.

preemption Constitutional term from the Supremacy Clause, which provides that the federal government preempts state law where such preemption was intended or where the federal regulation is so pervasive that it prevents state regulation.

preferred stock Nonvoting shares of a corporation entitling its holders to dividend preference above the common shareholders.

Pregnancy Discrimination Act Federal law prohibiting discrimination in hiring or promotion decisions on the basis of pregnancy or plans for pregnancy.

preliminary hearing In criminal procedure, the hearing in which the prosecution establishes there is sufficient evidence to bind the defendant over for trial.

pretrial conference Meeting among lawyers and court to narrow issues, stipulate to evidence, and determine method of jury selection.

prevention of significant deterioration (PSD) areas Clean air areas given special protection by the EPA regarding the maintenance of air quality.

price discrimination Charging a different price for different customers on a basis other than different marginal costs.

price fixing Agreement among horizontal competitors to charge a uniform price.

prima facie **case** A case establishing all the necessary elements; without rebuttal evidence from the defendant, entitles the plaintiff to a verdict.

primary offering In securities, the initial offering of the security for sale.

principal The employer or master in the principal-agent relationship.

private law The law of contracts and the intrabusiness laws such as personnel rules.

Private Securities Litigation Reform Act of 1995 Federal law passed with the goal of reducing litigation against companies in the form of class action suits by shareholders.

privity Direct contractual relationship.

probable cause Sufficient cause or grounds for the issuance of a search warrant.

probate courts Specialized courts set up to handle the probate of wills and estates and, generally, issues of guardianships and conservatorships.

pro bono Represented without fee, as when a lawyer agrees to represent a client without compensation for the representation.

procedural due process Constitutional protection that gives litigants in civil cases and defendants in criminal cases the right to notice in all steps in the process and the right of participation.

procedural laws Laws that provide the means for enforcing rights.

process servers Individuals licensed by a state to deliver summonses and subpoenas to individuals.

product disparagement Defamation of a product.

product liability Generic term used to describe the various contract and tort theories for holding parties liable for defective products.

product market Relevant product market for a firm; used as a basis for determining monopoly power.

professional corporation A statutory entity that permits professionals such as lawyers and doctors to incorporate and enjoy limited personal liability on all debts except for those arising from malpractice.

profit corporations Those corporations seeking to earn a return for their investors.

promissory estoppel A promise that causes another to act in reliance upon it; if the reliance is substantial, the promise is enforceable.

promulgation The process of passing administrative agency rules.

proper purpose A shareholder's legitimate interest in accessing a corporation's books and records.

prospectus A formal document describing the nature of securities and the company offering them; an ad or other description of securities.

proximate cause An element of negligence that requires a connection between the breach of duty and the type of form of injury/damages that resulted.

proxy Right (given in written form) to vote another's shares.

proxy solicitation The process of seeking voting rights from shareholders.

public comment period In administrative rulemaking, the period during which any member of the public can comment on the rule, its content, and potential efficacy.

public law Law passed by some governmental agency.

publicly held corporation A corporation owned by shareholders outside the officers and employees of the firm.

puffing Offering opinion about the quality of goods and products; not a basis for misrepresentation; not a material statement of fact.

pump and dump Practice of buying a stock, touting it to many who then buy it, and then selling the stock at an inflated price; not a new practice, but it is easier and faster over the Internet.

Q

qualified privilege A defense to defamation available to the media that permits retraction and no liability so long as the information is not printed or given with malice or with reckless disregard for whether it is true.

quasi-contract A theory used to prevent unjust enrichment when no contract is formed; the court acts as if a contract had been formed and awards damages accordingly.

quotas Affirmative action plans that dictate a specific number of minority or female applicants be accepted for jobs, graduate school, and so on. Outlawed by U.S. Supreme Court; can only have affirmative action goals, not specific quotas.

R

Railway Labor Act The first federal labor legislation that controlled strikes by transportation employees.

ratification A principal's recognition of a contract entered into by an unauthorized agent.

record Expanded form of documentation that qualifies as a "writing" for purposes of contracts under the UCC.

red herring prospectus A prospectus issued in advance of the effective date of a securities registration statement; permissible to release these before the registration statement is effective so long as a disclaimer that it is not an offer to sell securities is noted in red on the prospectus.

redirect examination Plaintiff's questioning of his own witness after defendant's cross-examination is complete; or vice versa when defendant's witness is involved.

regional reporter Series of volumes reporting the appeals and supreme court decisions of state courts; grouped by geographic region; for example, Pacific Reporter for the western states.

registration statement (S-1) Requirement under the 1933 Securities Act; a filing with the SEC that discloses all the necessary information about a securities offering and the offeror.

Regulation A Short form offering regulation under 1933 Securities Act.

Regulation D A regulation of the SEC governing the small offering exemptions under the 1933 Securities Act.

Regulation Z The Federal Reserve Board's regulation for the Truth in Lending Act; specifies disclosure requirements and offers examples of required forms.

Regulatory Flexibility Act Reform act for federal agency rules promulgation; requires publication of proposed rules in trade magazines so that industries and individuals affected can properly respond during the public comment period.

Rehabilitation Act of 1973 Federal law prohibiting discrimination by federal contractors on the basis of a handicapping condition.

relevant market Term used to describe the market studied to determine whether a particular seller has a monopoly.

remand Term used to describe the action an appellate court takes when a case is sent down to a lower court for a retrial or other proceeding on the basis of the appellate court decision.

rent-a-judge Means of alternative dispute resolution in which the parties hire a former judge and a private hearing room and have the judge determine liability.

repatriation Reaffiliating as a citizen of a country after having renounced that citizenship through expatriation.

request for admissions Discovery tool in which one side asks the other to admit certain facts as proven in a case.

request for production Discovery tool in which one side asks the other side to produce documents relevant to the case.

requirements contract Contract in which the buyer agrees to buy all requirements for her business from one seller.

resale price maintenance Practice of manufacturer attempting to control the price at which a product is sold at retail level.

rescission Process of rescinding a contract.

Resource Conservation and Recovery Act of 1976 (RCRA) Federal law governing the transportation of hazardous materials; requires a permit for such transportation; also encourages environmental cleanup.

Resource Recovery Act Federal law that gave aid to state and local governments with recycling programs.

respondeat superior "Let the master answer"; doctrine holds principal responsible for torts of agent in scope of employment.

respondent On appeal of a case, the party who is not appealing; in a petition for a divorce, the party against whom the petition is filed.

Restatement A summary of existing common law on a particular topic; for example, *Restatement of Contracts.*

Restatement of Agency A summary of the majority view of the states of the law of agency followed by courts in resolving agency issues and disputes.

Restatement (Second) of Contracts General summary of the nature of common law contracts in the United States.

Restatement § 402A Portion of the *Restatement of Torts* that deals with product liability.

reverse Action of an appellate court in changing the decision of a lower court because a reversible error has been made.

reversible error Mistake made in lower court proceedings that is ruled as improper by an appellate court and that requires a reversal of the case and possible retrial.

Revised Uniform Limited Partnership Act (RULPA) New version of the Uniform Limited Partnership Act that includes changes in the rights of limited partners and distributions on liquidation.

Revised Uniform Partnership Act (RUPA) Newest uniform revision of law on limited partnerships.

revocation In contract law, the retraction by the offeror of an outstanding offer.

RICO Racketeer Influenced and Corrupt Organizations Act; federal statute regulating enterprises involved in gambling and other businesses that tend to attract organized crime figures.

right-to-sue letter Letter issued by the EEOC to a complainant after all necessary administrative steps have been taken in the case; permits the complainant to pursue court action.

right-to-work laws State laws providing employees with the right to work even though they are not union members.

Rivers and Harbors Act of 1899 A federal law revitalized during the 1960s and 1970s (prior to the enactment of specific federal legislation controlling emissions) to control water pollution.

Robinson-Patman Act Federal law that prohibits price discrimination.

rule of reason Standard for evaluation of antitrust activity that allows the court to consider various factors and does not require an automatic finding of a violation of antitrust laws.

Rule 10b-5 SEC antifraud rule.

Rules 504, 505, and 506 *See* **Regulation D;** the rules governing small offering exemptions under the 1933 Securities Act.

runaway shop Employer economic weapon in which work is transferred to another plant to avoid the impact of a strike.

S

Safe Drinking Water Act Federal law passed in 1986 that sets standards for drinking water systems and requires states to enforce them.

scheduled injuries Under workers' compensation systems, listed injury for which certain payments are to be made to the injured worker.

scienter Mental intent; under 10(b) of the Securities Exchange Act of 1934, a requirement of intent to defraud as opposed to a standard of negligence.

scope of employment Phrase used to describe the liability limits of the principal for the agent; an act must be committed within this scope for the imposition of liability on the principal.

search warrant Judicially authorized document allowing the search of individuals' or businesses' premises.

Section 10(b) Antifraud provision of the Securities Exchange Act of 1934.

Section 16 Section of the Securities Exchange Act of 1934 that regulates sales and purchases of shares by directors, officers, and 10 percent shareholders.

securities Investments in a common enterprise with profits to come largely from the efforts of others.

Securities Act of 1933 The federal law governing the initial issuance and sale of securities to the public.

Securities and Exchange Commission (SEC) Federal agency responsible for enforcement of federal securities laws.

Securities Exchange Act of 1934 The federal law governing secondary sales of securities, the markets, and the firms dealing with securities.

security agreement Contract that creates a security interest.

security interest Lien in personal property; created under Article IX of the UCC.

self-incrimination Protection provided under the Fifth Amendment of not being required to be a witness against oneself.

separation of powers Principle of U.S. Constitution that divides authority for various governmental functions among the three branches of government.

sexual harassment Unlawful suggestions, contact, or other advances in the workplace; prohibited under federal law.

shelf registration Process of obtaining advance registration of securities offering and then waiting, or putting it on the shelf, until the market is at its best rates for issuance; can be valid for up to two years with regular filings such as the 10-K.

Sherman Act Original federal antitrust law; prohibits monopolization and horizontal trade restraints, such as price-fixing and boycotts.

shopkeeper's privilege A defense to the tort of false imprisonment for storeowners; allows reasonable detention of shoppers upon reasonable suspicion of shoplifting.

short-swing profits Profits made by corporate insiders during a period of less than six months between purchase and sale.

Sixth Amendment Amendment to U.S. Constitution that guarantees the right to a jury trial in criminal cases.

slander Tort of oral defamation.

slander of title Slander of business.

slowdown Economic weapon that interrupts the employer's business but falls short of a stoppage or strike.

small claims court Specialized court designed to allow the hearing of claims of limited monetary amounts without the complexities of litigation and without attorneys.

small-company doctrine Exemption from merger prohibitions that permits two smaller firms to merge in order to compete better against other, larger firms in the market.

social responsibility Theory of corporate social responsibility under which managers serve society by being accountable to society, not shareholders.

Social Security Act of 1935 Federal legislation that provides for the benefits of Social Security and the payment mechanisms through FICA deductions.

sole outlet Manufacturer's only designated seller in a particular area.

sole proprietorship Method of business ownership; one person owns business, receives all profits, and is personally liable for all debts.

Solid Waste Disposal Act Federal law that provided money to state and local governments for research in solid waste disposal.

Sonny Bono Copyright Term Extension Act (CTEA) Federal law that amends copyright law to extend period of protection for copyrighted works.

sovereign immunity Doctrine that provides that courts in one country are that country's law and cannot be reversed by decisions of courts in other countries; for example, a U.S. court cannot reverse a finding of not guilty by a court in Germany.

special warranty deed Deed that offers title protection only for grantor's period of ownership.

specific performance Equitable remedy in which party asks for performance of the contract as damages.

standing Right to bring suit; party who has experienced damages.

stare decisis Latin term for "Let the decision stand"; the doctrine of following or distinguishing case precedent.

state codes State laws passed by legislatures.

state implementation plans (SIPs) State plans for attaining federal air quality standards.

statute of frauds Generic term referring to statutes requiring certain contracts to be in writing.

statute of limitations Generic term referring to various state statutes controlling the time periods in which suits must be brought by plaintiffs; time varies according to the nature of the suit; for example, contract statutes of limitations are generally four years.

statutory law Law codified and written; passed by some governmental entity.

stipulated means In contracts, a method of acceptance specified or stipulated in the offer; if followed by the offeree, the mailbox rule applies for the timing of the acceptance.

stock restrictions Restrictions on the transfer of stock in a corporation; must be noted on the shares to be valid.

strict liability Degree of liability for conduct; an absolute standard of liability.

strict tort liability Standard established under the *Restatement of Torts* that holds product manufacturers and sellers liable for injuries resulting from their products regardless of whether they knew of the danger that caused the injury.

strike Economic weapon of employees; refusal to work for a given period of time.

Subchapter S corporation or S corporation A form of corporation for tax purposes that permits the direct flow-through of income and losses to the shareholders.

subject matter jurisdiction The right of a court to hear disputes involving certain areas of law and/or amounts.

subliminal persuasion A method of advertising using subtle and undetected means to persuade consumers to make purchases.

submarket In antitrust law, a segment of a market examined for purposes of determining either the impact on competition of a merger or the market strength of a competitor (e.g., tennis court shoes as a submarket of the tennis shoe market).

substantial evidence test Basis for challenging the actions of an administrative agency on the grounds that the rule promulgated was not based on enough evidence.

substantial performance Contract defense for performing a contract slightly differently from what was agreed upon; justification for substitute but equal performance; generally applicable in construction contracts.

substantive due process Constitutional protection that requires laws to apply equally to all and not to deny property or rights without prior notice.

substantive laws Laws that give rights and responsibilities to individuals.

summary judgment Method for terminating a case at the trial court level when there are no issues of fact and only a decision on the application of law needs to be made.

summary jury trial A private method of alternative dispute resolution in which the parties present a summary of their evidence to a private jury and then agree to abide by their decision or settle, depending on what the jury concludes; held privately and can often save the cost of going to court for a real trial.

summons Court document issued to the defendant in a lawsuit that explains the requirement of filing an answer and the time period in which it must be done.

sunset law Law that places an ending date on an administrative agency; if not renewed, an agency terminates at sunset on a particular date; the sun sets on the agency.

Superfund Federal fund used to clean up toxic waste disposal areas.

Superfund Amendment and Reauthorization Act Federal legislation extending CERCLA's authority and the liability of property owners and waste handlers for the cleanup of polluted lands.

superior skill, foresight, and industry Defense to monopolization based on "building a better mousetrap" and customers flocking to your door.

Supremacy Clause Constitutional provision allowing federal laws to preempt state laws where Congress intended or where the regulation is pervasive.

Supreme Court Reporter Series of volumes reporting the decisions of the U.S. Supreme Court.

Surface Mining and Reclamation Act of 1977 Federal law that requires restoration of surface coal mining land.

T

Taft-Hartley Act Labor Management Relations Act; federal law governing management in union relations.

takeover Process of one firm taking over another firm.

tangible property Form of personal property that includes goods, but not intellectual property such as stocks, bonds, patents, trademarks, and copyright.

tender offer Offer to more than 10 percent of the shareholders of a firm for the purchase of their shares; generally part of a takeover effort.

10-K form Annual report filed with the SEC; required of all 1934 Act firms.

10-Q form Quarterly report filed with the SEC; required of all 1934 Act firms.

theft Crime of taking property away from another permanently.

three-day cooling-off period Under Regulation Z, the period a buyer has to change his mind about a transaction initiated in the home.

tippee Party who is privy to inside information about a corporation or its securities and uses the information to trade securities profitably.

title insurance Insurance purchased for buyer's benefit; insures the land title from recorded defects.

Title VII Portion of the Civil Rights Act of 1964 prohibiting employment discrimination.

tombstone ad Ad run in newspapers announcing an upcoming securities offering; permissible after the registration statement is filed but not yet effective; must indicate it is not an offer for sale.

tort Private intentional or negligent wrong against an individual.

tortious interference with contracts Conduct by one party that results in another's breaching her contract with a third person (applies also to corporations).

toxic pollutant EPA classification of pollutant that requires the highest level of treatment prior to release.

Toxic Substances Control Act (TOSCA) Federal statute governing the control of the release of toxic substances into the environment.

trade dress The look, color, and decorative design of a business.

trade fixtures Personal property used in a trade or business that is attached to real property but is considered personal property.

trade libel Libel of a business.

trade name Name of a firm or product; entitled to federal protection for exclusive use.

trade restraints Obstacles to free and open competition.

trade secret A protected method for doing business or an item crucial to a business's success (such as a customer list).

trademark The symbol of a firm; entitled to federal protection for exclusive use.

traffic court Lesser trial court, in which traffic cases and violations of other city ordinances are tried.

transfer restrictions Limitations on the resale of shares of a corporation.

treaty In international law, an agreement between two or more nations.

treble damages In antitrust law and securities law, a civil remedy that permits successful claimants to recover three times the amount of their actual damages.

trial Process in a court of presenting evidence for a determination of guilt, innocence, or liability.

trial court First stop in the judicial system when a suit is filed; the court where the case is presented and witnesses testify.

trial *de novo* Latin for "trial again" or "trial anew."

Truth in Lending Act (TILA) The Consumer Credit Protection Act; affords disclosure protection for consumer debt.

tying sales Anticompetitive behavior requiring the purchase of another product in order to get the product actually needed.

U

ultra vires Action taken beyond the scope of authority; with federal agencies, action taken that is beyond the congressional authority given in the enabling statute.

unauthorized appropriation The use of someone's name, likeness, or voice without permission for commercial advantage.

unconscionable Term used to describe contracts that are grossly unfair to one side in the contract; a defense to an otherwise valid contract.

underwriter In securities transactions, the brokerage house offering the shares in a company to the public.

undue influence Contract defense based on one party taking advantage of a relationship of trust and confidence.

unemployment compensation Funds paid to individuals who are without a job while they attempt to find new employment; a federal program administered by the states.

unenforceable contract A contract that cannot be enforced because of a procedural error.

unfair labor practice An economic weapon used by an employer or employee that is prohibited under the federal labor laws.

Uniform Commercial Code (UCC) Uniform law adopted in forty-nine states governing sales contracts for goods, commercial paper, security interests, documents of title, and securities transfers.

Uniform Computer Information Transactions Act (UCITA) Uniform law that governs sales of software, databases, and other products used on computers.

Uniform Domain Name Dispute Resolution Policy (UDRP) Policy of ICANN that provides the means, timing, and rules for resolving disputes over domain names.

Uniform Durable Power of Attorney Act Act that allows individuals to set up a power of attorney that takes effect only if they are incapacitated.

Uniform Electronic Transactions Act (UETA) Uniform law for states that provides the rule for formation of electronic contracts.

uniform laws Series of laws drafted by groups of businesspeople, law professors, and lawyers; adopted and codified by states to help attain a more uniform commercial environment for transactions.

Uniform Partnership Act (UPA) Uniform law adopted in 49 states governing the creation, operation, and termination of general partnerships.

Uniform Unincorporated Nonprofit Association Act (UUNAA) Uniform law that governs liability and other issues related to nonprofit organizations.

unilateral contract Contract in which one party promises to perform in exchange for the performance of the other party.

unincorporated association A group of individuals that acts as an entity but has no legal existence.

union shop A plant or business controlled by a union.

United Nations Convention on Contracts for the International Sale of Goods (CISG) U.N. version of Article II on sales of goods for international transactions.

United States Code (U.S.C.) Statutory volumes of congressional enactments.

United States Reports Official U.S. government reporter for Supreme Court decisions.

Uniting and Strengthening America by Proving Appropriate Tools Required to Intercept and Obstruct Terrorism Act (USA Patriot Act) Federal law that permits expanded warrant and investigation techniques for federal agencies as well as the sharing of information about suspected terrorists; also imposes control on large cash transactions for banks, real property, and vehicles.

universal treaty A treaty accepted and recognized by all countries; for example, the Warsaw Convention on air travel.

unscheduled injuries Workplace injuries without specific award amounts covered in the workers' compensation statutes.

UPA Uniform Partnership Act.

U.S. Constitution The cornerstone of the federal government's structure and the basis of private citizens' rights and protections.

U.S. Court of Appeals The appellate court of the federal system; hears appeals from lower federal courts.

U.S. Department of Homeland Security Federal agency that is an umbrella for several existing agencies that was designed to bring together all the functions related to emergencies, immigration, border security, and antiterrorism efforts.

U.S. Government Manual Book published by the U.S. government that includes descriptions and organizational charts for all federal agencies.

U.S. Supreme Court The highest appellate court in the federal system and also the highest appellate court for state appeals.

usury Charging interest above the statutory maximum.

V

venue Geographic location of a trial.

verdict The outcome or decision in a trial.

vertical merger Merger between a manufacturer and a retailer; a merger between two companies in the chain of vertical distribution.

vertical trade restraint Trade restraints among firms in the distribution system.

void contract In contracts, a contract that neither side is required to perform; for example, an illegal contract is void.

voidable contract In contracts, a contract one side can choose not to perform; for example, a minor can choose not to perform his contract.

voir dire Process of questioning jurors to screen for bias and determine whether a lawyer wishes to exercise her peremptory challenge.

voting trust Arrangement among shareholders to gain uniform voting and some power by signing over voting rights on shares to a trustee; shareholders still get dividends, but trustee votes the shares; must be in writing and recorded with the corporation.

W

Wagner Act National Labor Relations Act; federal law governing the rights of unions and establishing the NLRB.

Wall Street Reform and Consumer Financial Protection Act *See* **Dodd-Frank Wall Street Reform and Consumer Financial Protection Act.**

warrant Court document authorizing an arrest or a search.

warranty A promise of performance or guarantee of quality on a good or service.

warranty deed Highest level of title protection in real property transfer; greatest number of warranties.

warranty of merchantability Warranty given in all sales by merchants that provides that goods are of average quality, are packaged properly, and will perform normally.

Warsaw Convention Agreement among various nations on the liability of air carriers for injuries, accidents, loss of luggage, and so on; an international agreement.

Water Pollution Control Act of 1948 First federal law directed at water pollution; authorized the surgeon general to study the problem.

Water Quality Act (1965) First federal law to set water quality standards.

watered shares Shares for which par value was not paid; shareholder is liable for the difference between what was paid and the par value per share.

Wheeler-Lea Act of 1938 Amendment to the FTC Act that permits prosecution under Section 5 if a consumer is injured, even though there is no injury to a competitor.

whistleblowing Act of an employee of a company disclosing to a regulatory agency or the press any violations of laws by his or her employer.

white-collar crime Crimes committed in business administration and/or professional capacity; the so-called paperwork crimes.

Williams Act Federal law governing the tender offer process.

work product An attorney's thoughts, research, and strategy in a case; nondiscoverable.

Worker Adjustment and Retraining Notification Act of 1988 (WARN) Federal plant-closing law requiring advance notice of plant closures and layoffs.

workers' compensation State system of providing for payment for workers injured on the job to avoid having liability suits by employees against employers.

working requirements Non-U.S. countries' patent requirement that the process or product be placed on the market within a certain time after the patent is granted, or the patent protection is lost.

writ of certiorari Order of the U.S. Supreme Court for hearing a case; *see* **certiorari.**

Z

zero-based budgeting Process of agency budgeting in which the budget starts with a figure of zero rather than at the level of the previous year's budget; effect is to require an agency to justify its functions and expenditures for each budget period.

Table of Cases

C

Table of Products, People, and Companies

Index